Lost Chords

Lost Chords

White Musicians and Their Contribution to Jazz,
1915–1945

Richard M. Sudhalter

New York Oxford
Oxford University Press
1999

Oxford University Press

Oxford   New York
Athens   Auckland   Bangkok   Bogotá   Buenos Aires
Calcutta   Cape Town   Chennai   Dar es Salaam   Delhi
Florence   Hong Kong   Istanbul   Karachi   Kuala Lumpur
Madrid   Melbourne   Mexico City   Mumbai
Nairobi   Paris   São Paulo   Singapore
Taipei   Tokyo   Toronto   Warsaw

and associated companies in
Berlin   Ibadan

Copyright © 1999 by Richard M. Sudhalter

Published by Oxford University Press, Inc.
198 Madison Avenue, New York, New York 10016

Oxford is a registered trademark of Oxford University Press

Library of Congress Cataloging-in-Publication Data

Sudhalter, Richard M.
Lost chords : white musicians and their contribution to jazz,
1915–1945 / Richard M. Sudhalter.
p.   cm.
Includes index.
ISBN 0–19–505585–3
1. Jazz—History and criticism.   2. Music and race.   I. Title.
ML3508.S85   1999   781.65'089'13—dc21   97–42470

Set in Joanna and Gill Sans
Design by Adam B. Bohannon

1 3 5 7 9 8 6 4 2

Printed in the United States of America
on acid-free paper

For Shirley and Biffly, who gave a lot more than just a damn . . .

Contents

Preface

Shortly after beginning work on this volume I realized that I was actually writing two books in one. First, of course, I was telling a story—or, more accurately, many stories; the style is standard exposition, combining biography, reminiscence, commentary, and even, in places, a form of narrative.

But musicians make music, and it follows that a book about musicians, especially one setting out a case for their creative importance, must also address the specifics of their achievements. That means entering the house of music scholarship and adapting some of its methods and techniques.

Inevitably, a hybrid textual form took shape, balanced between and blending the two disciplines. A chapter on Bobby Hackett, for example, while attentive to the facts of his life and character, also had to discuss and analyze his cornet style and improvising methods. That took an act of faith—an exhortation to the reader to stay with me: though I might pause to reflect on the felicities, say, of Hackett's famed "Embraceable You" solo or his extraordinary half-chorus on "Small Fry," I have intended that the narrative should never become lost in the particulars of music-making.

In general, the two lines of development survive comfortably side by side. Readers not interested in transcriptions of solos can move ahead with no fear of missing something crucial; musicians and students of music, meanwhile, can stop, analyze, reflect—and, if I have wrought well, gain enhanced understanding of what made Hackett (or anyone else so treated in the text) unique.

In that connection, I've adopted at least one variation which departs from common practice: transcriptions of solos, rather than being presented in concert key, are rendered in the *written key* of the instrument on which they were played. Therefore, if Hackett played his sixteen bars on "Small Fry" in concert E♭, they are presented here in F. The reason is clear: few instrumentalists think in concert pitch when playing solos on transposing instruments. Hackett, playing in concert E♭, was thinking a step higher, in F; had his part been written out for him, it would have been written out in that key.

Similarly, Jimmy Dorsey's 1927 alto saxophone chorus on "Sensation Stomp" is transcribed here not in concert A♭ but in his saxophone key of F. Frank Trumbauer, on the other hand, played the C-melody sax; for reasons explained at the appropriate point in the text, transcription of several of his solos, notably "For No Reason At All in C," appear in concert key and in the register in which they sound.

Solo transcriptions bear metronome markings, which provide easy indication of tempo to specialists and laymen alike. Two signs are given: a note value, indicating the basic unit of pulse, and a number, telling how many of these pulses occur within a minute. A marking of ♩ = 126, for example, tells us that the quarter note is the principal unit of pulse, and that at this tempo they go by at a swift rate of 126 per minute.

Some inconsistencies in the spelling of various names also require explanation. Trombonist George Brunies, for example, was later known as George Brunis and, for awhile, even as Georg. In general, I have opted for the spelling as it was in the 1920s, when he rose to prominence: in New Orleans and Chicago, he will be George Brunies. Later, in company with Eddie Condon, he may be Brunis. Similarly, Connie Boswell only became "Connee" in the 1940s, after the text stops tracking her.

Reliance on phonograph records has been constant and heavy. This does not entirely please me: having made records myself, I am only too aware of the ways in which studio conditions do *not* represent a natural playing environment. This was especially true in the early days of recorded jazz, when a combination of factors—mechanical, temporal, atmospheric, acoustic, and especially supervisory—could make the environment downright inhospitable for the kind of spontaneous interaction which lies at the heart of all good jazz. Even in those days, the crack-of-dawn scheduling of so many sessions often collided head-on with exhaustion—and, let us admit, acute hangovers, themselves enough to thwart effective performance. That so many memorable records resulted from so imperfect a circumstance is not only a small miracle but a tribute to the resilience of both music and musicians.

Records were, and are, a flawed index. But in the end, what other way do we have of hearing so many early jazzmen play? Beginning in the 1930s, "live" aircheck (off-the-radio) and concert recordings were available, finding the musicians at their evening best, on the job, relaxed and often adrenalized in a way impossible to imagine at ten in the morning. But no such representations of in situ hot music in the 1920s and earlier have yet surfaced. Sadly, jazz before 1917, the year it was first recorded, must forever remain an aural no-man's-land.

In the course of a quarter-century of jazz writing and research, and even before setting to work on this book, I'd been able to amass a large number of taped interviews, many with musicians now no longer living. Their names appear in the acknowledgments section, alongside those others who gave freely of time, memories, and insights during the nine-year preparation of this book. I am grateful to them all.

With a handful of exceptions, the text cuts off around the end of World War II. This was not orginally my plan; I began with every intention of writing an all-encompassing study, bringing the story right up to the present. But as research deepened and broadened, and I realized the scope and diversity of the subject, it soon became clear that this would not be possible. Too many musicians, too many evolving musical peaks; to scant one would be to scant all.

Better by far, I reasoned, to emulate Gunther Schuller, in his exhaustive and valuable study *The Swing Era*, and declare Part II a coming attraction. That meant deleting, for now, material on the vigorous Los Angeles traditional jazz scene of the late 1940s; on Clive Acker and his estimable Jump record label; on such distinguished individual players as bass saxophonist Joe Rushton and clarinetist Rosy McHargue; on Jack Webb's cornetist Dick Cathcart, in the *Pete Kelly's Blues* movie and radio and television series.

It meant deferring a lengthy, exhaustive, and long-overdue assessment of trumpeter Harry James. Though he won his first fame in the 1930s and experienced great commercial success in the World War II years, James only reached full artistic maturity as a jazz soloist in the 1950s. Records made in that decade reveal an improviser of resourcefulness and eloquence—and, of course, stunning technical command.

The band of Charlie Barnet, consistently popular throughout the 1930s and home to many outstanding sidemen and arrangers, may be conspicuous to some through its absence from this roll call. The omission can best be explained by citing George T. Simon's identification of this estimable unit as "the blackest white band of them all."

> The men make no bones about the fact that they're aping Duke Ellington, copying many of his arrangements, adapting standards and some pops to his style, using his sax section setup of two altos, tenor and baritone and his growling trumpet and trombone . . . the white boys are trying to master in one jump what it took the colored lads [sic] a long, long time to develop.[1]

The Barnet orchestra's emulation of Ellington, Basie, and other top black bands left it with little that could be identified as a style of its own—and a chronicler with the problem of assigning it a place in the ranks of white jazz ensembles. Regrettably, and with all respect for its musicianship (and that of its leader), I have left it out.

Another sacrifice was the San Francisco–based "revival" movement spearheaded by trumpeter Lu Watters, which began in 1940 and achieved wider public notice late in the decade; evaluation of the Watters band can hardly be separated from discussion of its two most distinguished alumni, trombonist Turk Murphy and trumpeter Bob Scobey, both of whom came into their own in the '50s.

Similarly, admirers of the latter-day Eddie Condon circle, and in particular the irrepressible cornetist Wild Bill Davison, will look for them here in vain. Though he came of age earlier, Davison found his true moment in the late '40s and '50s. So, too, did trumpeter Johnny Windhurst, pianist-trumpeter Dick Cary, and such clarinetists as Bob Wilber and Kenny Davern.

For all these omissions, and for any others, I offer regrets and promise redress in the future.

Some readers will notice repetition, from chapter to chapter, of words or phrases used to describe an individual or band. The sheer size of this book, the very proliferation of names and places, made this unavoidable.

And, finally, a word about structure. The migration, interaction, and biracial cross-fertilization which are such hallmarks of the early jazz years made a beginning-to-end chronological approach not only impractical but often down-right impossible. Aesthetic evolution is never neat or calendrical, but full of back-and-forth episodes. Consequently, I've chosen to group individuals and ensembles by stylistic and personal affinity—and, here and there, by contribution to the overall fabric of the music. I think the logic of such groupings will be self-evident as the reader moves through the text.

Thanks are in order to many people. Paramount among them are two old friends, jazzman and peerless sound restorer John R. T. Davies and record producer Michael Brooks. Without their resources, expertise, and unstinting generosity it's unlikely that this enterprise could have ever gone forward. However rare the record or recondite the information, they found ways of supplying it quickly and accurately; I stand eternally in their debt. A network of collectors and enthusiasts, including the late Bob Hilbert, helped locate otherwise hopelessly obscure recorded performances.

Dan Morgenstern, Ed Berger, Vince Pelote, and the rest of the staff at the Rutgers Institute of Jazz Studies gave patiently of time and effort, even when my requests were for matters of, to say the least, finely drawn detail. Bruce Boyd Raeburn placed the full resources of Tulane's William Ransom Hogan Jazz Archive at my service and displayed supreme magnanimity in granting me access to his superb doctoral dissertation.

Some fellow-musicians became unofficial consultants: saxophonist-arranger-historian Bill Kirchner helped clarify many an idea or concept during late-night telephone marathons and checked the musical side of things for logic, consistency, and accuracy. Marty Grosz, master of acoustic guitar, remained patient and informative in the face of my interminable questions about the history and techniques of his instrument. And, too, there was the nonpareil cornetist Ruby Braff: clear of eye, pure of heart, he steadied my focus time and again, reminding me of the incalculable value of wonder, of remembering how to dream.

S. Frederick Starr—historian, clarinetist, and author of distinction—read and offered invaluable comment, as did his friend and colleague John Joyce. James T. Maher undertook the Herculean task of distilling to manageable proportions a manuscript originally the size of a Doré Bible. Barbara Lea, as exacting with the printed word as with a song lyric, provided the detailed index; Sonia Jacobsen, herself an accomplished composer, typeset the musical examples.

India Cooper managed a titanic copy-editing enterprise with wit, wisdom, and—dare I say it?—unsinkable good cheer. Appreciation, too, to Joellyn Ausanka, not least for unerring diplomacy in handling an author's often intemperate defenses of his every precious word and phrase.

All thanks to the Lynde and Harry Bradley Foundation, to the late Shirley Katzenbach, and to "Biffly," without whose timely financial assistance these labors would never have reached completion, and to Malcolm Addey, for generosity far above and beyond the call.

My gratitude, as well, to Dorothy Kellogg, whose forbearance and evenness of vision still astonish me.

Finally, a word of thanks to Sheldon Meyer of Oxford University Press, who thought of this book, commissioned me to write it, watched indulgently and helpfully as it grew, and—most important of all—never ran out of faith.

My indebtedness to them all knows no bounds.

Southold, New York
January 1, 1998

Introduction

The past slips from our grasp. It leaves us only scattered things. The bond that united them eludes us. Our imagination usually fills in the void by making use of preconceived theories.

—Igor Stravinsky
Poetics of Music, 1956

Addressing a National Archives conference in 1971, the distinguished historian Barbara Tuchman identified two opposing viewpoints on the study of history. A pivotal issue, she said, was the role granted the present—its values, mores, attitudes—in assessing the past.

Are we entitled to judge another age from the viewpoint of our own, informed as it is by knowledge of the outcomes of past thought and practice? Or is such a method basically refractive, creating distortion by imposing the perspectives of one time arbitrarily on another? Tuchman came down unequivocally against the practice of second-guessing the past. "In order to identify with the period," she said, it is "essential to eliminate hindsight."

I try not to refer to anything not known at the time. According to Emerson's rule, every scripture is entitled to be read in the light of the circumstances that brought it forth. To understand the choices open to people of another time, one must limit oneself to what they knew: see that past in its own clothes, as it were, not in ours.

Such a view, she added, was bound to be contested bitterly by those historians who were (in a phrase Tuchman herself might have deplored) outcome-oriented. "According to their view, History is properly the interpretation of past events in terms of their consequences, and in the light shed upon them by present knowledge and present values."[1]

The relevance to current studies in American culture, particularly where race and gender are concerned, is obvious. Scholars across a broad range have used it as a stick with which to beat culprits as disparate as H. L. Mencken and Philip Larkin, Christopher Columbus and John F. Kennedy.

The history of jazz, particularly its growth in the racially segregated America of the early twentieth century, offers fertile ground for such hindsight-generated assessment. As an element of popular culture, jazz inevitably reflected the prevailing system: if musicians themselves were relatively color-blind (and indeed they were), their managers, agents, customers, employers, audiences—and particularly critics—were not. Beyond dispute, the machinery of the music business was not interested in social reform, and its chief beneficiaries were white.

Though the situation of black musicians may not always have been quite so desperate as has often been represented, life for members of the Duke Ellington, Count Basie, Jimmie Lunceford, Cab Calloway, and Chick Webb orchestras was neither as comfortable nor as well rewarded as it was for Benny Goodman, Artie Shaw, or Dorsey Brothers sidemen.

Change, though inevitable, was a long time coming. The rage for "multi-culturalism" in the arts—as in society at large—has led to the reassessment of, and often elevation of, artistic traditions of non-European and non-white cultures. With it has come recognition of many black artists and writers whose achievements long stood hidden from public sight.

Applied to jazz history, such thinking has spawned a view of early white efforts as musically insignificant and—particularly in the 1920s and '30s—vastly overpublicized. Jazz, says the now-accepted canon, is black: there have been no white innovators, few white soloists of real distinction; the best white musicians (with an exception or two) were only dilute copies of black originals, and in any case exerted lasting influence only on other white musicians.

In its more extreme forms, this canon maintains that black musicians, even those who worked for whites, seldom regarded them (again, exceptions) as true peers; that major black players took inspiration from whites only when no other models were available. And, finally, that black musicians, by some combination of instinct, heritage, and genes, were naturally more adept at the game. To this day, the underlying assumption, however casually felt or tacitly expressed, is that jazz is, *ipso facto*, more "authentic" when played by black musicians.

Some see this as just, arguing that more than a few white musicians got rich and famous by exploiting the innovations of black colleagues, and that true redress, in the natural order of things, demands no less than a shoe-on-the-other-foot exchange. Such reconception can even be seen to feed a noble goal: granting American blacks, particularly black youth, the worthiest of birthrights, a lineage brimming with estimable role models, a means by which every black child growing up in the United States in the next century can place himself at the very core of what is best in American culture.

But a growing body of scholarly research into the origins and early development of jazz has already yielded quite another conclusion: that the music may not be so much a black American experience as an *American* experience, with various racial and ethnic groups playing indispensable and interlocking roles. Not just a handful of white musicians, but many, now appear to have been decisive in the making of jazz. The canon, however, remains in place, and recognition continues to be denied, a situation that can only skew perception of both the music and its history.

Historian Arthur M. Schlesinger Jr., in *The Disuniting of America*, addresses the dilemma head-on:

> People live by their myths, and some may argue that the facts can be justifiably embroidered if embroiderment serves a higher good, such as the nurture of a nation or the elevation of a race. It may seem more important to maintain a beneficial fiction than to keep history pure— especially when there is no such thing as pure history anyway. This may have been what Plato had in mind when he proposed the idea of the "noble lie" in *The Republic*.[2]

Schlesinger goes on to say that zealots are "all too likely to confuse 'noble lies' with reality." In the case of jazz, certainly, the "noble lie" is achieved at great cost. The true losers are neither the neglected white musicians of the past nor their descendants, now laboring against such currents. The true losers are the young: the message they will receive is of a black cultural preserve, invaded and exploited by white America, and now being "reclaimed." In other words, a message of fragmentation, of separation—junk food history for young minds.

How much more laudable, and ultimately more beneficial, if they should learn that, in at least one important field, black and white once worked side by side, often defying the racial and social norms of their time to create a music whose graces reflected the combined effort. Multiculturalism, then, not as an encoded synonym for black America "getting its own back from Whitey"—but as living proof that the races and ethnic groups *can* cooperate to the common good.

To borrow a simple metaphor, only by peering through both lenses of a stereopticon can a viewer win the depth perception essential to appreciating the three-dimensionality of the scene depicted. Either lens, taken by itself, grants only a two-dimensional effect, flat and lifeless.

Why, then, a book on white musicians? Doesn't that focus also imply fragmentation, working against inclusiveness or three-dimensionality? Several possible answers present themselves. A counterweight to the "white men can't jump" approach embodied in the jazz history canon. A corrective to the neglect suffered by some extraordinary musical figures. A spur to further investigation (the records are, after all, real and available) and research. An act of pure utility, supplying the second lens that will render the picture three-dimensional.

All are applicable. Mounting scholarly evidence indicates that a distinct, significant, and creative white presence has existed in jazz from its first days; at almost every stage of the music's history the matter of "influence," so highly valued by jazz scholars, has been incontrovertibly two-way; many white individuals and ensembles have had powerful and lasting effect on the music, and on their black colleagues.

Early black jazzmen were unhesitating in expressing respect for Bix Beiderbecke, Adrian Rollini, Jack Teagarden, Miff Mole, Frank Trumbauer, Steve Brown, Dave Tough, Bud Freeman, Pee Wee Russell, and numerous other white musicians. More than once, Louis Armstrong hailed Bunny Berigan as his favorite among fellow-trumpeters. Coleman Hawkins advised young fans to listen to his favorite band, the Casa Loma Orchestra. Other similar testimony is plentiful and well-documented.

As for purported resentment of whites as "interlopers" or exploiters, hear trumpeter Adolphus "Doc" Cheatham: "That stuff about black musicians being envious of the whites because of money and such, that's been kind of exaggerated . . . If musicians were good, we learned from them, and they learned from us."[3]

The prominent white clarinetist-saxophonist Bob Wilber is even more forceful in dealing with matters of racial orthodoxy. As early as 1948, when he was doing his jazz apprenticeship as a pupil and disciple of the Creole jazz pioneer Sidney Bechet, "the idea was being sown by some jazz critics that the white man was merely an imitator of the black man, that jazz was the black man's music, and that any white man who tried to play it was naturally inferior because he was white. I'd never heard this idea expressed before, but I recognized it at the time as racial bullshit, just as it is racial bullshit today."[4]

In the 1940s and earlier, as Wilber and countless others have attested, the matter simply seemed less important—at least to musicians. Even if apocryphal, Louis Armstrong's oft-quoted remark to Jack Teagarden, "You an Ofay, I'm a Spade—let's blow!," enjoyed a rich contextual resonance. The music was the thing: if it worked, the rest—including the races of the players—hardly mattered. Certainly there was nothing of "You play all right—for a white man" in Armstrong's deep and frequent expressions of love for Teagarden, or for Bobby Hackett's lyrical cornet style.

Why, then, does the black creationist canon persist? Why the continuing notion, especially widely held among chroniclers and critics, that white musicians, no matter how accomplished and influential, are, in James Lincoln Collier's phrase, "only in it on suffrance?"

Part of it appears to involve the blues, particularly the degree to which its accents, inflections, and emotional thrust are deemed indispensable to jazz. Writer-canonist Albert Murray's Stompin' the Blues, for example, revives the thesis, much discussed and written about in the 1920s, that what has come to be called jazz music is only an outgrowth, an extension, of the blues. Such an assertion puts him in some unexpected company. Paul Whiteman, now regularly and ret-roactively demonized by jazz canonists as a popularizer-exploiter of ersatz jazz, affirmed in 1926, "Somebody, whose name has been lost to posterity unfortu-nately, declared illuminatingly that 'Jazz is blues and blues is blues.' I feel a good deal the same way and so does anybody who knows jazz and blues."[5]

Murray describes Lester Young and Coleman Hawkins as "the two great touchstones of the blues-idiom tenor-sax statement." And here he is on Duke Ellington:

> The preeminent embodiment of the blues musician as artist was Duke Ellington, who, in the course of fulfilling the role of entertainer, not only came to address himself to the basic imperatives of music as a fine art but also achieved the most comprehensive synthesis, extension and re-finement to date of all the elements of blues musicianship.[6]

As Murray reads it, the blues is not only central to but actually defines the essence of the American black experience. And if jazz is the blues, does it not follow that what we call jazz is but a permutation of that same essence?

Beyond argument, the blues in all its manifestations—urban and rural, secular and sacred—carries in its ebb and flow the ultimate majesty of black expression. Its might, its diversity, its mixture of great complexity and simple declaration, give it an eloquence unique in cultural history.

Identification of the expressive vocabulary of the blues as the *sine qua non* of jazz is more problematic. For many white musicians, the blues may indeed have been, in LeRoi Jones's phrase, a "learned art," but that is also true of a great number of prominent black jazzmen, among them Teddy Wilson, Art Tatum, Fats Waller, and even—*pace* Murray—Coleman Hawkins.

French composer, historian, and critic André Hodeir, writing more than four decades ago, brought the matter into focus. Use of harmonic alteration in con-structing a solo line, he observed, often all but prohibits use of the blues vocab-ulary. "Hawkins realized this very well when he made a radical choice in favor of alterations in his famous [1939] improvisation on *Body and Soul*. There is not the slightest allusion to the characteristic melodic lines of the blues in this solo." Hodeir further notes, in what almost seems a preemptive rebuttal to Murray-style canonic theorizing, "either Hawkins' work is not really jazz, or else the melodic language of the blues is not an essential part of such music. Common sense indicates which of these choices is the one to make . . . It cannot be repeated too often that the blues are one of the sources of jazz, but they are not [the whole of] jazz."[7]

The problem, then, appears to be synecdochical: the blues has indeed been a rich ingredient in what came to be called jazz—but not the entirety, and cer-tainly not equally indispensable to all styles. Other formative components include ragtime, Tin Pan Alley, late nineteenth-century European concert and dance mu-sic, grand opera, vaudeville and the minstrel traditions of both races, the white folk music of Appalachia, and—perhaps most of all—the concert bands so ubiq-uitous on village greens and in town dance halls in turn-of-the-century America.

When Casey waltzed "with his strawberry blonde and the band played on," the players were probably appearing in the town gazebo.

In light of this, the idea that without the blues (or any other single ingredient) jazz is not jazz seems at best a subjective conceit, unsupported by evidence. Accepted *a priori*, it begs too many questions, leaves too much unanswered. It is simply not possible to write off so large and diverse a body of music—not to mention the performances of several generations of accomplished players—as merely failed aspirations to a single ideal. How was it possible, as in the case of the white New York circle of 1920s jazzmen, to evolve a full and coherent system of rhythmic improvised music with almost no reference to the blues vocabulary? What explains the utterly blues-free virtuosity of the Harlem "stride" piano style?

If not the blues, and absent objective documentation, what *can* be adduced to support the idea of jazz as a uniquely black music? Has some metaphysical, hereditary or even genetic predisposition made black musicians better at this form than their white counterparts? In any other context, such a claim would be dismissed out of hand as a racialist atavism, a thinly disguised variant on "they all got rhythm." Can color, or even the historical experience of a racial group, legitimately be invoked as a determinant for artistic endeavor without summoning the unwelcome shade of Comte Joseph Arthur de Gobineau? Thin ice, indeed.[8]

Where, then, is the reality? Was there any such thing as "white jazz" or "black jazz," beyond the titles of a couple of numbers recorded by the Casa Loma Orchestra in 1931? Come to that, is "white jazz" necessarily the same thing as jazz played by whites? What explains obvious differences in sound, texture, emotional content, between Hoagy Carmichael's "March of the Hoodlums," as whooped and hollered by the composer's Indiana band, and the same piece as read dutifully by Duke Ellington's orchestra? Between the diverse treatments accorded Jelly Roll Morton's "Black Bottom Stomp" by the Red Hot Peppers and Red Nichols's Five Pennies? The different, but equally striking, emotional payloads in solos by Johnny Dodds (black) and Leon Roppolo (white), both clarinetists born and brought up in New Orleans?

The only way to find out was to investigate; and, as investigations will, this one swelled to unanticipated proportions. Everywhere I looked—and listened—I found evidence of white musicians in the game from the start: as innovators, admired and influential virtuosi, members of style-setting ensembles, groundbreaking arrangers, iconoclasts and individualists.

The story of jazz was emerging as a picaresque tale of cooperation, mutual admiration, cross-fertilization; comings-together and driftings-apart—all *despite*, rather than because of, the segregation of the larger society. For the musicians themselves, questions of jazz "legitimacy" seldom, if ever, had racial implications: some played well, others did not. Skin color was not an adequate explanation for either.

One of the risks of attempting to restore either an individual or a corpus of work to public regard involves the evaluative methods driving that attempt. Professor Carol Muske of the University of Southern California addressed it in reviewing a series of books which sought to rescue the poet and self-declared mystic Laura Riding from decades of obscurity:

> Riding's resurrection, in particular, raises . . . the unasked question: are we operating in the absence of a criticism sufficiently detached to guard against the false inflation of reputation?[9]

Application to this volume is plain. How good *were* these musicians? Who is to say that they were as important as their champions will have you believe? Is there the possibility that the advocate is falsely inflating their reputations for the sake of making an ideological point? The answers are right in front of us, in a full legacy of testimony and recorded music. There is no shortage of evidence attesting to what these men and women created, with whom and how well. These are not yet the "scattered things" of Stravinsky's doleful formulation: the bond holds. It is still possible to hear on records, and esteem, the skill and musicianship of such pioneer groups as the Georgians and the Original Memphis Five; the originality of Rollini and Mole, the grace of Sidney Arodin, the embracing creativity of Red Norvo, the audacious imaginativeness of the Boswell Sisters.

Though this is not a book about black musicians, they are a consistent and necessary presence throughout, helping to shape the work and attitudes of the white players as surely as white traditions, attitudes, and musicianship helped shape theirs. Such a study is anything but an exercise in one-upsmanship or retaliation: any attempt to look at the music without regard to such seminal figures as Armstrong, Ellington, Coleman Hawkins, Lester Young, Henry Allen, Sid Catlett, Benny Carter, and the rest would be folly. Their primacy, and the reverence in which they are held, belong to the unquestioned foundation on which the entire edifice rests.

But we must also hear Bud Freeman—not in a stylistic context determined by Coleman Hawkins but as an independent and eloquent tenor sax voice. Dave Tough as, in Lionel Hampton's words, "the most imaginative drummer we ever had in the business." Bob Crosby's orchestra not as a "dixieland" variant on the swing formula of the 1930s but as a highly motivated ensemble packed with vivid soloists, playing often memorably imaginative arrangements with a rare communality of musical thought.

Did the Casa Loma Orchestra's 1931 "Maniac's Ball" swing in *the same way* as Ellington's "Rockin' in Rhythm" or Henderson's "Sugar Foot Stomp," made the same year? Assuredly not; but swing it did, and on its own terms.

Many white musicians found black ways of swinging—and the blues idiom—irresistible and set out to incorporate them; to that degree it can be said that whites indeed *learned* to swing in this loose, relaxed manner. But so, too, did black soloists and ensembles absorb precedents in harmony, form, melodic and thematic organization, timbre, texture, tonal color, and blend from white musicians. No dishonor attaches to this, no sense of deficiency: it is in the nature of mutuality of art, a grand colloquy in which each participant brings something to the table.

My purpose is not to replace one exclusionist canon with another; nor do I affix any comparative judgment or value system to the matter of difference. I have attempted, using available evidence, an accurate portrait of the white contribution to jazz; and if that provokes sufficient curiosity to send a reader directly back to the music, I will have done my job. That is, after all, where we all should have been in the first place.

In the
Beginning
New Orleans to Chicago

1

Bands from Dixieland

Climbing off the train at La Salle Street Station, Ray Lopez couldn't help shivering as the Lake Michigan wind sliced easily through his light overcoat and suit. As a kid growing up in New Orleans he'd known some nippy days, but never anything quite like this.

Windy city, eh? Why the hell had he and his four companions ever come to this God-forsaken place? Sure, it was work: a job offer too good to turn down. But the cold—if this was May, what must December be like? He shook his head, picked up his cornet case and grip. This damn weather would be the death of him, he later recalled thinking.

Thus, on May 13, 1915, did white New Orleans music officially arrive in Chicago.[1]

The odyssey of Ray Lopez (1889–1970) had begun some weeks before, when, as cornetist and *de facto* manager of trombonist Tom Brown's five-piece "ragtime" band, he'd signed a contract with Gorham Theatrical Enterprises of Chicago. They would open May 17 at Lamb's Café, in the basement of the Olympic Theater building at Randolph and Clark, for six weeks at $105 per week for the band, renewable at the end of the fourth week.

Lopez and Brown (1888–1958) had done pretty well at home, providing music for dances at Tulane University, at the stately homes of the New Orleans Garden District, at such prestigious locations as the Young Men's Gymnastic Club; they played regularly for picnics and parties out at Lake Pontchartrain—and even the occasional evening down in "the District," known to posterity as Storyville, home of bars, brothels, and various other nocturnal amusements.

Mardi Gras was always especially busy, providing up to three jobs a day when times were good. But it was always a short-term feast: the arrival of Lent invariably brought such activity to a halt. Even at the best of times, dance music in New Orleans could hardly be depended on for a steady, reliable living. It's therefore not surprising that Tom Brown and most of his band members and friends were basically avocational musicians, with little or no professional training. The trombonist and his bass-playing younger brother Ted (known to friends as Steve) were tinsmiths. Clarinetist Gus Mueller (1890–1965) made much of his income as a plumber; drummer Bill Lambert (1893–1969) tended bar. They were young, unmarried, and footloose, children of a new century.

New Orleans in the years just before America's entry into the European "Great War" was coming face to face at last with reality. The boom economy built on cotton and other trade, which had made the Louisiana city a focus of world attention in the nineteenth century, had long since peaked. The port was losing out to Biloxi, Mississippi, and even up-and-coming Miami, Florida, jobs dwindling almost by the day. For thousands of laborers, the industrial cities of the North were the new Meccas, offering myriad opportunities for both skilled and unskilled work. When, in 1917, the black weekly Chicago Defender instituted its "Great Northern Drive," to attract southern blacks to the city, a mass exodus began in earnest.

Ray Lopez was the only one in his immediate circle who depended on music for a livelihood. As he explained it, he'd made a dollar a day as a shop worker for the Southern Pacific Railroad and found he could earn up to three times that for much shorter hours playing the cornet. As Steve Brown (1890–1965) later put it, not unkindly, Lopez became a professional musician because "he wanted to sleep in the daytime."[2]

Colleagues remembered Ray as forever hustling work, and photos of him in these years indeed show a young man on the go: handsome and alert, hair carefully slicked, he faces the camera with a confidence bordering on defiance. His enthusiasm and ambition would make him naturally curious about the wide world beyond the north shore of Lake Pontchartrain. A job in Chicago? A miracle, no less.

As Lopez recalled it, the band was doing a "ballyhoo" job, riding around downtown New Orleans on the back of a wagon, advertising a prizefight. "We'd stop at different corners in the heart of town and start playing," he said in a memoir published in 1976. "People would start dancing. I would pass out cards. That would go on for about three hours. Then we'd go to the club where the fights were being held and play between fights and get five dollars for the ballyhooing and fight, which wasn't bad in those days."[3]

At the corner of Canal and Royal streets, at the edge of the French Quarter, they ran smack into fate, in the form of vaudeville performers Johnny Swor and Charlie Mack. "Boys, y'all got steppin' music, y'hear me?" Mack called out to the band. "What do you boys call this music?" "New Orleans music," Lopez replied, unable to think of anything more original. Swor piped up: "This music has got to travel, man! How about coming north with us?"*

For the moment, at least, that seemed pretty far-fetched. A trip north would have to be based on more than just vague hopes and would have to be discussed, planned, worked out. But these two big-timers were a potential contact: Lopez gave them his card, cementing a friendship which was shortly to bear considerable fruit.

(Until recently, most reminiscences of New Orleans musical life in the century's first two decades have been highly romanticized. Emphasis was on black and Creole musicians, with whites assigned a secondary, carbon-copy role. A growing body of research has now begun to place early accounts by all parties in an accurate temporal and factual matrix. One effect has been a shift in balance: Storyville, long thought a jazz seedbed, is now seen as far less important than, for example, the turn-of-the-century brass band movement. Such figures as the cornetist Buddy Bolden, once imbued with almost superhuman powers, have been gradually stripped of their veneer of legend. It is in the work of such scholars as Karl Koenig, the late Henry Kmen, S. Frederick Starr, Don Marquis, Bruce Raeburn, Lawrence Gushee, Curtis Jerde, and Jack Stewart that the true history of New Orleans jazz has begun to emerge.)

Someone else had heard Lopez and Brown on what was fast turning out to be their lucky day. His name was Joe Gorham, and he was in town as manager for another vaudeville attraction, exotic dancer (actually more of a stripteaser) Myrtle Howard. Intrigued, he alerted his friend Smiley Corbett, manager of Lamb's Café in Chicago and a man always on the lookout for new and different talent. Swor and Mack, in their turn, also got in touch with Corbett, and with his boss, John Wilmes.

ARE YOU SURE BROWN BAND RIGHT FOR OUR PLACE? a puzzled Wilmes wired Gorham on March 27. ANSWER ME IF YOU CAN HAVE THEM COME ON. They signed in early April, back-dating the contract to March 1; on or about May 12, Lopez, Tom Brown, Gus Mueller, Bill Lambert, and pianist Edward "Mose" Ferrer, filling in temporarily for Arnold "Deacon" Loyocano (1889–1962), boarded the Chicago-bound Panama Limited with five round-trip tickets, bought with money sent by Corbett.

Their decision, though prescient, was not without cause. By this time, work for musicians of both races in New Orleans was beginning to dwindle with the economy. Dance orchestras still played for picnics, outings, and parades, and for balls and other social events in the large houses lining tree-shaded St. Charles Avenue, heart of the city's affluent Garden District. But there seemed no growth, little expansion of opportunity. For a while, both black and white bands had found plenty of seasonal employment at the beachfront restaurants, pavilions, and cabarets lining the south shore of 635-square-mile Lake Pontchartrain, less than five miles north of the city. Tom Brown's band was even one of the few that got

---

*Swor and Mack specialized in blackface comedy: within a few years, illness would force Swor to drop out of the act. He was replaced by Bill Moran. As Moran and Mack, the team became the Two Black Crows, one of the star show business attractions of the '20s.

to play on the excursion steamers that took tourists to the more exclusive north shore. But Pontchartrain's heyday ran in cycles, subject to sometimes violent weather and changing fashion. It ended forever when, in the mid-1920s, construction began on a seawall to extend the existing shoreline out several hundred feet, protecting it from storms and flooding—and leaving the former resort area stranded inland.

Chicago by 1915 had become the nation's second-largest city, with a population edging toward two million. The transcontinental railway system, completed in the mid-nineteenth century, had helped make it a major transport center and focus for industry. Its rapid growth, particularly after the disastrous fire of 1871, had attracted vast numbers of black and white laborers.

After the Civil War, according to one summation, "Chicago settled down to packing meat, shipping wheat, and making a fortune for Armour, Swift, Pullman, McCormick, William B. Ogden, and Marshall Field . . . its diverse manufacturing, shipping and export sales constituted a formidable economic base, and between 1860 and 1890 Chicago business flourished."[4]

In historian Charles Nanry's phrase, Chicago was "a city of violence and unrest, a city of action." Even before Prohibition turned bootleg liquor into a growth industry and spurred the rise of organized crime, Chicago was a "toddlin' town," a city—as native son Nelson Algren later put it—"on the make."

In those days, too, it still had something of the frontier about it, as if a post–Industrial Revolution urban landscape had been superimposed on a far simpler, more rural, image. That was the image seen and recorded by Jessie Binford, colleague of social activist Jane Addams, arriving from Marshalltown, Iowa, on a steamy July day in 1906. "Every other place was a saloon," she told oral historian Studs Terkel. "The streets were dirty. The air was heavy."[5]

Noisy, rough, teeming with energy and promise, it was—in the words of S. Frederick Starr—

> not only an economic center but also the most popular entertainment center in the Midwest. The many musicians who moved there from New Orleans to seek their fortunes found a fast life, a "sporting life" . . . Here musicians could live not as semipros, working at a "day job" to support themselves, but as full professional musicians.[6]

But to the five newcomers from New Orleans on that chill spring day in 1915 it seemed harsh, forbidding. "We felt scared, sober and alone," said Lopez. "When we hit Chicago we went directly to the Commercial Hotel at Wabash and Harrison. It was a dump! The 'el' made a turn right past our window . . . Lordy, it was cold. The damnyankee air cut through our thin suits . . . Everything was rush, rush, rush."[7]

The five "ragtime lugs," as Lopez affectionately remembered them, showed up at Lamb's, nervous but natty in silk suits and matching dark caps. They introduced themselves to Corbett, whom Lopez described as "big, fat and happy."

Not for long: "Where's your sheet music?" the manager asked. "In our heads," the cornetist answered with a grin.

He wanted to hear a sample . . . We played "Memphis Blues." We kicked off, and twisted that number every way but loose. We worked it up to the pitch that used to kill the folks back home—and found our way back as smooth as glass. We were right in there. It sounded fine.

But Corbett was white as a ghost. He roared: "What kind of noise is that! You guys crazy—or drunk?" Well, we played our novelty tune, "Livery Stable Blues." The cashier made faces and held her ears.

Corbett seemed to like that one. "Okay, men," he said. "You open tomorrow night. How do you want to be billed on the sign out front?" Brown's Band From Dixieland, they said. The sign, when it appeared, read only "DANCING HERE."[8]

By that time, the terms "Dixie" and "Dixieland" had long been understood as synonyms for the South. Whether taking its origins from the Mason-Dixon Line or, as various scholars have maintained, from a French-derived slang name for an old Louisiana ten-dollar bill, "Dixie" was in use well before the Civil War. The idea of "Dixieland," especially antebellum, as a lyrical paradise was central to the songs of Stephen Collins Foster, a key feature of late nineteenth-century minstrelsy, and persisted as a current in early twentieth-century popular songs. In wide public consciousness it was long a way of identifying things southern, related to a mythical Elysium—and it included various kinds of characteristic music. (This is discussed further in chapter 12.)

The Lamb's Café engagement started out dismally. The expected crowds didn't materialize. A string orchestra (which included a young French-born pianist named Jean Goldkette, of whom more in good time) quit in protest at the new band's raucous sounds, hurling at it the pejorative word "jazz." Loyocano recalled that "Smiley Corbett wouldn't even speak to us, he was so mad."

An outdoor photo probably taken that summer shows Loyocano on string bass, plus Brown, New Orleans clarinetist Larry Shields, Lopez, and Lambert, with vaudeville dancer-comedian Joe Frisco out front. They're smiling broadly, but the smiles are deceptive. The situation at Lamb's had been close to ruin only a short time earlier.[9]

Hearing that Swor and Mack were back in town, Lopez lost no time in getting over to the Palace Theater and telling his benefactors how badly things were going. The vaudevillians ("all you need is somebody to break the ice; that's the way it goes in this business") took quick remedial action, renting the entire restaurant one night after a performance of their Shubert show, Maid in America, bringing along its entire seventy-five-member road company cast. According to Loyocano, Charlie Mack also made a point of talking again to café owner Wilmes, urging patience and reassuring him that Brown's band represented something new, different—and bankable.

After that, at last, the word started to get around. Show people talked up Lamb's and the band, and the public, ever curious, came to investigate. The management obliged by adding a ten-cent cover charge and finally changing the sign outside to read BROWN'S BAND FROM DIXIELAND—DANCING.

What happened next, Lopez said in letters home to Steve Brown, was amazing: customers lined up for nearly two blocks every night, clamoring for a chance to get in; guest celebrities dropped by, making sure they were seen. The five boys from New Orleans were suddenly on the map in a big way.[10]

Loyocano remembered Lamb's as "a beautiful place, with tile floor and marble all around the sides; every note you'd hit would reverberate back about six times." It was a place for drinking and dancing: guests included dance innovators Vernon and Irene Castle, who spent an evening happily on the dance floor. "She had a live monkey on her shoulder," said Loyocano. "They danced a couple of times to the music, and said it was great: we could have gone with them, but who wanted to go?"[11]

Around this time the word "jazz" made its first official Chicago appearance as applied to the music dispensed nightly by Brown's band. Not surprisingly, accounts vary as to exactly how it came about—and even when it came into use among black musicians. A September 30, 1916, *Chicago Defender* article refers to a "jass band" led by black pianist-songwriter H. Benton Overstreet ("There'll Be Some Changes Made"), accompanying vaudeville singer Estella Harris. There is evidence of a black "Original Jazz Band," so billed, at the Dreamland Café the following year. Various musicians, among them whites Lopez, Brown, Loyocano, and their New Orleans colleague cornetist Dominick James "Nick" LaRocca (1889–1961), have offered different—sometimes contrasting—accounts of the word's use in billings.

Historian Dick Holbrook spent years researching the origins of the word, publishing his findings in *Storyville* magazine and other specialist periodicals. Among his conclusions:

- The word "jazz" seems to have been used, with or without explicit sexual connotations, in the San Francisco area well before the end of the nineteenth century. Actor William Demarest, growing up as a young musician, heard it there around 1908 as an exhortation to play with more energy. It was from Demarest, appearing in a New Orleans vaudeville theater in 1913, that Ray Lopez said he first heard it.
- A March 3, 1906, sports item in the *San Francisco Bulletin* refers to a promising baseball player as "very much to the 'jazz.'" Its meaning, as explained by the author, is somewhere between "pep" and "enthusiasm," and it turns up increasingly in such sports feature stories. Bert Kelly, Chicago banjoist, bandleader, and later club owner, also reported hearing it in turn-of-the-century San Francisco.
- An April 5, 1913, *Bulletin* article by Ernest J. Hopkins, under the headline "In Praise of Jazz," devoted nineteen column inches to this "futurist word which has just joined the language." By that time, according to many of Holbrook's sources, "jazz" was in common use throughout California, Arizona, and New Mexico and as far east as New England.
- Young white toughs in the notorious "Irish Channel" section of New Or-

leans were using the word early in the century as an undisguised synonym for sexual intercourse. Some brothels in that city were referred to as "jays'n houses."
- S. Frederick Starr states categorically that the word sprang from the Old Testament "jezebel," used in the late nineteenth century as a synonym for "prostitute." New Orleans usage soon shortened it to "jazzbel" or "jazz-belle," identifying pimps and other related males as "jazzbo" or "jazzbeau."
- The word surfaced in Chicago in late 1914 or early '15 and was widely documented at that time. Clarinetist Bud Jacobson later said he recalled seeing it advertising Art Arseth's local band at the Arsonia Café in 1914.[12]

What emerges from the various accounts and Holbrook's research is that (a) the new music, black and white, generated strong response, some of it of a decidedly sexual nature, in many who heard it; (b) the term "jass" (or "jazz"), whether as noun or transitive verb, was in wide common use by 1915; and (c) at least some of the time it was applied to various forms of dance music, alternately as an expression of enthusiasm and of disparagement.

Sometime in July clarinetist Gus Mueller got an offer to join Bert Kelly's six-piece band, playing for roller-skating and dancing over at White City amusement park. Kelly, from San Francisco, is now remembered mostly as owner-proprietor of Kelly's Stable, where clarinetist Johnny Dodds played a memorable engagement during the '20s. But in those days he was a new force in Chicago dance band circles.

Kelly wanted Mueller, and "Gussie," lured by the prospect of making more than three times what he was earning with Brown and Lopez, wanted to go. Finally, after much negotiation, Kelly sent to New Orleans for clarinetist Larry Shields (1893–1953), who impressed his new boss with his bright tone and fluid execution. But, in common with many early musicians of both races, he was a "faker," who couldn't read a note. Kelly, perhaps feeling he'd been had, was about to send the clarinetist home when someone suggested a compromise: why not simply swap reedmen? Mueller agreed, joining Kelly at White City while Shields came to work at Lamb's.[13]

The idyll didn't last long. On August 28, Corbett closed the café for renovations and enlargement, leaving the band scratching for work. Billing themselves "the Ragtime Rubes" (Al Williams replacing Bill Lambert on drums), they played some vaudeville houses with Joe Frisco, then accepted agent Harry Fitzgerald's offer to book them in New York as part of *Dancing Around*, a Broadway revue scheduled to feature Al Jolson.

The show never opened—but the "Rubes" picked up some New York casuals: two weeks in the foyer of the Century Theater, on Central Park West just north of Columbus Circle; a party at the Astor Hotel thrown by the legendary railroad mogul and bon vivant Diamond Jim Brady; a smattering of vaudeville dates. In the end, even these ran out, and "Brown's Band From Dixieland" officially split up.

Loyocano told New Orleans jazz historian Dr. Edmond Souchon in 1956 that the proprietors of Reisenweber's Restaurant, just down the street from the Century, were prepared at that point to hire the band. But all they could offer was twenty-five dollars per man per week, half of what the five musicians had been earning at the theatre, and far below what they'd wound up making after Lamb's had hit the jackpot in Chicago.

After some discussion they turned the offer down. Little more than a year later, the more practical Nick LaRocca took the Reisenweber's job; as will shortly be recounted, it made the Original Dixieland Jazz Band the talk of New York City. "We could have had all the gravy that the Dixieland Band got, because we were there before them," said Arnold Loyocano, with more than a hint of reproach at his colleagues' failure to recognize opportunity when they saw it.[14]

Black musicians, playing ragtime music, are known to have been active in Chicago as early as the first decade of the twentieth century. Novelty clarinetist Wilbur Sweatman, who later claimed to have made the first "jazz records" in 1912, is mentioned in print there in 1906. Ferdinand "Jelly Roll" Morton was working on the South Side in 1914–15. Perhaps most significant, the "Original Creole Orchestra," a transitional ragtime-based group whose members included cornetist Freddie Keppard and, at various times, clarinetists George Baquet and Jimmie Noone, is known to have played the Grand Theatre, on the South Side, in February of 1915. The flamboyant cornetist did well enough, in fact, to make Chicago his new home. New Orleans trombonist George Filhe had played at various South Side cabarets, and sometime between 1915 and 1917 Creole cornetist Manuel Perez reportedly led a band at the DeLuxe Café which included the respected New Orleans clarinet teacher Lorenzo Tio Jr.[15]

Chicago, burgeoning almost by the day, offered a better, freer life than had been available—especially to non-whites—down south. Clarinetist Johnny Dodds, who had married into a comfortable Baton Rouge Creole family, invested in Chicago real estate soon after his arrival at the start of the 1920s. Trombonist Honore Dutrey, his bandmate in King Oliver's Creole Jazz Band, was among several others who also owned property.

But up north, perhaps even more than in New Orleans, the races inhabited two different worlds: Chicago, like New Orleans, had segregated musicians' union locals (no. 10 for whites, no. 208 for blacks), and its jazz development followed similarly separate paths. Black cultural and social events covered generously in the weekly *Defender* seldom turned up in the white press.

Still, by 1916 the Original Creole Orchestra was sufficiently well known to have been approached—or so it was later claimed—by the Victor Talking Machine Co. to make records. Freddie Keppard, reportedly skeptical of the newfangled industry, turned the offer down.[16]

Tom Brown's success at Lamb's alerted white Chicagoans to what was, in content and effect (if not in exact performance style), the same kind of syncopated dance music as that dispensed by the Creole Orchestra. The sound of it, the ragtimey rhythm, was new, dynamic, and eminently marketable.[17]

Chicago promoters and proprietors rushed to find their own "bands from

Dixie." One of them, Harry James, remembered another little group he'd heard on a New Orleans visit; he got in touch with its drummer, Johnny Stein (né John Philip Hountha), offering ten weeks at the popular Booster's Club. Stein, well known at home as an organizer, brought a quintet to Chicago. On clarinet was Alcide "Yellow" Nunez (1884–1934), descendant of islenos (Canary Island immigrants), who had worked in early groups with Papa Jack Laine (of whom more presently), among others. On trombone was Eddie "Daddy" Edwards (1891–1963), another Laine alumnus; the pianist was Henry Ragas (1897–1919), with whom Stein had played jobs around town. On cornet was the aggressive and garrulous Dominick James "Nick" LaRocca.

By the time they arrived, in March of 1916, police had closed down the Booster's. But James, resourceful and persuasive, got them into the New Schiller Café, 318 East 31st Street on the South Side, only a block or two from what was shortly to become the Lincoln Gardens, headquarters of King Oliver's incomparable Creole Jazz Band.[18]

According to most reports it was little more than a dive; in the words of Ray Lopez "strictly a sawdust joint catering to a lot of pimps and whores." But if anything, that only added to the raffish charm of the whole enterprise, and Harry James's timing couldn't have been better. The perceived excesses of Chicago nightlife (later described in sometimes harrowing detail by journalists and social reformers) had loosed great indignation among guardians of public morals, among them the powerful Anti-Saloon League. By 1916, their campaign—which culminated four years later in the Eighteenth Amendment—was gathering steam.

On Saturday evening, April 29, a strike force of sixty upstanding Chicago ladies descended on café after South Side café, determined to beard the devil in his lair. One such den was Schiller's, by then featuring "Stein's Band From Dixie." "A line of taxi cabs radiated from the Schiller to the east, west, north, and south," one report said. "In front of the doors, a crowd of people fought for admission. A perspiring doorman held them back. 'Can't come in,' he shouted. 'We're crowded to capacity. Wait 'til some of the others come out.' " The ladies' "findings" duly appeared in the Chicago Herald, under the headline SIXTY WOMEN RIP MASK FROM VICE:

> It was impossible for anyone to be heard. The shriek of women's drunken laughter rivaled the blatant scream of the imported New Orleans Jass Band, which never seemed to stop playing. Men and woman sat, arms about each other, singing, shouting, making the night hideous, while their unfortunate brethren and sisters fought in vain to join them.[19]

For Stein, LaRocca, and company, this was advertising no money could buy. They were news, and such notoriety was sure to keep the customers coming. "After the sensation we created," said LaRocca, "other café owners sent to New Orleans for men who were supposed to play our kind of music. They imported anybody that could blow an instrument, and they all had 'New Orleans Jass Band' in front of their places."[20]

To an extent that was so—though it's remarkable how easily he "forgot" that Brown, Lopez, and three other guys had been there first and actually set the craze in motion. H. O. Brunn's dedicated but credulous *The Story of the Original Dixieland Jazz Band* mentions the Brown engagement at Lamb's as "a textbook of failures," which it clearly was not. It was, however, a story of opportunities not grasped because not recognized. Nick LaRocca, by contrast, knew the main chance when he saw it: and that, in turn, leads into a chain of events culminating in the sweeping popular success of the Original Dixieland Jazz Band.

Personality conflicts, reportedly between LaRocca and Stein, split the quintet up in May, shortly after the *Herald* vice-raid article appeared. LaRocca, Nunez, Edwards, Ragas, and newly arrived drummer Anthony Sbarbaro (1889–1969) went off to work elsewhere for Harry James. Stein reorganized with more New Orleans men: Larry Shields on clarinet, Jules Cassard (best remembered as composer of the pop song "Angry") on trombone, multi-instrumentalist Sigmund "Doc" Behrenson on cornet, and pianist-songwriter Ernie Erdman ("Toot Toot Tootsie, Goodbye"), who had been playing intermissions at Schiller's.

All were part of a broad pool of white ragtime musicians active in New Orleans before 1920; at its social and musical center was the drummer and musical contractor Jack "Papa" Laine. Born George Vital Laine in 1873, he realized early that anyone organizing a social event that needed music would have to turn to someone who could supply musicians to order, in groups large and small. He would be that "someone"—and some of the best white musicians in the city gravitated into his orbit. A few among very many: cornetists Johnny Lala, Manuel Mello, Pete Dietrans, Gus Zimmermann, Abbie Brunies, and Emile Christian (who later toured on trombone with the Original Dixieland Jazz Band); brothers George and Henry Brunies on trombones, clarinetists Shields, Nunez, and Nunzio Scaglione, and the Brown brothers, Tom (trombone) and Steve (tuba).

While Laine's were not the only good white bands in the city, they were among the most prominent. Laine even, tantalizingly, claimed to have sent a band to play at the great St. Louis Exposition of 1904. His "Reliance" bands were particularly active in the seasonal social life of the Lake Pontchartrain south shore. At one point, Arnold Loyocano reported, Laine ran a "kiddies' band" made up entirely of teenagers, which rehearsed in his front room while "Mama" Laine made certain they got enough to eat and drink.

In later life, until his death in 1966, Laine claimed to have had one of the only two bands in New Orleans to play in the ragtimey, cusp-of-jazz style. Similarly, he was loath to admit that black musicians had had any effect on his music—an attitude paralleling the claims of some black musicians that whites had no influence on them. To suggest that either group worked in isolation from the other contravenes an overwhelming body of scholarly and anecdotal documentation about New Orleans life, musical and social.

In this connection it is significant that several light-skinned blacks and Creoles, among them the admired trombonist and utility brass man Dave Perkins, worked regularly for Laine even while also playing in "colored" ensembles. Nor was he an isolated case: the clarinet-playing brothers George and Achille Baquet were among others who worked both sides of the racial street.

Laine's prominence as a contractor and organizer should not obscure his considerable abilities as a percussionist. A skilled bass drummer, he is also said by some to have developed the first bass drum pedal, a baseball on a stick attached to a rocker arm, and pioneered the use of wire brushes with a trap set.

Further Chicago engagements, at such spots as the Del'Abe Café, in the Hotel Normandy (Clark and Randolph streets) and the Casino Gardens (Kinzie and North Clark), reinforced both the group's cohesion and LaRocca's ambition. Nunez, apparently no paragon of personal reliability, clashed with the cornetist and left;[21] his replacement was Larry Shields.

According to Brunn, Nunez returned briefly to New Orleans, only to reappear in Chicago with a band including Stein, Behrenson—on trombone this time— Emile Christian on cornet, and Eddie Shields, clarinetist Larry's kid brother, at the piano. It appears to have been typical of New Orleans bands that many players were skilled on several instruments: Behrenson, for example, was also an excellent clarinetist, who recorded in New York with trumpeter Phil Napoleon and others.

The Casino Gardens ("The Theatrical Profession's Most Popular Rendezvous") drew good crowds and more than a few celebrities, among them Ziegfeld Follies headliners Fanny Brice, Will Rogers, and Bert Williams. Word about the new quintet was getting around, and among those who stopped in to hear what all the fuss was about was a fast-rising star named Al Jolson. Back in New York, he sang their praises to theatrical agent Max Hart—who promptly traveled to Chicago to hear them.

Or at least that's the way Brunn tells it in The Story of the Original Dixieland Jazz Band. Whatever the exact circumstances, January 1917 found LaRocca, Shields, Edwards, Henry Ragas, and Tony Sbarbaro in New York working a two-week tryout at Reisenweber's, the very deal that Tom Brown had spurned.

Therefore, and not without a certain irony, it was they, not Brown, who were the first to record the emergent New Orleans music. What, meanwhile, did Brown's "Band From Dixieland" sound like? It can't have been much different in substance from (though perhaps smoother in execution than) the jagged ensemble textures and nervous drive heard on the 1917–18 Original Dixieland Jazz Band records.

In a letter to Dick Holbrook, Ray Lopez's son Bert quoted his father as saying Brown's band differed from many others in that its musicians "tried to support each other and produce something melodic and rhythmical, instead of trying to drown each other out and make a lot of noise. Someone would come up with an improvised passage and they would work it into a sort of harmonious counterpoint behind the lead, who would be improvising off the melody."[22]

(Accurate description of jazz band ensemble textures presents some potential semantic confusions. The interweaving of cornet, clarinet, and trombone can be termed "counterpoint" only if the word is understood in its more modern sense, as "the horizontal aspect of music." This definition is found in Grove's Dictionary of Music and Musicians, which goes on to say that the word is used "more precisely . . . to describe music in which the chief interest lies in the various strands that make up the texture, and particularly in the combination of these strands and their relationship to each other and to the texture as a whole. It is the antithesis and at the same time the complement of harmony."[23] For scholars who prefer to use "counterpoint" in its more historical sense—i.e., the idea of a cantus firmus embellished by secondary lines—an alternative for jazz band use might be "polylinearity"; as a neologism, it has the singular advantage of being free of all historical baggage.)

Some recorded evidence of Brown and his musicians does in fact exist. The trombonist, for example, made records beginning in 1920, with Ray Miller's Black and White Melody Boys. His ensemble figures on their "Beale Street Blues," recorded for OKeh, are delivered in a broad manner very like that of Eddie Edwards on the Original Dixieland Jazz Band Victor records. "Beale Street Blues" also has that rarity, at least for 1921, a solo chorus. As the other horns provide a tango-like background figure, Brown plays an expansive twelve bars, as evocative of (the later-recorded) Kid Ory as of Edwards.

He is also with other bands on such slightly later records as Johnny Bayersdorffer's 1924 "The Waffle Man's Call" and Norman Brownlee's "Dirty Rag," made the following year. His marching-band conception of trombone as a kind of ground bass remained much the same for the rest of his life, as can be heard on records made in 1950 by a band led by New Orleans historian-guitarist Dr. Edmond Souchon and cornetist Johnny Wiggs, so it's reasonable to assume it hadn't changed much between 1915 and 1924.[24]

Lopez, too, made records. In contrast to Brown, he seems to have been an improvising player from the start, with a full tone, sound melodic conception, and relatively smooth rhythmic delivery. His recording career is discussed later in this chapter.

But it was Nick LaRocca who understood, from early in his career until the end of his life, the golden rule of promotion, advertising, and public relations: anything, repeated often and pervasively enough, will be believed, regardless of accuracy. Again and again he told his story in magazine and newspaper articles, in interviews, in countless letters to journals in and outside the music business, and finally to the all-too-believing ear of H. O. Brunn.

Accordingly, and because they were good, it was LaRocca and this band—the ODJB, as it has come to be known—that caught the public ear. This was the band that musicians came from near and far to hear and, because they'd never heard anything like it, admire and emulate. This was the band that prompted the brother musicians Jim and Fred Moynahan and their pal, jack-of-all-instruments Brad Gowans, to drive from Boston to Manhattan in a blizzard to catch them at Busoni's Balconnades. This was the band that would inspire Phil Napoleon, Miff Mole, and other young players to try the new ways with bands of their own; it would prompt countless "Fives," white and black (as well as white advertised as black in record catalogues), to emulate their recorded example; and that would so captivate young Leon Beiderbecke, growing up in Davenport, Iowa, that he had to go out, find a cornet, and teach himself to play LaRocca's kind of thrusting, inspiriting middle-register ensemble lead.

The influence of the ODJB on New Orleans musicians of both races has been extensively documented. "Dink" Johnson, drummer with the Original Creole Orchestra, confessed in a 1950 interview that he "had always wanted to play the clarinet since hearing Larry Shields." Joe Oliver and Kid Ory, still at home, fired the respected multi-instrumentalist and teacher Manuel "Fess" Manetta because, said Manetta, "they wanted to follow the format of the Dixieland Jazz Band and use only five pieces." Various other accounts tell similar stories.[25]

The irony is that LaRocca almost hadn't come north at all. Johnny Stein had assigned Eddie Edwards to find a cornetist for the Booster's Club engagement. The trombonist's first choice, he said in a 1959 interview, was capable, versatile Emile Christian. But Christian had taken a parade job and couldn't back out. Others were similarly indisposed or disinclined. So, said Edwards, they turned to brash, fiery LaRocca. "He was willing to go, [we] couldn't get anyone else who would go in a hurry, and we had to have him. But Nick was a good worker: never complained about working, never took the instrument down."[26]

Ray Lopez corroborated that account, adding some detail of his own: "I asked Edwards why he brought Nick along, when there were so many good hot cornet players he could have gotten, like Emile Christian, his brother Frank, Pete Dientrans, Joe Lala or Harry Shannon. Why Nick? He told me that Nick furnished the transportation, and Edwards guaranteed he would pay it back. It cost $125 for the five-man railroad fare to Chicago."[27]

LaRocca had begun his apprenticeship in New Orleans music, Steve Brown recalled, by sitting alongside Lopez on jobs and watching him play, then imitating him. Like Lopez, he even held the cornet in his right hand, fingering it with his left, instead of the more common reverse.

For a time, at least, Ray seemed to regard this hot-headed son of a Sicilian shoemaker as something of a protégé—though LaRocca, in fact, was his elder by several months. Only later did relations between them go sour—and prompt, one suspects, the dismissive tone so apparent in some Lopez remarks about the ODJB cornetist.

But it can truly be said that Edwards and Stein scarcely realized—at least at first—the value of their choice. LaRocca may or may not have been the best cornetist white New Orleans circles could offer, but he had something else, something every bit as valuable: a driving ambition, coupled with an instinctive understanding of *carpe diem*. None of the others seemed to grasp the potential of the situation in which they found themselves. And no other band ultimately benefited so much from the timing of events outside its compass.

Chicago was still wide open to southern hot musicians, with restaurants and cafés clamoring for New Orleans (or at least New Orleans *style*) bands. With this in mind, Tom Brown, Larry Shields, and Ray Lopez headed straight back to Chicago after the "Band from Dixieland" folded in Manhattan. "Deacon" Loyocano went home—only to return later in 1916 with yet *another* band, this one led by trombonist George "Happy" Schilling.

Before 1920, white musicians from the Louisiana city regularly joined the columns of blacks marching northward. Merritt Brunies (cornet) and Emile Christian (on trombone this time) were in the "Original New Orleans Jazz Band" that played Chicago in 1916–17. Christian's cornetist brother Frank was one of the "Five Southern Jazzers," which also included pianist-songwriter Ernie Erdman. "Yellow" Nunez stayed awhile before heading for New York, where he organized his cornet-less "Louisiana Five"; Tom Brown himself was in a five-piece band led by banjoist Clint Brush, which played Chicago in 1919. All used the cornet-clarinet-trombone-piano-drums instrumentation popularized by Brown's original band, and by now widely imitated by both black and white ensembles.[20]

Yet the reputation and preeminence of the ODJB persist, and with them a decided ambivalence in the way history seems to view its members. To their partisans, particularly those who heard the band in person in those first, heady days, they'll always be heroes. Listen to "Livery Stable Blues" and "Dixie Jazz Band One-Step," Rudi Blesh wrote in 1967, and "try—I dare you!—to *really* believe that it happened fifty years ago. I heard the Original Dixieland Jazz Band at Reisenweber's in 1917, and let me tell you—fifty years later I still don't believe it!"[29]

Whether in Blesh or in such musicians as Jim and Fred Moynahan, Phil Napoleon, Miff Mole, Brad Gowans (who remained a lifelong fan), or even the young Beiderbecke, this kind of breathless nostalgia is easy to understand. The epiphany—the moment of discovery, when it all comes together and makes sense—is deep and lasting, becoming more sharply etched in memory as years pass.

With LaRocca leading the way, the ODJB capitalized on its momentum. No one, if *he* had anything to do with it, would ever be allowed to forget that these five musicians were the first to put genuine hot music on records. His playing, like that of Shields and Edwards, was nimble and energetic. Even after more than three-quarters of a century, listening to the fierce drive he generates in the ensembles can be a heady experience.

Would that he had left it at that. In later years, after the band's reputation had faded (and a late-1930s reunion tour with comedian Ken Murray had flopped), he took another tack. In a flood of letters, magazine articles, and personal interviews he accused younger, more prominent musicians of trying to "cash in on this jazz craze started by the Original Dixieland Jazz Band." He also expressed contempt for anyone who tried to credit black jazzmen with any part in the creative process.[30]

Later outbursts became even more intemperate, as age, disappointment, and jealousy made their inroads. In growing rage, LaRocca watched as, led by Louis Armstrong, black musicians garnered increasing prominence as pioneers and innovators. Without doubt, memories of his own youth, saturated with the pain of growing up in New Orleans as part of the hated Sicilian underclass, came back ever more sharply in these years to haunt him and fuel his bitterness.

LaRocca kept up a drumfire of calumny until his death in early 1961. His personal papers, on file at Tulane's William Ransom Hogan Jazz Archive, are full of splenetic outbursts, dismissals of and attacks on blacks, and progressively fantastic claims for the Original Dixieland Jazz Band as the originators of jazz.

Popular views of jazz history in recent years, fueled by shifts in racial attitudes, have made it easy to disparage LaRocca's testimony as less the cri de coeur of a bitter and disillusioned man than simple racialist bluster. From there it's only a short step to discrediting the ODJB altogether as a noisy, unmusical novelty band which became famous and successful by little more than hustling and being white.

Such an interpretation, however widely held, is no more reflective of historical truth than LaRocca's more outrageous assertions. The Original Dixieland Jazz Band *was* important—and not only because it was the first to record.

Any attempts at assessment must begin with contemplation of the degree to which its first records are representative of the situation in which the musicians found themselves at their moment of initial popularity. Such performances as "Dixie Jass Band One-Step," "Livery Stable Blues," "Tiger Rag," and the rest are routined party pieces, delivered with a manic intensity which reflects the postwar times, the experience of having played to rapturous audiences in Chicago and New York—and, if Rudi Blesh is to be credited, a matter of recording-studio technical realities.

Talking with Blesh about his visit to Reisenweber's, fellow-writer James T. Maher asked why the band had taken its tempos so fast. "Rudi looked at me and said, simply, 'They didn't,' " Maher told the author. " 'When they went in the studio, they were given a choice: cut one chorus or play the whole thing faster.' He told me they didn't play as fast at Reisenweber's as they did on those first recordings."[31]

Or did they? The role of dancing in determining tempo is one of the factors least often considered in assessments of this band—and of much hot music recorded during subsequent years. As long as records were to be used "for dancing," as many labels announced, form was bound to follow function.

From myriad sources we know that dance steps popular at any given time influence the tempos at which orchestras played on records. But to what extent, if any, did the *time* restrictions on records influence the tempos at which bands played? And did this, in turn, influence what happened on the dance floor?

Jazz chroniclers have been singularly unhelpful, preferring to treat the music as something intended chiefly for listening—which it demonstrably was not. The interests of variety alone—not to mention the limits of dancers' physical endurance—would suggest that an average dance-floor number cannot have lasted much longer than three and a half or four minutes. (Broadcast airchecks of the 1930s, presenting bands on the job at ballrooms, dance pavilions, and restaurants, seem to confirm this. Rather than being a limiting influence, the time restrictions seem often to have compelled ensembles and soloists to condense and distill arrangements and to edit potentially discursive solo performances.)[32]

One factor which could not transfer from dance floor to recording studio was, of course, that of pure inspiration: with things going well, and the crowd's intensity level mounting, a band's tendency would be to keep playing, cranking the excitement to fever pitch. This was of course not possible on records until the advent of tape, and with it the long-playing record, in the 1950s.

Far from an incidental consideration, the matter of tempo and performance length is central to retrospective assessment of early jazz. If records constitute the only index—and apart from anecdotal material that is often the case—and the records do not represent a band's night-to-night performances, inaccuracy and misinterpretation are inevitable.

Within this context it is imperative that we listen well to Eddie Edwards as he tries to make an interviewer understand that the Dixielanders "often played soft: the clarinet would remain in the lower register, the drums would take to wood blocks and bass drums, the trumpet used a 'shell,' while I used a homemade mute on trombone." The band, he said, "often played soft and ratty—pronounced by the boys 'raddy'—so that the shuffle of [the] dancers' feet could be heard."[33]

None of this sounds like the band which careens and whoops its way through the 1917–18 Victor records. Similarly, the records yield little evidence of the beauty of Shields's clarinet playing, praised so rhapsodically by Gowans, Moynahan, clarinetist Rosy McHargue, and others. Overall, little about these records squares with the superlatives heaped on the band by those who heard it in the flesh.

Bruce Boyd Raeburn introduces yet another possible variable when he suggests that New Orleans bands away from home

> were removed from the context which had nurtured the style and changed accordingly to *suit their new audiences* [emphasis added]. Whether in live performances or on record, then, these bands were no longer tied to the functional imperatives of their hometown, and in seeking new functions in new places, they made numerous stylistic concessions.[34]

The daemonic energy of the ODJB's Victor records is consonant with the public mood of the World War I years. Again, Raeburn:

> Indeed, the band had caught the doughboys coming and going, first as the hottest ticket in New York City 1917–18 when the city served as a major port of embarkation, and later in London in 1919 at the Hippodrome and the Armistice Ball, where they played for the returning servicemen and their generals.[35]

The "Great War" left a new generation of disillusioned, worldly-wise Americans, determined to enjoy the pleasures of youth, and damn the consequences.

As John F. Carter's oft-quoted declaration in the September 1920 *Atlantic Monthly* so eloquently put it:

> The older generation had certainly pretty well ruined this world before passing it on to us. They gave us this thing, knocked to pieces, leaky, red-hot, threatening to blow up; and then they are surprised that we don't accept it with the same attitude of pretty, decorous enthusiasm with which they received it, 'way back in the eighties.[36]

What better vehicle to express the indignation and sense of independence those words implied than five musical roughnecks from down south, making such a racket that Mom and Pop, and just about everyone else over twenty-five, retreated in horror and dismay? Rock and roll, 1918 style.

Seventeen titles recorded by the band during its 1919–20 British tour reinforce Blesh's remarks about the differences between the band he'd heard at Reisenweber's and its Victor records, as well as Edwards's memories of dynamics and mood. The trombonist himself, called up for military service, couldn't go. In his place the band took Emile Christian, the same Emile who'd been asked to come north as *cornetist* back in 1916. He proved to be just as good on the deeper horn, filling in ensemble parts with verve and accuracy.

The English Columbia records, twelve-inch discs with a playing time of between four and five minutes, have been available only intermittently in this country and are therefore worth considering in detail for the performance clues they provide.[37]

On "I Lost My Heart in Dixieland," for example, the band drops to a nicely executed *pianissimo*, with LaRocca leading, Shields bubbling along merrily under his volume level, and Christian providing staccato punctuations in a manner immediately recognizable to anyone familiar with George Brunis's later work.

They handle the quasi-oriental accents of "The Sphinx" (Shields, stating the verse, seems to prefigure "Lament for Javanette," which Billy Strayhorn wrote and New Orleans–born Ellington clarinetist Barney Bigard recorded more than two decades later) with considerable polish and an unexpected variety of colors.[38]

"Tiger Rag" and "Sensation Rag" are set pieces, performed with little variation; but other numbers, including several pop songs, offer more latitude. "Satanic Blues" rolls along at an easy medium tempo ($\quarternote = 90$), making good use of ensemble dynamics. Shields's tone is broad and pure, his connection to such slightly later players as Sidney Arodin and Rosy McHargue easy to spot.

The ODJB addresses two waltzes, "I'm Forever Blowing Bubbles" and "Alice Blue Gown," with surprising delicacy: it never stops being a jazz band, the three-horn front line interacting exactly as on a 4/4 number, but the musicians work together here quite gracefully, a reminder that such skills were part of playing for dancing in these years. The testimonies of those who remembered King Oliver's Creole Jazz Band at the Lincoln Gardens not for its hot specialties, but for genteel renderings in 3/4 time, come readily to mind. There are some lovely moments, including Shields's low-register solo on "Bubbles" and a rather affectionate cornet lead on "Alice." How different, the atmosphere of these two numbers, from the clangor of the early Victor records!

The band's sixteen months in Britain witnessed the signing, on June 28, 1919, of the Treaty of Versailles. It was engaged to provide dance music for the Victory Ball, held at the Savoy Hotel and attended by such dignitaries as Marshal Ferdinand Foch, General Henri Pétain, American commander General John J. "Black Jack" Pershing, King George V and the rest of the British royal family, and many other crowned heads of Europe.

Brunn's account is particularly charming: "While the teddy bear atop Tony Sbarbaro's huge bass drum waved a miniature American flag, the New Orleans musicians opened the dance program with 'The Star-Spangled Banner,' astounding the multitude of guests by playing nearly as loud as the much larger [150-piece] Marine Band. When they stopped playing, cries of 'Bully!' and 'Viva!' echoed from the gaily decorated rafters of the hall."[39]

Back in New York, the band began recording again for Victor late in November 1920, with Bennie Krueger added on alto sax. This concession to current fashion, and the decision to record "Margie," a new popular song by the band's Indianapolis-born pianist, J. Russel Robinson (who had replaced Henry Ragas after the original pianist's sudden death), seem to have originated with the influential Victor executive and recording manager Eddie King. Though respected by industry colleagues for his market acumen, King has become something of a *bête noire* in the reminiscences of jazz musicians. No fan of jazz in general, he apparently nursed a special dislike of "hot" trumpet (and cornet) players—a distaste which was to have profound consequences in his mid-1920s relations with Bix Beiderbecke and others.

King's influence is readily discernible on "Margie" (which also, in traditional medley fashion, introduces Robinson's "Singin' the Blues"). LaRocca stands back from the recording horns (is he also muted?), playing the melody in near-unison with Krueger's much more prominent alto (or C-melody) sax. On the B side of the issued disc was another Robinson composition, the *faux*–Near Eastern "Palesteena." Together they added up to a hit record—and a formula soon duplicated in the unison melody passages of "Broadway Rose."

"Jazz Me Blues," recorded the following May, marks a return to a more straightforward format. LaRocca's lead is clear-toned, without growls, buzzes, or other tricks; just chime-like attacks, phrases placed neatly and economically on the beat, prefiguring Beiderbecke's OKeh record of seven years later. Even his second-chorus break has an almost Bix-like quality.

In the third chorus, Shields weaves a light-toned, supple obbligato around Krueger's straight alto lead, in familiar New Orleans fashion. No less interesting is his two-chorus clarinet solo on "St. Louis Blues," recorded three weeks later. No squawks or "laughing" glisses here: it's straightforward blues playing. "As far as I'm concerned," kid brother Harry Shields—also a clarinetist—told an interviewer in 1961, "there never has been a chorus played like that, before or since. I play it identically, note for note, even now: to me, it's one of the greatest [clarinet] choruses in jazz music."[40]

Most striking about this, as about "Royal Garden Blues" and the other late titles, is their relaxed, even elegant rhythm. The basic unit of measure is now unmistakably the quarter note, and Sbarbaro's full drum kit is clearly audible, laying down the broad four-to-the-bar which within the decade became associated, via records, with such New Orleans drummers as Paul Barbarin, Zutty Singleton, and Baby Dodds.

It's even more pronounced on the titles recorded for OKeh in 1922–23. There are passages—particularly in the closing choruses of a medium-tempo, swaggering "Tiger Rag"—when the ensemble achieves a rolling momentum comparable to that of the King Oliver band on its Gennett and OKeh records of the same years. Instead of the cut-time ($\rfloor$ = 127) feel of 1918, the tempo of this "Tiger Rag" is now better expressed as ($\rfloor$ = 220). Such changes had occurred not only for internal musical reasons but because fashions in dancing had changed.

Among the most neglected of all ODJB records are the six Victor big band titles of November 10, 1936. LaRocca was long since back in New Orleans, working in the construction business, when he got a call from New York agent William Morris: would he be interested in reorganizing the old band for a guest appearance in a Hollywood musical, to be called *The Big Broadcast of 1937*?

He turned it down. But the call got him thinking: perhaps, contrary to what he'd come to believe, the public *hadn't* quite forgotten the Dixieland Band and its postwar popularity. They were all still relatively young men, well under fifty. Why *not* give it a try?

He rounded up Shields, Edwards, and Robinson; all three had by now stopped playing music professionally. Only Sbarbaro, now known as Tony Spargo, was still working as a musician, playing with Phil Napoleon in New York.

They rehearsed, LaRocca put out the word, and on the evening of July 28, 1936, a reunited Original Dixieland Jazz Band made its debut on Ed Wynn's NBC radio show, winding up with a rousing "Tiger Rag." The fan mail poured in. According to H. O. Brunn, the band had "pulled more listeners for the Ed Wynn show than guest stars on fourteen previous programs." A comeback just might be in the offing.

At first, though, they'd have to adjust to changing times. Big swing bands were the rage, so LaRocca augmented his personnel with some young musicians and unveiled a fourteen-piece "Original Dixieland Band," of three trumpets (plus the leader), two trombones (Edwards not included), three saxes (plus Shields), and a four-man rhythm section.

An anomaly, yes, but a surprisingly listenable one. Shields embellishes and solos in a manner sometimes reminiscent of Benny Goodman—who, as a kid growing up in Chicago, had taken inspiration from him. His chorus on "Clarinet Marmalade," for example, is almost "modern." (The clarinetist is even better on six quintet titles, all remakes of the band's original "hits," issued around the same time under the name "Original Dixieland Five." On a small-band "Marmalade," he sets his solo entirely in his instrument's dark, handsome low register; his chorus on the 1936 "One-Step" employs an attack and gritty tone reminiscent of fellow New Orleanian Edmond Hall.)

LaRocca is another matter. The word most often used to describe his playing

21

on the early records is "ragtimey": it's usually meant as a synonym for stiff or stilted in the manner of marching-band players, typified (in its most extreme form) by Freddie Keppard on such records as the 1926 "Messin' Around," by Cookie's Gingersnaps, or "Stock Yards Strut," by his own Jazz Cardinals.

Though not adapting entirely, LaRocca has managed to smooth out the marching-band conception. The first eight bars of his "Clarinet Marmalade" solo, on the big band version, are almost Bix-like (or perhaps simply reflect that aspect of Beiderbecke's playing that was most LaRocca-like):

Nick LaRocca solo, "Clarinet Marmalade," 1936.

Consideration of the ODJB's entire recorded output is indispensable to understanding its historical role. A rather more versatile group than its detractors would have us believe, it handles a variety of material with musicality and even charm. The London records, and quite a few of the later Victors and OKehs, lead one seriously to question Gunther Schuller's assertion that "unlike jazz in general and many Negro musicians in particular, the ODJB was not able to absorb into its style the new popular songs coming out of Tin Pan Alley *en masse* in the early '20s."[41]

How, otherwise, to explain the grace of "I'm Forever Blowing Bubbles" or the restrained, careful dynamics of "I Lost My Heart in Dixieland"? Here, as in so many other instances, it is as if Schuller and other writers had only heard the first Victor records and were allowing the flummery and hype of marketplace promotion to take up the slack.

Responsibility for much of this can be laid squarely at LaRocca's door. The very absurdity of some of his later claims (inventors of jazz, originators of swing), coupled with his vitriolic racial pronouncements, has made him an easy target in a way far beyond anything generated by that other (and in some ways quite similar) master of rodomontade, Jelly Roll Morton.

(Not surprisingly, two of the most scornful dismissals of the ODJB came from Mister Jelly and Sidney Bechet, both men of Brobdingnagian egos and even larger assessments of their own roles in jazz history. Both, too, were New Orleans Creoles, who may well have grown up with the contempt for Sicilian-Americans so common in early twentieth-century Crescent City life. Furthermore, as British trumpeter-commentator Humphrey Lyttelton has observed, "it must always be borne in mind that black musicians who watched white contemporaries collect the richest rewards . . . are not exactly disinterested witnesses.")[42]

The testimony of such veterans as trumpeter Adolphus "Doc" Cheatham seems closer to the mark. "That stuff about black musicians being envious of the whites because of money and such, that's been kind of exaggerated," he said. "Some players might have felt that way, but most musicians I knew and worked with just accepted that *society was that way* [emphasis added]. If musicians were good, we learned from them, and they learned from us."[43]

There's also the matter of Bix Beiderbecke. Visiting Bix in 1931, his old friend Dick Turner found him bitter and disillusioned, complaining that life had passed him by, that there was no one on whom he could depend—and that hot music held no further charms for him. "Hell," he told Turner, "there are only two musicians I'd go across a street to hear now, that's Louis and LaRocca."[44]

Why LaRocca? Clearly, there had to be enough to the ODJB to engage a musical mind as demanding and questing as Beiderbecke's.

One of the most colorful, if comic, episodes linking the Original Dixieland Jazz band to Tom Brown and Ray Lopez before them concerns authorship of the "Livery Stable Blues."

In 1917 "Yellow" Nunez, who had played clarinet with the band in its Johnny Stein days before going on to form his own Louisiana Five, had the piece, with its characteristic barnyard effects, published in Chicago, listing himself and Lopez as co-composers. LaRocca countered by having Leo Feist, in New York, publish the piece (as "Barnyard Blues") with him as composer; he also filed suit against Chicago music publisher Roger Graham, who had published the Nunez version.

The hearing was held in U.S. Federal Court, Northern District of Illinois. Accusation, distortion and contradiction, charge and countercharge, saturated the entire ten days, all in a tone of unremitting venom. At times the heated exchanges veered close to farce. "Expert" witnesses produced learned analyses of the squawks and horse-whinnies used in the number. One critic took the stand to suggest that all "blues numbers" were alike anyway and could be played simultaneously with "perfect harmony."

Chicago newspapers had a wonderful time with it. DISCOVERER OF JAZZ ELUCIDATES IN COURT, proclaimed the *Daily News*, gleefully describing everything from a Nunez declaration that "Jedge, blues is blues" to LaRocca's purple-striped shirt and green jacket.

In the end federal judge George A. Carpenter, weary of such antics, threw the whole matter out, unresolved. Perhaps the most lasting effect of the furor, in fact, was a lifelong, unstinting hatred between Ray Lopez and Dominick James LaRocca.

Who wrote the "Livery Stable Blues"? Who, in the end, cared? The piece, like the brouhaha surrounding it, quickly sank from view. It surfaced briefly again in 1924, when Paul Whiteman opened his February 12 *Experiment in Modern Music* at Aeolian Hall with "Livery Stable Blues." Whiteman clearly intended it as illustration of how "primitive" jazz had been before he and his orchestra came along to civilize it—but right away he was worried.

"The audience listened attentively to everything and applauded whole-heartedly from the first moment," he wrote. "When they laughed and seemed pleased with 'Livery Stable Blues,' the crude jazz of the past, I had for a moment the panicky feeling that they hadn't realized the attempt at burlesque—that they were ignorantly applauding the thing on its merits."[45]

Back in Chicago in 1917 after his New York adventures with the "Ragtime Rubes," Ray Lopez called on old pals Gus Mueller and Bert Kelly and soon found himself working for Kelly at Al Tierney's Auto Inn, at 338 East 35th Street, near Calumet, on the South Side.[46]

(Contrary to widely held impression, the South Side in those pre-1920 years was not a black ghetto. Some of the most elegant white homes were to be found on Prairie Avenue and Grand Boulevard, only two blocks east of the predominantly black neighborhoods of State Street and Indiana Avenue. The checkerboard pattern held, too, in the dance halls and clubs along State Street. Some, like the Auto Inn, featured white entertainment, while others, such as the Royal (later Lincoln) Gardens, at 459 East 31st Street nearby, offered black bands. A bit later, the Grand Terrace ballroom booked black bands, but its clientele remained white.)

When, late in 1916, Tierney announced he was temporarily closing the Grand Auto Inn, Lopez, as usual, had an ace in the hole: he'd met and become friends with vaudeville star Benny Fields, who now steered him into a job at the Wyn-Clif Inn, the rathskeller of the Windsor Clifton Hotel in the Loop. "The Wyn-Clif Inn became a ball of fire, same as the Lambs [sic] had been," he told Dick Holbrook. "All the show people that were in town would come down and keep the joint 'jumping with joy.' " They backed the trio of Fields, Jack Salisbury, and Benny Davis and had plenty of featured spots as well.

Before long, the whole troupe began doubling down the street at the prestigious Keith's Majestic Theatre. In letters to Holbrook, Lopez described their opening night, with himself featured with the pit orchestra during the Fields-Salisbury-Davis specialty numbers.

Blossom Seeley, the headliner, was in her dressing room when they went into their routine, he said, and it wasn't long before the cheering and applause reached her ears.

> She came running to see who we were, and hearing the band playing like they never played before or since. They were doing their last number, which was *Darktown Strutters' Ball* . . . a big hoo-rah jam number where I stood up on a chair in the pit and waved a derby hat over the bell of my cornet, producing a weird effect (so I've been told) . . . I had transformed that staid pit band into a really hot jazz band—me and my little old cornet . . . she signed us up then and there and said she would send for us as soon as she got back to New York and arranged for a new act to open in the fall. This she did.[47]

That association carried Lopez far afield in the next four years as a member of Blossom Seeley's traveling act. It's clear from the billing that he was being presented not as an accompanist but as "Mister Jazz Himself," an attraction in his own right. An advertisement in the *New York Clipper* for August 22, 1917, announcing their appearance at the New Brighton Theater in Brooklyn, identified the Seeley troupe as "a distinct combination comprising class, originality and the highest extreme in musical and vocal ability. *Not a jazz band* [emphasis added], but a Group of Talented Artists. Every one a Star."[48]

Not a jazz band. By this time, the craze set in motion by Brown's band in Chicago (and subsequently taken to unprecedented heights by LaRocca and the ODJB in New York and London) had already become sufficiently widespread—and, presumably, sufficiently noisy—to prompt Miss Seeley and her handlers to distance themselves from it.

Five-piece instrumental groups had blossomed from Bangor to Bakersfield, many among them blatant attempts to emulate the bells-and-whistles "nut" side of the ODJB, and an even more boisterous quintet led by New York drummer Earl Fuller at Rector's, on Broadway. Most, judging from numerous records of this type made by both white and black groups between 1919 and 1922, seemed to have little to commend them save exuberance.[49]

Blossom Seeley didn't record until 1921, said Lopez, and

> [i]n the meantime, all the other gals were grinding out hit after hit and established themselves as recording artists. Furthermore, the Trio had offers to make some records without Seeley, but she stopped that, which brought on a lot of dissension. The act was a hell of a hit from coast to coast and no doubt the Trio would have been a big hit on records, but they never had a chance to show.[50]

In receiving featured billing, "Mister Jazz Himself" may have been the very first jazz *star*—that is, the first hot player accorded a featured role in vaudeville outside an organized band, and singled out as such by the press. The ODJB certainly generated more attention, but largely as an ensemble. LaRocca, Shields, and the rest never got the kind of individual billing accorded Lopez.

In 1920, after three years on the road in vaudeville, "Mister Jazz Himself" returned to Chicago, joining banjoist Clint Brush, for whom Gus Mueller had worked before quitting to join Paul Whiteman that spring. Lopez had done well in Chicago, and it had done well by him. But once a southerner, always a southerner: he'd never really adjusted to either the weather or the ways of the North. And one snowy evening in December 1920, destiny reached out again—as it had with Swor and Mack, and again with Benny Fields—to change his life.

"I had fought my way to an El station in the middle of a blizzard," he told Holbrook, "when I heard a fellow calling me. I looked around. I didn't know him. He called me over and we went into a Thompson open-all-night restaurant and he told me who he was and asked me if I would like to be in California on a night like this."

The stranger turned out to be Mike Lyman, whose brother Abe, a drummer, had contracted to lead a band at the Sunset Inn in Santa Monica. They needed a cornetist, and if "Mister Jazz Himself" was interested the job was his, at a handsome $150 a week plus tips. If Lopez hesitated it wasn't for long; the cold, and his doctor's advice to seek a warmer climate or risk chronic pneumonia, quickly overcame any doubt. A week later he boarded a train for Los Angeles, sunshine, and the next phase of a career that continued well into the 1930s.

Though never a strong reader, Lopez seems to have been technically proficient enough to become a favorite of both Lyman and, later, Gus Arnheim. He was professional, likable, and capable of graceful, even elegant, "hot" playing.

He is on Lyman records made between 1922 and 1926, soloing often and well. On "Those Longing for You Blues," done for the rare Nordskog label in mid-1922, Lopez works his derby hat in what is surely his "Mister Jazz" fashion, delivering his figures with a ragtimey even-eighth-note syncopation redolent of early LaRocca. His best moment is a descending break in the final ensemble, notable for its articulation and drive.

Given the rancor and low comedy of the "Livery Stable Blues" dispute with LaRocca, it's perhaps gently ironic that Lopez gets composer credit on the label of "Weary Weasel," an obvious "Tiger Rag" spinoff made by Lyman for Brunswick on July 27, 1923. His break and plunger solo are rhythmically "hot," in the dotted-eighth-and-sixteenth manner of the early '20s, with little trace of the stiff execution of the 1922 date.

Lopez himself cited Lyman's February 1, 1926, "Shake That Thing" as one of his best records. Both he and the band play with surprising abandon, the new technology of electrical recording bringing his tone across with enhanced clarity. On "Twelfth Street Rag," something of a hit for Lyman, he tears off a half-chorus similar in concept to that of fellow New Orleans cornetist Natty Dominique.

But perhaps Ray Lopez's most tantalizing record is "New St. Louis Blues," done the same day. If his solo is a bag of period mute tricks, redolent of what Louis Panico had been doing with Isham Jones, his counterlines in the beginning and closing ensembles are quite another matter; played open, they leap and dart around Howard Fenimore's lead with grace and agility.

The contrast between these two sides of Lopez's playing suggests that the various devices and muted tricks were conventions, expected and appreciated by audiences which, after all, paid the salaries of such bands. Panico, discussed fully elsewhere, presents a parallel: a fine and accomplished trumpet player, widely respected by fellow-musicians, whose main contribution to the Jones orchestra usually involved growls, smacks, whinnying laughter, and other novelty trappings.

As with the ODJB, the funny-hat stuff came with the job, part of the function of a dance band as an entertainment unit. Panico and Lopez, good journeyman professionals both, understood their roles. The jazz cultist's idea of the hot musician as a being apart, an uncompromising specialist who viewed the idea of entertainment with ill-disguised scorn, lay far ahead.[51]

The departure of Ray Lopez brought to an end the first flowering of hot music in Chicago, at least as played by whites. Whatever the nature of their music, the men of "Brown's Band From Dixieland" and of the ODJB had helped open a roadway between New Orleans and the sprawling, disorderly metropolis on the Lake Michigan shore. As work opportunities down south dwindled, ever more musicians of both races came to view the "toddlin' town" as a place of virtually limitless promise. They came and kept on coming, and promise soon enough became reality—a reality beyond Ray Lopez's wildest imaginings.

2

The New Orleans Rhythm Kings

Winter 1919 was a restless time for Americans. The Great War might be over at last, but life across the United States was far from peaceful.

More than four million white workers walked off the job nationwide, many protesting mass black immigration from the South, which had flooded the industrial North with cheap labor. Resentment flared into bloodshed as race riots swept twenty-five U.S. cities between April and October, killing thirty-eight in Chicago alone and prompting NAACP spokesman James Weldon Johnson to speak of the "Red Summer" of 1919.

His phrase cut two ways. National hysteria, fed in large part by the riots, turned against foreigners—in particular anyone suspected of sympathy with the Bolsheviks, who had overthrown the government of Russian czar Nicholas II. Red summer spawned, at least for a time, a nationwide red scare.

Zealots were out in force. The temperance movement had won a constitutional amendment banning sale and consumption of alcohol, effective in January. But suffrage, too, had triumphed: it looked as though 1920 would bring women the vote at last.

U.S. Army Captain E. F. White made headlines by flying nonstop from Chicago to New York. Jack Dempsey became heavyweight champion of the world, and the "Black Sox" scandal rocked baseball. Theodore Roosevelt and Andrew Carnegie died. H. L. Mencken tickled readers' fancies with his spirited *The American Language*; Sherwood Anderson published *Winesburg, Ohio*. In September, President Woodrow Wilson, disappointed and drained after Versailles, suffered a stroke that left him an invalid.

And in New Orleans, Albert "Abbie" Brunies got a telegram.

It was from his friend, drummer Mike "Ragbaby" Stevens. In common with dozens of other local musicians, Stevens had gone north to Chicago looking for better work than New Orleans could provide. He'd landed a job for a band at a place called the Campbell Gardens, at Campbell and Madison just west of the Loop—so named for the great downtown circuit of the city's elevated railway.

His first thought in putting a band together was of Abbie, who had been playing cornet and leading bands for "Papa" Laine at the Bucktown and Milne-burg resort areas on the Lake Pontchartrain south shore. Come on up, he wired, and bring the kid brother with you. The "kid brother," two years Abbie's junior, was George, who at age eight had played his E♭ alto horn in Laine's Junior Band, then switched to trombone as soon as his arms were long enough to reach the slide positions.

The kid, just seventeen, was keen to go, but Abbie had his doubts. He was doing okay driving a taxi part-time and had just begun playing at the Halfway House, out on City Park Avenue. Why toss it all over for what could easily turn out to be an expensive and time-consuming wild goose chase? As George succinctly put it many years later, "He didn't want to walk [railroad] cross-ties back."[1]

Abbie turned it down. Hey, he said to the kid, how about asking Paul Mares? Bet he'd be game to try something. Born in 1900, Mares was nineteen and had been in the marines briefly during the war. He'd come home and gone to work in his father's muskrat pelt business, all the while playing casual jobs around town on trumpet. He just might jump at a chance to travel.

"So I says Paul, I says, Abbie don't want to go to Chicago and I'm kind of leery, I'm afraid," George recalled. "Paul says, 'Man, give me that wire. I'll go.' So Paul went up [to Chicago] and introduced himself to Ragbaby Stevens and Ragbaby liked him . . . and Paul got the railroad fare from his father and sent me $60.

"I took my little mackinaw, my cap, my cowlick, and my horn in this big piece of paper, newspaper—I didn't have a trombone case then, I'd bought the horn in a hock shop—and I came on to Chicago and went right to the Campbell Gardens."

His excitement at being there almost cost him the job on his very first day. "We played the first set and went over pretty good," he said. On his first break he went outside for a breath of air—and gasped in astonishment. "It was snowing like the dickens," he said. "I [had] never seen it. I [had] seen it on Christmas cards, but I thought it was fictional. So I started rolling around in the snow and clowning and throwing snowballs and having a ball.

"So the boss comes out and says, 'You're on,' and so I says, to hell with the job, I says. I quit. I didn't have a dime in my pocket, [but] I was so happy. So the guy says, 'Well, all right, have a little fun and then come in and play.' So I missed a set and I went back in, and from that time the job was all right."[2]

Then and there, the kid from New Orleans decided he liked life up north. During an after-hours visit to the Blatz Palm Garden on North Avenue (shortly to become the Pekin Cabaret-Theater), he and Mares met drummer Frank Snyder, pianist Elmer Schoebel, and C-melody saxophonist Jack Pettis, in from Danville, Illinois. He also met a young Chicago cornetist named Francis Joseph Spanier,

29

Kid Muggsy to his friends: he knew very few tunes, said George, but oh boy, did he love boxing.

Not long after that, another group of young white New Orleans musicians hit the road, but in a slightly different direction and under rather different circumstances. Vaudeville "Shimmy Queen" Bee Palmer opened her 1921 tour of Orpheum theaters throughout the Midwest backed by trombonist Santo Pecora, drummer Johnnie Frisco, clarinetist Leon Roppolo, and, on cornet, seventeen-year-old Emmett Hardy. She called them her "New Orleans Rhythm Kings."[3]

Beset with public criticism and bad reviews, mostly aimed at the risqué side of Miss Palmer's onstage antics, the troupe broke up in Peoria, Illinois. Pecora went on to Chicago, but Hardy and Roppolo doubled back to Davenport, where they found work with local bandleader Carlisle Evans.[4]

By early summer several of the young New Orleans men were playing aboard Streckfus Line riverboats working the upper Mississippi as far north as Minnesota. Accounts differ as to who made the contact and which musicians were involved on which boat, but George Brunies remembered working at first with Mares and Pettis "and some guys from St. Louis." In Davenport, the Carlisle Evans band finished up for the summer and Hardy left town, apparently to join Brunies and others playing for drummer Albert "Doc" Wrixon on the Streckfus stern-wheeler *Capitol* (the same vessel that had brought Louis Armstrong north with Fate Marable's band two summers before). It's unclear whether Roppolo joined his pals on the *Capitol* right away or hung around Davenport, where he reportedly had a girlfriend.

By the end of June, Brunies, Hardy, Roppolo, Pettis, banjoist Louis Black, and perhaps Mares appear to have been working in and out of the Davenport–Rock Island–Moline area, at least part of the time on the riverboats.

Mares was already on the lookout for other opportunities. He went often to Chicago, staying at the home of Tommy Harrison, a police captain whose "beat" was the Loop. Harrison numbered among his friends Mike Fritzel, manager of the Friars' Inn, a cabaret at 343 South Wabash Street in the Loop, and through him had become aware of the still-healthy market for New Orleans music.

Fritzel had been managing Chicago clubs for some time and knew the value of a good band. As proprietor of the Arsonia, at 1654 Madison, near Ashland, he'd used both black and white units. One such included riverboat trumpeter Tony Catalano, Earl Wiley on drums, and the talented, if forgotten, clarinetist Roy Kramer; another was reportedly an instrumental ragtime ensemble featuring such New Orleans Creole musicians as cornetist Manuel Perez and clarinetist Lorenzo Tio Jr.[5]

Harrison got Mares together with Fritzel, and the result was an offer: if the trumpeter could put together a band of good New Orleans men, he could work at the Friars' Inn six nights a week, for a very decent ninety dollars a week per man.[6]

(Other accounts have Fritzel booking Bee Palmer into the Friars' Inn, backed by Mares and a band of New Orleans musicians. After a few weeks of so-so business she and her husband, pianist Al Siegel, reportedly decamped, leaving Mares to make of the job what he could.)

Ben Pollack recalled hearing Miss Palmer's original "Rhythm Kings"—Hardy,

Roppolo, Pecora, Siegel, and Frisco—jamming at a Chicago area theater, and on another occasion working at the Cascades Ballroom in a slightly different combination that also included Brunies and Mares. "They literally 'rocked us over,' " he said in a 1936 reminiscence.[7]

Marshall Stearns, writing in *Down Beat* the same year, quoted Pettis, Snyder, and others as saying that various of the musicians had been working at such spots around town as the Erie Café and Blatz Palm Garden, and that the Friars' Inn group took shape gradually, almost from job to job. At first, they said, the clarinetist was riverboat musician Johnny Provenzano; Roppolo was still in Davenport. Other witnesses, Catalano among them, seem to reinforce this view of a circle of musicians getting to know one another through working together in various configurations over a matter of weeks.[8]

One way or another, Mike Fritzel's Friars' Inn ("Land of Bohemia Where Good Fellows Get Together") presented a major opportunity, and Mares apparently grabbed it. From Wrixon's *Capitol* riverboat band he got Brunies and Roppolo. Soon, Arnold Loyocano, who had been in Chicago on and off since coming north with Tom Brown six years before, signed on. Though he'd played piano with Brown, he was equally able on bass and stepped happily into the job. Loyocano then summoned banjoist Lou (sometimes Lew) Black from Davenport. "He jumped at it like a hungry fish after the bait," the bassist said. Pettis, Schoebel, and Snyder were available and willing.[9]

A single rehearsal made it clear that only pianist-composer Schoebel could read music with any speed or accuracy. Accordingly, he became *de facto* arranger and straw boss. "He'd give them a note," said Loyocano, "and say, 'This is your note and this is your note,' and so they'd blow it. He'd pick out the different notes that the different instruments would play in harmony."[10]

Elmer Schoebel is a key figure in Chicago jazz. Born September 8, 1896, in East St. Louis, Illinois, he served his musical apprenticeship in silent-movie houses and as accompanist to vaudeville singers. Several of his compositions, among them "Blue Grass Blues," "The House of David Blues," and "Railroad Man," were widely played by early bands; a few, including "Prince of Wails" (a punning salute to the future king Edward VIII, who in the '20s was a jazz fan and avid amateur drummer), became jazz standards. He collaborated with Gus Kahn and pianist Ernie Erdman on the pop song "Nobody's Sweetheart," introduced at the Friars' Inn more than a year before its 1924 publication. Like Jelly Roll Morton, Schoebel worked for the Chicago-based Melrose Music Co., writing arrangements and plugging songs.[11]

The new band called itself the Friars Society Orchestra, and from late 1921 until they left the Friars' Inn early in 1923, it was a pivot of Chicago's growing jazz life. What it played was hot music, and clearly for dancing; it may not have sounded like what Isham Jones and his star trumpeter Louis Panico were offering at the College Inn, or the music of the Benson Orchestra of Chicago or any of the other white bands around town with "hot" aspirations. Nor did it much resemble the rattle-and-clang of the Original Dixielanders and their imitators.

This band was more relaxed, looser. In contrast with the insistently "peppy" rhythm of so many other groups, these musicians generated momentum by riding the beat; collectively and individually, their phrasing seemed closely related to the blues, but in both its texture and airy buoyancy it was also quite unlike that of the King Oliver Creole Jazz Band, which started making records for Gennett a few months later.

Drummer Ben Pollack, then working casuals around town, had been an admirer of Brunies, Pettis, and Mares since jamming with them out at Fox Lake, Illinois, a popular resort area up near the Wisconsin state line. His soon became a familiar face around the Friars' cellar bandstand at Wabash and Van Buren. Other young whites were frequent visitors: nineteen-year-old Bix Beiderbecke, then faring none too well at Lake Forest Academy, would bring his battered cornet along and ask to sit in playing "Angry." At times, said Mares, it seemed to be the only song he knew.

Don Murray, newly enrolled at Northwestern, often showed up with his tenor sax; Hoagy Carmichael, ostensibly studying law at Indiana University but clearly more interested in playing hot piano, took over the keyboard now and then from Schoebel. In his autobiographical *Sometimes I Wonder*, published in 1965, Hoagy furnishes a vividly evocative description of a night at the Friars' Inn:

> The place smelled just right—funky, run-down, sinister and dusty. Leon Rapollo [sic], the clarinet player, was wiggling into action in his seat . . . then George Brunies, the trombonist, picked it up and blasted his notes jerkily, with penetrating brassy tones. The notes surprised me at unexpected times and in unexpected places . . . George bounced in his seat like a trained seal, watching my reaction. I was biting on my tongue and looking very serious and idiotic.[12]

There were personnel changes: Frank Snyder left, supplanted by the more adept Pollack. When Pettis went on tour with a vaudeville troupe Pollack got a friend, the talented Voltaire "Volly" De Faut, to replace him. At one point Arnold Loyocano took a couple of nights off; his sub—permanent, as things turned out— was Tom Brown's brother Steve, shortly to emerge as the most admired of early New Orleans string bassists, white or black.

At eight pieces, a four-horn front line and four-man rhythm section, they were the real thing, an honest-to-goodness New Orleans–style ensemble, and any white musician in Chicago with even a passing aspiration to play hot music had to hear them. For dozens of music-happy teenagers all over the city they were a revelation: Jimmy McPartland, Frank Teschemacher, Bud Freeman, Benny Goodman, Dave Tough, Gene Krupa, Joe Sullivan, and others, none older then seventeen, came to listen, bought their records, and avidly tried to reproduce what they heard. They also adopted "Nobody's Sweetheart" as a kind of unofficial anthem.

Researching a magazine piece on Don Murray, historian Warren Plath reported questioning a variety of Chicago musicians: "It was noted that no mention was made by informants of the oft-reported almost ritualistic treks to the South Side where so many of the great black stars of the day held forth. While there were indeed some visits south of the Loop, another club had just opened up that fascinated the youths. It was the Friars' Inn . . . and a new group, to be known later as the New Orleans Rhythm Kings (NORK), was astounding the locals".[13]

But what was it, exactly, that they were hearing? The first records, eight titles done for Gennett August 29–30, 1922, and issued as the "Friars Society Orchestra, direction Husk O'Hara [sic]," reveal a band working comfortably within a well-defined idiom—an idiom, moreover, familiar to all of them.[14]

(The first New Orleans bands recorded in their home city two years later by Ralph Peer [discussed in detail in chapter 4] are unmistakably working the same way, using much the same repertoire. Heard in tandem with those records—by cornetists Johnny DeDroit, Johnny Bayersdorffer, and Stirling Bose, clarinetist Tony Parenti, pianist Norman Brownlee, and others—the Friars Society Gennetts are clearly part of a common, shared musical outlook.)[15]

The repertoire on the first Gennett session included three old standbys often played in New Orleans ("Panama," "Tiger Rag," and the much fought-over "Livery Stable Blues"), two Schoebel originals ("Oriental," "Discontented Blues"), one collective effort ("Farewell Blues"), and, as an opener, a number ("Eccentric") penned by J. Russell Robinson, pianist with the Original Dixieland Jazz Band, although the ODJB never recorded it.

The ensemble is light, supple; the tenor saxophone, far from rare in New Orleans bands, adds body and softens the texture—though on those titles where Pettis plays C-melody ("Panama," "Livery Stable Blues") he blends rather less well.

Mares clearly admires Joe Oliver and wears his admiration proudly. Nothing remarkable here: it is what jazzmen have done throughout their music's history, taking inspiration from a favorite player in building a personal style. The players of 1922 had few available role models; the smorgasbord available to novice instrumentalists only a decade later did not yet exist. Jazz, moreover, was not yet a soloist's domain, and few truly distinctive styles had emerged. Oliver's terse, punchy lead playing spoke to Mares most forcefully, as it did to young Louis Armstrong, to Tommy Ladnier, and to George Brunies's boxing buddy, Kid Muggsy Spanier.

The Friars band achieves considerable drive in such moments as the final ensemble of "Tiger Rag." But it is above all a tuneful band, its center of gravity melodic before it is rhythmic. Tone and intonation play key roles: on the whole, the Friars Society records are more consistently in tune than anything recorded by the Oliver ensemble.

The notion of tunefulness implies particular attention to the aesthetics of sound. The tutti passages on "Farewell Blues," with their echoes of railroad whistles, the carefully arranged interludes and fadeout ending on Schoebel's unusual "Discontented Blues," bespeak rehearsal and behind-the-scenes work aimed at achieving a polished and varied band sound. Nothing on any record by a black band of the early '20s is anywhere near as aesthetically venturesome.

Marshall Stearns, among the most prescient of first-generation jazz historians, observed in his September 1936 *Down Beat* article that the music of the Friars Society Orchestra "was a new genre," characterized by "an improvement in technique, less glissando to cover unsure attack, less vibrato to hide errors in pitch, less forcing, and inevitably less emotional fervor and intensity. It has always been the white musician's gain and loss, that with improved technique, less of the primitive emotion exists. The explanation of this may be found, perhaps, in the difference in temperament."[16]

Clarinetist James "Rosy" McHargue, discussing the subject in a 1988 conversation, remembered the 1923 Oliver band in person as sounding "kind of raucous and rough to me. No organization. The parts didn't fit . . . they weren't always in tune, there were wrong notes." He went on to laud such groups as the Original Memphis Five, in which the parts fit very well indeed, but which were noticeably short on visceral intensity, what Stearns termed "primitive emotion."[17]

The Friars' Inn band seldom played loudly, said Loyocano, because the room's acoustics made extremes of volume impossible. "You could almost reach up and touch the ceiling. If you played loud you'd drive everybody out of the place." So from the start the band got used to making its point without raising its collective voice, achieving intensity at moderate volume. Mares, in fact, played most of the evening with an old felt hat draped over the end of his trumpet, and a slice cut out of it to let the air through.[18]

Above all, there was Roppolo. In the context of 1922, with the art of jazz solo playing still in its infancy, his solo choruses on such numbers as "Tiger Rag" are small marvels. Shapely, melodically coherent, rhythmically smooth, they are free of both the ragtimey angularity of Larry Shields's work with the Original Dixieland Band *and* the awkwardness of line that plagues Johnny Dodds with the Oliver Creole Band.

A listener hearing these first solos—including "Farewell Blues" and the rocking low-register chorus on "Panama"—for the first time can be forgiven for not at once apprehending their significance. After more than three-quarters of a century, the sound and function of a clarinet solo within this small band idiom is a commonplace, so familiar as to be a cliché. Yet it had a beginning, a point before which it simply did not exist—at least on phonograph records.

While records made in 1921–22 by the Original Memphis Five and Georgians sometimes contain solo passages, there is seldom the sense of an individual player given a "window" in which to create something discernibly his own. Among notable exceptions: Larry Shields's memorable two choruses on the ODJB's 1921 "St. Louis Blues," discussed in chapter 1.

Did the practice originate with Roppolo? On balance, given evidence supplied by white, black, and Creole New Orleans musicians, the answer seems to be no. Without doubt, Roppolo is the result of a tradition that sprang, at least in part, from the obbligato function of the clarinet in concert and marching bands. But there is also no doubt that his is the first distinctive solo clarinet style to be

captured on records—and, if the testimonies of fellow-musicians are to be credited, it may also be the best.

Certainly it is no exaggeration in this context to suggest that Roppolo's work
in both ensemble and solo has been a model, a foundation, for the *use* of the
clarinet in many subsequent jazz developments. He is the first great jazz soloist
to appear on records, anticipating Louis Armstrong ("Chimes Blues," with Oliver)
by eight months, Sidney Bechet ("Wild Cat Blues," with Clarence Williams) by
eleven.

Hear, in this connection, "Tiger Rag." His chorus—balanced, melodically
serene, alternating fluid runs with long, singing held notes—almost singlehandedly lifts "Tiger Rag" to a new emotional plane.

Leon Roppolo, "Tiger Rag" solo, 1922.

Roppolo's "Tiger Rag" chorus made a deep—and apparently lasting—impression on fellow-musicians, on both sides of the color line. In an arrangement of "Milenberg Joys," written six years later for McKinney's Cotton Pickers, Don Redman uses part of it, scored for clarinet trio, as an ensemble counterline.

The band's hours at Mike Fritzel's basement cabaret ran long and late. As Brunies remembered it, they'd started the engagement working from eight P.M. until about two A.M. But brisk late-evening business soon dictated a change; from then on the music began at ten P.M. or even later, with Vic Benning's six-piece band doing the early shift. "We played as long as customers were there," Loyocano recalled. "We used to have fellows throw us hundred-dollar bills to keep us playing."[19]

Sometimes, said Brunies, the band would surprise Fritzel with its own treatment of a semi-classical piece like Rimsky-Korsakov's Song of India. "He says, 'Man, you guys play that thing like it wasn't written . . . but it's good.' He was a great café man, boy, [and] did more for jazz guys in those days than a lot of people today. People don't realize it."[20]

The Friars' Inn was popular with more than just young musicians. Mares recalled seeing Al Capone, Dion "the Florist" O'Bannion, and other big-time mobsters on more than one occasion. The setup was simple: tables, a small dance floor, space for about three hundred customers. "Something happened every night at Friars'," the trumpeter said. "There was a post on one side of the bandstand, and [Roppolo] used to play with his clarinet against it for tone. He used to like to play into a corner, too."[21]

Ben Pollack proved a boost for the rhythm section. Accounts of his later adventures (and misadventures) as a bandleader have tended to draw attention away from his real and lasting achievements as a drummer. But before the emergence of the second generation of white percussionists, among them Chicagoans Dave Tough, George Wettling, and Gene Krupa, his reputation for a rock-steady beat, enhanced with shading and texture, was unchallenged.

The limitations of acoustic recording make it all but impossible to actually hear the early drummers at work. Forbidden to use any equipment that might knock the delicate cutting stylus out of its groove, drummers were usually confined to woodblocks, cymbals, and an occasional small tomtom. The best index of Pollack's value to the Friars' Inn band, as in so many other situations, lies in the overall feel he lends to a rhythm section. The same can be said of Warren "Baby" Dodds with Oliver, and later as a member of Louis Armstrong's Hot Seven.

In a 1936 Down Beat Pollack described his approach to playing with the band. At first, he said, "novelty was still the thing. So I thought up some stunts that I thought were the nuts. First I palmed an iron drum key under the cymbal and got a ciss [a sizzle effect]. All the drummers thought I had split my cymbal to get the effect, so all the drummers split their cymbals. Then I tried a fly swatter on a bass drum to get a bass-fiddle buzz. So all the guys bought fly-swatters."

But one night, he said, a master of ceremonies complained that all the "fancy stuff" was throwing off one of the variety acts that periodically played the Friars' Inn. "So I just played rhythm, and the guys were so amazed with the easy way they could swing they wanted more drumming like it. So I discovered the secret of solid drumming, that is, to feed rather than overshadow—to send the other guys rather than play a million different beats."[22]

George Brunies remembered these events—and Pollack's joining the band—a little differently. "Pollack used to hang around the Friars' Inn a lot," he said. "One night he heard us talkin' about how Frank Snyder couldn't make it, and he walks up to me and he says, 'Do you mind, Mister Brunies,' he says, 'if I sit in?' I says, 'How you play?' 'Oh,' he says, 'I play pretty good.' 'Well, all right, sit in, I says, 'but don't give me no fancy damn beats. Just hold a good old New Orleans dixie beat.' So he sat in, and then made good from then on."[23]

Pollack's reminiscences shed light on an otherwise underdocumented chapter in the band's brief history. For a while, New Orleans bands playing "jaz" or "jass" had been all the rage and had made money for the owners of cabarets and dance halls. Well before 1920, it was possible to hear the large Charles Elgar Creole Orchestra at Paddy Harmon's Dreamland Ballroom, New Orleans cornetist Manuel Perez at the Pekin Café, Doc Cooke's band at Riverview Park with Jimmie Noone on clarinet and Freddie Keppard blasting away on trumpet.

The fad soon ran its course, and many proprietors, looking to an increasingly well-heeled clientele, began upgrading and expanding their entertainment policies with floor shows, chorus lines, comedians, and dancers. It happened at such spots as the Green Mill, the Bismarck Gardens, and the Valentino Inn, where owner Danny Baroni fired twenty-year-old Bix Beiderbecke because his hot cornet choruses distracted the dancers in the floor show. Even the Friars' Inn became part of the new look, as Fritzel added singing acts, comedy, and dancing.

All the jamming and hot music was fine, he seemed to be saying, but the band should also be able to play things straight for the customers and back up the acts. That meant arrangements and, for a band of non-readers, more long and arduous rehearsals. "The boys argued like hell against it," Pollack said, "and their chief argument was, 'What would we do if the lights went out?' Mike's idea was still arrangements, though; he wanted us to play tunes like 'Meditation' from Thaïs.

"So we quit. $50 a week [per man] was good money, but we got the breaks. We went to work in a ballroom four nights a week for the stupendous sum of $100 a week!" Fritzel finally hired them back, presumably with offers of a raise and a promise to augment the band. According to Pollack, he sent Roppolo to New Orleans to find some compatible men, and the clarinetist returned with cornetist Emmett Hardy, clarinetist Nunzio Scaglione (b. 1890), and the admired bassist "Chink Martin" Abraham (b. 1886).[24]

These events probably occurred toward the end of 1922. Around the same time, the Midway Gardens, a popular dance hall at 60th and Cottage Grove Avenue, near Washington Park on the South Side, bought up the old Merry Gardens nearby, tearing down the walls and hedges between them and combining the two in one larger Midway Dancing Gardens, a short-lived Frank Lloyd Wright architectural improvisation with plenty of outdoor space for dancing, winter and summer. Its management hired Schoebel away to form a brand-new, purpose-built house orchestra which could play hot dance music in a way that would satisfy its mostly young, working-class customers.[25]

Schoebel had his own ideas about running a dance band. At the Friars' Inn, it had taken a lot of patience, persistence, and arduous rehearsal to frame the jamming within polished arranged passages. He'd expended much effort on a group which not only could not read music but seems to have fought him all the way in matters of rehearsal.

This time he chose his men carefully, starting with trumpeter Arthur "Murphy" Steinberg, who, though part of the Friars' Inn circle, was a good reader and disciplined bandsman. For his rhythm section he simply snapped up the team with which he felt at home—the Friars triumvirate of Lou Black, Steve Brown, and Frank Snyder. Not unexpectedly, their first recordings are firmly in the Friars manner, even to some very Mares-like Steinberg lead and Roppoloesque low-register clarinet, possibly by Phil Wing. According to violinist Otto "Peanuts" Barbino, Mares was actually present on at least one of this band's recording dates; but in a conversation with John Steiner, Barbino dismissed a suggestion that the trombonist on the first session, never positively identified, may have been Brunies.[26]

Back at the Friars' Inn, Mike Fritzel was apparently uncertain what to do about his entertainment policy. Bix Beiderbecke, en route home after a brief visit to New York, dropped in and told him Nick LaRocca and the Original Dixieland Band might be interested in returning to Chicago. Bix's letter to LaRocca, dated November 20, 1922, leaves no doubt that Fritzel (perhaps remembering the ODJB's 1916 success at Schiller's) may have felt the time was right for a revival:

> I saw Mike Fritzel last night and he sure seemed impressed when I told him about you boys wanting to come [back] to Chi and that you would consider the Friars' Inn if everything—"Do" [dough] and hours were satisfactory. I sure poured it on thick, well Nick Mike wanted to know the dope . . . all I knew was that you were the best band in the country. Well he expects a letter from you Nick.[27]

In a postscript he added that "Ropollo [sic] and the band are leaving in about a week," but they had no immediate plans to go to New York.

What happened next can only be surmised, but presumably Mares changed his mind and talked Fritzel into a stay of execution. The Friars band remained a short while longer, with an expanded personnel including Mares, Hardy, Brunies, Roppolo, Scaglione and perhaps a third reed, pianist Mel Stitzel (doubling at the Midway Gardens), Martin on bass, and Pollack on drums.

"With the added men," Pollack's memoir says, "there was a terrific 'bang' in working with such new and novel effects as two cornet breaks, three sax riffs, etc. but funny as it seems, breaks and riffs were the only things they could play together."[28]

It's clear from Pollack's description that the band was now musically all but rudderless. The older and more experienced Schoebel, in departing, had taken order and discipline with him. Without him the Friars Society Orchestra was a jam band; it's therefore only too easy to understand Mares's later assertion that "we used to try to hold rehearsals, but no one would show up. So we did our rehearsing on the job."[29]

Anyone familiar with the practical aspects of running a band knows what that means: constant cutting up on the stand; lots of bickering over what songs to play; heavy reliance on tried-and-true material; emphasis on what Pollack termed "breaks and riffs"; and hastily worked-out routines. But mostly the heady, enjoyable—and ultimately self-indulgent—dynamic of the jam session.

Sometimes such methods yield inspired music; just as often the result is a kind of "let's have a ball" atmosphere which may please the musicians but all too often disorients and alienates the customers. Addition of extra men may have compounded the problem. Even at the start, said Mares, there had been "lots of fun and lots of clowning around in the band. I remember we used to put oil of mustard on each other's chairs on the stand. Fritz[e]l could never figure out what all the confusion was about at the beginning of a set."[30]

Voltaire "Volly" De Faut, who had replaced Pettis, remembered the clowning around, the practical jokes—and the lack of musical organization. "All the boys stated, 'My playing would be spoiled if I could read music,' " he told John T. Schenck. "Paul Mares directed the band into the right key by signaling what valve he would press first on his cornet."[31]

These were, after all, young men in their early to mid-twenties, still full of adolescent high spirits. Some of the musicians have spoken of frequently "getting high" on marijuana. It must have been great fun: Mares and Hardy playing two-cornet New Orleans–style breaks, three reed players improvising together.

Fritzel, his gaze firmly on the cash register, must have viewed such high jinks rather differently, and it can't have been long before things reached a crisis. Whether as a result of factors within the band, or just that the boss had had enough, the Friars' Inn idyll came to an end in March 1923.

Brunies, at least, remained on good enough terms with Fritzel to help him line up a replacement band, led—no surprise, this—by his trumpet-playing brother Merritt and including their eldest (and best-trained) brother, Henry "Henny" Brunies, on trombone. Judging from its records, made for OKeh and the rare Autograph label the following year (including a version of "Angry"), it was a rather more orderly and professionally run ensemble, able to back the floor shows and punctuate even the jam numbers with carefully worked-out arranged passages.

Some of the former group, Brunies and Martin among them, joined a new band at the nearby Valentino Inn (on East Adams, between State and Wabash), led by saxophonist Dale Skinner, who had been with Vic Benning's warmup unit at the Friars' Inn. Gene Caffarelli was on cornet, and Bill Paley, nephew and namesake of the CBS founder, on drums. Bix, getting stronger all the time, also played briefly with Skinner before being dismissed by owner Danny Baroni.

The end of the Friars' Inn job left Paul Mares with a big headache. He had talked Gennett into a second two-day recording session, scheduled for Monday and Tuesday, March 12–13, but now he had no band; his personnel was scattered. Strictly speaking, there no longer was a Friars Society Orchestra. He solved the problem by going back to basics, making the records with a quintet, billed on the label as the "New Orleans Rhythm Kings" and composed of himself, Roppolo, Brunies, Stitzel, and Pollack. That he did is a blessing, giving posterity a model performance by the now-standard instrumentation of trumpet, trombone, clarinet, piano, and drums—and showing by contrast how much musical coherence the Original Dixieland Jazz Band had sacrificed in recasting itself as a novelty act.

At least five of the recorded titles were either copyrighted by or handled by the brand-new Melrose music publishing house. Perhaps because it was a Chicago operation, therefore far from Tin Pan Alley, Melrose has been relatively little documented. What mention it has received in jazz histories is generally only in connection with Jelly Roll Morton, who worked for the firm as an arranger and songplugger.

It began in 1923 as a sideline, a natural outgrowth of the music shop run by the brothers Walter and Lester Melrose and their partner Marty Bloom at 6350 South Cottage Grove, a few blocks south of the Midway Gardens. At first they published sheet music, then quickly drew on the talents of Morton, Schoebel, and others to make the songs available as "stock" orchestrations for local dance bands.

As David A. Jasen notes in his *Tin Pan Alley*, the first important Melrose songs were Morton's "Wolverine Blues" (recorded by the Friars' Inn band, whose photo appears on the cover of the original sheet music), the band's own "Tin Roof Blues" (of which more presently), and Art Kassel's "Sobbin' Blues," which they recorded in July, a month after King Oliver's version.[32]

By mid-decade Melrose Music all but controlled the Chicago popular music publishing world. Such jazz classics-to-be as Charlie Davis's "Copenhagen" and "Jimtown Blues," Schoebel's "Prince of Wails" and "Spanish Shawl," Gene Rodemich's "Tia Juana," and Oliver's "Doctor Jazz" were all part of Melrose's burgeoning lists. As Jasen points out, their folios of Morton compositions and Armstrong's *Fifty Hot Choruses* are landmarks of jazz publishing. From the start, Chicago historian John Steiner has said, Walter Melrose "played a major role as a liaison man, manager, agent, promoter and all-round friend to most of these musicians. He got them jobs, tied in recording and publishing deals—he did a lot."[33]

Whether the Melroses approached Mares or he courted them, it's clear that this second of the two-day recording sessions was closely tied in with—perhaps underwritten by—the new firm.

Despite the familiar instrumentation, the records are quite new in character and texture: if this five-piece combination lacks the nervous *frisson* of the Original Dixieland Jazz Band, it more than compensates in finesse. On "That's a Plenty" and "Maple Leaf Rag," the horns play together with clarity, roles well defined in the New Orleans polylinear setting. Brunies, for example, is quite spare, his parts often consisting of little more than whole and half notes; even the quarters are often delivered with a broad legato attack familiar from concert band music.

"Maple Leaf," in fact, may be the first recorded example of a band successfully converting a ragtime piece into a jazz band vehicle, and it's surprisingly subtle. They play the "A" and "B" strains, in fact, very respectfully, keeping attack and ensemble texture light, then open out the "C" strain into a broad fourto-the-bar, pianist Stitzel and drummer Pollack laying down a beat broad enough to compensate for absence of banjo and bass. Roppolo then moves forward with a flowing, bubbling *chalumeau* solo against a spare muted trumpet lead, Pollack carrying the rhythm along on a chugging, propulsive eighth-note tattoo. They end "Maple Leaf" with a driving, decidedly un-raggy, jam ensemble.

Roppolo, soloing this time on "Wolverine Blues," "Weary Blues" (neither of which is a blues at all), and especially "Tin Roof Blues" (which is), continues to arrest attention. Brooding, private, a dark melancholy pervading even his brightest moments, he is quite unlike anyone else in jazz of these years. Various scholars, among them Bruce Boyd Raeburn, have pointed to an "Italian Connection," a tie to traditional Sicilian clarinet methods. Other Italian-American New Orleans reedmen, among them Nunzio Scaglione and Charlie Cordilla, also hint in this direction.

The English critic and scholar Max Harrison has called Roppolo's *Affekt* "spectral"; indeed, there is something of phantasm, something wraithlike, in the very sound Roppolo produces. It is at its most ghostly in the altissimo concert F with which he begins the "Tin Roof" solo. "Sometimes," clarinetist Kenny Davern has said, "he just seems not of this world."[34]

Much of it has to do with vibrato. Fast, narrow, it runs throughout each note, from attack to release, in the manner of European string playing; this quality renders it quite distinct from the end-of-tone, or *terminal*, vibrato integral to so many of the major jazz solo styles from Louis Armstrong on. The very speed of Roppolo's vibrato lends it an expressive urgency comparable to that of the French *chanteuse* tradition later epitomized by Edith Piaf.

Three takes of "Tin Roof Blues" exist, three opportunities to listen to Roppolo's mind at work, arranging and rearranging the pieces of his elegaic little statement. He begins all three on his high G (concert F), ends all three on the same two-bar resolution. But the differences in between, matters of tone, dynamics, and shading as much as specific notes, are spellbinding.

This solo, in each of its three variants, contains many "bent" notes, the exact pitches of which resist attempts at formal notation. In certain cases, such as bar 3 of version -3, a sustained note will have both a ♯ and a ♭ above it, indicating a progression from one pitch variation to the other, in the order given.

Leon Roppolo, "Tin Roof Blues" solo, three takes, 1923.

"Tin Roof Blues" began life, Brunies said, as a routine the band often did at the Friars' Inn. Their name for it was "The Rusty Rail Blues," until Walter Melrose came along looking for publishable properties. "He liked the tune," said Brunies, "gave us a $500 advance on it. So he says, 'You don't mind if I do anything with it, do you?' "

But he needed a better title, something evocative of New Orleans. So they named it after the Tin Roof Café, on Baronne Street back home, later known as the Suburban Gardens. They put all their names on it, "because we didn't figure it was going to do anything."[35]

A generation later, with a new title and lyric and an eight-bar release added, it hit the 1953 pop charts as "Make Love to Me," much to the surprise of the surviving musicians—though the presence of eight names on the composer credits (including that of Melrose) guaranteed that no one person would get rich on royalties.[36]

"Sweet Lovin' Man" is one of three numbers recorded by both the New Orleans Rhythm Kings and the King Oliver Creole Jazz Band (the others are Art Kassel's "Sobbin' Blues" and Morton's "London [Café] Blues"). What's striking here is not how much the Rhythm Kings and Oliver performances resemble one another, but how little. Lil Hardin's "Sweet Lovin' Man" (a.k.a. "Sweet Smellin' Man") is something of a genre song, similar in harmonic structure, shape, and feel to "You've Got to See Mama Every Night," "How Come You Do Me Like You Do?", and even Bob Carleton's widely popular "Ja-Da."

It's also not far from the blues; the verse, in fact, is a twelve-bar blues, thinly disguised with a few bits of harmonic gingerbread; Johnny Dodds, taking his solo on the Oliver OKeh version, strips away the trappings, delivering what is in effect a written blues chorus (he plays it, then repeats it). The tempo is a brisk four-to-the-bar, with Armstrong playing muted lead in the two strutting final choruses and Oliver turning in some eloquent breaks. Though Mares echoes Oliver, the Rhythm Kings' feel is quite different: in taking the number marginally slower, the band seems to be emphasizing its melodic side, playing it somewhat as a blues-flavored song.[37]

What happened after these record sessions is unclear. At least some of the time, Brunies and Chink Martin were with Skinner at the Valentino; Stitzel continued at the Midway, and Pollack picked up what he could around town, all the while resisting parental entreaties to give up music and go into their family fur business.

Mares and Roppolo, meanwhile, struck out for New York, where they joined pianist Al Siegel in a small band working at a Greenwich Village nightspot called Mills' Caprice. By July they were back in Chicago, preparing for another series of Gennett recordings under the New Orleans Rhythm Kings name, scheduled for Tuesday and Wednesday, July 17 and 18. Roppolo and Brunies were ready and willing; Jack Pettis was in town and available. The rhythm section would be Martin, Pollack, Skinner's pianist Kyle Pierce, and banjoist Bob Gillette, a Friars' Inn regular.

There were also some guests, and it is at this point that conjecture must assist documentation. Two extra saxophonists, Don Murray and Glenn Scoville, were present and are heard in various combinations. But it is not their presence, or even that—in a strictly non-playing role—of Murray's pal Beiderbecke, that has made this two days of recording fascinating to historians. It is, rather, the participation of Jelly Roll Morton.

For the public, at least, popular music in 1923 was still rigidly segregated. Black and white musicians might play together on riverboats or after hours in South Side joints; they might hang out together, even—if the accounts of Mezz Mezzrow, Vic Berton, and others are any indication—drink and smoke "muggles" together. But interracial appearances on the job or in a recording studio were strictly off limits. (If the point needs underscoring, it can be noted that the Gennett studios in Richmond, Indiana, were also the scene of recording sessions by members of the Ku Klux Klan.)

Some Creoles and light-skinned blacks had crossed the color line. Trumpeter Bill Moore, for example, worked regularly with such top white bands as the California Ramblers and Ben Bernie's Orchestra, billing himself as "the Hot Hawaiian" on those occasions when suspicion might be aroused. Singer Eva Taylor told of the scrim curtain hung between her and the band when she broadcast with the Original Memphis Five over New York radio station WEAF. But even then, such mixing was rare.

The NORK men all knew Mister Jelly. As Paul Mares's brother Joe told it, Morton—sufficiently light-skinned to "pass" as a Latin-American when entering all-white establishments—actually had come to the Friars' Inn to talk to the trumpeter and Roppolo about recording some tunes he'd written, which Melrose was planning to publish.[38] If Walter Melrose was underwriting this date, as he had the last, it's not beyond supposition that he set some conditions, among them that most of the tunes recorded would be Melrose properties, and that Morton, a Melrose artist, would be given a crack at performing his own compositions.

That seems to be the way it worked out. How much did Morton play on these dates? Historians disagree, and Gennett's muddy acoustic sound doesn't facilitate easy identification. He's clearly audible on "Milenberg Joys" and on his own "Mr. Jelly Lord" and "London Blues." What little piano can be heard on "Sobbin' Blues," a number popular with both black and white bands, could be Morton.

Kyle Pierce is most likely the pianist on his own "Marguerite" and probably on "Mad ('Cause You Treat Me This Way)," both Melrose songs. That leaves two band staples, "Angry" and "Clarinet Marmalade"—and another mystery. Chink Martin told various interviewers he remembered three pianists—Morton, Pierce, and Mel Stitzel—taking part in these recordings, each playing on his own arrangements.[39]

Given the nature of the sessions, and Stitzel's own connections with Melrose (it published his 1924 "Doodle Doo Doo," written in collaboration with Art Kassel), it's not impossible. But what substantiation? What musical evidence? Stitzel had certainly played both "Angry" and "Clarinet Marmalade" many times with this band and others, but there's nothing solid linking him with these performances.

Based on a collection of sources, including the Gennett master ledger for the two dates and Warren Plath's research as published in Storyville magazine, the sessions may have run as follows:

Tuesday, July 17: Full eight-piece personnel plus Morton and extra saxophones Murray and Scoville. The band plays "Sobbin' Blues" (two saxes) and "Marguerite" (three reeds) with Morton or Stitzel as pianist on the former, Pierce on the latter. Morton then records his own "King Porter" and "New Orleans Joys" as piano solos. The band then returns, Stitzel (or Pierce) at the piano, for "Angry" and "Clarinet Marmalade" (Murray on tenor?). Morton then takes over with the band for "Mr. Jelly Lord," to finish the first session. While the musicians are packing up, Roppolo and Martin, both accomplished guitarists, record a pair of guitar duets, "Bucktown Blues" and a reprise of "Angry." Regrettably, neither was ever issued, and the masters were apparently destroyed.

Wednesday, July 18: Morton opens by recording four piano solos: "Grandpa's Spells," "Kansas City Stomp," "Wolverine Blues," and "The Pearls." Kyle Pierce then records two solos, his own "I Forgave You" and the "St. Louis Blues." By this time the band has arrived and records Morton's arrangement of his "London Blues" with the composer and at least one extra saxophone, plus "Milenberg [more accurately "Milneburg"] Joys," which is the band's "Golden Leaf Strut" with an intro by Morton. Pierce (or Stitzel) returns for "Mad" to round out the day's activity.

One notable feature of the band's performances is its choice of tempos. "Milenberg Joys," for example, is taken considerably slower than bands later came to play it. Rather than try to generate the frantic excitement of what George Brunies in later years deprecated as "race-horse tempo," the Rhythm Kings opt for a broad fox-trot in the New Orleans manner. According to Chink Martin, medium tempos always elicited better response from the crowd. "People would move better with the music when it was played at correct tempos," he told interviewers, "but they'd just applaud politely for something played fast."[40]

(On the first take of "Milenberg," Morton is clearly and busily audible, almost swamping Roppolo's delicate-toned clarinet; the next take, by contrast, finds the piano subdued, noticeably avoiding conspicuous background figures. Could the clarinetist or someone else in the band have suggested to the extrovert Mister Jelly that he please tone things down just a bit?)

In the case of the added saxophones, the recording quality and lack of balance all but eliminate any chance of determining who plays what and where—though the low-register clarinet chorus on "Mr. Jelly Lord" could well be Murray, as Warren Plath suggests. It does not sound like Roppolo.

Back in New Orleans eighteen months later, Mares did two further sessions under the Rhythm Kings name; the first, for OKeh (January 23, 1925), used Roppolo, Martin, clarinet–tenor sax doubler Charlie Cordilla (sometimes Cordella), trombonist Santo Pecora, and the rhythm section of the band then working at the Halfway House. By any standard they are outstanding, distillations of all that must have made life at the Friars' Inn a nightly feast for musicians.

Pecora's "I Never Knew What a Gal Could Do" (later recorded as "Zero" by Wingy Manone) opens with a fully textured four-horn ensemble reminiscent of the early Gennett recordings. Mares's full chorus shows him moving toward a more flowing sense of line, but it is Roppolo, working his low register for thirty-two bars, who stands out. He's even better on "She's Crying for Me," playing two soaring, singing blues choruses.[41]

But the day's masterpiece is "Golden Leaf Strut" (a.k.a. "Milenberg Joys"), taken faster than on the Gennett. Roppolo forsakes the "Tiger Rag" changes of the trio strain entirely, instead playing two extraordinarily dark blues choruses, rendered more urgent by that peculiarly fast vibrato. As Max Harrison remarks, the solo is "introverted despite the fast tempo . . . a rarified achievement of a sort not widely associated with early jazz." Few, indeed, seem to have possessed this ability to create an island of serenity amid the genial high spirits of an up-tempo performance. Bix Beiderbecke's 1928 solo on "Tain't So, Honey, Tain't So," with Whiteman, comes readily to mind, as do the quiet deliberations of Irving "Fazola" Prestopnick, a Roppolo disciple, on "Diga Diga Doo," with Bob Crosby a decade later.[42]

The final ensemble works up a good head of steam, Mares and Pecora cranking up tension by going into mutes for the second of the two choruses. This throttling back for greater intensity, a familiar practice among early New Orleans bands, is now an all-but-lost ensemble art. It requires a tightly disciplined control over dynamics and an understanding of listener response, too often drowned out in the loud-louder-loudest puerilities of latter-day "dixieland" bands.

"Baby," the seldom-reissued final title, offers thirty-two bars of Roppolo on alto sax, with a tone and pronounced vibrato not unlike those of Sidney Bechet's soprano. Equally absorbing is a full-chorus Roppolo-Cordilla saxophone duet, carrying over into a fully textured final ensemble. (They do it again, even more effectively, on "Pussy Cat Rag," by the Halfway House Orchestra, discussed elsewhere.)

These two sessions, and the titles recorded by Roppolo as a member of Abbie Brunies's Halfway House Orchestra, brought the story of the Friars Society Orchestra home, just where it had started the day in 1920 that "Ragbaby" Stevens's telegram arrived from far-off Chicago.

The musicians who had created the Friars Society Orchestra were now scattered, their role as trailblazers behind them. Paul Mares returned to Chicago, where in 1935 he made one more batch of records with a refreshingly eclectic (and racially mixed) personnel. In the late '30s he and his wife ran the "P & M New Orleans Barbecue," fondly remembered as a musicians' meeting place and scene of many a late-night jam session.

Roppolo, never emotionally stable, spent his latter days in mental institutions. At this remove, it is hard to say what demons beset him and whether they might have been treated successfully with modern medications or techniques. He is known to have organized and played the saxophone in a band in a Louisiana hospital and to have been released briefly in 1940, playing two nights with Santo Pecora. He died, still a young man, October 5, 1943.[43]

Ben Pollack was off to California, where he started the dance band which was to imprint his name in the jazz history books. George Brunies and his Chicago pal, Kid Muggsy Spanier, hit the road with Ted Lewis and later became part of the circle of musicians surrounding guitarist Eddie Condon.

Steve Brown joined Jean Goldkette, where alongside Bix, Murray, Frank Trumbauer, and others he shortly achieved his own immortality. When the Goldkette band broke up in late 1927, he was one of several who moved on to Paul Whiteman's popular orchestra.

Jack Pettis went east with Ben Bernie. Elmer Schoebel, Mel Stitzel, Kyle Pierce,

Lou Black, Volly De Faut, Frank Snyder, and the others continued to make livings great and small out of hot music.

The Friars Society Orchestra existed for less than two years, only part of that time as a regularly constituted and employed unit. Two of its three record dates were done when the band was out of work, and with different formats and personnel. Yet there is a continuity to its efforts, an irresistible *esprit*—and with it a discernible and enduring identity as the first band of musical depth and substance to record and disseminate white New Orleans jazz. In Leon Roppolo, moreover, it had one of the first important jazz soloists: even confined by the imperfect sound of the acoustic records, the band's impact on what was shortly to become known as Chicago jazz was profound and enduring.

3

Emmett Hardy

Jazz, in common with so many other forms of art, reserves special affection for the ill-starred, the too-soon dead. Bix Beiderbecke, Clifford Brown, Frank Tesche-macher, Charlie Christian—each seems all the more beloved for having been cut down in youth, ere his moment of full blossoming.

Beyond argument, early death is cruel, summary. Yet is it not also somehow tantalizing, in its offer of an alternative to a long life too often prosaically lived? It frees us from the need to ask whether Wilfred Owen, had he survived the Great War, would have realized the early promise of his poetical gifts. Instead he becomes an image suspended in time, an antidote to the exquisite horror of a new century's new evils. Does it not thrill the romantic imagination that his brief life ends with the cry

O what made fatuous sunbeams toil
To break earth's sleep at all?[1]

James Joyce addressed the matter directly in "The Dead," the final episode of *Dubliners*. Gabriel Conroy, having discovered his wife's love for the long-dead

Michael Furey, is forced into contemplation of early death, contrasting it with the process of aging and loss, compromise and failed promise, which his own life has become. Gretta Conroy's passion, carried throughout the years of her marriage to Gabriel, remains inviolate, fixed at the long-ago moment of young Furey's death. It can neither tarnish nor decay but lives on as it was then, ardent and eternally pure.

In this setting, early death is transformed from destroyer, end of all things, to protector and preserver, from tragedy to triumph: "Better pass boldly into that other world in the full glory of some passion," muses Conroy, "than fade and wither dismally with age."

Seen thus, isn't the golden hero, dead in the flower of his youth, a bearer of consolation? Does his swift and brilliant passage not somehow vindicate and focus our travails by presenting an idealized alternative to the grim spectacle of mutability, attrition, and ultimate oblivion?

Bix Beiderbecke invites such reflections, and so, too, does an almost exact contemporary, whose thoughtful ways may have foreshadowed him. That is the New Orleans cornetist Emmett Hardy, who died in June 1925, four days into his twenty-third year. Extravagant claims have been made for Hardy by musicians who knew him and were his friends. Yet because he never made phonograph records he remains an enigmatic figure, easily romanticized.[2]

Emmett Louis Hardy was born June 12, 1903, in Gretna, Louisiana, in Jefferson Parish across the Mississippi from New Orleans. The family home, at 237 Morgan Street, was full of music: Emmett's father, Harry Hardy, played the tuba in the local Shriners band; his mother, the former Lillian Kennedy, was an accomplished amateur pianist. His uncle, R. Emmett Kennedy, also played the piano and was "well known for his entertaining lectures on Negro subjects presented in Negro dialect and featuring vocal renditions of early Negro spirituals," according to the Louisiana historian Dr. Karl Koenig. Of the Hardy children, Elinor both played the piano and sang. There were two elder sons, Hilton and Connell, but it is not known whether they were musical as well.[3]

Young Emmett was apparently a delicate child who took to music early, first through the piano and guitar, then, around age thirteen, the cornet. According to his friend drummer-cornetist Arthur "Monk" Hazel, the boy took lessons in nearby Algiers with the highly regarded Creole multi-instrumentalist Manuel "Fess" Manetta, who among other things taught him to play such current songs as "Panama." He also reportedly had six months of music tutelage with the respected local bandmaster Professor George Paoletti.

He attended the Delgado Trade School, where he learned machinist's skills. Banjoist Bill Eastwood, who would soon work alongside Hardy in a band led by pianist Norman Brownlee, recalled handing out tools in a shop class to him and to fledgling drummer Ray Bauduc.

Emmett had been studying the cornet little more than a year when, around 1917, he began playing at house parties and dances around Gretna and surrounding communities on the Mississippi's west bank. Clarinetist Harry Shields, whose elder brother Larry had made history first with Tom Brown's band and then as the clarinetist of the Original Dixieland Jazz Band, recalled meeting Hardy on what may have been the cornetist's first professional job—a dance pavilion at Midway Park, in nearby Harvey.[4]

Described by Martha Boswell, of the singing Boswell Sisters, as "slim and dark and rather reserved," Hardy seems to have been a thoughtful and courteous young man. Clarinetist Sidney Arodin, born in the West Bank community of Westwego, played with him on a few dances and street parades and remembered him as "a gentleman, as well as the greatest musician I've ever known." Even allowing for an element of exaggeration, it is clear that the youth was talented and well liked.[5]

In a 1940 Down Beat reminiscence, Martha Boswell told of Emmett's first visit to the musical Boswell home, at 3937 Camp Street near the city's affluent Garden District. His sister Elinor was the main attraction, she said, and "we awaited [the] cornet solo (by Emmett) with no anticipation whatsoever."

Daughters of a prosperous businessman, the three Boswell sisters were something of a local sensation. They could play classical music—Connie on the cello, Martha the piano, and Helvetia the violin—then switch instruments, "Vet" picking up a banjo and Connie an alto saxophone, for some lively ragtime. Perhaps a little put off (or intimidated) by his "confident manner and professional air," they decided to teach Elinor's big brother a lesson by playing their "number five," a trickily arranged version of "I Wish I Could Shimmy Like My Sister Kate," which they normally used as "a gag on unsuspecting musicians to sound them out."

To their astonishment, Emmett listened to "number five" with something not far short of contempt. Almost offhand, he asked Martha whether she knew "Ma, He's Making Eyes at Me," whistled impatiently while she quickly ran through the chords—and then began to play. "It was fascinating," she said. "We were overwhelmed. We've never forgotten it—it was the thrill of a lifetime."

Hardy and the Boswells became close friends, he and Martha ultimately more than that. "As we grew to know him better we admired his keen, philosophic mind, his wit and genial nature," she said. "He was always helpful, and his praise and encouragement gave my sisters and me the confidence, later, to go into the professional field ourselves. He insisted we were original in our musical ideas; by that I mean he emphasized the importance of an artist expressing himself and not others, developing and perfecting his own work rather than take the easier road and merely copy what successful artists in the same field are doing," she said.[6]

Soon after finishing at Delgado, Hardy went to work as a machinist at the Johnson Iron Works, in Algiers. Fellow-trumpeter Henry Corrubia, who worked alongside him there, recalled the young man turning his own mouthpieces on a lathe during breaks, trying out different cup and bore designs. In Corrubia's view, the exhaustion of working days at the foundry and playing late into the nights weakened Hardy's constitution and may have helped bring on the tuberculosis that contributed to his early death.

*　　*　　*

In those days, the Mississippi tended to divide the New Orleans region socially, along lines having little to do with race. For those whites, blacks, and Creoles living on the West Bank, a trip into New Orleans was something of an odyssey, involving slow, often irregular ferry service. If such West Bank youngsters as Emmett and Elinor Hardy wanted to pay a Monday evening social call on the Boswell girls, their trip had to be planned carefully around the ferry schedules.

The physical isolation of such West Bank communities as Gretna, Westwego, Harvey, and Algiers inevitably produced a social and cultural life distinct from that of New Orleans. White youngsters such as Hardy and his pal Monk did most of their playing, like their socializing, on their side of the Mississippi. Black trumpeter Henry "Red" Allen, growing up in Algiers, restricted much of his early musical activity to that area, where his father led a prominent brass band. Students from New Orleans coming to study with "Fess" Manetta often had to make a day of the pilgrimage. This remained true until the 1930s, when the Huey Long Bridge, in Westwego, finally linked the two banks.

One of Hardy's first regular associations was with a band led by Algiers pianist Norman Brownlee, whose regular sidemen included Harry Shields and Bill East-wood. Shields recalled a trip to Kansas City, Missouri, to play at a Shriners convention with a band that included himself, his pianist brother Eddie, Hardy, and several other local musicians. But he was unsure of the date. In early 1921, at age seventeen, Emmett Hardy went on the road for the first time, as part of a quintet in the Original Dixieland Jazz Band style, backing singer-dancer Bee Palmer; also along were eighteen-year-olds Leon Roppolo on clarinet and Santo Pecora on trombone, plus drummer Johnnie "Mulefoot" Frisco. The musical director was Miss Palmer's husband, pianist Al Siegel.[7]

The now-forgotten Bee Palmer plays a surprisingly important role in accounts of white jazz of this period. An attractive and glamorous blonde of about five feet, seven inches, she seems always to have had a retinue of male admirers close at hand. "She was a wild chick," New Orleans pianist Horace Diaz has recalled. "But talented—wow! A terrific entertainer."[8]

A photo of her taken around 1921 (and autographed "with kind thoughts" to bassist Steve Brown) reveals an extremely pretty, curly-haired woman swathed in furs but showing a pair of shapely legs. "She was really built," said Santo Pecora. "Everyone wanted to get in her pants."[9]

Born in Chicago sometime around 1898, Bee Palmer made her first major show business impact in 1918 as one of two performers (Gilda Gray was the other) who introduced New York vaudeville audiences to the Shimmy, described as a sinuous and suggestive undulation of hips and shoulders. It turns up in the titles and lyrics of dozens of songs written around this time, perhaps the best known of which is the jazz band standard "I Wish I Could Shimmy Like My Sister Kate."

Abel Green and Joe Laurie Jr., writing in *Show Biz: From Vaude to Video*, trace the Shimmy's origins to the good-time dens of San Francisco's Barbary Coast. It was scandalous, controversial, and, to many, obscene. It seemed, said Green and Laurie, "even more indecent when performed in the bare-legged, revealing costumes in vogue during the [First World] War's final year." Only with some difficulty, *Variety* reported with obvious glee, could it be danced *without* seeming lewd.[10]

Capitalizing on controversy, Bee Palmer took to billing herself "the Shimmy Queen" and included a generous amount of shaking and wiggling in her traveling act. Wherever she went she was news, particularly when—as in the Davenport–Rock Island–Moline area during her 1921 tour—she ran into trouble with local guardians of decency.

Miss Palmer appears to have made several test recordings for both Columbia and Victor, beginning in 1918, none of them ever issued. Her final, and probably most interesting, attempt came in 1929, when she recorded "Singin' the Blues" and "Don't Leave Me Daddy" for Columbia under Paul Whiteman's sponsorship, backed by Frank Trumbauer and a group of Whiteman musicians. On their evidence, Miss Palmer is clearly a polished, sure performer; but her voice seems shrill, unbalanced—better suited, perhaps, to a noisy vaudeville theatre than to the clinical silence of a recording studio.

As has already been seen, Bee Palmer had a hand in the formation (and naming) of the New Orleans Rhythm Kings; presently, she also employed Jimmy McPartland, Bud Freeman, Eddie Condon, and other youngsters of their circle in 1928, and seems to have played a part in bringing New Orleans guitarist Edward "Snoozer" Quinn into Whiteman's orchestra the following year.

She and Siegel split up, personally and professionally, toward the end of the 1920s. The pianist, apparently something of a hustler, soon attached himself to a new and fast-rising singer, a former stenographer from the New York borough of Queens named Ethel Zimmermann. In 1930 she burst like a roman candle on the entertainment world, singing a show-stopping "I Got Rhythm" in the Gershwin brothers' Broadway hit *Girl Crazy*. By then she was Ethel Merman and on her way to stardom, with Al Siegel as her coach and accompanist.

The 1921 Palmer tour got off to a fast start, with appearances booked at theaters in the Orpheum chain throughout the Midwest. Sometime in late January they hit Davenport, Iowa, and in the audience at the Columbia Theater were two young hot music fanatics, both budding cornetists: Esten Spurrier and his quiet, moody chum, Leon Beiderbecke. "We didn't miss a performance, the music was so great," Spurrier told Philip R. Evans.[11]

Not surprisingly, more than distance separated New York audiences from those in the apple-pie Midwest. Miss Palmer's onstage antics quickly got her in trouble with local educators, clergy, and indignant parents. Their outcry seems to have spooked theatre managers enough to force cancellations, and not long afterward Siegel and Miss Palmer decided to call off the tour.[12]

Stranded by the Palmer debacle, Emmett Hardy and Leon Roppolo made for Davenport, where they joined the local band of Carlisle Evans in time for its February 13 opening at the Coliseum dance hall. The band included trombonist Tal Sexton, saxophonist Myron "Rookie" Neal (best known for his later work with Curt Hitch's Happy Harmonists), drummer Jack Willett, and, on banjo, Louis Black, shortly to become a founder-member of the Friars Society Orchestra.[13]

They stayed three months, and Hardy apparently spent more than a little time with Beiderbecke, three months his senior but far less experienced, discussing the cornet and giving him playing tips. From the time the Palmer tour first hit Davenport, said Santo Pecora, Bix regularly came to the rooming house where the musicians were staying and would "practice with Emmett because he liked the way Emmett played."

But Beiderbecke played so poorly, the trombonist said, "that he gave me a headache. I couldn't sleep or do anything. I asked Emmett why he didn't kick the kid out of there, but Emmett said he was a nice kid. They were smoking all that weed and stuff, and I didn't care for that—so I had to get out of the room."[14]

Spurrier and Beiderbecke hung around the Coliseum a lot. When they could scrape together the seventy-five cents per person admission charge they'd go in; otherwise, Spurrier said, they'd slip around to the side of the single-story wooden building to listen and watch at the windows. But years later, in a letter to Philip R. Evans, Spurrier said he doubted whether those visits constituted the foundation of a major stylistic influence.[15]

Little solid documentation of these weeks exists, but there's plenty of anecdotal material, full of what is obviously affectionate exaggeration. An example is a story told by several New Orleans men, drummer-brassman Monk Hazel among them, describing a Sunday afternoon aboard the Streckfus excursion steamer Sidney, when Hardy and twenty-year-old Louis Armstrong appeared in bands opposite one another and allegedly got into a challenge, or "cutting contest."

The story is remarkable for having been seized upon and disseminated by people who were not present and had themselves heard it only at second or third hand. Embroidered more in each telling, it ends with Hazel swearing that Hardy played so hard he "split his upper and lower lips inside. When he blew water out of his spit key blood came out."

As a sometime cornetist himself, Hazel should have known better: perhaps a later Louis Armstrong, playing endless high notes in front of a band five shows a night, finally drew blood. But a three- or four-hour afternoon encounter aboard an excursion boat? This account has young Louis conceding defeat to Hardy after a climactic "High Society," telling him, "Man, you're the king." Armstrong later denied any knowledge of the event, insisting that the only white cornetist with whom he ever jammed was Bix, and that at the Sunset in Chicago.

Such stuff is easy to dismiss as hyperbole, even out-and-out fabrication, aimed at enhancing Hardy's reputation. But a certain quantity of evidence, however circumstantial, indicates that the story may not be totally apocryphal. During most of 1921 Armstrong was indeed playing for Fate Marable's orchestra aboard the Streckfus steamers Sidney and Capitol. Marable, a native of Paducah, Kentucky, was a trained musician who worked comfortably with both black and white—and sometimes mixed—groups. In fact, as early as 1907, he had played with a band on the Streckfus ship J.S. alongside white cornetist Tony Catalano, violinist Emil Flindt, and drummer Rex Jessup.

Recollections of such mixed ensembles are relatively plentiful. Trumpeter and violinist Peter Bocage recalled seeing Marable with a Streckfus band in which "Fate was the onliest [sic] colored boy in the band—all the rest was white boys."

White drummer Earl Wiley recalled playing in a riverboat band including black pianist Charlie Mills. "Even back in those days there were mixed bands and nobody seemed to think anything of it," he said in a 1945 magazine interview.[16]

Both the *Sidney* and *Capitol* called at Davenport regularly beginning in mid-spring, often adding local bands for Sunday excursions. Hardy and Roppolo, working with one of the region's leading groups (Carlisle Evans), would surely have done at least some of these jobs.

Marable, moreover, reportedly had helped rehearse Bee Palmer's backup band before the tour left New Orleans, and therefore knew the two teenaged musicians. It's not beyond probability, given his prominence and seniority in the Streckfus organization, that he was responsible for booking the kind of two-band Sunday session described in the "cutting contest" story.

In other words, there's nothing factually improbable about an Armstrong-Hardy meeting. Some kind of give-and-take, even involving the kind of musical jousting described by Hazel and others, could have occurred between the two bands. Armstrong in 1921, though still in many ways an apprentice (Marable and mellophonist Dave "Professor" Jones were helping him with his reading), was already being talked up among musicians as a player to hear.

But it is essential to remember that jazz in 1921 was still largely an ensemble music. If a contest of any sort occurred, it was most likely a matter of one band trying to generate more dance-floor steam than the other. The idea of two soloists squaring off in gladiatorial combat seems not only improbable in view of the relative obscurity of the two brassmen but wildly anachronistic as a musical event.

What, then, did Emmett Hardy sound like? By what standard can the size and persistence of his reputation in the accounts of so many early New Orleans jazzmen (most of them in oral history interviews on file at Tulane University) be judged? Our inability to confront the matter head-on illustrates the degree to which reliance on recordings has shaped perception of jazz history over many decades.

Recording, in 1921, was still relatively new, its technical quality unreliable, little more than an approximation of actual sound. Yet we have nothing else: however imperfect, records are the only way of knowing anything at all about how bands or individual musicians sounded at specific points in their development.

More dismaying still is the fate of the player who for one reason or another did not record. Posterity, again in the absence of any other evaluative method, favors those who did, consigning the unrecorded to a kind of limbo. As a matter less of conscious effort than of inadvertent effect, those who recorded—regardless of how inexact a representation the records may be—tend to assume a more important place in assessments of their times than those who did not.

In most standard texts, Emmett Hardy gets little more than passing mention, usually to the effect that he was highly regarded, that many claims were made for him, that he died young and made no records. Bix Beiderbecke, by contrast, survived Hardy by a crucial six years, which saw the emergence of the soloist in jazz and allowed Bix and others to record. For all the insistence of colleagues and admirers that the records captured little of him, that "you just had to hear him" in person, the electrically recorded Victor, OKeh, and Columbia performances featuring Bix give at least some indication of his brilliance. Beiderbecke, therefore, has historical substance; Hardy, unrecorded, has none.

What if Bix had never entered a recording studio? If all accounts of his musicianship—the sense of line, the balanced phrasing, the carillon tone—had come down only in the rapturous accounts of men who knew, played with, and admired him? "Aw, you think Hackett played beautifully—you should've heard Bix!" Or, "You know, Bix taught Jimmy McPartland everything he knew; when he left the Wolverines, they got together and Beiderbecke showed the kid a whole bunch of little tricks."

All the stories, all the reminiscences—Eddie Condon's description of a tone "like a girl saying yes," Hoagy Carmichael's memory of collapsing on a sofa after hearing Bix play three notes—depend on the corroboration, however imperfect, of the records. We can only imagine the same statements, the same romanticized homage, with no "Singin' The Blues" or "I'm Comin', Virginia" to cite as proof. Without them, it's likely that he would have achieved little of the prominence he enjoys in jazz history as the first major white soloist, avatar and prime exponent of the ballad sensibility.

Emmett Hardy did his most significant playing between 1919 and 1923, before the arrival of electrical recording and before any of the major solo styles (with the possible exception of Sidney Bechet's) had emerged. Those cornetists and trumpeters who did record at that time were chiefly ensemble players: even in taking solos, their approach was functional, an extension of the melodic lead.

This is true of Joe Oliver, of Paul Mares, whom he inspired. Of white cornetists Dominick James "Nick" LaRocca, Ray Lopez, and Johnny Bayersdorffer; and of Thomas Morris, Freddie Keppard, and Natty Dominique among the blacks. It is true, in fact, of almost everyone—with the possible exceptions of Johnny Dunn and Louis Panico, both of whom stressed (on records, at least) their skills as instrumental showmen, adept at the sorts of tricks that seldom failed to entertain audiences. Even allowing for the probability that live performances, free of the constraints of the recording process, offered more latitude to individual players, it's still unlikely that Hardy or anyone else had evolved a distinctive solo style that early.

Still, Emmett Hardy has to have had something that set him apart from his fellows. Hear, on that subject, the voices of colleagues and friends: Monk Hazel, remembering Hardy's tone as "pure and wonderful, and it sorta rolled forth, except with a drive like I've never heard anyone else get." A drive, he said, allied with "that legato style . . . [more] than it is a staccato style." Hear Norman Brownlee attest that Hardy was the first cornetist he'd heard to get "wah-wah" effects with a plunger. Frank Mackie, bassist with the New Orleans Owls, remembered Hardy's clearly articulated lead and fine tone. George Brunies, who played alongside Hardy at the Friars' Inn in 1923, came as close as anyone to a detached assessment in saying that Hardy "didn't blast much. He just played little variations and stuff around [the melody]."[17]

Emerging from all this is the probability of a controlled, thoughtful way of playing, cleanly articulated and smoothly executed, which must have contrasted sharply to the more extrovert ways of many other New Orleans men. That places Hardy, by implication, in the vanguard of those who anticipated, even spearheaded, a move away from the melodic and rhythmic conventions of ragtime. The raggy phrasing of many other early New Orleans cornetists, LaRocca and Keppard among them, heightens speculation about this aspect of Hardy. The "legato style" cited by Hazel could well have been an augury of lyrical, vocalized ways to come, placing Hardy far ahead of most of his contemporaries of the pre-1920 period.

It's easy to see how these qualities suggest comparisons to Beiderbecke, even if particulars of phrase shape or content differed greatly. Steve Brown, who worked with both men, declared that Hardy "had a style of his own, too, and both of 'em were good styles and [both] were well liked. But I wouldn't say that Hardy phrased like Bix at all." Most of Brown's experience, it must be remembered, is with Bix at full maturity, in the Goldkette and Whiteman orchestras. By this time Emmett Hardy was dead, and Beiderbecke's style bore little resemblance to what it had been in 1922. Brown's only memories of Hardy dated from that earlier time.[18]

Like Beiderbecke, Hardy apparently had a keen pitch sense and a sharp ear. "He could listen to a record and tell you what key they were playing in," said Monk Hazel. "He was another one of those guys like [Jack] Teagarden—you go way in the back room and hit a chord, and he'd tell you what chord and the notes in the chord." Hazel also cited Hardy's fondness for playing in difficult keys and finding unusual modulations in and out of them.[19]

It's not hard to see how Bix, still something of a beginner when Hardy came to Davenport, would have taken to him—or to imagine the two of them sitting together in the rooming house, Bix playing and Emmett commenting and responding. It's equally easy to imagine nights at the Friars' Inn with Bix, his confidence building, asking to sit in. "Paul Mares and Rap [Roppolo], they used to fluff him off," said Monk Hazel, "and Emmett didn't; Emmett told them, 'Aw, let the kid play.' "

Mares, particularly, was zealous in championing Hardy and denigrating Beiderbecke. "Get this straight," he told Dave Dexter Jr., in 1940, "Emmett Hardy as far back as 1919 was playing almost the identical stuff that Bix played with Goldkette and Whiteman nearly 10 years later—except that Emmett was even more sure of himself, had more ideas, and played with a push and drive that Beiderbecke never attained. It's high time Hardy received the acclaim he deserves."[20]

Even allowing for the hyperbole of partisanship, Mares seems too ready to disregard the process through which a jazz style is formed. To vouchsafe that Bix learned from Emmett Hardy is to comment only on the forces that helped shape him as a player; it says nothing about what Beiderbecke did with the raw materials, about the probing harmonic sense, the emotional layering, the gift for musical architecture, that are his glories.

Mares's remarks seem particularly ungracious coming from a man who himself clearly drew inspiration and direction from another—in his case Joe Oliver. Jazz solo playing, moreover, came a long way between 1919 and 1928; while it's possible that Hardy, had he lived, might have evolved along lines similar to those of Beiderbecke, at the beginning of the 1920s neither man could have played with the harmonic sophistication that became the hallmark of Bix's later playing and composition.

Mares's declaration that "it's high time Hardy received the acclaim he deserves" seems to get at the key issue. In 1940, what may be called the "Bix legend" was at an early peak; Bix Beiderbecke had become, in Benny Green's apt phrase, "jazz's number one saint," the "young man with a horn," reaching for notes (as explored so fancifully in Dorothy Baker's *Young Man With a Horn*) that weren't there.

All things to all people, Bix was the idealized young hero for all seasons, the tortured, self-destructive genius; the soft-spoken, polite young man, the Fitzgeraldian icon; the regular guy, ready to "peel a couple of C-notes off a roll" and press them into Jimmy McPartland's hand upon learning that "the kid" was broke and needed money. And, finally, the little boy lost, singing through his horn with the voice of angels.

The romance persists. The very idea of Bix—so golden, so young, so brilliant, and so lost—still has the power to tantalize, and to console. It feels almost *good* to have him there, the artist trying desperately to give form to seraphic music heard only in his head, misunderstood and ultimately undone by a prosaic, obtuse day-to-day world.

And, as noted earlier, perfectly preserved, unsullied by age, by accommodation, by the sober mechanics of survival in the music marketplace. We play his records and dream of golden yesterdays: that they may be fictionalized yesterdays, images of our own making, hardly seems to matter.

Emmett Hardy, meanwhile, sank into obscurity, cherished by a small circle of New Orleans friends and by Martha Boswell, who remained in love with him, even having a stone monument erected to him in 1934 at Point A la Hache, downriver from New Orleans. Little wonder, then, that Paul Mares was indignant, ready to make seemingly inflated claims for his gracious, doomed friend.

Within a very narrow context, Mares's remarks probably carry some truth. Bix's first records with the Wolverines, made in 1924, show a player not yet fully formed; the elements are in place, but the command and authority, and the emotional complexity, which dominate his performances of just three years later are glimpsed here only fitfully.

All the same, his playing is nicely organized, thoughtful, clean of tone, and smooth in its approach to the rhythm. It's not hard to imagine Monk Hazel turning up at the home of his ailing friend (by this time Hardy, weakened by tuberculosis, had stopped playing), clutching a copy of the Wolverines' first Gennett coupling, "Fidgety Feet" and "Jazz Me Blues." Hardy reportedly listened to it carefully, then said, "I know who that is. That's a kid from Davenport by the name of Leon Beiderbecke." The cornet solo, said Hazel, the ensembles—all showed a debt to Hardy.

It could be so, just as someone listening to Mares on the New Orleans Rhythm Kings recording of "Sweet Lovin' Man" can say, with accuracy, "I know who that is: it's that guy who worshiped Oliver." Players with developing styles are forever showing their indebtedness to others: far from being blameworthy, it's a badge of pedigree.

By 1927, Bix Beiderbecke had developed far beyond the diffident young man who made those first Gennett records. Comparison of his choruses on the two recorded versions of "Riverboat Shuffle" or "Jazz Me Blues," made only three years apart, tells the story. So swift was his progress that by 1928 he apparently regarded his own early work as little better than adolescent fumbling.

John Wigginton Hyman, who as "Johnny Wiggs" was a New Orleans cornetist who had heard and admired both men, emphatically contested any claim that Beiderbecke's style was little more than a copy of Hardy's. "Bix is the only [white] musician who created a separate and distinct jazz style," he said in a 1977 interview. "Bix pulled his style right out of the sky . . . [He] invented a new jazz style, full-blown, perfect in every respect, and laid it out before the people." Wiggs's own style clearly reflected fascination with the kind of "correlated" phrasing, thematically related phrases in pairs or groups of three, associated with Beiderbecke. He also spoke often about Hardy and the ways in which the two styles might have resembled one another. Some colleagues remember him on jobs, playing certain passages first in the style of Hardy, then in the style of Bix. "He was fascinated by the affinities and differences," said one, "a real nut on the subject".[21]

When the Davenport Coliseum closed for the summer on Memorial Day 1921, Carlisle Evans already had replacement work, and Hardy and Leon Roppolo were with him when he opened at Electric Park, in Waterloo, not far from Davenport. But the cornetist had other plans: on June 19 he left to join George Brunies in a band led by Albert "Doc" Wrixon aboard the Streckfus steamer *Capitol*. Bix, Brunies recalled, was playing on the Streckfus *Majestic* during this time and would occasionally sit in on the *Capitol*.

Hardy probably stayed around Davenport the rest of the summer, working the boats and picking up what extra work he could. But by autumn, when Brunies, Roppolo, and Black went to Chicago to join Paul Mares in a new band at Mike Fritzel's Friars' Inn, there seemed little choice for him but to go back to New Orleans.

For the next year the trail becomes indistinct. There is some indication that Hardy went back to work at the Johnson Iron Works, playing evenings around the West Bank with Norman Brownlee and others. But little is heard of him until late 1922, when Roppolo came back to town briefly to recruit extra musicians for the Friars' Inn.

Pianist and straw boss Elmer Schoebel had decamped to the new, remodeled Midway Gardens, taking several Friars' Inn men with him. Mares and Roppolo had talked owner Mike Fritzel into trying a reorganized, expanded house band, featuring two cornets and three reeds. Hardy headed north again, along with bassist "Chink Martin" Abraham and reedman Nunzio (sometimes identified as "Charlie") Scaglioni.

Chicago clarinetist Voltaire "Volly" De Faut remembered the cornetist as something of an original. "He wore an unusual outfit around town made up of a pair of brown-button shoes, brown derby, a tight-fitting pinch-back coat, and he carried his cornet around in a green sack, not a case," De Faut told interviewer John T. Schenck. Hardy, he said, played "in a much softer style" than Bix— perhaps something of a surprise to those who have characterized Beiderbecke as a withdrawn, even diffident, player.[22]

The larger band played for awhile—perhaps as much as a month—at the Friars' Inn, and from all indications the musicians had great fun. Mares and Hardy, particularly, enjoyed working out two-cornet passages in a manner that is more familiarly associated with King Oliver and Louis Armstrong but seems to have been a convention among New Orleans men of both races. Drummer Ben Pollack, alas, later described the group as disordered, able to get together only on "breaks and riffs." Without a Schoebel to guide and organize things, the ten musicians had fallen naturally and inevitably into loosely structured jamming.

Scaglione, a good reader, had no trouble getting into Chicago local 10 of the musicians' union. Martin, after some initial trouble, also got in. There is no indication how Hardy fared with the local; records for 1922–23 no longer exist to substantiate claims by some scholars (and by Hazel) that his failure to pass the union's admission test resulted in his departure from the Friars' Inn.

Whatever the case, the idyll didn't last long. By mid-spring, out of a job, Hardy was again on his way home. By this time his father was dead, his sister Elinor had married, and the two elder brothers were apparently out on their own. Emmett, accordingly, moved himself and his mother across the river to 2304 State Street, off St. Charles Avenue in New Orleans, near Tulane University.

From then on he seems to have remained largely at home. When Paul Mares came home from Chicago some weeks later, there were living-room jam sessions where the two men developed the two-cornet patterns they'd begun to work out during the month at the Friars' Inn. Clarinetist Raymond Burke recalled taking part in several such get-togethers. "They often called Leon Roppolo at his home so he could hear them over the phone," Burke told New Orleans historian George Kay. "[Roppolo] was very sick at the time and he wouldn't leave his house."[23]

Hardy's own health, never strong, began to fail as tuberculosis set in. It became rapidly clear, in the first months of 1924, that he would not be able to continue playing much longer.

Tuberculosis was still a major threat in 1920s America, particularly in cities. In many cases, people had it and didn't even realize they had been ill until examinations in later life disclosed scars. The situation only changed with the development first of streptomycin, then of more sophisticated antibiotics, all but wiping out the disease in the 1960s, '70s, and '80s.

"But in the '20s," said New York City physician Dr. Gary Horbar, "there were few options. There was an operation called a thoracoplasty, in which surgeons went in through the rib cage and crushed the portion of the lung that was tubercular. But that was rare, and held no guarantee of success." Much more common was the kind of treatment described in Thomas Mann's *The Magic Mountain*: a sanatorium in some country climate, often in the mountains, with plenty of fresh (preferably dry) air, rest, and good food.[24]

Hardy did what his doctors recommended. He moved to the semi-rural north shore of Lake Ponchartrain, between Mandeville and Covington, and spent more than a year convalescing. According to Monk Hazel the treatment was successful, and when he returned to New Orleans early in 1925 he seemed well on the road to recovery.

But shortly thereafter he was back in the hospital, this time with acute appendicitis. "He was weak from being in bed all that time," said Hazel, "so he couldn't take ether. So they had to give him a local anesthetic: in other words, he lay up there and watched them cut his guts open."[25]

He came through that crisis, too, his friend said. But not long after that—Hazel estimated it as between a month and six weeks—peritonitis (infection of the membrane of the abdominal cavity) set in, perhaps as an indirect result of the appendectomy. Hardy's constitution, weakened by both the tuberculosis and the surgery, obviously couldn't endure a new crisis. At eight A.M. on Friday, June 16, 1925, just four days after turning twenty-two, Emmett Hardy died.

A story persisted among fellow-musicians that Hardy celebrated his birthday with a party, surrounded by Monk, the Boswells, trumpeter Leon Prima (brother of Louis), and other close friends, and that at some point jamming began. "We were playing," Hazel said, "and I could see him arguing with his mother, because the doctors had forbidden him to touch the horn.

"So finally he goes in the closet and comes out with this square case—his Conn Victor model cornet. So he takes it out and his mama sits at the piano and they start playing. His mama starts hitting those church chords, you know, and they start playing the blues. They wound up with us sitting around the floor, crying like babies."[26]

Another romanticized, heavily embellished, bit of jazz bathos? The doomed young man playing the blues one last time before giving his body up to the gods? It's easy enough to read it that way; but even allowing for an element of exaggeration, it hardly strains plausibility that he knew, after having been through so much, that he might not survive longer. After playing, said Hazel, he packed the cornet back in its case and handed it to his friend with a remark to the effect that "I won't have any more use for this."

His funeral party was so large that the ferry had to cross the Mississippi four times from Jackson Avenue to Gretna to accommodate all the mourners and their cars. "It was the longest funeral I ever saw," said Hazel. "I mean, the party left the house, and by the time they got to the Jesuits' church at Loyola—what do they call it, the Little Flower?—there was people that still hadn't left the house." He was buried at the Hook and Ladder fireman's cemetery in Gretna.[27]

Hazel says Hardy's mother kept two pieces of correspondence—a postcard from Louis Armstrong, proclaiming her son "the King," and a long letter from Bix, written in late 1925, full of gratitude for all Emmett had done for him.

"Emmett was the greatest musician I have ever heard," the letter reportedly said. "If ever I can come near your son's greatness I'll die happy."[28]

Regrettably, neither document has been found. Also missing is an Edison home recording cylinder of "Wang Wang Blues," which Hardy is said to have made in 1920 with a small group including Brownlee, guitarist Bill Eastwood, and violinist Oscar Marcour.

Interesting, too, is a remark attributed to Jimmy Dorsey: "I roomed with Bix in New York, and I recall how he used to practice, often commenting on Hardy, and how terrific he thought Hardy was. Hardy was Bix's idol and Bix gave Hardy credit for teaching him."[29]

Martha Boswell's devotion to him remained undimmed. Indeed, Emmett Hardy, dead at twenty-two, might well have become her—and jazz history's—Michael Furey, as in Joyce's "The Dead," singing his sweet doomed song for all eternity beneath her window.

That is, had it not been for Bix Beiderbecke. Some of Hardy's advocates, in defending his reputation, seem to fall not far short of blaming Bix for also dying young and becoming an object of near-idolatrous admiration among later generations of fans.

Through no fault of his own, Beiderbecke achieved a higher profile (though not all that high) at a later and more accessible time, performed on a wider stage, had the good fortune to make records—and died under far more melodramatic circumstances.

Self-destructiveness, moreover, exerts its own morbid fascination, easily surpassing illness and inclement destiny in its appeal to the darker side of our emotions. Guitarist Eddie Lang, age thirty-one, dies needlessly after what should have been a routine tonsillectomy urged on him by his friend Bing Crosby. Chicago clarinetist Frank Teschemacher is cut off cruelly by an automobile accident; Leon Roppolo, his mind a demented shambles, wastes away in a Louisiana sanitarium. Another gifted clarinetist, Don Murray, expires in a Los Angeles hospital just when he seems about to recover from an auto accident.

All their deaths arouse a deep sense of loss, of regret—but none equals the emotional responses summoned by the very thought of Beiderbecke, struggling vainly against God knows what forces of inner darkness, seeking oblivion in alcohol, and dead at last in a squalid Queens apartment, screaming deliriously about Mexicans with knives.

Emmett Hardy, by contrast, died a sad, quiet, almost intimate little death. Also, to his eternal bad luck, he came and went a bit too early; too little of him remains on view—and, alas, he never made records.

Above all, his fate is just too similar to that of Bix. The romanticist early history of jazz may be too narrow a conceit to support more than one such beatification. Hardy would in effect have had to supplant Bix as the beautiful doomed youth of 1920s jazz; his life and early death seem too frail a vessel to do that.

It is probably just this for which Hardy's New Orleans friends never forgave Beiderbecke. It is hardly surprising that the grieving process should also involve selective remembrance of Bix only as the hero-worshiping, fumbling kid who hung around the band, and for whom Hardy kindly spared time and patience.[30]

That the kid should have been eulogized as a fallen hero, while his once-upon-a-time mentor was all but forgotten, must have been intolerable to those many in his home town who loved Emmett Louis Hardy.

4

White New Orleans Jazz in the 1920s

> You'll never know how nice it seems,
> Or just how much it really means . . .
> —Song: "Basin Street Blues"
> (words and music by
> Spencer Williams, 1928)

The early history of jazz often seems nothing so much as a litany of arrivals and departures. Arrivals of new populations and heroes, new ways of thinking and wanting and doing. And departures, leave-takings, mass flights of people and music to other germination points.

It's in the peripatetic nature of the music, hence in the lives of those who played it. Nomads, some of them, wandering wherever fortune, the railroad, or a beat-up Model T happened to take them. Young men on the make, following the imperatives of heart, hope, and hormones. Workers—husbands, fathers, even grandfathers—uprooting themselves for the sake of enough work to keep food on the family table, a roof overhead.

Often unspoken, *Auswanderung* is written into the story of jazz. And as centers of population and pullulation shift, so does the music, leaving behind—what? A ghost town, populated only by those too unimaginative, too faint-hearted, too conservative to take the big risk? An artistic wasteland, deserted by its best minds and talents? Empty streets, their faint echoes lost around the corners of the passing years?

The question seems particularly relevant applied to New Orleans. With or without the mythology constructed so long and lovingly around its early days, accounts of New Orleans jazz in the 1920s have always exuded a "been here and gone" flavor. No more Joe Oliver or Sidney Bechet, no Leon Roppolo or Paul Mares, no Dodds or Brunies brothers. Above all, no Louis Armstrong. Fun's over, gentlemen; the party has moved on.

For all the celebration and reverence accorded the activities of New Orleans musicians in distant cities, the home front has received relatively little attention. That seems regrettable: examination of what went on in the post-exodus Crescent City, and attention to the many records made there beginning in 1924, yields valuable clues to how the travelers sounded before they left; how typical the various recorded bands were of music heard in New Orleans before the advent of recording. Clues, also, to the very origins of the styles, individual and collective, that shaped the ultimate character of what has come to be called jazz.

Gradually the work of such scholars as Karl Koenig, Henry Kmen, S. Frederick Starr, Bruce Boyd Raeburn, Lawrence Gushee, Curtis Jerde, Jack Stewart, and numerous others has altered our perception of how the music that became jazz emerged. Even with all the results not yet in, it seems safe to assume that white, black, and Creole were present and active from the start, as both creators and innovators. Evidence abounds.

Though unmistakably a southern city, New Orleans was not entirely of the South, not even of the rest of Louisiana. Its century of French and Spanish rule, its status as a seaport, dealing with the Caribbean and Central and South America, even in a curious way its reputation as a sporting city, helped set it apart. This also extended to its population distribution. Racial and ethnic ghettos, as they existed in New York and other northern cities, were virtually unknown. People lived where they lived, in jumbled neighborhoods which seemed to reflect no grand design, no apprehension of order. "More often than not," says historian William Ivy Hair,

> black and white working people lived on the same block, frequently under the same roof in double-occupancy rectangular wooden cottages. Some of these dwellings were two-story structures, with families of different races alongside each other both upstairs and downstairs; they were neighbors but seldom friends, living side by side not out of preference on the part of either, but from economic necessity.[1]

So it was that bassist Pops Foster lived in Adams Street, only a couple of houses down from Italo-American clarinetist Leon Roppolo. That the Shields family, including clarinet-playing brothers Larry and Harry, shared a two-family house with Buddy Bolden, legendary cornetist of the earliest days of jazz. Cornetist-leader King Oliver was a tenant in a house whose landlord was a German who played cornet in a brass band.[2]

Musicians, too, were well aware of one another. Guitarist Danny Barker and many others have cited occasions out at the Lake Pontchartrain shore when "colored and white bands battled (or bucked) frequently from opposite lake-front camps." Similar accounts are found in the reminiscences of cornetist Johnny DeDroit and even pioneer drummer-organizer Jack Laine, who speaks of hearing a black band on a neighboring wharf practicing phrases his own band had just played, then—perhaps the following week—playing them right back. Karl Koenig suggests that the reverse was equally likely to have been true.

Overall, the role played by the 635-square-mile saltwater lake in the city's musical life cannot be underestimated. Its south shore, a six-mile train ride from downtown New Orleans, housed five major resort communities: Spanish Fort, Milneburg (celebrated in the jazz standard "Milenberg [sic] Joys"), West End (immortalized in Louis Armstrong's "West End Blues"), Little Woods, and the rather less reputable Bucktown. The south shore, running forty miles west to east, included boardwalks, amusement parks, restaurants, dance pavilions, theatres, movie houses, shooting galleries, ice cream parlors, private cottages, outdoor bandstands, picnic grounds, and numerous private social, rowing, and yachting clubs, all serving black, white, and Creole patrons. Beginning in the mid-nineteenth century, music was an integral part of south shore resort life.

According to various estimates, as many as twenty bands might be playing at once on a given Pontchartrain Sunday afternoon, and some have put totals for an entire weekend as high as seventy. Sidney Bechet and other early musicians have credited the lakeshore as the real cradle of jazz, far outweighing the Storyville red light district.[3]

Despite burgeoning research, much of what we know of the development of jazz before 1917, the year of the first Original Dixieland Jazz Band records, still rests on hypothesis, educated guesswork, supposition and conjecture, supported by personal recollection. With the added resource of the phonograph, inquiry is immediately on firmer ground. Similarities between the 1923 records of King Oliver's Creole Jazz Band and those made in New Orleans a few years later by Oscar Celestin's Tuxedo Orchestra, for example, lead to valuable conclusions about the conventions of New Orleans ensemble playing, conventions which might not have been available with only the Oliver records as evidence. Recordings by the society orchestra of Armand J. Piron, and by the bands of cornetist Sam Morgan and riverboat "Professor" Fate Marable, reveal much about the currents that shaped the music even before arrival of the phonograph.

Such, too, is the case with white New Orleans musicians in the 1920s. And in this connection, if the early saga of New Orleans jazz has any true heroes beyond the ranks of musicians, a leading candidate must be a young Columbia Graphophone Co. employee named Ralph Peer. As an artist-and-repertoire man based in New York, he appears to have been the first to recognize commercial potential in the Original Dixieland Jazz Band. He brought them in to record two test selections on January 30, 1917, a month before they ever entered a Victor studio. Columbia executives, unimpressed, fluffed their music off as ludicrous cacophony. History, as ever, moved on, and the Victor Talking Machine Company reaped the rewards.

Peer, too, moved on and by 1924 was working for OKeh records as a roving talent scout; sometime during the week of March 9 he arrived in New Orleans with mobile recording equipment and crew, setting up shop at 123 Carondelet, in the offices of the Kimball Piano Co.

According to discographies and OKeh ledgers, they began recording on Saturday, March 15, and ran virtually nonstop throughout the weekend. Given America's present end-of-century vogue for viewing history through the prism of racial politics, it would be easy to read meaning into the fact that four of the five bands recorded on this first visit were white. Clear-eyed assessment yields a simpler conclusion: OKeh was looking for organized bands, either well known or at least regularly employed, bands that could be counted on to play well together instantly and enjoyed enough of a popular following to assure the company of selling some records. Many of the city's best black bands were absent: Joe Oliver was in Chicago, as were Armstrong, Kid Ory, Jelly Roll Morton, the Dodds brothers, Jimmie Noone, and others. The highly rated band of violinist Armand J. Piron had been in New York since early the preceding year, at the Roseland Ballroom on Broadway, and had recorded for OKeh, Columbia, and Victor.

As Bruce Boyd Raeburn notes, Peer could as easily have recorded any number of local men (examples include cornetists Chris Kelly and Buddy Petit, not to mention Manuel Perez, who had played Chicago with Charles Elgar in 1915); but whether such men were not affiliated with regularly employed bands or whether—an all-important factor—Peer simply doubted their names would sell records, even in the regional southern market, is now impossible to determine.

Peer and his OKeh technicians returned the following winter for another recording marathon beginning on Thursday, January 22, 1925. The gates were now open: within the next months, Columbia and Victor followed, sending their own mobile units to capture a wide variety of both black and white New Orleans bands. Victor, arriving that March, recorded essentially the same reconstituted New Orleans Rhythm Kings that Peer had recorded for OKeh in January.[4]

The OKeh records of 1924–25 remain the most significant, in that they afford history its first concrete documentation of New Orleans jazz in situ. Whatever the selection process, there can be no doubt that these are accomplished musicians, and that the conventions governing ensembles, rhythm, and—to what limited extent they exist—solos are truly those of Crescent City music.

Despite differences of individual tone and approach (and, too, of ability), they are all playing generally the same kind of music, and in much the same manner. Sound and approach are closely related to those of the New Orleans Rhythm Kings, raising an obvious question: is this a matter of "influence," of emulation? Or (as is far more likely) are all these groups, the Friars' Inn gang included, drawing from a pool of commonly shared understanding of how things are done?

Paul Mares's oft-quoted comment—"We did our best to copy the colored music we'd heard at home . . . but naturally we couldn't play real colored style"—might have been so in some cases. But the other, unspoken, half of the trumpeter's statement is no less telling: whatever their original motivations, the white musicians quickly developed their own distinctive way of doing things. Emotionally more restrained, perhaps (though not without exception), rhythmically less intense (again, not without exception), it displayed a consistent, identifiably melodic character and a clarity of tone and execution.[5].

Cornetist Johnny DeDroit (1892–1986), leading off on March 15, was himself something of a trailblazer: in 1918, while the Original Dixieland Jazz Band was igniting showbiz pandemonium in New York City, DeDroit quietly landed a job for his sextet at Kolb's, a restaurant on fashionable St. Charles Avenue, a stronghold of white, polite New Orleans society. That very June, the *New Orleans Times Picayune* had decried "jass" music, along with dime novels and doughnuts fried in grease, as "manifestations of a low streak in man's tastes that has not yet come out in civilization's wash." The editorial went on to all but deny that "this particular form of musical vice" had originated in New Orleans at all.[6]

But there, amid all this righteous indignation, Johnny DeDroit and his "jass" band not only opened at Kolb's but did first-class business, and stayed on for the next eight years. DeDroit, whose technical assurance and versatility had made him a favorite of "Papa" Jack Laine, also worked at the Suburban Gardens, which as the Tin Roof Café had left its name on the New Orleans Rhythm Kings' "Tin Roof Blues."

"I was always working, always busy," DeDroit told Myra Menville in 1976. "Where did I play? You name it—nightclubs, Carnival balls, theatres, private parties, conventions, hotels, Tulane and LSU fraternity parties, political meetings, Club Forest, Suburban Gardens, The Orpheum and The Saenger [theatres], the old Liberty Theatre, vaudeville, country clubs, the New Orleans Symphony just to prove I could, Kolb's Restaurant . . . the Cave and the Forest Grill rooms in the old Grunewald Hotel which is now the Fairmont"—and just as many spots in Chicago and New York.[7]

DeDroit seems to have been active as early as 1912, when a newspaper account has him leading a "military" band at a parish fair on the more rural Pontchartrain north shore. But what were he and his colleagues playing at so distant a time? What kind of music entertained the customers at Kolb's? Probably pretty much the same transitional form of small-band, ragtime-flavored music as Tom Brown's 1915 "Band From Dixieland," if doubtless somewhat more polished.

By 1924, when DeDroit faced OKeh's recording horns at last, he had obviously moved with the times. His solid middle-register cornet lead dominates a tight little band, with the rhythm laying down a steady four-to-the-bar. If their "Panama" is neither as relaxed nor as free as the Friars Society Gennett recording of nineteen months earlier, it is nevertheless working easily within the same frame of reference. On "Nobody Knows Blues," in fact, trombonist Russ Papalia's choice of ensemble figures closely parallels that of George Brunies with the NORK.

Resemblance to the Friars' Inn band is even more marked on "Number Two Blues," the name by which "Tiger Rag" was known among both black and white New Orleans musicians; they take it at an attractive, strutting tempo—more on the order of what the Original Dixieland Jazz Band might have done in a less fevered atmosphere than that of 1917 New York. Clarinetist Henry Raymond plays sixteen Roppolo-like bars in his low register, then shifts to a bright-toned high range reminiscent of the ODJB's Larry Shields.[8]

Leading an even more forceful band was cornetist Johnny Bayersdorffer, a regular at the Tokyo Gardens, at Spanish Fort on the lakefront. Though his personnel usually included two saxophones, for this maiden recording effort he pared things down to a basic instrumentation. The band plays hard, generating lots of energy in the final ensembles; but in both the rhythm and in Bayersdorffer's fiery lead there's more than a trace of the old even-eighth-note ragtime feel, a bit passé even in 1924, which also dominates the playing of Freddie Keppard—and from which Nick LaRocca had gradually emancipated himself between 1917 and 1923.[9]

All the same, these are informative records, offering a taste of Tom Brown's strong ensemble trombone and—perhaps best of all—the elegant and supple clarinet of Nunzio "Charlie" Scaglione. In Max Harrison's telling phrase, Scaglione "possessed a fine contrapuntal sense and maintained unflagging melodic independence." Unhappily, these two titles, little circulated at the time of issue, are his only appearance on record. Save for them, his name might have been lost altogether, consigned, like that of so many early New Orleans colleagues, to a perpetual half-light of anecdote and reminiscence. He's undeniably a vivid presence, driving and filling out the ensembles; his solo on "The Waffle Man's Call," especially, is fine jazz clarinet playing.[10]

Its beauty and authority make clear that what posterity celebrates as the characteristic New Orleans clarinet style had many more white exemplars than merely Roppolo and Shields. Alongside the names of Dodds, Noone, Bechet, Bigard, Nicholas, and the rest must be set others, including Scaglione, Charles Cordilla, Irvine "Pinky" Vidacovich, Raymond Burke (of whom more presently), and in all probability Larry Shields's younger brother, Harry, who also recorded little in those early days (but who more than made up for it in later life).[11]

Reference to Roppolo, Scaglione, and Cordilla inevitably brings up the role, still underdocumented, played in the development of jazz by musicians from the city's populous Italian, largely Sicilian, working class. Between the close of the Civil War and the end of the nineteenth century, the number of foreign-born Italians in New Orleans is estimated to have jumped from fewer than two thousand in 1870 to somewhere between fifteen and twenty thousand. The majority of these by far were from the region of Palermo, in Sicily, drawn to New Orleans by the similarity of climate, by family ties, by the city's Roman Catholic heritage—and by what seemed to be both quantity and variety of employment opportunity.

(Though Irish and black workers monopolized the best waterfront jobs, Sicilians found work as fishermen, stevedores, fruit and vegetable peddlers, importers and exporters. But even at this relatively early date, they also had become associated in the American mind with crime and violence; fear of the "black hand" was widespread. A bloody clash in May of 1890 between members of the rival Matranga and Provenzano factions fed growing public outrage and resentment; and when, that October 15, the popular young police chief David Hennessy, who had handled the case, was shot down outside his home, the anger burst into the open.

Then followed the infamous Italian lynchings, now entirely overlooked in standard jazz histories. Nineteen Italians were rounded up and charged; nine were tried. Six were acquitted outright, and the jury could reach no verdict on the other three. But by now public outrage was at fever pitch, and on the evening of March 14, 1891, a crowd estimated at between five and twenty thousand—including many prominent citizens—marched on Orleans Parish Prison and shot or clubbed to death eleven of the nineteen Sicilians originally arrested.

Even the race riot of 1900, in which a black laborer named Robert Charles shot twenty-seven whites, including seven policemen, before being gunned down, did not wound the city's sense of harmony as deeply as, and in quite the way that, the Hennessy affair had done. As capstone to an ongoing series of violent events, and continued fear of the sinister and shadowy thing known as "the Mafia," it left an anti-Sicilian animus that pervaded New Orleans life at all levels and made of the southern Italian immigrant population a hated underclass.

The sheer quantity of Sicilian names in the ranks of early New Orleans jazzmen—LaRocca, Roppolo, Veca, Almerico, Giardino, Bonano, Barocco, Capraro, Prima, Lala, Coltraro, Davilla, Loyocano, Manone, Gallodoro, Federico, Cordilla, Guarino, Scaglione, Pinero, Schiro, Parenti, Mangiapane, Liberto, Franzella, Papalia, Mello, Palmisano, Pecora, Provenzano, Sbarbaro—attests to the role Italo-Americans played in the music's first years. It is a field ripe for further research.[12]

*   *   *

The abiding question, of course, remains that of the true origins of what came to be known as "jazz." Almost from the start of research in the mid-1930s, the music's earliest days have been a thicket of contradiction, a playground for social reformers, political ideologues, and cultural romantics. Too often, supposition has posed as research, opinion as documented fact. Creation mythology postulated a central role for the Storyville red light district and invested such early figures as cornetist Buddy Bolden with near-superhuman powers.

Until relatively recently, little attention was paid to such significant—if less fanciful—prime causes as the vast national mania for band music, set in motion in post–Civil War days by Patrick Sarsfield Gilmore and his heir, "March King" John Philip Sousa. It reached its apex at the end of the nineteenth century and beginning of the twentieth, not coincidentally the same fertile period that spawned jazz. Band popularity knew no barriers of class or even race but had equal impact throughout all strata of society. As Margaret Hindle Hazen has noted:

Inspired by the professionals, amateurs by the hundreds of thousands took up the art form. Factory workers, miners, railroad employees and cowboys played in bands sponsored by employers or labor unions. Members of men's clubs joined bands. So did newspaper carriers, orphans and schoolchildren. In response to the widespread nineteenth-century belief in the rehabilitative and healthful effects of music, penitentiaries, hospitals and even a Hawaiian leper colony promoted band activities for their inmates.[13]

The breakup of countless military bands after the Civil War had flooded the market with cornets, trumpets, trombones, and other brasswinds. Instrument companies quickly joined the vogue by producing wide ranges of "student horns," priced well within the reach of even the most modest of incomes. Music publishers, whether headquartered in New York, Cincinnati, or Oskaloosa, Iowa, saturated the national market with band arrangements: everything from transcriptions of symphonies and operatic arias to sentimental ballads and the latest popular marches, could be bought for pennies, and everyone played them.

A band, said Ronald L. Davis

> was as essential to community pride as a fire department . . . On practice evenings the players scurried home from work, bolted down a quick meal, snatched up their instrument cases, and sped off to the firehouse or city hall, where they rehearsed in shirt sleeves. During the summer months the band normally played a free evening concert once a week for the community and afternoon concerts on holidays . . . A wooden bandstand had been erected in the part or town square, usually circular or octagonal and big enough for the band's eight to twelve players . . . There were also military bands, industrial bands, Salvation Army bands, circus bands, and school bands. In 1893 seventy-one different bands marched in the inaugural parade for Grover Cleveland, while 136 bands paraded in the Knights Templar conclave in Boston two years later.[14]

The movement found a hospitable environment in New Orleans and its environs. Bands of whites, of blacks, of Creoles, were plentiful. There were Italian bands, highlighted by the fluid, richly ornamented Sicilian style of clarinet playing; German bands, French bands. As New Orleans historian Dr. Karl Koenig has remarked, a Louisiana town, great or small, that did not have a brass band was an anomaly. They played for concerts, for picnics and company excursions, for lawn parties and dances, weddings and funerals. At Mardi Gras time it often seemed a band could be found on every street corner, contributing mightily to the festive atmosphere.

That many of these bands, in New Orleans and elsewhere, were playing ragtime quite early is well documented on records. Researcher Jerome Shipman notes, that "Many of the characteristic features of early jazz—sliding trombones, upper register clarinet figures, snare drum and woodblock percussion, not to mention breaks—could be heard in the military bands, piano-percussion duets, and banjo trios before 1917."[15]

Other influences entered the New Orleans mix: tangos and habaneras from the Caribbean; rhythmic folk music from Martinique; Baptist and Methodist hymns from New and old England; piano ragtime and popular ballads; spirituals, a tradition now known to be shared almost equally by black and white.[16]

Many compositions later incorporated into the jazz repertoire began as brass band selections: the march "High Society," for example, dates from 1901, "Panama" from 1911. Latter-day jazz bands incorporated large portions of them, often including original ensemble parts, into their performances. S. Frederick Starr has pointed out that Kid Ory, performing S. B. Stambaugh's 1911 "Gettysburg March" in later years, still played the printed trombone line. Even the famed "High Society" clarinet obbligato was taken from the piccolo part of an earlier published arrangement.[17]

If the memories of those musicians who survived into the age of taped interviews and oral histories are to be trusted, all sorts of bands took early to "ragging" or "syncopating" melody lines, even on non-ragtime selections. The public culture may have remained racially segregated, but it would be folly to contend that such universals as music and dancing, marching and singing, were not the property of all New Orleans).

* * *

Ralph Peer's second New Orleans visit, in January 1925, yielded another batch of outstanding records, including four titles by a reconstituted New Orleans Rhythm Kings, with both Leon Roppolo and Charlie Cordilla* present on reeds. The two also appear together on a pair of titles by the Halfway House Orchestra, under the leadership of cornetist Albert "Abbie" Brunies.

These are the first in a series, spanning a three-year period, which clearly define the functional role of jazz as a *dance* music in New Orleans social life. They are not self-consciously *hot* in the manner of the Bayersdorffer sides; instead, the improvised solos and rhythmic elements—and, on many of their records, all-stops-out final ensembles—seem an energizing, contributing ingredient in what is essentially a straight dance band. It is probably closer to the way such bands sounded on the job, playing in roadhouses, restaurants, and dance halls.

The idea of a hot band playing for dancing, without concession to the full range of dancers' needs, is one of the by-products of the romantic view that many authors, beginning with Ramsey and Smith in 1939's *Jazzmen*, have taken of jazz history. In this context it is useful to remember that (a) most of the seminal hot records of the '20s were made by such *pro tem* units as the Armstrong Hot Five and Seven, Bix Beiderbecke's "Gang," and Jelly Roll Morton's Red Hot Peppers, which existed only in front of recording studio microphones; (b) regularly working bands, whether Oliver's in Chicago or Bayersdorffer's in New Orleans, stressed the hot aspects of their repertoires at the behest of record producers; and (c) the working libraries of such admired ensembles as Fletcher Henderson's orchestra included at least twenty publishers' "stock" arrangements of dance selections and current hits.

The writers' emphasis on hot jazz as somehow an entity apart has been to skew perception among fans and historians as to what actually constituted a night's work; to categorize working bands as "sweet" or "hot." The simple reality was that a band playing for dancing, if it expected to hold its job, had to satisfy many tastes, hot music only one among them.

The Halfway House still stands at the corner of City Park Avenue and Ponchartrain Boulevard (Louisiana Route 10), paralleling the New Basin Canal; situated about halfway between downtown New Orleans and the lakefront, it was often known among musicians as "Chris's," after co-owner Chris Rabensteiner.

Abbie Brunies got the job there in 1919. By 1924, his regular band included Cordilla on clarinet and tenor, Mickey Marcour as pianist, Bill Eastwood on banjo,

---

*Disagreement still exists as to the spelling of Charlie Cordilla's (or Cordella's) name. For the purposes of this work he will be Cordilla.

and Leo Adde on drums. Roppolo was never a member, but his presence on the band's maiden record date is not surprising: he was Cordilla's friend, much admired among white New Orleans musicians. To have him there must have been looked upon as something of an honor. A photograph of the group at that time shows both reedmen, plus left-handed trombonist Joe "Hook" Loyocano.*

Perhaps it's Roppolo's presence that makes "Pussy Cat Rag" and "Barataria," with their loose structure and jam ensembles, the hottest of the Halfway House records—though even here the band positions its jamming within an overall arrangement. Among the features of "Pussy Cat," for example, is a Roppolo-Cordilla "straight" saxophone duet. "Barataria" uses clarinet (Cordilla) and alto sax (Roppolo) in the ensembles. But the full-chorus clarinet solo is unmistakably Roppolo. It's reasonable to assume that Cordilla simply deferred, confining his own clarinet work to the tutti passages.

"The band," William J. Schafer wrote in 1980, "echoes the NORK style in many ways, and it is clear that this group of white musicians who grew up playing together had developed a habitual feeling for the music. They also had strong feels for small-band styles, like the New Orleans Owls, keeping an open, ad hoc approach to their playing. The two bands come as close to the ideal of simultaneous relaxation and tension in the best black jazz of the era as any better known recording groups."[18]

The personnel remained essentially the same, minus Roppolo, in September of '25, when Columbia brought in its own mobile equipment to record a selection of New Orleans bands, including the Halfway House Orchestra. The repertoire was diverse, to say the least: Fats Waller's just-published "Squeeze Me," Scott Joplin's "Maple Leaf Rag," the old barbershop favorite "Let Me Call You Sweetheart," and a hot original by local pianist Bill Whitmore called "New Orleans Shuffle."

This last sets the pattern for many subsequent records by this band: opening ensemble played straight, a solo or two hewing close to the melody, then an all-out, high-voltage jam finale. Musically, too, this is a halfway house, staking out ground between the needs of the dancers and the pleasure of the musicians. Their tempos, for example, remain quite consistent: approximately $\lrcorner = 116$ on the fast numbers, $\lrcorner = 116$ on the slower ones, in keeping with the fox-trot dance steps in vogue at the time.

Also heard from during Columbia's September recording spree was a new group, formed out of what had been the Invincibles String Band. With an instrumentation including violin, mandolin, guitar, banjo, and ukulele, the Invincibles had been popular throughout the previous decade. Like the equally popular Six-and-Seven-Eighths band, they epitomized an important, if underdocumented, sub-genre in New Orleans musical life. Often directly inspired by bands with more conventional horns-and-rhythm instrumentations, these groups nevertheless played a form of syncopated dance music readily identifiable as jazz.

As historian Frederic Ramsey Jr. has written, "there was a lot of string jazz

---

*According to Al Rose and Edmond Southon in *New Orleans Jazz: A Family Album*, Joe "Hook" Loyocano is not the same man as Erasmus "Joe" Loyocano, who played alto saxophone with the Halfway House band in 1927–28. They were apparently not even related.

music in New Orleans in the years between 1910 and 1925, but very little of it was recorded." A set of 1949 records by the Six-and-Seven-Eighths, including historian Dr. Edmond Souchon on guitar, were, in effect, "the first recordings of an entirely string jazz group in the city." For a time, said Ramsey, the Six-and-Seven-Eighths unit was "the official band about town when 'not too noisy, but hot' music was wanted. The college groups and the 'silk stocking' element both adopted them, and even Assistant Secretary of the Navy, Commodore Ernest Lee Jahnke, made them official band for pleasant weekends aboard his sumptuous houseboat, 'Aunt Dinah.' "[19]

The Invincibles, unlike the Six-and-Seven-Eighths Band, elected in 1922 to transform themselves into a standard dance unit, adding horns and changing their name to the New Orleans Owls. Overall they resemble the Halfway House Orchestra, duplicating that band's emphasis on neatly played "straight" arrangements which open out on to energetic jamming (hear "Stomp Off! Let's Go") in the finale. Occasionally, as on "Oh Me! Oh My!" the Owls achieve an attractive collective looseness, what William J. Schafer has rightly called "a powerful feeling of amateur cheerfulness."[20]

Columbia engineers returned to New Orleans in April 1926, this time with their brand-new electrical recording equipment, and the difference in sound is remarkable: playing for microphones able to pick up a broader frequency range, Abbie Brunies has added "Chink Martin" Abraham on tuba to the Halfway House personnel, and his firm pulse lifts the band.

What strikes the ear is the clarity, each part defined, floating atop an unusually buoyant, unembellished 4/4 rhythm; Cordilla, an excellent journeyman musician, seems to improve as a soloist from date to date. On "Won't You Be My Lovin' Baby" (1927), a medium-tempo "hot" item built on the same sixteen-bars-with-tag sequence that underpins "How Come You Do Me Like You Do?" and other genre standards, Cordilla takes two solos: here and on the other side, the faster "I Don't Want to Remember," he's long-lined and fluent, with a rhythmic attack that has a certain parallel in the playing of Johnny Dodds.[21]

These were Cordilla's last Halfway House records. His replacement was one of the truly exceptional musicians of early New Orleans jazz, clarinetist Sidney Arodin. Born Sidney Arnondin on March 19, 1901, he grew up in Westwego, across the river from New Orleans, and began playing clarinet at fifteen. He soon developed close friendships with three young local trumpeters—Joe "Wingy" Manone (b. 1904, and so called because he'd lost his right hand in a streetcar accident as a boy), Louis Prima (b. 1911), and Joseph "Sharkey" Bonano (b. 1904). All three employed Arodin frequently and used him on record dates, in the decade between 1925 and 1935.

His career has not been easy to document. A restless man, he traveled often and widely, spending long periods of time away from home with such "territory" bands as those of Charles "Sunny" Clapp and Mart Britt. There are entire periods, sometimes as long as three years at a stretch, when he is simply not to be found. Some accounts of him speak of a recurrent alcohol problem, but there is little substantiation.

Married at eighteen, Arodin apparently moved his wife and infant daughter to New York in 1922, falling in at once with a circle of local musicians who recorded frequently for Plaza Group labels (Regal, Banner, Domino) as the "New Orleans Jazz Band." Their "Tin Roof Blues" of January 1924 follows the NORK record closely, faithfully reproducing everything from Mel Stitzel's piano introduction through note-for-note recreations of the George Brunies and Leon Roppolo solos by Mike Martini and Arodin, respectively. "It Had To Be You" and "Down Where the South Begins," recorded two months later, afford Arodin several solo spots: Roppolo is still obviously the model as he plumbs a cavernous, dark low register.[22]

Between late 1924, when he made his last records with this group, and a December 2, 1927, Vocalion date in New York with Wingy Manone, Jack Teagarden, and some other southern pals, there is no sign of Arodin. A 1969 article in the *Second Line* magazine makes general reference to his having been in St. Louis, Kansas City, and Chicago but gives no specifics.

Wherever he'd been, he was back in New Orleans in time for three days of Columbia recordings beginning Wednesday, April 25, 1928. This is fortunate, for it is on these sessions, beyond all others, that Sidney Arodin's lasting reputation as a master of jazz clarinet is based.

His is indeed a sound unto itself, full, rounded, sweet without cloying. If any comparison is to be made, it will be to New Orleans clarinetists of the next generation, whose moments came *after* his, especially Irving "Fazola" Prestopnik* and Eddie Miller, the latter best known as a tenor saxophonist. While Leon Roppolo's melodic sensibility exists as an element in Arodin's work, there is no clarinetist active at the time who can be cited as a direct inspiration. He certainly has little in common with Dodds's broad attack or Jimmie Noone's *portamento*-saturated sentimentality.

The closest resemblance is to Omer Simeon, a New Orleans–born Creole who grew up in Chicago and is best known for his work on the Jelly Roll Morton Red Hot Peppers records of 1926–28. A student of the fabled Lorenzo Tio Jr., Simeon employed the same sort of rounded sound and easy melodism that distinguish Arodin's work in this period. But he never worked in New Orleans, making any effect on Arodin doubtful at best.

"I don't know where he got his style," pianist Armand Hug said of Arodin. "He didn't sound like Rap [Roppolo] or anybody else. Couldn't read a note, either. But he had a beautiful tone and ideas to match." To fellow-clarinetist Harry Shields he was "one of the finest I ever heard." Many others, among them trombonist Santo Pecora, echoed such assessments.[23]

The New Orleans Owls, meanwhile, had acquired their own clarinet soloist in Irvine "Pinky" Vidacovich (1904–1966). His work on such titles as "Pretty Baby" (in a Roppolo-like low register) and "West End Romp" (a remarkable full-chorus duet with guitarist Rene Gelpi), both recorded April 14, 1926, marks him as a fine

*In the interests of clarity, he will henceforth be referred to as Fazola, or the more conventional Irving Fazola.

journeyman clarinetist in the Cordilla manner. While his solos and the exhilarating final ensembles lend great charm and variety to many Owls records, the band still suffers overall from both rhythm section unevenness and a top-heaviness brought on by reliance on what seem to be publishers' "stock" arrangements.[24] The Halfway House Orchestra, working with smaller personnel, a better rhythm team, and simpler arrangements, escapes the snares that thwart even the best Owls performances.

Taken as a whole, the recordings of April 25–27, 1928, provide an index to the ways in which white and black New Orleans styles had taken on distinct identities by the late 1920s. Part of the difference seems to have been the white players' absorption, via recordings, of influences from the North, specifically the Beiderbecke-Trumbauer and Nichols-Mole partnerships (both to be explored later).

Though "Panama" and "Dippermouth Blues," recorded April 25 under pianist Johnnie Miller's name, belong to the New Orleans canon, their treatment here is highly melodic, with a tidiness of execution closely associated with the northern players. Yet the rhythm is pure New Orleans, broad and relaxed, and the combination is irresistible.

"Panama" opens with a whole-tone ensemble passage that could have been lifted from a Red Nichols record. Hal Jordy, on alto, has clearly noted both Trumbauer and Jimmy Dorsey, and Steve Brou's single-string banjo similarly acknowledges Eddie Lang and Dick McDonough. Arodin's sunny clarinet solos on both numbers evoke Don Murray with Bix, and though Sharkey Bonano's three trumpet choruses on "Dippermouth" follow the Oliver model, his lyrical *bel canto* manner and structured phrase-building lend them quite another, almost songlike, cast.

From his first solo break on "Panama," he seems able to blend Bix Beiderbecke and Louis Armstrong in a single melodic utterance. Bonano in 1924 had auditioned unsuccessfully to replace Beiderbecke with the Wolverines; on the basis of his playing here (and on the even more startling Monk Hazel date of the following December), the setback seems regrettable. Even on "Peculiar" and "Dirty Rag," recorded under Norman Brownlee's name only four months after his ill-fated Wolverines audition, Bonano is solid and assured.

The next two days brought Abbie Brunies and the Halfway House Orchestra in front of the Columbia microphones to do six titles. Chink Martin played tuba the first day but brought his string bass on Friday, driving the ensembles in a manner immediately reminiscent of his old friend Steve Brown.[25]

Arodin sets out the melody on "Love Dreams" with assurance and tonal beauty, contributes elegant choruses to "I Hate Myself for Lovin' You" and "Let Your Lips Touch My Lips," and adds full-toned low-register obbligatos to Johnnie Saba's vocals (how like England's Al Bowlly he sounds!) on "I'll Go Back To That Dear Old Pal" and "Tell Me Who." On "Wylie Avenue Blues," perhaps the most consistently hot number of the batch, Martin bows behind Arodin's first solo and slaps behind the second, with equal potency.

Overall, the clarinetist's finest moments are on the band's last session, done

75

December 17, 1928. His obbligato lends the opening ensemble of "Just Pretending" a patterned, needlepoint texture; his solo, woven around Loyocano's alto sax melody statement, is a study in lyrical balance. His use of a concert B-natural on the second beat of bar 28, anticipating the G7 chord which follows, is an especially piquant touch.*

The single weakness in these performances lies in Abbie Brunies's own conception. Rhythmically and structurally he is still rooted in the ragtime-derived phrasing heard on the 1924 records. It is as if he has remained oblivious to the solo possibilities opened by both Armstrong and Beiderbecke and reflected so strongly in Sharkey Bonano's work on "Panama." Brunies's lead is strong and sure, an excellent "ride" in the ensembles (listen to the closing moments of "Love Dreams" and "Just Pretending"), but his solos ("Tell Me Who" is typical) seem unable to escape a raggy "jazzing" of the melody, which seems increasingly archaic alongside the flowing conception of Arodin.

The influential northern (or "futuristic," as musicians called it at the time) style came to New Orleans in person on Sunday, October 28, 1928, when Bix Beiderbecke and Frank Trumbauer played the St. Charles Theatre with Paul Whiteman's orchestra. After the concert's first half passed without so much as eight bars from either man (curious programming, considering the location), an *ad hoc* delegation of local musicians led by drummer-mellophonist Arthur "Monk" Hazel reportedly bearded the "King of Jazz" in his backstage lair, all but threatening mayhem if he didn't feature the two hot soloists. He complied, bringing them out front to do "Singin' the Blues" and some other specialties.

The visit, and a party at Paul Mares's home following the concert, left a deep impression on the New Orleans men, and most remembered it vividly the rest of their lives. Armand Hug, for example, told proudly how Bix leaned over the piano that night and showed him how to voice the chords of "In a Mist." Several of the others, with the apparent complicity of Beiderbecke and Trumbauer, took it upon themselves to make sure Whiteman heard a local hero, guitarist "Snoozer" Quinn. It worked: Quinn spent part of 1929 with the orchestra.

When, that December, a band led by Monk Hazel (1903–1968), and including both Arodin and Bonano, recorded four titles for Brunswick, the musical language was explicitly that of the New York musicians. A boyhood friend of cornetist Emmett Hardy, Hazel was active around town on cornet, mellophone, and occasionally drums. He'd recorded with clarinetist Tony Parenti and cornetist Johnny Wiggs and subbed at the Halfway House. He may, in fact, have been the drummer on "Barataria" and "Pussy Cat Rag," the first Halfway House records.

---

*The alto-and-clarinet configuration surfaces repeatedly on New Orleans–style records of the period. Perhaps the best-known of such pairings is the team of clarinetist Jimmie Noone and the sugary-toned alto saxophonist Joe Poston (later replaced by Eddie Pollack), as evidenced on many records made for Brunswick between 1928 and 1931. Boston-born multi-instrumentalist Brad Gowans, an avowed ODJB admirer, plays clarinet in the Larry Shields manner around Jim Moynahan's straight alto lead on "Four-Leaf Clover," recorded for Gennett January 20, 1927. Other examples of this particularly New Orleans convention abound on record.

By the end of 1928 he was leading the band at the roof restaurant of the Bienville Hotel, on St. Charles Avenue at Lee Circle, one of many places in town then featuring white jazz groups. "I played cornet in that band," he told the historian Bill Russell in 1959. "But I didn't have guts enough to make a record [with it], so I hired Sharkey. Sharkey didn't play [regularly] with that band." Why then, asked Russell, did the label read "under the direction of Sharkey Bonano?" Hazel waved the question aside. It was Bonano's first chance to be viewed as a leader, he said, and "I gave him the break."[26]

It's also unlikely that Arodin or Hal Jordy, both busy freelancers around town, played full-time with Hazel's band at the Bienville Hotel. But together with Sharkey they make a strong front line, easily equal to the intricacies of guitarist John Capraro's Red Nichols–like "Sizzlin' the Blues." Sharkey salutes Bix in his two first-chorus breaks, drawing on some chromatic patterns unusual in 1920s jazz; his solo leading into the final ensemble blends Bix and Louis: it's hard to think of any other trumpet soloist of the period, with the possible exception of Rex Stewart, who fused the two approaches as effortlessly.

"Get Wit It" offers more of the same, as does "Ideas," a reworking of Norman Brownlee's "Peculiar," recorded by Sharkey in 1925. The trumpeter moves comfortably throughout the whole range of his horn, Hal Jordy solos on both alto and baritone saxes, and Hazel, apparently bashful no more, picks up his mellophone for eight neatly turned bars.

Dozens of New Orleans white jazzmen had taken to the harmonically more complex, form-conscious music coming out of New York. Cornetist John Wigginton Hyman (who soon shortened his name to Johnny Wiggs) never concealed his admiration first for Red Nichols and later, after the 1928 Whiteman visit, for Bix. His first coupling under his own name, "Ain't Love Grand" and "Alligator Blues" (1927), is marred a bit by lapses of tone and execution; but two titles with clarinetist Tony Parenti's New Orleanians, done almost exactly a year later, show a cornetist well in charge of what he wants to do. Both "In the Dungeon" (interpolating a theme that strongly resembles W. C. Handy's "Ole Miss") and "When You and I Were Pals" have about them a strong Five Pennies flavor, with Parenti's alto evoking Jimmy Dorsey and trombonist Charles Hartman showing his awareness of Miff Mole.

Tony Parenti is a singular New Orleans figure. A child prodigy, he was a "reader," who studied clarinet with the respected Professor Joseph Taverno and did his ensemble apprenticeship in a concert band led by his teacher. He could also "fake"—play and improvise by ear—and not long into his teens worked for Jack Laine and played jobs alongside Johnny Stein and Nick LaRocca, who apparently invited him to go north with them. Because of his training, Parenti was equally at home in little hot groups and large theatre orchestras. Leading his own small band, he played such high-profile locations as the Liberty Theater and the Lavida Dance Hall, both on St. Charles, and made his first records for OKeh in January 1925.

By the end of 1928, he'd made up his mind to move to New York. Two records made shortly before his departure show him to be a good, if rhythmically somewhat stiff, clarinetist and an excellent alto saxophonist. His alto solos on "Pals" and "You Made Me Like It, Baby" (1928) are coherent and technically assured, with a tonal brilliance which bespeaks legitimate training.

Once in New York, Parenti entered a long career as a radio studio musician, and at one point led a saxophone quartet playing intricate arrangements of popular and "light classical" selections. He returned to small-band jazz in the 1940s and spent the rest of his career playing clarinet in various groups around New York.

Sidney Arodin, meanwhile, also hit the road. He is easily recognized on two titles recorded in Memphis September 13, 1928, by Mart Britt's "territory" band and is rumored to be (though not audible) on some mid-1929 Sunny Clapp selections.[27]

In late 1929, during one of his "at home" periods, Arodin played on one of the most significant record dates of his career—not least because it was racially mixed. The band, co-led by black cornetist Lee Collins and saxophonist Dave Jones, was working regularly at the Astoria Hotel and Ballroom, South Rampart Street and Gravier, above Canal Street. Arodin fits in as comfortably with this somewhat rough-and-ready hot ensemble as he does with the smoother Halfway House Orchestra or the musical intricacies of the Monk Hazel recording band.

Perhaps it is this very adaptability that has fueled a contention, often repeated, that Arodin was actually a "Creole of color," passing for white. On a record ("Let's Have a Jubilee") made in 1934, trumpeter Louis Prima calls out, "Why cook my beans if it ain't bayou Pom Pom Arodin! What's on your mind there, Creole?" Joe Robichaux, pianist on the Jones-Collins session, told British discographer Brian Rust categorically that Arodin was "passing," but Collins himself referred to him in a 1958 interview as "a white clarinet player."[28]

The four titles recorded on Friday, November 15, 1929, in the glistening "live" acoustics of Italian Hall, have been of interest to scholars on a number of levels. First there is the instrumentation, combining Collins's Armstrong-like trumpet with a clarinet and two saxophones. Testimony by Collins and others implies strongly that Teddy "Wiggles" Purnell, who plays alto sax on the date, was a poor clarinetist. To avoid bruising his bandmate's ego, the cornetist appears to have induced the recording director (was it Ralph Peer?) to ask for Arodin.

The clarinetist is as good as could be hoped. His solo on "Astoria Strut" is in the classic New Orleans manner, swinging as hard as Jones or Purnell on alto. For the second of his two solo shots on "Duet Stomp" he takes to his lower register, illustrating graphically the points at which Roppolo and Johnny Dodds intersect. But his most impressive showing in this company is on "Tip Easy Blues," where his single chorus rivals even Collins's brooding, Armstrong-like majesty.

Shortly after this date he was on his way again. Eddie Miller, who had been playing clarinet and alto with the New Orleans Owls, told of setting out for New York in an old Model T with Arodin and two others. Four days, four nights, and one major snowstorm later they got there, leaving the battered car in a parking lot when they discovered how much they'd have to pay to get it out.[29]

Among Arodin's new friends in New York was an emigrant from Indiana, a pianist and fledgling songwriter named Hoagy Carmichael. And it was he who took a liking to a tune the clarinetist had been playing on jobs around town, supplying lyrics, a title, and a publisher. Hoagy recorded it with a band of New York jazzmen in November 1930, thereby ushering "Lazy River" into the ranks of American popular song standards.[30]

Arodin next surfaces in autumn 1934, returning in a burst of recording activity with boyhood chums Louis Prima, newly arrived in New York, and Wingy Manone. Where was he in the meantime? His playing on the Prima numbers is, for him, rather tense—perhaps in response to the tighter feel of the New York rhythm section of Claude Thornhill (piano), George Van Eps (guitar), Artie Shapiro (string bass), and veteran drummer Stan King. They push the beat, in a way quite different from the wide, steady groove of the New Orleans players. While enhancing the visceral excitement of Prima's Armstrong-based style, it also seems to force Arodin to harden his approach.[31]

He's sometimes abrupt, breaking off phrases, and there's a rasp in his tone quite in contrast to the purity of 1928–29. The overall result is to lend this normally most flowing of clarinetists a guttural, piping quality reminiscent (as on "Long About Midnight") of Pee Wee Russell. Yet the minute the tempo relaxes or slows down, the old qualities reappear. He opens "Star Dust," for example, with a reflective low-register melody statement, and mines the blues potential of another Carmichael tune, "Sing It Way Down Low."

Things with Manone are a bit different. The atmosphere is rather less frenetic, and the band (billed as the "New Orleans Rhythm Kings") is full of old Crescent City friends: alongside Wingy and Brunies (or, on a later date, Pecora) are pianist Terry Shand and bassist Bennie (sometimes identified as "Bonnie") Pottle, Arodin companions in several territory bands; guitarist Hilton "Nappy" Lamare, who had just quit Ben Pollack, was in New York (with Eddie Miller, Ray Bauduc, and others) scuffling for work.

Another outstanding clarinetist in this New Orleans circle is the all but unsung Meyer Weinberg. Also known as Gene Meyer, he appears only in discographies and in three photos printed in the Al Rose–Edmond Souchon *New Orleans Jazz: A Family Album*. Unlike such early figures as Emmett Hardy and Nunzio Scaglione, who recorded little or not at all and are known chiefly through anecdotes, Weinberg is now remembered through some three dozen record titles, mostly with Prima, Sharkey, and Santo Pecora.

Unlike Arodin, he plays with a punchy, almost Chicagoan tone and attack. Especially good representatives from 1937 include "The Love Bug Will Bite You," "I Just Can't Believe You're Gone," and "Rhythm on the Radio" (Prima), and "Danger, Love at Work" and an unusually bright-tempo "Tin Roof Blues."

Colleagues clearly thought well of him. "He was a fine musician," said Pecora. "He didn't sound like anybody but himself . . . He didn't sound like Artie Shaw or Benny Goodman." Johnny DeDroit agreed, adding that Weinberg "should go down in posterity." In New Orleans he's perhaps best remembered for having stepped in at short notice when Joe Dixon didn't turn up for a May 5, 1946, New Orleans concert by an Eddie Condon group. His performance that night, widely praised, won him a photograph in Esquire magazine's jazz year-book.[32]

Though Louis Prima recorded widely and well throughout the '30s, achieving great popularity and visibility, his name is often conspicuous by its absence from standard jazz histories. Dealing with him seriously means confronting one aspect of New Orleans jazz which chroniclers, almost as a point of honor, seem to find distasteful.

That, of course, is the matter of showmanship. The flamboyance of Prima's latter career, in which his identity as a trumpeter became almost totally subordinate to his role as a high-energy showman, seems to offend those who would represent jazz as an art music of solemnity and unstinting high purpose. The Las Vegas image, the raucous sound of Sam Butera and the Witnesses, the risqué badinage with singer Keely Smith—such make it all too easy to mistake this showbiz aspect of Prima for the creative substance, ignoring his past achievements and core musicianship.

Far from being exclusive to such as Prima, the idea of hot music as an arm of highly commercialized show business runs throughout the early years. It's present in the singing, dancing, and impromptu comedy skits of the dance bands, including those that prided themselves on their dedication to jazz. Its absence is a root cause of the failure of the great Jean Goldkette orchestra, an ensemble which either stubbornly resisted advice to "put on a show" or acquiesced in a manner landing somewhere between perfunctory and downright hostile.

For New Orleans musicians, especially, showmanship was—and remains—a fact of life. Was it not Louis Armstrong, above all, who understood the relationship between music and entertainment, and never wavered in his application of it, even in the face of critical hostility? "You'll always get critics of showmanship," he told British critic Max Jones. "Critics in England say I was a clown, but a clown—that's hard. If you can make people chuckle a little; it's happiness to me to see people happy, and most of the people who criticize don't know one note from another."[33]

Prima, in common with his two hometown friends Wingy Manone and Sharkey Bonano, accepted—as had Nick LaRocca before them—that they were, above all, entertainers; they might now and then get together for their own enjoyment, and even (as in the case of the 1928 Monk Hazel titles) make music to suit themselves. But where the public was concerned, the paying customers always came first. By his own lights, and by the laws of the box office, Prima was doing what he properly should be doing, and with resounding success. It is only regrettable that the nature of his fame in later years has drawn attention away from his skills as one of the most accomplished, often thrilling, of New Orleans trumpet men.

He arrived in New York in 1934 and right away landed a job at the Famous Door, a 52nd Street club popular with—and owned by—musicians. At first Sidney Arodin was his clarinetist, but when Arodin left to work with Wingy elsewhere in town, his replacement was Pee Wee Russell, who'd played with Louis's elder brother Leon (also an excellent trumpet player) in a Texas band headed by pianist Peck Kelley.

Things started happening. Broadway columnist Walter Winchell took note. The little band was featured on a coast-to-coast CBS radio hookup. Society folk, ever on the lookout for novelty, "discovered" Prima. He fit the role admirably, dispensing an early form of the high-voltage fare which was still sending the customers into orbit twenty years later at Vegas and Tahoe. Critics, predictably, couldn't resist sniping: the formidable John Hammond, while praising Russell, complained that Prima "persists in playing identical solos night after night"— this from a man who never complained when Billie Holiday sang the same predictable embellishments for three decades. Another commentator found Prima performances to be "all on one level."

Whether or not that was so, audiences hardly seemed to mind. The Famous Door did turnaway business—and provided inspiration for a cluster of other tiny places that began opening along "Swing Street." Executives of the American Record Co., clearly viewing both Prima and Manone as potential competitors for Louis Armstrong, signed them both, the former on Brunswick, the latter for the thirty-five-cent Vocalion label alongside fellow–Crescent City trumpeter Henry "Red" Allen.

Between September 27, 1934, and July 17, 1937, Louis Prima recorded some fifty-four titles, mostly backed by small jam groups. What strikes the listener now is the overall excellence of the bands (Pee Wee is the clarinetist on some, with Arodin, Weinberg, and Eddie Miller on others), the ease with which Prima handles a wide variety of material—and the incendiary brilliance of his trumpet work. Again and again, he fires off compelling, technically assured solos, fluent throughout the entire range of the horn.

The records (and those of Manone) tend to follow a pattern: more or less straightforward melody chorus, Prima vocal in what one musician called "that hoarse, horny voice of his," solos by a sideman or two, then the leader's trumpet back for the big finale. Within that, there are consistent peaks, including tough and exhilarating Russell solos on "Chasing Shadows," "The Lady in Red," and "Cross Patch."

Prima, for all his gaudy ways, stands up well. There's no denying the pervasive Armstrong flavor, but what's refreshing here is how freely he's able to work within that vocabulary. There are moments, particularly when he descends into his low register, when his figure shapes and sense of drama recall those of Bunny Berigan.

Manone, too, often surprises. His work on dozens of 1930s titles—while displaying nothing comparable to Prima's technical command—is crisp and assured. On "Swing, Brother, Swing" (1935) he easily paces hard-driving solos by

Miller (on tenor) and clarinetist Matty Matlock. He opens "Jazz Me Blues," from a September 12, 1934, date with Arodin and Brunies, with a quite Armstrong-like cadenza.

Both men made the jump to radio and movies, and their subsequent careers have been well documented. Their travels, taking them far afield in both a geographical and musical sense, continue the *Auswanderung* of the earliest jazz days, the arrival-and-departure cycle woven into the fabric of New Orleans life. Not that some outstanding musicians didn't stay home: such players as admired clarinetist Raymond Burke, cornetist Wiggs, and pianist Armand Hug are but a few among many. Others, Irving Fazola among them, came home after growing tired of ceaseless travel.

Burke, in particular, inherited the lyrical tradition so beautifully exemplified by Arodin and, before him, by Roppolo. Even in later life, he seemed able to astonish younger colleagues with a poised elegance in solos and ensembles. Born Raymond Barrois on June 6, 1904, a nephew of the previously discussed brothers Jules and Leo Cassard, he was self-taught on clarinet and remembered admiring Shields, Roppolo, Dodds, "Yellow" Nunez, Jimmie Noone, and even Benny Goodman. He was eighteen when, in 1922, he replaced Charlie Cordilla with Tom Early's locally popular "Harmony Band."

Alongside the leader on string bass, this all but undocumented group included brothers Herbie (trumpet), Eddie (trombone), and Clifford (drums) Rosenmeyer, all respected local figures. Emmett Hardy, said Burke, sometimes worked with the Harmony Band, improvising second cornet parts to Herbie Rosenmeyer's lead.

Burke moved on to another New Orleans unit now lost in obscurity, Alfred "Pantsy" Laine's "Wampus Cats." Son of "Papa" Jack Laine, Alfred (he took extreme umbrage if anyone dropped the t from his nickname) played trumpet and often used such local favorites as Joe "Hook" Loyocano on trombone, Chink Martin's brother Willie Abraham on banjo and Sanford Mello (brother of cornetist Manuel) on drums.

Such bands as these are filled with the names of white New Orleans men, all capable journeymen (and often considerably more than that), who have not found their way into the standard histories: trombonists Avery Loposer and "Big Boy" Lay; pianists Johnny Riddick, Julius Chevez, Roy Armand, and Eddie Mitchell; drummers Charlie Stowe and Blaise Finkley; trumpeters Red Bolman, Bill Naquin, "Handsome Johnny" Coltraro, Bill Gallity, and "Blind" Gilbert Meistier; reedmen Lester Bouchon, Roland Leach, and "Chick" Johnson; brothers Henry (guitar) and Bill (bass) Waelde; guitar-playing brothers Joe and Angelo Capraro; and scores of others. They played in an equally numerous assortment of locales: the Brown Derby, White Star, Radio Café, and Las Marinas Club on Decatur Street, the Shamrock on Bienville, the College Inn on Rampart Street, and such grander venues as Pete Herman's Club Plantation, which had its own radio wire and was the scene of many an after-hours jam session with local and visiting musicians. As Norman Brownlee put it in a 1961 reminiscence, in those days "you couldn't go anywhere in New Orleans and not run into a good band." What emerges is a simple, incontrovertible fact: far from being a minority presence in early New Orleans hot jazz, white musicians were everywhere, contributing strongly from the music's beginnings.

Apart from a brief Kansas City sojourn in the '30s, Raymond Burke seems not to have strayed far from New Orleans. But because of various factors, most of them a matter of simple luck, the clarinetist remained all but unknown outside his home town, where he ran a "rabais," what today might be referred to as a "collectibles" or "memorabilia" shop.

Things began to change in 1949, when he made his first records. From then on he recorded regularly—to the astonished delight of listeners everywhere who had scarcely known of his existence. Here was a pure New Orleans clarinet style, seemingly unaffected by Benny Goodman and his instrument's other pervasive and influential stylists, going his elegantly serene way. New Orleans historians Al Rose and Dr. Edmond Souchon, writing in *New Orleans Jazz: A Family Album*, refer to him as "one of the greatest creative artists jazz has produced." Hyperbole aside, it provides clear indication of the regard in which this relatively unsung clarinetist was held by colleagues and friends.

And it may not be far from the mark. Perhaps as a result of having lived his entire life in the Crescent City, Burke appears to have fused the city's two major streams of hot clarinet playing: the Creole, as carried forward in the disciples of Lorenzo Tio Jr., and the white, as exemplified by the Sicilian (Roppolo, Scaglione) and the more forceful lyricism of Arodin, Fazola, and Miller. It all comes together on a ten-inch LP made for Joe Mares's Southland label in 1955. His solo on a medium-tempo "At Sundown" recalls the almost perfumed cadences of Albert Nicholas; on "St. Louis Blues" he brings Edmond Hall (and his younger brother Herb) to mind; the reflective "Blues for Joe," by contrast, gives us echoes of the "spectral" Roppolo. Yet there is no imitation here, no measured eclecticism, but something far simpler—and more intriguing. In Raymond Burke the lines of development have met at last, interacted, in what may be the most complete of New Orleans clarinet styles.

New Orleans remained, as ever, a place of arrivals and departures. The diaspora that had begun in World War I days continued, musicians of both races carrying the special ways of their home town abroad in the land. Often it was little more than a flavor, a spice, blended into some larger dish to enhance its flavor; but it was strong, distinctive, easily discerned—and indispensable.

And when groups of them gathered far from home, the result was invariably something of a private club, a homeboys' reunion, which often crossed racial lines in ways unthinkable at home. New Orleans expatriates in New York formed the nucleus of two pivotal big bands, the Luis Russell Orchestra of the late 1920s and the no less memorable Bob Crosby unit of the following decade. New Orleans men, wherever they were, made a point of hiring their own, for casual work as well as for radio and record dates. Many, tired of wandering, came home in later life.

By the end of the 1930s it was clear that the days of New Orleans as a jazz gestation center belonged to the past. It was perhaps timely, and fitting, that when NORK trumpeter Paul Mares organized a band of New Orleans and Chicago men to record for OKeh as his "Friars Society Orchestra" in January of 1935, one of the numbers should have been built on the chords to "Basin Street Blues," but without the melody, and bearing a new title.

Mares called it "The Land of Dreams."

5

White Chicago
Jazz, 1923–1926

Not much of 1923 had gone by when the city of Chicago awoke one morning to the news that Mayor William Hale "Big Bill" Thompson—Republican, entrenched—had decided not to run for reelection.

Big Bill had come to power in 1915 as a reformer—"cannot be bought, bossed or bluffed," said his campaign posters. In truth he could be—and was. Over two four-year terms he'd cozied up nicely to the city's top racketeers. It seemed anything was okay in Thompson's Chicago, as long as the right people got rich off it.

Now, plagued with scandal and accusation, Thompson had had enough—at least for the moment. Abdicating, he left the field open for increasingly strident discussion of cleanup, of restoration of old-fashioned virtues—though it is now easy to wonder how many Chicagoans really cared. The reformers, after all, had had their day in 1920, and Prohibition was now the law of the land, at least officially. "The business of evading it and making a mock of it," commented H. L. Mencken, "has ceased to wear any aspects of crime, and has become a sort of national sport."[1]

In Chicago, as in other American cities, a wedding of Prohibition and City Hall corruption had been conspicuously good for business. New York alone, someone estimated, had close to five thousand speakeasies, where most forms of alcohol were readily available. Could Chicago be far behind?

As Humbert S. Nelli put it in *The Business of Crime*: "Dry Laws or not, Americans wanted their drinks, and were ready to do business with anyone who could supply them. The network of [underworld] contacts with police, politicians, and members of the legal profession developed during decades of illegal gambling activities, prostitution, and labor racketeering, readily adapted to the new situation . . . Much of the general public accepted and condoned law-breaking when it involved the manufacture and distribution of liquor and beer.''[2]

Thompson had formed an apparently invulnerable constituency of Irish, Italian, German, and black voters. He'd been good to proprietors of nightclubs and dance halls (even livening up his campaigns with vaudeville entertainers and jazz bands of both races). Wendt and Kogan, in their *Big Bill of Chicago*, quote him as shouting, "Get a horn and blow loud for Chicago . . . Put on a big party! Let the jazz band play! Let's show 'em we're all live ones!''[3]

With Thompson in power, Chicago nightlife had been booming. All over town, proprietors of dance halls, ballrooms, and nightclubs could well have been intoning the slogan popularized by the nation's new Dr. Feelgood, Frenchman Emile Coué: "Day by day in every way I am getting better and better."

Thompson's one-term successor was William Dever, a reform-minded Democrat and ardent believer in Prohibition. His "beer war," unleashed soon after he took office, revoked thousands of operating licenses—most of the revocations immediately overturned on technicalities or restraining orders. Even with Big Bill out of office, things managed to go on pretty much as usual.

It's difficult now, at such a remove, to convey what "as usual" meant. Part of it, certainly, included the sheer numbers of regularly employed bandsmen and other entertainers, especially on the black South Side. There's nothing even roughly comparable today: sometimes it seemed every block had a theatre, a dance hall, a cabaret with a band, or some combination of all three.

A 1924 photo taken at the Sunset Café, one of the hottest of South Side hot spots, tells the story as well as any. On the bandstand, in front of a painted faux-Oriental backdrop, violinist Carroll Dickerson leads an eleven-piece band including jazzmen Buster Bailey, clarinet, and Rudy Jackson, saxophone. In front of the stand, part of what looks to be an elaborate floor show produced by actor Clarence Muse, are blues singer Mary Stafford, a chorus line, and, doing the splits in the center, singer-dancer Frankie "Half-Pint" Jaxon.

Part of the success was tied directly to a new and widespread enthusiasm for social dancing. William Howland Kenney remarks that young working-class men and women "were no longer content to sit passively and watch vaudeville musicians, vocalists, and dancers perform exciting new dance demonstration numbers on stage; they wanted to get closer to their musician-heroes, and even to play, sing and dance to the new songs themselves."[4]

The result, for white Chicago at least, was what Kenney has termed "a widespread, grassroots social dance movement," which by the mid-'20s had established Chicago as, in one veteran's words, "the dancin'est city in the country." It had been in large part responsible for the Chicago success, a decade earlier, of such New Orleans ensembles as Tom Brown's "Band From Dixieland" and the Original Dixieland Jazz Band.

Business at the expanded Midway Gardens was as good as had been hoped. On Monday, April 2, 1923, Elmer Schoebel's new and enthusiastic band drove out to Richmond, Indiana, to make its first records for Gennett.

What the musicians had played or heard night after night at the Friars' Inn stamps these performances, and not only in the rhythm section, dominated by Steve Brown's bass and Louis Black's strong banjo. Arthur "Murphy" Steinberg's trumpet recalls Paul Mares; the clarinetist and trombonist are clearly aware of Leon Roppolo and George Brunies.[5]

The hand of Schoebel, listed as composer of all four selections on the date, is everywhere discernible: it's easy to suppose that this is the direction the Friars Society Orchestra might have taken had he stayed on—and if the New Orleans horn players, who could not read music, had been as flexible and disciplined as these Chicagoans appear to be.

"There's No Gal Like My Gal" illustrates the effectiveness of alternating freedom with organization, Steinberg delivering his solo with attractive lift over the strong rhythm section. Schoebel's "Blue Grass Blues" bristles with arranged breaks for horns in combinations: trumpet and trombone, two saxes, trumpet and two low-register clarinets, solo banjo. Yet none of it gets tricky enough to arrest the forward momentum of the piece, whose chord structure occasionally resembles that of "Wolverine Blues."

By May 30, when they record for Columbia, Schoebel has enlarged his personnel, with three reed players clearly audible. They take a second crack at "Blue Grass Blues" and work through the leader's "House of David Blues." Named for a headline-making scandal involving sexual goings-on within a midwestern religious cult, "House of David Blues" is no blues at all, but instead a sixteen-bar strain along the lines of "How Come You Do Me Like You Do?" Steinberg hews close to the melody, embellishing only slightly and using muted effects in a Mares-out-of-King Oliver manner. But the highlight of Schoebel's arrangement is a full chorus for clarinet trio, one of the earliest recorded examples of this device in a jazz setting, and clearly predating similar efforts by both Morton and Don Redman.[6]

The band's energy and spirit are a reminder, overall, of how many talented young white musicians around Chicago in the early 1920s aspired to play hot music. It was dance music, of course: black or white, all the players involved considered themselves dance musicians, as anyone who ever spent a night at the Dreamland or the Sunset could attest. As drummer Warren "Baby" Dodds put it, even King Oliver's Creole Jazz Band "played for the comfort of the people [emphasis added] . . . not so they couldn't hear, or so they had to put their fingers in their ears . . . Sometimes the band played so softly you could hardly hear it."[7]

It was dance music and, to greater or lesser degree, it was hot jazz. And it was in the Chicago air: young musicians all knew where the best bands were playing, and made a point of hearing them. "I think that jazz, as such, was pretty universally understood at that time to be what blacks were doing on the South Side, and what the New Orleans Rhythm Kings, as they came to be called, were playing at the Friars' Inn," said Chicago jazz historian John Steiner. "That was understood to be the most genuine jazz.

"Lots of musicians around town, sometimes entire bands, would go to listen to these groups and pick up on what they heard. The Rhythm Kings, remember, had made records beginning in 1922, and they had some stars. [Leon] Roppolo, for example, was something of a legend among musicians."[8]

This trend parallels another: the emergence of the dance orchestra of the early '20s as a discrete, identifiable entertainment attraction. The postwar New Orleans vogue had helped get it started, with every theatre and cabaret touting its own novelty or "nut" band, patterned more or less after the more excessive side of the Original Dixieland Jazz Band. For awhile, as pianist Vincent Lopez later described it, there seemed no dearth of "whining and whistling clarinets, trombones that guffawed, trumpets that buzzed and fluttered, pianists that gyrated, and acrobatic drummers."[9]

But the main impetus seems to have been the success of Paul Whiteman's orchestra, which by 1923 had enjoyed a series of million-selling Victor records and had appeared at such prestigious venues as the new Ambassador Hotel in Atlantic City and the Palais Royal in New York, not to mention the greatest showcase in vaudeville, the Palace in Times Square.

Whiteman had moved along a path opened in pre–World War I days by the pioneering San Francisco bandleader Art Hickman: rhythmic presentation of pop songs by a group usually including three brass and two (or even three) saxophones, divided into sections. As the research of James T. Maher and others has made clear, this is the true birth of the modern dance band—and by extension hot big band—instrumentation.

By adding the saxophonists Bert Ralton and Clyde Doerr to his personnel in 1919, Hickman created an ensemble which included not only counterlines to the brass statements but even afforded orchestrated "breaks," interruptions in the rhythm which the saxophones filled with a syncopated figure, usually voiced in thirds or sixths. And in the hands of so skilled an arranger as pianist Ferde Grofé it became the key to a world of possibility. The sections worked together in tutti and as independent units; solos, usually "jazzing" the melody, punctuated the ensembles.

The "break" device, for example, had enormous implications for hot jazz, as Oliver and Louis Armstrong were to demonstrate some years hence. In such cases, phonograph records supply plenty of evidence that even the "spontaneous" moments on the Oliver records (and of those by such New Orleans bands as Oscar Celestin's) were worked out carefully in advance.[10]

Ferde Grofé, his arrangements pivotal in Hickman's success, joined forces with Whiteman in 1920; their aim, expressed forcefully in the Victor recording of "Japanese Sandman," was to develop a large-ensemble concept which to some degree captured the loose intensity of a small improvising ensemble. Some numbers, such as Gus Mueller's "Wang Wang Blues," even achieved a polylinear texture by weaving solo clarinet in and out of the arranged ensembles.[11]

One result of ongoing research by Maher, Thornton Hagert, and others is to show conclusively that Don Redman, widely credited as the preeminent innovator in adapting jazz band textures and sonorities for larger groups of instruments, was working within an already established frame of reference in writing for the Fletcher Henderson Orchestra of 1923–25. There is no questioning the quality or significance of his work; but his uses of brass and reed sections on Henderson recordings ("The Gouge of Armour Avenue," July 31, 1924), or such devices as the clarinet trio ("Copenhagen," Oct. 30, 1924), rather than innovations, are developments of techniques firmly in place since the start of the decade. Saxophone scoring on such earlier Henderson efforts as "Old Black Joe's Blues" (1923) and "Chicago Blues" (1924) is conventional within the practices of the time, and "The Dicty Blues" (1923) is made up almost wholly of jam ensembles. Within this context, the work of Schoebel, like that of Roy Bargy and Don Bestor for the 1923 Benson Orchestra of Chicago, and the still-unidentified arranger responsible for the Jean Goldkette Victor recording of "It's the Blues (March 27, 1924), emerges as easily equal to Redman's.

By 1925, pioneer arranger Arthur Lange had published chapters of his Arranging for the Modern Dance Orchestra in Metronome, an up-to-the-minute codification of scoring practices that sold out in book form the following year and became "the arrangers' bible." It was Lange who, as early as 1920, announced that he would thereafter supply original saxophone parts for dance bands, ending the practice of using cello parts—and thus heralding the arrival of the saxophone era in dance music. A now-forgotten figure in dance band scoring, Lange appears as arranger on countless publishers' "stock" orchestrations of the early 1920s, regularly using trios of saxophones (two altos and a tenor) and clarinets as organic sectional units. Arthur Lange went to Hollywood in 1929 as director of music at Metro-Goldwyn-Mayer, where he pioneered precisely cued film scores.

Within a very few years after World War I, dance orchestras had become entertainment units. Besides being useful accompaniment for cabaret and vaudeville acts, a band could be an act on its own, a self-contained variety show: it could serve up the latest hot novelties, present excerpts from the classics (Mike Fritzel's desire to hear the Rhythm Kings play the "Meditation," from Massenet's opera Thaïs, belongs here), play for dancers, even recruit singers, vocal ensembles, and comic acts from within its own ranks.

Nowhere was this more evident than in Chicago. "Chicago," James T. Maher has said, "was without doubt the great dance band city of the '20s. New York simply didn't measure up." Dance halls sprouted all over the North and South sides. Andrew Karzas, best known as a builder of theatres and movie palaces, erected the lavish Trianon Ballroom at a cost of a million dollars and prospered: Whiteman was his opening attraction—disappointing for the dancers, it turned out—appearing for six nights at a reported fee of twenty-five thousand dollars.[12]

There were many bands, many venues, and many dancers to fill them. They catered to different clientèles; some establishments featured black performers but enforced a whites-only policy among the customers. Others were favorite haunts for black dancers. Among places where white bands worked were such favorite venues as Al Quodbach's Granada Café, the Rendez-vous, the Marigold, the Terrace and Rainbo (without w) Gardens, and the ballroom at White City amusement park. With all this going on, it soon became clear that a resourceful entrepreneur could book many bands at a time, all playing under his name.* It was good business, while providing employment for dozens of musicians. Cope Harvey and Bert Kelly had been booking bands since the war years, and they were soon joined by such newcomers as "Husk" O'Hare and former cellist Edgar Benson.[13]

Edgar Benson's main ensemble, the Benson Orchestra of Chicago, quickly became a potent force in the dance band world of the early '20s. Based at the Marigold Gardens—Grace, Broadway, and Halstead—on the near North Side, it was relatively forward-looking in its arrangements, which featured sectional scoring, and in the latitude given soloists against orchestrated backgrounds.

The Benson orchestra came of age musically with the arrival, in 1923, of C-melody saxophonist Frank Trumbauer. His chorus on the June 14 Benson record of "I Never Miss the Sunshine," discussed elsewhere, was quickly snapped up and imitated by both black and white reedmen. Trumbauer sets out the melody on "Nobody Knows but My Pillow and Me," from the same date, revealing many of the hallmarks of his later style: legato, almost vibrato-less delivery; use of swoops and glisses in introducing phrases. He's also heard in eight nicely turned stop-time bars on "Mean Mean Mamma," recorded August 21.

Trumbauer apart, the Benson orchestra's chief strength lay in its arrangements. Bestor and his predecessor, pianist Roy Bargy, seem to have grasped basic notions of section writing as firmly as did Don Redman. Recorded evidence indicates that, rather than black precedent and white imitation (or its reverse), this appears after a time to have been a matter of independent and spontaneous gravitation toward universally accepted principles of ensemble organization.

The Benson record of "Wolverine Blues" (September 10, 1923), for example, has saxophones providing syncopated counterpoint to a legato violin statement of the trio theme. "Forgetful Blues" (November 4, 1923) offers three choruses of arranging variation: reed section melody with muted brass punctuations, then

---

*Which opens a window on a key subject, as yet relatively ignored by jazz chroniclers: the central role played by the bookers in creating an ever-expanding network of opportunities for bands—and their jazz soloists with them—to play. As Maher has put it, jazz writers since the early 1930s have practiced a "tooth fairy" approach, which seems to imply that hot jazz "came out of a hedgerow at midnight and the world took it to its heart . . . and on the seventh day it bloomed like wildflowers all around the place." When the bookers, marketers, ballroom owners, and other businessmen have been acknowledged at all, they are usually demonized as exploiters, aesthetic troglodytes who viewed musicians only as a way of making money. Yet, as Maher points out, bands "did not 'just happen' to arrive at a dancehall, a hotel ballroom, a radio, TV or recording studio, a movie lot, or wherever they were contracted to perform; nor did a dancehall, a hotel, a movie lot and so on 'just happen' to pop up overnight for the convenience of the bands and their followers."

Maher credits such show business figures as Florenz Ziegfeld, Edward Albee, Paul Salvin, and others, as well as Ernie Young and his partner Jules C. Stein in Chicago, with the realization that dance music could be, in itself, a new and valuable entertainment commodity. But he reminds us that "jazz purists came to loathe the idea of jazz ever being part of a business transaction. God only knows how the 'authentic jazz' fan ever came to grips with the fact that, like other human animals, the jazz musician had to eat . . . in the purist's view, the presence of the vulture-businessman hangs like a pall of evil over the saintly act of creating jazz." Clearly, future examinations of jazz history must include a reassessment of this indispensable side of the music business. (James T. Maher, letter to the author, April 23, 1996.)

a closely voiced ensemble of what sounds like trumpet, trombone, and two middle-register saxes, making free use of chords of the ninth; in the third chorus, the trombone takes the melody while reeds decorate.

(A regular Benson figure was pianist Jean Goldkette, who had been a member of the house ensemble at Lamb's Café supplanted by Brown's "Band from Dixieland" in 1915. Recognizing the leadership and business potential behind Goldkette's Continental accent and charm, Benson put him in charge of an engagement at the prestigious Detroit Athletic Club. Goldkette, in turn, booked a band into the brand-new Book-Cadillac Hotel there; more opportunities presented themselves, and by mid-decade the pianist was owner of Detroit's sumptuous Graystone Ballroom and proprietor of a major regional booking agency. Its flagship band, featuring Trumbauer, Bix Beiderbecke, and other hot jazz soloists, became, as will be seen, the talk of the music business.)

Arguably the most influential Chicago dance orchestra of the early '20s, and musically perhaps the best, was that of Isham Jones. Born January 31, 1894, in Coalton, Ohio, Jones arrived in Chicago in 1915 as a young and highly capable saxophonist and soon was working around town, leading first his own trio, then a dance orchestra.

Not too long into the decade, as Albert McCarthy observes in *The Dance Band Era*, Jones had established himself as a popular favorite in Chicago. His 1921 Brunswick record of "Wabash Blues," written by and featuring trumpeter Louis Panico, sold as many copies as Whiteman's landmark "Whispering." Where the novelty gimmick of Whiteman's record had been Warren Luce's slide whistle, "Wabash Blues" had Panico's "laughing" effects on his horn. All the same, the band showed more obvious affinity for hot rhythm and phrasing than was evident with Whiteman's band.[14]

In mid-1922 the word got around that Joe "King" Oliver had brought his Creole Jazz Band back from a tour of California and was once again in residence at the Royal Gardens Café, 459 East 31st Street on the South Side. In the tight little world of Chicago hot music, this was news: Oliver had arrived from New Orleans in 1918 and quickly made an impact on South Side musical life. By the time his band, including clarinetist Johnny Dodds and pianist Lillian Hardin, headed west, it was a musicians' favorite.

They reopened at the Royal—now renamed the Lincoln—Gardens on June 17. By the second week in August the new, expanded personnel had a second cornet, a kid from New Orleans who worshiped King Joe and had been something of a protégé back home. It didn't take very long before the Oliver band, enhanced by the power, drive, and flexibility of "Little Louis" Armstrong, was drawing musicians, black and white, to hear for themselves. "You've got to hear Joe Oliver" was Isham Jones's exhortation to fellow-bandleader Art Landry, then a newcomer. "The whole Jones band would go over there to listen," Jim Breyley, longtime Jones manager, told James T. Maher, "because the Old Man [Jones] believed that Joe Oliver had one of the best dance orchestras in Chicago."[15]

Jones, Louis Panico, and the other sidemen, in fact, appear to have been frequent visitors to the Lincoln Gardens. Panico's phrasing on the Jones record of "Aunt Hagar's Children Blues," done that November, is in an Oliver idiom, and the ensembles move along with a drive reminiscent of the Creole band.

It's important to remember that in 1922–23 "jazz" was widely understood less as any sort of free-standing musical entity than as an atmosphere, a feeling. If Joe Oliver billed his octet as a "Creole Jazz Band," it was chiefly to give the public some thinly coded information. "Creole," like "dixie" and "dixieland," implied that these were musicians from down south, and "jazz" told potential customers they could expect a lively, good-time atmosphere for dancing—which in turn meant far more than just stomps and rags.

It was as just as important that the band at the Gardens, whether Midway or Lincoln, be able to render a waltz in suitably sentimental fashion or capitalize on a new dance vogue such as the tango. Joe and young Louis Armstrong might wow fellow-musicians—and younger dancers—with their lively two-cornet breaks on "Snake Rag" or some other hot novelty; but it was the variety of the dance band craft he'd perfected playing for the cotillions and garden parties along St. Charles Avenue in New Orleans that kept the paying customers happy.

"Black or white," Maher has said, "the [Lincoln] Gardens was a fashionable place if you loved to dance." The clientele, he added, always seemed to include a healthy percentage of white couples—not slumming or seeking exotic doings among the black-and-tans, but simply because the dancing was first-rate.[16]

Jones and his men also frequently visited the Friars' Inn—and understood what they were hearing, as their January 1923 Brunswick record of "Farewell Blues" demonstrates. Panico's lead is right out of Mares, and clarinetist Al Mauling fares well in reproducing Roppolo's brooding clarinet sound. The Jones band is a disciplined ensemble, making good use of dynamics and shading. "Farewell's" final two-chorus tutti, at a broad, walking tempo, actually swings in a handsome, even modern, fashion, over a solid pulse laid out by John Kuhn's tuba and Joe Frank's drums.

Panico is a particularly interesting musician. Not yet twenty when these records were made, he'd already achieved technical mastery on trumpet, beginning solos easily on cleanly articulated high notes, firing off rapid-fire tonguing with ease, executing long and complex passages on few breaths. On records where he plays open ("Never Again," of January 1924, is an example), his tone sounds large and controlled.

Panico "told me that when he joined Isham Jones he was carrying a large case," said John Steiner. "In fact, you might have been surprised that a trumpet player in those days would carry a case that big. When he opened it, all his mutes tumbled out and everybody broke up laughing. What was he doing with twelve mutes? Well, that was part of the act, part of what he did—and that probably has a lot to do with why people so easily took to labelling him a novelty trumpet player, rather than a very fine band trumpet player, which is what he really was."[17]

Jazz fans and chroniclers, when they've dealt with Panico at all, have found it easy to dismiss him as a purveyor of tricks, typified by the "laughing" trumpet on "Wabash Blues" or the "wah-wah" tomfoolery on Jones's record of "Memphis Blues." But this skilled trumpeter must not be judged by such unrepresentative moments. "I heard him a lot," said veteran jazz trumpeter Adolphus "Doc" Cheatham, who arrived in Chicago when the Jones band was at its early peak. "It was the first time I'd ever heard trumpet played like that. He was so good technically. He had a great tongue, and could growl in the high register like no one else. Don't let anybody tell you he wasn't a jazz musician. He was like Johnny Dunn, another one I admired a lot in those early days. For me, guys like that were pioneers of jazz trumpet playing. They were my idols."[18]

Pianist Jess Stacy, who played in Panico's band at Chicago's Canton Tea Gardens in the late '20s, agreed. "He could really play," the pianist said. Frank Teschemacher was in the band, too, and "a couple of times Louis really surprised Tesch. Played sort of—well, not exactly like Bix, but on that order. He really could play in a very attractive hot style."[19]

Panico plays his solo on "Mama Loves Papa" (October 12, 1923) into what sounds like a derby, and the overall effect is indeed not unlike that achieved by Beiderbecke on records later in the decade. On "Somebody's Wrong," he growls into his plunger in a way that seems to foreshadow "Bubber" Miley. Panico, in short, knows how to turn on the heat. His playing is rhythmically forceful, driving the ensembles (for example, "Forgetful Blues") powerfully.

In later years, said John Steiner, Panico denied he was a true jazzman, because he'd never really improvised. "He played with mutes and he played with embellishments that were almost textbook figures, and made no effort to swing the band," the historian said. But it is well to remember that in the context of the early '20s dance band—and this applies equally to black bands and white—trumpet players *were* melodic embellishers, rather than improvisers. For the pre-Armstrong New Orleans hornmen, as for Louis Panico, the task was to play a strong, lively melody lead. Even Oliver, on the evidence of records and the recollections of colleagues, seems to have been above all a strong player of lead lines.[20]

"They embellished," said S. Frederick Starr. "They ornamented. For example, in playing a hymn or otherwise foursquare piece, the cornet lead would 'rag,' or syncopate, the melody." Other players became adept at "improvising" inner parts, creating *extempore* second and third lines to reinforce the lead and fill out the ensemble texture.[21] The practice is still widespread in society dance orchestras. The lead trumpet, trombone, and saxophone set out their lines, usually following phrasing standard to the idiom; players on the lower parts "find" their chordal voices and follow the lead man's phrasing. This skill, born equally of a fast ear and familiarity with the formal aspects of the style, allows ensembles of up to twenty pieces to play an evening's dance without reference to written music. It is also, obviously, what enabled Louis Armstrong to fashion second parts to Joe Oliver's leads at the Lincoln Gardens.

"Authentic" jazzman or not, Louis Panico enjoyed much respect among fellow musicians, including those with aspirations to play hot jazz. One such was Bix, then still a teenager none-too-happily enrolled at suburban Lake Forest Academy; he and classmate Samuel "Sid" Stewart visited the College Inn one night and heard Panico with Isham Jones. Bix, Stewart recalled, "sat there for hours and just listened. We thought it was just wonderful."[22]

Cavalier dismissal of Panico by the jazz faithful reveals some curious anomalies in musical evaluation. His use of the plunger is not unlike Oliver's; his "talking" sounds—growls, buzzes, wah-wahs—anticipate both Miley and Jabbo Smith; and none of it, black or white, is all that removed from the tricks subsequently popularized by trumpeter Clyde McCoy a decade later on his first of countless turns through "Sugar Blues."

It's impossible to escape the conclusion that such effects simply belonged to the standard dance band (and in some respects "hot") trumpet vocabulary of the period. Any distinction between one application and another appears to be the result of retrospective, and to a great degree subjective, evaluation. With the exception of Duke Ellington—his fertile mind made imaginative use of such devices—all bandleaders and soloists appear to have employed gimmicks to please their crowds. Panico, as a dance band trumpet player of his time, was simply doing his job.

Jones and his orchestra prospered. The influential Chicago drama critic Ashton Stevens, best remembered as the man who coined Guy Lombardo's "sweetest music this side of heaven" slogan (and, according to some, the model for the character of Jed Leland in Orson Welles's Citizen Kane), "discovered" the band and started touting it in his Hearst newspaper columns. Conductor Frederick Stock invited them to perform at a Chicago Symphony rehearsal.

Jones, meanwhile, was making a national name as a songwriter. Among the standards he turned out between 1922 and 1924 alone were "On the Alamo," "Swingin' Down the Lane," "I'll See You in My Dreams," "It Had To Be You," "Spain," and "The One I Love (Belongs to Somebody Else)."

Equally skilled as an arranger, Jones used a rather unconventional instrumentation—trumpet, two trombones, violin, and three reeds, including himself—in a style that stressed a "singing" delivery of long, smoothly melodic lines. By the late '20s he'd developed an ensemble sound rich in mid-range sonorities. Trumpeter Ziggy Elman, looking back, spoke for more than a few top-rank musicians in declaring it "the greatest sound of any of the dance orchestras."[23]

Jones had helped set a standard for Chicago-based dance bands, and others soon followed. Charley Straight, a prominent music business figure since pre–World War I days, had played vaudeville and recorded piano rolls in the novelty ragtime style popularized by Zez Confrey, Felix Arndt, and others. He'd written popular songs and such instrumental confections as "Buddy's Habits." In later years he took to claiming that the band he ran at the Rendez-vous Café, West Diversey and Broadway, was a forerunner of "swing."

Interestingly, several of Straight's hotter records come close to bearing him out: "Hobo's Prayer," done for Brunswick in 1926, is a blues with orchestral gift-wrapping. At one point, Straight backs a rather agitated hot trombone solo with chiming upper-register chords, while Joe Gist's tuba maintains a steady four-to-the-bar rhythm on the bottom. The effect is exquisite. Trumpeter Gene Caffarelli also solos here much in the manner of Beiderbecke (who spent four months in Straight's band in 1925), even to the ringing tone and bell-like attack. Such records as "Hi Diddle-Diddle" and "Too Busy" show him off handsomely.

By the mid-1920s, even those groups not specifically known for it boasted a hot soloist or two, able to "get off" where occasion demanded. Trumpeter Frankie Quartell sparked the band led jointly by Dan Russo and songwriter Ted Fio Rito; Sol S. Wagner had a capable and flexible hornman in Nate Bold; saxophonist Johnny Provenzano, who had worked the Mississippi riverboats, led the band at Ralph Capone's Hawthorne Inn, in Cicero, that featured Charley "Nosey" Altiere on cornet and pianist-arranger Art Gronwall; brothers Merritt (cornet) and Henry (trombone) Brunies, who succeeded the New Orleans Rhythm Kings at the Friars' Inn, came of a distinguished New Orleans jazz dynasty and featured the excellent Volly De Faut on clarinet. "Murphy" Steinberg, Roy Kramer, Harry Greenberg, Earl Baker, and others were busier than ever around town. New faces, some of them still teenagers, were turning up regularly and would shortly be heard from: they included Jimmy McPartland, Muggsy Spanier, Benny Goodman, Dave Tough, Frank Teschemacher, and Bud Freeman.

But what gave white Chicago jazz its first national—and, soon, international—profile in the early 1920s involved none of these men. It sprang instead from the energy and brash insouciance of three amateurs: Jack Bland, a former soda-jerk who played banjo in his spare time; Dick Slevin, who liked to hum through a kazoo he'd picked up in a five-and-dime store; and William "Red" McKenzie, who had worked awhile as a jockey, spending his off-hours in places where bands played. His specialty was what he called "blue-blowing," singing hot choruses in falsetto through a comb-and-paper, and what set him apart wasn't so much the oddity of his "instrument" as how good he was at it. Though untutored, he seemed to have a firmer rhythmic and melodic grasp than many professionals trying to master the idiom.

Sitting around a table one night in a St. Louis restaurant, they'd somehow got to making music together. It was a peculiar sound—squeaks and gargles, in one musician's phrase—but fun; before long they were doing it at parties, for money, billing themselves the "Mound City Blue Blowers" in deference to their St. Louis origins.

Frank Trumbauer, in transit between the Benson orchestra and a job with Ray Miller, tossed some work their way, including a party for Alice Busch, of the famed brewing family. He also apparently got his former boss Gene Rodemich, who had a recording contract with Brunswick, to listen to them. Rodemich, intrigued, offered to slot them in for a featured chorus on one of his records, scheduled to be made in Chicago in early 1924.

At this point the story takes a curious turn. A night or two before they were to record with Rodemich (discographical deduction would place it at Tuesday or Wednesday, February 19 or 20, 1924), they dropped by the Friars' Inn to listen to the house band. They got to talking and before long were invited to sit in for a couple of numbers.

"Right in the middle of our second number a fellow walked out on the floor and said, 'What kind of music is this?' " Bland said in a reminiscence. "It happened to be Isham Jones . . . We told him that we were going to take a chorus on a record with Gene Rodemich the next day. He told us to go to a Turkish bath and 'get yourselves hoarsed up so you can't play those freak instruments.' And he pressed some folded money into McKenzie's hand, and said, 'I will get you a date on Brunswick records by yourselves.' "[24]

Sure enough, he did. On February 23, McKenzie, Slevin, and Bland recorded two songs, Spencer Williams's "Arkansas [spelled "Arkansaw" on the label] Blues" and their own "Blue Blues," for Brunswick. Three weeks later they recorded again, this time with their benefactor Trumbauer added on C-melody sax for the currently popular "San" and his own composition, "Red Hot."[25]

They were an unalloyed success, "Arkansaw Blues" alone selling more than a million copies. Not long afterward, bandleader Ray Miller—perhaps on a word from Trumbauer—came to hear them and signed them to go to New York. They played the Beaux Arts in Atlantic City, the State Theater in Jersey City, the Palace in Manhattan.

And somewhere during this time they met guitarist Eddie Lang, who started recording with them in December. Early the following year (1925), he went to England with them to play the fashionable Piccadilly Hotel, and there's no doubt that his effect on the little group was salutary. "He had the best ear of any musician I ever knew," said Bland. "He could go into another room and hit 'A' and come back and play cards for fifteen minutes, and then tune his instrument perfectly. I've seen that happen."[26]

Even with Lang, the Blue Blowers were reminiscent before all else of the "spasm bands" of homemade instruments that had entertained on street corners in turn-of-the-century New Orleans. But they had their virtues: on "Arkansaw Blues," for example, McKenzie's comb solo shows good natural phrasing, though Bland's rhythm on banjo is often erratic.[27]

Things go rather better on their next coupling, the presence of Trumbauer a stabilizing force. Rather than mix into the somewhat helter-skelter ensembles, he provides bass lines, and with them a rhythmic center missing from the first date (his full chorus on "San," in fact, was widely imitated by other saxophonists, as was his solo on "I Never Miss the Sunshine," discussed elsewhere in this volume).

By January 26, 1925, when they recorded for Vocalion as "McKenzie's Kandy Kids," the Blue Blowers had begun to reach out a bit. Lang opens a slow-tempo "Best Black" with some fine single-string solo playing, memorably transcending Bland's rather clunky banjo. On the blues "Happy Children," McKenzie sings through his comb in an unaccustomed lower register, obviously attempting to play "trombone" to Slevin's "trumpet" lead on kazoo. He sounds as though he's been listening hard to—and understanding—the blues singing of Bessie Smith.

Though really little more than a novelty act, the Blue Blowers were nonetheless "playing" hot jazz, with considerable brio. That alone was enough to put them in touch with dozens of eager and talented young musicians just getting into circulation. And it was here that Red McKenzie's true strength soon emerged:

however adept his "blue-blowing" and capable his ballad singing (his pleasing high baritone voice ultimately won him a job with Paul Whiteman), he seemed infallible in his ability to generate and promote work for both himself and other musicians. Many musicians now revered as jazz greats owe their initial breaks to McKenzie's quick patter and persuasive manner.

The Mound City Blue Blowers remained a potent hot jazz force throughout the rest of the '20s. They surface again later in this volume.

A 1922 photograph of Sig Meyer's Druids, house band at White City ballroom, provides a nice cross-section of white Chicago jazz generations in the early '20s: bassist Arnold "Deacon" Loyocano was thirty-three, and had come from New Orleans in 1916 with Tom Brown's band. Saxophonist Floyd Town, a dance band man, was keenly interested in the new music burgeoning around him, as was banjoist Marvin Saxbe, and was picking it up on the job. Also in the picture are two teenagers: Arkansas-born saxophonist Voltaire "Volly" De Faut, eighteen, and on cornet sixteen-year-old hometown boy Francis "Muggsy" Spanier.

One of ten children in a poor family, Spanier had broken in the year before, playing part-time with a band led by Elmer Schoebel at the Blatz Palm Garden. There he'd met young George Brunies, newly in from New Orleans. Muggsy, said Brunies, knew very few songs at the time besides the Dixieland Band's "Sensation Rag." But he was tough and spunky. The two young musicians, both boxing fans, took to one another right away—with unanticipated results.

"[There were] these two racketeers, bouncers and hoods—after the night was over they took us to an athletic club, and they made us put the boxing gloves on," said Brunies. "I said, 'Man, I don't want to hurt this man. I just met him . . .' [but] they made us do it—you know how they do in Chicago—they made us do it, and we boxed for about two hours."[28] This rather exotic initiation rite resulted in small injuries for both combatants—and cemented a friendship that endured the rest of their lives.

Toward the end of 1922, saxophonist Jack Pettis left the Friars' Inn to tour in vaudeville, bringing in Volly De Faut as his replacement. Muggsy, developing fast, worked for Town, Straight, and other sympathetic bandleaders. He and De Faut stayed in touch and on February 25, 1924, teamed up for what are probably the first small-band hot jazz records by an all-Chicagoan white group.

"The Bucktown Five" (the name celebrating a Lake Pontchartrain honky-tonk community none of the musicians had ever seen) made seven titles for Gennett. Besides Spanier and De Faut the quintet included Marvin Saxbe on banjo, pianist Mel Stitzel, and Charley Straight's trombonist Guy Carey. In a departure from the standard five-piece format, there is no drummer, and it's a tribute to Stitzel and Saxbe that none is missed.

From the first bars of "Steady Roll Blues" (not a standard twelve-bar blues but a slow-tempo Stitzel original) it's clear that these men are doing something new. They don't play in the bouncy collegiate manner of the Wolverines, who had recorded for Gennett just a week before. Nor do they emulate the almost stately cadences of the New Orleans Rhythm Kings. No, this quintet comes out slugging, ready for a scrap. There's something tough-minded here, edgy, a little aggressive. Something, in other words, very Chicago.

Spanier and Art Kassel share composer credit on "Really a Pain," an up-tempo exercise loaded with solo and duo breaks, melodic strains of irregular lengths and structures. The band negotiates its intricacies with cocksure, "hey look at me" high spirits, riding things home on a stomping ensemble.

Muggsy contributes a hot, Armstrong-like break to "Chicago Blues" and tears loose for a full chorus on the driving "Hot Mittens." At this point he's still more comfortable in the ensembles: his concept of line hasn't yet jelled, and it's hard to avoid the feeling that he's just lining up licks one after the other, like books on a shelf.

De Faut has developed further, as he shows on "Someday Sweetheart," with its extraordinary clarinet-guitar duet. This graceful and fully realized thirty-two bars is the work of an accomplished jazz clarinetist. Nor is it a fluke: his playing on two fine 1925 trio titles with Jelly Roll Morton, and on the earlier, even rarer duets with singer Kitty Irvin on Gennett, is no less impressive.

A ubiquitous figure in 1920s dance band Chicago, De Faut was in the group Merritt Brunies took into the Friars' Inn to replace the New Orleans Rhythm Kings; he also worked with Ray Miller, Isham Jones, and Jean Goldkette before settling down to a Depression-era job as a radio staff musician. Colleagues deeply respected his fluency, rhythmic command, and overall musicianship. He is remembered with affection by all who heard him.

Yet his name has all but vanished from view. Part of it may be timing, simple bad luck; De Faut came up in the shadow of Roppolo, whom he greatly admired, playing only saxophone in the Friars' Inn band. Then, just as he was emerging as a clarinetist, along came a slightly later generation, whose leading lights were Benny Goodman and Frank Teschemacher. Yet as his work on these and other records shows, Volly De Faut was a soloist of coherence and grace.

Spanier is even more forceful in kicking off "Why Couldn't It Be Poor Little Me?" and "Everybody Loves My Baby," made seventeen months later under the name "Stomp Six," with Joe Gist added on tuba and Ben Pollack on drums. He's still not fully formed, and fighting to control a runaway vibrato. But he's come under Louis Armstrong's spell, and it's beginning to shape him; his "Everybody" chorus, especially, bursts with Armstrong licks and rhythmic mannerisms, as if Louis had shown him a way to build a solo line—which, in a way, he had.

De Faut, as usual, is a model of poise, and Pollack, who shortly would head west to start his own band, nothing less than a treat. The electric recording, however primitive, allows the drummer to be *heard* rather than just felt, and he more than lives up to his reputation (Louis Armstrong and others hailed him at the time as the "best drummer in Chicago"), kicking the "Everybody" rideout chorus home with engaging verve.

These records are at once both an end and a beginning: they close out the New Orleans–influenced early 1920s in white Chicago jazz—and announce, unequivocally, that the city on Lake Michigan has now spawned a style, a jazz voice, uniquely its own.

II

The Sophisticates

*New York and Its
Hot Jazz Chamber Music*

6

Miff Mole
and the Original
Memphis Five

I t's hard now to remember who spotted him first. Just an old-looking guy in an old-looking overcoat, standing there beside his big, old-looking trombone case. No mistaking him, though: wire-rimmed glasses just a little askew on a leathery, seamed face. The look—still, so many years later—of a slightly quizzical owl.

Miff Mole. Mister perfection himself. He of a thousand hot-lick surprises, leaping off countless old records with a "Gee, ain't this easy?" insouciance.

He'd been invited, this hero from the past, to appear at the 1960 Newport Jazz Festival. If you knew enough to care, the very idea that Miff Mole, the genuine item, was going to be playing there was an event in itself.

In Newport Festival annals, 1960 is remembered as the year the roof fell in. The year things got so unruly that the City Fathers finally decided they'd had enough, didn't really need to have their old-money purlieu overrun every Fourth of July by gangs of beer-swilling college kids.

"They came to drink, raise hell, and release their inhibitions," said Festival historian Burt Goldblatt. "It was a substitute for panty raids and had replaced the Ft. Lauderdale beach scene in spring."[1]

He was sixty-two and hadn't played regularly in ten years. Repeated operations on an infected hip had undercut his health and depleted what savings he had. The jazz world of the time, embroiled in its usual intramural squabbling, neither knew of him nor gave a damn. Yet some important people, John Hammond among them, had remembered enough to find him and get him practicing again.

There was also internal strife. Festival founder-organizer George Wein had angered some musicians by engaging pop, folk, and rhythm-and-blues performers. Bassist Charles Mingus and drummer Max Roach seceded altogether, announcing their own concert series at nearby Cliff Walk Manor.

The Festival began Thursday evening at Freebody Park, while revelers by the carload streamed into town. By Saturday their numbers had swollen to an estimated twelve thousand; that night order broke down entirely, as hordes of them stormed the park's perimeter fence.

From there it was only a step to full-scale riot, with state police, tear gas, cries of "Kill the cops! Get the bastards!" all but drowning out musicians' attempts to play. At two A.M. the National Guard arrived. Heads were broken, arrests made.

He was to appear on Sunday, the final evening. It would be recorded, with radio and TV attendance. It looked for all the world like comeback time at last for the man Tommy Dorsey had once called "the Babe Ruth of the trombone."

At 9:20 Sunday morning, the Newport City Council met in emergency session. After hours of shouting and accusation, they put it to a vote: the Jazz Festival was finished.

Workers at Freebody began dismantling stage, tent, lights, chairs, sound system. Journalists, standing around the press tent, wondered why, for jazz, it was always a matter of one step forward, two steps back.

And into the middle of all this, steadying himself with a cane as he lugged the big trombone case, shuffled the gray, stooped figure of Miff Mole.

"It was like seeing an apparition," said Dan Morgenstern, in those days a twenty-nine-year-old freelance jazz writer. "He hadn't been listening to the radio. Didn't know about any of it. He'd just gone to Port Authority Station and taken the bus up to Newport."[2]

Photographer-archivist Jack Bradley spotted him right off. "He sat down on one of those folding chairs, just sat," said Bradley. "People kept walking by. Nobody even stopped to talk to him. He seemed utterly lost."[3]

He asked for a cigarette. Asked to speak to Hammond. "I've been practicing for weeks for this thing," he said to no one in particular. "My lip is in good shape—whatever that means."

Morgenstern remembered it with terrible clarity. "What went through my head was 'My God, he doesn't know. He doesn't know what's happened here.' But he seemed so old: he was only sixty-two—I'm sixty-three now—but here he was, on this windy, kind of chilly July day, dressed like an older person, several layers of clothing. And clearly exhausted."

There's a record, one of hundreds he made in those years, that explains Miff Mole instantly and with an eloquence no words can match. It's a performance of the "Original Dixieland One-Step," recorded for OKeh on August 30, 1927, and issued under the name "Miff Mole and His Little Molers."

In common with much of the early jazz band repertoire, it's something of a circus piece, set up in three strains like a march. Most performances of it begin like this:

"Original Dixieland One-Step," first four bars, as written.

In Miff Mole's performance, this is what the trombone plays at the beginning:

"Original Dixieland One-Step," first four bars, with Miff Mole trombone break.

Tightly packed, impeccably executed, those two bars are precisely what Miff Mole intended to play—and the sort of thing that made him, at least before Jack Teagarden arrived in New York, the envy of just about every hot trombonist around.

In 1927, such ambitious solo playing was still relatively new to hot music. Most trombonists of either race seemed to accept their instrument as a kind of musical Falstaff, its contribution ranging from the sound of lowing cattle (as in the ODJB's "Livery Stable Blues") to the sort of roughly executed foundation parts characteristic of Honoré Dutrey, Kid Ory, or, among the whites, Eddie Edwards and George Brunies.

In a way it's curious, in that the trombone, like the cornet, boasted a solo virtuoso tradition, which had reached its zenith in the years before the Great War. The extraordinary Arthur Pryor and other soloists had opened possibilities in range, flexibility, and speed to compare with those achieved by the star cornetists. New York, moreover, boasted such internationally famous teachers as Gardell Simons and Ernest Clarke, brother of cornet king Herbert L. Clarke.

Two factors seem to have kept such sophistication from making itself felt sooner in hot music. First, most of the early players were audodidacts, who had learned by trial-and-error or imitation of records. Although many could read music, the man who even thought of going to a teacher was a rarity.

Early hot jazz, moreover, was basically an ensemble music: the concept of the virtuoso soloist did not yet exist. Each instrument played its strictly defined ensemble role: the cornet set out the melody, the clarinet decorated and provided counterpoint, the saxophone played parts similar to those of alto and baritone horns in a brass band, and the trombone replicated its marching function as a foundation, a ground bass. A few moments spent listening to the brass and woodwind parts of any Sousa march tells much about early jazz band ensemble playing.

Change was in the air. Clarinetist Leon Roppolo had converted his instrument's obbligato function into a solo role with surprising ease. Adrian Rollini, using the otherwise awkward bass saxophone, managed—on the September 1923 California Ramblers record of "Sittin' in a Corner"—a full-chorus improvised solo, uniting rhythmic vitality, melodic coherence, and considerable technical mastery. When, the following year, Louis Armstrong began contributing long-lined, supple, and rhythmically relaxed solos to Fletcher Henderson records, musicians everywhere listened in amazement: it had never occurred to them that things could be done that way.

On trombone, the role of discoverer-innovator seems to have fallen to shy, bespectacled Irving Milfred Mole. Born March 11, 1898, he grew up in Roosevelt, Long Island, about an hour outside New York City.

As an eleven-year-old he took violin lessons and taught himself the piano, soon becoming skilled enough on both to work professional jobs. According to biographer Richard DuPage, he bought his first wind instrument, an E♭ alto horn, at age thirteen, and then—after watching a brass band parade through the streets of Roosevelt—sent away for a mall-order trombone.

At first he taught himself: DuPage has described young Mole striking a note on the piano, then testing positions on the trombone until he found one that worked. Eventually the hunt-and-peck methods yielded results—and an appetite for knowledge about the instrument beyond what he could find out for himself. He sought out, and found, his man in the person of Charlie Randall, a good all-rounder whose background included both Sousa's concert band and a hitch in a dance orchestra called the Merry Melody Men, which ultimately became the California Ramblers.[4]

The boy was a quick and diligent student: by early 1917, as newly reelected President Woodrow Wilson issued the order for the first wave of U.S. soldiers to join the Great War raging in Europe, nineteen-year-old "Miff" Mole—the nickname just a corruption of "Milfred"—was on his professional way as a confident and versatile trombone player.

He joined scores of other New York musicians flocking to the "400 Room" of Reisenweber's Restaurant, on Columbus Circle, to hear the "Original Dixie Land Jazz Band." It was at one of these noisy evenings that he met a young trumpeter who combined prodigious talent with ambition and a flair for business.

Born Filippo Napoli in Brooklyn on September 2, 1901, he'd been both a cornet prodigy and something of a rebel; as a twelve-year-old he'd run away from home, winding up in New Orleans, where he heard and fell for the local music. By the time the Original Dixielanders hit New York, he'd become Phil Napoleon—and was right there in the first row, listening.

And learning. He was already working jobs with a quintet of his own, including his chum Frankie Signorelli at the piano and an assortment of clarinetists, trombonists, and drummers. He called it his "Memphis Five"—largely, he said later, as a tribute to W. C. Handy, whose Memphis-based society orchestra was well known throughout the country.

At first the group's personnel and fortunes were closely intertwined with those of the ODJB. New Orleans multi-instrumentalist Emile Christian, who substituted for "Daddy" Edwards on trombone on the band's 1919 British tour, worked single jobs with Napoleon. Signorelli, on the other hand, sat in for J. Russel Robinson with the Dixielanders. On at least one occasion in 1922, Napoleon himself filled in for Nick LaRocca. In later years, ODJB drummer Tony Sbarbaro (or Spargo, as he came to be called) was a regular member of various Napoleon-led bands.[5]

Miff and Phil took to one another at once, and before long they were working together. Out of this alliance came the band known to jazz history as the Original Memphis Five. No band of the earliest jazz years recorded more frequently; no band was more skillfully managed. No band was more universally popular, more admired on musical grounds.

"In 1921–22 the band we all were listening to, the only band worth listening to, was the Memphis Five," one veteran of the era remarked. "They had the arrangements, they were smooth—they all could play. They played music. The Original Dixieland Jazz Band? We thought they were noisy, old hat. Corny."[6]

So ubiquitous were their records that *Variety*, not fully with tongue in cheek, reported that "the Original Memphis Five have had the distinction of being the only orchestra to record for every phonograph company in existence."[7]

For all that, the Original Memphis Five was for many years one of the most underdocumented of the early jazz ensembles. Only within the last decade has the work of Horst H. Lange in Germany and the late Bob Hilbert in the United States begun to fill in the wide gaps in knowledge of this seminal band.

It's been an uphill climb. There is still next to no literature. Though Napoleon, clarinetist Jimmy Lytell, and others lived long, active lives, no oral historians saw fit to interview them. Their records, though plentiful, appear seldom in reissue packages. They remain, for all practical purposes, invisible. The standard received view of the years 1919 to 1922 seems to be of a kind of jazz hiatus, with history holding its breath and waiting for something to happen. The Dixieland band has made its impact and sailed for Europe; Joe "King" Oliver is on the West Coast, young Louis Armstrong still playing the riverboats. The men who will shortly become the New Orleans Rhythm Kings are touring in the Midwest, some of them with singer Bee Palmer, before coming together at the Friars' Inn.

It is precisely this perceived gap that the Memphis Five so admirably fills.

To better understand the context of those early years it is useful to consult the tape collection *The Becoming of Jazz*, compiled by Swiss jazz scholar Arnold Bopp and cited in chapter 1. By compiling dozens of obscure and forgotten records, instrumental and vocal, he reveals the extent to which bands of both races, especially in the East, were working at overcoming the same handicaps, including stilted rhythms and melodically disjunct phrasing left over from ragtime—not to mention a shared weakness for the barnyard effects, klaxons, whistles, and other vaudeville trappings of the "nut jazz" craze.

This was especially noticeable in New York. "Royal Garden Blues," by Mamie Smith's Jazz Hounds (black), and "Beale Street Blues," by Ray Miller's Black and White Melody Boys (white), both recorded for OKeh in January of 1921, stumble over the same tripwires in the same ways. Trumpeters Johnny Dunn, with Smith, and Earl Oliver, with Miller, play spirited but clearly rag-oriented leads.

Black and white learned a lot, and equally, from one another in these years. Clarinetist Garvin Bushell, with Mamie Smith, told of having been impressed by the ODJB's Larry Shields, and his *playing on "Royal Garden Blues" reflects that exposure. In his autobiographical* Jazz: From the Beginning, *he also avers that "Dope" Andrews, an uncle of trumpeter Charlie Shavers, played "more or less the New York trombone style—also similar to what they played in the circus bands."*[8]

Toward the end of his life, Phil Napoleon became very reluctant to talk about "the old days." He was preparing his memoirs, he said, and parried most questions with a coy "I think I'd better save that for the book." No book was ever written. Nor did he, apparently, even commit any information to notes or tape. Most of what he knew died with him, at age eighty-nine, in September 1990.

This is particularly regrettable in view of the esteem in which the Original Memphis Five—and especially Miff Mole—came to be held by fellow musicians. Napoleon's feeling, as quoted by Bob Hilbert, was that the Original Dixieland Jazz Band "never knew what was going on, that—as businessmen, at least—they would have to introduce themselves to each other after each song."

Not so the Memphis Five. On June 26, 1922, they even filed incorporation papers, registering themselves (in the manner of a professional brass band of the day) as the "Original Memphis Five, Inc.," for the purpose of furnishing "music and entertainment at hotels, cabarets, dance halls and private parties, and to engage in vaudeville entertainments either as an orchestra band or soloists."

A stockholders' meeting elected Napoleon president and Signorelli secretary-treasurer. Each participating musician, moreover, signed a contract obligating him to the company for a year. There were stock issues, by-laws, fines for such infractions as talking on the bandstand, complaining on the job, or "not doing their best while playing their instrument."[9] It may seem excessive now, but such formality resulted in a smoothly functioning band, as coherent in its musical policy as in matters of administration and conduct.

"If we played the ODJB tunes, people would say we were copying them," Napoleon told the host of a Florida radio station. "So we were smart enough to go into the dime store and learn the new popular tunes, like 'Last Night on the Back Porch' and 'Down Among the Sheltering Palms.' "[10]

In a telephone conversation with the author, he let slip a tantalizing hint about how things were between his band and LaRocca's in those early New York days. "We carved up the territory," he said. "We agreed that those guys would play their own stuff, their originals and the jazzier novelties, and we'd concentrate on the pop tunes. That way we'd never be in direct competition with each other."[11] It brings a smile, this image of two Sicilian-American leader-cornetists, meeting like Mafia dons to decide spheres of influence, lines of musical demarcation, in the interests of peaceful coexistence.

With Mole on trombone, the Memphis Five hit the road, touring the Orpheum theatre circuit as accompanists for the dance act of Vi Quinn and Frank Farnum. A stopover in Chicago, he said, included a visit to the South Side, where he sat in with Joe Oliver.[12]

The date of the Quinn-Farnum tour is uncertain. Bob Hilbert places it in the winter of 1917–18. At that time, according to Oliver scholar Laurie Wright, Papa

Joe had recently arrived in Chicago and was working with the bands of trombonist-turned-bassist Bill Johnson and trumpeter Lawrence Duhé, at the Royal (later Lincoln) Gardens and Dreamland Café respectively. If Miff sat in with the King, said Wright, it could only have been at one of these two locations.[13]

The act broke up in Los Angeles, apparently after a quarrel between its head-liners, and the others headed back east. Miff, intrigued with California, hung around awhile, joining a band at Mike Lyman's Sunset Inn in Santa Monica that included the owner's brother Abe on drums and Vincent Rose, composer of "Avalon," at the piano.

Napoleon, back in New York, jobbed around (with Charles Panelli filling in on trombone); in early 1919, when Miff finally returned, the two of them joined Sam Lanin's popular dance band at Roseland Ballroom. It's unclear whether Lanin snapped up only Napoleon and Mole or whether he hired the Memphis Five entire, as Paul Whiteman tried to do some years later with Red Nichols's Five Pennies. What is certain is that Lanin, businessman to his finger-tips, understood the commercial potential of the "dixieland" craze unleashed by the ODJB.

"Sam," said bassist Joe Tarto, "was always a great guy for talent. As soon as somebody would come around, or someone would mention somebody to him, he'd get right on it. It would have been just like Sam to hear them and go book them, right on the spot. He was the sharpest of the Lanin brothers, knew talent when he saw it. On the whole, quite an operator. And he recognized he potential of the Original Memphis Five: you can bet he did."[14]

It was under Lanin's aegis that, in late summer of 1921, a revamped Original Memphis Five, featuring Napoleon and Mole, faced recording studio equipment for the first time. The two titles they did that day, "Shake It and Break It" and W. C. Handy's "Aunt Hagar's Children Blues," were released on the Emerson label under the name "Lanin's Southern Serenaders."[15]

Not surprisingly, Mole's playing on both titles still reflects the broad ensemble style of the ODJB's Eddie Edwards. Even here, however, there are passages exe-cuted with an ease and cleanliness beyond the reach of the older man.

Also on this date, playing clarinet, was New Orleans–born multi-instrumentalist "Doc" Behrendson. Like alto saxophonist Loring McMurray, he seems to have been a member of Lanin's regular band during this period, re-cording just enough to remain a tantalizing, even mysterious, figure.

McMurray is even more arresting. Originally from Kansas, he appears on about a dozen record dates, one of them under his own name. His alto on "Haunting Blues," made for Gennett in June 1922 and issued under the name "McMurray's California Thumpers," displays a full, controlled tone and fluidity of execution. His conception seems far more developed than that of any other "hot" alto saxophonist, white or black, in 1922 and to an extent foreshadows the solo work of Frank Trumbauer during his late-'20s association with Bix Bei-derbecke.

McMurray's alto (or C-melody) choruses on the Memphis Five's "Gypsy Blues" and "Eddie Leonard Blues" (neither actually a blues in any but a titular sense) hew close to the melody in the "legit" manner popularized by Rudy Wiedoeft—though he also takes a most Trumbauer-like "hot" break on the latter title, a pop song strongly reminiscent of Leonard's own "Ida, Sweet as Apple Cider."[16]

His obbligato to the trombone melody on "Satanic Blues" (altogether a smoother, more flowing rendition than that of the ODJB) possesses the vocalized quality so attractive on "Haunting Blues." Other impressive work includes "Doo Dah Blues," with a beautifully realized melody statement, some fancy counterline playing, and a well-constructed break.

Even at this early stage, McMurray seems to have achieved a coherent sense of line which, coupled with rhythmic smoothness and singing tone, makes him a singular figure. Little else, alas, is known of him. Jim Moynahan, Boston clarinetist, writer, and loyal friend of both the ODJB and OM5, mentions him glowingly in a 1937 *Saturday Evening Post* article—but adds no supplementary information. McMurray is known to have died young, apparently of blood poisoning, in 1923 or 1924.[17]

By 1923, Napoleon and Mole were at the center of a growing circle of jazz-minded white New York musicians. Extended listening to their records yields several conclusions:

- The Memphis Five appear to have "routined" their arrangements in advance and in detail, even down to supposedly *extempore* "hot" solos. A routine on one number not only doesn't change from take to take but remains similar from session to session. This was a more widespread practice than has been generally acknowledged: others who regularly "routined" solos included Coleman Hawkins and Frank Trumbauer.
- At their best, the OM5 achieve enviable cohesiveness and teamwork. They come across as a chamber ensemble, with great attention to blend, dynamics, and the tone colors, weights, and textures possible in the instrumentation.
- Napoleon, Mole, and clarinetist Lytell are an exceptionally compatible front line. They seem keenly aware of their roles in respect to one another, working for a close, balanced ensemble weave.
- At first, in 1921–22, their concept seems a refined version of the ODJB, with the jagged edges planed off, but the ragtimey, even-eighth-note execution still vestigially in place. This begins to change almost immediately, supplanted by an attractive legato quality. All the same, Napoleon never wavered in his praise of the ODJB. "In those lean days," he wrote later to LaRocca, "we, the Memphis Five, had only the Dixieland band to copy from and try to play the many things you all gave to the world. For without your band how would we have been able to make the little success we were able to get?"[18]

In addition to the pop tunes, the Memphis Five regularly "covered" specialty numbers written or popularized by other bands. Their "Tin Roof Blues" (1923), for example, is rhythmically crisper than the NORK's own version and works interesting variations in the ensemble melody statement. Lytell's clarinet chorus doesn't even try to capture the mysterious, fey quality of Roppolo's original. No one could.*

They seem to have been the first band to record Jelly Roll Morton's "Jelly Roll Blues," in September 1923, anticipating the composer's own first recording by nine months. They take it fast, sacrificing the natural elegance evident in Morton's own treatment for a strutting drive, distinctive in its steady 4/4 way. They also appear to have been the first band to record "I Wish I Could Shimmy Like My Sister Kate," which remained a lifelong Napoleon favorite.[19]

On such records as "He May Be Your Man," the band achieves a collective lilt quite different from any of the southern or midwestern bands, white or black. Lytell plays the twenty-bar melody (a kind of "Sister Kate" with the final four bars extended to eight) in his low register, singing all the way. This is not Roppolo, all shadows and inner mysteries: but it's *bel canto* clarinet all the same, drawing on the same roots, with the melodiousness of a Neapolitan street singer.[20]

But a surprise is in store, as Lytell shifts down a step, from E♭ to D♭, and delivers a bright-hued blues chorus over a Signorelli accompaniment loaded with "modern" passing chords.

By "Shufflin' Mose," in December that year, Napoleon is playing a broader, more relaxed lead; but, as his solo on "Maybe She'll Write Me, She'll Phone Me" in February 1924 shows, he's not yet learned to *ride* the beat instead of playing against it. His problems here are similar to those of New Orleans hornmen Bayersdorffer and DeDroit, discussed in chapter 1. The old ways were hard to shake: within this frame of reference, the first four bars of "Sister Kate" could be played in even-eighth-note ragtime values, the tied-note syncopations providing the rhythmic thrust:

"Sister Kate" melody line, first four bars, ODJB-style.

or it could be "jazzed" by exaggerating the eighths almost to the point of dotted eighths and sixteenths:

"Sister Kate" "jazzed" melody line.

---

*"Tin Roof Blues" seems to have caught on widely. Cornetist Johnny Sylvester's Original Indiana Five recorded it that November for Paramount, with trombonist Charles Panelli (also a frequent OM5 member) reproducing the Brunies solo and clarinetist Nick Vitalo taking a clarinet solo in much the spirit of Lytell's. New Orleans master Sidney Arodin is reportedly the clarinetist on another version, recorded by the "New Orleans Jazz Band" (otherwise all New Yorkers and pretty stiff) the following February; he gets Ropollo's notes—and even a bit of the substance.

The idea of swing, of treating eighth-note execution as though it were actually written in triplets, implying a time signature of 12/8, arrived in explicit
form with Armstrong and, in a rather more restrained fashion, with Beiderbecke.

"Sister Kate" "swung" melody line.

Lytell is another matter. Born James Sarrapede in New York, December 1,
1904, he was a cousin of pianist Frank Signorelli. While still a teenager he heard,
and fell under the spell of, Larry Shields, even working briefly with both the
ODJB and the Original Indiana Five. By the time he joined the Memphis Five he
had become Lytell—the name borrowed from that of a popular actor of the day—
and blossomed into a strong and well-schooled clarinetist.

What is remarkable about Lytell's playing, in fact, is the degree to which it
does not reflect any of the familiar clarinet antecedents. Certainly not Roppolo.
Nor Dodds nor any of the other New Orleans men of either race. Even his debt
to Shields now seems only general, discerned in brightness of tone and forth-
rightness of delivery.

Mostly, Lytell just goes his own way. Brad Gowans, another Shields disciple,
exhibits some of the same flavor on his 1927 "I'm Looking Over a Four-Leaf
Clover." Rosy McHargue, appearing for the first time on records shortly
thereafter, also seems part of this line of development, as does Don Watt, his
predecessor in Ted Weems's band. Clarence Hutchenrider, clarinet soloist with
the Casa Loma Orchestra, was a lifelong Lytell admirer; in later years he worked
for the elder man in NBC radio orchestras.

Between 1926 and 1928 Lytell recorded some eighteen solo titles for Pathé,
usually accompanied by piano and banjo or guitar. They show steady development, keeping pace with the increasingly sophisticated harmonic and melodic
vocabulary of the time, while remaining curiously inert rhythmically.

His phrasing is quite foursquare, tidy patterns that always conform to the
two- and four-bar phrases of the songs and invariably land on the downbeat of
a bar. Its effect is comparable, perhaps, to that of a prose passage constructed
entirely of declarative sentences in subject-predicate-object order. There are moments when the ear longs for a subordinate clause, alternation of phrase lengths,
anything asymmetrical.

Still, this was a common method of phrase-building in the early jazz years.
Both Jimmy Dorsey and, in his less serpentine moments, Frank Trumbauer,
though more advanced soloists than Lytell, frequently exhibit the same kind of
thinking.

Later clarinetists, notably the Chicagoans, Benny Goodman, and, most of all,
Pee Wee Russell, opened out phrase lengths, carrying figures across the natural
barriers of stanza and bar lines into a greater sense of both variety and forward

movement. All the same, Lytell is a highly musical soloist, with a sure command of his horn in all its registers and a seemingly infallible ear. His choruses on the attractive "Why Be Blue?" (1927) or throughout the poised "Sweet Emmaline" (1928) mark him as exceptional.*

The overwhelming quantity of Memphis Five records, and duplication of titles from label to label, make comprehensive listening—even collecting—a time-consuming, often maddening, challenge. Reissue packages have been rare: an exemplary three volumes of Ladd's Black Aces on the English Retrieval label, an LP of Cotton Pickers Brunswicks on the Dutch Grannyphone label, a single OM5 LP on the American Folkways label are among very few.

At random, it's helpful to report that Lytell interpolates two well-shaped blues choruses into "Sister Kate" (Cotton Pickers, Brunswick, September 1922); that "Way Down Yonder in New Orleans" sports unusually fine-tuned ensembles; that "Do Yo' Dooty, Daddy" shows Napoleon smoothing out his phrasing; that his muted lead opening "St. Louis Gal" (all 1923) displays an almost spectral delicacy; that on "Prince of Wails" (1924), Miff Mole emerges at last as a nimble and quite assured trombone soloist. But this only scratches the surface, and the listener is left with the feeling that, were there world enough and time to hunt down and examine the entire scattered Memphis Five *oeuvre*, many such revelations might lie in store.

What, for example, of Napoleon's insistence that Leon Roppolo recorded with the OM5 during a brief stay in New York, that he "went bad on us, and he decided he didn't like New York so he went back to New Orleans"?[21] Could this have been during those weeks, following the end of the Friars' Inn engagement, when the clarinetist and Paul Mares were reportedly playing with Al Siegel's band at Mills' Caprice in Manhattan? And if Roppolo did record with the Memphis Five, even identifying the performances would require untold hours of listen-ing—provided the records could be found.

Phil Napoleon went on to become, in the late '20s, a versatile broadcasting and recording musician, and, still later in life, leader of a popular "dixieland" band. But to the end of his playing days, his style remained proudly insular, taking note of neither Louis Armstrong nor Bix Beiderbecke. According to his friend Bob Nance, a Boston businessman and amateur cornetist, Napoleon was little impressed by either man.

As the critic Otis Ferguson put it, Napoleon's approach to hot playing—rhythmically precise, tonally pure—seemed to fall "between a good heavy ride and good melodic line, missing both." Perhaps—but Ferguson knew little of the older melodic traditions of the brass band; it was there that he would have found the essence—and an explanation—for Phil Napoleon.[22]

*   *   *

---

*Lytell spent many years as an NBC staff radio musician, graduating in the '40s to the post of musical director for several key variety shows. He reentered the jazz field at the beginning of the '50s, recording with old friend Napolean and contributing exceptionally graceful—and variegated—playing to an LP by singer Connee Boswell. Lytell died in 1972.

As impressive as the Memphis Five, and now even less remembered, are the Georgians, formed in mid-1921 as what is surely jazz history's first "band within a band." They were the creation of Pennsylvania-born leader Paul Specht, whose liberal musical policies and prescient grasp of promotion did much for hot music in the early '20s.[23]

Playing at Detroit's Addison Hotel, Specht began featuring his six-piece (sometimes seven) "hot" combination in two thirty-minute sets each night. They proved popular enough with the dancers to win a shot, on June 29, 1922, at recording on their own, under the name "Specht's Jazz Outfit" ("Specht's Society Syncopators" on some issues).

Two sides for the Plaza Group, issued on the Banner and Regal labels, did well enough to alert Frank Walker, the Columbia Records talent scout responsible for coaxing Bessie Smith into a recording studio for the first time. He signed the band to record for Columbia as "the Georgians," presumably because hot music with a Deep South connection still sold records. Their immediate success seems to indicate that the word "jazz" may have been used at that time not only in its generic sense of lively, "peppy" dance music but also—at least occasionally—to identify a specific kind of band playing in an identifiable way.

Specht was a pioneer in another sense. In 1920, when few orchestra leaders were even aware of the brand-new phenomenon of radio, his ten-piece unit was broadcasting regularly over Detroit station WWJ. Relocating in New York in 1922, he continued a friendship begun in Detroit with radio pioneer Lee DeForest and soon was being heard over WJZ.

When the station decided, later that year, to experiment with on-site "remote" broadcasts, it chose Specht's orchestra, then at Manhattan's Alamac Hotel, as performers. The small band, a regular feature of the Alamac broadcasts, soon won a show of its own on competing station WEAF, surely the first exclusively "hot" unit to broadcast on a regularly scheduled basis. "Radio," Specht told the *New York Clipper* in the mid-'20s, "is the greatest method for exploiting anything man has ever invented. It is the one perfect medium for bringing out the best artists and music."[24]

In view of all that, it seems extraordinary that the Georgians' records have been so little reissued. Polished, musical, they impress with a strong ensemble swing, a maturity of concept—and, perhaps above all, through the commanding trumpet of the group's *de facto* leader and yet another in the pantheon of pioneering Italo-American brassmen, Frank Guarente.

Born October 5, 1893, at Montemiletto, a village in the southern Italian province of Avellino, near Naples, Guarente came to the United States in 1910, landing in Philadelphia and proceeding to Allentown, where his elder brother Alphons had settled. Before long he was touring with a concert band.[25]

In 1914 (some accounts say 1913) he played in New Orleans and, according to a 1951 reminiscence by Specht, fell in love with the city's "Old World glamour" and decided to stay. Belgian writer Robert Goffin, one of the trumpeter's early champions, suggested illness as a cause for his decision.

One way or another, the twenty-year-old musician found himself in a major gestation center for hot music, and at the best possible time. Working in a bank by day, he spent his evenings listening to bands and meeting local musicians. Among these, leading one of the most popular dance bands in town, was the seemingly ubiquitous King Oliver.

The two men became friends, spending a good deal of time together in what appear to have been mutual coaching sessions. "Guarente could teach Oliver the basic concepts of music reading and the methods and techniques of European classical brass playing," said Horst H. Lange, something that gave the King a technical edge on his New Orleans competitors. He apparently returned the favor by coaching the young Italian in the nuances and subtleties of "hot" improvisation. According to Lange, Oliver even played for his new friend's twenty-first birthday party, on October 4, 1914.[26]

Word was getting round, and soon the young trumpet player had enough band work to quit the bank. He worked at Kolb's, one of the city's most prestigious restaurants, did some marching-band work, and played outdoor events at Milneburg, Spanish Fort, and other lakeside resort areas. Clarinetist Tony Parenti reported working with Guarente in a six-piece band at the Triangle movie theatre, at Dauphine and Iberville in the French Quarter.[27]

Guarente apparently left New Orleans in 1916 to freelance around the Southwest, saw service with the U.S. Army during World War I, and ultimately headed back north. En route he played briefly with Charlie Kerr's Philadelphia-based band, where his path crossed that of two young Italo-Americans, the violin-and-guitar team of Giuseppe Venuti and Salvatore Massaro, shortly to be known as Joe Venuti and Eddie Lang.

He joined Specht in Atlantic City in mid-1921. The leader, responding to the continuing appeal of the music first popularized in the East by the ODJB, decided to expand his five-piece personnel, mandating Guarente to bring in four new players: trombonist Ray Stilwell, banjoist Russell Deppe, drummer Chauncey Morehouse, and clarinetist Johnny O'Donnell.[28] By early 1922 they'd played the Addison, been fired from New York's Astor Hotel for "playing too loud," done a few months at the Monte Carlo theatre-restaurant on 51st Street, and wound up at the Alamac, Broadway and 71st Street.

In all, quite an odyssey. On the evidence of the Georgians' records, Guarente was by this time a strong and assured trumpeter, effective in solo and able to provide a fiery, rhythmically supple ensemble ride. Most important, he appears to have moved beyond the angularity of ragtime eighth-note patterns, substituting a broad, flowing sense of line, a freedom reminiscent of those New Orleans men, black and white, then active in Chicago.

The Georgians' "Chicago" (1922) climaxes in a powerful tutti, steady and smooth in 4/4. Guarente's lead and O'Donnell's lithe bass clarinet (surely the first such use of this instrument in recorded jazz) are highlights of "Nothin' But"; "You've Got to See Mama Every Night" (1923) generates a collective momentum to rival even the Friars Society band's socko finale of its Gennett "Tiger Rag."

This is clearly a band with ideas. They take "Farewell Blues" even slower than the Friars record, achieving a lonely, haunted atmosphere wholly in keeping with the melody and title of the piece. Their "Land of Cotton Blues" (1923) features what must be the first jazz drum solo on record, Morehouse working over band "stop-time" figures.

They conceive of James P. Johnson's "Old Fashioned Love" as something of a ballad (this a full three and a half years before Bix, Tram, and "Singin' the Blues"), O'Donnell getting off a highly vocal clarinet solo; here and there his style foreshadows that of Don Murray, both tonally and in the slightly dotted-eighth-and-sixteenth feel of its long strings of eighth notes.

His alto chorus on "Way Down Yonder in New Orleans" (1922) comes across as a legato preview of Frank Trumbauer's solo on the 1927 OKeh of the same song; "Lovey Came Back" (1923) culminates in a particularly forceful ride-out, over a rolling rhythm much like the Wolverines' "sock time" of 1924.

This is unmistakably good and expert jazz, full of little forward-looking touches: ensemble breaks utilizing whole-tone scales and other "modern" devices of the day; short contrapuntal passages pitting different combinations of instruments (trumpet and saxophone vs. clarinet, tenor, and trombone) against one another.

Horst Lange makes a point in commending Guarente for not falling victim to "soloist hysteria; he played his choruses as a lead trumpeter, never pushing himself to the foreground or trying to 'cut' or overshadow his fellow-musicians. Every note had a musical value in terms of the whole; Guarente combined a robust improvisational technique in the Oliver style with a subtle, essentially European, lyricism long before Bix Beiderbecke became known for this same thing."[29]

Gilbert Erskine is clearly thinking similar thoughts when he draws the beginnings of a comparison between Guarente and Beiderbecke and suggests that the link between them might have been the young—alas, unrecorded—Emmett Hardy. On the evidence, what similarity exists seems rooted neither in tone nor specifics of phrasing but in the overall feel of the solo as it rides the beat.

Guarente, who never seems to miss a note or be in any doubt what he wants to play, contributes several quite capable solos: on "You've Got to See Mama Every Night" (1923), his plunger technique lends credence to tales of mutual "pro sessions" with Oliver; on "Barney Google," he solos with what sounds like a glass held loosely in front of his bell, achieving an intimacy and tonal warmth which does indeed seem to prefigure Bix.

He's at his best on "Dancin' Dan," done the same day as "Lovey Came Back." Working with what is probably a hand-held cup mute, he sets out the melody in expansive fashion, again with more than a touch of the bel canto expressiveness found so often in Lytell, Roppolo, and other Italo-American jazzmen.

The Specht orchestra spent the summer of 1923 in England, doing residencies at Lyons Corner House restaurant, Coventry Street and Shaftesbury Avenue, and at the Royal Palace Hotel, in West London's fashionable Kensington district; the Georgians, as usual, were featured twice an evening. So deluged was Specht with offers that he began selling the small group as a separate attraction. They quickly caught on in London's West End, and when the Claridge Hotel, in Paris, asked for a Specht orchestra to open its 1924 fall season, the Georgians got the job.[30]

In May 1924, Guarente took a sabbatical and returned to Europe. His first destination was Italy, where he sought out and, on June 30, married a childhood sweetheart in their home town of Montemiletto. Later in the summer he would go to Paris and meet up with the men who were to form the rest of a "new" Georgians unit for the Claridge.

These were happy days for him, but from the viewpoint of his stateside recognition as a "hot" trumpeter his timing couldn't have been worse. In his absence, Louis Armstrong arrived in New York to join Fletcher Henderson's orchestra at Roseland, startling local musicians with intense, rhythmically free solos. Bix and the Wolverines opened at the Cinderella Ballroom, a few blocks down Broadway—handled, incidentally, by Specht's newly established Consolidated Booking Exchange.[31]

By mid-1924, cornetist Red Nichols, fast, clever, and ambitious, had established himself in New York; he was in the Sam Lanin orchestra which shared the Roseland bandstand with Henderson's men, all the while establishing the business connections which would make him, within two years, one of the busiest musicians in the city.

It was a time of ferment, of seminal activity. The Original Memphis Five were turning out records by the dozen. By year's end, Armstrong and soprano sax pioneer Sidney Bechet had recorded together for Clarence Williams. Bessie Smith and Ethel Waters were heard more and more on records, laying the foundations on which their later reputations would rest.

Frank Guarente, meanwhile, was overseas. Leading his reconstituted Georgians, he worked in Paris, in Belgium, in Holland, Germany, Switzerland—and, finally, back in England. Their appearances on the Continent met with universally enthusiastic reception. "No matter how one feels about jazz," wrote a rapturous Swiss critic, "one must confess that these Georgians are splendid representatives of their art . . . each is a master of his instrument, and trumpeters of the quality of the man with this troupe don't exactly grow on trees."[32]

Guarente soon became a respected figure in English dance band circles, recording often with the Savoy Orpheans and other leading units. But again, it kept him away from New York during a crucial period. Before his return, in 1928, Bix, Armstrong, and Nichols had reached peaks of expression and influence, and such significant brassmen as Jabbo Smith, Sidney De Paris, Henry "Red" Allen, Cootie Williams, Rex Stewart, and Jimmy McPartland had made their strong presences felt.

In effect, what had happened to Guarente is comparable to the fate that befell Sam Wooding, who led the first black American hot band to tour widely abroad: by the time Wooding returned home, at the end of the '20s, he discovered to his dismay that his fame—and the music—had passed him by. His band now sounded dated, his ideas about orchestration long since superseded by such young arrangers as Don Redman, Benny Carter, and Duke Ellington. Guarente was apparently aware of the risks in remaining abroad too long: arriving in London at the end of 1927, fellow-trumpeter Sylvester Ahola recalled Guarente warning him to keep his visit brief, lest he lose his contacts and prominence in New York.[33]

As a schooled trumpeter, Guarente was still able to find top-of-the-line work in New York—but not as a jazzman. On four 1928 titles recorded under his own name for Harmony, he restricts himself largely to straight melody and ensemble leads, though his phrasing on the last chorus of "When Polly Walks Through the Hollyhocks" is light and rhythmically crisp.

From 1928 to 1930 he worked with Specht, and from 1930 to 1936 with Victor Young, in each case as *lead* trumpet. By a supreme irony, Specht's "hot" trumpet soloist in the late '20s was a young Connecticut musician named Charlie Spivak, soon to win respect as one of the outstanding lead men of the '30s.

Guarente did well enough during the '30s in radio and recording studios. He's present on record dates featuring Bing Crosby, Smith Ballew, Chick Bullock, the Dorsey Brothers, the Boswell Sisters, Jack Teagarden, and on dozens of instrumental sessions as part of the pool of house musicians working under Victor Young's direction for ARC-Brunswick. But he seldom solos, and few among the many who worked with him in those units seem to have been more than dimly aware of the role he'd played as a pioneer jazzman little more than a decade before.[34]

The final chapter in Guarente's story is odd and profoundly sad. By mid-1941 it had become increasingly clear that the United States could not avoid being drawn into the war then engulfing Europe. When America did enter the war, Benito Mussolini's Italy, closely aligned with Nazi Germany, would be an enemy. Guarente, though a naturalized American citizen, was of Italian birth, hence—as seems always to be the case in wartime—suspect.

He'd been active in radio, working as a staff musician on such regular network shows as Lucky Strike's *Your Hit Parade*, *The Aldrich Family*, and *The Lone Ranger*. But apparently the presence of an Italian-born bandsman made some executives, including music director Harry Salter, nervous. Guarente was let go, apparently with only the clumsiest of explanations. According to Lange, "even though Guarente had long been a U.S. citizen, the influential and powerful Salter saw to it that the trumpeter became unemployed and stayed that way."[35] The precise facts behind this case are now hard to ascertain, though histories of the World War II years offer countless examples of discrimination against American citizens born in Axis countries, notably Germany and Japan.

Tommy Dorsey, for whom Guarente had worked in the early '30s, offered the trumpeter a chair in his 1942 band. If this seems remarkable, in view of the stylistic direction the band was taking at that time, it is also typical of the younger Dorsey, a man of strong will, long memory, and unswerving loyalty to old friends.

In any case, it never came to pass. Frank Guarente died of an unspecified illness, perhaps cancer, on July 21, 1942. He was forty-eight. His death followed by less than three weeks that of Bunny Berigan, another old Dorsey friend whom the trombonist had tried to rescue by making a place for him in his brass section.

Miff Mole, meanwhile, left Sam Lanin in May 1924, to join Ray Miller's orchestra. He was by now among New York's most sought-after hot trombonists, strong and agile in solo, and the Miller band gave him plenty of chances to shine.

Ray Miller was a drummer whose first records by his "Black and White Melody Boys" in 1920 had included New Orleans trombonist Tom Brown. Surprisingly little is known of him now, save that his band recorded regularly for Brunswick throughout the '20s and was regarded highly enough to have played long engagements at such spots as the Beaux Arts Club in Atlantic City (where Mole joined him) and the New York Hippodrome. According to Mole, the band even played for President Calvin Coolidge at the White House, accompanying Al Jolson.

Along with Isham Jones, the Benson Orchestra of Chicago, and very few others, Miller's seems to have been one of the first commercial dance bands of the early '20s to incorporate with any success the accents (and various exponents of) "hot" improvisation. Solos by Mole, Frank Trumbauer, and pianist Rube Bloom abound on Miller's 1924–25 Brunswick records. Arrangements, many by the gifted Tom Satterfield, are generally crisp and to the point.[36] Miff's duet with Trumbauer on "Mama's Gone, Goodbye" presages the saxophonist's forthcoming "chase" choruses with Bix; his solos and breaks on "Lots o' Mama" and "Nobody Knows What a Red-Headed Mama Can Do" (all 1924) show him negotiating his horn with a dexterity unmatched at the time.

On Sunday, September 7, 1924, Bix and the Wolverines descended on the Hippodrome *en masse* to hear the Miller band. When Miff stood to take a chorus on "Limehouse Blues," they cheered him so lustily that ushers, thinking them hecklers, threw them out. "I thought you guys were giving me the bird" was Mole's reaction afterwards when they met backstage. Trumbauer and Mole returned the favor, dropping by the Cinderella to hear Bix and his band of midwestern pals.

Bix made his last, and best, records with the Wolverines October 7 at Gennett's East 37th Street studios. Three days later he was back, this time to do two sides with Trumbauer, Mole, and Bloom (plus Wolverines Min Leibrook on tuba and Vic Moore on drums). Trumbauer's slow, bluesy "I'm Glad" and Bloom's up-tempo "Flock o' Blues" (the same tune widely recorded the following year, by Fletcher Henderson, Louis Armstrong, and others, as "Carolina Stomp"), issued under the name "Sioux City Six," are performances of some significance. Trumbauer, at twenty-three, was already the most listened-to and influential reedman of the day, and Mole's work with the Memphis Five had conferred something of the same celebrity on him; Bloom was quickly achieving a dual reputation as pianist and composer.

Gennett 5569 seems an almost casual record: but hear the lightness and ease of Miff's solo on "I'm Glad," never raising his volume level beyond a *mezzo-forte*, and Bix's lead on "Flock o' Blues," so pliant it seems an exercise in legato playing, though even the acoustic recording can't muffle his ringing attack. And what of the ensemble give-and-take on the same number, Miff and Tram adhering to and adorning the cornet line?

Yes, the Georgians excelled in ensemble unity as well; yes, the last chorus of Oliver's "Chattanooga Stomp" achieves a momentum wondrous to behold. But those are the recorded efforts of regularly constituted bands, who achieved their cohesion by working together night after night. The musicians, moreover, are chiefly ensemble players, as yet (*pace* Lange) impervious to the lure of "soloist hysteria."

"I'm Glad" and "Flock o' Blues" give us something new: three horn players, all with personal, identifiable solo styles, coming together to play as a band. In its quiet way, this record is a summit meeting, the first "all-star" unit put together expressly for a record date.

Beyond argument, the Armstrong-Bechet recorded encounters of that winter, under Clarence Williams's name and that of the "Red Onion Jazz Babies," produced more musical electricity. But they now seem gladiatorial events, two titans battling for supremacy on the upper slopes of Olympus. For all their grandeur, they show little sign of the camaraderie which characterizes the Sioux City Six titles. Where "Cake-Walkin' Babies From Home" comes across as competition, full-frontal confrontation, "I'm Glad" is the work of a team taking the field together.

Mole's "I'm Glad" solo, though to some extent buried by the other two horns in an awkward recording balance, offers vivid illustration of how far he'd brought his instrument from its circus-style ensemble role.

"I'm Glad," Miff Mole trombone solo and melody line (two staves), 1925.

Essentially a paraphrase, it works the elements of the melody into new and more unified shapes. Rather than repeat the figure of the first two bars (which returns three times, lending the piece a structural blockiness and holding up any melodic development), Miff transforms the first two bars into a little melody of his own, then varies it just enough to round it off and dismiss it.

He turns bars 9–10 into an even more ingenious variant on the theme by the simple expedient of leaving out the triplet, then finally alludes to it in 11–12 in a way that integrates it into a figure which culminates in a descending triplet passage. Miff's final, almost stately figure in bars 15–16 comes to rest on a concert D, third voice of the tonic, and Bix, in a charming flourish, resolves the phrase for him to a concert B♭.

Mole spent the winter of 1924–25 with Miller at New York's brand-new Arcadia ballroom. But by then the word was out, and offers were coming in faster than he could deal with them. No one on trombone could execute "hot" solo passages more cleanly, better in tune, with smoother slide work and more incisive attack in all registers of his horn, than the bespectacled young man from Long Island. "He made everything sound easy," said Gunther Schuller, "at a time when most trombonists could barely struggle to play some inane tailgate lick in tune and on time."[37]

When Miller went on the road in early 1925 Miff left the band, convinced that he could make just as good a living staying on New York. By early summer he was in an orchestra formed by multi-reed virtuoso Ross Gorman for the third edition of the *Earl Carroll's Vanities* revue, opening July 6 at the New Amsterdam Theater on Broadway.

It was an outstanding unit, drawn from the cream of New York's hot-oriented white players. Perhaps their most famous record was one of the show's big production numbers, Charles Gaskill's "Rhythm of the Day." Richard DuPage describes the scene onstage, with Mole playing a hot solo on the "futuristic" chord sequence, "lights flashing madly and other chaotic effects all designed to give the illusion of Hades and to frighten the chorus girls." The climax came when the girls, appearing terrified of the "weird" trombone effects, leaped one by one into the orchestra pit (the band had been moved to a box, stage left), followed by the trombonist himself.[38]

Heard now, "Rhythm of the Day" sounds far less audacious than it must have sounded in 1925, but it *is* unconventional. The first half of its thirty-two-bar principal strain (structured ABAC) is built along the lines of the later "Sweet Georgia Brown," except that the first two chords (in B♭ a G7 and C7) are expressed as augmented sevenths. As a result, Mole's solo improvisation is based on the whole-tone, rather than diatonic, scale; its use in this manner anticipates by at least eight years the great Coleman Hawkins–Fletcher Henderson collaboration "Queer Notions," with its whole-tone trumpet solo by Henry "Red" Allen.

"Rhythm of the Day" is also unusual in that its first three eight-bar episodes (ABA) are rooted firmly in the key of B♭. But its last eight bars pull a surprise, resolving the C7 augmented to an F major chord, making it the subdominant of a familiar cadence pattern resolving to C major.

In the context of 1925, these are radical departures from pop song chordal norms, but Miff, the record's only soloist, handles them with disarming ease.

"Rhythm of the Day," Miff Mole trombone solo, Ross Gorman Orchestra, 1925

It was in the *Vanities* orchestra, directed during the show by Donald Voorhees, that Miff Mole first played alongside, and became friends with, Red Nichols. In later years, with both men's reputations in eclipse and their records all but unknown to whole generations of jazz listeners, it might be easy to overlook the significance of this encounter.

But significant it certainly was. Nichols had supplanted all others (excepting perhaps Armstrong and Beiderbecke) as the cornetist most in demand in New York; he recorded constantly, was widely listened to and emulated. If his hot solos lacked the depth and sheer beauty of Bix's, he was undeniably a far more polished and versatile instrumentalist. Like Mole, he was fast, clean, and in tune; his attack was crisp, his tone light and controlled, impeccable in all registers.

Nichols himself had admired Mole since hearing him with the Original Memphis Five in Atlantic City, and from all evidence the feeling was mutual. It seemed a foregone conclusion that they would team up: and so they did, on a February 26, 1925, record date for the ever-perspicacious Sam Lanin. It was the first of many, in groups large and small, for a variety of labels and under an array of names to challenge even the encyclopedic permutations of the Original Memphis Five.

Nichols, Mole soon realized, was a go-getter, a pint-sized dynamo with boundless ambition, unlimited energy, and a fingertip sense for business. In the vocabulary of a distant future, he was also an indefatigable networker, who knew how to parlay one contact into ten, spreading his name and reputation across an ever broader front.[39]

With Red doing the talking, the pair soon found themselves at the epicenter of white hot music activity in New York. Excellent foils, they were fast, clever, and harmonically sophisticated and seemed to get better with each record date.[40]

The team quickly became the cynosure of a more-or-less consistent group of musicians: pianist Arthur Schutt, star of the Georgians; guitarist Eddie Lang and, occasionally, his violinist partner Joe Venuti; Vic Berton, respected widely as one of the key percussionists of the age; Jimmy Dorsey, whose spare, bright-toned alto sax solos were being imitated everywhere.

And in the quiet eye of the hurricane was shy, studious-looking Miff Mole. In Otis Ferguson's description, "he could raise the tension of any band with a four-bar break, he could swing into the pattern of the trumpet solo with a middle eight bars, he could take thirty-two by himself and double that, and keep the line of interest clear and free. What is more, he was old reliable himself in studio work: he could play straight when he had to and when you wanted something else it was there."[41]

They were a team and they were good, and the evidence is right there in the records. Max Harrison quotes Nichols as saying that "the principal aim was to turn out something which met the approval of your fellow musicians right there in the recording studio," and—remarkably—just about every record bears him out. Beginning with the Red Heads' "Fallen Arches" and "Nervous Charlie" (1925) it is a departure, music intended as much for listening as for dancing: thoughtful, sophisticated, intelligently devised—and faultlessly played.[42]

Harrison is right in remarking that such care could also result in performances "overcrowded with incident"—too much detail packed into too small a space, often leaving an impression of clutter. It's a problem chronic in the early days of jazz on record: such "art" ensembles as Armstrong's Hot Five, Trumbauer's various groups, Morton's Red Hot Peppers, and the various Nichols-Mole units are wont to overfill the three minutes offered by a standard 78 rpm disc. Too much incident, and the music stops breathing.

All the same, there is much to treasure: Miff's solo on the Red Heads' "Wild and Foolish" (1926) is particularly nimble; he charges determinedly out of a brisk opening ensemble on "Alabama Stomp" (and an introduction of some complexity), sustaining interest throughout a full chorus; on "That's No Bargain" (taken much slower than the more familiar Five Pennies Brunswick) he's drily humorous and to the point.

In this period, especially throughout 1926, each solo seems to find Mole a bit more realized, more focused. His emotional range is greater, enabling him—as musicians like to put it—to tell a better story. His technical grasp is ever more secure: there seems nothing he *can't* do, popping out his notes dead center. Again, Otis Ferguson:

> With everybody else muffing weaknesses with shakes, slurs, repeated phrases, and high notes, he sticks to a rounded phrase of notes struck dead center. His slide is as easy and noiseless as a trumpet valve without sacrificing that typical and exhilarating capacity of the instrument for rolling into a note; more, he knows, as few have discovered, how to use the full lower register to give a phrase an upward spring. He never tries something he can't pull off, and yet there seems to be little he can't pull off.[43]

Tommy Dorsey idolized him and is said to have kept a manuscript book of Mole solos, faithfully transcribed from records, and in later years talked of having them published. Recorded evidence shows how many other colleagues on both sides of the racial divide were listening with equal attentiveness: Glenn Miller, out in Chicago with Ben Pollack's new band; Bill Rank, with Goldkette in Detroit; Claude Jones, shortly to star with McKinney's Cotton Pickers; "Big" Charlie Green, with Henderson (as the Dixie Stompers' 1926 version of "Nervous Charlie" graphically illustrates).[44]

Everybody seemed to want Miff. The Martin Instrument Co. published, as an advertisement, an endorsement letter he'd written praising the "action and mellow tone" of their "Dansant" model. Plans were announced to publish a folio of Mole's "hot breaks and choruses" for aspiring trombonists. Roger Wolfe Kahn, twenty-one-year-old son of millionaire banker Otto Kahn, hired him for good money to play in an all-star band he was putting into the Biltmore Hotel. Miff stayed with Kahn eighteen months—on condition that he could also continue to record as a freelancer.

And the records kept getting better. That spring he and Red recorded as "the Six Hottentots" for Banner, with Joe Tarto's tuba giving needed bottom to the rhythm section. By this time the Goldkette orchestra, with Bix and Trumbauer its key soloists, had been to New York, and Nichols's playing on the Hottentots dates shows how deeply he'd been moved by Beiderbecke's ungimmicked lyricism: the lead is broader, sparer, riding the beat rather than jostling it.

Perhaps most revealing of the evolution going on in all of them, and the level Miff's playing in particular had attained, comes in the Hottentots' May 1927 "Memphis Blues." Red opens with four Bix-like *a capella* bars, and the band glides into the W. C. Handy favorite, not in the rough-and-tumble manner popularized by latter-day bands but with a thoughtful, lilting elegance, treating it primarily as a *song*.

Accordingly, their solos are not on the blues section, but on the melodically richer sixteen-bar verse: Miff takes his time in an almost affectionate statement;

Red, in his turn, muses on the value of a melodic line. But another surprise is in store: when they do get to the blues they treat it almost kiddingly, in the razz-matazz manner of Ted Lewis. Jimmy Dorsey's "growl" clarinet break, in fact, could almost have been lifted from the "top-hatted tragedian of jazz."[45]

Nichols had also signed a contract with Brunswick to record under his own name, and in December of 1926 he, Miff, Dorsey, Schutt, Berton, and Lang made their debut on the label as "Red Nichols and His Five Pennies." The name, reportedly tossed out by Berton as a joke, stuck: for the rest of the trumpeter's career, he would lead groups called—regardless of size, which sometimes swelled to as many as fifteen—the "Five Pennies."

More wheeling and dealing resulted in an OKeh contract to record as "Miff Mole and His Little Molers." On Columbia they simply took over the label's house name, the Charleston Chasers; on Harmony, Columbia's acoustically recorded dime-store subsidiary, they were the "Arkansas Travelers," on Pathé "the Red Heads." Victor billed them as "Red and Miff's Stompers."

There seemed no end to the aliases. At the same time, the same men were appearing with and recording for Kahn and other dance band leaders. When Nichols and Donald Voorhees, for whom he'd worked in the pit of *Earl Carroll's Vanities*, jointly took over musical directorship of radio station WOR, one of their first acts was to hire Miff Mole.[46]

Miff, in short, had it made, and there's plenty of recorded evidence to prove it: he seemed incapable of playing a poor or even mediocre solo. "He was very steady, very consistent," said drummer Johnny Blowers, who knew Mole well during the '30s. "He'd always had that reputation. That's why he did so well as a studio man at NBC later on. But Miff—you know, he was kind of shy. Retiring. He was just as happy to play, leave the business to others. I never knew him to be any kind of businessman."[47]

With Red as front man, the Nichols-Mole partnership—and Mole's own prominence as a hot trombone soloist—hit its peak in 1927–28. Paul Whiteman, anxious to add substance to his "King of Jazz" reputation, tried to hire the basic Five Pennies group—Red, Miff, Jimmy Dorsey, Vic Berton, and Eddie Lang—entire. According to some reports, there were plans also to add Joe Venuti.

In the event, only Red, Dorsey, and Berton joined. Miff simply carried on as before, though in retrospect it seems curious that he, with his lack of interest in the business side of his trade, hadn't accepted Whiteman's offer and the job security that went with it. Jean Goldkette, too, had tried to get him. But Mole, said friends, didn't want to travel.

His solos on records of this time show how far his basic concept had evolved. Their balance and trumpet-like accuracy of attack prompted some trombonists of the period to suggest that Miff must actually be playing valve trombone; no slide work, they insisted, could be *that* clean.

His chorus on "A Good Man Is Hard to Find," with the Red Heads, embodies all the virtues, including an almost Bix-like sense of structure. What is lacking from the following transcription—and must be heard to be appreciated—is the exhilarating *snap* of his delivery.

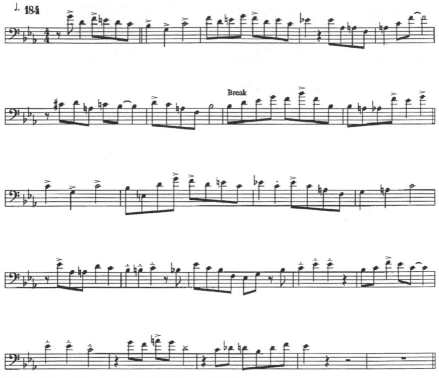

"A Good Man Is Hard to Find," Miff Mole solo, 1927.

Among small felicities: his use of an E♮ in the pickup run into the first bar, anticipating the C7 chord which begins the chorus. His mid-chorus break is a complete two-bar episode, compounded of crisply played eighth notes without a hint of syncopation or *rubato*. They sit more or less foursquare within the structural framework imposed by bar lines and two- or four-bar phrases.

There is also not a hint of the bent notes, between-the-pitches intonation, and other colorational features characteristic of the blues vocabulary. While little claim can be made for the blues (contrary to the insistence of some latter-day commentators) as the *sine qua non* of a jazz style, there is no denying the blues as a personalizing, emotionally enriching element.

Without doubt, moreover, Mole (in common with many of the other New York white jazzmen) tended to *play* the beat, rather than play *with* it, in the manner of Armstrong, Bechet, and other major black soloists; his chief interests lie, rather, in matters of form and melodic organization. Inevitably, such traits confer on his choruses a sense of tidiness—deft, purposeful, with energy and plenty of forward motion. But, listening even to Miff's best choruses one after the other—The Molers' "Original Dixieland One-Step," "The New Twister," "Honolulu Blues," and the three remarkable takes of "Alabama Stomp" with the Pennies come readily to mind—it's also not hard to understand why the arrival of Jack Teagarden had such an impact on New York jazzmen.

Teagarden, too, had speed and flexibility: but he used it in the service of a more vocalized, blues-rooted delivery, which conferred on every phrase he played an immediacy seldom achieved by Mole. Miff's choruses, even at their best, never quite escape a sense of having been *devised*, rather than rolling out of some inner consciousness. Rhythmically, too, they evince a certain constraint, even stiffness of execution.

By the end of the 1920s, with Teagarden and Jimmy Harrison in place, Joe "Tricky Sam" Nanton working his plunger with Ellington, and J. C. Higginbotham shouting and hollering exuberant choruses with Luis Russell's band at the Saratoga Club, the trombone picture had changed drastically. Miff's way, though still widely admired, was but one of several.

There was still work aplenty. But sometime in the spring of 1929, under circumstances which have never been made fully clear (but are not hard to guess), the Nichols-Mole partnership came to an end. The last record date on which the two appear together is the February 16 Five Pennies session which produced "Allah's Holiday," "Roses of Picardy," and a striking "Alice Blue Gown."

Had Miff been more alert, a better judge of his friend's motivations, he might have seen it coming. On a July 6, 1928, Molers date, they'd used four newcomers from Chicago: clarinetist Frank Teschemacher, pianist Joe Sullivan, banjoist Eddie Condon, and young Gene Krupa on drums.

Listening now to "Shimme-Sha Wabble" and "One Step to Heaven," it's not hard to imagine that the raw energy of the young Chicagoans must have been, for Red and Miff, something of a shock. Nichols was obviously entranced. His sixteen-bar solo on the Molers' "Crazy Rhythm," done three weeks later, is, for him, almost manic. Miff's chorus works with a wider palette, including use of "blues" timbres and across-the-bar-line phrasing.

Red, nothing if not pragmatic, began hiring the Chicagoans and their friends whenever and wherever he could. He began using Benny Goodman on clarinet. Invited to organize a pit orchestra for the Gershwin brothers' new Broadway show, *Strike Up the Band*, he included Benny and trombonist-arranger Glenn Miller, both of whom had come to town with Ben Pollack.

Goodman, Miller, Krupa, and—perhaps most significant—Teagarden were on hand when, on April 18, just two months after the "Allah's Holiday" date, Nichols assembled a band at Brunswick to record three titles. Two of them, "Indiana" and a medium-slow "Dinah," made history, largely because of Teagarden.

Miff, with characteristic lack of competitiveness, had even sent the newcomer in as a "sub" on a Roger Wolfe Kahn date in March of 1928. Teagarden's chorus on "She's a Great, Great Girl," generally considered his recording debut, created a sensation when it was issued—and did much to fix the Texan in the minds of potential employers for whom, before this, the "hot" trombone men of choice were Mole and Tommy Dorsey.

Mole simply carried on: he continued to make records for OKeh under the Molers name, with Phil Napoleon, his old associate from Original Memphis Five days, now playing most of the trumpet. In late 1929 he went to work at the National Broadcasting Company as a staff musician, all while recording for Ed Kirkeby, Irving Mills, Adrian Schubert, and other leading contractors.

125

Taken together, the last Molers dates are something of an oddity. Miff, playing with a broader tone and softer attack, seems to be examining his own musical identity. There are even moments when his playing resembles that of his disciple, Tommy Dorsey: his cup-muted melody statement on "Lucky Little Devil" (1930), for example, could have been Dorsey as he sounded throughout the early '30s.

Napoleon, too, has changed. The calm, neatly distributed phrases of just a few years before have given way to an agitated, often rough-toned manner which strongly resembles no one's more than Tommy Dorsey's in his cut-and-slash trumpet incarnation. The result, particularly on "Navy Blues," is a curious sense of multiple personality, as though Tommy were standing alongside his own trumpet-playing *Doppelgänger* on the front line.

Mole's style obviously was evolving, and it might have been interesting to follow his progress, had he continued to make jazz records throughout 1930 to 1935, years of great ferment and change in hot music. But after the Molers date he was silent for five years.

At NBC he was branching out more and more into general studio work. According to one story widely circulated among musicians and cited by Mole chronicler Richard DuPage, conductor Hugo Mariani brought him in for a 1934 broadcast of Ravel's *Bolero* because he couldn't rely on the orchestra's regular man to deliver the solo trombone entrance on a high B♭, coming after many bars' rest. Mole, said DuPage, played the solo impeccably. He also performed under Bruno Walter and Fritz Reiner, and, when the network organized its NBC Symphony Orchestra for Arturo Toscanini, Mole reportedly was offered—but declined—the first trombone chair.

From time to time he'd also run into Paul Whiteman, who never lost an opportunity to remind him that the invitation of 1927 was still open. Finally, at the end of 1938, he said yes, and spent two years in Whiteman's brass section.

On Whiteman's "Bouncing Brass" date of April 6, 1939, he shows he's lost none of his flexibility. His obbligato to the opening ensemble of "Rose Room" is particularly noteworthy. But it's his eight bars on the ballad "Now and Then," played by Whiteman's "Swing Wing," that command attention with their striking *rubato*, a departure from the tidy, foursquare Miff of the '20s.

It's even more in evidence when he solos on "A Good Man Is Hard to Find," as part of Milt Gabler's four-part *Jam Session at Commodore* of March 23, 1940. Though the song is the same as his 1927 Red Heads effort, the slow-tempo treatment makes it something a world apart. From both the sound of him and various photographs taken at the date it's obvious that he's playing a bigger-bore horn, a Martin Imperial, and getting a broader, earthier sound.

The most arresting feature is the degree to which Miff has absorbed a melodic and rhythmic vocabulary only hinted at on the Whiteman records. Presumably the main source has been the universally admired Teagarden, with his bluesy tone and phrasing (though such distinctive stylists as Dicky Wells, Jack Jenney, Vic Dickenson, and Lawrence Brown also may have had some effect). But leaving it at that hardly describes a solo of—literally—breathtaking rhythmic complexity. It is almost a cadenza over a steady pulse, so unrestrained are its phrases by beat or bar line.[48]

The phrase beginning bar 11, for example, involves nine sixteenth notes, grouped as three triplets, spread *ad lib* across two beats. It is notated in transcription as accurately as possible, but in the end—as with that greatest of all *rubato* masters, trumpeter Henry "Red" Allen—hearing is the only guide.

It's impossible, listening to Miff here and grasping the implications of what he's playing, to disagree with Max Harrison when he senses "a potentiality of imagination" in Mole that might have led him, in a different time and context, into a world of discovery and even innovation.[49]

"A Good Man Is Hard to Find," Miff Mole solo, 1940.

But that was not to be. He spent a year with Benny Goodman, six more at Nick's, leading bands which brought together veterans of New York, Chicago, and New Orleans, playing an increasingly static repertoire in ever more routined ways. There were fine solo moments, as on his April 28, 1944, "Peg o' My Heart" feature for Commodore. But there is in all his work from here on an inescapable sense of possibility not explored, potential allowed to slip away.[50]

Later records show him seemingly content in a standard "dixieland" framework, his ensemble style often recalling the broad accents of his first inspiration, the ODJB's Eddie Edwards. It's as if the man who took jazz trombone out of the circus has found sanctuary back under the big top. "I just got lazy, I guess" was his rather rueful explanation to interviewer Pat Harris in 1951.[51]

Bassist Jack Lesberg, who worked with Mole in New York during the 1940s, remembered him as sounding "like a guy who had started out as a legit player and come to jazz from there. A lot of trombone players at that time had different little tricks, ways they'd found of getting around things. Miff went at it straight, head on: that slide was always in motion, all those maneuvers of the positions. Sometimes, watching him, I thought the slide was going to come right off the trombone.

"He was determined to get things right. If he wrote an arrangement he wanted you to play it just the way he'd written it. No great liberties or 'improvements.' He knew just what he wanted, and wanted you to play things just so."

Sometimes, said Lesberg, that led to amusing consequences. "One time on a record date he wrote out a part for Pee Wee [Russell], and Pee Wee looked it over and, very serious, pointed to one note and said, 'Hey, chum, that note's not on the clarinet.' Miff was shocked. He says, 'What note?' And PeeWee says, 'This note,' and hits the note, big and loud as you please. It was probably the low concert D, the lowest note on the horn. Even Miff had to laugh."[52]

He moved to Chicago and worked for six years in the house band at Bill Reinhart's club, Jazz Ltd. His technical command of the horn remained impeccable, winning admiration from colleagues—particularly those with long memories. "He played about everything you can play on a trombone," pianist Art Hodes once said admiringly. "Some things he does, other players can only stand around and listen to."[53]

In 1954 an old hip injury flared up, and Miff returned to New York for a series of operations, which left him in more or less constant pain. He continued to work occasionally around town, even leading jam sessions at a small neighborhood club, the Mandalay, in Bellmore, Long Island, not far from his home town of Roosevelt.

"Those were fun," said Johnny Blowers, a regular. "Miff—well, he didn't really run things as much as just let them happen. Everybody turned up at one time or another: Bobby Hackett used to come out, sometimes with Billy Butterfield. Both of 'em. And Miff? Well, he still played great. Some nights he could scare you to death."[54]

But by 1960 he'd slipped again from sight. The invitation to play at Newport apparently surprised and delighted him, and he began practicing in earnest.

His disappointment at the way things worked out that Newport Sunday, said Dan Morgenstern, was a thing so vivid, so palpable, you could almost touch it. He tried to find John Hammond, for explanation, for reassurance. Anything. But Hammond was off fighting for the life of the festival; he never even knew, until afterwards, of the small drama going on in the press tent. In the end they got Miff back to the bus station, and he returned to New York.

Some time later—days? weeks?—trombonist Eddie Bert, who had taken lessons from Miff back in 1941, reported seeing him somewhere on upper Broadway, selling apples in the street. The story has circulated in several forms: some accounts place him near the 59th Street Bridge, selling pretzels. In another version it's peanuts. Another, pencils.

Fans, colleagues, admirers rallied in support. *Record Research* magazine published a special Miff Mole issue, its centerpiece an exhaustively researched, intelligent, and sympathetically written biographical article by Richard DuPage on which this chapter has drawn. Jack Crystal, who ran regular jam sessions at the Central Plaza, scheduled a "Miff Mole Night" benefit concert for late February 1961, the proceeds to help Miff move to Arizona, where he might find a new life, another chance, teaching in a healthier environment.

Crystal (father of the comedian Billy Crystal) asked Benny Goodman to take part, and the clarinetist readily agreed. When out-of-town engagements intervened, Crystal rescheduled the date for March, then for April, and finally for May 22.

It never happened. On April 29, 1961, Miff Mole suffered a cerebral hemorrhage at his 250 West 88th Street apartment. He was dead by the time medical help arrived.

7

Red Nichols
and His Circle

The late musicologist and lexicographer Nicolas Slonimsky, an unlikely commentator on jazz, once said of Red Nichols:

> Heuristic exegetes of European hermeneutics bemoaned the commercialization of his style, giving preference to his earlier, immaculate, jazzification.[1]

Translation and distillation: insiders, who claimed to understand the true artistic nature of hot music, cried "Foul!" when Nichols, in the late '20s, began acknowledging a responsibility to someone more than just fellow-musicians and hot music initiates.

For all its willfully Nabokovian opaqueness, Slonimsky's declaration identifies and isolates an attitude long prevalent among followers of jazz and, to greater or lesser degree, among musicians themselves. To play for one another, it holds, appreciated chiefly by the few, is admirable; to bid for wider public acceptance is selling out, betraying both the covenant and, in some not-quite-defined way, the music itself.

It's nonsense, of course, but it's been part of jazz throughout the long, self-conscious climb from simple *Gebrauchsmusik* to perceived artistic respectability. Clarinetist Frank Teschemacher, sometime in the mid-'20s, complained to Mezz Mezzrow:

> You knock yourself out making a great new music for the people, and they treat you like some kind of plague or blight, like you were offering

them leprosy instead of art . . . That's always the way it is with a *real artist*
[emphasis added] who won't put his talents on the auction block to be
sold to the highest bidder.[2]

He might be playing music in public, but his audience had to seek him out
and understand the gift he offered them. "You knock yourself out, making a
great new music for the people," and—to carry his sentence to its real, implied
conclusion—the people are ultimately too benighted, too obtuse, to come and
partake of it. Poor artist! The notion that even a jazzman might have a responsibility to meet "the people" halfway—to attempt, howsoever he could, to find
a receptive public and woo it just a bit—had no place in Teschemacher's thinking,
at least at that youthful point.

At its beginnings, what came to be called hot jazz was functionally a form
of entertainment, of diversion. Louis Armstrong and others never tired of reminding all and sundry that a musician took a bandstand or stage to play to an
audience which had paid to see and hear him. It belonged to his calling, therefore,
to give the people, in the age-old show business formulation, their money's
worth. Yet the dichotomy, the gulf between the needs of the public and the
musician's declared need, no less compelling, to see himself as something more—
better—than simply a paid entertainer, haunted this music throughout its adolescent years and in some ways haunts it still.

It's a perception that seems particularly keen in the young. And as Neil Leonard and others have observed, the young jazzman's sense of being isolated in a
wasteland of ignorance has lent an almost gnostic, revelatory—and quite insular—quality to the very ability to play hot music. Anyone betraying the trust,
acknowledging that the musician might owe his audience more than the simple
act of playing before them, risks ostracism, even outright vilification.

Yet from the start there were jazz musicians who perceived the duality of
artistic and commercial responsibility more clearly than others, attempted to serve
both ends—and paid a high price for their trouble. As Slonimsky might have
suggested, no case illustrates the pitfalls of such a course better than that of Ernest
Loring "Red" Nichols.

He was a cornetist, an excellent one, and a strong and positive force in
producing and disseminating a body of music which can still astonish with its
subtlety, ingenuity, harmonic and technical brilliance. It's hardly stretching a
point to contend that much of what became the "modern" and "progressive"
jazz of later decades had its origins here.

Yet few hot musicians of the early years have been so consistently fought
over, have polarized critical opinion so violently, as Red Nichols. Throughout his
sixty-year lifetime he was both extravagantly overpraised and cruelly vilified, as
much by fellow-musicians as by critics. Since his death in a Las Vegas hotel room
in 1965, his music has remained in eclipse, all but unknown to latter-day listeners. Yet any investigation of that music yields the inescapable conclusion that
Nichols *mattered*: his achievements are real and substantial.

Born in Ogden, Utah, May 8, 1905, he arrived in New York in 1924 a fully seasoned professional. He'd toured widely throughout the Midwest, recorded for Gennett and Edison, played such prestigious venues as the Ambassador Hotel in Atlantic City. Before long he was one of the busiest freelancers in town, working regularly for Sam Lanin, George Olsen, Harry Reser, Bennie Krueger, and dozens of others. A quick and accurate reader, he impressed employers with his ability to turn in a clean, capable job in almost any situation.

He worked for Lanin at Roseland, playing opposite Fletcher Henderson's orchestra and listening with awe to Louis Armstrong, who reciprocated by showing great interest in his younger colleague. "Louis and I used to play for each other in the musicians' room downstairs," he told a *Down Beat* interviewer. "He was very interested in the false-fingering ideas I was working out and I showed him how it was done. *The jazz musicians of that day were a kind of fraternity—all working together to promote and advance the music and each other. It's quite different now*" [emphasis added].[3]

Nichols was a go-getter, with a fast business sense and a flair for self-promotion. It didn't take him long to establish a solid network of contacts with recording studios, dance band leaders, Broadway contractors, and other potential work sources. For a time, in 1925, he even played with the California Ramblers, until Ed Kirkeby got tired of having to sub out his chair every time Red went off to do a more lucrative date on his own.

There's no doubting how good he was. His tone was bright, attack incisive; he had speed, dexterity. He could play lead or section parts with equal facility, and when a hot solo was needed, he'd deliver something snappy, polished. If the solos were a mite precious, too dependent on such contrivances as the "false-fingering ideas" referred to above, they were in any case always highly musical.

But it took a chance meeting, in the brass section of Donald Voorhees's *Earl Carroll's Vanities* orchestra of mid-1925, to turn Red Nichols into something more than just a capable all-round sideman. Miff Mole, on trombone, was already considered a musicians' musician: with the Original Memphis Five he'd set a new technical standard for hot trombone playing, easily outdistancing both white and black rivals. He'd worked for Lanin and Ray Miller, made records with Bix. He, too, was fast and accurate, with a flawless ear.

They fell in with one another right away and before long were working as a team. Natural partners, they seemed to think as one, anticipating one another's moves, all with a clean-lined, rhythmically crisp approach, which remained coherent even at the fastest tempos.

Sam Lanin, ever alert, was one of the first to get them together in a recording studio. Their "Five Foot Two, Eyes of Blue" (1925), done for Columbia under the name "Lanin's Red Heads," offers a good preview of coming attractions, Nichols showing beyond doubt that he's listened hard to Bix. It was probably inevitable that his ordered mind would seize first on Beiderbecke's sense of form, his "correlated" phrasing. The first four bars of Red's solo on "Five Foot Two," for example:

"Five Foot Two, Eyes of Blue," Red Nichols solo (first four bars), 1925.

immediately bring to mind Bix opening his great "Singin' the Blues" chorus of fifteen months later:

"Singin' the Blues," Bix Beiderbecke solo (first four bars), 1927.

Both solos deal in form and emotional understatement. But where Beiderbecke's restraint emphasizes the layered richness of emotions held in check, Nichols appears to make it an end in itself. This and many other Nichols solos seem less a main text than a genial and occasionally mildly ironic commentary. The two men are, in short, quite different creatures.

But that's in the natural order of things. In so subjective a music as jazz, even emulation is a highly personal matter: the sound and style of Bix, like that of Louis Armstrong, emerges quite differently when filtered through the minds and responses of his various admirers. In Jimmy McPartland it takes on a certain astringency, quite in keeping with his youth as a Chicago street kid; the young English cornetist Norman Payne explored its gentle, even tender side; Chelsea Quealey, sitting beside Payne in Fred Elizalde's orchestra, seemed to have built an entire style on Beiderbecke's chiming, almost military up-tempo attack. Andy Secrest, Stirling Bose, Leo McConville, Rex Stewart: the essence passed through each sensibility and was transformed accordingly.

By the start of 1926 Red and Miff were doing pretty much what the Memphis Five had done before them: recording for many labels under many names. Full of sparkle and wit, the records were much admired, widely imitated. So attractive was this way of doing things that more than a few brassmen admitted to having had trouble making up their minds whether to emulate Nichols or opt for Beiderbecke's earnest lyricism.

Even so ostensibly remote a figure as Roy Eldridge was quoted several times as saying that as a very young trumpeter he'd been drawn to Nichols's polished fluency. What's notable about this declaration is that it was made without apology: Eldridge was saying not that he admired Nichols because he couldn't find anyone better but that Nichols was an excellent cornetist, able to execute anything he felt like playing.

By mid-decade Red and Miff had become the axis, the driving force, around whom were gathered some of the most creative white jazzmen of the day: Jimmy and Tommy Dorsey, Joe Venuti, guitarists Eddie Lang and Dick McDonough, pianist Arthur Schutt, drummers Vic Berton and Stan King. Each was a top player, known and respected by colleagues. With its jauntiness and sense of slightly ironic detachment, their music was "cool," fully three decades before that term became popular. No other bands, white or black, preceded them in exploring this new psychological territory.

Their records are a delight: varied in tone, color, and texture, full of unusual combinations of instruments, unafraid to import harmonic and structural devices from European music, each performance offers some surprise, some unexpected felicity.

Yet no other major jazz figure, no body of work, has been more consistently and arbitrarily disparaged than that of Red Nichols. Ordinarily, differences in past critical assessment do not belong to the process of serious evaluation: different ears, after all, hear different things, and judgment proceeds from widely diverse assumptions and criteria.

But the case of Nichols is unique, in that the vilification has taken on a life of its own, tainting all judgment. Among critics and historians he stands almost alone as an object of scorn—little of it directly connected with the specifics of the music, except insofar as it takes the music to task for not being something other than what it is. As a result, any attempt to deal with Red Nichols means addressing the negative aura surrounding him, trying to understand it and see through it to the reality of the music itself.

Disparagement takes many forms, both in what is said and what is *not* said. One prominent critic, writing notes for an LP anthology devoted to early jazz trumpeters, dealt with Nichols simply by not dealing with him. Each player got a paragraph, discussing his career, influence on others, and the specific record included in the collection. All, that is, except Nichols; the writer simply skipped his name.[4]

Gunther Schuller, assembling *Early Jazz* in the mid-1960s, also ignored Nichols and associates. To his credit, he corrected the omission a decade later in *The Swing Era*, hailing the Nichols-Mole groups for their ensembles, which were "truly astonishing" in the context of the 1920s. "Wonderful, too, is the variety that these groups packed into their performances—variety in many respects: instrumental, formal, textural, harmonic, even dynamic. And though their recordings represent a specific and well-defined collective style, within that style there is to be found an amazing amount of personal liberty and diversity." Schuller also compliments Nichols on his "ringing tone and springy, punchy rhythmic drive" and a "succinct, uncomplicated solo style, maintained with remarkable consistency . . . he was a dazzling perfectionist in his way and believed intensely in the intrinsic beauty and validity of improvised jazz."[5]

The widespread animus toward Nichols appears to have various sources. First, and perhaps most pervasive, is the fact, encountered again and again in autobiographical reminiscences, that the group of white jazzmen who arrived in New York during the late 1920s, mostly from Chicago, simply did not take to him.

Very young men, scarcely beyond adolescence, they viewed themselves with the characteristic self-indulgence of the young, tellingly articulated by Frank Teschemacher: as a unique and embattled minority, possessed of precious insights and skills, forever at the mercy of a benighted public. Anyone who tried to have it both ways—to represent himself as part of the minority while trying to court the public—was *ipso facto* suspect. Benny Goodman put the matter in focus by observing in 1939:

> Musicians who played hot were pretty much of a clique by themselves. They hung around in the same places, made the same spots after work, drank together and worked together whenever they had the chance . . . None of us had much use for what was known then and probably always will be, as "commercial" musicians [emphasis added].[6]

It was as if anyone not willing to camp out in a sleazy hotel room while awaiting a chance to make music his own way was somehow being dishonest, betraying the idealism of his fellows. You could take a job with a commercial band in order to pay the rent, as long as you didn't take it seriously. Red Nichols, by contrast, paid attention to business, worked hard at generating jobs, was a sharp man with a buck. How *could* he be a real jazzman?

"In the opinion of our group," said Bud Freeman, "Nichols was a synthetic player. He was a clever musician and made a lot of records, but he was a very mechanical player."[7]

The choice of words is revealing. "Our group" defines a demarcation line. Even so otherwise neutral an adjective as "clever" is read here in its pejorative sense, laden with connotations of trickiness and artifice.

Freeman, Teschemacher, Eddie Condon, Dave Tough, Jimmy McPartland, and the rest were unique in that they'd become professional musicians for *the express purpose* of playing hot jazz. Unlike Nichols, Mole, the Dorseys, and the rest, they hadn't come up through dance bands, had never faced the necessity of meeting music business realities at least halfway. They could still pursue their goals with that particular single-mindedness that is the luxury of youth—a single-mindedness which all too easily shades off into intolerance.

Trumpeter Max Kaminsky, kindred soul to the Chicagoans, toured with them under Nichols's leadership in 1929. "Nichols loathed us and we returned the compliment" was his summation. Mezz Mezzrow, whose opinions were seldom less than categorical, declared, "We had always thought Nichols stunk, with or without his corny Dixieland Five Pennies." Eddie Condon, reminded by a friend that Red loved Bix Beiderbecke perhaps as much as he did, remarked that Nichols "thought he played like Bix, but the similarity stopped the moment he opened his case."[8]

Whatever Nichols thought of these opinionated and often unruly young men, he recognized their talents and—something few of them ever quite got around to admitting—kept them working during a time when work was scarce, allowing them as often as possible to play pretty much as they liked.

Approached by George Gershwin to form a pit orchestra for *Strike Up the Band*, for example, he hired a reed section of Goodman, Pee Wee Russell, and Babe

Russin; the larger group for *Girl Crazy* the following year also included Charlie Teagarden and Gene Krupa. When it became clear that Robert Russell Bennett was not available to arrange some music from the show as an entr'acte, Nichols made sure the Gershwins hired Glenn Miller, who had been writing for Five Pennies record dates.

Retrospective critical dismissal of—and contempt for—Nichols has much to do with the prominence he and his associates enjoyed in the '20s. Because they were recording widely, their records well distributed both here and abroad, an entire generation of listeners came to identify jazz largely through them.

For many, hot music *was* Red and Miff playing "Hurricane" or "Feelin' No Pain," Joe Venuti and Eddie Lang "Kickin' the Cat," Bix and Tram steaming through "Clarinet Marmalade." To some degree this took place at the expense of records by black musicians, usually made for a label's "race" series and distributed largely in black neighborhoods. Those few whites in American cities who knew about Armstrong and Dodds, Henderson and Ellington, Bessie Smith and Clarence Williams, often had to go hunting in other parts of town to find them.

The situation abroad, slightly different, has relevance here. Parlophone and HMV, European outlets for OKeh-Columbia and Victor respectively, pursued a policy of "cross-coupling" American hot records. One side, in most cases the A title, would be devoted to a white band, the other to a black; thus Louis Armstrong's "West End Blues" wound up backing Eddie Lang's "Freeze and Melt," Luis Russell's "Mugging Lightly" paired with the Casa Loma Orchestra's "San Sue Strut," Duke Ellington's "Down in Our Alley Blues" with "Delirium" by the Red-and-Miff Charleston Chasers.

With the exception of Armstrong, who appeared to be an entity apart, the white recordings were generally those most often discussed and written about. The view, as expressed as late as the 1970s by veteran musicians and collectors in Britain, was that the technical gloss and organization of the white groups, their restraint and subtlety, their attention to matters of form, somehow reflected deeper values and set them above their more dionysian black counterparts.

They thus satisfied more exactly the musical criteria inherent in their listeners' own musical educations. Nichols and Mole, exemplars within this frame of reference, were bound to rank high with listeners. Jimmy Dorsey, with his lightning technique, was no less a favorite. Adrian Rollini, strong and assured on bass sax; Venuti and Lang, making music of sculpted delicacy; Fud Livingston, writing Debussian harmonies into his musical miniatures—this was music at once creative and civilized, challenging and reassuring. Unthreatening.

The result, overall, was an unbalanced situation: Nichols, as cynosure and avatar, captured disproportionate attention. Each new record was hailed as an event, discussed and dissected by musicians and reviewers.

Reassessment was inevitable, and when it came it was with all the intemperate zeal of any backlash. Hearing Armstrong, Ellington, Coleman Hawkins, and other black musicians touring Europe in the early '30s jolted many listeners who had not suspected the eloquence and sheer emotive power they commanded. Almost overnight, writers and fans who had praised Red, Miff, Rollini, Dorsey, and the rest to the skies now seemed at pains to belittle them.

Their denunciations carried just the slightest *Duft* of the lover betray'd—as if they'd been duped, seduced. But such epiphanies are seldom characterized by moderation or level-headed assessment: suddenly it wasn't enough to admit that Nichols's sometimes phlegmatic stylings were less immediately thrilling than Armstrong's flights of rhapsody, or that the alto playing of Johnny Hodges cut rather more deeply into the emotions than did Dorsey's. There seemed a need to go farther, express the point in more extreme terms. Hugues Panassié, in *The Real Jazz*, proclaimed belated realization that "most white musicians were inferior to colored musicians" and identified Red Nichols among the chief villains.

There *were* differences. Where Armstrong's 1926 record of "Heebie Jeebies" had been an unrestrained romp (highlighted, of course, by the trumpeter's not-quite-accidental scat vocal), the Red Heads version took a rather more reserved view of the same material. Jelly Roll Morton's Red Hot Peppers careened through "Black Bottom Stomp" with headlong momentum; Nichols and friends had driven more carefully—and in so doing missed the *frisson* of excitement.

Such differences were of temperament, of personality. That they were represented for so long, and in so many ways, as measures of inherent quality is regrettable—and unfair. To revile Nichols and his associates for what they are not, underestimating the value of what they *are*, seems as pointless as holding Buster Bailey to account for lacking the emotional depth of Edmond Hall, or plunger master Joe "Tricky Sam" Nanton for being a relatively clumsy open-horn soloist.[9]

Taken on their own merits, the records made by Nichols and his various groups between 1926 and 1930 remain an extraordinary body of music. It is a rare performance which does *not* offer some solo or ensemble passage, some felicity of arrangement or execution, to please the ear and stimulate the mind.

In the words of pioneer jazz scholar Marshall Stearns:

> The ensembles are crisp and cohesive, the solos nimble and abstract. It is as if, at an exhibition of modern painting since Cézanne, you turned the corner and walked smack up to a Mondrian; bright, precise designs in complex geometrical patterns. In its own way and on its own terms, a Mondrian can't be beaten because nobody can go any further in that direction.[10]

A random sampling of records might include the Charleston Chasers' version of Nichols's own "Five Pennies," with intense cornet and Miff's trombone like a human voice over the lilting ensemble; the Pennies' justly-esteemed "Ida," Red and Miff soloing thoughtfully before Pee Wee Russell barges in like Groucho crashing one of Margaret Dumont's society parties; Nichols's impassioned lead (entering on a strong, sure high concert A♭) after a shapely half-chorus by Mole on the Molers' "My Gal Sal"; a 1929 "Alice Blue Gown" on Brunswick, with Rollini (home on leave from England) playing a mischievous Puck to Jimmy Dorsey's alto; the Molers' 1927 OKeh "New Twister," building through emphatic solos by Mole, Nichols, Russell, and Rollini to a deliciously strutting ensemble; Miff's bright agility on the Red Heads' "Baltimore," over high-register chimes by Schutt.

Red's opening solo on the Arkansas Travelers' 1927 "Ja-Da" is a thoughtful paraphrase of the melody, organized with a composer's precision. It's also something of a precis of the salient points of his approach to medium tempos, which changed little over the following three and a half decades.

Nichols was least comfortable on the faster numbers, where he often reverted to the more mechanical side of his cornet training. Certainly the snappy triplets opening his solo on the Molers' "Honolulu Blues," regardless how cleanly executed, don't quite add up to a hot jazz break; the rest of the chorus, too, never wholly escapes the trumpet method book. Even late in life, Red was never entirely able to loosen up rhythmically: his up-tempo solos march before they swing. Somehow he's always the Culver military cadet of his youth, standing to attention. It's only on the slower tunes that he seems able to play more expansively, with some rhythmic elasticity.

He is beyond argument an excellent and versatile cornetist, who now and then produced a solo of truly transcendant quality. Consider, for example, his sixteen bars on "Crazy Rhythm," recorded by Mole's Molers on July 27, 1928. Taut and spare, it delivers its message with emphasis and economy; indeed, in moments such as these, Nichols's work as a hot improviser stands very solidly on its own merits.

"Crazy Rhythm," Red Nichols solo (sixteen bars), 1928.

It is particularly striking that each of the men in Nichols's immediate circle was an outstanding musician in his own right. "They were top-notch technicians, who could execute anything they felt," Marshall Stearns wrote in 1961. "They worked out a balance between arrangement and solos that made each number an artistic unit, and they played together with one mind and one heart. The result is a high level of precision and clarity."[11]

Arthur Schutt, for example, commanded a full, powerful piano style, developed during his long tenure with Paul Specht's orchestra and its band-within-a-band, the Georgians. He was an able composer: his own "Delirium," especially popular with fellow-musicians, was recorded widely in the late '20s and issued in a well-crafted publisher's "stock" arrangement. Schutt's chorus on the Charleston Chasers version blends chordal substitutions and whole-tone inflections with disarming ease. His 1934 "Georgia Jubilee" features a lilting melody and rich harmonic texture, part of which takes the form of an unusual countermelody. Nicknamed "the Baron" for his aristocratic manner and elegance of dress (always a carnation in his lapel), Schutt was liked and admired across lines of style and race. "He was a musician's pianist," said singer Joey Nash, jobbing around New York in those years as a saxophonist.

Nash told of an afternoon drinking session at a Seventh Avenue gin mill— interrupted only when someone remembered that the group at the bar was supposed to be en route to Westchester for a country club date. "We all piled into cars and drove like madmen," he told Michael Brooks. "Someone remembered that we had no arrangements, so Artie, drunk out of his mind, sat in the back seat, pulled out sheets of manuscript, and while we were tearing along at 60 mph he calmly dashed off about ten arrangements—and they were perfect."[12]

The story may be apocryphal, but the skill and breadth of talent it portrays were real. According to Nash, Schutt's admirers included Fats Waller, James P. Johnson, and even Art Tatum, who reportedly modeled his key-changing variations on "Tea for Two" after something the Baron had devised.

Schutt seems to have taken a while to master the problems of playing easily and rhythmically at faster tempos. His solos on such '20s records as the Molers' "Feelin' No Pain" (OKeh) or the Five Pennies' "That's No Bargain" (1926), however adept, tend to lumber; they seem forever shackled to his early apprenticeship playing ragtime novelties in silent movie houses.

But time, and frequent exposure to such men as Fats, James P., and Willie "the Lion" Smith, seem to have helped. An unissued piano solo, "Bring-Up Breakdown," recorded for ARC in 1934, finds him loosening up, incorporating "stride" rhythmic elements and bounding along with a freedom quite beyond anything the Baron had displayed in the '20s.

That aside, Schutt must be respected as a harmonically sophisticated and inventive musical thinker, whose briefest solos bristled with cross-rhythms and chordal implications. "There was nothing," tuba player and arranger Joe Tarto once told the author, "that he couldn't play." Schutt spent the '40s and '50s as a Hollywood studio musician; he died in San Francisco in 1965.[13]

No less inventive was the circle's regular drummer, Vic Berton. He is a true pioneer, both for the timekeeping methods he introduced and for his role in determining the very equipment on which all subsequent drummers would play. Before he came on the scene, for example, drummers' top cymbals were suspended on a leather thong fastened to a kind of S-hook mounted atop the bass drum. It was adequate for single strokes or for situations where a drummer actually held the cymbal with one hand and played rhythms on it with the other, achieving color and texture by alternately choking and releasing it.

At some point Berton decided he wanted to play steady rhythm on his cymbals. So, his brother Ralph reported, he devised a vertical rod on which the cymbal could sit, fixed in place with a nut, but with enough play to ring freely. Snapped up by manufacturers, it quickly became standard equipment, opening myriad new options to future generations of drummers.

In another burst of experimentation Berton reportedly mounted two small cymbals together facing one another on a vertical rod and connected with a spring device; using a foot pedal, he could whack them together on afterbeats, providing a rhythmic counterbalance to the heavy first and third beats marked by the bass drum, a kind of "boom-CHICK, boom-CHICK" effect. The device, which he called a sock cymbal, eventually developed into the modern hi-hat.[14]

Born Victor Cohen in Chicago in 1896, Berton had already enjoyed broad-based success as a percussionist by the time he became involved with Red Nichols, Miff Mole, and their crowd. He'd played in the U.S. Navy band under "March King" John Philip Sousa; studied tympani with Josef Zettelmann of the Chicago Symphony; taken over and even run the Wolverines during Bix Beiderbecke's tenure as their cornetist; starred with bands led by Roger Wolfe Kahn, Arnold Johnson, and other prominent leaders; and even played briefly with Paul Whiteman in early 1927, but had fallen out with the "King of Jazz" in a clash of egos which erupted in a men's-room fistfight between leader and sideman.

As a timekeeper, Berton provided a firm, often propulsive beat, rendered with great technical polish. He also found a way, using change-of-pitch foot pedals, of playing rhythmic bass lines on a pair of tympani; though sometimes a bit clumsy, it was an imaginative and colorful effect. He uses his "tymps" with particular buoyancy behind singer Annette Hanshaw on "I'm Somebody's Some-body Now" (1927), even contributing a sixteen-bar "stop-time" solo.[15]

Discussion of this circle must also include Jimmy Dorsey, whose influence in the late '20s easily rivaled—and occasionally exceeded—that of Red and Miff. He was by common agreement one of the most versatile and accomplished sax-ophonists of his time. His tone, bright and a little hard, almost without vibrato, was distinctive in itself: at a time when the alto model was still the string-based French style, with its sugary tone and lush vibrato, Dorsey's leanness of concept was quite new, unprecedented—even revolutionary.

Dorsey's best hot solos are studded with unusual and ear-catching touches. His chorus on the Molers' "Davenport Blues" (1927) begins with two matched four-bar phrases which, though ostensibly simple paraphrases of the melody, manage—merely by changing a few key notes—to imply greater harmonic com-plexity. Typical is the matter-of-fact, almost offhand manner in which the second phrase (bar 7) comes to rest on the thirteenth:

"Davenport Blues," Jimmy Dorsey alto solo (eight bars), 1927.

No less intriguing are his first four bars on the Five Pennies' "Alabama Stomp," with Berton galumphing along on his tymps like *Tyrannosaurus rex* chasing lunch. Reedmen of both races seized avidly on Dorsey's latest variations; only Frank Trumbauer elicited comparable attention and respect. Benny Carter recalled listening attentively to both men; Lester Young, too, has been widely quoted as saying that he had trouble deciding which of the two to emulate, and after much consideration finally chose Trumbauer, because "he told a little story."

If less consistently a storyteller, Dorsey could captivate nevertheless. When his full-chorus, party-piece solo on the chords of "Tiger Rag" appeared, first on Nichols's "That's No Bargain" and then interpolated into Don Redman's arrangement of "Sensation" for Whiteman, saxophonists all over the country learned it note for note.

Taken at a fast clip ($\bullet = 160$) it's a model of fleet, assured playing, full of swooping, hill-and-dale phrases, nimble "false" fingering, and other tricks of the saxophonist's trade:

"Sensation Stomp," Jimmy Dorsey alto solo (thirty-two bars), 1927.

Rehearsing for a 1976 Whiteman commemorative concert under the author's leadership, saxophonists Al Gallodoro (Whiteman alumnus), Johnny Mince (soloist with Tommy Dorsey's 1930s orchestra), and Eddie Barefield (star of the Cab Calloway and Chick Webb bands) astonished fellow-bandsmen by reeling off the chorus from memory, in faultless unison. "Why, of course *everybody* picked up on that one" was Barefield's explanation (even, to judge from the false-fingered written C's in bars 9–14, Lester Young).

The Brunswick coupling of "Cornfed" and "Mean Dog Blues," recorded in the last week of June 1927, finds these musicians in characteristic form. Dorsey is at his most "modern," with elevenths and thirteenths in odd combinations and intervals which, delivered with his bright, hard tone, could almost be said to presage the early Charlie Parker. Nichols is Bix-like in his rather clinical way, Rollini bumptiously forceful. Berton has fun with both cymbals and pitched tymps, while Lang rides foursquare on the beat. "Cornfed" is a dense, variegated performance; at the end, a listener has the feeling that these six men have mined Phil Wall's composition to the fullest.

For years, saxophonist-arranger Bill Kirchner has used "Mean Dog Blues" as an example in demonstrating to his arranging and composition classes the sophistication and musical ingenuity of the Nichols circle. Each episode introduces some new color, weight or texture, uses the seven-piece instrumentation in a new and different way. Among the confections: bass sax theme statement over syncopated horn riffs; sustained-chord cushion for single-string guitar solo; interaction between Berton's tuned tymps and the ensemble; Schutt's surprisingly Ellington-like piano solo (with even, at one point, a faint echo of "Black and Tan Fantasie"); surprise shifts of dynamics and textures in the final ensemble.

Thinking man's jazz, music for the mind. Gunther Schuller put it well in declaring, "Although the worked-out (or arranged) ensembles are mostly quite sophisticated and technically tricky of execution, there is hardly a performance which is less than faultless." Just so.[16]

When larger instrumentations were called for, Nichols drew on an even wider, consistently first-rate, musician pool: trumpeters Leo McConville and Manny Klein (both able improvisers in their own right), mellophonist Dudley Fosdick, reedmen Pee Wee Russell and Fud Livingston, pianist Lennie Hayton, and guitar-banjo virtuoso Dick McDonough.

As new musicians—including the Chicagoans—arrived in town, Nichols was quick to sense their potential and incorporate them. In short order, Goodman, Freeman, Krupa, Jack and Charles Teagarden, Babe Russin, and Glenn Miller turned up on Nichols records alongside Dorsey, Rollini, and the rest of the old guard.

His openness and receptivity weren't exactly altruistic. As the Chicagoans never tired of pointing out, Nichols was keenly attuned to the music business, in particular the need to have something new ready for a fickle public. Success on that front invariably entailed a kind of *Realpolitik*—a willingness, if need be, to sacrifice old loyalties in the interests of staying power.

From that perspective, the Five Pennies Brunswick session of April 18, 1929, incorporating Goodman, Jack Teagarden, Sullivan, Krupa, and others, can be seen to signal the end of the Mole-Schutt-Berton alliance. Nichols had made a change, and in so doing inevitably left behind a detritus of ill-will. Some musicians, mindful of the ongoing pragmatism required to stay afloat in the music business, simply let it go and moved on. But the lingering rancor expressed toward the cornetist by more than a few erstwhile colleagues indicates that some old grievances die hard.

The opening ensemble of "Indiana," from the April 18 session, rides high on Krupa's aggressive four-to-the-bar. Goodman stabs and punches, Red snaps out a crisp, Bix-like chorus in a derby; but it's Jack Teagarden's fiercely declamatory two-bar phrase in the new key of A♭ that really heralds the new spirit.

Anyone seeking to understand why Teagarden supplanted Miff Mole, not only in Nichols's affections but as the hot trombonist of choice around New York, would do well to study his twenty-four bars on "Dinah." The relatively leisurely tempo ($\quarternote = 128$) affords Teagarden an opportunity to recast the pop song's lines and content as a blues. That's its vocabulary, its accents and inflections. The simple figure that dominates the bridge, ripping from concert F to C above, is played three times with increasing urgency, puncuated by a flurry of sixteenth notes, then repeated once more with great emphasis before a broad *rubato* figure brings in the ensemble. Even then he doesn't stop, but carries the flavor through the last eight bars of band riffing.[17]

The third number done that day, Isham Jones's "On the Alamo," has been relatively little reissued. Again, Teagarden is the key figure, playing lead in the opening ensemble and contributing an eloquent muted obbligato behind "Scrappy" Lambert's rather lifeless vocal. On a second, non-vocal take, Goodman fills the vocal slot with a contemplative chorus, and young Babe Russin, deeply under Bud Freeman's spell, contributes sixteen agitated bars, with Krupa rattling temple-blocks and tomtoms behind him.

Nichols, it must be noted, takes relatively few solos. Suggestions that he felt outclassed are groundless, in light of his prestige, musical track record, and penchant for self-promotion. His generosity in sharing the spotlight seems motivated only by a desire to give talented new voices—even players of his own instrument—a chance to be heard.

It is significant that, even at those moments when Nichols most offended the "heuristic exegetes of European hermeneutics" by playing to the marketplace, he did so on his own terms. If Brunswick wanted twelve-inch "symphonic jazz" arrangements, he gladly supplied them—all the while making sure that *someone* (Jimmy Dorsey, Teagarden, Goodman) got a chance to play some jazz somewhere along the way.

But there were also good, straightforward "hot" numbers, with liberal space for soloists. Teagarden, Freeman, and Pee Wee Russell turn June 1929's "Rose of Washington Square" into a free-wheeling romp, urged on by Dave Tough's juggernaut beat. "After You've Gone" is pretty much a feature for Teagarden, singing and playing, Krupa pushing him along by whacking feverish backbeats on his choke cymbal.

Again, as with the earlier recordings, the sheer plenitude of first-rate performances is dazzling—in truth, as Gunther Schuller suggests, "one of the glories of late '20s jazz." Among other highlights: Teagarden's slam-bang opening salvo on "I Want to Be Happy"; Dorsey's thoughtful half-chorus on "Tea for Two"; Glenn Miller's flirtation with boogie-woogie in his "Carolina in the Morning" arrangement; Charles Teagarden's impassioned opening to "Peg o' My Heart" (Nichols does the double-time passage near the end); brother Jack bursting in on the puerile ballad singer of "The Sheik of Araby" with his "What in the world are you doin'? Don't you know that's all out of date?"—then going on to sing and play in most memorable fashion; the extended transcription version of "Sweet Georgia Brown," with manic Freeman, dancing Rollini, and Goodman shapely and poised on an interpolated "I Ain't Got Nobody."[18]

"China Boy" opens on an ear-catching Teagarden cadenza, then moves swiftly through solos by Nichols (at his best, a well-turned summation of his view of Bix), Goodman (whirling and cascading, driven by Chicago boisterousness and sustained by his limitless technique), and two stomping Sullivan choruses backed ardently—if a tad raucously—by Krupa.

Nichols's best records divide easily into two major groupings, 1925–28 and 1929–30, and constitute a valuable index to what happened to white jazz in New York in the five years they represent. In the earlier group, the efforts of Mole, Dorsey, Schutt, Lang, Berton, Rollini, and Nichols himself display a common approach to rhythm and the mechanics of hot playing. Even allowing for the cross-fertilization that went on throughout most of the decade, their ways remain insular, recognizably not those of the black jazzmen.

One distinguishing feature lies in the relationship among musicians—soloist and rhythm section, horn players on a front line, rhythm players with one another. On most of the pre-1929 New York records the sense of form seems uppermost, producing what is in effect a hot chamber music ensemble: miniatures, vignettes, cameos, finely crafted and studded with small jewels of invention—but with rhythm playing a decidedly secondary role.

Relatively absent, too, is the element in which the work of so many of the early black ensembles of the period excels: call it visceral interaction. There is among the black musicians a sense of easy colloquy, personal and emotional, not at the forefront of the music-making process of these white groups. In that particular the Nichols units resemble the Original Memphis Five—less a matter of organic interaction than of individual players fulfilling roles, sometimes brilliantly, within a formalized context.

Anyone looking to see the difference writ large need only consult the December 5, 1928, Louis Armstrong–Earl Hines duet record of "Weather Bird," with its lightning repartee and high-speed competitiveness. The same qualities are present on the memorable "Cake-Walkin' Babies From Home," recorded by the Clarence Williams Blue Five in 1925; Louis Armstrong and Sidney Bechet volley across the net like a couple of tennis pros; independently and together, they play off the rhythm as well, stretching it, pushing and being pushed by it, hanging back on it, elasticizing it. But this is more than just musical sport: there is a strong personal dimension as well, driven by a lifelong rivalry, social as well as musical, between the two great New Orleans pioneers.

The arrival in New York of white musicians from other parts of the country began a perhaps inevitable process of cross-pollination. Jazzmen from Chicago, from the South and Southwest, had heard and absorbed the rhythmic vitality and easy informality of their black counterparts. It suffused their own playing, made it more interactive.

All this belongs to a familiar pattern, the infinitely complicated black-white symbiosis central to the social history of twentieth-century American society. White culture forever finds in black culture those elements it perceives as lacking in itself; black musicians, meanwhile, admired the technical command and control of the whites, their harmonic inventiveness, the ingenuity and ease with which they dealt with melodic creation.[19]

Little by little, the eastern ethos blended with the more uninhibited styles from the heartland, both white and black: rhythm sections became more elastic; the blues, hitherto conspicuous by its relative absence, made itself increasingly felt; even the principal soloists began to change, each at his own rate of speed. The collective chamber style the New York whites had built so carefully during the '20s, as exemplified in such recordings as "Mean Dog Blues," seemed to melt into, become absorbed by, a larger whole—and not without loss of some of its more attractive qualities. While it lasted, however, it achieved refinement, great subtlety, and—within its own frame of reference—considerable creative freedom.[20]

Much credit for that goes to reedman-composer-arranger Joseph "Fud" Livingston, who first attracted attention in the mid-'20s as a tenor saxophonist in the light-toned style popularized by Jack Pettis. Born Joseph Anthony Livingston on April 10, 1906, he and his elder brother Walter learned both piano and reeds in their native Charleston, South Carolina.[21]

They seem to have moved around quite a bit in the early '20s: Walter achieved celebrity among musicians in 1924 for a nimble break on "Somebody Stole My Gal," recorded by the Ted Weems Orchestra on its first Victor date. Fud played briefly with Ben Pollack in California in mid-1925, briefly with the California Ramblers later that year, briefly with Jean Goldkette in Detroit in 1926, then rejoined Pollack when the drummer's new band moved to Chicago.

It was a good time to be there. The city, especially the South Side, was full of hot music; a new generation of white musicians had emerged and were making their presence felt in bands all over town. Livingston quickly got to know Muggsy Spanier, Jimmy McPartland, Jess Stacy, Bud Freeman, Joe Sullivan, Dave Tough,

Gene Krupa, "Mezz" Mezzrow—and, perhaps most important of all, clarinetist Frank Teschemacher.

It's hard to know what Fud sounded like on clarinet *before* he met Tesch; he never soloed on it with Pollack, at least on records, that distinction being the exclusive province of sixteen-year-old Benny Goodman. But innumerable records of his work on the instrument *after* that time display the hard attack, brittle tone, and angular figure shapes characteristic of Tesch and his admirers.

Trombonist Al Philburn, who knew Livingston well, insisted that, rather than having learned from the Chicagoans, Fud deeply affected them. "He was playing like Benny and Tesch when those two were still in short pants," he told Michael Brooks in 1970. "Only the booze got to him, and he never developed.

"I can remember seeing him in a recording studio, trying to play sounds that he was hearing, jumping up and down, flapping his arms and screaming with rage because he couldn't transpose from his brain to his instrument. So he hit the bottle to dull out all that beauty he couldn't share—and Christ, how he drank! I've never seen anyone drink as much as Fud and survive for so long."[22]

Alas, Livingston played only tenor with Pollack, soloing occasionally, contributing "hot" arrangements, while trombonist Glenn Miller did the ballads. "Singapore Sorrows," recorded in New York April 6, 1927, after he'd left the band, is a characteristic Livingston score, mixing colorful faux-Oriental bits with aggressive "hot" passages. Goodman and McPartland as chief soloists further enhance the flavor.

Fud recorded the same arrangement in London almost exactly a year later as a member of Fred Elizalde's orchestra—only this time taking the clarinet solo himself, in a punchy, "Chicagoan" manner—which just might lend weight to Philburn's words.

Sometime in the early months of 1927, Livingston gave Pollack his notice and set out for New York. He seems to have fallen into regular work almost immediately and by August was recording—and drinking regularly—with Nichols, Mole, Rollini, and their crowd. His arrival coincided almost exactly with that of Pee Wee Russell, whose clarinet style, formulated far from Chicago, displayed many of the same surface features as Fud's own.

But Livingston's chief impact on this circle of musicians, and on the music in a more generalized sense, lies in his skills as an arranger and composer. His aptly named "Imagination," recorded for OKeh under Mole's name, for Columbia under the "Charleston Chasers" pseudonym, and for Brunswick under Nichols's own name (1928), is typical of his work.

He's thought carefully about matters of form and come up with a finely tooled, architectonically sound chamber composition. Few writers at this time had achieved this degree of ease within the hot jazz idiom. Hoagy Carmichael's "Boneyard Shuffle" and "Manhattan Rag" demonstrate similar preoccupations but far less skill. There is little in the recorded work of either Duke Ellington or Don Redman at this early point to suggest a comparable degree of accomplishment in scoring.

"Imagination" represents a set of preoccupations more commonly found in the branch of popular instrumental music now widely—and judgmentally—identified as "novelty" music. The piano compositions of Rube Bloom and Zez Confrey, for example, regularly address such matters of structure and thematic development. Such vignettes as Arthur Schutt's "Piano Puzzle" and Willard Robison's "Eight Ball" work some of the same soil. Bix Beiderbecke's four piano compositions, published as a suite by Robbins in 1928, also lie within the concept.

The common thread is an obvious fascination with European music, particularly the melodic and harmonic conventions of the French Impressionists: use of sequential augmented chords and the whole-tone scales out of which they are formed; reliance on the chord of the minor ninth as part of the basic vocabulary; regular employment of elevenths and thirteenths as melodic color tones.

The final ensemble chorus of the up-tempo "Feelin' No Pain," from the Mole date of August 30, 1927, even displays a touch of *Klangfarbenmelodie*. That device, so beloved of followers of twelve-tone European music, brings different tone colors (as represented by different instruments and registers) to bear on the same pitch or sequence of pitches; the result is a "melody" constructed as much out of tones and textures as of pitches.

Since the 1924 success of the *Rhapsody in Blue*, George Gershwin had been experimenting with hybrid forms, wedding the accents and inflections of what he perceived as jazz to European technique and tonality. Various writers and arrangers were writing "modernistic"—i.e., *faux*-Impressionist—pieces for jazz ensembles. Trumpeter Donald Lindley's *A Rhythmic Dream*, recorded by Fletcher Henderson's orchestra at the same 1927 session which produced the loosely swinging "Hop Off" but not released at the time, is typical—especially in that it never transcends the artificiality of its basic concept. Henderson's musicians cope gamely with Lindley's score, but the performance fails to come to life.

Livingston seems almost alone in having incorporated such conventions successfully into what was unequivocally a jazz context. There is no mistaking his "Humpty Dumpty," recorded by Trumbauer and Beiderbecke (1927), as anything but the work of a jazzman's—and Fud Livingston's—mind.[23]

This is no less the case with "Imagination." The Charleston Chasers performance begins with an eight-bar introduction, half of which consists of tenor sax breaks by Russell; the band then states the major theme, a twenty-eight-bar creation based on a bass line descending in whole tones, which breaks down into four-bar units: 8 (theme A—descending bass line); 4 (A), 4 (transition), 4 (A recap), 4 (trans), 4 (A recap).

An eight-bar piano interlude brings on the next episode, eight bars built around an ascending melodic line full of chromatic surprises,

"Imagination," first passage (eight bars), 1927.

which establishes the key of F-major long enough for a four-bar Russell clarinet solo. A four-bar transition (based on a descending chromatic scale)

"Imagination," second passage (four bars), 1927.

ushers in eight bars in which the tonal center shifts again to G, setting up a four-bar solo by Nichols. The rest of the composition consists of a sequence of two-bar episodes in which the prior themes are recapitulated.

Livingston's clarinet work, highly regarded by fellow musicians throughout the late 1920s, is often overlooked—not least because it is so often mistaken for that of Pee Wee Russell. He is the soloist (and presumably arranger) on Nichols's "Nobody's Sweetheart" (1928). Taken at an unusually slow tempo ($\quarternote = 168$), it does indeed sound "Chicagoan" in its approach. He's heard skipping along at a faster tempo on "Avalon," is bright and incisive on "My Angeline," by a pickup group called the Mississippi Maulers (and featuring Venuti, mellophonist Dudley Fosdick, and ex–California Rambler Bill Moore on trumpet), the Molers' 1928 "Crazy Rhythm," the Chasers' "Melancholy Baby," and Elizalde's "Nobody's Sweetheart," made at the same London date as "Singapore Sorrows."

Livingston's clarinet is showcased perhaps best of all on "Old Fashioned Girl" and "Anytime, Anyday, Anywhere," by a quartet under Lennie Hayton's name. His playing is sufficiently "Chicagoan" here to have been included among possible undiscovered Frank Teschemacher solos on a Time-Life records set of the early '80s.

His arrangements were in steady demand. "Oh Baby," part of a series of 1927–28 records for Victor under Nat Skilkret's direction (as the "All-Star Orchestra"), alternates passages of almost pastoral woodwind scoring—making full use of Max Farley's skills as a flutist—with "hot" episodes, the most effective of which is a nicely framed sixteen-bar cornet solo for Jimmy McPartland.[24]

There's no telling what Livingston could have achieved had he been more attentive to business. Had more compositions of the inventiveness of "Imagination" and "Humpty-Dumpty" found their way onto records, for example, it's not unreasonable to assume that Livingston might have won some of the kudos now lavished on Jelly Roll Morton as an innovator in small-ensemble jazz composition. Certainly he was a composer of infinitely greater range and harmonic sophistication than Morton, while no less skilled at integrating solo and ensemble in original ways.

But Fud, in common with Bix and so many others, was by the late '20s an irretrievable alcoholic. Stories of his inconsistency and unreliability are legion.

Jimmy Dorsey, starting his own band in 1935, hired his old friend Fud to play saxophone and arrange; he stayed until the beginning of 1938. When Bob Zurke left Bob Crosby's band in mid-1939 to launch his own group, he turned to Fud for arrangements. As with Dorsey, the results were excellent, crisply and cleanly written in the large-ensemble dixieland idiom associated with Crosby.

He spent most of the '40s in California, eventually moving back to New York, where he died, victim of chronic alcoholism, in 1957.

Gunther Schuller makes the point that, for all the brilliance of its individuals, the unique creativity and sophistication achieved by the New York white jazzmen of the '20s was at least equally the product of a collective instinct, a meeting of minds. Beyond dispute, the situation in which Nichols and Mole came together and were able to join forces with Schutt, Berton, Rollini, and the rest afforded them all a rare degree of latitude.

Nothing embodies that latitude better than the partnership of violinist Joe Venuti and guitarist Eddie Lang. As the third major "team" of the New York chamber jazz circle, they worked as a unit, sometimes on their own, sometimes under the leadership of others. Each, moreover, played a major individual role in lending the New York music its distinctive identity.

They grew up together in working-class South Philadelphia. As the careful and thorough Norman Gentieu has ascertained, Giuseppe Venuti was born there

September 16, 1903—not on the high seas and not in Italy, as he later claimed at various times. He appears to have studied violin with Michel Sciapiro, who played with the Philadelphia Orchestra under Leopold Stokowski.

He became friends with Lang, then known as Salvatore Massaro, when they were both pupils at the James Campbell Public School, 8th and Fitzwater streets. Young Massaro, too, was a violinist: Venuti, in fact, seems to have had a hand in convincing him that he should take up the banjo.[25]

At first they pursued individual careers, coming up through a succession of dance bands: both put in time with Charles Kerr's Philadelphia-based unit, where Georgians trumpeter Frank Guarente met them on his way to New York, and with Bert Estlow's band in Atlantic City. Massaro (by this time he'd become Eddie Lang, after an early basketball hero) worked awhile with the Scranton Sirens, most memorable of the Pennsylvania "territory" bands, then joined Red McKenzie and the Mound City Blue Blowers; Joe, in his turn, played for a succession of leaders, including Jean Goldkette, in Detroit.[26]

But their paths kept crossing, and each seemed happiest and most creative when working with the other. By the mid-'20s they were a regular team, doing cameos on other people's record dates. Arrangers, learning they were going to be present, would just leave sixteen or thirty-two bars open, knowing Joe and Eddie would find the best way to fill them.

Each had technique to burn: Venuti was by any standard a superb violinist, with a clear, singing tone, true intonation, and seemingly limitless facility. He'd listened to the Original Dixieland Jazz Band and other early groups, but there is every indication that he had just figured most of it out for himself. Certainly there was no precedent on his instrument, no handy *Vorbild* of how to cope with the special problems of bowing, attack, and tone coloration inherent in playing hot violin solos. Like Adrian Rollini addressing the rather daunting bass saxophone, he seems to have sized up the situation and experimented until he found something that worked. His earliest recorded solos, with Goldkette in 1924, are balanced, melodically coherent, and free of the slightest trace of rhythmic atavism.[27]

Lang, too, seems to have bypassed most of the growing pains. By the time he appears on record with the Mound City Blue Blowers in 1924, he has mastered both straight rhythm and single-string solo playing, as well as a style of accompaniment which seems to blend the two. And, unusual for a white guitarist at this early stage, he soon proved he could hold his own with, and sometimes even outdo, most bluesmen at their own game.

But it is in playing together that Venuti and Lang are at their most revolutionary. Violin and guitar are, of course, natural partners, tonally compatible. But these two carry things farther: they seem to think together, to function as two halves of a complete entity, anticipating one another's moves, intuiting each other's thoughts in advance.

At first, Venuti told an interviewer, "we used to play a lot of mazurkas and polkas. Just for fun we started to play them in 4/4 . . . then we started to slip in some improvised passages. I'd slip something in. Eddie would pick it up with a variation. Then I'd come back with a variation. We'd just sit there and knock each other out."[28]

They were obviously still doing it on September 29, 1926, when OKeh first recorded them as a featured attraction. "Black and Blue Bottom" and "Stringing the Blues," their first two titles, introduce most of the mannerisms, devices, and idiosyncrasies which were to become the duo's hallmarks.

Both numbers, as usual for them, are built on familiar chord sequences, minus the melodies: "Stringing the Blues," for example, is a thinly disguised "Tiger Rag." Both that and "Black and Blue Bottom" abound in small worked-out breaks and other bits of teamwork. On the latter, Lang ad libs a twelve-bar whole-tone solo passage, giving Joe time to detach the hairs of his bow from their mooring and turn the bow upside down, anchoring the hairs with his hand. This lets him play all four strings at once, achieving a variety of four-voice chordal effects; it's an extraordinary sound, an innovation, and Joe Venuti's unique contribution to the flavor of jazz.[29]

By 1927 Venuti and Lang were dominant figures on the New York dance band and recording scene. It would take many hours spent with discographies, history books, and interview transcripts to compile anything like an accurate reckoning of their activities between 1926 and 1930. They just seemed to be everywhere. Lang, particularly, had his pick of the most lucrative work around, from theatre orchestras to dance bands to backing vaudeville performers and all manner of singers. "Under the Moon," recorded in June 1927 by the teenaged Annette Hanshaw, is a fine example of his technique and imagination as an accompanist.

Added to the Goldkette orchestra in 1926 for recordings ("People know who they are, and they'll help sell the records"), they enhanced such performances as "Sunday" and the memorable "My Pretty Girl."[30] Venuti solos with great dash alongside Frank Trumbauer, Bix, and the rest on "I'm Gonna Meet My Sweetie Now" and "Four-Leaf Clover." Venuti and Lang are at their most electrifying on "Look at the World and Smile" in February 1927, where they team with the great New Orleans bassist Steve Brown for a sixteen-bar hot "window" in an otherwise monochromatic arrangement.

Three takes of that number exist. On each, the trio takes off like thoroughbreds from the gate; by any standard, at any place, in any period, it is brilliant hot jazz, swinging hard in the kind of energized, utterly relaxed 4/4 commonplace a decade hence, but all but unprecedented in the '20s.

It's the buoyant swing generated by these three that helps lift that September's "Clementine" into the pantheon of truly memorable—and prescient—jazz moments on record. Even without its exquisite Beiderbecke cornet chorus, this would have been a landmark: no other record by any other band, black or white, even begins to approach the rhythmic elasticity and lift, the modernity of sound and smooth four-to-the-bar rhythm, achieved here by the Goldkette musicians.

Lang's powers as an accompanist also help shape the great Trumbauer-Beiderbecke OKeh record of "Singin' the Blues," made February 4, 1927. It's all the more remarkable for the fact that, apart from the guitar, there is effectively no rhythm section: no bass instrument is present, and the early electric recording (or, more accurately, conservative recording engineers—the equipment, it turned out, could handle more) limits drummer Chauncey Morehouse to little more than a woodblock and a couple of cymbals; Paul Mertz's piano, never rhythmically incisive, is little more than a distant, ghostly presence. Lang carries it with charm and winning intelligence: his ascending arpeggio in bar 26 of Bix's chorus, meeting a descending one played by the cornet, is stunning, topped only by a second, in triplets this time, at a similar place in the closing ensemble.

Where did it come from, this original, fully conceived way of playing the guitar? Inevitably, subscribers to the black-as-originator, white-as-accolyte dogma have suggested that Lang learned from the great black guitarist Lonnie Johnson, with whom he recorded (under the pseudonym "Blind Willie Dunn") for OKeh's "race" catalogue. There's no doubt, listening to their interplay on such 1928–29 duet records as "Blue Room Blues," that they share an affinity for the blues.

But Lang's work on scores of records made long before his encounters with Johnson makes clear that he came to those sessions with his conception already firmly in place. It seems far more likely that Lang's approach to his instrument, like those of Armstrong, Beiderbecke, Teagarden, and the other innovators, was a product of his own sensibility and response to the musical world around him. Both he and Venuti, moreover, could draw freely on the rich and varied traditions of string playing brought to this country in the great turn-of-the-century waves of Italian immigration. It is no less important to them than the Sicilian clarinet tradition was to the formation of Leon Roppolo, Nunzio Scaglione, and other early white New Orleans reedmen. Venuti never lost an opportunity to depict his friend as a true pioneer. "Who else was there?" he asked, rhetorically, in 1973. "Eddie started it all."[31]

To a man, fellow-musicians remembered Lang with respect and deep affection. "He was the swellest guy that ever lived, the best disposition," said guitarist Jack Bland, with whom Lang worked in the Mound City Blue Blowers. "You couldn't make him mad. He was about five feet eight and a half inches, curly dark hair—and one of the best card players in the country."[32]

Lang "could lay down rhythm and bass parts just like a piano," Lonnie Johnson said in a 1939 Down Beat interview. "He was the nicest man I ever worked with. He never argued. He didn't tell me what to do. He would ask me. Then, if everything was okay, we'd sit down and get to jiving." Their shared affinity for the blues, and the give-and-take that it produced, make their joint performances deeply satisfying.[33]

He had a photographic memory and perfect pitch. Frank Trumbauer recalled that Lang kept the important cues in his Whiteman orchestra parts on the back of a business card, the rest in his head. Venuti was at pains, however, to deny any suggestion that Lang was not a good sight-reader.

Off the bandstand, the two were quite different personalities. Venuti, of course, was one of the great "characters" of jazz, given to the kind of flamboyant behavior which is bound to inspire storytelling. As in the case of Bix, anecdotes about him have taken on a life of their own, which sometimes obscures their flesh-and-blood subject from view.

Not that the stories aren't true. For anyone who knew and spent any time with Venuti in later life, many of them have at least more than a faint ring of authenticity. Joe playing the circus, close enough to the horses to tickle their private parts with his bow—with startling results; Venuti phoning up every tuba player in town (some versions say string bass) for an alleged job, then watching from hiding as they all converge on one street corner; Venuti auditioning for the Goldkette office by dressing up as an Italian immigrant speaking broken English and playing a tarantella instead of the expected jazz number; Venuti and some cronies dumping a piano out a hotel room window, allegedly to determine what its predominant tonality would be when it hit the ground below. On and on, as fond reminiscence unchains imagination and unhinges common sense.

There's no doubt that Venuti had a roisterous, rebellious side. Anyone who understands the tedium and frequent frustration which are as much part of a musician's life as the actual making of music will understand the occasional urge to cut up. As Artie Shaw put it in a conversation about the so-called good old days, "You can't imagine some of the garbage we sometimes had to play, and for what idiots. It was *worse* than being bored. It made you wish you were any-where else. And I *mean* anywhere."[34]

Too often forgotten amid the yarn-spinning is the simple fact that no one would even have bothered telling whoppers about Joe Venuti had he not been an extraordinary, larger-than-life musician. In common with the rest of what for convenience's sake can here be called the Nichols circle, he was a highly accom-plished virtuoso, who could play a ballad melody line with poise and passion to rival those of such reigning concert artists of the day as Fritz Kreisler. According to historian Richard DuPage, his playing with the Goldkette orchestra in 1924 earned so much respect that he was offered a chair with the Detroit Symphony. True or not, it's a useful gauge of his stature.

Colleagues remembered the long practice hours he put in daily, the attention to details of technique. When Venuti broke his bowing arm in a California auto accident during the filming of The King of Jazz, he worked with single-minded ferocity at retraining it, altering his entire technique to regain his former facility.

He was intense, highly charged, with an often volcanic temper and a mouth to match. By contrast, Lang was quiet, understated, a natural gift for diplomacy counterbalancing his partner's excesses. An excellent businessman—though unlike Nichols no self-promoter—he was the ideal counterweight, onstand and off, for the mercurial violinist. "Eddie brought order out of the chaos of Joe's inventions and only Eddie could placate Joe," DuPage wrote. "Venuti always demanded fantastic pay and was incensed at offers he considered unworthy. When Eddie would obtain a higher figure than the offer (though lower than Joe's) Joe would loudly proclaim Eddie's shrewdness."[35]

Venuti and Lang appeared together on Red Nichols records starting in March 1927 and from then on were a fixture, separately or (more often) together, on most hot recordings of consequence made in New York.

Adrian Rollini, free of his commitment to the California Ramblers, joined them at OKeh on June 28, along with "Baron" Schutt, for the first of a series of titles issued under the name "Joe Venuti's Blue Four." From the first notes of

153

"Kickin' the Cat," the alliance worked, Rollini's quick intelligence and cavernous tone providing the ideal foil for Joe and Eddie's two-part inventions. Moreover, his experiments with the "goofus" and "hot fountain pen" clearly appealed to Venuti's sense of fun.

So happy was the union that, even after Rollini's departure for England in late 1927, Venuti retained the low saxophone as bass voice on Blue Four records; with no comparable bass saxophonist around they turned to baritone, using Don Murray, Jimmy Dorsey, and the gifted Pete Pumiglio, later to come into his own as a member of the Raymond Scott Quintet. On the particularly fetching "Running Ragged" and "Apple Blossoms" (1929), they even drew on the comic potential of the bassoon, as played by Frank Trumbauer, for a pair of performances with especially wide emotional range.

The Blue Four records are masterpieces, high points of New York chamber jazz of the '20s; original compositions, credited to both men, bearing such names as "Beatin' the Dog" (also with Rollini), "Pretty Trix," "The Wild Dog," and "Wild Cat," they're fully realized, finely wrought musical miniatures, harmonically and texturally rich; yet they leave plenty of latitude for improvisation and swing fiercely.

"The Venuti-Lang Quartet performances," Richard Hadlock has written, "represent a pioneer effort to present chamber jazz with a minimum of unmusical effects or superfluous vocals and without any pretense of its being anything but music for listening."[36]

Sometimes they are essays on pop tunes of the moment ("Blue Room," "Little Girl") or jazz band standards ("Dinah," "I've Found a New Baby"); whatever the material, the Venuti-Lang touches—introductions, interludes, modulations, interpolated strains—easily carry each performance into its own category. Sometimes Venuti and Lang develop a number as a party piece: the uptempo "Four-String Joe" (1927), as its title suggests, showcases the violinist's dexterity playing all four strings at once with the upside-down bow. Recycling, too, is part of the game: what was "Cheese and Crackers" on OKeh reemerges on Victor as "Really Blue"; "Little Buttercup," with a Gus Kahn lyric added, becomes "I'll Never Be the Same."

Altogether it's dazzling music, the product of a real and lasting meeting of minds. Nothing else in '20s small-group jazz even begins to challenge its consistent intelligence. Venuti may not cut as deeply emotionally as Bix—but then, who did? Even among the other major soloists of the era, only a handful—above all Louis Armstrong—laid bare the depths and complexities of feeling present in Beiderbecke's best work. But on record after record Venuti and Lang left a testament of excellence hard even to challenge, let alone surpass.

There can be no doubt that of the two Lang was the more broadly influential, largely because his was the more common instrument. The subsequent history of jazz guitar abounds with conventions which entered the vocabulary as Lang innovations. Marty Grosz, himself an outstanding guitarist in an idiom owing much to Lang, has written with great insight on the subject. He draws attention to Lang's rich, resonant sound, party the result of a guitar with violin-style F-holes in the top, rather than the customary single round or oval-shaped hole.

If Lang's picking sounds a bit stiff by modern standards, it should be noted that he is playing an acoustic instrument with high action, i.e. one in which the strings are raised away from the finger board in order to increase volume and produce more punch. [Grosz wrote in his notes to a collection of Lang records issued by Time-Life.] The higher the strings, the more pressure required to push them down for clean notes. Furthermore, Lang used heavy strings to achieve his rich, round tone."

Most guitarists of the era, says Grosz, used lighter, thinner strings, which, though tinny-sounding, were easier to control, particularly on the note-bending and coloration so vital to jazz.[37]

With the exception of the Grosz and DuPage notes and an excellent chapter on Lang by Richard Hadlock in Jazz Masters of the Twenties, there has been little serious writing about Venuti and Lang, separately or as a team. Yet almost every record they made contains something of surpassing musical interest. Witness Lang's easy, Bix-like use of alterations and upper chordal voices in his own "Get a Load of This," recorded with Nichols, Schutt, and Berton for Pathé—and expanded into a full-length guitar solo, renamed and recorded for OKeh four months later as "Eddie's Twister."

Then, too, there is his interplay with Trumbauer's C-melody sax and Bix's piano in "For No Reason At All in C," a paraphrase of the pop song "I'd Climb the Highest Mountain." Within the context of the 1920s (and even the 1930s) it is a startling concept, presaging bebop; Trumbauer and Lang create solo essays on the chord structure, referring to the melody only allusively and tangentially. Lang's full-chorus solo creates a brand-new and quite appealing melody, which Marty Grosz used as a basis for an entire performance on a record made twenty years after Lang's death. This, too, like "Clementine," is a performance free of the constraints of time and place (discussed fully in chapter 18).

On "It's Right Here for You" (1928), one of a series of trumpet solos recorded for OKeh by Tommy Dorsey, Lang reaches deep into his knowledge of the blues for a plangent full-chorus solo against a wheezing (and somehow rather winsome) harmonium background by Schutt. As in "For No Reason At All in C," he creates a new melody on the outlines of the old, flavored with highly vocalized "bent" notes.

These same qualities saturate his contribution to "Knockin' a Jug" (March 5, 1929), hallowed as the first hot record by a racially "mixed" band. It's a slow blues in B♭, eloquently stated by Louis Armstrong, Jack Teagarden, Lang, Joe Sullivan, drummer Kaiser Marshall, and tenor saxophonist Happy Caldwell. Louis, predictably, dominates, but Lang's solo and rhythm backing, knitting together Marshall's wobbly, overrecorded drumming and Sullivan's all-but-inaudible piano, are impeccable.

In contrast to the push-the-beat insistence of the Chicagoans (as exemplified in the excellent, generally underappreciated rhythm playing of Eddie Condon), Lang sat squarely—sometimes perhaps a bit too squarely—on the pulse, conveying a feeling of comfort rather than urgency, relaxation before tension. Whatever rhythmic problems he may have had, however, had been solved by October 22,

155

1931, and the "Joe Venuti–Eddie Lang and Their All-Star Orchestra" titles with Goodman, the Teagarden brothers, and a rhythm section of Frank Signorelli, bassist Ward Lay, and drummer Neil Marshall.

Beautifully recorded, widely written about and praised, they show the extent to which black and white rhythmic approaches had merged into one by the end of the 1920s. They're loose, elastic, with intense ensembles bookending strings of solos, repertoire chosen from pop tunes beloved of hot musicians ("Someday Sweetheart," "After You've Gone"), the blues (W. C. Handy's "Beale Street Blues"), and such earlier bands as the Friars Society Orchestra ("Farewell Blues").

"Farewell Blues" is a juggernaut. Goodman works through his registers, Venuti tosses off double-stop passages with disarming ease—then the elder Teagarden takes the stage with a simple four-note phrase that seems to unlock hidden stores of energy in the rhythm section. It all culminates in two choruses of spirited ensemble riffing. Jack sings engagingly on "After You've Gone," then jumps aside just in time as Venuti dives, swoops, and plunges through a full chorus, pausing only for a hair-raising mid-chorus break before goading the final ensemble into a last manic burst of intensity.

Lang doesn't solo, save for a four-bar introduction to Teagarden's "Beale Street Blues" vocal. He duets with Joe on "Someday Sweetheart" but for the most part seems content to control and drive the rhythm.

Critic Leonard Feather, listening in the early 1970s, hailed this as "one of the most exciting sessions of its kind ever produced" and found it hard to believe that so exciting a group of recordings could date from so early a time. Indeed, they seem at a stroke to have left behind the conventions of the '20s and established a new set of ground rules, especially in matters of rhythm.[38]

As the 1930s got under way, Venuti and Lang were beginning to move in different career directions. Bing Crosby, who had become a devotee and close personal friend of both men during the months with Whiteman, offered Eddie a job as his regular accompanist. It meant a spectacular leap in income—a thousand dollars a week basic salary, plus six films at fifteen thousand dollars each—and a kind of visibility that not even Whiteman, for all his popularity, could offer.

Lang accepted. He was with Bing on theatre appearances, radio shows, and record dates; he's onscreen (and even has a couple of speaking lines) in the movie *The Big Broadcast*, where he accompanies memorably on "Please," "Here Lies Love," and Crosby's theme, "Where the Blue of the Night (Meets the Gold of the Day)."

He continued to record regularly. In early 1932 he broke new ground yet again by joining Carl Kress for a pair of guitar duets, whimsically titled "Pickin' My Way" and "Feeling My Way." These are carefully worked-out miniatures, first of their kind to be preserved on record, with the two guitarists playing complementary roles: where Lang and Lonnie Johnson had found a common denominator in the blues, he and Kress are united by strong similarities of conception. Five years Lang's junior, Kress had learned much from him, but his chordally based statements are easily distinguished from the veteran's single-string solo lines.

"April Kisses," recorded in 1927 with Arthur Schutt at the piano, shows another side of Lang's personality. It's a waltz, idiomatically similar to the salon pieces being dispensed at the time by such saxophonists as Rudy Wiedoeft, Clyde Doerr, and Whiteman's Chester Hazlett. After a *rubato* introduction reminiscent of classical master Andres Segovia, Lang creates a musical *gateau*, decorated with romantic flourishes and showing off the strength and beauty of his tone.

He and Venuti still found time to record together in the familiar chamber jazz setting, turning out buoyant, flavorful performances. Rollini, home from his London sabbatical, joined them for a revival of the original Blue Four personnel: as "Ragging the Scale" and the blues-tinged "Put and Take" more than attest, the chemistry still worked.

Rollini was there, too, for their last date together: the Blue Five session of May 8, 1933. From a strictly musical viewpoint it's an artistic culmination, apotheosis of the form: Venuti, Lang, Jimmy Dorsey, Rollini, and pianist Phil Wall perform on a variety of instruments, making music that sounds the way summer sunlight looks on water, plays of color punctuated by sudden flashes of brilliance. These are masters of their craft, making music of a high order—intricate, varied, devised with care, full of humor—yet beyond any doubt hot improvised jazz.

One of the four selections is a remake of "Raggin' the Scale," jumping Edward Claypool's old rag through an up-tempo steeplechase, with bright-toned alto sax from Dorsey and a cleanly executed pizzicato solo by Venuti. Rollini plays vibes on the Fields-McHugh "Hey, Young Fella," while Jimmy picks up his cornet for a Bixish muted solo chorus.

They bring great style to the aptly named "Jigsaw Puzzle Blues," each chorus a jewel in a different and effective setting: Lang, for example, solos magically over the shimmer of Rollini's vibes. The old barroom favorite "Pink Elephants" occasions some witty Dorsey alto and exultant ride cornet at the whoop-it-up finish.

It was to be a valedictory. Less than a month later, Eddie Lang went into the hospital for what should have been a routine tonsillectomy. In one of those strokes of fate that defy any attempt at understanding, he developed an embolism and died without ever regaining consciousness. He was thirty-one years old.

Venuti was thunderstruck, dazed. How to explain it? How, finally, to carry on? How to go on making music with only half of you left intact?

He moved on, of course, because he had to. For awhile Dick McDonough, close friend of both men and a supreme guitarist, filled in. Just how well can be heard on the sessions of May 8 and October 2. The playing on the latter in particular, also featuring Rollini, Benny Goodman, and Bud Freeman, is excellent, often rising to great heights (as in "Jazz Me Blues" and the closing chorus of "Doin' the Uptown Lowdown"). McDonough is superb, particularly playing ensemble lead on "Sweet Lorraine" and taking a two-chorus chordal blues solo on "In de Ruff," a renamed "Dippermouth Blues."

For a while, Venuti teamed up with the talented guitarist Frank Victor. In a series of 1934 duo transcriptions for Muzak, they revived "Wild Cat," "Pretty Trix," "Running Ragged," and some of the others in upbeat, satisfying performances, with Victor fully equal to the task. Only when they are heard in comparison to the originals does it become clear how very much Eddie Lang took with him in departing so abruptly on March 26, 1933.

Many years later Venuti was standing backstage at a jazz festival in Europe, waiting to go on. A fellow-musician took the opportunity to ask a long-nurtured question. "Eddie Lang died forty-two years ago," he began. "Do you ever miss him?"

Venuti didn't laugh. Didn't growl some dismissive epithet or otherwise fluff the questioner off. Instead he simply stopped, lost in reverie, and after a long moment looked up.

"Every day," he said.

8

Adrian Rollini
and the California
Ramblers

On Easter Sunday 1925, New York radio station WGBS serenaded listeners with a program of hymns, played by a dance orchestra called the California Ramblers. It was decorous, reverential, eminently innocuous.

Or so the station management thought. Calls from irate listeners swamped the tiny WGBS switchboard; over the next few days, protests swelled the letters columns of newspapers. One such, in the *New York Herald-Tribune*, cursed the participating musicians for a bunch of ill-educated clods, too ignorant to realize the offense they'd caused.

For Wallace T. "Ed" Kirkeby, their manager and agent, that tore it. Offended sensibilities could be dealt with. Even allegations of incompetence. But nobody was going to impugn the educational credentials of the California Ramblers and get away with it.

"The personnel of the orchestra," he said in a riposte published Thursday, April 16, "are of an intelligence and social standing comparable to the average collegian."

In those few words, perhaps without even realizing it, Kirkeby had identified the core, the single most important factor, in the immense popularity of the California Ramblers throughout the early and middle 1920s.

No society cotillion, no college prom, was complete without them. Their Westchester County headquarters, the Ramblers Inn in Pelham, was the place to go for dinner and dancing outside Manhattan. Top-of-the-line restaurants and exclusive resort hotels vied for their services.

In all, they were as much a part of the popular image of '20s life as raccoon coats, hip flasks, and the cartoons of John Held Jr. College students loved them because they *recognized* them: having them for your prom or tea dance was like having a band full of fellow-students: highly professional, yes, and talented, but fellow-students all the same. If the lyrics went "Collegiate, Collegiate, Yes we are collegiate," it was the eleven-piece California Ramblers who supplied the accompaniment.

Perhaps for that very reason, the California Ramblers have been neglected badly by historians of jazz, as if their popularity disqualified them from serious consideration as a musical force. As record producer Michael Brooks has put it, there's a stigma, "which almost makes an apology mandatory in a California Ramblers liner note." Discussion of their records invariably falls back on such implicitly dismissive phrases as "interesting period piece" or "dated, peppy dance music."[1]

Yet many—perhaps even most—of the major New York–based white jazz-men of the 1920s spent time as members of the California Ramblers. Among the band's countless records, made for dozens of labels under a bewildering variety of pseudonyms, are many no-compromise, first-rate hot jazz performances, bursting with solos and ensembles that easily lift the Ramblers and their various smaller units from the status of social phenomenon to that of musical landmark.

And at the center, as anchor and ace-in-the-hole, catalyst and musical guiding deity, is one of the most gifted and seminal of the period's hot music figures—the bass saxophonist, vibraphonist, pianist, and multi-instrumental virtuoso Adrian Rollini.

Between 1922, when Rollini began appearing on their records, and 1927, when he left to strike out on his own, the Ramblers drew the crowds, determined the fashions, and set a musical pace among New York City–based hot dance bands. His musical consistency, one of the most remarkable of the era, made the band consistent; combined with Kirkeby's business sense and an extraordinary flair for publicity, it was a surefire formula for success.

The name, to start with, was an out-and-out fraud, if a canny one: the California Ramblers were no more from California than the Original Memphis Five had been from Tennessee. Most of the original members, in fact, were from Ohio and Pennsylvania. But, as banjoist-founder Ray Kitchingman later confessed, in those days a California association was eminently good for business.

In 1920, two California bands had set off a revolution in the dance band world. Arranger Ferde Grofé, by dividing Art Hickman's San Francisco–based band into autonomous sections (including the saxophone team of Bert L. Ralton and Clyde Doerr), shaped the modern dance orchestra and laid the foundation for the entire field of big band writing, foreshadowing even the swing bands of the 1930s. As arranger Robert Haring Sr. told James T. Maher, "Everybody—and I mean players, arrangers, and leaders of bands—was talking about Hickman. What he was doing was utterly unprecedented."[2]

Paul Whiteman, ambitious and alert, was watching and listening. Building on early successes in San Francisco and Los Angeles, he brought his orchestra east in the spring of 1920, opening at the Ambassador Hotel in Atlantic City—and featuring carefully worked-out arrangements by Ferde Grofé.

In electing to call themselves the California Ramblers, then, the young collegians were buying into what was newest and most exciting in the dance band field. Atlantic City, scene of Whiteman's first East Coast triumph, seemed the place to start: so they worked at Rendezvous Park, and in the fashionable Café de Paris, before heading for New York City.

It was almost a case of too much, too soon. They floundered, picking up work where they could, but by year's end things had pretty much dried up. Then, at the eleventh hour, destiny strode onstage in the person of Ed Kirkeby.

Born in Brooklyn in 1891, Kirkeby had tried his hand at a number of things, including selling and playing banjos. He'd plugged records for the Columbia Graphophone Co., graduating to the post of assistant recording manager by 1914. Intrigued with the new phenomenon of "hot" music, he'd helped organize the Earl Fuller Jazz Band (with young Ted Lewis on the clarinet) as Columbia's answer to the Original Dixielanders on Victor. He'd helped get Phil Napoleon, Frank Signorelli, and their Original Memphis Five into a studio for the first time under the nominal aegis of bandleader Sam Lanin.

Bright, brash, he knew a prospect when he saw one, and this group of ersatz Californians—clean-cut, good-looking, well-spoken, and musically no worse than anyone else—was definitely a prospect. He put them into the Palace Theatre on Broadway, backing singer Eva Shirley, "the Galli-Curci of Vaudeville," and Al Roth, "the boy who dances on his ankles."

They moved with the show to Poli's Theatre in Boston in time for release of their first record, a performance of the brand-new "The Sheik of Araby" on the Vocalion label. A Boston newspaper review praised their "syncopation . . . of the lingering and crooning kind that no one would tire of hearing" and noted that the band had taken nine curtain calls.[3]

In a 1938 interview, Kirkeby claimed to have been in at the very start, even to have been responsible for the California Ramblers name; he built the band, he said, out of the remnants of the Merry Melody Men, a little-known group which recorded extensively for a variety of labels between March 1920 and October 1921. Among the members of this early and rather obscure band, only Frank Banta, composer of many popular piano novelties, and Charles Randall, trombonist who taught the young Miff Mole, are remembered today.

It's worth noting that the California Ramblers began recording immediately after the Merry Melody Men stopped. As Kirkeby tells it, the first edition of the Ramblers consisted of a mixture of the two groups. At one point, probably in early 1922, there was a split; Ramblers violinist-leader Oscar Adler departed, taking several musicians with him. Kirkeby seized the opportunity to reorganize, retaining Kitchingman and saxophonist Jim Duff and adding a complement of new men.[4]

To front the band he hired a young socialite named Arthur Hand; good-looking, charming, and well connected, he played enough violin to know which end belonged where. But his function, as Kirkeby made clear in later years, was not musical. Real estate magnate J. C. Hand, in fact, had at first tried to discourage his son from entering the *infra dig* dance band world and even cut him out of his will. But later, impressed with the Ramblers' popularity in society circles, he relented—and left the young man a generous inheritance.

Kirkeby pulled every string, exploited every contact he had, to get the band established. He leaned on his old pal Pete Shanley for a booking at the Shanley family's popular restaurant, on Broadway between 43rd and 44th streets. He also went to work in earnest scouting talent and hustling jobs, looking for ways to sell his band and open doors to top-quality work. He found his *open-sesame* in a colleague of Hand's who had been working with the violinist at Healey's Restaurant, 96th and Broadway, as a xylophone soloist.

Adrian Rollini was eighteen, five feet, five inches tall, and already something of a prodigy. At age four he'd attracted attention by playing a fifteen-minute Chopin piano recital at the Waldorf-Astoria Hotel. In 1917, when the boy was fourteen, the family (of French-Swiss extraction) moved from Astoria, Queens, to Larchmont, in well-to-do Westchester about twenty miles north of New York City. Soon he was leading his own little band, and at sixteen had recorded a series of piano rolls for the Republic Company.

Saxophonist Arnold Brilhart, soon to play alongside Rollini in the Ramblers and numerous other bands, recalled a job they worked together as youngsters in nearby Mamaroneck. "He played the piano and the xylophone," said Brilhart, respected in later life as a maker of widely sought-after saxophone mouthpieces. "Even as a kid, from the very beginning, he was a natural musician, a guy who could do just about anything. He had perfect pitch, probably a keener ear than anybody I've ever worked with."[5]

It's unclear whether Rollini took up the B♭ bass saxophone specifically at Kirkeby's urging (as Kirkeby later claimed) or whether it was his own idea, based on the realization that with the departure of their tuba player, one Otto Yedla, the band needed a solid rhythmic bottom. "He just came home with it one day," said his younger brother, tenor saxophonist Arthur Rollini. "He never took any lessons on it or anything. Didn't say much about it. Just went to work in his room learning it, and in about three weeks he had it under his fingers. After that he never brought the horn home. He just figured it out as he went. It all came easy to him. He was a quick study, a natural."[6]

Arnold Brilhart concurred. "He seemed to have a built-in embouchure. It was as though he'd just figured out in his head how the thing should be played, then gone ahead and done it. That simple."[7]

His choice of the bass saxophone was itself a departure. Most dance orchestras of the period used either the E♭ tuba or (double) BB♭ sousaphone for a broad, if rhythmically inflexible, foundation. Whether in the pre-microphone conditions of dance halls and hotel ballrooms, or facing the conical horns of an acoustic recording studio, the brass bass was the only one that could be heard. The string bass, used widely in early New Orleans combinations, was rhythmically more flexible but had not yet caught on in New York bands, presumably because leaders felt it lacked the volume and amplitude needed to be heard in larger units playing dance halls and ballrooms. That was the prevailing opinion until the arrival, later in the decade, of bassists Wellman Braud, George "Pops" Foster, and, above all, Steve Brown, all raised in New Orleans.

Though part of the original "family" of instruments devised by Belgian pioneer Adolphe Sax, the bass saxophone seemed to have achieved little practical use outside marching bands and such novelty vaudeville acts as the "Six Brown Brothers." There certainly was little evidence, and no solid precedent, to determine whether it would be any more effective in dance orchestras than the brass bass. The exact circumstances that prompted Adrian Rollini to learn it, therefore, may be irretrievably lost to inquiry.

But learn it he did. He first appears on Ramblers records in April 1922, dutifully marking the first and third beats of the bar in the manner of a tuba. He doesn't solo until "My Sweetie Went Away," recorded for Columbia more than a year later, on July 12, 1923. Becoming adept—and strong—enough to sustain a bass line was one thing, but what did one *do* in approaching a solo on so large and potentially unwieldy an instrument? The snap of a muted trumpet, the flow of a clarinet, even the caricatured braying of a trombone—such qualities fell naturally within the normal playing scope of their instruments. But the bass saxophone, for anyone interested in using it as a solo vehicle, was *terra nova*.

New York in 1922 was the capital of America's popular music industry. Tin Pan Alley was cranking out new songs at the rate of about five hundred a week, and publishers, understanding the promotional value of the phonograph, saw to it that as many of them as possible got recorded and endorsed by contract artists. New dance orchestras were sprouting up everywhere, satisfying a growing generation's appetite for entertainment and the publishing industry's appetite for new outlets.

There was little about the California Ramblers at first—at least on the basis of their early recordings—to set them apart from dozens of other competent outfits, in New York and elsewhere. For example, "When You're Near," recorded for Perfect October 3, 1922, is a straightforward and rather faceless performance of an undistinguished tune, featuring melody solos by saxophonist Jim Duff, trombonist Lloyd "Ole" Olsen, and trumpeter Frank Cush.

But Ed Kirkeby's mind was at work. Figuring that a classy band deserved a classy and well-heeled clientele (and perhaps with some prodding from Rollini), he concentrated his efforts in affluent Westchester. Finally the Post Lodge, on the Boston Post Road in Larchmont, agreed to take them on November 16.

They were an instant success. "The California Ramblers, comprising one of the really famous orchestras in the country, literally knocks 'em for a goal," bubbled the *Yonkers Herald.* "Applause last night sounded like the thunderous roar of a battery of howitzers . . . encore followed encore until it seemed that they would be forced to play through half the night."[8]

If there had been any doubt in Kirkeby's mind what his next step would be, that night dispelled it. While the band was filling winter dates in and outside New York (including a year-end holiday run in Montreal and two weeks subbing for Paul Whiteman at the Palais Royal on Long Island), he was wheeling and dealing: on Friday, May 18, 1923, the California Ramblers opened at what had been the Shanley family's Pell Tree Inn, on Pelham Shore Road only half an hour up the newly built Pelham Parkway from midtown Manhattan. For the occasion they renamed the big old house the California Ramblers Inn and advertised "Cool breezes, spacious dance floor, shore dinner à la carte."

The *New York Evening Standard* for May 26 described "ten snappy chaps . . . double-barreled musicians in the truest and best sense of the word." The report is a milestone, in that it heralds both the beginning of the Inn as Ramblers headquarters and the band's emergence as a force in New York dance band circles.

Its playing at this early stage has been referred to (and disparaged) often in print as, in Gunther Schuller's later assessment, "slightly jerky, bouncy, carefree music, full of Charleston syncopations." What's central here is less whether such a characterization is true than the fact—not mentioned by Schuller but obvious from countless records—that every other dance orchestra in New York at that time, white and black, also played "slightly jerky, bouncy, carefree music," many of them with considerably less charm and verve than the Ramblers.[9]

Such records, chosen at random, as "Aggravatin' Papa" by Vincent Lopez, "St. Louis Gal" by Gene Rodemich's orchestra, or Fletcher Henderson's "Linger Awhile" and "Feelin' the Way I Do" (1924) display an equally awkward approach to rhythm and solo playing, bound by the same exaggerated dotted-eighth-and-sixteenth phrasing heard on Ramblers performances.[10]

That only began to change in 1924, a year of two significant events: first, the arrival of the Wolverines, with Bix Beiderbecke on cornet, at the Cinderella Ballroom on Friday, September 12; then, a month later, the opening of the winter season at Roseland, a few blocks further up Broadway, featuring Fletcher Henderson's Orchestra. In his trumpet section, reading the third book, was twenty-three-year-old Louis Armstrong.

(It would be both stimulating and comforting to think of these two master innovators working in the same area at the same time, hot jazz history in the making. But it is, alas, not so: on Monday, October 13, when Henderson opened at Roseland, Beiderbecke had left the Wolverines and was on a train headed for Detroit and a job with Jean Goldkette's orchestra.)

Records made by both these ensembles at this point show how fast developments were moving: Louis's solos—linear, rhythmically relaxed, rooted firmly in a 12/8 conception of the beat—fairly leap out of the hidebound ensembles of Henderson's "Nasty Man" or "Go 'Long Mule"; is there any more startling contrast than that between the stick-figure band on the Southern Serenaders' 1925 "I Miss My Swiss" (a combination of Lanin and Henderson men?) and Armstrong's elastic, startlingly "modern" sixteen-bar solo in the final chorus?

Similarly, Beiderbecke's choruses on such Wolverines records as "Sensation," "Tia Juana," and "Big Boy" (all 1924) sing along smoothly on the beat, without even vestigial trace of dotted-eighth-and-sixteenth phrasing. They are the work of a thoughtful, lyrical soloist, as compelling in their logic and compositional balance as Armstrong's are in their visceral excitement and swing.

*   *   *

In Ed Kirkeby's scrapbook, on file at the Rutgers University Institute of Jazz Studies, is a sixteen-page typewritten prospectus, carefully outlining a promotion campaign for the California Ramblers throughout one calendar year. It includes exploitation of radio, newspapers, popular magazines, and trade journals; deals with instrument companies and music publishers (the last aimed chiefly at getting the band's picture on the covers of new song sheets); suggests ideas for publicity stunts, product tie-ins, hometown pitches focused on individual band members, and much more. In the context of the 1920s—or of any period—it is an extraordinary marketing document, prepared by a man whose grasp of publicity and the communications media was decades ahead of its time.

Among Kirkeby's promotions was a series of well-publicized, high-profile weekly theme nights, featuring guest celebrities. For a "George White's Scandals Night" in August, he brought in Winnie Lightner, Lester Allen, Johnny Dooley, and other stars of the revue then playing to capacity audiences on Broadway. He scheduled it for midnight, allowing performers ample time to make the drive from midtown Manhattan—*and* guaranteeing that the crowds would arrive early enough to listen to the band and then stay for the show.

There was a "Celebrity Night," a "Radio Night," and even a pair of "Texas Guinan Nights," featuring the flamboyant nightclub proprietor and entertainer with a troupe which included a slick little guy billed as "Georgie Raff, the world's greatest Charleston dancer"—soon to become Hollywood's George Raft. But Kirkeby's September 27 "Blues Night" was, at least for history, his most adventuresome: Bessie Smith headed an all-star, all-black roster which also included Clara Smith, Clarence Williams, trumpeter Johnny Dunn, and others. A daring move in 1923—and from all indications an immensely popular one.

On October 17, the Ramblers opened at the Monte Carlo theatre-restaurant at 51st Street and Broadway, downstairs from Roseland Ballroom. The trumpets were Frank Cush and Bill Moore, a light-skinned black most often billed as "the Hot Hawaiian" in specialty acts.[11] Olsen was the trombonist. Bobby Davis, an able improviser with a full, "legit" tone, had replaced Jim Duff as third alto. Arnold Brilhart was playing lead, with Fred Cusick on tenor. Irving Brodsky was the pianist, Ray Kitchingman still on banjo, plus Rollini and drummer Stan King, who had come in from Barney Rapp's New England–based band.

Rollini had by this time begun taking solos on Ramblers records, and they are at once a revelation and a mystery. The band is still very 1923 in its phrasing and rhythm, yet Rollini stands apart, his solo statements smooth, melodically coherent. On "Sittin' in a Corner," for example, he delivers a full-chorus counterline to Cush's wah-wah melody lead. As a Columbia Records catalogue of the time rather archly put it, "the part that gets us most is where the saucy cornet tries to chatter down a bouncing big bass sax, as it punches out a rhythm that would rock Gibraltar."[12] The trumpet dates, but the bass sax does not. Rollini's phrases move along sparely and coherently, with an engaging forward thrust.

But how? Where did he get it? Where did it come from? According to the

X-begat-Y-begat-Z formulations so beloved to chroniclers of jazz history, Rollini makes no sense. Was he aware of records by the Friars Society Orchestra or Oliver Creole Band? There's no evidence that he was. He may well have been familiar with the Original Dixieland Jazz Band and its legions of imitators, but his playing on "Sittin' in a Corner" betrays no hint of it.

Such theorizing, with its strong implication of "monkey-see, monkey-do," leaves no room for the possibility of simple individual initiative, a talent able to work out the problems of continuity in an improvised solo pretty much on its own. More plausible is the suggestion that Rollini, like Bix and Eddie Lang, Jack Teagarden and—most remarkable of all—Louis Armstrong himself, just *got* there.

"It was the times," said cornetist-guitarist Bill Priestley, who as a young man newly arrived in New York was a frequent visitor to the Ramblers Inn. "The fascinating thing about the years 1923 to 1929 was that each year a new person or orchestra would appear and immediately influence a whole new batch of people . . . I can't see how any era, musically, could have been more creative than those few years."[13]

Rollini shows every sign of having simply addressed the problems of rhythm and line and solved them his own way, much as he solved problems of intonation and flexibility on the often recalcitrant bass saxophone. "He was breaking ground," said Spencer Clark, who took up bass sax after hearing Rollini at the Inn. "Just like Jack [Teagarden] on trombone, he was opening the way for others, doing things that just hadn't been heard before. Funny thing is, I'd gone up there at first to hear him because he was known as a fine xylophone player. I remember standing on cartons, or crates or something, peering in the back window of the Ramblers Inn watching him play 'Nola' with four mallets. Four mallets! I couldn't even do it with two, and here was Rollini flailing around with four sticks."[14]

At some point Rollini discovered that by using the slightly smaller baritone saxophone mouthpiece and reed (and later a specially constructed neck), he could increase his control over the bass sax without sacrificing power. The baritone mouthpiece also enabled him to use altissimo harmonics, notes above the instrument's normal playing range achieved by unusual combinations of fingerings.

This practice, said Arnold Brilhart, was catching on quickly among those investigating the lower saxophones. "I owned and played a bass saxophone in my high school band days," he said, "and even at that time the instrument, when played using a regular bass sax mouthpiece, sounded very stuffy and out of tune." Substitution of a baritone mouthpiece and reed made all the difference, he said.[15]

Rollini also replaced the springs in some of his instrument's higher keys with extra-thick piano wire, his brother Arthur said, to prevent leakage of air. And when Brilhart, in his eighty-ninth year, looked back on a long and distinguished career in music and declared that Adrian Rollini "was one of the two or three most astonishing musicians I've ever known, and certainly the best bass saxophone player," his words were not to be taken lightly.[16]

Rollini's penchant for the unusual also led him to begin experimenting with what might otherwise have been dismissed as toys, or at best children's instruments. One such was the Couesnophone, developed by the Couesnon Instrument

Co. of Paris and marketed here as a novelty. In essence it was a kind of harmonica in the shape of a toy saxophone, with a bank of spring-fit keys which could be lifted in combinations to sound chords. When blown, it sounded like a cross between a harmonica and a small concertina. According to Walter C. Allen and other historians, Kirkeby soon dubbed it a "goofus."

Rollini quickly became adept enough on it to play solos, and soon the piping sound of the goofus was a regular feature of Ramblers performances, especially popular with college audiences. In a bid to capitalize on such popularity, Don Redman began playing the goofus late in 1924, often using it in conjunction with Coleman Hawkins's efforts on the bass saxophone. Several Henderson records, including "Pensacola" and "Nobody's Rose" (1925), illustrate this emulation of Rollini by leading black musicians.[17]

Such was the renown Rollini achieved with the instrument, in fact, that later models were sold with the word "goofus" actually embossed in script under "Couesnophone" on the body. More surprising yet, Percy Scholes's tenth edition of the august and traditional-minded *Oxford Companion to Music*, first published in 1938, contains a one-paragraph entry, listed under "Goofus," describing it and commenting, "It can be held to the mouth like a saxophone or laid on the table and blown through an india-rubber tube."[18]

Another novelty instrument that became something of a Rollini specialty was a ten-inch miniature clarinet, pitched in A♭, with eight holes and no keys, and blown through a tiny mouthpiece fitted with a cut-down E♭ clarinet reed. Rollini called it a "hot fountain pen," playing solos on it in something of the manner of an ocarina or tin whistle. He uses it with much charm, for example, on the May 7, 1930, Joe Venuti Blue Four record of "Put and Take."

"We guarantee the California Ramblers as the best band that has played here," said a sign in the lobby of Proctor's Theatre, in New York, after a particularly successful Ramblers engagement. And so it was: on January 14, 1925, they opened at one of the city's most prestigious locations, the Congo Room, on the twentieth floor of the Alamac Hotel, Broadway and 71st Street, best known as home base for the popular Paul Specht orchestra.

As usual, publicity wizard Kirkeby was on the job. Read one advertisement:

The cannibal drum
Says "Come! Come!"
So as you hear its weird BOOM!
Answer with a trip to the CONGO ROOM!

By now the California Ramblers were recording regularly, for an increasing variety of labels; in 1925 alone, they appeared as the Golden Gate Orchestra, the Palace Garden Orchestra, Meyer's Dance Orchestra, Ted White's Collegians, the Baltimore Society Orchestra, Rialto Dance Orchestra, Southampton Society Orchestra, Imperial Dance Orchestra, and dozens more.

It took some ingenuity. Unlike Whiteman, Henderson, Isham Jones, and many other prominent dance orchestras of the time, the Ramblers had no resident arranger to feed them a regular diet of custom scores on pop tunes or hot specialties. They relied instead on publishers' "stock" orchestrations, which they doctored in seemingly inexhaustible ways.

Though a decided operating advantage, the practice also had a negative side. Stock orchestrations, usually published at the same time as the sheet music of a new song, were functionally conceived and written to be played by any combination of instruments, at any level of competence. Form inevitably followed function, and sections were scored so that the top two parts would sound consonant even by themselves, a third part filling in remaining chordal notes. While effective, that all but ruled out unusual voicings of the sort that later set many bands, notably that of Duke Ellington, apart. Instrumental "doubling," moreover, was rare in stocks—again, on the assumption that such resources might not be universally available; that, too, limited the variety of textures and sounds that helped make such units as Paul Whiteman's late '20s orchestra so distinctive.

Many bands of the 1920s and early 1930s used "customized" stocks to great advantage, especially for recording. Louis Armstrong's classic 1931 OKeh record of "Star Dust" is based on a stock, as are such Fletcher Henderson items as the 1927 "Baltimore" (Dixie Stompers) or the 1931 Victor "Roll On, Mississippi, Roll On."

But among the most prominent bands only the Ramblers relied almost exclusively on stocks—which, for all their flexibility, tended to be faceless in sound and design. Soon enough, the successes of the Casa Loma Orchestra and other bands would result in transcriptions of their most famous numbers (with some adjustments in section voicing to conform to the norms of "stock" scoring) being published as "rhythm specialties," greatly upgrading the quality of available material. In the 1920s, though, such "specials" were still the exception. All too often, Ramblers records come across as well played (sometimes considerably more than that) but with no strong identifying feature beyond the unmistakable bark and bite of Rollini's bass sax.

Still, their "customizing" of stocks (from all indications a cooperative enterprise) was often quite resourceful. On one version of a song the introduction and opening chorus would be retained, but a vocal inserted and one or two choruses of scoring stripped away, replaced by soloists. In another, the vocal would begin the piece, *sans* intro, then another *tutti* would be reinserted, and space cleared elsewhere for solos. On small-band records often only intro, ending, and rhythm section parts would remain intact, the rest given over to solos.[19]

Between 1924 and 1926 a succession of New York's finest hot musicians passed through the California Ramblers. Reedmen Fud Livingston and Jimmy Dorsey, trombonists Abe Lincoln, Tommy Dorsey, and Al Philburn, trumpeters Chelsea Quealey, Red Nichols, and Sylvester Ahola, among many others, turn up on Ramblers records and in the numerous photos taken of the band in this period. Kirkeby's own meticulous diaries have helped discographers sort out who played what, and for how long.

Throughout this time the overall band sound—or, more exactly, the lack of one—changed little. Rollini apart, the California Ramblers remained a band play-ing stocks. The many fine solo choruses on these records do little to personalize a sense of ensemble anonymity, regardless how well-executed.

By 1925 they'd begun to find a solution: most records by the full band, for Columbia and other labels, remained relatively formal, dotted here and there with hot solos. But small groups from the personnel, recording for minor labels as the "Goofus Five," "University Six," "Varsity Eight," or "Five Birmingham Babies," could afford a looser, more relaxed approach.

Small labels, with small budgets, small distribution and sales expectations, seemed less subject to the constraints governing major-label policy. The resultant small-band performances, infrequently reissued and often hard to find, are the real key to understanding the Ramblers in 1920s hot music: anyone judging the band solely on the basis of its full-strength commercialized efforts for Columbia, Perfect, or Edison is getting only half the picture.

"Desdemona," of September 18, is the first University Six title for Harmony, and it's quite a departure. The small band charges into the little-known Maceo Pinkard song with surprising ferocity; Rollini, prominently recorded, pushes the rhythm and solos with brio. Bobby Davis, on alto, shows creamy tone and clean execution.

Here, as in "Camel Walk" from the same session, the band generates a drive and overall sound quite like that of such titles as "Spanish Shawl" and "Florida Stomp," as recorded in November (also for Harmony) by Fletcher Henderson under the pseudonym of the Dixie Stompers. On those latter titles Coleman Haw-kins plays bass sax with the same massive thrust Rollini brings to the instrument, but with neither the tone nor the finesse. He often sounds as if he's trying to wrestle this large, uncooperative instrument into submission, in hopes of making it behave as flexibly as his tenor.

On "Dustin' the Donkey" (1926), Rollini leaps in with an agile break, then plays a full chorus with the band riffing Charleston figures behind him. He drives hard on "Tiger Rag" (where trumpeter Chelsea Quealey paraphrases Bix's cornet solo from the Wolverines record), and on "San" backs the ensemble with an intricate, technically demanding syncopated figure. There's also a solo by the formidable trombonist Abe Lincoln, who brought to Miff Mole's agile approach a power and sense of humor which were later to make him a valued figure on the Los Angeles traditional jazz scene.[20]

Again and again, listening to Rollini here, the mind asks, "How? How did he figure that out? How did he come to understand that this instrument could provide a bass line with the weight of a tuba, yet with the elastic syncopating power of a string bass—even while emerging as an independent solo voice?" The implications of such questions, weighed against commonly held assumptions of how "influence" is passed on in jazz, are vast.

On another date, they take the Friars Society Orchestra's "Farewell Blues" at an insinuating, medium-slow tempo, affording Rollini one of his most imagi-native solos. Their "After You've Gone," of June 24, hits the ground running,

Rollini driving like a man possessed, and Chelsea Quealey (like a rather militaristic Bix) laying down two solo choruses including a long, complex, impeccably articulated phrase over a four-bar mid-chorus break:

"After You've Gone," Chelsea Quealey solo break, 1927.

By late spring of 1927, Rollini was sufficiently in demand on his own to have decided it was time to make a move. He gave Kirkeby his notice and right away began recording regularly with an expanded circle of associates, which included the best white players then working around New York.

In terms both of quantity and overall quality, it's a remarkable burst of activity. Without exception, each record date he did within this four-month period produced at least one performance now considered an indispensable feature of recorded white jazz in the '20s. With the Red Nichols Brunswick sessions of June 20 and October 26 as bookends, here's what Adrian Rollini was doing in recording studios in between:

Monday, June 20 (Brunswick): Red Nichols and His Five Pennies (Nichols, Mole, J. Dorsey, Venuti, Schutt Lang Berton)

Cornfed / Five Pennies

Tuesday, June 21 (Pathé): Annette Hanshaw (voc), with the Four Instrumental Stars (Venuti, Lang, Rollini, Berton)

Under the Moon / Ain't That a Grand and Glorious Feeling
I'm Somebody's Somebody Now / I Like What You Like
Who-oo? You-oo, That's Who!

Friday, June 24 (Pathé): The California Ramblers

Vo-Do-Do-De-O-Do Blues / Heart-Breakin' Baby
Goin' Home Again Blues / After You've Gone

Saturday, June 25 (Brunswick): Red Nichols and His Five Pennies (as above)

Mean Dog Blues

Tuesday, June 28 (OKeh): Joe Venuti and His Blue Four (Venuti, Lang, Schutt, Rollini)

Beatin' the Dog / Kickin' the Cat

Wednesday, August 10 (OKeh): The Goofus Five (Quealey, Philburn, Davis, Sam Ruby, J. Russin, Rollini, others)

Clementine (from New Orleans) / Nothin' Does Does . . .
I Left My Sugar Standing in the Rain

Monday, August 15 (Brunswick): Red Nichols and His Five Pennies (Nichols, Manny Klein, Leo McConville, Mole, Russell, Rollini, Lennie Hayton, McDonough, Berton)

Riverboat Shuffle / Eccentric
Ida (Sweet as Apple Cider) / Feelin' No Pain

Thursday, August 25 (OKeh): Frankie Trumbauer and His Orchestra (Beiderbecke, Rank, Trumbauer, Murray, Rollini, Riskin, Lang, Morehouse)

Three Blind Mice / Blue River
There's a Cradle in Caroline

Tuesday, August 30 (OKeh): Miff Mole and His Little Molers (Nichols, Mole, Russell, Livingston, Rollini, Schutt, Lang, McDonough, Berton)

Imagination / Feelin' No Pain / Original Dixieland One-Step

Thursday, September 1 (OKeh): Miff Mole and His Little Molers (as above)

My Gal Sal / Honolulu Blues / The New Twister

Thursday, September 8 (Pathé): Annette Hanshaw (voc) and Her Sizzlin' Syncopators (as above)

It Was Only a Sun Shower / Who's That Knockin' at My Door?

Tuesday, September 13 (OKeh): Joe Venuti and His Blue Four (as above)

Cheese and Crackers / A Mug of Ale

Wednesday, September 28 (OKeh): Frankie Trumbauer and His Orchestra (Beiderbecke, Rank, Murray, Trumbauer, Bobby Davis, Rollini, Signorelli, Lang, Venuti, Morehouse)

Humpty Dumpty / Krazy Kat / Baltimore

Friday, September 30 (OKeh): Frankie Trumbauer and His Orchestra (as above)

Just an Hour of Love / I'm Wonderin' Who

Wednesday, October 5 (OKeh): Bix Beiderbecke and His Gang (Beiderbecke, Rank, Murray, Rollini, Signorelli, Morehouse)

At the Jazz Band Ball / Royal Garden Blues / Jazz Me Blues

Tuesday, October 25 (OKeh): Bix Beiderbecke and His Gang (Beiderbecke, Rank, Murray, Signorelli, Rollini, Morehouse)

Goose Pimples / Sorry / Since My Best Gal Turned Me Down

Same session: Frankie Trumbauer and His Orchestra (add Russell, Venuti, Lang)

Cryin' All Day / A Good Man Is Hard to Find

Wednesday, October 26 (OKeh): Frankie Trumbauer and His Orchestra (exact personnel uncertain, but Trumbauer, Rank, Rollini among those present)

Sugar / Did You Mean It?

Wednesday, October 26 (Victor): Red Nichols's Stompers (Nichols, B. Ashford, Rank, Russell, Trumbauer, Rollini, others)

Sugar / Make My Cot Where the Cot-Cot-Cotton Grows

Quite a list, and it seems obvious that Rollini had a more than salutary effect on his surroundings. Each small entente—Bix-Tram, Nichols-Mole, Venuti-Lang—had made excellent records before and would do so again. But there was something in the sound Rollini contributed, the way he dealt with matters of rhythm and ensemble, above all in his sheer musical *presence*, that seemed able to spur his companions to exceed even their own high standards. "He had a strong, surprisingly aggressive way of playing," said Spencer Clark. "He'd approach a phrase, an attack, with great gusto. And the sound, so sonorous and beautiful. That was something brand-new for me, and I have to assume for lots of other musicians, too. He was just a kind of catalyst."[21]

In Rollini's hands, wrote Michael Brooks, the bass sax "became the musical equivalent of a modern football player, a 300-lb. running back mowing down everything in its path." Herb Weil, who took Stan King's place on drums with the Ramblers, agreed. "He made you *want* to play. His intonation, attack and creative ideas were inspiring."[22]

Everyone was listening, including many prominent black jazzmen. Saxophonist-arranger Budd Johnson confessed to a lifelong admiration for Rollini and an awe for that "sound as big as a house." Eddie Barefield declared that Rollini "was, along with Bix and Trumbauer and Jimmy Dorsey, one of the guys we all listened to." Harry Carney, whose majestic baritone sax anchored the Duke Ellington orchestra for more than four decades, told Stanley Dance he "tried to make the upper register sound like Coleman Hawkins and the lower register like Adrian Rollini."[23]

Through a business connection, Rollini got a line on plans to open a new club at 48th and Broadway, in a space which had been, back in 1924, the Cinderella Ballroom. For hot music lovers it was a hallowed spot, where Bix and the Wolverines had played their maiden New York engagement, and where the

Charleston, introduced in *Runnin' Wild* on Broadway the year before, had really caught on. The Cinderella had eventually folded, reemerging in early 1927 as the "Club Whiteman," one of the ever-expanding business ventures of the "King of Jazz."

Paul Whiteman was one of several show business figures who had decided to take a plunge in the nightclub business: Jimmy Durante, Texas Guinan, and Whiteman's self-declared rival, Vincent Lopez, were among the others. Despite a lot of financial backing and an unending stream of celebrities among the well-publicized guests, the place didn't last long. By early summer Whiteman had pulled out, and the club that bore his name soon disappeared.

The word now was that the space, just three blocks from Roseland Ballroom, would be remodeled and reopened as the Club New Yorker, and that the management was looking for a band: by acting fast, Rollini might snag the job.

His first move was to Atlantic City, where the Jean Goldkette Orchestra was appearing at Ernie Young's Million-Dollar Pier. Everyone knew Goldkette was in trouble. While no one would question the band's excellence, it still seemed to appeal more to fellow-musicians than to the public. The obvious disdain of the sidemen for "hokum," the sort of entertainment most bands of the 1920s considered routine, had done little to bring in work. Not for them the sort of impromptu vaudeville that had made Ted Weems and the Coon-Sanders Nighthawks major attractions in the Midwest.

Music alone, went the thinking in the 1920s, doesn't play to Mr. and Mrs. Everyman. Goldkette and his associate Charles Horvath, in fact, were coming to see the all-star unit as little more than a self-indulgent, high-priced liability. It wasn't paying its way, so it would have to go.

Rumors of an impending breakup were all over New York. Paul Whiteman, they said, had already moved in, offering Bix, Trumbauer, and a few of the others jobs at top salaries. But Rollini, figuring he had an inside track, made his pitch anyway: his would be an all-star hot band, the *crème de la crème*. He was also working on supplementary appearances, record deals. It would be like the hot side of the Goldkette band, and no funny-hat stuff.

The men, loyal to Goldkette and to their own *esprit de corps*, held him off, at least temporarily. "We didn't want to see it fold," saxophonist Stanley "Doc" Ryker said, "and were only too willing to give Jean every chance to pull it out."[24]

But on Sunday night, September 18, the Goldkette Graystone Ballroom Orchestra played its final engagement, and four days later Adrian Rollini and his New Yorkers opened at the brand-new club. As promised, it was an all-star mixture: Bix, Trumbauer, trombonist Bill Rank, clarinetist Don Murray and drummer Chauncey Morehouse from Goldkette's band; Bobby Davis, Sylvester Ahola, and Rollini himself from the Ramblers, plus Joe Venuti, Eddie Lang, and veteran Memphis Five pianist Frank Signorelli.

Musically it may have been an idyll, but as business ventures, "musicians' bands" seldom work out; this one was no exception. It lasted little more than a month, during which the band recorded four times for OKeh under Trumbauer's name, with widely varying results. Some of the records, such as Fud Livingston's

"Humpty Dumpty" of September 28 and "Crying All Day" of October 25, are jazz classics, with fine, often ingenious, ensembles and outstanding solos by Bix, Tram, Rollini, and Pee Wee Russell in place of Davis. Others, such as "Just an Hour of Love," are little more than straightforward pop tune performances, enlivened here and there by solo moments from Bix, Tram, and the others.

OKeh Records recording director Tom Rockwell, convinced that Beiderbecke was more than just another hot cornet player, gave him a chance to do some small-band titles for issue under his own name. It paid off: the results, with Rank, Murray, Morehouse, Signorelli, and Rollini, appeared as "Bix Beiderbecke and His Gang" and found the cornetist at his relaxed best.[25]

But the New Yorker job was clearly doomed, and Rollini was working overtime at finding further work for the band. Trumbauer, meanwhile, entered into a brief agreement with Red Nichols, under which they would share record dates and even sidemen. The partnership produced only two rather curious records of the Yellen and Ager tune "Sugar" (not to be confused with the Maceo Pinkard standard of the same name).

The Nichols version, recorded for Victor on Wednesday morning, October 26, 1927, features some Five Pennies regulars plus Trumbauer, Russell, Rank, and Morehouse, in addition to a booting first chorus from Rollini. Trumbauer's version, done in the afternoon for OKeh, spotlights a cornet soloist who is definitely neither Beiderbecke nor Nichols, and whose identity remains unknown to this day. Sylvester Ahola, lead trumpeter in the New Yorker band and a meticulous diarist, was categorical in his insistence that he was not present.[26]

The Rollini band soon fell apart. The Trumbauer-Nichols collaboration died aborning. Soon Bix, Tram, and Bill Rank were on their way to Indianapolis to join Paul Whiteman.

And, finally, sometime during the following weeks, Adrian Rollini accepted an offer from Manuel "Lizz" Elizalde to join a band being put together by his pianist brother Fred, to open at London's Savoy Hotel. He rounded up Davis and Quealey, and they sailed in early November, opening at the Savoy shortly before New Year's, 1928.

Federico "Fred" Elizalde is a figure unique in dance band history. Born to a prominent Manila family in 1907, he spent much of his youth in the United States, studied music under Maurice Ravel, and distressed his parents by chasing around after bands. He even made some now very obscure records with a group of his own, which included his brother Manuel "Lizz" Elizalde on alto sax and the excellent Los Angeles trumpeter Ted Schilling. Perhaps in an effort to discourage such indulgences the family sent Fred and "Lizz" to Cambridge University—where they promptly organized another band. It recorded for Brunswick as Fred Elizalde's "Varsity Band" and for His Master's Voice as Elizalde's "Cambridge Undergraduates." By this time he'd become an excellent jazz pianist and arranger and made a formidable reputation among London musicians. He later abandoned the dance band business entirely and turned to "serious" composing.

The California Ramblers, meanwhile, carried on much as before. In young Spencer Clark they'd found a talented replacement for Rollini, and Pete Pumiglio had taken over Davis's hot alto book. Finding a trumpeter to replace Quealey proved rather more difficult; Bill Moore filled in temporarily, as did Mickey Bloom and a handful of others before the arrival of Fred Van Eps Jr., brother of guitarist George, saxophonist John, and pianist Bobby.

There were still good records: "The Pay Off," for example, has crisp work by Van Eps and Pumiglio (possibly a more fully realized improviser than Davis) and some vigorous bass sax from Clark. But it was getting harder to keep a stable personnel. On July 20 Clark, too, left for Europe, sailing on the Île de France with a band led by banjoist George Carhart. Among its other members were saxophonists Bud Freeman and Babe Russin and the brilliant, eccentric trumpeter Jack Purvis (of whom more later).

Clark's departure left the Ramblers without a bass saxophonist and at the mercy of an increasing number of personnel substitutions. Some alumni, trumpeters Frank Cush and Roy Johnston and both Dorsey brothers among them, plugged the holes briefly. Phil Napoleon and Miff Mole joined for record dates, as did Glenn Miller and Whiteman veteran Tommy Gott. Stan King came back. But the Ramblers were floundering, and their 1928 records show it.

Rollini and friends, meanwhile, became instant stars of the band at the Savoy. "We were just amazed at how extraordinary a musician Adrian was," said London violinist George Hurley. "We all had a rather high regard for ourselves—I mean, this was a hand-picked band and all; but hearing Rollini every night—why, it was like going to school again. The Americans were virtually being teachers without knowing it. They were enjoying themselves, and we were learning, because this was entirely new."[27]

British journalist Stanley Nelson, a regular visitor to the Savoy at that point, recalled that the Elizalde band "thrilled me by its ensemble, there being a fine homogeneity about it—mainly because of Rollini's bass sax . . . I can remember the great punch and drive which characterized [their] playing."[28]

Elizalde, characteristically, had firm ideas about the directions in which hot music should go. In an article titled "Jazz—What of the Future?" which appeared under his byline in 1929, he postulated a music that made free use of various time signatures, abandoned the traditional verse-chorus structure of pop songs, and even dismissed the idea of melody as "an entirely secondary consideration."[29]

Sometimes his band's performances of its more "modernistic" arrangements at the Savoy appeared to reflect such ideas. According to Nelson, customers were quick to protest that they couldn't hear the melody; others complained of having to stand around during long, out-of-tempo introductions. Some took particular— and loudly expressed—umbrage at the leader's refusal to accede to their requests for waltzes and other old favorites.

The management, conscious of its priorities, leaned on Elizalde a bit, and he quickly compromised, adding violins (including Hurley) and hiring a handsome singer-guitarist, just in from the Continent, named Al Bowlly. For the hot music fans he'd bring Rollini, Davis, and Quealey out front now and then to serve up specialties. All in all, it seems to have worked: in mid-1928, while the band was fulfilling a six-week engagement in Paris, the Savoy renewed Elizalde's contract.

Suddenly New York and Prohibition seemed very far off. As Hurley and others remembered it, there was a lot of drinking; Rollini seemed particularly good at holding his liquor while still functioning at peak efficiency, but Davis and Quealey were more erratic. Elizalde, for his part, chose simply to overlook the occasional lapses of decorum and punctuality for the sake of having three outstanding guests in his band.

"The Americans 'ran' the band, of course," Nelson wrote. "Fred was the leader, but it was never in his nature to be a dictator. And he was far too good a musician and easygoing in temperament to act in a manner comparable with the businessman-leaders who ran others' bands and who in the main were jealous of him." He'd sooner spend his mornings playing piano-violin duets with Hurley, early evenings entertaining friends, many of them royalty, in his Mayfair home, and nights after the job drinking and socializing with his bandsmen.[30]

Rollini hadn't been at the Savoy long when he received word that his father was ill with cancer and not expected to last much longer. He sailed for home, staying just long enough to get married (with the old man's deathbed blessing), attend the funeral, do a record date for OKeh with the Dorsey brothers, and head back for London.

Life at the Savoy was comfortable, well paid, musically satisfying. There seems no doubt of Elizalde's dedication to hot jazz, or of his creativity in dealing with it. The punch and drive to which Stanley Nelson refers all but saturate the band's records, even those on which the hot potential is kept relatively under wraps. The presence of the Americans energizes their very first records with the band: "Calling Me Home" and "Under the Moon," of January 15, 1928. But the easy highlight of that session is Bill Challis's arrangement of "Sugar," recorded by the Paul Whiteman Orchestra in New York a month later. A Goldkette holdover, it had been passed to the New Yorker band and brought across by Rollini.

Listeners used to the crisp precision of the Whiteman record will find this performance a surprise. Loose, almost casual, it rides along powerfully on Rollini's bass sax. Quealey delivers a Bix-like, if rather brittle, solo, and Bobby Davis veers as close to Trumbauer as might be expected, given both the arrangement and the effects of having sat next to Tram for a month the previous autumn.

Davis's work here, on the whole, is considerably freer and more intense than on his American records. His choruses on "Arkansas Blues" and "Tiger Rag" by the small hot combination are especially memorable, the latter evoking Jimmy Dorsey in its use of false fingerings and other Dorsey hallmarks. On "The Dark-town Strutters' Ball," he solos on clarinet in a hard-toned, almost Chicagoan, manner.

Overall, these small-band performances constitute a logical extension of the earlier Little Ramblers and Goofus Five efforts. Again, there's no mistaking Rollini as the driving force, his bass sax prominent, powerful, and assured. He contributes a surprisingly expressive "hot fountain pen" chorus to "Somebody Stole My Gal" and dominates the dreamy "Dixie," an original dedicated to his new wife and built on a series of diminished chords.

The larger band performances, though more formal, also have their attractive touches. On "How Long Has This Been Going On?" (not the Gershwin song), recorded after Rollini's return in April, the seventeen-year-old English cornetist Norman Payne delivers thirty-two muted bars which announce him as a fresh new voice in the Beiderbecke manner. Impressed, Rollini later asked Payne to return to the United States with him; though tempted, the cornetist remained in England. His sculpted, gently lyrical contributions to such recordings as "Blue, Turning Grey Over You," with the British composer-arranger Spike Hughes, and "Allah's Holiday," with Ray Noble (as the "Night Club Kings"), show what a loss to American jazz his decision was.

The Elizalde band is probably at its most representative on "Blue Baby," recorded in July. With "Tiny" Stock playing the bass lines on tuba, Rollini is free to roam the ensemble at will, opening out new depths of texture and density. The arrangement is presumably by the leader himself and bristles with whole-tone devices and extended chordal voicings. Quealey and Davis exchange eights, much in the manner of Bix and Tram on "Just an Hour of Love," and Rollini comes up slugging briefly toward the end.

The Savoy band was a hit, the idea of guest Americans turning into a craze. Violinist Reg Batten went to New York looking for musicians for the Savoy Orpheans, alternating with Elizalde at the hotel; he returned with three men, among them trumpeter Sylvester "Hooley" Ahola, who had played alongside Bix in Rollini's New Yorkers. Bert Ambrose, about to open at the May Fair Hotel, dispatched his Boston-born banjoist, Joe Brannelly, on a similar prospecting trip to the States.[31]

For Elizalde, the only thing better than four American stars was double that number. So it was that Rollini (with Lizz Elizalde in tow) turned up again in New York in February of 1929, did a record date for Bert Lown, and sailed for Southampton March 9 aboard the *Berengaria*, bringing with him three saxophonists: Fud Livingston, Max Farley, and seventeen-year-old kid brother Arthur Rollini. In his autobiographical *Thirty Years With the Big Bands*, the younger Rollini described how the orchestra split itself into two units, which alternated playing four P.M. Savoy tea dances. Adrian led one group, his bass sax set up in front, Bobby Davis the other.[32]

Like the Paul Whiteman orchestra, which it occasionally resembled, the Elizalde band was devoting more and more of its efforts to large, lavish "symphonic jazz" arrangements. A notable exception is its April 12, 1929 "Nobody's Sweetheart" by a ten-piece hot unit; based on a sketch they'd rehearsed on the ship, it consists of a tightly arranged opening chorus (the lead mostly in the tenor sax, voiced in the middle of the ensemble) and a succession of solos. While Quealey is ruminative, Fud charges through his half-chorus in a manner that recalls Al Philburn's claims for him as the uncredited author of the Chicago clarinet style. Davis is bright-toned and upbeat in the Dorsey manner; Art Rollini sounds like Fud on tenor, his own fleet, rhythmically agile approach yet to come. Not surprisingly, the elder Rollini dominates things with a sinewy, fully realized sixteen bars.

Sometime in the week of June 16, Quealey and Livingston disappeared. They'd been rehearsing for one of Elizalde's "symphonic jazz" presentations and afterwards had gone out drinking. Their pub crawl apparently became an epic bender, and they awoke—or so they swore ever after—aboard a New York–bound ocean liner.

The rest of the band soldiered on—until the October stock market crash froze Elizalde's assets. As usual, Rollini made the decision: "Pack up, kid," he told his brother, "we're going home." They sailed soon after on the giant German luxury liner *Leviathan*. Davis and Farley stayed a few more months, but by mid-1930 all Elizalde's peregrines had flown.

Rollini picked up plenty of work around New York; his reputation was intact, and the old magic was still there. So, too, was his old association with Ed Kirkeby. A Ramblers Inn advertisement published around 1930 shows the two as joint managers. A bit later the band moved to new quarters; now it was: "The California Ramblers, Under the Direction of Adrian Rollini, announce the gala opening of their new home, the CALIFORNIA RAMBLERS INN, On Pelham Parkway on the site of the old Castilian Royal."[33]

But times were changing: the landscape was full of bands with distinct and personal styles, steered by skilled and creative arrangers. Gene Gifford's scores for the Casa Loma Orchestra were pointing toward a new concept of ensemble writing; Benny Carter had emerged as a major creative force, writing for saxophones in a manner that was both novel and natural. Duke Ellington had turned his orchestra into a kind of laboratory for an arranging concept at once powerful and exotic. A band playing stocks, regardless how good, just couldn't compete.

Electric recording and amplification—and the example of Steve Brown, Wellman Braud, and others—had helped string bass supplant the tuba as most bands' rhythm foundation of choice; guitar, similarly, was steadily eclipsing the banjo. The bass sax, to appropriate the phrase of a much later day, stood on the threshold of a major identity crisis.

If it was not part of the rhythm section, where did it fit? Played strongly and surely, it could add breadth and depth to any saxophone section or full ensemble, as Rollini had demonstrated. But the way dance orchestra instrumentation was evolving, the baritone sax was a much more supple anchor, easier to master and blending more readily with the higher-voiced instruments.

Nor did bass sax quite belong in small jazz ensembles. If a saxophone was to be added to the standard trumpet-clarinet-trombone triumvirate, it was more likely to be a tenor. Chicagoan Bud Freeman, for one, had become a master of this style and already had disciples, "Babe" Russin among them. Eddie Miller, with Ben Pollack, was emerging as a major voice on the instrument. Art Rollini, too, quickly began evolving in that direction.

Another problem lay in the bass sax itself. Rollini apart, many otherwise capable men still found it awkward and hard to keep in tune. Former tuba player Min Leibrook, who used it with Whiteman, never transcended his instrument's tendency to sound like a dyspeptic bullfrog. A handful of Rollini admirers, Joe Rushton and Spencer Clark paramount among them, did well with it; but in general, by 1932 the bass sax had become a character actor in search of a role.

This was not lost on Rollini. Ever alert as both musician and businessman, he appears to have understood what was happening; as the 1930s got under way he drew on his mallet training and devoted increasing attention to the vibraharp, an instrument whose solo potential was yet to be exploited by improvising jazz-men.

The field was wide open. Red Norvo, also a former pianist, had used it sporadically but chosen to develop his unique skills on the xylophone and ma-rimba. Lionel Hampton, playing drums with Les Hite's Los Angeles–based band, had plunked out a few chords on a studio vibraharp at a 1930 Louis Armstrong record date; but it would be some years before he addressed the instrument seriously.

The vibes, as musicians called the instrument, had hitherto been used largely for effect: a pulsating chime, lingering beyond a final orchestral chord; a brief interlude between ensemble and vocal in some production number. But Rollini seems to have conceived of it from the start in solo terms, bringing to bear the formidable mallet technique that had impressed Spencer Clark back in Ramblers days.[34]

There was still plenty of bass sax work, including radio and record dates with Bert Lown, Freddie Rich, Richard Himber, and others. Rollini continued to play the instrument well into the '30s but incorporated the vibes more and more into every performance. His work on the Venuti Blue Five OKeh date of May 8, 1933, discussed elsewhere in this volume, is typical.

With the same speed and intelligence that had characterized his progress on the bass sax, he now worked out a solo style on vibes. How well he did it is obvious in his agile, swinging full-chorus solo on "Charlie's Home," recorded for Columbia June 12, 1933, under his own name: he solos again on "Happy as the Day Is Long" and uses the vibes to create a shimmering, crystalline tonal tapestry behind the introduction to "Blue Prelude."[35]

Quite a few Rollini records of the early '30s are signal events. His Decca date of October 23, 1934, for example, teamed him with Jack Teagarden, Benny Goodman, and others, with predictably happy results. Their version of Bix's "Dav-enport Blues," for example, adds an introduction and coda which immediately became standard features of all performances. "It Had To Be You," made the same day but first released many years later, presents a newcomer, Scottish-born Ella Logan, singing a vocal chorus with surprisingly Armstrong-like phrasing.

Never at a loss for enterprise, Rollini opened his own club, Adrian's Tap Room, in New York's Hotel President just above Times Square, in mid-1935. Various recordings by his sometimes racially mixed "Tap Room Gang" com-memorate the association: on the June 14, 1935, "Bouncin' in Rhythm," for example, he plays a light, almost delicate bass sax counterpoint to trumpeter Wingy Manone and clarinetist Joe Marsala. "Bugle Call Rag" and "Old Fashioned Love," of March 17, 1937, feature Rollini on both his instruments, as well as intense work by black trumpeter Jonah Jones, at that point the toast of 52nd Street.

Beginning in 1936, Rollini also began appearing with his trio, alongside guitarist Frank Victor and bassist Haig Stephens, broadcasting for NBC four times a week and recording regularly. For a pair of early 1938 sessions, he augmented that group with two new talents: teenage drum whiz Buddy Rich and Rhode Island–born cornetist Bobby Hackett. The results of the second session, particularly, are remarkable and enduring music, Hackett's soft-edged tone and Bix-like phrasing blending exquisitely with Rollini's vibes (see chapter 25).

Though he continued to work for many years thereafter, Rollini was clearly no longer a central figure. This is puzzling, in view of his pioneer work on vibes. He was the first to play jazz successfully on the instrument (using four mallets rather than the standard two, which predated the innovations of Gary Burton by three decades), the first to compose for it in the jazz idiom. Such published solo specialties as "Vibrollini," "Gliding Ghost," and "Preparation" sold widely and did much to popularize the vibraharp—all well before Hampton's leap into fame as a feature attraction with Benny Goodman.

But Rollini remained something of an insider, his reputation strongest among fellow-musicians. Under the headline PUBLIC DOESN'T APPRECIATE ROLLINI!! an article in a 1939 Down Beat lamented that "outside of musicians and a small gathering of hot jazz exponents, [he] isn't nearly as well known as he should be. Yet he has been banging around the country with [more of] the nation's best leaders and side men than your correspondent can recall."[36]

In the early 1950s, reportedly discouraged at the changes taking place in the music business, Rollini moved to Florida, where he ran a hotel, the Driftwood Lodge, at Tavernier, a few miles south of Key Largo. He died on May 15, 1956.

Though the official cause of death was listed as a combination of pneumonia and cirrhosis of the liver, complicated by a severe fracture of his right ankle, the exact circumstances remain surrounded in contradiction. There have been hints of foul play, of possible involvement with organized crime. One article appeared under the headline WAS ADRIAN ROLLINI MURDERED? In it, the diligent and thorough researcher Norman Gentieu examined newspaper accounts, individual testimony, and doctors' and coroners' reports, concluding that the answer was an emphatic no. But the late Bob Hilbert, no less even-handed, interpreted Gentieu's information differently, pointing to contradictions and inconsistencies in the various accounts.[37]

The full story may never be known. Overall, it is far more dismaying to note that Adrian Rollini was only six weeks shy of his fifty-second birthday when he died and had spent the last half-dozen years of his life in an obscurity ill-befitting a musician of his talents and accomplishments.

Ironically, his death preceded that of Frank Trumbauer by only a month. Both men, so gifted and once so prominent and influential, had seemed simply to melt away, their outlines, ever less distinct, gradually lost to view.

III

The Hot
Lineage
Chicago and Its Descendants

9

Revolutionaries from the Suburbs

Eddie Condon had it just about right. By the mid-'20s, he wrote, there was so much hot music in Chicago that a visitor to the corner of 35th and Calumet, on the South Side, "could hold an instrument in the middle of the street and the air would play it."[1]

That celebrated intersection was the site of the Sunset Café, where in early 1927 Louis Armstrong supplanted Carroll Dickerson as leader of the house band. But it was also something of a focal point for South Side black and white nightlife. Almost directly across 35th was the Plantation Café, where King Oliver led his Dixie Syncopators from 1925 to 1927 (and which, as Al Tierney's Grand Auto Inn, had featured white New Orleans cornetist Ray Lopez in 1916).

Above that, upstairs, was the Apex Club, formerly the Nest, where clarinetist Jimmie Noone and alto saxophonist Joe "Doc" Poston serenaded after-hours customers with New Orleans–style clarinet-and-alto-sax duets. Within a radius of only a few blocks, between 1924 and 1927, it was possible to hear brothers Johnny and "Baby" Dodds, Albert Wynn, Kid Ory, Omer Simeon, Natty Dominique, Albert Nicholas, Barney Bigard, and dozens of others.

"The New Orleans musicians had everything wrapped up" was the way trumpeter Adolphus "Doc" Cheatham remembered it. Cheatham, from Nashville, hadn't been in town long when he discovered that the Crescent City men were a tight and exclusive clique, and breaking in was going to take time and patience. Rather than hang around, he moved on; but while there he made the rounds, hearing everything he could, listening to Oliver ("He had a nice, quiet tone, and he knew what he was doing every minute"), Freddie Keppard ("very loud . . . reminded me of a military trumpeter playing jazz"), and a white favorite, Louis Panico ("what a wonderful trumpet player he was!").[2]

Musicians from other cities were arriving all the time, some just passing through, others to stay. Pittsburgh-born pianist Earl Hines, tired of touring vaudeville houses, was one of the few non-southerners who found immediate acceptance with the New Orleans clique. He was with Louis at the Sunset, then crossed 35th to work with Noone and Poston at the Apex.

When black bandleader-columnist Dave Peyton, writing that September (1923) in the Chicago Defender, proclaimed that there were ten thousand jazz bands in the United States, his clear implication was that a good many of them could be found right there in the lakeside city, particularly south of the Loop. By 1923 records and radio were also bringing the newly inflected dance music into more and more homes. Inevitably its energy, its unrestrained and rebellious spirit, caught the imaginations of the young.

The message landed with striking potency in middle-class homes; parents, brought up according to strict Victorian (or church-dictated) values, hated it. Educators (especially music teachers) and clergymen had little good to say about it, particularly in that it seemed one more factor aggravating the more-or-less chronic problem of school truancy. Much of it, moreover, still bore the tang of the forbidden, of smoke-filled ballrooms, of drugs, booze, and illicit sex—all the supposed, exotic mysteries popularly demonized by the last generation to come of age in a Victorian world.

Among youngsters drawn to the music were more than a few who decided early that just listening wasn't enough: they'd have to play it as well. "Their greedy ears," clarinetist Mezz Mezzrow has written,

> drank in the music like suction pumps. The sprawling outside world, they found, was raw and bubbling, crude, brutal, unscrubbed behind the ears but jim-jam-jumping with vital spirits; its collar might be grimy and tattered, but it was popping with life and lusty energy, ready for anything and everything, with a gusto you couldn't down. And jazz, the real jazz, was its theme song. These kids went for that unwashed, untidy world, and they made up their minds to learn its unwashed, untidy music.[3]

Even allowing for the excesses of Mezzrow's prose (or that of his "ghost," novelist Bernard Wolfe), it's obvious that many white Chicago teenagers were ready to burst the confines of their well-ordered lives, and that hot jazz and its ambiance seemed purpose-built to help them do it.

Their parents, more often than not, had come here as immigrants, some from other, often economically depressed, parts of the United States, many from even worse conditions abroad. Chicago was America, the dream of something, however small, for everyone. Just being here, in this sprawling, unruly, burgeoning, ever-surprising metropolis was cause for rejoicing, and they attempted to bring their kids up in a comfort and security they themselves, few of them, had ever enjoyed. But kids, as kids will, look for their own ways: often, eternally, they find their parents' ways overbearing, confining, stifling. In a word, not their own. And Chicago in the 1920s was no exception.

Even so, little of Mezzrow's febrile compulsiveness seems to have been in the air the day in late 1922 when a stack of Friars Society Orchestra Gennett records materialized beside the wind-up Victrola at the Spoon and Straw, an ice cream parlor in the well-manicured West Side suburb of Austin. Jimmy and Richard McPartland, stopping in for an after-school soda, found them first; soon they were joined by their pals Jim Lanigan, the brothers Lawrence and Arny Freeman, and shy, bespectacled Frank Teschemacher. All between fourteen and sixteen, they'd been drawn together by an enthusiasm for music, dance bands in particular.

Jimmy, curious, picked up the top record—in later years he would remember it as "Farewell Blues"—placed it carefully on the turntable, cranked up the machine, and dropped the heavy tone arm into place.

"Boy, when we heard that—I'll tell you we went out of our minds," he said. "Everybody flipped. It was wonderful. So we put the others on—'Tiger Rag,' 'Discontented,' 'Bugle Call' and such titles. We stayed there from about three in the afternoon until about eight at night, just listening to those records one after another, over and over again. Right then and there we decided we would get a band and try to play like these guys."[4]

A 1945 *Jazz* magazine article by Catherine (Mrs. Bud) Jacobson, based on an interview with Richard McPartland, gives a rather less romanticized account. In this version it was Freeman who came up with the first record. With his earnings as a part-time clerk at Sears Roebuck, he bought a copy of "Tiger Rag" and "Panama" and rushed over to the McPartland home to share his discovery.

Jim Lanigan was dating Ethel McPartland, the boys' sister, and was frequently there. The four of them, said Richard, had often spent time together "debating the relative merits of current dance bands such as Paul Biese, Isham Jones, Paul Whiteman and Ted Lewis. They were completely unimpressed by the popular [Original] Dixieland Jazz Band which was also in circulation."

But the Friars Society record stimulated their interest, prompting the McPartland brothers to risk their father's wrath and ask for instruments—and to try to persuade Lou Freeman, who made a rather less-than-handsome living as a garment-cutter, to invest in a C-melody saxophone for his son Lawrence, even then nicknamed "Bud."[5] This squares well with Bud Freeman's own account of going every Sunday as a fourteen-year-old to the Senate Theatre, a movie palace that featured a pit orchestra led by Paul Biese, who played a diamond-studded saxophone.

One way or another, and even allowing for a certain amount of embroidery, the excitement of discovery comes through. These Gennett records by an eight-piece white band, half the musicians from New Orleans and the other half from the Midwest, didn't sound like what was being dispensed as "hot" music by Whiteman, Jones, and the other dance bands. These were loose-limbed and buoyant, mixing flowing solos with tightly knit, propulsive ensembles. It sounded free, worldly, intensely personal; for a bunch of teenagers, huddled breathlessly around the Victrola, it was revelation and rebellion.

Most accounts of this transformation have suggested, or at least left the impression, that it happened in a vacuum; that this group of schoolboy chums made their discovery alone, amid unheeding parents and complacent, uncomprehending classmates. Nothing, said Teschemacher's Austin High classmate Bud Hunter, could have been farther from the truth. Quite a few musically inclined kids got hooked in the same way, at about the same time, he said, and by the same records.

In a 1943 magazine interview Hunter, himself an accomplished jazz tenor saxophonist, named Bud Prentiss and Stan Kassler (saxes), Bob Downey (piano), and drummer Lyle Kelly as part of another "Austin High Gang," a small band that played occasionally for socials at the school; they, too, he said, were aware of what was going on at the Friars' Inn and other off-limits places around town. They, too, were trying to "play hot."[6]

What distinguishes the McPartland-Teschemacher-Freeman circle is that they seem to have resolved together that they were going to be a band. Jimmy McPartland was a brash youngster who had spent his earliest years on the near West Side, in a far tougher neighborhood than Austin, and been dumped into an orphanage for a while in 1912–13 when his parents were temporarily divorced. Bud Freeman remembered the elder McPartland as "an alcoholic and a rough guy," and Jimmy grew up "fast and strong . . . he could have been a professional athlete." McPartland instead chose music, selecting the cornet, he said in later years, because it was the loudest and "that made me the natural leader."[7]

Richard, two years his senior, took up the banjo. Freeman, still in love with Paul Biese's shiny saxophone (and, presumably, with his image of himself, on-stage, playing it in the spotlight), was dispatched to McPartland père—a music teacher and leader of a small local concert band—for lessons.

Teschemacher, son of a railroad worker, seems to have been the quick one. One summer, while his family was vacationing at Paw Paw, near Lake Michigan, his pal Orville "Bud" Jacobson had come to visit, bringing an alto sax with him. "We spent hours fooling with it," he told Dave Dexter Jr., and within a short time Frank, age fifteen, had mastered the basics of fingering. "First thing we knew, Tesch was borrowing saxes right and left, and after that he bought his first horn." He was soon playing banjo, violin, and occasional saxophone alongside Bud Hunter in a little student band at Austin High.[8]

Not surprisingly, youngsters who shared the passion quickly found one another. Over in nearby suburban Lakeview, sixteen-year-old Joseph Michael O'Sullivan practiced such hits of the day as "Margie" and "San" on the parlor piano when his father, an alderman, was out of the house. He'd taken lessons at Chicago Conservatory but dismayed his parents by turning his newly acquired skills to playing in dance halls, amusement park pavilions, and speakeasies. He soon became friends with a young drummer named George Wettling, who had moved to Chicago from Topeka, Kansas, and was at Calumet High. At Lakeview, a year or two behind O'Sullivan, were pianist Oro "Tut" Soper, alto saxophonist Bill Dohler, and drummer "Dash" Burkis, all eager and ready. At Crane High, Bud Jacobson had his own circle, which at one time included Dave North, shortly to become pianist in the McPartland-Teschemacher-Freeman crowd.

Regardless of neighborhood or economic circumstances, the process of discovery was much the same everywhere: Benny Goodman, growing up poor in the Near West Side Jewish ghetto, remembered his elder brother Louis bringing home a wind-up Victrola, and with it at least a few jazz records, presumably by such groups as the Original Dixieland Jazz Band and Original Memphis Five.

Jimmy McPartland, playing an afternoon social in the Austin High gym, heard somebody mention "a kid who could play drums. He was from Oak Park High School, which was just the next suburb, and the kid's name was Davey Tough. He got some drums from somewhere and came in and man, that was it! He was just great."⁹

William Howland Kenney, writing of Chicago jazz, attributes this outburst of enthusiasm to both the "excitement of urban life" in Thompson-era Chicago and a "sense of defying the dull and predicable lives prepared for them by parents and school."¹⁰

Well, yes: but when have such impulses not animated adolescence? This ferment also belongs to something larger: to the wave of social change that swept the United States in the years immediately following World War I. Though not always expressed as resentment or open revolt, it was in the air, the very atmosphere breathed every day by American youngsters growing up in the 1920s. Victorian morality was under siege, and with it the authority it had carried until and through the Great War.

Since the unexpected, and unprecedented, New York success of the Original Dixieland Jazz Band in 1917, the musical counterpoint to all this had been the raucous, seemingly anarchic, even subversive, sound of hot music. All the same, if played by black or white bands, or whether it was "genuine" improvisation or simply peppy renderings of pop songs.

Bassist Milt Hinton has pointed out that alongside the growing numbers of young whites taking up hot playing there were substantial numbers of young blacks as well, and for some of the same reasons. In many such cases, the confining force in the home was less a matter of Victorian mores than the all-controlling—and no less pervasive—influence of religion. In each case the effect of liberation was much the same.

Critic-essayist John McDonough observes that the superheated appeal of the first Original Dixieland Jazz Band records fostered "a sense in the culture that art and morality had certain and subversive linkages. As an aspect of a larger canvas of modernism, jazz was part of that growing sense of early postwar tension between small town traditional values in America and urban cosmopolitan sophistication."¹¹

Also, it is not without significance that the first records to catch the attention of this group of young whites were not by black bands but by a white ensemble. The growing divide separating them and their passions from the world of their parents was not specifically racial but primarily sociological and generational. At the outset, the idea of finding a *white* band playing such music, and available through nothing more dangerous than a visit to the Loop, was irresistible. That many of the musicians they soon discovered and came to admire were black, and could only be found on the South Side, added special tang to fruit already forbidden.

Overall, it hardly strains credibility to imagine that, for the parental generation, the gulf separating the Friars' Inn from the Lincoln Gardens was nowhere near so great as that separating the well-ordered streets of Austin, Oak Park, or Lakeview from the deeply subversive, sin-drenched city life represented by all such "jazzy" music.

In early September of 1922, only days after the Friars Society Orchestra made its first records for Gennett, a young Iowa cornetist named Leon Beiderbecke came through Chicago en route to a ballroom job in Syracuse, New York. Known from childhood as Bix, he'd been captivated by the Original Dixieland Jazz Band and taught himself to play the instrument by slowing down the turntable and imitating Nick LaRocca's ensemble leads. At the piano he often seemed lost in a world of his own, experimenting for hours at a time.

He'd been such a problem at home in Davenport that his parents had sent him to Lake Forest Academy, only an easy train ride from the downtown Chicago Loop. Though still unformed, he'd managed to impress many local musicians with a kind of lyrical thoughtfulness. He was clearly something special in the making.

With time to kill before their train left for Syracuse, Beiderbecke and his bandmates headed for the College Inn, in the Sherman Hotel, to hear Louis Panico with Isham Jones's Orchestra. Eddie Condon, the sixteen-year-old banjoist with the Syracuse-bound group, was dubious: Beiderbecke didn't look terribly impressive, he thought, in a beat-up overcoat and a rumpled, equally disreputable-looking cap. How would they ever get beyond the front door?

There, and later at the Friars' Inn, the reaction was "as if free drinks had been announced . . . The players fell all over themselves greeting Beiderbecke. Have I got to buy a cap to make good, I thought?"[12]

Bix seemed to have that effect on people. Young Jess Stacy, playing piano with trumpeter Tony Catalano's band on the Streckfus riverboat *Capitol*, was, as he put it, "just blown away. [Bix] came on board and he sat in, playing piano," Stacy said. "The chords he hit, the way he got this nice little rhythm thing going—I said to myself, 'God, I'd like to be able to play like that.'"

Growing up in Cape Girardeau, Missouri, Stacy had first fallen for music after hearing Fate Marable's Orchestra on the *Capitol*, with Louis Armstrong on second cornet and Baby Dodds on drums, in 1921. "I remember one tune they played even now," he said. "It was 'Whispering,' the thing Paul Whiteman had recorded. They just played the hell out of it. That was the big thrill for me—at least until I met Bix."[13]

When Jess got to Chicago, at the end of 1924, eighteen-year-old Art Hodes was already there. Born in Russia, he'd come to Chicago as a boy, learned the piano, and quickly been assimilated into his new environment, working with bands around town. Among his early pals was a character whose background was worlds apart from his, New Orleans–born trumpeter Joe "Wingy" Manone. Though no older than the rest of them, he'd been around: he knew Oliver, Johnny Dodds, and other hometown musicians and could expect a warm welcome anytime he went to hear Armstrong. "Wingy had such personality, could be so funny, and above all could really play then," said Hodes. "He had a beat you couldn't get away from."

For all of them it was a process of total immersion, slow and sometimes arduous. "Our mistress was music," said Hodes. "We worshipped her as a god. In the morning, when we'd start in on the vic[trola] till late at night when we were exhausted and had to sleep, we had but one desire—to play, to play better this minute than we had the last, to hear something played that would knock us out."[14]

Jimmy McPartland, too, told of group sessions around the Victrola, learning note by painstaking note. "Just starting, as most of us were, we'd make so many mistakes that it was horrible on people's ears," he said. "We had to move around because neighbors couldn't stand it too long."[15]

Frank Teschemacher's mother, quoted in 1939, confirmed that part of the recollection—but added that she, in common with most of the other parents, took it lightly. "My, what a racket those boys made," she said. "I thought it was terrible. But my husband and I never scolded them. We figured they were just having a lot of fun and that nothing would come of it."[16]

Each learned at his own pace, with Freeman (whose chief ambition in those days was to be an "eccentric" dancer in the style of Joe Frisco) definitely bringing up the rear. "It was murder those first weeks," said McPartland. "Tesch used to get disgusted with him and say, 'Let's throw that bum out.' But I said, 'No no no don't. He's coming on, he's playing' . . . He began by just playing rhythm, getting on one note and . . . swinging it, just that one note. He didn't change the harmony or anything, and we used to get so mad at him, you know. We'd yell at him: 'Change the note!' "[17]

The "Austin Blue Friars," as they styled themselves in homage to the band at the Friars' Inn, played together as often and wherever they could. They played tea dances and parties, socials at church and school; played for anyone who would hold still long enough to listen. Nights were for pilgrimages to the Friars' Inn (where most of them stood outside listening because they were too young to get in) or to rather less strict establishments on the black South Side. Everywhere they went, they found other young whites from other neighborhoods, different parts of town, all drawn by hot music.

Their studies suffered, and most dropped out well before finishing high school; even bookish Frank Teschemacher, who stuck out nine semesters at Austin, racked up an academically poor record and never graduated. But in matters of evening attendance they were honor students. At one South Side venue, Bud Freeman said, "there was a big fat doorman, a black doorman. The guy must have weighed 400 pounds. And we'd all come up, all well-dressed from high school. And he'd say—and he was so nice—he'd say: 'I see you [white boys] are all out here to get your music lessons tonight.' ''[18]

Whether Freeman's account refers to the Lincoln Gardens' towering bouncer "King" Jones or (as Chicago historian Dempsey Travis suggests) Bill Summers, flamboyant guardian of the portals at the Sunset, is hardly important. Freeman and his pals were there to soak up every note, every phrase.

When Elmer Schoebel, pianist at the Friars' Inn, moved to the expanded, remodeled Midway Gardens with a new band, the youngsters came in force to check them out. If someone said there was a good band at a Chinese restaurant somewhere, a delegation would descend on it to sample both the chop suey and the music; black or white, it made no difference. All it took was a report from someone, anyone, that a place had a good quartet, or that some dance band was featuring a hot soloist: whether it was Erskine Tate at the Vendome Theatre, or Doc Cooke's large orchestra at Paddy Harmon's Dreamland Ballroom, at Paulina and Van Buren, with Freddie Keppard on cornet and Jimmie Noone providing the tracery on clarinet, the kids knew about the place and, where possible, would turn up in person.[19]

Muggsy Spanier, though their exact contemporary, was professionally far ahead of them. He'd sat in on cornet with Schoebel and Brunies at the Blatz Palm Garden in 1921, worked at White City with Sig Meyers the following year—and had become a familiar face ringside at the Lincoln Gardens, listening hard to "Popeye" Oliver's no-frills lead. The King, he said, even let him sit in on "Dippermouth Blues," and Kid Muggsy returned the favor by playing the master's famous three-chorus solo "exactly like Joe. If you don't play the 'Dippermouth' like Joe," he told Ralph J. Gleason in 1958, "it's not the 'Dippermouth.' ''[20]

Spanier also told of buying records in a little bookshop at 31st and Calumet, down the street from the Sunset, the Apex, and the rest; his two favorites, he said, were the Friars' group ("now that was a band!") and the Creole Jazz Band. Muggsy's solo style abounded ever after with pet phrases learned from both.

By early 1924 the word was out about "that wild West Side mob" and their passion for hot music. Promoter "Husk" O'Hare got them a job playing as the "Red Dragons" on radio station WHT (so labeled, it's said, for the initials of William Hale "Big Bill" Thompson), later renamed WBBM. They worked, as had Bix, for Bill Grimm on the Lake Michigan excursion boats; pianist Charles "Murph" Podalsky found them jobs. They played for Palmer Cady at the Cascades Ballroom, as had George Brunies and Leon Roppolo before the Friars' Inn came along.

Working at a Lost Lake, Indiana, resort in the summer of '24, Tesch started noodling one day on Bud Freeman's brand-new clarinet. Bud, just learning, recalled his difficulties in getting it back—and how short a time Teschemacher took to outdistance him in proficiency.

Benny Goodman, younger than most of them by several years, sat in with them and displayed an already formidable technique, though Freeman said later that young Benny "wasn't much of a melody player—he was what we called a noodler." On such occasions, with another clarinetist sitting in, Teschemacher would quietly retreat to violin or saxophone.[21]

Goodman had come out of the Jane Addams Hull House band, one of three such organizations run by charities or newspapers as antidotes to truancy and street crime in poor Chicago neighborhoods. Louis Panico and fellow-trumpeter Charlie "Nosey" Altiere were alumni of the *Chicago Daily News* Boys Band; on the black South Side, the *Chicago Defender* band proved an incubator for Lionel Hampton, bassists Hayes Alvis and Quinn Wilson, and other black jazzmen.

They played at picnics, parades, football and baseball postgame parties, and even occasional socials and dances. In *The Kingdom of Swing*, Goodman recalled the competition between the Hull House and *Daily News* groups, a rivalry that sometimes took on extramusical dimensions. "The idea was to play louder than any of the other bands, and drown them out," he wrote. "If we couldn't outplay them, we'd get into a scrap and bang up their instruments. Even if we didn't play the best, we had the smartest uniforms—red with blue trimmings, with long pants and regular military caps."[22]

By mid-1924, the world in which these young musicians lived was changing fast. Paul Whiteman's February 12 Aeolian Hall concert in New York, featuring everything from a parody of the Original Dixieland Jazz Band to George Gershwin's *Rhapsody in Blue*, had widened public awareness of "jazz." The young Washington, D.C., pianist Edward Kennedy Ellington, "Duke" for short, had taken over a little-known band called the Washingtonians and had just begun working with lyricist Jo Trent on music to be used in a new edition of the popular *Chocolate Kiddies* revue.

On Friday, September 12, the Wolverine Orchestra of Chicago, so-called, with Bix Beiderbecke on cornet, opened at the Cinderella Ballroom, at 48th and Broadway in New York City. They were a septet, drawn largely from among the young midwesterners who had hung around the Friars' Inn, and had begun recording for Gennett that February. The records had made the twenty-one-year-old cornetist something of a celebrity among the new generation of white musicians all over the country.

"He became like a god to us," a saxophonist in far-off Boston recalled. "When those first records—the Wolverines—came out, we listened to him with our mouths open. He sounded like everything we'd always wanted to sound like. He had tone, taste, a nice, easy way of playing right on the beat: you just couldn't get enough of it." The Wolverines influence saturates "Tell Me Dreamy Eyes," done for Gennett in late 1924 by the Boston band of saxophonist Perley Breed, featuring Brad Gowans—later to be known as a valve trombonist—on clarinet.[23]

Though their admiration for the Friars' Inn musicians, as for Oliver, Dodds, Noone, and Armstrong above all, was boundless, the young Chicago musicians found in Beiderbecke something different, and somehow more immediate. His intensity and thoughtfulness, the beauty of what he played—the fact that he was like *them* (white, middle-western, and middle-class) yet unlike them, inhabiting some private inner universe—made him a combination mentor and kindred spirit, embodiment of what each of them would have liked to be. "I think Bix was the perfect player," said Bud Freeman, "not only a master of his instrument but an artist who loved the theatre, loved to read, who loved the aesthetic life."[24]

Not long into the Cinderella engagement, Beiderbecke accepted an offer to join Jean Goldkette's Orchestra in Detroit, and the Wolverines went looking for a replacement. They auditioned New Orleans trumpeter Sharkey Bonano, who for reasons never clearly explained didn't work out. Nor did Fred Rollison, an Indiana musician admired for his work with Curtis Hitch's Happy Harmonists. Still looking, pianist-business manager Dick Voynow sent a telegram to seventeen-year-old Jimmy McPartland.

CAN YOU REPLACE BIX BEIDERBECKE WITH THE WOLVERINES? $87.50 A WEEK. WIRE YES OR NO. ANSWER IMMEDIATELY. Jimmy went. He met Bix, spent time with him, did the audition—and got the job. After finishing out their Cinderella contract they hit the road for Florida, aglow with the promise of lucrative work among the winter resorts.

McPartland's lone recording with them, made December 5, shows him coping gamely with what is, without Bix, a pretty turgid bunch. From the opening bars of "When My Sugar Walks Down the Street," the rhythm section plods along in leaden lockstep, and the two reeds, tenor saxophonist George Johnson and clarinetist Jimmy Hartwell, seem unable to stay out of each other's way.

They modulate from G into the far less common key of D-concert for McPartland's solo. Hartwell was supposed to play it, said Jimmy, but "couldn't find the notes in that key, so he said, 'You take it, kid.' And I was stuck with it—in my key of E. In those days, you played in C, F, G, a few of the flat keys. But what the hell: I took the solo, did a good job. They were happy."[25]

Things in Florida fizzled, and before long the teenage cornetist was on his way back north. But the Wolverines were too well known to simply vanish; best to keep things going, he and Voynow agreed, even with other players. As George Johnson told it, they struggled along through the spring, mostly in Indiana, but after that the trail becomes unclear. Reminiscing in 1938, the saxophonist mentioned jobs at the Valentino Inn and other Chicago spots during the summer. At one point, he said, drummer Ralph Snyder (brother of the NORK's Frank) worked with them, as did clarinetist Jimmy Lord. They soldiered on into September, with only himself and Voynow left of the original personnel, he said. Then they broke up.[26]

But neither Johnson nor Voynow was among the "Wolverines" who played the opening of the 1925 summer season at Riverview Park, in Des Moines. "The ballroom has been enlarged and beautified," an undated newspaper clipping, found among Jimmy McPartland's papers, proclaims. "It will be opened with one of the best dance orchestras in the country. This is 'Husk' O'Hare's famous Wolverines, direct from the Midway Gardens, Chicago, where they have played a long engagement."

The item gives no personnel, save for a small headshot of young, dapper Dave Tough. But a group photo, apparently taken onstage at Riverview, shows a youthful-looking Jimmy McPartland, flanked by a solemn-looking Tesch and Freeman (the latter with a full head of hair) on one side, Dick McPartland and trombonist Floyd O'Brien on the other, with Tough, bassist Jim Lanigan, and pianist Dave North brooding in the background.*

Soon, however, this episode was over, and the young musicians found themselves face to face with some music business realities. As a dance band sideman you could take a hot chorus now and then, and jam after hours in any number of places. But when it came to playing pure hot music for the public, or putting it on records, the gates were as good as locked.

It must be repeated, and stressed, that the very term "Jazz Age" does not necessarily refer to improvised hot music. Young people—they were not yet a discrete sociological group identifiable as "teenagers"—might prefer the hot instrumental specialties, but they did not pay the rent and maintenance bills at ballrooms, hotels, and restaurants. Dance orchestras, large and small, had to play, in Baby Dodds's exquisite phrase, "for the comfort of the people." That meant, for the most part, music that would appeal to the adults, those who had come of age before the postwar social rebellion began; those to whom music for dancing meant waltzes before it meant the Charleston, and for whom a bit of exotica like the tango or rumba might be far more stimulating than a two-step. Things might be a little different on the South Side, but certainly not as different as has been imagined; if the testimonies of Dodds and many other black musicians are to be believed—and there is no reason for not believing them—things were pretty much the same everywhere, even in dancing Chicago.

"Chicago was really kind of a corny town," said Jess Stacy. "[Customers] went for people like Ace Brigode, Wayne King, Art Kassel. There was really no audience for what we were doing."[27]

They had a friend in Kassel. He'd come up through the dance bands playing alto and clarinet and had been in Elmer Schoebel's first Midway Gardens band, taking over leadership when the pianist went to New York with Isham Jones. He'd written "Sobbin' Blues," recorded by the New Orleans Rhythm Kings and, a bit later, King Oliver, as well as the Midway band. Goodman, Spanier, Stacy, and others worked for him at the Gardens; and when, in early 1926, he took a band into Detroit's Graystone Ballroom, his sidemen included Freeman, McPartland, Jacobson, and Tough. They appeared opposite Fletcher Henderson's Orchestra, affording Freeman his first chance to hear the impressive Coleman Hawkins. He was later at pains to make clear that, while he admired Henderson's tenor sax star, he did not find Hawkins's surging, powerful approach to the saxophone something he chose to emulate.

Kassel, all agreed, was a good leader and a fair-minded man; but, McPartland added, he and his coterie of young jazzmen represented two very different points of view where professionalism was concerned. "We played more or less what

---

*One musician who heard them that summer was eighteen-year-old Rod Cless, who had just moved to Des Moines and was trying to decide whether to risk a career as a clarinet and saxophone player. The music helped convince him: by 1928 he was in Chicago, playing alongside Bud and Tesch. Shortly thereafter he married Freeman's sister.

we wanted to play," the cornetist said, "and Art would stand there and make a face, as if to say, 'What can I do with these guys?' "28

The "wild West Side mob," meanwhile, was expanding. Eddie Condon, the fast-talking Indiana banjo player who had played Syracuse, New York, with Bix in 1922, had moved to Chicago Heights. In every way, said Bud Freeman's younger brother Arny, he cut quite a figure.

> The first time I saw him I was 13 or 14 years old, and, although he was no more than 4 or 5 years older, he appeared to me to be a glittering, sophisticated man of the world. He had straw-colored hair, slicked down with Stacomb, and parted in the middle. He wore a "Norfolk" [jacket] suit, with four buttons and a half-belt, knickers and very expensive shoes, and the inevitable (I learned later) bow tie. He was the sharpest thing I had ever seen, outside of John Held's drawings in *College Humor*. He talked out of the side of his mouth in a voice that had the quality of a side-show barker, and he was very witty. He played the banjo, an instrument to which his personality and appearance were so ideally suited one won-dered which came first—Eddie or the banjo. Both were brash, brassy and clamorous.29

A similar, if more raffish, brand of worldliness also guaranteed instant entree for Milton "Mezz" Mezzrow (né Mesirow). Born in 1899, he was six years older than Condon and considerably more streetwise; he'd been to reform school, where he'd met and become tight with trumpeter "Murphy" Steinberg. He knew bookers, bootleggers, and other shady characters, including suppliers of "mug-gles" or "gage," slang of the day for marijuana.

Like Condon, he seemed to be on a first-name basis with everyone who mattered in the little world of hot music. He'd worked with Bix, hung out with Armstrong, knew his way around the South Side. He played some clarinet and saxophone. In all, he was a racy, colorful guy, given to affecting southern black speech patterns, mannerisms, and musical tastes.

He also held strong opinions about music. For him, "authentic" jazz was black, and anything white musicians did had to be ersatz, a pale (in both senses of the word) simulacrum. Said Jimmy McPartland: "We didn't take Mezz too seriously that way. We just let him talk. He was good company, knew everybody. Played a little. So it was okay."30

Opinions or not, Mezzrow's company had a salutary effect on these young musicians. "Mezz never spent enough time on his instrument to make the splash that he could have," said Freeman, ". . . but he understood what we were doing and what we wanted and he gave us more inspiration and influenced us more than it seemed any single man could do . . . It's funny how much his encour-agement and interest did to give us confidence in ourselves and our style."31

Some of Mezz's descriptions of events and people in *Really the Blues* are vivid in their evocation of time and place. Dave Tough, for example, was a little bit of a guy, no chubbier than a dime and as lean as hard times, with a mop of dark hair, high cheekbones, and a nose ground fine as a razor blade, and he popped with spirit until he couldn't sit still. It always hit me to see that keyed-up peanut crawl behind the drums, looking like a mouse huddled behind an elephant, and cut loose . . . the beat really moved him, and he jumped from head to toe, then back again.[32]

Art Kassel moved on to a successful dance band career, and tenor saxophonist Floyd Town took over the Midway band, hiring Tesch, Muggsy Spanier, and several of the others. The piano chair was up for grabs, and Muggsy quickly alerted Jess Stacy.

"It was winter," said Jess, "and I had no overcoat. So I got on the El wearing just my tux, and walked the rest of the way to the Midway. It must have been 26 degrees. I felt near to freezing to death." When he arrived, the band was playing "Poor Little Rich Girl." Stacy didn't mind, and warmed his hands playing the Noël Coward hit. Town hired him on the spot. George Wettling took over on drums soon after, and Floyd O'Brien came in on trombone.

"We had a good band," said Stacy. "I was with them for eighteen months, and always enjoyed it." He, Spanier, Tesch, and Wettling were also regular after-hours visitors at the Sunset, where Louis Armstrong and Earl Hines were appearing with Carroll Dickerson. But Stacy rejected any suggestion that he built his own style by copying Hines, the Pittsburgh-born master.

"Sure, I'd listen to him," he said. "But to tell the truth I was more interested in playing myself." He elaborated on the point with his biographer, Keith Keller. "My mind," he said, "would be on cajoling [Hines] into the kitchen or some back room to have a drink or a rest so that I could get to play with Armstrong."[33]

Mid-1926 found Tesch, Spanier, Stacy, and Wettling at the Midway, McPartland, Jacobson, Freeman, and Tough with Art Kassel. Joe Sullivan (the O' had been dropped when he got his local 10 musicians' union card) was jobbing around town with Sig Meyers, Louis Panico, and others. Eddie Condon fell into a long stand at the Vanity Fair Café with pianist Jack Gardner and bassist Thelma Coombs, shortly to become the widely respected leader Thelma Terry; often Gene Krupa, who had by then made up his mind not to complete his studies for the priesthood, was the drummer. On days off a bunch of them would get together, round up Mezzrow (who owned the only car), and drive seventy-five miles to Hudson Lake, Indiana, where Bix, Frank Trumbauer, and clarinetist Pee Wee Russell were with a summer-contract Jean Goldkette unit.

Good times—but as yet no records to show for it. Between mid-1925 and early autumn of 1927, in fact, Chicago white musicians (as distinct from those from New Orleans who happened to be in Chicago) seem to have recorded little by way of hot music.*

*Among the few exceptions are records made for Autograph and OKeh by Merritt Brunies's Friars' Inn Orchestra, with Volly De Faut on clarinet. Merritt, on trumpet, and brother Harry, on trombone, acquit themselves well, but it's De Faut who commands attention. His obbligato on an unissued "Up

For Chicago-based black jazzmen, meanwhile, 1926 was a landmark year. For the first time they broke through the resistance of white musicians' union local 10 (and its president, James Caesar Petrillo) and began working downtown, in the cabarets and hotels of the Loop. Louis Armstrong even played briefly at that all-white *sanctum sanctorum*, the Blackhawk Restaurant.[34]

Nor was that all: 1926 was also the first golden age of black hot jazz on records. Armstrong recorded the greatest of his Hot Five OKehs, including "Heebie Jeebies," "Cornet Chop Suey," "King of the Zulus," and "Irish Black Bottom"; Jelly Roll Morton's Red Hot Peppers bequeathed "Black Bottom Stomp," "Sidewalk Blues," "Doctor Jazz," "Grandpa's Spells," and others to posterity; Johnny Dodds made his admired New Orleans Bootblacks and Wanderers records; King Joe Oliver, leading his expanded, revamped Dixie Syncopators, did "Deep Henderson," "Snag It," and a magnificent "Someday Sweetheart"; Freddie Keppard belted out "Stock Yards Strut" and "Salty Dog" for Paramount. Even such relatively minor efforts as "That Creole Band" by Albert Wynn's Gut Bucket Five (featuring the excellent Dolly Jones on cornet) and "Plantation Joys" by Luis Russell's Heebie Jeebie Stompers, both on OKeh, all but leap off the grooves with energy and powerful, on-the-beat rhythm.

So compelling were the results that musicians everywhere began talking about a "Chicago sound" and "Chicago rhythm" as identifiable qualities. In its issue of November 1927, the British magazine *Rhythm* offered an explanation of "the Chicago beat:"

> It is new and yet it is old. It consists of four beats in the bar on the bass drum applied to a hot, but *pp* solo on, say for example, the baritone saxophone. If you get your pianist and banjoist to do it with you in conjunction with the Sousa, it's very effective indeed. Try dropping the snares and playing the steady four in a bar on the side drum also. It forms a good solid foundation for a hot solo and you'll like it.[37]

Four equally demarcated, steady beats to a bar—and this nearly a decade before the Count Basie Orchestra's much-celebrated arrival in New York! This rhythmic idea, just as enthusiastically embraced by the young whites, is one of many amply documented instances of an alleged "innovation" which was actually more or less common practice long before its reported "discovery." It also helps expose decades of argumentation among fans about distinctions between "two-beat" and "four-beat" rhythm as little more than ill-informed nonsense.

In New York, as 1927 got under way, Bix Beiderbecke was making hot records (and occasionally getting label billing) for OKeh with Frank Trumbauer, Don Murray, and other Goldkette men; Red Nichols, Miff Mole, and their circle were all but living in recording studios, sometimes doing three dates a day for three

Jumped the Devil" (November 14, 1925) and his solo on the issued version of the following March 2, look back at the graceful New Orleans conception of Roppolo and forward to the hard attack and slightly brittle tone shortly to become identified with Teschemacher and his admirers.

different labels; OKeh had begun to record the hot chamber music of Joe Venuti and Eddie Lang; records by various California Ramblers units, usually featuring Adrian Rollini's supple bass sax, were impressing both white and black colleagues.

But in Chicago, all the brave young men were still waiting their turn. All the listening, all the rehearsals and little jobs, had helped them find their own way of playing together and had cemented friendships between them—friendships based equally on shared interests and a sense of fighting the tide.

Though the case has often been overstated, there is no doubt that these young musicians and their many friends around town "clung to their music with a seriousness bordering on fanaticism," as one account put it. The dance bands in which they often worked didn't go out of their way to nurture or promote hot music. Working for Joe Kayser, Ted Fio Rito, Sol Wagner, Del Lampe, and others, you might get a shot at a hot chorus now and then, but most of the time you were producing, in one leader's words, "perfect sustained tones."[36]

Al Quodbach, at the Gingham (68th and Cottage Grove), had heard, liked, and hired a syrupy band from London, Ontario, led by genial Guy Lombardo; before long the band—and the place, upgraded and renamed the Granada—were the talk of dancing Chicago. Saxophonist Wayne King, who while a sideman with Del Lampe had taken some clarinet lessons from Jimmie Noone, opened at the Karzas brothers' top-of-the-line Trianon ballroom playing waltzes. Even Art Kassel, so receptive to the efforts of the young rebels, took the field with a conventional band, playing long stands at the Trianon and its new North Side twin, the Aragon.

Facts of life: the way record companies (and to a major extent dancers) saw it, if you wanted musicians who could really heat things up you looked south of the Loop. The market (and the clientele in many South Side dance halls) was predominantly white, and its appetite for hot instrumental music definitely finite. Why should a record company be interested in white musicians—particularly young, untried ones—playing hot, when so many expert South Side men were readily available?

All the same, a breakthrough finally happened, and largely thanks to Dick Voynow. After the Wolverines fell apart, the pianist had gone to work for Brunswick, scouting talent and producing records. One of his first projects was an "Original Wolverines" date featuring Jimmy McPartland and a few other youngsters around town, including seventeen-year-old Maurie Bercov on clarinet. Fresh out of Lindbloom High School, he'd heard Johnny Dodds and the rest on the South Side but worshiped Teschemacher and had subbed for him at the Midway, emulating his tone, attack, off-center figures. It's a small irony that, thanks to Voynow, he wound up recording two months before his idol.

Only two of the four titles done at the Columbus Day 1927 session were issued at the time; heard now, they sound like dress rehearsals for what is shortly to come. McPartland pitches his cornet solos on "The New Twister" and "Shimme-Sha Wabble" with confidence and great verve—though nervousness takes its toll on his coherence. But the little signatures are here, including the exclamatory "flare" (the horns hold a *sforzando* chord, and the drummer kicks the

197

rhythm ahead) and the "explosion" (two-bar, all-in eruptions between choruses), shortly to be identified with the white Chicago style. The rhythm section—Basil DuPre on bass and the Wolverines' original drummer, Vic Moore—lay down a "Chicago shuffle," identified by its characteristic even eighth notes; it's quite different from the dotted-eighth-and-sixteenth-note variety popularized in the 1930s by Jan Savitt and other bandleaders.

Better known by far are the OKeh records of three months later. They came about, at least the way Condon later told it, because Red McKenzie wandered in one night to the Three Deuces, a basement joint at 222 North State Street that had become a musicians' hangout. He'd made records with the Mound City Blue Blowers, played for high society, toured abroad. A talker to rival either Condon or Mezzrow, he was also a natural salesman, who seemed to have the ear of some pretty influential people. He and Condon took to one another at once, talking and comparing musical tastes. When McKenzie praised some New York records he'd heard by Red Nichols and Miff Mole, Condon, never one to resist expressing a categorical opinion, summarily dismissed such efforts as contrived and mechanical.

"Do you know anyone who plays half as good?" he recalled McKenzie saying.

"I know a dozen guys who can play twice as good," was his reply. Condon rounded up some of his pals; they played, and McKenzie listened. Then he went to Tom Rockwell, in charge of recording at OKeh, and turned on the charm. Okay, said Rockwell: one record. Two sides only. If they do all right they can do two more. If not, quit bothering me.[37]

Privately, Rockwell had his doubts. The market didn't *need* these guys, particularly since nobody knew who they were. Also, it didn't do much for his confidence to walk into OKeh's studios, just off Clark Street, the day of the session to find young Krupa setting up a full kit of drums.

Electric recording was brand-new, and engineers had little experience as yet with what microphones and cutting heads could take. One widely held assumption, left over from acoustic methods, was that too great a range of sound, or anything resulting in sudden boosts of modulation (such as a particularly emphatic thump on a bass drum), would produce an impulse strong enough to knock the cutting head out of the groove and ruin the wax master disc.

At first there had been a tendency to err on the side of caution. Bands set up carefully, various instruments distanced from the microphones much as they had been from the acoustic recording horns. Grand piano, for example, remained in the near background. Large drums, particularly the oversize bass drums in use during the 1920s, were simply *verboten*; tomtoms, with their shallow bodies and hide heads, were all right if used discreetly. Best of all were cymbals, temple blocks, and other light, trebly sounds.

Krupa, enthusiastic and impulsive, was having none of it: a drummer played his drums, not a collection of toys and rattles. McKenzie and Condon, sensing a crisis, proposed a compromise: if Krupa would move his kit halfway across the room, muffling it with overcoats and anything else handy, he could pound away as he wished. The result, to posterity's utter delight, was a full and rhythmically powerful band sound. Apprehension quickly gave way to euphoria as the playbacks came through, climaxing with Rockwell's announcement: "We'll have to get some more of this. Can you boys come back next week?"

They did two more titles on December 16. For all the later critical talk of imitation, the young Chicagoans on these first records sound only like themselves. They are playing hot music, and playing it their own way. Because these records are a debut, and unlike anything recorded up to that time, they have been submitted to practically bar-by-bar scrutiny. The combination of edginess and relaxation, aggressiveness and lyricism, a certain devil-take-the-hindmost ardor and cockiness, is brand-new and very attractive. And theirs.

And, overall, there is the pervasive spirit of Beiderbecke. As British trumpeter-journalist Humphrey Lyttelton has observed, "To say that the style revealed by the young Chicagoans in their early records is simply a bad attempt at New Orleans style is to turn a deaf ear to the Bix influence in every bar."[38]

It's not just a matter of licks, phrasing, or other questions of shape and delivery, though, but something on an almost spiritual plane. Though only three years older than both Freeman and Tesch, Beiderbecke remained a being apart, a distinct and pervasive identity, and more than a little mysterious. To many of these brash young men he often seemed, in Benny Goodman's phrase, "like a man from another planet," or in Max Kaminsky's formulation, "everything we wanted to be."[39]

Mezz Mezzrow told of watching Bix as the cornetist listened to a band in which he was playing:

> There was a dead-serious, concentrated look on his face that I got to know years later as his trademark—I've never seen such an intense, searching expression on anybody else. With that pokerface mask of his and his left eye half closed, he looked like a jeweler squinting at a diamond to find out whether it's phony or not. He seemed to be looking right through us.[40]

"Tesch idolized Bix, worshiped the ground he walked on," said Jess Stacy. "He even tried to walk like Beiderbecke, copy his movements, his little mannerisms. Complete hero worship . . . I saw them jam together at the Three Deuces. Bix would take a chorus and Tesch would just sit there in a trance, looking as if he were about to faint."[41]

Ardor, adrenaline, and more than a little nervousness are the engines driving "China Boy" and "Sugar," recorded at the first McKenzie-Condon OKeh session. Everyone is trying perhaps a little too hard to impress, and the results (as in the rideout to "China Boy") occasionally lose focus and coherence. Coming out of the bridge in his solo, Tesch bats out six concert G's that are flat enough to be quarter tones, falling right between G and G♭. They've given rise to a small piece of jazz mythology, the suggestion that Teschemacher had a chronic problem staying in tune. Generations of writers who would have trouble finding middle C on a keyboard have discoursed with great authority about alleged deficiencies in Teschemacher's technique and intonation.

The statute of limitations on such armchair analysis has run out. Though he takes some liberties with pitch and tone quality, Teschemacher is no more "out of tune," in any general sense, than such diverse and distinguished stylists as Johnny Dodds, Henry "Red" Allen, cornetist Rex Stewart, or his own cognate spirit on clarinet, Pee Wee Russell. Why, then, single him out for criticism, particularly on the evidence of little more than a few passages?

(Without placing undue emphasis on a tu quoque defense, it must also be said that there is regularly far more wayward pitching on records featuring Dodds, Ory, or many of their less celebrated colleagues, such as the saxophonists "Stump" Evans and Joe Clark, than on those involving Tesch. Intonation lapses are regular features, moreover, of records by the New Orleans Wanderers and Bootblacks, Freddie Keppard Jazz Cardinals, and even the King Oliver Creole Jazz Band.)

For all their importance, the McKenzie-Condon OKehs are first records, made by youngsters scarcely out of their teens. Nervousness, the sense of make-or-break that powers them, more than accounts for lapses in intonation (lapses which also affect Freeman and especially McPartland, who is below pitch throughout both "China Boy" and "Sugar"). Tesch, increasingly at ease with recording, shows up better and better on later records. McPartland soon comes into his own with Ben Pollack. Freeman takes longer; but his voice, when he finds it, is among the most distinctive in all hot music.

The first wave of jazz writing, notably French critic Hugues Panassié's 1934 Le Jazz Hot, heaped extravagant praise on various white players, often scanting their black counterparts. Panassié, for example, lauded Teschemacher as "incredibly good" and "always highly inspired . . . his performance . . . sweeps the rest of the orchestra along by its eloquence, its amplitude and its force."[42]

But by 1942, when Panassié wrote The Real Jazz, much had changed. In the latter book he takes Teschemacher sternly to task for "too many choppy, rough phrases" and cites Beiderbecke as a particularly pernicious influence. The key to this volte-face comes in his preface. "Since jazz is a music created by the colored people, it is very difficult and, in fact, almost impossible for a white man to get to the heart of it at first shot . . . the number of white musicians who have succeeded in assimilating the musical inspiration of the Negroes . . . is far smaller than I believed a few years ago."[43]

Whence this change of heart on the part of a white writer, this embrace of the gospel according to Mezz Mezzrow? The two men were friends: the Frenchman had visited the United States in 1938 and supervised two record dates with mostly black bands (Freeman is the only white) organized for him by Mezzrow.

To some degree, it could have begun with visits to Europe, in the early and mid-1930s, by Armstrong, Duke Ellington, Benny Carter, Coleman Hawkins, Rex Stewart, Bill Coleman, and a host of other major black jazzmen. But such exposure by itself would surely only have broadened the writer's perspective, allowing him to see each group of musicians in context with the rest. Neither that nor the friendship with Mezz really accounts for so categorical a repudiation of earlier views, and with it so cavalier a dismissal of the efforts of so many widely respected musicians, particularly on the grounds of race.

There was yet another factor, which now, viewed from the political perspective of the final decade of the twentieth century, seems almost the stuff of fantasy. The sixth Congress of the Communist International, meeting in Moscow in mid-1928, had come to some unprecedented conclusions. A document bearing the imposing title *Theses on the Revolutionary Movement in Colonial and Semi-Colonial Countries* identified southern American blacks as a separate people and proposed an independent "black republic" within the southern United States, from Virginia to Texas. This would demonstrate—and promote—southern Negro culture as a separate, free-standing entity, and its music as an "authentic" folk music. Jazz, according to this doctrine, occurred in both "bourgeois" (urban, commercialized, northern, and spurious) and "proletarian" (southern, folk-based, authentic) societies.

The Comintern adopted the document as official policy—meaning, as S. Frederick Starr points out in his excellent *Red and Hot*, it also became official policy for the U.S. Communist Party. By the mid-1930s a new generation of American writers, many of them closely associated with the left, had begun to write seriously on jazz. Among them was Charles Edward Smith, best known as co-author (with Frederic Ramsay Jr.) of the pioneer text *Jazzmen*. Basic to their work was a new emphasis on the importance of black musicians.

The black writer Albert Murray remarks in *The Omni-Americans* that as a result of such ideologically based theorizing,

> blackness as a cultural identity was all but replaced by blackness as an economic and political identity . . . U.S. Negroes, that is to say, were in effect, no longer regarded as black people. They were now the Black Proletariat, the poor, the oppressed, the downtrodden minority. Sometimes, as a matter of fact, it was as if white left wing intellectuals had deliberately confused cultural issues with questions of race.[44]

Above all, it is necessary to consider the times and circumstances within which the early jazz theorists were working. Panassié, in fact, is in at least one way a singular case: Hitler's Wehrmacht, rolling easily westward en route to complete domination of continental Europe, had overrun France in May of 1940, and on June 14 occupied Paris. Life had become increasingly unhealthy for Jews and for blacks, branded *Untermenschen* in the racial doctrines set out in *Mein Kampf*. Nazi propaganda regularly depicted jazz as "Jew-Nigger music," a form of "Entartete Kunst"—degenerate art. Given such circumstances, it is hardly surprising that Panassié (and his colleague Charles Delaunay, if more moderate, was not *that* far behind) would so vehemently renounce a work which so one-sidedly appeared to favor whites over blacks. It is even possible, though a bit of a reach, to suggest that the fact of Beiderbecke's and Teschemacher's German extraction in some way helped drive Panassié's almost violent repudiation of both men.

*   *   *

"Nobody's Sweetheart" and Condon's own "Liza" followed "China Boy" and "Sugar." Brand-new, brashly vivid, they now seem to amount less to a formalized, discrete style than a collection of accents and inflections—a patois before a free-standing language. "We were just a bunch of musicians who got together," Joe Sullivan told Richard Hadlock. "The so-called critics invented Chicago style."[45]

To be sure, there are a few innovations besides the previously mentioned flares and explosions. In one effective device, the ensemble pulls its volume down to *pianissimo*, then works a gradual crescendo over a chugging "Chicago shuffle." It's generally used in the first half of a chorus, building gradually to an "explosion," in which the drummer slams cymbal and bass drum on the fourth beat of bar 16 and everybody drops out for a beat or two, sneaking back in and building again to an all-stops-out finale.

But these are mainly embellishments. The chief difference lies in the realm of personality, of ethos. The New Orleans men had a measured elegance, an almost stately way of riding the pulse quite in keeping with the character of their home city. But these players are young men in a hurry, crowding the front of the beat like rush-hour commuters muscling their way into a subway car. The New Orleans men, it must be remembered, were playing for their audiences, in a city whose long and varied tradition of showmanship continues to this day. For the young Chicagoans the audience was at best an inconvenience: if they understand and like us, fine—if they don't, to hell with them. The difference is real, and discernible in every phrase.

The effect, overall, replaces the inner poise of the New Orleans players, black and white, with a bright surface tension. It's Chicago as "second city"—bustling, a little cheeky, growing fast and grabbing at a chance to strut its stuff, have its say—prove itself to New York and to the world.

Of the dozens of hot records made in Chicago around this time by black bands, few if any were composed entirely of local, home-grown musicians. New Orleans ways—accents, flavors, rhythm—saturate the performances. The pace and tension of Chicago make themselves felt, perhaps, but chiefly as an energizing factor.

Nowhere on any black record of the period is there anything that sounds like the two-bar ensemble kickoff to Bud Freeman's tenor chorus on "China Boy." McPartland plays a simple two-bar figure:

"China Boy," Jimmy McPartland transition, 1927.

but rather than give the eighth notes equal value he accents the B♮'s (concert A's), turning the A♯'s and G's into little more than what musicians call x notes, felt rather than actually played. It imparts to the brief passage an energy that sends the band careening into Freeman's solo.

Recognizing a good thing, McKenzie ran with it: by March he'd talked his way into another date, this time for Vocalion. McPartland and Freeman were gone, playing in New York with Ben Pollack, so Spanier and Mezzrow took their places; with Dave Tough barnstorming around Europe, young Krupa was again the drummer. But for reasons now lost to history the date was not a success, and the sides were scrapped. Undeterred, Red cadged another date from Jack Kapp, and on April 6 they recorded two sides for Brunswick; two more for Paramount, this time as "the Jungle Kings," followed within days.

Tesch and Muggsy, meanwhile, recorded for the same label with Charles Pierce, who made most of his living helping manage his family's butcher shop but played good hot alto and kept finding places for bands to play. As Max Kaminsky remembered him, Pierce was "a great big fat guy with a genial, expansive nature and a mean, swinging tone on his horn."[46]

Unlike the OKehs, the Pierce records are as relaxed and sociable as their leader. On the Pierce "China Boy," Spanier jumps right out of the opening ensemble (it sounds as if it was intended to be an Oliver-Armstrong two-cornet break, but that second man Dick Feige muffed his part) to deliver sixteen punchy, rhythmic bars. Tesch, in on a jack-in-the-box entrance, is better organized here, less febrile than on the Okeh.

And in tune. The two choruses with which he kicks off "Bull Frog Blues" show no trace of random pitching or other technical lapses. They also show little debt to Dodds: Teschemacher's tone is lean, tart, without the latter's plummy center and fast, prominent vibrato. If his phrase-building owes anything to anyone, it is to Beiderbecke's logic.

Spanier, too, is his own man. Though both he and McPartland are at root Irish sentimentalists, Spanier cloaks his in a tough-guy image; it's as if Jimmy Cagney, in *Public Enemy*, had sung "Oh Promise Me" to Mae Murray instead of pushing a half-grapefruit in her face.

"In a certain way," said Chicago jazz historian John Steiner, "[Jimmy] McPartland was hardly a part of the Chicago style. He was . . . too melodic to be at the center of it." British trumpeter Humphrey Lyttelton reaches much the same conclusion, declaring that "in view of the widely accepted image of Chicago jazz as hard-boiled and tough, McPartland's cornet playing is surprisingly soft-centered. Its main attraction, clearly absorbed from Bix, is its unpredictability." It is perhaps telling that, almost without exception, McPartland's strongest performances on later records are on ballad material.[47]

Muggsy opens his "Bull Frog Blues" solo by quoting a familiar Earl Hines phrase (it begins one of the pianist's choruses on "Apex Blues," with Noone). Alternating singing held notes with stabbing, across-the-beat accents, Muggsy shows how far his conception has come since the Bucktown Five and Stomp Six records of 1924–25.

Two Charles Pierce Orchestra performances, "Jazz Me Blues" and "Sister

Kate," made a few weeks later, were for years assumed to feature rather substandard Spanier and Tesch. Then, in the late 1960s, a European collector found a copy of the same Paramount record bearing two quite different versions of the same numbers, Spanier and Teschemacher recognizable and at their best.*

Muggsy erupts from a sax section *soli* on "Jazz Me Blues" like a welterweight charging out of his corner for round one. He bobs and weaves, tossing phrases like punches, until Tesch elbows him aside with an energetic, almost belligerent, clarinet chorus.

"Sister Kate," apart from some sax section backgrounds behind Jack Reid's opening trombone solo, is all ad lib. Spanier sings one out in a manner owing as much to John McCormack as to Joe Oliver; Tesch finishes out a chorus on alto, then switches to clarinet for some "let's get this show on the road" fills (and one bustling double-time break split with Muggsy) during the last ensemble.

But it is in the Pierce reading of "Nobody's Sweetheart," third title made that day, that things come really into focus. In some not-quite-definable way, and more emphatically than the OKeh titles, this fuzzily recorded three minutes and five seconds sums up the defiant spirit of white Chicago hot jazz, all insolence and innocence, barroom sentimentality with a thin crust of tough-guy bravado. As the late Bill Esposito put it in a 1988 appreciation:

> There is a sequence in James T. Farrell's *Studs Lonigan* trilogy where Studs visits Louisa Nolan's dance emporium on a Sunday afternoon and tries his hand at being a big shot on the dance floor. You read that and, between the lines, you can hear Charley Pierce's band playing "Nobody's Sweetheart" with Frank Teschemacher's clarinet solo followed by Muggsy's horn. Farrell was there and so was Muggsy.[48]

It's just that good. After a first ensemble, saxes reading dutiful and straight over chugging rhythm, Tesch—what? Takes over? Lets the sunshine in? Charges up San Juan Hill? Becomes Red Grange, in the clear, bearing down on the end zone? Well, maybe. Maybe a little bit of all those things.

Listen to the rhythm section, suddenly energized, perk right up. Listen as Muggsy, sliding in off his top-of-the-staff B♭ (unusual for him and for most other horn players of the time), keeps things popping, at once both sweet and aggressive.

And listen best of all when, midway through the last chorus, the whole band lets out a mighty, shouting flare on an E♭ augmented chord and heads for home. (The only thing on a record of this period to surpass it is Louis Armstrong's jubilant high C [concert B♭] into the rideout on "Willie the Weeper.")

Esposito had it just right: a startlingly visual image, all dancing and exuberance, Spanier and trombonist Jack Reid punching away for all they're worth and

---

*Charlie "Nosey" Altiere is the cornetist on the first coupling. Maurie Bercov's clarinet solos on the Pierce titles, as well as on the Original Wolverines' "Limehouse Blues" and "Dear Old Southland," and on "My Gal Sal," by Danny Altier's Orchestra, show how carefully he listened. Bercov jobbed around Chicago with dance bands until 1937, when he became a CBS staff musician.

Tesch firing off rockets overhead. Want to know what it was to be young and full of beans, playing hot music in Chicago amid the wonders of discovery? Have a listen to this incomparable record.

Altogether, April 1928 was the month which—even more than the previous December—finally put the innovative young white Chicagoans on the map. Within a period of two weeks they recorded "I've Found a New Baby" and "There'll Be Some Changes Made" for Brunswick, and "Friars Point Shuffle" and "At the Darktown Strutters' Ball" for Paramount, using much the same personnel: Teschemacher, Spanier, Mezzrow, Sullivan, Condon, Lanigan, and Krupa, with McKenzie as vocalist.

The band is smoother, more cohesive, than on the OKeh dates. Even the erratic Mezzrow, for all his rhetoric, turns in a well-organized, almost Bixish tenor solo on "I've Found a New Baby." Brunswick's better-quality electric recording picks up the overall timbre of the band quite well, particularly Teschemacher's tone, which on the Paramounts has a screechy, almost whistling, quality. Bix's concept of "correlated" (i.e., paired, structurally balanced) phrases, question-and-answer, point and counterpoint and summing up, governs every note of Tesch's chorus. See, for example, the beginning of the second eight bars, built on sequential use of a four-note motif:

"I've Found a New Baby," Frank Teschemacher solo (second eight bars), 1928.

Pianist-theoretician John Mehegan also has called attention to the intricate, eventful nature of the ensembles, which he terms "more florid" than the New Orleans model. He hears this as "an inevitable result of the expanding concepts of melody, harmony and rhythm."[49]

Certainly the concept of individual role within the ensemble, so formalized in New Orleans bands, has given way here to an intense form of interaction. In a New Orleans front line, it was generally understood that the trumpet or cornet would supply a straightforward, lightly embellished lead; that the clarinet would play a decorative, sometimes arpeggiated, counterline; that the trombone would confine itself to a ground bass function derived from its marching-band use. Saxophone, if present, was left to fend for himself.

The New Orleans Rhythm Kings records of August 1922 show Paul Mares, Leon Roppolo, and George Brunies working, with considerable grace, within these rather strict role definitions. Saxophonist Jack Pettis, by contrast, can't make up his mind whether to play an independent, clarinet-like counterline (as on "Panama," where he all but smothers clarinetist Roppolo) or opt for a spare, subordinate commentary (as on the rather more successful "Tiger Rag"), leaving more latitude for the clarinet.

The white Chicagoans changed all that. Under the new rules, the cornet laid out a flexible (sometimes quite free) lead line, clarinet played off him, and tenor (trombone was not much of a factor in these bands, at least on records, until later) worked in tandem with the clarinet. The thrust, for everyone, was urgently, aggressively forward.

The success of such a formula depended in large measure on the abilities of the participants. Mezzrow, despite some fine moments, is in general a rather dismal ensemble player: the final *tuttis* of both "I've Found a New Baby" and "There'll Be Some Changes Made" evolve into an increasingly fervent dialogue between Spanier and Teschemacher, with the tenor mooing and mooning somewhere in the middle distance.

For another Paramount date in April, Teschemacher and Mezzrow teamed up with a third reed player, twenty-year-old Rod Cless. "Singin' the Blues," probable homage to Bix, was lost; but a pressing of "Jazz Me Blues" survived, and it is remarkable.

Tesch lays out the melody on clarinet, setting the mood and determining the flow. He then grabs an alto and jumps right into a solo. As guitarist Marty Grosz remarked in a 1982 essay, it is "a safe bet that he could have been picked out of a crowd of 100 contemporary alto sax players." His sound and approach don't conform to the sugary, "legit" model popularized by Rudy Wiedoeft; nor does he resemble either Jimmy Dorsey's diamond-cut brilliance or the rather more florid ways of the great black soloists, among them Johnny Hodges and Charlie Holmes.

Perhaps it's best to say that Teschemacher on alto sounds exactly like what a hot Chicago alto would be expected to sound like: slightly acidulous tone, annunciatory attack; trumpet-like clarity; push-the-beat rhythm; and, inevitably, the Bixian phrase-building. Cless, who takes a half-chorus on alto a bit later, plays in much the same manner, if rather less emphatically.

Most assessments of Teschemacher have worked from the inference that he stood alone, unique and inexplicable, and that anyone who sounded like him did so through imitation. Yet there is evidence to suggest that the elements of his clarinet and saxophone styles were to some degree Chicago conventions, firmly in place by the time he got into a recording studio.

Certainly Volly De Faut's solos on "Why Couldn't It Be Poor Little Me?" and "Everybody Loves My Baby," with Spanier and the Stomp Six, point in that direction, as does his work on "Wolverine Blues," from a seldom-heard, racially mixed Jelly Roll Morton Trio date, also made for the Autograph label in mid-1925.

Similar tone and mannerisms turn up in the clarinet of Joseph "Fud" Livingston, who had played in Chicago with Ben Pollack. Livingston's solo on the Red Nichols recording of "Nobody's Sweetheart," made in New York at the end of

February 1928, demonstrates palpably "Chicagoan" qualities. Where, and from whom, did he adopt them?

Wade Foster, from Moline, Illinois (directly across the Mississippi from Bix's home town of Davenport), recorded "Downright Disgusted" and "Fare Thee Well" with Wingy Manone in Chicago in September 1928 and sounds uncannily like Teschemacher on both. So, too, do Bercov and Bud Jacobson, though it's regrettable that the latter is not more extensively heard on the few records he made during the '20s. And what of Jimmy Lord, heard once dimly on record and soon dead of the effects of tuberculosis? How did he come to sound as he did?

There are still other records made around the same time by lesser-known white Chicago bands quite unrelated to these musicians. An example is "When Sweet Susie Goes Stepping By" and "Tin Roof Blues," done for Paramount in July—again 1928—by a group billed as the Midnight Serenaders. Next to nothing is known of them: Brian Rust (in *Jazz Records, 1897–1942*) lists a personnel including trombonist Frank Lhotak, who had recorded in New York at the end of the previous decade with the New Orleans Jazz Band. But Chicago historian John Steiner, proprietor of the Paramount catalogue in later years, has contested this, suggesting that the "Serenaders" were probably the house band at a Near South Side dance hall called the Midnight Frolics. While nowhere near the same level of accomplishment as Teschemacher or even Bercov, the unidentified clarinetist is playing in what is clearly the same style.

Then, too, there is Pee Wee Russell, who spent next to no time at all in Chicago during the '20s (though Jess Stacy remembered him coming to visit at least once at the Midway Gardens and jamming with the band afterwards), and whose highly idiosyncratic clarinet style shares certain traits with Teschemacher's.

Tesch is beyond contest an exceptional musician. In Eddie Condon's words, "of all the people generally associated with me in early Chicago he was the most musically talented, with the exception of Bix, whom he idolized." Without questioning his brilliance, it is also useful to hear his playing within a context, especially if it helps others be perceived as more than just imitators.[50]

In a way, Benny Goodman stands in counterpoint to Teschemacher. On January 23, 1928, while playing at the Blackhawk Restaurant with Ben Pollack's band, he recorded two titles under his own name for Brunswick. He used Jimmy McPartland, who had just joined Pollack, and local man Bob Conselman on drums; the rest—Glenn Miller, Vic Breidis, Dick Morgan, and brother Harry Goodman—were Pollack sidemen.

Here, too, the resident deity is Beiderbecke. It turns "A Jazz Holiday," a bit of period razzmatazz by the composer of "There'll Be Some Changes Made," into a contemplative tone poem. Goodman's solo, especially, is steeped in Bix. This is even more apparent on "Blue (and Brokenhearted)," made that June in New York by essentially the same unit. Goodman, soloing on alto sax, produces a chorus which grasps perfectly Beiderbecke's unique structural sense.

In doing so he surpasses even McPartland, whose resemblance to his idol is more a matter of attack and delivery. As music critic Irving Kolodin observed in a long-ago record sleeve essay, such Goodman solos could have been transferred to Beiderbecke's cornet with little or no alteration and remained utterly in character.

Soloing on Bud Freeman's "After Awhile," Goodman allows himself a certain grittiness, redolent less of Tesch than of Pee Wee, whom he had by this time heard in New York. But in playing "dirty," Goodman is employing a device, part of a vocabulary, for the effect it will produce. Even when he openly celebrates Bix, there is a sense of having listened and absorbed, then carefully applied what he has learned.

Goodman's stature, the virtuosity and emotive force of his playing, are beyond challenge. But there is a fundamental difference, a gulf of intent, between his approach to style and that of Teschemacher. Benny's solos on these early records are products of a musically alert mind, drawing on an ever-expanding reservoir of device for whatever is necessary to get his point across.

To a certain degree the methods are those of the theatre: learn the lines, understand the role—then tap into available emotional reserves to lend impact, weight, authority. It is a highly sophisticated way of doing things, a virtuoso's prerogative, applied to the matter of playing jazz.

When, late in life, Goodman told the author that "some of the guys I played with in those days didn't go around learning more about their instruments from an intellectual point of view," he was revealing as much about himself as about them. "*All they wanted was to play hot jazz* [emphasis added], and the instrument was just the means . . . but I've always wanted to know what *made* music. How you do it, and why it sounds good."[51]

Frank Teschemacher seems to have been one of those to whom Goodman alluded, and it is this that sets them apart: the horn not as an end but as a means. The way Teschemacher plays is the way he plays, the only way, natural and unself-conscious, subject to wide vicissitudes of mind and body, mood and circumstance. Though his later records show growing ease with the clarinet, and the testimony of colleagues leaves no doubt that he was an expert, schooled musician, there is also no doubting the forces that drove him.

Goodman, as was his wont, learned by listening and by study. It's therefore not surprising when Jess Stacy recalls catching sight of him in the shadows at the Midway Gardens. "Benny was working at the Southmoor Hotel with Ben Pollack," said Stacy. "He used to come over and stand behind a post . . . He didn't want to be seen, this great prima donna, listening to Teschemacher. Tesch was blowing him away, you see."[52]

In early summer of 1928, Red McKenzie and Eddie Condon landed in New York, ready to join McPartland and Freeman in taking on the big time. Instead they found their pals out of work: the Pollack band's first job, at the Little Club, had folded; the musicians had forsaken their fancy Mayflower Hotel digs and were sustaining themselves through regular attendance at cocktail parties, where, as Jimmy put it, "at least the hors d'oeuvres were free."

They hooked up with singer Bee Palmer, who was getting ready to open at a new club. Still as partial to hot musicians as when she had brought Emmett Hardy and Leon Roppolo north from New Orleans, the "Shimmy Queen" promised to help find them work. At her urging the club's proprietor agreed to include Condon and friends on the bill.[53]

Eddie went home to Chicago, managed to extricate Teschemacher, Joe Sullivan, and Gene Krupa from their regular dance band jobs, and headed back east. But things quickly went awry: Miss Palmer and her husband, pianist–vocal coach Al Siegel, had one of their many fallings-out (resulting, inter alia, in a torrid, if brief, affair between the singer and cornetist McPartland), and the club manager fired the band without ever having hired them; a theatre job backing a dance team died at birth ("We just couldn't play for that arty, highbrow dance stuff," said Sullivan), and the musicians went their separate ways, Freeman joining Dave Tough as a ship's musician on the Île de France.[54]

For the moment, Sullivan, Teschemacher, Krupa, and Condon were on the loose—and broke—in New York City. Again thanks to Tom Rockwell, they landed a couple of OKeh record dates, one for the four of them as a quartet (Tesch especially effective on alto) and another in tandem with Red Nichols and Miff Mole.

At its best, the kind of jazz Red and Miff represented was melodically imaginative and harmonically forward-looking, but emotionally a little detached, the "cool" modern jazz of its time. For them, hearing the young Chicagoans must have been a bit like stepping out their front door into a force ten gale. They'd had some preview: both Fud Livingston and Pee Wee Russell had been absorbed into their circle after Jimmy Dorsey elected to remain with Paul Whiteman. They'd heard Goodman and McPartland with Pollack. The McKenzie-Condon records, moreover, had become widely known in the East.[55]

All the same, "One Step to Heaven," made July 6, is a jolt, a fascinating collision of concepts, Nichols and Mole drawing energy from their companions like an automobile battery getting a jump start. As for Teschemacher, here's what guitarist Marty Grosz has to say:

> Nichols and Mole leave him an opening for a break, into which he drops
> suddenly and mysteriously as though he had stepped into a hole in the
> arrangement and was about to disappear forever. Far from it. He rebounds
> into an extraordinary solo, delivered mostly in the middle register and
> with some deliberation, yet with a suggestion of tremendous force. He
> is by turns ruminative, harsh and strident, and from time to time he
> slants off into some private train of thought that seems unrelated to what
> he is doing yet is actually part of his total conception.[56]

The second side, "Shimme-Sha Wabble," is even more notable for the effects of this pro tem alliance on Red and Miff. Both men catch fire, even during the technically intricate arranged ensemble following the Chicagoan's clarinet solo, and Red's last-chorus lead is a shouting departure from his usual composed manner.[57]

Condon, McKenzie, and Krupa were in New York to stay. Others, Freeman and McPartland among them, would spend the next years shuttling back and forth between there and home; but Teschemacher, homesick and seeking financial stability, wandered back to Chicago and stayed there. He was, said Freeman, "the best player of the lot. But he then didn't pursue the jazz directions he could have followed. He went into big bands and dance halls, and he was concerned with making a living, and he could read well. I have the feeling that he might have gone into the studios and have become that kind of musician . . . Tesch was that way about money."[58]

Things in Chicago went on much as before—some good work and some not so good, punctuated now and then by a record date. A few good players, such as Iowa-born clarinetist Jimmy Cannon and trumpeter Al Turk, never got to make records and are all but forgotten today. Ohioan Bill Davison, who arrived in 1927, made some interesting records (e.g., his chorus on "Smiling Skies," with Benny Meroff) but is best known for much later work, by which time he had become, emphatically, "Wild Bill." Others, Wade Foster, tenor saxophonist George "Snurps" Snurpus, and drummer Augie Schellang among them, recorded very little.

"You gotta understand," Jess Stacy said. "At that time, when jazz musicians walked in to play their stuff—say, into a recording studio—you almost had to go in the back door. They'd say, 'Here come that scum, that bunch of drug and boozeheads.' You could just see it, feel it. 'You're lucky we'll even let you in to play,' they seemed to say.

"I think a lot of 'em must have thought, 'Well, all this kind of music belongs to black people. What the hell are you guys doin' playin' it?' And that wasn't any kind of compliment: what they meant was that if you were a jazz musician you were automatically connected with marijuana, gin, gangsters, all that stuff. The only places we got to play was at the gangster joints; they liked the way we played. But the whole thing had this air of unrespectability to it."[59]

Dave Tough, back at last after tasting the bohemian life in Europe (where he'd reportedly known F. Scott Fitzgerald and other expatriate literary figures), jobbed around New York, did a New England tour with Red Nichols, and came home to Chicago sick and depressed. Between 1930 and 1935 he seems—with the exception of a patch with Joe Kayser in early 1931—hardly to have played at all. To Stacy, who saw him occasionally, he sometimes appeared the very incarnation of the degenerate image referred to above. "He looked like a bum and he hung out with bums. He'd go along Randolph Street and panhandle, then he'd buy canned heat and strain off the alcohol and drink it."[60]

Dave Tough remains one of the most puzzling and contradictory of early jazz figures. Bright, articulate, learned, he belongs—with Jo Jones, Sid Catlett, and Chick Webb—to the very greatest of jazz drummers who came of age between the world wars. His way of seeming to drive a band from within, forsaking showy effect or technical display, consistently amazed those who worked with him. Along with Jones, he is responsible for transferring the focus of jazz drumming from the snare and bass drum to the cymbals, thus paving the way for decades of "modern" timekeeping.

But Dave Tough was a man in conflict, dedicated to making music yet beset by private demons; straining against the intellectual and artistic limitations of the musician's life and taking refuge in alcohol and vagrancy. The acknowledged intellectual mainspring of his circle of young musicians, he inducted Bud Freeman into the world of art and legitimate theatre, winning the saxophonist's lifelong admiration. "Dave Tough," said Max Kaminsky, "wouldn't be in a band a week before he had the whole band showing up for work with books under their arms."[61]

Tough's unspectacular but irresistible beat swung the Tommy Dorsey, Bunny Berigan, and Benny Goodman bands of the 1930s and Artie Shaw's wartime navy band—which encountered living conditions in the Pacific theatre that left the drummer, never robust, in perilous health. For Lionel Hampton, "he was the most imaginative drummer we ever had in the business . . . Everything he ever hit was musical. If he tapped on the floor, it was musical."[62]

Bud Freeman took that even farther. "Dave," he said, "was a little beyond being a drummer. That was a hell of a deep mind working there. I don't think an ordinary man could play that well."[63]

Tough stayed friends with most of his early associates—though old ties must have been strained a bit when in 1946, at the height of his success with Woody Herman's first "Herd," he was quoted as declaring the music the Chicagoans played little more than "harmonically infantile, devoid of embellishments and interesting connecting chords and, all in all, scaled to the level of musicians with meager technique."[64]

Alcohol was a chronic problem, complicated in later years by epileptic seizures. Gene Lees, in his biography of Herman, goes so far as to suggest that Tough's fear of the seizures was "one of the underlying causes of his drinking." Despite many attempts (and with the unstinting assistance of a devoted wife) to curb the alcohol, to eat well and live a more balanced, temperate life, he somehow always tumbled back into the abyss. Musically he continued to grow, to probe: in the '40s he listened to, and made great efforts to absorb, the new concepts of bebop. Bassist Chubby Jackson and other alumni of the Woody Herman band still speak of him with undisguised awe.[65]

Tough at one point told fellow-drummer Louis Bellson that he wanted to study tympani and develop better "legit" technique. Yet this, like his attempts to curb the drinking, came to nothing. One cold December morning in 1948, Dave Tough was found, unconscious, on a street in Newark, New Jersey. He died the next day. He was just forty.[66]

Even when times were good, with the South Side booming and hot music in the air, white jazzmen faced a problem that refused to go away. The more popular, the better-paid a dance band, the less interested it seemed in featuring its hot soloists. Only in roadhouses, joints, and such decidedly *infra dig* venues as the Midway Gardens did they find anything like freedom to do what they did best. "Hot musicians," said Muggsy Spanier, "weren't wanted because all the commercial bands were doing all the business the 'corny' way, which seemed the easier way to them because the public readily swallowed whatever it was fed.''[67]

The decline of cabaret life in Chicago toward decade's end, the rapid growth of radio (and its apparent preference, in the words of a *Variety* writer, for ''melody stuff over hot breaks and tricks''), and the rise of nationally based booking agencies all contributed to what was beginning to look like a famine for hot musicians, and not only the whites. Some simply packed and moved to New York. Others, reluctant to leave, tried compromise.

It was a situation not without with irony. Because black musicians were so closely identified with ''hot'' music, radio's emphasis on more conservative fare meant that fewer black bands got a chance to broadcast. William Howland Kenney, in *Chicago Jazz*, quotes a *Chicago Defender* column by Walter Barnes protesting that black bands were versatile and complaining that ''it seems to be the belief among whites that The Race is still in the cotton fields and cannot sing or play anything else but cotton songs or blues. This is a great mistake. We are music lovers and enjoy all types and forms of music.''[68]

Muggsy Spanier, for example, participated in an October 22, 1928, Vocalion record date by what had been the Midway Gardens band and was now working with Floyd Town at the mob-owned Triangle Café. Issued under alto saxophonist Danny Altier's name, the record finds the jazzmen struggling in the embrace of non-rhythmic, vibrato-laden arrangements clearly aimed at doing business ''the corny way.''

All the same, ''My Gal Sal'' gives Spanier a broad-toned, rocking chorus, almost defining his style of the time: its roots may be in Oliver and Armstrong, but Muggsy's own sensibility comes through. Jess Stacy also gets a precious sixteen bars here, his first on record. All the familiar features of his style—the little right-hand tremolos, a touch which makes the notes sound almost as though they're on springs—are instantly recognized. Bercov, on clarinet, and Altier, on alto, solo convincingly, both very much in the Teschemacher manner. But overall, considering the number of jazzmen present (George Wettling on drums, Pat Pattison on bass, Ray Biondi on guitar), it's a dismayingly inert performance, achieving no tension, no momentum.

Chicago's hot music craze, whatever it may or may not have been, was drying up. When Ted Lewis came through town he took George Brunies's advice and heard Spanier, then playing with Ray Miller at the College Inn; before long, Kid Muggsy was on his way to San Francisco to join the ''High-hatted Tragedian of Jazz.''[69]

Wingy Manone, meanwhile, hung on in Chicago. He got a job at the Club Royale, on North Clark Street, then parlayed it into a record deal with Vocalion. On September 4, 1928, he used Krupa, Freeman (in town on a visit), and Wade Foster on clarinet, plus Biondi and pianist ''Jumbo'' Jack Gardner. Two titles, ''Downright Disgusted'' and ''Fare Thee Well,'' bristle with the old roughhouse spirit.

By the time Wingy returned, three months later, to the Vocalion studios, Krupa and Freeman were gone; in their places he hired George Snurpus and drummer Augie Schellang, a New Orleans native (and nephew of clarinetist Tony Parenti) who was tending bar in a joint on the South Side. On clarinet was none other than a newly returned Frank Teschemacher.

"I remember asking Wingy at the record date how I should play when Tesch took his chorus," pianist Art Hodes said in reminiscence. "Play like you always play" was the trumpeter's brusque reply. Powered by stabbing Teschemacher solos and Manone's vigorous lead, "Isn't There a Little Love?" and "Tryin' to Stop My Cryin' " have "made in Chicago" stamped all over them. But the freedom and irreverence they represent (down to the four-bar coda: two bars lifted from Louis Armstrong, two from Stravinsky's *Petrouchka*) resonate with echoes of a younger, more carefree time.

The Coon-Sanders Nighthawks, a Kansas City dance band whose "jazz" novelties had become, at best, a bloodless parody of hot music, had over moved in at the Blackhawk Restaurant and were broadcasting nightly over WGN, the powerful *Chicago Tribune* radio outlet. What passed for "hot" was usually novelty material like "Here Comes My Ball and Chain" and "Kansas City Kitty" and had little in common, even distantly, with these Manone records—or with anything heard half a decade before at the Friars' Inn.

Once in a while a trumpeter or saxophonist might pop out of an ensemble to "get off" for eight bars; but even then the public seemed to recognize no distinction between the solo efforts of dedicated hot players and those of journeyman dance band men. The result was functionally the same, and the soloists remained largely anonymous.

Things on the South Side were winding down as well. The brand-new Savoy Ballroom, at 47th and South Parkway, was doing fine, thanks to the growth of Jules C. Stein's Music Corporation of America (MCA) and other nationally based agencies; but more and more, such places were bringing in "name" bands (Fletcher Henderson's was one) from outside. Small theatres closed or converted to movies-only policies. Many key musicians, Armstrong, Morton, and even Oliver among them, had long since gone to try their luck in New York. Those who stayed, including the venerated Jimmie Noone, were scuffling; the clarinetist continued to make records for Brunswick, but they were now devoted increasingly to such pop material as "Through (How Can You Say We're Through?)" and the old reliable "My Melancholy Baby."

In Chicago historian Dempsey Travis's words, "the Pullman Cafe, the Vendome, and the Grand Theatre that had shone in brilliant splendor were now shady ladies with unpainted faces. Rising above the ruins was the Binga Arcade Building, standing on the northwest corner of 35th and State like a giant tombstone in the midst of a commercial graveyard."[70]

Sam Beers, whose State Street speakeasy, My Cellar, paid Wingy Manone's salary for a while around decade's end, liked hot music and the guys who played it. He was a rarity in a city which, as Frank Teschemacher had observed, neither knew nor cared about what the disciples of Louis, Bix, and King Joe were trying to do.

What Muggsy Spanier termed "the corny way" had prevailed. Only a year

213

and a day separate the OKeh "Nobody's Sweetheart" session and Wingy's second Club Royale date. "Isn't There a Little Love?" could have been both title and lament; less and less of the music it exemplifies was to be heard in the cafés and dance halls of its own home town.

The Depression, when it arrived, was almost an anticlimax. The party, however heady it had been, was over, and most of the revelers had moved on.

10

Chicago Jazz in the 1930s

There's a certain easy melancholy in the notion that by the end of 1929 hot music was finished in Chicago. That the good players had moved on, mostly to New York, leaving behind a host of lesser lights who simply winked out one by one. As Charles Edward Smith put it, "the musical spirit of the Chicagoans was swallowed up in the maw of something bigger and considerably less great than itself, the popular music business."[1]

Well, yes—though it wasn't that neat and it certainly wasn't that final. If Chicago in 1929 was no longer a town with a hot little combination on every street corner, it was far from a musical Sahara. All very well for Mezz Mezzrow to lament the change "from a frolic-pad into a mortician's icebox [when] King Jazz had packed his trunk and made his get-away." But, as Jelly Roll Morton might have put it, there was still plenty life and plenty music.[2]

It was just that the rules had changed. More than ever, thanks to network radio, Chicago was still the nation's dance band center. For every musician who had left town there seemed to be two who had stayed, and there was plenty of work. Not hot jazz work; not the free-and-easy, jam-or-croak existence of the mid-'20s. But work nevertheless.

Even the stock market crash seemed to make little impression on the crowds showing up at the Blackhawk and the Granada, the Aragon and the Trianon. Ben Bernie's Orchestra packed them in at the Sherman Hotel's College Inn in the first months of 1930. The Drake, the Stevens, the Palmer House, the Morrison and Edgewater Beach hotels offered music for dancing every night of the week.

Smaller places had it tougher. Some, finding the extra expense of paying a band not reflected at the cash register, dropped music entirely. Police closed Bert Kelly's Stables, long the home of the Dodds brothers, on New Year's Day 1930. Shortly thereafter, Paramount Records, which had meant so much to hot music in Chicago during the '20s, went out of business.

For young jazzmen in their mid-twenties it meant the end of a happy and carefree adolescence. Time now to grow up: as professional musicians they had to earn a living, to seek employment where they could. Any guy who owned a tux, could read reasonably well, and could "get off" glibly in an occasional solo could find a place in dance bands around town. It might not always please his soul, but it allowed him to play regularly and keep the creditors happy.

Even with the Depression biting deep it wasn't a bad life. All the same, families by the hundreds were coming up "empty rent-handed" at the end of every month as unemployment soared. Evictions were a daily South Side occurrence. Musicians, in general, still worked, and when they went out prowling after hours they could still hear Jimmie Noone, Earl Hines and George Mitchell, Natty Dominique, or even the Dodds brothers, who had found work in a 31st Street Chinese restaurant.

There were even still places to jam, and no dearth of good people with whom to do it.

True, the class of '27–28 had fled. Jimmy McPartland and Benny Goodman were in New York playing for Ben Pollack. Gene Krupa, Bud Freeman, and Joe Sullivan were working there for Red Nichols. Eddie Condon and Red McKenzie clung doggedly to their hot-music-or-nothing credo, picking up dates around New York where they could, chasing work as far south as Florida. Muggsy Spanier and George Brunies were on the road with Ted Lewis, Paul Mares back in New Orleans; reedmen Volly De Faut and Maurie Bercov had found comfort and security in the radio studios.

Jim Lanigan, still living at home, was headed toward a career as a symphony bassist. Frank Teschemacher, having decided that scuffling in New York wasn't for him, had made his peace, playing violin and saxophone—and even doing a bit of singing—with the commercial bands of Jan Garber and Joe Kayser.

Jess Stacy, unperturbed, just kept doing what he'd always done, playing piano in dance halls and speakeasies, usually in bands led by Floyd Town, Danny Altier, Louis Panico, and other old friends. He spent a year with Eddie Niebaur's Seattle Harmony Kings, a good, hot-inflected unit which had at various times provided regular employment for clarinetist "Rosy" McHargue and cornetist "Wild Bill" Davison.

Things in those years, he said, weren't really much different from the way they'd always been. There always had been a few who appreciated hot music, "but the greatest audiences were always for those entertaining bands that put on funny hats, and played cornball [dance] music."[3]

The most consistently rewarding hot music listeners were the gangsters, "with their hair slicked back, and all of them wearing the most expensive clothes. We soon found out that they would kill you just as soon as look at you . . . but they did like rhythm. What they did not like was corny music played by musicians wearing funny hats."[4]

Funny-hat music, especially as a daily diet, could be pretty dismaying—making it all the easier to look back fondly on a time, just two or three years before, when a guy could play hot jazz in at least a few places and get paid for it; could jam until dawn at the Deuces, drive Art Kassel nuts by mangling his stock arrangements, and salt the bands at White City or the Midway Gardens with young musical subversives ready to play things their way.

It's easy to suspect that much of the mythology surrounding the brief career and early death of Bix Beiderbecke grew out of this kind of post-adolescent *Sehnsucht*. There was poor Bix, hot music prophet and free spirit, bound and gagged and dying by stages in Paul Whiteman's brass section. That Beiderbecke might actually have enjoyed the challenge of so schooled and sophisticated an orchestra, and the wide musical life it represented, seemed beyond the ken of all but a few of his idolators.

It seemed more consoling by far to remember an earlier Bix, barnstorming with the Wolverines, camping out with Pee Wee Russell amid the flies and empty milk bottles at Hudson Lake, making magic with his beat-up cornet (it had to be beat-up) every night at the nearby Blue Lantern Inn.

> Youth was mine,
> Truth was mine;
> Joyous, free and flaming life, forsooth,
>   was mine . . . [5]

found its resonance with a generation of fans and admirers who had arrived on college campuses in the late 1920s, a generation that helped make an icon of Bix and, even many years later, never stinted in its reverence for the cultish small-band hot music of the period.

But it's not without significance that such keepers of the flame were lawyers, advertising men, and corporate executives, financially secure enough to indulge themselves forever in the passions and obsessions of youth. A working musician, alas, pursues his sustenance at a rather more mundane—and economically far more perilous—level than this. It was all very well to dream about the good old days when you got together after hours, or play a tune that evoked memories of Bix. But more important by far was to get a gig, to work, to pay the rent.

Bud Jacobson, for example, found work with bassist Thelma Terry at the Golden Pumpkin (where the sitters-in often outnumbered the paying customers), with Floyd Town out at the mob-owned Triangle Café, and with Wingy Manone at My Cellar, Sam Beers's State Street speakeasy. It wasn't a great living, but at least he got to see and play with old friends—Bill Davison, Bud Hunter, Johnny Mendel, Jack Gardner, Ray Biondi, Floyd O'Brien—and a new crop of young players, many barely out of their teens, among them two sets of brothers, Harvey (guitar) and Boyce (alto) Brown and Joe (clarinet) and Marty (cornet) Marsala.

Some of the big-time commercial dance band leaders found it useful to keep a few such men around; one or two apparently even enjoyed it. But none seems to have appreciated hot music more, and been more aware of its benefits to the musical profile of a band—and to have been more respected by musicians in return—than Ted Weems.

Born Wilfred Theodore Weymes in Pennsylvania in 1901, he'd formed his first unit in 1922 in partnership with his trumpet-playing brother Art. Their first Victor record, "Somebody Stole My Gal" (1923), created a stir in dance band circles, largely due to a widely imitated alto sax break by Fud Livingston's elder brother Walter.

One of the first bandleaders to be booked by Jules Stein's Music Corporation of America, Weems attained great popularity throughout the Midwest. As late as 1990, nearly three decades after its leader's death, a "Ted Weems Orchestra" was still playing one-night stands throughout Ohio, Indiana, and Illinois.

Instinct and experience had made Weems a canny judge of audience tastes, able to mix entertainment and comedy with light-on-its-feet—and often engagingly hot—dance music; during a long residency in the Plantation Grille of Kansas City's Muehlebach Hotel, they alternated with the Coon-Sanders Nighthawks and were at home playing to the same audiences. Their broadcasts over station WDAF reached an ever-widening public, and in late 1929 the Weems band took on Chicago, opening at the Granada.

"We weren't exactly, or officially, what you'd call a hot band," said clarinetist Don Watt. "But there were always several guys in the band who were fine hot players. Joe Haymes did the arrangements, mostly, and he gave them plenty of chances to play."[6]

Haymes is an intriguing, all too often overlooked figure. Born in Missouri in 1908, he started writing for Weems at the Muehlebach, and when they moved to the Granada he came along as second pianist and staff arranger. His scores, full of unusual voicings and daring modulations, reflect an admiration for the innovative writing Bill Challis had done for the Detroit-based Jean Goldkette Orchestra.[7]

On the Weems Victor record of "Nothin' on My Mind," for example, he works in ensemble "pyramids" and gives cornetist Merrill Conner a Bix Beiderbecke–like solo over sustained saxophones. He uses a clarinet trio to good effect on "If You Want the Rainbow"; on "Me and the Man in the Moon" he scores as a homophonic tutti what is in effect a hot solo line—all 1928 recordings.

Besides Watt and Conner, the Weems band of 1929 included lead alto saxophonist Dick Cunliffe, who also doubled on mellophone for jazz solos. But it's the rhythm section, dominated by Joe "Country" Washburn's supple tuba and the lithe drumming of Ormand Downes, that commands attention.

"Country was just a magician on bass," said Watt. "He made everything so light, not like most other guys who played tuba. Also, he had a knack for filling in at the ends of phrases, in a way that made you think there was an extra sax or trombone in there. That band was the biggest-sounding ten-piece band I ever heard, and it was mostly because of Country."[8]

Washburn, Downes, and trombonist Pete Beilmann later became popular figures on the post–World War II "dixieland" scene in Los Angeles, recording for Clive Acker's Jump label; so, too, did Chicago bass saxophonist Joe Rushton, who spent time as a Weems sideman before moving to California in the early '40s.

"Joe and I were good friends in those days," said Don Watt. "In fact, I think he took up bass sax because I had one. In those days he was jobbing on clarinet around town. Played well—but as soon as he got interested in that bass sax he just went to town on it.

"He came from Evanston, up on the North Shore. Wealthy family. Those kids from up there—there were a bunch of them—they had a good deal. They used to buy secondhand cars. All the people who lived around there were millionaires, and they'd trade their cars in regularly. The kids would practically steal 'em; they'd be driving around in Cadillacs, Lincolns, Packards. Joe for a while was my driver—that is, he'd always volunteer to drive me out when we played one-nighters outside Chicago."

Watt, Conner, and other Weems sidemen, delighted to be in Chicago, spent much after-hours time making the rounds, often jamming with local men. "There was still lots of hot music going in Chicago at that time," Watt said. "One time I saw Teschemacher playing with Wild Bill Davison for some sort of dance marathon on the West Side. I remember hearing Jimmie Noone a bunch of times at little joints. I especially liked the way he played. I think both Jimmy Dorsey and I learned a lot from listening to him."[9]

Note Watt's nimble sixteen-bar clarinet solo on "Man From the South," recorded December 2, 1929. Here, as in most of the band's performances, what impresses is the ensemble's *feel* for rhythm and hot phrasing. "They weren't what you'd call a burn-'em-down hot band," said Rosy McHargue, who replaced Watt as clarinet soloist in 1934. "Not like Ben Pollack's band, anyway. But then, you gotta remember that Weems was playing to a different public, and they wouldn't have been as interested in a band like Pollack's, regardless how good we—the musicians—knew it was."[10]

As Warren Vaché Sr. put it in a particularly trenchant record sleeve essay: "It wasn't enough that a band was capable of playing good dance music—this much was taken for granted—but in addition it had to be entertaining and able to put on a good show all by itself. It had to develop a personality—a collective spirit that colored the band as a unit distinct from the others—unusual vocalists, novelty songs, original arrangements, outstanding instrumentalists, as many and as varied as possible."[11]

The Weems orchestra excelled in each particular; and that, ironically, seems to have taken it right out of the running as far as connoisseurs of hot music were concerned. Entries on the Weems band seldom appear in histories of big band jazz: it's almost as though any band that didn't play just hot music couldn't be taken seriously.

Musicians knew better. When Bix Beiderbecke, hopeful of rejoining Paul Whiteman, stopped off in Chicago in February he made a point of visiting the Granada. He'd been listening to Weems on the radio in Davenport and was particularly taken by Joe Haymes's arrangements. He sat in, much to the delight of the musicians, and was sufficiently impressed that when Haymes told him he was thinking of forming a band of his own and offered him a chair, he accepted with enthusiasm.

He attended a couple of rehearsals, playing both cornet and piano. But, said Haymes, "he kept having nervous spells, during which it was sometimes hard for him to finish a chorus, especially on piano." Bix, the shadows around him lengthening, went on to New York.[12]

The outstanding feature of Weems hot performances is the rhythm, particularly Washburn's tuba. Where Henderson's June Cole and others anchor and push the pulse, Washburn makes it dance; he underpins the *tutti* passages with the dexterity of a wide-toned second trombone, kicks things forward with across-the-beat accents reminiscent of Adrian Rollini's bass saxophone, then lays out a driving four-to-the-bar during a clarinet or trombone solo.

"He played that thing like a trumpet sometimes," said Watt. "He and Orm [Downes] had plenty of volume and played a beat that was as firm as a rock, but it stayed light. And he had a great sense of where to put in a lick and where not to."[13]

Haymes is again the star on "What a Day!," made the following June. It's easy to imagine Bix, sprawled on couch or easy chair in his family's Davenport parlor, listening happily to this performance on the radio. The rhythm, steered by Washburn and Downes, skips along in a smooth four-to-the-bar, and Watt's clarinet solo leaps out of an imaginatively scored band interlude of six bars, rather than the customary four or eight.

Downes is especially skilled with brushes, not a common feature of late-'20s dance band drumming. As early as "Baby Doll" he's working his brushes lightly and propulsively behind Bob Royce's piano solo.

Other Weems records of the period yield ample evidence of the band's hot music skills. Examples include Haymes's score on "Remarkable Girl," Washburn's "walking four" on "Miss Wonderful," and his four-string skill on the eponymously titled "Slappin' the [string] Bass."

Frank Teschemacher, meanwhile, had settled into Chicago dance band life, taking whatever came his way. When he soloed—as he did frequently in the bands that employed him—the fire still sometimes burned bright.

In the crowd one night at the Aragon, listening to him with Joe Kayser, was a seventeen-year-old Chicago clarinetist named John Muenzenberger, shortly to become Johnny Mince. "I'd never heard anything like [Tesch] before," he said. "He blew with such enthusiasm, such fire, that even when he squeaked accidentally nobody minded because he was swinging so hard. In those days we all tried to play hot, but Tesch was the hottest."[14]

Ted Lewis came through town in August 1929 and stopped to make some records. Don Murray, who had been with him since early 1928, had been killed in Los Angeles in June, and the leader, stunned by the loss, was picking up reedmen where he could. Muggsy Spanier and George Brunies were quick to recommend Tesch.

They did two titles. As was becoming more and more often the case, both harked back to the "good old days" of the early '20s. "Farewell Blues," a Friars' Inn anthem of 1921–23, had been the very number which, six short years before, had drawn the clarinetist and his high school buddies into hot music. "Wabash Blues" was Louis Panico's tune and feature and had been his big record hit.

"Tesch was always nervous about making records," Bud Freeman once told the author. "He never sounded his best in a recording studio. There was always a tension." Perhaps it was the sheer absurdity of the date, Lewis mooing and squawking away on his saxophone while Muggsy, Tesch, and Brunies did their best to keep straight faces, that helped relax him. His solo on "Wabash Blues," particularly, has a most engaging lilt, a relaxed, ruminative quality quite new in hot music of the time, at least on records.[15]

Nostalgia for the early '20s also permeates an October 18 Brunswick session under Elmer Schoebel's leadership. By then the pianist of the Friars' Inn was heavily involved in commercial music; he'd done well as a songwriter and had risen in the Melrose organization as a composer and arranger.

For his Brunswick date he chose two Melrose catalogue items, "Copenhagen" and "Prince of Wails." In all, the session has a curiously anachronistic feel. Even Schoebel's arrangements seem a bit out of touch; Joe Haymes's scores for the Weems band over at the Granada had more "modern" voicings, more out-and-out swing, than anything heard here, on what was supposed to be a "pure" jazz date.

Indiana bandleader Charlie Davis had written "Copenhagen" in 1924, and it had been recorded that year by Bix and the Wolverines. Schoebel treats it almost as a piece of jazz repertory, down to having Tesch and Floyd Town paraphrase the solos played by Jimmy Hartwell and George Johnson on the Wolverines record (and incorporated in the Melrose stock orchestration). Cornetist Dick Feige, who had played alongside Spanier on the first Charles Pierce Paramount records, shows himself here to be a devotee of both Muggsy and Bix, and trombonist Jack Reid, another Pierce regular, gets off some lusty work.

There's nothing much about these performances to tie them to the "Chicago style" of the McKenzie-Condon records. No flares or explosions, no get-off-my-note impulsiveness in the ensembles. Not even any real rhythmic spark or sense of urgency. In a broad sense, these records could have been made by any octet of capable hot music sympathizers in any number of cities in 1929.

Chicago in early 1930 was still attracting musicians from all over the Midwest. Bill Davison was from Defiance, Ohio; pianist Floyd Bean from Davenport, Iowa, where he'd picked up harmony from Bix. Stirling Bose, from Alabama by way of New Orleans, had played opposite Beiderbecke in St. Louis.

Kenneth Norville (soon to be known as Red Norvo) had done an apprenticeship as a teenage xylophone wonder in vaudeville and appeared briefly with Ben Bernie at the College Inn. By 1930 he was playing NBC radio shows in Chicago alongside Volly De Faut and pianist Dave Rosenberg (soon shortened to Rose). In May 1931, he opened with Paul Whiteman at the fashionable Edgewater Beach Hotel, and he stayed with the "King of Jazz" nearly two years.

Iowan Rod Cless, married to Bud Freeman's sister, was comfortably settled in Chicago, sometimes working for Panico. Drummer Earl Wiley had worked the riverboats with Tony Catalano before 1920; Danny Alvin, who had played drums for Sophie Tucker in Reisenweber's Crystal Room while the Original Dixielanders were breaking it up next door, was back in town and working for Joe Kayser.

Trombonist Floyd O'Brien was in and out. Jovial Charley Pierce still landed occasional jobs and could be relied upon to hire as many of the old guard as were still around. Clarinetist Joe Marsala, though the same age as McPartland and Freeman, had been slower in developing into an accomplished stylist in the fleet-fingered manner pioneered by Jimmie Noone. His younger brother Marty played cornet and drums; like his trumpeter friends Johnny Mendel and Carl Rinker, his style had been shaped by admiration for such black masters as Natty Dominique, George Mitchell, and the granddaddy, Joe Oliver.

They constitute a reminder that not all young Chicagoans had fallen equally under Bix's spell. Art Hodes, for all his friendship with Wingy, Tesch, and others, remained apart, both in his tastes and associations. So, too, did the gifted and enigmatic pianist Franklyn Taft "Kansas City Frank" Melrose.

Born in 1907 into the same family as music publishers Walter and Lester Melrose, Frank was from childhood bright, fast, and apparently quite rebellious. Jelly Roll Morton fascinated him, as did such South Side pianists as Clarence Williams and Jimmy Blythe. At sixteen, fresh out of high school, he hit the road, drifting first to St. Louis, then to Kansas City, playing where he could, but most often just listening.

It's been estimated that late-'20s Kansas City, under the wide-open regime of boss Tom Pendergast, boasted the country's largest concentration of speakeasies and cabarets. As a Nebraska columnist wrote with mingled censure and awe, "If you want to see some sin, forget about Paris and go to Kansas City." On 12th and 18th streets alone, pianist Mary Lou Williams later estimated, there must have been upwards of fifty joints featuring live music.[16]

Coming home from one such visit, Melrose went right into a Brunswick record date set up for him by elder brother Lester. The two titles, done with South Side drummer Tommy Taylor, reflected the hard-hitting styles he'd heard on his travels—enough to prompt Brunswick to issue "Jelly Roll Stomp" and "Pass the Jug" as part of its 7000 "race" series and identify Melrose on the label as "Kansas City Frank." The nickname stuck.

For Frank Melrose, "Mister Jelly" sometimes seemed little short of a god. As John Steiner has written, "Jelly and Frank saw each other frequently, jammed together in South Side clubs, exchanged fellowship, and the satellite advanced far along the paths his mentor showed him."[17]

Melrose's way of playing piano, like Morton's, was rhythmically forceful, heavily blues-flavored, and sometimes none too accurate technically. But it covered the keyboard in a way few Chicago pianists could approach, and it swung hard.

Equally at home among musicians of both races, he hired black cornetist Herb Morand for his first band date under his own name, for Paramount in 1929. Yet

Melrose also seemed to enjoy working with white cornetist Pete Daily, a pal and drinking buddy, at out-of-the-way joints in such rough areas as Calumet, on the far South Side, or in the industrial suburbs of Hammond and Gary, over the state line in Indiana. He was also a frequent sitter-in at the Three Deuces. When Sam Beers, who had run the Deuces, opened My Cellar, at Clark and Randolph, and hired Wingy Manone to lead the house band, Kansas City Frank got the piano chair.

Manone, whose knack for falling into good gigs was exceeded only by his skill at losing them, soon tangled with his new boss and found himself out of a job—but not before he'd wangled a record date at Brunswick. Both Teschemacher and Bud Freeman were around and available, as were Melrose and George Wettling. The only doubtful factor in "the Cellar Boys," as Manone called the band, was Frank Melrose's kid brother Charlie on accordion.

Accordion or no, these are extraordinary performances which, unlike the Schoebel titles, couldn't have been recorded anywhere but in Chicago. Somehow the sound of Wingy's Louis-like horn and Melrose's Mortonesque piano alongside Tesch and Freeman epitomizes the unique musical cross-fertilization of hot music in Chicago.

"Wailing Blues" isn't a blues at all but a thirty-two-bar song, its D-minor chorus adapted from Armstrong's "King of the Zulus." The "Barrel House Stomp," on the other hand, is actually a fast blues with a sixteen-bar verse. Both titles, issued in multiple takes, offer Teschemacher and Freeman in a raw, hotly blues-flavored vein. Bud, particularly, plays it down and dirty, with a tone that wouldn't have been out of place in a 1950s rock-and-roll band.

And that was it. No more records, no more good times. Just a sense of gathering darkness. On August 6, 1931, Bix Beiderbecke died at age twenty-eight, victim of pneumonia, drink, and the demons raging within him. Not seven months later, in the early hours of February 29, 1932, Frank Teschemacher was killed in an auto crash.

He and Bill Davison had gotten a band together for an engagement at Guyon's Paradise Ballroom. With a hand-picked personnel and arrangements by West Indian composer Reginald Foresythe ("Dodging a Divorcee"), it seemed a sure winner.

The night was cold, and the clarinetist huddled in his heavy overcoat, hands in pockets, as Davison's open Packard roadster bounced along quiet streets on the way home. According to Bill's account they'd just entered the intersection of Magnolia and Wilson when a taxi, headlights off, hit them broadside. Teschemacher was hurled over the windshield, landing head first on the concrete sidewalk. He was pronounced dead at a local hospital.

Both Bix and Tesch were still in their twenties when they died; both had only begun to explore their potential as musicians. Their deaths, coming so close together, seemed to many a rite of passage, a signal to move on and start coming to terms with life. To accept, as Teschemacher himself had said to Mezz Mezzrow, the fact that no one really knew or gave a damn what they and their kind were trying to do.

* * *

The story from there has a certain morning-after quality. By the end of 1933 Prohibition was over, with former speakeasies reopening as restaurants or straightforward nightclubs, some with music. Inevitably, as it always does, that meant work for musicians. Not always good work: the hours tended to be long, the money poor. If you were Jess Stacy, working with a little band in a joint called the Subway Café at Grand and Wabash, it was a sure bet that the piano you played on wasn't going to be a Steinway concert grand.

Frank Snyder, still playing good drums, had hired Jess, Jacobson, Carl Rinker on cornet, and George Lugg on trombone. "It was very easy to get lost in the Subway," said Lugg, who had spent part of the '20s touring outside the country, "because it was so vast, so mobbed, and so mysterious, with its low ceilings and scores of catacomb-like alcoves and passageways. I can recall times when I might be talking with someone only to find the person completely engulfed and carried away by the crowd before we could finish a few words of our conversation."[18]

Boasting what its management claimed was the longest bar in the world, the Subway stayed open twenty-four hours a day and lasted, remarkably, until mid-1935, when it closed over what Bud Jacobson termed "gangster-protection trouble."

Things were equally loose at Johnny McGovern's Liberty Inn, at Clark and Erie on the Near North Side. During Prohibition it had been the Breakfast Club, and Wingy Manone had worked there with Art Hodes, who called it "the last of the bucket-of-blood joints that we read about in the history of many a town." But, he added, it "was unique because it kept running and being itself at a time when all other places had lost all identity—had just become upholstered sewers."[19]

Earl Wiley was the house drummer—except when he could find Dave Tough or talk Don Carter into subbing. Mel Henke and Tut Soper were among the regular pianists, Manone was often on trumpet, and when Muggsy Spanier was in town he'd invariably turn up, too. The Inn had a floor show, with dancing in between, said Wiley, so "the piano never stopped . . . it was a great place, never a lull. Three fights on week nights and five on the weekend; if there was no fight nobody had any fun."[20]

One of the most familiar faces at the Inn belonged to a slight, scholarly-looking fellow who'd just as soon discuss poetry or philosophy as play his alto sax. But when he did get around to playing, it was with an urgency, a perfervid creativity, that held listeners spellbound.

His name was Boyce Matthew Brown. Born April 16, 1910, he'd been at John Marshall High School when McPartland, Tesch, and their pals were already out working as pros. He'd courted them, jammed with them, and in mid-1927 played his first professional job, at a Capone-run joint called the Amber Light.

Though he could read music, poor vision kept him out of larger bands; he spent most of his career in Chicago working in small groups, often with his guitar-playing elder brother Harvey. A photo published in *Down Beat* in 1940 shows the two of them during a 1928 engagement at the Midwest Athletic Club, in a band including Don Carter and violinist-guitarist Ray Biondi.

"He was a loner," said Jimmy McPartland. "He read a lot, was always writing poetry—little sonnets and things. Lived at home with his mother all his life. But boy oh boy, he sure could play!"[21]

As Dave Dexter Jr. and others have remarked, the effect of listening to Brown is something like that of hearing the early Charlie Parker. Indeed, the long phrases, chromaticism, altered chords, and alternative scales that pepper his choruses might almost qualify this retiring, bookish man as a sort of proto-bopper.

At up-tempos, for example, he'd come charging into a solo, generating irresistible momentum out of long, looping chains of eighth notes bound together with triplets. His tone is hard, bright, and a little sour, attack aggressive. For all his gentle and scholarly nature, Brown is a remarkably unsentimental, even tough-minded, soloist.

His debut on records came in early 1935. Trumpeter Paul Mares, restive in New Orleans, had returned to Chicago; taking advantage of a flurry of musical activity surrounding the city's "Century of Progress" exposition, he talked the management of Harry's New York Bar, on Wabash downtown, into having a jazz band. He got old New Orleans sidekick Santo Pecora on trombone, plus Stacy (replaced at the Subway by "Tut" Soper), George Wettling, bassist Pat Pattison, guitarist Marvin Saxbe, and, on alto, Boyce Brown. Almost right away he negotiated a session with OKeh, bankrupt but still in business.[22]

"We wanted to have a clarinet on the date," Stacy said, "and somebody came up with the idea of using Omer Simeon, from the South Side. He was working with [Earl] Hines at the Grand Terrace and used to come up after he finished down there and sit in with us."

Born in New Orleans, Simeon had moved to Chicago as a boy and studied clarinet with Lorenzo Tio Jr. when the famed Creole teacher was working with trumpeter Manuel Perez at a succession of South Side venues. He'd been active on the Chicago hot music scene since 1920 and was a pivot of the great Victor recordings by Jelly Roll Morton's Red Hot Peppers. Though racial divisions had relaxed considerably by 1935, it was still relatively unusual to find a black (or Creole) player sitting in with a white band.

More unusual, perhaps, for northerners than for the New Orleans men. Mares, it must be remembered, had recorded with Jelly Roll Morton in 1923. "We didn't think much about that," said Stacy. "We loved the way [Simeon] played, and when Paul got the date we just said, 'He's our man.' "

They recorded four sides on January 7. But something went wrong with the balance; so just short of three weeks later, on the twenty-sixth, they came back and remade all four. Both sets have been issued at various times. The format is loose jamming, held together with the sketchiest of head arrangements. "Paul was kind of a limited trumpet player," said Stacy. "Didn't read. Didn't know any harmony. Didn't have much of a lip. But he played a fine ride lead, just punched it out."[23]

Again, as on the Schoebel and Ted Lewis dates, the mood harks back to glories and good times past. OKeh labels identify the group as "Paul Mares and His Friars' Society Orchestra," itself an explicit reference to the heady days of 1922–23; no coincidence, too, that a slow blues featuring Simeon and Stacy is titled "Reincarnation."

Musically the performances are as hybrid as their personnel would suggest. Mares and Pecora clearly favor the broad-based New Orleans approach; in form and method, in fact, the trumpeter's way of playing a strong ride lead hasn't changed much in the dozen years since the Gennett records. Brown and the rhythm section are just as discernibly Chicagoans, bounding and rattling along with high energy. Simeon's long, vigorously executed phrases (how strongly they resemble Sidney Arodin's!) seem at home with both camps—though his occasional attempts to match the saxophonist's "funny notes" result here and there in harmonic missteps.

When the music dies away it is Boyce who is most clearly remembered, galloping out of the opening ensemble of an up-tempo "Nagasaki," for example, like a racehorse out of the gate.

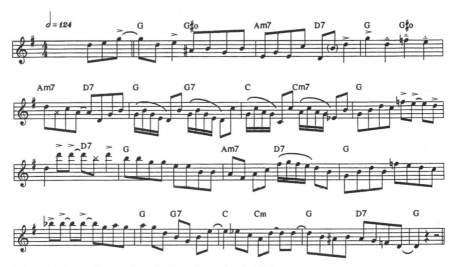

"Nagasaki," Boyce Brown alto solo (first sixteen bars), 1935.

On the January 7 version of "Maple Leaf Rag" (another nostalgic choice: the NORK, in 1923, had been the first jazz band to record it), his second solo begins with eight bars of almost boppish length and intricacy. In the medium-tempo "Land of Dreams" (an AABA song so named, presumably, because its eight-bar "A" section is based on the chord sequence of "Basin Street Blues"), he builds an attractive, Bix-like descending phrase which pivots neatly on the thirteenth.

Boyce next recorded in February and March with a racially mixed band led by Charles La Vere, who played piano like Stacy and wrote attractive songs. Neither session was issued, though test pressings have circulated for years among collectors. Boyce opens La Vere's own "I'd Rather Be With You" with a melody statement which manages to be at once romantic and unsentimental. The pianist solos effectively on "Smiles," from the same session, which also features some robust tenor from young Chicago prodigy Joe Masek, a Hawkins admirer.

Hugues Panassié, writing in Hot Jazz in 1936, declared Boyce Brown to be "the best of all white alto players at present, and probably the greatest of all, apart from Johnny Hodges." He would soon enough (in The Real Jazz) recant such judgments, having "discovered" Benny Carter and Willie Smith, not to mention a host of decidedly lesser lights, among the black jazzmen of the day. But his original assessment, for all its aura of hyperbole, remains perceptive:

> [Brown's] solos give an impression of an immense power and total mastery, as well as . . . enthusiasm . . . Assuredly Boyce Brown uses many notes in his solos, but they are no less simple, direct and impregnated with a spirit analogous with Bud Freeman's . . . entirely attached to the Chicago style.[24]

Around the beginning of 1935 Jimmy McPartland came home, his life in disarray, his marriage to Dorothy Williams, of the singing Williams Sisters, on the rocks. His cornet embouchure, never consistent, was shot; alcohol had become a problem, and he was broke. So when his guitar-playing brother Richard, married and well-established in town, wired him with a job offer, he took it without delay.

Richard had been working a lot in upscale hotels with a quartet he called his "Embassy Four," and when trumpeter Jack Ivett left the group it seemed logical to get in touch with Jimmy. They went into a lounge in the Palmer House and spent the next eighteen months in relative tranquility while the younger McPartland rebuilt both his chops and his personal life.

Help also arrived from another source. Edwin M. "Squirrel" Ashcraft III was a lawyer, living in well-to-do suburban Evanston. In the late '20s he'd been a central figure in the jazz-crazy Princeton crowd that venerated McPartland's own hero, Bix. During school vacations he'd frequented all the North and South Side haunts where hot music was to be heard. He knew the musicians, played piano (and a bit of accordion) himself.

In the mid-'30s he helped found (along with Canadian-born Helen Oakley) the Chicago Rhythm Club, bringing together the city's best hot players in public jam sessions. One widely discussed 1936 event run by Ashcraft and his Evanston neighbor Jack Stewart teamed NORK alumni Mares, Snyder, and Jack Pettis with Rod Cless, Boyce Brown, bassist Pattison, and other kindred spirits.

Sessions at the Ashcraft home quickly became regular affairs, usually on Monday evenings, ancestors of and inspiration for the jazz parties of a later day. Participants usually included top professionals, both Chicago residents and musicians passing through, plus a sprinkling of talented amateurs.

Joe Rushton, by now strong and proficient on bass sax, was a regular. "Where did Chicago Style Jazz go after 1930?" Rushton's wife Priscilla wrote many years later in an LP sleeve essay. "The answer is simple—it went out to Squirrel Ashcraft's house . . . nearly every Monday night from 1930 to 1942, the elite of jazz in Chicago at the time could be found in Squirrel's living room."[25]

There's much truth in that. The Ashcraft sessions offered a welcome for musicians, a chance to play with friends and peers in a relaxed, congenial atmosphere. Accordingly, significant musical moments were regular occurrences. It was at an Ashcraft gathering, for example, that Bob Haggart and Billy Butterfield worked out the shape of the trumpeter's band feature "I'm Free"; with a Johnny Burke lyric added, it later became the popular standard "What's New?"

Ashcraft sessions "often threw unlikely guys together," Eddie Condon wrote. "One night Brad Gowans and Joe Rushton just played duets, and valve trombone and bass saxophone is a strange combination but it sounded all right. On another night Bud [Freeman] and Pee Wee [Russell] traded instruments and sounded like each other, and on another night Bobby Hackett and Jimmy McPartland met for the first time. They kept their mouthpieces but exchanged horns and played Till We Meet Again for about twenty minutes, exchanging choruses."[26]

That encounter, at least, was recorded and issued. Though a bit far into their cups to be at their best, the two hornmen radiate an engaging bonhommie.

Beginning in 1935, when trumpeter Bobby Burnet (like Ashcraft, the child of a wealthy family) brought along a portable recording machine, the sessions at Squirrel's were regularly preserved on acetate discs. In later years, the precise and history-minded John Steiner functioned as engineer-in-residence.

Pianist Bob Zurke, musing in impressionistic, Bix-like fashion, was captured for posterity. So, too, was Boyce Brown, probing the melodic and harmonic implications of "Blue Skies." Wade Foster, the clarinetist from Moline who had recorded with Wingy Manone, came one night and sounded far less like Teschemacher than had been the case in 1928. Rosy McHargue and drummer Orm Downes, both with Ted Weems, were regulars, as was Bill Priestley, an architect who had studied in Europe with Mies van der Rohe, and who played both guitar and Bix-flavored cornet.

One notable part-timer was bass saxophonist Spencer Clark, friend and admirer of Adrian Rollini (and his replacement in the California Ramblers), a respected professional before leaving full-time music; often, when he and Rushton were at the same session, the latter would turn to his beloved metal clarinet.

Jimmy McPartland attended so often that he became, along with McHargue and Downes, part of the "Monday Knights," a sort of house band for the sessions. Some of his playing on these occasions, captured on the home recording discs, is indeed close to his warm and genial best, without the nervousness which often afflicted him in recording studios. There's much beauty in his work here, phrasing balanced and shapely in his Bix-like manner.

Ashcraft himself played a self-effacing role, gladly surrendering the piano stool to Zurke, Jack Gardner, or any of the other top men who attended the sessions. The parties continued on a more-or-less regular basis until World War II, then resumed (at Bill Priestley's home) in the early '50s. Some highlights, recorded by John Steiner, were released on custom ten-inch LP pressings: though occasionally uneven and often unmistakably bibulous, the music remains inspiriting.

For all the good times, Ashcraft's most keenly felt achievements may lie in his activities as adviser and behind-the-scenes "angel" to McPartland and more than a few other jazzmen. "I used to go up to his house all the time and tell him my problems," the cornetist said. "He knew I was busted up, and he often helped me."[27]

Soon after Jimmy's homecoming, Ashcraft presented him at a public jam session with a dozen of the city's finest, then followed up by staking him to a record date at Brunswick. Billed as "Jimmy McPartland's Squirrels" in obvious homage to its benefactor, the band was a composite: tenor saxophonist Dick Clark and trombonist Joe Harris were playing with Benny Goodman at the Joseph Urban Room of the Congress Hotel; McHargue and Country Washburn were with Weems. Rounding out the rhythm were Richard McPartland on guitar, Jack Gardner on piano, and his old buddy George Wettling on drums.

The music moves sunnily along, particularly on "I'm All Bound Round With the Mason-Dixon Line," a graceful, unjustly forgotten 1917 tune suggested by McHargue. Jimmy's cornet is quite confident, indication that his problems were well on their way to solution.

Chicago, meanwhile, remained a dancing town, a good location for traveling bands. Benny Goodman's stand at the Congress was long and successful. The Grand Terrace regularly featured Earl Hines, Fletcher Henderson, and the other major black bands. At the Blackhawk, owner-manager Otto Roth took a chance and brought in first Red Norvo's soft, subtle band, then Bob Crosby's New Orleans–flavored outfit, reconstructed from the remnants of Ben Pollack's band (which had itself played there earlier in the decade).

It was intrepid programming, in view of the Blackhawk's earlier reputation for musically conservative entertaining and novelty bands. The Coon-Sanders Nighthawks had done five successful seasons there; two years of Blackhawk broadcasts had made Hal Kemp a national name; bespectacled Kay Kyser launched his "Kollege of Musical Knowledge" on the Blackhawk's Monday evening radio remotes.

But Roth was quick to spot a changing market. Goodman's success, above all, had driven home the point that swing bands—i.e., dance bands playing big band jazz—were now good for business.

College students flocked to Sunday afternoon jam sessions staged by the Bobcats, Crosby's band-within-a-band, featuring trumpeter Yank Lawson, tenor saxophonist Eddie Miller, and clarinetist Matty Matlock. Radio listeners enrolled in the "Bobcat Club" and tuned in faithfully to the band on station WGN.

Metronome magazine's George T. Simon came, listened, and rated them "A." He especially admired "a certain atmosphere around this band that you won't find in any other . . . a unanimity of purpose, of thought, both musical and otherwise, plus a sense of freedom and play—all combined with an air of maturity— that you won't find in any other orchestra."[28]

Crosby made the Blackhawk his band's unofficial headquarters for the next three years, moving to New York only when an offer came to take over the popular coast-to-coast *Camel Caravan* radio show from Benny Goodman. To a man, his musicians looked back on their Chicago time as the most enjoyable in the band's illustrious history.

The city's hot jazz life, meanwhile, went its quiet underground way. George Avakian, a Yale English literature major with a flair for Renaissance poetry and a yen to produce hot records, visited in 1939 on a two-week tour of midwestern cities, in company with fellow-scholar Marshall Stearns. In a long *Down Beat* article, he praised Rod Cless, then working with Muggsy Spanier and George Brunies at the Sherman Hotel, and pronounced Bud Jacobson with sweeping certainty "the no. 1 clarinetist in the U.S. at the moment." He and Stearns also dropped in at the Liberty Inn to catch Boyce Brown with Earl Wiley's trio.

"Boyce," Avakian wrote, "is possibly the Ellington of the alto sax—you can't say he's playing jazz and he doesn't always swing either. What does he do, then? Well, they're still trying to find an answer for Ellington, and when they do they'll be able to say the same for Brown. That both are great cannot be denied, and both have their place in jazz. This automatically makes Boyce Brown the best white alto saxophonist."[29]

The results of Avakian's visit became apparent later that year when he began assembling bands for his first major record project, a Chicago jazz album to be issued by Decca—and the first jazz *album* devoted to one theme (as opposed to reissue compilations). For a group led by Jimmy McPartland, he filled out the front line with Brown and Bud Jacobson, adding a rhythm section that included adoptive Chicagoan Floyd Bean, who had worked often with the saxophonist. Gordon Darrah, writing in the punningly titled British magazine *Eye Witness Jazz*, described hearing the two of them a year or two later at the Preview Lounge, on Randolph Street:

> Boyce's choruses never faltered, and, like Floyd's, always showed vivid ideas and imagination . . . He never seemed to work, or to give the appearance of working—none of the familiar bending back on the knees or making faces to indicate passion for the music . . . His fingers seemed to fly over the keys without effort, and the outward indication he gave of interest in the music was occasionally closing his eyes as he played.[30]

On bass was Jim Lanigan, by then well established as a member of the Chicago Symphony Orchestra. Richard McPartland was the guitarist, Hank Isaacs on drums. The results came far closer to the original Chicago feel and flavor than had the 1936 session, right down to flares, shuffle effects, and the rest of the old devices.

They rehearsed regularly at the Ashcraft and Priestley homes until the band was sounding tight and full of pep. A date was set. Then, only then, did bad luck seem poised to again blight McPartland's efforts.

> When I woke up that morning I couldn't open my mouth; [I] had an infected wisdom tooth, and my jaws were all swollen. When Bud [Jacobson] came in he said: "We'll get some brandy down you and see if

we can loosen it up." I kept sipping on this brandy till I'd drunk about a pint. My mouth began to open, and boy! I felt good.[31]

McPartland's playing belies such travails. He leads well, solos with almost serene lyricism on "Sugar" and "The World Is Waiting for the Sunrise." Brown and Jacobson both manage to raise the shade of Teschemacher, the saxophonist with his push-the-beat attack and affinity for "funny" intervals, and the clarinetist with his sour tone and slashing approach to the rhythm.

Boyce's full chorus on "Sunrise," in fact, is as unconventional as Avakian's *Down Beat* pronouncement indicated. It doesn't quite swing in any usual sense; its phrases, with their long chains of eighth notes, jostle and crowd one another in an inexorable forward push. In the end, it sounds like no one else but Boyce Brown. On "Sugar," his phrase construction and choice of notes are particularly startling. In the chorus's last eight bars he makes free use of diminished and augmented chords (and whole-tone scales) as *substitutions* against the unaltered diatonic harmonies of the rhythm section:

"Sugar," Boyce Brown alto solo (last eight bars), 1939.

Brown's appearance with McPartland on the four Avakian titles attracted unexpected attention. He won the 1940 *Down Beat* readers' poll in the alto sax category, edging out such competition as Benny Carter, Johnny Hodges, and Jimmy Dorsey. But it was all little more than a prelude to obscurity. On February 12, 1940, the saxophonist did two numbers for the small, limited-circulation Collector's Item label as part of a quintet led by a refulgent Bill Davison. And that was all: they were his last records, until a final, disappointing LP in the late '50s, and they are among his best. His solos on "I Surrender Dear" and "On a Blues Kick" are angular, idiosyncratic, harmonically and melodically probing.

"Brown was perhaps the most philosophical of numerous philosophic musicians I have met down through the years," Dave Dexter wrote in 1964. "To him, jazz was purely metaphysical, and he sincerely believed that the instrument he played actually absorbed part of himself and was more than an inanimate object."[32]

So much did Brown believe this, Dexter said, that he named his alto saxophone Agnes and once explained one of his less notable performances by saying that "I failed to communicate with Agnes. It was my fault, not hers."[33]

231

Boyce's way of expressing himself verbally was as singular as on his instrument. In a letter to *Down Beat*, for example, he declared:

> Attempting to understand himself emotionally and to effect a moderate self-discipline in accordance, and making a real effort to diversify his interests should keep a musician on an even keel mentally. I adhere closely to a diet, evading acid-forming foods among other things. And I try to get some exercise every afternoon, and at least eight hours' sleep every 24. I don't really feel that night-club work is any less healthful than office work.[34]

He continued to play around Chicago in the 1940s, at the Liberty Inn, the Club Silhouette, and other small rooms, frequently in company with pianists Chet Roble or Floyd Dean. Over time, inevitably, he began to feel he was going nowhere, and that communicated itself strongly to friends and colleagues. His eyesight, never good, worsened, cutting him off little by little even from his beloved books, the world of poetry and philosophy which was his solace.

He continued to write verse. In a "Sonnet on Jazz Music," he observed:

> Musicians of today must grow to learn
> That superficial praise and spotlights tend
> To fetter freedom and distress the mind.

In "Christmas Anthem" he reflected:

> Upon the keyboard of Eternity
> The aged, outstretched fingers of the years
> Now recapitulate the harmony
> Of peace, long alien to human ears.

Retreating ever deeper into contemplation, surrounding himself with the music of Delius and Debussy, Boyce Brown was baptized a Catholic in 1952, and entered a Servite monastery the following year as Brother Matthew, a title taken from his middle name.

He emerged once more, in 1956, to appear on television and record an LP with Condon, Davison, and other pals from the old days. It's a saddening affair; Boyce is rusty, out of shape and out of tune, the once rapid flow of unorthodox ideas all but gone. Condon and friends, obviously feeling no pain, have their usual good time, with Eddie contributing a particularly raffish running commentary.

The LP sank from sight with merciful swiftness, and after a burst of publicity surrounding Brother Matthew and his jazz past, Boyce Brown disappeared, too, into the monastery outside Granville, Wisconsin, where he died of a heart attack January 30, 1959.

"Looking back, I think he's just as interesting now as I thought he was then," George Avakian said recently. "The things he did, people are doing that kind of thing much more now. But at that time almost nobody was: the element of surprise was a big factor. People hearing him for the first time were just flabbergasted. I know I was. Where did this guy *get* this odd way of playing? Where did it come from? I guess there was a rather mysterious quality in all that. Part of what makes it so interesting."[35]

It's one of the strengths of the whole short, rapid evolution of jazz that new styles and approaches seem to supplement, rather than supplant, their predecessors. If by 1939 the way of playing represented on these records belonged to the past, it was a past still alive and healthy.

Only a dozen years had passed since the McKenzie-Condon OKeh session, and not many more than that since the glory days at the Friars' Inn. Bix and Tesch were only recently dead. Yet jazz had swept on; new heroes had emerged, and with them new ways of playing and thinking.

By October 11, 1939, when Jimmy McPartland and his friends recorded "The World Is Waiting for the Sunrise," the Count Basie and Duke Ellington orchestras were riding high as jazz forces. Billie Holiday and Lester Young had made epochal records together; Benny Goodman had conquered Carnegie Hall (demolishing some racial barriers along the way); Dizzy Gillespie was attracting attention with Cab Calloway, and Charlie Parker with Jay McShann, both with solos full of fascinatingly "wrong" notes.

And on the very day, perhaps at the very moment, that McPartland was celebrating his music's past with "Sugar" and "Jazz Me Blues," tenor saxophonist Coleman Hawkins, in a New York recording studio, was helping shape its future with an extemporaneous, end-of-session "Body and Soul."

Yet there would always be musicians, comfortable in the older ways, who saw no reason to change; they'd continue to play as they always had, honing and refining. Younger players, attracted by the sound and emotional aesthetic, would come along to join them.

Jazz has always traveled these two parallel roads. If Hawkins, protean and ever-restless, spent the great part of his career tearing apart and reinventing his style, there is no obloquy in acknowledging that Ben Webster devoted equal effort to polishing and reducing his to its essentials.

For some, the quest is all: surely Bix, had he lived, would have followed exploratory instincts which were already leading him away from the hot jazz of his youth, and even from the cornet. Yet Louis Armstrong, jazz icon and exemplar, spent four decades of his life shaping and simplifying a style he'd perfected in his twenties.

Benny Goodman never stopped deepening his technical mastery of his instrument, yet never strayed from the jazz style that had dazzled contemporaries when he was a sixteen-year-old boy wonder with Ben Pollack's band. Artie Shaw, by contrast, studied, understood, then absorbed the harmonic advances of bop into an ever-evolving musical conception.

But a certain need to celebrate its own past, forever glancing back over the shoulder, seems built into the mechanism of white Chicago jazz—and to a certain degree into early white jazz in general. Paul Mares, if unwittingly, identified it by choosing "Reincarnation" as a title on his 1935 OKeh date. But reincarnation of what? And why? It had been only a dozen years since the long, great nights at the Friars' Inn, not a long time by anyone's measure. Yet he saw fit to celebrate it all the same.

An easy answer lies in citing the commercial interests of record companies. The original Friars Society Orchestra and New Orleans Rhythm Kings records were already collector's items: why not capitalize on the name and the nostalgia of all those for whom the basement cabaret on Van Buren Street had become something of a shrine? But how many such records did a company expect to sell? These were not, after all, pop confections, pressed in the hundreds of thousands to be snapped up by a mass audience.

And what of George Avakian's motivations in wanting to devote an entire album to white Chicago style while the original records, made only a decade before, were still, as it were, hot off the presses?

One clue, perhaps, lies in the fact that, as a form of dance music, hence entertainment, hot jazz was subject to the same generational forces that shape all forms in American popular culture. As young Americans of post–World War I days had embraced the Original Dixieland Jazz Band as emblematic of their rebellion, their rejection of their parents' legacy, so did succeeding generations find new spokesmen, new theme songs to voice their comings-of-age. The children of the turbulent 1960s, who warned their contemporaries never to trust anyone over thirty, were part of a process little different from what had gone on in 1918: 1923 and 1940 may have been separated by only seventeen years on the calendar, but to generation-conscious Americans it was as good as a lifetime.

It's useful, moreover, to note that there was no parallel movement among black musicians, no attempt to re-create or revive such pivotal early ensembles as the Oliver Creole Jazz Band or Morton Red Hot Peppers, least of all by the original participants, who seemed content—even eager—to put their pasts behind them. Exhumation of that music came about only in the '40s, when white bands such as that led in California by trumpeter Lu Watters spearheaded a New Orleans jazz "revival."

When, in 1938, Johnny Dodds made his first records in almost a decade, it was with a band that included members of the then currently popular John Kirby Sextet. Their versions of even such chestnuts as "Wild Man Blues" and "Melancholy" are firmly, even resolutely, anchored in the present. Charlie Shavers's treatment of "Wild Man Blues," in fact, sounds for all the world as though this twenty-year-old trumpet whiz did not know Louis Armstrong had made a classic of the number eleven years before—"back then." Even Dodds himself, as heard on the record, seems to be avoiding so much as a perfunctory nod in the direction of earlier ways of playing.

By the time Mares did his 1935 OKeh date there had been other exercises in "Reincarnation." When, in 1927, Bix Beiderbecke recorded "At the Jazz Band Ball" and "Jazz Me Blues" for OKeh, he was by his own declaration celebrating Dominick James LaRocca and the Original Dixieland Jazz Band. Elmer Schoebel's curiously anachronistic Brunswick date of October 18, 1929, discussed earlier in this chapter, saluted the Friars Society Orchestra and drew on numbers popular in the early '20s.

By contrast, the Fletcher Henderson Orchestra recorded its 1928 "King Porter Stomp" arrangement again in 1932, this time billing it as the "*New* King Porter Stomp." It was as if to say, "Don't worry, folks—none of that old-fashioned '20s stuff here. This is brand-new, up-to-date, fresh as today." James T. Maher recalled bringing up the subject of early Henderson records one night in a conversation with Coleman Hawkins. "What do you want to listen to that junk for?" was the tenor saxophone pioneer's immediate and annoyed response.[36]

A Chicago Rhythm Club concert at the Winona Gardens, January 24, 1937, featured a Friars' Inn reunion with Mares, Loyocano, Snyder, and pianist Kyle Pierce, plus guests Rod Cless and Bud Hunter; by contrast, Earl Hines, appearing as a guest star, seemed most anxious to plug his latest vocal discovery, Ida James, whom he'd picked up at a Philadelphia club.[37]

Half a century later, with major revivals on record, and nostalgic festivals getting under way in both classic jazz and tap-dancing, initial reactions of black and white performers to such archaeological exercises differed markedly. Where the whites, in the main, approached the older forms with curiosity and a desire to re-create the spirit, veteran black players and hoofers alike resisted. Their attitude was best summed up in Hawkins's remark to Maher, and echoed in fellow-saxophonist Budd Johnson's nonplussed "Why would you even *want* to go back to that old stuff?"

The answer, surely, lies in the tangled sociology of black-white relations and the layered meanings which the past—separate, shared, intertwined—carries for both groups. In many respects, the two groups had inhabited two different pasts: for whites, looking back was often a sweet experience, equal parts pleasure and the melancholy of recalling times that seemed better, purer, more carefree. For too many blacks, that same past meant memories of poverty, frustration, anger, and—perhaps above all—iron-willed determination to fight clear of the legacies of slavery. In this house, nostalgia was at best a stranger.

George Avakian admitted to more than a little outright sentimentality in putting together his 1939 *Chicago Jazz* album. While still at Yale, he'd suggested the idea to Jack Kapp at Decca as a way of illustrating the spread, influence, and dissemination of Chicago jazz (later albums to be devoted to Kansas City and New Orleans). He'd record three different bands, all composed of native or adoptive Chicagoans, all playing songs they'd recorded back in the '20s.

The album, as it turned out, was even more revealing than its creator had foreseen; the three groups produced quite different results, illustrating in aggregate fashion what had happened to the music, its spirit, and its practitioners in a single decade.

The band at the first session was, in essence, Bud Freeman's Summa Cum Laude Orchestra under Eddie Condon's leadership, Joe Sullivan replacing Dave Bowman at the piano. The musicians were all just into their thirties, the open possibilities of the future still outweighing the foreclosed options of the past.

Listening to their four titles half a century later, Avakian heard them as adaptation rather than re-creation, "an extension of the music these guys were playing [at that time] back toward the direction of the Chicago style." Dave

Tough, for example, went right to Baby Dodds, playing on his drum heads, using cymbals only for accents. By then his usual style, heard on countless records with Tommy Dorsey (and with essentially this same group on Columbia's *Comes Jazz* album of half a year later), focused heavily on his cymbals, particularly his big, deep-toned Chinese ride cymbal.[38]

The front line (New Englanders Max Kaminsky and Brad Gowans, Chicagoan Freeman, and southwesterner Pee Wee Russell) functions, as usual, like a precision instrument: while there are a few of the musical details that characterized the first records—a stop-and-start mid-chorus explosion in "Nobody's Sweetheart," for example—Chicago is mostly in the flavor, in *how* they go about things.

McPartland's group, by contrast, goes for the spirit *and* the letter of the earlier style. Its four selections display all the trappings, even to a neatly executed ensemble shuffle, explosion, and drop to *pianissimo* in the last chorus of "Jazz Me Blues." This little band had obviously done its homework and a lot of conscientious rehearsing.

"I think they took to the idea as enthusiastically as they did because it was very close to them," Avakian said. "I don't think any of those guys, except Jimmy himself, had traveled very much. They were Chicago musicians in Chicago, and they had been working there all their lives, often with each other. It made a difference."[39]

The third series of four titles, by a band under George Wettling's leadership, had the potential to be as rewarding as the other two. Avakian's nomination for clarinet was Joe Marsala, who had left Chicago for New York in the early '30s but still reflected the many nights he'd sat listening to Jimmie Noone. But who, then, would play tenor?

"We had Floyd O'Brien on trombone," he said, "but had to have a tenor, for the flavor. There was no one around who was really suitable. So Joe decided to play tenor himself, which he did wonderfully, and we got Danny Polo on clarinet."

It was a fortuitous choice. An Indiana native, Polo had worked for Elmer Schoebel at the Midway Gardens and subbed for Don Murray in the memorable Jean Goldkette Orchestra of 1927. He'd spent years in Europe, famously with Bert Ambrose, returning to widespread admiration in bands led by pianists Joe Sullivan and Claude Thornhill. In Thornhill's band he played alongside New Orleans fellow-clarinetist Irving Fazola: the two men, both using Albert system instruments, were—in their awed words of one Thornhill alumnus—"two of the most beautiful-sounding clarinets in the world." Among Polo's most devout admirers was a young saxophonist-arranger named Gerry Mulligan, who in the 1990s still spoke of Polo with reverence, calling him "the first truly modern-sounding clarinet player I'd heard who encompassed all the qualities of the clarinet that had gone before."[40]

Avakian's attempts to recruit Muggsy Spanier foundered on RCA's refusal to let the cornetist out of a newly signed Victor contract. His surrogate was Charlie Teagarden, younger brother of Jack and a fine trumpeter in his own right, playing in what Max Harrison has termed, aptly, the musical equivalent of a classic prose style. But in some not-quite-definable way the records misfire; Teagarden's decorative, and decorous, manner never quite jells with the rhythmically more aggressive Chicagoans. There's a difference in concept—subtle, but enough to dilute the effect.

Not that "I've Found a New Baby," "Darktown Strutters' Ball," and the others are less than fine performances; they just don't come off with the punch, with the clarity and unity of purpose, that distinguish the others.

The gulf between Teagarden and his companions—especially Marsala, O'Brien, Polo, Stacy, and Wettling—is itself a kind of identification of the white Chicago way of playing. Just as Avakian and Marsala recognized the need for a soloist of a special kind to play the ensemble tenor parts (a Ben Webster or Chu Berry, however accomplished, would not have fit), so, too, did the lead horn role demand a specific—a punchy Muggsy Spanier—orientation.

Beyond dispute, those young white Chicagoans who emigrated to New York in the late '20s carried the substance and creative thrust of their music with them. It's felt as a catalyst, an energizing factor, in many records made there beginning in 1928. Red Nichols's June 12, 1929, Brunswick version of "Rose of Washington Square," for example, could not have been made two years earlier; Freeman, Sullivan, and Tough, aided by Pee Wee Russell and Jack Teagarden, seem to shoot a bolt of electricity through the performance.

Mixed with elements of other approaches, notably the unbuttoned intensity of such black players as trumpeters Sidney DeParis and Frankie Newton, trombonists Sandy Williams and J. C. Higginbotham, and such new Orleans emigrés as Henry "Red" Allen and "Pops" Foster, this music ultimately evolved into New York "dixieland" of the late '30s and '40s. Eddie Condon, ever garrulous, became a kind of spokesman and media champion.

At home, the Chicago brand of tough-minded, crowd-the-beat lyricism persisted among white musicians. Bud Hunter and Joe Rushton were on hand when, in 1941, a young New York collector and fan named Bob Thiele came to town determined to make his own "genuine" Chicago-style records. He'd consulted Avakian, who had suggested Hunter, Joe Rushton, and Bud Jacobson, plus veterans Earl Wiley on drums and Frank Melrose at the piano; the cornetist was Carl Rinker, whose style had been formed by such South Side players as Natty Dominique and Herb Morand.

Bud Jacobson's Jungle Kings (named, of course, after the band on the Spanier-Teschemacher "Friars Point Shuffle" date) recorded first on January 13, 1941. It took two sessions to get both the balance and Thiele's patchwork equipment working; even then, neither is entirely successful. Occasionally, as in the ensembles of the two-part, curiously named "Blue Slug" (issued not by Thiele but by John Steiner), the band churns so violently it sounds about to fly apart.

Yet there's no denying that these primitive recordings capture a certain continuing vitality. "Blue Slug I" and "Laughing at You" are the same song, written in 1926 by Jacobson and Eddie Condon, and taken at two different tempos. On the fast version ("Blue Slug"), Jacobson's tone and attack evoke Teschemacher, but it's Austin High irregular Bud Hunter who commands most attention; his bustling tenor solos suggest, but never ape, the early Freeman.

He also dominates a rather manic "Clarinet Marmalade," opening the solo

237

round with sixteen bars on tenor, then switching to clarinet for an equally thrust-ing solo. Rushton, also on clarinet, is softer-toned, a little reminiscent of Volly De Faut.[41]

The rhythm section is raw but powerful. Melrose, in common with his old friend and hero Jelly Roll Morton, delivers a fully chorded, thumpingly forceful brand of piano—though as John Steiner has observed, "the flamboyant dynamics contributing so much to Jelly's ultimate charm seem neglected in Frank's per-formances. Frank was as deft, but he was not as loud where Jelly was loud, not as soft where Jelly was soft, not as furious or buoyant in climactic passages."[42]

Though no one realized it at the time, these free-wheeling records turned out to be the true final act in Chicago's two and a half decades as a hot jazz gestation center. At 7:30 on Labor Day morning 1941, police found Frank Mel-rose, thirty-three, battered and dying on the corner of 130th and Oglesby on the far South Side, not far from his home.

His face had been so mutilated he was all but unrecognizable. Only his over-coat could be positively identified. A hit-and-run driver? An attack by hoodlums? No one could tell. A Down Beat article commented that, "typical of the plight of so many truly gifted jazzmen, Melrose has never seemed to make a decent living at his art, but occasionally found work playing in taverns and joints of the Calumet region, southeast of Chicago."[43]

There was a certain irony in the manner of his death: throughout the thirteen years of Prohibition, with gangsters all but running the city and mayhem likely at any time, jazzmen had lived and worked in relative safety. They kept their noses clean, kept playing, and nothing befell them. But here, eight years after repeal, on a lonely street corner in a grubby section of town, Franklyn Taft Melrose met violent death at the hands of assailant or assailants unknown, calling out to his old friend Bud Jacobson for help.

Only the music, echoing now in stillness, remained.

11

Bud Freeman
and the Tenor
Saxophone

*"If I want to hear a good saxophone, I'll find out
where Bud Freeman is playing."*
— John O'Hara, The Flatted Saxophone

Every Sunday, Bud Freeman remembered, there were special matinees at the
Senate Theatre, a rather grand picture palace on Madison Avenue, on Chi-
cago's heavily residential West Side. And every Sunday the audience included
Bud, age fourteen, his brother Arny, twelve, and various cousins.

"In those days, the better cinemas carried a pit orchestra that played a kind of
overture made up of the current popular songs," he told John Bainbridge in a 1979
New Yorker profile. "The orchestra at the Senate Theatre was led by Paul Biese."

Though a name scarcely remembered today, Paul Biese was a key dance band
leader in the germinal, still relatively underdocumented years around 1920. His
records sold well, and he had appeared at Chicago's popular College Inn.

"Biese was a saxophone player," Freeman said. "He played alto—and his
saxophone was *diamond-studded*. I remember they used to pin this lone spotlight on
him, so everything was dark except Biese and his saxophone, shining and sparkling. The sound of the saxophone and the shininess of it—it's difficult to explain,
but it just got me," he said. "I thought, I must have one of these one day."[1]

What documentation does exist, and all available discographical information,
indicates that Biese played not alto but tenor saxophone. He had worked widely in
vaudeville, hotels, and ballrooms, sometimes for the seemingly ubiquitous booker-

bandleader Edgar Benson, often with a novelty trio heavy on the squeals, squawks, and "laughing" effects of what was briefly called "nut jazz." Songs bearing such descriptive titles as "Chili Bean" and "Happy Hottentot" were staples of his repertoire. Biese recorded regularly, for a variety of labels, from 1919 to 1924.

If Bud Freeman had wished to concoct a romantic myth around his first encounter with the instrument that became his life, he could hardly have bettered this one. Sitting there in a darkened theatre, bedazzled by the sight—the entire mise-en-scène—of it all, he dreamed his dreams.

Reality turned out to be another matter: the awkward but well-documented facts indicate that Lawrence Freeman, born in Chicago April 13, 1906, and known from childhood as Bud, didn't take to music easily. Among his music-obsessed boyhood chums he was the slow one, who took longest in getting his chosen instrument under his fingers.

Not that the Freeman home was without music. His mother played the piano, as did her five sisters and two brothers. But Emily Fernette Freeman spent her last years in a sanitarium and died when Lawrence was sixteen, leaving her husband Louis, a garment cutter, to bring up the children himself—Lawrence, his younger brother Arnold, and elder sister Florence.

It proved a formidable undertaking: at some early stage the boys apparently decided they were going to be "artists"—no specifics, no strong motivation to study or excel at any given endeavor. They'd simply live and behave in the way they fancied artists lived and behaved; the rest, presumably, would take care of itself. Image and reality, again, inhabiting adjacent, but quite different, worlds.

Perhaps realizing he had no choice, no way of enforcing any real discipline, Freeman père seems to have acquiesced. "You boys don't have to worry," he told them. "You have the house. There will always be food for you. Go on and do what you want to do. Be happy. But make sure that what you do is what you want to do."[2]

But they never seemed to do anything. Neighbors, alarmed, would telephone or knock on Lou Freeman's door to ask why Lawrence and Arnold seemed always to be hanging around, never going to school—or even out to work. "And Dad would say, 'You don't understand. My boys are artists. They're crazy. They're different from other boys . . . And you're going to hear about them some day.' "[3]

Once in a while, when neighborly concern pricked his conscience, Lou overcame his resignation enough to challenge his sons. One morning, bursting into their bedroom, he demanded they get out of bed and go out looking for jobs like "other normal people." Arny, said Bud, drew himself up and "in stentorian Shakespearian fashion said, 'Sir, how dare you wake us before the weekend!' "

According to Freeman's own testmony and that of such friends as cornetist Jimmy McPartland, his image-chasing went through phases: he was going to be an eccentric dancer in vaudeville, an actor on the English stage, an aristocratic country gentleman—all, presumably, until he learned that work and sustained effort, even potential hardship, might be involved.[4]

"If I had been forced to earn a living I would not have laid off the instrument as often as I did," he said of his first efforts on the saxophone. "I would have taken more jobs . . . I was a spoiled brat, and so was Arny, but he was tougher.

He worked very hard at being an actor but I didn't work as hard at being a musician. I *wished* that I were a musician [emphasis added] more than I worked at becoming one."[5]

Arny, in fact, did go into the theatre, becoming a respected character actor with many Broadway stage roles to his credit. Bud, meanwhile, made slow, sometimes excruciating progress on the saxophone—often to the dismay of the tight little circle of friends who included him somewhat begrudgingly in their efforts to turn themselves into a band. The most precocious of them, by far—and the least patient with Freeman—was bespectacled Frank Teschemacher, the clarinetist. "Let's throw that bum out!" he'd yell in despair after more than one practice session disrupted by saxophone honks and squeals and one-note solos.

The oft-told story of this group of boys, usually known as the "Austin High Gang" because of a neighborhood school they hardly attended, appears elsewhere in this volume. Suffice here to say that hot music was their mania, that it was readily available all over Chicago, and that they were far more assiduous in searching it out than in attending classes. They made no distinctions between white or black, authentic or ersatz: be it the Friars Society Orchestra at the Friars' Inn, King Oliver's Creole Jazz Band at the Lincoln Gardens, Isham Jones and Louis Panico at the College Inn, or Doc Cooke's big orchestra at the Dreamland Ballroom, they grabbed it where and however they could.

Freeman, the slow starter, had the furthest distance to travel, but eventually, after many setbacks, the instrument began to yield to him. His way wasn't any easier for the fact that he'd chosen a horn with virtually no solo tradition in the "hot" idiom. Neophyte clarinetists could go to Jimmie Noone and Johnny Dodds among the South Siders, Leon Roppolo and Volly De Faut among the whites, hear Larry Shields on records. Cornetists had Joe Oliver, Freddie Keppard, Johnny Dunn, Paul Mares—and the glorious example of Oliver's commanding protégé, the fast-developing Louis Armstrong.

Tenor saxophone offered more limited options. Biese and Isham Jones may have been fine, accomplished players, the latter even something of a virtuoso: but they were not hot improvisers. For that, Freeman looked to Jack Pettis, who played tenor and the lighter-toned C-melody with the Friars' Inn band. "Nobody seems to know about Jack Pettis," he said in reminiscence, "but he was the first swinging tenor player I ever heard. Since there was no one before him, playing that style, I have to call him a master. It must be realized that there was a Chicago school of tenor. There were many players who played in that style and didn't become well-known. Pettis was the king of that style. They called the style Northwestern then. It had the cool sound . . . Lester Young, though he may not have known Pettis, was influenced by that particular school of tenor."[6]

There's more than a little evidence on records to bear him out, at least in a general way. Besides Pettis, solos by Don Murray, George Johnson, and Fud Livingston display many common traits: a fluid attack and loping beat, generating momentum through chains of eighth notes; a pure, light-textured tone which at its best is quite vocalized but at other times seems unable to escape the instrument's natural tendency, when played this way, to low a bit.

Overall, it's a concept that seems to have sprung from the clarinet. Comparison between Pettis's ensemble lines and those of clarinetist Leon Roppolo on "Eccentric" (1922), the Friars Society Orchestra's first record, reveals a similarity of conception and execution. What's lacking here—and what Coleman Hawkins brought so dramatically into play in these years as a member of Fletcher Henderson's New York–based orchestra, was a conception of the tenor saxophone as a separate entity, with a voice—and technical properties—of its own.

Freeman became aware of Hawkins very early. What impressed him most, he said, was less the emergent Hawkins style than the *idea* of the style. "I had not known what a powerful solo instrument the tenor could be until I heard Hawkins with Henderson in 1925 or 1926 in Detroit at the Graystone Ballroom," he told Ira Gitler. "I was just amazed by the way the man handled the instrument and the power of the instrument. Hawkins, in those days, did not play the way he plays today. He played very much on the beat, tongued a lot of things, and had a powerful beat and terrific drive and sound." Freeman was impressed, he said, "by the idea that a man could play with such powerful authority . . . But I never tried to play like Hawkins."[7]

In common with his friends, Bud learned as he went along. Their little band seldom used a trombone, so he got used to finding a third voice in the front line, a more mobile one—given his instrument—than a trombone could have supplied. "I loved the idea of being able to play around the melody and get in and out of the way of the [others]," he said. "So when I was playing between the voices I wasn't aware that I was doing it. It was instinctive."[8]

And, a step at a time, something began to evolve. A sound and approach. A language. And it sounded like no one else: not like Pettis or Murray or Livingston; not like Hawkins; not like Prince Robinson, shortly to become tenor soloist with McKinney's Cotton Pickers, or Benny Waters with Charlie Johnson's band at Smalls' Paradise. It sounded like Bud Freeman. It's there on his first records, made in late 1927 with McPartland, Teschemacher, and the rest of the little band that called itself, for the occasion, McKenzie and Condon's Chicagoans. His solos on "Nobody's Sweetheart," "China Boy," and the rest are rough in spots, sometimes disjointed, technically unfinished. But they are undeniably, indisputably, jazz tenor saxophone solos.

The tone is lean, a little coarse, quite without the mellifluousness of the white "Northwestern" players and with a harder, more percussive attack. Yet it's a linear style, owing little either to Pettis's clarinetlike noodling or Hawkins's arpeggiated arabesques (this latter, and occasional chordal lapses, make clear that Freeman's harmonic sense still lagged behind his fingers). Where, then, did it come from? A clear answer seems to lie with another instrument—the trumpet.

"Too much Armstrong," said Teschemacher of Freeman's solo on "Nobody's Sweetheart." What constitutes "too much" is for the listener to decide. There is no doubt that Armstrong's attack, rhythmic vitality, and bravura manner affected the young saxophonist profoundly. But there's a second motivating force, more specific because closer to the sensibilities of all these young men, which makes itself felt in every note they play, every phrase. That force is Bix Beiderbecke.

Bix. Friend and mentor, at once youthful (only three years their senior) and very old, innocent and wise beyond his years, he was everything they aspired to be. He was—by temperament rather than by design—the artist both Bud and Arny Freeman had tried to be. And the *sound* he made: people listening to records today, Freeman told Max Jones, "can't really hear Bix. If they could have heard Bix as I did, in person, and played with him, then they would have known that he was probably the genius of our times."⁹

He was, in William Howland Kenney's apt formulation, "a middle-class Mid-westerner become ill-fated artist." Everything about him made sense to them, embodied what they wanted to think about themselves. If Bix listened to Stravin-sky's *Firebird* or Ravel's *Daphnis et Chloë*, so did they. His phrasing—linear, com-positional, less emotionally charged than Armstrong's but more layered, more complex—challenged the intellect as readily as the heart. Teschemacher worshiped him; McPartland emulated him—and replaced him in the Wolverines; Freeman, spellbound, listened and learned.

"I don't recall ever saying, 'I want to be different. I don't want to play like anybody else,' " Freeman told his literary amanuensis, Robert Wolf. "My style was just the result of so much listening I don't think I was conscious of its unique character until people came to me and said, 'How does it happen you don't sound like anybody else?' "¹⁰

How unlike anybody else is obvious on a record done for Columbia October 30, 1930, under Red McKenzie's name but not issued until many years later. For the first time, Bud Freeman and Coleman Hawkins stand side by side in a re-cording studio, and on "Girls Like You Were Meant for Boys Like Me," each gets a chance to solo. A confident Freeman opens with a full chorus, stating the melody in the manner of a trumpet leading a jam ensemble. After a spirited comb-and-paper chorus by McKenzie, Hawkins takes over for thirty-two bars.

The comparison is tantalizing: where Freeman phrases right on the beat, even pushes it a little, Hawkins plays with it, elasticizes it with *rubato*; where Freeman's concept is almost Bix-like in its restraint, Hawkins is garrulous, expansive; Free-man's tone is austere, a little dry—Hawkins's ripe, full-blown. A conclusion is ob-vious: this moment, this marker along the road, defines two clear, intensely person-al, unmistakably different, ways of playing hot jazz on the tenor saxophone.

Bud Freeman went to New York in the spring of 1928, playing alongside Jimmy McPartland and fellow-Chicagoan Benny Goodman in Ben Pollack's band, only to leave that summer to work for George Carhart aboard the liner *Île de France*. He seems to have spent the rest of the year trying to make up his mind where he wanted to settle: sometimes he was in New York, working with Condon and Red Nichols, doing society jobs for Meyer Davis and Roger Wolfe Kahn, and more than a few times he returned to Chicago.

He recorded there for OKeh December 3, this time under his own name and using some local friends, among them clarinetist Bud Jacobson, trumpeter John Mendel, trombonist Floyd O'Brien, and pianist Dave North. One of the two se-lections was his own "Craze-o-logy," loaded with portents of things in store. It had been only a year since the manic but not-quite-formed solos of the McKenzie-Condon records, but Bud Freeman had come a long way.

243

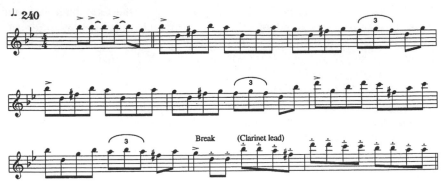

"Crazeology," Freeman's first eight bars, 1928.

Here, in raw form, is the foundation of the mature Freeman style: there is a new ease with arpeggiated phrases, delivered on the beat and stitched together with triplets; he'd begun to work out little variations—altered notes, chordal superimpositions, characteristic runs and rhythms. The slow learner had hit his stride: he was developing fast. The rest was polishing and refinement.

He's easily recognizable on a clutch of records made between 1929 and 1933. His rather wild chorus on "Rose of Washington Square," made with Red Nichols on June 12, 1929, includes a figure in bars 15–16,

"Rose of Washington Square," Freeman solo (fifteenth and sixteenth bars), 1929.

which by using a concert D♮ against an F7 chord creates the tonality of a B♭ minor triad, and with it the illusion of harmonically exotic goings-on. It was a bit of musical sleight-of-hand, *trompe d'oreille*, which was to permeate Freeman's work more and more. Much the same thing happens in bars 7 and 8 of his half-chorus "Bessie Couldn't Help It," made September 15, 1930, with a group led by Hoagy Carmichael (and marking Bix Beiderbecke's last appearance in a recording studio).

Even at this early stage Freeman was developing a second, parallel, conception, which finds expression on ballad material (and on slow blues). Its hallmarks are restraint (more Bix here, perhaps?) and, emerging gradually, a dry humor which seems very much his own ingredient. On his own "After Awhile," recorded under Benny Goodman's name August 13, 1929, he sings out the appealing melody, with the ardency of a radio crooner. (This duality is hardly unusual. Hawkins, too, developed rather different methods of dealing with different material. Where his solo on the fast "Hello Lola" is agitated, his attack percussive to the point of brutality, his treatment of "One Hour," on the reverse of the 1929 record, is warmly sensual, deeply romantic, full of *rubato* flourishes quite absent from his up-tempo manner.)

As the 1930s got under way, Freeman kept polishing what he'd developed and gradually attracted a cadre of followers, saxophonists who found his agility and gutty attack appealing; with sometimes more enthusiasm than skill they adopted his delivery, his triplet-and-arpeggio manner, and even some of the "funny notes."

Prominent among them was Pittsburgh-born Irving "Babe" Rusin (later Russin), who as a seventeen-year-old had sat beside Bud in Carhart's Île de France band. His rather breathless contributions to such 1930 Red Nichols records as "Shimme-Sha Wabble," "Peg o' My Heart," and "I Want to Be Happy" attest to his ardor in picking up the tonal and rhythmic accents of his mentor's playing. He developed into a full-toned, probing stylist who can be heard to excellent advantage on Tommy Dorsey's 1938 "Milenberg Joys" and backing Billie Holiday on her May 11, 1938, "You Go to My Head." Russin in later life became one of the most formidable of reedmen working in the Hollywood film studios. Those few occasions when he emerged as a jazz soloist never failed to surprise and delight listeners who had simply overlooked him.[11]

Illinois-born Larry Binyon, whose place Freeman had taken temporarily in Pollack's band, worked in something of the same idiom, with perhaps a more explicit nod to the "Northwestern" style cited by Freeman. A quiet man, he was a solid and versatile professional, who doubled on flute and other woodwinds—yet could turn out excellent, heartfelt hot choruses on tenor.

More than a few musicians of the era, in fact, rated him very high. Before Freeman came east to stay, said trombonist Al Philburn, "there were only two tenor men who counted for anything in New York: Coleman Hawkins with Henderson and Larry with Ben Pollack. He was responsible for that big, full sound that later guys like Herbie Haymer and Georgie Auld used. But he was a modest guy and never pushed himself.

"I remember asking him why he never took a solo on all those Dorsey brothers records they did for Brunswick in the '30s, and he said, 'You've got three minutes, and there's Tommy and Jimmy and Bunny and Manny and Joe [Venuti] and Dick [McDonough] and Fidgy [McGrath] and sometimes a vocalist. How the hell do you expect me to fit in? Besides, I'm usually too busy laughing at the other guys.' " Binyon's twenty-four bars on the Dorsey Brothers' 1933 "Old Man Harlem" is typical of his authoritative playing.[12]

In 1933 Bud Freeman recorded another piece of his own devising, a kind of sequel to "Craze-o-logy." He called it "The Eel," first of an icthyologically-titled oeuvre which also eventually included "The Sailfish," "The Disenchanted Trout," "The Eel's Nephew," and the melodically intriguing "Margo's Seal." He recorded it at least four times, twice that first year, again in 1939 and finally in 1971.

It's basically little more than an E♭ blues, bookended by a sixteen-bar B♭ strain based on a simple harmonic structure: eight bars of tonic, four of D♭9 (or, without the root, A♭m6), and four more of tonic. But the agile, at times chromatic and harmonically suggestive melody he placed atop this simple foundation became an index, a primer of his rhythm style, for the rest of his career. A fascinating exercise, it reveals much about its author's methods and thought processes. The following transcription is taken from the 1939 version, recorded for Bluebird.

"The Eel," Freeman thirty-two-bar melody statement, 1939.

The figure dominating the first two bars, recurring throughout the piece, declares the game: rhythmic displacements, juxtaposition of a three-beat figure against a 4/4 rhythm, frequent alternation of major and minor intervals—and, in bars 22–24, exploitation of the rich possibilities in chromatic upper and lower neighbors. All without sacrificing a strongly propulsive sense of swing.

If the overall impression left by up-tempo Freeman is of exuberance and whirligig high spirits, Freeman's alternative *persona*, used on medium and slower tempos, is an exercise in understatement. It's close, in fact, to the manner he cultivated off the stand: witty, a little detached emotionally, "cool" with an aristocratic, faintly ironic mein. In one commentator's apt phrase, a dry sherry to Hawkins's fuller-bodied old port. It's there for the sipping on the "A" take of another E♭ blues, "Home Cooking," made the same day (October 21, 1933) as the first exploration of "The Eel."

The duality persisted throughout the '30s. Bud Freeman at fast tempos was most often the *attack* soloist, tone coarsened, drawing heavily and often imaginatively on the vocabulary of "The Eel." But the other Freeman, the debonair Freeman, emerged on the pop songs, the medium- and slow-tempo arrangements. He spent 1936 and '37 in Tommy Dorsey's reed section, and Dorsey records of those two years are full of him: "Little White Lies," "Keepin' Out of Mischief Now," "Sleep," "Stop, Look and Listen," "Beale Street Blues," "Twilight in Turkey," "A High Hat, a Piccolo and a Cane," and the outstanding "At the Codfish Ball," which manages to blend attack and amenity in a manner that evokes the image of John Steed, the suave character played by Patrick MacNee on the TV series *The Avengers*.

Not everyone was captivated. No other saxophone soloist of the '30s, in fact, seemed as able to polarize opinion as did Freeman: the very mention of his name in the trade magazines could bring on paroxysms of intemperate letter-writing.

"In the first place," sputtered an anonymous *Metronome* magazine reader in 1937, "I think Bud Freeman is just about the world's worst tenor man . . . How you gentlemen can rave about a lot of meaningless and out-of-tune tenor is beyond me." Return fire came a month later from another correspondent, also nameless, lauding a "finesse that . . . overshadows all instrumentalists on the tenor sax." And so it went.[13]

Both are of course exaggerations. What's beyond dispute is that Freeman, unlike Hawkins or Lester Young, seemed able to generate such wildly contradictory feelings. Part of it may have had to do with how he was perceived, both on the stand and off.

His friendship with Dave Tough, begun when they were teenagers, had directed Freeman toward literary and artistic tastes, a life of the mind. He often expressed impatience with fellow-musicians for shutting themselves off from such experience. Bud never forgot the time Dave took him to the Chicago Art Institute to see an exhibition of paintings by Paul Cézanne.

> Now I confess that I'd never heard of Cézanne, but I said, "I'd love to go." So I saw this painting, *The Fruit on the Table*. The piece of fruit was a sort of purplish green color, which made it seem to stick out from the table. I said to Dave, "I wish I could say something about this magnificent work," and Dave said, "That's the best thing you'll ever say about it." He hated the idea of words for art.[14]

Freeman often disparaged the "vulgarity" of American culture and made little effort to disguise his preference for Europe and its traditions, frequently affecting British speech and dress. "He was always talking about the theatre, or art, or some book nobody else had read," said Jimmy McPartland, "or about how Americans were really jerks who didn't know anything. I used to say to him, 'If you love England so much, why don't you move over there?' "[15]

For a while during the '70s he did, living in London and appearing as guest soloist with cornetist Alex Welsh's fine septet and other European groups. He could often be seen, impeccably tailored, rolled-up umbrella in hand, strolling along Charing Cross Road. For pianist Keith Ingham, a frequent accompanist, this too was role-playing. "Somehow you knew that this great Anglophilia of his had come right out of the movies—Ronald Colman, people of that sort," said Ingham. "To him, *that* was England. Midnight in Mayfair. Afternoon tea at the Ritz. Bond Street, Simpson's in the Strand. I think he was rather surprised to come up against the average Anglo-Saxon lout. That wasn't exactly what he'd envisaged, and I doubt he had any idea how to deal with it. So he just ignored it."[16]

Even on the stand Freeman had an air, a mien: those partial to him saw in it his love of theatre; others, taking less charitable views, looked on him as a *poseur* and heard his playing as mannered, a series of roles played for various occasions, more image than substance.

Freeman may have invented his musical *personae*, but there's no denying that he inhabited them fully. His solos, especially from 1935 on, are always forceful, compelling, the vocabulary readily identifiable as his alone. The figure-shapes, little chromatic and enharmonic conceits, the distinctively fast, pronounced vibrato—not to mention a whole arsenal of honks, purrs, and other characteristic sounds—make Freeman solos on record immediately recognizable, full of surprise and ingenuity.

On an October 2, 1933, date with Joe Venuti's Blue Six, he punches out his chorus on "The Jazz Me Blues" in an almost Bix-like manner, the effect enhanced greatly by Adrian Rollini's bass sax in the rhythm section. He's quite percussive on "In de Ruff," which is just "Dippermouth Blues" traveling under a flag of copyright convenience, and even evokes Hawkins a bit with his rhapsodic "fills" in the opening chorus of "Sweet Lorraine."

Freeman seems particularly effective on a certain kind of up-tempo, minor-key solo. On "Sendin' the Vipers," from Mezz Mezzrow's band date of May 7, 1934, he delivers a plangent, rhythmically intense chorus in D-minor. If Bunny Berigan's majestic trumpet takes the gold medal at the memorable Gene Gifford small-band session of May 13, 1935, Freeman easily qualifies for the silver: his whirling, stabbing contribution to "New Orleans Twist" (this time in E♭-minor) is one of his best.

He tops that one on Mezzrow's March 12, 1936, date, spinning out a chorus of even greater vitality and forcefulness (in D-minor) on "The Panic Is On." After a piano solo by Willie "the Lion" Smith, Freeman complements Frankie Newton's strong, spare trumpet lead with a succession of plunging, pirouetting ensemble figures over George Stafford's powerful drumming.

With his vocabulary now in place, Bud—in common with Webster, Goodman, Roy Eldridge, and countless others—began a long and rewarding process of refinement. Unlike Hawkins, who seemed driven throughout his life to discard each language as soon as he'd perfected it, Freeman worked with the elements he'd created, forever varying and shaping. He began to mix his placements and accents, dynamics and tonal shading, use space in new ways. His tone deepened and broadened.

Freeman recorded "China Boy" many times. It was with him at the start and became, like "You Took Advantage of Me," "Exactly Like You," and a handful of other standards, a familiar vehicle for his style. Three Freeman "China Boy" choruses, recorded in '27, '39, and '57 respectively, show the constants and the variables: the shapes and favored note-combinations remain recognizable, but the refinement process is clear.

(continued)

"China Boy," three Freeman choruses on three staves, 1928, 1939, 1957.

In bar 9 of his 1927 chorus, for example, he reaches for a high B♮ to begin a downward-tracking figure, but that figure is only half-realized. By 1939, he's developed it to a point where he can execute the entire pattern over four bars—but allows it to lead him into the self-indulgence of an exercise-book conceit. He uses much the same material in the 1957 chorus but distributes it in far more measured fashion.

The figure with which he opened his '39 bridge even turns up verbatim elsewhere in '57, in a melodically more coherent role. His treatment of bars 27–28 is similar in the '39 and '57 versions—but by extending the phrase into bar 29 in the latter chorus he gives the entire episode more weight, imparting greater melodic continuity to the entire eight bars.

A growing body of critical opinion hears Freeman's as one of the three significant tenor styles of the '30s, alongside those of Coleman Hawkins and Lester

Young, and the hardest of the three to reproduce. "It's funny," said historian Loren Schoenberg, himself a polished tenor stylist. "I can integrate elements of the styles of Lester, Hawkins, or Ben Webster into a coherent solo of my own. It's a matter of figuring out what parts of their various vocabularies are relevant to what I'm trying to do, the story I'm trying to tell. But I can't do that with Bud Freeman. Sure, you can approximate a bit of him now and then, but only the most superficial aspects. You can never really get into it. His melodic vocabulary is unique, and so is his sound. Harmonically he's as advanced as anyone— but it's his own harmonic system.

"Mostly, I think, it's rhythm: he has a fascinatingly different approach to rhythm, one which works perfectly for him. The odd thing is, when you listen to those records what he does sounds easy—simple, straightforward, on the beat. It's just when you try to reproduce it that you discover how subtle it is, and how far beyond reach."[17]

By the mid-1930s the list of tenor sax players using Freeman's style as a point of departure had lengthened considerably. Pee Wee Russell, recording on tenor with the Rhythmakers in 1932, approached rhythm playing in the same vigorous, gutty manner. His solos on such records as "I Would Do Anything for You," "Who's Sorry Now?" and "Mean Old Bed Bug Blues" are unmistakable in their provenance. Forrest Crawford, a frequent associate of Bunny Berigan, seemed to blend Hawkins's broad sound and Freeman's way of attacking a phrase; Art Rollini and Dick Clark, both featured with Benny Goodman, found the triplet-and-eighth-note figure patterns so prominent in "The Eel" a handy and light-footed way of dealing with fast tempos. Rollini's striking half-chorus on Goodman's 1936 record of "I've Found a New Baby," for example, is a study in such chain-link phrasing.

Tony Zimmers, with Larry Clinton's late-'30s orchestra, sometimes carried this manner even further, producing choruses that felt as though they'd been conceived on a trampoline; his solos on such 1937 Clinton records as "Swing Lightly," "I Cash Clo'es," "Military Madcaps," and "Shades of Hades" show him at his most typically saltatory. It makes Zimmers easily identifiable and adds great lift to the sometimes static and repetitive Clinton arrangements. On slower performances, Zimmers displays a different manner: his thoughtful chorus on "How Am I to Know?" is quite reminiscent of Freeman's ballad side, tone rounded yet capable of delicate shading.[18]

"I still consider Tony Zimmers one of the fine tenor jazz stylists of our time," said Larry Clinton, "and you might be surprised at how many latter-day savants and studio jazz men agree." Big band historian George T. Simon, who saw and admired Zimmers on many occasions during the '30s, certainly did, and has said repeatedly that the saxophonist was not accorded sufficient credit. "He really played his horn excellently," Simon said, "and his solos always swung. I never could understand why he didn't get noticed more. Probably it was just a matter of too many tenor players in the field—with guys like Hawkins, Lester Young, Bud Freeman around, it was probably inevitable that lesser guys, no matter how good, would be taken for granted." Tony Zimmers was killed in action in World War II.[19]

Skeets Herfurt, who replaced Freeman in Tommy Dorsey's reed section and had been a mainstay of the earliest Dorsey Brothers band, presents his own version of the Freeman "attack" style on the 1938 Dorsey Clambake Seven's "Chinatown, My Chinatown." His mid-chorus break and the four-bar hill-and-dale phrase that follows it could have been lifted out of some "Freeman's Fifty Hot Licks" book, so closely does it hew to the precedent.

Dave Harris, best known for his work with the stylistically hybrid Raymond Scott Quintet, displayed a strongly Freeman-oriented tone and attack. His solos on such fancifully titled Scott records as "Powerhouse," "Reckless Night on Board an Ocean Liner," and particularly "Dinner Music for a Pack of Hungry Cannibals" draw extensively on the same vocabulary.

Chicagoan Joe Marsala was chiefly a clarinetist, for whom saxophone playing, either on alto or tenor, was very much a subsidiary activity. Yet, as noted earlier, when George Avakian approached him in 1939 to play with a band led by drummer George Wettling as part of Decca's projected Chicago Jazz album, he volunteered to play tenor. "I suspect Joe was intrigued by the challenge of playing Bud's role in a Chicago ensemble," the producer said.[20]

Marsala filled it admirably. His ensemble work is a model of integration with Danny Polo's clarinet, Charles Teagarden's trumpet, and Floyd O'Brien's terse trombone; his solos, particularly on "I Found a New Baby" and "Darktown Strutters' Ball," combine Freeman mannerisms with his own softer tone and attack.[21]

Arranger Deane Kincaide, on his few outings as a tenor soloist, showed himself quite adept at Freeman impersonation; Tony Pastor, friend and sidekick to Artie Shaw, displayed Freeman traits, particularly on ballads; Bostonian Nick Caiazza mixed Freeman, Hawkins, and Young in a particularly eclectic style; such others as Ray McKinstry and Bernie Billings, both of whom worked with Muggsy Spanier's little "Ragtimers" band of 1939, used Freeman's attack and rhythmic sense as components in various ways.[22]

But after Freeman, the outstanding white tenor saxophonist of the '30s, to the point of being almost an independent force, was unquestionably the diminutive, New Orleans–born "Little Prince," Eddie Miller. Unlike the Chicagoan, he began with clarinet: as a teenager, working around his home town, he idolized Leon Roppolo, and clearly remembered one night when the brooding, emotionally troubled clarinetist of the New Orleans Rhythm Kings showed up to hear him play. Eager to please, the youngster unleashed a solo full of technique and showy phrases.

"Hey, kid," the older man said reprovingly. "It's not how many notes you play, it's how you play 'em." Miller, a modest and thoughtful man, never forgot: his style, as it matured, became a model of economy, balance, and grace. Nowhere in any Miller solo on record, on either instrument (or on alto or baritone, both of which he played commendably), is there a superfluous note, a throwaway passage, a phrase dropped in for effect. Whatever the the tempo or setting he's poised, coherent, with a rich, singing tone.

Arriving in New York in 1930, he jobbed around the hotel and freelance circuit awhile, playing alto and clarinet (he remembered his awe at one dance job on which the trumpets were Bix and Bunny Berigan), then joined Ben Pollack's Orchestra, replacing Babe Russin in the tenor chair. Though the larger instrument was new to him, he quickly made himself right at home on it: his solos on such 1933 Pollack records as "Two Tickets to Georgia" and Wingy Manone's "Swing Out" show him playing easily and forcefully.

The remains of the Pollack orchestra, of course, became the foundation of the brand-new Bob Crosby band, dealt with at length elsewhere. "The Little Prince" was easily its most popular musician and, along with clarinetist Irving Fazola, most highly regarded soloist.

He is most often compared to Freeman and cast in a decidedly secondary role. But comparing these two outstanding tenor saxophonists of the '30s is hardly that simple and must be undertaken carefully. Similarities between them, overall, rest in matters of delivery and effect rather than content. Both play clean, rhythmic phrases, riding high on the beat and quite without the rubato effects basic to the mature style of Hawkins and his admirers. True, Chu Berry also tended to ride the rhythm, but in a far less elastic manner—and with a heavy tone and legato attack which often creates the impression of a solo being played on ball-bearings.[23]

Miller and Freeman solos, particularly on faster numbers, are most often direct and exuberant. Freeman at his most nimble (as on Tommy Dorsey's thrill-a-minute "Maple Leaf Rag") could produce a jiggling, almost manic intensity. It is this aspect of his style that seemed particularly to affect such admirers as Chicago alto saxophonist Boyce Brown.

Both Freeman and Miller were masters of small-band ensemble playing. No one has ever bettered either at finding the interstices in the trumpet-clarinet-trombone mesh and filling them in interesting and melodically varied ways. As Commodore Records founder Milt Gabler has said of Freeman, "A band really came to life when he was in the bottom booting it! Just like he's giving rim shots there, when he's playing the background underneath."[24]

Clarinetist Joe Muranyi remembered vividly a conversation he had with Freeman in 1977, on joining the rather hyperbolically named World's Greatest Jazz Band of Yank Lawson and Bob Haggart. "I'd been wondering how it was going to work out," he said. "No charts. What's going to happen? How should I play with him in the ensembles? Busy? Spare? How am I going to avoid bumping into him? Well, it was as though he'd been reading my mind. 'Joe, don't worry,' was all he said. 'Play anything you want. I won't get in your way.' And you know, he didn't. I just went and played and it was uncanny: nothing I could do interfered with him. We never crossed, never bumped into one another."[25]

The two saxophonists' methods differed somewhat: for illustration, it's useful to listen to Bud working with Max Kaminsky, Pee Wee Russell, and valve trombonist Brad Gowans on "There'll Be Some Changes Made," recorded under Eddie Condon's leadership in 1940. He appears to roll off the backs of Kaminsky's on-the-beat phrases: there's seldom a place, in fact, where Freeman attacks a phrase or pattern head-on, simultaneously with the lead. Instead he waits—perhaps one or two beats, perhaps more—then places his phrase to emerge as that of the cornet is tapering off.

Eddie Miller, by contrast, plays a modified clarinet role, finding a third voice to complement and sometimes parallel the declarations of trumpet and clarinet and leaving the trombone to work independently, often in the traditional New Orleans "tailgate" manner; but he achieves much the same effect as Freeman by extending his phrases, carrying them over into the gaps. That's especially clear on such Bobcats records as "Stumbling," where he develops a melodic counter-line to Lawson's lead, "Coquette," and the exuberant final ensemble chorus of "Hindustan."

In later life the two men appeared often together at festivals and jazz parties. One of their most satisfying meetings came in Hard Times, Good Times, presented at New York's Town Hall during the 1983 Kool (later JVC) Jazz Festival. During the afternoon rehearsal, as friends and fellow-musicians listened in delight, Freeman and Miller got into an exchange on "Royal Garden Blues" which began as friendly bantering and quickly opened out into a more probing conversation. Each, it seemed, was reiterating a credo, setting out belief and conviction about playing jazz on tenor sax. It was an exhausting, exhilarating experience, quite surpassing anything that happened during the concert itself.

What emerged in that exchange was an inventory of similarities between the two men—and, more numerous, dissimilarities. Most of the latter seemed to result directly from the way each had come to his instrument.

Freeman, from the moment he saw Paul Biese in that theatre spotlight, had wanted to play the saxophone, and it was the saxophone with which he began—though he did take some early lessons from a Chicago Symphony clarinetist. Miller, by contrast, was an accomplished clarinetist: his clarinet solos on various Crosby records show him to be a full-toned, liquid improviser very much in the New Orleans tradition of Roppolo, Sidney Arodin, and above all his sectionmate Fazola.

The last-named three played the Albert system clarinet, an instrument whose simple fingering and dark, woody sound made it a favorite among early hot soloists of both races. Edmond Hall, Barney Bigard, Omer Simeon, and Albert Nicholas were among other New Orleans men who persisted with the Albert instrument even after it had sunk into oblivion elsewhere.

Miller's clarinet chorus is a highlight of the Crosby band's "Wolverine Blues," building from its low register with limpid ease and tonal beauty. On "Stumbling," Miller takes a full chorus on tenor, then picks up the clarinet to finish out Bob Zurke's piano chorus. His concept on the two instruments is almost the same: it's easy, listening to the two solos, to understand that Miller's approach to the saxophone was essentially a built-out version of his way of playing clarinet.

Freeman did it the other way round. His few recorded clarinet solos (the most notable are "The Buzzard" and "Tillie's Downtown Now," from his John Hammond session in 1935, discussed presently), are examples of his saxophone style pared down and shaped to fit a rather restricted clarinet technique.

Where Freeman was often an object of controversy, even vituperation, Miller appears to have been universally loved. "He was a sweetheart, every inch a gentleman," said big band historian George T. Simon. "Personally he was the warmest, most genuinely caring of human beings, an absolute joy. I don't think he had a mean or nasty bone in him."[26]

That carries over into the music. There is little sense in Miller of Freeman's risk-taking, the sense of operating on the edge that gives his work its special *frisson*. Not that Miller is without forcefulness: once away from the easy *bonhommie* of the 1935 Crosby band (cf. "Swing, Brother, Swing" and "Nickel in the Slot" with Wingy Manone), his playing often takes on a bite that brings it closer to that of Freeman.

Freeman had recorded "Nickel in the Slot" (as "In the Slot," conferring a slightly different shade of meaning) with Manone half a year earlier. His solo, predictably, is harder-hitting than Miller's, but perhaps less melodically rich. Freeman is even more forceful on "Rhythm Is Our Business," also with Wingy, but his two choruses lose some melodic coherence as a result.

Eddie Miller is above all a melodist straight out of the white New Orleans clarinet tradition, a prime song-singer on both instruments. Which, inevitably, suggests comparison to Lester Young. Critical discussion of Young most often centers on how his work differed from the prevailing Hawkins-influenced tradition of black tenor playing. According to this interpretation, Lester burst, fully formed, into view with the Jones-Smith "Shoe Shine Boy" and "Lady Be Good" of 1936, upsetting the hegemony of Hawkins and his desciples. A departure, an original, he'd found his own way and developed it in the black territory bands of the Southwest.

What seems odd about all this is not how different he was from Hawkins, Webster, and the rest—he was indeed that—but how *similar* he was conceptually to the white saxophonists. In matters of tone, rhythm, melodic conception, he shares much with Freeman, Miller, and the overall aesthetic they exemplify.

Yes, no black tenor saxophonist before 1936 played the way Lester Young played. But all the components of his style are present in the work of his white colleagues: his debt to Trumbauer (and, through him, Bix) is obvious and widely acknowledged. No less striking is a clear rhythmic tie to the buoyancy of Freeman and Miller.

Young never hid his disdain for the heavy-breathing effusions of the Hawkins school ("Some of you guys are all belly") or his fondness for the records of such white pop singers as Frank Sinatra, Jo Stafford, and Doris Day. George Hoefer, writing in *Down Beat* in 1952, described a visit by Lester to the Long Island home of club proprietor Bob Maltz during which the saxophonist spent the evening listening to and admiring Bud Freeman records. He liked Freeman, Lester once told an interviewer, "because nobody played like him. That's what knocked me out."[27]

Pianist Jimmy Rowles, who played with Young frequently during the '40s and '50s, said the saxophonist always named Bud Freeman among the players he liked most. Several record collectors remembered being asked, "You have any Bud Freeman records?" when Lester visited their homes.[28]

Young's way of riding the beat, particularly at fast tempos, immediately recalls the dancing-on-springs approach of the white tenor men. He uses almost no *rubato* but plays squarely on the beat, generating momentum, like Freeman, through long, nimbly played, eighth-note phrases, pivoting here and there on a triplet. Here, for example, is Young's half-chorus on the Teddy Wilson Brunswick record of "I've Found a New Baby" (transposed from his original key of F), contrasted with Freeman's treatment of the same material on a 1939 broadcast with Joe Marsala.

(Note: Young transposed from written key of F)

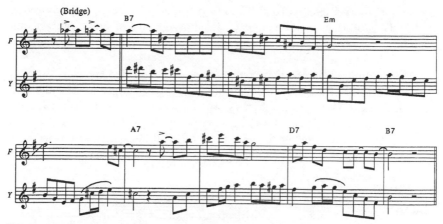

"I've Found a New Baby," Bud Freeman/Lester Young solos, 1939/1937.

Perhaps Young's key indebtedness to the white tenors lies not in rhythm or phrase construction but in aesthetic choices—where he positions himself emotionally. His solos on the Teddy Wilson–Billie Holiday "I Must Have That Man" and "Foolin' Myself," two examples among many, couple restraint and emotional layering in a manner not only redolent of Bix but far removed from Armstrong's operatic bravura, the sentimentality of black cornetist Joe Smith, or the extravagant floridity of Sidney Bechet.

As early as "Home Cooking" in 1933, Bud Freeman had established a reserved, "cool" *persona*, light of touch, economical, with a certain emotional *Abstand*. His alternation of textures and timbres and use of chromaticism (a quality basic to Trumbauer as well) also clearly attracted Young. As George Hoefer put it in a 1952 *Down Beat* article, "Pres was fascinated by the yearning quality inherent in the lightness of tone and the sensitivity of the white jazz tradition."[29]

There is a relation here, extramusical, abstract, between the way Young's and Freeman's styles work. Part of the delight of hearing Young on Basie records rests in the contrast between the band's riff-based blues orientation and the saxophonist's insouciant, even occasionally satiric, solo excursions. Herschel Evans (and later Buddy Tate), ripe-toned, embellished, fit the context admirably. They are within and of it. Young is quite another matter: he often seems a kind of Astaire, top hat at a rakish angle, the band his stage set as he dances around and outside it.

And if Young is Astaire, Freeman is Nöel Coward, natty in ascot and smoking jacket. Each, in his way, is onstage, playing a role, speaking in aphorisms: it's a theatrical phenomenon, one that both men carried over into day-to-day life, if in quite different ways. But in those early days they lived in quite different environments, which expected different things of them.

Mid-1930s America was still segregated America. However close they might be after hours, black and white musicians still viewed one another across a wide social gulf. Both Bud and Lester might be critical, even disdainful, of the societies surrounding them, but it's inevitable that their criticism would take different

257

forms, socially and intellectually. It's easy to suspect that Young's introspection, his need for privacy, found expression in idiosyncrasies of dress, carriage, and speech, a way of distancing himself from the insensitivities of the environment in which he lived and worked.

There is little likelihood that Young consciously emulated Freeman, except in the most general of ways. It's enough to say that what he played and the ways in which he played it, creative as they were, stood on well-established foundations. Here is "Honeysuckle Rose," as interpreted by Young (Benny Goodman Carnegie Hall concert), Eddie Miller (as part of "Call Me a Taxi," by Four of the Bobcats), and Freeman, on a recording made in December 1945.

"Honeysuckle Rose," Bud Freeman/Eddie Miller/Lester Young, three staves.

In bar 6, playing against B♭ and B♮ diminished chords, Freeman and Young opt for much the same figure shape and much the same note order. In bars 7–8 Young seems to draw a wriggle or two from "The Eel" in setting up an intensely rhythmic episode. Bar 2 of the bridge, similarly, has Bud and Lester relying on the same sort of sequence; but where Young chooses one of his familiar one-note "rides" going into the last eight, Freeman and Miller play melodic paraphrases which, though structured differently, clearly spring from the same kind of conception of the song.

While Eddie Miller spent most of the 1930s with the Bob Crosby band (and its predecessor, the Ben Pollack Orchestra), Bud Freeman moved around. He put in a few months with Roger Wolfe Kahn, a year with Joe Haymes, and was with Ray Noble's new American band when it opened the Rainbow Room, on the sixty-fifth floor of newly built Rockefeller Center, in 1935. His cliff-hanging solo flights, said George T. Simon, kept trombonists Will Bradley and Glenn Miller happily occupied. "Betcha a couple of drinks he doesn't come out of this one," Bradley reported Miller saying. "And I'd say, 'Two drinks he does.' I almost always won, too!"[30]

That December (1935), record producer John Hammond got Freeman a date of his own. The saxophonist remembered the circumstances vividly. He'd finished work with Noble at the Rainbow Room and headed for 52nd Street, where Bunny Berigan was playing at the Famous Door. "The place was packed," he recalled. "Humphrey Bogart and Bea Lillie were there; they were jazz fans. One of the first people I saw was John Hammond, and he called me right over." In the early years of the Depression, with American record companies either out of business or on the edge of bankruptcy, Hammond had struck a deal with English Parlophone to make records with American jazz artists for issue in England. This arrangement had enabled him to record Goodman, Teagarden, Fletcher Henderson, Benny Carter, Mildred Bailey, Billie Holiday, and others throughout those lean years.

For the Freeman date he wanted a racially mixed band: Cozy Cole on drums, young Grachan Moncur (a Hammond "discovery") on bass, plus Berigan, Freeman, Condon, and, from Noble's band, the brilliant pianist Claude Thornhill. Freeman readily agreed—though, as he remembered it, Thornhill took some coaxing, insisting he wasn't a good enough jazz pianist for that kind of company.

The four titles made in a tiny, cramped Seventh Avenue studio once used by Decca are memorable chiefly for the surprisingly tough, gloves-off interplay between Freeman and Berigan. No debonair Bud here, no Noël Coward ascot and Amontillado. Berigan is in a slugging mood, and Freeman more than meets him halfway: the usually smooth tone is coarsened, with a return to the gritty attack of Chicago days. On the two up-tempo numbers especially, "The Buzzard" (based on the chords of "Basin Street Blues") and the 1925 Jolson favorite "Keep Smiling at Trouble," they're like sparring partners, bobbing and feinting, punching and counterpunching as they dance around one another.

The date brought a surprise bonus. Condon and Hammond together persuaded Bud to play the clarinet. He'd used the instrument on a 1929 date (at which Jack Teagarden also doubled on trumpet) but seldom thereafter, except for section work. Though he was under no illusions about his skills as a clarinetist, the clarinet solo with which he opens "The Buzzard" is a revelation. It could have been lifted bodily from the tenor, an effect heightened by the fact that he keeps to the low register. The turns and twists of phrase, especially in the -B take issued in the United States by Decca, are characteristic Freeman, riding the beat hard, yet with a light, attractive mobility. He's warm, even tender, on the slower

"Tillie's Downtown Now," with a limpid, almost Roppolo-like tone. It's a plaintive melody, based on the changes of "Take Me Back to My Boots and Saddle," by Billy Hill, Boston-born composer of "Wagon Wheels," "There's a Cabin in the Pines," and other faux-western genre standards.[31]

The date, said Hammond, "was an utter joy. I'd always thought Bud was sort of an unsung hero, and I was delighted to hear him prove me right."[32]

"Introducing our new addition to the Clambake Seven, Bud Freeman and his tenor sax, 'At the Codfish Ball.' Take him away, Davey." With that command to drummer Dave Tough, singer Edythe Wright served notice, on an April 15, 1936, record, that Tommy Dorsey's Orchestra had gained a new tenor soloist. The trombone-playing younger Dorsey brother had launched his own band in late 1935, buying out Joe Haymes's band and making some personnel adjustments, such as adding Tough at his first opportunity. He'd wanted Freeman from the start, but Ray Noble was paying well, and the Rainbow Room was a high-profile job. Eventually Dorsey got his way, as he invariably did, and by April of 1936 Freeman was sitting in the trombonist's reed section.

Dorsey loved his playing, featured him often. Like Duke Ellington, he seemed to take private delight in bringing his chosen soloist out front, ostensibly for a chorus or two, then keeping him there for as long as fifteen minutes, egging him on to wilder and wilder flights of fancy. Freeman, delighted to be playing again with his friend and mentor Dave Tough, took to it with relish. "Even though Tommy was very unhappy about the way I played in the saxophone section," Freeman said, "my solos pleased him so much that he was able to forget about my independent way of playing." Independent, that is, of the way the rest of the reed section phrased: Freeman, for all his solo gifts, was never a strong section player.[33]

But he soloed on nearly every Dorsey record of the period, and the records tell the story: beginning with the beautifully poised full tenor chorus on "At the Codfish Ball," with the Clambake Seven, they represent an impressive body of solo work. Among the memorable ones, the whimsical "Keepin' out of Mischief Now," a plaintive "What'll I Do?," an elegant "Beale Street Blues"—and perhaps best of all, his single-handed transformation of the old Dorsey standby "Stop, Look and Listen."

With Tough as willing accomplice, he delivers two choruses of stops, starts, punctuations, pregnant pauses, shifts of mood and dynamics, which amount to a free-standing work, recomposition of the composition. There's else nothing quite like it on record—save perhaps Freeman's own solo on Raymond Scott's exotic "Twilight in Turkey," with Dorsey's small unit, the Clambake Seven. Again, as with "Stop, Look and Listen," his solo seems less a jazz improvisation than a monologue, a humorous commentary in the manner of Robert Benchley or James Thurber.

A set of six LPs, issued in 1985 by California-based Sunbeam Records, provides an especially vivid account of Freeman's value to Dorsey. Drawn from

1936–37 Raleigh-Kool radio broadcasts, they show the band far looser, more powerfully swinging, than on its commercial recordings—and Bud Freeman as an imaginative, invigorating, and quite unpredictable soloist.

E. Y. Harburg's "You're a Builder-Upper," for example, has Tommy leading off with a muscular chorus, Dave Tough's cymbals swishing and swooshing him along. The superb clarinetist Johnny Mince, too often taken for granted in that clarinet-happy decade, blazes through a chorus (again, prodded and nudged by Tough), before Freeman pushes off for a sixteen-bar turn on the high trapeze. He's looser on "Weary Blues" and "Ja-Da" than on the Victor records, debonair on "Way Down Yonder in New Orleans." He uses his high register attractively on "You Took Advantage of Me," a repertoire staple in later years, and takes a vigorous "Dippermouth Blues" over the top, backed prominently by Tough's tomtoms.

It was Tough who induced Freeman to make, in early 1938, what he later called "the biggest mistake of my life": to leave Dorsey and join Benny Goodman. At first things seemed much as they'd been with Dorsey. "When Bud joined the band," said Art Rollini, playing the other tenor chair, "on solos Benny would say, 'Take another one, Bud,' then another and another. Bud blew his brains out."[34]

That wasn't a situation destined to last long. In Benny Goodman's band, Benny was the main attraction, and trumpeter Harry James an established star. It quickly became obvious that, while Bud Freeman worked for Goodman, he would not be accorded the same prominence—or treated with the same deference—he'd enjoyed with Dorsey.

Goodman airchecks spell it out graphically. The first weeks offer some extended Freeman solos: a superb "Roll 'Em" from an April 4, 1938, *Camel Caravan* broadcast (on which Benny is heard introducing "our new saxophonist Bud Freeman"), a supercharged "Ti-Pi-Tin," even a "Don't Be That Way," in which the saxophonist is allowed extra solo space before the drum break and explosive rideout.

But that seems to subside, and soon enough Freeman's only appearances are in solos written into the arrangements. There are some gems: in a certain sense, the more disciplined surroundings, and Goodman's rationing of his solo space, seem to have forced Freeman to edit himself more rigorously than had sometimes been the case in Dorsey days. His solos on Goodman's Victor records of "Ciribiribin" and the Basie classic "Topsy," and even brief appearances on "Could You Pass in Love?" and "Sweet Sue," are like gourmet treats, precisely concocted, delicious on the palate.

Scholar and tenor saxophonist Loren Schoenberg seems right in asserting that Freeman and Tough were, at this point, one of the most satisfying of jazz partnerships. He hears them as a tonic to Goodman's orchestra, invigorating after three years of the superheated but rather brutal reign of drummer Gene Krupa. Freeman and Tough, reunited with old Chicago friend Jess Stacy, had a singular and salutary effect on the leader: often, on these records, Benny's solos seem closer to the hot music spirit of Chicago days, the intensity and focus that illuminated his work with Ben Pollack. The difference is subtle: with Krupa behind him, Goodman had risen to remarkable heights of virtuosity—but now, surrounded by men who had shared his formative years, there was something else, something more focused. Hotter, in the original, early sense of the word.

Freeman later referred to his time with Goodman as "big band factory work," which may have had as much to do with the greater demands on his section reading as on his relations with Goodman. Certainly his solo playing didn't suffer: it's enjoyable to hear him taking the familiar tenor spots on such Goodman favorites as "Lullaby in Rhythm" and "Sometimes I'm Happy" and bringing his own distinctive accents to "One O'Clock Jump" and even "Sing Sing Sing."

It must also be said that Bud was probably not blameless. Ever the aspiring thespian, he had at his command virtually numberless ways, some subtler than others, of drawing attention to himself onstage. In later years, fans delighted in watching him while colleagues were playing; whether a matter of facial expression, body language, or such seemingly innocent gestures as adjusting a reed or shooting his immaculately tailored shirt cuffs, Bud Freeman was almost always "on" in a theatrical sense.

Goodman, a complex and in some respects not very sophisticated man, may have sensed some of this, may have made a point of treating his old friend as just one of the sidemen. If so, said Dorsey guitarist Carmen Mastren, that has to have made a difference. "I roomed with Bud," said Mastren. "All you had to do to keep him happy was tell him how great he was. He'd pick up his horn, start with a low B♭ and go right on up to the highest note, then look at you and say, 'Am I getting sharp?' Even if he was, I'd say, 'No, Bud, your intonation was perfect.' He loved that—just tell him he was great and you were in. I think he needed that; it was almost as if under that smooth manner of his he was really like an insecure kid, needing his daddy's approval. He sure got it from Tommy— but not from Benny."[35]

Goodman, too, had his insecurities, and the idea of having three guys, three peers, who had known him since childhood may have bothered him at some very basic level. "When we were kids Benny was a wonderful guy," said Freeman, "but he was a genius, and no genius can really handle a band and remain a good guy. Benny was not cruel, he just lived in a kind of egomaniacal shell."[36]

There were still brilliant moments, as on the October 11, 1938, aircheck recording of "Bumble Bee Stomp," but by December he was out, replaced by Jerry Jerome. Another factor feeding his discontent with Goodman was surely the fact that during these months he was recording regularly for Milt Gabler's brand-new Commodore label, with all the autonomy and musical freedom he could have asked.

He helped set the tone at Commodore's January 17, 1938, maiden session, the morning after Goodman's historic Carnegie Hall concert. In deference to that event (and presumably because Benny had let Jess Stacy out of a rehearsal to make the date), they titled the first two sides, both blues, "Carnegie Drag" and "Carnegie Jump." In common with most of what appeared on Commodore over the next decade, the playing is loose, informal, bursting with genial high spirits.

With some time left over at session's end (and perhaps with Goodman's small groups more or less in mind), Gabler decided to experiment. Why not do a number, he said to Freeman, with just Stacy and drummer George Wettling? The result, a hot, rattling-good "I Got Rhythm," was enough to encourage him to try a couple more: "You Took Advantage of Me" and a blues they decided to call "Three's No Crowd."

It worked. On these, and on the two Bud Freeman trio sessions that came about as a result, Bud plays with freedom and heart-lifting abandon. His final chorus on an up-tempo "My Honey's Lovin' Arms," for example, wriggles and snaps in a most "Eel"-like fashion, with great rhythmic velocity. Much credit to Wettling, who, like Dave Tough, seemed to know how to drive Freeman (and Pee Wee Russell, Bobby Hackett, and the rest of their circle) into an adrenalized frenzy.

Bud recorded several times again that year for Commodore, with salutary results. On "Meet Me Tonight in Dreamland," he rides Wettling's press roll like a tobogganist on a downhill run; his half-chorus on Jack Teagarden's feature, a 4/4 reading of the old Erno Rapee waltz "Diane," is a pointed reminder of his skills as a ballad player. He solos last on " 'Life' Spears a Jitterbug," a free-form romp on the changes to "Song of the Wanderer," and swings hard over backbeats laid down by pro tem drummer Marty Marsala.[37]

Stacy's chorus on the trio's "Blue Room" is an unaffected masterpiece, combining a spare lyricism and his own dancing kind of swing. It's worth producing as Exhibit A the next time some benighted soul wants to write Jess off as derivative of Earl Hines. These sessions were particularly good exposure for Stacy. Teddy Wilson got to do the trio and quartet numbers with Benny—but as superbly as he did them, there are times when one wishes to hear Stacy's simplicity and understated forcefulness, what Whitney Balliett has called his "quiet, firm inner voice," in the small combinations.[38]

On October 10, Freeman joined Louis Armstrong, Jack Teagarden, Fats Waller, and others in an all-star jam session organized by radio station WNEW, and hosted by *Make-Believe Ballroom* disc jockey Martin Block. Recorded on acetate discs and issued many times over the years, it finds the saxophonist very spirited among his peers. His solos on "Tiger Rag" and "I Got Rhythm" hurtle along with the same intensity that distinguishes the best of his Commodore work.

It was also through Milt Gabler's efforts that Freeman got a rare chance to indulge his penchant for the theatre, and in particular for Noël Coward. One afternoon, at Gabler's Commodore Music Shop, Freeman was "putting on his Shakespearian British accent and expounding on jazz . . . just improvising, and he had this great spiel," said Gabler. They got to talking about it, and the result was a studio date at which Freeman and actress Minerva Pious, best known as "Mrs. Nussbaum" on the Fred Allen radio show, did a satire on Coward's *Private Lives*, scripted by advertising copywriter and lyricist ("Oh, Look at Me Now") John De Vries, with piano and cornet effects by Joe Bushkin and radio-style announcing by Everett Sloane, of Orson Welles's Mercury Theatre group. "Private Jives," as it was called, sold an estimated 150 copies, said Gabler, mostly to friends. Full of insider allusions and sophomoric jokes about digestive processes, it's memorable now largely for the degree to which it allows Lawrence Freeman, actor manqué, to become his own Laurence Olivier.

With some prodding by press agent Ernie Anderson, Freeman agreed to become nominal leader of a loose alliance of musicians who had been working with Eddie Condon at Nick's, on Seventh Avenue in Greenwich Village. Most were Commodore regulars: clarinetist Pee Wee Russell and trumpeter Max Kaminsky had been Freeman associates since the '20s, and Bostonian multi-instrumentalist Brad Gowans had become a familiar figure on the Manhattan jam session scene. Gowans had recorded on cornet during the '20s, on clarinet for Commodore's revival of the Original Dixieland Jazz Band, and was now specializing in what he called his "valide" trombone—a valved instrument of his own invention, with an auxiliary slide which could be brought into play for glisses and other characteristically "trombonish" figures. Most important, he was a skilled arranger, able to strike the kind of elusive balance between organization and ensemble freedom which had distinguished the work of Jelly Roll Morton a decade before.

Condon's incisive four-string guitar dominated the rhythm section, which also included pianist Dave Bowman (a Stacy admirer who had at one time toured Europe with British bandleader-impresario Jack Hylton), several bassists, and a variety of drummers, including Morey Feld, Al "Zip" Sidell, Fred Moynahan (younger brother of Boston clarinetist Jim), '20s veteran Stan King, and, best of all, Dave Tough.

Retitled (thanks to Condon's wife Phyllis, a prominent advertising copywriter) Bud Freeman's Summa Cum Laude Orchestra, the band was a cooperative, musically and financially. It enjoyed a two-year, up-and-down life—and, before it broke up, more than lived up to its name. It struck a balance between the freewheeling jamming of Chicago days and a more polished ensemble profile shaped by Brad's arrangements.

They began with a long run at Nick's, which had become a kind of spiritual home for Condon and his circle. "All these men were strong individualists," Kaminsky wrote, "but despite high-voltage temperaments and the Chicago guys' style of letting loose with caustic, cutting remarks which were hard to take, we somehow or other worked things out as we went along."[39]

Among the fans crowding Nick's on opening night were representatives of several record companies, bearing offers. "We took the best one, which was Victor," said Freeman. The four titles they recorded for Victor's Bluebird subsidiary on July 19, 1939, included a new, snappy version of "The Eel," a Gowans original called "Easy to Get," which became the band's theme, and two throwbacks to the '20s, "China Boy" and "I Found a New Baby." Gowans added introductions and endings to both; two arranged band passages on the latter title, one a four-bar descending chromatic line, the other a simple riff formula, gave the old Spencer Williams–Jack Palmer a fresh-minted feel. Freeman's "China Boy" chorus, transcribed earlier in this chapter, is among his best—in Max Harrison's apt phrase, "tightly packed" in its clear sense of organization.[40]

Repertoire, at Nick's, quickly became a problem, one that would plague musicians within this style for years to come. "We did a lot of dixieland numbers," said Condon, "because the customers identified them with our music and asked for them; we could have played the most recent popular hits, giving them our interpretation, but many of the listeners would not have believed they were hearing jazz."[41]

(Broadcast recordings by the band bear him out. On one, from the Panther Room of Chicago's Hotel Sherman in May of 1940, they do an extended dance medley, arranged by Gowans, including such songs of the moment as "Shake Down the Stars," "Sierra Sue," and "Secrets in the Moonlight.")

Erik Charell, who had successfully revived Ralph Benatzsky's operetta *The White Horse Inn* in Vienna in 1930, announced plans to stage an updated, jazz version of Shakespeare's *A Midsummer Night's Dream*, with a book by Gilbert Seldes (an early champion of hot jazz), an all-star black cast—Louis Armstrong as Bottom, Maxine Sullivan as Titania, Butterfly McQueen as Puck, among others—songs by Jimmy Van Heusen and Eddie de Lange based on Mendelssohn themes; Don Voorhees conducted a full pit orchestra, and, doing instrumental specialties from the boxes, were two jazz sextets—the popular John Kirby group from 52nd Street and Benny Goodman's unit with guitarist Charlie Christian. For some reason Kirby withdrew; his replacement was the Summa Cum Laude band.

For all its potential the show was a flop, running only fifteen performances. The band, unable now to return to Nick's (other groups were booked), worked briefly at Kellys Stable, then landed a job at a place on West 47th Street called the Brick Club, described by Freeman as "a real rough dive, sort of an underworld rendezvous." Lee Wiley, with whom Freeman, Kaminsky, and Russell had recorded albums dedicated to songs by Rodgers and Hart and the Gershwins, then helped get them the Panther Room job in Chicago, sharing a bill with her and a little band co-led by violinist Stuff Smith and trumpeter Jonah Jones.

Before they left, they did an album for Decca, set up for them by Milt Gabler. The theme: songs associated with the Wolverines, Bix's first recording group. "I wondered, as we were cutting the sides, how many of the tunes Bix would have been playing if he were alive," said Condon. All the same, it was an outstanding album—in a sense a precursor of the jazz repertory movement which would make its impact half a century hence. Max Harrison has called it "jazz about jazz," which seems right on target: there is no attempt to re-create the old, acoustic Wolverines records (made, it's sobering to realize, only fifteen years before). Gowans instead, and with relatively few touches, has applied fresh coats of high-gloss paint to such repertoire staples as "Fidgety Feet" and "Sensation" and presented some of the lesser-known Wolverines numbers—"Big Boy," "Tia Juana," and the charming "I Need Some Pettin' "—in a manner permitting both tidiness and ensemble freedom. Occasional allusions to figures played on the earlier records establish historical pedigree, but these are free-standing performances, saturated with the personality of the Summa Cum Laude band and its individuals.

(The Bob Crosby Orchestra and its band-within-a-band, the Bobcats, were up to much the same sort of thing at this time. Arrangers Bob Haggart, Deane Kincaide, and Matty Matlock incorporated elements of earlier records into their scores on such Armstrong-related material as "Savoy Blues" and "Come Back, Sweet Papa" and such Bix-associated numbers as "Royal Garden Blues." Often, said Haggart, they "wrote the lines out that way because we didn't know the original melodies. We only knew those things from what we heard on the old records." Again, jazz about jazz.)

Fine solos abound: Kaminsky setting out the melody of "Oh, Baby!" (a neglected Walter Donaldson gem, not the oft-played Owen Murphy song from *Rain or Shine*) against sustained band chords; Bowman personalizing Jess Stacy's springy touch on "Susie," Russell's extraordinary low-register essay on "Fidgety Feet."

But Freeman is the easy solo hero of his own date. He comes dancing out of the ensemble on "Sensation Rag," equal parts wit and earnestness, swinging hard. No posturing: this is a chorus to define his "third stream" of hot tenor, owing nothing to either Hawkins or Young. The way he *sings* the melody in the trio section of "Tia Juana" or works some chromatic derring-do into his mid-chorus break toward the end of "Copenhagen" belongs to his personal signature.

The ensembles, too, are textbook lessons on how to play this style. Kaminsky's lead is straightforward and spare, leaving plenty of room for Gowans' trumpet-like counterlines (the valve trombone tends to promote that kind of figure-building), Freeman's arabesques, and Russell's unpredictable punctuations. Drummer Morey Feld, at twenty-five a youngster fresh from the bands of Ben Pollack and Joe Haymes, knits well with Condon, Bowman, and bassist Pete Peterson.

Then they were off to Chicago. The Panther Room job lasted a month and, musically at least, was great fun. "We did two broadcasts a night and we also played for the floor show, which included a clown who handed out balloons to the patrons and had them participating in kiddie cart races, and a Spanish dance team for whom we played bullfight music," Kaminsky recalled. Gowans, meanwhile, would sit up all night writing arrangements of the new pop tunes publishers kept bringing around.

Airchecks of these broadcasts have circulated among collectors for years, appearing occasionally on small independent labels. In addition to the medleys mentioned earlier, there are loose, exuberant renderings of the Wolverines material—"Oh, Baby!," "Susie," "I Need Some Pettin' "—and superb jam versions of such standards as "After I Say I'm Sorry," "I Ain't Gonna Give Nobody None of My Jelly-Roll," and Gowans's solo specialty on "Ja-Da." Solos are uniformly excellent, with Russell and Freeman especially outstanding.[42]

The Chicago job ended on June 6, 1940—and with it, for all practical purposes, the career of what Eddie Condon sometimes called the "Some Come Loudly" orchestra. They tried to find other work: Freeman even wired Bing Crosby, who replied that Los Angeles was "still a hillbilly town." At last they returned to New York and went their separate ways—but not before recording one last album, on the twenty-third; it turned out to be their best.

John Hammond was in charge, and he insisted on bringing Jack Teagarden in on trombone in place of Gowans. Equally important, the band finally got to use Dave Tough, who teamed with Teagarden to elevate what would in any case have been a good record date into a great one. The eight titles, issued as Columbia's *Comes Jazz* album, define this style as fully and lastingly as the small Ellington units and the Billie Holiday–Teddy Wilson–Lester Young–Buck Clayton collaborations (also Hammond productions) define their respective genres.

Some of the participants may have played at their personal solo best elsewhere (this is arguably true of both Freeman and Russell), but the sense of combined effort, of unity and teamwork, and the collective swing on display here, remain unsurpassed. To single out one moment is to slight another, but it is well to listen to Tough as he energizes, electrifies, boosts into orbit, the old Chicago favorite "Shimme-Sha Wabble." From chorus to chorus, he uses his three cymbals and hi-hats the way a painter uses brushes on a canvas: broad strokes and tiny details, strong motives and telling background touches.

He plays on his closed hi-hat under Bowman's piano intro, then opens the aperture with a splash of his tiny top cymbal when the band hits the C-minor verse, lending the whole operation a loose, swashbuckling sound. Yet once into the C-major chorus he throttles back, working on closed hi-hat, keeping embellishment to a minimum with so much going on in the horns. More splash and he's on his large Chinese cymbal behind Bud, switching to a smaller, lighter ride cymbal to accommodate Pee Wee's wispier sound. Teagarden's solo precedes the final ensemble, so Tough repeats the process with which he opened the record: closed hi-hat behind the trombone, with a few punctuations on the hi-hat post, then opening the sock cymbals with a great splash to drive the band home.

The B♭ blues "47th and State," named after the corner, on Chicago's South Side, which was the epicenter of late-1920s black night life, is no less fascinating. The way Tough builds the intensity behind Bowman's five effervescent solo choruses is a primer in the *musical* side of jazz drumming: from straight time on closed hi-hat in chorus one, he moves to triplets in chorus two, opens up a bit in chorus three, all the way in four, moves briefly to his Chinese cymbal in five to let things breathe a bit, then ends the episode where he began, on closed hi-hat, setting up Bud's entrance. But he outdoes even this when it's time for Teagarden's two choruses: Tough bears down on his Chinese, punctuating with rimshots, driving the rhythm section with a relentlessness that suffers no laggards.

He's playing far up on the beat—bringing to mind Bob Haggart's remark that "he seemed ahead of everybody. When he played, it was as if he was saying, 'Go with me or else!' " He generates a momentum, a dervish intensity—and when the ensemble (minus Kaminsky, who was apparently late for the session) takes over and Tough returns to his half-open hi-hats, he's so far forward he sounds almost as if he's rushing. Yet it's not the tempo that picks up but the energy, transcending even the high plane it's achieved so far.[43]

During and after the World War II years, with jazz styles changing radically around him, Bud Freeman remained a busy freelancer, recording widely. But in common with Pee Wee Russell and Jack Teagarden, he seems to have been one of those soloists who, though accorded critical and artistic respect, have not been lastingly or broadly influential among musicians of later generations.

In the '50s, the undeservedly neglected Sam Margolis drew on both Freeman and Young in fashioning solos of often considerable eloquence. British saxophonist Danny Moss acknowledged Bud and Ben Webster in a particularly expressive manner. Michael "Peanuts" Hucko, perhaps best known as a clarinetist, is a tenor soloist of great warmth, his debt to Freeman clear; it seems a pity that as of this writing he had abandoned the instrument entirely. Freeman, Young, and Miller turn up side by side in the best work of Abe "Boomie" Richman.

What remains is an innovative stylist widely noted in his youth yet virtually without echo in today's increasingly fragmented and diverse jazz world. Perhaps Dan Morgenstern is correct when he suggests, in his notes to Mosaic Records' massive Commodore reissue package, that "if Bud's skin [had been] of a darker hue, more of the attention he merits would be paid to him."

The elements of Coleman Hawkins's style—the embellishments, "vertical" chordal orientation, mahogany tone, heavy attack, use of rubato and the rest— found their way easily into the playing of others. Sometimes it was as trace elements, but more often a single component of the original formed the basis for someone else's entire concept. Thus it was that out of Hawkins came Ben Webster, Chu Berry, Herschel Evans, Buddy Tate, Don Byas, Eddie Barefield, and hundreds of others. So, too, with Lester Young's linear, or "horizontal," conception, as the styles of many saxophonists—from Wardell Gray and Paul Quinichette to Stan Getz and Zoot Sims—have demonstrated. Some—Dexter Gordon, Lucky Thompson, and Gene Ammons among them—drew from both sources, with generally salutary results. Both lines carried over easily into a broad and diverse range of contemporary styles.*

Bud Freeman's influence was far less generalized than those of either Hawkins or Young. Overall, the particulars of the Freeman tenor style remained inseparable from the Freeman persona: Freeman figures remain Freeman figures, intact, regardless where they occur. Like those of Pee Wee Russell, they resist transition from the specific to the general.

Johnny Mince, who sat beside Freeman in Tommy Dorsey's reed section, told with much affection how he was onstand one night at London's 100 Club when Bud walked in. "I took a chorus on alto sax," he said, "and put in every Bud Freeman figure I could think of. He came up to me afterwards and said to me, 'Johnny, I didn't know you played alto that well.' And I said, 'Well, I was trying to think of as many Bud Freeman things as I could.' And he said, completely seriously, 'Johnny, that's why it was good.' "⁴⁴

*Musicians regularly use the terms "vertical" and "horizontal" in describing styles played on single-line instruments. A "vertical" style is one with a heavily chordal bias, spelling out and using as many notes of each chord in a sequence as possible, if sometimes at the expense of melodic coherence. A "horizontal" style, by contrast, will use only those chordal voices which are necessary to construct a flowing melodic line, one which moves, in other words, in a horizontal direction.

Freeman's vanity, his sense of himself, sometimes took on epic proportions: a Ptolemaic universe with himself, blithely unconcerned, at its center. "He was consummately egocentric," said cornetist Ruby Braff, who worked with Freeman frequently beginning in the mid-'50s. "I really think he believed all the world revolved around him, and around every note he played.

"But make no mistake: he played so *wonderfully* that it really doesn't matter. It was wonderful anytime to play with him: he had this tremendous, contagious enthusiasm that made you care almost as much as he did, even if"—and here he paused for a small, engagingly affectionate laugh—"even if you didn't love him quite as much as he loved himself. There was always this search, with him as with Louis and all the great ones, for a line, a way of putting things together as artistically and beautifully from a melodic point of view as possible."[45]

After the Summa Cum Laude band broke up, Freeman spent some time back in Chicago, leading a band that included local alto saxophonist Bill Dohler. Drafted in 1942, he experienced the war largely in the Aleutian Islands (where he busily cultivated the detective novelist Dashiell Hammett, who edited a base newspaper, the *Adakian*, and to whom Bud referred ever after as "Red," in recognition of his political views). Back in New York at war's end, he recorded "The Atomic Age," an intriguing tenor-and-drums duet with Ray McKinley, and showed on yet another version of "I Got Rhythm" that the elements of the Freeman style were still in place, still evolving.

There was a marriage, and with it a short-lived move to Chile. A period of immersion in Zen. A "block," where he could not produce a sound, led to three months' study with pianist-guru Lennie Tristano—though Bud confided afterwards, "I was not influenced by him in any way . . . we just reviewed what I had known as a kid—scales and intervals. Of course, he did give me terrific confidence."[46]

He recorded frequently and well, sometimes with such old friends as McPartland and Russell, sometimes in company as diverse as Hawkins and former Ellington trumpeter Harold "Shorty" Baker. One of the most remarkable Freeman records of this later period is *Something Tender*, recorded in 1962 with guitarists George Barnes and Carl Kress. Tapping into the subtle, melodic—and melodious—side of Freeman's playing, it's an album deserving of careful study.[47]

"It's no exaggeration to say that Bud Freeman was—is—one of the best writers of instrumental music, jazz music, that there is," said Ruby Braff. "He was a composer of wonderful, beautiful melodic lines. Take a look at 'Margo's Seal,' 'The Sign of the Dove,' some of those things—those are high-grade compositions, almost Tchaikovskian in their melodic invention. He had everything, had it all—yet people didn't know, never did recognize and properly exploit his talents."[48]

(In the late '60s Freeman joined Yank Lawson and Bob Haggart as a member of their "World's Greatest Jazz Band," touring widely. On *The Compleat Bud Freeman*, an LP done with a contingent from the band, Bob Wilber fashions an arrangement of "Just One of Those Things" from a series of characteristic Freeman figures, scored as a duet for his own soprano and Freeman's tenor. The performance is an exquisite *pas de deux*, an elaborate arabesque within an idiom having far more to do with Bud Freeman than with Cole Porter.)

French critic Hugues Panassié, writing before the abrupt *volte-face* which resulted in his repudiation of all white jazz as spurious, remarked: "Not enough justice has been done Bud Freeman. He is a far greater musician than is generally realized. I owe him some of the greatest musical enthusiasms of my life." He went on to advise neophyte hot tenor players to study Freeman's style closely, appreciating its combination of simplicity and intelligence.[49]

But the most meaningful expressions of respect for Freeman came from those fellow-musicians who were themselves secure and original stylists. Shortly before his death in 1973, the great tenor saxophonist Ben Webster delivered himself of the following thoughts during an afternoon conversation in his Copenhagen apartment:

> The guys who matter, the real ones, are the guys who never mooched off somebody else's stuff, who did something completely their own and never gave a shit about showin' everybody how much or how fast they could get over it. Lester was like that. Benny Carter, too. And so was Bud Freeman; everybody keeps forgetting about him. But, man, you hear him play two notes, and you know, no mistake, who's in town.[50]

You always did. And you always smiled, in the vision they conjured up of the man who *was* the sound, whose simple yet ever-curling figures were so apt an expression of his now-you-see-it, now-you-don't personality. Clarinetist Kenny Davern, forever intrigued by the paradoxes, often tried to get behind the façade, to elicit Freeman's views on a range of potentially controversial subjects. But "he was like a squid in the water," the clarinetist said. "Talking with him, you'd get close to something, and he'd squirt ink at you and vanish."

But from time to time, at an unguarded moment, the mask would slip. Davern remembered strolling along London's Oxford Street with Freeman one day in the '70s. "He looked ever so spiffy in his khaki twill slacks and blue blazer, his light blue shirt and ascot," the clarinetist said. "You know, camel's hair coat. Sartorially impeccable. Mr. Savile Row.

"Well, right there in the middle of Oxford Street he stops and says to me, 'You never heard King Oliver in person, did you?' He knew damn well I hadn't. And he went into this dance; he was mesmerized, in a trance, going 'happa-doo-dah, doo-doo-DAH!' scatting along, carrying on that way, doing all this stuff, like a soft-shoe, on the street. Here are people walking by—you know the English—trying their best not to look at this snappily dressed guy who looked as if he had the St. Vitus dance.

"He was really carried away—sort of reliving, in his mind, the thrill of that first time he heard Oliver's band. Imagine, being a teenager, impressionable and self-conscious, and walking into the Lincoln Gardens and hearing that music for the first time," Davern said. "Outrageous. He'd never realized that something could sound like that. And here he was reliving it, there in the middle of the street."[51]

He lived the last decade of his life in Chicago, occasionally honored, toasted by such hometown celebrities and fans as author Studs Terkel. Visited there, he seemed content, playing the gentleman of a certain age, in a manner faintly reminiscent of his idol John Barrymore in *Grand Hotel*.

"Do you think people will actually remember my playing?" he asked with a typical rhetorical flourish in a 1941 interview. Yes, Bud, one might answer, drawing on Carmen Mastren's example. Yes, Bud—you're the greatest. People will remember. Indeed they will. Really. I promise.[52]

And so they have. At least some of them.

And in Valediction

Lying there on the bed, so frail and wan, so diminished, he is, beyond mistaking, a man soon to die. How strange: above the covers the familiar, clean-lined face, grey moustache neatly trimmed; below, so very little.

I've been warned: his mind wanders, he's in and out. He may not recognize you. If he does, he may blank out altogether in the middle of a sentence. Or fall asleep. Any number of things. Be prepared.

Yet as I enter the room he brightens. Smiles. "Why, it's Dick Sudhalter, dapper as ever," he says, and despite myself I have to laugh: it's something he's said just about every time we've met, a little unspoken joke between us. I wear clothes well, I'd always protest, look pretty good in most things. But by no stretch of imagination could I ever be called a sharp or natty dresser. Dapper? Me? Never. Not like that. Not like you, Bud.

But there it is. Bud Freeman, gravely ill, failing, his mind an incoherent jumble of half-formed, badly pasted-together memories. Yet he remembers style: recognizes and comments. Makes, again, his little sartorial joke.

And the memories come flooding back. Bud over dinner, going on and on about some girl he's seeing—a girl who, it inevitably occurs to me, hasn't the faintest idea who Bud Freeman is and what he means to so many people in so many places. Bud waxing lyrical about how some book he's reading—Flaubert's Parrot, perhaps?—is just a masterpiece, a towering work of contemporary literature. And then, suddenly, all contrition: "But enough about me, Dick. What about you?"

And me loving every minute of it, lapping it up, because he's Bud Freeman—and all he has to do is play one note, one of those improbable, slithery phrases, and I'm his friend and acolyte for life.

He died, finally, on Friday, March 15, 1991, two days after Jimmy McPartland. Wednesday morning I'd woken early from a starkly imprinted dream: in it, I'd hired Bud to play at a concert in New York City—made the arrangements, flown him in, gone to the airport to meet him. Driven him into town to meet the organizer.

As soon as we entered her office I knew something was terribly wrong. "I'm so sorry," she began. "I tried to reach you. We didn't get our grant. There's no money. We have to cancel the concert, the whole series. There's nothing we can do. I'm so sorry."

No, no, I protested. It can't be. This isn't just any concert. Don't you understand? It's Bud Freeman. It's important. It has to go on. He's been sick. We may never have another chance. Please.

At which point Bud, calm and poised as ever, laid a gentle hand on my arm. "It's all right, Dick. Don't worry. It's finished anyway."

And I awoke. I lay there awhile thinking about it, trying to make sense of it—then, despairing of that, tried to talk myself back into sleep, to recapture the vivid images. All to no avail.

At length I got up, washed the sleep out of my face—and was halfway downstairs when the telephone rang. It was Marian McPartland, to say that Jimmy had died perhaps an hour before— just about the time Bud was telling me, "It's finished anyway."

And, two days later, he too was gone. Marian believes—believes with a cool certainty which brooks no suggestion of doubt—that between these two boyhood chums it was in the natural order of things that Jimmy should go first. Should resolutely take his leave, then square his shoulders and march off to round up his old friend Bud.

Think of it. Big, jovial Jimmy McPartland, the tough street kid who took up the cornet because with it he'd always be the leader; Bud the dandy, the self-conscious "artist," content to follow. Who else to lay the gentle hand on Bud's arm, to say softly but firmly, "Okay, pal, it's all over. Let's go."

Once upon a time, asked about some colleague or other, Lester Young declared in that oblique way of his that "the President likes smart music." No mistaking what he meant: the phrase, in both its graphic and implied senses, is deliciously self-explanatory. Bud Freeman played—was the very personification of—smart music.

And I, unabashed, will always love him for it.

273

12

Dixieland

World War I turned out to be a major bonanza for popular songwriters. From 1917, when America entered the war, until 1919 and Versailles, Tin Pan Alley operated at capacity, turning out such topical trivia as "Hello, Central, Give Me No Man's Land," "Just Like Washington Crossed the Delaware, General Pershing Will Cross the Rhine," "Goodbye, Broadway, Hello, France"— and, occasionally, more durable efforts, "Roses of Picardy" and "Avalon" among them.

The war once over, the Alley returned its attention to that staple of popular mythology, the antebellum American South: it was Paradise Lost, a time of simpler, clearer values, when man was better able to perceive the gentler side of his nature. A time of community, when life seemed more in balance.

NO MORE MORAL ATTENTION SONGS, proclaimed signs posted on the backstage walls of vaudeville houses across the land. After the anxiety and jingoism of the "Great War," the slogans and relentless patriotic appeal expressed so well by James Montgomery Flagg's I WANT *YOU* recruiting poster, here was the backlash— a desire, a need, to turn away.[1]

What better anodyne than a resurgent preoccupation with pre–Civil War Dixie, reinvented as a time of lazy, magnolia-scented days and soft, moonlit nights, the melodious (if safely distant) singing of contented "darkies" floating on the velvet air?

Part of its appeal was its living proximity. In 1919, after all, the Civil War was not long past; many Americans still had at least one grandparent who remembered Shiloh and Bull Run, Appomattox and the assassination of Lincoln at Ford's Theatre. They were still connected with those paroxysmal events: by implication, the time just before it must have been an idyll, a moment of tranquility. Eden before the Fall.[2]

Driving all this was a pervasive sense of frustration and disappointment. The humanist tradition and the Industrial Revolution had obviously not united to turn the twentieth century into the Golden Age anticipated by so many late Victorian writers. On the contrary, life now seemed more complicated, more dangerous, more intimidating—and less clear—than ever before.[3]

Into the breach galloped the troops of the Brill Building, Manhattan nerve center of the popular songwriting industry. It's still surprising how many thousands of popular songs written between 1918 and 1930 celebrate the virtues of a halcyon and largely fictional South, prescribing a prompt return there as medicine for all modern, big-city melancholy. Consider "Alabamy Bound," "I'm Goin' South," "When It's Sleepy Time Down South," "When the Midnight Choo-Choo Leaves for Alabam," and dozens of others.

The word "Dixieland" (sometimes abbreviated to "Dixie") is a regular feature of such songs: "Mister Lindbergh made Paree/But I'm in God's own heaven, you see/'Cause there ain't no land like Dixieland to me"; "Tuck me to sleep in my old Kentucky home/Cover me with Dixie skies and leave me there alone"; and, perhaps, the ultimate sentiment, title of a 1916 favorite by the composers of "The Japanese Sandman": "(They Made It Twice as Nice as Paradise) And They Called It Dixieland."[4]

Nor were such pastoral longings the exclusive preoccupation of the white pop music establishment. Black writers became equally adept at grinding out instant musical paeans to an Elysium south of the Mason-Dixon Line. The case of the brothers Leon and Otis René is instructive: New Orleans–born Creoles, they moved early to California, where they jointly owned both a publishing house and a record company and collaborated on several successful songs, among them "When It's Sleepy Time Down South" and "That's My Home," both popularized by Louis Armstrong, who made the former his theme song.

From a latter-day social perspective it's tempting to claim that they were merely playing the white man's game, tongue firmly in cheek, laughing all the way to the bank. But that hardly explains the ardor Louis brings to his performances of both songs. When he sings, "Where the folks say 'howdy-do'/And they mean it, too," in "That's My Home," his sincerity is obvious—and comes with an emotionally loaded subtext.

Of the many blacks (and whites, if Ray Lopez's remarks are to be credited) who came north during the century's second decade, drawn by the prospects of plentiful and well-paid work, a surprising number returned home, or wished to. For them, the North was a cold, inhospitable place; many, overcome by homesickness, returned south.[5]

The terms "Dixie" and "Dixieland," of course, had been long understood as synonyms for the South. The idea of "Dixieland"-as-paradise was central to the songs of James Bland ("Carry Me Back to Old Virginny") and of Stephen Collins Foster ("The Old Folks at Home," "My Old Kentucky Home"), who died while the Civil War still raged. It was a central feature of late nineteenth-century minstrelsy and persisted as a current in early twentieth-century popular songs.

The enormous and ubiquitous success of the Original Dixieland Jazz Band only reinforced word and concept in public consciousness, while sounding the overture for an eruption of national Dixiemania: in 1920–21 alone there were "Alabama Moon," "Goodbye, Dixie, Goodbye," "I Love the Land of Old Black Joe," "I'd Love to Fall Asleep and Wake Up in My Mammy's Arms," "Dear Old Southland," "Down South," "Down Yonder," "I'm Goin' South," "My Sunny Tennessee," "Swanee River Moon," and "Tuck Me to Sleep in My Old Kentucky Home."

"Dixieland," in this context, was handy shorthand for Utopia—and record companies, promotional arm of the popular music publishing industry, got the message right away. For the next decade, "Dixieland" and "Dixie" were used freely to identify bands of both races playing any music even distantly reminiscent of a southern Arcadia. Hence the "Dixie Daisies" (white), "Dixie Four" (black), "Dixie Instrumental Four" (white), "Dixie Stompers" (black), "Dixieland Rhythm Kings" (white), and "Dixieland Thumpers" (black). Even the venerated King Oliver (whose "Creole Jazz Band" was also so named in identification with the South) recorded for Vocalion with his "Dixie Syncopators."

By the late 1920s, the word "Dixieland" had begun to take on some additional freight. Though record companies were still marketing performances by the all-black "Dixieland Jug Blowers" and "Dixie Washboard Band" for their "race" catalogues, use of the word among northern, urbanized blacks had fallen off sharply. Pittsburgh-born Roy Eldridge spoke often of hearing Louis Armstrong for the first time and being tempted to dismiss him as a "southern trumpet player." For him, "southern" in that context meant bucolic, rustic, even "hick"—in short, the very antithesis of the hip urban mentality Eldridge valued and so passionately espoused.

So, too, with "Dixieland." Though personal ties, to home and one another, remained strong among southern black musicians, especially those from New Orleans and environs, their musical focus had shifted north—first to Chicago and ultimately to New York. In general, black musicians seemed disinclined to revisit or in any way commemorate the past—their own or that of the music they played. A combination of social and historical reality militated too strongly against it.

The situation among whites was different. Given an opportunity in 1927 to make records under his own name, Bix Beiderbecke chose to perform an act of homage to Dominick James LaRocca and the Original Dixieland Jazz Band, who had so animated him as a teenager. All three titles recorded at his first OKeh date in 1927—"At the Jazz Band Ball," "Royal Garden Blues," and "Jazz Me Blues"—are from the ODJB repertoire.[6]

With the exception of Jelly Roll Morton, whose 1926 Red Hot Peppers records for Victor ordered and to some degree codified the music he had played while growing up in New Orleans (and whose Library of Congress recordings were exuberantly, sentimentally, retrospective), there appears to be no motivation in black hot music of the '20s or early '30s comparable to the fealty to the past that drove Beiderbecke's *hommage* to LaRocca.

(Morton, it must also be remembered, was a product of the highly Europeanized New Orleans Creole culture—a culture which, but for a caprice of law, might well have remained, in both a *de facto* and *de jure* sense, part of that city's white population. It also seems relevant that by 1928, when Morton arrived in New York, the majority of younger black musicians fluffed him off as a curio, an anachronism. Some New Orleans emigrés, Henry Allen notable among them, dealt with him respectfully, even with affection. But for many others he was, in one veteran's phrase, just "an old ragtimey piano player who ran his mouth all the time." Morton's compositions, bearing such evocative titles as "Mississippi Mildred" and "New Orleans Bump," were backward-looking in a way unlike anything else written by musicians "of color" working in New York at the time.)

Matters of style apart, the overall lineaments of early small-band hot music (polylinear ensembles, instrumentation, solos bookended between all-in *tutti* passages) remained common to both black and white small groups throughout the '20s. Though musicians of the two races still couldn't appear on bandstands together, toward decade's end they began to record together with some regularity, and with salutary results. Louis Armstrong led the way in 1929 with his landmark blues "Knockin' a Jug," alongside Jack Teagarden, Eddie Lang, and Joe Sullivan (white) and drummer Kaiser Marshall and tenor saxophonist Happy Caldwell (black). Coleman Hawkins appeared on dates led by Red McKenzie, alongside such leading white musicians as Jimmy Dorsey, Pee Wee Russell, Muggsy Spanier, Benny Goodman, and even, as discussed earlier, the distinctively original tenor saxophonist Bud Freeman. Jack Teagarden played the blues with great eloquence on a date led by Eddie Condon and featuring several musicians from Charlie Johnson's great Harlem band, including the St. Louis trumpeter Leonard "Ham" Davis. In these and other cases the prevailing jam (i.e., non-arranged) format was what an only slightly later age would be quick to label "dixieland."

Among the outstanding small-band record sessions of the time are those by "the Rhythmakers," done for the American Record Company in spring and summer 1932. They mixed whites (Condon, Sullivan, Russell) and blacks (Allen, Fats Waller, drummer Zutty Singleton) with results seldom short of thrilling. Using such standards as "Margie," "Who's Sorry Now?," and "Yellow Dog Blues," this loosely confederated *pro tem* group produced some of the most carefree hot playing ever recorded by all participants. In matters of organization and approach they were something of a throwback, the kind of unrestrained jamming that in another, earlier, time would have been known—without disparagement—as "dixieland."

Some circles of musicians who had kept regular company in the '20s, through both musical affinity and the segregated nature of the music business, continued to play together often. Nowhere was the blend of musical and personal association as pronounced as among those musicians associated since the late 1920s with the white "Chicago style." At its center was a five-foot, five-inch human dynamo who played four-string guitar and had a way with snappy repartee. His name was Eddie Condon.

Eddie Condon's banjoistic guitar playing epitomized the style—its rhythmic urgency, devil-take-the-hindmost ensembles and lyrical, heart-on-sleeve approach to soloing; neither his belief nor his advocacy ever wavered; and both traits consistently attracted fellow-musicians.

Among them, ultimately, were fellow-Chicagoans (Bud Freeman, Muggsy Spanier, Joe Sullivan, Gene Krupa), players from New England (cornetists Bobby Hackett and Max Kaminsky, valve trombonist Brad Gowans), New Orleans (trombonist George Brunies, cornetist Stirling Bose), the Midwest (Jess Stacy, George Wettling), the Southwest (Ernie Caceres, Pee Wee Russell, and Jack Teagarden), and just about anywhere else. Many made livings in big dance bands, others in studio orchestras; but all gravitated in their leisure hours to Condon's kind of free-wheeling small-band music.

Born in Goodland, Indiana, November 16, 1905, Albert Edwin Condon was scarcely twenty when his family moved to Chicago Heights. He fell in almost immediately with a circle of eager young musicians that included the McPartland brothers, Bud Freeman, Frank Teschemacher, Dave Tough, and an ever-expanding network of sympathizers. He was soon fast friends with another fast talker—the singer and hot comb player Red McKenzie: together they became the front men, the deal-makers, spokesmen and agents, con men and true believers, unsurpassed at finding jobs and record dates—all the while talking up their musical philosophy, converting the doubters, and rustling up a few bucks when they were needed.

Condon's guitar of choice was a four-string instrument, legacy of his beginnings on the banjo, which could produce neither the depth of sound nor the harmonic richness of the conventional six-string instrument. "It was a little thin" was the way bassist Jack Lesberg, a frequent Condon associate in the 1940s, put it. "Mostly Eddie would play just the top ends of the chords. But he never got in the way—knew the right changes to the songs. And his time, once he fell into it, was just fine. He wasn't hard to play with—except maybe when he'd had too much to drink."[7]

Condon played well, even without the technique or versatility of Lang, Kress, McDonough, and the rest. Never a soloist, he preferred to lay out a strong, clear pulse that energized many an otherwise torpid rhythm section. Cornetist Bobby Hackett, an exacting judge, called him "the greatest rhythm guitarist you ever heard"—a superlative which, though it appears to scant many superb players, nevertheless attests to Condon's skills as a timekeeper.

But it's not for his prowess as a guitarist that Eddie Condon is best remembered. Blessed with a ready wit and an unerring ability to exploit an opportunity when he recognized one, he became organizer, manager, and spokesman for a cadre of musicians not otherwise noted for their abilities in those areas. Trumpeter-commentator Digby Fairweather sums it up well:

> It would be hard to overestimate Condon's jazz contribution. He created an image for Chicago jazz and, more important, a collection of faultless recorded jazz music. He was fiercely loyal to the musicians he loved, created a professional frame for them to shine in, and was a fine judge of humanity who liked the good things about people: genuineness, creativity, humility.[8]

* * *

"Dixieland," meanwhile, began to take on connotative meanings quite beyond its original, southern, association. Perhaps it had to do with the lasting and vivid impression made by the Original Dixieland Jazz Band; perhaps it stemmed in part from the tendency of white musicians to celebrate the past in a way their black colleagues did not; perhaps it was to some degree racial—white associating with white, black with black. Or even a matter of repertoire choices. Whatever the specific causes, by the mid-1930s the word "dixieland" was being applied freely to certain circles of white musicians, first by the trade press, then by the public.

Often such compartmentalization ignored the very sound of the music. When a 1937 pickup group led by Teddy Wilson recorded the 1926 standard "I've Found a New Baby," with Buck Clayton, Buster Bailey, and Lester Young as the horns, it was heard and discussed as "small-band swing." When, two years later, Bud Freeman's Summa Cum Laude Orchestra, with Max Kaminsky, Pee Wee Russell, and Brad Gowans in the front line, recorded the same number in much the same manner, it was "dixieland."

The two performances, similar in structure and feel, draw on ensemble polylinearity and band riffing. Both spot rhythmically vigorous solos: Freeman and Young seem equally to enjoy the tune, with its minor-and-major chordal mix. As Bud put it many years later, "You can't say to a jazz performer, whose talent is worth anything, that he plays avant-garde, or dixieland, or that he is a modern or even a proponent of the Chicago style. A substantial musician will say, 'I just play.' "[9]

Yet the "dixieland" label, once applied, stuck to the white players; by the end of the decade it had all but lost any direct "southern" association and acquired meaning on two distinct levels. For admirers it identified a general repertoire, played in loosely collective manner by Condon and his associates, by descendants of the Original Memphis Five, Original Dixieland Jazz Band, and New Orleans Rhythm Kings; by such Crescent City veterans as Wingy Manone and Sharkey Bonano; by the Bob Crosby Orchestra, with such soloists as trumpeter "Yank" Lawson, Matty Matlock, Ray Bauduc, and Eddie Miller.

In the years after World War II, a period beyond the scope of this survey, the situation became even more confused. Such black and Creole musicians as clarinetists Edmond Hall and Barney Bigard, New Orleans men who had spent most of the 1930s in big bands, found their way comfortably into "dixieland" surroundings. Trumpeters Rex Stewart, Buck Clayton, and Charlie Shavers fit easily in such bands, as did trombonists Vic Dickenson and Benny Morton. Brothers Wilbur (trombone) and Sidney (trumpet) DeParis became fixtures at Jimmy Ryan's, a club with long-standing "Dixieland" associations. On clarinet was Omer Simeon, a New Orleans–born adoptive Chicagoan who had recorded with both Jelly Roll Morton and Paul Mares.

* * *

In the mid-1930s, Eddie Condon worked regularly on 52nd Street, often in company with McKenzie and Bunny Berigan. The trumpeter's signature treatment of "I Can't Get Started," in fact, appears to have originated one evening at the Famous Door, with Condon contributing a series of modulatory cadenzas, played against four-bar sustained chords by the band, that follow Berigan's vocal.

From 1937 until the mid-'40s, when he opened his own club, the guitarist was a more-or-less regular figure at Nick's, a Greenwich Village nightspot that nurtured small-band hot music. Condon and owner Nick Rongetti shared a belief in this kind of jazz, but their theories of advocacy and promotion differed dramatically.

> "Play the music," Nick said. "Play the music and talk about it," I said. "Talk about it to the right people. Get pictures and articles in newspapers and magazines. Get it played on the radio." "Get up on the stand and play that guitar," Nick said.[10]

Ever quick with a wisecrack, Condon seems, indeed, to have attracted prominent figures, especially those from the communications media and other branches of the arts, to his cause. Above all he was a doer who, once seized with an idea, would brook no obstacles to its execution. When public "jam sessions" began to spring up all over town (admission usually free), Condon was in the thick of things. As he himself put it:

> You often have the best times when you get a bunch of guys together who don't play together regularly. As often as not in the thirties and into the forties they were not playing at all, so jam sessions provided a remedy for both these problems. The best ones were often in the homes of musicians or their friends; there have been a few in my living room where everyone was unsorted and disorganized. Sometimes the music turns out bad, sometimes awful, but if the mood is good and there is enough to drink only the good memories last.[11]

Eventually, inevitably, jam sessions went public. Whether held in 52nd Street clubs on off days, or in empty recording studios, or, later, in the ballrooms of Manhattan hotels, they proved a consistent draw for fans eager to see their favorite hot musicians, in unusual combinations, let their hair down.

For a while, Condon teamed up with advertising men Ernest Anderson and Paul Smith (the latter shortly to become his brother-in-law), staging Friday afternoon sessions in the otherwise unused ballroom of the Park Lane Hotel, on Madison Avenue. A typically heterodox "Friday Club" lineup might include Bobby Hackett, Oran "Lips" Page, Bud Freeman, Sidney Bechet, Henry Allen, Pee Wee Russell, pianist Arthur "the Baron" Schutt, Leo Watson of the Spirits of Rhythm, Jimmy Dorsey, and pianist Willie "the Lion" Smith. No racial lines here, no compartmentalization of the participants into "swing" and "dixieland" musicians. Just some different and often stimulating combinations, with often memorable results.

One ardent jam session habitué was Milt Gabler, who owned and ran the

Commodore Music Shop, at 144 East 42nd Street between Lexington and Third avenues, a gathering place for hot music fans. He'd been issuing decade-old collector's items on limited 78 rpm pressings (under the imprimatur of the loose nationwide network of United Hot Clubs of America); now, realizing the strength and vitality of what he was hearing every week, he had begun to think hard about recording some of it on a label of his own.

No one else, least of all Columbia, Victor, and Decca, had shown any but desultory interest in doing it; yet the demand, if restricted in numbers, was obvious and consistent. Gabler and Condon became friends and began talking seriously about making records with none of the restraints, either of form or repertoire, imposed by the major commercial labels.

For weeks, Gabler went through the same frustrating cycle: he'd book studio time, then try to get some musicians together for that day. Each time, something would intervene, thwarting his plans. Pianist Jess Stacy, a favorite, was in Benny Goodman's band; drummer George Wettling was with Paul Whiteman. Both were as often on the road as in New York. There were other, no less thorny, problems in scheduling some of the others he had in mind.

But there came a day, at last, when everything seemed ready to go. The date was set for Monday, January 19, 1938, the morning after Benny Goodman's Carnegie Hall concert, in which Stacy and cornetist Bobby Hackett were among the participants. But on Friday, three days before the session and two before the concert, the blow fell. "Eddie walked into the store and said, 'Jess can't make it Monday—he's recording with Benny before they leave town.' "

For Gabler, that tore it. He'd been patient, flexible, tolerant; but this was too much. He needed Stacy on this maiden date, and he would have him. No Jess, no date—and probably no label. It was time for direct action. He marched over to Carnegie Hall, where the Goodman band was rehearsing, and confronted the clarinetist on a break. It was a spectacular moment: both men had been born into modest circumstances, pulling themselves up by sheer stubbornness and strength of will. Neither was about to back down to the other. In later years both were vague about exactly what passed between them; but in the end, remarkably, Benny relented and canceled his Monday date.

Milt was in business, and with him Commodore Records, the first label wholly devoted to recording hot jazz of any sort. Its success paved the way for other enterprises, among them Harry Lim's Keynote and Alfred Lion's Blue Note, and marks the beginning of the small independents which, in times of major-label torpor, have again and again been a salvation in documenting jazz styles.[12]

It also helped that several mass-circulation magazines were squarely behind Condon and Commodore and the hot music cause in general. "Eddie, of course, was one of the most hustling, promotion-minded men I ever met in my life," Gabler told Dan Morgenstern. "And a delightful man. Every writer loved him. Newspaper people adored him. As well as disc jockeys and anybody."[13]

Jim Moynahan, active in the 1920s as a Boston-based hot clarinetist (and a pal of multi-instrumentalist Brad Gowans, q.v.), was working as a writer-editor at *Time* magazine. Alexander King, photo essay editor at *Life*, was a devotee: in its issue of August 8, 1938, for example, Life ran an eleven-page feature on what it labeled "Swing," prominently highlighting photos taken at a Condon Commodore session among those of other prominent figures. There was no reference to "dixieland."

Over the following decade, Commodore amassed a catalogue a key portion of which presented Condon among ever-shifting personnels and under various nominal leaderships. They included cornetists Max Kaminsky, Bobby Hackett, Muggsy Spanier, and, beginning in 1943, "Wild Bill" Davison; trombonists Jack Teagarden, Brad Gowans, George Brunis, and Miff Mole; reedmen Freeman, Russell, Joe Marsala, and Ernie Caceres; pianists Stacy, Joe Sullivan, Joe Bushkin, and Gene Schroeder; and drummers Wettling, Zutty Singleton, Sid Catlett, and, on a pair of trouble-plagued sessions, Dave Tough.

Gabler's taste and musical perceptiveness also resulted in Commodore dates by other artists, which now rank among the era's keystone performances: the Kansas City Six recordings featuring Buck Clayton, Lester Young, and a contingent from the Count Basie Orchestra; a session of ex–Fletcher Henderson sidemen dominated by Benny Carter, Coleman Hawkins, and Roy Eldridge which revived the old "Chocolate Dandies" name and left a body of extraordinary music; dates by groups led by Mel Powell (featuring, behind the pseudonym "Shoeless John Jackson," Benny Goodman, for whom the pianist was working at the time), Red Norvo, Teddy Wilson, the DeParis brothers, Catlett, Lips Page, and numerous others; nonpareil performances by Bille Holiday, among them the unique "Strange Fruit."

A striking feature of the Condon Commodore records is their choice of material. By this time a more or less standard "dixieland" repertoire had emerged, one identified (in the minds of fans, at least) almost exclusively with white, small-band musicians. It included numbers associated with the ODJB ("At The Jazz Band Ball," "Tiger Rag," "Clarinet Marmalade") and NORK ("That's a Plenty," "Tin Roof Blues," "Farewell Blues"). There was an admixture of old marches and dance numbers from New Orleans days ("High Society," "Panama"), pop songs from the '20s and before, including some ("I've Found a New Baby," "Sugar," "China Boy") that had been musicians' favorites from the outset.[14]

Condon made little secret of his growing revulsion for such already trite numbers: "They're bleeding, they're bloody, we play them every night," Gabler quoted him as saying. Some "Dixieland" numbers do turn up now and then on Commodore records, but they are relatively rare. Audiences at Nick's, Ryan's, and other venues might have clamored night after night for "That's a Plenty" or "Fidgety Feet," but when the musicians were on their own time things were different.

Part of the credit goes to Gabler. Selling records and dealing with music publishers had sharpened his taste for good songs—songs old and new, some familiar and beloved, some quite out-of-the-way. It's at least partly his doing that, for every turn through "Royal Garden Blues," there's a Commodore record of a standard by Berlin or some old half-forgotten barroom ballad ("Save Your Sorrow," "Don't Leave Me, Daddy") or even earlier ("Meet Me Tonight in Dreamland," "Alice Blue Gown").

The performance level was consistently high, with a degree of personal involvement seldom found on commercial records, even those by the same men. Their treatment of the old waltz "Diane," Teagarden's feature at the April 30, 1938, date, is representative. The trombonist's opening melody statement, cushioned by Stacy's buoyant piano, is beautifully considered—affectionate, relaxed, yet moving along in a surprisingly quick ($\downarrow$ = 105) 4/4. It sets a romantic tone, picked up by Freeman for a half-chorus solo.

But the truly indelible moment here is the lilting *tutti*, led by Hackett. In its clarity, rapport, and unanimity of purpose it is a model for jazz ensemble playing: the four horns—cornet, trombone, tenor, and clarinet—are like a piece of multicolored fabric, each strand easily discernible, but so finely woven together as to be inseparable one from another. No line clashes or tramples on another, but each complements the rest, finding a placement that allows it to come together with the others *and* emerge momentarily in someone else's breath points. These men are used to playing together, know each other's ways; understand that the key to successful ensemble playing is a generosity of spirit, allowing the individual to subordinate himself to the whole with no loss of identity. They are one mind, one consciousness out of several.

A slightly different, though no less attractive, ensemble spirit saturates a November 30, 1939, Condon date. Done in the glistening acoustics of Manhattan's Liederkranz Hall, site of some of the finest recordings of the 1920s and early '30s, it substitutes Kaminsky for Hackett, Brad Gowans for Teagarden (yielding, with Pee Wee Russell, three-quarters of the front line of Bud Freeman's Summa Cum Laude band of the time), Joe Bushkin for Stacy. Again, the band punches together with a sense of teamwork and collective spirit.[15]

It's especially notable in the final ensemble of "Strut Miss Lizzie," a bit of 1921 erotica ("Won't you strut Miss Lizzie/Get busy/I wanna see you walk") by "After You've Gone" composers Henry Creamer and Turner Layton. Gowans is the chief soloist on Perry Bradford's 1920 "It's Right Here for You," first recorded by the Original Dixieland Jazz Band. His chorus, quite trumpet-like in construction and execution, shows his admiration for Bix—less a valve trombone solo than a cornet conception, moved down an octave and played on the larger instrument.

But that's hardly surprising. Choice of the song, and this way of treating it, are characteristic of Gowans, surely one of the music's greatest characters—and one of its most critically neglected major figures.

Born December 3, 1903, in Billerica, an outlying Boston suburb, Arthur Bradford Gowans was still a teenager when he first heard the Original Dixieland Jazz Band. With no one around to tell him otherwise, he reacted in typically extravagant fashion: he admired Larry Shields, so he became an adept clarinetist; he translated his esteem for Nick LaRocca into a punchy cornet style; he did homage to Eddie Edwards by adapting what he'd learned to the trombone.

His first records were as a clarinetist: sure enough, on "Tell Me Dreamy Eyes," by Boston saxophonist Perley Breed's Shepherd Colonial Orchestra (1924), he sounds much like Shields. The resemblance is even more explicit on "I'm

Looking Over a Four-Leaf Clover," (1927), issued as "Gowans's Rhapsody Makers": while Jim Moynahan plays the melody on alto sax, Gowans weaves a liquid, graceful clarinet obbligato.

That's pure New Orleans and can be found on the much-admired Jimmie Noone–Joe Poston Brunswicks and in the teamwork of Sidney Arodin and alto saxophonist Joe Loyocano on the Halfway House Orchestra Columbia records of the same period. Gowans's clarinet here, in fact, strongly resembles that of Arodin, whom he replaced in drummer Tommy DeRosa's New York–based "New Orleans Jazz Band" in 1925. What's remarkable is that the "Four-Leaf Clover" duet is not the work of New Orleans expatriates but of two musicians from faraway New England.

No less adept on cornet, Gowans charges through a chorus on the 1926 "I'll Fly to Hawaii" with daunting intensity. He was sufficiently adept on that instrument to be invited to participate in a Red Nichols date two weeks later, contributing a pair of solo breaks to "Heebie Jeebies."

Nichols, hardly a man given to exaggeration, remembered Brad's arrival at the Pathé studio in some detail. His account, told to Richard DuPage in the '50s, vividly captures the New Englander's eccentric ways:

> Brad just pulled in from Boston wearing a baseball cap and a raccoon coat that went all the way down to the floor. He had on one black shoe and one tan shoe, no sock on one foot and one spat on the other—he wasn't kidding either. The coat had special built-in pockets for his sawed-off cornet and a jug of gin. Brad whipped out his cornet and was all ready to go.[16]

(Among those impressed by Gowans's "Heebie Jeebies" breaks was reedman Fud Livingston, who turned one of them into the opening phrase of his own composition "Humpty Dumpty," recorded by Beiderbecke and Trumbauer the following September.)

Brad "had a wonderful way of playing the cornet, real hot cornet," said Max Kaminsky. "That's now a mystery phrase. No one knows what 'hot cornet' means any more—but in those days it had to come out hot. It wasn't the song you were playing. It was the way you did it, and Brad knew how to do it."[17]

Gowans was firm in his conviction that the early white New Orleans men had a sound, an essence, all their own, quite different from the black musicians and no less appealing. At various times throughout a career which ended with his death in 1954, he organized and propelled revivals of the ODJB, usually with himself on clarinet.

"Dixieland—the Original Dixieland band—was his big thing," said alto saxophonist Nuncio "Toots" Mondello, eight years Gowans's junior, who played with him in the New England–based band of Mal Hallett. "He knew all the parts. When we were with Hallett—he was playing cornet, I think—he used to show me things Larry Shields had played on the clarinet.

"Personally—well, Brad was something of a free thinker, what we might now call a hippie. In those days he didn't adhere to convention very much.

Wouldn't shave, was rather careless about bathing, dressed rather casually, if you know what I mean. Brad hung around a lot with Arthur Karle, the tenor player, and a trumpet player named Warren Hookway. They were all kind of wild guys." But, said Max Kaminsky, none of that should be allowed to obscure the fact that Gowans was also "a sweet soul and an extraordinarily talented musician."[18]

Jim Moynahan elaborated. Brad, he said, "used to be the 'one-man band' in Mal Hallett's orchestra. That is, he used to stand up and play, in turn, cornet, trombone, clarinet, saxophone, banjo, drums, piano." And, said Moynahan, he played them all to a standard that both amazed and impressed his fellow-bandsmen.[19]

Gowans spent the early 1930s with Hallett and other dance bands around the Northeast, shuttling back and forth among his various instruments. Often, his companion in small-band ventures was the young Rhode Island guitarist Bobby Hackett, who had lately taken up the cornet. Critic George Frazier heard them together at Boston's Theatrical Grille in 1936. "A good many of [Brad's] solo ideas are monotonous after one's heard them a few times," Frazier wrote in *Down Beat*, "but his backgrounding, which happens to be dixielandish as hell, fits in perfectly and sends the rest of the guys. Gowan[s], like Hackett, is one of those unbelievable guys who plays all instruments with rare skill."[20]

(It's worth noting that both Mondello and Frazier have used the word "dixieland" with a specific meaning in mind: an approach to small-band hot playing whose textures, repertoire, and general allegiance reflected the ODJB. As editor-producer Orrin Keepnews has said, "in those days we said 'dixieland' to distinguish a certain kind of small-group jazz from what the big dance bands were doing. We had two terms, 'dixieland' and 'small-band swing,' which were supposed to mean different things but which actually overlapped all the time. The truth of it is that nobody really thought much about definitions then. It was just a kind of verbal shorthand.")[21]

In common with Hackett and other New England jazzmen, Gowans soon headed for New York, where on November 4, 1938, he recorded for Vocalion with the cornetist and with that other unclassifiable individualist, Pee Wee Russell, whom he'd met in Boston. He wrote arrangements, played trombone and occasional saxophone (alongside Pee Wee) with Hackett's short-lived big band of 1939.

And, perhaps inevitably, he gravitated to the Condon circle, whose free-wheeling approach to hot music (and, it must be added, to alcohol consumption) allowed him a kind of latitude he hadn't enjoyed working in larger bands. While perhaps not as vividly personal a stylist as Teagarden or as agile as Mole, Gowans was far from the "monotonous" player described by Frazier. In common with Hackett, Russell, and Ernie Caceres, his solos—lyrical, melodically rich, intelligently structured—worked off a rather simple harmonic concept but used upper chordal voices imaginatively as color tones.

His "Ja-Da" solo feature is a case in point. Taken at ballad tempo, and fleshing out the song's rudimentary sequence with chromatic passing chords, it is something of a *tour de force*. Blending upper chordal voices—ninths, elevenths, and thirteenths—into a coherent melodic line, it foreshadows the efforts of later generations of musicians, and in particular valve trombonist and composer Bob Brookmeyer.

Far from a random improvisation, Gowans's "Ja-Da" is very much a composition-within-a-composition—and, on the evidence of several recorded performances, a perpetual work-in-progress. But its origins were just as obviously spontaneous, products of the way his ears heard intervals and chords. The chorus transcribed here is from a live radio broadcast, aired during the 1940 summer engagement of Bud Freeman's Summa Cum Laude Orchestra at the Panther Room of Chicago's Hotel Sherman.

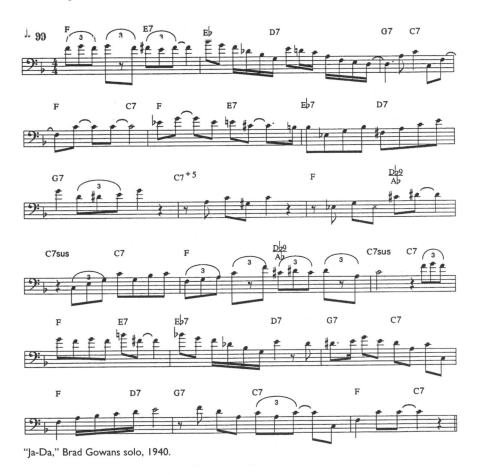

"Ja-Da," Brad Gowans solo, 1940.

Gowans's use of the C♯ against the E7 in bar 5, or the leap to the B♮-F♯ figure in bar 13, is a bit reminiscent of composer-bandleader Ray Noble's enharmonic writing in the bridge of "Cherokee." In both cases, chordal extensions are incorporated into the basic melodic vocabulary so casually that the ear does not resist, or even identify them as dissonances.

He'd learned largely through listening, through exploring what his acute ear told him—and through a flair for invention. "When I first used Brad on a job he was playing trombone," Jim Moynahan said. "He brought an instrument and a pocketful of pipe fittings. Every time we changed key, Brad changed plumbing. He had joints of every length to change the key of the trombone."[22]

Whatever inner curiosity drove Gowans to such explorations found expression off the bandstand as well. "Brad loved to tinker with machines," said bassist Jack Lesberg, a frequent Gowans associate in the 1940s. "Engines fascinated him, and he was good at it. One time he built a car right out in the street, at Sheridan Square in the Village. Nobody stole anything in those days: he'd just come round every day and work on it."[23]

In view of all that, it's no surprise to learn that Gowans devised and built the very horn he played, a combination valve and slide trombone. The "valide," as he called it, proved a remarkable enough invention to warrant an illustrated feature in *Popular Science* magazine in 1946.

"On the valide," said the text, "28 notes can be played in one position without changing the embouchure." It went on to describe, in appropriately meticulous detail, the permutations available through combinations of slide and valves. A sample:

[The valide] can be used as a slide trombone in seven keys by locking down the valves in different combinations, as a valve trombone in four keys by locking the slide in one of its four positions, as a valide by using both methods at once or one in conjunction with the other. The thumb of the left hand operates the valve lock to add the fifth, sixth and seventh positions to the four-position slide.

There was more in this vein, and the article concluded by noting that Gowans, a lifelong baseball fanatic, had also "perfected a realistic parlor baseball game," and was "installing a 91-cubic-inch, eight-cylinder racing engine in a British Standard Swallow" automobile.[24]

Though without formal training in harmony, Gowans developed into a capable, often imaginative, arranger, who seemed to understand the balance between structure and the improvisational freedom demanded in jazz band writing. His sketches for Freeman's Summa Cum Laude Orchestra are models of the genre: clear, neatly ordered, yet leaving plenty of room for individual solo efforts.

"The Summa Cum Laude wouldn't have been a band at all if it hadn't been for Brad," said Max Kaminsky. "He knew all the parts, especially because he could play all the instruments. So everything he wrote out made sense."[25]

Early in World War II Gowans played briefly with Ray McKinley, took a reconstituted ODJB on tour with the Katherine Dunham dance troupe—but spent the rest of the war working in a defense plant near Boston. In April 1946, he was back, to do a Victor album which still stands as the definitive showcase for his arranging skills. Included in his "New York Nine" for the date were Billy Butterfield, Joe Bushkin, and, recording for the last time in his short life, drummer

Dave Tough. Using Paul Ricci's bass sax for both color and rhythmic force, Gowans achieves a remarkable play of ensemble textures.

He contributes a vigorous full-chorus trombone solo to "Stompin' at the Savoy," arranged with the density and variety of an Ellington small group, and builds "Carolina in the Morning" from Art Rollini's demure tenor sax opening to a triumphal, Armstrong-like ending featuring Butterfield's trumpet over a thickly scored chordal carpet. Arrangement and soloists (notably Joe Dixon's almost ethereal clarinet) imbue "I'm Comin', Virginia" with a hushed, elegiac quality just hinted at in the famed Beiderbecke-Trumbauer recording. "Poor Butterfield" is a recycled, dolled-up version of Gowans's own "Easy to Get," used by the Summa Cum Laude band as a signature theme.

"I really think he bordered on genius," said Dixon. "This wonderfully inventive mind, all the different things he could do. I got to know him in '36, when I sat in with him and Bobby Hackett at the Theatrical Club in Boston. They were very similar in conception: I was absolutely awestruck by the way they played. The only time I'd ever heard that kind of harmonic thinking was on the old Bix records."[26]

In 1950, tired of New York and with the amount of available work apparently dwindling, Gowans drove cross-country to California, where he lived the remaining four years of his life, recording superbly for Clive Acker's Jump label in company with such old friends as bass saxophonist Joe Rushton and clarinetist James "Rosy" McHargue.

"It was a thrill for me to play with Brad," said McHargue. "He knew how to keep the trombone part from intruding on the clarinet part. Today, too often, when I'm playing with some band, playing the part that I think is the clarinet part, there's the trombone playing it, leaving the clarinet with nothing to do except go high."[27]

Brad Gowans died of cancer, age fifty, September 8, 1954.

On Saturday, May 20, 1944, Eddie Condon began a series of weekly concerts at Town Hall (later transferred to the Ritz Theatre); widely publicized, they were broadcast on NBC's "Blue" Network, shortly to become the American Broadcasting Co., and on the Armed Forces Radio Service (AFRS). (Radio "jam sessions" were nothing new: some of the best of them, held at the St. Regis Hotel in 1938 with British reporter Alistair Cooke as host, were not even heard in this country but beamed to England by the British Broadcasting Corp.)

Condon's idea, developed with friend and publicist Ernie Anderson, was simple: assemble between seven and nineteen musicians, add a couple of "name" guests (Gene Krupa, an old Chicago pal, was a regular), and present a program of good songs, giving each participant a chance to shine.

The personnels were often a roll call of Condon musical cronies: Hackett, Kaminsky, and Billy Butterfield among the trumpets; Ernie Caceres on baritone; Russell, Joe Marsala, and Edmond Hall on clarinets; plus such familiar faces as Stacy, McKenzie, and Miff Mole. The Dorsey brothers dropped in, singly of course; trumpeters Jonah Jones and "Lips" Page put in striking cameo appearances; Muggsy Spanier turned up, as did Willie "the Lion" Smith, James P. Johnson, Joe Bushkin, Wingy Manone, and even trombonists Jack Teagarden, Benny Morton, and, from Woody Herman's band, Bill Harris.

Among notable absentees were Gowans and Bud Freeman, the latter by this time stationed, courtesy of the U.S. Army, in the Aleutian Islands. But, the Noël Coward of the tenor saxophone assured Condon later, he was a faithful listener via AFRS.

The concerts have now been released on records in their entirety, and what's most remarkable is their consistency: outstanding performances are frequent, with Hackett and Caceres particularly good. It's perhaps pointless to single out individual moments from among the hours of music, though a three-part "Clarinet Chase" on a B♭ blues, featuring Caceres, Russell, and Marsala, is memorable.

On drums, except on those days when Krupa felt like putting in a guest appearance, was the often inspired George Godfrey Wettling.

George Wettling had been (with Tough and Krupa) part of the original Chicago circle and, like them, spent most of the '30s playing in big bands. His were the brushes backing Bunny Berigan's vocal on the best-selling "I Can't Get Started," his the steady but non-intrusive beat that lifted the bands of Artie Shaw, Red Norvo, Paul Whiteman, and others. A well-schooled musician, he'd worked regularly in radio and commercial recording studios.

But Wettling seemed happiest by far in the small, unfettered jam groups which were Eddie Condon's specialty. Overshadowed to some degree by Krupa's flamboyance and Tough's sheer brilliance, Wettling more than matched them in his ability to unify and steer a rhythm section. Like Krupa, he'd learned by listening to Baby Dodds, Ben Pollack, and other pioneers and had retained the flavor, the ability to *blend* into an ensemble. Wettling's small-group work, with Condon and countless others, is remarkably subtle in its sense of mood and pace, its control of a finely calibrated sense of abandon. In Burt Korall's authoritative words:

> "His time was firm; it bubbled and danced. His breaks had an inner life and logic. His solos were well-crafted bursts of energy. Wettling had a fine touch, ample technique, and a distinctive sound on the snare drum. He was a good listener and responded inventively to ensembles and solos. He would change the background behind each soloist, adapting, giving and taking, building, serving as a time center and as another interesting voice in the ensemble.[28]

His propulsive drumming enlivens hundreds, even thousands, of records, and those with Condon are among the best. It's Wettling's accented press roll, a Baby Dodds legacy, that carries Bud Freeman to the very edge of anarchy on the Commodore "Meet Me Tonight in Dreamland," Wettling's drive that sends the normally demure Bobby Hackett careering through the final ensemble of the uptempo blues "Carnegie Jump," Wettling's and Jess Stacy's quiet prodding that gets Pee Wee Russell rocking happily on "Rose of Washington Square."

Wettling was a master—some would contend *the* master—of that overused and frequently misunderstood hallmark of so many "dixieland" performances: the four-bar end-of-performance drum break. Following a final tutti, especially at faster tempos, it's a kind of eight-bar melody reprise, the drummer taking the first four bars and the band returning, all pistons firing, to finish out the cadence. In some bands it becomes a sixteen-bar reprise, drummer and ensemble taking eight apiece.

Done right, it functions as both tension release and "kicker" in the journalistic sense: the punchy last line that leaves the reader's senses sharpened, tingling. Some drummers—Cliff Leeman, Nick Fatool, Ray McKinley—have understood this and done it with masterly finesse. Depending on the player, that means either a display of technique, a witty or imaginative "four" in the bebop sense, or even (Fatool is outstanding at this) a melodic paraphrase.

But in George Wettling's hands this modest device became a small-scale work of art. Again and again he'd seem to hurtle out of an ensemble and into the break with a force, an irresistible momentum, that swept the band right along with it. There was no sense of an ensemble stopping for the drummer to do some little trick before the horns returned: a Wettling break was part of the action—in a way it *was* the action.

Examples, a few among dozens: "The World Is Waiting for the Sunrise" (from *Brother Matthew*, ABC-Paramount), "I've Found a New Baby" (*Eddie Condon's Treasury of Jazz*, Columbia), "Runnin' Wild" (*Dixieland in Hi-Fi*, Columbia/Harmony)—which also offers a nimble full-chorus Wettling solo; "China Boy" (*The Roaring Twenties*, Columbia).

Perhaps the definitive example of Wettling's ability to energize a band is on a ten-inch LP issued by Columbia in 1951 under his own name. It's a Condon unit, of course, with "Wild Bill" Davison, Edmond Hall, and other regulars. Each of the eight titles works steadily, inexorably, to a climax of drive and almost demonic energy. Wettling's four-bar break at the end of a swaggering "Memphis Blues" employs a kettledrum to great and humorous effect. "Collier's Clambake" (basically the chord sequence of "St. James Infirmary" at a medium-bright tempo) starts at a high intensity level, Davison punching out the kind of virile, aggressive lead that earned him his nickname. Even by the standards of Condon groups, "After You've Gone" is extraordinary. Like "Clambake," it opens hot: "They sound as if they've been playing the number for five minutes, heating up to this pitch, before turning on the microphones," pianist Dick Hyman has remarked. That's largely Wettling's doing. He hits it hard and keeps cranking things up, through solos by Sullivan, Hall, and trombonist Jimmy Archey (Condon's guitar strong and audible behind them), to a stomping final ensemble.[29]

This is no random collection of seven men playing together: it's a *band*, a team, component parts fused into a splendid performance engine fueled by Wettling and cornetist Davison; bars 13–16, for example, are a furious ensemble explosion, Davison tearing up to his high E♮ and cascading down over four bars, to be deftly caught by Wettling's bass drum "thwack" on the last beat of bar 16.

(Among Wettling's fans was the great American abstract painter Stuart Davis, whose brand of modernism was as stubbornly individualistic as the styles of the jazzmen he liked to hear. The two men struck up a friendship, and before long the drummer, a gifted amateur painter, had become a Davis student. By 1950 he'd mastered a style which, though strongly influenced by his teacher, was skilled and vigorous on its own, winning him several well-received exhibitions in the '50s. Adorning the Columbia album cover was a photograph of the band, superimposed on a Wettling painting representing the same scene. It's good work, strongly in the spirit of such jazz-influenced Davis canvases as "The Mellow Pad," "Rapt at Rappaport's," and "Something on the Eight Ball," from the same period. Though Pee Wee Russell's paintings later attracted more publicity, it is Wettling who is the superior craftsman.)

With the exception of such singing instrumentalists as Jack Teagarden and "Lips" Page, few vocalists turned up on Condon's Town Hall evenings. One exception to the rule was Condon's old friend and crony Red McKenzie.

As noted earlier and in detail, he'd gotten off to a fast start in the early '20s with the Mound City Blue Blowers. Though musically uneducated, he had a sharp ear and understood jazz phrasing: to hear his comb-and-paper "blue-blowing," swinging hard alongside Russell, Spanier, and Coleman Hawkins, on "At the Darktown Strutters' Ball" and "Hello Lola," or wringing real pathos from "Georgia on My Mind" or "One Hour," is to recognize a genuine, if unconventional, hot stylist at work.

Also a fine intuitive ballad singer, McKenzie landed a job with Paul Whiteman in 1932 as a replacement for Bing Crosby. He sings such pop songs as "Three on a Match" and "I'll Follow You" with Whiteman, "Lovable" and "Just Friends" on his own, in a strong, confident—and not a little sentimental—baritone.

But McKenzie's drinking, and the bursts of temperament it usually brought on, coupled with an apparent inability to capitalize on many opportunities that crossed his path, ultimately proved his undoing. Though he always surrounded himself with top-of-the-line musicians, achieved mid-'30s popularity on 52nd Street, and made many fine records, he never achieved the recognition or financial success his talents might have brought him.

In later years his voice deepened, and his sense of aesthetic balance seemed to fail him: what had been a charming vein of sentimentality in his singing slipped more and more often into excess. His performance of Willard Robison's mawkish "Little High Chairman" on an October 21, 1944, Town Hall broadcast is, by that time, all too characteristic. But Condon stuck by him—even until his death, of cirrhosis, on February 7, 1948.

If the Town Hall concerts, and Condon's circle in general, had an official "house vocalist," it was surely Lee Wiley. Born in Fort Gibson, Oklahoma, October 9, 1915, she'd come to New York around 1930 and been noticed almost at once. Tall, striking of figure and feature, with long, corn-colored hair, she was a woman bound to attract men even before they realized she could sing.

Attract them she did. Stories of her romances, her passions and trysts and flings, still circulate among older musicians. At the mention of her name, more than one seen-it-all veteran has been known to roll his eyes skyward in mute acknowledgment that Lee Wiley "was some little number."

More important, she sang superbly, a fact not lost even on those men who were drawn to her sexually. "Miss Wiley has a little thing going for her called class," the columnist and jazz devotee George Frazier once wrote in the notes to a Wiley LP, confessing himself "extremely eager to go to bed with her—but in a nice, noble way, you understand." Musical theatre historian Stanley Green waxed no less euphoric, declaring, "I loved Lee Wiley even before I had any idea who she was."[30]

But sexuality alone, at least in the musical world of the '30s, would not have brought Lee Wiley the respect that soon came her way. Her singing quickly won over Leo Reisman (with whom she made her first records), Johnny Green, Paul Whiteman, and Victor Young. Her relationship with Young, on-and offstage, proved to be one of her most durable. "Victor kept her for years," one musician's wife was quoted as saying. "Apparently he was able to put up with her antics with other men."[31]

By 1935 Lee Wiley was something of a radio star. ("Radio has once more opened its portals to beauty—this time from Oklahoma," a newspaper in New Bedford, Massachusetts, rather breathlessly proclaimed.) She'd recorded with the Casa Loma Orchestra and with the Dorsey Brothers. Bunny Berigan, trumpeter on the Dorsey sessions, soon became one of her romantic conquests.[32]

Larry Carr, whose skills as a singer and pianist lent deeper authority to his work as a music historian and record producer, got quickly and directly to the heart of Wiley's singing—particularly its appeal to jazz musicians. "Early on, Lee decided that less is better, and this conviction never changed," Carr wrote in a record sleeve essay. "Her love of simplicity was evident in everything about her; her chic appearance, the way she wore her hair, and, of course, her singing. All reflected her innate taste." To Carr's ear, Wiley's unique diction was "an intriguing amalgam of Oklahoma, Park Avenue and 52nd Street."[33]

With Mildred Bailey and Connie Boswell, she was one of the three premier white singers of the '30s. If her smoky vocal timbre and languorous phrasing reflected a certain admiration for Ethel Waters, Wiley also possessed an intrinsic stylishness, as unadorned and elegant as the single strands of pearls she often wore. As Britain's Digby Fairweather has put it, "her intimate, veiled voice, precise, almost tutored, diction and stroking approach to a note seemed guaranteed to turn strong men to jelly."[34]

Wiley left a small footprint on jazz history in 1939–40 by recording the first "composer albums," collections spotlighting the work of a single songwriter. With such albums now so commonplace as to be a cliché, it's hard to imagine someone doing it for the first time. But so it was.

Her backing for the Gershwin set, produced by Ernie Anderson and issued by the Liberty Music Shop, was by Condon, Kaminsky, Russell, Freeman, Wettling, bassist Artie Shapiro, and Bushkin, with an unbilled Fats Waller taking over the keyboard on some titles. There were also albums devoted to Cole Porter (Berigan and Bushkin among the supporting cast), Harold Arlen (Hackett, Butterfield, Caceres, Wettling, pianist Dave Bowman, and others), and Rodgers and Hart (Kaminsky, Freeman, Gowans, Bushkin, Shapiro, Wettling).[35]

"The only way she sings is the right way," Condon said, introducing the singer at a Town Hall concert. "Good and right." Her records are plentiful and reveal much. Even such early efforts as "I'll Follow My Secret Heart," recorded with a large Victor Young orchestra in 1934, have an unadorned directness that arrests both mind and emotions.

"How did you learn to project the inside meaning of each word in your songs while virtually never articulating a hard consonant?" Richard Hadlock asked rhetorically in a 1977 essay. "You couldn't have absorbed the tricks of bel canto at 15, but you guessed the right way to combine something like it with a lovely Oklahoma softness and a jazz master's sense of time."

Still apostrophizing the singer, Hadlock went on to deliver himself of some trenchant views on Wiley, the Condon musicians, and the parochialism which had even then come to minimize their achievements:

> I've long been annoyed by those pinheads who associate you with "Dixieland" musicians. I suppose it's because people you knew and admired, like Jess, Bunny, Pee Wee, Bud, Hackett and Teagarden really listened to one another and liked to play off the wall without too much written stuff. And, of course, it is a fact that you recorded some with Eddie Condon. But, then, most of the pundits forget that Eddie's one ear was a pretty good ear; he embraced any jazz musician who had a personal and beautiful sound, provided the performer was skilled at improvising and could swing. That's why Eddie never stopped talking about people such as Beiderbecke, Armstrong, Bechet, Holiday and Wiley.[36]

The composer albums are first-rate performances all around ("the best thing," said Condon, "that ever happened to the Liberty Music Shop"). Hear how comfortably Wiley floats on the buoyant rhythm laid down by Waller and Wettling on "I've Got a Crush on You" and lends "Baby's Awake Now" a deliciously morning-after feeling that would surely have won Larry Hart's enthusiastic support. Quality stuff, almost unique in the way it interacts with its jazz accompaniment, and equalled at the time by few singers of either race.[37]

As Roy Hemming and David Hajdu remarked in Discovering Great Singers of Classic Pop, the Gershwins' " 'Sweet and Lowdown' could well have been written for her. It wasn't, of course, but Lee sang it often—and better than anyone before or since, with a particularly distinctive mixture of cool elegance and warm succulence." TV personality Dave Garroway, a lifelong Wiley fan, likened her vocal sound to "running your hand over a piece of fine Harris tweed—and they both tickle."[38]

At the start of the 1950s, Wiley joined Hackett, Bushkin, and a string quartet to create Night in Manhattan, a ten-inch Lp which may be one of the finest of all jazz-related vocal albums. Here, as elsewhere, her alto voice projected an intimacy which was at once erotic and, to use Frazier's word, exalted, limned by Hackett's softly glowing cornet obbligatos. Critic Max Harrison has referred to her "exquisite aloofness" and called her, not quite facetiously, "the jazz equivalent to Louise Brooks."

Overall, it's quite certain that, given her background in radio, her beauty, the unique qualities in her singing, Lee Wiley could have gone on to major stardom. But there was something perverse, willful, in her character that forever refused to play the games, laughed at the kind of posture and self-importance inherent in the very idea of stardom. She'd rather, as Max Kaminskly put it, "just be a barrelhouse chick, singing with a bunch of guys whose playing she liked."

"I always sang the way I wanted to sing," she said once. "If I didn't like something, I just wouldn't do it. Instead, I'd take a plane to California and sit in the sun." Such independence always comes at a price. Whether by accident or design, Lee Wiley's every brush with opportunity wound up subverted either by her stubbornness or by plain bad luck.[39]

She was married for a while to pianist Jess Stacy, one of the mildest of men, and in the words of one onlooker "just ate him up." The union lasted five years; though Stacy looked back on it with something less than relish, it did yield at least one truly memorable performance: a twelve-inch Commodore record of a blues called "Down to Steamboat Tennessee." Lee, Jess, and Muggsy Spanier are the only performers on this poised, lustrous updating of a format immortalized by Bessie Smith's great blues records of the 1920s—singer and pianist in close tandem, the horn as commentator and confidant.

Not surprisingly, Wiley appearances at Condon Town Hall concerts are almost casual, disarmingly relaxed. Typical is an August 12, 1944, "You're Lucky to Me," with a startling half-chorus solo by Russell. Several times she sang "Wherever There's Love," a rather fetching collaboration by Condon and John De Vries. Among her best Town Hall moments is a nicely judged "Don't Blame Me," done October 14, 1944. Beginning with an out-of-tempo verse (played with great delicacy by Stacy), she builds depth and involvement until, at length, the horns and rhythm join her in a quietly rocking finale.

Wiley was in and out of music during the late 1950s and '60s, recording a few LPs. Her performances on *West of the Moon* (RCA) and *A Touch of the Blues* (RCA) have good moments: a reading of Benny Carter's "Blues in My Heart," cushioned by Bill Finegan's spare, imaginative reed tapestry, is direct and affecting. On "A Hundred Years From Today," her pronunciation, even her vocal timbre, strongly recall those of an old friend, Texas-born Jack Teagarden.

But however well, however sensitively, Finegan, Al Cohn, and Ralph Burns might write for her, Lee Wiley still seemed most at home in a small group, supported by a horn or two. Whether Hackett (on *Night in Manhattan*), Ruby Braff (on the Storyville Rodgers and Hart LP), or Russell and the various other participants in the Condon groups, this setting was sure to bring out the best in her.

She did one final LP, for Monmouth-Evergreen, in 1971. By that time the once supple contralto had deepened and coarsened, the vibrato widened. But she makes it work for her, as if age and illness had bequeathed a dimension, a depth of understanding only hinted at earlier. If "A Woman's Intuition," as sung on *Night in Manhattan*, was a reproach to a wayward lover, this version is an acknowledgment, accepting—without humiliation or bitterness—that lovers will be wayward and that's the way of the world. Even "I'm Comin', Virginia," a song she'd sung hundreds of times over the years, is less an expression of homesickness here than a valedictory, transition and farewell—and poignant into the bargain.

Her last public appearance was at Carnegie Hall, in the summer of 1972. Hackett was there, as were Teddy Wilson (with whom she'd never worked) and an all-star quintet. From the sound of the capacity crowd when she is introduced, it is clear that, even in retirement, Lee Wiley remained a much-admired, even beloved, figure.

She died, of cancer, on December 11, 1975.

In December 1945, Eddie Condon stopped talking about opening a place of his own and finally did it. Located in an old town house at 47 West 3rd Street (a speakeasy during Prohibition and, more recently, a transvestite bar called the Howdy Club), it was an immediate and resounding success, a late-night oasis at which celebrities and fellow-musicians frequently vied with paying customers for a clear view of the tiny bandstand—and an excellent bully pulpit for its proprietor's advocacy of what someone had begun to call "Americondon music."[40]

(Another factor, frequently overlooked, behind Condon's entry into the nightclub business—as the Town Hall concerts before it—was a 20 percent federal tax, levied early in World War II, on profits of any establishment providing "entertainment," which in this context meant music for dancing. Without dancing, a room could offer live music but dodge the tax—a condition which did much to promote the rise of "jazz clubs," in which customers sat and listened while eating and drinking. This, in turn, freed bands from having to tailor tempos and lengths of numbers to the needs of dancers, providing a fertile climate for far-reaching changes in jazz style and presentation.)

In the words of critic-historian Leonard Feather, Condon "had become a fashionable personality, patronized by prominent figures from the book, magazine and art worlds and publicized widely in many articles that identified him as a one-man crusade for jazz." Among regular customers at his club: writers John O'Hara and John Steinbeck; artists Stuart Davis and Mischa Resnikoff; such old music friends as Bing Crosby and Johnny Mercer; and even actors Robert Mitchum, Yul Brynner, and Kirk Douglas (who received coaching there at first hand for his role in Hollywood's *Young Man With a Horn*).[41]

Condon was eminently quotable. People who had never heard him or his bands play repeated his one-liners ("Beboppers flat their fifths, we drink them") and snappy rejoinders ("What's the difference between New Orleans and New York?" he was once asked: "About a thousand miles," came the reply). Long before the era of the sound bite, he was an expert at it.

Though many musicians worked at Condon's during its decade-and-a-half existence, its musical profile remained pretty much the same as in Chicago days: hard-hitting ensembles, a tendency to push the beat, tough-tender on the ballads.

And, always, an air of ease and informality, a bond (and a certain amount of alcohol consumption) taken for granted. A determined, sometimes compulsive youthfulness—some, less indulgently, called it adolescence—of outlook.

And, too, a tendency to lapse into formula. The nine-to-four, night-after-night grind of the professional jazz business (not to mention daytime record sessions and other jobs) made that an inevitability, and it's certainly not a phenomenon confined to this style of music. As any working jazzman will quickly admit, it's asking a lot to conjure up inspiration on a nightly basis, particularly with the audience clamoring to hear a short list of tunes again and again.

Singer Barbara Lea, whose career has been closely intertwined with musicians of this style, referred to workaday jazz as "the most demanding and unsparing of all businesses. I can't think of any other performer who's required to be 'on,' creatively so, as much and as often as jazz players. In a way, I'm often surprised that more of them didn't fall into routine, or run out of creative steam, a lot earlier."[42]

After a while, it was easier to oblige all the requests for the "Original Dix-ieland One-Step" and "Tin Roof Blues" than to resist, especially if obliging meant keeping the customers coming back. "At Nick's," Condon told an interviewer, "we did a lot of dixieland numbers because the customers identified them with our music and asked for them. We could have played the most recent popular hits, giving them our interpretation, but *many of the listeners would not have believed they were hearing jazz* [emphasis added]."[43]

The listening audience, moreover, was aging; in that generational way peculiar to American fans, it embraced the music more tenaciously, and less for strictly musical reasons than personal and psychological. It symbolized their youth, the well (if selectively) remembered time in their lives when the future seemed limitless, immortality theirs for the asking. Reminded them of a *Zeitgeist*, vivid and enjoyable, before time and change edged it into memory.

To examine what happened to this music, to those who played it and those who witnessed and embraced it, is to uncover a vein of deep melancholy not far below all the surface *bonhommie*. The poet Philip Larkin, a hot music fan since his undergraduate days at Oxford in the '30s, caught it deftly when he described "men whose first coronary is coming like Christmas; who drift, loaded helplessly with commitments and obligations and necessary observances, into the darkening avenues of age and incapacity, deserted by everything that once made life sweet."[44]

George Frazier, celebrating a long-ago evening at Nick's, also understood. "The beers are short and there never is a moment when you can't cut the smoke with the crease in your pants," he wrote in a 1941 *Down Beat* column,

> but there are still those of us who . . . in days to come will think of it and be stabbed, not with any fake emotion, but with a genuinely heartbreaking nostalgia. We will think of this place at 7th Avenue and 10th Street, and all of a sudden the fragrant past . . . will sneak up on us and for a little while we will be all the sad young men.[45]

Other factors, too, were at work. The World War II years had seen the rise of bebop, a new and technically demanding—and increasingly politicized—jazz form; its creators and high priests were young black musicians, among them saxophonist Charlie Parker, trumpeters Dizzy Gillespie and Miles Davis, pianist Bud Powell, bassist Charles Mingus, drummers Kenny Clarke and Max Roach. They, and countless followers, eager for dignity and respect as "artists," were at pains to distance themselves from the show business conventions of the past.

"Dixieland," as they understood it, *was* that past. Upbeat, relaxed, it romanced its audiences. It was often played for dancing or as light entertainment. Harmonically simple (though certain of its individual soloists were anything but that), it used pop songs as basic material and still clung to the idea of ensemble polyphony. Above all, its aesthetic foundation was still the romanticism of the late nineteenth century.

Its days as social rebellion long gone, its players approaching middle age, "dixieland" was increasingly perceived as a music played by white musicians (a far from accurate assessment) for largely white audiences. The new core jazz audience turned away, following new prophets and leaving Condon and those who believed as he did in something of a cul-de-sac.

Matters didn't improve when traditionalist fans (or "moldy figs") sounded off in the pages of their favorite monthly, the *Record Changer*, against demonized moderns, as represented by *Down Beat* and *Metronome* magzines. Though most of the polemic of those days now seems puerile and musically irrelevant, it was taken seriously enough—at least in lay perception—to deepen a schism between "modern jazz" (representing progress) and Luddite "dixieland."

A new generation of young, mostly white, musicians who had aligned themselves with the older forms spoke out against such thinking. "One of the common misconceptions about jazz history," said saxophonist-clarinetist Bob Wilber, "is that a style which started in a certain era is then superseded by another style which makes the first one obsolete, and then that style is superseded by a third, and so on."[46]

Ever more pervasively identified with white, middle-class American society, "dixieland" found itself on the wrong end of an emerging consciousness that was part racial, part social, part artistic: its very buoyancy of attitude, its straightforward tunefulness, tough-and-tender emotional stance, set ill with those who equated solemnity with seriousness, anger with moral authority. Scholars and commentators who should have known better consigned "dixie" to a kind of semantic limbo and were promptly followed by casual listeners. Gradually, inexorably, an entire generation of expert jazzmen, marginalized and maligned, disappeared from wide view.

When Condon's 3rd Street lease ran out, he moved his club to a new site in the Sutton Hotel, at 330 East 56th Street. That lasted eight years, perhaps a healthy run by New York nightclub standards but never a comfortable fit for the old Village crowd. More and more, attrition was claiming friends and coevals: Brad Gowans dead at age fifty, in 1954; George Wettling in 1968, at sixty; Pee Wee

Russell, sixty-three, in 1969; Edmond Hall, sixty-five, in 1971; trombonist Bob "Cutty" Cutshall, fifty-six, in 1968; Jack Teagarden, fifty-eight, in 1964.

With repertoire and routine increasingly calcified, Condon and his friends kept producing music now too often sustained by a kind of dogged energy—and hyped to death as "good-time" party music by the promotional machinery of journalism and public-relations. It takes only a brief look at the covers of "dixieland" LPs issued in the late 1950s and early '60s to see the result: straw hats and candy-striped blazers, such album titles as *That Happy Dixieland Jazz* and *Dixieland, My Dixieland*; breathless sleeve notes likening bands playing this form of jazz to barbershop quartets, Stanley Steamers, and Fourth of July fireworks displays.

Some jazzmen, sick of it all, simply drifted away. Pee Wee Russell began making records of Thelonious Monk tunes. Bobby Hackett and Dick Cary put together an intrepid little band to play a wide and diverse repertoire—only to find themselves victims of "dixieland" stereotyping on their sole commercial record date. Various others sought—and found—solace and stimulation in other contexts and company.

A 1961 NBC-TV special, *Chicago and All That Jazz*, reunited Condon, Freeman, Russell, Gene Krupa, Jimmy McPartland, Jack Teagarden, Joe Sullivan, and bassist Bob Haggart for another backward glance. But there was little chemistry; the participants seemed unable to crank up more than superficial enthusiasm for "China Boy," "Nobody's Sweetheart," and the rest of the aged-in-malt standards. Russell, visibly ill at ease, played especially listlessly, both on the soundtrack and on a Verve LP made around the same time.

Condon still took groups out to festivals and on tour abroad. There were always good men about, some of them representing newer generations, eager to play and share the spirit of the music. Pianists Dick Cary and Dick Wellstood, reedmen Bob Wilber and Kenny Davern, trumpeters Johnny Windhurst and Ruby Braff, and others were skilled, often brilliant, in translating what they'd learned into vivid, personal solo styles. But it was over. Something had gone out of the music, and Condon seemed to know it. Was it youth, with its sense of limitless promise? Idealism? Belief in itself? Or had time and change, demographics and political demagoguery, the simple process of aging, carved the heart out of his musical way of life?

Eddie Condon died of cancer on August 4, 1975, and some will say that his music, whatever it was or was not, died with him. Young musicians still play the songs, still generate firepower enough to get a listener's pulse racing for a moment or two. But as any of them will readily admit, it's just not the same. The world, the social circumstance, in which Eddie Condon lived and made music is now only a memory.

"If you could only have heard it back then," clarinetist Jack Maheu said recently, wonder edging his voice. "You'd open the door to some little club where those guys—Eddie, and some of his cronies—were playing. And that music would hit you like a fist, a blast of superheated steam. It was *powerful*." Maheu, now in his middle sixties, grew up in upstate New York and came downstate to the city as soon as he was able. "I mean, lots of guys today play well. But back then there was something else—in Pee Wee, Bud, Wild Bill, Teagarden, George Wettling . . .

"Take Wettling, for example. One of those breaks could just lift you off your chair. They had a fire to them. The records? Yeah, some of them capture it a bit—but you should have heard what it sounded like live. You wouldn't have believed your ears. It was the most emotionally powerful kind of jazz I've ever heard. But that's gone now."[47]

Perhaps Glen McNatt, writing in the *Baltimore Sun*, got to the heart of the matter in declaring that "the major creative forces that drove the development of jazz from the early part of this century . . . appear to have exhausted themselves . . . Jazz emerged as an expression of the modern age against the stuffy conventions of the Victorian world that preceded it. A cynic might say that it simply has outlived its usefulness."[48]

Listening to the records now, particularly those by three decades of Condon-organized groups, it's difficult not to be struck by the polish and emotive power of the soloists and, perhaps even more, by the close-mesh texture and rhythmic verve of the ensembles. This last, surely, is an art that reached its fullest flower with these musicians and, as Maheu and others seem to be suggesting, may have died with them. But what to call it? Is "jazz" enough? Do such terms as "Chicago style" still mean anything to anyone? Is there nothing better than tired, politically beleaguered old "dixieland?"

"We called it music," said Condon, bestowing a title on his 1947 autobiography. As usual, he'd found the best way of saying it.

IV

The Big Bands I

Creating a Tradition

13

The Jean Goldkette and Ben Pollack Orchestras

On Tuesday, February 1, 1927, the Jean Goldkette Orchestra recorded "The Stampede," an instrumental stomp composed by Fletcher Henderson and recorded by his orchestra the previous May. From all reports, it was an outstanding performance, with fine solos by Bix Beiderbecke on cornet and Frank Trumbauer on C-melody saxophone. The Victor Company chose not to release it, and the masters were destroyed.

Rex Stewart, cornetist with Henderson at the time, recalled that the leader wanted to record a medley of waltzes with the word "rose" in the title, a consistent favorite at the whites-only Roseland Ballroom, where the band played regularly. Recording executives turned down his offers to do so.

Bix Beiderbecke and his six-piece "Gang" recorded three small-band titles during a Frank Trumbauer OKeh session on Tuesday, October 25, 1927. The company released one of them, Fats Waller's "Goose Pimples," as part of its "race" catalogue, identifying the band only as the "New Orleans Lucky Seven."

When the Casa Loma Orchestra's December 6, 1930, OKeh record of its instrumental "Casa Loma Stomp" showed signs of widespread popularity, it reappeared concurrently on Columbia, by now OKeh's parent company, as played by "Louis' Harlem Stompers."

The early history of jazz on record abounds with such paradoxical situations, all proceeding from an implicit set of marketing assumptions made by the record companies: that "hot" jazz, in common with the blues, was best received by black record buyers, whose social and sexual mores were widely assumed to be more "natural," less restrained, than those of whites; and that whites, by contrast, preferred their "jazz" on the polite side, peppy rather than sensuous, and not too intense. If a few white record buyers wanted really hot music, there were plenty of black bands around to supply it.

Not only were such stereotyped assumptions not supported by evidence, but they directly contradicted what people outside the offices of record company executives knew to be true: that in a significant number of cases the exact reverse applied. A great part of the core audience for "hot" music was to be found among whites, especially on the college campuses, and "sweet" dance music such as waltzes of the sort Henderson wanted to record found great response among blacks.

But the front offices of the record companies were a world of their own, and in that world—especially at Victor, the most conservative of the major labels—no one was going to be much interested in a white band whose specialty was hot instrumentals. No wonder that jazz oral histories of the 1920s abound with complaints by musicians, veterans of such groups, that record supervisors "never let us play our best stuff."

Paramount among these bands, if the testimony is to be credited, were the Jean Goldkette Victor Recording Orchestra of 1926–27 and the Ben Pollack band of 1927–30. In both cases, the complaint recurred with remarkable frequency: the records *never showed more than a fraction of what the band could do*. They—the recording directors—*never let us record our best arrangements*. Most of the records were, at best, *compromises, watered-down arrangements of lousy pop tunes*.

In the minds of the Goldkette and Pollack musicians, their respective bands were as good as, perhaps even better than, the corresponding black ensembles; but they—the black bands—were permitted, even urged, to record the very sort of hot instrumentals that were off limits for the whites.

The result, many have protested, has been second-banana status for bands that were actually, by acclamation and common consent, at the top of the heap. "We wuz robbed" might sum up the oft-heard plaints.

But latter-day scholars have approached such claims with a certain skepticism. The gulf is simply too wide, goes the received consensus; the music, as represented on records, fails to live up to its billing. "A band like nothing you ever heard," the phrase most often applied by Goldkette alumni to their short-lived orchestra, fails to emerge from its recorded performances. The result is at best a standoff, final judgment reserved. Partisans cling to their loyalties, skeptics remain unconvinced. The resulting vacuum is quickly filled by those other bands whose recorded performances *do* live up to, and sometimes even exceed, anecdotal evidence.

Verbal testimony to the excellence of both the Goldkette and Pollack ensembles is abundant. A large and compelling body of anecdotal documentation insists that they were, as hot units, easily on a par with the best black orchestras of the day. All accounts agree that Goldkette's Detroit-based unit clearly and cleanly bested that of Fletcher Henderson in a climactic "Battle of Music" held at New York's Roseland Ballroom in late 1926, and that Pollack's collection of young jazzmen, spearheaded by Benny Goodman's clarinet and Jack Teagarden's trombone, were as esteemed in Harlem as downtown.

"Not one of [our] records really takes off the way we were able to," said Pollack's cornetist Jimmy McPartland. "None of 'em really swings the way we did on the job. The band on the records sounds a lot stiffer than I remember it."[1]

Goldkette trombonist Newell "Spiegle" Willcox: "The records never sounded the way we did in person. They're just a shadow, a hint. Bix—well, you can't begin to imagine, listening to those records, what his tone *really* sounded like. You had to be there. You could never imagine it without hearing it for yourself."[2]

Understanding the disparity between reputation and recording demands knowledge of record company policies in the 1920s. By mid-decade, records were well established as a promotional arm of the music publishing industry. The publishers, in turn, were constantly identifying new markets for different kinds of song material—then seeing to it that material was recorded and sold to those markets. In 1920, OKeh had recorded Mamie Smith singing her own "Crazy Blues"—and been astonished when it took off among black buyers, selling nearly eight thousand copies a month for close to a year.

Mass migration of blacks to northern cities during the wartime decade just ended had been a major contributing factor in this case, creating a large body of people, concentrated in large urban areas, working, earning money, and spending at least a part of it on entertainment. The idea of a special "race" catalogue, produced and aimed at these buyers, priced within their means, proceeded naturally from Smith's success.

As so often happens, the specific quickly—and mistakenly—became a general policy. Such orchestras as those of Henderson, Charlie Johnson, and numerous others were encouraged to record their hottest numbers for this apparent market; most often they were not even distributed in communities where whites lived; white fans (or musicians) looking for new releases by Louis Armstrong, King Oliver, or Bessie Smith had to go to black neighborhoods to find them.

Conversely, as Rex Stewart observed, "although the Henderson band played a variety of music on the tours, the record executives characterized [his] band as a stomp band. They didn't accept the fact that a Negro band could play sweet, though as a matter of fact, we used to get tremendous applause at Roseland and other places for playing waltzes beautifully."[3]

According to the stereotypes, the white market could use an occasional rhythm specialty or "hot" treatment of a current song. That being the case, it was easy enough to fill the need by tossing a Henderson or McKinney's Cotton Pickers record into the "mainstream" catalogue. Either way, the black bands could keep the hot music market supplied.

That left white bands, at least those with hot inclinations, in a dismaying situation. Both Goldkette's and Pollack's orchestras, with their often illustrious jazz soloists, were valued by the record companies—Victor in these two cases—chiefly as commercial dance bands. Many officials—Victor's all-powerful recording director Eddie King is but one example—regarded the jazz ambitions of such bands, and even their chief soloists, with something not far short of distaste. Goldkette's arranger, Bill Challis, recalled a typical encounter with King:

> When we went to Victor a few days before the date to check out the tunes we'd selected with them, we discovered King had already selected the songs he wanted us to play. He gave 'em to [band manager Charles] Horvath, who gave 'em to me with an apology and said to arrange them as best I could. But boy, were they ever dogs! Charlie argued with him, and told him the tunes weren't what the band did nor what they wanted. But King won the argument . . . He told Charlie that if we didn't like his selection he'd find another band to do the tunes. So we got together for one rehearsal before the recording date, and you should have seen the guys' faces. I mean, those songs were the worst![4]

What's striking here is the gulf between the band's sense of what it did best and the concept represented by King and his selection of songs. In the words of Goldkette's lead alto saxophonist Stanley "Doc" Ryker, "I don't really know why [King] hired the band at all. The stuff he didn't want—why, that was our style."[5]

Stylistically, the Jean Goldkette Orchestra of 1926–27 was built around three men: Beiderbecke, Trumbauer, and arranger Challis. Flanking them were some outstanding journeymen: the bright-toned Chicago clarinetist Don Murray, who had recorded with the New Orleans Rhythm Kings; the great New Orleans bassist Steve Brown, whose slap technique and percussive drive had dazzled both white and black musicians; drummer Chauncey Morehouse, whose solid beat had energized the Paul Specht Orchestra and its band-within-a-band, the Georgians; Bill Rank, a trombonist in the strong and nimble style pioneered by Miff Mole.

Challis, a Pennsylvanian, had begun as a saxophonist and done some arrangements while in college at Bucknell. He found his true gift in an ability to convert the figures pouring out of Beiderbecke's horn into elegant, shapely full-band scores. By 1927, such Challis arrangements as "The Blue Room," "Baby Face," and "On the Alamo" were widely known among musicians and rated with the efforts of Don Redman, Fud Livingston, and a few others in establishing standards by which the flexibility and freedom of small-band jazz found its way into larger ensembles.

Jean Goldkette himself was less a participant in his band's efforts than a benevolent—and indulgent—*paterfamilias*. Born March 18, 1899, in Valenciennes, France, and brought up in Greece and Russia, he'd come to the United States in 1911 hoping for a career as a concert pianist. Settling in Chicago, he found an easy source of income playing in dance orchestras; he was, as noted earlier, the pianist in the Lipschultz ensemble at Lamb's Café, which quit in protest, sight unseen, when Tom Brown's "Band From Dixieland" opened there in May 1915.

"Sometime later," he wrote in a 1955 letter, "I had a chance to come into the café and for the first time in my life I heard jazz music played. It made such a profound impression on me, also gave me ideas as to its unlimited possibilities that as you well know, this event changed the entire destiny of my career."[6]

Goldkette's combination of musicianship and business acumen, sweetened with Continental charm, impressed bandleader and music contractor Edgar Benson; before long he was a trusted Benson lieutenant, leading units on key society engagements in the Chicago area. When Benson decided to expand his operation to Detroit, he dispatched Goldkette to oversee and coordinate the operation.

Already enriched by the burgeoning automobile industry, Prohibition-era Detroit was well positioned as a social and entertainment center. Flowing right by the city was the Detroit River, the national border between the U.S. state of Michigan and the Canadian province of Ontario. For all practical purposes, the city of Windsor, Ontario, was simply East Detroit. Windsor's Hiram Walker distillery was, in fact, clearly visible from downtown Detroit.

There was no Volstead Act in Canada, no Prohibition. Perhaps even more than automobiles, Detroit's big business was smuggling, most of it controlled by the Purple Gang, a kind of Jewish equivalent of Capone's Chicago operation, and every bit as deadly. Residents of communities within earshot of the river were often heard to complain—not always ill-humoredly—of trouble sleeping amid the racket of motor launches crossing back and forth, back and forth, with their cargo of bottles and barrels.

It didn't take Goldkette long to develop the Detroit operation into an agency of his own, supplying orchestras for single events and maintaining full-time units at the popular Graystone Ballroom and Book-Cadillac Hotel. He soon entered into a partnership with Charles Horvath, brother of the man who had conducted the band at Lamb's, and by 1924 their organization was growing fast in the Motor City.

It's also probable that Goldkette or Horvath, pragmatists both, reached a working arrangement with the Purple Gang soon after setting up shop. There is no proof—but neither is there any evidence of a Goldkette entertainment operation encountering the least trouble with the city's mobsters.

A pet Goldkette project involved formation and promotion of a flagship band, to be resident at the Graystone. How handsomely he succeeded is obvious from the orchestra's March 27, 1924, Victor record of "It's the Blues." This is a capable, polished dance band, quite at home—remarkably so, considering the date—with a jazz-oriented score. It's hard, in fact, to think of any 1924 unit of comparable size, white or black, delivering this kind of material this well.

(Certainly not that of Henderson, still groping after an ensemble style, its phrasing stilted, its rhythm still hopelessly locked in the conventions of ragtime. It would be another half-year before the arrival of Louis Armstrong transformed this into the pioneer unit now taken for granted by historians—and even then the process did not happen overnight. What makes "It's the Blues" remarkable is the ease with which Goldkette's ensemble appears to have simply bypassed the problems of both individual and ensemble execution with which Henderson's musicians, and so many others, were grappling.)

Goldkette had recruited his men from both the Midwest and the East, forming a personnel which was to remain stable throughout the orchestra's entire three-and-a-half-year history. Here were trumpeters Fred "Fuzzy" Farrar and Ray Lodwig, trombonists Tommy Dorsey and Bill Rank, the saxophone team of Murray (whom he'd heard on the Lake Michigan excursion boats), Jimmy Dorsey, and lead alto Stanley "Doc" Ryker. Violinist Joe Venuti, pianist Paul Mertz, and banjoist Howard "Howdy" Quicksell were already in place.

Regrettably, the amount of attention given the band after Beiderbecke and Trumbauer joined in 1926 has all but eclipsed such earlier efforts; what's abundantly clear in "It's the Blues" is that the Goldkette orchestra was an extraordinary unit from its very inception, a remarkably fine-tuned ensemble.

The recording opens, unconventionally enough, with "Irish" Henry's tuba "walking," four-to-the-bar, through an entire chorus, with the reeds supplying punctuations in a way that eerily foreshadows King Oliver's "Snag It" of two years hence. The arranger, whoever he is, understands how to break the band into sections, operating independently of, and in tandem with, one another. There are effective "call-and-response" passages, a neatly executed double-time chorus (hot clarinet obbligato by either Murray or Dorsey), and a low-register clarinet trio which predates on record the sort of thing Don Redman wrote for Fletcher Henderson's Orchestra that appeared on records made later that year. Joe Venuti contributes a chorus in his four-strings-at-a-time manner, highlighted by an impeccably executed break.[7]

Here, in March of 1924, is a full dance band playing what is clearly jazz, with an assurance and unanimity of conception all but unrivalled elsewhere. Yet, as a direct result of Victor's musical policies (and perhaps influenced by Goldkette's personal penchant for "semi-classical" specialties), this orchestra recorded few other performances of this sort.

Goldkette was alert to what was going on around him. He knew of the Wolverines, their popularity that spring on midwestern college campuses, their light-textured and rhythmically vibrant records for the tiny, Indiana-based Gennett label. Above all, he knew about Bix Beiderbecke. Though unreliable as a reader, the young Iowa cornetist already had demonstrated a solo style quite new in its lilting, unforced elegance.

And, that September, shortly after the Wolverines opened at the Cinderella Ballroom in Manhattan, Goldkette paid them an unannounced visit. He came right to the point, offering Beiderbecke a chair in his orchestra at a salary the Wolverines couldn't hope to match.

Bix accepted the offer and in late November spent a short time as a Goldkette sideman. His sixteen-bar solo on "I Didn't Know" is a gem, clear-toned and earnest. Not unexpectedly, it displeased Eddie King, whose aversion to the trumpet in general (and "hot" trumpets in particular) was already well known among musicians. The performance lay entombed in Victor's archives until its rediscovery and release on an LP nearly four decades later. Beiderbecke stayed with Goldkette only a few weeks, leaving in December. (In January 1925, he "borrowed" Goldkette sidemen Tommy Dorsey, Mertz, Murray, and Quicksell for a date of his own at Gennett's Richmond, Indiana, studio. The results included the first re-corded version of his own "Davenport Blues.")

Goldkette had drawn quite a few of his men from the Scranton Sirens, an excellent band based in Pennsylvania coal-mining country. Formed in 1919, it was one of the best of the white "territory" bands, constantly on the road throughout the central Atlantic seaboard states.

It recorded little, and its records, though competently played—an increasingly familiar pattern, this—offer little to corroborate its reputation as a "hot" unit. The Sirens have lived on largely in the accounts of their alumni, most notably the Dorsey brothers, who joined Goldkette in 1924. Other Sirens men who found their way to Detroit and Goldkette's payroll included lead trumpeter Farrar, trombonist-arranger (and, later, bandleader) Russ Morgan, pianist Irving "Itzy" Riskin—and Bill Challis.

"They were a small band," Challis said. "Everything was faked, including ensembles. Nothing written out. Everybody took a solo. But they were very, very popular as a road band." Other notable Sirens graduates included trumpeter Vic d'Ippolito and bassist Mike Trafficante, mainstays of Paul Whiteman's Orchestra; New York studio musicians Charlie Butterfield (trombone) and Alfie Evans (sax-ophone); and guitar great Eddie Lang. One Sirens admirer then working in the region as a trumpet player was Bob Stephens, later a recording director at OKeh and Decca and a key figure in recording many key jazz bands—including those of the Dorsey Brothers and, later, Count Basie.[8]

The Jean Goldkette Orchestra appears not to have recorded again until an eastern tour brought it to New York, and Victor's studios, on January 27 and 28, 1926. Most of what resulted was straightforward dance music, save for Russ Morgan's arrangement of the currently popular "Dinah." Victor by this time had switched to an electric recording system, and the microphone brings Steve Brown's slap bass, accompanying a Don Murray clarinet solo, thundering out full and strong.

The personnel by this time was Farrar and Ray Lodwig on trumpets, Rank and Newell "Spiegle" Willcox on trombones, and Ryker, Dorsey, and Murray on reeds, with a rhythm section of Brown, banjoist Quicksell, and drummer More-house. Pianist Mertz doubled regularly between the Graystone and the Book-Cadillac Hotel, alternating with Lou Longo.

Beiderbecke and Trumbauer joined that autumn, after working the summer with a smaller Goldkette unit at the Lake Michigan resort of Hudson Lake, Indiana (that idyll has been chronicled at length and in detail in *Bix: Man and Legend* and elsewhere). After a few days' rehearsal they left for a three-week tour of New England ballrooms, including the Music Box, on Boston's busy Huntington Av-enue. "The lines of tuxedos in front of the bandstand ran about fifteen or sixteen deep," said Boston saxophonist Al Sudhalter. "And when Bix stood up to take a four-bar break, the great yell that went up in that room would have dwarfed the wildest screaming of '60s teenagers for the Beatles or the Rolling Stones."[9]

Culmination of the tour was a fortnight at New York's Roseland Ballroom, opening with a widely advertised "Battle of Music" with Fletcher Henderson's resident orchestra. While audience assessment of such encounters usually depends on individual partisanships, all accounts here agree that Goldkette's musicians had surprise on their side. No one, least of all Henderson's somewhat cocky sidemen (playing on their home turf), expected them to be as good as they were.

Cornetist Rex Stewart, astonished and charmed, wrote of "this band of Johnny-come-latelies from out in the sticks" with affection and undisguised admiration. "We kept makin' excuses," Stewart said, "but we knew we'd been licked. That was all there was to it."[10]

From trombonist Bill Rank comes a particularly vivid account. "We were very nervous," he told researcher Philip R. Evans in a 1960 letter. "Fletcher Henderson's band was on the stage. We shared the same stage. As you faced the bandstand, our band was on the right, Henderson on the left. We got set up to play and noticed that the Henderson band didn't get off the stand. They just sat there. They wanted to hear us. We looked out into the audience and here were lots of guys in tuxedos, and we knew they were musicians that had come over to hear us."[11]

With Trumbauer fronting, they opened with the 6/8 specialty "Valencia," a surprising change of pace that only heightened the tension and sense of expectation in the ballroom. When, right after that, Goldkette's musicians tore into "Tiger Rag," the battle was on—and a hot music legend had been made.

The band deeply impressed all who heard it. Many years later Artie Shaw, indignant at the omission of the Goldkette orchestra from the Smithsonian Institution's large and lavish Big Band Jazz record reissue box (selections by Martin Williams and Gunther Schuller), vented his ire in a letter to a curator at the Institution. "I'm absolutely dumbfounded . . . at the unaccountable omission of the great—actually landmark—Jean Goldkette band from the record album," he wrote. "What a sickening injustice to one of the first truly important big bands that ever appeared in this country!"[12]

Xylophonist Red Norvo, who heard the Goldkette orchestra in situ at the Graystone, said he never got over the experience. "I'd never heard anything like that in my life," he said, the memory still vivid. "It was a shock to me. I'd heard lots of small jazz groups, both black and white, on the riverboats. But this was different: it was a hot band, yes, but it was a big band, and so clean and precise and swinging. The feeling was—well, just overwhelming.

"People today don't know, can't imagine, how good it was. Trumbauer, Bix, Steve Brown—and don't forget Don Murray. He's been all but forgotten, but in those days he was just a marvelous clarinet player. Joe Venuti told me that Benny Goodman used to come in, come down by bus from Chicago, and just stand in front of the bandstand listening to Don."[13]

(Lead alto man "Doc" Ryker remembered with amusement that Bix was too unreliable a reader to hold down the second trumpet chair. So Ray Lodwig, whom he otherwise would have replaced, stayed on. "Bix would fill in where he could—he could always find another note—and take the hot solos," said Ryker. "Funny: when we came to New York, most of the bands there were using two trumpets. Here they saw this band with three, and not knowing the reason why, they all went out and got an extra trumpet so they could have three trumpets.")

Yet most of the Goldkette records only hint at "a band like nothing you ever heard." Perhaps in order to make sense of the disparity, early jazz writers—as writers will—invented categories. "Big band jazz" usually referred to the output of black bands, playing specialty hot instrumentals for the recording studio microphones. Their white counterparts, with very few exceptions, were identified as "hot dance" units.

In a strictly musical sense, such a distinction is nonsense. But it is useful as a way of identifying a matter of form, a compromise between two imperatives: the need of publishers (hence of record companies) to peddle pop songs, and the need of musicians whose primary language was hot jazz to express themselves. The result was a hybrid, consistent throughout thousands of records made by dance orchestras, and not only white ones, during the 1920s and early Depression years.

Roughly expressed, a characteristic "hot dance" performance went like this: first an ensemble chorus (and often verse) setting out the melody, played more or less straight, scored as well as an arranger could manage. Then a vocal, lyric and melody clearly defined, usually by a contract singer whose trademark was clarity: a cadre of such performers—Harold "Scrappy" Lambert, Dick Robertson, Irving Kaufman, Smith Ballew, Franklyn Baur, and many others—made excellent livings in recordings, though they were often at musical odds with the spirit of the young musicians accompanying them.

The rest of the record usually belonged to the band—as long as things didn't get out of hand. If there were going to be hot solos, fancy arranging touches, even all-out swinging, it would happen here. The casual listener has only to examine a selection of "hot dance" records of the late '20s—"Forgetting You," by the Dorsey Brothers Orchestra; "Dancing With Tears in My Eyes," by a group led by Joe Venuti; "Smile, Darnya, Smile," by Ben Selvin's studio orchestra; and, directly to the point, "Hoosier Sweetheart" by the Goldkette orchestra and "Bashful Baby" by Pollack—to understand how it worked.

Black bands, too, sometimes conformed to this pattern, especially when recording for the "mainstream" market, itself driven by the (then) conventions of ballroom dancing. The only major black orchestra that seemed largely exempt was that of Duke Ellington, house band at the Cotton Club. Its job when recording was to present Cotton Club songs and "jungle" specialties (as well as occasional material Irving Mills was plugging) to a wider public. That Ellington was able to work so creatively, be so innovative, within that constricting frame of reference is to his eternal credit.

Now and then, a lenient recording director would allow a white band to "loosen up" before the microphones. Sometimes, as with "The Stampede," the results never saw issue. On other occasions, especially if the material was a recognizable pop song, the increased musical freedom produced memorable results. The Goldkette orchestra's "I'm Gonna Meet My Sweetie Now," for example, combines a lean Challis score with some crisp and spirited solo playing.

Given the quantity of anecdotal material surrounding their Roseland encounters, it may be useful here to compare the results of the January 31, 1927, Goldkette recording date with a session done just ten days earlier by the Henderson orchestra. Between these two sessions, on January 24, the two bands had met again at Roseland Ballroom, with Jimmy Dorsey filling in for an ailing Don Murray. This second contest seems to have been a more equally matched encounter. "We weren't about to be taken twice," Henderson clarinetist Buster Bailey said of that night. "We really tore the place down, played over our heads. But those guys were also getting better all the time, too. You can bet there was a lot of great music that night."[14]

On January 21, Henderson's men recorded Redman's arrangement of "Rocky Mountain Blues" and a Tin Pan Alley concoction called "Tozo" (Fletcher Henderson listed as co-composer and lyricist), using a personnel about the size of Goldkette's, including trumpeters Russell "Pop" Smith, Joe Smith, and Tommy Ladnier, trombonists Benny Morton and Jimmy Harrison, reedmen Redman, Bailey, and Coleman Hawkins, and a rhythm section of the leader's piano, banjoist Charlie Dixon, June Cole on tuba, and Kaiser Marshall on drums.

Despite the weight of Cole's tuba, Redman's arrangement of "Tozo" stays light on its feet, rhythmically relaxed. Midway through a straightforward opening ensemble Hawkins tears off a break which clearly demolishes any notion that old Tozo, "That Hottentot Sheik," is going to be dealt with respectfully. His sixteen-bar solo is forceful and driving, in his most agitated mid-'20s manner. Tommy Ladnier's clear-toned, almost heraldic trumpet dominates the verse, and after a tongue-in-cheek Redman vocal the band returns for a hot ensemble passage led by Hawkins and also including at least one trombone. (According to one report, quoted by *Hendersonia* author Walter Allen, the recording appears, spinning on a turntable, in the 1927 Janet Gaynor film *Sunrise*, directed by F. W. Murnau.)

This is a performance of a pop tune by a hot band, one apparently under no restrictions in matters of style save the need to *somewhere* set out the melody and to include a vocal (and Redman's singing, however charming, cannot be cited as a model of clarity either for melody or lyrics). There is the decided impression that Henderson's men are having a good time with an admittedly mediocre song. Still, Columbia considered "Tozo" a mainstream item and issued it in its standard catalogue.

The January 31 Goldkette date included an equally undistinguished pop trifle, the punningly titled "Hoosier Sweetheart," arranged by Challis. True to convention, Spiegle Willcox's trombone, played through a megaphone, sets out the melody with little distraction save a few discreet muted brass punctuations. Moving into the verse, the band remains on its best behavior, like schoolboys with a substitute teacher; Bix, given a pair of four-bar solo spots here (cadences after a strong band melody statement), chimes out his phrases in a manner not unlike that used by Ladnier on the Henderson record.

Ray Meurer, a studio vocalist supplied by the company, puts across the lyric with a kind of ardent sobriety quite unlike the good-natured kidding that characterizes Redman's "Tozo" vocal. Only then, its duty done, can the band open up a bit. A transition passage based on a whole-tone scale (much like one used by Redman on "Tozo") launches Trumbauer on a solo chorus, skipping jauntily across the top of Brown's bowed rhythm and spurred along by a simple but effective dotted-half-note ensemble background. His two-bar, end-of-chorus break (with something of the same sense of agitation found in Hawkins's break on "Tozo") is a springboard for Bix, who leads fellow-trumpets Farrar and Lodwig through a sixteen-bar scored hot *soli* which somehow manages to include *three* statements of a five-note figure widely understood by musicians at the time as an encoded way of saying "You're a horse's ass" (sometimes "Oh, you horse's ass!")! Just, presumably, to make sure no one listening was in any doubt as to the musicians' opinion of the song. Brown, slapping now, manages to lay down a strong and propulsive beat *and* perform a function typical of early New Orleans bassists and taken over in later years by big band drummers: throwing in "bombs," across-the-beat accents that kick the rhythm forward.

Bill Rank takes the bridge, playing cleanly and rhythmically in the manner of Miff Mole, and the ensemble swings "Hoosier Sweetheart" home, even pausing to quote "Back Home Again in Indiana" before a four-bar, devil-take-the-hindmost tag—all of which, just for a moment, gives the listener a hint of what this band may have sounded like on the Roseland bandstand.

In both cases, the bands were dealing with inferior material. Comparative listening makes clear that Henderson's musicians were free to do pretty much what they wanted with it (as long as melody and lyrics were part of the treatment), while the Goldkette men had to play things by the rules for most of the record. What, one wonders, would this performance have been if Eddie King had been in charge, and not the more tolerant Nat Shilkret?

On its date, the Henderson orchestra reads crisply and easily through Redman's rather complex score on "Rocky Mountain Blues," which includes a beautiful Joe Smith trumpet solo over sustained clarinets, and brief statements by Hawkins, Ladnier, and trombonist Benny Morton. Overall, the band is genial, a bit aggressive, deliciously confident of its own prowess.

That's also the case on the Goldkette performance of "I'm Gonna Meet My Sweetie Now." A well-played, straight ensemble sets out the melody of this somewhat better-than-average pop song, before a four-bar transition brings on solos by Trumbauer (16 bars), Rank (8), Bix leading the trumpets (8), Jimmy Dorsey (16, playing the verse as a hot baritone sax solo), Willcox (8, played straight), Venuti (16 and 8, with Brown prominent behind him), and a final, shouting ensemble featuring Bix darting around the melody and Dorsey taking the bridge on clarinet.*

What impresses first, and remains longest, is a sense of enthusiasm, a true *esprit*. These musicians were proud of their band, proud of its soloists and ensemble precision, and of the regard in which it was held by colleagues.

Both the Henderson and Goldkette orchestras swing handsomely, but in distinctly different ways. On the whole, the Henderson rhythm section finds a groove and relaxes into it, letting intensity build naturally. Goldkette's men, led

---

*Venuti and Eddie Lang, though not regular Goldkette sidemen at this point, were added regularly for record dates. Because of their popularity as a team, their presence was assumed to have commercial, as well as musical, value. Needless to say, they were always welcome.

by Brown (and, when he's playing, Lang), seem to play higher and further forward on the beat, producing an impression of great verve and sparkle.

In its broadest application, it is this very difference in *attitudes* toward keeping time that distinguishes the efforts of the white Chicago bands of the 1920s from their black South Side counterparts. There *are* differences, at least in the context of the period. They began to blur after 1930, with black and white musicians playing together more frequently. But given the way things were being done in 1927, it is doubtful that the Goldkette "Stampede," had a pressing survived, would have sounded much like Henderson's.

Recent years have brought new evidence of what the Goldkette orchestra sounded like in its purely hot music element. In mid-1927, as it became clear that Goldkette was planning to disband, Bill Challis accepted an offer to join the large popular orchestra of Paul Whiteman. His new boss gave him *carte blanche*, encouraged him to get to know the ensemble by writing for it, whatever and however he liked.

Challis began by carefully and faithfully reproducing the best of the Goldkette hot specialties for Whiteman's musicians, in most cases using instrumentations of comparable size to retain the weight and flavor of the originals. Whiteman never recorded these arrangements, but they were played occasionally and rest today in the Whiteman Collection, on file at the Williams College Library in Massachusetts.

Here, for the scholar's examination, are scores and parts for "Blue Room," "On The Alamo," "St. Louis Blues," "Tiger Rag" and numerous others; also such items as "Ostrich Walk," "Riverboat Shuffle" and "Since My Best Gal Turned Me Down," recorded in cut-down fashion by Trumbauer and Bix on their OKeh dates. Whether performed or merely studied, they supplement the records, fill in the gaps, and furnish yet more evidence of the Goldkette orchestra and its chief arranger as peers of Henderson, Don Redman, Benny Carter, and other key black figures of the time.[15]

Informed by such understanding, a listener can approach such heavily compromised efforts as "Slow River," "Sunday," "In My Merry Oldsmobile," "Four-Leaf Clover"—and quite a few even more frustrating efforts than these—with new appreciation. One can hear them as rather subversive performances, with Challis and the Goldkette musicians doing everything in their power to inject the band's unique spirit into sanitized arrangements of sometimes embarrassingly poor songs. "You're a horse's ass," indeed!

The Goldkette orchestra made only two unequivocally hot records. By a supreme irony, both were based not on Challis arrangements, not on original compositions, but on edited, customized publishers' "stocks" of pop songs. The driving "My Pretty Girl," made the same day as "The Stampede," features solos by Venuti, Trumbauer, and clarinetist Danny Polo, taking over for Dorsey while Murray was indisposed. Bix leads the brass tutti passages with great verve. The sense of teamwork, and the irresistible momentum it achieves, go far toward explaining the astonishment of Henderson's musicians on that fateful Roseland evening.

But the undisputed star of "My Pretty Girl" is Steve Brown's prominently recorded bass. Whether slapping or bowing, he's an irresistible rhythmic force, reaffirming his stature as the leading pioneer of New Orleans–style bass playing. Even in a field rich with such topflight talent as John Lindsay, Wellman Braud, and Pops Foster among the blacks, "Chink Martin" Abraham and "Deacon" Loyocano the whites, Brown remains the dominant figure. If the testimony of colleagues, fully supported by his records, is to be credited, he is also one of his instrument's true innovators.

"Steve Brown was the one everybody listened to," bassist Milt Hinton has assured us. He recalled his own youth in Chicago, standing outside the Midway Gardens, unable to enter because blacks were not allowed. "But you could hear him loud and clear, even from outside. What a beat that man had! He was doing things, cross-rhythms and stuff, that I've never yet heard anyone else do. He was the best, and we all knew it. Don't ever let anybody tell you different." Wellman Braud, Ellington's superb bassist, also cited Brown as his favorite on his own instrument.[16]

The Challis arrangement of "Tiger Rag," on file at Williams College, includes a full chorus solo for Brown; on his part, scrawled hastily in pencil, is the exhortation "Go the limit, Steve—Atta Boy!" Musicians remembered him being regularly featured with both Goldkette and with Whiteman, coming out front to do solo specialties—perhaps the first bassist to be granted such an honor; one of the "lost" Goldkette records, done for Victor on May 23, 1927, but never released, was a piece identified only as "Play It, Red." A feature for Brown, "Red" to his friends? We may never know.

In a 1958 conversation, Brown described his technique for historian William Russell. Sometimes, he said, he'd pluck his gut strings with two and three fingers at once. "Mine were heavier strings than ordinarily used on the string bass," he said. "They weren't soft and pliable. I couldn't finger as well as a legitimate man could, because those strings were so heavy, but I had to have 'em heavy on account of the body, to produce all that heavy instrumentation we had."

He described how he would both pluck a string, then slap it back against the fingerboard with his palm, producing the effect of a drummer's backbeats and accents. Many bass players, he said, were reluctant to play that way. "It's too troublesome to the bass player," he said. "It creates a lot of trouble, puts too heavy an indentation in the fingerboard."[17]

Few latter-day bassists have cultivated the techniques for which Steve Brown is known. Hinton adapted them to the needs of his own distinctive style, and late in his long career was still charming listeners with slap-style solos. The late Sherwood Mangiapane of New Orleans was, by common consent, Brown's one true heir, playing with a wide variety of local bands until his death in 1992. Some latter-day white players, Vince Giordano and Greg Cohen outstanding among them, have studied Brown's records and learned how to use his snap-

and-slap methods to drive a band. But in this era of thin metal strings, lower (closer to the fingerboard) action, amplification, and lightning finger technique, there seems little likelihood Brown's ways will find any home except as historical exotica.

Beyond dispute, the Goldkette orchestra's finest moment in a recording studio came on Thursday, September 15, 1927, at its final Victor session. In the context of what other groups of comparable size and configuration, white and black, were doing at that time, "Clementine (from New Orleans)" is little short of miraculous.

By this time Challis was with Whiteman; as Goldkette sidemen remembered it, musically lenient Leroy Shield (best known as composer-orchestrator of soundtrack music for Little Rascals and other comedy films of the era) was in charge, the atmosphere quite relaxed. Someone had brought in a "stock" on the song, a new novelty by Harry Warren and "After You've Gone" lyricist Henry Creamer. What followed can best be called an exercise in collective editing.

"Doc" Ryker was in charge. "I sent the brass section out to one room, the saxes to another, to work out their choruses," he said. "I think, in fact, the saxes went to the ladies' room. The idea was that each section would work out part of the arrangement, and then we'd put it all together. That way, a part of everybody's style would be sure to get into the arrangement."[18]

Thanks to the crystalline acoustics of Liederkranz Hall, the performance is a model of handsome sound and tonal balance. The rhythm section, Lang's guitar alternating with Quicksell's banjo, lays down a solid four-to-the-bar which would have been quite in keeping on any swing record made a decade later. Even Chauncey Morehouse, still without a full set of drums (only three months later, record producer Tommy Rockwell began his Chicago experiments with Gene Krupa), manages well with woodblock and cymbals.

Beiderbecke is something of a free agent in the opening ensemble chorus, dodging and swooping, filling holes between phrases, finding "another note"; the overall effect is of great cheer and geniality, as though this were not an orchestra playing but a group of friends, singing together.

After a verse statement highlighted by a pair of Eddie Lang solo breaks, the sax section (Trumbauer's lead is unmistakable) deliver a full chorus which, like the best of Benny Carter's sax section scoring, appears to lie easily and naturally under the fingers. Then it's time for Bix, snapping out a characteristic ascending break to begin a solo which, in effect, recasts the melody; with grace and simplicity he "sings" through his horn, giving us a brand-new song.

Joe Venuti skips through the bridge with customary aplomb, Lang and Brown digging in nicely behind him. But this moment belongs to Bix and, in general, to the Goldkette orchestra. It is, at its eleventh hour, a superb ensemble showing what it can do when allowed the latitude and assuring its place in the hot music hierarchy. Yes, it is an anomaly among Goldkette records, and because of that a valuable index, a point of reference; a graph, or chart, with "Clementine" at one end and the dreary "Just One More Kiss" at the other, shows clearly what was sacrificed to recording company policy.

Musical riches, however, don't always make for good business, and the Gold-kette Victor Orchestra seems to have been far more successful in impressing fellow-musicians than in winning a consistent public. The band's earnings, never spectacular, were dropping steadily, and Goldkette seemed unable to reverse the trend. Eddy Sheasby, hired by the Goldkette office to front the band during tours, simply disappeared one night that June, taking with him the entire library. The arrangements could be replaced, but Sheasby's defection only deepened an atmosphere of foreboding.[19]

At root, the problem rested with the band itself. Goldkette may have enjoyed billing himself as "the Paul Whiteman of the West," but in matters of presentation and basic musical philosophy his orchestra fell far short of the musical leviathan led by the "King of Jazz."

"We were strictly a musician's band," "Doc" Ryker told writer Amy Lee in 1940. "We played the way we wanted to, and didn't care whether the people liked it or not. The boys just couldn't—and wouldn't—do hokum."[20]

By "hokum," the saxophonist referred to the sorts of novelties and comedy routines which were the stock-in-trade of nearly every successful band, black or white, that played the great dance palaces. As various Goldkette sidemen recalled, their occasional attempts in this direction varied from simple flops to outright embarrassments.

Where they had bested the Henderson band the first time at Roseland just by outplaying them, Goldkette's musicians fared poorly in musical encounters with such modest competition as the New England–based, entertainment-oriented bands of Barney Rapp and Mal Hallett. As Spiegle Willcox rather wryly put it, "we got our hand from the musicians, but Hallett got his from the crowd."[21]

A dance band, more than simply a purveyor of music, was a traveling show, almost a branch of vaudeville, and the ballroom customers fully expected to be treated to an evening's entertainment. "We sang, we danced, we did comedy routines," the late saxophonist Eddie Barefield once told the author. "Everybody did it. People expected it of us; if you didn't entertain them you were out."[22]

According to James T. Maher, the success of King Oliver at Chicago's Lincoln Gardens had as much to do with his ability to do "hokum," to put on comedy effects (e.g., playing with the bell of his cornet in a bucket of water), as with his skill at playing dance music. It is hardly surprising that this side of Oliver fails to emerge in the accounts of the young white jazzmen who flocked like pilgrims to hear him, any more than does the side that could play waltzes so softly "you could hear the feet shuffling on the floor." For the young zealots, such stuff was little more than an annoyance, to be endured for the sake of "Snake Rag" or the other hot specialties in the King's repertoire.

Goldkette's youthful sidemen were, at root, no different. It may even be said that by leaving control of his flagship orchestra to its musicians Goldkette was assuring its early demise. For them, and for most devotees of hot music, the concept of putting on a show for the customers was the antithesis of making good music.

"They just don't understand" was a rallying cry—and, all too often, justification for abandoning any attempt to *make* them understand. Neil Leonard has explored the almost gnostic aspect of this adversarial sense of separation in his excellent *Jazz: Myth and Religion.* Jazz initiates, he observes,

> Consist of adolescents, apprentice musicians, ethnics, or artists (sometimes all at the same time) in the fissures or on the edges of the received order. Flourishing in egalitarian, simply organized groups and guided mainly by peers, they operate at a remove from many ordinary responsibilities and preconceptions and freely question conventional standards of behavior and belief. Their climate is charged with potency and potentiality that encourages experimentation, spontaneity, improvisation, and imagination in art and in conduct.[23]

But a dance orchestra, regardless of its skill or musical orientation, is a business. And without a regular and faithful audience it becomes little more than a conceit, an exercise in self-indulgence.

By mid-1927 things had reached a point where the Goldkette orchestra was attracting less and less high-paying work; its parent organization was no longer able, or willing, to meet a three-thousand-dollar weekly payroll. Shortly after the "Clementine" recording date the band broke up, with Bix, Trumbauer, Murray, Rank, and Morehouse joining bass saxophonist Adrian Rollini in a brief, ill-fated band at a New York nightclub before throwing in their lot with Paul Whiteman.

Business for Goldkette went on largely as before. Impressed with Henderson appearances at the Graystone, he hired Don Redman away to build and shape a black band, to be resident at the Graystone. The result was McKinney's Cotton Pickers, a superb ensemble owing much to the precedent of the Victor orchestra — but also, unlike its predecessor, a first-rate entertainment unit.

Goldkette also helped form a staff band at Chicago radio station WGN, a band which made its own excellent records for Victor in 1928–29. In its personnel was cornetist Stirling Bose, a Bix admirer since playing opposite Beiderbecke and Trumbauer in St. Louis two years before. So Bix-like was his work at this point that early collectors regularly mistook his obbligatos behind the vocals on the Goldkette records of "So Tired" and "Just Imagine" for Beiderbecke. Bose is outstanding in his two long solos on "My Blackbirds Are Bluebirds Now," which also features brief appearances by alto saxophonist Larry Tice and trombonist Vernon Brown.

Another Goldkette ensemble, the Orange Blossoms, soon became the Casa Loma Orchestra. (The story of that highly influential band, and of its trend-setting arranger, Gene Gifford, is discussed in the next chapter.) The three ensembles combined cost him no more than had the Victor band.

But for those who heard it, particularly musicians, there was only one "Goldkette Band"—that matchless combination of individuals which for one brief year captivated the world of hot dance music. It was a team, an ensemble band, its soloists contributing brilliantly to the combined effort. In this regard it differs considerably from the band organized by drummer Ben Pollack in late 1925, which soon ripened into the other major "hot dance" unit of the 1920s.

*   *   *

Pollack's story differs in almost every particular from that of Goldkette. Unlike the Detroit-based pianist-entrepreneur, he was first a jazz musician, one of the most innovative and respected drummers of his era. He brought to the organization of his ensemble less a businessman's steady hand than a musician's vision—which proved to be both its glory and its ultimate undoing.

Born in Chicago June 22, 1903, he came of age just around the time the craze for New Orleans bands was catching on in the city's speakeasies and dance halls. Dark, intense, and ambitious, he developed quickly into an adept band drummer—much to the dismay of his parents, who would have been far happier to see him take over the family fur business.

The young man was too caught up in music to care. He'd begun jobbing around town for such contractors as "Husk" O'Hare when one night his path chanced to cross that of a group of young white musicians from New Orleans. Hearing trumpeter Paul Mares, trombonist George Brunies, and the others was, as he later described it, something of an epiphany. "Before that," he wrote in the mid-'30s, "jazz was just a lot of jumping around and throwing of sticks, but these boys had rhythm and a definite style that was very fine . . . they literally rocked us over."[24]

The admiration seemed to be mutual. They jammed several times together, and soon he had replaced Frank Snyder with their band, known first as the Friars Society Orchestra, later as the New Orleans Rhythm Kings. Their story is told earlier in this volume.

As long as he was working and bringing home a steady paycheck, Pollack heard little from his parents about responsibility, respectability, and the fur business—though Mama Pollack never quite got used to the idea of her son going to work at one A.M. and coming home with the dawn. Sometimes he'd double elsewhere, perhaps with cornetist "Murphy" Steinberg at the Midway Gardens—meaning he'd be gone from early evening through early morning, then sleep most of the following day.

When the Friars' Inn engagement finally sputtered out, it found Ben Pollack, age twenty, facing the prospect of a winter at home, trying to hustle work and having to listen to the family's none-too-subtle hints about better—i.e., more secure—ways to make a living. Pollack *père* and *mère* seem to have understood that an ultimatum at that point would yield only rebellion. Instead, they made their son an offer: if he'd curtail the drumming and late hours, and agree to join his father in the family business, they'd bankroll a three-month summer vacation for him in California.

If he balked at all, it wasn't for long: California in the '20s seemed, at least from afar, some kind of mythic, vaguely sybaritic fairyland, alive with opportunity. The meteoric rise of the movie industry had made Hollywood a symbol of everything new, energetic, up-to-date. It was a young place, seemingly without entrenched social hierarchies—or even the sorts of pressures which might impel a young man who wanted to play the drums to forsake it all and go into the fur trade.

Ben agreed and dutifully bided his time; come June, with a couple of pals (saxophonist Maury Hicks and trumpeter Fred Ferguson, who'd been working with Art Kassel's band alongside a stern-faced young trombonist named James Caesar Petrillo, later czar of the musicians' union) as company, he headed for Los Angeles.

In retrospect the Pollacks seem as astonishing in their naïveté as had been the parents of Bix Beiderbecke in sending their son to boarding school in a Chicago suburb. Did they actually believe he would *avoid* seeking out music and musicians, particularly in a city brimming with chances to play?

Arriving in Los Angeles, Pollack was delighted to find that a reputation of sorts, based on the New Orleans Rhythm Kings records, had preceded him among local musicians; calls to play began coming in almost at once. After working briefly with clarinetist Larry Shields, alumnus of the Original Dixieland Jazz Band, Pollack landed a regular job playing out at Venice Beach, a kind of southern Californian equivalent of Atlantic City.

But the "summer vacation" was passing quickly. Impressed with the newcomer, leader Harry Bastin urged him to stay on; not surprisingly, his stay stretched through autumn, then winter and into spring of 1925. "By this time," said Pollack, "my folks wired me that they would disown me if I didn't return home, so I left Los Angeles to return to Chicago."[25]

It took only a day or two working for his father for the young drummer to realize that mink was not his métier. Within a week, with his parents apparently resigned at last to the inevitable, Ben Pollack headed east for an exploratory visit to New York.

There, too, his work with the Rhythm Kings had made him something of a celebrity in local hot music circles. But before he could do anything about it a cable arrived from California: bandleader Bastin had fallen ill, and his musicians had nominated Pollack as his replacement—all at the handsome salary of $165 a week. Pollack caught a westbound train and alighted in Los Angeles a bandleader.

He set about reorganizing Bastin's band along more hot-oriented lines. From Carl Allen's band at the Rendezvous he plucked another Chicago friend, saxophonist Gil Rodin, and with an ear for talent which was to stand him in good stead through the years began building his personnel. Ironically, even the sudden death of an elder brother contributed to the process; back in Chicago for the funeral, Pollack and Rodin found sixteen-year-old Benny Goodman playing clarinet at the Midway Gardens and offered him a job on the spot. In later years Benny remembered it well.

"He [Rodin] began talking about glamorous California . . . The more he talked about it the better it sounded to me. Go west—the idea of going out there on a train, seeing places like Santa Monica, all beautiful hotels and glamorous people and places. It sounded too good to be true." Pollack and Rodin agreed to put their case to Goodman's parents directly; after a heated conversation, much of it in Yiddish, Mama and Papa Goodman agreed, and the boy wonder of the clarinet headed west.

His illusions barely survived the train trip. "Oh boy," he told the author. "It was the sleaziest place. Rides, roller coasters and all that. I just looked around and I thought, 'What the hell did I come here for?' But there I was—and the band was very good, after all.''[26]

Pollack kept building, swapping, adding. Before long the new band was being talked about, and he and Rodin started thinking about Chicago. Los Angeles might be a place to make beginnings, but it was far from the real centers of hot music ferment, far from the action. Chicago, by contrast, was a dance band town, the liveliest in the country. A combination of geography, business, bootlegging, and especially the introduction of remote-control broadcasts from various of the city's dance halls, had made it fertile ground for an aspiring bandleader.

Every ballroom had at least one band, and there was work in speakeasies, restaurants, hotels. Pollack was ready: he had nineteen-year-old Fud Livingston, also a skilled composer-arranger, alongside Goodman in the reeds; he'd picked up two more arrangers in trombonist Glenn Miller, fresh out of the University of Colorado, and pianist Wayne Allen. Harry Greenberg, a Chicagoan with a punchy style reminiscent of Muggsy Spanier's, was his hot trumpet man. And, apart from any musical consideration, he and several of his men—young Goodman presumably among them—were getting homesick.

What did such a band sound like? In late 1925, the most commercially successful white orchestras playing for dancing, apart from Paul Whiteman's, were those of Roger Wolfe Kahn, Ray Miller, Isham Jones, and the New York–based California Ramblers. Though scoring for such groups had come far in five years, arrangers still tended to overwrite: ensembles were often cluttered, rhythmically stiff. The notion of soloist and ensemble as a synergy, the *yin* and *yang* of one basic concept, was only beginning to evolve, and the last vestiges of ragtime drumming were still hobbling the easy flow of the emergent four even beats to the bar. When Goodman, remembering 1925, assessed Pollack's band as "very good," he was more likely remembering the overall competence of the musicians than any specifics of the sound. It seems never to have occurred to Pollack that he might have trouble booking regular work for a brand-new, untried and unrecorded eleven-piece band. With high hopes and great expectations, he and his "Californians" boarded a train for Chicago—and found no work. The quality places, those doing the kind of business that would sustain a band of this size, were in effect a closed shop. They had their regular favorites, and no established leader was about to step aside to admit a newcomer.

It left Pollack's men in a quandary, and not for the last time. Goodman, already well known around town for his versatility and prowess, picked up casuals and fell into a job at the Uptown Theatre with Bennie Krueger, who had recorded on C-melody sax with the Original Dixieland Jazz Band. According to Goodman's autobiographical *The Kingdom of Swing*, published in 1939, the Pollack band continued to rehearse occasionally "on the chance that something might turn up."

It did, in the form of two weeks at A. J. "Toots" Marshall's popular Castle Farms ballroom outside Cincinnati, with an option to extend—an option which somehow, much to Goodman's dismay, had evaporated by the time the band arrived. They did the fortnight anyway and returned to scuffling in Chicago.

Benny went back to Krueger—but his sense of having been deceived over the Castle Farms affair left him with an abiding distrust of Pollack.

Pollack kept hustling, tracking down leads. Finally he talked Paul Ash, a prominent bandleader and impresario known as "the Rajah of Jazz" (presumably after Whiteman's no less hyperbolic "King"), into "presenting" the Pollack orchestra at the Venetian Room of Chicago's Southmoor Hotel. Goodman, perhaps still smarting over Castle Farms, opted for the security of the Krueger job and turned the Southmoor down; Pollack filled his chair with a capable local man identified variously as Lenny or Lou Cohen.

But this one seemed to stick. Perhaps it was Ash's prestige, or timing, or some other, less definable factor, but the band caught on. They stayed eighteen months, bringing in a respectable $1,050 a week. Goodman soon rejoined, at least partly through some diplomacy by Rodin, by now Pollack's adviser and lieutenant.

Benny's younger brother Harry came in on tuba—but only after having to learn string bass in the style of Steve Brown, with whom Pollack had played at the Friars' Inn. Record producer Jack Kapp dropped by and, impressed, offered Pollack a recording contract with Brunswick; but Victor, reportedly alerted by an ever-astute Jean Goldkette, had also made an approach. Pollack obviously found the higher profile and bigger sales potential more compelling and signed with Victor.

The band recorded for the first time September 14, 1926, but the three titles made that day were lost. Another try in December produced four titles, two of which are particularly revealing. " 'Deed I Do" bears out various recollections that Miller—or was it Livingston?—fashioned his arrangement after the successful New York society band of Roger Wolfe Kahn, who employed such top jazzmen as Miff Mole and the violin-guitar team of Joe Venuti and Eddie Lang.

(There is considerable doubt as to who was responsible at this point for the Pollack band's arrangements. George T. Simon, writing about Miller in 1974, quoted Gil Rodin and others to the effect that "Glenn had been living in the Pollack band under the shadow of Fud Livingston . . . most of the time, Glenn, instead of writing the kind of jazz arrangements he really wanted to write, was kept busy arranging corny ballads and trite novelty tunes that the band needed for commercial reasons.")[27]

As Goodman put it in The Kingdom of Swing, the Kahn band's arrangements "were pretty complicated. They might not sound so now, but they were for us, especially as [our] level of reading ability wasn't very high." As Benny told it, the band finished at the Southmoor at two A.M. the night before the date, then started rehearsing the new scores. "It took us until 6 a.m. to get them in shape," he said. The session was scheduled for nine.[28]

Sure enough, the sound is clearly on the Kahn model, replete with a pair of violins played by Pollack's cousin Alex Beller and a prodigy named Victor Young, who had studied at the Warsaw Conservatory in Poland and already gained experience on the international concert-hall circuit. It's a well-crafted score, though the introduction, built on whole-tone scales, seems at first to lead nowhere; it just stops, and the saxes then state the melody over muted brass punctuations and a violin counterline. Greenberg's trumpet, playing in a style not unlike that of Jimmy McPartland (who soon replaced him), gets a piece of the verse before Pollack's relentlessly cheery vocal.

With a rather contrived sense of symmetry, Livingston (or Miller) brings back the whole-tone motif for an eight-bar transitional passage (also spotlighting a bit of Goodman clarinet) to set up a tenor solo by Livingston. Miller's own Miff Mole–like interjections in the bridge reinforce the sense of similarity to the Kahn band.

Only Goodman seems unaffected by such self-conscious doings, delivering his half-chorus solo with lift, sharp attack, and an engaging brightness of tone over Pollack's loose-limbed cymbal beat. From the opening bars of this, his first solo on record, it's clear that a new and formidable hot clarinet talent has arrived.

Perhaps without the passion and unruly creativity of Frank Teschemacher, or the idiosyncratic charm of Pee Wee Russell, Goodman even at this early stage (he was seventeen) clearly possesses a poise, technical mastery, and fluency of expression far beyond that of either man. If he echoes Noone or Dodds, Roppolo or Shields, or even Don Murray, it is only in the sense of having heard them and absorbed aspects of their work into an overall synthesis of style.

There's more of the same on "He's the Last Word," with Goodman's solo and Pollack's support again providing the highlights. "Let's face it," Harry Goodman said in 1991, "we had a great drummer in Pollack. He was the heartbeat of the band . . . the rhythm was so solid."[29]

Pollack's drumming, in fact, compares very favorably with that of Henderson's Kaiser Marshall on such 1926 records as "Clarinet Marmalade" and "The Henderson Stomp." But there's a difference: where Marshall's beat, however crisp, remains in strict conformity with the rest of the rhythm section in its cut-time subdivision of the bar, Pollack's is the one that streamlines things, emphasizing all four beats equally.

The way he plays his top cymbal behind Goodman on " 'Deed I Do" and "He's the Last Word" goes far toward explaining the enthusiasm of cornetist Jimmy McPartland, who joined the band the following year. "Now there was a drummer, one of the finest that ever lived," he told British critic Max Jones in 1954. Pollack, he said, "produced as fine a beat as I've ever heard. When he got behind you, he'd really make you go; yes, he'd send you."[30]

McPartland was an old pro of twenty when he went with Pollack. He'd tasted the big time, or something close to it, at seventeen, by replacing Bix with the Wolverines. He'd dropped in several times to listen to the Pollack band at the Blackhawk Restaurant, where they'd been since May 1927, and say hello to Goodman, whom he'd known since their days playing college dances with "Murph" Podalsky's band.

The band McPartland joined "really swung. We didn't play all jazz, naturally: had to play popular tunes of the day for the customers. But everything we did was musical. The intonation was fine, the band had tonal quality . . . it played nice, danceable music."[31]

The cornetist did his first record date with Pollack December 7, 1927, the day before the initial McKenzie and Condon's Chicagoans session for OKeh—and nearly a year to the day after " 'Deed I Do." Comparison between that earlier title and "Waitin' for Katie," done on the seventh, shows how extensively things had changed. No more emulation of Kahn or anyone else: Pollack's band was beginning to go its own way.

Goodman jumps out of the introduction to "Katie" with a full solo chorus backed nimbly by the rhythm and using the melody as little more than a reference point. He's fluent, rhythmically agitated in what can safely be identified as a Chicago manner—and also, unusual for him, just a bit below pitch.

Miller's scoring of the verse—and it's more than likely, with Livingston long gone to New York, that it was Miller's work—is exceptional, splitting the four-man brass team in half, two to state the theme and two for a counterline. The cornet trio (Al Harris, Jimmy McPartland, Benny Goodman) that follows indicates, moreover, an awareness of Bill Challis's writing for Bix Beiderbecke and his Gold-kette sectionmates.

Listening to Goodman's one-bar cornet break after the bridge later fetched an affectionate chuckle from McPartland. "We used to do that often with the band," he recalled. "We'd be playing out in front, Benny, Glenn [Miller], and myself, playing choruses on 'Bugle Call Blues' or some such thing, and Benny would take my cornet and I'd take his clarinet. I could play a little in the low register on the clarinet: well, the people thought we were just wonderful because we could switch instruments.

"At the session, after we'd rehearsed this thing a couple of times for sound balance, Benny whispers to me, 'Hey, Jim, let me take the pickup on the cornet going into your solo.' And I said, 'Sure, go ahead.' What the hell—everything was fun to us."[32]

McPartland's solo on "Memphis Blues" reflects his strong admiration of Beiderbecke, who had played a similar chorus three years before on a Wolverines record of "Royal Garden Blues." Goodman, on clarinet, and Miller (trombone) also solo forcefully, but the main event here is the arrangement. In getting a larger band to play what is normally a small-band number, Miller has succeeded in retaining the textural clarity of a small-band performance. If his score shows occasional clutter, it is nonetheless full of felicitous touches.[33]

One little-remarked feature of both "Waitin' for Katie" and "Memphis Blues" is their rhythmic foundation. "That rhythm you hear," said Harry Goodman, "we created it. Every band was marking two—one and three with the tuba—but we played four. I played four on the tuba, and Pollack did it on his bass drum. And it worked."[34]

In dance bands of the early '20s, brass bass (and bass drum) usually marked the first and third beats of each bar, leaving accentuation of the second and fourth, the "after" or "back" beats, to piano or other rhythm instruments. The practice, descended from marches and early dance rhythms, set up a firmly rocking—if not very elastic—platform, ideally suited to pre-1920 fox-trots but less to the one-step and later dance rhythms. Pianists and banjo/guitarists soon found that by accentuating all four beats of the bar (even while the tuba was marking only beats one and three) they could do much to smooth out the rhythmic texture.

The role of the bass also evolved for physical reasons: it's difficult to sustain playing all four beats of a bar comfortably on a tuba or bass saxophone. Even those tuba players able to play a four-beat "walking" bass line cleanly and lightly were bound to fall victim sooner or later to fatigue and the inherent physical problems of any large-bore wind instrument.

A handful of wind-bass players became skilled at alternating between two and four beats to the bar, with considerable delicacy and no loss of drive. Cyrus St. Clair, with Charlie Johnson's band at Smalls' Paradise in Harlem, and the remarkable Joe "Country" Washburn, with Ted Weems, were two outstanding exponents—and, on the basis of these records, so was Harry Goodman. From the first notes of Benny's clarinet solo on "Waitin' for Katie," the feeling (accentuated by Dick Morgan's well-miked guitar) is an evenly played four to a bar.

Goodman may be right in contending that Pollack's was the first rhythm section to do this regularly. Only such Goldkette performances as "Clementine," buoyed by Steve Brown's string bass and Eddie Lang's guitar, offer a comparable foundation.

Duke Ellington's orchestra by this time was using the more supple string bass, as played by Wellman Braud in a style similar to that of his New Orleans colleague Steve Brown. By October of 1928, Braud was playing four-to-the-bar on records of such slower numbers as "The Mooche," and even behind solos on the "Tiger Rag"–based stomp "Hot and Bothered." This is nearly a year after "Waitin' for Katie" and "Memphis Blues," lending some credence to Harry Goodman's assertion—though again, what was being put on records may not always have represented what was happening nightly on the bandstand. In late-'20s hot music circles, news traveled fast; it was a time of discovery, and all musicians, black and white, were keenly aware of what their colleagues were doing.)

The following advertisement appeared in the February 29, 1928, issue of *Variety*:

"THE BIG ORCHESTRA WITH THE LITTLE LEADER"

BREAKING INTO THE BIG CITY
At The LITTLE CLUB, New York, March 6
BEN POLLACK
and his CALIFORNIANS
(Victor Records)

The Little Club, in the basement of the Nora Bayes Theatre on West 44th Street, had formerly been the Club Alabam, where Fletcher Henderson's orchestra had made its debut some five years before. Not inappropriately, then, the band Pollack brought in to open there was loaded with jazz talent: Bud Freeman had come in on tenor sax beside Goodman and Rodin, replacing Larry Binyon. McPartland and Bostonian Al Harris were on trumpets, Miller on trombone. The rhythm, besides Pollack, was Harry Goodman, guitarist Morgan, and pianist Vic Breidis.

It was a good start, and Pollack's musicians fell into it with enthusiasm. McPartland and Freeman took rooms at the stylish Mayflower Hotel, on Central Park West. "We all moved into nice places to live," the cornetist told Max Jones, "and we spent our money fast." There were record dates along the way. On March 21, McPartland, Goodman, and Miller were part of an "All-Star Orchestra" assembled (presumably by Fud Livingston, who did the arrangements) for a date at Victor. McPartland's half-chorus solo on "Oh, Baby!" is particularly good.

At an April 6 Pollack Victor date, the band got through three takes of "Singapore Sorrows" (a bit of Chinoiserie closely related to "Limehouse Blues") and one of "Sweet Sue (Just You)," before giving up for the day. They remade both titles, with more success, on the twenty-sixth.

Their enthusiasm didn't survive the season. As Goodman remembered it, Pollack came up with a chance to play the new Broadway show *Say When*, scheduled to open June 26, and gave his notice to John Popkin at the Little Club, closing on May 5. Vocalist Smith Ballew, who heard Pollack's band at the basement room (and had worked with it briefly in Chicago), hinted that there may have been other problems. "Strangely enough, that fine band of Ben's was not too well received in New York," he told an interviewer. "People there seemed to prefer the society-type orchestra over Chicago-style jazz. So Ben didn't last too long at the Little Club."[35]

One way or the other, fate then intervened—in the form of local 802, American Federation of Musicians. Because Pollack's was still officially designated a "traveling band," it would not be allowed to accept theatre employment as a unit because that would take a big chunk of work away from New York musicians; local 802 would have an insurrection on its hands.[36]

So by mid-May Pollack's musicians, out of work, were stuck in New York City with lots of free time (there were a few theatre dates, a radio broadcast here and there) and almost no money coming in. Miller and a couple of the others hooked up with Paul Ash for a run at the Paramount Theatre. McPartland and Freeman, unable to pay the rent at the Mayflower, moved to the more modest Whitby Apartments at 325 West 45th Street, between Eighth and Ninth avenues, where Goodman, Rodin, and Miller were already domiciled.

Their sustenance, McPartland remembered, came through regular attendance at cocktail parties where the hors d'oeuvres, at least, were free. At one such event he ran into Bix, in town with Paul Whiteman's orchestra for a Brooklyn theatre engagement and a fortnight of daily recording sessions under its new Columbia contract. Hearing the "kid" was out of work, Beiderbecke peeled a couple of hundred-dollar bills (on another occasion Jimmy remembered it as five fifties) off a roll and handed them to the younger man with instructions to "pay me when you can."

Benny Goodman had done well with his first small-band record date for Brunswick back in Chicago; now he talked Walter Melrose into letting him have one in New York. ("We can get some money, buy some food, eat!") One of the numbers they recorded on June 4 was an original titled "Room 1411," wry acknowledgement of their communal digs at the Whitby. Around this time, Eddie Condon and Red McKenzie got into town and looked up—and moved in with— their old pals; they, too, quickly became part of a floating circle of young, largely unemployed hot musicians.

Pollack, meanwhile, had been hustling and scored with a few weeks at Young's Million-Dollar Pier in Atlantic City (owned by Chicagoan promoter-booker Ernie Young), where the Goldkette orchestra had played its final engagement the previous August. He started assembling his men—and ran right into trouble. Miller was about to get married, he told his boss, and Ash was paying him good money; he couldn't jeopardize so good a chance. He'd keep doing arrangements, but Pollack had better find himself another trombone player.

It proved easier than anticipated. Everybody was talking about a newcomer from Texas, an easygoing guy named Jack Teagarden, who didn't sound like Miff Mole or any other trombone player in New York. Word had spread fast on the musician grapevine, accounts of Teagarden's playing taking on almost mythic proportions. Where Miff and his disciples, Miller among them, favored an agile, even calisthenic, approach, the twenty-three-year-old Texan played long, highly vocalized lines. Where Mole's phrases often jumped around, in one musician's words, "like hoptoads," Teagarden's rolled. He played naturally and easily, elasticizing the beat. He'd subbed for Miff on a March 14 Victor date, and his chorus on "She's a Great, Great Girl" had created a stir.

And, everybody said, *you ought to hear him play the blues.*

According to Pollack's account—one of many—of what happened next, he found the trombonist in an ancient, dimly lit hotel room, asleep in his clothes on a cot, while New Orleans cornetist Johnny Bayersdorffer read a newspaper.

"Can he read?" Pollack asked Bayersdorffer.

"He's the best," the cornetist replied.

"Well, I got a job for him," said Pollack. After some further conversation they managed to rouse an ill-tempered Teagarden and get him to understand that no less a person than *Ben Pollack* was offering him a job. He went to Atlantic City with the band—and stayed with it thereafter.

The exact personnel of the group that made the trip is harder to pin down. Gil Rodin was recovering from a tonsillectomy, in those pre-antibiotic days still a major piece of surgery. On the recommendation of McPartland and Freeman, Pollack reportedly sent to Chicago for Frank Teschemacher. How sweet, the thought of the "Austin High Gang" front line complete for three weeks in Ben Pollack's orchestra. But it may not have worked out exactly that way.

In May the band had shared a bill at Brooklyn's Metropolitan Theatre with their old friend from Chicago days, "Shimmy Queen" Bee Palmer, who reportedly liked what she heard. After a backstage discussion, she proposed that Jimmy, Bud, Condon, and some of their friends become her backup band at the Chateau Madrid, a new nightspot to be run by Lou Schwartz, who had turned the Club Richman into a Manhattan bonanza for extrovert entertainer Harry Richman.

At this point the sequence of events is not clear, though researcher Trevor Tolley has gone far toward establishing a chronology. From accounts by Condon, Mezzrow, and others, it seems likely that McPartland and Freeman left Pollack for this venture and that Condon went back to Chicago to fetch Teschemacher, Joe Sullivan, and Gene Krupa.

According to Condon (in *We Called It Music*), the musicians auditioned, but Schwartz, unimpressed, dismissed them out of hand. Condon, characteristically, persevered: now that their "gang" was together again, why not try to find jobs as a unit? At one point, he said, they worked the Palace Theatre, backing (or, more likely, jamming behind) the dance team of Barbara Bennett and Charles Sabin. Reviews ranged from "rather dreadful" to "the poorest seven-piece orchestra on earth."

Recent work by Dutch-based researcher Horst Bergmeier indicates that a few days into the Palace job McPartland and Freeman got an offer from a friend, a playboy and sometime banjoist named George Carhart, to join him in a band he was putting together for a European tour, beginning with passage as ship's musicians on the brand-new liner Île de France. According to Bergmeier, Freeman accepted, hoping to hook up overseas with his old friend Dave Tough.[37]

McPartland, questioned, remembered little of this time—save that Bee Palmer had been feuding with her husband, pianist and vocal coach Al Siegel, and avidly welcomed the young and handsome cornet player into her bed. It's equally likely that this situation influenced both his decision to turn Carhart down and, when Pollack phoned about Atlantic City, to decline that offer as well. Trumpeter Earl Baker clearly remembered coming in from Chicago to do the engagement, thereby meeting Jack Teagarden for the first time.

Freeman apparently left Pollack, went back to Chicago briefly (where he worked with pianist Zez Confrey), then returned to New York in time to sail around July 18 on the Île de France. Mezz Mezzrow, in *Really the Blues*, claimed to have filled in for Rodin, with Teschemacher playing Freeman's tenor chair—an assertion at least circumstantially strengthened by the former's presence on tenor for the September 29 Dorsey Brothers and "Big Aces" OKeh date. Sam Lanin's band replaced Pollack's at the Million-Dollar Pier in late August, and—as a photo of this band attests—Teschemacher simply stayed on.[38]

In and out, from band to band, grabbing the work as it became available, the "hot" musician tended to be that kind of peripatetic, a twentieth-century wandering minstrel. One commentator has termed accounts of such peregrinations "a whirlwind family album of survival," and as any veteran musician will attest, the description is right on target.

Pollack's orchestra opened September 28 at the Florentine Grill of the Park Central Hotel, Seventh Avenue at 55th Street. In the tenor chair, sitting beside a newly recovered Rodin, was the talented and versatile Larry Binyon. At the management's request Pollack had added two violins (one of them Alex Beller) and a 'cello and had supplemented his book of Miller and Fud Livingston scores with some arrangements bought from Don Redman, by then working for Goldkette in Detroit.

And on October 15, two weeks later, they recorded for Victor; the changes, as reflected in overall performance, are dramatic. The band is full, confident, rhythmically charged, even playing unadventuresome arrangements of second-rate songs in the standard "hot dance" fashion. Teagarden solos directly after Belle Manne's Betty Boopish vocal on "Buy, Buy for Baby," showing in sixteen bars that none of his advance billing among New York musicians was exaggerated. His easy swing and linear phrasing make even excellent efforts by McPartland and Goodman seem stiff by comparison. The other selection, "She's One Sweet Show Girl," gives Jimmy McPartland a chance to ring and shine over an attractive descending background figure scored by Miller for trombone and bass (or baritone) sax.

McPartland's work here, and on such titles as "Add a Little Wiggle" and "Oh, Baby!" by the All-Star Band, as well as Pollack's "Sentimental Baby," "Louise," and numerous small-group numbers, is of high quality. While not a soloist of startling originality—his debt to Beiderbecke is constant and pronounced—he establishes his own strong musical presence. He is more sentimental, yet in a way more emotionally austere, than his hero; among titles warranting consideration are "Since You Went Away," recorded October 16, 1928, under Irving Mills's name by a small Pollack unit, and the several versions of "Whoopee Stomp," appearing on a variety of labels.

Still, the restrictions of "hot dance" make the Pollack records seem hidebound compared to those made around the same time by some of the black bands; "Walk That Thing," for example, made for Victor in September by Charlie Johnson's ten-piece Smalls' Paradise Orchestra, exhibits none of the constraints so apparent in the Pollack performances. From Benny Waters's opening tenor chorus it's a hot jazz original, with fine solos (notably by Jimmy Harrison on trombone and Sidney DeParis on trumpet) and high-stepping rhythm from George Stafford's drums and Cy St. Clair's tuba.

"Just listen to those tunes we did," said Jimmy McPartland. "Glenn [Miller] did what he could with 'em, but what the hell can you do with 'Buy, Buy for Baby?' They wouldn't let us record the stuff we were playing every night, stuff we knew sounded great. These things—we'd only get a chance to run 'em down once or twice before recording 'em. We weren't even familiar with them yet. If we'd at least had a chance to play them on the job a few nights we would've been able to smoothe things out and get 'em to swing. But here—well, it was no better than sight-reading."[39]

His words echo those of the Goldkette musicians: what happened in front of the microphones was little more than a faint echo of what happened every night on the bandstand. With this band, as with Goldkette's, there's plenty of corroboration from participants and spectators alike to back that up.

But the two bands differed in at least one major particular. Miller's arrangements, however well crafted, demonstrate little of the sense of surprise and discovery inherent in Challis's work, and there is little indication that Pollack's musicians ever strove for the kind of ensemble teamwork that distinguished the Goldkette orchestra. Chicagoans in spirit, their priorities lay in what they could do as soloists.

"We used to do numbers on the stand that would go on for five, ten, fifteen minutes—'I Want to Be Happy,' things like that," said McPartland. "We'd start out with the full band, then I'd play maybe two or three choruses, and Benny would play ten, fifteen, or twenty, with Pollack on the drums, and those guys would get to swingin' like mad. Also, Pollack had a thing where he used the fly swatters—brushes—on the bass drum, and he and Benny would just go at it, playing chorus after chorus, just inspiring each other."[40]

According to Ruby Weinstein, who replaced Al Harris as lead trumpet,

> all the real good arrangements that we played with Pollack were head arrangements. Pollack's band cannot be rated with Goldkette's, Roger Wolfe Kahn, Casa Loma, Henderson, McKinney's, etc. These bands were all ensemble bands and all great. Pollack's band was . . . strictly a soloist's band. Goodman, McPartland, Teagarden and the rest were always featured and each played as long as he wanted to, with the rest of the orchestra playing a rhythm behind the solo. When they were tired we'd end the piece with a riff and that was it.[41]

For the young jazzmen in its ranks, at least for a while, Pollack's band on the bandstand seemed a kind of paradise, foreshadowing the looseness and freedom of the Count Basie Orchestra of a decade hence. But it's only too easy to imagine the reaction of the Little Club's customers—no college students, these, but more likely their parents—at such self-indulgence. It's also not difficult to infer that Smith Ballew, an experienced bandleader, had it just right: Pollack's Broadway deal was only part of the reason the band didn't last long at the Little Club. Long strings of improvised solos, with only token concession to the needs of the dancers, must have done little to endear this band of Young Turks to John Popkin and the rest of the Little Club management.

Or, for that matter, to the Victor Company's executives. "The producers gave you the songs that had to be recorded, and they worked together with the publishers," Harry Goodman said. "So when you had a session you'd have four songs. If the leader didn't like it, he could say, 'I'd like to record one of my instrumentals instead of that.' And once in a while the instrumentals got put in. But Pollack—well, let's just say he wasn't very assertive that way."[42]

For all his allegiance to hot jazz, Pollack was coming to realize that if he expected to make a success of his orchestra he'd best play the game the way Eddie King and other Victor bosses wanted him to play it. Whatever happened on the stand at night, things in the studio had to be done by the prevailing rules. That meant, alas, not holding out for the occasional instrumental specialty, not taking his sidemen's part in fighting the limitations on what his band played and how. In other words, accepting it all—in a way sure to bring him into conflict with his young, headstrong musicians.

He surely rationalized this by reminding himself that other circumstances afforded plenty of opportunities to stretch out. At least partly through Pollack's efforts, the band was booked solid (usually through Irving Mills) with dates for small companies such as the Plaza group, whose thirty-five-cent Banner, Romeo, Lincoln, and Cameo labels sold in a variety of outlets, including five-and-dime stores. On these sessions, issued under Mills's name or bearing such colorful pseudonyms as "The Lumberjacks," "The Dixie Daisies," "Jimmy Bracken's Toe Ticklers," "Goody's Good-Timers," and others even more fanciful, rules were few. If a studio once in a while supplied a singer, vocals were just as often by Teagarden or even guitarist Dick Morgan, the latter using a nonsense "icky" (i.e., corny) language of his own invention.

These unrestricted small-band efforts, which did not have to appeal to the wider dancing public (and, in fact, were within a price range that made them affordable to younger buyers), were at least relatively unrestricted, with Pollack often playing drums himself. "Whoopee Stomp," "Bugle Call Rag," and Teagarden's blues feature, "Makin' Friends," were long among the most sought-after of collector's items. Goodman solos frequently and well on both clarinet and alto sax, and McPartland's work is uniformly fine.

Ironically, "Whoopee Stomp," recorded November 27, 1928, for Columbia's low-priced Harmony subsidiary, probably is a more typical Pollack band performance than most of those recorded under the leader's own name. It consists of sixteen-bar solos by Freeman (back from his European adventure), Goodman, Teagarden, and McPartland, bookended by an arrangement that is little more than a sketch.

Start to finish, it is, in McPartland's phrase, "full of good feelings," closer to the cornetist's description of evenings at the Park Central. And, true to his memories, it swings deliciously. "Somebody would play something nice, and the guys would turn around and say, 'Hey, that was great!' " Nor were these musicians above a little hokum: when they played "Tiger Rag," Harry Goodman donned a carnival tiger head and leaped, roaring, onto the dance floor.[43]

Sometime in late autumn Pollack stopped playing the drums at the hotel, largely because, as he later told George T. Simon, he was "sick and tired of having people come up to the band and asking [sic] when Ben Pollack's going to come in." He replaced himself with Ray Bauduc, a New Orleans man who had been around New York since 1926, working for Fred Rich and other leaders. While neither as buoyant nor as creative as Pollack, Bauduc played drums with a firm beat and fit in well.[44]

"Ben wanted to be real big time" was McPartland's way of putting it. "All sorts of people had his ear. They told him he needed a manager—so he got a manager, this guy Bernie Foyer . . . a real manager type, one of these horrible guys with a cigar stickin' out of the side of his mouth. A backbiter, too. He was the one who told Pollack he should quit playin' the drums, stand up there in front of the band, sing through a megaphone, wave a baton like Paul Whiteman or Rudy Vallee or someone who was a big hit.

"It was the worst thing he could have done. First, he didn't sing too well. Also, he—well, he changed. He'd always been terrific: as a leader, drummer, and as a person, he'd always been one of the guys. We'd always been a pretty close-knit bunch—loved our music and loved to play . . . played handball and stuff together, went swimming. But when Foyer came along and started treating us like sidemen, well—Pollack seemed to change, too."[45]

Foyer seems also to have been responsible for Pollack's insertion of a sim-pering "May it please you, Ben Pollack" as a signoff line on records made in 1929. An attempt at a signature, a personalizing touch to make each performance readily identifiable? Probably, in view of Annette Hanshaw's pert "That's all!" and other similar devices of the day. Not surprisingly, it was greeted with scorn by Pollack's sidemen—and apparent indifference by the public. He dropped it later that year.

As 1929 got under way it was clear that Pollack's was a band philosophically divided. The young musicians, with little sympathy for their leader's ambitions, saw themselves as responsible for (and indispensable to) his success; at a very personal level they read Pollack's change of course as a defection, even a betrayal, putting him in a class with the widely loathed Red Nichols. That he might have been attempting, however clumsily, to avoid the unhappy fate of Goldkette's "musicians' band" did not seem to occur to them.

As the musicians saw it, Pollack would have remained a regular guy and lived happily ever after, jamming off into the sunset with his boys, had the cigar-chomping tempter not slithered into Eden to dangle commercial success in front of him.

But simple experience with the day-to-day travails of keeping a band em-ployed had shown Pollack that successful orchestras, at least in 1928, did not spend their evenings jamming onstage and were not successfully led from behind a set of drums. The era of a Gene Krupa or Buddy Rich, drumming in the spot-light, still lay far ahead. In order to compete in the big time, he'd have to be out front, presenting a recognizable and personable image to the public.

In time, such sidemen as Goodman, Miller, the Dorsey brothers, and Artie Shaw also came to understand that being a leader also meant standing apart from the rank-and-file; the public had to be able to draw a distinction between a commanding officer and his troops, a leader and his—ultimately fungible—side-men. It's significant, too, that those players who tried to have it both ways, stepping out front while also trying to remain "one of the boys" (Teagarden and Bunny Berigan are two among many), were not notably successful as bandleaders. For the leader, having a band meant meeting a payroll—and payday came once a week.

Without a Bernie Foyer at his shoulder it's all too likely that Pollack would never have thought to create such distinctions. He remained, at heart, a jazz drummer. Just how totally emerges in Ruby Weinstein's words: "We were sup-posed to be through at the [Park Central] hotel at 2 A.M. Just about that time [Pollack] would get behind the drums and with brushes alone give that band a drive that was just sensational. Never used sticks. We would play almost an extra hour, and it was something to hear and be part of. Nobody ever complained of playing overtime without being paid."

But Pollack seems to have been somewhat less adept at handling his men. As Benny Goodman recalled with some asperity, the leader "always seemed to be doing something wrong . . . He just wasn't the kind of guy to stop and reflect, and ask himself, 'What am I? Who am I? Where am I going and why?' No objectivity, no insight. And no sense of humor about himself. Wasn't able to think, 'I'm doing well. I ought to treat these kids well'—meaning us—'accept ideas from them and encourage their confidence.' "[46]

On balance, it seems likely that he *was* asking himself these questions but coming up with answers not in line with his sidemen's notions of how things should be run. He was not the only leader trying to reconcile the often contradictory demands of playing for dancers (and for increasingly jazz-oriented younger listeners) while serving the record-buying public as well. But as Goodman seems to suggest, Pollack never took a clear and consistent stand: in the end, this denied him the kind of authority that would have let him enforce his will without sacrificing respect. Shaw, the Dorseys, and, in a curious sense, even Goodman ultimately brought it off—though, it must be added, not without a certain cost to relations offstand.

Like a teacher trying to overcome nervousness in front of a recalcitrant class by imposing excessive discipline, Pollack overdid things. His sidemen responded in kind, with defiance, pranks, and schoolboy misbehavior. "We just gave him a hard time" was McPartland's summation more than half a century later.

And Pollack gave *them* a hard time in return. "Once in a while I'd get a job in Williamstown or someplace, say with Bix," Goodman said. "I'd say to [Pollack], 'Look, Ben, they're offering me an awful lot of money to go up there and play. Maybe four times what you pay me. Do you mind if I go?' And he'd get furious, you know. I'd say, 'Well, I don't think you should be furious about this. You can get a good substitute for a night or so.' But he didn't see it that way— didn't *want* to see it that way."[47]

All he saw, in fact, was an ever more dogged pursuit of commercial success. When songwriters Jimmy McHugh and Dorothy Fields hired the band to play in the pit of their new musical *Hello, Daddy*, Pollack went after—and won—the long-withheld local 802 approval; they opened December 26 at the Mansfield Theatre, while still doubling at the Park Central.[48]

It made for a long night, at the hotel (with a radio broadcast) from 6:30 to 8:00 P.M., then at the theatre from 8:30 to 11:00, then back to the Park Central until nearly 2:00 A.M. For the show, moreover, Pollack returned to his drums, leaving conducting chores to the more experienced Max Steiner.

All this, plus records and other extras, added up to a busy schedule. As the rest of the nation, and much of the entertainment business, slid into the Depression, Ben Pollack and his orchestra were working steadily and making all the money they needed. But this doesn't seem to have expressed itself as any sense of well-being within the band: the rift between Pollack and his men kept widening.

Picking up his megaphone to sing "Let's Sit and Talk About You" one night at the theatre, Pollack discovered that persons unknown had smeared its inside with strong-smelling Limburger cheese. There was a particularly ugly set-to between Bauduc and the leader. The tone became increasingly juvenile: Pollack recalled, with obvious distaste, one night when "I caught the boys trying to give me the so-called finger."

Ruby Weinstein was now the lead trumpeter, bringing added authority to the brass. He was in place for two Victor recording dates the first week of March; whatever may have been going on behind the scenes, the band sounds comfortable and relaxed.

McPartland sets out the melody of "Louise" in his attractively lilting Beiderbecke manner, with Goodman and Teagarden adding brief solos; Pollack sings, none too convincingly, on "My Kinda Love," but Goodman and McPartland are effective, and Teagarden, turning the song into a blues essay, achieves real eloquence. A Vitaphone movie short of the band, made in 1929 at Warners' Brooklyn studios and recovered in the '80s, reveals much. Pollack stands nervously out front, performing exaggerated gyrations with an overlong baton and singing in a manner best described as unctuous. Overall, it's hard to escape the impression of a little man trying very hard to be visible in front of his own band.

Goodman, by contrast, comes across as almost cocky, while Teagarden, who even does some singing after Pollack's vocal on an overblown "production" arrangement of "My Kinda Love," seems very young. "Why, they're just boys!" one wants to exclaim. And, in the opinions of Goodman and more than a few others, they never quite grew up.

With the Park Central closed for the summer, Pollack lined up parties and theatre dates to tide them over while he worked on something for the autumn at the Silver Slipper, a club reportedly controlled by mobster Owney Madden. A WEAF radio wire added greatly to its appeal. They also continued to make good records. On "Bashful Baby," Goodman charges through a full chorus, one of his most fluent, fully realized recorded solos of the period. The ensemble playing is crisp throughout, the rhythm buoyant. Yet the arrangement, presumably by Miller, never really takes off: it is good journeyman work but little more, with nothing to elevate it above the level of a publisher's stock orchestration.

Therein lies the same factor that hobbled the Goldkette orchestra on most of its records: in most particulars, "Bashful Baby" is indistinguishable from dozens of performances by the studio orchestras of Ben Selvin, Fred Rich, and Bert Lown, on which brief hot solos liven up a business-as-usual atmosphere. Overall, the impression is of a first-rate band held back by second-rate material. There is merit in the later suggestion by several of the participating musicians that Miller, deeply sensitive to the demands of the marketplace (as witness the unprecedented success of his own band a decade hence), was simply doing his job with maximum efficiency. To him, the kind of subversion that had characterized Challis's work with Goldkette was unthinkable; if the assignment was a clean, commercial rendering of a pop tune, with room for a couple of hot solos, that's what would be done.[49]

Certainly there is no doubt that Miller understood hot arranging. His scores for Red Nichols, notably "Dinah," "I Want to Be Happy," and the extraordinary "Carolina in the Morning," confirm that. When it became clear that someone would have to be hired to arrange some "hot" passages in the Gershwin show Girl Crazy, he got the nod. But for these Pollack records his job was to play it straight. Posterity listens to "Bashful Baby," "Louise," or "On With the Dance" and longs to hear more. But this was the Victor Company, and the bosses sub-scribed to their own stereotyped market mythology. The situation takes on poign-ancy when these records are set beside accounts of what the Pollack orchestra sounded like in person, on the job, at its best (and on various of its small-band, small-label efforts).

What would Pollack's musicians have sounded like had Victor given them the same latitude afforded Duke Ellington, had the band been allowed to record better scores, such as those contributed by the able and creative Fud Livingston? It can almost be argued—not without a certain attendant irony—that white bands eager to play undiluted hot music would only have achieved their goal had they been allowed to record for the "race" market; obviously, there were more than enough black bands available to keep that an unlikely option.

By summer 1929, relations within Pollack's band had gone into a tailspin. Goodman, in the leader's rancorous words, "was getting in everybody's hair, taking all the solos." McPartland's laxity in making rehearsals was by now chron-ic; the pranks and general cutting up were at an all-time high.

About this time Pollack also discovered that Benny and guitarist Morgan had approached the Park Central management with an offer to give them "Ben Pol-lack's band without Ben Pollack," for a price undercutting what the leader had been charging. He scotched the deal—but his fury at what he saw as the clari-netist's perfidy and ingratitude had reached the breaking point.

The explosion came one night during a Brooklyn theatre date, when Pollack chewed McPartland out for coming to work with his shoes dirty (or his socks drooping, or his garters missing, depending on the account) and fired him; Good-man promptly chimed in with his notice.

The specific incident is less important than the undeniable fact that things simply couldn't have gone on as they were: Pollack's ambitions for himself and his band had all but blinded him to any need for consistent diplomacy in running a collection of bright and headstrong young musicians. The players, for their part, were unable—and unwilling—to understand their leader's side of things.

Once rid of the "mutineers," as he called them, Pollack carried on as before, but his troubles were far from over. During the Silver Slipper engagement, Wein-stein recalled, the leader "decided that his style of music was not popular . . . and since Guy Lombardo was doing well he decided to emulate that orchestra. [He] had simple straightforward chorus arrangements made and put most of the good arrangements in the back of the book."

The musicians kept their heads down and played their parts, even joining in the spirit of things when Pollack hired a dancer to develop a comedy routine in which various bandsmen would come out front and imitate a chorus line.

The death blow came in a way worthy of a Hollywood B movie, when Pollack fell in love with—and hired—a singer named Doris Robbins. Though he later insisted her presence had helped make the band more saleable, many of the musicians remembered her only as a disruptive force; some threatened to quit.

Pollack dug in his heels. Let them go, he said: there were plenty of good men around who would be grateful for a chance to work steadily. His knack for finding talented newcomers never failed him: by mid-1933, he was leading what would soon become the nucleus of the Bob Crosby orchestra—Bauduc, Rodin, clarinetist Matty Matlock, saxophonist Eddie Miller (whom Pollack had encouraged to switch from alto to tenor), cornetist Stirling Bose, guitarist Hilton "Nappy" Lamare, and others. A 1935 Pollack band introduced Dave Matthews on alto and tenor, trombonist Bruce Squires, and a lean trumpeter from Texas named Harry James. But again, as always seemed the case, other leaders came along to pluck the choicest apples off Pollack's tree. The case of James was particularly galling, in that the raider was none other than Pollack's old protégé-turned-nemesis, Benny Goodman. And when Harry struck out on his own a few years later, Squires, Matthews, bassist Thurman Teague, and other Pollack alumni were in his band.

By the mid-1930s, "swing" had become a national craze, with none other than Benny Goodman at its forefront. Pollack, though still respected, was becoming a figure increasingly associated with the past. With mounting desperation, he kept looking for the magic formula, the "Open Sesame" that would bring him at last the real, lasting success he felt he deserved. In its July 1935 issue, Down Beat ran ' a brief item under the headline BEN POLLACK'S ORCHESTRA SUCCUMBING TO COMMERCIALISM:

> One of the few leaders who have always had a real "ride" aggregation, fine musicianship and arrangements, is definitely going commercial. Ben Pollack, of all the swell guys, is featuring an amplified Hawaiian guitar effect that is calculated to set the band "apart" from the multitude in the mind of the great radio listening "poohblic" and brand it as "distinctly different." It succeeds in doing just that too. It sets a once mighty fine band APART! There are flashes of the old time Pollack "swing" but they are entirely too rare. Ben told us that he had missed several fine commercials because he had stuck to his Dixieland, and he was tired out being just on the outside and wanted something he could build into a little cash.

All this happened just as public taste, fueled by Goodman's explosive success, was starting to turn around. Pollack took note—and soon took to billing himself as the "father of swing," a title not without a certain truth. But little by little Ben Pollack was moving out of the picture, scarcely able to conceal his anger, a sense of having been ill-used by those to whom he'd been most generous. What had he done wrong, he seemed to ask, that he should have been denied the rewards due the "father of swing"—all while his musical progeny were becoming millionaires and international celebrities?

In a final, futile gesture, he tried to bring suit in 1939 against Goodman, Bob Crosby, Paramount Pictures, Victor Records, and Camel Cigarettes for five hundred thousand dollars—his estimate of what had been denied him in proceeds of his efforts at commercial success. The suit died in the courts.

The rest of Ben Pollack's life was a patchwork of schemes that always seemed to misfire, business ventures that got off to fast starts, then collapsed. He continued to play drums around Los Angeles, always leading groups of promising young musicians—who invariably left him to pursue successful careers. An appearance in Hollywood's *The Benny Goodman Story* in 1955 brought renewed attention—but somehow even that somehow came to nothing. In the late 1950s he ran a restaurant, the Pick-a-Rib, on Hollywood's Sunset Strip. It ultimately failed.

Finally, on June 7, 1971, came a dispassionate statement of a tragic event, torn off a teleprinter:

> PALM SPRINGS, Calif (UPI)—Former bandleader Ben Pollack, who was known as the "father of swing" during the 1930s and '40s, hanged himself Monday in the bathroom of his home here . . . Police said the 67-year-old Pollack had left two notes complaining of despondency because of financial and marital problems.

And so it ended. It seems doubtful that either Pollack's band or Goldkette's will ever win full and equal due from chroniclers of hot music, and certainly not from "politically correct" cultural historians. Too many forces were ranged against them. But both deserve substantially more than the secondary status to which history—and the misconceptions of the Victor Company—have consigned them. There is every reason to believe that on the job, at their height, they were indeed as good as their partisans remembered them.

Of course, Harry Goodman has observed, the black bands "had their style, we had ours. But there was no better or inferior. It was just different, and I think it—what we did—stands the test of time very well."[50]

14

Casa Loma Stomp

To the day he died, Clarence Hutchenrider remembered with undimmed clarity the first time he ever heard the Casa Loma Orchestra.

"We were working in Cincinnati," the clarinetist said in 1985. "It was late '29, maybe early '30. I was with the Clevelanders, a cooperative band that had been Austin Wylie's orchestra, at Miller's Swiss Gardens in Cincinnati. The Casa Loma guys were scheduled to appear at Castle Farms, outside of town, and had to pass our place to get to theirs. Some of them stopped in to listen to us and were very complimentary.

"Later on, after we finished for the night, some of us drove out to Castle Farms to hear what they sounded like. We sat in the car and listened to them, there in the night air, and I'll tell you, they sounded just great. They were well rehearsed, that was clear, and had this really compact sound, everything cleanly played, everybody on their toes reading the notes. Very intricate, or at least it sounded that way to us. But all the same it was a hot band.

"I think the main thing is, it didn't sound like any other band I'd ever heard. It was all class, and in a class by itself; something to remember."[1]

Not long after that night the old laundry van carrying the Clevelanders' band library caught fire and burned. Many instruments were damaged, and the arrangements destroyed. The musicians held an emergency meeting, largely to discuss whether to continue.

Then, as though heaven-sent, came a telegram. Spike Knoblauch, saxophonist and newly elected president of the Casa Loma Orchestra—also a cooperative—

had a brass section opening. Would Grady Watts, the Clevelanders' "hot" trumpet man, be interested? Watts said yes, on condition his pal Hutchenrider be included in the deal.

So it was that in the last weeks of 1931 Grady and Clarence joined the Casa Loma Orchestra at the Necho Allen Hotel, in the northeast Pennsylvania coal-mining town of Pottsville, birthplace of writer John O'Hara.

They entered an ensemble already firmly aware of where it belonged and where it was going. Between 1930 and 1935, before swing became a national religion, with Benny Goodman among its high priests, the Casa Loma Orchestra dominated the dance band world with a blend of intensely played hot jazz specialties and smoothly scored ballads. No other band of the day, whatever race, could rival it for popularity, precision, and team spirit, or for the ability to bring dancers to the floor and raise the temperature of any gathering. No band of those years was more frequently discussed, more widely admired or emulated.

They'd begun in the mid-'20s, as one of many bands organized and managed by Jean Goldkette's Detroit-based National Amusements Corp. Goldkette, who liked to think of himself as the "Paul Whiteman of the West," had bought and renovated the large Graystone Ballroom, using it as a showplace for his talent-packed Victor Recording Orchestra, for McKinney's Cotton Pickers, and for various featured guest units.

At one point Goldkette's office, under Charles Horvath's stewardship, had as many as six full orchestras working under its name around Detroit. One such, led by society trumpeter Henry Biagini, called itself the Goldkette Orange Blossoms, after a cocktail popular at the time. At this early point there's no indication that it was anything but a competently straightforward dance band in standard mid-1920s fashion: peppy rhythm, three-man sax section striving for a silky blend, a "hot" soloist or two for the rhythm numbers. If they emulated anyone, it was more than likely the Goldkette Victor band itself, dominated by such stars as Bix Beiderbecke, Frank Trumbauer, and arranger Bill Challis.

In autumn 1927, National Amusements dispatched Biagini and his Orange Blossoms to Toronto to fulfill a commitment at the Casa Loma luxury hotel. Built between 1911 and 1914 as a private residence for soldier-turned-financier Sir Henry Mill Pellatt, the Casa Loma (the name translates from Spanish as "the House on the Hill") was a castle-builder's conceit, a vision worthy of M. C. Escher; a vast jumble of gables, turrets, and arches, it cost Sir Henry a total of five million dollars to build and furnish.[2]

It boasted its own private telephone network, sixty bathrooms, an indoor swimming pool, a ventilation system of daunting complexity, electric elevators connecting the three main floors, five thousand electric lights, a 165-foot shooting gallery in the basement, and the largest wine cellar in North America, according to research done in the 1960s by historian Frank Driggs. Its operating costs included a staggering twenty-two thousand dollars a year for domestic staff alone.

With the death of Lady Pellatt in 1923, Sir Henry seemed to lose interest in running this immense Xanadu, and by 1927 a corporation had taken it over and opened it as a luxury apartment hotel. The Orange Blossoms were there as an enticement—classy, hot dance music to help lure big spenders.

Accounts vary as to just how much of the engagement the band actually played. Lead trombonist Billy Rauch, who joined soon after this episode, insisted that, as he'd heard it, the band never even went to Toronto but were canceled out in advance. Other reports have them in residence for as long as eight months. According to most accounts, they did play: things started off well, but before long it was clear that the hotel wasn't drawing enough customers to meet its costs. The band went home, and soon afterwards the Casa Loma venture folded. The building still stands, a monument to the follies of another age.

Things back in Detroit looked no more promising. Goldkette had over-extended himself, and various of his operations were in trouble. He'd never made back the four hundred thousand dollars he'd sunk into the Graystone Ballroom; the McKinney's Cotton Pickers band, into which he'd poured a lot of capital, hadn't yet begun to pay for itself; worse yet, the Victor Recording Orchestra, however musically rewarding, had proved a financial disaster—not least because its musicians, wedded to hot jazz, seemed unwilling to put on the kinds of shows (singing, novelties, comedy sketches) that had made Ted Weems and others so popular throughout the Midwest. In September of 1927, as recounted earlier, Goldkette closed the band down, giving Paul Whiteman his chance to snap up Beiderbecke, Trumbauer, Challis, and others.

If the Orange Blossoms were to stay in business and not be just another Goldkette casualty, they'd best try going it on their own. Among other things that meant taking on responsible management, establishing a distinctive musical profile and even a more glamorous image. They found the key to all these things in Spike Knoblauch.

Born June 7, 1906, in Metamora, Illinois, Glen Gray Knoblauch had learned saxophone while working days as a freight handler for the Illinois Central Railroad. By the time he joined the Goldkette office he was an accomplished journeyman musician and a fast and accurate music copyist. Smart, personable, he was tall (six feet, five inches), good-looking (wavy hair, radiant smile, William Powell moustache), and—perhaps most significant—he had a good feel for business. While friends bought on margin and played the bull market, he'd been quietly investing in such steady, proven winners as AT&T and putting his earnings away. He exuded confidence and common sense.

Among Spike's friends was Francis "Cork" O'Keefe, just getting started in the booking side of the Goldkette operation. By 1929 Cork had done well enough to move to New York and go into partnership with the visionary OKeh Records executive Tom Rockwell, who had produced the Armstrong Hot Five and Seven sessions, the McKenzie-Condon dates, and countless other landmarks. Their Rockwell-O'Keefe booking agency had become an overnight force in the band business.

Knoblauch (the name, often misspelled as "Knoblaugh" in print, is simply the German word for garlic) figured—correctly, it turned out—that the new agency would welcome a chance to handle a new, potentially hot band. He got in touch, and before long O'Keefe came up with a few bookings. Quickly renamed Goldkette's Casa Loma Orchestra (capitalizing, with official blessing, on both the Toronto job and the Goldkette cachet), the band played Young's Million-Dollar Pier in Atlantic City, a few nights in Pennsylvania, and wound up at New York's Roseland Ballroom under the nominal sponsorship of the young millionaire bandleader Roger Wolfe Kahn.

Along the way there were changes. Walter "Pee Wee" Hunt came over from another Goldkette unit to join Billy Rauch on trombone. Indiana-born cornetist "Dub" Schoefner, an avowed Beiderbecke idolator, joined the brass. But perhaps the most significant addition to the newly renamed orchestra was its banjo player and arranger, a soft-spoken Georgian named Harold Eugene "Gene" Gifford.

Gifford was something of a banjo virtuoso, able to play single-string solos with Harry Reser–like dexterity. But his true métier, it soon emerged, was arranging: trained as a draftsman, he had developed a concept of ensemble writing almost mathematical in its order and balance. He'd done a tough musical apprenticeship in the South and Southwest, playing with and writing for various white "territory" bands, including that of Blue Steele. He'd also led (and presumably arranged for) his own groups in Texas during the '20s.

He brought to his new job a style of ensemble writing that seems, at this early point, to have been little short of revolutionary: rather than an outgrowth of dance band arranging conventions developed by Ferde Grofé and others in the early '20s (and developed by many major pathfinders of the time), Gifford's Casa Loma scores sound, even on the band's earliest records, like swing arrangements. In their use of sections as antiphonal blocs, fused through call-and-response patterns into an ensemble sound, they look forward to the later '30s.

If records are to be trusted as evidence, few bands of either race had done much with this formulation at this time. The writing of Fletcher Henderson, Don Redman, and Benny Carter among the black arrangers, Bill Challis, Fud Livingston, and Glenn Miller among their white colleagues, was still either homophonic (all parts moving together to the same rhythm) or expanded from the polylinear concepts of the small Dixieland ensembles.

There is next to nothing in the hot dance band ensemble writing of 1929–30 to prepare a listener for the antiphonal chorus-building of "Casa Loma Stomp," or the last, all-in ensemble riffing of "White Jazz," brass and reeds interacting in a way that foreshadows the Goodman and Basie bands of 1937–39. "How is it," Gunther Schuller wrote of "Casa Loma Stomp," "that an obscure white guitar and banjo player, Gene Gifford, could create, . . . seemingly in one musical stroke, the full-blown progenitor of hundreds of swing-style offspring—in effect tantamount to the national anthem of 1930s jazz?"

Schuller goes on to hypothesize that Gifford's innovative style shows the influence of a black arranger, John Nesbitt, who played trumpet with McKinney's Cotton Pickers at the Graystone: "Since both men were working in Detroit for Goldkette-managed bands, and since Nesbitt's scores precede Gifford's by (in some cases) two and a half years, it is at least a supposition for further research that Gifford must have been strongly influenced by Nesbitt's work."[3]

But by his own account, based on documents submitted to critic Leonard Feather for the original edition of the Encyclopedia of Jazz and on statements to Down Beat and other magazines during the '30s, Gifford was traveling with Blue Steele during 1928 and most of '29, the period when Nesbitt was most active with the McKinney band. According to a "Hot Box" story by jazz chronicler George Hoefer in the July 2, 1947, Down Beat, Steele played the Graystone in 1929, at which time Gifford "made a connection with the Goldkette orchestra chain. He wrote arrangements that were circulated to all the Goldkette units."

"By the end of 1929," Schuller wrote, "the McKinney's Cotton Pickers' decline had become swift and alarming, as [Don] Redman turned the band more and more into a 'sweet' dance band, virtually unrelated to jazz . . . gradually even Nesbitt could no longer overcome the tawdry material he was assigned, his last good arrangement being of Fats Waller's 'Zonky' (in early 1930)."[4]

Schuller's niggling tone resembles that of scholar-historian Marshall Stearns, who, while praising Gifford in The Story of Jazz, suggests that the Casa Loma Orchestra could have taken its example from the 1932 Victor records of the great Bennie Moten band of Kansas City—ignoring both chronology and the unequivocal testimony of Eddie Barefield, saxophonist and arranger with Moten, that "we all admired the Casa Loma band, and tried to ape them."[5]

George Hoefer more plausibly asserts that, while with Steele, Gifford was surely aware of records by a wide range of groups, including the Goldkette Victor band, McKinney's, Sam Lanin, Ray Miller, and many others. Certainly the harmonic innovations of Fud Livingston made a deep impression on him, as they did on all arrangers of the late '20s, black and white. No one worked in a vacuum: in common with most of his colleagues, Gifford heard what was going on and incorporated what he chose to in his work.

(A 1947 Hoefer column connects Gifford to a Gennett date of April 22, 1929, issued under the name of pianist Johnny Burris, a Goldkette office regular. Sure enough, the band on "So Comfy" and "I'll Never Forget" sounds like Orange Blossoms in transition, with solos by Hunt, tenor saxophonist Pat Davis, and presumably cornetist Schoefner. The relatively straightforward arrangement seems to derive from Challis, who spoke of contributing scores periodically to the Casa Loma library beginning in its Detroit days; brass and sax section passages in "So Comfy" could easily be his work: yet the introduction and between-chorus interludes, the backgrounds to the clarinet and trombone solos, seem equally typical of Gifford's Casa Loma writing.)

The orchestra's first Okeh records under its own name (including "Happy Days Are Here Again," unluckily recorded on Black Tuesday, October 29, 1929) are less than impressive; the musicians sound tense, sometimes not quite in tune. Of the soloists, Schoefner comes off best, emulating Beiderbecke in the same slightly stilted manner adopted by Nesbitt on the McKinney records. Their "Sweepin' the Clouds Away," done February 6, 1930, features a good hot mellophone solo, also presumably by Schoefner.

But it's only on February 11 that things begin to come together. "China Girl," a 1924 relic written at the height of the *chinoiserie* craze, is recast as a hot instrumental. Billy Rauch, talking with Frank Driggs, recalled that the arrangement was his; whoever wrote it, it's polished work, and played with assurance. There are brief, competent solos by Hunt, an unidentified trumpeter, alto saxophonist Ray Eberle (no relation to the singer) and Pat Davis. But the focus is on ensemble teamwork: "China Girl" builds through its two final choruses with an increasingly layered sound, moving up steadily from the key of F (D-minor) to G (E-minor) to A♭ (F-minor). It never quite takes off rhythmically, hampered by bassist Stan Dennis's stolid bowing, but achieves intensity through attack and a sense of collective lift, which were to become Casa Loma hallmarks.[6]

"San Sue Strut," done at the same session, is another matter. A hot specialty related harmonically to "Sister Kate" and first recorded by New Orleans–born trumpeter Joe "Wingy" Manone, it becomes in Gifford's hands a primer and role model for big band riff writing down to the end of the decade. It is safe to say that, as of February 11, 1930, there was not another band in the United States playing arrangements of this character.

"San Sue Strut" is intricate, technically demanding, and flawlessly executed, bearing witness to the Casa Loma's reputation for tireless rehearsal. It builds as it goes, combining ensemble and solo voices, achieving variety through canny use of backgrounds. Of special interest are the question-and-answer patterns of choruses nine and ten, beginning with simple two-bar exchanges and escalating into ever-greater complexity.

This was not an ideal time to be launching a band, however good that band might be. One of the Depression's earliest and most visible casualties had been the entertainment business. Musicians who only a year or two before had lived comfortably off the proceeds of dances and parties were jostling one another for a limited number of staff jobs in the radio studios. Red Nichols, ever astute, formed and led pit orchestras for two Gershwin shows, *Strike Up the Band* and *Girl Crazy*, furnishing steady work for Benny Goodman, Gene Krupa, Glenn Miller, and a clutch of other jazzmen—many of whom returned the favor by vilifying him whenever the chance presented itself.

Things were leanest for touring bands. Even Paul Whiteman, who had dominated the 1920s with an orchestra sometimes numbering more than thirty instrumentalists and singers, was forced to cut his personnel to eighteen pieces in order to play New York's Roxy Theatre. Fletcher Henderson's pace-setting band, which had always worked regularly despite its leader's dilatory ways, made but four records in all of 1930.

With O'Keefe supplying bookings, the Casa Loma Orchestra took to the road. Said Knoblauch, "It was a matter of either staying in Detroit and building ourselves up or going to New York and doing our climbing right there in the big city. We chose the latter, and for three years barnstormed around the country." It wasn't any easier for them than for any other up-and-coming band of Depression days. Whether getting stuck in snowdrifts, blizzards howling around them, or being arrested on suspicion of bank robbery in Kentucky by overzealous state police, it was an arduous life.[7]

As cornetist Grady Watts remembered, though the band labored through 101 consecutive weeks of one-night stands between mid-1931 and mid-1933, morale remained high. "I think you can compare it very much to a young football team with a bunch of rookies," he told historian Ray Hoffman. "All good, and with good arrangements—blending together, enjoying each other's company. Good friends. And nothing was too tough for us to do because we wanted to hold it together and make it a success."[8]

There had been internal changes. Soon after reaching New York they'd fired Biagini, the Goldkette front man, for reasons having nothing to do with music. "It was Rockwell and O'Keefe who decided they didn't want [him] as the leader," Rauch told Ray Hoffman, "because he spoke with such an accent—'dese' and 'dose.' He really did that, [but] now that I look back at it, it probably wasn't as bad as it seemed."[9]

The musicians turned the band into a cooperative, with O'Keefe as business manager and Knoblauch—around this time he dropped the awkward surname and become plain Glen Gray—as president and leader. Frank Driggs, writing in 1970, summarized the corporation's structure and function with accuracy:

> The musicians shared the band's income equally, and as the band pros-
> pered their weekly shares increased. Because the corporation held salaries
> to a reasonable limit, it eventually had money left over after meeting all
> expenses. Any surplus was paid out in annual or semiannual dividends
> or invested . . . The stockholders met whenever necessary and wherever
> they happened to be to set rules like the fine ($50) for showing up for
> work drunk and to consider admissions of new members. Nobody got
> into the band unless he was someone the sidemen considered to be not
> only a first-rate instrumentalist but also personally congenial to the group.
> A writer of the period called Casa Loma "the band that's organized like
> a corporation and run like a college fraternity."[10]

Much of their work was in New England, under the benign aegis of brothers Sy (or Si) and Charlie Shribman. Owners of prominent dance pavilions and ball-rooms throughout the region, they helped many bands stay afloat and gave others their first breaks. Black and white bands alike benefited from regular employment at Shribman venues; all admired the brothers' honesty and the respect they brought to their dealings with musicians.

The Casa Lomans were improving, and their December 6, 1930, session, their last for OKeh, shows it. Schoefner evokes Bix on "Little Did I Know" with a long solo over a Challis-like sax section "carpet"; his plunger choruses on "Royal Garden Blues" recall King Oliver's famed "Dippermouth Blues" solo. Good, re-laxed ensembles and a smoother four-to-the-bar in the rhythm section dominate "Put On Your Old Gray Bonnet," which also sports an engagingly lusty vocal by Pee Wee Hunt.

But it is above all to "Casa Loma Stomp" that attention turns; even more than "San Sue Strut" it defines both the Casa Loma *sound* and Gifford's immense, even incomparable, contribution to jazz arranging. It quickly became something of an anthem, identifying the band to its public *and* creating a sensation among fellow-musicians. A publisher's "stock" version of the orchestration sold widely.

After a four-bar introduction kicked off by a sharply articulated Charleston figure (and dropped from later performances), the band launches into a sixteen-bar ensemble passage melodically derived from "Oh, Susannah! (Dust Off That Old Pianna)," establishing the sectional riff patterns individually and together. Hunt and Davis (trombone and tenor sax) solo buoyantly, the former sounding like a rough-hewn version of Miff Mole. A shift from B♭ down a step to A♭ begins a gradual buildup on a sixteen-bar sequence chordally identical to the trio strain of the '20s "dixieland" standard "That's a Plenty." (Later small-band performances of that repertoire staple returned the compliment by incorporating one of Gifford's riff choruses.)

After punchy solos by trumpeter Schoefner and clarinetist Eberle (the latter over an attractively percolating background figure), the ensemble drops to a well-executed *pianissimo* and builds steadily through a series of riff choruses, one of them incorporating a call-and-response pattern. It's easy to understand Bill Challis's comment that "those guys would rehearse and rehearse—then they'd take a break and go off and rehearse some more." That kind of drilling was necessary to execute arrangements as demanding as this, especially in a band which included some less-than-proficient sight-readers.

(The record sold well, a fact not lost on Columbia, which had absorbed Otto Heinemann's OKeh company in 1926. While keeping the Casa Loma OKeh in current issue, the company also reissued the same performance on its parent Columbia label under the name "Louis' Harlem Stompers"—backed, to compound the irony, by Fletcher Henderson's Orchestra playing white arranger Archie Bleyer's published stock orchestration of his rhythm specialty, "Business in F," based on the Casa Loma precedent. The company thus had it both ways: "Casa Loma Stomp" by both white and—nominally, at least—black bands, on sale at the same time.)

In later years, as other bands encroached on its territory, the Casa Loma Orchestra took to playing "Casa Loma Stomp" and the other Gifford instrumentals at ever faster tempos. Precision and energy always carried the day, but, listening to this first record, with its relaxed medium-tempo drive, it's clear that something was lost in the process of acceleration.

In the first week of May 1931, Bill Challis and Cork O'Keefe visited the orchestra during an engagement at Boston's Metropolitan Theatre. With them was Bix Beiderbecke, fresh back from a rest cure and looking fit, enthusiastic. It wasn't entirely a social call: Dub Schoefner had been a problem for some time, his drinking sufficiently out of control to warrant prolonged absence from the band during 1930. He was increasingly unreliable, and there was talk of dropping him. Bix, having left Paul Whiteman and washed out of *The Camel Pleasure Hour*, needed a job, and Challis was determined to find him one.

In retrospect, the idea of bringing him into the Casa Loma Orchestra to replace

345

an unreliable alcoholic trumpeter (one whose role model in this, as well as a musical sense, had been Bix) seems particularly daft. True, they all admired him, and for the moment, at least, he was on the wagon; it's understandable that Challis and O'Keefe might have looked to the Casa Lomans' discipline and camaraderie to keep him there.

Billy Rauch, among others, saw the danger and warned against the move. The Casa Loma was full of heavy drinkers, and, in Rauch's words, "every night was party night in our suite of rooms at the Metropolitan Hotel in Boston." Beiderbecke's newfound resolve wouldn't survive the first night.[11]

Bix was also dubious—but more on musical grounds. Never a strong section player, he feared the exacting rehearsals and technically demanding parts. The Goldkette and Whiteman orchestras had given him some section reading, but under quite different circumstances. Much of Challis's Goldkette book had been built around him; with Whiteman he'd been featured only on certain selections and had been given—at least before the orchestra began doing its regular Old Gold shows—ample time and assistance in working out his parts. As a Casa Loma member he wouldn't have that luxury and would be expected to pull his weight on every number.

Challis and O'Keefe were persuasive, and on Friday, May 22, 1931, Bix Beiderbecke joined the Casa Loma Orchestra. Though Rauch enlisted fellow-trumpeters Bobby Jones and Joe Hostetter in helping him through the first rehearsal, it was slow going. Bix found after-hours solace with Schoefner, who produced a jug— and the rest unfolded with a terrible inevitability. By the following Monday Bix was on his way back to New York. He died two months later.

By mid-1931 the orchestra was the talk of the band business. As Marshall Stearns put it, "virtually alone, they played swinging jazz—mixed with a large amount of engaging sweet music . . . on phonograph records, in ballrooms and on the air."[12]

Writer-historian James T. Maher, then a boy of fifteen, recalled being "utterly astonished" the first time he heard them on the radio. "I came on them by accident," he said. "I was just roaming the dial, and all of a sudden I heard this wonderful, exciting sound. I'd heard Duke Ellington's band, and that was my favorite—but this was different. They were so precise, and played with such tremendous verve. When they were finished I turned off the radio and covered my ears as I walked through the house; I wanted to go on hearing them in my head forever."[13]

At this historical remove, with so little left of the music business as it was at the dawn of the '30s, it's difficult to appreciate the full impact of the Casa Loma on dance bands nationwide. Musicians knew and appreciated the pioneering work of Ellington, Redman, Carter, Nesbitt, and other ranking black arrangers; a limited section of the public understood what Challis, Livingston, and others had accomplished in writing jazz arrangements for large groups of instruments. But it was left to the Casa Loma Orchestra to break through in a major way. It could dazzle listeners with the regimented perfection of the jazz instrumentals, then turn around within the same set and play smoothly scored ballads, highlighted by the strong baritone voice of Kenny Sargent.

"The band strove for perfection," said Hutchenrider. "We worked hard at it. For myself, I liked the ballads better than the flagwavers. But it was all very influential. Everybody was copying what we were doing."[14]

Certainly the influence of the Casa Loma—and of Gifford in particular—saturates dozens of records by black and white bands made between 1931 and 1935. It is clearly evident in the writing of Will Hudson for Fletcher Henderson ("Hocus Pocus"), Jimmie Lunceford ("White Heat"), and Benny Goodman ("Nitwit Serenade"), among others; the work of the Mills Blue Rhythm Band ("Harlem Heat") and the Bennie Moten Orchestra ("Toby," "Lafayette"); European bands led by Lew Stone in England and James Kok in Germany. Henderson himself recorded "Casa Loma Stomp"—less precisely than the originals, perhaps, but with undeniably greater swing.[15]

Henderson's star tenor sax soloist, Coleman Hawkins, made no secret of his admiration for the Casa Lomans. He's quoted by John Chilton, in *The Song of the Hawk*, as telling one friend they were "my favorite band" and recommending to another that he give them serious attention.[16]

"Serious attention" was the key. More than any other unit of its time, the Casa Loma Orchestra helped free dance bands, black and white, from their traditional secondary role as traveling vaudeville units, the very requirement that had helped undermine the Goldkette Victor Orchestra of the mid-'20s. For the first time, the music—and an inherent elegance of presentation—seemed to be enough: here was an ensemble which, in its faultless dress and demeanor, its dazzling "Wurlitzer Window" array of instruments, its ability to satisfy any dancer's wishes, was a show in itself. No group vocals; no vaudeville pratfalls or funny hats. Just music.

In March 1931, it switched to the Brunswick record label, re-recording both "Put On Your Old Gray Bonnet" and "Alexander's Ragtime Band." The three months since the OKeh versions had brought a sharp increase in confidence and poise. Intonation is more consistent, blend better, rhythm more secure. Hunt's feature, "When I Take My Sugar to Tea," establishes him as a genial jazz vocalist; the two final ensemble choruses of Gifford's up-tempo "White Jazz," fierce in their momentum, have not dated a bit.

That brand of excitement went down particularly well on the campuses of the big eastern colleges. "The college crowd—boy, it was maddening!" Rauch told Ray Hoffman. "We played Cornell thirteen times. They had some big dances up there with three name bands at once, and our band would be jumpin' so bad they'd have to stop us, to get the people to stop bouncing so!"[17]

The Casa Loma Orchestra was a sensation and easily dominated the big dance band field until the mid-'30s. At its peak it was discussed, admired, fought over, and often decried. The pages of *Down Beat*, *Metronome*, and other music business periodicals were full of news and heated opinion about them.

It was deliberately an ensemble band, though the soloists more than held their own. Cornetist Grady Watts, who joined with Hutchenrider, commanded a

347

firm if unspectacular middle-register solo style, which he demonstrates attractively on "Thanksgivin,' " a little-known Hoagy Carmichael tune. If Pee Wee Hunt, on trombone, lacked the eloquence of a Teagarden or the rip-snorting drive of a J. C. Higginbotham, he was nonetheless easily on a par with many others of the day, black or white, and an effective singer in the bargain. His two blues choruses on "Black Jazz," for example, are notable for their agility and drive. Hunt's sectionmate Billy Rauch commanded a range and technique rivaled at that time only by Tommy Dorsey's. His high F-concert at the end of Gifford's arrangement of "Smoke Rings" was one of the standards by which all trombonists of the '30s judged one another.

Pat Davis is a bit more problematic. His tenor solos on the early records, often stressing surface agitation at the expense of content and tone, led to his nickname "Honker" but are nonetheless effective in driving the performances, as his chorus on "Indiana" shows. On prolonged listening, particularly at medium tempos, Davis often seems to fit best among such black tenor men of the era as Albert "Happy" Caldwell and Prince Robinson, a star of McKinney's Cotton Pickers. Later he developed a more standard swing style, reminiscent of Charlie Barnet's tone and attack. Bandleader Les Brown, reminiscing in the '50s, praised Davis as a fine all-round player and even a convincing jazzman.

Beyond argument, Clarence Hutchenrider was the Casa Loma Orchestra's premier jazz solo voice. Born in Waco, Texas, June 13, 1908, he found his first musical inspiration in the records of two early white clarinetists, the Original Dixieland Band's Larry Shields and the Memphis Five's Jimmy Lytell.

"I first wanted to be a saxophone player," he said. "I got some brochures . . . and it just looked beautiful to me. And of course I'd heard [Rudy] Wiedoeft." His musical talents attracted the attention of three maiden aunts; they went en masse to a local bandmaster, who suggested that clarinet would be a better foundation than saxophone. So the boy began on an Albert system clarinet and soon also acquired an alto sax as well.

As a teenager, Hutchenrider barnstormed with bands around the Southwest and Texas, where he first heard the Teagarden brothers, Jack and Charlie. "In those days, Texas—west Texas especially—was pretty wild country, with more than a touch of the frontier about it," he said. "Everything was cars. No train rides. Just take off across the prairie, and have a few cans of beans in case you get hungry, because you're not gonna run into any all-night restaurants."

They heard lots of "territory" bands, he said, all of them white: the black bands, though working some of the same turf, seemed to exist in a parallel, separate world. "We just never crossed paths with them. It was funny: Sammy Price, the pianist, lived in Waco, where I grew up—but I never met him until many years later."[18]

While playing with the now-forgotten Larry Duncan band at the Washington Hotel in Shreveport, Louisiana, Clarence met and became friends with saxophonist-arranger Lyle "Spud" Murphy. They soon joined a band led by reed virtuoso Ross Gorman, who had made his mark by creating the opening clarinet glissando on George Gershwin's Rhapsody in Blue at its Aeolian Hall premiere.

Traveling with Gorman ultimately took them to Cleveland, where they both joined Austin Wylie during a long residency at the Golden Pheasant restaurant, on Prospect Avenue in the Playhouse Square theatre district. "A lot of my success in those days was due to Spud touting me to bandleaders," Hutchenrider told Ray Hoffman. "He would get into a band and then get me into it—or the other way around sometimes."[19]

Wylie's band was both a way station for musicians en route east and an incubator for up-and-coming talent, much of it recruited by Murphy. Among other Wylie alumni were trombonist Jack Jenney; trumpeters George Thow, Nate Kazebier, Billy Butterfield, and Dale "Mickey" McMickle; pianist Claude Thornhill; and multi-instrumentalist (and composer) Joe Bishop, the latter soon to be an anchor of the Isham Jones band. And, probably most important of all, Artie Shaw, whose chair Hutchenrider inherited. The Wylie band of 1929–30 never recorded, and that seems regrettable. With the excellent Murphy writing arrangements and the ranks full of able hot soloists, it appears to have been a musically fertile ensemble, one of several fine white regional units that have gone all but undocumented.[20]

From the moment Hutchenrider joined the Casa Loma Orchestra he played a dominant role, his gracefully fluent clarinet solos featured more and more. He shows peppery attack and much drive playing the blues on Gifford's "Black Jazz"; he's punchy and agitated on "Clarinet Marmalade," elegant on "Indiana." It's a singular style, which seems to owe little to either New Orleans or Chicago. Hutchenrider doesn't sound like Benny Goodman, though he often exhibits a comparable fluidity; nor Frank Teschemacher, despite a certain grittiness in his up-tempo work. Tonally he has reminded some listeners of Edmond Hall, though the resemblance seems superficial at best.

If Hutchenrider's work can be compared to any contemporary's, it is probably that of Kentuckian Matty Matlock, another alumnus of the territory bands active in the South and Southwest in the '20s and '30s. There are moments when the New Orleans master Sidney Arodin, who also spent time in some of these bands, sounds this way. A "white territory style" of hot clarinet? Could be: the subject is ripe for research.

Other fine Hutchenrider solos of this period include a full chorus on "Ol' Man River," two spots on "Copenhagen," and a thirty-two-bar essay on "Linger Awhile." He also takes two supple (and rather clarinet-like) baritone sax choruses on "I Got Rhythm," made December 30, 1933.

Around this time, Gene Gifford gave up his guitar chair, reportedly because he wanted to devote full time to writing arrangements. But statements by various Casa Loma men indicate that his increasing alcohol problem ("He really didn't want to do anything but get drunk," said Billy Rauch) had begun to affect his reliability. Jack (or Jacques) Blanchette, late of Isham Jones's orchestra, was his replacement.

The band made an eastern swing in mid-1933, highlighted by an extended engagement at Atlantic City's Steel Pier. O'Keefe had promoted it well, and the ballroom was loaded with college kids from Baltimore, Philadelphia, all over New

Jersey, and points as far distant as New York and Boston. Among them was writer–band historian George Piersol, who described his first impression of the band as "truly magnificent. Not only were all fourteen musicians impeccably groomed, but they were a collection of very good-looking men. This orchestra reeked with class."

Their playing, he added, was "both crisp and precise . . . The band programmed each set with versatility. They mixed such sentimental ballads as Kenny Sargent crooning 'I Love You Truly,' which brought squeals of delight from the female contingent in the crowd, to ending the set with a rousing 'killer diller' such as 'Maniac's Ball.' When the program ended, we all filed out of the Steel Pier convinced that 'Casa Loma Stomp' had become the collegiate national anthem!"[21]

That led to an equally successful appearance at the brand-new Glen Island Casino, on Long Island Sound in Mamaroneck, north of New York City, and thence to the Colonnades Room of Manhattan's fashionable Essex House Hotel, facing Central Park. The Casa Loma band was signed for regular appearances on NBC's *Camel Caravan* radio show, the first band to be regularly featured on a network commercial radio series.

By this time they had gained another outstanding soloist in trumpeter Sonny Dunham. A native of Brockton, Massachusetts, strong and technically assured, he could work easily in his high register, producing solos full of drama and brash excitement. He also doubled on trombone, affording Gifford the option of expanding that section to three. On "Wild Goose Chase," for example, Dunham picks up a trombone to join Rauch and Hunt in a fast and precisely executed trio passage which proved so popular that it appeared in exact transcription in the published stock orchestration.

Grady Watts stayed on in the trumpet section, taking an occasional solo. "Sonny was far beyond Grady in technique and range," said Hutchenrider, "but each one had his message," and Watts's quiet, shapely choruses provided good counterweight to the newcomer's grandstanding.

Dunham opens his own arrangement of "Chinatown, My Chinatown," recorded September 17, 1934, with eight blasting, annunciatory high concert B♭'s, as if marking out territory. His solos on this and on such other performances as "Ol' Man River" and "Walkin' the Dog" occasionally resemble the flashier side of Louis Prima and even Bunny Berigan, full of lip trills, sudden ascents to vertiginous high notes, dramatic bursts of volume and technique. But where Berigan achieves majesty, it might be said, Dunham most often seems to find grandiloquence. All the same, he adds excitement and *frisson* to many an arrangement, and his solo feature, "Memories of You," later became a hit record for the band.

Up-tempo flagwavers were hardly the sole basis of the Casa Loma's popularity. Gifford, if anything, had an even greater flair for ballads, drawing on a varied palette of instrumental colors. "That was the thing that never came through on the records," said James T. Maher. "In person they always came across with this wonderful depth and richness. The sheer *sound* of it was what got you. Sometimes he'd voice things with two trombones on top, a trumpet or two in the middle, and, say, bass clarinet or bassoon on the bottom. The result was something beautiful to hear, and sounded like no other band, at least in those days."[22]

An example is the January 31, 1933, recording of "Blue Prelude," a moody song in minor by Joe Bishop (with a rather self-pitying "Gloomy Sunday"–like lyric by Gordon Jenkins). Its opening chorus—muted trombone carrying the melody over darkly scored low clarinets, with plunger comments from the trumpet—sets a mood heavy with foreboding. As the arrangement develops, Gifford varies his textures, pitting solo voices against sections in ever-shifting variety. Even Hutchenrider's sixteen-bar clarinet solo seems ominous, punctuated by growls from Hunt's plunger-muted trombone.

Gifford's tone-painting reaches its zenith with his own "Smoke Rings," featuring Hutchenrider. "We were playing somewhere out Allentown way," the clarinetist recalled. "We had a night off. Gene [Gifford] called me up to his room. 'Bring your clarinet up,' he said. Well, he'd written out some notes. 'Here, play this melody.' He took his banjo and I played it. He scored it with Billy [Rauch] on lead, Pat [Davis] and me on clarinets under him. We didn't use it as a theme at first. At that point we were using 'Was I to Blame for Falling in Love with You,' a thing by Victor Young. But when we got the Camel show—well, it kind of seemed appropriate [as a theme song], wouldn't you think?"[23]

The most frequent complaints about the Casa Loma in those days were directed at its rhythm section. Blanchette apart, the other three—pianist "Joe Horse" Hall, bassist Stan Dennis, and drummer Tony Briglia—had been together as a team almost from the beginning. They knew how to work with the band, and the rest of the players liked them. "I really didn't think the rhythm section was a weak spot at the time," Hutchenrider said. "In fact, when we first heard them at Castle Farms, I remember thinking the rhythm was tremendous."[24]

But with the coming of new, looser forms of timekeeping, the more upright Casa Loma rhythm began to sound stilted, at least to some listeners. Hall's piano solo on the 1934 "Linger Awhile," moreover, seems curiously archaic, particularly compared with Teddy Wilson's elegant chorus on the Chocolate Dandies' "Once Upon a Time," recorded the previous October.

Briglia, too, seems to have been caught in a time warp, with Sid Catlett, Dave Tough, Chick Webb, Gene Krupa, and others changing the face of jazz drumming almost daily. Yet Buddy Rich, who would soon come to dominate the field, listened carefully to Briglia in those years. "He was a bitch," Rich told Leonard Feather, "because that band was a bitch. If you have ever listened to some of the things that they've made, you'll know that was the most together band ever."[25]

Rich elaborated in conversations with his friend, singer Mel Tormé. "They were so hot. And so hip! They wore tails at night," Tormé quotes the drummer as saying in *Traps: The Drum Wonder*. "My ambition was to meet that band. And particularly Tony Briglia. He never played hi-hats! Only press rolls on the snare drum. He was a bitch! I loved the way he played . . . They used to broadcast from [the Essex House] every night around eleven, eleven-thirty. I'd be sitting downstairs in our house, with a pair of brushes in my hand, ready to play. Kick it off, Glen! . . . I played along with them. I was hot! . . .'cause I knew all the charts. All of them!''[26]

Nor was he the only musician thus impressed. Trombonist Sandy Williams, reminiscing on his days with Chick Webb at Harlem's Savoy Ballroom, recalled that, with the exception of Duke Ellington, ''the only other band that gave us a headache was the Casa Loma band. I hate to say it, but they outplayed us. We used to have an arrangement on 'Chinatown' that featured Taft Jordan, and he'd end up on high C, or something like that. The Casa Lomans came in after we finished, playing the same tune, but their trumpet man [Dunham] started where we left off and went on up. And then they started swinging their tails off. That was a big letdown that night.''[27]

Grady Watts elaborated on matters of presentation. ''You put full dress suits on those boys and have them walk in, lots of class,'' he said. ''Then they'd sit down and get into some of those wild flagwavers—it would make for a great contrast.''[28]

By 1933 the billing had become ''Glen Gray and the Casa Loma Orchestra,'' though Gray himself was still in the sax section and violinist Mel Jenssen fronting. That was obviously not a situation that could last long. As one theatre manager, quoted by Frank Driggs, put it, ''I'm not paying thousands of dollars for Glen Gray and his Casa Loma Orchestra if he's not out there in front of the band where everybody can see him!''[29]

Eventually Jenssen left, and Gray—tall and handsome, but utterly inexperienced as a conductor—came out front. ''He was awful,'' said Grady Watts. ''It got so we wouldn't pay any attention to him.'' Saxophonist Art Ralston recalled that ''we would see that downbeat come down three seconds late, so we stopped following his lead, and eventually he started following us.'' All the same, Gray was a friendly, diplomatic man who seemed eternally able to smooth over potential conflict. In later years musicians spoke of him with fondness and affection.[30]

The Casa Loma Orchestra remained big news in the trade press. Throughout 1935 and '36 it seemed impossible to open a copy of Down Beat or Metronome and not find some prominently displayed article on their travels, records, or personnel. Lee Wiley, Connie Boswell, and Mildred Bailey, the three best white vocalists of the day (all three deeply admired by jazzmen), made a point of recording with them; the twelve-inch Boswell–Casa Loma record of ''Washboard Blues'' is still one of the best readings of the Hoagy Carmichael standard.

Yet for all the attention, they seemed unable to please the growing corps of writers for the jazz magazines. ''From the start,'' Albert McCarthy wrote in Big Band Jazz, ''the records of the Casa Loma Orchestra were poorly received by jazz enthusiasts, and, in over thirty-five years of reading the international jazz press, I can recall less than half a dozen favorable references to the band.''[31]

Typical was a front-page Down Beat blast by outspoken New Englander George Frazier, who would ''make no bones about my intense distaste for, not only the Casa Loma itself, but for all the meaninglessness it represents as well as for all those goops [sic] who seek to interpet that meaninglessness as something unfor-gettably spirited."[32]

But why such an animus for so accomplished, well-presented, and popular a band? Part of a reason may lie in the very scale of their success. Frazier's piece appeared little more than a month after the news that the Casa Loma Orchestra had taken in a record-breaking fifty-five thousand dollars in revenues for one week at New York's Paramount Theatre. Many writers have bridled, especially with the luxury of hindsight, at the disparity between the financial circumstances of this major white band and those of its black counterparts.

Anti–Casa Loma diatribes took many forms. Some concentrated on technical matters: Gifford's writing was too busy, too mechanical; the band's very precision made it seem soulless; the rhythm section didn't swing; the soloists, Hutchenrider and Dunham excepted, were undistinguished. Comparable criticisms, singly or collectively, could have been leveled at many other bands throughout the decade: at Goodman's (and Gene Krupa's) volume and brashness, Basie's ensemble slop-piness, Lunceford's militaristic precision, and even the sometimes random into-nation and phrasing of the Ellington band. But *tu quoque* isn't much of a defense—especially when something quite other is at issue.

Much early jazz journalism emanated from writers on the political left; what seems to have nettled many of them was the notion that a white band could have wielded such absolute influence over white and black bands alike. Add to this a desire to see jazz in general represented as a black creation, expropriated and exploited by whites, and the animus becomes only too comprehensible.

Even today, writers chronicling the development of big band jazz tend to ignore the pioneering work of Gifford and the Casa Loma Orchestra, minimize it, or dismiss it out of hand. Hsio Wen Shih, writing in the otherwise outstanding anthology *Jazz* (edited by McCarthy and Hentoff), deals at length with Henderson, Redman, and Ellington and touches on Lunceford, Bennie Moten, and Luis Rus-sell. No white band is mentioned. His underlying assumption seems to be, as enunciated by Hugues Panassié in *The Real Jazz*, that "there have never been any large white orchestras comparable to the Negro groups."[33]

Albert McCarthy was one of the few to deal seriously with the Casa Loma Orchestra. In *The Dance Band Era*, he observes: "It is the mechanical quality of the Casa Loma recordings that has attracted most criticism, and certainly *at times* [em-phasis added] the swing of the band sounds somewhat laboured, but the ines-capable fact is that for the early '30s these were remarkably advanced scores, and were played with an ensemble precision that was at the time virtually unique."

McCarthy is worth quoting further on Gifford's techniques: "A more valid criticism of Gifford's writing was that he frequently—but not always—failed to use riffs satisfactorily at the close, so that after a technically arresting opening and middle section there followed a succession of repetitive phrases that represented an anticlimax to what had gone before."[34]

For all the complaining, the Casa Loma Orchestra remained a fine, eminently marketable band, which looked as good as it sounded. They seemed, in James T. Maher's phrase, "like royalty." They could dazzle with virtuosity, and they could entertain. In the phrase of a later time, they "had it all covered." Why, then, should they not be popular?

"I still find the anti–Casa Loma attacks in the jazz press baffling and provoking," Maher declared. "All I can assume is that the writers were basing their criticism entirely on a few recordings. The band always sounded better in person: richer, even looser . . . They never felt that stiff on the job. I just don't think the jazz writers were listening closely. It wasn't Basie, but damn it, it swung in its own way. Buddy Rich was right!"[35]

As the orchestra developed, so too did its arrangements. Rhythm numbers displayed less and less reliance on simple riff patterns: such scores as "Avalon," "Stompin' Around," and "Chant of the Jungle" abound with unusual voicings and textures, dynamic subtleties mixed with exuberant shout passages.

By the end of 1934 the rhythm section had all but shed its old-fashioned clunkiness and was functioning as a smoothly integrated unit. Hall, Dennis, Blanchette, and Briglia continued to think of themselves only as a background team, discreetly supporting the ensembles and soloists and never coming forward, never drawing attention away from the horns or from the arrangement.

Though Hutchenrider was still the leading soloist, the others also had come far. Pee Wee Hunt's trombone solos, as his plunger chorus on the 1934 "Jungle Fever," were polished and versatile; Pat Davis had shed much of the honking agitation of his earlier work and moved smoothly into a deeper-toned style. Occasionally, as on "Who's Sorry Now?" (1935) he showed signs of having reciprocated Hawkins's attention.

"Avalon," in fact, tells a lot about the band's direction at this point. It consists of five choruses, played smooth and fast: the first, in concert E♭, features two muted trombones and bass clarinet in a clipped, tongue-in-cheek melody statement almost Ellingtonian in its attack and texture. The second moves to A♭ for an essay in pastel voicing, featuring cup-muted trumpet over three clarinets and bass clarinet. The third has the brass fanning their hats in a "doo-wah-doo-wah" pattern behind a Davis tenor solo. Hutchenrider gets the next one to himself, beginning with some Roppolo-like low-register comments and moving with poise through his middle and upper registers. Finally the band riffs things home in a beautifully executed diminuendo.

A shaped, even sculpted, quality in such performances sets the Casa Loma Orchestra apart from Goodman and others who rode the swing wave. The thrust is different: a Goodman performance of the same song, at the same fast pace, would have generated great excitement, with roof-raising trumpet by Berigan (or, later, Harry James), crowd-pleasing drumming by Gene Krupa, and a generous helping of virtuosic clarinet by the leader—all at substantial volume.

The Casa Loma performance is different, based on a more orchestral concept. Though it did its share of adapting to the conventions of swing, the Casa Loma Orchestra remained an entity apart, as surely as did—albeit in quite another way—that of Ellington.

"They had a very distinctive sound," said bassist Bob Haggart, who replaced

Stan Dennis for a week of *Camel Caravan* shows, in addition to his regular duties with the Bob Crosby band.

> It really opened my eyes. I found there was a whole lot more music to this band than the guys in our crowd had ever given them credit for.

> What I discovered was that all their charts were interesting, smooth, well rehearsed. Very complete. It was a real contrast with the Crosby band, which was basically an expanded jazz band. I don't know what other band you could compare them to. They were something, a law unto themselves. I remember the first time I heard some of those charts: things like "Dance of the Lame Duck" caught my ear. It's hard to explain—it was a fascinating concept, though I don't think I would have written that way myself, wouldn't have thought to make a band I was writing for sound that way.

> But they were so elegant. I don't know why this sticks in my memory, but I remember one of those broadcasts, just before we went on the air, there's Billy Rauch out in front of the band, up on this little box with his own microphone, ready to go into "Smoke Rings." He's standing there, waiting. All at once, he takes out his watch, a pocket watch on a fob, in his vest pocket—they all wore them—checks it casually and puts it back. Then sets himself to begin. You want to know the difference between their band and ours? There it was, right there.[36]

By mid-1936, Gene Gifford was off getting cured and Larry Clinton had come in as chief arranger. Ironically, some of the criticism directed at Gifford's work seems to apply better to such Clinton specialties as "Shades of Hades" (thematically related to both "The Dipsy Doodle" and "Bugle Call Rag"), "Zig Zag," and "Jungle Jitters," longer on repetitive riffs than on thematic content.

Yet Clinton's "A Study in Brown" (a mistitling apparently resulting from a recording executive's unfamiliarity with the expression "a brown study"), "Two Dreams Got Together" (ravishing unison clarinets), and the exquisite "Drifting Apart," with its play of textures and colors, show that Clinton had other dimensions. On "Drifting Apart," Rauch's singing tone leads a darkly scored combination of trombones and reeds, giving way to a particularly fetching, broad-toned contribution from Hutchenrider and a richly hued *tutti* in the "Smoke Rings" manner. Even the normally extroverted Pat Davis contributes eight thoughtful bars toward the end.

Clinton didn't stay long, particularly after Victor offered him a chance to record under his own name. His replacement, after a brief interregnum, was Oregon-born Larry Wagner. "Believe me," Wagner said in 1983, "when I say the Casa Loma band was the only band for me. I was 101 percent for Casa Loma and was just crazy about Gene Gifford's style. It was an honor for me to be asked to arrange for them. I lay their pace-setting nature, their popularity and importance, all to Gifford . . . He started that way of writing, and it was responsible, the way I hear it, for the whole scene that came later. You can hear patterns in the work of all sorts of arrangers who started out then that trace right back to Gene."

As a youngster growing up in the early '30s, Wagner said, he worshiped the Casa Loma Orchestra—bought its records, listened to it regularly on the radio. They were so well known that "you'd hear kids saying things like, 'Let's go home and listen to Casa Loma.' " And when he first arrived in New York, Wagner lost no time in getting to know Gifford.

"My gosh—to walk down the street with him was to be talked to by every music man everywhere in Tin Pan Alley. 'C'mon, Gene, I want you to hear this new tune.' 'C'mon, Gene, we need you to make this arrangement for us.' They were always after him, the music publishers."[37]

Gifford tended to make light of his arranging achievements, sloughing off compliments by claiming that what people perceived as innovations were merely solutions to problems occasioned by limitations in the band's instrumentation. "Sleepy Time Gal," for example, features a passage with the sonority of a trombone quartet but is actually Gray on baritone joining trombonists Rauch, Hunt, and a newcomer, Murray McEachern. Canadian born, equally skilled on trombone and alto sax, McEachern had come over from Benny Goodman's band; he brought impressive technical mastery and a warm lyricism, both of which are displayed magnificently in his full-chorus "Sleepy Time Gal" solo.

Though Goodman and others had cut deeply into the Casa Lomans' market (Benny's band replaced them on the *Camel Caravan* radio show in 1936), the orchestra remained popular, with a knack for holding onto its fans. "This was the greatest band in the country for making friends," saxophonist Art Ralston told Frank Driggs. "Whenever we'd go into a town, the guys would call up the people they had met the first time they were there, and those people never forgot it . . . During the eight years I was with the band, I never remember a dance we played that wasn't absolutely packed, and [at] most of them they had to turn people away from the door. This is all through the time when Goodman and the others were riding high, too."

Most of the time, Larry Clinton added, the welcomes were so enthusiastic that "none of the guys ever had to eat in restaurants, and often they slept in private homes."[38]

And, as such scores as Wagner's "No Name Jive," from 1940, amply illustrate, the Casa Lomans had no difficulty with the vocabulary of some of the other, black-influenced, swing bands. This is a blues, one of the few recorded by the band, a series of riff patterns taking up both sides of a ten-inch 78 rpm record and featuring adept solos by Hutchenrider on clarinet, McEachern on alto sax, Watts and Cy Baker on trumpet, and—unexpectedly, a brief, gutty Hutchenrider encore, this time on tenor sax.

Why tenor? "Hard to say," Wagner said. "He probably did it on the job one night and it sounded so good that the guys said, 'Hey, let's do it that way all the time.' He used Danny D'Andrea's tenor on the record—didn't own one himself."[39]

"No Name Jive" sold well, giving the Casa Loma Orchestra a major swing hit. It's particularly interesting to note the degree to which the rhythm section has smoothed out its concept, laying down a rocking swing 4/4 under solos and ensembles.

By 1938 the Casa Loma library boasted swing arrangements by Deane Kincaide, Jimmy Mundy, and Red Bone, alongside scores by Wagner and Dick Jones and the old Gifford favorites. All the same, Glen Gray understood that trying to compete solely as a swing band in a field dominated by Goodman, Charlie Barnet, the Dorsey Brothers, Basie, Ellington, Artie Shaw, Jimmie Lunceford, and numerous others would have amounted to musical suicide. At best, the Casa Loma would have found itself forever trying to keep up, chasing the trends.

Instead, wisely, the band drew on a duality that had been in place from its inception, emphasizing its ballad, or "sweet," side. The band business of the 1930s, with its arbitrary (and too often mindless) division into "hot" and "sweet," categories, offered some intriguing options to the enterprising leader. The "sweet" category was actually something of a misnomer: it might more accurately have been labeled the "not strictly for the swing fans" category. Paradoxically, it offered greater diversity of style and texture: more than a few of the major "sweet" bands, quite able to hold their own on the jazz numbers, chose not to be judged solely by them.

Most chroniclers of the period, particularly those with a pronounced jazz bias, have ignored this marketing distinction, or just missed it. In Albert McCarthy's words: "The trade papers and fan magazines of the day enthusiastically supported the swing bands and tended to condemn the others, but such a blanket dismissal of the 'straight' dance bands is manifestly unfair"—and badly skewed history into the bargain.[40]

Overall, the distinction worked in the Casa Loma Orchestra's favor, allowing it to compete—or not compete—on various fronts. Casa Loma led the "sweet band" category in *Metronome*'s 1939 readers' poll; yet the same year the orchestra recorded an outstanding Hoagy Carmichael album with Louis Armstrong as guest soloist, and Sonny Dunham wound up beside Bunny Berigan and Harry James on the first Metronome All-Star swing band recording session.

George T. Simon, who organized and supervised the date, recalled that "none of the other guys on the session—[Tommy] Dorsey, Jack Teagarden, Eddie Miller, and the rest—really knew Sonny. Somehow the Casa Loma was a thing apart, its own closed little circle. They didn't hang out with anyone else; they weren't on the scene. So Sonny kept to himself—and from the flashy way he played on 'Blue Lou,' after Bunny had soloed, I got the impression he was trying to prove something. A kind of attitude, as they say today."[41]

Other accounts reinforce the sense of insularity implied in Simon's account. Asked why Casa Loma musicians didn't appear as freelancers on records done for other leaders in the '30s, Hutchenrider laughed. "I did a record date—I no longer remember who with—but it was frowned on in the band, on account of us being a corporation. We were gonna try to keep the sound within our circle, you know, so we gave up on doing any outside work."[42]

This extended to after-hours jamming and hanging out as well, and it seems regrettable. Not only were Hutchenrider, Hunt, Watts, Dunham, and the others excellent musicians who would have fit comfortably into any number of recording units, but it seems likely that exposure to a wider variety of styles would have helped offset a certain inbred quality discernible in some of their work.

The Casa Loma Orchestra remained popular until World War II, when a combination of the draft, thinner bookings, a recording ban, and the lure of network studio jobs depleted its personnel. Gray carried on, traveling and recording with some excellent new men; cornetist Bobby Hackett was briefly a member, recording the striking "If I Love Again" in late 1944; Red Nichols came and went, as did guitarist Herb Ellis, trombonist-arranger Ray Conniff, and others.

But they finally called it a day in 1947, with the exception of an ill-advised eight-month comeback bid three years later. Spike retired to his home in Plymouth, Massachusetts (he, Hunt, and trumpeter Joe Hostetter had married Plymouth girls), emerging in the mid-'50s to collaborate with Larry Wagner on LPs of big band re-creations for Capitol Records, using crack Hollywood musicians. He died of cancer, age fifty-seven, in 1963.

Pee Wee Hunt had a pair of unexpected record hits with deliberately tongue-in-cheek Dixieland versions of the old chestnuts "Twelfth Street Rag" and "Oh!" Clarence Hutchenrider freelanced around New York as an admired and consistently sought-after jazz clarinetist until his death, at eighty-three, in 1991. Sonny Dunham, after leading his own bands for several years (including an ill-concealed half-life as one of the few known gay musicians in the jazz business of the time), retired to a trailer in Florida, playing occasional jobs on trombone and railing bitterly about the injustices of the music business. He died on June 18, 1990.

Beyond argument, the Casa Loma Orchestra was the most influential white band in the United States between 1930 and 1935, and the band which, in Glen Gray's words, "made swing commercial." It is, as Albert McCarthy has suggested, "forward-looking, adventurous," linking such hot dance bands of the '20s as Goldkette's and Pollack's with the swing bands that dominated the industry from mid-decade on. Its spirit, its level of musicianship, and the quality of its arrangements set a standard for bands of both races which can only be admired—and ought never to be ignored or belittled.[43]

Certainly, as Gunther Schuller proposes in The Swing Era, the Casa Loma Orchestra should "in the future be accorded more than the condescending footnote it has had to be contented with in the past."[44]

15

Dorseys
and Boswells

I t's not that they didn't love each other. They did, with a loyalty that knew neither stint nor exception. But whatever force bound Jimmy and Tommy Dorsey together as brothers came fully outfitted with tripwires and triggers.

They fought. All the time. Anywhere and at the slightest provocation. Invariably one would take a poke at the other, and they'd scrap right there, onstand or off, like kids in a sandlot.

For a while every musician who'd ever worked with or for either brother seemed to have a favorite account of some epic brawl between them. As such stories will, they've survived both subjects and tellers; more than a few now have about them the exaggerated knockabout violence of a Tom-and-Jerry cartoon.

At root, it remains more than a little mysterious. Two brothers, both extravagantly gifted, both highly charged; two contrasting temperaments, one mercurial and explosive, the other restrained; two personalities, one blunt and outspoken, the other guileful, indirect. Together, in the same business. In the same studio. On the same stand. United and divided.

Not, overall, a formula for collaboration. Yet Tommy (1905–56) and Jimmy (1904–57) Dorsey launched their first bandleading partnership on records in 1928, and six years later were confident enough of it to give it a try in the rough-and-tumble world of ballrooms, buses, and bandstands.

To be sure, that venture didn't last long. A quarrel, reportedly over nothing more consequential than a tempo, ended it abruptly in 1935. But while it lasted it produced some extraordinary music. There are many, fans and fellow-musicians alike, who still cite the Dorsey Brothers Orchestra as one of the most musical and original of the early 1930s.

Though both are now remembered as bandleaders and virtuoso instrumentalists, Jimmy and Tommy Dorsey made their first reputations as jazz soloists, in the vanguard of New York's hot music scene of the late '20s and early '30s. Neither has done particularly well at the hands of jazz writers and chroniclers. The word most often applied to Jimmy is "technician"—as though his facility on the alto saxophone, widely admired by white and black musicians of the day, were all he had to offer. The fact that Tommy, on trombone, chose to emphasize his lustrous ballad playing is widely viewed as an admission that he couldn't cut it as a hot trombonist. For both brothers the reality is more complex; in Tommy's case, it is symptomatic of a fascinating musical dichotomy.[1]

Jimmy Dorsey was born February 29, 1904, in Shenandoah, fifty miles south of Scranton in the heart of Pennsylvania coal country. His brother Tommy came along November 19 of the following year, when the family was living in nearby Mahanoy City. They then moved to Lansford, where Dorsey senior led a concert band and gave music instruction to local children—including cornet lessons for both his sons. It was a musically rich area, full of town bands, concert bands, and small dance orchestras, and by the time the boys were in their teens their reputations as up-and-coming talents—Jimmy on the clarinet, Tommy the trombone—had spread.

They worked together with the Scranton Sirens, a seminal "territory" band (discussed more fully elsewhere in this volume) and incubator for topflight professionals. They were together with Jean Goldkette in Detroit, with the California Ramblers in New York, and a bit later (if briefly) with Paul Whiteman.

"Jimmy went first and then sent for Tommy" was the way their mother described it to writer Amy Lee in 1940. "That's the way it's always been. Whenever Jimmy joined a band he'd always tell the leader about the kid brother, the trombone player."[2]

Tommy would come, and they'd be together again, at least for a while. No one—not their mother, not their colleagues or close friends—ever quite understood the dynamic between them. When they were together Tommy was "Mac," Jimmy "Lad." Their mutual devotion was beyond question; so, too, were the battles, which could erupt, it seemed, over any trifle.

"We were working for Sam Lanin at Roseland" was how saxophonist Arnold Brilhart began one of his familiar "you should have seen 'em" anecdotes. "Jimmy came in with a brand-new Selmer saxophone. Well, somebody said something, and before you know it they're on the floor, a real knock-down, drag-out fight right there on the stand. Tommy—I'll never forget it—Tommy got up and jumped all over Jimmy's brand-new saxophone. Made scrap metal of it. Jimmy grabbed his brother's trombone and just wrapped it around his knee, slide and all. Ruined it."

But woe betide the man who tried to intervene. "It didn't matter whose side you took," said Brilhart. "If you tried to separate them they'd gang up on you together and beat the blazes out of you. They just had to be left alone to fight their own fight in their own way."[3]

Cornetist Jimmy McPartland was one of those rash enough to try to referee a Dorsey scrap. "I was pretty tough in those days," he said in a 1983 conversation. "But when it came to those two guys—they both jumped all over me. And all I was tryin' to do was separate 'em, for Pete's sake, before they killed each other!"[4]

By 1928, the brothers' versatility, technique, and reading skills had placed them among the busiest of New York's first-call radio and recording musicians. It was hardly unusual for one man to do as many as fifteen radio shows a week and maintain a full recording schedule. As Jimmy recalled it, "Sometimes, when we finished a broadcast, a lot of us would get up, dash down the hall, and take our places in another orchestra starting the next program."[5]

Inevitably, a certain amount of this work involved hot jazz. Unlike many of the young firebrands then arriving from Chicago and other points south and west, Jimmy and Tommy Dorsey hadn't taken up their horns just to play hot choruses on them. They hadn't done musical apprenticeships in the sorts of cabarets and dance halls that nurtured the "play-hot-or-croak" spirit in the breasts of the newcomers.

But they'd done their listening and learning. Both belonged to a tight circle of jazz players which also included Red Nichols, Miff Mole, Adrian Rollini, Joe Venuti, and Eddie Lang. Regular visitors uptown, they'd spent many an evening listening to Louis Armstrong and to the orchestras of Fletcher Henderson, Charlie Johnson, and the rest. Each, moreover, had played and recorded with Bix Beiderbecke, patron saint of the young "Chicago jazz" zealots.

Of the two, Jimmy was in those days the more influential, combining prodigious technique with a flair for the unexpected—unusual intervals, a way of suggesting harmonies well beyond what his accompanists might be playing. "He was the pace-setter, he and [Frank] Trumbauer," said Iowa-born Eddie Barefield, who made his substantial reputation as a saxophonist-arranger working with Bennie Moten, Cab Calloway, Henderson, Chick Webb, and other major black bands of the '30s.

"If you wanted to keep up, you followed those two guys. You didn't think, 'Are they white, are they black'—or 'colored,' as we called it then. They were the ones doing the most interesting stuff; that's all we cared about." Jimmy Dorsey's solo on the "Tiger Rag" chords, recorded several times between 1926 and 1936, was widely imitated. A transcription appears elsewhere in this volume.[6]

Tommy, too, was admired. Working within the nimble style perfected by Miff Mole, he's recognizable on countless records, playing solos with a genial, slightly gruff tone. His chorus on the California Ramblers' "I Ain't Got Nobody," done in 1928 for Edison, is understated, even a bit ironic; on "St. James Infirmary," done for Columbia in 1930 under the leadership of pianist-songwriter Rube Bloom, he shows that he'd been listening seriously to Jack Teagarden as well as Mole.[7]

Dorsey's trombone solos are at all times the work of a smart, versatile musician; cleanly executed, musical, they speak in an instantly recognizable voice. Yet it's been consistently suggested in print that "Mac" was not really a jazz trombonist. Even as perceptive a commentator as Gunther Schuller declares that "there is hardly a jazz solo or background obbligato during the 1928 to 1932 period on which Dorsey does not run into some note trouble, what musicians call 'fluffs' or 'clams.' " He claims to hear a "sense of uncertainty and lack of melodic invention" in Dorsey's trombone solos.[8]

Dorsey solos on scores of records made in that period, under a wide assortment of leaders, show the inaccuracy of such pronouncements. As for "clams," it would be instructive to see such revered black soloists as trumpeters Rex Stewart and Jabbo Smith taken so sternly to task on the basis of fluffed (or just wrong) notes, or lapses in melodic invention. In truth, few brassmen of the era are as free of such blemishes as Tommy Dorsey.*

His trombone, in fact, is like a character actor in an early movie: reliable, familiar, always part of the team. And that's where matters might stand—until one further element is factored into the equation. That is Dorsey's trumpet work, powerful and distinctive enough to force a listener to listen to the trombone from a new perspective.

Tommy Dorsey the trumpet soloist is everything the trombonist is not: rough, rugged, passionate, badgering his way to center stage with a style animated by the example of Louis Armstrong. Dorsey's trumpet solos on late-'20s records can startle with their urgency. He opens the Dorsey Brothers' "My Melancholy Baby" on trombone, setting out the melody in no-nonsense fashion. Then, when he picks up a trumpet for a break into the verse, things get really interesting. Where his phrases on trombone were rounded, balanced, on trumpet they seem torn out of him, hot and stabbing.

Paul Whiteman was between hot trumpet soloists when, in mid-1927, he had Tommy Dorsey deliver two pungent four-bar trumpet solos, muted, and a Louis-like cadenza, open, at the end of "It Won't Be Long Now." It arrests attention, not least because it sounds, in its barely controlled intensity, like no other hot trumpet player—white, at least—making records at the time.

But it was little more than a preview of coming attractions, as borne out by the Dorsey trumpet solos recorded for OKeh at two sessions under his own name, in late 1928 and April 1929, and a third under Eddie Lang's name a month later. Using a straight mute in the opening chorus of Perry Bradford's "It's Right Here for You," Dorsey announces the melody in brusque phrases, tone throbbing with a fast, intense vibrato. With Lang laying down his customary full accompaniment and Arthur Schutt wheezing away endearingly on a studio harmonium, Tommy Dorsey is quite a commanding presence.

There's no doubt these solos are the work of a well-developed hot sensibility,

*For examples of Dorsey's hot trombone playing in this period try "Dust," recorded April 21, 1930, under Ben Selvin's name; "He's So Unusual," for Fred Rich, November 15, 1929; or, perhaps best of all, his excellent, ferocious solos on two 1931 versions of "When I Take My Sugar to Tea": the Sunshine Boys, on February 23, and the Boswell Sisters, on March 19, 1931.

an impression emphasized with startling force on "Bugle Call Rag," with Lang. The rhythm section—Lang, Schutt, Joe Tarto on string bass, and Stan King on drums—generates a loose 4/4 drive as Dorsey solos first (clam-free, it might be noted) on trombone. Leo McConville's trumpet chorus is out of Bix by way of Nichols—melodic, clean of line and tone, played by a musician whose gifts as an improviser, like those of his friend and fellow-trumpeter Manny Klein, were often obscured by his prowess as an all-purpose studio musician.

After Schutt's piano solo, it's Dorsey on trumpet—with a vengeance. Abrupt, guttural, he cuts and slashes, singlehandedly transforming a jaunty performance— if only for a moment—into a near-riot. Something quite different, even revolutionary, is afoot here.

An Armstrong flavor saturates Dorsey's long, rangy D-minor trumpet solo on the slower "Hot Heels"; he's clearly thinking about Louis's 1926 "King of the Zulus," all the way up to a spectacular high concert F. It's messy, emotionally unbuttoned, dripping blues feeling—and quite exciting. With the exception of Jack Purvis, whose style was not fully formed before 1929, Dorsey seems to have been the only white trumpeter during the '20s to have traveled this path.[9]

"Tommy loved Louis," said drummer Ray McKinley. "I remember one time—it was just before I went into the service in World War II—I visited him out in California, in Los Angeles. Here we were sitting in a booth at the Brown Derby, with all these movie stars around us, singing Louis's choruses to each other—you know, trying to top each other. We both knew 'em note for note. All those other people were looking at us as though we were crazy."[10]

On the strength of these late-'20s trumpet solos it seems regrettable that Dorsey all but forsook the instrument, at least on records, in the following decade. Now and then, late in a ballroom date, he'd borrow Bunny Berigan's (or Pee Wee Erwin's, or Ziggy Elman's) horn and knock off a chorus or two. But with the exception of one 1937 Clambake Seven title, and "Back to Back," in 1939, he never recorded on trumpet again.[11]

Yet here, unmistakably, is the key to Tommy Dorsey as a jazzman: his work on trombone, polished and consistent, seemed more and more an index of his professional musicianship, its very evenness of temperament guaranteeing it could fit in anywhere, play any role, with verve and bonhommie. Not a particularly original hot trombone soloist (any more than Claude Jones, Sandy Williams, and Jimmy Archey are particularly original trombone soloists), he is nevertheless (as they were) a fine one. The near-universal regard in which he was held throughout the '30s—and not merely a matter, as Schuller would suggest, of ballad phrasing and breath control—attests to that. His solos on "Honeysuckle Rose," from the "Jam Session at Victor" date (1937) and on "Beale Street Blues," "Mendelssohn's Spring Song," and "Milenberg Joys" with his own band leave no doubt that he could swing hard and authoritatively when the need arose.

But the trumpet, as heard on a surprising number of late-'20s records, cuts closer to the temperamental core of the man who, for his public's (and his own musical) sake, became the "sentimental gentleman of swing." Impulsive, hot-tempered, sarcastic, equally disposed to thoughtless cruelty and great generosity, he seemed, on trumpet, to be playing no role but himself. It only takes hearing his caustic, thrusting horn on "Forgetting You" (1928) to know Tommy Dorsey well.

Together on a New York radio program in 1978, former Dorsey sidemen Pee Wee Erwin, Carmen Mastren, and Johnny Mince discussed their former boss at length and with candor. How was Tommy rated as a jazz trombonist? Mastren laughed: "He rated himself. He used to tell me, 'I never played anything original in my life. Everything I play is Miff Mole.' "

"In truth, he was a better jazz trumpet player than jazz trombone player. He loved to play trumpet," said Erwin. "Played it quite a bit with the band. On the last set he'd go back there in the brass. There wouldn't be too many people in the crowd. He'd say, 'Lemme have your horn, Harve.' He called everybody 'Harve.'

"He didn't have the facility on trumpet, and that limited him. As a trombone player he was technically the very best. I'm a brass player, and I'll tell you, that man had one of the best air columns I've ever seen. It was unbelievable: the control he had was phenomenal."

(Marcel Tabuteau, revered oboist of the Philadelphia Orchestra, reportedly advised his chamber music classes at Curtis Institute to listen closely to "Tom-mee Dor-see." The trombonist's sense of phrase, his control of his air column, were a textbook example of how a wind instrument should be played. Others hailed Dorsey's skills at sight-transposition, pitch placement, and singing tone. Arranger-conductor Frank Black once told a reporter that Dorsey was one of four players—the others were Jack Jenney, Will Bradley, and the lesser-known Jack Lacey—responsible for changing the American approach to the trombone.)[12]

Carmen Mastren chimed in. "Trombone players would come to him and say, 'How do you do this, Tommy, how do you do that?' So he'd pick up his horn and do it. That's not to say any of 'em would learn that way, because they couldn't ever do it the way he did. Yet when it came to jazz, all he could talk about was Miff Mole and Jack Teagarden."[13]

"[But] in truth," said Erwin, "all that tremendous technique on trombone probably limited his true jazz feeling. On trumpet he had real limitations, and as a consequence he'd play rhythmic as all getout. Punchy, a good brand of jazz. And he blew hard." There's every indication that Tommy Dorsey, ever the prag-matist, understood the great potential of his trombone mastery and manipulated it in the interests of professional success. But if he is to be evaluated accurately as a hot music figure, both sides of this fractured musical personality must be known and appreciated.

Jimmy Dorsey's case is somewhat different. Schuller vouchsafes that Jimmy's clar-inet playing on his 1929 "Praying the Blues" is "remarkably beautiful" and "authentic" and goes on to wonder, "If he could produce one such distinguished, convincing true sample of jazz, why not more often?" The comment may say less about Dorsey's skill as a jazzman, alas, than it does about the writer's listening experience.[14]

"True samples of jazz" abound on the numerous records made by the elder Dorsey throughout the late '20s and early '30s. It takes only a hearing of his alto on "Alice Blue Gown" with Nichols, his clarinet on the aforementioned "Bugle Call Rag," his nimble baritone opening the Venuti-Lang "I've Found a New Baby," to realize that.[15]

Visiting London with Ted Lewis in 1930, Dorsey did a solo date with a rhythm section organized by English composer-arranger Patrick "Spike" Hughes: it's as good an index to his worth as a jazzman as can be found. He opens "After You've Gone" on clarinet, plumbing his instrument's *chalumeau* register in a lovely, ruminative melody statement that carries on behind Alan Ferguson's Lang-like guitar solo. On "Tiger Rag" he tosses off some nimble, Jimmie Noone–like clarinet figures, then switches to alto for a disquisition that culminates, on one of two issued takes, in his oft-quoted set piece solo.

But Dorsey is perhaps most impressive on "St. Louis Blues": playing clarinet throughout, he builds steadily from a delicate, thoughtful opening through a succession of choruses, undeterred even by Bill Harty's intrusive drumming. No shortage of "convincing true samples of jazz" here.

A factor that seems to have hampered appreciation of Jimmy Dorsey's jazz skills is a certain partiality for virtuoso effects, notably the kind of double-and triple-tonguing so evident on the 1930 "I'm Just Wild About Harry" with Red Nichols and 1933's "Pink Elephants" with Venuti. This sort of alto playing enjoyed great popularity in the '20s, embraced by all technically equipped saxophonists, regardless of race. According to the late Eddie Barefield, he and Otto Hardwick, of Duke Ellington's orchestra, were especially adept at the game; Barefield's solo on the 1934 Cab Calloway recording of "Moonglow" more than substantiates the point.[16]

But Schuller errs when he cites such Dorsey showpieces as "Oodles of Noodles" and "Beebe" as "flashy Wiedoeft-style solo numbers . . . which were at a considerable remove from anything one might call jazz." A touch of Wiedoeft, yes, but both "Beebe" and the up-tempo section of "Oodles" (basically a blues with an eight-bar release) draw clearly and unequivocally on a jazz vocabulary:

(continued)

"Oodles of Noodles," opening strain.

Its slow center section, a melody of commanding beauty, later became Dorsey's theme song, "Contrasts."

"Oodles of Noodles," middle strain.

Schuller concludes his dissection of Jimmy Dorsey's playing with the curious declaration, "By the early and mid-thirties the Wiedoeft influence [in Dorsey] had been partially replaced by a sincere admiration for Johnny Hodges"—albeit, he hastens to add, a pallid, imitative one. This is nonsense: Dorsey appears to have been almost alone among those saxophonists of his age *not* extensively affected by the Wiedoeft approach and its violin-based techniques. He was one of the few alto saxophonists of his time who did not come to the instrument by way of the violin but rather from the cornet; it is hardly a quantum leap of imagination to hear his annunciatory, bright-toned playing and attack as legacies of these brass-instrument beginnings.

Any notion that Dorsey, like a repentant sinner, forsook his prior ways in a futile atttempt to emulate Hodges collapses with a hearing of recordings by the two men. There was no need for Dorsey to alter his basic approach: while he knew and respected Hodges, Benny Carter, and the other premier black saxophonists, Jimmy Dorsey had staked out territory of his own. On musical grounds alone there is no reason to suppose he would relinquish it.

"Everybody listened to him and Trumbauer," saxophonist Eddie Barefield declared. "We wrote out his 'Tiger Rag' solo from the Whiteman record [see "Sensation Stomp" transcription, chapter 7] in four-part harmony and played it that way. He was just as much admired by black musicians as by white; though a lot of the black musicians went for Trumbauer because of his style, Jimmy was in some ways just as good."[17]

Despite the often volatile chemistry between them, the Dorsey brothers invariably wound up working together—and in 1928 they tried their hand at a jointly led band. The "Dorsey Brothers Orchestra" was a recording unit only, drawn from the New York studio pool for a series of dates at OKeh. Its champion and guardian angel was recording director Bob Stephens, a Pennsylvania trumpet player the brothers had known since Scranton Sirens days.[18]

Though the first Dorsey records are largely uneventful dance band efforts, they still have the capacity to surprise: "Breakaway," for example, has emphatic trombone and trumpet by Tommy (as well as a fine opening trumpet solo by Leo McConville), alto and clarinet by Jimmy. Bing Crosby takes a guest vocal on "Spell of the Blues," and arranger Glenn Miller uses an introductory figure later recycled in his excellent "My Kinda Love" score for Ben Pollack; the final tutti, trumpets punching over unison trombones and Jimmy's clarinet playing a counterline, is a highlight. "My Melancholy Baby" offers not only Tommy's swashbuckling trumpet but generous solo space for Adrian Rollini's bass saxophone.

All these performances benefit from the buoyant rhythm of California Ramblers veteran Stan King, drummer of choice on countless New York hot record dates of the '20s. "The Dorseys worshiped him," said singer Joey Nash, who knew King well. "But he was a terrible drunk, always stank of booze . . . He hated authority, particularly bandleaders, but he was such a good drummer that they'd put up with him."[19]

Unlike drummer Vic Berton, King didn't read music. But his natural drive, allied with a quick ear, more than compensated for this lack. It's King who whips up the rhythm section behind Tommy's trumpet lead on "Bugle Call Rag" or sends "Man From the South," by Rube Bloom's Bayou Boys, careening through its final moments. Also a fair hand with novelty effects, he developed a device he called the slapstick, described by Dorsey chronicler Herb Sanford as a small plank, split and hinged. King would wave it up and down in rhythm, open and back, producing a resounding "thwack!" on beats two and four of each bar.[20]

By 1932, OKeh was bankrupt, and Bob Stephens had gone to work for Irving Mills, running recording sessions at Brunswick; not surprisingly, he came through with some dates for the Dorseys. Small budget, small band: just Tommy and Jimmy, plus Larry Binyon on tenor and old cronies King, guitarist Dick McDonough, pianist Fulton "Fidgy" McGrath, and Artie Bernstein on bass. On trumpets were all-rounder Manny Klein and a kid from Wisconsin who had come to New York two years before and established himself as the most commanding and versatile of soloists. Bunny Berigan seemed to have everything: strength, limitless endurance, a huge, singing tone. His hot solos fused Beiderbecke's lyricism with Armstrong's sense of drama. More consistent than Jack Purvis, more inventive than Klein, he seemed to achieve expressive heights few trumpeters, black or white, had approached before.

Berigan's solos alone would have made the Dorsey Brothers' March 14, 1933, Brunswick session memorable. But he's far from the only attraction: by any standard, "Mood Hollywood" and "Shim Sham Shimmy" are outstanding performances. They use only five horns—Berigan and Klein, the two Dorseys, and Binyon—but the combination of tight scoring and light-footed playing make them seem twice that number.

Berigan swaggers into his "Mood Hollywood" solo with an assurance quite surprising for a relative newcomer to the big time. Working over a nudging shuffle figure, he covers the full range of his horn with ease and no sense of strain. As Steve Lipkins, one of the major lead trumpets of the '30s, later put it, Bunny "was the first jazz player I'd heard at that time who played the trumpet really well from the bottom to the top, very evenly all along the line."[21]

Both Dorseys solo well, as does tenor saxophonist Binyon, one of many white soloists on the instrument clearly animated by the serpentine fluidity of Bud Freeman; he's good on "Mood Hollywood," even better in a longer, bright-toned outing on Hoagy Carmichael's "Old Man Harlem," recorded June 8.

Between 1931 and 1933 the Dorsey brothers were something of an axis, around which revolved much of the most important white jazz activity of the time. They provided accompaniments on record for singers Mildred Bailey and Lee Wiley. Bing Crosby made more records with them, as did Ethel Waters, then starring on Broadway in As Thousands Cheer.

And, perhaps most significant of all, they were accompanists of choice for the Boswell Sisters, Martha (1905–58), Connie (1907–76), and Helvetia (or "Vet," 1911–88). The Boswell Sisters are unique, a vocal trio which at the start of the 1930s was on the creative cutting edge of hot jazz. They existed as a unit only until 1936, but their innovative, often audacious treatment of popular song material still has the impact of the unexpected.

They grew up in New Orleans, among such friends as Louis and Leon Prima, Leon Roppolo, "Monk" Hazel, Tony Parenti, and the short-lived cornetist Emmett Hardy. The family was musical, and all three girls had classical training, becoming proficient on a variety of instruments. "They had a little trio," said Hazel. "When they played classical, Connie would play the cello, Martha would play the piano, and Vet would play the violin. When they played jazz, Vet would play the banjo, Martha played the piano and Connie would play the saxophone."[22]

Singing together was a natural outgrowth. "We could be in different rooms in the house," Vet Boswell told New York radio personality Rich Conaty in 1982. "I'd be in the bedroom, Martha'd be in the kitchen, and Connie in the living room, and we'd start singing the same song at the same time in the same key. That's how in tune we were to each other."[23]

Various accounts of their early years have made much of the fact that the family had black servants who sometimes sang to the girls at bedtime, or that "Vet" Boswell spoke of visits to the New Orleans French market, where the sisters would hear black singing that could "tear your heart out." Some of these reports have a vaguely forced quality, as if the various Boswell chroniclers were looking for an admission that the sisters learned to sing the way they did by simple imitation of black precedents. Vet Boswell, in a 1987 interview, recalled seeing a French newspaper "that had a drawing of three black girls listed as The Boswell Sisters."[24]

But the simplest explanation is also the most plausible: Connie, Vet, and Martha Boswell grew up in New Orleans, subject to the same musical crosscurrents that helped shape all the city's young jazz musicians, regardless of color. They went to black churches and theatres, heard bands everywhere. They bought records: Connie told George T. Simon she particularly admired blues singer Mamie Smith and tried at one point to sing like her. "And you know what," she said, "I also tried to sing like [Enrico] Caruso . . . Caruso probably influenced me more than anyone else. Of course I don't sound like him, but I used to sit and listen and be amazed by his breathing. Then I'd try to do what he was doing. I'd take a long breath and hit a lot of notes."[25]

By the mid-1920s the sisters were singing together as a unit, and thinking—despite their father's opposition—of trying it professionally. A pair of 1925 performances, acoustically recorded and issued by Victor, shows them still groping for a coherent approach. On "I'm Gonna Cry (Cryin' Blues)," Connie sounds like a combination of Mamie Smith and vaudeville "Shimmy Queen" Bee Palmer. The Boswells' attempts at double-time ensemble scatting are reminiscent of nothing so much as the squawking of Red McKenzie's comb and Dick Slevin's kazoo on the first Mound City Blue Blowers records, selling well nationally at the time.

"Heebie Jeebies," recorded by OKeh in Los Angeles in late 1930, shows that much has changed. They use a variety of devices—tempo shifts, ensemble scatting, a bluesy solo chorus by Connie—to maintain interest in what is basically not a very interesting tune. At the end they demonstrate, with a brief and explicit reference, that they've been listening to Louis Armstrong's famed 1926 Hot Five record of the song.[26]

By early 1931 the Boswells were in New York, had broken into network radio, and had signed a contract with Jack Kapp to make records for Brunswick. It is to Kapp's eternal credit that, beginning with their first Brunswick date on March 19 and continuing throughout most of the next three years, he let them choose their own backings, and that the bands turned out most of the time to be Dorsey Brothers units.

It's hard to imagine a better partnership. Personnels might vary a bit from date to date (sometimes Berigan was on trumpet, sometimes Manny Klein, and at least once Jack Purvis), but the musicians understood what the trio was up to, and often proved to be inspired accompanists. "They were just the greatest bunch of fellows to work with," Connie told Michael Brooks. "Crazy, but all wonderful musicians who understood exactly what we were trying to do."[27]

And what they were trying to do was in its implications truly startling. It is no exaggeration to say that Boswell Sisters treatments of popular song material extend far beyond anything covered by the simple term "arrangement." On record after record, they fragment, alter, reharmonize, recompose, interpolate, free-associate their way into a concept which in the context of the early 1930s had no name—and had the power to terrify such conservative listeners as Jack Kapp.

All three sisters apparently took a hand in the arranging process, though Connie seems to have been the prime mover (with Glenn Miller as silent partner, helping score the instrumental sections). When she told George Simon that "we revolutionized trio and group singing," she was not exaggerating. Before they came along, most popular vocal ensembles stuck to more or less straightforward renderings of the songs. Even the Rhythm Boys, rhythmically flexible as they were (and driven by Harry Barris's fertile imagination), seldom took real structural or harmonic liberties with the songs.[28]

(Female singing groups, though not exactly a commonplace, had existed throughout the 1920s. But the Brox Sisters, Trix and Keller Sisters, and the rest were content to sing the songs as written, squarely on the beat, and usually in the high, thin Helen Kane–like voice in vogue at the time. The idea of tampering with or in any way customizing the material, not to mention incorporation of hot jazz elements, was without precedent.)

For the Boswells, it seemed, nothing was immune to alteration—or, to stretch a point just a bit, to deconstruction. A song was only an arbitrary construct, a sequence of ideas, assembled in accordance with a canon of prevailing conventions. Those conventions could be bent, even discarded, if that suited the overall needs of interpretation.

The Boswells' records, some seventy-five in all, tell the story after that: ever-shifting tempo changes ("Roll On, Mississippi, Roll On"), reharmonization of an entire chorus ("We Just Couldn't Say Goodbye"), switching a song's tonality from major to minor, then fragmenting and abstracting its lyric for use as a blues

("There'll Be Some Changes Made"), wholesale reconstruction of melody, harmony, and lyrics ("Got the South in My Soul"), wordless "hot instrumental" vocalizing ("If It Ain't Love"), halving the note values of a song ("Down Among the Sheltering Palms"), extending the note values and chorus length by doubling consonant sounds—the sisters called it their "gibberish"—in the lyrics ("It Don't Mean a Thing"), interpolation of fragments of other songs ("Yes, Sir, That's My Baby" dropped into "Ev'rybody Loves My Baby"), or even smoothing out a potentially awkward melodic line (the last two bars in the bridge of "Sophisticated Lady") with no loss of innate character.

All this, moreover, in close interaction with the musicians. On "Nothing Is Sweeter Than You," Connie's humming and Tommy Dorsey's muted trombone become two halves of a single expression, the melody moving freely back and forth between them. On "It's the Girl" and "Put That Sun Back in the Sky," Jimmy Dorsey's fast, Noone-like clarinet provides dynamic counterthrust to the singers' sustained-note lines. On "Doggone, I've Done It!" Connie solos like a trumpet over a sustained-chord "carpet" of voices and instruments. On "Whad'ja Do to Me?" Connie and Martha have a duet passage that's among the finest bit of true vocal interaction on any record of the era.

The most remarkable feature of all this, as Will Friedwald has observed (in Jazz Singing), is that none of it, not even the frequent swapping of lead and voicing within the three-part vocal ensembles, ever jars the listener or sounds "anything less than completely natural." The very ease with which it strikes the ear makes realization of what they're doing, dawning slowly over time, all the more amazing. It's comparable, if in a distant way, to watching a master magician with unwavering attention, looking for the momentary illusion, the decoy, the key bit of sleight-of-hand—and still missing it.

Nor did the Boswells slight the solo abilities of their accompanists. Bunny Berigan's half-chorus on "Ev'rybody Loves My Baby," at a rocking medium tempo, is among his most deliciously abandoned. Jimmy Dorsey's alto is at its edgy best on "Sleep, Come On and Take Me," while Tommy plays the blues on "Hand Me Down My Walking Cane" with Teagardenish authority. Elsewhere there are fine moments from Joe Venuti (violin), Eddie Lang (his guitar backing to the verse of "It's the Girl" is particularly delectable), guitarist Carl Kress, and trumpeter Manny Klein, whose considerable skills as a jazzman never fail to surprise.

There is hardly a Boswell Sisters record that does not yield some audacious dismantling and reassembling of the component parts of their materials, often with a result richer and more provocative by far than the original. And even that, at least according to Connie, wasn't the extent of it. You should have heard, she told Rich Conaty, the things that they weren't allowed to record: it is obvious that careful thought and preparation went into every bar of these performances—all of it informed by a natural and deepgoing understanding of the process of hot improvisation.

(Though he recognized the sisters' obvious abilities, Jack Kapp apparently never quite got used to their treatment of their material. Several times, said Vet Boswell, he had them retool and re-record particularly unorthodox arrangements in more conventional fashion, threatening more than once not to record them at all unless they simplified things. Later, as chief of American Decca, he went so far as to bring in an arranger to put their records together. The results were bland, even predictable, with little of the sense of adventure that still makes their earlier efforts such heady listening.)

It is instructive to select one Boswell Sisters record of this time and follow it carefully from start to finish. A particularly absorbing example is "Forty-Second Street," recorded April 11, 1933, with a group including Berigan, both Dorseys, and guitarist Dick McDonough. After a straightforwardly harmonized opening chorus in B♭ minor (obbligatos by Berigan and Jimmy Dorsey), things shift to B♭ major, and sixteen bars of the lyric over a chord structure akin to that of "Between the Devil and the Deep Blue Sea." But not for long: Tommy Dorsey takes the bridge muted, and Berigan returns to B♭ minor for six solo bars, interrupted by a tempo break and move to A♭ minor for the verse, sung out of tempo (and with perfect precision) by the three voices, McDonough providing the sparest of accompaniments. Back to B♭ minor for four bars of quasi-gospel group vocal, giving way to Connie in a "preaching" blues mode.

In the record's most remarkable passage, the sisters sing the bridge against a *marcato* band backing, evoking both "Brother, Can You Spare a Dime?" and "Ten Cents a Dance," opening out a vista of emotional implication. No mere tourist thoroughfare, teeming with stereotypes, this 42nd Street is a street of sorrows, gritty and shadowed, full of "rough and tough guys" and dreams gone awry. Small wonder that they end it as a dirge, dark and downbeat. The Boswells have taken a good look behind the high-stepping façade, to show us a slice of real life. No hearing of "Forty-Second Street" will ever again be the same.

Collective efforts aside, the sisters had another, no less important, strength in the solo singing of Connie Boswell. Of the three white female singers active in early '30s jazz band settings, she may be the most compelling, and the most lastingly influential.

From the start, she seems to have had the easiest way with rhythm: where Mildred Bailey seems relatively stiff by comparison (even in such otherwise outstanding efforts as "Shoutin' in That Amen Corner" and "Is That Religion?"), and Lee Wiley treats even rhythm numbers ("Got the South in My Soul," "I Gotta Right to Sing the Blues") as ballads, Connie Boswell addresses the beat as an instrumentalist would. She phrases her solo chorus on "When I Take My Sugar to Tea" (1931) like a female Jack Teagarden; when she sings the blues on "There'll Be Some Changes Made" and "Hand Me Down My Walking Cane," it's with a rhythmic incisiveness rare in *any* singer of the time, black or white. Not until the arrival of Billie Holiday on records at mid-decade, and the maturation of Mildred Bailey at about the same time, did female singers—whether nominally "jazz" or not—catch up to this kind and degree of rhythmic ease.

Concurrent with the Boswell Sisters records of 1931 to 1933, Connie was also making solo discs for Brunswick. Many were ballads, backed by studio groups (usually with the Dorseys), on which she had little to do but sing the melody and lyric. Her reading of "Time on My Hands" (1931), verse and chorus, is musically letter-perfect, cleanly and intelligently phrased; but a young, nervous Lee Wiley, recording it the day before (and at a faster tempo) with Leo Reisman's Orchestra, gets at its erotic core more directly.

(Comparisons of Boswell, Wiley, and Bailey, while perilous, are not without a certain usefulness. Each had her unique strengths. Wiley's readings of love songs, whether "Hands Across the Table" or "You've Got Me Crying Again," convey a sensuousness relatively rare in Boswell's work and almost totally absent from Bailey's. Bailey, meanwhile, brings to such vehicles as Carmichael's "Snowball" and Willard Robison's " 'Round the Old Deserted Farm" a nurturing quality and a feel for the resonances of everyday American life. Boswell seems most comfortable in more rhythmically oriented situations and those which objectify emotion, depicting it before they participate in it. The stark landscape of "Washboard Blues," for example, seems to suit her: her March 16, 1932, record with the Casa Loma Orchestra is still a standard by which performances of this Carmichael masterpiece are measured.)

Not surprisingly, Connie Boswell's strongest solo performances of this period are the jazz ones. From the first notes of the verse to "Concentratin'," made the same day as "Time on My Hands," she's at ease and swinging—easily outdoing Bailey, who recorded it with a Whiteman unit a month later. "Horn-like" phrasing in female vocals, later stylized by Billie Holiday, probably originated in the way Connie Boswell handles "Concentratin' " here.

She's at the top of her game on "Me Minus You," driving hard with a solid four-to-the-bar beat, while Berigan and Tommy Dorsey add obbligato touches. After a nudging, insistent Berigan solo (and good Jimmy Dorsey in the bridge), she comes back punching, the horns first riffing quietly behind her, then shaking out into a jam ensemble as she stomps the tune home. It's hard to think of any other singer in 1932 working with this degree of rhythmic ease and abandon.

Despite their continuing success (radio, records, movies), the Boswell Sisters broke up in 1936. Other vocal groups, among them the vastly successful Andrews Sisters, followed, crediting the Boswells as an inspiration. Some sang well, but none approached the Boswell combination of vocal excellence (each had an excellent voice and faultless intonation), originality of arrangement, and musicianly sophistication.[29]

Connie carried on, forging a successful career as a solo singer. Several of her records achieved considerable popularity: "Whispers in the Dark" and "Sand in My Shoes," backed by studio groups, and "Martha," with Bob Crosby's Bobcats. Other outstanding moments included a pair of 1937 duets with Bing Crosby, on "Basin Street Blues" and "Bob White."

During World War II she toured the country singing at military training camps. But her offers to sing abroad were rejected: she was paralyzed from the waist down, result of a childhood accident. Though she could and did stand on occasion, and even walk several steps, the government was unwilling to take the risk: she stayed home.[30]

By 1976, when Connie (or, by that time, Connee) Boswell died of cancer, she had left her imprint on several generations of singers. Kay Starr's approach to the beat and Keely Smith's substitution of "ah" for the word and vowel sound "I" are among her legacies. Best known, perhaps, is the young Ella Fitzgerald's declaration that Connie Boswell was her original inspiration. "I know," she was quoted as saying, "that Connee Boswell was doing things that no one else was doing at the time. You don't have to take my word for it. Just check the recordings made at the time and hear for yourself."[31]

By 1934, records by the Dorsey Brothers Orchestra had been appearing for five years and had done reasonably well. Perhaps inevitably, Jimmy and Tommy now turned their thoughts to the notion of starting a full-time band of their own.

Not that they had to: Depression or no, it was easy enough to make a secure living in radio and recording studios, doing occasional dates under your own name on the side. The Dorseys had been playing the game that way, as had confrères Goodman, Rollini, Joe Venuti, Artie Shaw, Red Norvo, and others. But that life, however comfortable, also could be mind-numbing: "You'll never know some of the stuff we had to put up with on a regular basis, the garbage we had to play," said Artie Shaw. "There were times when it was so unbearable that you wished you were anywhere else, doing anything else."[32]

The popularity of the Casa Loma Orchestra had shown that a dance band could exist solely for the purpose of playing good music. No funny hats, no novelties or gag vocals, comedy skits or pratfalls. Just music, much of it out-and-out jazz. All at once it seemed a number of prominent studio musicians were thinking hard about taking full-time bands out into the land of theatres, ballrooms, and long bus trips.

With the help of Glenn Miller, who had been so invaluable to the Boswells, Tommy and Jimmy formed an ensemble, incorporating some men from Smith Ballew's newly defunct band. Its instrumentation was unusual: one trumpet (Berigan at first, George Thow later), two trombones (Miller and Don Matteson) augmented to three when Tommy joined in, three saxes (Jimmy on alto, Skeets Herfurt and Jack Stacey on tenors), and a rhythm section of pianist Bobby Van Eps, guitarist Roc Hillman, bassist Delmar Kaplan, and, on drums, a lean twenty-four-year-old Texan named Ray McKinley.

The idea, as McKinley remembered it, was to build a band sound around the middle-register sonority of the trombones and tenors, a kind of instrumental cognate to the vocal timbre of Bing Crosby. "Bing was the biggest thing around in those days," said McKinley. "There was nobody who sang like him. The Dorseys had often played for Bing, and they felt—or the Rockwell-O'Keefe Agency felt—that they could achieve something if they pitched their sound like his."[33]

McKinley's drumming was an integral part of the ensemble sound. Fellow-drummer Cliff Leeman recalled catching the band at a ballroom in Massachusetts. McKinley, he said, "was just as good in person as he was on the radio. His drums had a marvelous sound; they were tuned to what seemed like different intervals. He used the set in a most musical way. I recall he played a lot of top cymbal and his rim shots were clean, sharp and well placed."[34]

Writer-drummer Burt Korall has lauded McKinley's team-player approach to

375

timekeeping, observing that he used the various components of the standard drum kit to create "a rhythmic climate that is simultaneously stimulating and comforting."

George T. Simon, too, responded instantly to McKinley's "tremendous drive . . . the way his style fit right in with that of the horns, the sound he got from his instrument and the light, subtle wit that permeated his playing."[35]

George Thow, if no Berigan, was nevertheless a capable trumpeter, Harvard educated, who had done his apprenticeship under the watchful eye of Isham Jones. Bob Van Eps was a skilled and resourceful pianist, part of a family of skilled and resourceful musicians. In Herfurt and Stacey the Dorseys had two versatile reedmen, one a fine hot soloist, the other able to join Jimmy doubling on cornet for six-brass tutti passages.

"What they really needed," said McKinley, "was an arranger who understood and could exploit that baritone-register sonority. But they never got it. I don't really think Glenn was the one: he'd studied with [Joseph] Schillinger, but I don't think he was at that time what you'd call a really accomplished, expert arranger. A lot of the stuff we did was heads—head arrangements—so many of 'em you wouldn't believe it. 'Honeysuckle Rose,' 'St. Louis Blues,' all those. They were searching frantically for an identifying sound, and heading off in all kinds of directions at once."[36]

Sound or no, the band showed every sign of catching on. Cork O'Keefe, who had helped build the Casa Loma Orchestra into a national attraction, booked them into venues where they were bound to reach younger dancers. There was plenty of radio time and a contract with Jack Kapp's newly formed Decca label, whose thirty-five-cent price tag made it accessible to a wide range of Depression-era buyers.

Musicians who heard the band at this point spoke of it with respect. George T. Simon caught them at Nuttings-on-the-Charles in Waltham, outside Boston, and rhapsodized in *Metronome* about "one of the slickest, most exciting musical aggregations ever to enter our musical lives." It swung more than the Casa Loma, he said, also pointing out that the emphasis on low brass and saxes gave the ensemble "a round-bellied resonance we'd never heard before." James T. Maher, growing up in Cleveland, was struck by "their easy, swift lightness, their transparency."[37]

Simon, Maher, and many others admired the attention to detail: the sculpted dynamics, use of carefully calibrated fade-outs (this long before the era of the recording studio "board fade") and sometimes unusual sectional voicings. For example, the band's theme song, Bonnie Lake's evocative "Sandman," begins with a dotted-eighth-and-sixteenth shuffle figure which later became a familiar (and overworked) device in the performance of such standards as "Blue Moon" and "Heart and Soul." Low reeds announce the melody, with punctuations by cup-muted brass, and the full ensemble in the bridge shows off the middle-register focus. Kay Weber's vocal, delivered in a hushed, almost fragile voice, heightens the mood.

"The guys were really enthusiastic about their band," Bonnie Lake later said.

"They knew they had something special, really believed in it." And right from the start, when they opened at the exclusive Sands Point Bath Club on Long Island, "the people responded, accepted them right away."

But, she said, "they fought all the time; sometimes it would make people nervous just to be around them. You never knew when the explosion would occur. It didn't matter where. Rehearsal, recording session. One time they got into a terrible scrap right in the middle of the Onyx Club, on 52nd Street. Tommy, I think it was, threw Jimmy down a flight of stairs. Nothing was sacred: they'd bust up each other's instruments, anything. And usually, it was over something pretty inconsequential, even stupid."[38]

On "Dippermouth Blues," George Thow delivers a faithful account of the three King Oliver cornet choruses. The band is particularly crisp on "Tailspin," a Jimmy Dorsey–Frank Trumbauer collaboration (also recorded by the latter with Paul Whiteman), on which Tommy plays a long-lined melody reminiscent of a legato theme from Beiderbecke's "In a Mist." Miller seems to be reaching for a kind of chamber sound on "Milenberg Joys," another '20s holdover, with some imaginative reed writing featuring flute.

Jimmy plays a cornet solo on "That Eccentric Rag," his work on the instrument (also to be heard on several Joe Venuti–Eddie Lang records) as beholden to Bix as his brother's is to Armstrong. "Jimmy was technically a better trumpet player than Tommy," said Ray McKinley. "He didn't keep an embouchure up— but there were a few times out at Glen Island Casino when he picked up a trumpet and played some great stuff, just flyin' all over the horn. Tommy never could do that."[39]

The band is at its nimblest on "St. Louis Blues," which ends in a beautifully turned Tommy Dorsey trombone cadenza, and on "Weary Blues," sporting handsome solos by Jimmy, Bob Van Eps, and George Thow. Yet these records constitute a relatively small percentage of the Dorsey orchestra's output during its brief existence. For every "Stop, Look and Listen," there seemed to be two or three faceless performances of tunes with such names as "Tiny Little Fingerprints" or "I Threw a Bean Bag at the Moon." They might record Bonnie Lake's melodically subtle "Gracias," but there would also be "I'd Like to Dunk You in My Coffee," "The Farmer Takes a Wife," and "I'm Goin' Shoppin' With You."

This is hardly unusual. To greater or lesser degree every band, black or white, was at the mercy of the publishers who determined what got recorded, and the market they hoped to reach. Many bands had managed, usually through the skill of their arrangers, to subvert the process to some degree by imposing personal touches on arrangements of even the dreariest songs (witness the Goldkette orchestra of the mid-'20s, "customizing" the likes of "Hoosier Sweetheart"); whatever its reasons, the Dorsey Brothers Orchestra remained rigidly compartmentalized. On "the good stuff," they were everything George T. Simon and others remembered—lively, original, often quite inventive. On more mundane material they could have been any band anywhere, laboring through a publisher's stock orchestration. Like Tommy Dorsey's split musical personality, the duality was absolute, not to be bridged.

All the same, they did well—until Decoration Day (now known as Memorial Day) 1935. The story of what happened that day has been told often enough to blur all distinction between fact and fancy: onstand at the Glen Island Casino, Tommy calls "I'll Never Say 'Never Again' Again," in an arrangement that has Jimmy switching from baritone to alto, and then to cornet for some three-way stuff with Thow and Jack Stacey. Say, Mac, says Lad. Isn't that tempo just a little fast for all that? Without a word, Mac picks up his trombone and walks off the stand, never to return.

People tend not to question their pet legends. For decades, the official story of Bix Beiderbecke's demise involved a Princeton Prom and a snowstorm—supposedly at the end of July. But it was years before anyone wondered enough to say, "Now wait a minute. That makes no sense." So, too, with the Dorseys. The actual event may indeed have happened just that simply, just over a tempo. But given the ever-volatile relations between these two, it's more than likely that the pressure, as in all volcanic eruptions, had been building for some time.

"The question of who was really the leader was never really settled," said Ray McKinley. "Tommy was the one who sort of assumed leadership. But Jimmy—well, he never did settle for any idea of what his status was." At an attempted reconciliation in the office of Tom Rockwell, Tommy put it quite succinctly: "He didn't say anything wrong. He just bawled me out with his eyes."[40]

Cork O'Keefe called a joint meeting in one last attempt to mend the split. Tommy, iron-willed and not without a certain streak of cruelty, showed up, rebuffed them all with threats and imprecations, and walked out. Herb Sanford described the scene:

> Jimmy had been looking out the window. He turned to Cork, tears in his eyes.
>
> "What'll I do?"
>
> "From now on, you're the boss."
>
> It was the end of the Dorsey Brothers Band, little more than a year from its beginning. But it was not the end for the Dorsey Brothers. It was a new beginning.[41]

And so it was. Both Dorseys went on to lead bands of their own, and with great success, both drawing heavily on musical elements first worked out by their joint orchestra. Tommy executed what might now be termed a hostile buyout of Joe Haymes's band, added some choice sidemen, and ran an ensemble full of star jazzmen, which also highlighted his seamless ballad solos. As his theme he adopted George Bassman's "I'm Getting Sentimental Over You," which he'd recorded twice with the Dorsey Brothers Orchestra.

For hot instrumentals, things were much as before: "Weary Blues," "Milenberg Joys," "Beale Street Blues," "Stop, Look and Listen," "Royal Garden Blues." Before long such old Dorsey pals as Bud Freeman, Dave Tough, and Bunny Berigan were in the band.

Jimmy, too, borrowed liberally from the Dorsey Brothers precedent. He kept Ray McKinley and the rest of the original personnel, got young Bobby Byrne to play trombone solos, and brought in a cadre of talented arrangers, including Fud Livingston and young trumpeter Salvador "Tutti" Camarata. And with the addition of singers Bob Eberle and Helen O'Connell in the late '30s he had all the elements for major success.

But along the way something had happened to the Dorsey brothers as jazz figures. Both played as well as ever and turned up regularly at jam sessions and, now and then, on jazz records. But Benny Goodman's 1935 breakthrough, playing arrangements by Fletcher and Horace Henderson, Lyle "Spud" Murphy, Deane Kincaide, Jimmy Mundy, and others, had established a fashion. "Swing," as defined by its audiences and by the trade press that served them, sounded like Goodman—and, by extension, like the Hendersons and, soon enough, like Count Basie and the countless other bands springing up in their image.

In running their own bands, both Dorsey brothers took inspiration from what they knew, from the earlier hot jazz idiom that had brought them to prominence in the 1920s. The Tommy Dorsey Orchestra of the late '30s, featuring such soloists as Bud Freeman, clarinetists Joe Dixon and Johnny Mince, trumpeters Berigan, Pee Wee Erwin, and Yank Lawson, and even that most versatile of drummers, Dave Tough, sprang from roots in that earlier soil.

In Jimmy's band the line of descent may not have been quite so clear, but it was there nevertheless. Such instrumentals as "Dorsey Stomp" and its descendant, "Dusk in Upper Sandusky," "Parade of the Milk Bottle Caps," and the popular "John Silver" are legacies of Dorsey Brothers days.

That both bands could swing handsomely was beyond question. Each had outstanding soloists and turned out a succession of excellent records. The instant and lasting popularity of the Bob Crosby Orchestra, moreover, proved beyond doubt that the audience for "dixieland"-style big band music was large and loyal. Yet retrospective appreciation for both Dorseys and their orchestras, particularly from critics and historians, has been oddly muted.

The judgments of Gunther Schuller are representative. He criticizes Tommy's mid-'30s band by observing, "Jazz standards for Dorsey meant things like Milenberg Joys or Tin Roof Blues. He, for example, never performed or recorded Stompin' at the Savoy, One O'Clock Jump, Take the 'A' Train, or any number of other later jazz standards." Schuller goes on to cite this as proof that Dorsey had little concern for "composition and creativity in the jazz sense."[42]

The suggestion that a collection of repeated blues riffs such as "One O'Clock Jump," or such attractive but fundamentally unremarkable standards as the Sampson and Strayhorn compositions, in some way constituted a higher level of musical achievement than the earlier pieces is risible. What objective or intrinsic quality in Basie's riffy, blues-based "Jumpin' at the Woodside" or "Doggin' Around" elevates it above such "dixieland" performances as "Wolverine Blues," as played by Crosby's orchestra, or "Beale Street Blues" by Tommy Dorsey's?

Perhaps the best demonstration of the Tommy Dorsey band's powers emerges on airchecks of its Raleigh-Kool radio broadcasts. On the Harold Arlen–E. Y. Harburg–Ira Gershwin "You're a Builder-Upper" (1937), Dorsey and clarinetist Johnny Mince solo with fervor over Tough's kicks and cymbal splashes, and Bud

Freeman, batting cleanup, lines the ball far over the right-field fence. By any standard it's thrilling, and very hot, jazz, played with great swing by a superb band.

Both brothers had their moments, their hits, and it's likely such records as "Marie" and "Song of India," "Green Eyes" and "Amapola," will be played and reissued as long as a market exists for big band popular music. What is less certain is how posterity will judge the two brothers.

There's no disputing that between 1925 and '35 both of them *mattered* in jazz circles, in ways they never again recaptured. "Jimmy," said Ray McKinley, "may have sometimes thought he was better than he really was; the shadow of Benny was always there, hanging over him. And maybe neither one of them was a really great jazz player in the sense that Benny and Jack Teagarden were. But then, who was? They were very, very good—maybe better than that—all the same; Tommy, especially, loved jazz and knew what was good. And it goes without saying that both of them were excellent all-round musicians."[43]

Throughout their years as individual bandleaders the brothers maintained an uneasy, on-again, off-again truce; that's probably the only aspect of their story captured with any accuracy in Hollywood's otherwise fictionalized 1947 effort, *Those Fabulous Dorseys.*

Tommy hid little. In one colleague's words, "what you saw was what you got." And if the younger Dorsey got steamed up enough to take a poke at someone—such as Benny Goodman, on the set for *A Song Is Born* in 1948—most often he'd do it. Jimmy, by contrast, kept his feelings under wraps. When Tommy complained that his elder brother "bawled me out with his eyes," he was probing at something very basic. As Cork O'Keefe, who remained friends with them both, put it, "Tommy would raise hell, Jimmy would insinuate it."

Insinuation strikes different people in different ways. Kitty Kallen, who followed Helen O'Connell as vocalist with Jimmy's band in 1943, remembered him as "a very hostile man," consumed with envy for his brother's success. "And when he drank," she said, "he was a different person. He had to have a bodyguard with him all the time."[44]

Yet Jean Bach, who knew and dated Jimmy (and was married for a time to a favorite Dorsey soloist, trumpeter Shorty Sherock), told of thinking one day, "How many bandleaders can you name who were liked, really liked, by the guys in their bands? Well, I thought of Basie, and Charlie Barnet, and poor, dear Bunny Berigan. And then it occurred to me that the winner, the real, absolute champion, had to be Jimmy. They all loved him."[45]

Trumpeter Irvin "Marky" Markowitz, veteran of a later Dorsey band, concurred. "One of the best," he said. "A kind, sweet man—and could he ever play!"[46]

Assessments of Tommy, like the man himself, tended to be less subtle. Love him, hate him, kindnesses and cruelties. As Pee Wee Erwin put it, "Tommy either liked you and you got along with him, or you didn't want to be within five hundred miles of him."

Johnny Mince vividly remembered playing a solo one night that incorporated a few Jimmy Dorsey–like licks. "Tommy turned to me—even while I was still playing—and said in my ear, 'Johnny, don't play like brother.' And he wasn't kidding."[47]

Yet even throughout the years of separation and rivalry the two brothers remained bonded in ways few outsiders could begin to understand. Whatever enmity there was between them existed in its own, hermetically sealed universe. After their fashion, they remained loyal to one another, and to their mother, who watched over both with concern—and outlived them both.

Finally, in 1954, with ballrooms closing and the wreckage of big dance bands littering the music business landscape, Tommy and Jimmy Dorsey swallowed their differences and teamed up again. Until Tommy's sudden death at the end of 1956, the reconstituted Dorsey Brothers Orchestra (actually Tommy's band using a combined library, with Jimmy as featured soloist) played to regular and enthusiastic audiences.

There was never any doubt who was in charge. Sidemen, including trumpeter Lee Castle, remembered Tommy as the one who led and gave the orders, Jimmy as the sometimes reluctant follower.[48]

Their TV *Stage Show* appearances in 1954–55—first as summer replacement for Jackie Gleason, then on their own—were particularly rewarding. An aircheck recording of "Dippermouth Blues," for example, has both brothers soloing fiercely, then joining Castle for a spirited band-within-a-band jam ensemble before drummer Louis Bellson kicks the full band in.

One day in 1954, Bonnie Lake got a call. "It was from Jimmy. I think it was right after their father died. They'd gone back together again and were playing at the Café Rouge, in the [Hotel] Statler, and were inviting me to come down.

"I did, and on the way I got to thinking about 'Sandman.' They'd played it a lot back when they had a band together, but after they broke up, neither of them ever played it. Each was afraid it would associate him with 'the brother.'

"So here I come walking into the Café Rouge, and what do you think? They'd had somebody make a brand-new, utterly gorgeous arrangement of 'Sandman,' and here they were playing it, just for me. I was thrilled—both by the music and by what it brought back. Looking at them up there together, playing this tune they'd both left alone since the old days, I realized a lot of things about them, myself, all of us," she said.

"Above all, I guess, I realized how very much those two guys loved one another. It shook me. Still does."[49]

On Thanksgiving Day 1956, Tommy Dorsey, age fifty-one, choked to death in his sleep. Jimmy, already ill with lung cancer, lasted barely half a year longer. As their friend Herb Sanford put it, they'd grown up with and "helped steer the course of jazz in its formative years." Now, with breathtaking suddenness, they were gone. It's no exaggeration to say that an age departed with them.

16

The Bob Crosby Orchestra

"**A**bove all," Bob Haggart recalled, "we were like a family. We worked together, socialized together. Thought musically together. Most other bands—well, to tell the truth, we didn't pay much attention to what everybody else was doing. To us most of the time, they just sounded as if they were trying to steal from one another."

Meet that wonder of the musical 1930s, the Bob Crosby Orchestra. In the whole colorful decade there wasn't another band like it, and in certain ways there may not have been another nearly so good.

For chronicler George T. Simon, they were an ensemble "with tremendous spirit, one filled with men who believed thoroughly in the kind of music they were playing and, what's more, who respected and admired one another as musicians and as people."[1]

Few bands, however brilliant, approached that degree of unanimity with any consistency. It extends beyond mere skill, beyond originality—even beyond a leader or arranger's inspired vision. Neither Benny Goodman's virtuosity nor the faultless precision of his orchestras ever quite transformed their efforts into the expression of a single collective will. Artie Shaw came closer, his various bands driven by the strength and singularity of his vision: but Shaw's musicians remained his employees. Much the same could be said even for Red Norvo's extraordinary 1937 band, breathing, whispering, exulting as extensions of both its leader's xylophone sound and Eddie Sauter's ensemble concept.

The Crosby orchestra had an extra dimension. It lives in such words as "ensemble," when describing tightly knit group acting, or "team," in the finest athletic sense; the idea of a collective entity, each component interacting constantly and creatively with the others to shape, to determine the whole. *Gestalt*, a single consciousness compounded of many.

In that rarified context only the Duke Ellington Orchestra comes to mind as in any way comparable. But an Ellington orchestra, any Ellington orchestra, assumed its finished shape through the leader's (and often Billy Strayhorn's) codification of an ongoing fusion and fission among its individual members. The Crosby orchestra, by contrast, began with unanimous, shared dedication to a single stylistic ideal. Its name, most often popularly (and imperfectly) identified, was "dixieland." But the word fails to describe either a stylistic predisposition or a rhythmic foundation, not to mention a wide palette of orchestral color and texture.

Better by far, and more accurate, to remember that the band led by Bing Crosby's younger brother was built around a core of New Orleans musicians, whose shared background and affinity determined its musical direction.

Historically, New Orleans jazzmen away from home shared a bond, a camaraderie, that seemed to transcend class, education, politics, even race. Meeting in New York, Chicago, or Los Angeles, they were often simply homeboys together, carrying their environment with them in a way that seemed to render differences among them irrelevant, or at least secondary. It may be that way with musicians from St. Louis, Boston, or San Antonio, but not to that degree; and on the evidence it's anything but that with New Yorkers.

Crescent City jazzmen seemed to recognize one another, even gravitate toward one another's company both on and off the stand. When clarinetist Joe Darensbourg, a Creole, says of guitarist Hilton "Nappy" Lamare, a white, "if everybody was like Nappy this would be an awful nice world," he's talking New Orleans. The sight of Eddie Miller and Kid Ory crawfishing together in a stream on the outskirts of Los Angeles says less about race relations or social ecumenism in jazz than about their shared home town and its ways.[2]

In this connection the Bob Crosby band has a strong cognate, perhaps even a forebear, in the great Luis Russell Orchestra of 1929–30. Henry "Red" Allen on trumpet, bassist George "Pops" Foster, drummer Paul Barbarin, and clarinetist Albert Nicholas had known each other back home, and they were at the heart, musically and socially, of an extraordinary band. Others, such as Russell himself (born in Panama but raised in New Orleans), Georgia-born trombonist J. C. Higginbotham, and Bostonian alto saxophonist Charlie Holmes, quickly got to (as the title of one of their best records put it) "Feelin' the Spirit."

"We worked seven days a week and we loved it," said Foster. "Russell's band was romping so good in twenty-nine we had everything sewed up around New York . . . playing the same style we played back in New Orleans." For Allen, Russell's was "the most fiery band I ever heard . . . There was more group spirit, more friendliness, and star temperament was never a problem. It was a real happy band and we created a lot of things." To Holmes, "it was a different type of music to me altogether. They'd [the band's New Orleans contingent] been playing that stuff for years, and it was born in them."[3]

"That stuff," of course, was New Orleans music. Pops Foster is emphatic (and perhaps a little resentful) in declaring,

> When we left the Saratoga Club [in 1931], Luis decided to change his style. We started fooling around with big arrangements and quit romping and playing what you call Dixieland. While we were playing Dixieland we were great. When we started playing like the other bands, finding work got rough. Why should they hire you when they've already got the same thing?[4]

To Foster, "dixieland" was synonymous with the loose, contrapuntally textured music played regularly in New Orleans by musicians of both races. His remarks are striking in their similarity to the statement by Bob Haggart, bassist and arranger of the Crosby orchestra, quoted above. Why play like everyone else, and risk disappearing into the crowd, when you already stand out with something distinctively your own?

Like the Russell band, the Crosby unit had New Orleans musicians—Lamare, drummer Ray Bauduc, tenor saxophonist Eddie Miller, and, slightly later, clarinetist Irving Fazola—at its core, alongside a cadre of avid fellow-travelers, among them Long Islander Haggart, Kentucky-born clarinetist Julian "Matty" Matlock, and Missourian John "Yank" Lawson on trumpet.[5]

As with the Russell band, Crosby's men were never in doubt or disagreement about what they wanted to play and how they would do it. Even with a slightly larger instrumentation than Russell's, they were doing what they'd known "down home." In this connection, all the Miller-Lamare banter about "po' boy" sandwiches and other local delights that opens the Crosby record of "Way Down Yonder in New Orleans" tells its own affectionate story. As the guitarist put it in a 1940 interview, "white musicians as well as the colored seem to have the right ideas down there."[6]

Whatever it was, and by whatever name its music was known, the band had sparkle, spontaneity, and lift and left a legacy of distinctive records, which have easily withstood the shifting winds of musical fashion.

The Crosby orchestra owes its origins to Ben Pollack, whose skill at assembling fine bands nearly matched his gifts as a drummer. By mid-1934, when his first group broke up, it included Miller, Matlock, Bauduc, Lawson, Lamare, pianist Gil Bowers, and trombonist Joe Harris. To a man, and perhaps unfairly, musicians laid the blame squarely on Pollack, endlessly chasing the "Open Sesame" of commercial success; he'd fallen for a young singer named Doris Robbins and begun taking an almost Svengali-like control of her career.

Records made by the band in the six months between December 1933 and May 1934 tell a dismal story: on the final date even such promising songs as Walter Donaldson's "Sleepy Head" and the Arlen-Koehler "Here Goes" sound as if they're being played by fifteen men crammed into one musical straitjacket. The arrangements are faceless enough to have been "stocks," and vocals dominate. Every element that might have distinguished Pollack's band from others in the field has been suppressed.

The earlier "Two Tickets to Georgia" is another matter. Like a movie trailer, it offers an explicit preview of a style in the making, good things to come: vigorous solos by Miller, Matlock, Jack Teagarden, and cornetist Stirling Bose; scored passages featuring tenor and clarinet in octaves, collective small-band-style riffing, the broad New Orleans beat—even a high-pitched, exuberant vocal by Lamare. Something was clearly afoot, if Pollack would only give it room to breathe.

But Pollack had other things in mind. Just as his rather extreme plunge into commercial self-promotion had run afoul of his spirited young band in 1929, so did history repeat itself in 1934. If a booking didn't seem likely to advance Doris Robbins's career, Pollack didn't take it. On those he did accept, he insisted she get star billing. He took to joining her in "romantic" vocal duets: several of these have been preserved on Vitaphone movie shorts and are little short of embarrassing.

"That girl is this band's meal ticket!" an angry Pollack retorted when a sideman, well-meaning, suggested things had slid out of balance. Little wonder that after a Los Angeles foray, with Pollack sparing no expense to get his *inamorata* into the movies, his musicians decided they'd simply had enough. They handed in their collective notice—but only after they'd met in secret and decided that the degree of teamwork they'd achieved was worth preserving.

"We wanted to stay together," said Eddie Miller. "There were good jobs available in the movie industry, but we were all young fellows then and wanted to do our own thing." So several of them headed east, stopping off for family visits before a planned regouping in New York. Another defector, Pollack's saxophonist and longtime band manager Gil Rodin, became business manager by acclamation.[7]

Once back in Depression-era New York, the "Pollack Orphans," as they soon became known, began to pick up work. Bassist Harry Goodman joined his brother Benny's new band, broadcasting nightly for the National Biscuit Company. Trumpeter Charlie Spivak garnered respect as a freelance lead man. Red Nichols, still hustling, was good for an occasional week's—or night's—work. Fellow-trumpeter "Wingy" Manone, an old New Orleans crony, hired as many of the "orphans" as possible, as often as he could, for record dates. Miller and Matlock are especially forceful on "Send Me" and—reunited with Lamare, Gil Bowers, Bauduc, and Harry Goodman on "Swing, Brother, Swing" and "Nickel in the Slot"—generate a high-stepping, almost swaggering drive.

Occasionally they'd get together to rehearse arrangements by Matlock and Texas-born saxophonist Deane Kincaide. Sometimes trombonist Jack Jenney was in the personnel, sometimes Glenn Miller or Neil Reid. Within a two-week period in March 1935, they made a few records as the "Clark Randall Orchestra," with Miller on trombone and contributing some arrangements.

From the content of the ten selections it's obvious that the band hasn't yet found a successful formula. "Troublesome Trumpet" and "Jitterbug" feature good Kincaide arrangements, characteristically agitated Lamare vocals, and intense solo work by Lawson, Eddie Miller, and Matlock. "When Icky Morgan Plays the Organ," for all its novelty touches (gag Glenn Miller arrangement, band vocal), also boasts propulsive work by the three soloists.

Things had changed somewhat by month's end and the third and final "Randall" session. The last four titles, issued this time as "Gil Rodin's Orchestra," are facelessly discreet, with the "hot" content kept to a minimum. Lamare sings on "Here Comes Your Pappy With the Wrong Kind of Load" but even he sounds comparatively restrained. Frank Tennille does most of the singing in his pleasant, straight tenor.[8]

But little of any substance happened until music publisher Jack Bregman dropped by a rehearsal one day, later telling his friend Tom Rockwell what he'd heard. Rockwell, who in the '20s had recorded and promoted countless major jazzmen of both races for OKeh, now headed (with Francis "Cork" O'Keefe) the powerful Rockwell-O'Keefe booking agency, handling the Dorsey Brothers and Casa Loma orchestras, and was ever on the lookout for new talent. He went to listen, agreed that the band showed promise—but confessed he didn't begin to know how to promote them.

Part of an answer lay in the Casa Loma example. They'd formed themselves into a cooperative, a corporation, in which each musician had the option of either becoming a shareholder or remaining a salaried employee. As front man they'd installed six-foot, four-inch Glen Gray, whose charm and suave good looks greatly enhanced the band's image. That idea appealed to the "Pollack Orphans." But when none among them volunteered to be "leader," the search began for someone who could "lead" the band, charming the public in a way that thirteen men with instruments could never manage on their own.

Rodin, O'Keefe, and the musicians considered, then discarded, several candidates: corpulent trumpeter Harry "Goldie" Goldfield, who in his Paul Whiteman days had entertained audiences with droll comedy routines; Johnny "Scat" Davis, who had clowned and played trumpet with Fred Waring; Frank Tennille, who had come east with the "orphans" and was a friend; even old Texas pal Jack Teagarden, musically a favorite but, alas, under contract to Paul Whiteman. A suggestion about New Orleans trumpeter Louis Prima, newly arrived in town, fell on deaf ears. New Orleans men, clearly, had strong notions about fellow homeboys.[9]

At length someone thought of Bob Crosby, an easygoing twenty-one-year-old who had done some singing for the Dorsey Brothers and had fallen foul of Tommy's hair-trigger temper. He even sounded a bit like his elder brother Bing—though as things turned out, there was never any need to draw on the family connection. He didn't know much about music, or even how to start off a number. "You count the band in how[ever] you like," Bauduc told him. "I'll make sure they come in at the right tempo." Above all he was a likable presence, happy to leave music to the musicians.[10]

*   *   *

Musical policy, at least at the outset, was also problematical. Jack Kapp had signed the band to make records for Decca—but he seemed to have no clearer an idea than Rockwell and O'Keefe just what to do with them. Their first release coupled two ballads, "In a Little Gypsy Tea Room" (vocal by Crosby) and "Flowers for Madame" (vocal by Tennille). Between June 1, 1935, and March 19, 1936, they recorded only pop songs, mostly ballads; each of the twenty-eight titles features a vocal.

It helps to remember conditions in the dance band business at that point. The Crosby band did its third Decca session ("Thanks a Million," "Tender Is the Night," and two other competently played but largely featureless titles) on Monday, August 19, 1935. *Two days later* and three thousand miles away, Benny Goodman's band opened at the Palomar Ballroom in Los Angeles, setting in motion the national dance band craze shortly to be known as "swing."

Musical fashions, like most news, traveled slowly in 1935. Goodman's success took a while to spread, even longer before it enabled other bands to depart from music marketing ideas that had been in place since the '20s. Jack and Dave Kapp, no takers of risks, clearly thought it best to keep their enthusiastic young Crosby band on a short leash, recording such neutral fare as "Here's to Romance" and "What's the Name of That Song?"

On location appearances things were inevitably a little different. Their debut engagement, at New York's Roseland Ballroom, was well received. "Unlike Ben Pollack," opinion-maker John Hammond wrote in *Down Beat* that summer, "Bob Crosby has a healthy respect for the musical whims of his band and allows the boys to blow as loud or as soft as they may wish. As a result their performance is many times better than when Ben Pollack was scowling at them last year, waiting for Doris Robbins to sing a chorus." Hailing young Bob Haggart as "a world-beater," Hammond also praised Deane Kincaide's arrangements, the band's overall enthusiasm, and Crosby himself, for being discreet enough to keep his vocals to a minimum.[11]

More of the same was waiting for them when they hit the road; whether at the Cherry Hotel in Wilson, North Carolina; the Adolphus Hotel in Dallas; or the Netherlands Hotel in Cincinnati; the New Orleans–style instrumentals seemed to click. During a stand at Tybee Beach in Savannah, bassist Haggart finished his first arrangement for the band, an adaptation of the famed Louis Armstrong Hot Five record of "Heebie Jeebies" for the larger instrumentation. Saxophonist Fud Livingston, one of the most imaginative hot arrangers of the '20s, heard it at Tybee and singled it out for praise. "That sort of set the seal of approval on it," said Haggart. "After that I was encouraged to write for the band as much as I could."[12]

There's nothing quite like a year on the road, playing dates in far-flung locations and interacting with dancers, to shape a band. By April 1936, when they went into Manhattan's New Yorker Hotel on a brief trial booking, the Crosby orchestra was ready to take on all comers. And it was there that George Simon—recent Harvard graduate, amateur drummer, and, for the last year, a writer at *Metronome* magazine (transforming it, in effect, into a jazz journal)—experienced them for the first time. With characteristic zeal he hailed them as "not only one of the swing greats of the country today, but . . . one of the smartest and neatest all-around performing units heard in a long, long time." To which, in retrospect, he has added:

> Seldom in all the years that I reviewed for *Metronome* did any band hit me as hard. It was one of the most exciting evenings of my life, and I, of course, gave it a rave review, one with which not all readers agreed. To some, two-beat [i.e., New Orleans–style] jazz was and always would be old-fashioned and corny, so that in essence most of their arguments were beamed not so much at the band in particular as at the style of music in general.[13]

Simon's enthusiasm for the band's *esprit* and musicianship had collided head-on with an already well-entrenched set of prejudices among his readers. Still, there was no denying the powerful, broad beat of the rhythm section or the strength of the band's three vivid soloists: Matlock, on clarinet, played a more angular style than Benny Goodman, whom he'd replaced with Pollack in 1929; Yank Lawson, on trumpet, had grown up listening to both Bix and Louis, fusing them in an often perfervid solo style of his own. But above all there was Eddie Miller, the one his bandmates called "the Little Prince," whose courtliness of manner matched the finesse of his playing.

Three band members, moreover, were now sharing the arranging. Kincaide, Texas-born, had grown up in Illinois, where he became an able saxophonist, joining Pollack in 1933. Matlock's inspiration to arrange had been Fud Livingston, himself a Pollack alumnus. "Fud was very underrated," said Bob Haggart. "Those things he wrote for [Red] Nichols, 'Imagination' and the rest, were way ahead of their time. They still sound fresh even today. I'd even go so far as to say that it was Fud who was responsible for the kind of scoring that later became the Glenn Miller sound. But poor Fud—he never got the credit for any of that."[14]

Haggart, the third arranger, had studied guitar with George Van Eps (who remembered him as a prodigy), played respectable trumpet, and had learned bass to get himself into his high school orchestra in Douglaston, Long Island. So, too, with arranging: he'd just picked it up, becoming expert within weeks.

Despite some differences in method and conception, all three aimed for a unified, recognizable band sound; many a Crosby road trip found them in agitated discussion about how to score some ensemble passage. That often led, said Haggart, to an intriguing division of labor. "Pop tunes would come in where we had to get something done fast, so we'd split up the arrangement: I'd do the intro, say, Matty the first chorus, maybe Deane the last chorus, and me the coda. Something like that. I don't know how many we did that way, but there were quite a few."

Kincaide "had perfect pitch, the kind where he'd sit there in a bus or train, a score pad on his lap, and whistle a chord right up from the bottom to some piccolo-range note on top. Not only did he have terrific ears, but he had really thorough knowledge of Ravel, Debussy, that sort of thing. He especially liked the *Valses nobles et sentimentales.* Deane didn't go in for discussing things to quite the extent Matty and I did; more often the two of us would sit together on trips and pull each other's scores apart, just to see what each guy had done, how he'd handled this situation or that."[15]

All three agreed that the Crosby band should sound only like itself. "All the other bands seemed to be in the same sort of mindset, all looking for riff tunes," said Haggart. "We hated riff tunes, thought they sounded ordinary, musically stupid. We avoided playing stuff like that wherever possible."[16]

A statement in *Metronome* by Eddie Miller reflects the fervor with which the rest of the Crosby musicians shared this view. "You know," he told George Simon, "that marching dixieland is still the real swing. You can take ninety percent of this so-called Harlem swing (not all of it, for some of it is really fine), and you can just swing it into your East River and let it sink there. It was that stuff they used to parade to down in Noo Ohlins [sic] that really swung right out."[17]

Then as now, the popular record business was a marketplace, responsive to familiar supply-and-demand imperatives. If "this so-called Harlem swing" sold records and the riffy "Christopher Columbus" was riding high, why not urge your most promising new band to take a shot at it? The Crosby band recorded it. Not surprisingly, their record is crisp, capably played—and relatively lacking in identity: save for brief solos by Lawson and Miller, there's little to set it apart from any number of other groups active at the time.

It was becoming clear, even to the brothers who headed Decca, that this was one group of musicians who would have to do things their own way—and if George Simon's *Metronome* review is any index, by April 1936 they were on their way to doing just that.

> [Their] type of swing is, for the most part, enlarged dixieland that swings right out with a sock, and which, though arranged, bears no resemblance to the harnessed kind of stuff that so many bands nowadays unfeelingly call, and think is, swing.[18]

Though Haggart, Matlock, and Kincaide often incorporated standard "swing" touches in their writing, they were clearly working off a different foundation. Rather than thinking in terms of strict brass-and-reed divisions, they seemed to hear the linear three- and four-voice contrapuntal textures of a small New Orleans–style band.

In counterpoint, says *The Harvard Concise Dictionary of Music,* "each of the several lines sounding together retains its character as a line," as opposed to those "in which one line predominates and the remainder are clearly subservient"; heard thus, the three- and four-part "dixieland" ensemble is most certainly contrapuntal, wholly linear, its texture dependent on the melodic parity of its components. The bloc-based "sectional" writing of the swing bands, whether in the formulae of Gifford or Henderson, the repetitive riffing of the Basie band, or the martial scores Sy Oliver was writing for Jimmie Lunceford, most often sacrificed this linear parity in the interests of ensemble power and rhythmic momentum.[19]

While Crosby reeds show up sometimes as a sax section in the Henderson or Jerry Gray manner, they just as often work as a clarinet trio or quartet (with Miller or Rodin on bass clarinet for depth); sometimes tenor and clarinet are in unison, sometimes in octaves. Even when (as in the final moments of Haggart's "Diga Diga Doo" arrangement) the ensemble falls into riffing, it is for momentary effect, soon giving way to the basic polylinear independence.

Rhythmically, too, the band made a strong and personal statement. If Ray Bauduc lacked the inventiveness of a Chick Webb, the catalytic drive of Dave Tough, or the relaxed subtlety of a Jo Jones, he compensated with an *élan* perfectly suited to the band's aims. His percussion effects, like those of Paul Barbarin with Luis Russell, were right out of the New Orleans parade band tradition: behind Miller, for example, he'd often play a tattoo on the wood rim of his bass drum for an especially resonant sound.

Haggart's "Heebie Jeebies" arrangement proved both innovative and prophetic. By 1936, the Armstrong Hot Five record was a decade old, and a revered classic among hot music fans. By using it as model, both preserving its essence *and* leaving latitude for solo and ensemble, he established a precedent. Soon the Crosby band repertoire was full of such updatings, rethinkings of seminal records: "Savoy Blues" and "Come Back Sweet Papa" echoed Armstrong; "Dixieland Shuffle" clad King Oliver's "Riverside Blues" in stylish new raiment; Kincaide's ensemble lines on "Royal Garden Blues" are drawn directly from the 1927 Bix Beiderbecke OKeh record; and the melodic line on "Fidgety Feet" echoes the Wolverines.

Sometimes, said Haggart, it was not strictly a matter of homage. "Quite often we wrote the lines out that way because we didn't really know the original melodies; we only knew what we'd heard on the old records. Some of those things by Louis's Hot Five, for instance: all I knew was what Louis had played—and to me that was gospel, the way the tune should be played."

The three arrangers added New Orleans standards ("Panama," "High Society") and numbers associated with both the Original Dixieland Jazz Band ("Mournin' Blues, "Palesteena") and New Orleans Rhythm Kings: on "Tin Roof Blues," trumpeter Lawson borrows liberally from the line played by Paul Mares on the 1923 Gennett record, and Matlock's clarinet solo evokes the delicacy of much-admired Leon Roppolo.

So thoroughly did this sense of the jazz past, however recent, saturate the band's work that musical allusions to earlier records turn up even in unlikely places. The end of a rousing "Pagan Love Song," for example, finds Lawson firing off King Oliver's "Dippermouth Blues" breaks; Haggart's arrangement of the otherwise forgettable "A Precious Memory" seems to have taken the title seriously, sneaking in a reference to Louis's 1926 "Cornet Chop Suey."

In looking back this way, Gunther Schuller remarks in *The Swing Era*, "the Crosby band became in a way the first 'jazz repertory orchestra,' and the first to recognize that, even in 1935, jazz already had a venerable history and a worthy accumulated artistic tradition." Perhaps. But what sets these Crosby performances apart, keeps them fresh on the ears, is that they are not re-creations but adaptations. Respectful, yes—but what makes the Crosby ensemble not a jazz repertory band is its personal freedom and sense of involvement. Each performance is a continuation of the very tradition it salutes.[20]

Other groups—Goodman, Henderson, Tommy Dorsey, the Casa Loma Orchestra—would occasionally play, even update, an arrangement from the '20s. But that usually had more to do with the lasting popularity of the piece or (as in Dorsey's 1938 *Evolution of Swing* radio broadcast) a specific commemoration.

Duke Ellington, as always, went his own way, forever revising such early pieces as "Rockin' in Rhythm" and "Black and Tan Fantasy [or Fantasie]." But the Ellington standards were eternal works-in-progress, subject to the endless refractions of their composer's vision. Ellington's orchestra became, and remained, a repertory orchestra for itself, its collaborative identification with its leader's compositional processes absolute and exclusive.

Though quite different from Ellington's ensemble, the Crosby orchestra shared one of its cardinal traits: so strong was its sense of identity that it could imbue almost anything (perhaps, intriguingly, even an Ellington piece) with its own, immediately recognizable, flavor—as long as it was allowed to do things its own way.

The beginning of 1937 brought the Crosby band its first really important personnel change. Gil Bowers, one of the original "Pollack Orphans," had left in mid-1936; his replacement, eagerly awaited, was to have been the hard-hitting Chicago pianist Joe Sullivan. Arriving from Los Angeles, where he'd been working with Bing Crosby, Sullivan joined in September—only to discover that he had tuberculosis, an ailment that was to plague him the rest of his life. He returned to California and entered a sanitarium, leaving the Crosby orchestra looking for a pianist of comparable stature.[21]

They found him in Bob Zurke. Born Robert Zukowski in Detroit, Zurke had been a child prodigy, performing at age ten for the great Polish pianist-statesman Ignace Jan Paderewski. As a young man he'd worked around the Midwest with regional bands led by Oliver Naylor, bassist Thelma Terry, and society trumpeter Henry Biagini, father of the Casa Loma Orchestra.

Zurke's personal idiosyncrasies, whether epic consumption of alcohol or inattention to personal details from finance to hygiene, were legion. But what made him memorable, ultimately, was the way he overcame what was almost a physical handicap to become one of the most original piano stylists of the '30s. His hands were tiny, with unusually short, stubby fingers: where many pianists of the era routinely reach a tenth (and sometimes, as in the case of Fats Waller, considerably more), Zurke had trouble even spanning an octave; in practice, this meant that the left-hand accompaniment basic to all early stylists, from Earl Hines to the Harlem "stride" men, and refined by players as disparate as Sullivan, Teddy Wilson, and Jess Stacy, was simply not open to him.

Zurke found his own way of achieving the same ends, modifying the standard root-chord, root-chord pattern, and blending it with what is probably the first regular use of independently moving lines in the history of jazz piano. "[Zurke's] contrapuntal sense made things interesting for a bassist," Haggart said. "It was probably a good thing that he couldn't reach tenths. Piano players then were playing left-hand tenths all the time, and from a bass player's standpoint it didn't leave you much to do: you were locked into what the piano player was doing. Zurke's small hands meant he had to work on a different principle, and I kinda prefer that. Leaves things open."[22]

Crosby records abound with superb Zurke solos. He opens his chorus on "Call Me a Taxi," a 1938 quartet exploration of the chord sequence of "Honeysuckle Rose," with a thematically simple right-hand figure. Left hand picks up a complementary statement, and both build to a tumbling climax in bars 23–24, ending with a lower-register recapitulation using material selected from earlier points in the solo. It is represented here in a superb transcription by Dick Hyman.

(continued)

"Call Me a Taxi," Bob Zurke full piano chorus, 1938.

Other Zurke highlights can be found on "Squeeze Me" (1937), "Stumbling" (an aircheck of April 1938 gives him a full-chorus solo, rather than the half-chorus of the 1937 Decca record), and Kincaide's "In a Minor Mood," unrecorded commercially but featured in a broadcast version of April 28, 1938. It's a simple chord structure, similar to Fats Waller's "Zonky" but *sans* melody, and bookended by the introduction to Rachmaninoff's *Prelude* in C♯ *Minor*. Kincaide

393

keeps interest high with varying ensemble textures and frequent modulations; within three minutes band and soloists have played in C-minor (Zurke, Miller), D-minor (Fazola), G-minor (Lawson), then eight ensemble bars apiece in Ab-minor, A-minor, Bb-minor, and B-minor, with an exultant wind-up in C-minor.

Zurke was a perfect fit. Such features as his variations on "Tea for Two" and energized boogie-woogie interpretations ("Honky-Tonk Train Blues") made him a Crosby band attraction. "I never thought he played with the swing, or the kind of feel, that Sullivan or Jess [Stacy] had," Haggart said. "But he was a sensation: people still remember that today, and talk about it. You could hear only a bar or two, and you'd know it was Bob Zurke. He knew just what he wanted to do, and played with a completely different sound, a lot of intensity."[23]

With Zurke in place, and the strong trumpet section of Lawson, Billy Butterfield, and lead man Charlie Spivak matching the drive of the rhythm, the Crosby orchestra achieved a lustrous, widely envied consistency. But there was also something else, harder to define. Historian John Chilton, himself a fine jazz trumpeter, got close to it in remarking that "the Crosby band existed in an atmosphere that was a cross between a family and a highly successful sports team."[24]

The camaraderie is obvious, saturating their treatments of even such unlikely vehicles as "The Old Spinning Wheel," a cowboy-style melody by Billy Hill, a Bostonian who had found his market with such similarly faux-naïf items as "Wagon Wheels," "The Last Roundup," and "There's a Cabin in the Pines." The arrangement is a collaboration, with Haggart, Matlock, and Miller all taking a hand. Rather than lampoon Hill's sentimental melody, the performance plays to its strengths, letting it sing with winning sweetness over Bauduc's broad New Orleans beat.

After Matlock and Lawson split a chorus, Zurke takes one, his first on record with the band, mixing twisting counterpoint with hard-stomping barrelhouse passages. The final tutti, devised by Haggart and Miller, is as simple as a folk song yet generates considerable force, Matlock's clarinet flashing brightly over the ensemble.

At the same session they recorded Haggart's arrangement of "Between the Devil and the Deep Blue Sea." "I think I spent more time, gave that one more thought, than just about anything else I wrote for the band around that time," he has said. "It still sounds good to me today." No wonder: from its opening bars, brass punching out the melody in Eb over a bouncing unison reed figure, it's full of incident, changes of pace, texture, and key. Haggart varies the harmony underpinning Matlock's Bb solo, replacing the tonic-dominant pattern of the song's first four bars with a more interesting D7-G7-C7-F7 sequence. After the full band (trombones to the fore) finishes out that chorus, he deals a surprise: he has Miller play the first eight bars of the melody in Bb and the second in Db, setting up the final ensemble. So easily, so naturally, is it done that the ear doesn't register right away that a modulation has occurred.

By the end of 1937, every major band seemed to be presenting its own small unit, usually a jazz group, drawn from within the larger one. It made musical sense, affording sidemen—and often leaders—more breathing room than the

1. Tom Brown's "Band from Dixieland" in vaudeville garb, New York City, 1915. L to R: Bill Lambert (dms), Brown (tbn), Larry Shields (clt), Ray Lopez (cnt), Arnold "Deacon" Loyocano (bs). *Frank Driggs Collection.* 2. Original Dixieland Jazz Band, publicity photo, 1917. L to R: Henry Ragas (pno), Larry Shields (clt), Eddie Edwards (tbn), D. J. "Nick" La Rocca (cnt), Tony Sbarbaro (dms). *Frank Driggs Collection.*

Instrument abbreviations: arr = arranger; as = alto sax; bjo = banjo; bs = bass; bsn = bassoon; bsx = bass sax; C-mel = C-melody sax; clt = clarinet; cnt = cornet; dms = drums; fl = flute; gtr = guitar; ldr = leader; picc = piccolo; pno = piano; ss = soprano sax; tbn = trombone; tpt = trumpet; ts = tenor sax; vcl = vocal; vln = violin.

3

4

3. New Orleans Rhythm Kings, Chicago, 1922. L to R: George Brunies (tbn), Frank Snyder (dms), Jack Pettis (C-mel), Elmer Schoebel (pno), Leon Roppolo (clt), Paul Mares (tpt), Arnold Loyocano (bs). *Duncan Schiedt Collection*. 4. Carlisle Evans Orchestra, Davenport, Iowa, 1921. L to R: Jack Willett (dms), Myron "Rookie" Neal (ts), Evans (pno/ldr), Emmett Hardy (cnt), Leon Roppolo (clt), Lew Black (bjo), Tal Sexton (tbn). *Duncan Schiedt Collection*.

5. Sidney Arodin and Friends, New York City, 1935. L to R: Arodin, Wingy Manone (tpt), George Brunies (tbn), Bob White (dms). *Frank Driggs Collection.* 6. Louis Panico, with Isham Jones's Orchestra, Chicago, 1922. *Duncan Schiedt Collection.* 7. Original Memphis Five, c. 1922. L to R: Frank Signorelli (pno), Phil Napoleon (tpt), Jimmy Lytell (clt), Miff Mole (tbn), Jack Roth (dms). *Duncan Schiedt Collection.*

8

9

8. The Georgians, Alamac Hotel, New York City, 1924. L to R: Chauncey Morehouse (dms), Arthur Schutt (pno), Russell Deppe (bjo), Frank Guarente (tpt), Johnny O'Donnell (as), Dick Johnson(?) (clt), unknown (tbn). *Duncan Schiedt Collection.* 9. Red Nichols Five Pennies, c. 1926. L to R: Nichols (tpt), Bill Haid(?) (pno), Jimmy Dorsey (clt), Vic Berton (dms), Fred Morrow(?) (as), Miff Mole (tbn). *Frank Driggs Collection.*

10

11

12

10. Adrian Rollini, c. 1925-26. *Ed Kirkeby Collection/Institute of Jazz Studies.* 11. Adrian Rollini, English cartoon, c. 1928. On floor: his "Goofus" and "Hot Fountain Pen." *Jim Shepherd.* 12. Joe Venuti (violin, front, 3rd from L) and Eddie Lang (guitar), with Paul Whiteman's Orchestra in scene from *The King of Jazz,* 1930. Mike Pingitore (bjo) is to Lang's right. *Herman Rosse Collection, Chapin Library, Williams College.*

13

14

13. The "Austin High" Gang, in a non-musical moment, Chicago, c. 1925. L to R, standing: Eddie Condon (bjo), Dave Tough (dms), Dick McPartland (gtr), Dave North (pno), Bud Freeman (ts), Frank Teschemacher (clt). Front: Jim Lanigan (bs), Jimmy McPartland (cnt). *Marian McPartland Collection*. 14. Jimmy McPartland's Band recording in Chicago, Oct. 11, 1939. L to R: McPartland (cnt), Bud Jacobson (clt), Boyce Brown (as), Hank Isaacs (dms). Not shown: Floyd Bean (pno), Dick McPartland (gtr). *Marian McPartland Collection*.

15. Two Chicagoans and their Tommy Dorsey Bandmates, Texas, 1936. L to R: Max Kaminsky (tpt), Jack Leonard (vcl), Axel Stordahl (arr), Dave Tough (dms), Bud Freeman (ts). *Frank Driggs Collection.* 16. Eddie Condon and Friends at Carnegie Hall, Jan. 14, 1942. L to R: Condon (gtr), Bud Freeman (ts), John Kirby (bs), Gene Krupa (dms), Max Kaminsky (tpt), Pee Wee Russell (clt). *Charles Peterson Photo, courtesy Don Peterson.* 17. Members of the Jean Goldkette Orchestra, jamming for photographers at the Bronx Zoo, New York City, autumn 1926. L to R, front: unknown, "Howdy" Quicksell (bjo), Bix Beiderbecke (cnt), Fred "Fuzzy" Farrar (tpt), Bill Rank (tbn), hidden behind snake handler. Rear: Ray Lodwig (tpt), Irving Riskin (pno), Don Murray (clt), Steve Brown (bs), Newell "Spiegle" Willcox (tbn), Frank Trumbauer (C-mel). *Richard M. Sudhalter.*

18

19

20

18. Ben Pollack Orchestra, from Vitaphone movie short, 1929. Front, L to R: Vic Breidis (pno), William Schuman (cello), Ed Bergman, Alex Beller (vln), Benny Goodman (clt), Larry Binyon (ts), Gil Rodin (as). Rear, L to R: Harry Goodman (bs), Dick Morgan (gtr), Jack Teagarden (tbn), Jimmy McPartland (cnt), Ruby Weinstein (tpt), Ray Bauduc (dms). *Frank Driggs Collection.* 19. Boswell Sisters, 1935. L to R: Connie, Helvetia "Vet," Martha; Bobby Sherwood (gtr). *Frank Driggs Collection.* 20. Tommy Dorsey, soloing on trumpet, his jazz horn of choice, c. 1938. *Courtesy of Mrs. Neil McCaffrey.*

21. Bob Crosby's Bobcats, Hickory House, New York City, 1937. L to R: Ray Bauduc (dms), Yank Lawson (tpt), Warren Smith (tbn), Matty Matlock (clt), Eddie Miller (ts), Bob Haggart (bs), Bob Zurke (pno), Hilton "Nappy" Lamare (gtr). *Frank Driggs Collection.* 22. Irving "Fazola" Prestopnik, c. 1939. *Frank Driggs Collection.*

23

24

23. The Wolverines, onstage at Palace Theater, Indianapolis, summer 1924. L to R: Vic Berton (dms), Dick Voynow (pno), Bob Gillette (bjo), Min Leibrook (tuba), Jimmy Hartwell (clt), Bix Beiderbecke (cnt), George Johnson (ts). *Duncan Schiedt Collection.* 24. Frank Trumbauer, combining music and aviation, c. 1929. *Melody Maker.*

25. Jack "Jacques" Purvis, entry card for travel to Mexico, June 20, 1932. *Duncan Schiedt Collection.* 26. Bunny Berigan and Gene Krupa, at Roseland Ballroom, New York City, 1938. *Frank Driggs Collection.* 27. Dick McDonough and Carl Kress, duo guitars, onstage at Imperial Theatre concert, May 24, 1936. *Charles Peterson Photo, courtesy Don Peterson.*

28

29

28. Artie Shaw, Chick Webb, Duke Ellington, at jam session, March 14, 1937. *Charles Peterson Photo, courtesy Don Peterson.* 29. Brad Gowans (tbn), Bobby Hackett (cnt), Pee Wee Russell (clt), at Jimmy Ryan's, New York City, Jan. 19, 1941. *Charles Peterson Photo, courtesy Don Peterson.*

30

31

30. Ernie Caceres, prince of the baritone sax, at 1957 recording session. *Photo: Popsie Randolph, Frank Driggs Collection.* 31. Red Norvo Swing Sextet, Famous Door, New York City, Feb. 1936. L to R: Herbie Haymer (ts), Pete Peterson (bs), Norvo (xylophone), Dave Barbour (gtr), Don McCook (clt), Stew Pletcher (tpt). *Charles Peterson Photo, courtesy Don Peterson.*

32

33

32. Red Norvo Orchestra with Mildred Bailey, Hotel Commodore, New York City, 1938. *Frank Driggs Collection.* 33. Mutual Admirers: Jack Teagarden and Tommy Dorsey, at Club El Rio, New York City, Oct. 21, 1938. L to R: Teagarden, George Wettling (dms), Milton "Mezz" Mezzrow (clt), Dorsey. Not shown: Frank Signorelli (pno). *Photographer unknown.*

34

35

34. A Sublime Team: Bobby Hackett and Jack Teagarden, at *Jazz Ultimate* record session, New York City, 1957. *Photo: Popsie Randolph, Frank Driggs Collection.* 35. George Barnes Octet, Chicago, 1946. L to R: Barnes (gtr), possibly Eddie Swan (bsx, bcl, clt), Hal Taylor (bs), Tommy Miller (fl, clt, picc), unknown (bsn), Phil Wing (clt/oboe), Frankie Rullo (dms). *Institute of Jazz Studies.*

36

37

36. Lee Wiley, singing at Gjon Mili jam session. L to R: Eddie Condon (gtr), Jess Stacy (pno), Wiley (vcl), Sid Weiss (bs), Cozy Cole (dms). Figure in background, to right of Cole, unknown. *Institute of Jazz Studies.* 37. Members of Casa Loma Orchestra visit a Texas music store and pose for *Down Beat* cover, November 1938. L to R: vocalist Kenny Sargent (as), leader Glen Gray (contrabass sax), trombonist "Pee Wee" Hunt (holding ears), trumpeter Sonny Dunham (antique rotary valve fluegelhorn). *Institute of Jazz Studies.*

larger context allowed; and it was wise programming as well, a valuable break from the heft and volume of the full band.

Benny Goodman's Trio and Quartet were virtuoso units, well matched to his instrumental mastery. Artie Shaw's Gramercy Five, featuring Johnny Guarnieri's harpsichord, was a child of its leader's ever-restless imagination. Duke Ellington's various small recording groups—often under nominal leadership of such sidemen as Johnny Hodges, Rex Stewart, or Cootie Williams—reflected his resplendence off new surfaces.

No surprise, then, that the Crosby small group, which made its first records while the band was playing the Los Angeles Palomar Ballroom, was an eight-piece, concentrated version of the larger group's collective outlook. Lawson, Matlock, Miller, and trombonist Warren Smith made a close-knit front line, playing with and off one another with a cohesiveness rivaled only by Muggsy Spanier's 1939 "Ragtimers" or the Bud Freeman Summa Cum Laude Orchestra of the same time. The smaller format, moreover, made it possible to hear in fine detail Bauduc's full range of percussive textures and colors in fine detail and to appreciate the two-handed complexity of Zurke's solo lines.

Zez Confrey's 1922 "Stumbling" might have seemed an atavism, an odd repertoire choice for a 1937 jazz band; but from the repeated concert F's of the introduction, straining forward like racehorses at a starting gate, it's clear the Bobcats found the old melody more than congenial. Both here and on an aircheck version of the following April 25, the band hurtles forward with great brio: Miller solos on tenor and clarinet, centering his clarinet chorus in the instrument's fluid low register.

Fans and collectors have wondered why, with so able a clarinetist as Matlock standing beside him, Miller took both solos here. "When there was something with a New Orleans taste," he told John Chilton, "they'd usually call me out front." And Matty, almost as gracious and self-effacing as Miller himself, would have been the last to complain. It was also typical of them both that when New Orleans–born Irving Fazola, whom they both admired, joined in early 1939, Matlock simply turned more to arranging and Miller concentrated on tenor.

The rest of the Bobcats titles done that day—"Who's Sorry Now?," "Coquette," "Fidgety Feet," and two others, plus three selections as accompaniment to vocalist Connie Boswell—also leave no doubt as to the importance of trumpeter Lawson in the overall impact of both the large and small bands. His is a shouting, commanding lead, often (to extend Chilton's sports analogy) like the voice of a coach, exhorting his team to greater and greater effort on the field. Its chief inspiration is clearly Louis Armstrong, but the manner of expression is just as palpably Lawson's own.

He opens Haggart's "Dogtown Blues" with a chorus over low reeds, at once plaintive and impassioned; the effect deepens when, after a clarinet section episode, he returns for a stop-time chorus. It clearly moved Eddie Miller: his two clarinet choruses (the first over instrumental choirs and Haggart's bowed bass, the second with brass and a Bauduc tomtom ostinato) are among his best, with a growing fervor of expression which carries easily into a glorious final ensemble. Here is Haggart the master orchestrator, drawing on a wide range of densities and shadings to achieve a cumulative, gospel-like intensity.

"I used to buy records by Mitchell's Christian Singers," he said, "and I was crazy about the voicings they used. They knew nothing about [formal] music— but all their performances had this kind of wonderful dissonant sound. Very exciting. I think there's a little of that in the way I voiced things at the end." (His admiration emerges most explicitly in his arrangement of "I'm Prayin' Humble," an almost verbatim adaptation of one of the selections for which the Mitchell singers were best known.)[25]

Part of the dissonance rests on simple devices: within the B♭ ensemble chord opening the first of the final choruses he has both concert D and D♭ strongly represented, with open fourths and fifths prominent; the sound is evocative of a southern gospel "shout." Though less widely known than its session-mate, Haggart's "South Rampart Street Parade," "Dogtown Blues" is musically more important in what it shows of Haggart's ability to marshal tonal resources in a vivid and fully integrated musical statement.

It's worth remembering here that the Crosby orchestra existed as a regularly constituted unit for only seven years; what might have been the result if Haggart, with his idiomatic knowledge and grasp of tonal potential, had been able to write for a stable, highly compatible personnel over seven times that period, as did Ellington?

The cohesiveness of the 1937–38 Crosby ensemble finds expression on dozens of records, in peaks and memorable episodes: Lawson's shouting exposition of the verse of "At the Jazz Band Ball," Miller's poised tenor choruses on the quartet's "I Hear You Talking," a mile-a-minute series of variations on the changes of "Oh, Lady Be Good"; the teamwork and shared love of idiom so obvious in the way they play Matlock's "Wolverine Blues" arrangement.

Yet such closeness carries risks. To again borrow Chilton's analogy, what happens to a championship baseball team when its star hitter or pitcher signs with another club? Is there a point at which interdependence becomes as much liability as strength? It happened to the Crosby orchestra in late 1938, when Tommy Dorsey came shopping for a trumpet soloist. Pee Wee Erwin, who had taken over so strongly from Bunny Berigan, was leaving, and Dorsey turned his gaze on Yank Lawson.

Herb Sanford, in his *Tommy and Jimmy: The Dorsey Years*, has recounted in detail the various subterfuges used by "the Sentimental Gentleman" to woo Lawson away from Crosby. It was in every way "an offer he couldn't refuse," and he accepted, taking lead trumpeter Charlie Spivak with him. The Crosby musicians were stunned; morale, so crucial to this band's on-the-field success, took a nose-dive.

It wasn't readily apparent in the band's recorded performances. The recent arrival of Fazola had brought in another eloquent solo voice. The trumpet section, too, had an ace in the hole: with Lawson playing most of the solos and Spivak (or Zeke Zarchy) the lead, twenty-year-old Billy Butterfield had been given little to do. Now, suddenly, he had a chance to show every night that he was a gifted jazzman, a peerless ballad player, *and* a strong, sure lead man.

Dorsey's band was loaded with talent: Johnny Mince was one of the most admired clarinet soloists of the decade, Bud Freeman, on tenor, even more so, unique and imaginative; in Dave Tough, Dorsey had one of the grand masters of jazz drumming, able to energize a band from within.

If the Crosby band resembled a sports team, Dorsey's more closely approximated a small corporation, run by a tough (and occasionally benevolent) CEO. "If Tommy liked and respected you," guitarist Carmen Mastren explained, "he let you alone. But if he didn't—well, I've seen him make life miserable for a lot of guys."[26]

Lawson, from all indications, was not one of them. After a few preliminary solo appearances (such as "Ya Got Me," on which he paraphrases the Oliver "Dippermouth Blues" breaks), he comes into his own on "Tin Roof Blues" and "Down Home Rag," and no wonder: they're both Deane Kincaide arrangements, creating a strongly Crosby-like ambiance. Yank's thrusting plunger solo is the focus of "Hawaiian War Chant," another Kincaide score, over Moe Purtill's tom-toms (again, with an allusion to "Dippermouth"), leading to a strong rideout.

The rule seems to hold: when soloing in someone else's arrangement (as in "Angels with Dirty Faces" and others), Lawson is clean, efficient, sometimes more than that. But when Kincaide is the arranger, replicating the Crosby environment, he seems at his best, charging his surroundings with electricity.[27]

The best evidence, and a moment of real climax, is surely the, two-sided "Milenberg Joys," one of Kincaide's best scores for Dorsey. Dave Tough had been out of the band, grappling with alcohol and a collection of personal demons, for nearly a year. But now he was back, and the difference was thrilling. "I sat right next to him," said Lawson, "and it was a great experience. His taste—well, he knew just when to play and when *not* to play. Never flashy or anything—but as close to perfect as you can imagine."[28]

Tough's inspiriting drumming, Kincaide's arrangement, and solos by Lawson, Mince, Dorsey, and tenor saxophonist Babe Russin combine to make "Milenberg Joys" one of the decade's signal records. "Little Davey" rides his Chinese cymbal hard behind Yank's two choruses, and the drive they generate together is something to behold. It's not that the trumpeter does anything technically spectacular: he stays in his middle register (his highest note is a concert A♭ above the staff), generating intensity through attack, tonal density, and a fast, urgent, terminal vibrato.

"Tommy was generous to me in a thousand ways, and we lived very well, better than with Crosby," said Lawson, who clearly enjoyed his time with Dorsey. He was free at last, he said, of the Crosby band's internal management system, with its endless friction between those who were corporation members and those who were not. The non-corp men, he said, made full salaries, nothing withheld. Shareholders like Lawson often surrendered part of their wages to the corporation for operating expenses—which meant usually coming out short on payday. Business manager Rodin most often deflected complaints with standard rhetoric about "investment in the company."

"I must have been in the [Dorsey] band two or three months before I even knew how much money I was making," he said. "I never talked about money with Tommy at all. When I went with the band he just said, 'Just draw whatever you need and we'll talk about it later,' or something like that. So I did, and believe me, I drew a lot. But Tommy never griped about it. Finally he said to me, 'What do you want? We'd better talk about salary.' And I told him laughingly, 'Well, I just want whatever the top money is in this band.' And he said, 'Okay.' Just like that."[29]

The picture Lawson paints of Dorsey is of a thoughtful man, kind to many, but forever masking it behind a rough, side-of-the-mouth exterior. "He was very generous, and certainly doesn't deserve all the knocks he's taken. On paydays, for instance, there'd be a line of people outside the door, people he was taking care of—old trombone players and such—and he'd give 'em money every week."

At one point Lawson contracted Bell's palsy, a disorder of the nerves and muscles of the face, often the result of sitting in a draft or leaning up against a cold window in a heated bus. It sidelined him for several months. "Tommy paid my salary the whole time," he said.

Billy Butterfield, meanwhile, quickly became one of the Crosby band's great strengths. Haggart's "I'm Free" showcased his silvery tone and soaring conception—and occasioned a rip in the band's social fabric. "I had the trumpet parts marked with each musician's name," Haggart said. "When Charlie [Spivak] saw that the lead part was to go to Billy, he asked, 'Isn't there some mistake?' And Billy, who knew I had written the song for him, simply said, 'It says "Billy," doesn't it?' That was the start of a rift . . . that I think never fully healed."[30]

"I'm Free," of course, soon gained a memorable lyric (by Johnny Burke) and a new title. As "What's New?" it has won a secure place as one of the great popular ballads of the '30s. Perhaps Bob Crosby wasn't straining credibility overmuch in suggesting that his bassist "could have been another George Gershwin if he'd channeled all his talents into composing."[31]

The Crosby orchestra recorded "I'm Free" and thirteen other titles during a three-day recording marathon at Decca's Chicago studios, October 19–21, 1938. Taken together, they furnish an invaluable cross-section of the band and its many strengths. On "I'm Prayin' Humble," Pollack veteran Stirling Bose brings his distinctive plunger style to a trumpet solo originally intended for Lawson; Zurke shows off his boogie-woogie mastery in personalizing Meade Lux Lewis's "Honky-Tonk Train Blues"; Eddie Miller contributes one of his most elegant choruses to "Swingin' at the Sugar Bowl," based on the chord sequence of "Honeysuckle Rose."

The genesis of that one, Haggart explained, was the popular *Harold Teen* comic strip. "Carl Ed, who drew it, used to come in all the time to hear us when we were at the [Hotel] Blackhawk, in Chicago. And he regularly put us in [the strip]—me and Bauduc. The Sugar Bowl, of course, was the soda shoppe where

Teen and his pals all hung out; I guess this was our way of saying 'thank you' to him."

It's in solos such as this that Miller demonstrates how dissimilar his style was to that of his admired friend and colleague Bud Freeman. His tone is warmer, attack less rugged. He makes more frequent use of his high register. His basic conception, discussed more fully elsewhere in this volume, proceeds from the Albert system clarinet, instrument of choice for so many New Orleans reedmen.

A Miller solo can be intense ("Pagan Love Song"), hard-swinging ("I Hear You Talking"), infinitely graceful ("Cecilia"). It can be a thing of warm, almost erotic beauty, as his own "Slow Mood" (or, as it came to be called, "Lazy Mood"). Whatever the setting, it never loses a certain stateliness, as fundamental to New Orleans reed playing as a prodding, edgy attack is to Freeman, Frank Teschemacher, and their fellow-Chicagoans.

The first October session ends with the old favorite "Diga Diga Doo." Clarinetist Irving Fazola displays a tone like poured sunshine; Miller, on tenor, is upbeat; and Zurke's solo is a whirlwind, loaded with surprises. But Haggart's writing is the real star of this two-part treatment of the Jimmy McHugh–Dorothy Fields collaboration first heard in *Lew Leslie's Blackbirds of 1928*. It is a virtuoso arranging turn, endlessly combining ensemble weights and textures in a steady thematic development.

Above all, Haggart shows (especially in the closing ensemble, where he borrows a figure from the Pollack band's "Two Tickets to Georgia" arrangement) that even riff writing can be intelligent and absorbing. In contrast with the many riff-based pieces then in vogue, each episode here bristles with melodic interest; the twisting, downward chromatic reed figure with which he ends "Diga Diga Doo" is a masterstroke.*

Among the outstanding moments of the second day was another Haggart composition, also originally intended for Butterfield. But Decca had announced its intention of turning a dozen of these performances into a record album, *A Bob Crosby Showcase*, to feature various members of the band. The Ohio-born trumpeter already had "I'm Free," but there was nothing to show off Fazola—except Haggart's new piece.

They wound up calling it "My Inspiration." Informally, said Haggart, "we called it 'Big Mouth.' That was Faz's slang term for gin, and we told him that just to get a rise out of him." But inspiration it certainly is: a thoughtful melody that fits Fazola's broad tone and flowing conception perfectly.

The clarinetist's full name was Irving Henry Prestopnick; "Fazola" seems to

---

*The band was also lucky enough at this point to have something of a freak hit record with "The Big Noise From Winnetka"; it's a Haggart-Bauduc duo, little more than a series of patterns on a G-minor chord, climaxing with the drummer beating on the bass strings while Haggart fingers the notes with his left hand. The story of its genesis, a Sunday afternoon jam session at Chicago's Blackhawk, has been told again and again. The piece has become an industry standard, bassists and drummers (some of whom have never heard of Haggart and Bauduc) still performing it at jazz concerts worldwide. Its role in the popularity of the Crosby band is unquestioned: musically, however, it is really little more than a footnote.

have been a nickname, conferred on him by Louis Prima and probably having something to do with the "fa-sol-la" of solfeggio studies. He'd grown up in New Orleans, enchanted (as were Eddie Miller and most of the other young white clarinetists) with the limpid playing of Leon Roppolo; like Miller, Sidney Arodin, Barney Bigard, Jimmie Noone, Nunzio Scaglione, Edmond Hall, and most other New Orleans clarinetists, he took to the Albert system instrument, rather than the more complex, but easier to finger, Boehm system.

Explaining many years later why he finally switched from Albert to Boehm, Eddie Miller said that "even the third clarinet parts contained fingering that was just too fast for my old [Albert] clarinet. But I still think the Albert system suits jazz playing more than the Boehm; you get a bigger tone out of an Albert."[32]

Fazola, by contrast, tried Boehm for a while but returned to Albert, playing it for the rest of his life. He brought to it an ease, tonal beauty, and simplicity of execution which were widely and genuinely admired, even by musicians (such as tenor saxophonist Jerry Jerome, who worked with him in Glenn Miller's first band) who nursed no great love for the "dixieland" style.

By all accounts "Faz" was neither a thinker nor even particularly likable. Chronically overweight, slovenly in matters of personal hygiene, he often seemed a social liability. But his clarinet playing had long been a major attraction for musicians visiting New Orleans; pioneering cornetist Johnny DeDroit, with whom he worked in the '20s, especially remembered Fazola's purity of tone. Ben Pollack, indefatigable as a talent scout, finally prised the clarinetist loose from his home town in 1935.

National recognition followed directly. John Hammond, writing of Pollack's band, adjudged Fazola a "great musician"; George Frazier, in Down Beat, hailed him as "one of the great artists of 1936." His solos on such 1936 Pollack records as "Jimtown Blues," "Peckin',t" and "Spreadin' Knowledge Around," the last by a small unit labeled "the Dean and His Kids," broadened his reputation still further.

Even at faster tempos, Fazola seems to speak in a tranquil voice, his choruses small pools of serenity amid the uproar of a band performance. But the tranquility is in no sense a dead spot or lull: a Fazola solo moves along freely and lightly, even with a certain gaiety, while never calling attention to itself. In this sense Fazola is the mirror-image of Yank Lawson, who in all but his most reflective moments seems forever shouting at the listener.

Consider, for example, the two B♭ choruses with which the clarinetist opens the 1938 "Milk Cow Blues," one of his first recorded efforts with the band: he seems at once composed and emotionally involved. His eight-bar introduction and full chorus on "Spain" (1940), with the Bobcats, seems less to play the old Isham Jones melody than to caress it. He's no less effective on a Haggart adaptation of Emil Waldteufel's "Skaters' Waltz," his two choruses gliding with all the grace of one of the patineurs of the title. On pianist Joe Sullivan's up-tempo feature, "The World Is Waiting for the Sunrise," Fazola enters with the simplest of devices— a half-note concert G, followed by a six-beat concert C—which has an immediate calming (but in no way dampening) effect.

*   *   *

Having weathered Lawson's departure, the Crosby musicians were better prepared when, in early 1939, Bob Zurke announced he was leaving to start his own band. In a statement to *Down Beat*, he hinted that friends and fans had been after him for months to strike out on his own. But Crosby bandmates, seeing the headline HELL, THEY'VE DRIVEN ME TO IT, wondered whether "they" was in fact just the ever-expanding roster of the pianist's creditors.

Zurke put together a good band, which began recording immediately for Victor. Again, as had been the case with the Dorsey-Kincaide-Lawson alliance, it sounded much like a Crosby unit, playing arrangements by Fud Livingston and featuring Stirling Bose, who had left Crosby to join the pianist. The thirty titles they recorded between July 18, 1939, and May 8 the following year include some of the pianist's—and Bose's—best work.

The trumpeter has incisive solos on "It's Me Again," "Nickel Nabber Blues" (which must have brought a certain grim amusement to the Crosby musicians, from whom Zurke had borrowed hundreds of dollars in very small increments), and Livingston's clean-lined refurbishing of "I've Found a New Baby." The pianist steps out handsomely on his own "Hobson Street Blues"—not a blues at all, but an attractive thirty-two-bar strain built on a chord sequence related to both "There'll Be Some Changes Made" and "Honeysuckle Rose." He redoes "Honky-Tonk Train" and reprises "Tea for Two" in much the same arrangement used with Crosby, tenor saxophonist John Gassoway turning in an Eddie Miller–like solo. Bose sings the eight-bar blues "Peach Tree Street" and plays a couple of particularly engaging plunger choruses in a manner reminiscent of Muggsy Spanier.

For all its talent, the Zurke band lasted less than a year. Its story resembles that of cornetist Bobby Hackett's short-lived big band of about the same time: too much drinking (Bose, drummer Stan King, Livingston, and fellow-trumpeter Chelsea Quealey could match Zurke shot for shot), too much debt (including, in Zurke's case, delinquent alimony payments), and insufficient attention paid overall to business.

Zurke went back to playing solo piano, first in Chicago (where a *Down Beat* news item had him expressing relief at "no payroll worries, no killing one-nighters, no personnel headaches and none of the lousy kicks every band leader has to die of"), then back to Detroit. Ultimately he wandered west to Los Angeles, working—ironically, perhaps—at the Hangover Club. He died, age thirty-two, in 1944.[33]

The Crosby band's piano chair, meanwhile, was well occupied. After a brief interregnum, during which Chicagoan Floyd Bean filled in, Joe Sullivan returned, apparently free of the tuberculosis that had sidelined him in 1936. He had earlier won admiration for his stomping accompaniment to Bing Crosby on Hoagy Carmichael's "Moonburn" in 1935 and on various dates with Joe Venuti ("In de Ruff"), Red Nichols ("China Boy"), and Eddie Condon (the blues "Home Cooking," among others). His rolling blues chorus on "Spider Crawl," with the Rhythmakers, uses elements of Earl Hines, Fats Waller, and James P. Johnson, with force and gruff individuality.

Unlike Zurke, Sullivan had unusually large hands, which could—and often

401

did—play the tenths that his predecessor couldn't reach. In the words of commentator and Sullivan friend Richard Hadlock, those hands were capable of

> playing music as sensitive and lovely as ever was heard in Sullivan's chosen field, jazz. They could also hammer out solos of astonishing power and unparalleled crispness—every note struck as though by a bell clapper. Serving this magnificent jazz technique was a creative impulse that made Sullivan one of the most adventurous, least hackneyed pianists in his profession, a musician consistently honored with superlatives from colleagues and audiences alike.[34]

But Sullivan's return engagement as a Crosby sideman lasted only four months. In later years, various reasons were cited: alcohol, personality clashes with Crosby, even the tight cliquishness of the New Orleans men at the core of the Crosby band. Mary Anne Sullivan, the pianist's wife, suggested to Hadlock that he "was also being less than faithful to me, and the boys didn't like that. They were quite particular about personal commitments. Finally, he just went too far and Gil [Rodin] let him go."[35]

This last explanation rings true. The Crosby band was, as its members have said, something of a family; couples were frequently as close off the bandstand as the individual musicians were on it. But whatever happened, the esteem in which the Crosby musicians held Joe Sullivan was never in question. He plunges and stomps on the Bobcats' "Love Nest" and is even more daring on "Till We Meet Again," pummeling the old waltz into new rhythmic and harmonic shapes. Hadlock is again right on target in remarking that Sullivan

> leads the listener into reacting with the whole body rather than just the sort of steady foot-patting that ordinarily goes well with Crosby music. The pianist worries the beat and takes chances beyond the call of the job, almost playing himself into an impossible corner with eccentric bass lines in the middle of his solo but returning to the straight pulse for the next soloist.[36]

Perhaps most rewarding of all is the lovely old 1920 ballad "Feather Your Nest," which gets an almost perfumed exposition from Fazola and thoughtful half-choruses from Miller and Butterfield; Sullivan's thirty-two bars open with unaccustomed delicacy, in a manner reminiscent of Teddy Wilson's crystalline touch, before building to a rolling, barrelhouse finish. Unaccountably, "Feather Your Nest" was never issued by Decca, appearing only on a collector LP in the '80s.

Sullivan's replacement was the no less respected Jess Stacy. Fresh from four years' indenture with Benny Goodman, he seemed an even better complement to the rhythm section than either Zurke or Sullivan. Crosby, ecstatic, told Down Beat that the Missouri-born pianist had "put us back in the right groove. His work with the band has been one of the most revitalizing things ever. Jess is playing today like he never did before. Don't take my word—ask Jess."[37]

Stacy's time with Goodman had been very much a mixed blessing. As pianist with the most popular band in the country he had a visibility equaled by few others, but within his visibility he remained curiously invisible. Teddy Wilson, appearing with the Goodman Trio and Quartet, got the spotlight, leaving Stacy as what Otis Ferguson called, in the title of a now-celebrated *New Republic* article, the "Piano in the Band."

With a few exceptions, Stacy's most vivid playing at that time was not with Benny but in small independent groups, particularly those that began recording in 1938 for Milt Gabler's new Commodore label. They find Stacy at his best, whether rippling and cascading behind Jack Teagarden on "Diane," swinging buoyantly on "My Honey's Lovin' Arms" with Bud Freeman and George Wettling, or thoughtfully exploring Bix Beiderbecke's masterpiece, *Candlelights*.

He'd had at least one unforgettable—and unexpected—triumph with Goodman, toward the end of the January 18, 1938, Carnegie Hall concert. Benny, Gene Krupa, Harry James, and the rest had taken their turns on a tumultuous "Sing Sing Sing," each playing to the grandstand. For reasons he scarcely remembered later, Benny turned things over to Jess—who, beginning with a simple A-minor chord, fashioned a two-minute elegy of timeless, meditative beauty. It is preserved on recordings of the concert, as dumbfounding now as on that winter night more than half a century ago.

After many problems with Goodman, joining Crosby relocated Stacy at center stage, featured as much as Miller, Fazola, and the rest of the regulars. Haggart wrote arrangements of the pianist's own "Complainin' " and "Ec-stacy" and of the engaging "Burning the Candle at Both Ends" to frame his solo talents; even his ensemble contributions seemed to be highlighted—something which quite astonished him at the time.

"All the guys were nice," he told an interviewer. "Nobody was pushing. Nobody was jealous. Most of them were about ten years younger than me, and on the road I had now graduated to having my own room in hotels." He especially enjoyed the Bobcats, which he later described as "pure fun, and music undiluted."[38]

Stacy is all over Crosby records beginning in November 1939. His solos, his customary right-hand tremolos (thumb and pinky stationary, second and fourth fingers creating the effect), are particularly effective on such numbers as "Do You Ever Think of Me?" The rhythm section seems lighter, even the often overbearing Bauduc displaying new suppleness.

But it's the pianist's opening chorus on "Where the Blue of the Night Meets the Gold of the Day" (a curious choice, given the nature of its association with another Crosby family member) that makes his value to the Crosby band unmistakably clear. He sets the melody out in octaves with a Bix-like clarity, left hand adding bounce to the phrases, and all over a closely voiced, four-clarinet chord cushion. If the February 1940 Decca record is good, an aircheck performance of a month later, from the Terrace Room of the Hotel New Yorker, is even better, with an almost bardic urgency in the pianist's delivery. His "Embraceable You," again from the New Yorker, is almost as eloquent, with ruminative contributions from Miller and Fazola along the way.

Good music isn't always a guarantee of success. There was trouble at the box office, growing evidence that the Crosby "dixieland" policy was wearing thin with the public. Several other bands, Tommy Dorsey's among them, had veered away toward different, more black orientations. Still other groups were specializing in rather mechanical renderings of the Crosby sound and style.

A growing revival of interest in older small-band jazz, moreover, seemed to dilute the band's following still further: those who had clung to the Bobcats when they were the sole standard-bearers for their musical philosophy now embraced a number of groups, including Spanier's "Ragtimers" (with George Brunis on trombone and Rod Cless on clarinet) and Freeman's excellent Summa Cum Laude Orchestra, with Max Kaminsky, Pee Wee Russell, and Brad Gowans.

Nor did a growing chorus of complaint in the trade papers help matters. *Metronome*'s Barry Ulanov, for example, scolded Ray Bauduc for, among other things, his "irksome rim-work and the block-work he fills in with." Editor George T. Simon, meanwhile, faulted the band for the alleged colorlessness of their arrangements and repertoire choices.

The musicians were at first puzzled, then angry. John Chilton relates one incident in which the normally affable Matty Matlock dragged an unidentified critic (Ulanov, perhaps?) up to the bandstand during a performance, demanding that he listen, then haranguing him with a shouted "What's wrong with *that* rhythm section?"

There were strains within the band as well. A fistfight between Fazola and trombonist Ray Conniff over some trifle brought the clarinetist's sullen resignation. Billy Butterfield left, ostensibly to spend more time with his wife and infant son. Good replacements were on hand, in Hank d'Amico and Muggsy Spanier (with Matlock resuming some of the hot clarinet work himself), but discord, overall, was in the air.[39]

Rodin, ever mindful of business, decided it was time for a major change and announced in *Metronome*: "We're going to have a more versatile outfit. It's true that we all feel the two-beat type of jazz more, but there's no getting away from it that many of the kids who come to hear us want us to play some four-beat, so we're going to give it to them from now on."[40]

He hired a vocal quartet called the Downbeaters, on the model of Tommy Dorsey's Pied Pipers, rechristening them the Bob-o-Links. He commissioned some arrangements from pianist Phil Moore, perhaps best known as an originator of the locked-hands "block chord" style later popularized by George Shearing. There were more out-and-out novelty numbers, more Crosby vocals. Above all, there were more standard swing arrangements, many along the very riff-saturated lines the Crosby men had sworn never to play.

"The way it was going was pretty discouraging," said Haggart. "All the white bands were trying to sound like Ellington and Basie and Lunceford. I always wondered why the hell we went to the trouble of arranging and recording some of that stuff, because everybody else did 'em so much better. I used to wonder, 'Why go through this exercise?' We went through a whole bunch of arrangers;

some of 'em did make the saxophone section sound good—at least like a standard sax section. But in the end our heart wasn't in it, and it sounded like that too."[41]

Lawson, who returned to the band in 1941, concurred. "I didn't care for some of the arrangements that had been added," he said. "They certainly didn't do anything to establish a new style for the band. Rather, they tended to make us sound like most of the other bands who were around at that time."[42]

The band's treatment of such Phil Moore originals as the two-part "Brass Boogie" and the Ellington-flavored "Blue Surreal" and "Black Zephyr" from 1942 is respectful, eminently musical; but these performances never quite escape a sense of anomaly, like a man in a clothing shop trying on suits whose cut or fit isn't quite comfortable.

It's not entirely the arrangements, and certainly not a matter of dependence on the "dixieland" texture. Indeed, it seems likely that the strong personalities of Miller, Matlock, Stacy, and Lawson could have left an imprint on an ever-broader range of material, as long as it was written with these specific musicians in mind. "Blue Surreal," for example, is a nicely crafted atmosphere piece; but it could have been written for *any* good band—and, not surprisingly, the Crosby musicians sound like any good band in performing them.

A clearer glimpse of the musicians' breadth of possibility comes with Haggart's own "Chain Gang," recorded at the "Blue Surreal" session. Issued on a twelve-inch 78 rpm record, it's an imaginative piece of tone-painting, drawing on the specific colorational resources of the Crosby band without recourse to "dixieland."

Using Lawson's ferocity and increased skill with the plunger, Haggart (who later developed considerable range as a painter) covers his canvas with dark colors and large, ominously hulking chordal shapes. At times his reed voicings may recall Duke Ellington, but overall, this tonal palette is his alone.

"To me there is a definite parallel between composing a piece of music and painting a still life," he commented in 1984. "The play of light in figurative art is very similar to the play of counterpoint in music. As one attempts to create these effects of light and shade, music and painting seem to go hand in hand."[43]

These impulses find musical expression in "Chain Gang," taking on an intensity which is as much visual as auditory. "I was getting into more complex harmonies at that point," said Haggart. "Trying out thicker textures. I remember one night some of the guys from Paramount Pictures came in, and they really liked it. It was quite a departure from what we'd been doing."[44]

What might have happened had he continued to experiment along such new and complex lines? There have been some hints through the years. Haggart's adaptations of the scores of *Porgy and Bess* and *South Pacific* for mid-'50s jazz LPs show flashes of brilliance in their economy and use of ensemble. Even "Sudan," done for an LP tribute to the music of the Original Dixieland Jazz Band, seems poised to plunge into the shadowland of "Chain Gang," again with Lawson as the anguished cry-in-the-wilderness, before veering off sharply into convention as if seeking the safety of higher ground.

The 1942 "Milenberg Joys" returns to the format of the late '30s—though even here Haggart is thinking imaginatively, casting the Lawson–Matlock–Miller–Floyd O'Brien front line as a kind of *concertino* against the full ensemble *ripieno* in a *concerto grosso* format. So taken was Gunther Schuller with the tightness and cohesion of the four horns that he transcribed their entire chorus in his massive survey *The Swing Era*.

Matlock's arrangement of "Jimtown Blues," from the same date, gives that 1924 chestnut a brightly nimble workout, highlighted by clarinet-led reeds. Eddie Miller is relaxed against punchy (and rather Glenn Millerish) brass figures, and Matlock steps out attractively. Throughout this session, Ray Bauduc eschews the rim-and-woodblock effects characteristic of his work, restricting himself (even behind Miller) to relatively staid, straightforward timekeeping. Did he keep a copy of *Metronome*, perhaps, hidden under his pillow?

Clearly, the band was happy and comfortable reclaiming this musical ground. But it does no disservice to suggest that such familiar terrain may represent less a recovery than a retreat, and that the continued challenge of new colors and forms might have brought its own stimulation and renewal. It's not without significance that shortly after World War II Bob Crosby organized a band that intentionally—some would have even said self-consciously—avoided any "dixieland" association at all, concentrating instead on a Basie-derived feel and sound. The venture proved mercifully short-lived.

The men who had shaped the Crosby orchestra's identity in the '30s remained socially and musically close, playing together often. Matlock and Miller settled in California, worked in film studios together, recorded together often, usually in company with other like-minded veterans. Lawson and Haggart, in New York, were also frequent associates. Their Lawson-Haggart Jazz Band of the '50s was an often jubilant extension of the old alliance, with Billy Butterfield, clarinetist Bill Stegmeyer, and other ex-Bobcats as regular sidemen. Haggart, especially, became an august, deeply respected elder statesman: bassist, songwriter, arranger, painter, and leader, with Lawson, of the immensely successful "World's Greatest Jazz Band," he remained active and vital well into his eighties.

Nappy Lamare and Ray Bauduc ran a small band together for a while. Crosby, for his part, could be relied on for periodic, often spirited Bobcats reunions, both on record and on the stages of clubs and concert halls. His very name remained synonymous with "dixieland," as played impeccably by top-of-the-line musicians—until changes in the politics of the music business, and of race relations within it, made even the music a matter of controversy.

But in 1937, or at any other time in the early years, such a future—and its attendant ironies—lay far ahead, over a distant horizon. "We were all very young," Lawson wrote to Scottish writer-admirer Ken Gallacher, "and we thought very little about how we were going to be a part of the history of jazz. All we did was try to get the best people we could . . . [and] I think, looking back, that we had pretty good taste in our selections."[45]

In retrospect, the Bob Crosby Orchestra stands as a powerful, singular force. At its best, which was often, it was an ensemble like no other, injecting the characteristic flavors, rhythms, and textures of New Orleans into the dance band world of its times. And as "Chain Gang" and other pieces show beyond doubt, it was an ensemble well stocked with gifted and versatile individuals, steered by inspired arrangers. "Pretty good taste in our selections?" It was more, more by far, than that.

V

Individual Voices

17

Bix Beiderbecke and Some of His Friends

He had music in a way of invention that is only found when you find a good song, inevitable, sweet, and perfect.

Otis Ferguson, 1940

"**B**ix was a mystery to us," cornetist Jimmy McPartland once confessed. "We all knew him, admired him, thought he was a great guy. But in a way we didn't know him at all. He wasn't really like us." McPartland spoke for many: even now, more than six decades after Bix Beiderbecke's death, he remains a being apart, an enigma.[1]

Beiderbecke is one of the most ardently, tirelessly documented of all early jazz figures. Philip R. Evans, in researching Bix: *Man and Legend*, seemed determined to account for every day in his subject's brief life and came remarkably close to achieving his goal. Such diverse writers as Otis Ferguson, Benny Green, Charles Wareing, Max Harrison, Burnett James, Humphrey Lyttelton, Gunther Schuller, and even, in rather different ways, Eddie Condon and Mezz Mezzrow (or their literary "ghosts") have captured aspects of him in print.

Bix Beiderbecke played the cornet and the piano, lived twenty-eight years and five months, and died alone, victim of alcoholism and pneumonia, on August 6, 1931. He made some 250 records, each of which has been subjected to endless scrutiny, as though hidden clues to a life could be prised from every bar or phrase. As early as the 1940s, his best-known cornet solos were lovingly transcribed and published, to be reproduced by generations of devotees. Beiderbecke's four piano compositions have been, and still are, performed in myriad settings, including full, sometimes overcooked, arrangements for symphony orchestras.[2]

From the standpoint of fact, little of Bix Beiderbecke's life and music remains in shadow: we know about him, can read about him, view the familiar photographs and listen to him on countless reissue albums. He has been safely enshrined as, to borrow Benny Green's apt phrase, jazz's number one saint.

Even various revisionist attempts to stress the preeminence of early black jazzmen to the virtual exclusion of their white peers seem willing to make an exception for Bix. Ann Douglas, in her widely praised but frequently misinformed *A Terrible Honesty*, singles him out—but is sure to remind readers that he "played brilliant apprentice, not robber, to black music."[3]

Somehow, when the verbiage falls away, we know this quiet, deferential young man as little as we did before the documentation began. The reality of him—motivations, perceptions, conflicts, the complex machinery that drives a human being this way or that—remains just beyond camera range, tantalizingly out of focus.

There is a point at which all accounts of his life, however scrupulous their attention to accuracy, begin to read like fiction, a plot worked out by some Faulknerian novelist. At its center is the gifted but ultimately flawed golden boy, driven to his own destruction by—what? The pressures of an uncomprehending society? The conflict between "art" and the marketplace? Or was it dark, nameless forces within him? Some tragic secret locked away in his past?

Had Bix been born black and poor, had he grown up in the toils of segregation, the whole matter might have been easier, more accessible. How relatively painless it's been, after all, to cast Charlie Parker, Lester Young, and others as racial victims, rather than having to gaze squarely at their characters and draw thornier conclusions.[4]

But no. From the moment of his birth, in Davenport, Iowa, at two o'clock on the morning of March 10, 1903, Leon Beiderbecke was a child of privilege. Family, financial security, social mobility, ease of passage: all were his for the asking. He seems at first to have been a fairly unexceptional child: well-mannered, polite, eager to please, amiable but relatively unmotivated. In the Beiderbecke household, the boy's obvious musical gifts were remarked upon (not without a certain pride, as is obvious from an early local newspaper item) but seem not to have been taken with great seriousness.

All that changed drastically the first time the fifteen-year-old ninth-grader heard "Tiger Rag" and "Dixie Jass Band One-Step," as played by the Original Dixieland Jazz Band. His elder brother, conscripted in the latter days of World War I, had brought home a Victrola and a pile of records as unanticipated trophies of military service. Nick LaRocca's cornet, however obscurely perceived through the frenetic ensemble muddles, was enough to ignite a sense of purpose and direction in a hitherto unfocused Leon Beiderbecke. The story after that is a familiar artifact of jazz history: he learned fast and within two years was good enough to play with bands of local youngsters; soon he was totally absorbed in playing hot jazz, and it is with hot jazz that he is now most strongly identified.

He made his first records on February 18, 1924, his last six and a half years later, on September 20, 1930. Less than a year after that he was dead. This brief span houses three clear peaks of creativity, at least on records, each defined roughly by a calendar year: 1924, with the emergence of the "Wolverine Orchestra" as one of the seminal bands of early jazz; late 1926 to late 1927, apogee of the nonpareil Jean Goldkette Victor Orchestra (see chapter 13); and 1928, which brought the successful incorporation of Beiderbecke's talents into Paul White-man's large light music ensemble.

(Regrettably, neither Frank Trumbauer's much-revered St. Louis band of 1925 nor its musical successor, a small Trumbauer-led Goldkette unit that played at the resort of Hudson Lake, Indiana, in mid-1926, both including Beiderbecke and clarinetist Charles "Pee Wee" Russell, ever recorded. After 1928, ill health and advanced alcoholism took Bix away from Whiteman's orchestra, away from reg-ular performance, away from critical scrutiny. His subsequent appearances on record are uneven at best.)[5]

It is a measure of Beiderbecke's gifts that records made during these three pivotal years left so great and lasting an impact. They herald not only the arrival of a major solo voice, a distinctive and appealing instrumental stylist, but a sea-change in the development of the entire field of musical activity we now identify as jazz.

To understand the latter it is useful to examine the hot music landscape before Bix Beiderbecke's presence began to be felt. By the mid-1920s, jazz had begun its evolution from an ensemble music into a soloist's art. Louis Armstrong and Sidney Bechet, a New Orleans black and a Creole of French extraction, had brought a grandeur, an eloquence, to improvised solo playing. Armstrong's al-most operatic melody lead in the last chorus of "Pickin' on Your Baby," Bechet's exegesis of "Kansas City Man Blues," their thrilling gladiatorial encounter (as much sociological as musical) on "Cake-Walkin' Babies From Home," all with Clarence Williams, make that clear.

Clarinetist Leon Roppolo, with the New Orleans Rhythm Kings (see chapter 2), had explored a more introspective solo approach. Such innovators as Miff Mole, Jimmie Noone, Frank Trumbauer, and Coleman Hawkins were expanding vocabulary and range while pointing the way to greater emotional complexity.

That complexity found its avatar, its embodiment, in Bix Beiderbecke. Even his early solos, on such Wolverines titles as "Riverboat Shuffle," "Royal Garden Blues," and the delicious "I Need Some Pettin'," are products of a sensibility new to hot jazz. Its orientation, in common with those of Bechet and Armstrong, is melodic: recasting and de facto recomposition of a given melodic line through embellishment, vocalization, rearrangement and redistribution of phrase. But it is in two distinct particulars that the differences are apparent:

First, both Armstrong and Bechet are—even at this early stage—instrumental virtuosi. Technical mastery of their respective horns has opened worlds of expressive potential to them. A listener is never in a moment's doubt that each man is creating through an instrument, thereby pushing back the frontiers of common understanding of what that instrument can do. In Armstrong's case it is the matter of range, of endurance, length and arc of phrase, density and amplitude of sound. Bechet's achievement, no less awe-inspiring, is to convert this ugly duckling of Adolphe Sax's instrumental family into a princess, whose tonal and rhythmic breadth, and sheer evocative power, are little short of charismatic.

None of this applies to Bix Beiderbecke. At no point in his brief career, at least as represented on records, is there any indication that he considered the cornet anything more than a conduit, an outlet. His technique and tone, though polished—and occasionally of surpassing beauty—seem at no time any greater than is sufficient to execute his musical intentions. Never, even at its most nimble, can his playing be described as virtuosic in the Armstrong or Bechet sense.[6]

Beiderbecke's province is altogether more subtle. Even in his Wolverines solos, and certainly more so later, in the landmark choruses with Trumbauer and Whiteman groups and those issued under his own name, there is a new, and quite surprising, sense of what may be termed emotional layering. For the first time, a "hot" improvisation, regardless of length, seems able to speak on several levels and arouse in the listener a mixture of responses.

Such complexity was of course an innate feature of European formal music, in composers as diverse as Beethoven, Brahms, Wagner, and Schumann, and in such twentieth-century "moderns" as Stravinsky, Bartók, and Hindemith. The French Impressionists, for whom Beiderbecke evinced a special fondness, dealt in suggestion, in emotion implied as well as expressed. Painters explored responses suggested by the play of light on a subject rather than the subject itself. The poets Rimbaud, Verlaine, and Mallarmé used sounds of words to capture impressions and evoke feeling. In Mallarmé's oft-quoted words, "To name an object is to sacrifice three-quarters of that enjoyment . . . which comes from the guessing bit by bit. To *suggest* it—that is our dream."

Application to music of the idea of *suggesting* rather than stating found its champions in the abstractions of Claude Debussy, the gauzy color palettes of Maurice Ravel, even the whimsy of Erik Satie. The result often seemed a striation of emotional content, in which the strata bled into one another at their points of juncture.

Even so brief and familiar a composition as Ravel's *Pavane pour une infante défunte* illustrates the point. The major motif

contains elements of sunlight, of happiness remembered—but saturated with a melancholy, an aching sense of loss. Like the harmonics produced by the sympathetic oscillations of two consonant pitches, the overlapping of these two extremes yields further, subtler gradations of evocation. Even the composer's use, in the final exposition, of a childlike quasi-Alberti bass seems to intensify and further complicate the emotional images.

It is this kind of heterogeneity that finds its way decisively into jazz through Bix Beiderbecke. Though the comparison should not be driven too far, it is worth noting that even the most magnificent of Armstrong solos on record—the exultant "Willie the Weeper," the grieving "West End Blues," the majestic "Star Dust," the aria-like "That's My Home"—are emotional monoliths; they make their statements plainly, unequivocally, unalloyed by contrasting or contradictory impulses.

Beiderbecke, even in his earliest efforts, is anything but monolithic. Admirer and fellow-cornetist Jimmy McPartland consistently cited Bix's chorus on the Wolverines' 1924 "Royal Garden Blues" as a shaping influence on his own style. He even attempted emulation, on a 1927 record of "Memphis Blues" with Ben Pollack's Orchestra.

In the jazz context of 1924, the Beiderbecke solo is indeed a small miracle. Played at a tempo considerably slower ($\bullet$ = 152) than what was already the standard for this piece, it floats, airborne, above the rhythm, carried aloft on one initial whole note, a top-of-the-staff written G. Structurally, the twelve bars are of a piece, all heralded by that first, lilting note.

"Royal Garden Blues," Bix Beiderbecke solo (twelve bars), 1924.

It is also significant that this chorus, while harmonically a blues, is not a blues in either a melodic or emotional sense. It uses little of the standard blues "vocabulary": no flatted thirds or sevenths, no figures redolent of such blues-based cornetists as Joe Oliver or Paul Mares. It is a song-form improvisation, one of economy and considerable beauty.

Various other solos on Wolverine records are appealing and informative as indexes to Bix's way of playing jazz on the cornet: "Tia Juana" foreshadows the chiming attack of "Ostrich Walk" and the other 1927 utterances; the aforementioned "I Need Some Pettin' " offers a melodic exposition rich in what Gold-kette alto saxophonist Stanley "Doc" Ryker called Bix's "sweet-hot" quality; his final ensemble lead on the originally issued -A take of "Susie" rides the beat with gaiety and relaxation.[7]

But "Royal Garden Blues" provides the major clue to Beiderbecke's unique sensibility. It is a way of looking within every piece of material, regardless of tempo or surface character, to find and expose a core as variegated as the realm of all human emotion. Humphrey Lyttelton, himself a trumpeter of great distinction, describes Armstrong and Beiderbecke as moving

> in diametrically opposite directions. Louis Armstrong's music expanded outwards, as if violently impelled by centrifugal force . . . he took off on an exploration into the unknown. Bix, seemingly more cautious by temperament, took the opposite course, staying within the musical conventions of his time, but digging deeply into them and upturning little gems of subtlety and fresh discovery every inch along the way.[8]

Benny Green's astute formulation recognizes Bix as "a modern, modernism being not a style but an attitude." Others, inevitably, speak of Bix and his followers as representing a "cool" approach—which, Lyttelton remarks with admirable scrupulousness, "implies no lack of warmth or intensity in their music, [but] simply that they seem to us to have sought tranquility rather than turbulence."[9]

However it is defined, Bix's way has become so universal, so integral, so diversified in its expression in jazz that the idea of its having begun with a single musician can be hard to grasp.

If Bix's musical development was steady during 1925–26, his career path was somewhat less so. His inability to read music quickly and accurately cost him jobs in several bands, including an early opportunity with Jean Goldkette. On one occasion, the manager of a Chicago nightspot objected to his playing improvised "bum notes" in dance arrangements and ordered bandleader Dale Skinner to "get rid of that guy" or consider his whole band fired. Bix went.[10]

The turning point came in Bix's association with Frank Trumbauer. Already a celebrity among musicians of both races for his pioneering work on C-melody saxophone (see chapter 18), "Tram" was also a polished bandsman, capable leader, and reliable businessman, who found Beiderbecke musically appealing and relatively easy to handle.

After the summer at Hudson Lake, the two became regular members of Goldkette's Victor Recording Orchestra, Trumbauer soon emerging as its musical straw boss. He ran rehearsals and even fronted occasionally, while Bix, content to improvise section parts and play occasional solos, quickly became popular among his bandmates.

On Monday, January 24, 1927, the Goldkette band opened its second engagement at New York's Roseland Ballroom. Again, as the previous October (see chapter 13), the midwesterners were sharing bandstand and billing with Fletcher

416

Henderson's acclaimed orchestra—only this time, challengers no more, they arrived as champions in their own right. Enthusiasm and *esprit* saturate records made by Goldkette musicians beginning on the twenty-eighth, and no one shows it more graphically than Bix. His solos bristle with confidence. He bites into his sixteen solo bars on "Proud of a Baby Like You" with incisive assurance; his break in the final chorus of "I'm Looking Over a Four-Leaf Clover" shoots a bolt of electricity through the band; his lead lifts "I'm Gonna Meet My Sweetie Now," "Hoosier Sweetheart," and the supercharged "My Pretty Girl" into high orbit.

But it is the small-group dates for OKeh, under Trumbauer's nominal leadership, that best show Beiderbecke as a revolutionary musical figure. The numbers are more congenial, including—"Riverboat Shuffle" and "Ostrich Walk" are examples—cut-down versions of "hot" arrangements done for the full Goldkette ensemble by Bill Challis. Bix plays a full chorus on almost every title: they are an aggregate masterwork, the playing for which he is best known, most respected, most lastingly beloved.

Musically this body of recorded work, beginning on February 4 with "Singin' the Blues" and "Clarinet Marmalade" and carrying through the rest of 1927 into 1928 and membership in Paul Whiteman's orchestra, defines Bix Beiderbecke. Each performance has been scrutinized, analyzed, debated almost bar by bar.

"Singin' the Blues" is the touchstone. The tone is that of a brass-band cornetist—clean, ringing, silvery, every note struck head-on. Colorational devices familiar in the work of the great black soloists—growls, buzzes, smears, half-valve effects—occur seldom; even vibrato, where present at all, is feather-light, dramatic contrast to its expressive prominence in the work of Armstrong, Bechet, Johnny Dodds, and others.

But it is in matters of structure that the difference between Bix and the rest of his peers is most noticeable. His "Singin' the Blues" solo is less an improvisation than a *composition*: almost as if it had been planned in advance, it has a clear exposition, a middle, and an ending. Unlike the great recorded Armstrong solos, it does not develop serially, theme-and-variations style. If Armstrong sings arias, Bix is a master of *Lieder*. Where Louis paints on a Delacroix-size canvas, Bix's is the near-miniature of Erasmus, as painted by Hans Holbein the Younger. It is, in James Lincoln Collier's good formulation, "calligraphy, rather than great, sweeping strokes; the sonnet rather than the epic."[11]

"Singin' the Blues" also demonstrates what Beiderbecke himself termed "correlated" phrasing. His solo's first four bars consist of two one-bar phrase fragments, perfectly matched and closely related, then a two-bar phrase incorporating them into a coherent statement. Bars 5 and 6 extend the thought of the first four, and the two-bar phrase in bars 7 and 8 wraps up the entire episode, preparing the ground for a new idea sequence.

Bix's matter-of-fact use, in bars 9–12, of the ninth voices of both the G7 and C7 harmonies is also striking. This, like the use of augmented chords and whole-tone scales, is not new in hot music; but as givens, basic components of an instrumental solo style, they are indeed without precedent. The mid-chorus break, dominated by a descending run of sixteenth notes, again easily incorporates the ninth. As the author noted in Bix: Man and Legend:

> For the remainder of the 32 bars Bix moves through a series of emotionally evocative, vocal phrases to an emphatic and poignant conclusion, built around a chromatic ascent to the dominant which was a Beiderbecke hallmark. It was one of those mannerisms most recognizable as Bix, and therefore most often seized upon by other, lesser cornetists attempting to evoke the superficials of his sound and phrasing.[12]

"Singin' the Blues," Bix Beiderbecke solo (thirty-two bars), 1927.

Though Bix at age twenty-three was all but unknown to the general public, his name already meant enough to fellow-musicians (and a scattering of hot music fans) by early 1927 that the original OKeh label of "Singin' the Blues" bears the credit line "Frankie Trumbauer's orchestra with Bix and [Eddie] Lang." "You couldn't go anywhere in New York," said Goldkette drummer Chauncey Morehouse, "without hearing some guy trying to play like Bix. They copied his tone, his attack, his figures. Some guys tried to take his stuff right off the records."[13]

(Trumbauer's opening C-melody sax solo was accorded perhaps even greater reverence at the time—result, at least in part, of his wider fame. Saxophonists learned his "Singin' the Blues" solo as assiduously as cornetists and trumpeters learned the Bix chorus; in arranging the song for Paul Whiteman's orchestra (and that of Fletcher Henderson), Bill Challis scored the Trumbauer solo for the entire reed section. Only from the vantage point of more than six decades of musical history does Tram's chorus seem rather more contrived than Beiderbecke's. See chapter 18 for further discussion.)

Each of these records exposes some other dimension of Beiderbecke's singularity. His solo and ensemble lead on the current pop hit "I'm Comin', Virginia," like his treatment of "Singin' the Blues," follows his self-declared practice of "playing 'round the melody." Almost without exception, Beiderbecke solos are melodic paraphrases; there are very few instances in which he is clearly playing primarily "on the changes."

Emotionally, "I'm Comin', Virginia" is a strongly layered performance. It is dark, elegaic, saturated with brooding melancholy, but the gloom is seldom absolute: in bars 13–16 of the final chorus, for example, Caravaggio-like shafts of light pierce the darkness. "Way Down Yonder in New Orleans" reverses the situation: its basic mood is upbeat, tone optimistic. But at certain moments (bars 9–12 are typical) doubt, even anxiety, seem to cast a shadow.

Though various commentators have somehow heard in Bix's creativity a debt to Armstrong, the connection is hard to discern in the young Iowan's work on these records. The only identifiable jazz "influence," in fact, is that of Nick LaRocca, of the Original Dixieland Jazz Band. LaRocca's way of playing through an improvised ensemble, keeping to his middle register and pushing the beat along with rhythmic and melodic bursts, seems to have shaped Bix's own ensemble concept. When Bix "rides" a single, repeated concert B♭ in the final chorus of his 1927 version of "Royal Garden Blues," it's easy to hear echoes of LaRocca's lead in the ODJB's 1918 "Tiger Rag."[14]

Inflated budget and the uncompromising attitude of its musicians contributed to the end of the Goldkette Recording Orchestra in the autumn of 1927. Resisting, at least temporarily, the offers of Paul Whiteman, Bix and Tram joined bass saxophonist Adrian Rollini's all-star unit at the Club New Yorker. Located at Broadway and 48th Street, on the site of what had been the Cinderella Ballroom, the club didn't last long; nor did the band exist for long enough to live up to its spectacular potential. Even its records, however good, are little more than tantalizing hints at what could have been.

Fud Livingston's "Humpty Dumpty" (1928), for example, comes replete with "modern" harmonies, chromaticism, shifting tonal centers. Bix's eight-bar solo near the end is audaciously sophisticated, if intuitive, in its treatment of the chord sequence. In the first two bars he ignores Livingston's F-A7-D7 progression, choosing instead a figure based squarely on an F6; rather than appear to clash, it gives him a strongly declarative opening, related to the key of the solo. In bars 3–4, with the band sustaining a D♭7 chord, he plays a figure ostensibly built on a written F-minor (concert E♭) triad. In this case, Bix's C and D♮, far from "wrong," are simply a superimposed major seventh and lowered ninth, respectively, and occur frequently in contemporary harmony. In the words of music editor Jay Arnold, writing in 1944, "the effect is colorful and not the least bit unpleasant."[15]

"Humpty-Dumpty," Bix solo (eight bars), 1927.

Bix's best work is studded with such surprises. His contribution to the Trumbauer-Morehouse "Krazy Kat," made the same day as "Humpty Dumpty," yields something in each of its sixteen bars. Jay Arnold's analysis, published in 1944, is particularly good, worth quoting in its entirety:

> The third and fourth notes of measure 1 are the upper and lower neighbor of the root of the chord, which when reached, has become the fifth of the G7 chord of the second half of the measure. In measure 4, the dotted quarter note (D♮) is an anticipation of the seventh of the E7 of measure 5. However, Bix has already left the note by the time the chord of which the D is a part is sounded. The G♮ is the Negroid [sic] lowered third, the F♯ used twice is the ninth. The construction in measure 6 is very ingenious. The E♯ is the lower neighbor of the thirteenth (F♯) which follows it. G is the seventh of the chord, followed by a passing note leading to the root of the chord (A) which is not sounded until several notes later, giving the figure an element of suspense. The D is the eleventh of the A7 chord, the B is the ninth. At the end of the measure there is a restatement of the lower neighbor of the thirteenth and the thirteenth itself. The measures 7 and 8 are a "break" that is charming in its simplicity. In measure 9, E♯ is the lower neighbor of the third (F♯) of the chord D. The E♮ is the upper neighbor of the fifth of the G7 chord. Measures 10, 11, and 12 show a disregard for the ornamental harmony of the background. In measure 13, F is the upper neighbor of the chord root. Measures 14 and 15, also, are rather independent of the background harmonies.[16]

"Krazy Kat," Bix solo (sixteen bars), 1927.

In these months it seemed Bix Beiderbecke could not play a solo that was not fresh, bright, stimulating. His chorus on "Clementine (from New Orleans)," at the Goldkette orchestra's final date, is an enchanting melodic paraphrase. The small-group sessions issued under his own name by OKeh are modeled on, and draw heavily on the repertoire of, the Original Dixieland Jazz Band. Such performances as "The Jazz Me Blues," "Royal Garden Blues," and "At the Jazz Band Ball" can almost be heard as acts of homage to LaRocca, though with a greatly expanded melodic and harmonic vocabulary.[17]

Almost every Beiderbecke solo on records made around this time period repays careful study. A Pathé date, for example, produced a second version of Morehouse's "Three Blind Mice," done some weeks earlier for OKeh. Bix's solo on the -A take easily incorporates unusual intervals, chordal extensions, and chromatics and comes to rest matter-of-factly on a major seventh, a startling and audacious departure even among 1927 "moderns."

Another moment to treasure comes with "Cryin' All Day," based on the opening phrase of Trumbauer's "Singin' the Blues" solo and obviously a follow-up to the quite unexpected sales success of the earlier record. Perhaps it is, as George Avakian once punningly suggested, "a far cry from the original"—but it boasts glories of its own. Among other points it is rhythmically more secure than "Singin' the Blues," thanks to the presence of Adrian Rollini's bass saxophone. It also gives Pee Wee Russell his lone chance on record to show both his admiration and thorough understanding of Bix.

Beiderbecke and Russell split a solo chorus, and it is striking how accurately the clarinetist catches and continues the cornetist's musical and emotional arc. To illustrate the point, both solos are presented in the following transcription; Russell's sixteen-bar contribution appears an octave below where it sounds, for the sake of comparison with Beiderbecke's phrase-building methods.

"Crying All Day," Bix cornet solo (sixteen) and Pee Wee Russell clarinet solo (sixteen), 1927.

In its "correlated" structure, tonal clarity, and blending of European and American musical values, it is a music—jazz—of a high and creative order. It is the music of Bix Beiderbecke, bringing a classicist's methods to bear on a Romantic sensibility, the mind holding the emotions in check for great, and variegated, impact.

With no work in prospect, Rollini's band broke up. The leader, his alto-playing friend Bobby Davis, and trumpeter Chelsea Quealey sailed for England. Most of the others went back to freelancing. And, on October 27, Bix Beiderbecke and Frank Trumbauer flew to Indianapolis to join the orchestra of Paul Whiteman.

*   *   *

Bix's two years with Whiteman are a source of perpetual contention among fans and scholars alike. Benny Green, so incisive in so many ways, decried the thought of

> this gifted musician about to bestow on a mediocre vaudeville act his own talent, a musician so far above the jazz standards of almost all his contemporaries that today we only tolerate the horrors of Whiteman's recordings at all in the hope that here and there a Bixian fragment will redeem the mess.[18]

Yet several factors—Bix's growing interest in more formal aspects of musical expression, his disregard for his own musical achievements, and even a growing dissatisfaction with jazz in general—can lead to another conclusion.

At first, when the Jean Goldkette Orchestra was still the talk of hot music circles, there is every indication that Bix joined fellow-musicians in making sport of the three-hundred-pound "King of Jazz." Boys will be boys, after all, and in 1927 Bix Beiderbecke was but twenty-three years old. Whiteman, moreover, made a generous target. A 1926 New Yorker profile comes readily to mind, describing him as "a man flabby, virile, quick, coarse, untidy and sleek, with a hard core of shrewdness in an envelope of sentimentalism." The night in Atlantic City that Whiteman led the Goldkette orchestra on the "St. Louis Blues" with flamboyant gestures and less than inspiring musical results must have provided plenty of ammunition.

But when the Goldkette band had collapsed, and Adrian Rollini's Club New Yorker deal fizzled, Bix—perhaps with a bit of coaxing by the more practical-minded Trumbauer—wound up with Whiteman. Without a diary or some other, equally reliable, means of following his thoughts, we can only guess at the process through which the young cornetist began to realize how valuable his move had been, how much he could learn musically from his new surroundings.

Almost overnight, he was in day-to-day contact with, and accepted as a peer by, some of the outstanding popular instrumentalists of the day, men whose standing among fellow-musicians all but eclipsed his own. Ferde Grofé, a leading architect of the modern dance orchestra; Chester Hazlett, of the faultless saxophone tone and control; trumpeter Charlie Margulis; and reed doubler Charles Strickfaden—men with few peers among orchestral players.

Colleagues have testified that, far from feeling bound or stifled by the Whiteman orchestra, as Green and others have suggested, Bix often felt a sense of exhilaration. It was like attending a music school, learning and broadening: formal music, especially the synthesis of the American vernacular idiom with a more classical orientation, so much sought-after in the 1920s, were calling out to him.

Evidence of this turn of mind has never set comfortably with those who would canonize Bix as a hot jazz martyr, sacrificed on the altar of Whiteman's commercial success. To those faithful, the thought of Beiderbecke actually *enjoying* the concert extravaganzas of George Gershwin and Ferde Grofé has always seemed a kind of apostasy: more comfortable by far to imagine a disgruntled young man marking time back there among the automatons in the brass section, his drinking increasing in inverse proportion to the ever-leaner solo scraps tossed him by the arrangers.

Such a fiction, in order to be credited, had to have a villain, and what better malefactor than Whiteman himself? Even the "King of Jazz" sobriquet, creation of a press agent's imagination, has been held against him with surprising tenacity: Whiteman the mountebank, the trivializer and remorseless hypocrite, who—perhaps in the way large corporations buy up promising small ones in order to put them out of business—hired Bix Beiderbecke, then killed him with studied neglect.

Stifled. Restricted. Smothered. Buried. Suppressed. Muzzled. Stultified. Such has been the lexicon throughout many decades of jazz chronicling, all nurturing the same slice of popular mythology. That such theorizing is ill-informed and, in its most extreme form, mean-spirited, hardly bears further repetition here. A large and compelling body of evidence militates against such vilification. Bix was in Whiteman's orchestra because he wanted to be there. Because it interested him. Because, ultimately, he enjoyed it.

In a long and perceptive Whiteman footnote in *Early Jazz*, published in 1968, Gunther Schuller refers to many Whiteman scores as "marvels of orchestral ingenuity," which made full use of the ensemble's textural and colorational potential. He rightly praises the ensemble's "excellent intonation, perfect balances and clean attacks" and goes on to remark that "there is in the best Whiteman performances a feeling and a personal sound as unique in its way as Ellington's or Basie's. It was just not based on a jazz conception. For this we cannot automatically condemn it. At their best, Whiteman's musicians played with a richness and bounce that has its own validity."[19]

It is no quantum leap to infer that this environment set free at last the part of Bix that was drawn to formal music, a part reaching beyond the rather modest disciplines of hot improvisation into areas which had long fascinated him from afar.[20]

On an everyday level, Bix's presence seemed to transform the Whiteman orchestra—at least that aspect of it concerned with "hot" arrangements of popular songs—almost overnight. Bill Challis, whose scores had shaped the Goldkette orchestra in Beiderbecke's image, was contributing regularly to the Whiteman library. Fellow-arranger Tom Satterfield, whom Bix had met while working in St. Louis, quickly proved himself adept at incorporating the sounds and flavors of both Beiderbecke and Trumbauer. Violinist Matt Malneck, soon to emerge as a gifted songwriter, also contributed congenial, often witty, arrangements.

The Whiteman ensemble recorded almost daily throughout the first weeks of 1928, and Beiderbecke got to solo often. Sometimes, as in "Dardanella" or "From Monday On," he'd be given a full chorus. More often his solo "window" would be sixteen bars or an eight-bar release, toward the end of the performance. It's no exaggeration to say he made the most of such opportunities, usually placed in the arrangements like precious stones in carefully wrought settings, great paintings in often ornate frames.

On the Walter Donaldson song hit "Changes," Challis has Bix soloing, muted, for half a chorus over a sustained-tone "carpet" of seven voices; "Lonely Melody" brings him on after a full-ensemble statement of the verse, to heightened dramatic effect; on "Smile," Bix leads the brass in rousing counterpoint to a plummy baritone sax solo by Charles Strickfaden. Other arrangers, too, understood the value of Beiderbecke's sound and attack as a flavoring agent: Malneck's arrangement of "(What Are You Waiting For) Mary" is almost programmatic in its interplay between the jazz-flavored "new wave" (Bix, Tommy, and Jimmy Dorsey) and Whiteman's more strait-laced "old guard," as embodied in trumpeter Henry Busse.

Beiderbecke's solos on these records are models of clarity, balance, melodic organization, delivered with lift and assurance; Victor's microphones, and the natural acoustics of such rooms as Manhattan's Liederkranz Hall, even go far toward capturing some of the silver in his tone: it's discernible, certainly, in his final eight bars on "Back in Your Own Back Yard" or his lead on the brass trio section of "Coquette."

Again, what is most striking about these solos is their inner balance. Each is a small composition, a melodic paraphrase of almost lapidary precision—yet without any loss of spontaneity. Fortunately, multiple takes exist of many of these performances and show Bix's mind ever at work, turning his material to let different surfaces catch the light. If an overall structure falls into place early, its details are forever subject to modification and exploration.

"Louisiana," for example, finds Bix playing into a derby, producing an almost saxophonic tone. On take -1, the original issue, he spends his first eight bars investigating a kind of serpentine phrasing characteristic of Trumbauer. But rather than follow where that leads him, he seems to tire of the experiment, resolving to a rather foursquare two-bar declaration. But on take -3, issued during the '30s, he's exploring the asymmetry farther, producing a fluid, adventuresome variant on the same thought process. (See music example on next page.)

Often he returns to the "correlated" or paired phrases so obvious in "Singin' the Blues." He ends his eight bars on take -3 of "There Ain't No Sweet Man (That's Worth the Salt of My Tears)" with a neatly tongue-in-groove couplet:

"There Ain't No Sweet Man," Bix break (two bars), 1928.

"Louisiana," Bix solo (sixteen bars) with Whiteman Orchestra, two versions, double staff, 1928.

In May 1928, Whiteman began recording for Columbia. A newsreel film sequence, unearthed in the early 1990s, shows Bix standing during a brass soli—as if Whiteman, without identifying him by name, wanted to draw attention to him. The viewer is struck by his extreme youth; even sporting a moustache, he seems little more than a boy, visibly ill at ease, at one point sneaking a "how'm I doin'?" glance at his sectionmates.

His musical assurance is quite another matter. Challis's arrangement of the faux-naïf Willard Robison song " 'Tain't So, Honey, 'Tain't So" gives him two solo openings. The first, a pass through the release, is straightforward and uneventful, but the second, a verse statement over a rhythmic sax section figure, is a show-stopper. Full of chromaticism, consistently defying the bar line, it seems to bring forward the broadly rubato concept first heard on the 1924 "Royal Garden Blues" solo.

" 'Tain't So, Honey, 'Tain't So," second Bix solo (sixteen bars), 1928.

This rhythmic freedom, and the harmonic implications in his solos on "Sweet Sue (Just You)" and "China Boy," show a deepening of thought and content. And the Whiteman Orchestra, even in its overcooked "symphonic jazz" efforts, somehow seems the most fertile environment he could have asked for in his quest to explore these depths.

One incontrovertible truth dominates the reality of Bix Beiderbecke's brief life and career, and it's one that those who admire him most as a jazzman least like to face: though Bix is clearly a product of hot jazz, and brought to it a set of qualities it had not possessed hitherto, it was not at the center of his musical aspirations. When Jimmy McPartland, quoted earlier, remarked that Bix "wasn't really like us," he was grasping, albeit intuitively, at this reality.

The tragedy of Bix Beiderbecke, if his early death and lapsed potential can be viewed as tragedy, lies not in the allegedly corrupting influence of Whiteman and his associates, not (as Pee Wee Russell and others have contended) in the hard-drinking "friends" who wouldn't let Bix alone; not in any of the other putative villains invoked to explain Beiderbecke's steep descent and destruction.

More convincingly, the tragedy lies in Beiderbecke himself, in the Aristotelian notion of greatness undone by flaws within itself. By inner conflict, perhaps having little to do directly with music, which he simply lacked the strength of will or character to resolve.

Much has been written about Beiderbecke in the more than six decades since his death, but surprisingly little of it has addressed this matter. An approach to understanding requires a major digression, a side trip into the larger popular music world, and its *Zeitgeist*, in which Leon Beiderbecke lived and worked.

Recognition among formally trained musicians that hot improvisation was a language, with its own vocabulary, grammar, distinctive inflections, and wide expressive potential, seems to have come early. But from the start, the question was what to do with it: how to use it, incorporate it, offset its intrinsic evanescence, lend it staying power and substance.

One of the consistent responses of "legit" musicians of both races in the '20s seems to have been an urge to codify, expressing the emergent jazz language in compositional terms. Throughout the decade, therefore, running alongside the efforts of the improvising soloists, is a parallel stream of vigorous compositional activity, drawing on the selfsame vocabulary.

It includes, among much else, the efforts of European and American composers, from John Alden Carpenter (*Krazy Kat*, 1922) to Darius Milhaud (*La Création du monde*, 1925) to Maurice Ravel (*Five O'Clock Fox Trot*, 1925) and Georges Antheil (*Transatlantic*, 1930), to incorporate jazz inflections and rhythmic devices into their works.

Nor was the appeal of formalization in any way restricted to white musicians: Duke Ellington was working toward essentially the same goal in such early miniatures as "Black and Tan Fantasie [or Fantasy]" and "East St. Louis Toodle-oo." James P. Johnson used an expansive canvas for such works as *Yamecraw* (1928) and *Symphonie Harlem* (1932). In general, the need to conserve, to render permanent, seems part of the overall context of the time, logical reaction to a basically fugitive idiom.

The development of arranging methods for dance orchestras seems also to have been a by-product of such need. In the work of Grofé, Don Redman, Benny Carter, Fud Livingston, Bill Challis, Art Gronwall, John Nesbitt, Arthur Schutt, Bob Van Eps, and countless others of the period (including such capable Whiteman staff men as Malneck, Satterfield, and Hayton) it's possible to hear the trial-and-error process as it gets under way.

The works of composers working from outside hot music circles seemed always to be running a step or two behind the efforts of the arrangers. Gershwin's *Rhapsody in Blue*, viewed in 1924 as a great leap forward, is manifestly the work of a musician approaching the language from an external point, in this case Tin Pan Alley and the Broadway stage. While he knew and admired such pianists as James P. Johnson and Charles Luckeyeth "Luckey" Roberts, Gershwin's own vocabulary, as expressed in the *Rhapsody*, is closer to that of the Original Dixieland Jazz Band, as represented on its 1917–18 Victor recordings. But by 1924, even Nick LaRocca and his associates were approaching the basics differently, having moved steadily away from their foundation in ragtime. In the hot music context of 1924, as defined by King Oliver and the New Orleans Rhythm Kings—and, presently, by Bix—the raggy working vocabulary of *Rhapsody in Blue* already seems an anachronism.[21]

The need to adapt the language and vitality of improvised jazz to composed music produced some curious and attractive hybrids. Such composed instrumentals as Willard Robison's *Jubilee*, recorded in orchestrated form in 1928 by Bix and Frank Trumbauer, or trumpeter Donald Lindley's *A Rhythmic Dream*, recorded for Columbia by Fletcher Henderson's Orchestra (but not released at the time),

428

contain not a single note of improvisation—though their rhythmic, melodic, and harmonic vocabulary is that of the hot improviser.

One particularly successful effort is an orchestral rendering of Rube Bloom's piano solo *Soliloquy*, recorded September 6, 1927, by a unit under the leadership of Don Voorhees and including Red Nichols, Miff Mole, and other major figures in the New York white jazz circle.*

Beautifully recorded, the eleven-piece ensemble reads Arthur Schutt's arrangement with a relaxed, natural idiomatic flair. The performance never begins to "swing," and, again, not a note is improvised; yet it is in conception and execution unmistakably a jazz composition. *Soliloquy* is distinctive, too, in that its melodic and harmonic frames of reference are directly consonant with those of Bix Beiderbecke. It is in no way extending the point too far to contend that much of Bloom's piece, especially in this setting, could have sprung from the same thought processes as Bix's *In the Dark* or superior, through-composed *Candlelights*.[22]

There is ample evidence that Bix was thinking in these directions almost from the start. Numerous colleagues recalled him at the piano, "fooling around with modern stuff," in the words of trombonist Newell "Spiegle" Willcox, seemingly at every opportunity. The piano compositions can hardly be written off as flukes, aberrations in some pursuit of hot music. Rather, they seem to be the substance. As early as 1925, when saxophonist Damon "Bud" Hassler noted with admiration Bix's attempts to incorporate elements of Ravel's *Daphnis et Chlöe* ballet suite and Debussy's *Prélude à l'après-midi d'un faune* into his probings at the keyboard, Beiderbecke (in common with quite a few of his contemporaries) was heading toward a musical conception in which hot improvisation was but a component part.

(These 1925 months, working with Trumbauer in St. Louis, were a time of heightened musical awareness for Beiderbecke. It was at this point that Bix consulted symphony trumpeter Joseph Gustat about taking lessons in "legitimate" technique. He also demanded of Hassler, who was doing most of the band's arrangements, to "give me regular B♭ parts. I've got to learn to read properly." In Hassler's recollection, it was Bix who nudged the band's sound in the direction of more complex harmonies.)[23]

If the European moderns, the "novelty" piano conventions of the '20s and the emergent hot jazz language helped shape Beiderbecke and resulted in his piano compositions, so too—perhaps even more directly—did the musings of the American composer Eastwood Lane.

Lane is all but forgotten today. His music remains out of print, seldom found even at auctions and collectors' secondhand outlets. Were it not for the thor-

---

*It was done the same day, in the same studio, and with almost exactly the same personnel, as a quite successful Charleston Chasers session which produced two performances of unquestioned jazz pedigree: Nichols's impassioned solo reading of his own "Five Pennies" and a crisp "Sugar Foot Strut," highlighted by a well-turned clarinet solo by Pee Wee Russell and a flawlessly executed brass trio by Red, Miff, and second trumpeter Leo McConville.

oughgoing and rigorously scholarly research of Philadelphia historian Norman P. Gentieu, there seems little doubt that all memory of him would have disappeared entirely.

Born in upper New York State in 1879, Eastwood Lane attended (but did not graduate from) Syracuse University and lived outside New York City during the '20s. According to Gentieu, he was very much an insiders' favorite and "a true eclectic in the matter of friends and acquaintances." He included among his close associates critic Deems Taylor and the self-proclaimed literary lions—critic Alexander Woollcott, writers Dorothy Parker and Ring Lardner, humorist Robert Benchley, director George S. Kaufman, and the rest—who constituted the much-publicized "round table" at the Algonquin Hotel. Paul Whiteman, too, was an admirer.

Lane's visits to Manhattan were most often in his capacity as assistant to fellow-composer Alexander Russell, head of the Department of Music at Princeton and director for the highly regarded Wanamaker Auditorium concert series. His widow, Modena Scovill Lane (whom he married, after a long professional association, in 1933), told Gentieu that during these times Bix Beiderbecke was a frequent caller. On such occasions, she said, Bix demanded, "Now you play for me! I don't care what you play . . . improvise, but keep playing and I'll just lie right here on the couch and listen." The listening sessions sometimes went on for up to three hours, with Bix, silent on the couch, lost in reverie. He was quite fond, she said, of both the *Adirondack Sketches* and Lane's *Five American Dances*, especially "The Crap Shooters," which opens the *Dances*.

"Ragtime and the game of craps have much in common; each is a particularly racial expression," Lane wrote, expressing himself within the verbal conventions of the day. "Each is ardently loved and indulged in with great zest by the negro. In the playing of either, the Afro-American is without a peer." Pointing out his use of an old "coon song" as part of his thematic fabric, Lane went on to say that he had sought to "catch the spirit of the ragtime band and the game of craps."[24]

Eastwood Lane's effect on Bix is at its most discernible in the six-part *Sketches*. Some writers have alluded to the parts titled "The Legend of Lonesome Lake" and "The Land of the Loon" as representative. But it is best to listen to the suite in its entirety: in matters of thematic construction, structural unity, and above all a bittersweet, emotionally layered atmosphere, the consonances with Beiderbecke's work are impossible to miss.

Eastwood Lane died, age seventy-two, January 22, 1951. In Norman Gentieu's words, "what Bix Beiderbecke discovered and found great pleasure in during the twenties still retains its freshness and its power to entertain us; if we continue to ignore this heritage, the loss is ours."[25]

As a member of Paul Whiteman's Orchestra Bix importuned Grofé, Roy Bargy, and other "legit" arrangers to write him into their scores whenever possible. He's clearly audible, for example, in Grofé's *Metropolis* suite and contributes with noticeable enthusiasm to a fourth-movement *fugato* section. The story also persists that it is Bix, not lead trumpeter Charlie Margulis, who performs the long, taxing second movement solo on Whiteman's 1928 recording of the Gershwin *Concerto in F*. Though some veteran symphony trumpeters have since questioned the likelihood of a self-taught jazz cornetist being entrusted with so critical a passage on a major recording, Bargy and others who were there stuck by their assertion that Bix was the soloist.

How extreme a process his musical development was, and how fast it was moving, emerges with indisputable clarity in an incident related by Beiderbecke's friend and fellow-cornetist Richardson "Dick" Turner and quoted in *Bix: Man and Legend*. Turner tells of visiting Bix in mid-1928, in a hotel in Harrisburg, Pennsylvania. Idly, he picked up Bix's new Vincent Bach cornet and played a few bars of his friend's solo from the Wolverines' record of "Riverboat Shuffle," made just four years earlier. Beiderbecke's reaction was immediate—and unexpected.

"What on earth did you play that for?" was his petulant reply. He went on to dismiss the Wolverines and his own work with them as crude, simple-minded, lacking dimension or depth. He expressed affection for the Original Dixieland Jazz Band, but in a way which led Turner to conclude that his remarks were motivated as much by nostalgia as by musical taste.

Such testimony points to a profound, if unfocused and only dimly perceived, sea-change. Formal music, and the possibilities of incorporating into it the language and aesthetics of hot jazz, appear to have become, for Bix, an obsession.

Such information has done little to alter Bix Beiderbecke in the perceptions of hot jazz devotees, or to explain why his life ended so soon, and the way it did. Why the quality of his playing dropped off so sharply after hitting its 1927–28 peak. Why his drinking became so blindly compulsive, even at a time when success, respect, money, even a measure of fame—and the opportunity to pursue his passion for formal music—were his for the taking. And, too, why he seemed unable to take any pleasure in the prominence he had achieved among his musical peers.

Little enlightenment is to be found in the by now rather shopworn notion of the "artist" as a being apart, subject to different rules and standards of judgment. It's been a consolation since the days of the *L'Art pour L'Art* movement epitomized by Stéphane Mallarmé and Théophile Gautier and handed down to us as a legacy in countless forms. But in Bix Beiderbecke's case it seems little more than a way of avoiding any fruitful engagement with the reality of the man. It's been easier for colleagues, chroniclers, and votaries alike to continue viewing him in the abstract, even in the face of such efforts as Philip R. Evans's exhaustive and detailed chronology of his twenty-eight years. It's almost as if by accepting Bix as *special*, as independent of place and time, we're spared having to understand him as a human being, with responsibilities to himself and to others; a human being who just happened to have made beautiful music.

Testimony of friends and colleagues agrees that outside the embrace of his music Bix seemed remarkably indifferent, content to let life find him where it might. It's hard to imagine him "networking" his way into lucrative business arrangements with promoters or record company chiefs, as did his admirer Red

Nichols. A curious lack of substance attends the character identified as "Bix Beiderbecke" in the lore of jazz. Did he read newspapers? Was he aware of the Darrow-Bryan clashes at the Scopes "Monkey Trial"? Did he and Bill Challis discuss the relative guilt or innocence of Sacco and Vanzetti?

We know he read Wodehouse, laughed at the misadventures of Wooster and Jeeves. But, truth to tell, that's pretty light stuff, and it was in vogue at the time. But did Bix, like Eastwood Lane, admire Benchley, Woollcott, and the other Round Tablers? Did he read Mencken, worry about the implications of the 1923 Munich Beer Hall *Putsch*, reflect on Radclyffe Hall and *The Well of Loneliness*?

Most likely not. "He was always talking music, telling us, 'Let's play this chord,' or 'Let's figure out some three-way harmony for the trumpets after the job tonight,' " Wingy Manone recalled of him. "It seemed to us he didn't want us to enjoy our life."[26]

Or Mezz Mezzrow: "He had an air of cynicism and boredom about most things, just sitting around lazy-like with his legs crossed and his body drooping, but it wasn't an act with him. Even in his teens he had worked out the special tastes and interests that he carried all through his short life . . . Not that he was dull or sluggish; nothing like that. That kid could get as lively and hopped-up as anybody you ever saw, but it took something really stirring, something really good, to get a rise out of him. Music is what did it mostly."[27]

He lived, it most often seems, entirely in the abstract. In his 1974 memoir *Remembering Bix*, Ralph Berton depicts Beiderbecke as a directionless and emotionally stunted man who found a kind of shelter in hot music, at least for a while.

> I suppose we may assume that Bix loved jazz but there are many kinds
> of love: joyous, zestful, desperate, anxious; there is a kind of love that is
> a gloomy, confused dependency, a continuum of almost-satisfaction and
> frustrations, never fulfilled and therefore insatiable, a love that asks more
> of its object than it can give. I seldom felt, even in Bix's best moments,
> that his love of jazz had much merriness in its composition. I did feel
> even then—and more surely now—that what Bix wanted from music,
> jazz never truly gave him; and that his fumbling overtures to classical
> music were an indication that he hoped to find it there.[28]

There is evidence, most of it necessarily circumstantial and even inferential, to buttress this view. At one point, Berton refers to Bix's "elaborate defensive system of alcohol/jazz/nomadism/solitariness/introversion" and wonders aloud what would have happened if some tough, skilled psychiatrist had been able to go to work at unraveling—or at least understanding—its complexities.

The idea of Bix on some Freudian couch, pouring out a litany of resentment against parental rigidity, defining himself in terms of "dysfunction" and "lowered self-esteem," seems remote and more than a little risible. But Berton's vision of him, with its implications of pathology, seems congruent with available testimony. It asks, as few have asked, why Bix, as an intelligent and probing musician, did not avail himself of opportunities to perfect his reading, learn theory and explore composition, study the piano, especially once he'd been in Whiteman's orchestra a while and saw the opportunities.

More than a few of Bix's friends apparently recognized his inability to take those steps. But no one except Challis seems to have done anything about it. "All of us," says Berton,

> each for his own reasons—tact, indifference, defensiveness, preoccupation—simply failed to face the fact, root out the trouble and cure it. I feel in my heart, today, that the chance was there, for anyone who would have had [sic] the wit and understanding to seize it, to help Bix get over that boulder in his path—and we all missed it, we all failed him as he failed himself, to the lasting remorse of his legion of mourners.[29]

That's a rare and courageous admission, one of several in a book which, however flawed, offers what may be the only serious attempt we have at understanding the forces that drove Bix Beiderbecke and ultimately killed him. It deserves to be reissued, and to remain in print.

Berton also addresses another issue, one that has remained at the far fringes of discussion on Beiderbecke. In *Remembering Bix*, he contends that his brother Gene enjoyed a fleeting homosexual liaison with Beiderbecke. Eugene Berton was by all accounts a cultured and sensitive man, well versed in classical music and ballet. That Bix would have been drawn to him intellectually hardly strains credibility. But a physical dimension?

Protest, even anger, greeted Berton's disclosure, especially among those fans for whom Bix Beiderbecke remained an idealized all-American boy. Yes, even though he dated girls and even had a few romances, he always seemed preoccupied, his thoughts somewhere else. But it was the music, wasn't it? Just the music.

Such resistance, and an absence of documentary evidence, made it inevitable that Berton's contention would be dismissed or, at best, studiously ignored. William J. Schafer, one of the few writers to even acknowledge it, ridiculed Berton's account as "coy" and a "weird kamikaze endgame move."[30]

Yet viewed objectively, the incident, if it happened, seems at least consistent with Bix Beiderbecke's apparent unconcern with—and self-imposed isolation from—anything outside his direct musical life. Berton suggests as much when, in the moment of revelation, he has his brother say,

> Homosexual? Is that the word we're avoiding? Bix was about as "homosexual" as you are, brother. I mean let's face it—it meant *absolutely nothing* to him one way or the other [emphasis added]. I don't even know how much girls meant to him, if it comes to that—or let's say sex. You know his favorite phrase: "What the hell." That was about where he stood, on nearly everything but his music . . . For God's sake, Rafe, you must know yourself Bix would do just about anything you suggested to him—if it didn't take him away from his God damn horn too long— just because he couldn't think of a really good reason *not* to. Isn't that true?[31]

What is it, then, about this preoccupied, oddly disconnected young man that makes his presence so tenacious? How to account for the durability of a musical figure so briefly among us, artistically so little realized, personally and motivationally so obscure?

One of the most distinctive traits of a jazz solo is that it seems to speak on two levels. One, up front, incorporates such qualities as power, range, tone, attack, majesty, melodic felicity, simple prettiness, drive, or swing. These are the face and features, enabling listeners to establish the identity and characteristics of a soloist.

Behind that, like the corporeal reality behind the mask on a sarcophagus, is another; more elusive, deeply personal, its very existence is noted chiefly in a listener's reaction to it. Call it the "inner voice." Yet critics, and musicians themselves, disagree on how the process works. Some challenge the notion of *anything* inherent in a piece of music, viewing all response as subjective and reactive.

Igor Stravinsky appears to endorse this view when he suggests, in his 1936 *Chroniques de ma vie*, "If music appears to express something . . . this is only an illusion and not a reality." British critic Alexander Waugh expands the point by declaring, "The art of listening to music relies, not on searching for emotion among the notes where it cannot be found, but creating external emotions and meanings to which the music can then be applied."[32]

But if music is so neutral, and the listener brings everything to the listening experience—and that is surely what both Stravinsky and Waugh are suggesting— why do certain pieces of music, and certain individuals, inspire, over time, so uniform a pattern of reaction and recognition in so wide and diverse an audience?

The concept of the "inner voice" in literature is obvious and universally accepted. Moving through the constructs, imagery, and idiosyncrasies of language, the reader discerns a cadence, and through it "hears" a voice. It is that voice, heard silently in the mind, that draws and holds attention.

Otis Ferguson, one of the first to write well about jazz, is said to have affected a hard-boiled, Chandlerian kind of public image, extending even to manner of dress. Teddy Wilson recalled seeing him togged out in the gangster-movie mode of the '30s: black shirt, cream-colored tie, slouch hat, cigarette dangling from a corner of the mouth. "For a long time I didn't even know he was a writer," said Wilson. "He never talked about it. He just talked about the [Goodman] band, and about music and musicians, all in this pseudo–tough guy way. I was really surprised when I found out he was a writer."[33]

Yet whether the subject was jazz, movies, or the humanity in Jimmy Durante's comic style, Ferguson's prose spoke in quite other accents: steady, worldly-wise but incorruptibly idealistic; sweet, even sentimental—yet never maudlin or bathetic.

Given this, it's hardly surprising that the very sound of Bix should have appealed to Ferguson, and that the latter should have been the first to describe him with eloquence and aesthetic accuracy. He wrote about him a lot—not just the two well-loved *New Republic* pieces, "Young Man With a Horn" (the phrase, his coinage, was shortly to become the title of Dorothy Baker's novel) and its sequel, "Young Man With a Horn Again," but a series of fragmentary musings, unpublished until the 1970s. "Perhaps you will have to hear him a lot," Ferguson wrote in 1940:

perhaps you won't have any ear for the jazz music that grew up around you and in your time, and so will never hear the voice, almost as if speaking; but there is something in these records that goes beyond a mere instrument or the improviser on it, some unconquerable bright spirit that leaves no slops even in confusion and defeat and darkness gathering; some gallant human thing which is as near to us as it is completely marvelous . . . something, grown in this country out of the Iowa dirt, that didn't die and could not be buried so long as there should be a record left in the world, and a turntable to spin it on.[34]

Whatever Ferguson heard, his prose—his voice—captures it for us.

"Like a girl saying yes" was Eddie Condon's way of trying to explain the indefinable quality in Beiderbecke's playing, and as descriptions go it's not bad. The "yes" is there in Bix's exquisite four-bar cornet phrase ending his "Georgie Porgie" solo with Whiteman, and in the six-note ascent that brings him in on "Love Nest." Yes, yes; voice of sweet vulnerability. Yes, yes, yes—as light, as incomparably transitory, as the scent of lilacs on a warm spring night. Yes.

But can we isolate an inner voice, measure it, chart its amplitude and oscillatory curve? If not, how to explain the ardor of the Bix idolators, the annual March 10 get-togethers of Rotarian types from Bangor to Bakersfield, with their bumper stickers and bass saxes and birthday cakes, all sporting BIX LIVES lapel pins in the image of some OKeh or Victor record label? How to account for the existence of a "Bix Beiderbecke Memorial Society," or even a jazz band of otherwise competent and responsible musicians calling themselves the "Sons of Bix's" [sic]?

Above all, how to explain a woman in Hastings-on-Hudson, New York, who knew little of jazz and rather disliked what she did know, listening to Bix on the Chicago Loopers' "Three Blind Mice" for the first time and responding to him with surprisingly powerful, and quite intimate, emotion? "What I find . . . perplexing," she wrote, "is how hearing a Bix solo (even for the nth time) can be such an electrifying experience. And if I respond to Beiderbecke so profoundly, why am I not similarly moved by performances of other, 'better' music?"[35]

Why, indeed—unless the inner voice, however fugitive and problematical, is taken into account. How else to account for clarinetist James "Rosy" McHargue's contention that Bix "didn't seem to play loud, but all the same you could hear everything he played"? Or Ralph Berton: "Every note went through you like a shaft of light, making you feel all clear and clean and open"; and comparable flights of verbal fancy from Condon, Mezzrow, Goodman, Bud Freeman, Carmichael, and so many others.[36]

By 1930 Bix Beiderbecke was a sick man. A combination of illness, injury, and alcohol had left him shaky, inconsistent, given to bouts of mood and even—though little was known about the condition at the time—something that sounds like clinical depression. A return to Whiteman's orchestra, with its pressure and punishing schedule, was out of the question. A blackout during a broadcast put paid to a job on radio's *Camel Pleasure Hour*.

His last records, made between May and September, are a portrait in light and deep shadow. If sheer energy lifts his chorus on "Barnacle Bill, the Sailor" (May 21), with an all-star band assembled by Hoagy Carmichael, into the sunlight, his work on an Irving Mills date ten days later is saturated with melancholy. Two takes of the Trumbauer-Hayton "Loved One" reveal much: on both solos Bix begins strongly, tone and phrasing easily recognizable, but soon loses his footing through either technical slips or lapses in imagination. The exquisite structural sense is only intermittently in evidence.

One sublime moment was still in store. For a September 8 recording date at Victor he hired Benny Goodman, Pee Wee Russell, and Jimmy Dorsey—reportedly because he found the three of them together at Plunkett's, a midtown musicians' hangout, and couldn't bear to choose one at the expense of the others. The rest of the band included tenor saxophonist Bud Freeman, violinist Joe Venuti, and Gene Krupa on drums. Of the three titles recorded that day, "Deep Down South" has strong, confident playing from Bix and Goodman; "I Don't Mind Walking in the Rain" offers a short, choice, Russell statement.

But it is for "I'll Be a Friend (With Pleasure)" that this date will be remembered. When played at a medium to brisk tempo the song can be a pleasant vehicle for jazzmen, its chord structure particularly suited to improvisation. But the band here takes it very slowly, at a tempo that can only be described as lachrymose; vocalist Wes Vaughan milks the lyric for every drop of self-pity.

Somehow all this energizes Bix. Two takes, -2 and -3, were released at the time, and it is the former that commands attention. If a Beiderbecke "inner voice" indeed exists, it speaks here in grieving, valedictory accents. The figure in bars 7–8, especially, achieves a remarkable, and lasting, poignancy.

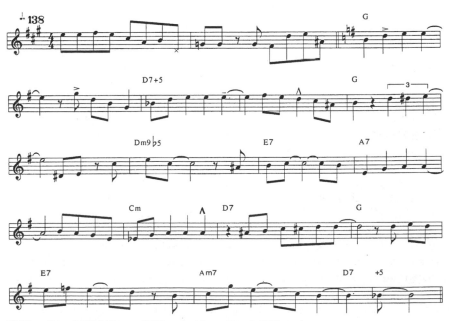

"I'll Be a Friend (With Pleasure)," Bix solo (sixteen bars), 1930.

436

*   *   *

All the attention lavished on Bix Beiderbecke has tended to obscure, and often minimize, consideration of the musical surroundings in which he came of age. Standard jazz histories regularly treat him either as an entity apart or in the context of New York, where he did most of his recording, or Chicago, where he spent time on and off before joining Jean Goldkette.

In common with a surprising number of his hot music contemporaries, Beiderbecke was a product of neither city, though both played roles in his musical development. He grew, instead, out of the fertile environment of the Midwest, in particular the states of Indiana, Iowa, Illinois, Ohio, and Michigan; taken together, they form a center of vigorous jazz activity throughout the 1920s.

Bands of both races proliferated, playing dance halls, theatres, restaurants, and roadhouses, lakeside summer resorts by the dozens; each college had at least one campus group full of keen, often quite adept young musicians. They knew about, made regular pilgrimages to, Chicago, especially to hear the New Orleans men who had settled there.

A focal point—some, remembering the energy and numbers of musicians, would call it an epicenter—of activity appears to have been Indiana. Hoagy Carmichael evoked the times and the enthusiasm with vivid poignancy in two memoirs, *The Stardust Road*, in 1946, and the rather less breathless *Sometimes I Wonder* of two decades later. As he put it:

> In the farmlands among the Indiana-Iowa corn, and from the cow-pasture universities, there sprouted a beardless priesthood of jazz players and jazz composers. Instead of buttermilk and Blackstone, we were nurtured on bathtub gin and rhythm . . . It just happened, like a thunder cloud. It may sound sentimental to say that young men caught fire in a quest for beauty, that they dedicated themselves to its realization, starving and striving, laughing, dreaming, and dying. So it's sentimental, but I think it's true.[37]

Duncan Schiedt, in his remarkable *The Jazz State of Indiana*, addressed the matter in rather more measured terms. Collector of records and rare jazz photographs, and a capable amateur pianist into the bargain, Schiedt is a Hoosier with a lifelong passion for the hot music history of his state and its surrounds. His thorough yet lively book takes a close-focus view of the growth and development of midwestern hot music.

Indiana, says Schiedt, "was not a root-source of jazz, as were New Orleans, the rural South, or the great show-business capitals of New York and Chicago. Its particular place was earned by its development of a *style*—its interpretation of music from other places.

"The style might be called, for lack of a better name, 'Midwestern Jazz.' Predating the well-known 'Chicago' style by several years . . . it was an authentic 'hot' style, so evident in the number and variety of college bands which embraced it, beginning about 1920."[38]

Such "regional" bands as those of Charlie Davis, Curt Hitch and Emil Seidel,

Marion McKay, the "Miami Lucky Seven," and the Royal Peacocks among the whites, "Speed" Webb and the Ohio-based Clark F. Hampton Family band pre-eminent among the blacks, developed a distinctive way of playing—and functioned as incubators for a large and varied talent pool. Many musicians who later became major figures in New York, Chicago, and Los Angeles were midwesterners who brought their distinctive regional accents with them.

Indiana jazz is surely best known for Hoagy Carmichael, in those days something of a "hot" piano player, who led an enthusiastic campus band at Indiana University and seemed always at the center of collegiate jazz activity. His friendship with, and devotion to, Bix has been chronicled lovingly and often, both in Carmichael's own books and elsewhere.

It saturates his early musical efforts, both as composer and performing musician; his first issued record of "Star Dust," made for Gennett October 31, 1927, with a contingent from Emil Seidel's Indianapolis-based orchestra, shows the affinity most profoundly. The melody line of the verse, especially, could have been an abstract of a Beiderbecke cornet solo—especially as trumpeter Byron Smart plays it on the record; even more explicit is Carmichael's full-chorus piano solo, redolent in its harmonic devices and melodic organization of both Bix the cornetist and Bix the pianist.[39]

Hoagy seems to have had a hunch this date would be something special. He cabled his banjo-playing chum Harry "Buzz" Wernert, then living in Toledo, that he was expecting Bix and Frank Trumbauer, who had just arrived to join Paul Whiteman at the Indiana Theatre, to be present. As things worked out, the Whiteman orchestra left on the twenty-ninth for St. Louis. The birth of "Star Dust" went on as scheduled, but unattended by its spiritual godfather.

(Not that the song's decidedly jazz orientation began and ended solely with Bix. The phrase spanning bars 3 and 4, in fact, appears to have been lifted entire from bars 25–26 of Louis Armstrong's stop-time solo on the OKeh Hot Seven record of "Potato Head Blues." Given the degree to which Louis was admired, his records known, among jazzmen everywhere, the possibility of coincidence seems remote.)

As played and recorded by Carmichael, "Star Dust" is not a rag, as some commentators, hearing the brisk tempo, have concluded. It springs from a jazz conception and emerges at first as a composition in four distinctly interrelated episodes: verse, melody statement, piano solo paraphrase, and finally an arranged ensemble chorus, another paraphrase more closely modeled on Beiderbecke's "correlated"—i.e., thematically interlocked—phrasing.

Hoagy's piano solo incorporates structural, melodic, and even harmonic aspects of both Bix the cornetist and Bix the pianist. The shape and harmonic direction of bars 9–12 are especially revealing. The arranged final chorus, no less interesting, develops much in the manner of a jazz solo—all in the unusual, at least for hot jazz of this period, key of D-major.

"Star Dust," Bud Dant–arranged passage (eight bars), and original melody, 1927.

Several other records made between 1927 and 1930 clearly use this arrangement, written by cornetist Charles "Bud" Dant and circulated by Carmichael himself, among others. The first significant departure is the Victor Young dance band arrangement for Isham Jones, recorded for Brunswick May 16, 1930, followed by Louis Armstrong's celebrated OKeh record of eighteen months later.[40]

That the "midwestern" hot jazz style has been so well documented is thanks largely to Gennett, one of the most remarkable of early record labels. The Starr Piano Company, headquartered in the small town of Richmond, Indiana, began making records in 1915—largely, it seems, because its successful piano-making operation suited it well to turn out the cabinetry in which the new record-playing machines were housed.

Founded in the 1870s, it occupied a generous thirty-five acres along the gorge of the Whitewater River, in east central Indiana. By 1915, when it started its small record operation, the company was turning out fifteen thousand pianos a year. As employer of 750 persons locally, and another four hundred nationwide, Starr was decidedly an advantage to any community—and fostered considerable pride both in Richmond and throughout the rest of the state.

As historian Rick Kennedy describes it:

> Two long rows of factory buildings, divided by a secondary railroad spur, for hauling materials and finished products within the complex, covered more than 300,000 square feet. Impressed by the self-contained, modern manufacturing complex, trade magazines in the early 1900s praised the massive industrial park in Starr Valley as a model of scientific efficiency.[41]

By the early 1920s, Gennett (from the name of the family that owned the company) had recorded a vast and formless roster of artists, from the National Marimba Orchestra to classical violinist Scipio Guidi, from hillbilly folk singer Wendell Hall (his "It Ain't Gonna Rain No Mo' " was a hit for the label) to Ku Klux Klan chief David Curtis Stephenson. William Jennings Bryan recorded his

439

famed "Cross of Gold" speech for Gennett, and Gonzales' Mexican Band played South-of-the-Border specialties.

One evening in 1922, Fred Wiggins, manager of Starr's Chicago music show-room on South Wabash Avenue, dropped in at the Friars' Inn, around the corner on Van Buren Street. He liked what he heard and talked the musicians up to Fred Gennett, one of the three sons of Starr patriarch Henry Gennett. Wiggins and Gennett went to hear the band together, made them an offer, and scheduled a recording date for August 19. The Friars Society Orchestra, as they called themselves for the occasion, set a key chapter of jazz history in motion.

Thereafter a seemingly endless procession of hot bands, black and white, from Ohio, Indiana, Illinois, Michigan, and other surrounding states made the trip to Richmond, cranking out their best party-pieces in the recording "studio," a 125-X-30-foot, board-paneled room in a single-story gray building, tucked away toward the rear of the Starr complex. Richmond was ideally located for such activities: 235 miles from Chicago, 66 from Indianapolis, and 60 from Cincinnati, it was central to just about anything going on in the region.

In contrast to such well-known (and marketable) Gennett artists as Bryan, gospel singer Homer Rodeheaver, or the entire Cincinnati Symphony Orchestra, some lesser-known or untried musicians weren't paid for recording. On the contrary, they (or someone sponsoring them) bought the time—the company's way of giving new talent a break while covering their production costs.

By early 1924, Fred Wiggins had been promoted to supervisor of Gennett's day-to-day operations—including the choice of who got to record for the label. Hot jazz had become a craze all through Indiana, with the rest of the region not far behind, and one of the first bands to record at Richmond under Wiggins's tenure was the "Wolverine Orchestra of Chicago."

Their connection with the lakeside city was slight. Though they'd all listened hard to the band at the Friars' Inn, they didn't *sound* like them. Nor was there anything in the way they played that could be traced directly to such popular units as the Isham Jones or Benson orchestras or to the great South Side bands. Born in late 1923, on a roadhouse job near Hamilton, Ohio, not far from the Indiana state line, the Wolverines can best be said to typify the hot music life of the region. Ohio-born cornetist "Wild Bill" Davison spoke often and fondly about good musicians and bands active around Cincinnati, a musical center all but undocumented in standard jazz histories. Bix, too, worked and spent time there in 1924, and some of Davison's memories of their after-hours adventures together, as related to fellow-cornetist Tom Saunders on a 1991 video, are vivid and entertaining.

As Davison and many other musicians of the time have attested, the Ohio-Indiana-Illinois belt had its own identifiable style, a band sound and rhythmic outlook quite apart from those found in Chicago, Kansas City, or St. Louis. Where the New Orleans musicians, black and white, had achieved a broad, rolling, almost stately rhythm foundation, the midwesterners bounced; ardent fans defined the way they played as "sock-time," giving the impression of being at once tight and relaxed. It could generate excitement, as the crowds at scores of college proms discovered, but not through the needling, nervous energy that drove the white Chicagoans of the later '20s: no pushing the beat, none of the hurrying insistence of "China Boy," as recorded by Eddie Condon (Indiana born, but Chicagoan by adoption), Frank Teschemacher, and their brash young associates.

But what was it? How to define it? Merrill Hammond, in later life a diplomat who served with distinction in Europe, was in those days an undergraduate at DePauw University, near Indianapolis. He played drums with a campus jazz band, and because DePauw was not far from Bloomington, where the Wolverines played frequently for dances and fraternity parties, he heard lots of "sock-time" at first hand.

In conversation with Duncan Schiedt, he characterized "sock-time" as "a medium tempo with a heavily-accented first beat, with two and four light, and three somewhere in-between." The final ensemble chorus of the Wolverines' "Susie" is as good an example of this as any: it's neither the strict "oom-pah" characteristic of most dance bands of the time nor the evenly demarcated four-to-the-bar of the New Orleans musicians.[42]

Another Wolverines admirer, quoted in *Bix: Man and Legend*, observed that "all the instruments of the band emphasized each of the four beats of the measure, whereas only the rhythm sections of other bands had done it in the past." Others speak of a crispness, a buoyancy.

But none of this really sets the midwesterners apart. It can as easily be said that the four horns of the Oliver Creole Jazz Band emphasized all four beats of the bar; that saxophonist Perley Breed's Boston-based Orchestra, recording at Gennett's New York studios in November of '24, achieved all the crispness and bounce of a midwestern ensemble.

It had more to do with a certain sunniness of outlook and a lyrical emphasis, even in the ensembles. Some scholars, S. Frederick Starr among them, attribute this—at least in part—to the collegiate environment. A world of difference existed, they seem to be saying, between playing a campus dance for generally affluent youngsters at a small liberal arts college and making yourself heard over the hubbub of a dance hall on Chicago's tough West Side. Chicago might have been, in Nelson Algren's oft-quoted phrase, "a city on the make," but such college communities as Oxford and Yellow Springs, Ohio, or Greencastle and West Lafayette, Indiana, certainly were not.

Though Bix inevitably stands out as the only soloist of real stature, records by the Wolverines are quite similar in attitude to those made around the same time by pianist Curtis Hitch's "Happy Harmonists," based in Evansville, and by a host of lesser-known groups, among them a little-known unit led by Dud Mecum, the Wolverines' first pianist, which recorded for the obscure Rainbow label (owned by Homer Rodeheaver). On "Angry," a favorite Beiderbecke tune, Mecum's personnel reportedly included Wolverines tenor saxophonist George Johnson and might even have almost had Bix, who—at least according to one account—canceled out at the last minute. Such were the regional similarities that more than a few listeners, hearing Marion McKay's 1924 "Doo Wacka Doo," mistook cornetist Leroy Morris for Bix.[43]

On Hitch's 1925 "Cataract Rag Blues," the ensembles and rhythm section strongly resemble those of the Wolverines, and Fred Rollison (briefly considered as a replacement when Beiderbecke left the band) contributes a strongly Bix-accented cornet solo.

The Wolverines records, and those by Hitch, Emil Seidel, and so many others, do sound different and are recognizable as distinct in sound and style. It all comes into focus in the person of Hoagland Howard Carmichael. Born in Bloomington, on November 22, 1899, he'd enrolled at Indiana University to study law but had little save hot music on his mind. He'd met Bix one night at the Friars' Inn, and they'd taken to each other at once. But it was only after Hoagy had heard Bix play the cornet that the friendship really blossomed.

"It's hard to say what got to me so much," Carmichael said, looking back in wonder. "Just four notes, some little thing—and I *knew* it was right. Not a matter of, 'Hey, what was *that* he did?' Nothing like that. It's just that those few notes sounded like something I might have been waiting for, searching for, all my life—without even knowing that they were what I was after."[44]

The Wolverines recorded Carmichael's first composition, a three-part stomp called "Free Wheeling," for Gennett, promptly changing its name to "Riverboat Shuffle."[45] Curt Hitch, whose Happy Harmonists were also recording for the label, loved it, and when his band scheduled a Gennett date for May 19, 1925, he asked Hoagy for another "hotsy-totsy" item just like it. "Hoagmichael," as friends had taken to calling him, could even play piano on the session if he wanted.

If he *wanted?* Nothing would keep him away. But what to write? He'd been working on something, an asymmetrical little theme which, the way he played it, wound up seventeen bars long. Yet it had something—a bit in the middle, superimposing five groupings of three quarter-notes on four 4/4 bars. George Gershwin had used a similar device on "Fascinatin' Rhythm" in London around the same time, though Hoagy, perched at an old upright piano in Bloomington, Indiana, had no way of knowing that.

He added a verse, a kind of secular hymn tune rising scalewise from tonic and resolving in some Bix-like descending arpeggios; for an interlude, or "patter" section, he cobbled together a four-bar descending figure and a twelve-bar blues. He called the result "Washboard Blues."

For the requested "hotsy-totsy" number, the young pianist devised a stomp bristling with little "modernistic" touches: whole-tone scales, irregular thematic structures, even a three-against-four phrase borrowed from "Washboard Blues." He called it "Boneyard Shuffle," and as a hot jazz specialty it's quite innovative: little in the output of either black or white bands of 1925 compares with its way of making the unconventional seem perfectly natural. As the work of a tyro, which Carmichael certainly was, it's spectacular.

"Washboard Blues" almost didn't get recorded at all—at least not at the Hitch date. After they'd run it down, recording supervisor Ezra Wickemeyer came out from behind his double-thick pane of glass and shook his head. Too short. Too short by twenty seconds—which when you're making a three-minute record is about 11 percent of your total time, an eternity.

Steady, avuncular, Hitch didn't miss a beat. "Hoagy will put in a piano solo," he said. The musicians filed out for a smoke, leaving the composer to his thoughts. In his own account, he thought about everything he could—about his family, a three-year-old sister dead of diphtheria, his mother playing hymns on the piano; about Bix, about various college pals, especially artistic, surrealist Bill Moenkhaus. And, by the time they got back, he had something. A bit of the blues, some double-time—and, in bars 5 and 6, an elegiac little phrase he'd later extract for use at the heart of the beloved "Lazy Bones."

Twenty-two seconds by the clock. They dropped it at midstream—and had themselves a record.[46]

Nor did the saga of "Washboard Blues" end there. Red Nichols and Miff Mole recorded it twice within a month, spreading it far beyond Indiana. In the meantime it picked up a lyric, thanks to Fred Callahan, a stonecutter and part-time poet who lived in Bedford, some fifty miles south of Bloomington. On November 20, 1927, Hoagy himself recorded the result, piano and vocal, closely attended by Bix, the Dorsey Brothers, and the rest of Paul Whiteman's Orchestra.

Far more than the straightforward and largely conventional "Riverboat Shuffle," "Washboard Blues" represents Hoagy Carmichael's real debut as a composer. It is one of the most singularly extraordinary pieces of music to emerge from the hot jazz ferment of the 1920s. Half popular song, half dramatic recitative, it draws entirely on the twinned aesthetics of jazz and the blues: not Tin Pan Alley, not the Broadway stage, not even the rich folk heritage of Appalachia, the South, and the Southwest. "Washboard Blues" could only have been written by a musician positioned, as was Hoagy Carmichael, in the thick of hot jazz, and as such it is a pioneering work.

On May 2, 1928, Carmichael brought an eight-piece group back to Richmond to do six titles. Among his men were some old cronies (banjoist Arnold Habbe, from Hitch's Happy Harmonists), Indianapolis pros (bassist Jack Drummond), and new faces (IU freshman cornetist Charles "Bud" Dant). They'd prepared six tunes, including a piano-and-voice version of "Star Dust," this time outfitted with Hoagy's own lyrics and backed only by Ed Wolfe's fiddle.

Fred Wiggins, who for all Carmichael's new prominence still seems to have viewed him with some misgivings, issued only two of the six titles the band recorded that night. "Star Dust" he disposed of with the written instruction: "Reject. Already on Gennett. Poor seller." The rest, including what may have been an ebullient reading of "Shimme-Sha Wabble" (by then a staple of the Chicago and New York jazz band repertoires), suffered similar fates and have been lost. Two band sides survived, and they are exceptional.[47]

Taken together, Hoagy's own "March of the Hoodlums" and "Walkin' the Dog," by Shelton Brooks (composer of "Some of These Days" and "At the Darktown Strutters' Ball"), endure as definitive examples of midwestern hot jazz. Musical roman candles, they crackle and flash, firing off sparks of sheer youthful exuberance.

"Jazz was so new in those days," Dant told Rick Kennedy, "and we just thought going over to Richmond with Hoagy would be a kick . . . He was older and the most talented among us, but we still considered him one of us . . . He would write out basic head arrangements, but you had to transpose them for your instrument. Mostly, you went on Hoagy's explanations and we were pretty used to doing that."[48]

On alto sax Carmichael had Kerval Chauncey Goodwin, who came from Brownstown, not far from Bedford. He'd been a freshman at DePauw, majoring in music and playing impressive alto and trumpet in campus groups, when Hoagy first heard him, and shortly thereafter he transferred to Bloomington. He was, said Carmichael years later, "just the best around."

"March of the Hoodlums," a Hoagy creation, weds dixieland march, à la "Tiger Rag," and college fight song (which part of it later became). They take it fast ($\downarrow$ = 140), in a style that can only be described, without a trace of obloquy, as 1920s manic, picking up momentum as they go. Dant's cornet lead is bright and sure; the rhythm charges gaily along in purest "sock-time." And, when Goodwin's alto bursts out of the scored trio section, he seems to lift the whole thing into the air. Based on the "Tiger Rag" chords, his thirty-two-bar solo owes much to Jimmy Dorsey's well-known display piece on the same sequence.

(Goodwin played in Carmichael's band during a late-1928 engagement at the exclusive Columbia Club in Indianapolis, then moved on to Detroit, where he worked with a number of Jean Goldkette units. Ray Conolly, cornetist at the Columbia Club, told Duncan Schiedt that "saxophone players from all over [Detroit] would come to catch him. He was amazing!" Kerval—or "Chance," as he preferred being called—headed west, working with the Henry Halstead band throughout the Mid- and Southwest, including stands at the Muehlebach Hotel in Kansas City. By 1932 he was with the Jimmie's Joys Orchestra, one of the finest of the white "territory bands," where fellow reedman Gilbert O'Shaughnessy remembered him as a soloist "way out in front," sounding like an ancestor of latter-day alto giant Paul Desmond. Apparent mental instability led to a breakdown in the mid-'30s and a diagnosis of paranoid schizophrenia. Goodwin ended his days at California's Camarillo State Hospital, best known for its treatment of another prominent alto saxophonist, Charlie Parker, early in the following decade. Kerval Chauncey Goodwin died at Camarillo May 5, 1942.)[49]

"Walkin' the Dog," if not quite up to the same voltage level, is no less satisfying. Goodwin, opening over band stop-time chords, shows he's listened to both Trumbauer and Jimmy Dorsey. But Hoagy is the show here, knocking off sixteen bars on cornet (tone and embouchure leave something to be desired, but the conception is pure Bix) and bookending some perilously manic scat vocalizing within two reflective piano excerpts from Edward MacDowell's *To a Wild Rose*.

It's music quite different in texture and attitude from the stuff being made in Chicago and other cities by either white or black bands. Looser than the Nichols-Mole New York miniatures, more relaxed than the devil-take-the-hindmost hustle of the Chicagoans, less thoughtful than the Bix-Tram collaborations, it's pure, undistilled exuberance. But polished, with a clear, confident idea of where it's going and how it wants to get there.

Perhaps, indeed, it could only have been made by young, affluent whites, growing up in a well-defined, secure world. But it seems churlish to take Carmichael and his friends to task because, as youngsters enjoying themselves, they weren't out to plumb any great political or artistic depths. Better by far, to listen to Hoagy's scatting on "Walkin' the Dog" or Goodwin's tearaway alto on "Hoodlums" and smile in affectionate enjoyment of their youth, the boundless optimism of their perceived immortality.

Their musical snapshot captures a precious moment in the emotional life of the American heartland, as vivid as a Thomas Hart Benton painting or a passage from Sinclair Lewis's *Main Street* or Sherwood Anderson's *Winesburg, Ohio*. Generations will change, and with them the social and moral ways of a people—and even the brightest memory fails. But once, long ago, young men in blazers and straw boaters, or tuxes, or plus-fours, or just shirtsleeves, got together in a stuffy little room by a railroad track in Indiana and made music that leapt and sang, celebrating life eternal. The day, the musicians, the lives and good times, are lost now, save for a few images, fast blending into a golden twilight.

But the music. Ah, the music. Play "March of the Hoodlums" and it's 1928 all over again, denying time and mortality. "Hot *dawg!*" it fairly whoops across the years. "We're young, it's spring in Indiana, and we're playing hot jazz. The sky is bright blue, Bix is with Whiteman, and we haven't a care. What could be nicer?"

18

Frank Trumbauer:
The Divided Self

It's easy enough to wax lyrical about Bix Beiderbecke. Posterity loves him: in death, he has become an American icon, transcending the hermetical peer culture of hot jazz as he never did in life.

Some of his associates have fared less well—as if the beatification process required defoliation of the musical landscape around him. Poor Bix, many assessments seem to say, hobbled by second-raters and wannabes, their only glow a pallid reflection of his.

Sober listening reveals that the confederates, often companions of choice, were anything but satellites. Some, especially bass saxophonist Adrian Rollini and the ill-fated clarinetist Don Murray, were outstanding on their own. Bill Rank's recorded solos easily attest to his skills as, in Digby Fairweather's phrase, a "brilliantly agile, full-toned" trombonist.

At least one Beiderbecke compatriot, C-melody saxophonist Frank Trumbauer, is considerably more than even that and can be counted a significant innovator—a major contributor to jazz on his own.

He's a problem figure, an awkward fit for romantics and clear-minded analysts alike. From all reports he lived the kind of temperate, socially and professionally conscientious life seldom found among early jazzmen. Married at age twenty, he spent the rest of his life with the same woman, saved his money, did not drink, always showed up on time for work, looked responsibly after family and friends.

Even his chosen instrument was a thing apart. Pitched in concert, or piano, key, between the E♭ alto and B♭ tenor, the C-melody saxophone enjoyed great popularity in the 1920s: instrument makers stressed the ease with which an amateur player could read piano music right over his accompanist's shoulder. No fussy transposition, no tangling with music theory: with a C-melody *anybody* could become a saxophone player in just a few easy lessons.

But the instrument found few champions among professionals, perhaps due to a built-in crisis of identity. Was it a "C-tenor," as parts in some published stock arrangements indicated, or a lowered alto? Even early design seemed to reflect the dilemma: some C-melodies look like miniature tenors, with that instrument's distinctive crook neck. Others resemble large, slightly ungainly altos.

Tonally the C-melody often seemed to *moo*, achieving neither the muscularity of the tenor nor the unique singing quality of the alto. Yet it was the instrument most often used by Rudy Wiedoeft, incontestably the chief popularizer of the saxophone in America between 1917 and 1927, and in his hands achieved considerable expressive power.[1]

It found its major pioneer jazz voice in Trumbauer, who converted its weaknesses to strengths: rather than struggle with the C-melody's inconsistencies of pitch, he finessed them by eliding and glissing; rather than resist the bovine tone quality, he often exploited it for humorous effect.

The result was a style and tone uniquely his, uniquely recognizable, neither *faux*-alto nor emasculated tenor—or even typical C-melody. Just Trumbauer.

It confronted any other jazzman approaching the instrument with a potentially deadly choice: either succumb to the C-melody's technical weaknesses and neither-fish-nor-fowl identity by forcing it into alto or tenor postures, or wind up sounding like Frank Trumbauer. Perhaps partly as a result, there were no legatees, no C-melody stylists, when hot jazz began to codify and coalesce at the start of the 1930s. Like the bass saxophone, which found its only major stylist in Rollini, the C-melody simply had nowhere to go.

But there was more to it than that: Frank Trumbauer, in common with his between-the-markers instrument, was himself an identity divided, two stylists in one.

Orie Frank Trumbauer was born May 30, 1901, in Carbondale, Illinois, into a family related, at various degrees of distance, to both Charles Dickens and the ownership of the Winchester Firearms Company. He grew up in St. Louis, trying violin, trombone, and piano before hearing the saxophone, played by a local man named Ray Reynolds, at the Arcadia Ballroom and deciding that it was what he wanted for himself. He persuaded his mother, a film theatre pianist, to buy him an instrument, and under her supervision made quick progress.

By the time he left the navy and returned home after World War I, the young man was a proficient "ear" player on a variety of instruments. But he'd no sooner landed a job at Cicardi's Café than he realized to his horror that he'd have to learn to sight-read. His diary, published in the Philip R. Evans–Larry Kiner study *Tram*, records the result:

I made up my mind that I was going to study. I worked at the café every night and spent at least eight hours on my instruments. Study! Study! Study! I lost weight, I had very little sleep, but in nine months I could read and transpose any part. Flute parts—trumpet parts—trombone parts—clarinet parts—cello parts—anything at all.[2]

Over the next few years Trumbauer worked for a succession of prominent dance band leaders, among them Joe Kayser, Gene Rodemich, Ted Jansen, Edgar Benson's Benson Orchestra of Chicago, and, in 1923–24, Ray Miller (whose "Black and White Melody Boys" of 1920–21 had included the pioneering New Orleans trombonist Tom Brown). With the experience came an enviable reputation as all-rounder, blessed with near-virtuosic technique, equally skilled at reading and "faking"—playing improvised "hot" solos.

There is no indication where, or how, he learned to do it, no account of having listened to other musicians. Historical speculation could have him hearing Charles Creath, William Thornton Blue, Leonard Davis, and other St. Louis–based black jazzmen, or records by the Original Dixieland Jazz Band and other early groups, but evidence is absent. His diary is silent on the subject.

On Rodemich's 1921 record of "By the Pyramids," Trumbauer and Bennie Krueger play a two-part harmonized saxophone break, apparently one of the first on record. If that attracted some attention among colleagues, it was nothing compared to what happened when Victor released the Benson orchestra's "I Never Miss the Sunshine," recorded June 14, 1923. Saxophonists everywhere, white and black, devoured it, studying and copying Trumbauer's full-chorus solo; dozens, among them such major jazzmen as Benny Carter, later remembered the effect it had on them.

Using a smoothly vocalized tone, and with only a light, slow vibrato, Trumbauer delivered an unhurried, economically melodic paraphrase. Its sound, delivery, and symmetrical phrasing are at once redolent of the remarkable but now-forgotten Loring McMurray, heard on various Memphis Five and Sam Lanin records of the pre-1924 period and discussed elsewhere in this survey. There is no direct indication that Trumbauer knew about McMurray, but testimony from several musicians active in the early '20s, including Boston clarinetist James Moynahan, suggests that McMurray was more widely known than is now supposed.

At Detroit's Graystone Ballroom, Jimmy Dorsey interpolated the Trumbauer chorus in an arrangement of "I Never Miss the Sunshine" played by Jean Goldkette's house orchestra. Don Murray, on tenor sax, faked a harmony part, then wrote out a third voice for Stanley "Doc" Ryker. It was, said arranger-pianist Paul Mertz, a giant step forward in "concerted sectional playing of jazz."[3]

Musicians all over the country suddenly seemed to know who "Tram" was, and when, the following year, he joined the Mound City Blue Blowers on their second Brunswick record date (March 14, 1924), the news got around fast. They played the currently popular "San" and backed it with Trumbauer's own composition "Red Hot." His full chorus on "San" became as widely imitated by other saxophonists as "I Never Miss the Sunshine" had been.

But even at this early stage, a split can be discerned in Trumbauer's musical *persona*. He often exhibits a sense of device: phrases, "licks," clever in conception but unrelated to any emotional sense of song or moment, seem to have been fitted together for maximum effect. "This'll wow 'em," he seems to be saying— and wow 'em he does. At bright tempos, moreover, he reels off strings of un-syncopated eighth notes, which often emerge sounding like method-book exer-cises.

Yet running parallel is another, at times contradictory, track: an ability to plasticize and smooth out a melodic line, lending it grace and coherence with long held notes, gentle arcs of phrase, and a logic of development rare in hot music of the early '20s. Only clarinetist Leon Roppolo, of the New Orleans Rhythm Kings, comes to mind as a comparably endowed (if quite different-sounding) melodic soloist on a reed instrument.

This melodic sense is apparent in Trumbauer's solo, a half-chorus and breaks, on "Jimtown Blues," with the Cotton Pickers. Also present is a repertory of "novelty" effects—rapid tonguing, hill-and-dale phrase patterns, an angular ap-proach to rhythm—which link him clearly to Rudy Wiedocft—or at least one aspect of him.

No assessment of saxophone playing in the '20s, in or out of the limited precincts of "hot" improvisation, can be accurate without reference to Wiedoeft, so pervasive was his influence. Born in Detroit in 1893, he began as a violinist, switching to clarinet after breaking his bowing arm in a bicycle accident. By 1910 he was in California, attracting attention as a clarinet soloist of enviable technique. Shortly after moving to Chicago in 1912, he "discovered" the saxophone, and by the time he arrived in New York, four years later, he had become known as a soloist, specializing in the C-melody.

Wiedoeft recorded often, for many labels. He played frequently on the radio. His name became widely identified with the instrument, his compositions ever more widely performed. Instrument companies approached him for advice in improving and redesigning their saxophones. By 1920 he was running his own publishing firm, and such solos as "Valse Erica," "Valse Llewellyn," and the ubiquitous "Saxophobia" were reaching musicians everywhere.

Wiedoeft's appearances in vaudeville (sometimes in cowboy outfits and other costumes) drew capacity audiences. His column, "Rudy Wiedoeft's Counsel to Saxophonists," was a regular feature of *Metronome* magazine. A monograph, *Three Talks to Saxophonists*, was published by the Henri Selmer Instrument Co. and sold well. He was possibly one of the first (in 1920) to use four saxophones together on a recording as a section. As early as 1919 he redesigned part of the saxophone's key mechanism to improve its low register. On April 17, 1926, Wiedoeft and three colleagues staged a saxophone concert at New York's Aeolian Hall, where Paul Whiteman had introduced George Gershwin's *Rhapsody in Blue* two years ear-lier. He appeared in London, where critics hailed him as the "Fritz Kreisler of the Saxophone."

Everywhere, it seemed, saxophonists were copying the Wiedoeft tonal conception and manner of execution. Such disciples as Clyde Doerr (with Art Hickman's seminal orchestra), Andy Sannella, Chester Hazlett, Merle Johnston, Arnold Brilhart, and Alfie Evans, though none a C-melody specialist, acquired followings of their own. As saxophone player-historian Ted Hegvik has observed, Wiedoeft "took the saxophone—an instrument without a style, a literature, or an artistic example—and, in supplying it with all of these, created the 'saxophone craze' of the '20s." No saxophonist of any aspiration, black or white, disregarded his example: it is even present in the tone or technique, attack or vibrato, of such men as Johnny Hodges, Otto "Toby" Hardwick, and Charlie Holmes.[4]

In common with his playing, Wiedoeft's compositions demonstrated a neatly bifurcated personality, in which "Saxophobia," "Sax-o-Trix," and other novelty contrivances lived side by side with such elegiac, melodically rich, Kreislerian salon pieces as "Dans l'Orient" and "Valse Vanité." His dual identity seems to have had profound effect on Frank Trumbauer. It is not without significance that the latter's first OKeh recording date in association with Bix Beiderbecke includes both "Singin' the Blues," a masterpiece of legato attack and logical phrase-building, and his own "Trumbology," with its Wiedoeftian double-tonguing effects.[5]

Tram's records of 1924–25 show some awkwardness dealing coherently with fast tempos. His half-choruses on "Tessie! (Stop Teasin' Me)" and "Red Hot Henry Brown," with Ray Miller, seem somehow imprisoned by the beat; he fares better on the slower "Mishawaka Blues" with the Cotton Pickers, where a legato approach buffs the jagged edges off his rhythmic execution.

It is against this frame of reference that the true importance of Trumbauer's meeting and four-year association with Beiderbecke becomes clear. Bix and Tram, as they quickly became known to colleagues, first recorded together in New York on October 10, 1924. Their partnership, nurtured during an eight-month engagement in St. Louis (at the same Arcadia Ballroom where Trumbauer had first heard Ray Reynolds) and reaching full flower with the orchestras of Jean Goldkette and Paul Whiteman, is one of the peaks of hot jazz in the '20s, and in the very history of jazz itself. It has been chronicled, examined, analyzed, venerated, and fought over. In more than six decades, its records have seldom been out of catalogue.

But attention has always focused on Bix. Those Whiteman performances that feature only Trumbauer have seldom been reissued and remain known to few outside collector circles; he brings clarity and melodic insight, for example, to a full chorus on the 1928 Paul Whiteman record of Rodgers and Hart's "Do I Hear You Saying (I Love You)?," recorded the day before the far better known "You Took Advantage of Me."

Trumbauer's stance on most records of the late '20s is elegant, debonair, a little above it all, commenting on the proceedings rather than participating in them directly. Even in ostensibly rhythmic situations—"Ol' Man River" and

"China Boy" with Whiteman, for example—he floats on the beat, never attempting to drive it, using it mainly as a point of reference.

The key to this *persona* is Bix, and Trumbauer's reaction to him. The cornetist's every recorded solo, regardless of length or setting, seems to project a range of identifiable emotions: a bittersweet yearning; a fresh, almost girlish innocence; even, though admittedly at a stretch, something foredoomed, more than a little fey. On a purely reactive level, Trumbauer seems to seek contrast, to balance attic with antic. Where Bix is metaphorical Tram is matter-of-fact; when Bix plays Hamlet, Trumbauer gives us Polonius; Bixian high seriousness fetches whimsy from his musical partner.

Between "Singin' the Blues" and the end, in late 1929, of the Bix-Tram association, the saxophonist cultivated a manner, a musical deportment, that informs all his work, whether in tandem with Bix or on his own. Sometimes—as on such otherwise unmemorable Whiteman efforts as "Dancing Shadows" and "I Can't Give You Anything but Love"—the manner seems even more important than the actual content of what he plays.

Without doubt, "Singin' the Blues" brought the Bix-Trumbauer partnership sharply into focus and wrought a permanent change in the way musicians everywhere, whatever their race, thought about playing jazz solos. With unconcealed wonder, the clarinetist Kenny Davern has told of a day when tenor saxophonists Eddie Barefield and Don Byas dropped by the New York workshop of reed repairman Saul Fromkin. "They stood out in the hall, got their tenors out, and in unison played Trumbauer's 'Singin' the Blues' chorus—and *perfectly*. When they walked in, I asked how it happened that they knew it. '*Everybody* knew that chorus' was all they said."[6]

Bill Challis, arranging "Singin' the Blues" for Paul Whiteman's Orchestra in 1928, scored Trumbauer's chorus for the entire reed section. It got the same treatment on Fletcher Henderson's two performances of the piece: the reeds play Trumbauer together, before Rex Stewart renders Bix's equally famed thirty-two bars as a solo in the inflections and accents of his own style. It was the first time such homage had been delivered in so complete a fashion: individual musicians had quoted from certain favorite solos—Johnny Dodds's clarinet chorus on the Oliver record of "Camp Meeting Blues"; various choruses (or parts thereof) by Armstrong, Bix, Roppolo, and others—but no one had emulated *an entire record* in such a fashion.[7]

The Beiderbecke-Trumbauer duets, or "chase choruses," achieve moments of almost magical rapport; there can be few more rewarding episodes on record, for example, than the thirty-two bars they share on Whiteman's 1928 "You Took Advantage of Me." Yet their sequential, almost conversational communication appears rooted entirely in their differing solo styles; in contrast, those few occasions (the final chorus of "Riverboat Shuffle," for example) which find them together in an improvised ensemble reveal no special interaction.

*   *   *

Besides Trumbauer, the only other early jazz saxophonist to use the C-melody with any distinction was Jack Pettis, first heard on records in 1922 as a member of the Friars Society Orchestra. Later, as a member of Ben Bernie's reed section, Pettis recorded extensively, showing good rhythmic sense and command of his instrument. But unlike Trumbauer, he seemed stuck fast between his horn's alto and tenor identities.

Sometimes, as on "Nobody's Sweetheart" with his own "Pets," he sounds as if he's actually playing tenor, which was one of his doubles; on "Baby," made at the same Victor date, he may be using an alto. But Pettis's full-chorus solo on the January 19, 1929, "Freshman Hop" (one of innumerable recorded versions of his own piece) is clearly on C-melody: he's fluent and in tune—but the tone never quite escapes his instrument's bovine quality.

Another "Freshman Hop," done about a month later for Pathé, teams Pettis with nineteen-year-old Benny Goodman, and to revealing effect. Compared with Goodman's rhythmic flexibility and bright attack, Pettis seems almost dowdy, like a housemother chaperoning a—well, a Freshman Hop.

The saxophonist's career after the '20s is something of a mystery. After leaving Bernie in 1929 he freelanced a while, playing a few New York hotel residencies, then eventually moved to Los Angeles and there dropped from sight. Four 1937 sides made under his name for Variety bear scant resemblance to the hot performances of the '20s. There is little about the clarinet and saxophone work that can be positively identified as his.[8]

Perhaps it can be said of him that he was as much a phenomenon of the 1920s as the C-melody saxophone he played and, unlike Frank Trumbauer, was not a sufficiently original soloist on it to have much of an impact on other players.[9]

Symbiosis, says Webster's, is "the living together in more or less intimate association or even close union of two dissimilar organisms." Ordinarily, the definition continues, "the association is advantageous, or often necessary, to one or both, and not harmful to either." The Beiderbecke-Trumbauer relationship is at its most symbiotic in the exchanges on "You Took Advantage of Me," on "Borneo," and on "Just an Hour of Love," the latter two on OKeh under Tram's own name, or in those moments (such as "There Ain't No Sweet Man") when one picks up directly from the other. So often, they could be two halves of one consciousness, somehow blending at points of intersection.[10]

Almost equally illustrative of their kinship is the manner in which each man deals with the first sixteen bars of "China Boy," on the Whiteman record of May 3, 1929. The similarities in their methods of assembling component "correlated" phrases are striking. Both solos are rendered here in concert pitch, to facilitate comparison.

"China Boy," Bix and Tram solos, sixteen bars on two staves, 1929.

Perhaps Trumbauer's crowning achievement, however, lies in "For No Reason At All in C," an original composition recorded for OKeh May 13, 1927, in trio with Eddie Lang on guitar and Bix at the piano. More than even "Singin' the Blues," it illustrates the creativity inherent in Trumbauer's approach to improvisation.

Though based on the chord structure of "I'd Climb the Highest Mountain," a 1926 pop tune beloved of both Beiderbecke and (in later years) Pee Wee Russell, it never states the melody. It is a seminal effort, three choruses of invention and commentary which presage the methods (if not the substance) of bebop and yield numerous passages of striking melodic invention.

The melodic lines of the three choruses appear below, transcribed in their recorded sequence in concert pitch, and in the register in which they *sound*. Points of high musical interest include Trumbauer's alternation of E$\natural$ and E$\flat$ in the figure which occupies bars 17–20; the songlike construction of bars 25–32; the *Leitmotif* running through Lang's entire chorus; the triplet figure with which Trumbauer opens his final chorus, and the way in which he develops it and climaxes with a Bix-like exclamation in bars 7–8.

453

(continued)

(SAX)

(continued)

"For No Reason at All in C," entire record (Trumbauer and Lang solos), 1927.

Many of the best Trumbauer solos are minimally altered paraphrases of their parent melodies. His twelve-bar verse statement in "When," with Whiteman, or his full choruses on "My Heart Stood Still" and the superb, aforementioned "Do I Hear You Saying," epitomize the Trumbauer manner.

During the 1927–29 period there seems no such thing as a routine or uninteresting Trumbauer solo. "Reachin' for Someone" (Whiteman version), with its droll downward gliss; his sardonic transformation of "Japanese Sandman"; a spirited sixteen bars on "I'm Gonna Meet My Sweetie Now," with Goldkette— all speak in a voice at once amiable and lightly satiric, knowing yet somehow never jaded.

They are not, in the main, rhythmically oriented choruses. Trumbauer's solo on "Way Down Yonder in New Orleans," however melodically rich and widely admired, is rhythmically static in a way that Beiderbecke's is not. His phrases, like those of Jimmy Lytell and several others who came of age in the early '20s, demonstrate a foursquare on-the-beat quality, invariably resolving on half notes. Even at faster tempos, gliding along above and across the rhythm or even addressing it directly—as on "Clarinet Marmalade" and, with Goldkette, "My Pretty Girl"—he never breaks out of the two- and four-bar phrase boxes so evident on "Way Down Yonder in New Orleans."

But to find Trumbauer wanting as a swinger is to miss the point of his gift for melodic narrative; for canny, often mordant commentary; for a matchless ability to reshape the elements of a melody into a new song, in which the lineaments of the original remain clearly visible.

When Bix's drinking and faltering health caused him to leave the Whiteman orchestra temporarily at the end of 1928, Trumbauer carried on undiminished, recording some of his most eloquent solos. He brings just the right insouciance to Cole Porter's "Let's Do It," rides happily over a thrusting brass figure on "How About Me?," and leads the saxophones through a Challis orchestration of his "Singin' the Blues" solo on a performance, unissued and long thought lost, featuring vaudeville "Shimmy Queen" Bee Palmer. Singing the song's first four bars "straight," Miss Palmer then offers an innovation: a Ted Koehler lyric, set to the Trumbauer solo and anticipating by three decades a practice popularized by Dave Lambert, Jon Hendricks, Eddie Jefferson, and others. After scatting eight bars of

Bix's solo, she ends with a passage based on the last moments of the Beiderbecke-Trumbauer ensemble.[11]

"Don't Leave Me Daddy," also from the Palmer date, tops even these efforts. Trumbauer's solo is emotionally charged, with a strong narrative thread. It is also deeply revealing in its freedom from the beat: moving forward in a procession of *rubato* arabesques, it develops like a cadenza, propelled not rhythmically but melodically. This side of Trumbauer can be heard elsewhere—on "My Heart Stood Still," for example; but there is no other solo that comes so close to declaring the fixed pulse almost irrelevant.[12]

When Bix returned, it quickly became clear that he'd not be able to handle a full schedule of touring, broadcasting, and recording. One of his first decisions was to withdraw from Trumbauer's OKeh recordings. According to the saxophonist's diary, as quoted by Evans and Kiner, Beiderbecke concluded, "in his own mind, that he was not playing up to standard" and hesitated to be heard in that condition with major players. "He decided, after April 1929, not to make any more recordings with OKeh Records until he felt that he was returning to his old form."[13]

So it was that, when Tram convened an eleven-piece Whiteman unit on May 15, 1929, to make two small-band titles for Columbia, young Andy Secrest was playing what would have been Bix's book and taking the hot cornet solos. The earlier OKeh records had done well, at least partly due to Beiderbecke; even dealing with an increasingly commercial pop repertoire, the cornetist had been the driving force. Not surprisingly, then, Secrest got a solo on almost every Trumbauer OKeh title.

He rose to the task, handling a half-chorus on "Nobody but You" with aplomb, opening "Love Ain't Nothin' but the Blues" with a melody statement so strongly evocative of its model that many collectors attributed it to Bix himself. Hoagy Carmichael had written "Manhattan Rag" with Bix in mind, and Secrest tackled the showcase solo assignment with conviction.

Trumbauer, meanwhile, underwent an interesting, if subtle, metamorphosis. Where the pairing with Bix had cast him as a largely reactive, secondary figure, the newcomer precipitated a new situation, with new requirements. Andy Secrest might do fine *sounding* like Bix (hear him on "Deep Harlem"), but his style at that point in his career was just a simulacrum of its model. The creative force that had breathed life into the Beiderbecke-Trumbauer collaboration, given it weight, was on the wane.

Its absence is particularly noticeable when Secrest and Trumbauer trade phrases in a "chase" on another version of "Reaching for Someone." For the first time it's *Tram* who leads off, with Andy scrambling along after him. The allocation of bars, too, is revealing: in each eight-bar episode Tram plays four, Andy two, then Tram (or, the last time, Eddie Lang) finishes up the last two.

Born in Muncie, Indiana, in 1907, Andy Secrest had played widely around the Midwest while still a teenager, winning respect as a responsible journeyman musician and good soloist. In common with so many other Indiana and Illinois musicians, he worshiped Bix, rooting his own "hot" style in that adoration. He'd played alongside New Orleans–born Stirling Bose in 1927, when the Indiana Royal Peacock Orchestra briefly recorded as a Jean Goldkette unit; the two men's brief solos on "Here Comes the Show Boat" demonstrate their indebtedness to Bix.[14]

Whiteman first "borrowed" Secrest from Goldkette for a four-day Detroit engagement, liked what he heard, and quietly bought the young man's contract. Barely twenty-one, Secrest returned to New York with the "King of Jazz" and was in the personnel for a February 7, 1929, Columbia record date. A quiet, respectful bandsman, he remained aware that Whiteman had hired him as insurance, to "play" Bix, in solo and section, in case of trouble when the cornet soloist returned from a rest cure.

Denying that he ever directly copied Beiderbecke's recorded solos, Secrest nevertheless vouchsafed that "I idolized the guy . . . thought his style and tone were way ahead of the times. I started playing that way because it was the style that I wanted to obtain, and by the time I joined the [Whiteman] band I sounded a good deal like him."[15]

Bix, moreover, was still in the Whiteman brass section, still taking solos, still able—though less often now—to make the lights glow; some degree of residual energy, originating with him, still drove the Trumbauer band dates. Perhaps it is his absence-yet-presence, being there and not being there, that strengthens Trumbauer, recasts him as the dominant figure—and propels his 1929 work to a generally more emphatic level.

Trumbauer is in top form setting out the verse of "Turn On the Heat," waxing surprisingly cornet-like on "My Sweeter Than Sweet," and stretching out with a full (how well Lang accompanies him!) chorus before Mildred Bailey's vocal, her first on record, on "I Like to Do Things for You." Even handling the faster tempos of "Happy Feet" and "Sunny Side Up," the saxophonist never lapses into novelty effect or the stiff angularity of his earlier, pre-Beiderbecke work. Without exception, his solos on these performances are smoothly articulated, unhurried, tonally suave.[16]

"Sittin' on a Rainbow," with Tram easily transcending an otherwise stolid Ferde Grofé arrangement, provides an interesting look at his methods. He in effect recomposes the "A" section of the song's AABA structure, playing the paraphrase twice before an ensemble bridge, then recapitulating it afterward. He thus combines the practice of "routining" (working a solo to a high point of development, then presenting it more or less the same way each time) with a keen compositional sense.

Jazz listeners—fans, critics, historians—seem always to have resisted accepting, even understanding, such practices. From earliest days, the romanticized view of hot music has demanded that a solo be wholly extemporaneous, creation of a given moment's circumstance and stimuli. For many, the thought of a player working on a chorus over time, shaping and buffing it, then performing it like a theatrical set-piece, each time with the enthusiasm of first creation, seems profoundly disturbing. Some have been inclined to view musicians who practice such methods as not genuine, their creations at best a simulation of "the real thing."

The attitude differs little in kind or effect from the Rousseau-esque ("noble savage") primitivism once prevalent among fans and canonists of early New Orleans music; any musician who had studied his instrument, it seemed to say, or knew harmony, or could even read music was somehow contaminated, less authentic than his unlearned colleagues.

"Routining" came about for reasons intrinsic to the mechanics of professional music-making. Having to play nightly, sometimes repeating the same number, in the same arrangement, several times in an evening, can quickly sap inspiration. If the player is a featured attraction or bandleader, it becomes all the more necessary to deliver, each time, an inspired and convincing performance, easily recognizable as his work. The result, inevitably, is a distillation, gradual creation of a generic solo which, when completed, contains the player's essence.

Recording exacerbates the process. The need, in a studio, to deliver a quality performance for the microphone, the chance that any one of a number of "takes" will be chosen for issue, exerts pressure to have something ready—even though that something may not, strictly speaking, be improvised on the spot. Once in place, it is subject to infinite variation; but the shape and structure remain. If the player is feeling especially inspired he will take liberties; if not, he can still deliver the "routined" solo with appropriate *élan* and pass muster.

Neither false nor dishonest, this is an expedient, born of the conditions under which hot musicians of the '20s and '30s had to work. Multiple takes from famous record sessions, some issued years after the event, reveal that Beiderbecke, Trumbauer, Louis Armstrong, Coleman Hawkins, Lester Young, Adrian Rollini, Jack Teagarden, Harry Carney, and Bunny Berigan were among many others who worked oft-featured choruses into fixed shape and kept them there.

In the words of British trumpeter-commentator Humphrey Lyttelton:

> The creation of jazz is a more mysterious process than the mere pouring out of spontaneous ideas. The requirements of "improvisation" can be satisfied, in jazz terms, if an identical sequence of notes is played with the subtlest alteration in rhythmic emphasis, the slightest change in the use of dynamics or vibrato, the almost imperceptible raising or lowering of the emotional temperature. Likewise, "originality" in jazz lies not only in the pattern of notes that is produced, but also in the instrumental tone or "voice" in which it is uttered.[17]

(An enlightening instance, referred to elsewhere in this volume, is the monumental Bunny Berigan chorus on "Marie," with Tommy Dorsey's Orchestra. Dorsey airchecks of January 11 and 18, 1937, show Berigan working with the song, approaching the synthesis he so gloriously achieves at the Victor recording session of January 29. The pieces come gradually together, and, once in place, remain that way.)

Frank Trumbauer's case introduces another factor. His reactions to *extempore* situations appear to have been inconsistent: he's even quoted (in Evans and Kiner) as telling a friend that he did not generally enjoy jam sessions. More to his taste was a process of preparation, through which a given solo became a combination paraphrase, variation, and commentary—even exegesis—on its original material.

But if "Sittin' on a Rainbow" seems plotted in advance, his lilting melody statement and "fills" behind the vocal on a rhythmic "Bye Bye Blues" definitely do not. Secrest, too, fares well here, evoking Louis Armstrong as strongly as Beiderbecke.

There's every indication that, without Bix to function as *alter ego*, Trumbauer is prising open his emotional range. His half-chorus toward the end of the Whiteman "Nobody's Sweetheart" is especially noteworthy for forceful attack and delivery, and no loss of coherence—and even a few stabs at across-the-bar-line phrasing.

He's especially light-hearted, witty, playing in tandem with Chet Hazlett's subtone clarinet on "Should I?," another "lost" Whiteman item, and shows two contrasting faces on two Venuti Blue Four selections, made at OKeh the same day. "Running Ragged" finds him on bassoon, and he does well, though somewhat restricted in his ability to use awkwardly fingered accidentals. His C-melody verse statement on "Apple Blossoms," over sustained chords from the violin, achieves an almost perfumed quality.

When listening to him in each of these settings, it's easy to understand what caught Lester Young's fancy one snowy night in Bismarck, North Dakota, when Eddie Barefield first played him a copy of "Singin' the Blues." As Young told Nat Hentoff:

> I tried to get the sound of a C-Melody on a tenor. That's why I don't sound like other people. Trumbauer always told a little story. And I liked the way he slurred the notes. He'd play the melody first and then after that, he'd play around the melody.[18]

There seems little point in seeking direct links between Trumbauer and Young based on phrasing methods or rhythmic approach. As Bernard Cash established in a closely reasoned 1982 master's degree thesis, "the improvising methods of the two players are in most ways disparate." Cash seems to view Trumbauer's frequently discussed "influence" on Young as more a matter of tone and execution than of substance. It's a productive line of thought, but he doesn't follow it far enough. What Young seems to have derived from Trumbauer is the stance, the emotional positioning, a way of viewing himself in an aesthetic looking-glass—like the "method actors" of a later day.

It's worth remembering that Young, as reported by Eddie Barefield and others, was taken with *both* Trumbauer and Beiderbecke. When things turn serious (as on "I Must Have That Man" or the stunning "When You're Smiling," with Billie Holiday and Teddy Wilson), the manner may be Trumbauer, but the phrasing is Beiderbecke. It is not without significance that Lester's own composition "Tickle-Toe" borrows its last eight bars verbatim from Bix's solo on "When," with Whiteman.

Seven months separate the "My Sweeter Than Sweet" session from the next batch of Trumbauer OKeh titles. Whiteman's orchestra had wintered in Holly-wood, where it filmed Universal's Technicolor feature *The King of Jazz*, recorded for Columbia, kept up a full broadcast schedule for Old Gold cigarettes, and even toured briefly as far north as Vancouver, British Columbia.

Bix was gone, and it seemed doubtful he'd return. Secrest was doing well enough in the solo cornet chair, but there seemed less for him to do, with even the Bill Challis arrangements shifting away from a hot emphasis. Occasionally Trumbauer, Secrest, or clarinetist Irving "Izzy" Friedman got a chance to shine, but such moments were ever fewer: the occasional improvised solo was becoming just one flavor among many.

"Get Happy," done for OKeh under his own name, finds Trumbauer forsak-ing his C-melody for clarinet and cornet. On the former, his deadpan approach and absence of tonal coloration seem to foreshadow Lester Young's clarinet efforts of the late '30s. His way of addressing the cornet bears marked similarity to that of fellow-saxophonist Jimmy Dorsey: short-duration notes, somewhat guttural tone, vaguely Bix-like phrasing.

By a gentle, even bittersweet irony, Trumbauer recorded "Bye Bye Blues" for OKeh on the same day that Beiderbecke, back in New York after another rest cure at home, was at Victor committing "I'll Be a Friend 'With Pleasure' " to posterity. It's not too much of a reach, given content and flavor, to view the two perfor-mances as a paired prophecy: where Tram, understated as ever, radiates quiet optimism, Bix turns his solo on a dreary pop song into a sixteen-bar valedictory address, weighted with deep sadness. Within a year he was dead.

Early 1931 was an uncertain time for the American record industry. The Depres-sion was biting deep into entertainment business profits, and sales were down: millions of Americans had apparently decided it was easier to stay home and listen to the radio programs, which were plentiful and free, than to spend even thirty-five cents for six minutes of music on a disc.

Brunswick was among the labels hit hardest. Despite its roster of stars, among them headliners Al Jolson and Harry Richman, the company had been in almost continuous financial straits since the late 1920s. Brunswick-Balke-Collander, the pioneering parent firm, finally sold out in early 1930 to Warner Brothers; the studio was still pumping money into Brunswick, and looking to expand and diversify its catalogue, when Frank Trumbauer signed with them shortly after the first of the year.[19]

His first session, on April 10, used some Whiteman musicians—Secrest and Nat Natoli on trumpets, Bill Rank on trombone, violinist Matty Malneck—and a few Chicago freelancers, among them clarinetist and Trumbauer devotee Rosy McHargue. "I'd always admired him," McHargue said in 1988. "I thought he was the most original of all the saxophonists, very inventive. He never copied anybody. I knew all the famous solos—'I Never Miss the Sunshine' and the rest. It was—well, an honor—to record with him. I was—well, thrilled."[20]

Only one of three titles made at this date, the forgettable novelty "Bass Drum Dan," was issued at the time. But "Honeysuckle Rose," which surfaced in the mid-1990s, sheds light on Trumbauer's improvisation methods. It's a paraphrase, using elements of the Fats Waller melody to construct what is in effect a new song, more chromatic, atmospherically reminiscent of "Singin' the Blues." As the issued remake, done in late June at an even slower tempo ($\downarrow$ = 124 to the earlier $\downarrow$ = 144), confirms, it was carefully "routined," even *composed*. Any difference between the two is largely one of habituation: both the outline and inner structure of this small essay are set, solidified.

"Honeysuckle Rose," Trumbauer paraphrase and original melody, two staves, 1931.

The vocalist on the earlier version is Trumbauer himself. He seems never to have taken his singing too seriously, filling in on record dates when a contract singer either wasn't available or didn't show up. But his vocals are, in their way, quite effective: his bantering treatment of the Andy Razaf "Honeysuckle" lyric comes across more convincingly than Art Jarrett's Crosby mannerisms on the June 24 version.

Melodically and harmonically, "Crazy Quilt" is almost a gloss on Irving Berlin's "Puttin' On the Ritz," popularized by Harry Richman the previous year; Trumbauer bears down on the rhythm in a way he's not done on records since "Clarinet Marmalade," in 1927. But he seems uncomfortable, falling back repeatedly on an exercise-book triplet pattern. More successful by far is a considered "Georgia on My Mind," done at the same session: his statement of the melody—speculative, a little rueful—is first-rate storytelling. This is Frank Trumbauer's great strength, and there was no other jazz soloist who could rival him at it until Lester Young arrived at mid-decade.

There is no gainsaying the beauty and evocative power of this "Georgia" solo, any more than "Singin' the Blues" or "For No Reason At All in C" can be called into question. Comparing Trumbauer and Young, Gunther Schuller seems right on target in asserting that "in the context of 1920s jazz, Trumbauer's basically lyric, quite linear approach is perhaps more of a miracle than Lester's of a few years later."[21]

September found Paul Whiteman back with Victor Records. Columbia, headed for bankruptcy, apparently had found it easier to pay the popular leader fifty thousand dollars *not* to record for a year than to chance producing, marketing, and perhaps losing money on twelve months' worth of records.

Recording at Victor began again almost at once—but with a difference. Alongside the usual parade of ten-inch issues, the company inaugurated a series of twelve-inch medleys, up to five minutes of music on a side, featuring several songs and a variety of performers. It seemed good business, wooing record buyers with quantity, selling multiple songs at no significant increase in price.

Jack Kapp, at Brunswick, had pioneered the idea, recording a medley from the current Broadway edition of *George White's Scandals* (including the enormously popular "Life Is Just a Bowl of Cherries") on October 25, featuring Bing Crosby, the Boswell Sisters, and the Mills Brothers. Whiteman took the field with his own *Scandals* medley, vocals by Mildred Bailey, Jack Fulton, and the King's Jesters. The next months brought a "Popular Selections Medley" and potpourris from *Hot Cha* and Irving Berlin's *Face the Music*.

In view of all this, it's hardly surprising that Trumbauer's Brunswick date of April 5, 1932, yielded a "Sizzling One-Step Medley," combining such "hot" standards as "Dinah," "My Honey's Lovin' Arms," and "Nobody's Sweetheart," and a "Medley of Isham Jones Dance Hits," issued back-to-back on a twelve-incher. Both arrangements are from the Whiteman book (as were "My Sweeter Than Sweet," "Love Ain't Nothin' but the Blues," "What a Day!," and others), a good business move for the leader, who might otherwise never have seen them recorded.

Trumbauer doesn't solo on either medley, but he is clearly the author (and lead voice) of the unison sax section *soli* on "Dinah": written in an unsyncopated, even-eighth-note style, it's more like a saxophone method-book exercise than a hot improvisation—and foreshadows a reemergence of the "novelty" side of Tram's playing.[22]

Charles Horvath, who had managed the Goldkette orchestra in its mid-1920s heyday, approached Trumbauer in mid-April of 1932 about leaving Whiteman to front his own band. At first the saxophonist balked: Whiteman was paying him well, and regular employment meant a stable home life, with even the traveling done in comfort. Thanks, he told Horvath, but no thanks.

A few weeks later his old boss was back, this time with a firm offer, an eight-week stand at Kansas City's Bellerive Hotel. Trumbauer thought about it again. His diary, quoted by Evans and Kiner, records that Whiteman opposed the idea—but promised that, should he take the bait, his chair in the reed section would remain open. With the Whiteman ensemble due to begin a vacation in the first week of May, the auguries seemed overwhelmingly right.[23]

Setting up temporary headquarters in Chicago, Trumbauer put together some musicians and began rehearsing. Bing Crosby, in town for a run at the Oriental Theatre with Eddie Lang and Lennie Hayton, got in touch: he'd scheduled two days of recording at the end of the month. Could Tram do it, bringing along a few of the new sidemen to round out the personnel?

Bix Beiderbecke, though dead nearly a year, was clearly still on the minds of all four men when they squared off in front of the microphones on May 26. Bing's scatting on "Some of These Days" evokes Beiderbecke strongly, as do solo spots by Tram and Lang. "Love Me Tonight" presents Trumbauer at his best, in a gently ruminative, even sensual, solo. Crosby's singing, too, reaches expressive heights.

August found the new Trumbauer orchestra making records on its own. Kansas City had gone well, and they'd followed up with a string of one-nighters across the Midwest before heading back to Chicago. But the six titles recorded for Columbia on August 17 make odd, vaguely disquieting listening: though the band is tightly efficient, its focus seems skewed toward a self-conscious jokeyness. Much of the instrumental "Business in Q," for example (a sidelong reference to Archie Bleyer's riff-based "Business in F"), is built on the old, by now hackneyed "You're a horse's ass" gag. Trumbauer's two solos, replete with Wiedoeft-like triple-tonguing passages, are in effect a return to the methods and attitudes of "Trumbology."

What was his intention in preparing and presenting such displays? What was it about fronting his own full-time band that transformed the wily soloist of the Okehs into this dispenser of party tricks? "I've always thought that when he got a band of his own he put in a lot of time on the business end and neglected the saxophone," said Rosy McHargue. "In the first half of the time that I knew him he was very inventive, but later—like everybody who gets into the business of running a band—he kind of lagged back off."[24]

A folio, *Frank Trumbauer's Saxophone Studies*, published by Robbins Music in 1935, is informative in this connection. Much of it is given over to scales, arpeggios, and dexterity studies, some of them familiar from 1931–35 Trumbauer solos on record. At one point he prefaces a printed jazz solo with the observation that it "is based on exercises. In fact practically every phrase used is part of some exercise. You cannot spend too much time on these exercises as they are the foundation of improvising. Constructing an improvised chorus without them is almost impossible."[25]

With this declaration Trumbauer locates himself at a quite different spot on the musical map from that occupied by a Beiderbecke or a Pee Wee Russell. Other players might have "routined" choruses, but the use of exercise-book formula and device in their construction is quite another matter. In a certain distant sense it has much in common with a far later jazz development: introduction of almost formal, modally based pattern playing by John Coltrane and others in the early '60s.

The first independent Frank Trumbauer Orchestra lasted until autumn of 1933. On November 24, according to Evans and Kiner, Trumbauer had lunch in New York with Paul Whiteman, who offered him his chair back. At first the saxophonist declined, claiming he wanted to "test the waters" on his own. But within a week he'd changed his mind, and in mid-January he began recording again for Brunswick using Whiteman musicians.

Trumbauer's solos on two takes of "China Boy" in February 1934 and the earlier (January) "Break It Down" begin on the same F-major figure, intricate and carefully devised. Charlie Teagarden, on trumpet, leaves more to chance: his half-choruses on the two "China Boy" takes, while similar, show ongoing development. The alternate "China Boy" seems to precede the originally issued version, as evidenced by an ensemble introduction lifted note-for-note from Trumbauer's 1928 OKeh recording of "The Japanese Sandman." Did someone realize at the last moment that so generic a musical approach to the Far East simply wouldn't do? Whatever the case, the intro was quickly scrapped.

Jack Teagarden also sings effectively on " 'Long About Midnight," but the highlight here is a shrewdly observed Trumbauer solo. Understated, economical, it illustrates the continuing duality of this most paradoxical of sensibilities.

Martin Williams, writing in *The Jazz Tradition*, concludes that Trumbauer "got most of his ideas" from Bix and refers to "the shocking deterioration" in the saxophonist's playing after Beiderbecke's death. Such assertions typify the kind of oversimplified reasoning that still hobbles attempts at assessment of Trumbauer. When Williams declares that Tram "never had any swing, and his playing projects far less emotional expressiveness and conviction than Beiderbecke's," he's arguing synecdochically, as if the novelty side had become the substance and the more thoughtful Trumbauer had ceased to exist.[26]

On the contrary, the restrained and whimsical storyteller survived undiminished, unaffected by the multi-noted "novelty" *alter ego*; no other figure in the elliptical history of jazz seems to have functioned so consistently along both sides of a musical fault line. Which was the *real* Frank Trumbauer? The answer, in the end, may be "both."

Without doubt, the altered, looser rhythmic climate of 1934 finds Trumbauer often sounding isolated. He seems particularly uncomfortable on the appropriately named "Troubled" beside a particularly swaggering Bunny Berigan. But to cite his chronic rhythmic weaknesses as the basis of a "shocking decline" does considerable injustice to an accomplished, melodically fertile improviser. When Red Norvo warns younger listeners to "pay good attention to Trumbauer," he speaks out of an understanding that transcends such matters of fashion.

Trumbauer remained with Whiteman until 1936. Whiteman was the patron, in fact, when the saxophonist opened at Manhattan's Hickory House December 2, 1936, as part of an unusual and adventuresome new group, the "Three T's," also featuring Jack and Charles Teagarden, backed by a rhythm section including the remarkable harpist Casper Reardon.

Born in 1907, Reardon was a prodigy, a prize student of the great harpist Carlos Salzedo. As a teenager he won a scholarship to Philadelphia's Curtis Institute of Music, and by his twentieth birthday he had played with the Cincinnati Symphony and New York Philharmonic.

Even in these years, Reardon displayed great interest in, and skill at, applying the accents and vitality of jazz to his instrument. By the mid-'30s he was much in demand in New York radio and recording studios as a freelancer. His solo work on Jack Teagarden's 1934 recording of "Junk Man" is notable for the ease with which he borrows from the concepts of both piano and guitar in adapting the harp to the rhythmic needs of hot music.

465

"His big ambition," said a 1937 *Metronome* article, "is to do in a performing way what Gershwin did in a composing way—i.e. to educate the general long-haired public on the finer points of shorter-haired jazz and actually elucidate via concerts at Carnegie Hall."

In addition to his efforts for others, Reardon recorded fourteen titles under his own name between 1936 and 1940; they are notable both for the beauty of his work and the consistent inventiveness of their arrangements. A 1936 "Summertime" rests on an unusual and haunting ostinato figure; and "They Didn't Believe Me," done in 1940, makes poignant use of the high, pure voice of Loulie Jean Norman.

Singer-songwriter Bonnie Lake, a close friend, called him "a consummate musician," and most colleagues agreed. Reardon died suddenly in 1941, age thirty-four, of the effects of a liver ailment.

Reaction to the Three T's in the trade press was disappointing. Bob Bach, writing in *Metronome*, found their performances lifeless and uninspired. But his reaction was mild compared to that of John Hammond, the wealthy young man who had promoted Benny Goodman, "discovered" Count Basie, championed Billie Holiday, and been a friend to jazzmen—at least those jazzmen whose work he liked. Hammond's *Down Beat* review opens by asserting that "the polite thing to do would be to overlook the band entirely, were it not for the disgraceful waste of genuine talent and the fantastic ideas that went into the presentation."

He goes on to dismiss the arrangements as "lousy," the rhythm section as incompetent, and—perhaps most puzzling of all—harpist Reardon as "condescending." But Hammond saves his harshest words for Jack Teagarden: the trombonist, he says, "had the opportunity of his life on this job, for everybody in town was raring to hear him with a band that would 'send' him. He muffed his chance and he has only himself to blame if circumstances force him back into the Whiteman band, where he will be brought down for another few years."[27]

And there it rested until, in early 1978, acetates of several Three T's broadcasts from the midtown restaurant came to light and were issued on long-playing record. The group bears little resemblance to the travesty described by Hammond. It's tight, well rehearsed; each of the principals plays (and in the elder Teagarden's case, sings) quite engagingly. Several of the arrangements, among them " 'S Wonderful" and "I'm an Old Cowhand," are the same as used on the Trumbauer Brunswick records, but played with even greater zest.

"We had to get used once again to the idea of relaxing and playing improvised ensemble passages, which we hadn't done for so long, that it all seemed crazy at first," Charlie Teagarden said in a 1937 interview. "Then gradually, after a few nights, we felt ourselves getting back in the groove, and musicians who came in to listen told us how they noticed the improvement in the band since the opening night."[28]

Trumbauer's work here is of particular interest. The shade of Beiderbecke informs his languorous opening solo on "Where the Lazy River Goes By" and his lead in "Fare Thee Well to Harlem." Use of "Singin' the Blues" as the group's theme, with Tram reiterating his famed chorus and Charlie Teagarden playing Bix's solo as an obbligato against it, only deepens the atmosphere. Elsewhere, Reardon solos excellently on "You Took Advantage of Me," and the younger

Teagarden distinguishes himself just about everywhere, especially on a revival of the 1927 favorite "Did You Mean It?"

A "disgraceful waste of genuine talent"? Hardly. The real basis for Hammond's hostility to this group may never be known, but these recordings suggest that it wasn't simply musical. A perhaps more plausible explanation has to do with the writer's politics and convictions on racial matters: apart from little-publicized efforts on behalf of William Grant Still and Don Redman, Earl Hines, Fats Waller, and other prominent black musicians, Paul Whiteman was widely viewed (especially in the sorts of left-oriented circles Hammond favored) as a conservative when it came to breaking down the band-business color bar.

Zealous for integration and impatient with those he felt were holding things back, Hammond doubtless saw such caution as little short of racialist. On his deathbed, in the 1980s, he could still refer to such musicians as Adrian Rollini as "racists"—an absurdity, given how often Rollini played with black musicians and hired them to play at his Tap Room.

On both "Fare Thee Well to Harlem" and "Christmas Night in Harlem," moreover, Teagarden and Trumbauer indulge in a bit of minstrel-show hokum; it's not hard to imagine Hammond sitting in the audience, all too visibly fuming. In this connection it's also relevant to recall Otis Ferguson's comments on the young zealot's oft-expressed animus for the general run of white jazzmen:

> And when [Hammond] goes around saying "white musicians" the way you'd use the term "greaseball," he not only confuses his readers and upsets his own standards but starts the Jim Crow car all over again, in reverse. Some will tell you that you're not doing much to eliminate a color line by drawing it all over the place yourself.[29]

Hammond's fondness for Jack Teagarden's playing was well known—but so, too, was his oft-expressed conviction that the trombonist's long hitch in Whiteman's orchestra had damaged him musically. It's hardly unreasonable to assume that Hammond would have preferred listening to Teagarden as part of a racially integrated band of uncompromising (and, preferably, blues-oriented) jazzmen. As Ferguson put it, Hammond never hesitated to deliver himself of strong and categorical opinions on such matters. There are, he said,

> more ways of comparing two things than saying one stinks, and the less comparing a critic does, the better, anyway. And when he does say he doesn't like a thing, he's got to make the grounds for divorce very clear; and if he only dislikes it a little, he's got to mind his words, for they are going out in public where they'll do a lot of damage.[30]

By February 1937 two of the Three T's were gone, and the band had evolved into "Frankie Trumbauer and His Ensemble." Reardon was still present, but the Teagardens had been replaced by trombonist-vocalist Ford Leary and the capable trumpeter Al Stuart, who joined Charlie Barnet's band soon afterwards. A February 3 location broadcast emphasizes "dixieland" standards, with Trumbauer soloing somewhat in the bright-toned manner of Jimmy Dorsey.

Soon after this engagement, Frank Trumbauer moved to Los Angeles, where he found work in radio, then formed and co-led a relatively conventional swing band with trumpeter Manny Klein. A May 1938 *Down Beat* feature indicates that they'd put their group together in November, using arrangements by Jack Pettis's old associate, pianist Al Goering, by saxophonist Lennie Cohn (or Kahn), and, eventually, others, including friends Fud Livingston and Bobby Van Eps.

While waiting out union restriction time before their maiden engagement at the Biltmore Bowl of Hollywood's Biltmore Hotel, the band did more than three dozen radio transcriptions. Found and issued during the '80s, they show a tightly organized, already well rehearsed unit.

(Curiously, Trumbauer chose at this time to change the spelling of his name to "Trombar." The alteration has never been fully explained. Some have suggested that the saxophonist, feeling that the public associated him too strongly with the '20s, wanted to update his image. Perhaps, too, the change stemmed from awareness of current events: having grown up during World War I, he may have realized, as the shadow of Germany again fell across Europe, that a German-sounding surname could be a liability to a leader trying to win public favor with a brand-new band.)

Predictably, "Trombar's" C-melody and Klein's trumpet are the band's chief featured instruments. Klein, whose versatility and technique had usually kept him in the section on dates where others took the solos, emerges here as a strong and resilient jazz soloist in a style reminiscent of Bunny Berigan and, to a rather lesser degree, Harry James.

His solos on "Stars and Stripes Forever," "Ol' Man River," and the slow section of Trumbauer's "Tempo Takes a Holiday" feature make compelling listening. On the strength of these recordings, Klein's continued omission from discussions of outstanding jazz trumpeters of the '30s is hard to understand. He can be found, no less satisfyingly, on other Los Angeles records of the 1937–39 period. His solos, for example, on the Johnny Mercer "Last Night on the Back Porch" and Ella Logan "Jingle Bells" and "Oh, Dear, What Can the Matter Be?," both on Brunswick, are typical.

Trumbauer, for his part, seems at last to have streamlined his rhythmic approach; certainly his solos on "Stars and Stripes," "Midnight Oil," and "Raisin' the Roof" are witty and quite relaxed—and swinging, in a light-on-their-feet sort of way. With such examples factored into the equation, it becomes clear that what happened to Trumbauer in the early 1930s was less a deterioration than a kind of temporary disorientation.

With Trumbauer and Klein as co-leaders, brother Dave Klein as business manager, and the Rockwell-O'Keefe Agency as bookers, the band should have done well. A May 1938 advertisement for the Biltmore engagement bills "Trombar" as "King of The Sax" and Klein as "The Tops in Trumpets."[31]

But it didn't last. A *Down Beat* item of the time refers obliquely to the band's failure to "land the big jobs," and by early 1940 Trumbauer was back in New York, recording for the small Varsity label with a new and rather less polished group. Even these relatively undistinguished records offer unanticipated felicities, thanks to the leader. On "Wrap Your Troubles in Dreams," Tram (once again billed as "Trumbauer") fashions an attractive eight-bar paraphrase of the Harry Barris melody.

"Wrap Your Troubles," Trumbauer paraphrase and original melody, two staves, 1940.

That band, too, came and went, and in mid-1940 Trumbauer announced he was leaving music to take a full-time position as an inspector with the Civil Aeronautics Authority. He spent the rest of his life in aviation, working as a test pilot during World War II and returning to aeronautics thereafter. Now and then he'd emerge from self-imposed retirement: on a 1946 session for Capitol, he's quite at home on a front line with trumpeter Pee Wee Erwin and clarinetist Bill Stegmeyer, and with the four-to-the-bar pulse of the rhythm. His dry, nearly vibratoless tone and laconic phrasing anticipate the "cool" players of the '50s with uncanny accuracy.

There were guest appearances, most often in revivals of the great years with Bix. At such times he played faultlessly, tone and technique undiminished. But "Mister Tram" had left professional music, never to return. His death on June 11, 1956, less then a month after that of his colleague and friend Adrian Rollini, seemed, if anything, a postscript.

In a 1942 Down Beat interview, Trumbauer summed up his own musical credo by declaring that if music, whatever its style and orientation, "has tone, style, and beauty in phrasing, it will live." There seems no better evaluation of Frank Trumbauer's unique musical presence than that.

19

Jack Purvis

"He [was] one of the most gifted musicians I have ever come across . . . very much ahead of his time . . . and the swingingest white trumpet player I ever heard."

—Rex Stewart, 1967

"I want the public to know him as mother did—a carefree, lovable sort of guy, with not an ounce of common sense in his head, but with enough brains to get him where he wanted to go."

—Betty Lou Purvis, 1946

He was tall, maybe about six feet. Stocky. Nice looking, if running a bit to fat. He had come up to the stand after a set and introduced himself to cornetist Jim Goodwin. "My name," he said, "is Jack Purvis."

Goodwin knew some jazz history. He knew Jack Purvis by reputation as a brilliant, often wayward trumpet player whose adventures off the bandstand were almost as legendary as his daredevil solos. Who was to say the man standing there in a joint on the San Francisco Embarcadero *wasn't* who he said he was?

"We talked," said Goodwin. "He was the right age. Said the right things. Seemed to know a lot about the old days. I offered him my horn, asking him if he'd like to sit in. He kind of shrugged and said something like, 'Yeah, I used to play one of these, but that was a long time ago.' We talked a little, and he sat around listening to the music a while."

The man came back the following week, and they chatted again. "I remember him saying he wasn't in too good health, wasn't feeling well, though he looked fine to me," Goodwin said. "But that was it. I never saw him again."[1]

That happened in late 1968. What makes the encounter puzzling is that Jack Purvis—at least a man identified as Jack Purvis in a San Francisco death certificate—had been dead some six years at the time it happened.

However, the story is not inconsistent with the life of, and the often striking music made by, this flamboyantly innovative trumpeter, who flashed brightly around the beginning of the 1930s but spent most of his fifty-five years on the run, perhaps from himself. Mention Jack Purvis to any musician who came up playing hot music in those days, and the reaction was invariably pretty much the same: wonderful, sometimes brilliant. A madman, probably a con artist. But brother, could he ever play.

He's part of the mythology, one of those figures around whom musicians' tall tales seem to cluster the way they do around Joe Venuti or Jelly Roll Morton. Purvis near, Purvis far; Purvis fleeing the cops over rooftops in southern France; Purvis climbing the Alps barefoot, or running guns in Mexico; Purvis giving flying lessons in the South Pacific and "Greek dancing lessons" to scantily clad maidens in Miami.[2]

But that at least partly obscures—or at least deflects attention from—the more important reality of his playing. Rhapsodic, almost operatic in its breadth of conception, Purvis's trumpet, at its best, captures a sense of drama then rare in players of either race, even looks forward to harmonic devices which entered the jazz solo vocabulary only during the next decade.

Unconventional, against the grain, he danced to nobody's tune but his own. At a time when most white jazz trumpet men drew inspiration from either Bix Beiderbecke or Red Nichols, Purvis built an individual solo voice on a foundation that was pure Louis Armstrong. Though working in a succession of first-rate white bands, he longed to play with the black ones—and went to some surprising lengths to do so.

Jazz scholars through the years have tried to document Purvis, place him in perspective. Not surprisingly, he defies their efforts: every newly discovered fact comes gift-wrapped in a new inconsistency, another contradiction. He remains, finally, just out of reach.

All his known records, at least those featuring him to any degree, were made within a period of six years—December 1929 through December 1935. Taken by themselves, heard critically, they constitute a small but potent oeuvre, by any standard the' work of an exceptional musician.

Jack Purvis was born in Kokomo, Indiana, December 11, 1906, son of real estate agent Sanford B. Purvis and his wife, the former Nettie Jackson. According to researcher Harold S. Kaye, Nettie Jackson Purvis died early, and Sanford remarried. Unable to get along with his stepmother, young Jack became refractory, hard to manage. Despairing, his father placed him in a boys' training (vocational) school, where he first learned music.[2]

As a teenager he worked around Indiana, playing both trumpet and trombone, and in 1923 joined the band of trombonist Hal Denman. Errell Nutt, Denman's pianist, recalled Purvis as "awfully good—too good for us around here. He just had to go far."[3]

By 1926 he seemed to be on his way, touring New England with a band led by saxophonist Bud Rice and including Payson Ré, a pianist-banjoist later to play a major role in discovering Rhode Island cornetist Bobby Hackett. In late October he joined Whitey Kaufman's popular "Original Pennsylvania Serenaders." An item in the October 30 *Billboard* announces that Purvis will also be arranging for the band: "Jack has been very successful with his music," it says, "and has a number of pieces which he will shortly submit to the publishers. Jack hopes that Whitey will take a liking to some of his numbers and 'can' some of them for Victor." He's said to have recorded four titles with Kaufman in March 1927, but they were never issued and have never been verified.[4]

In July 1928, George Carhart, described by most who remember him as a *bon vivant* who played just enough banjo to make him look good with the ladies, landed a job on the newly commissioned liner *Île de France*. The band he organized included saxophonist Bud Freeman, brothers Jack and Irving "Babe" Rusin (later changed to Russin), cornetist Jimmy McPartland, and bass saxophonist Spencer Clark.

McPartland soon dropped out. Casting about for a replacement, Carhart found Jack Purvis, by then playing trombone (according to a photo in the June 23, 1928, *Billboard*) with Hal Kemp—whose elder brother, T. D. Kemp, had been Whitey Kaufman's manager. "He'd just come to New York from Pennsylvania with a new LaSalle roadster, a cornet, trombone and a pilot's license," Spencer Clark recalled. "We first met at rehearsal after the boat sailed, and we were all astonished at his prowess on the trombone. For a warmup he did 'Nola' at a pretty good tempo, in different keys."[5]

Research by Harold S. Kaye, Paul Larson, "Bozy" White, and Horst J. P. Bergmeier has summoned admirable detail in recounting the events connected with this cruise and its aftermath. Though the material is highly anecdotal and in no way immune to embroidery, a few highlights bear repetition here:

- In filling out his passport application, Purvis identified himself as "Jacques Fræmac Purvis," the *a* and *e* joined in diphthong form. This name does not appear on his birth certificate; his death certificate, issued in San Francisco March 31, 1962, lists several aliases, but this is not among them. According to historian "Bozy" White, he'd been calling himself "Jacques" for some time.

- Among the *Île de France* passengers were transatlantic aviators Bert Acosta and Charles Levine. After playing the first night, Purvis apparently talked them into letting him stay in first-class with them, and his fellow musicians didn't see him for the rest of the voyage. He reportedly got his musical kicks in the first-class lounge, sitting in with Ted Lewis's band, which included reed-man Don Murray and trombonist George Brunies.

- Playing with Carhart in a casino at the French alpine resort of Aix-les-Bains, Purvis (in company with Clark, Babe Russin, and the leader) one morning took a funicular railway up to a nearby hill, estimated by Clark at no more than a modest three thousand feet. Just for a lark, they started down on foot, and Purvis soon found he could make his way better *sans* his shoes. Hence Eddie Condon's widely quoted comment (and the source of another well-circulated bit of mythology) about Purvis climbing the Alps in his bare feet.

- Working with Carhart at the Hotel Negresco, on the seafront at Nice, Purvis fell in with some local Arab boys who sold everything from rugs to pornographic postcards, learned some Arabic from them, and wound up affecting Turkish garb on the stand, complete to fez and turned-up slippers.[6]

- Later, Clark and trombonist Eddie Norman were sharing a room on the top floor of a cheap hotel in Montmartre when, one night, Purvis—whom neither had seen in weeks—burst in, dashed through to the balcony, vaulted the rail, and leaped to the roof of the neighboring Bal Tabarin, all with the gendarmes in hot pursuit. "It seems they were after him for conning an American tourist out of his American Express travelers' checks" was Clark's laconic comment.

Back in the country in mid-autumn of 1929, he rejoined Kemp, this time on trumpet. Tommy Rockwell of OKeh, ever alert to new talent, apparently heard him around then and was sufficiently impressed to sign him up for a pair of titles with the band's rhythm section. It is here, with these December 17 recordings, that the story—and the mystery—of Jack Purvis really begin.[7]

The first title was a composition of his own, which he called "Copyin' Louis." Working his way through its opening C-minor strain, he sounds like no other white trumpet player of 1929. He takes chances, leaping great intervals to high notes, alternating sweeping declamatory utterances with asides that scamper all over his horn. He's passionate, dramatic—but at this point nervous, and his ideas incompletely formed. If both his conception and execution specifically resemble those of anyone else, it's the fidgety, often explosive Cladys "Jabbo" Smith, then being touted by Brunswick as an Armstrong rival. On both "Copyin' Louis" and its session-mate, the up-tempo "Mental Strain at Dawn" (echoing Jabbo's own "Jazz Battle" of the previous January), Purvis is hit-or-miss in the Jabbo manner: phrases begun and not carried through, notes attacked off center, questionable pitch, fragmentary ideas sprayed at random, audacious intervals and figure-shapes lunged at and sometimes fluffed.

Toward the end of "Mental Strain," moreover, he seems to run out of steam, as if his endurance weren't equal to the task he's set himself. He's hearing things still beyond his reach, in matters both of formation and execution. All the same, these two performances place Purvis alone in the field—with the possible exception of Tommy Dorsey, whose powerful, rough-hewn trumpet solos were clearly modeled on an Armstrong precedent.

Heard objectively, "Copyin' Louis" and "Mental Strain" are memorable chiefly in what they promise, what they reveal about how Jack Purvis is thinking on trumpet—broader, more expansive. New. Even if, at this point, the circuits don't quite close, the wiring is clearly in place.

He's rather less unruly, therefore more effective, on a rare non-vocal take of "Charming," made for OKeh the same day under the leadership of vocalist Smith Ballew, his ballad solo indebted to the Louis Armstrong of "Confessin'." Purvis is also in evidence on at least one later Ballew OKeh session. He takes a brief but immediately recognizable solo toward the end of "Sing, You Sinners," recorded the following February 25.[8]

Purvis was by now a recognizable presence. There's no doubt, listening to all the anecdotes, that his personal ways were as unbridled, as contrary, as vivid, as his way of playing his horn. "Purvis was one of the wildest men I have ever met in my life," Charlie Barnet declared in his autobiographical *Those Swinging Years*. "He was also one of the greatest trumpet players, certainly head and shoulders above most guys around then. He had great high-note ability, and he could play just like Louis Armstrong; but he could also turn around and hold down a chair in a symphony."[9]

Purvis's admiration for Louis seems to have been but one aspect of an overall infatuation with the sound of the black bands, particularly those working in Harlem. Many white musicians would go uptown to listen and occasionally sit in, but the trumpeter went them one better: he'd simply join the band, content to play in the brass section and take solos where the arrangement called for them. Several of Fletcher Henderson's men remembered Purvis playing with them this way at Roseland.

Black cornetist Rex Stewart, ever outspoken, characterized Purvis unhesitatingly as

> one of the most gifted musicians I have ever come across. He had an ear beyond belief. He used to come and sit down at Roseland and play a third trumpet part to "Beau Koo Jack." He may have just looked over someone's shoulder to get the rhythm, but then he'd just play a third part, without the music. He'd just play it! There were only two parts written for the doggone thing, but he'd come up with a third—and no mistakes.[10]

A story persists that the Henderson band used a Purvis arrangement on its record of "Baltimore," done for Harmony (as "the Dixie Stompers") October

24, 1927. The orchestration is in fact a publisher's "stock," written by Robert Haring Sr. But in view of the trumpeter's activities, it's easy to infer that Purvis was at the session and may have brought the arrangement with him.

Stewart, in fact, mentioned a Henderson rehearsal at which the band was running down a pile of brand-new stocks. Purvis, he said, walked in, took out his horn, and sat on the steps leading up to the bandstand. "He didn't get on the stand, he just sat himself on those steps going up to the stand, and he just improvised parts for himself on all those tunes. Now remember, they were new tunes, just sent in from Chicago, so he couldn't have known them beforehand—it was truly amazing. 'Smack' [Henderson] was very strict who he allowed on the stand, but Jack could always sit in at any time."[11]

Purvis's infatuation with the black bands seems to have driven him to some bizarre methods. George "Pops" Foster, bassist with Luis Russell's band of New Orleans expatriates, told of Purvis coming around to the Saratoga Club. "He wanted to play with colored bands so bad he stayed in the sun for hours getting tanned," Foster said, "and then he'd black his face." Charlie Barnet described much the same scene when he found Purvis playing with the black house band at Frank Sebastian's Cotton Club in Los Angeles.[12]

There's no denying Purvis's fondness for the grand gesture, for behavior which stopped just short of the edge—and in so doing couldn't help calling attention to itself. Trombonist Al Philburn, who played alongside him with the California Ramblers, said he drove the usually even-tempered Ed Kirkeby wild by missing rehearsals for key broadcasts, then turning up with moments to spare, usually offering some far-fetched excuse. "Then he sits down in his chair, coolly looks over the first trumpet parts," said Philburn. "The red light goes on and he plays like an angel."[13]

Colleagues remembered Purvis as a tall, handsome man who periodically wore a moustache, dressed like a dandy, and was always mooching money, which he then "forgot" about and never returned. One told of a time he rented a private plane after someone bet him he couldn't fly under all the New York City bridges; another revealed that at one point he had a "crush" on Martha Boswell, of the Boswell Sisters, and as a gift stole a horse in Central Park and tried to run it up a flight of stairs to her apartment.

It's hardly stretching a point to contend that this need for attention, whatever drove it, found expression in the showier side of his playing. There's a lot of incendiary but slightly off-kilter trumpet on records made with Kemp around the time of "Copyin' Louis." Hear him on "Navy Blues," firing off a buckshot blast full of missed notes, fluffed leaps—and an irresistible harum-scarum excitement.

He left Kemp in mid-January 1930. The band was scheduled to open in Coral Gables, several sidemen recalled, but Purvis insisted he couldn't go to Florida because he was wanted there by the law (in connection, perhaps, with morals charges generated by his involvement with a "Greek dancing school"). Despite entreaties from Kemp and fellow-bandsmen he refused to budge. His chair went, at very short notice, to the respected all-rounder Mickey Bloom.[14]

Purvis stayed in town, joining the California Ramblers. "I wish I'd kept a diary of those days," said Al Philburn. "It would have been a best-seller— only it would have to have come out as fiction, because no one would ever have believed the things Purvis did. He was a total lunatic—off the wall, as I think they call it now. Nothing fazed him: he was the arch con-man of all time."[15]

He recorded again under his own name for OKeh April 4, this time heading a racially mixed, and quite distinguished, seven-piece band. Sessions the previous year by Fats Waller, Louis Armstrong, Eddie Condon, and Red McKenzie, among others, had fractured racial barriers in the recording studios. Purvis, therefore, had something of a free hand in picking his men: Coleman Hawkins and Adrian Rollini as the saxes; J. C. Higginbotham on trombone; and his Luis Russell band-mate, Will Johnson, on guitar, with young New Orleans pianist Frank Froeba also in the rhythm section.

Again all the titles are originals, composed and arranged by Purvis. The chord sequences flow naturally, with just enough variation from normal patterns to make them interesting for soloists. There's no jamming, nothing left to random chemistry; he's clearly thought everything through carefully and worked it out the way he wants it.

Setting out the melody to his own "Dismal Dan," Purvis on trumpet is strong-er, surer now of where he's heading, and—perhaps not surprisingly—even more Armstrong-like in his own individual way than on "Copyin' Louis," especially on a flawlessly executed six-bar lip-trill on a high concert C. It's a well-realized, coherent performance also including, at one point, an Alphonse-and-Gaston duet by Hawkins and Rollini, two giants meeting as friendly peers.

Purvis knew his music, many colleagues attested, and the quotation from Grieg's *Peer Gynt* which opens the funereal "Poor Richard" seems to corroborate that. The trumpeter's minor-key solo excursion here echoes Louis's "King of the Zulus," a record that seems to have had a profound effect on many fellow-musicians. Tommy Dorsey's trumpet solo on "Hot Heels," with Eddie Lang, is patterned on it, and there are echoes of it in Jabbo's "Croonin' the Blues." Froeba's Hines-like piano solo further enhances the Armstrong flavor.

On "Down Georgia Way," Purvis achieves a real sense of drama, even majesty, the quality most sought after—and hardest to capture—in this brand of trumpet-playing. He also incorporates, verbatim, into the final bars of his stop-time solo the two-bar break with which Louis begins his 1928 "Knee Drops."

Purvis returned May 1 with most of the same men (the able Greely Walton in place of Hawkins) to record another batch of originals. The easy high point is "What's the Use of Crying, Baby?," with an exquisitely constructed Purvis solo.

"What's the Use of Cryin', Baby?," Jack Purvis trumpet solo, 1930.

Here is the first white trumpeter to develop his solos sequentially, in the Armstrong manner, rather than "compositionally," as did Bix and his admirers; the first, too, to make free use of embellishment; and, perhaps most significant, the first to employ *rubato* as an effective creative device.

Comparison of the above transcription of his "What's the Use of Cryin', Baby?" solo with the record reveals the lengths to which Purvis, like Henry Allen—whom he occasionally resembles—took his use of *rubato*. In almost every phrase note values are stretched, foreshortened, delayed, and bunched in ways which defy accurate notation. Bar 10, as played, is actually somewhere between what's represented above and something that could as easily be notated as:

Same, bar 10 only.

It's all a bit slapdash, a bit seat-of-the-pants, leaving a listener to wonder what Purvis might have achieved had he been able to harness and more effectively discipline so prodigious an imagination—and himself. But then, perhaps it was all of a piece: such unbuttoned, dazzlingly idiosyncratic playing may be inseparable from, and an expression of, the undisciplined character of the man. After all, it is Purvis's very unpredictability as a soloist that often makes him most tantalizing.

On "When You're Feeling Blue," Purvis mixes chattering double-time passages with long, arching phrases, to substantial dramatic effect. "Be Bo Bo" seems to anticipate swing, with nimble Rollini, swaggering Higginbotham (vocally and instrumentally), and driving trumpet from the leader.

Purvis was suddenly recording a lot, and quite a few otherwise straightforward dance band performances of 1930–31 burst into life with his trumpet solos. Sometimes, as on "The Stein Song," made March 18 by a Ramblers unit and issued under Kirkeby's "Ed Lloyd" pseudonym, he's mostly shooting off fireworks. But more often, as on "Whistles," made with Kemp a year later, he succeeds gloriously: jumping into his solo, he modulates from D to F (concert C to E♭) with an impeccably single-tongued ascending break:*

"Whistles," trumpet modulation, 1931.

He's even more startling on "St. Louis Blues," done for the obscure Crown label in October of 1930 with a Ramblers group identified as "Lloyd Newton and His Varsity Eleven." Perhaps this inexplicably little-known performance is the one that should have been titled "Copyin' Louis": Purvis's muted fills behind the unidentified vocalist and the shapely, restrained solo that follows constitute eloquent obeisance to Armstrong. But the best is yet to come: after a straightforward trombone solo (Philburn?), Purvis scrambles through two ascending bars to a pealed high concert D, leading the band through a double-time chorus in which he reproduces, with great fervor, Louis's rideout on his 1929 "St. Louis Blues" recording with Luis Russell. He also makes explicit and attractive use of the raised dominant, in this case a concert E♭ resolving to D, a tonality which found its fullest expression some years later in the work of Roy Eldridge—which in turn anticipated Dizzy Gillespie.

Purvis's Armstrong affinity also seems to place him on a May 24, 1930,

---

*By this time, Bunny Berigan was established as Kemp's jazz trumpet soloist. But Berigan is absent from the band for several early 1931 record dates, perhaps fulfilling radio and recording obligations to Fred Rich at CBS. Kemp appears to have brought Purvis in at this point as a substitute. His presence on "Whistles" is beyond contest, but Berigan is just as clearly the soloist on "Mary Jane," recorded a month later, on April 23.

Columbia date under the leadership of pianist-composer Rube Bloom. Ending his opening solo on "There's a Wah-Wah Girl in Agua Caliente," the hitherto un-identified trumpeter quotes the same "Knee Drops" break Purvis employs so effectively in "Down Georgia Way." It's too distinctive a feature to be fortuitous: what other white trumpeter in 1930 was mining the Louis vocabulary in this way?

On a little-known November 1930 date for Melotone with Columbia Artists executive (and sometime singer) Roy Wilson, Purvis again scales expressive heights comparable to those of "What's the Use of Crying, Baby?" His solo on "Deserted Blues" has a bit of everything: daredevil leaps to the high register, double-time outbursts, dramatic intensity. His stop-time chorus on "Swamp Blues" erupts from the introduction, saturating the performance with emotional electricity; he signs things off with a similarly intense coda.

Purvis spent July and August of 1930 in Europe, having convinced the U.S Passport Authority that he was not *really* an itinerant musician, likely to get strand-ed without funds, but a serious student. Hal Kemp's band was in Europe that summer, with Mickey Bloom and Bunny Berigan as the trumpets; arriving in Paris, whom should they run into but "Jacques" Purvis, dressing and acting "very French." At one point he even professed not to know the musicians when they greeted him, insisting that he did not speak "ze Eeenglish."[16]

Sometime in late 1931 Purvis joined Fred Waring, perhaps on the recom-mendation of Ed Kirkeby, who had helped the Pennsylvania-born leader get start-ed in the early '20s. Cornetist Bill Priestley, then playing guitar with Waring, told of Purvis's romantic infatuation with harpist Verlye Mills, who occasionally ap-peared with the band for concert engagements and records.

"She was a tiny little thing, very pretty and quite terrified of this wild man," Priestley told record producer Michael Brooks. "So Jack, thinking he was being subtle, goes to one of the music stores in Chicago, dead of night and all that, breaks a plate glass window, steals a harp, brings it back to the theatre and the next day asks Verlye if she'll give him lessons. She doesn't want to know, so next night he takes it back, bold as you please, and leaves it on the doorstep."[17]

It's hard not to feel affection for the almost childlike nature of a man who could pull such a stunt. "Just dare me!" he seems to say, waiting for someone to unlock the magic doors by expressing the slightest doubt that he'd do it. Charlie Barnet tells of another Waring incident in which Purvis was to be featured in a pinspot during the opening bars of the band's adaptation of the *1812 Overture*. The leader, exacting about his band's collegiate image, ordered the trumpeter to shave off his carefully groomed, well-waxed William Powell moustache. "At the next show," Barnet wrote, "Waring made his trek across the pit and gave the downbeat. When the spot hit Jack, he had shaved off not only the moustache but every hair on his head, and very uncollegiate he looked."[18]

Fellow-musicians made wide-eyed, generally uncritical, audiences for his ac-counts of his escapades. Had he really flown guns and ammunition across the Texas border to Pancho Villa's Mexican revolutionaries? Did he really escape a wife's bigamy charges by shipping out on an ocean liner as a cook? Did he really take friends up in his private plane, then whip out his horn and play for them while the plane dove and swooped with no one at the controls? Perhaps not—at least not in quite that way. Such stories (the Condon "bare feet" anecdote is an example) usually proceed from real-life events but pick up an ever-thicker encrustation of hyperbole as they make the rounds.

Beyond question, the "character" and risk-taker is present in the music as well. For illustration there's "Last Dollar," recorded for Columbia's rare Clarion subsidiary November 5, 1931, and released under the name of Eddie Droesch. Coming out of Dick Robertson's vocal, the trumpet sweeps up to a powerful high C (concert B♭) to deliver a solo popping with the kind of pyrotechnics only King Louis himself could match at the time. It's all in line with the "Look ma, no hands!" image of the kid tearing down the street on his bike, hoping that mother, neighbors, or playmates will see him and gasp in both horror and grudging admiration. Alcohol, ever present, only reinforces and exaggerates the bravado.[19]

The way Purvis apparently learned to fly illustrates the point. According to guitarist George Van Eps, he simply decided he was going to learn, bought an instruction manual, and spent his every waking moment studying it. "Jack was extremely bright," Van Eps said. "Not always very smart, maybe, but bright. He was with Kemp at the Manger Hotel at the time, and after studying the book for about three days he took Bobby Mayhew, who also played trumpet in the band, and went out to Roosevelt Field, on Long Island."

There, at the field where Charles Lindbergh had taken to the air in the *Spirit of St. Louis* for his historic transatlantic flight, Purvis talked someone into renting him a small plane. With only the manual for companionship, he rolled down the runway and lifted off.

"He actually *flew* the damned thing," said Van Eps. "He went six miles, and landed safely in a plowed field, going in the direction of the ruts so he didn't nose over." At that point Mayhew, who had been following on the ground, pulled up. "Hey, kid," Purvis called, springing out of the cockpit. "Get in—I'll teach you to fly!"[20]

Not surprisingly, he left Waring shortly after the 1812 *Overture* incident and headed south with Charlie Barnet. According to the saxophonist he talked himself into an appearance performing *The Carnival of Venice* with the New Orleans Symphony, sat in with Alphonso Trent's black territory band in Shreveport, ran into trouble with Mexican authorites in Juarez (lending possible credence to the Pancho Villa story), and wound up in Los Angeles, where he and Barnet jammed till dawn one night with Lionel Hampton, clarinetist Archie Rosati, tenor saxophonist Hubert "Bumps" Myers, and others.

He stayed in Los Angeles a while, his quick reading and all-round musicianship reportedly finding him steady employment with Georgie Stoll at Warner Brothers. According to some reports, he composed a long concert work for orchestra bearing the title *Legends of Haiti*. There's no trace of it, or any indication it was ever performed. Years later, Stoll told singer-songwriter Bonnie Lake that Purvis had once been arrested by California state police for standing in the middle of a heavily trafficked road tunnel and playing his horn. "It sounded so nice in there that I just had to play" was his explanation.[21]

There's little accounting for his whereabouts throughout late 1933 and 1934. Stories persist that he shipped out for the South Pacific as a ship's cook and that he was seen on the island of Bali. Other reports place him in Hawaii. Oddly, none of this seems far-fetched: clearly a man who lived by his wits, Purvis seemed to interpret norms of behavior and legality with great flexibility. Besides, jazz history has had its share of peripatetics, footloose characters whose innate restlessness and curiosity about the world prompted them to wander off now and then on sometimes lengthy hegiras. Witness the similar stories of such early figures as pianist Teddy Weatherford, trumpeter Arthur Briggs, and trombonist Herb Flemming.

That Jack Purvis was a man driven by often contradictory forces seems obvious. That the behavioral extremes welled up from some dark place, a place of torment and frustration, is equally believable. That such a man would attempt suicide—or want to be *seen* to attempt it—hardly seems out of keeping.

"Jack was always threatening to do that," said Al Philburn. "One night [in 1932] when he was with the Ramblers he calls up Ed Kirkeby in the dead of night and says he's gonna do himself in. Ed blows his top, tells him to get off the wire, and goes back to sleep. About ten minutes later the phone rings again and this time it's Victor Young. 'Ed, you'd better get round to Jack's apartment,' he says. 'I've just been talking to him and I'm sure he means it this time.' "

Turning up at Purvis's building, Kirkeby found a crowd, an ambulance—and the trumpeter being carried out on a stretcher after a botched attempt to gas himself. But even here the story takes a zany twist. "The cold air must have brought [Jack] around, for he sits up and yells, 'Hey, you guys, what the fuck do you think you're doing? Do you want me to catch pneumonia?' "

Purvis, said Philburn, got out of the hospital after Kirkeby signed a letter taking responsibility for his bandsman's subsequent actions. "So he moves in with Ed, and every night he'd wait until Ed was asleep, get up and try to throw himself out the window. Thing is, he'd always dress himself first, and he'd make so much noise falling around in the dark, trying to find his things, that Ed would always wake up and lead him back to bed."[22]

In late 1935 Purvis turned up again in New York, having apparently driven east in a baby Austin, towing a trailer full of luggage, instruments, and orchestral scores. Several musicians swore they'd heard that he ran out of gasoline at the entrance to the Holland Tunnel and lacked enough money either to refill his tank or pay the toll. An instrument company representative reportedly came to the rescue.

He went out for a month with Joe Haymes's orchestra. Helen O'Brien, who later married trumpeter Gordon "Chris" Griffin, was singing with Haymes at the time as part of a vocal trio called the Headliners. "Jack was very knowledgeable musically," she said. "A terrific, quick mind. Wonderful ear. He'd sit down with us and help us in getting our vocal arrangements together. He was nice—handsome, charming, you know—and played really beautifully."

"But he was also very, well, strange. There was a lot of talk that he'd tried to do himself in, turned the gas on," she said. "They said it was accidental, but who knew with him? We certainly never knew. He left the band after about a month, and Chris, whom I married, replaced him."[23]

Purvis was back in New York for a Christmas Eve 1935 session at Columbia put together by an old pal, pianist Frank Froeba. The three titles swing loosely in the standard 52nd Street manner, not substantially different in sound or feel from records made around the same time by fellow-trumpeters Wingy Manone and Louis Prima. Most of the solo space goes to twenty-year-old tenor sax whirlwind Herbie Haymer.

Purvis sings quite capably on the novelty "The Music Goes 'Round and 'Round," providing a bit of off-the-wall comedy as he chastises Froeba for "a'blowin' on that piano like you was huffin' an' puffin' at the reefer-smokin' ball."*

Here and on the instrumental "There'll Be a Great Day in the Morning," he keeps his trumpet solos short, perhaps in the interests of endurance; he hadn't, after all, been playing regularly. The Armstrong flavor seems to have evolved into an agile and rather personal brand of swing trumpet, with only the frequent lip-trills echoing his earlier manner.

These are good, lively records—and, incredibly, they are Jack Purvis's last. So far as is known, he never again set foot in a recording studio. He did a two-week run at the Club 18, on 52nd Street—then dropped out of sight.

There's been little solid information on where Purvis was and what he was doing during 1936 and early 1937. Various reports place him back in California; according to one, in early 1937 he walked into a club in San Pedro carrying a battered horn and identifying himself as "Jack Jackson." He reportedly told the bandleader, Johnny Catron, that he'd been working as ship's cook on a freighter and that police had confiscated his belongings in connection with a murder investigation.

Another account has him in Marysville, about fifty miles north of Sacramento, spending two weeks in jail in connection with a convoluted situation involving a suitcase full of glittering, but practically valueless, trinkets. He's reported up and down the West Coast during this time, playing occasionally, trying to get his compositions performed, among them an orchestral suite some musicians remembered as *Panama Canal*.

What is striking about all this is the frequency with which Purvis seems to have been in trouble or near-trouble with the law. Always the same pattern: extravagant claims, half-truths, slippery deals—and, inevitably, the quick getaway, leaving behind only the memory of some extraordinary behavior and even more formidable trumpet playing.

Driving across Texas sometime during 1937, singer Connie Boswell and her

---

*Two Purvis admirers, drummer Hal Smith and trumpeter Chris Tyle, argue that the voice heard here is the same which plays the "deacon" at the beginning of Bloom's "On Revival Day" on the May 1930 session and intones the words "Poor Richard" at the end of the Purvis OKeh record of the same name.

manager-husband Harry Leedy stopped at a small diner, miles from anywhere. "We were very tired and hungry," Leedy told Michael Brooks. "We sit down, and a guy comes over with the menu and says, 'Hi, Connie! Hi, Harry!' It was Jack. God knows what he was doing there—but I do remember that he was a fine cook."[24]

And, at some point around then, Purvis simply went too far, got into something over his head. According to various Texas musicians it was a robbery, and he was caught making for Galveston in hopes of hopping a ship for Europe. On July 31, 1937, Jack Purvis entered the State Penitentiary in Huntsville, Texas, two hundred miles south of Fort Worth.[25]

A pair of *Down Beat* articles in late 1938 described him leading a prison swing band in once-a-week *Thirty Minutes Behind the Walls* broadcasts, aired over Dallas station WBAP. According to writer Dick Hall, he was playing mostly piano and arranging and had even composed the instrumental theme, "Twilight and You," for the broadcasts.

"Prison's the best thing that ever happened to me," he was quoted as saying. "Why, I didn't amount to a thing when I was a free man. My physical and mental health were on the bad side." So popular did the broadcasts become, the article insisted, that one prisoner on death row even won a stay of execution so he could listen to "my pals" one last time.[26]

Another article the following May described Purvis leading both a jazz trio and a concert band and teaching music "to any prisoner who wants to learn. Most of his pupils are exceedingly anxious to improve their talents as they live with the constant vision of the day when they will be released."[27]

Purvis remained at Huntsville until his release on a conditional pardon in August 1940. From there his trail becomes indistinct. Though such researchers as Peter Kelley and Paul Larson have followed every lead, explored all available options, little of substance has emerged, save that Jack Purvis seldom stayed long in one place—and apparently never lost his ability to dazzle anyone willing to listen with his command of both trumpet and trombone.

George Hoefer, writing in his regular "Hot Box" column in the July 1, 1946, *Down Beat*, wondered what had happened to Jack Purvis. Was he still alive? Was he still playing? The column ended with a request for information.

Among the replies was a letter from a Betty Lou Purvis, who identified herself as the trumpeter's daughter. She was living in Pittsburgh, working as a disc jockey at a local radio station. Her attempts to find her father, she said, had been thwarted at every turn; she'd even written to Texas prison authorities asking his whereabouts, only to be informed that "we are not permitted to supply information requested." All she had was some music and an album full of photographs. Intrigued, Hoefer answered her; the exchange blossomed into a regular correspondence.

"Good news!" she exclaims, beginning a letter dated March 4, 1947. "I found my Dad . . . He's over in Europe now, doing some long, tall studying but will be back here in the fall. Call it miracles or just good, down-to-earth praying, but it worked! I have been writing to him and received my third letter today."[28]

Subsequent correspondence elaborated on the theme. "Dad" had seen the

Down Beat column, she said, and written to her. The letter, dated April 15, 1947, and poignant in its obvious delight, continues:

> He's doing some deep composing . . . working on a piano suite with umpteen different movements and has been spending a great deal of time on piano (The traitor! I'm strictly a brass gal!). His last letter was written from (hold your hats) Cairo, Egypt, and he's headed for the Pacific by way of India, the Philippines to Hawaii and then into San Francisco! Watta-man Purvis! Anything to be different! He's getting some great kicks from my being a jazz addict and can hardly wait to get home and beat out some good sessions with me! Hot dog! It'll sure be a great day then! It's almost like a fairy story; something I've dreamed about but that was all!

While all this was going on, Purvis was not abroad at all but back in Huntsville for parole violation, and corresponding regularly and openly with his wife, also named Betty, planning a family reunion. In light of this, Betty Lou's difficulty in locating her father is only too clear. Even the far-flung postmarks on his letters seem part of an elaborate ruse, accomplished possibly with his wife's complicity, aimed at sheltering an obviously idealistic young woman from an emotionally damaging reality.

According to an affidavit from J. C. Roberts, chief of the Bureau of Records and Information, Texas Prison System, dated September 25, 1952, Jack Purvis "was returned to Prison on September 30, 1946, as a parole violator and was (again) discharged by expiration of sentence on September 20, 1947. We have no record of the subject since his release."[29]

On October 27, Betty Lou wrote to Hoefer again, even more breathlessly than before. "Dad was home for a month and we had a rip-roaring time," she said. "He's down in Florida right now, working on his piano suite . . . He expects to be back in Pittsburgh by the first of next year."

She told Spencer Clark, living in Pittsburgh at the time, that "Dad" was intending to settle down and make his living as a carpenter—and was also looking around for chances to play. Delighted, Clark suggested the trumpeter come around to rehearsals of a part-time orchestra with which he and his wife were playing at the time. He never did.

"He did, however, turn up at my office one day and tried to put the bite on me for five dollars," the bass saxophonist said. "It seemed that he needed to get away for a while, had a job on a ship sailing from Baltimore, and needed the fare to get there.

"The visit was typical. He wandered in while I was out of the room, went up to one of my co-workers, a man of very small stature—five foot four, 125 pounds (I am five foot ten and 160 pounds), moustached and as unlike me as possible, and said, 'Hi, Spence, you haven't changed a bit.' I walked in as he said it and my friend turned and pointed to me. Jack never batted an eye, but strolled over and repeated: 'Hi, Spence, you haven't changed a bit.' Nothing ever fazed him."[30]

A letter from Betty Purvis to Paul Larson, dated November 30, 1974, and sent from an address in Fort Lauderdale, Florida, fills in details. "Three different times he came back," it says, "but he couldn't stay off the 'sauce' . . . he started drinking again, and Betty Lou was doing so well with her radio shows, mistress of ceremonies at large affairs, and also correspondent for *Down Beat* magazine, and I didn't want her career ruined by having a 'lush' for a father. So I put him out and told him never to come back until he could be worthy of such a lovely daughter."[31]

Three times? Where did he go between homecomings? Did he in fact ship out to foreign ports of call? According to John Chilton a man resembling Purvis was seen sitting in a garden in Honolulu sometime around the beginning of the 1950s, playing *The Flight of the Bumblebee* on trumpet and trombone. But, as so often, the account is unsupported by hard evidence.

Nothing after that, until March 30, 1962, when police were called to a rooming house at 309 Hayes Street, San Francisco, by a woman who reported smelling gas coming from an upstairs room. Forcing their way in, they found the body of Jack Purvis.

But even that final, sordid ending had a twist or two. An autopsy revealed that the dead man had actually succumbed not to gas inhalation but to cirrhosis. If he had entertained any thoughts of taking his own life, he'd apparently been foiled again, this time by nature.

According to his death certificate he'd last worked as a radio repairman but was unemployed at the time of his death. He was buried April 26 at Greenlawn Memorial Cemetery.[32]

That said, who was the man who introduced himself to Jim Goodwin that night in 1968? An impostor? Who would have taken the trouble to impersonate so obscure a figure as Jack Purvis? Was it in fact Purvis who died in that Hayes Street rooming house in 1962? Or could this, too, have been another bit of now-you-see-it, now-you-don't Jack Purvis trumpery?

Jack Purvis died, if indeed he did, as he had lived, in half-light. Nothing quite what it seemed. Everything evanescent, fleeting, without substance.

Through the years there's been a tendency to look at his various misadventures as evidence in casting Purvis as the Peck's Bad Boy of jazz. What new escapades has that wild and crazy guy gotten himself into this time? What a card! What a character! To be sure, it makes entertaining reading, but all the yarn-spinning seems to miss two vital points: first, whether breaking a showroom window, stealing a horse, smuggling guns, flouting aviation rules, or fleecing tourists out of their travelers' checks, much of the behavior in these off-the-stand capers is irreconcilably sociopathic. It seems less the efflorescence of a happy-go-lucky free spirit than the symptom of a pathology, shadowed and compulsive.

Second, and vastly more important, all the anecdotes effectively obscure the fact that for a few brief years, pivotal ones in the early development of jazz, Jack Purvis was a pace-setter, an adventuresome and creative trumpet soloist who ventured into uncharted musical territory and left behind more than a few vivid recorded examples of how brilliantly he succeeded. It is for this, above all—and

485

for the wasted potential embodied in the behavioral excesses—that he must be remembered.

Betty Purvis moved to Fort Lauderdale in 1965, after General Motors closed its Pittsburgh plant. She hadn't seen her husband since 1947, when she threw him out for the last time. "I guess," she wrote, "he loved the bottle more than he loved us."

In her letter to Larson she alludes to her daughter's having been "very ill with the same thing that took her daddy," presumably alcohol. But "with loving care she came through okay and has been quite well since, thank God."

Mother and daughter never stopped hoping Jack Purvis would come home, this time to stay. "I never married, hoping he would straighten out and come back to me the man I knew he could be," Betty wrote. "I am just so very sorry he died alone when two people who loved him so very much were waiting to share that love with him."[33]

Who, and what, was Jack Purvis? Gifted, refulgent, musician? Adventurer and "citizen of the world," who thrived on risk and challenge? Restless wanderer and small-time crook, driven by who knows what private demons? Mental Strain at Dawn, played out in day-to-day reality? Poor Richard and Dismal Dan, trapped in one unquiet mind?

The mystery of Jack Purvis remains. So, too, do his often illustrious records: for all their wild, frustrating inconsistency, there's nothing else in early jazz quite like them.

20

Bunny Berigan

If you could have seen him out on that stage in a white suit, with that shiny gold trumpet, blond hair and gray, penetrating eyes—well, if it didn't knock you over when he started to play, ain't nothing gonna knock you down.

—Joe Bushkin, 1982

In the half-century since his death, Bunny Berigan still inspires ecstasy in those who knew him, worked with him, and admired him from afar. It's in the Joe Bushkin utterance that begins this chapter, rapt acknowledgment of a reality quite beyond the events of an ill-starred trumpeter's life.

"Bunny hit a note—and it had *pulse*," said clarinetist Joe Dixon, a member of Berigan's band in 1937–38. "You can talk about one thing and another—beautiful, clear, big tone, range, power—and sure, that's part of it. But only part of it."

He gropes for the one elusive, all-encapsulating thought. "It's hard to describe, but his sound seemed to, well, *soar*. He'd play lead, and the whole band would soar with him, with or without the rhythm section. There was drama in what he did—he had that ability, like Louis [Armstrong], to make any tune his own. But in the end all that says nothing. You had to hear him, that's all."[1]

You had to hear him. Hyperbole and magic, pressed into service yet again to explain the inexplicable.

But what is the reality of this trumpet player, dead, emptied of life-force, at age thirty-three? Is Bunny Berigan, as more than a few chroniclers would have us believe, merely a very good musician whose significance has been exaggerated by generations of votaries? Or is something else at work in the minds and memories of those who heard him?

George "Pee Wee" Erwin, who followed Berigan into Tommy Dorsey's trumpet section, insisted: "I don't think you could ever really appreciate [Bunny] unless you stood in front of that horn and heard it. I've never heard anyone who could match it. When he'd hit a note it would be like a cannon coming out of that horn. And I'm not speaking of sheer volume—I'm speaking of the body of the sound."

(In illustration, Erwin told of recording "Who?" with Tommy Dorsey's orchestra on October 14, 1937. The arrangement, a follow-up to the immensely successful "Marie," assigned Erwin the full solo chorus, after the vocal, that had been Berigan's on the earlier record. Curious, he asked the Victor house engineer, Freddy Alsessor, where Bunny had stood for that vibrantly powerful effort. "He showed me," said Erwin. "Bunny was approximately thirty feet from the microphone. I stood about fifteen feet from it: that'll give you the difference in the actual body of the sound.")[2]

Steve Lipkins, who played lead trumpet with Dorsey and with Berigan's own band, declared him "the first jazz player we'd heard at that time who really played the trumpet well, from bottom to top, evenly and strongly throughout. Besides that, he had something special in the magic department—and you had to hear that to understand it."[3]

Many trumpeters had power, beauty, and density of tone. Manny (sometimes Mannie) Klein had near-perfect control in all registers, too; he could lip-trill the high notes just as adeptly as Berigan. Roy Eldridge was a more daring high-wire walker, leaping and swooping and racing around his horn like a clarinetist; Sonny Dunham, with the Casa Loma Orchestra, had a keen sense of drama; Harry James could whip audiences into a hysterical frenzy, and his Goodman band sectionmate Ziggy Elman was a powerhouse in both solo and lead. Henry "Red" Allen was probably more creative, Rex Stewart more abandoned. Cootie Williams—in his open-horn moments, at least—equally majestic (hear his opening chorus to Ellington's 1934 "Troubled Waters").

But it's hard to imagine any of those men, however accomplished, inspiring talk of "something special in the magic department." Berigan, then, can't be understood as simply an amalgam of skills and attributes. There is another dimension; even his less distinguished recorded work exudes a sense of something transcendental, unmatched by any other trumpet soloist of the 1930s.

The only comparison that comes to mind is the mighty, all-pervasive—and now increasingly mythic—figure of Louis Armstrong. And indeed, Armstrong was at pains to make clear that "my boy Bunny Berigan" was in a class by himself. "Now there's a boy whom I've always admired for his tone, soul, technique, his sense of 'phrasing' and all. To me, Bunny can't do no wrong in music."[4]

At the end of the 1920s, when Berigan arrived in New York, many white brassmen admired Louis Armstrong, but few attempted to emulate him. Jack Purvis had been the trailblazer with his recording of "Copyin' Louis," discussed in the previous chapter. Tommy Dorsey, who in those days doubled regularly on trumpet, brought to the horn an Armstrong-like intensity quite different from his trombone playing.

But most white trumpeters were under the spell of Bix Beiderbecke, whose introspective sensibility wedded romanticism with a classicist's sense of order and structure. Where Louis's solos were bold, emotionally dense statements, painted in bright primary colors, Bix's were more subdued, richly layered, nuanced.

That polarity created a dilemma for musicians who admired both men. Rex Stewart, one of Berigan's first friends in New York, confessed to being unable to make up his mind between Beiderbecke and Armstrong and embraced both in a most original manner. The solos of John Nesbitt, arranger and trumpeter with McKinney's Cotton Pickers, show the same sort of division.

But the duality found its most fully realized expression in Bunny Berigan.

Born November 2, 1908, in the small town of Hilbert, Wisconsin, Roland Bernard Berigan came of a musical family and by age twelve had moved through a succession of instruments to trumpet. He and his elder brother Don played in a community band led by their grandfather, and by age twenty the young man was working in dance units around Wisconsin and surrounding states.

He was playing at a roadhouse outside Madison when Hal Kemp's band came through in late 1927. Kemp and his pianist-arranger John Scott Trotter invited him to audition and were less than impressed: the kid had talent, yes—but he still had a way to go. In later years Trotter remembered him having a good beat but "the tinniest, most awful ear-splitting tone you ever heard . . . like a peanut whistle."[5]

Others remembered the incident differently, remembered that Kemp actually offered the youngster a chair, replacing the departing Earl Geiger. Remembered, too, that William "Cap" Berigan, Bunny's father, refused permission; there would be other opportunities to play, he said, but never another to finish high school.

Wisconsin-born trombonist Keith "Curly" Roberts, with Kemp at the time, added that the young trumpeter "played a good, solid horn and had a big tone. At that time Bunny played a Holton trumpet, but later he switched to a Conn—22B, I think it was called—which was the biggest horn they made." Others have also called his tone at the time good.[6]

In early 1928 Berigan landed a job at Janssen's Hofbrau restaurant in Philadelphia, with a band led by singer-violinist Frank Cornwell; they rehearsed in New York, affording the young brassman his first contact with a circle of musicians he'd soon come to dominate. He met cornetist Rex Stewart, who in turn introduced him to others, including Tommy and Jimmy Dorsey.

By September of the following year he was back in Manhattan to stay, working for Cornwell at the New York branch of Janssen's. The place had a radio wire, and word about the new trumpet player started to circulate. Musicians came to investigate. Before long, Berigan was an after-hours regular at Jimmy Plunkett's bar, hanging out with a circle of new friends, including Benny Goodman and the enterprising Dorsey brothers.

Kemp heard him again, and this time definitely liked what he heard. Left with an empty trumpet chair by the defection of ever-unpredictable Jack Purvis, he promptly hired the young man for a European tour. Wednesday, May 14, 1930, the day before they left, they recorded for Brunswick. On available evidence, "Washin' the Blues From My Soul" is Bunny Berigan's first solo on record, and by any standard it's an impressive debut.

On both issued takes he uses a straight mute for his opening statement of this minor theme (similar to the better-known Victor Young–Ned Washington "Got the South in My Soul" of the following year). Even at this early point he's unmistakably Bunny Berigan: the figure-shapes, rhythmic address, attack, and execution—even the sense of swagger in the entrances—are fully formed, recognizable.

"Washin' the Blues From My Soul," Bunny Berigan trumpet solo, 1931.

After the Skinnay Ennis vocal Berigan returns, open this time, for four uninhibited bars, taking for granted an easy use of the high register.

Same, four later solo bars.

In a total of twenty-eight solo bars, the young trumpeter has covered two octaves and a fourth, from his instrument's next-to-lowest note (a written G below middle C) to its firmly struck high C. Among jazz trumpeters in 1930, only Armstrong and very few others were working with such a span, and fewer still with such ease.

Others—Stewart, Purvis, and Jabbo Smith come readily to mind—used their high registers to sometimes striking ends. But their solos never escaped a sense of risk, the frisson of high-wire acrobatics; exciting enough in itself, such display belongs mainly to the realm of musical special effect. In this earliest of Berigan solos, and consistently thereafter, quite the opposite is true: Bunny takes for granted the possibility that his solos may lead him into extreme registers of his horn, and he deals with them as matter-of-factly as he deals with his rich middle register. As Steve Lipkins said, "from bottom to top, evenly and strongly throughout."

The day after that recording session the Kemp band sailed for England aboard the Majestic. So it was that Bunny Berigan, age twenty-one, found himself in London, playing at the Café de Paris and being courted by the local trade press (a Berigan chorus on the brand-new "On the Sunny Side of the Street," written out by some anonymous scribe, appeared in the August 1930 issue of the magazine Rhythm), as well as such influential figures as bandleader-arranger-composer Patrick "Spike" Hughes.[7]

By the time he got back to New York at the end of September, Berigan had become something of a celebrity among those jazz-oriented musicians who were doing most of the commercial recording work around town. His three short solos on Kemp's "Them There Eyes," recorded November 18, show why: though muted, he seems to burst out of the ensembles with irresistible force. Again and again he stabs at the rhythm, pealing out high Ds (concert Cs) in a way rivaled by no other white trumpeter of the time and by only Armstrong, Stewart, and Jabbo Smith among the black trumpeters.

As 1931 got under way Bunny Berigan was one of the busiest trumpet players in New York. Whether broadcasting and recording with Fred Rich's CBS house band or joining the Dorsey brothers and Jack Teagarden in the pit orchestra for the Broadway revue Everybody's Welcome (which lasted a modest 139 performances and bequeathed "As Time Goes By" to posterity), he was turning down as many offers as he took.

That meant leaving Kemp. His replacement was the ever-peripatetic Purvis, fresh back from a series of European escapades (he'd dropped in unexpectedly on the band in Paris). But for reasons now lost to history, Purvis is absent from Kemp's Brunswick session of April 23. His replacement, no surprise, is Berigan, who solos warmly and well on "Mary Jane."

Beginning in February, Bunny was a regular presence on records made under the Dorsey Brothers name: his brief solo on their July 30 "Parkin' in the Moonlight" demonstrates his unique combination of strength and lyricism. He could play lead, sparking the band with his sound and phrasing, deliver a forceful solo—then go right back to playing the lead book.

"He just seemed to have it all covered," said tenor saxophonist Eddie Miller, who worked several freelance jobs with Berigan during 1931. One of them, Miller said, was a Dorsey Brothers date at Yale, and Bix Beiderbecke was also in the band, along with trumpeter Bill Moore. "Bix hadn't been well," said the saxophonist. "He didn't look well and was playing far from his best. It was so sad: here was my idol Bix, and he was clearly on the way down. And here was Bunny, a young guy full of piss and vinegar—he had the technique, the chops, the heart and warmth going for him."[8]

Johnny Morris, drummer on a similar date at Amherst around the same time, recalled Bix as "very moody and despondent," even reluctant to solo—though when he did the crowd responded warmly. Berigan, playing lead that night, was clearly "the trumpeter of the day" but seemed content to remain just a face in the band. "Tommy had brought Bix along on the date to help him make a few dollars. It was quite apparent that Bix was professionally jealous of Berigan, but on that night Bix completely captured the audience and Berigan was definitely in the background."[9]

(Beiderbecke didn't last much longer. His death that August hit the entire community of hot musicians very hard. But Berigan continued to regard Bix's memory with the same deference and respect he had shown the man in life. It found expression in 1938, when Bunny recorded the four Beiderbecke piano pieces and "Davenport Blues" in small-band settings.)

In 1932 Bunny Berigan hit his stride. He's commanding and immediately recognizable on the Boswell Sisters' "Everybody Loves My Baby," even turning a "clam" at the beginning of his second eight bars into an arresting figure.

The rare "What Would You Do?," recorded March 1, 1932 by an ARC-Brunswick house orchestra under Victor Young, furnishes evidence of Berigan's impact on his fellow-musicians. Young, says Berigan biographer Robert Dupuis, "allowed Tommy Dorsey and the other regulars to work out the details of the music themselves . . . Usually, the publishers gave them stock arrangements that the band would proceed to cut, charting the introductions, changing keys, blocking in solos, setting a coda."[10]

Two takes were issued: on the first, the band plays the four-bar introduction as written and takes the first chorus straight. Bunny, recognizable in a cup mute, has half the sixteen-bar verse over reed backing, then contributes a punchy obbligato behind Scrappy Lambert's vocal. By the next take they've given him the first half of the introduction as an Armstrong-like solo break and dropped the verse entirely, substituting a full-chorus trumpet solo on the chords of the song. He stays close to the melody for half of it, but after the saxes take the bridge he's back, with eight bars as recognizably Bunny Berigan as anything he did later in the decade.[11]

His solos with Dorsey Brothers groups—the 1933 "Mood Hollywood" and "Shim Sham Shimmy," and "Is That Religion?" backing Mildred Bailey, to cite just a few—are alternately stately, eloquent, and hair-raising in their flair for the dramatic.

Berigan was now one of the most polished and versatile trumpet men in the music business. His range was big, glowing, and secure all the way up to his high G. His control of high-note lip-trills was nonpareil. His flexibility was remarkable even by today's advanced standards of technique: he could vault from the lowest to the highest reaches of his horn with the same matter-of-factness displayed on his records with Kemp, but with ever greater confidence and polish, and no loss of tonal size or quality.

He used this technical equipment in shaping solos often stunning in their power to move a listener—something special, as Steve Lipkins put it, in the magic department; it is this quality, above all, that sets Berigan apart from even such supremely gifted contemporaries as Roy Eldridge.

Comparison of Eldridge and Berigan is instructive. Each exploits the dramatic potential of his instrument, but to somewhat different ends. From his first appearance on record, the 1935 "(Lookie, Lookie, Lookie) Here Comes Cookie," with Teddy Hill's orchestra, Eldridge is clearly an unprecedented force in jazz trumpet playing. His ability to get around the horn is awe-inspiring, combining Stewart's flexibility and Jabbo Smith's daredevil acrobatics—but with greater accuracy and sense of purpose.

Nothing in any trumpeter's work up to that time remotely approaches the mile-a-minute stunt flying of "Heckler's Hop," "After You've Gone," or "Swing Is Here." But Eldridge (in common with Dizzy Gillespie, whom he directly inspired) did not form his approach out of the examples of either Armstrong's stateliness or Beiderbecke's introspection. He admired Red Nichols—but largely, he added, for the latter's fluency and command of his horn. It was in saxophonists, notably Coleman Hawkins, that Roy Eldridge found his role model. Though capable of eloquent moments at slow tempos ("Where the Lazy River Goes By," "Falling in Love Again," and, with Billie Holiday, "I Wished on the Moon"), the closest he gets to the brooding majesty of Berigan's utterances on the 1935 "Nothin' but the Blues" (under Gene Gifford's name) is his two sombre, grieving choruses on Teddy Wilson's 1936 "Blues in C♯ Minor."

But these two trumpeters are singers of quite different songs. Berigan was, in one colleague's admiring phrase, "the ultimate romantic." His every solo flight, so expansive in the Armstrong manner, so reminiscent of the great tenors of Italian grand opera, also includes (and here he differs sharply from Eldridge) something of the sentimental. Never dominant, seldom even rising to the surface (quite unlike the saccharine excesses of Harry James, Ziggy Elman, or, at times, Charlie Shavers), it's nonetheless an ingredient.

Eldridge's sharply honed competitiveness seems quite at odds with Berigan's more bardic tendencies. Unlike Roy, Bunny seems never to think in terms of effect, display or spectacle. In all his recorded work it's hard to find a solo, even a single phrase, that seems calculated to impress. Berigan doesn't compete: he prefers to follow his instincts as a teller of stories.

If, as in his astonishing break toward the end of "That Foolish Feeling," he leaps from his horn's next-to-lowest note, a concert F below middle C, two and one-half octaves to a concert C above, he's not doing it to show that he can do it, or to intimidate potential challengers; he's doing it solely because his sense of phrase, balance, and dramatic narrative tells him that's where he must go.

Relevant here, if unlikely, is an observation by Edgar Allan Poe. Setting out guidelines for the successful short story, he declares, "In the whole composition

493

there should be no word written, of which the tendency, direct or indirect, is not to the pre-established design." Granted, most jazz improvisers work to far more generalized, less "pre-established" designs than do writers; but the jazz-man's art as a (short) storyteller conforms no less strictly to Poe's stated criterion. Each part serves the whole; each phrase moves the story forward, furthers the grand design. This is obvious in the work of Lester Young, of Bix Beiderbecke, of Pee Wee Russell—master storytellers all. And it is richly, gloriously true of Bunny Berigan.[12]

Black jazzmen soon came to respect Berigan as well; Henry "Red" Allen, Jonah Jones, Rex Stewart, and Fats Waller were numbered among his friends and admirers. "He was always welcome uptown," said saxophonist Eddie Barefield. "He played great, was a nice guy. Nobody cared if he was white or black. Bunny could play. Who cared about the rest?"[13]

His friendship with Louis Armstrong was based firmly on mutual admiration. "Each one thought the other was the greatest trumpet player," his widow, Donna Berigan, later recalled. "That meant a lot to Bunny because Louis had been his idol when Bunny was coming up."

One night in Boston, drummer Zutty Singleton took him to a jam session at a black club; after declining invitations to sit in (and, presumably, show what he could do), Bunny finally took out his horn. A friend present recorded that he "really let 'em have it! When Bunny got done and sat down, that was the end. Nobody else would play."[14]

In late 1932 Bunny Berigan became a member of Paul Whiteman's orchestra. Bix Beiderbecke, dead barely a year, had joined the "King of Jazz" only five years earlier, and some have sought parallels in their actions. Few exist: though they played the same instrument (for this discussion cornet and trumpet will be re-garded as one), the two were quite different musicians, with different needs. Beiderbecke, the musical autodidact, saw in Whiteman's large orchestra an op-portunity for education and self-improvement. There's no evidence that he chafed at the relative lack of jazz solo spots. On the contrary, he appears to have taken pleasure in being written into Ferde Grofé's "symphonic jazz" pieces.

Ironically, the restlessness and unease attributed to Beiderbecke in his White-man days may better apply to Berigan—a possibility all the more likely in view of the changes the organization had undergone since its late '20s heyday. Perched atop the entertainment world of 1928, leading a large and well-paid ensemble, Whiteman had felt free to experiment. He could tell arranger Bill Challis to "write whatever you want—we'll play it," commission modern concert suites from George Gershwin and Grofé, have various hands, including his staff men, or-chestrate pieces by Eastwood Lane, Domenico Savino, and others. And he could afford to keep Bix on an already bloated payroll, even when the cornetist was physically absent.

The Depression had changed the rules for survival, and Whiteman had made adjustments: the 1932 orchestra was smaller, musically more conservative. As trombonist Bill Rank put it, "people were talking about such things as popularity ratings, so Paul often featured straightforward arrangements of popular songs or selections which allowed little scope for jazz."[15]

Still, Whiteman was more than generous in finding feature spots for his new trumpet soloist, even if it meant injecting Bunny into arrangements which otherwise had no solo space. An April 27, 1933, NBC broadcast from the Palace Theatre in Dallas finds Berigan frequently and strongly in the limelight. He punches out the verse in a pit-orchestra arrangement of "I Got Rhythm" (a spot apparently cleared for him by marking the passage *tacet* for the other brass), adds sixteen choice muted bars to "Look What I Got," and cuts loose handsomely for the entire opening chorus of "It Don't Mean a Thing if It Ain't Got That Swing." He also gets generous solo space in "Sing," "Fit as a Fiddle," and an exhilarant reading of Lennie Hayton's 1929 "Nobody's Sweetheart" score.

Bunny stayed with Whiteman a year, filling the gaps between tours with a steady succession of record dates. By this time he was enough in demand to have made an excellent living—particularly by Depression standards—from radio and recording alone, as Goodman, the Dorseys, Artie Shaw, and others were doing. But clearly he derived some comfort from membership in the Whiteman retinue.

It's at this point that Berigan's life off the bandstand becomes a factor. Married in 1931 to a dancer named Donna MacArthur, he'd settled down in Queens, and the following summer he became the father of a baby girl, named Patricia. Clarinetist Joe Dixon remembered Donna as "a sweet little lady, but naive. Both of them, Bunny and Donna, were naive. He was, after all, a hick from Fox Lake, Wisconsin."

From the start, Donna appears to have taken unwillingly to her stay-at-home role as the wife of a traveling musician and mother of his child. When he left on a long tour with Whiteman, she took baby Patricia to Fox Lake to stay with the Berigan family. Though accounts vary, relations seems to have been rather less than cordial. She was already pregnant with their second child and felt unwell much of the time—which may account, at least in part, for the reported friction between her and her in-laws.

Not yet twenty-five, Berigan was already a celebrity among fellow-musicians; his dramatic solo playing, coupled with matinee-idol good looks and a boyish charm, meant that he would scarcely go unnoticed by women during the band's travels. Donna, married at nineteen and barely old enough to vote, was about to become a mother for the second time.

They were, in many respects, not only "hicks," in Joe Dixon's word, but very young. The process by which musicians and other popular artists are romanticized by their admirers often obscures such simple realities. It's unlikely that Bunny and Donna Berigan were equipped to handle the increasingly complex demands on their lives, or the gulf steadily growing between them. Donna had been a dancer, part of a brother-sister act, had tasted enough of show business life to chafe at her enforced isolation.

There is every indication that despite all the traveling, all the drinking, Berigan was determined to have a stable home life with Donna and Patricia. That life sustained a mortal blow on November 2, 1933; the very day Bunny Berigan turned twenty-five, Donna gave birth to their second child, a baby girl. But Barbara Ann Berigan, born prematurely, didn't survive the day. Her father, never one to discuss his troubles openly, internalized the pain. "He kept his mind occupied," said Donna. "He never said too much about it."[16]

Unlike Beiderbecke, to whom he is so often compared, Berigan hardly seemed a man in conflict or at war within himself. There's little surface evidence of the kind of self-destructiveness that haunted Beiderbecke and such later figures as Lester Young and Charlie Parker. But he was drinking heavily now, and beyond argument that had an effect on his day-to-day reliability.

"You didn't know sometimes whether he was gonna show up for a session," said Manny Klein, who shared many dates with Berigan and whose own strong, shapely solos on records of the period have occasionally been mistaken for Bunny's. "That's the reason we had two, and sometimes even three, trumpets on some of those Boswell Sisters dates. But when he did show up—well, nobody played with the balls and with the beat he did."[17]

"He could be a mean drunk," said saxophonist Artie Drelinger, who later worked with Berigan at the Famous Door, on 52nd Street. "All those wonderful things you hear about him—well, they should be put in some perspective. Booze was his priority, and when he was stoned he could be a son of a bitch."[18]

Drelinger's rather sour recollections are in no way unique. And it's easy to wonder, finally, why *did* Bunny drink? Many of his colleagues did, and often to excess. Stirling Bose, Brad Gowans, Bobby Hackett, Pee Wee Russell, Adrian Rollini, Chelsea Quealey, Jack Teagarden, J. C. Higginbotham, Jabbo Smith, Dick McDonough, Joe Smith, Pee Wee Erwin—jazz of the 1920s and '30s is rife with men for whom alcohol was just a fact of life. It seemed to come with the package.

Pee Wee Erwin, for example, was once asked by an interviewer whether he and Berigan had ever appeared together. "Never," he said quickly. Then, "Well, yes—I'll take that back. We made regularly scheduled appearances at Hurley's Bar and Grille. In fact, the last time I saw Bunny was at Hurley's. We were having breakfast together—four martinis apiece."[19]

Part social, part occupational, drinking was companionable, fostered a sense of closeness, camaraderie, and well-being. It was also exclusive—or, more aptly, exclusionary—as such non-drinkers as Benny Goodman and Manny Klein quickly discovered. Drinking helped alleviate the day-in, day-out boredom which is an ever-present part of music business life; some early jazzmen have maintained they could only play well when drunk, a sentiment echoed a generation later by users of heroin.

According to one widely circulated, possibly apocryphal, anecdote, a colleague once asked Berigan how he managed to play so well even when hardly able to stand. "I practice drunk" was his alleged reply. The miracle seems to have been that it took so long for the drinking to affect the playing, the flights of lyric fancy, soaring on his big, burnished sound, that made him a hero to so many.

He recorded a lot in those early-'30s years, and if one quality distinguishes

Berigan's work it is the ease with which he seems to fire off one brilliant solo after another. Though he had played beautifully before, and would afterwards, these are arguably the peak years. Somehow the combination of popularity, good money, and superior musical surroundings drew from him a body of music still able to startle in the frequency with which it scales peaks of inspiration. Drunk or sober, he seemed able to make any performance, however pedestrian, glow brightly.

"I used to hear him on the radio," said Jim Maxwell, shortly to become a trumpeter whose power, range, and immense tone would rival Berigan's. "I was still in high school, and I'd sometimes stay home from school to hear him. I'd never heard anybody play so lyrically: a good deal like Louis, I felt, but looser. Armstrong at that point was inclining toward a more rigid, angular style.

"At that time, most of the white musicians liked Bix and Red Nichols, and the blacks liked Louis and the people who played like him—Henry Allen, for example. When I heard Bunny my thought was that here was a bridge, taking the race out of music and just playing music. He had the most gorgeous sound, big and beautiful from top to bottom, and the most beautiful, liquid vibrato."[20]

Recorded evidence, plentiful, can be sampled at random. On "Troubled," issued under Frank Trumbauer's name, Berigan enters by pealing out his high C$\sharp$ to begin sixteen bars whose effect, over an unvarying E-minor background, is like a giant searchlight beam piercing a night sky.

He comes in much the same way, and on the same note, to begin his half-chorus on "In a Little Spanish Town," with Glenn Miller. But the context is different: Berigan's outburst, following a particularly fussy bit of Miller orchestration, sounds for all the world like a mighty "Enough!"—the cry of a man at the limit of his patience.

It also illustrates a familiar Berigan trait. He hits that first C$\sharp$ with such force that in striking it a second time to begin a downward phrase he overshoots, resulting in an unexpected "clam," or missed note. "That was part of his charm," said Manny Klein. "Once in a while he'd get into the woods, foul up a little bit—but he always worked his way back right. And sometimes it was *better* than it would have been if he'd made what he was after in the first place."[21]

May 13 brought one of Berigan's landmark sessions. It was a pickup band, led by arranger Gene Gifford, who'd made his reputation scoring and composing for the immensely popular Casa Loma Orchestra: it included tenor saxophonist Bud Freeman and pianist Claude Thornhill, who were appearing nightly with Ray Noble at the newly opened Rainbow Room; Matty Matlock, on clarinet, and Ray Bauduc, on drums, who were with Bob Crosby's new band; and bassist Pete Peterson, guitarist Dick McDonough, and trombonist Morey Samel, all busy free-lancers. One surprise participant was New Orleans–born trumpeter Wingy Manone, hired for this occasion as vocalist.[22]

"We were all so thrilled to get a chance to play such good arrangements on a date like this that we almost ran into trouble with the recording people," Freeman said. "Usually, the A-and-R man will hope that you finish up what you have to do in the allotted three hours or whatever. But this time we were enjoying ourselves so much that we wanted to play the things over and over. They got good takes right away, but we just kept on playing."[23]

Gifford's arrangements are spare, uncluttered; each solo has its own setting, striking an attractive balance with the ensemble passages. Berigan opens "Nothin' but the Blues," for example, with a simple, almost heraldic eight-bar announcement, tone full and resounding over backbeats by the band. The background switches to marching quarter notes for Matlock's clarinet to set out the theme, and a bar-long C augmented seventh chord, played *tutti*, brings on Berigan.

Here, incontrovertibly, something happens in the magic department. Transcription can reproduce the notes, the phrase shapes, show a solo's architecture and sense of inner balance and development. Less successful is any attempt to capture on manuscript paper those elements—nuances of attack, dynamic, tone—that personalize it, lend it poignancy. Here is his first twelve-bar statement: the somewhat unorthodox notation of bars 1–2, and again of 5–6, is an attempt to approximate, within the rigidities of formal notation, figures built upon a keen sense of *rubato*.[24]

"Nothin' but the Blues," first Berigan trumpet chorus, 1935.

Bar eight, for example, could also be expressed this way:

Same, alternate transcription of eighth bar.

with Berigan creating the impression of the triplet by simply delaying the fifth note (his written D), associating it in the phrase with the F♯ above; it's an altogether more interesting choice than casting it as part of a straightforward run of four sixteenth notes. The effect in both cases is the same.

Berigan contributes a passionate blues solo to "Squareface," which also features an affecting Manone vocal; it's regrettable that Wingy didn't receive more such "straight," i.e., non-comedic, singing assignments—and a credit to Gifford for having recognized and exploited this side of the trumpeter's talent.

At the end of June, Benny Goodman, who had experienced Berigan's gifts as a musical catalyst again and again at first hand, brought him into his new band—in full knowledge of the newcomer's drinking problem—and paid him its highest salary, two hundred dollars a week.

"He'd done the *Let's Dance* programs with me for a while, and I knew what to expect," the clarinetist said. More than once, the ever-reliable Manny Klein had been called in at short notice when Bunny either didn't show up for broadcasts or might as well not have. Yet as far as Benny was concerned, the advantages of having Berigan around far outweighed such peccancy:

"You just had to hear the band with him in it. He'd take a solo and boy! It was like a bolt of electricity running through the whole band. He was so exciting, and so inventive in his own way that he just lifted the whole thing. And what a lead player! Beautiful sound, range, everything."[25]

Berigan was in the band on its trip West in summer of 1935, culminating in the now-fabled triumph at the Palomar Ballroom in Los Angeles. Canadian-born Helen Oakley, who heard them en route, wrote in a *Down Beat* review that Berigan "is, I believe, the only trumpeter comparable to Louis Armstrong."[26]

Even with success apparently theirs, Goodman said, he remained careful about Berigan. "We were supposed be at the Palomar only a month, but the engagement was extended, and we were doing radio broadcasts at night. They came and asked me, 'What time do you want to be on the radio? Do you want the 11:30 slot, or 12:30?' I told them I thought 11:30 would be good. The earlier the better—largely because if it were any later Bunny would usually be wiped out."

Berigan solos on most of the records made by the Goodman band during his four-month stay, and several of them number among his best recorded work. His entrance on "Jingle Bells," for example, brings Goodman's "bolt of electricity" remark vividly to mind. In a way it's set up for him: starting in G, Spud Murphy's fine arrangement moves chorus by chorus around the circle of fifths, with Benny's own solo getting considerable impetus from a modulation to C. Even bearing in mind the natural catapult of a shift up to F, Berigan's solo is exceptional. His annunciatory phrase, four notes spread over two bars, rivets attention in a way not accomplished by either the clarinet or Art Rollini's tenor, which follows. Part of it lies in a natural, unerring swing, a way of placing notes on the beat that conveys a sense of momentum and urgency even without the fervid quality so fundamental to Roy Eldridge's brand of excitement.

Berigan's is an innate grandeur of conception, lending a sense of inevitability to whatever he plays. If he arrests attention on "Jingle Bells," he does yet more on "King Porter Stomp," recorded the same day. Benny has just soloed, two good choruses with Gene Krupa whacking backbeats on a tiny splash cymbal. It's good, cheery hot clarinet at Goodman's usual high standard. But there's nothing in it to foreshadow what's about to happen.

"Pow!" goes Berigan, pealing out a single massive high concert D♭ to fill his first bar. Charleston beat in bar 2, an octave down. "Pow!" again, for a two-bar figure built from the top down. Then again, this time a four-bar summation, bringing the chorus to mid-point. Then two more terse two-bar phrases, each beginning on that same top D♭, and another four-bar comment to close things out.

It's both forceful jazz, simply and logically constructed, and superior trumpet playing. For a trumpet player to begin a solo on this kind of a *fortissimo* high note, then use it as a structural pivot, returning to it five times in sixteen bars *without strain, without a hint of effect for its own sake*, is notable by any standard.

But, as Gunther Schuller suggests in *The Swing Era*, lots of other men on the scene in 1935 could bat out the high ones. What's telling here is *how* Berigan uses them in the service of a higher aesthetic good. Therein lies the real mastery.

His sixteen-bar contribution to "Sometimes I'm Happy," if somewhat more nuanced, is no less striking. Its first half is a study in dramatic contrast, a simple phrase played low, then an octave higher, and capped with a leap to an exultant high D (concert C) and a long, descending arc of a figure with power and weight—and an almost Bix-like sense of structural logic.

But it's the next eight bars that capture the imagination: in several spots Bunny's line clashes with the harmonies of the song (the concert F♮ in bar twelve, for example, against a D♭ minor chord). But what he's playing has enough melodic and emotional momentum to establish its own precedence by a kind of aesthetic *force majeure*, over and above the harmonies of the Vincent Youmans song.[27]

Berigan left Goodman in September, joining his family in Wisconsin. A story persists that he sent his horn to Mark Warnow, director of the house band at CBS radio in New York (and brother of bandleader-composer Raymond Scott), serving notice in somewhat melodramatic fashion that he was again at liberty. Warnow, no fool, hired him immediately.[28]

The combination of studio work at CBS and freelancing with jazz bands around town seemed an ideal—and highly paid—existence. Bunny Berigan was the trumpet player of the hour, and no one recognized this more than his fellow-brassmen, including potential rivals.

"Everything he played had a line," said Jim Maxwell. "It was like a melody, even if it had a lot of notes in it. Sometimes I think that after Bunny left Goodman's band the brass section lost the really beautiful tone quality it had had. The guys who followed—Harry [James], Ziggy [Elman], and the rest—used Selmer trumpets and shallow mouthpieces and got that very bright, brittle sound. It was exciting, yes—but for me something had been lost."[29]

One successor, Gordon "Chris" Griffin, remembered Berigan with something close to awe. "His continuity was so great. With me, and with most players, you'll start a note or two and the phrase maybe comes to fruition, if it does, in a few notes. With Bunny, the phrases were long and beautiful. He was almost completely abandoned, took what I thought were a lot of chances. Of course he had accidents—but you could always tell how much he was putting into it . . . He was never imprisoned, never played the same chorus twice. And those long, beautiful phrases . . . it still gives me goose pimples to think about them."[30]

Though blue-blooded critic-entrepreneur John Hammond usually favored black musicians, when he assembled record dates in those years he made a regular exception of Berigan. Bunny contributes long-lined solos and great energy to Bud Freeman's Hammond-organized record date of December 4, 1935, particularly on the up-tempo "Keep Smilin' at Trouble," where he and the saxophonist are like two sluggers going at it in a sparring match.

"He picked up all those little patterns of mine, picked them up right away," said Freeman. "He was so quick. No self-consciousness, no friction. Just another guy on the date, and as a result we had a wonderful time and played very relaxed music."[31]

Two days later he was again in the cramped little studio ("the broom closet," musicians rather disparagingly called it) at 799 Seventh Avenue, this time joining alto saxophonist Johnny Hodges, pianist Teddy Wilson, and bassist Grachan Moncur in backing vocalist Mildred Bailey. (Those records, and the trumpeter's contributions to them, are discussed elsewhere.)

A week later, on December 13, it was Bunny's own turn, leading a racially mixed band that included Moncur, saxophonists Eddie Miller and Edgar Sampson, pianist Cliff Jackson, and drummer Ray Bauduc. Perhaps the day's highlight was Berigan's own version of "I'm Comin', Virginia," so closely associated with Bix Beiderbecke. He takes it faster, as if deliberately eschewing the bittersweet nostalgia of Bix's recording. Bunny here is thoughtful, affectionate, as if commenting with some detachment on Bix and the song.

In early 1936 he began supplementing his daytime income by working nights at the Famous Door on 52nd Street, usually with vocalist and comb-and-paper virtuoso Red McKenzie, guitarist Eddie Condon, and Forrest Crawford, an excellent tenor saxophonist from St. Louis. He had played "the Street" on and off during 1935, often jamming at Joe Helbock's Onyx Club with Goodman, the Dorseys, the Teagardens, and others. In fact, joining Benny that summer had meant turning down an offer from clarinetist Joe Marsala to play the Hickory House.[32]

The Berigan-McKenzie Famous Door band quickly became the talk of 52nd Street. Its pianist was a skinny nineteen-year-old named Joe Bushkin: son of Russian immigrant parents, he'd started by playing intermissions at the Door and graduated to the band. To him, history owes its most convincing account of how Bunny Berigan encountered the song for which he is best known outside jazz circles.

It was February. John De Vries—artist, advertising writer, occasional songwriter, and friend of many jazzmen—had been to see the brand-new *Ziegfeld Follies of 1936* at the Winter Garden, around the corner and a couple of blocks down Seventh Avenue. Passing through the lobby, he'd bought the sheet music to one of the songs in the show—melody by Vernon Duke, lyrics by Ira Gershwin—that had caught his fancy. Music in hand, he made for the Famous Door.

"He laid it on the piano," said Bushkin, "and we just read it down, playing it in the key it was in on the sheet. Bunny loved it from the first moment he heard it." Thus did "I Can't Get Started" fall into the hands of its most celebrated popularizer. McKenzie recorded it for Decca on April 3, with Bunny hewing close to the melody in a sixteen-bar solo.

They played it every night at the Door, and little by little a routine emerged. That was apparent on April 13, when Bunny got to record it at a Vocalion date under his own leadership. Going into the last chorus, for example, he used an idea suggested by Eddie Condon as a way of modulating from concert C half a step up into D♭. Simple, logical, it consisted of a series of five two-bar cadenzas, based successively on C-F7-B♭7-E♭7 and A♭7, which not only set up the key but boosted the emotional temperature in preparation for the finale.

This version of "I Can't Get Started" is the first of two performances recorded by Berigan sixteen months apart; many listeners prefer it to the latter, rather grander Victor version. It's quite unself-conscious, relaxed, almost carefree: let's just play the damn thing, Bunny seems to say here—if we get it, fine. If we miss, what the hell.

They don't miss. After a thoughtful opening *tutti*, Berigan sings a chorus in his high, light voice, his fast vibrato lending a sense of vulnerability. Crawford's tenor takes eight bars in a subdued ballad mood, and then it's all Bunny, playing at a bravura peak. Moving easily throughout the entire range of his horn, he climbs at the outset to a titanic high concert D♭ and E♭, only to plunge near the end to four broad-toned, *sotto voce* bars before a final climactic ascent.[33]

There's no minimizing the importance of this three-minute *tour de force*. It's the apotheosis of Bunny Berigan's art as a soloist in the grand tradition established by Armstrong and illustrates graphically why Louis, while praising Eldridge for his "chops" and others for their various "ingredients," as he was fond of calling them, singled out Berigan as the one who "can't do no wrong in music." He knew what he was hearing.[34]

If 1935 had been a good year for Berigan, it turned out to have been just a warmup to 1936. What's striking now is less how many records he made—quite a few others were recording regularly, some even more frequently—but the consistently high level of his work on them. When Billie Holiday began recording for Vocalion under her own name in mid-year, for example, Bunny was one of her accompanists, and his work is outstanding.

He enlivens "Did I Remember," "No Regrets," "One, Two, Button Your Shoe," and the rest with discreet obbligatos and powerful solos. A piquant moment comes on "A Fine Romance"; Billie's sensibility, refracted through her own life and experiences, converts the popular Dorothy Fields lyric from an expression of good-natured exasperation into a taunt, a coruscating indictment by a marital prosecutor.

Berigan, responding, bursts in on Irving Fazola's thoughtful clarinet solo with a five-note exclamation which seems to yell, "It's a FINE romance!" holding the word "fine" (a high concert C) for four long, emphatic beats. The rest of his solo is almost truculent, unusual for him but quite appropriate to the mood established by the singer.

His work behind Billie here epitomizes his own advice to accompanists, published as part of a *Metronome* magazine article the following year:

> Your best bet is to keep your fill-ins rather simple, especially if the number is medium or bright tempo. At a slow tempo you can put in a little more elaborate phrases. By all means be careful to avoid playing anything that will conflict with the voice, or attract too much attention from it. In other words the voice must hold the spotlight. Very often you will find it effective to play a little phrase that imitates what the vocalist has just sung . . . The general idea is to play a phrase in the open parts, or while the singer holds a long note.[35]

(There was a personal application as well. Among the regular sitters-in at the Famous Door was a willowy, auburn-haired singer from Oklahoma named Lee Wiley, who was immediately and irresistibly attracted to Bunny Berigan. The attraction was reciprocal and blossomed into an affair, which led in turn to a confrontation with Donna Berigan and a separation that turned out to be permanent. Stories of the liaison have circulated among musicians for years, including one in which Wiley—"that snake eyes," in Donna's phrase—kept the trumpeter virtual prisoner in a hotel room for many hours by the simple expedient of tossing his shirt and trousers out the window.)

Other examples of Berigan gloriously on record in this peak year: his charging, abandoned ensemble leads on "If I Had My Way" and "Swing, Mister Charlie"; his full-blooded break and solo on "Just Like a Melody From the Sky"; the long, legato phrases of his chorus on "Let's Do It"; the hair-raising transition and solo, mentioned earlier, on "That Foolish Feeling" (all issued under his own name); his flowing contribution to "Dardanella," by a Dick McDonough unit (also featuring able work from Toots Mondello on clarinet, Larry Binyon on tenor, and Adrian Rollini on bass sax and vibes).[36]

In a way the best example of Bunny's unique incandescence lies in a series of transcription recordings done for Thesaurus in mid-1936. It's obviously a pickup date, with the band laboring doggedly through a score of publishers' stock arrangements, edited here and there to make room for choruses by Bunny and several of the others.

His solos on "Dardanella," "On Your Toes," and an up-tempo "San Francisco" (from the Clark Gable–Jeanette MacDonald movie of that year) ring and flash. At times he seems to be pulling the whole sodden weight of the band along with him. Berigan is up to it, with power and verve to spare.

503

He played "I Can't Get Started" at the Joe Helbock Imperial Theatre swing concert that May 24, with Chick Webb as guest drummer. A *Down Beat* reviewer seemed too preoccupied with the trumpeter's occasional inconsistency to spend much time contemplating the material: "He can play marvelously for two or three selections and then get off on a tangent that would have the N.Y. Schools of Music—twenty-five¢ per lesson—sending out circulars."

But John Hammond, writing in the same issue, described Berigan's performance as one of the evening's two "surprise hits" (the other being an appearance by Red Norvo and Mildred Bailey); "Bunny's playing," he wrote, "is now so close to perfection that even a society audience at the opera would appreciate it."[37]

By this time the public was becoming aware of Berigan as well, especially after he began appearing regularly as guest soloist on the CBS *Saturday Night Swing Club* broadcasts. And when Henry "Red" Allen and some others from the Mills Blue Rhythm Band played as Berigan's "guests" on one of the shows, Bunny was on the sidelines, shouting (as an aircheck of the broadcast deliciously shows) encouragement.

It all began to point in one direction: sooner or later, Bunny Berigan was going to have to think about leading his own band. Benny Goodman's immense success had shown beyond doubt that the formula could work handsomely; the Dorsey brothers had gone their separate ways as bandleaders and were catching on. Louis Armstrong was appearing regularly in front of what had been the Luis Russell Orchestra; Count Basie, former pianist with Bennie Moten in Kansas City, had brought a band of his own to New York's Roseland Ballroom, featuring the light, supple tenor playing of Lester Young. Cab Calloway, Duke Ellington, and Jimmie Lunceford were doing fine, and the Casa Loma Orchestra was still riding high. Artie Shaw was experimenting with larger personnels; even Glenn Miller, after helping put together an all-star band for Ray Noble, was starting to think about doing it for himself.

At this point Tommy Dorsey, whose behind-the-scenes assistance to colleagues and fledgling bandleaders (even when they were clearly potential rivals) at times constituted a kind of second career, stepped in: if Bunny Berigan was going to lead a band he might as well do it properly. Dorsey got his manager, Art Michaud, to agree to help run Bunny's band too. And then he turned to the trumpeter himself: what better way to learn what bandleading really involved than becoming a *pro tem* Dorsey sideman? He'd play with them, broadcast with them, even do a bit of traveling with them—and above all, keep his eyes open. Watch how Tommy handled agents, bookers, ballroom managers; learn how to organize transportation and accommodations, work out an itinerary; learn how to deal with good crowds and bad—and above all, to keep everyone on his side.

It was the best of apprenticeships—and, as it turned out, one with immense musical rewards. "He amazed us all," said Dorsey's bassist Gene Traxler. "You know, he drank a lot, but he always delivered. Tommy gave him a lot of room, and the guys were delighted to have him aboard, they all admired him so much."[38]

Berigan's effect on the Dorsey band was immediate and profound. Arrangers wrote him into their scores. Openings at first assigned to other players wound up as Berigan solos. Dorsey, for his part, treated the trumpeter with the same mixture of affection and awe he reserved for Bud Freeman and Dave Tough, the band's two pet jazzmen. A large quantity of aircheck material from Dorsey's weekly Raleigh-Kool broadcasts still exists; on selection after selection, Berigan's solos sizzle and crackle, energizing even the most pedestrian arrangements.

He stayed with Dorsey just two months. As with Goodman, he left behind a body of recorded solos for the ages: brief and pithy on "Looking Around Corners for You" and "How Could You," riding handsomely atop Tough's Chinese cymbal on "The Goona Goo" and "Buy My Violets," and lighting up such exercises in "swinging the classics" as Rubinstein's "Melody in F," "Mendelssohn's Spring Song," and a thrilling sixteen bars on Liszt's "Liebestraum."

The Dorsey hitch also produced three recorded masterpieces. On "Mr. Ghost Goes to Town" Bunny comes out of his corner swinging, fashioning a twenty-four-bar solo rich in layered, rather complex phrases (and some figures in common with his half-chorus on "Sometimes I'm Happy"). Live aircheck versions of this and several others bear witness to Red McKenzie's admiring reference to Berigan as "a gambler." A January 31 radio performance of "Mister Ghost," particularly, comes off like the Fourth of July, Berigan firing rockets and roman candles in a solo that makes the Victor studio version, however good, seem little more than a rehearsal.

But without doubt the two crowning moments are the Dorsey records of "Marie" and a swing transformation of Rimsky-Korsakov's "Song of India," both made on January 29. In each case the arrangement has simply been opened up to accommodate a Berigan chorus, and each is an independent melodic statement, free-standing and compositionally balanced.[39]

Both solos quickly became part of the swing band canon. Berigan's "Song of India" chorus was incorporated, in note-for-note transcription, in the published stock version of the Dorsey arrangement. In a later Dorsey orchestra, trumpeter-arranger Sy Oliver (presumably at the leader's behest) scored the "Marie" solo for the entire trumpet section; it was a highlight of all subsequent performances of the number.

Strong evidence suggests that neither chorus sprang fully formed out of its creator's mind. Two Raleigh-Kool airchecks, from January 11 and 18, show Berigan's "Marie" solo to be very much a work in progress. The elements of the finished product are there, but he's still moving the pieces around, developing and turning phrases. The effect is quite similar to that of viewing the preliminary sketches for a great work of art, then revisiting the painting itself. Seldom has the creative process been so well and clearly defined.

(Certain figures, inevitably, recur. What Berigan plays in bars 6–7 of his "Mr. Ghost" solo is similar to bars 6–7 of his "Sometimes I'm Happy" solo with Goodman; and the group of four eighth-note triplets in bars 13–14 of the "Marie" solo also turns up, in various forms, in bars 7–8 of the "Liebestraum" solo, bar 4 of "The Goona Goo," and bars 4–5 of "Buy My Violents." Great soloists, in common with lesser ones, make use of stock figures—though Berigan, on the whole, did this somewhat less than others. It's of course how they're used that makes the difference.)

During his weeks with Dorsey, Berigan was hard at work organizing and shaping a band of his own. At first, not surprisingly, he drew on friends, reedmen Matty Matlock and Art Drelinger among them. They rehearsed at Haven Studios, on West 54th Street, and almost immediately landed a chance to do some records for Brunswick. Trombonist Walter Burleson remembered a momentary panic, when Bunny discovered that a specially prepared arrangement of "One in a Million" was of the wrong song, one of two by that name then current. He had no choice but to send out for a publisher's "stock" on the right one, doctor it up a bit, and record it on the spot. No one at Brunswick, said Burleson, was any the wiser.[40]

Its personnel stabilized, the new band tried a brief New England tour under the ever-indulgent gaze of the brothers Sy and Charlie Shribman, then four weeks at Frank Dailey's popular Meadowbrook, on the "Pompton Turnpike" in central New Jersey, known nationwide through network "remote" broadcasts. Participating musicians remembered the time with enjoyment, but the elements that contributed to the Berigan band's ultimate failure—and, indeed, to its leader's early decline and death—were already ominously in place. Bunny kept promising premium work and higher salaries, neither of which ever quite came through. And, as usual, there was the drinking: as lead trumpeter Harry Greenwald told Ian Crosbie, "Bunny used to drink hard liquor from a Coke bottle to fool the audience—he got a kick out of that."[41]

Berigan reorganized in March, this time with a larger group. It was an excellent band, with good, young sidemen, including such promising soloists as clarinetist Joe Dixon (fresh out of Dorsey's band) and Canadian tenor saxophonist Georgie Auld; above all, it had a leader who was respected, even revered, both by fellow-musicians and by the public.

But it takes more than respect to turn a good band into a successful one. An aspiring leader must understand that the second word of the phrase "music business" is as important as the first. He must be businessman—or politician—enough to cope with the offstand responsibilities, or surround himself with others who can guide him through that often frustrating and contradictory terrain.

Tommy Dorsey, to choose an outstanding example, was an excellent intuitive businessman. There is significance in hearing trumpeter Pee Wee Erwin say, with pride, that "no promoter ever lost money on Tommy." If the Dorsey band played a regional date, Erwin said, and the attendance failed to make the guarantee, Dorsey would seldom hold up the ballroom operator for the money. "That way he really helped every band, everyone in the music business, because he helped keep those promoters in business."[42]

There's a second consideration, more elusive than the simple outlines of a good business sense. Transformation from working musician into bandleader is a rite of passage, a personal shift of a surprisingly delicate nature. A man who has been a peer, a comrade-in-arms, sharing both musical experiences and off-the-stand bonding (including schoolboy pranks and other expressions of defiance of authority), now must in effect break ranks, distancing himself from his erstwhile colleagues.

He is, in effect, an ordinary corporate employee promoted to a managerial position, his advancement lifting him across the "us and them" line common to all labor-management situations. He now perceives differences between his interests and those of his men: he's in charge of them, responsible for them, working toward the same goal as before but charged with keeping them in line. He has the authority to hire and fire them at will: men who a short time ago were his pals, his equals, are now his employees, and things between them can never again be the same.

Some—Tommy Dorsey, Benny Goodman, Artie Shaw, and especially Glenn Miller—were better at it than others. Some chose to sidestep the issue entirely by using younger, untried musicians rather than established peers. The result was not unlike a benevolent form of military hierarchy, the authority coming, as it were, with the office.[43]

But for those who chose to lead bands stocked with former drinking pals, sectionmates, and fellow-campaigners, the bandleader-sideman relationship was more problematical. The example of Jack Teagarden is instructive: esteemed, beloved, he seemed to have little appetite for the disciplinarian-father-schoolmaster—or businessman—side of his new role. The Teagarden big band, while it lasted, had every break imaginable, largely on the strength of the regard in which its leader was held, but it failed. Cornetist Bobby Hackett, similarly admired, tried a big band—and populated it with most of those musicians in his circle able to drink him under the nearest table. Little wonder that it lasted only a year.

And then there was Bunny Berigan. "Bunny was a marvelous sideman," said drummer Johnny Blowers, who worked for him in 1938. "In fact, he was always a sideman, never a leader in the strict sense of the word. He was very lackadaisical about business: he wanted to play, drink, enjoy life. He was a fun guy—but not disciplined."[44]

Joe Dixon concurred. "Emotionally I don't think he ever thought of himself as a leader. It made him uncomfortable, isolated him from the men. You could say that Bunny did everything either consciously or unconsciously to reaffirm this thing, this camaraderie, he had with the guys in the band—that he was right there in the trenches with us."

Even his method of dealing with musical matters reflected an unwillingness to climb out of the trenches. As bassist Arnold Fishkind put it, "Tommy, Artie, Benny—they were disciplinarians, who knew what they wanted and how to go about getting it. Bunny? He'd do it all himself: he'd play his jazz choruses, and then when you wanted an out chorus he'd go back and stand with the trumpets and play lead, which was sensational, because nobody could play lead like he could. He'd be saying, in effect, 'This is the way to do it, so let's do it this way.' "[45]

"Don't think we didn't rehearse," said Joe Lipman, who came to the band in a swap that sent pianist Les Burness to Artie Shaw's band. "We rehearsed a lot. But it was the enthusiasm that carried it. There was a lotta love in that band: everybody wanted to play with Bunny. He could inspire people. God, could he! He was such a player—as good as anybody in the world."[46]

Joe Bushkin, who succeeded Lipman, remembered that Bunny "ran his big band much the way he'd run the little one. At rehearsals he'd always have whoever had done an arrangement rehearse the band, and he'd just come in and play his parts like one of the guys."[47]

For a while the band thrived on enthusiasm. "It wasn't always a very disciplined band," said Dixon, "but it had a sizzle, a real *élan*, that made up for it. It's a hard thing to describe in words: maybe Patton's divisions had it during the war, I don't know. But I'll tell you, when I listen to some of those records, the transcriptions especially, it's easy to think that we had to be the best band in the country at that time."

The records, at least those resulting from the first Victor dates in 1937, almost bear him out. Not unexpectedly, the band had to record its share of inferior songs. ("We were the low men on the totem pole at Victor," said Dixon. "Victor had all the bands, and they got all the tunes. We got the lousy ones.") But there were good ones as well, and good or bad, the spirit is there. Bunny's solos lift even such undistinguished Tin Pan Alley products as "You Can't Run Away From Love Tonight" and "The Image of You." He sings on " 'Cause My Baby Says It's So" in his endearingly bashful tenor, then leaps into his trumpet solo with a rip up to a concert high D which generates enough energy to keep half the lightbulbs in New York City burning.

(On March 31, the day before his band's first Victor date, Berigan joined Tommy Dorsey, Fats Waller, Dick McDonough, and George Wettling for *A Jam Session at Victor*. Recording director Eli Oberstein saw it as a great promotional opportunity, with Dorsey and Waller established as Victor artists, and Bunny about to launch his own band on the label after the triumphs of "Marie" and "Song of India." But Oberstein didn't reckon on Berigan showing up with a pint in each pocket, and Waller probably similarly fortified. Out of four planned titles they got only two; but both "Honeysuckle Rose" and a nicely turned E♭ "Blues" are good, spirited fun.)

The next day, on "Frankie and Johnny," Auld and Dixon solo with perhaps more agitation than content, but Berigan settles down on George Wettling's backbeats to deliver two effective middle-register blues choruses; on "Mahogany Hall Stomp" he perhaps pointedly makes no reference at all to Louis's famous solo (though on "Little Gate's Special," recorded two years later, he quotes it extensively). Then, too, there is the seldom-reissued "Swanee River," in a well-crafted arrangement by Larry Clinton. Berigan uses a straight mute throughout, and even the way he sets out the melody is enough: joy, and the *élan* Dixon recalled, seem to burst from every note.

On August 7, the Berigan band made what is probably its most famous record: "I Can't Get Started" was by this time both the leader's theme and his most frequently requested feature. Pianist Lipman, by this time doing much of the arranging, had scored it according to the routine set out on the 1936 Vocalion recording, adding a four-episode trumpet cadenza at the beginning over sustained chords, and a half-chorus sax section *soli* passage leading into Berigan's vocal. Two takes have been issued, and comparison makes clear that Bunny's way of playing the song had crystallized into a routine, as formalized and polished as a trumpet concerto; any variation was at best a matter of detail.

There had also been a subtle shift in his approach to playing it. Where the 1936 "I Can't Get Started" had seemed casual, almost tossed off, in its brilliance, the twelve-inch 1937 reading exudes an aura of *gravitas,* a self-conscious high seriousness. This "I Can't Get Started" is a grand gesture, not without a certain rather disquieting stridency. For the first time, Berigan seems aware that every time he solos he has to *deliver,* in a manner befitting (in Cole Porter's apt phrase) "the leader of a big-time band."

"The Prisoner's Song," appearing as the "flip" side of "I Can't Get Started," became something of a hit on its own. "Bunny ran it down and decided he liked it," said Dixon. "For most of us, it was a nothing arrangement on a nothing tune." Maybe: but the exuberance of the performance—bookended by growling plunger passages from Bunny and featuring vigorous solos by Berigan, Dixon, Auld, and veteran trombonist Sonny Lee—makes it hard to resist.[48]

The sinuous, eight-bar, hill-and-dale phrase which opens the second of his three choruses is the apex of Berigan's solo. Played in one breath, it starts high and descends by unusually positioned chromatic stages; in its length, chromaticism, and structure it seems to look forward to some of the innovations of bebop.

"The Prisoner's Song," first eight bars, second chorus of trumpet solo, 1937.

The Berigan band had its ups and down over the next two years, records good and (too many) not so good. Bunny's alcohol consumption was by this time consistent and immense, and in several instances cost his band important work. Their continuing Victor records, and an unusually large amount of aircheck and transcription material make it possible to follow their fortunes almost day by day.

When Bunny was *on*, which was still a good deal of the time, he continued to deliver powerful, electrifying (if also occasionally somewhat stentorian) solos. He sparks the band on such records as the much-reissued "Russian Lullaby," "Black Bottom," and "High Society" and especially on "The Wearin' of the Green" (an excellent Lipman arrangement, making resourceful use of three B♭ clarinets and Mike Doty's bass clarinet).

At one point late in the performance, Nat Lobovsky, a trombonist with an unusually clear, singing tone, plays the melody sweet and straight, sailing to an unforced high F. As the band picks up at the bridge, Berigan comes up over the near horizon on an eerie, massive high concert F, a full octave above Steve Lipkins's trumpet lead. It's almost preternatural drama—improbable, unexpected, emotionally shattering.

"It's not just playing high," said Dixon. "A lot of screechers today, they can play up there all they like, hit double C's whenever they feel like. But so what? They don't turn me on at all. Bunny, when he hit one of those notes it sort of vibrated, I mean *inside* you."

Berigan caps his triumph at the end when, during a reprise of the introduction, he joins trombonists Lobovsky and Ray Conniff for some three-part low-register harmony. His tone is broad enough to blend perfectly.

He's no less impressive on "Trees," done two days before Christmas 1937, at the same session that produced "Russian Lullaby" and "Black Bottom." It's based on a frequently quoted poem by the American Alfred Joyce Kilmer, killed at the Second Battle of the Marne in 1918. The melody, by Kentucky-born classical composer Oscar Rasbach, captures the aching introspection of Kilmer's verse—and Berigan somehow manages to do justice to both.

He chooses the trumpet's lowest register to begin a solo that after many hearings seems less an improvisation than a commentary on poem and melody alike. Especially poignant is a drop to his F♯ (concert E) in bar six, followed by a low F (concert E♭), a note not actually on the horn, but which Bunny "lips" into being. A sweep upward through two octaves ushers in a legato passage in his top register, culminating in a high F (concert E♭) which sounds less like a played note than a cry of deep, heart-rending anguish.

The sense of lamentation also saturates his two choruses on "Jelly Roll Blues," a number little played since Jelly Roll Morton, its composer, recorded it in the '20s. Berigan's treatment here finds emotional depths in the piece that even Morton himself probably never knew existed. The melody and chord structure, richer and with more inner movement than the normal blues changes, afford Bunny two sources of emotive strength: the basic force of the blues itself and the lyric intensity of song. He mines both in a solo rich in exquisite detail: his use of eighth-note triplets in bars 5 and 6 of the first chorus is typical, in the way he accents some and leaves others out in shaping a coiled spring of a phrase.

He's playing right across the warmest part of his middle register, going for no spectacular climaxes or effects, devoting everything to melody and emotion. His solo clearly affects the band, which returns with an intense, singing tutti, colored by use of four clarinets in the ensemble.[49]

The impetuous, carefree Bunny of the early '30s is gone, supplanted by a creator of craggy, epic soliloquies, declaimed as often as played. Comparison between his solos on "Nothin' but the Blues" and "Jelly Roll Blues" defines the change. Both are majestic utterances; but they appear to spring from two quite different perceptions, even two distinct times of life. Ordinarily the span between the two would be counted in decades, part of the natural aging process: in Berigan's case the difference is a scant three years.

There's been another, rather more alarming, change. Both the "Jelly Roll Blues" solo and the expressive "I Cried for You," from the same date, abound in little technical blemishes—fluffs, missed attacks, uncertainties of pitch which would have been unthinkable even a year before. Not that "clams" were anything new in his work. The testimony of the anonymous *Down Beat* writer after the 1936 Imperial Theatre concert attests to that. As Artie Drelinger put it, remembering nights at the Famous Door: "When he was right he was the greatest player I'd ever heard, but when he was stoned beyond a certain point I thought he sounded like a high school kid . . . the worst I'd ever heard. Nasty, terrible. He'd go for the high ones, all full of false courage, and wouldn't make 'em. Crack 'em. Awful."[50]

When he was stoned. And from all the evidence, as time went on and the demands on him intensified, Berigan was stoned a good deal more of the time. "There was definitely some deterioration," said trombonist Ray Conniff. "He was drinking too much, and he missed an awful lot."[51]

To be sure, said Joe Bushkin, Bunny could often turn his missteps into triumphs. "Take 'I Cried for You,' " the pianist said. "The goof becomes part of the piece. It was a wonderful kind of game, and we played it with him—how's he gonna get out of this one? And most of the time, he did."[52]

The single event that seemed to crack Berigan's confidence happened in Boston on Wednesday, September 21, 1938. No one living in New England at that time needs reminding of that date: like Pearl Harbor, the death of FDR, or the assassination of John F. Kennedy, it is etched in memory.

Trumpeter Bernie Privin remembered it well. At nineteen, he had run away from a home dominated by a tyrannical father and was beginning to catch on in the music business. He'd been happy to fill in for Steve Lipkins when the Berigan Band opened a two-week stand at the Roof Garden of Boston's swank Ritz-Carlton Hotel.

Bunny called a three P.M. opening day rehearsal. But as the musicians took their places under the Roof Garden's great striped awning, something was definitely not right. "It was the wind," said Privin. "It was making this kind of howling noise, and coming up in gusts. And the sky had gone a funny yellowish color. The air was heavy. It was scary."[53]

Berigan, none too steady on his feet, began counting off the first number. With a sound like a siren, a savage gust of wind tore a strip off the awning. The whole roof seemed to tremble. Attendants rushed to mend the rent, even as another gust tore an opposite end loose. The sky was darkening fast, the wind rising, driving sheets of rain before it.

511

"All at once there was this tremendous sound, like ripping and slamming together," Privin said, and a new, mighty blast of air tore the striped awning loose and whirled it away. The Roof Garden was suddenly a chaos of flying music, crashing music stands and chairs as fourteen terrified musicians dove for cover, leaving their leader, bemused, still trying to start the tune.

Unknown to Bunny Berigan—and to a network of fifteen government weather stations strung out along the U.S. eastern seaboard—a giant tropical storm had found a comfortable trough between two pressure fronts and churned north at express-train speed, picking up punch as it went. It had made landfall on Long Island at mid-day and at that very minute was bearing down on Massachusetts with winds clocked at well over a hundred miles an hour, spewing death and destruction across a wide area. The great hurricane of 1938 may not have been the biggest on record, but it hit New England with the force of utter surprise.

That could also be said for Bunny Berigan's orchestra. The band had spent much of its first year and a half on the road, largely because the long residencies in major hotels, bread and butter for name bands in the '30s, hadn't materialized. Though recommended by Benny Goodman, they'd lost a plum job at New York's Pennsylvania Hotel—largely, it turned out, because certain of the managers (and, presumably, executives at the Music Corporation of America, which controlled most of the venues) were apprehensive about Berigan's drinking.

Saxophonists Joe Dixon and Mike Doty, discouraged at a combination of sloppy management and flagging discipline, turned in their notices. Berigan, trying to win them back, promised that the band was about to land a spot on the brand-new Bob Hope radio show (Les Brown eventually got the job, and remained), that things would be better. "I told him flat out that he wasn't going anywhere because he was drunk all the time," Dixon said. "I had already turned down too many good opportunities."[54]

Bunny had had high hopes for the fortnight at the Ritz: a reversal of fortune, maybe? The first sign of a financial stability his band badly needed? What later came to be called "a wind to shake the world" whirled those hopes away as easily and mindlessly as it had whirled away the big striped awning. To many, saxophonist Gus Bivona among them, "it was more than [just] two weeks' work down the drain. It kind of broke Bunny's back. From then on everything seemed to be downhill."[55]

There were still good records, as "Jelly Roll Blues" more than shows—though some have found it easy to hear in those two grieving choruses a valedictory, foreshadowing ruination and early death. What's beyond dispute is that things for Berigan were sliding, and that he seemed powerless to stop them.

That November he used a nine-man personnel to record five Bix Beiderbecke compositions—In a Mist and the three other piano pieces, plus "Davenport Blues"—in arrangements by Joe Lipman. The idea, Lipman said, was to create a little band within the big band, as Goodman, Dorsey and the rest had done. They tried it out on a Saturday Night Swing Club broadcast, then took it to Victor.

Berigan's contributions to the date were above all reverential: he plays his parts with accuracy and concentration. If the performances never quite catch fire, it's probably because Beiderbecke's pianistic thinking doesn't quite translate to six horns, however carefully scored. Other arrangers, from Dick Cary to Michel Legrand, tackling this same material through the years, have encountered similar difficulties. All the same, there are poignant moments on In a Mist and even more on Candlelights, dominated by Berigan's wistful trumpet.

As from the start, Bunny was determined to remain one of the guys, never casting himself as the leader, never creating distance from his men. In Ray Conniff's words: "It was just one continuous good time, like a non-stop party. We were like a family of bad little boys, with Bunny the worst of them. He wouldn't hire anybody he didn't like. And you should've seen what went on in those hotel rooms!"[56]

Gus Bivona, Joe Dixon's replacement, takes up the narrative. "We'd check into a hotel, and the first thing we'd do was ask the porter to send up a hooker. We were just growing up then, you know. And Bunny—well, he liked to watch. I never saw him with a hooker, but he seemed to get a kick out of watching guys who were brave enough to perform in front of him."[57]

"We played Chicago," said Bivona, "the Panther Room of the Sherman. He was two or three weeks behind in our salaries. [Musicians' union czar James C.] Petrillo ordered all of us to be up in his office at a certain time one day. We all stood around this office, and he told Bunny, he says, 'You come up and stand in front of my desk.' And Petrillo really called him every name in the world, and said, 'Goddamn it, if you don't pay these guys I'm gonna knock that hotel down and put a parking lot there!' He was a pretty wild guy, and Bunny was scared to death. And don't you know, we all felt sorry for him: here he owed us money, and we were on his side when Petrillo was going at him!"[58]

For the public, the Chicago engagement was a hit. Chicago was close enough to Wisconsin to guarantee strong local support, and the four weeks ran easily to six. A few airchecks survive: on the Fletcher Henderson arrangement of "Sugar Foot Stomp," for example, Berigan plays an abandoned set of variations on the famed King Oliver solo. His power and range are intact, but there are inaccuracies, small goofs—and even a bit of random intonation, never before a Berigan concern.

There were other debts—to hotels, to the Greyhound Bus Company; Petrillo fined him a thousand dollars "for conduct unbecoming a member of the American Federation of Musicians." In late summer Berigan, hopelessly snowed under, declared bankruptcy—and, according to a front-page item in Down Beat, couldn't even scrape together the forty-dollar fee for the official petition.[59]

Everyone—colleagues, critics, fans—stayed firmly loyal. George T. Simon remembered the deference accorded Berigan when, in the early hours of Thursday, January 12, 1939, a band of Metronome readers' poll winners assembled at Victor's East 24th Street studios. "All the musicians worshiped this guy," Simon told the author. "And that night he was in fine shape. No problems at all. He just pitched in—and played great."[60]

It was certainly a band of friends and admirers—Benny Goodman, Tommy Dorsey, Jack Teagarden, Eddie Miller, Bob Zurke, Harry James, Charlie Spivak, and the rest. On "Blue Lou," Berigan is up first in the solo order: after a swaggering, four-bar opening phrase, he blasts out a high concert C. It's an affirmation, like a prizefighter who's been on the ropes a time or two bringing his gloves together over his head to proclaim, "See? I'm still the champ."

But two other takes of the same number, issued in recent years, show just how hard Bunny now had to work to win that reaffirmation. There was competition in the room, in the person of trumpeter Sonny Dunham, famed for his high-note displays with the Casa Loma Orchestra. Few of the others knew him, Simon said, and he was clearly out to prove himself in their company. His half-chorus, after spots by Teagarden and Miller, sounds almost defiant in its open challenge to Berigan.

Take -1 is a warmup, each soloist feeling his way—though Dunham can't resist a bit of rather untidily executed Roy Eldridge–style grandstanding. Take -2, the issued version, finds Bunny in assured form—and Dunham clearly stalking him around the ring. By take -3, Berigan has taken up the gauntlet, overdoes things—and Dunham, in response, screams out a shrill and rather querulous solo.

Early in 1940, Berigan abandoned the idea of leading a band altogether and found sanctuary in the very place that had begun his three bandleading years: in the trumpet section of his old friend Tommy Dorsey. He could still play, though by this time the erosion of tone, technique, and even the once effortless flow of ideas was all too readily apparent. It was often hit or miss.

But he could still come up with surprises, as Paul Weston, Joe Bushkin, and other veterans of that Dorsey band have attested. A recently discovered aircheck version of "I Found a New Baby," broadcast August 3, 1940, underscores the point: the rocking, medium-tempo Sy Oliver arrangement gives Berigan most of a full chorus, and he delivers—with a power and forcefulness easily equal to the best of his mid-'30s years.

Dorsey did his best to boost his old friend's name, giving him star billing (alongside Frank Sinatra and drummer Buddy Rich) in newspaper advertisements and even on theatre marquees. Sometimes, when Dorsey showed up late (or left early), he'd front the band. He took on a good deal of the lead book and, said Joe Bushkin, threw himself wholeheartedly into making this opportunity work.

And they had their fun. "Late at night, said Bushkin, "Tommy would want to play some trumpet. He'd grab Jimmy Blake's horn, and Bunny would toss me his—literally—from the brass section. I'd play it; Tommy and me, doing fours and stuff, while Bunny sat back there and enjoyed it."[61]

Berigan stayed with Dorsey five months; he recorded, and well, for the small Liberty Music Shop label, doing Cole Porter songs with Lee Wiley and a quartet including Bushkin. The entire session, breakdowns and all, has been issued: it shows Bunny still able to play at a high level—and functioning as peacemaker at a few of the singer's more temperamental moments.

But however good Dorsey's intentions, even so old a friendship couldn't survive the benders, the fallings on and off the wagon—and, most of all, the little disasters on the stand, to which Berigan seemed so prone. One night at the Hotel Astor, standing up to recapitulate his famed solo on "Marie," he fell backwards and out of sight: he'd eaten "supper" before the job, it turned out—a ham sandwich, washed down with twelve scotches. Ill-feeling grew between the two colleagues; there were arguments, reconciliations. More quarrels. Finally Dorsey, whose band was finding new popularity, decided he'd simply had enough. With much reluctance, he let Berigan go, replaced by the less inspired, but more reliable, Ziggy Elman.

The rest is sad beyond measure. A shrunken, enfeebled Berigan, taking out band after young band, straining and too often failing to recapture what had once come so easily; Simon and other friends scarcely able to conceal their dismay at the sight and sound of what seemed a "man trying to imitate himself."

Drummer Johnny Blowers never forgot an encounter around this time. "I was doing a kiddie show, on the twenty-second floor at CBS, at 485 Madison Avenue. I'm sitting outside in the hall, waiting to go in; suddenly someone kicks me in the bottom of the shoe. I looked up—and I wanted to cry. It was Bunny, but it took me a moment to realize that. He was thin, emaciated, almost unrecognizable. He was doing a guest shot on the Major Bowes show—Major *Bowes*, for pete's sake! We talked a while, and he said, 'C'mon, I want to have a drink.' I said, 'You know I can't do that.' It was ten in the morning. It all made me terribly sad. It still does. What a waste."[62]

Everybody rallied around him, helping out in fulfilling engagements, trying to keep a watchful eye. But it was all for nothing. Bunny Berigan died at New York's Polyclinic on June 2, 1942, with Tommy Dorsey, faithful to the end, at his bedside.

It's not enough, simply, to say that Bunny Berigan drank too much and that it finally killed him. To be sure, he was a jazzman at a time when most people in his business were drinkers, some of them to excess. But unlike Bix Beiderbecke, to whom he's so often compared, Berigan had a large and devoted support system, many of them people who were either non-drinkers or who had licked alcohol. Unlike Bix, he did not live his brief life half in shadow, hounded by private demons; he was a public figure, widely known and admired.

He'd had plenty of warning, moreover, of what might happen if he didn't cut back. As early as 1938, Berigan's doctor had told him he had cirrhosis of the liver and would be dead within five years if he didn't stop. "I drove his big Chrysler Imperial on the road once in a while, with him out cold on the back seat," Joe Dixon said. "There were times when he'd wake up from a dead sleep, all perspired and hysterical, and I'd have to head for the nearest bar or liquor store and get some brandy. He'd swallow between half a pint and a pint of the stuff before he'd calm down."

Some, unfairly, blamed Donna Berigan for not turning the miracle that would have saved her husband. Joe Bushkin cited the pressures of leading a band as at least a contributing factor. "He had no head for business. Didn't care about it. His idea of the perfect life was when he had that group at the Famous Door and was doing broadcasts at CBS during the days."[63]

From the day Bunny Berigan died, the adulation that had surrounded him in life seemed to transmute itself into the beatification which has colored subsequent evaluation of him. To that degree, Gunther Schuller and others are right: the mythologizing process too often distorts, and often all but obscures, the reality, as it has done for figures as disparate as Beiderbecke and Charlie Parker.

Berigan's recorded work, moreover, is not always easy to evaluate. The Victor records made in 1937 and thereafter, when he was leading his own band, have been far more accessible, reissued far more widely and for longer periods, than the much superior earlier material. The second "I Can't Get Started," for example, has appeared in countless forms, in anthologies and Berigan collections beyond number. Even now it's played regularly on the radio. The 1936 Vocalion, by contrast, was for years available in only one LP, often hard to find, and for a short time as part of a boxed set in the Time-Life *Giants of Jazz* series.

A similar fate has befallen the often thrilling performances with the Dorsey Brothers, Dick McDonough, Adrian Rollini, Paul Whiteman, Chick Bullock, Red McKenzie, the Boswell Sisters, Mildred Bailey, and the rest. Most evaluations of Billie Holiday records of the '30s place their emphasis on her work with Lester Young and his colleagues from the Basie band, passing lightly over her 1936 efforts with Berigan. The Fred Rich and Victor Young records cited earlier have seldom, if ever, been reissued.

The imbalance has resulted in a perception of Bunny Berigan's strengths and musical stature posited on the weakest portion of the evidence. No one, listening to the dozens of solos recorded by Berigan between 1931 and 1936, can fail to perceive their eloquence and consistent beauty, allied to great strength and technical command. To be sure, Roy Eldridge, Buck Clayton, Red Allen, Jonah Jones, Bill Coleman, Sidney De Paris, and the rest had their sublime moments. But it takes nothing from them to acknowledge that Bunny Berigan simply had something extra, something rare and striking, to set him apart. Something special, that is, in the magic department.

"If you met him," said Joe Bushkin, "and didn't have any idea he was a musician, you'd still know he was an intensely talented, gifted guy. There was just something about him—a kind of radiance. So intense about everything. Everything he did—well, you knew he did it all the way. His way. And there was nothing for you to do but go with him."[64]

And go with him they did, even when they weren't sure where it might lead them. "Remember, we were all very young, very eager to play and please Bunny," said Joe Dixon. "He had that about him, and it was great. We loved him, and for the moment, for a while, that was enough."

21

Guitars, Solo and in Combination

"**G**eorge, would you like to keep my guitar till tomorrow?" The youngster shook his head, uncertain he'd heard right. Was his idol, the great Eddie Lang, really offering overnight guardianship of his precious instrument?

"Well, how about it, George? Would you like to?" This time it was his father speaking, rousing him from a reverie equal parts incredulity and awe. "Well, sure," he managed at last, looking at both men. "Sure. I'd love to."

"Fine," said Lang, smiling. "I'll pick it up tomorrow on my way to work."

So it happened that George Van Eps, age twelve, found the expressive medium that would dominate the rest of his life—and whose destiny in jazz he, in turn, would help shape over more than half a century.

It wasn't exactly a shot in the dark. His father, Fred Van Eps, was a revered music figure, whose technique and imagination had lifted the banjo out of its folk and salon tradition into a new virtuosity. He'd begun recording on Edison wax cylinders in the 1890s, and since 1914 his Van Eps Trio had never stopped making successful records. Songwriters and fellow-musicians wrote specialty pieces for him, trying to push his skill to its limits. (One such vehicle, "Banjo Ballet," by the trio's pianist, Felix Arndt, took on a new name when Arndt found a surefire way of impressing a new girlfriend. As "Nola," it became a lasting popular favorite.)

All four of Fred Van Eps's sons, born in New Jersey at two-year-intervals beginning in 1907, were musical: Fred junior became a trumpet player; Bobby took to the piano, John the saxophone; George, the youngest, inherited one of his father's banjos.

An unusual family, they were at once musicians and precision craftsmen, fascinated with machines and how they worked—and why. A Van Eps had to be able to take a given device apart and rebuild it, improving on its design in the process. Watchmaking, passed carefully from generation to generation, was a family specialty.

Appropriately, this mechanical bent led George directly to Eddie Lang. "My brother Bob and I had built a little crystal radio," he said in clear, detailed reminiscence. "One of the first things we brought in was a broadcast by the Roger Wolfe Kahn Orchestra, playing in the Pennsylvania Hotel Grille. They were on the air every night, on WEAF/WJZ.

"Joe Venuti and Eddie Lang were in that band. Even as horrible as the sound was on our little crystal set, I could hear the sound of the guitar. It had a singing quality. Maybe it sounds strange to say it this way now, but the first time I heard that sound I decided, 'That's for me. That's what I want to do.' "[1]

In the mid-'20s Eddie Lang stood virtually alone in his use of the guitar as both accompaniment and solo instrument. He'd arrived there with difficulty: most dance band leaders preferred the more penetrating metallic sound of the banjo. Guitar, they'd say, was too soft, too easily drowned out by brass and reeds, and swamped in a rhythm section by piano, tuba, and drums.

When the electric microphone came along, its new clarity giving the guitar a chance to be heard on radio and records, Eddie Lang was among its earliest beneficiaries: on scores of discs made between 1925 and his sudden death in 1933, he introduced and perfected an accompaniment style combining the punch of straight rhythm with the variety of chordal and single-string melodic passages.

"For me, the records where Lang really shines," said latter-day guitarist Marty Grosz, "are the ones on which he has to accompany singers pretty much all by himself; it sometimes seems that the worse the singer, the more interesting and imaginative his accompaniment. It's as if he realized he had to be the whole show, and just rose to the occasion."[2]

Examples abound. Backing St. Louis blues singer Alma Henderson on "You Can't Have It Unless I Give It to You" and "I've Got a Daddy Down in New Orleans" in 1927, Lang's settings are models of variety and clarity. He joins King Oliver, Clarence Williams, and other masters behind Victoria Spivey on "My Handy Man" and "Organ Grinder Blues" on a 1928 issue. Williams's rather unsteady piano is audible throughout, but Lang effectively is the rhythm section, soloing briefly on the latter title and ending with a fetching G-to-E figure which he repeats, up an octave, as an easily executed acoustical harmonic.*

---

*In the interests of clarity, several guitar-related terms will be defined as they occur. Harmonics, in this context, are an acoustical phenomenon, based on the fact that a string, plucked or bowed, vibrates both as a whole and in two or three (or more) equal parts. Vibration of the whole string produces its fundamental, or basic note; shortening it produces higher pitches. Additionally, each vibrating length of string (or tubing, in the case of wind instruments) also can produce other overtones of substantially higher pitch, with a tone which has been variously described as "silvery" and even "ghostly." On

One of his best vocal accompaniments is on "Under the Moon," recorded in June 1927 with sixteen-year-old Annette Hanshaw. After a particularly rhythmic ensemble (by Lang, Joe Venuti, bass saxophonist Adrian Rollini, and Vic Berton's jaunty "hot" tympani), the guitarist fashions a decorous *rubato* introduction, then leads the obviously nervous young singer (she makes a false entrance) into her chorus.

"Lang was an excellent harmonist," said Van Eps. "He knew the fingerboard very well, and that big sound you hear on the records—that's no gimmick. He ... just positioned himself close to the microphone. He was the trailblazer for all of us."

Young George soon got a chance to meet his idol. By 1925 Van Eps *père*, not content merely to play banjos, was also manufacturing them. He'd set up a factory in Plainfield, New Jersey, and his instruments were popular from the start. "They were exquisite," his son said. "As you'd imagine, he was a good inventor and a fine craftsman. If he made a banjo, everybody just knew it was going to be tops."

That year, the nation's musical instrument makers held their major annual promotional exposition at New York's Pennsylvania Hotel. Each firm took a suite on one of the upper floors; dealers, musicians, educators, buyers would drop in, talk to the salesmen, and try out the latest products. Young George's job was to demonstrate the plectrum banjo, accompanied by his brother Bob at the piano. Their father, meanwhile, demonstrated the tenor and five-string models.*

"When dinnertime came around, as you can imagine, down to the Grille we went, and there was the Kahn band, this marvelous band with Arthur Schutt, Joe Venuti, Vic Berton, Alfie Evans—all those great guys in it. And Eddie Lang. There I was, looking right across the dance floor at my idol."

---

the guitar, violin, and other stringed instruments, these are most often obtained by exerting light pressure at the halfway point (and other divisions) of an open or stopped string during plucking or bowing.

*The long-necked five-string banjo, familiar from minstrelsy and early folk ensembles, is fundamental to the American vernacular tradition. Its strings are a low C, an octave below the piano's middle C, then a G-major triad, G-B-D, beginning with the G a fifth above the basic C. Pitched above that is an upper "drone" string, generally tuned to G above middle C, but mounted below the bottom C. By the beginning of the '20s, most dance band banjoists had discarded the drone string, not even mounting it on the instrument. The result was the four-string plectrum (so-named for the pick used in its playing) banjo, which soon replaced the five-string models in all but folk-related ensembles. Plectrum banjoists of the early jazz years included Jack Bland, of the Mound City Blue Blowers; Lew (or Lou) Black, with the New Orleans Rhythm Kings (shown in some photographs playing a five-string instrument *sans* the drone string); and Bob Gillette, with the Wolverines. Eddie Condon, originally a plectrum banjoist, kept its tuning when he switched to the four-string guitar.

The short-necked tenor banjo, coming into wide use in the 1920s, tuned its four strings in open fifths, beginning with the same low C. This C-G-D-A tuning, identical to that of the viola, gave it a broader open range than the plectrum and made it more accessible to string players—violinists, violists, mandolin players—who wished to play it in dance orchestras. Its higher chord voicings had greater penetrating and carrying power in that pre-microphone era but often lacked the plectrum's depth; easily identified in rhythm sections through its clanging, metallic sound, the tenor was banjo of choice for Dave Wilborn, of McKinney's Cotton Pickers; Fred Guy, with Duke Ellington; and Mike Pingitore, longtime fixture of Paul Whiteman's orchestra, among others.

Fred Van Eps had come prepared with a surefire way to entice not only Lang but the entire Kahn band up to his suite when they finished playing. "He made the most marvelous corn whiskey," said George. "Meticulously blended, as you'd expect, absolutely safe—and '200 proof.' He'd brought two gallons of the stuff in with him and served it with grapefruit juice to all the people he knew who came in to look at the instruments.

"On that first night, when the band finished at the Grille, why, up they came, fast as you could imagine." What started as an informal gathering soon developed into a jam session, the Van Eps boys joining in, and lasted into the wee hours. When things finally broke up, Lang was quick to notice young George eyeing his Gibson L-4 guitar. It was then that he asked the fateful question and got the boy's tremulous reply.[3]

"Naturally I didn't get any sleep that night," Van Eps recalled. "I had the guitar—and that turned out to be the end of the banjo for me. Not long afterward I went to a music store in Newark, where I'd been told I could get a discount. I bought a forty-dollar Martin guitar—I couldn't afford one of those Gibsons. But it was enough: I was on my way."[4]

Around the time young Van Eps was staring at Eddie Lang's L-4, another former banjoist was finding destiny in the form of a six-string guitar. Richard Tobin McDonough had come to the tenor banjo while a high school student on Manhattan's West Side via its close relative, the mandolin. He'd played banjo all through Georgetown University, and once back in New York had soon established himself as a capable sideman.

In mid-1925 he joined an orchestra led by Ross Gorman, the versatile reed-man who had devised and executed the opening glissando and clarinet solo on George Gershwin's *Rhapsody in Blue* in its Aeolian Hall debut the previous year. Gorman's unit, heard nightly in Earl Carroll's *Vanities* revue, also included such "hot" talent as Red Nichols on cornet and Miff Mole on trombone.

Sometime in the year or so he spent with Gorman, McDonough began playing guitar with some regularity. He's featured on "I'm Sittin' on Top of the World," both in a half-chorus solo and as a prominent rhythm accompanist in two passages with Red and Miff. The style is almost identical to that of Lang, both in the single-string solos and in the method of accompaniment—even to a two-bar whole-tone chordal substitution in the middle of a Nichols cornet solo.

Here and on such other Gorman records as "No More Worryin' " and "I'd Rather Be the Girl in Your Arms," he's quick, rhythmically agile, technically clean. From then on, McDonough is never far from recording and broadcasting studios; but there's little sign at first of the unique sound—a blend of single-line and chordal techniques—that identifies his later work.

Now a third figure enters the picture. Carl Kress, of Newark, New Jersey, was three years McDonough's junior and, like him, had started as a tenor banjoist. But when he switched to guitar it was on his own terms: first to tenor guitar, tuning its four strings in the open-fifths C-G-D-A pattern of the banjo, but pulling a variation by dropping the top A-string an octave to permit closer voicing of chords.

With this peculiar hybrid in hand, he showed up for his first big-time re-cording date, the January 12, 1928, Paul Whiteman Victor session that produced "San." It's hard to imagine how the twenty-one-year-old newcomer felt walking into Liederkranz Hall, on Manhattan's Upper East Side, and seeing such men as Bix Beiderbecke, Frank Trumbauer, and Jimmy Dorsey; though not yet widely known to the public, all three were heroes to any musician, white or black, who aspired to play hot music. Bill Challis, the arranger, had decided that "San," a musicians' favorite since its appearance in 1924, should be done by a cut-down "hot" combination, with rhythm guitar replacing the orchestra's regular banjoist, Mike Pingitore.

Interviewed years later, Whiteman described the scene: "We needed a guitar [especially] to back up Matty Malneck's hot fiddle chorus on 'San.' Kress . . . fished out of a dilapidated box what looked to me like a ukulele. I called Roy Bargy aside and told him we couldn't use a ukulele in our big band. Bargy only smiled. He knew how Kress played, and a few minutes later I realized too that this boy could make a four-string guitar sound like a harp."[5]

The sound of Kress behind Malneck's carefully programmed "San" solo is indeed high and a little uke-like, lacking the depth that would have been afforded by two extra strings. But the chording (including some whole-tone stuff) is firm, the rhythm supple. Kress soon graduated to a six-string instrument, retaining and extending the same banjo-oriented tuning he'd used on the smaller instrument. That remained consistent throughout his long career, determining the largely chordal solo style that became the Kress hallmark.[6]

Kress made his record with Whiteman only four days after an event that proved deeply significant for each of these men, and for the history of jazz guitar throughout the following decade. On Sunday, January 8, 1928, the great Spanish guitar virtuoso Andrés Segovia made his American recital debut at New York's Town Hall; many guitarists of serious aspiration, regardless of style, were in the audience.[7]

As music historian-lexicographer Nicolas Slonimsky has put it, Segovia "did much to reinstate the guitar as a concert instrument capable of a variety of ex-pression," and his playing that night opened new possibilities in the minds of players who until then had thought mostly in terms of accompaniment. It also inspired a new burst of popularity for "finger-style" playing, in which the gui-tarist plucks the strings with the digits of the right hand, rather than using a pick.[8]

As the 1930s began, the small circle of white guitarists dominated by Eddie Lang reigned supreme in hot music circles. Now and then an outsider, such as four-string converted banjoist Eddie Condon, would attract some attention; but on the evidence of most testimony, and of the hundreds of records made in New York in those years, the field clearly belonged to Lang, McDonough, Kress, and

Van Eps, with a retinue of capable journeyman players in their footsteps. Among the best of the latter were Tony Colucci, John Cali, Perry Botkin, Frank Victor, Darrell Calker, and California Ramblers alumnus Tommy Felline.

The role of black guitarists at this stage is less focused, therefore more difficult to chart. Will Johnson, with Luis Russell's band at the Saratoga Club, and Lawrence Lucie, arriving in 1931, were respected as unfussy, dependable time-keepers. Neither man seems to have had serious aspirations as a soloist, though Johnson now and then got off some good single-string blues choruses. Among slightly older players, New Orleans veterans Johnny St. Cyr and Bud Scott (both playing the six-string hybrid "guitar-banjo," combining the neck and tuning of the former with the body of the latter) understood their instrument's rhythm function well; but St. Cyr's solo efforts, typified by his sixteen bars on "Willie the Weeper," with Louis Armstrong's Hot Seven, show him not yet able to deliver a melodic solo without losing his rhythmic balance.

The one black guitarist of the 1920s most often cited as a seminal figure is Lonnie Johnson. Born in New Orleans, he spent a few years working the Mississippi riverboats, then settled briefly in St. Louis, where in 1925 he won a blues talent contest sponsored by OKeh Records. His prize was a chance to record regularly for OKeh, "placed" on records with Louis Armstrong, Duke Ellington, McKinney's Cotton Pickers (recording as "the Chocolate Dandies"), and numerous blues singers. He also recorded several duets with Lang (as "Blind Willie Dunn") for the label's "race" catalogue, marketed to black audiences.

In a sleeve essay to Columbia's two-volume *Fifty Years of Jazz Guitar* in 1976, blues historian Lawrence Cohn ranks Johnson with Lang as one of the two major guitar innovators of the '20s, an assessment echoed by Doug Caldwell in *Guitar* magazine. In view of Johnson's work on record, such claims seem altogether too inclusive in their implications of musical range and depth.

To be sure, such performances as his own "6/88 Glide" and "Four Hands Are Better Than Two," and his exchange of breaks with Armstrong on "Hotter Than That" (all recorded in 1927), show his playing to have been fluent and supple, but at the same time pattern-bound and lacking harmonic or melodic variety. "Star Dust," recorded with the McKinney group, finds him struggling with colors and textures, and a chord structure, quite beyond his expressive range. He attacks his half-chorus as if it were a blues, using accidentals which in the harmonic and melodic circumstances of "Star Dust" are simply wrong. The solo all but derails the rest of the performance.

Johnson is more comfortable in his blues duets with "Blind Willie Dunn," who lets him play most of the lead and solos on their nine selections (except on "Guitar Blues," where they alternate) and complements him with chordally and rhythmically varied backings. No wonder Johnson, in later life, remembered Lang as "the nicest man I ever worked with . . . He never argued. He didn't tell me what to do. He would ask me. Then, if everything was okay, we'd sit down and get to jiving. I've never seen a cat like him since. He could play guitar better than anyone I know. And I've seen plenty in my day."[9]

Lang, too, clearly enjoyed the encounters and may have picked up useful blues tips from them. But any suggestion that Johnson was a major shaping force on his *pro tem* partner outside the relatively narrow context of the blues seems to contradict a large and compelling body of recorded evidence.[10]

George Van Eps, meanwhile, was working regularly around New York as 1927 began, subbing for fellow-guitarists, and practicing with a kind of quiet, focused fervor. Then, a few weeks after the 1929 Wall Street crash, came a major break: Dick McDonough left Smith Ballew's band to go to Boston as part of the orchestra that conductor Donald Voorhees was organizing for Ruth Selwyn's new *Nine-Fifteen Revue*. Bob Van Eps, Ballew's pianist, quickly nominated his sixteen-year-old kid brother as a replacement.[11]

It was a good band, and Bobby a resourceful arranger, who used Ballew's eleven men in imaginative ways. Lead trumpeter J. D. Wade, for example, doubled on mellophone, which blended well with the four reeds. "Instead of tight clusters, though, he'd open things up so there would be these big open voicings," said George. "It would make the band sound much bigger than just eleven pieces. He'd use the mellophone in its lower register, for example—there was no trombone in the band. That could give us a sound like a chamber orchestra. Remember, with a few exceptions arrangers in the late '20s weren't thinking with a purely orchestral mind; they weren't too careful about the way they voiced things, about the weight they gave to different instruments in the voicings."

(Robert Van Eps played piano and arranged for several major bands, including the Dorsey Brothers unit of the early '30s. He later enjoyed a successful career as a California studio musician. A solo LP made toward the end of his life reveals a pianist of technique and imagination, reminiscent at times of Art Tatum. Yet this Van Eps brother remains perpetually in shadow, unknown even to many jazz enthusiasts. "Part of it was that Rob wasn't too fond of playing in front of a big audience," said George. "I think he lost a lot of opportunities to present himself in clubs and other places as a soloist because of that. And don't think he wasn't invited: he was, and often. But that's the way people are constituted, isn't it? The public really didn't know about Rob, but other musicians did. He was very deeply respected by guys who were in the know.")[12]

In late 1930 Ballew made an unconventional move. Joe Venuti and Eddie Lang were fresh back from California, where they'd filmed *The King of Jazz* with Whiteman. Ballew, a longtime friend and admirer, decided to add them to his band as a team, while retaining Van Eps. The young guitarist was delighted.

"Here I was all of a sudden, sitting beside my idol," he said. "Come to think of it, we were probably the first band in the United States to carry two guitars on a regular basis. I learned such a lot from him—and not just about the guitar. He was a marvelous man, a very kind, very thoughtful, very aware individual. And very intelligent. You couldn't help being in awe of him all the time."[13]

Recorded evidence of the association exists. On "You're Simply Delish," Venuti solos for sixteen bars over a rhythm section which clearly includes two guitars.

He lets the pair take the bridge, Lang laying down a solid accompaniment to Van Eps's chorded solo part, then returns to finish out the chorus.

An excellent ballad singer, Texas-born Ballew appears to have been a man of taste and sensitivity, willing to take a risk now and then in the interests of good music. Another beneficiary was Bix Beiderbecke, added to the band briefly in 1931. (George Van Eps remembered it as being in winter, possibly January or February. This appears to contradict other evidence placing the cornetist's time with Ballew in early summer.)

They were working at Salzman's, a restaurant on East 42nd Street diagonally across from Grand Central Station. Beiderbecke had spent more than two months at home in Davenport, Iowa, trying to dry out, and wasn't doing well. "He was starving to death," the guitarist said.

> Everybody was plying him with gin and he wasn't eating worth a damn. So Smith, being a nice guy, invited him to join, just to play jazz choruses.
>
> It was kinda sad. He'd stand up to play a solo, and it just wouldn't come out any good. He'd take the horn away from his mouth, fiddle with the valves—then hand it to J. D. Wade, our first trumpet player, and J. D. would check it over and hand it back to him, saying there was nothing wrong with it.
>
> But the funny thing is that during intermissions he'd sit at the piano—he was writing *Candlelights* at that time—and play *beautifully*. I mean impeccably. Of course it didn't involve anything as variable as embouchure, and his coordination at the keyboard was unimpaired. My brother Rob, as a piano player who'd grown up listening to Bix, was always there. Bix would finish something, improvising beautifully with that fertile harmonic mind of his, and he'd look up and say, "Where's Bobby? I want Bobby." And my brother would be there all the time, leaning on the piano on the bass side, as close as he could get without actually sitting beside Bix."[14]

The beginning of 1932 found Lang, McDonough, Kress, and Van Eps all freelancing around New York, in and out of radio and recording studios, and spending their evenings holding down steady jobs in dance bands. Van Eps has estimated that in a single year around that time he recorded more than twenty-two hundred sides, most as just an anonymous ensemble musician. If not an exaggeration, the figure may represent an aggregate total over several years. Whatever the case, there can be no doubt that he, and the rest of them, spent a lot of time facing microphones.[15]

Through their efforts, individually and collectively, it was now possible to think of guitar as both versatile accompaniment *and* solo instrument, able to sustain listener interest over long passages. Individual approaches differed, but largely in matters of technique, tuning, and detail. When McDonough solos on "In de Ruff" (a retitled "Dippermouth Blues") with Venuti, or Kress gets a full chorus on Frank Trumbauer's 1936 " 'S Wonderful," they're working off a common notion about the guitar and how it operates.

It's a concept rooted in understanding of strengths and limitations. By voicing chords with the melody note on top, for example, players could execute passages which were melodically attractive and completely harmonized, making the guitar in effect a miniature orchestra. Lang had opened the way to duo playing, teaming with Johnson in the '20s, then recording two widely admired duets ("Picking My Way," "Feelin' My Way") with Kress in 1932. They were by any standard a departure, symbiotic yet formal, each instrument's role worked out in terms of the other.

Guitar duets were a tradition in European music. There is evidence that the popularity of piano, four hands, in the late eighteenth century found at least informal parallel in combinations of two guitars. In both cases the assignment of roles is the same: one player is the "right hand," or carrier of melody, the other the "left," or accompanist. That two jazz guitarists in America should have essayed much the same thing was brand-new. But in this instance, too, the lessons of Segovia had been well learned: why not use the guitar this way?

In early 1934 Kress and McDonough took the process a step further with records of two duets: "Stage Fright" and "Danzon." Both are highly virtuosic, requiring deep understanding of the instrument's resources; so, too, with "Chicken à la Swing" three years later. At one point in "Stage Fright," McDonough and Kress play chordal glissandi (continuous sliding from one chord to another) in opposite directions, simply by moving the fingers of the left hand, grouped to form a chord, up or down the fingerboard; such effects, easily executed on the guitar, are not available to the piano.[16]

"The New York guitar players were, in general, very strongly affected by the classical tradition," said guitarist Art Ryerson, who arrived in 1935 from Ohio. "That and the Italian style, originating with the mandolin. It was a more—how shall I say it?—*guitaristic* style than, say, the blues guys or some of the single-string players."[17]

Throughout the early '30s guitarists everywhere were incorporating the New Yorkers' blend of single-string and chordal techniques. But elsewhere—in other cities, other regions, even other countries—local traditions modified and sometimes reconfigured the example. This is nowhere so clear as in the music called "western swing," which developed and thrived during those years in Texas, Oklahoma, and surrounding states.

Jazz chroniclers have long lavished attention on black "territory bands" of the Southwest: the sense of rhythmic and ensemble freedom they brought to the '30s; their role as incubators for major soloists. Saxophonists Lester Young, Herschel Evans, Ben Webster, Buddy Tate, and many other top jazzmen apprenticed in these bands, and their stories form a key chapter in the music's development.

Musicians who played in the "western swing" bands (or, as they were called in the 1930s, "hot string bands") of Texas and Oklahoma have been dealt with rather differently. All but ignored by jazz historians, they've been "rediscovered" and deeply researched by scholars of country music. Carefully documented articles have appeared regularly in such periodicals as the *Journal of Country Music*; reissues of records by Bob Wills, Milton Brown, Adolph Hofner, and other major figures appear regularly, but always aimed at country music buyers.

Yet as even cursory listening to the records of these groups reveals, the music they played was discernibly jazz, with improvising "hot" soloists, driving rhythm sections, and ensemble interplay. It's not long before any attempt to examine such artistic segregation runs into a thicket of social, class, and racial perceptions. Just as most of the blues-inflected territory bands are popularly understood to have been black (there *were* white ones, little documented, throughout the South and Southwest), the "western swing" units are widely considered not only a white phenomenon but a white "cracker" one. Scholars seem to perceive the two types of ensembles, and the music they play, as twin emblems of a segregated, Deep South mentality whose divisions remained in place long after the civil rights movement had begun to transform the rest of the nation.

Not surprisingly, given its geographic isolation, western swing is a unique hybrid, cross-fertilizing a variety of jazz and blues influences (many absorbed via radio and records) with the distinctive sounds and accents of Appalachia, the rural South and Southwest, and Mexico.

Guitarist Adolph Hofner brought things nicely into focus when he described listening with equal ardor to Bing Crosby and to the "singing brakeman" of the '20s, Jimmie Rodgers. C. G. "Sleepy" Johnson, guitarist of the Light Crust Dough-boys, a pivotal western swing unit, recalled going to furniture stores where "race" records were sold, copying the blues lyrics, and refitting them to melodies he and his colleagues thought more appropriate to their own playing styles.

(This situation is further complicated by the presence, also in Texas and Oklahoma, of a close-knit and surprisingly large circle of jazzmen working not in the western bands but in more conventional itinerant hot dance units. Among them were, at various times, trombonist Jack Teagarden, clarinetists Bob Mc-Cracken and Pee Wee Russell, and the Houston pianist John "Peck" Kelley. Such New Orleans–based musicians as trumpeter Wingy Manone and clarinetists Leon Roppolo and Sidney Arodin were also frequent members of these white territory bands. Their comings and goings seem to have paralleled but only seldom inter-sected those of the western swing musicians. Texas-born saxophonist Drew Page has left a vivid description of his early years in these bands in his autobiographical *Drew's Blues*.[18]

(Ross Russell, in his *Jazz Style in Kansas City and the Southwest*, remarks that white territory bands that concentrated on hot music generally had a tougher time than their black counterparts. "Black orchestras . . . were all doing well," he wrote, "but apparently the public refused to take the white jazz musician seriously." Most southwestern whites, he said, regarded jazz as "a typical and exotic style played by black musicians, and something of a novelty or musical joke when played by white men."[19]

(Many jazzmen active in this region, both in the western swing bands and in the "territorial" units, eventually settled on the West Coast, where they inter-mingled with other veterans on the California traditional jazz scene of the late '40s and '50s. Page's book, among others, shows the Southwest to be an area ripe for serious and exhaustive scholarly research in this field.)

Western swing bred several generations of musicians notable for proficiency and, in many cases, real originality. Easily the central figure in this movement, though not himself an improvising musician, was the violinist James Robert "Bob" Wills: from the mid-1930s until well into the '70s his "Texas Playboys" included such gifted soloists as Leon McAuliffe and Eldon Shamblin (guitar), Jesse Ashlock (violin), Danny Alguire, Benny Strickler and Alex Brashear (trumpet), and mandolinist Tiny Moore, the last-named equally skilled as a violinist.

In *San Antonio Rose*, his 1976 biography of Wills, Charles R. Townsend writes that the guitarists who worked for Wills in those years "deserve more credit for their pioneer efforts than the meager praise a few writers have grudgingly given them. Most writers have tended to overemphasize the influence on them of Djan-go Reinhardt and Charlie Christian and thereby overlook the innovativeness and creativity of Shamblin and McAuliffe."

Townsend is especially critical of an article in *Rolling Stone* magazine praising Shamblin but representing him as only a disciple, even imitator, of Christian and Reinhardt. "Shamblin's style had already matured before he heard Christian," he writes. "Charlie did not make any records until late in 1939; Shamblin recorded with Wills in the spring of 1938. Since Christian was playing in Oklahoma City at the very time Shamblin and McAuliffe were experimenting with guitar styles and helping make the instrument more significant in a popular dance band, it is just as possible that Christian learned a great deal in those years from listening to Wills's guitarists, especially Eldon Shamblin, over [radio station] KVOO and on recordings."[20]

Guitarist Les Paul added independent testimony to the suggestion that Sham-blin was far more important and influential than is generally acknowledged. In the late '30s, he said, he heard the Playboys on a late-night radio remote from Tulsa and was sufficiently intrigued to sub out his Chicago network job for a few days and hop a Greyhound to Oklahoma City to investigate what he'd heard. In the audience on one occasion, he said, was a thin black kid who asked—rather diffidently, Paul remembered—if he could try the visitor's guitar. "It was Charlie Christian, of course, and he was so good he surprised us all."[21]

Throughout their long career, the Texas Playboys walked a line between the string band tradition associated with the Southwest (though actually, in various forms, a national phenomenon) and a jazz approach incorporating the ensemble textures of small improvising groups and larger swing bands. Sometimes their records were pure examples of one style or another; just as often they were eclectic, a blend, always with attractive drive, spirit, and ensemble cohesion.

A glance at the Wills discography yields some extremes of repertoire: such small-band staples as "I Wish I Could Shimmy Like My Sister Kate" and "Basin Street Blues" and standard pop songs of the "Alexander's Ragtime Band" variety stand comfortably alongside "Downhearted Blues" and "Mississippi Delta Blues" and such out-and-out country material as "Beaumont Rag" and the leader's own "San Antonio Rose."

For a long time the idiom had no fixed name. Then, in 1941, Metronome magazine started calling it "western swing," and the name stuck. By then, Wills had achieved unprecedented popularity throughout the Southwest, national sales of his records competing well with those of the major swing bands. Cornetist Danny Alguire, later a staff artist with the Walt Disney Studios (and a founder-member of the boisterous Firehouse Five Plus Two dixieland band), recalled hearing the Playboys at the Trianon Ballroom in Oklahoma City in 1941. "It took me fifteen minutes to get upstairs," he told Townsend. "I never saw such a crowd in my life . . . There must have been twenty-five hundred people there."

The band, he said, "had a beat that wouldn't quit. If you couldn't dance that beat, you can't walk. Your ears started to prick up as you heard that swingin' beat. Gee, what a beautiful bunch of musicians. They played so well together." The band was divided in two, he said, "with horns and regular western setup. The sax section as a whole blended beautifully."[22]

Wills's band grew out of a quartet, the Light Crust Doughboys, which appeared on several Texas and Oklahoma radio stations in the early '30s; another alumnus of that group, vocalist Milton Brown, later led his own "Brownies," which some have hailed as musically the most innovative of the genre. It was short-lived, effectively ending with Brown's death in a 1936 auto crash.

Historian Gary Ginell marshals impressive evidence to support his contention that Brown, not Wills, deserves credit as the "father of western swing." Brown, he says, introduced slap-style bass and jazz piano (played by Wanna Coffman and Fred Calhoun, respectively) into the Texas string bands. Perhaps even farther-reaching was Brown's use in the Brownies of electrified steel (or Hawaiian-style) guitar.[23]

And it is at this point that the imposing figure of steel guitarist Bob Dunn enters the picture. According to historian Kevin Reed Coffey, Dunn electrified his steel guitar early, using the resultant power and amplitude in unexpected ways. "Not content with just being louder, Dunn experimented with ways to capture the brassy resonance of jazz horns. According to surviving contemporaries, he emulated musicians such as Texas trombonist Jack Teagarden and the great trumpeter Louis Armstrong, and his approach to the steel was based on their styles, their tone, their phrasing and attack."[24]

Dunn dampened his strings not with the left, or "bar," hand but with his right, or "picking," hand, allowing this to control the duration of his notes and match a staccato, trumpet-like effect with the sliding, trombonish sounds produced by the bar. If Charlie Christian heard Shamblin and others at this time, he surely heard Dunn; it's equally likely, says Coffey, that such southwesterners as Eddie Durham and Floyd Smith, both early converts to amplified guitar, heard Dunn on the radio.

According to Bill Malone in Country Music USA, Dunn "converted a standard round-hole Martin guitar into an electric instrument by magnetizing the strings and raising them high off the box. He then attached an electric pickup to the guitar, which in turn was connected to a Vol-U-Tone amplifier . . . Since the electrical amplifier was already being commercially distributed by 1934, it is highly possible that somewhere someone had already attached a guitar pickup to it." Dunn's first use of this equipment on record was at a January 1935 recording session in Chicago. Country fiddler Jimmy Thomason said that Dunn "ran into this black guy who was playing a steel guitar with a homemade pickup attached to it. He had this thing hooked up through an old radio or something and was playing these blues licks." Such experiments paralleled those of George Van Eps and, even earlier, Les Paul, discussed presently.[25]

Though said to be inconsistent when recording, Dunn is in top form on the Brownies' "Some of These Days" and "Fan It," and on "When You're Smiling" and "Old Joe Turner Blues" (very clarinet-like phrasing here), recorded for Decca with Cliff Bruner's Texas Wanderers in September 1938.

Brown's guitarist brother Durwood (sometimes spelled "Derwood") and banjoist O. C. Stockard also have attractive moments. Stockard digs in with a percussive single-string attack on "Brownie's Stomp," a pastiche coupling the breaks-all-around format of "Bugle Call Rag" with solos on the "Tiger Rag" chord sequence. Just how closely Durwood Brown has been listening to Eddie Lang is clear on "Do the Hula Lou" and the eight-bar blues "Just Sitting on Top of the World," where he underpins vocal and ensemble passages in much the same chord-and-bass-line manner used by Lang in backing Lonnie Johnson.[26]

Any doubt that the music played by these bands was truly jazz, and an exciting and original form of it, quickly evaporates on hearing such efforts as "Fort Worth Stomp," recorded in Dallas June 19, 1937, by a group calling itself the Crystal Springs Ramblers. Fort Worth's Crystal Springs dance pavilion was something of a musical and spiritual home for western swing in general and Bob Wills in particular. It also achieved momentary notoriety as a hangout for Bonnie Parker and Clyde Barrow, the "Bonnie and Clyde" of Depression-era legend. Of the musicians on the Ramblers date, hot fiddler Joe Holley was a frequent Wills associate, and all the others belonged to the same circle of players.

"Fort Worth Stomp" offers a driving rhythm section and a full-chorus solo by an excellent alto saxophonist (discographies list Earl Driver as playing tenor on the date, but the saxophone is clearly an alto). He's obviously listened to all the prominent alto men: Benny Carter and Johnny Hodges live side by side in his playing with Jimmy Dorsey and Frank Trumbauer. But the style, however hybrid, is his own.

Though capable hornmen emerged from the western swing bands (among them trumpeters Strickler, Brashear, and "Tubby" Lewis, and tenor saxophonist "Zeb" McNally), the idiom's most important soloists were the string players. Recorded solos by banjoist Stockard, guitarists McAuliffe and Shamblin, and mandolinist Moore are as startling now for their coherence and swing as they were in 1937.

(Just how close the work of the western swing musicians was at times to that of the great eastern jazzmen becomes clear on an early '70s LP, issued on the Flying Fish label. Titled *'S Wonderful*, it teams violin pioneer Joe Venuti with Shamblin, steel guitarist Curley Chalker and mandolinist Jethro Burns, best known as part of the "Homer 'n' Jethro" comedy team. Backed by a straightforward rhythm section, the four men have themselves a fine, compatible time.)

Though their influence on the jazz mainstream has been slight, western swing bands have been a potent force in the country field, and through it on pop music: an *Austin City Limits* telecast of the late '80s, for example, found country stars Willie Nelson, Merle Haggard, and Johnny Cash backed by an excellent western swing unit featuring Moore and an accomplished, but unidentified, hot cornet soloist.[27]

The historical importance of western swing and its best soloists seems beyond dispute. Whether as a matter of innovation (Dunn's adaptation of his instrument to the expanded possibilities of amplification), cross-fertilization of influences into a style transcending eclecticism, or just the straightforward ability to swing, these bands belong to any serious consideration of '30s jazz. Without them, the story lacks a colorful—and in several respects critical—dimension.

Among guitarists active in the South during this period, surely the most tantalizing is Mississippian Edwin MacIntosh "Snoozer" Quinn (1906–49), who spent most of his adult life in and around New Orleans. Friends boasted that he was better than Eddie Lang, and that his failure to record more in his prime robbed jazz history of one of its most original soloists. Some of the claims made for him, in fact, sound remarkably like those made on behalf of the short-lived and unrecorded New Orleans cornetist Emmett Hardy (chapter 3).

Unlike Hardy, Quinn *does* appear on records, most made during his eight months as a member of Paul Whiteman's orchestra. "It was Bix and Tram who were responsible for getting him into the band," said cornetist Johnny Wiggs. Whiteman had played the St. Charles Theatre in New Orleans Sunday evening, October 28, 1928, and after the show Beiderbecke and several others went to a party at the home of Paul Mares, cornetist with the New Orleans Rhythm Kings. There they heard Quinn play, and were hooked.

Back to the St. Charles they went, where they "contrived to have him begin an impromptu concert for the maestro." Whiteman, seated in a swivel chair backstage, whirled around after hearing a few bars of Quinn's "Tiger Rag" demonstration piece. "Man, what is that you're playing?" he bellowed, "and where have you been all this time?" He hired him on the spot, Wiggs reported.[28]

(Quinn's employment with Whiteman has generated one of those interminable wrangles among jazz chroniclers and discographers which often display all the passion and intensity of Talmudic disputations. Was he or wasn't he on records made by Whiteman and Trumbauer units of early 1929? For all its frustrating attention to minutiae, the argument has relevance in assessment of Snoozer Quinn's potential significance among jazzmen of his day. Outstanding guitar soloists were not a commonplace, and reports of a potential newcomer were cause for much stir among musicians. Moreover, news sometimes traveled slowly from one part of the country to another, lending accounts of regional virtuosi an almost mythic quality.)

Standard discographies identify Eddie Lang as the guitarist on small-band OKeh dates made under Frank Trumbauer's name in early 1929. Yet the standard Whiteman contract of this time stipulated that any band member making records on his own, under his own leadership, had to use other Whiteman musicians where possible. Therefore Trumbauer would have drawn his personnels from among his bandmates, except in those instances where Whiteman musicians could not supply what was needed. Freelance drummer Stan King, for example, could lay down a beat quite beyond the capabilities of Whiteman's regular man, George Marsh.

Between February and May 1929, Snoozer Quinn was a full-time member of the Whiteman entourage, the first time the "King of Jazz" had carried a regular guitar. Rhythm duties usually fell to banjoist Mike Pingitore, with trombonist Wilbur Hall doubling on guitar now and then, and Eddie Lang coming in for important occasions. Given, especially, that Trumbauer and Beiderbecke were directly responsible for Quinn's employment, it seems curious that the saxophonist, assembling sidemen for record sessions of his own, would *not* have used him. Yet all available discographical data, and Trumbauer's own diary, for the dates of March 8, April 17 and 30, May 15, 21, and 22, list Lang on guitar.[29]

That Quinn was popular with the Whiteman musicians is well established. Colleagues remembered the guitarist saying, after his return to New Orleans, that Whiteman had "worn him out taking him around to parties and other off-hour affairs." Tor Magnusson and Don Peak, writing in 1992, cite a report in the New Orleans periodical *The Prelude* that Quinn was back in his home city by May 10, 1929. He is known to have made a January 10 date at Columbia as part of a Whiteman unit backing singer Bee Palmer; he is definitely present on Bing Crosby's Columbia session of March 14 ("My Kinda Love," "Till We Meet") and may have made a Willard Robison date the following day.[30]

Even that narrow compass leaves open at least the theoretical possibility that Quinn, not Lang, is the guitarist on Trumbauer's recordings of "Futuristic Rhythm" and "Raisin' the Roof." If he remained in New York through April, he also could be on "Baby, Won't You Please Come Home?," "Louise," and "Wait Till You See 'Ma Cherie.' "

Documentation is more problematic. Magnusson and Peak quote jazz scholar Philip R. Evans in saying that when he interviewed Roy Bargy and others for *Bix: Man and Legend*, they did not remember Snoozer having been on the Trumbauer dates. Evans and Larry Kiner are categorical, moreover, in identifying the guitarist on these titles as Lang.[31]

Yet two kinds of evidence seem to speak for Quinn's presence. First, a simple matter of logic, cited by Magnusson and Peak: would Trumbauer, having helped bring Quinn into Whiteman's orchestra, have snubbed him repeatedly in organizing record dates—dates on which he was contractually bound to employ Whiteman musicians wherever possible—instead bringing in Eddie Lang, who was not at that point a Whiteman musician?[32]

Equally compelling is the evidence of the music itself. To the experienced ear, the guitarist on Trumbauer OKeh records made between March 8 and May 22, 1929, neither sounds nor *feels* like Eddie Lang—whereas the guitar on records made by similar groups beginning that September clearly does.

No two rhythm players hear their basic pulse the same way. Some (Eddie Condon and the other white Chicagoans come readily to mind) tend to play "high up" on the beat—i.e., at its front edge—creating a feeling of urgency, of tense excitement. Others "lay back," playing a fraction *behind* the basic pulse. The result, at its best, is a sense of relaxation, of "cool." This found its extreme apotheosis in white California jazz of the '50s, with its emotionally rather detached quality.

One of the salient features of Eddie Lang's rhythm playing is that it rides squarely on the pulse. To what degree becomes clear on "From Monday On," with vocalist and "blue-blowing" expert Red McKenzie, where Lang and Condon play together. Throughout the performance Condon's banjo pushes the beat, riding a hair's breadth ahead of Lang's guitar. They're obviously feeling—and demarcating—the pulse in two different places, and the disparity remains consistent throughout.

The guitarist on the spring 1929 Trumbauer records does not play squarely on the pulse, in the manner of Lang, but a fraction *behind*. It's particularly noticeable on "Shivery Stomp": for comparison of Lang's way of dealing with a similar tempo and feel, there is "Sunny Side Up," recorded by Trumbauer and many of the same musicians that October 10, after Quinn's departure. Lang is immediately recognizable, solidly on the beat, and his rhythm accompaniment abounds in all the little guitaristic touches associated with him—touches not evident on "Shivery Stomp."

Yet there is also the 1959 testimony of drummer-mellophonist Arthur "Monk" Hazel that Quinn stayed in New York no more than "a month, a month and a half." The guitarist had written to Hazel, complaining that "they never did put him in the band; all Whiteman used him for was to take him around to these parties, and entertain Whiteman's friends . . . he was telling me . . . that he was going to quit, that he just couldn't take it any more. They wouldn't let him sleep; he wasn't making any records, or things like that. So he quit Whiteman and he come [sic] on home, and never did go out of town any more after that."[33]

Young Les Paul, fascinated by reports about "this guy who's as good as Lang," paid Quinn a visit in New Orleans. "I found him on his front porch," said Paul. "He played for me, and he *was* remarkable. Could hammer out a solo with one hand, all sorts of stuff. But he had a lotta things going against him: for one thing, his face was deformed. It was—well, kinda crooked on his head. He was also sick a lot. But he was a really remarkable player; I just sat there and listened to him."[34]

Saxophonist Drew Page described an encounter with Quinn in an apartment in downtown Galveston, Texas: "[Quinn] had a favorite trick of playing a solo with one hand while lighting a cigarette with the other . . . Snoozer was a retiring sort of person, who lived with his guitar, carrying it around with him wherever he went. Some nights we sat out on a pier, listening to him play until sunup."[35]

Quinn is known to have recorded with country blues singer (and future Louisiana governor) Jimmie "Sunshine" Davis in 1931, but the guitar-playing on "The Davis Special" is in a rather rudimentary, rural blues manner. The guitarist of "My Kinda Love" is not discernible in this performance.

Illness forced Snoozer to stop playing professionally around 1940. Confined to a sanitorium, he recorded eleven titles in 1948 on a portable machine brought along by cornetist Johnny Wiggs. It is on the basis of these, above all, that he can be judged as an interesting and often original guitar stylist.

In at least one sense his solo style is as regional as that of the Texas men, combining a chordal approach reminiscent of Lang and Kress with the kind of blues delivery found in Lonnie Johnson. Even on ballad material he almost never indulges in *rubato*, instead reinforcing his single-string and harmonized melody lines with strummed rhythm chords. At times, as on an up-tempo "You Took Advantage of Me," the effect is not unlike that generated by the Lang-Johnson duets. Yet his "Snoozer's Telephone Blues" is redolent of the playing on the Jimmie Davis records.

These "location" recordings suggest that, had Quinn remained active during the '30s, challenged by others and recording regularly, he might have made a wider impact. There's a tantalizing rural blues strain in his work, quite unlike anything associated with Lang and the other white New Yorkers, and blending comfortably with the chordal and rhythmic sophistication of his jazz work.

But these are late performances. What changes had Quinn's playing undergone in the nearly two decades since his months in the New York spotlight? Was he, in 1929, the guitarist heard in 1948? The records with Jimmie Davis suggest, if Quinn is indeed the player, that the blues component was always present. But to what degree? And how expressed?

Snoozer Quinn died in 1949, and the answers to such questions appear to have died with him.[36]

Perhaps the farthest-reaching, most profound example of Eddie Lang's effect on guitarists of his time was acted out at a point even more distant from New York than Texas or New Orleans. Jean Baptiste "Django" Reinhardt was a Belgian gypsy, a self-taught guitarist who since the late '20s had been a familiar figure in the cafés and *bistros* of Paris. British bandleader-entrepreneur Jack Hylton heard him there in the autumn of 1928 and immediately offered him a job. But early on the morning of November 2, the wagon in which the guitarist lived near the city limits caught fire, and Reinhardt barely escaped with his life.

With his left, or chording, hand badly disfigured by burns, he relearned the guitar, developing—partly in compensation—a technique at once dazzling and unconventional. In the words of American guitarist Art Ryerson, a declared admirer: "He had that gypsy temperament. For him there were no restraints, no barriers: whatever the task, he just went ahead and did it. It was a kind of wildness, really, and in this case it produced amazing results."[37]

Photographs of Reinhardt indicate that two fingers of his left hand were badly burned, leaving two and a thumb to form unusual chord positions. But, Art Ryerson once warned, it would be a mistake to write off the two damaged fingers

533

altogether: "The third finger wasn't a hundred percent, but he could use it about two-thirds of the time, and he could even use the damaged fourth once in a while." He described various effects obtainable with a technique called "barring," in which one or two fingers are laid across the strings in the manner of a metal capo (or the solid bar of the Texas steel guitar) and another finger moves to vary the resultant pitch from there.

Simply retuning his guitar, as Kress had done, might have made things easier for him. But Reinhardt took another path: the instrument was a challenge, and he had no choice but to accept it. In a recent discussion, the young American guitarist Frank Vignola called attention to Reinhardt's distinctive chordal inversions: "They're things other players didn't use, because they didn't have to. There are records he made in the '20s, before his accident, and he's playing more or less standard inversions. I think it's safe to say he owes a lot of the uniqueness of his way of playing, ironically, to the handicap caused by the fire."[38]

Reinhardt's biographers tell of a night sometime in 1929 when Emile Savitry, an artist who had traveled widely, first played the guitarist a few American hot jazz records. "Ach moune! My brother!" he is reported to have exclaimed, tears in his eyes, after hearing Louis Armstrong for the first time. Also among the records he heard that night were several by the Venuti Blue Four, with Lang on guitar.[39]

Violinist Stephane Grappelly met Reinhardt when they were both members of a small tea-room band led by bassist-accordionist Louis Vola. Changing a string one day during a break, Grappelly began to tune up, playing fragments of songs as he went. Django, sitting in a corner, quickly fell in behind him. "I remember we did *Dinah*," the violinist said, "and we decided every day to do like Eddie Lang and Joe Venuti to amuse ourselves."[40]

Django and Grappelly quickly became the second major violin-and-guitar team in jazz. By the mid-'30s, their many recordings together, most of them as members of the government-sponsored Quintette of the Hot Club of France, had created a sensation among collectors and musicians on both sides of the Atlantic.

Reinhardt was something quite improbable, an original and vital hot stylist who had never set foot in the United States. Though initially inspired by Lang, he seemed to owe little direct debt to him or any of the other Americans: above all, his daredevil single-string solos, interspersed with rolls, glisses, rifle-shot punctuations, and biting chordal passages, seemed to reflect his gypsy heritage. Certainly his tone, vibrato, and attack bespoke that background: in his hands the guitar sang a passionate, rhapsodic song.

"Pay special attention to that vibrato," said Vignola. "It comes of pressure on the fingerboard. Your fingers have to be very, very strong. Sometimes it reminds me of the vibrato used by Piaf and the singers who followed her: fast, emotional, nothing hidden or held back. Vulnerable. The passion just jumps out at you."[41]

Reinhardt the jazzman was a curious mixture. His strengths as a soloist are beyond dispute: an irresistible drive, especially at fast tempos ("Lily Belle May June," March, 1935) and the technical command necessary to bring it off; a fertile, sometimes quite affecting, ability to make melodies of his solos ("Hot Lips," June 1937); a florid rhapsodic sense, particularly effective in his *a capella* solo guitar inventions.

Between 1934 and shortly before his death in 1953 he recorded often and well, turning out compelling solos by the dozen. There is the almost savage drive of 1936's "Limehouse Blues" or Walter Donaldson's "I've Had My Moments" in 1935; the tenderness of his opening solo and accompaniment for singer Jean Sablon on the 1934 "Je Sais Que Vous Êtes Jolie"; the infectious joy of his partnerships with such visiting Americans as Bill Coleman, Dicky Wells, Rex Stewart, Arthur Briggs, Eddie South—and, most of all, Benny Carter and Coleman Hawkins. In short, something for everyone. It is hard to imagine anyone, exposed to this creative dynamo, not falling in love with the very sound of him.[42]

A 1943 *Down Beat* article hailed him as "The Tatum of The Guitar," adding that unlike piano wizard Art Tatum, Reinhardt "seldom if ever succumbs to the temptation to sacrifice jazz instincts and principles for the sake of sheer exhibitionism."[43]

Django in a rhythm section could occasionally be somewhat less effective. Within the congenial setting of the Quintet, with two other guitarists (one of them often his younger brother, Joseph) and a bass laying down a chunky, backbeat-accented pulse (not unlike that of the western swing bands) he could be a kind of drummer's left hand, propelling things forward with accents and chordal "shots," leading from one chorus to another (as going into the final *tutti* of "Hot Lips") with three-against-four tremolo bursts.

In more conventional surroundings his rhythm playing sometimes became stiff and surprisingly inflexible. Behind Benny Carter's trumpet solo on "Sweet Georgia Brown," for example, he almost disrupts the 4/4 flow of Tommy Benford's drumming. And the idea of a smooth, unaccented four-to-the-bar in the manner of Freddie Green seems simply to have eluded him, as February 20, 1940, performances of "Panassie Stomp" and "Rock-a-Bye Basie" with saxophonist Alix Combelle's big band indicate.

Still, the sheer sweep of Reinhardt's playing, the emotive punch it packs, easily compensates for such lapses. It is fascinating to hear the relative simplicity of his early style evolving in adaptation to new harmonic complexities—but always on its own terms. The sheer quantity of material, and its duplication on myriad labels, can turn Django record-hunting into confused muddle; but Reinhardt compilations seem always to sell, and nothing remains out of catalogue for long.

He recorded his own composition "Nuages" (Clouds) often, and comparison of several performances is useful. The first, and probably best-known, version is from a December 13, 1940, session and features Django with a revamped QHCF. In Grappelly's place are two clarinetists, Combelle and Hubert Rostaing, with Joseph Reinhardt's rhythm guitar plus bass and drums. Django's solo begins with eight bars of carefully measured harmonics, before opening out into characteristic double-time runs and flourishes. He recorded it again in Brussels on May 8, 1942, this time backed by Stan Brenders' large studio orchestra. Hearing Reinhardt's imagination blossoming over a string-section is an experience not to be missed: the ear can almost follow his thinking as he discovers the expressive possibilities.

Reunited with Grappelly in London, he recorded another "Nuages" (January 31, 1946), this time with a British two-guitars-and-bass rhythm team as backing. Two takes done that day are startlingly different: on one he reverts to the pensive harmonics of the 1940 solo in a charming but unadventuresome way, but on the other he unleashes a torrent of ideas, of sheer *incident*, compelling in its urgency. In Max Abrams's felicitous observation, it simply "dazzles the thought of the listener and [challenges] him to follow Django's route."[44]

By August 25, 1947, when he recorded yet another version with a new group (including the excellent pianist Eddie Bernard), Django had been to the United States on what should have been a triumphal tour. But a combination of poor planning, Reinhardt's own irresponsibility, and his unfamiliarity with the electric guitar he was given to play turned it into something not far short of disaster. Even a month's engagement at Barney Josephson's Café Society Uptown fell short of expectation, critics complaining that the hero of so many exciting prewar records had failed to strike sparks in person.

In his 1947 "Nuages," Django all but turns his back on the past, charging into a fresh-sounding, unamplified solo with new zest. It is almost completely in double-time, save for one emphatic declarative passage shortly after mid-point, and explores the harmonic implications of the song as never before. Bebop has arrived, and Reinhardt is clearly aware, if only intuitively, of its expanded vocabulary. The feel, the conventions of execution, may still belong to his past style, but the chromaticism and harmonic frame of reference are new. There is even a point at which he boldly plays an unlikely sustained G against an Ab7 chord: it works because he takes it into an almost enharmonic realm, a series of figures constructed almost entirely of upper chordal voices.

A reunion in Rome with André Ekyan produced a "Nuages" that seems at first almost an affectionate backward glance. Django begins, as he did in 1940, with harmonics, but there's been an important change: he's now playing electric guitar and is already exploring the amplified instrument's ability to sustain notes. Unlike the 1946 and '47 versions, this solo displays no fireworks, no double-time bursts. This is a study in economy, full of relatively brief phrases, widely spaced.

He's still thinking along these lines in a February 1951 radio broadcast from the Club St. Germain in Paris. Surrounded by such "modern" musicians as the brothers Hubert and Raymond Fol (alto and piano, respectively), he further investigates the same terrain, this time even throwing in a couple of emblematic flatted fifths—as if to say, "Ach, *mon vieux*, nobody's going to slip anything by Django."

There is one final "Nuages," made March 10, 1953, only two months before his death. In its directness and simplicity, its avoidance of flourish, it is perhaps the most affecting of all. Reinhardt lets his lovely melody speak for itself, his mastery of the electric guitar complete: he understands how to make it work *for* him, accentuating his sound and inflections. It is a fitting valedictory to an extraordinary jazz career.

Django Reinhardt found many admirers, but few disciples, among American guitarists of his day. Art Ryerson and Les Paul were dedicated fans, and according to some musicians the little-recorded guitarist Zeb Julian emulated some of the Belgian's single-string approach. It's even possible to hear traces of Reinhardt in the attack and rhythmic thrust of Eddie Durham's electric guitar solos on the Kansas City Five and Six records of 1938. But elsewhere he remains, like Pee Wee Russell and Jack Teagarden, a unique identity, distinctive enough not to be easily assimilable into the styles of others through any means save outright imitation. For illustration it is useful to consider Charlie Christian, whose linear, saxophone-like approach proved sufficiently generic to find its way easily into the work of subsequent guitar generations.

The contrast between Reinhardt and the Americans finds vivid illustration in "Spring Fever," one of four duets recorded in London in 1935 by English guitarists Albert Harris and Ivor Mairants. Its opening strain, taken at a medium-fast tempo, is derived unmistakably from the chordally based duo efforts of the New Yorkers; but the slow middle section, in minor, is just as clearly inspired by Reinhardt's single-string virtuosity. The differences are striking and linger vividly in memory.

European imitators of Reinhardt were—and remain—easier to find. Canadian-born guitarist William "Diz" Disley, for example, carried his fealty to an extreme, slipping into the Django *persona* as if it were a new overcoat (even to playing the same model Maccaferri guitar) and working for a time with Stephane Grappelly. Among today's players, Frank Vignola has shown that it is possible to incorporate features of Reinhardt's style—tone, attack, certain phrase shapes and matters of conception—successfully into a highly personal manner *without* seeming to imitate. The gypsy Birelli Lagrene has displayed many Reinhardt-like traits—though they often seem as much the result of a shared cultural background as of direct influence.[45]

Any discussion of jazz guitar in Paris during this period must also include mention of Argentine-born Oscar Alemán, who arrived in Europe in 1927 and left in the early days of World War II. His crisp swing and stinging attack place him somewhere between Reinhardt and the blues-inflected guitarist Teddy Bunn. Alemán, too, seems to have been at home playing his instrument's European concert repertoire. According to several reports he gave recitals at which he would devote half the program to Bach, Fernando Sor, and others, then after the intermission turn to jazz with equal skill.[46]

By 1935, George Van Eps was well established among fellow-musicians as the "underground guru of the guitar," in Marty Grosz's colorful phrase: teacher and theoretician, innovator and virtuoso, he was also advancing the very technology of the instrument he played. When, that year, the Epiphone Company finally built a reliable and tonally distortion-free guitar amplifier, Van Eps was quick to respond: he bought one, began using it with the Ray Noble band.

"Noble didn't like it," he said. "But when we played one-nighters, especially in places with noisy crowds or poor acoustics, the things we did could now be heard. The piano didn't have to take the guitar solos."

Wisconsin-born Les Paul, another restless and inventive mind, had incorporated electricity early, probably around the time of Bob Dunn's first discoveries. Like the Texan, he adapted radios—and movie projectors and other devices—in designing an amplifier which would not distort the guitar's tone. Unlike Van Eps, he all but forsook the acoustic instrument, working instead toward an indigenous amplified sound and approach. This led him to a formidable array of sounds and timbres, many achieved on electronic devices of his own invention—sometimes even making use of the very tonal distortions Van Eps had sought to avoid.[47]

Where Paul confined his experiments to amplification and recording, Van Eps's curiosity about how things worked spilled over into other fields. In the garage of his home in Freeport, Long Island, he designed and built a full-size wooden flying boat. Though he had a pilot's license, he said, he was less interested in actually flying his creation than in the specifics of its design and construction.[48]

In the winter of 1938–39, George's technological interest in his instrument yielded a major breakthrough: a guitar with seven strings, rather than the conventional six. While he respected Carl Kress's playing, his friend's changes in tuning were not for him. "What Carl did was fascinating to listen to," he said, "but it didn't change much over the years, didn't develop. It couldn't: the voicings he'd locked himself into didn't allow him to change. Besides, I didn't want to destroy that beautiful classic six-string guitar tuning. After all, it had evolved over a long time. It hadn't been thought up by any one person but had come about naturally."

Instead, he decided to add a low A-string, giving the guitar both a bottom register adaptable to bass lines and a chord-voicing potential equal to that of Kress's altered tuning—but without the limitations. The three tuning configurations, then, afforded the following spans:

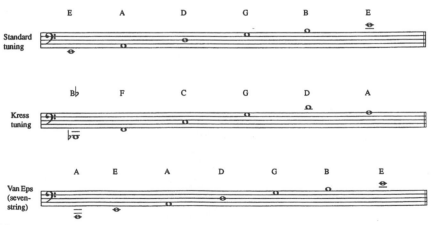

Guitar tunings: standard, Kress, Van Eps

Carmen Mastren, himself a polished and versatile soloist, spoke for most colleagues when he exclaimed that Van Eps "sounds like a piano when he plays. He gives you the bass, the melody, the treble and chords all at the same time." Even before adding his seventh string, George had become, in Mastren's phrase, the "guitar player's guitar player," taking the instrument to new heights of technique and mastery.[49]

In essence, guitarist Bucky Pizzarelli has said, "George did for modern-day Spanish [i.e., conventional] guitar what Segovia had done for classical guitar. Made it a complete orchestral instrument." Van Eps seemed eager to reinforce the point, referring to the seven-string guitar as his "lap piano."[50]

For all the records he played on in those years, Van Eps soloed but infrequently; there is a certain temptation to read this as evidence of a scientist's preference for his laboratory. Still, there is his sparkling duet with Red Norvo on "Honeysuckle Rose," discussed in chapter 26. Van Eps also is a key player on Adrian Rollini's memorable Decca session of October 23, 1934, and his sixteen-bar solo on "Somebody Loves Me" is a model of clarity. Like McDonough, he plays in what may be termed a *chord-supported* style: that is, blending some single-string passages with the almost exclusively chordal manner of Kress. Both Van Eps and McDonough mix elements freely: sometimes there will be a passage of harmonized melody, the guitar functioning like the saxophone section of a big band. Other times the thrust will be a single- or double-string line, reinforced and balanced by chordal punctuation.[51]

Ironically, Van Eps's finest expositions of his own solo style at this point appear to be on two records long credited to McDonough. Privately recorded in 1933 or '34, they were first issued in the '70s as part of an LP anthology devoted to McDonough and Kress. Things might have gone on that way indefinitely but for a chance remark in 1993 by Bob Haggart, Van Eps's former guitar student turned bassist, with younger guitarist Howard Alden in attendance.

They were on tour in Germany. Over dinner, Haggart got to reminiscing. Shortly after taking up the bass he'd recorded a couple of duets with Van Eps, but as far as he knew they'd not been issued at the time. He hummed a few bars of one of the numbers. Wait a minute, said Alden: I know that piece. He'd learned it off the anthology LP, which identified it as "The Ramble," played by McDonough and bassist Artie Bernstein. Van Eps, astonished, confirmed that he and Haggart had indeed been the performers.

A second piece on the anthology, also attributed to McDonough, also turned out to be Van Eps's work; that was "Chasin' a Buck," originally called "The Chant" (no relation to the 1926 Mel Stitzel piece of the same name). "George was even more surprised at that," said Alden, because "he'd recorded it privately on his brother's equipment and had no idea how it got into circulation." (A third guitar solo, "Honeysuckle Rose," which appeared on the same LP, was indeed played by McDonough.)

"It's true that the right-hand figures, the use of the plectrum, sounds a lot like McDonough," said Alden. "But listen to the left hand, the chordal movement. That's pure Van Eps. All the same, it's easy to see how people would have been fooled by it." With that new perspective, a listener can now recognize "The

539

Chant" as characteristic Van Eps, a finely tooled precision work in which the liberating influence of Segovia is keenly perceived, and the line defining "jazz guitar" as a separate entity blurs almost beyond recognition.[52]

Some of the most distinctive examples of the Van Eps style come not from its originator but from his star pupil. The name of Allan Reuss seldom arises in discussions of jazz guitar, chiefly because he is so little known as a soloist. His was the strong pulse that knit the somewhat disjunct (and in Gene Krupa's case, downright erratic) elements of Benny Goodman's rhythm section into a smoothly functioning team between 1935 and 1938.[53]

Van Eps had been Goodman's original choice and is present on most records made by the band between mid-1934 and autumn of 1935. But Glenn Miller, assembling an all-star American band (Bud Freeman, Johnny Mince, and Pee Wee Erwin) for Ray Noble to lead at the brand-new Rainbow Room, atop Radio City, made the guitarist an offer, which he took. "I delivered my prize pupil to Benny," he said. One of a small and gifted circle of Van Eps students, Reuss had been with the "underground guru" four years and absorbed every aspect of his technique. Like his teacher, he had come to terms with amplification, using it discreetly to boost his volume level when needed.[54]

Reuss takes a full solo chorus on Goodman's "If I Could Be With You One Hour Tonight," and, sure enough, the style is pristine Van Eps: chordal passages alternate with chord-supported single-and double-string figures to shape a small essay on the melody and chords of James P. Johnson's fetching little song. The coherence and structural balance of this solo seem to support Van Eps's assertion that he helped Reuss work out at least its shape, if not every point of detail.

Four years later, as a member of Jack Teagarden's big band, Reuss recorded his (and, by extension, his teacher's) masterpiece. "Pickin' for Patsy" is a *tour de force*, which does for the acoustic chordal style (discreet amplification is used) what Charlie Christian's "Solo Flight" with Goodman was shortly to do for single-string amplified playing.

After leading four clarinets through an attractive and quite chromatic melody statement, Reuss decides to mix and match; whether playing over a saxophone chord cushion or trading licks with the brass, he delivers his single-string and octave lines and chordal passages with incisiveness and punch. Finally he punctuates a chorus of band riffs and winds things up neatly on a broad *rallentando*. "Pickin' for Patsy" might have impressed musicians, but it seems to have missed the public entirely; it's among the least-reissued of all Jack Teagarden records— which must be counted a great loss to appreciation of a rich, varied guitar style.

(Perhaps the best chance to evaluate Reuss on record comes on an April 7, 1946, date for Harry Lim's Keynote label, featuring alto saxophonist Benny Carter and issued under the name of the excellent pianist Arnold Ross. Reuss, unamplified, solos on each of the four numbers; his combination of single-string and chordal passages is clearly derived from Van Eps, but the warmth and suppleness of conception are emphatically his own. Each of his solos is a standout: whirling and plunging on an up-tempo "Bye Bye Blues"; chatting amiably on "The Moon Is Low"; a lyrically contemplative half-chorus on "I Don't Know Why." Multiple versions of several numbers disclose development of the guitarist's choruses from take to take.)

Van Eps himself is both composer and focus of three band selections issued in March 1938, under the leadership of drummer Bill Harty, who had come to America with, and ultimately managed, Ray Noble. "Bill Harty Presents a George Van Eps Musicale," reads the label of each; indeed, all three are presented— staged, even—like salon showcases.

"Squattin' at the Grotto," for example, has been carefully worked out and arranged, figures and episodes fitting the overall mechanism like the wheels and gears of a timepiece. George and brother Bob deliver their parts impeccably, as do trumpeter George Thow, clarinetist Payton Legare, and the others. But at no point does the guitar play a solo of any length or containing any improvisation. "Squattin' " remains more exercise than expression.

For more extensive consideration of George Van Eps on record it's necessary to move forward to the late '40s and early '50s. As is usual with Van Eps, such performances as "Kay's Fantasy," "I Wrote It for Jo" (dedicated to daughter and wife, respectively), and two others done for Clive Acker's Los Angeles–based Jump label in 1949 are finely tooled creations. They show a style virtually un-changed since the '30s, as comparison with the guitarist's brief appearances on such Ray Noble records as "Dinner for One, Please, James" and "Bugle Call Rag" make clear.

Van Eps's later work on record illustrates the extent to which he thinks of the guitar orchestrally, as solo and accompaniment in one. His reading of "Once in a While," from the Jump session, is full of complexities—deftly executed single-string triplet passages, chordal underpinning rich in inner movement, full use of chromatics—not to mention the kind of open voicing afforded by the seventh string. Yet its logic, its utter clarity, makes even the most involved mo-ments sound simple.

Clive Acker chuckled every time he recalled Bucky Pizzarelli's remark as they sat listening, one night in a Texas motel room, to a test recording of Bix Bei-derbecke's *Candlelights*, arranged by Bill Challis for five top guitarists—Pizzarelli, Ryerson, Allen Hanlon, Barry Galbraith, and Howard Collins—with no loss of clarity. "Sounds like George, doesn't it?" said Bucky.

Compared to Van Eps, Dick McDonough is easy to find on records of the early and mid-1930s. He is given most of a chorus on "Honeysuckle Rose," from the March 31, 1937, *Jam Session at Victor*, and makes much of it. In substance, the solo consists of a series of four-bar episodes, each showcasing one aspect of Mc-Donough's way with his instrument: the first episode offers a melody line with supporting notes, the second a self-contained, guitaristic little set-piece built on ascending and descending triplets; the third is a closely voiced block chord figure, and the fourth a clanging ostinato, also chordally rendered, with a repeated A♭ on top.[55]

Unlike Van Eps, McDonough also recorded single-string solos. His tone, light-er and prettier than Lang's and softer-edged than Reinhardt's, is particularly attractive when it takes the lead over an ensemble. He does that on "Hiawatha's Lullaby," from Joe Venuti's first date after the unexpected death of Eddie Lang, setting out the melody in vocalized fashion, with Venuti's violin and Jimmy Dorsey's clarinet playing discreet supporting roles.

When the violinist convened a Blue Six session on October 2, 1933, to do four sides for John Hammond, he gave McDonough most of the opening chorus lead on "Sweet Lorraine." Again, violin and clarinet (this time Benny Goodman) furnish the harmony, with Bud Freeman's tenor adding comments at the end of every four bars.

The essence, the best distillation of the acoustic guitar style, lies in a combination of the four McDonough-Kress duets, recorded between early 1934 and early 1937, the 1934 Van Eps solos, and Kress's solo album of 1939, the first by a guitarist. In common with the "rhythmic novelty" piano instrumentals of the '20s and even the saxophone set-pieces of Jimmy Dorsey and others, these guitar pieces employ the full vocabulary of the jazz improviser. That they also happen to have been set down as formal music seems secondary, no more relevant than the fact that various of the great jazz soloists, black and white, found it useful to "routine"—shape and polish—solos on given numbers until they were, in effect, miniature works in their own right.

What, then, separates "The Chant" or Kress's elegiac "Afterthoughts" of 1939 (written as a memorial to McDonough, who died the previous year)—or, for that matter, the various unaccompanied "improvisations" and meditations of Reinhardt—from solos by such master-writers for the guitar as Villa-Lobos and Rodrigo? Very little, it seems. Guitarists, particularly the white masters of the acoustic school, seem to have felt unusually close kinship to their instrument's long and diverse tradition.

But the tradition exacted its compromises. Compared with the other instruments of the jazz band, the acoustic guitar seems a delicate, even fragile, expressive vessel. Without the power to make itself heard, its ability to sustain notes severely limited, it does not so much command attention as *invite* it. That Lang, Van Eps, Kress, McDonough, Reuss, Mastren, Dave Barbour, and other outstanding guitarists received the exposure they did, at a time when even miking their instrument properly was a problem, attests to the esteem in which they were held among colleagues.

With this in mind it's easy to appreciate the impact of electrification on young guitarists coming of age toward the end of the '30s. Suddenly, miraculously, they had a way of holding their own with the horns, able to sustain notes as well as (and in some cases better than) a wind instrument.

Shortly after Charlie Christian joined Benny Goodman's orchestra in 1939, his name appeared as author of a *Down Beat* article exhorting guitarists, "Wire for sound; Let 'Em Hear You Play." Electrification, he said, heralded the "dawn of a new era" and had given guitarists "a new lease on life." He singled out Allan Reuss's amplified sound on "Pickin' for Patsy" as an example of what could be gained. "Musicians have been aware of Reuss's ability for several years, but the instrument is subtle and the public probably would never have realized his ability if they'd had to strain their ears to catch the niceties of his technique and the beauty of his improvisations," he said. The *Down Beat* piece failed to mention that Reuss, like his teacher Van Eps, had used amplification only very discreetly, and that the improved microphones of the '30s had made unamplified acoustic guitar plainly audible on records and radio.[56]

Christian's exhortations found their target. Young guitarists, eager to be heard, plugged in and stepped up to new volume levels, concentrating more and more on the kind of single-string solos which were winning attention from such influential (though hardly disinterested) observers as John Hammond. The stampede left its casualties: as amplification spread, the orchestral guitar approach came to be regarded more and more as an anachronism, a backwater, explored only occasionally by younger players.

Among those features lost in the transition was the unamplified guitar's uniquely percussive rhythmic capability. McDonough, for example, used an adapted version of the drummer's accented "press roll" behind Jack Teagarden's trombone on the 1931 Charleston Chasers' "Basin Street Blues." On the Dorsey Brothers record of 1933's "By Heck," he uses his accented roll on the second beat of each bar, and is promptly imitated by drummer Stan King.

Eddie Condon accompanies cornetist Bobby Hackett on the 1938 "Carnegie Drag" with a continuous guitar tremolo; backing Pee Wee Russell on 1933's "The Eel," he generates momentum with a banjo-like "figure eight" rhythm. Django Reinhardt displayed, and all but patented, an entire lexicon of chordal "shots," rolls, and tremolos in driving the QHCF to ever greater levels of intensity.

Such effects are theoretically possible on an amplified instrument, but only minimally practical. More sensitive strings, placed closer to the fretboard, and the greater volume levels produced by amplification make even straight rhythm playing, however discreet, often sound ungainly and overbearing. Such problems, coupled with changing timekeeping methods introduced in the 1940s, led to the practice of "comping" (musicians' slang for rhythmic "accompanying") using chordal accents much in the manner of the piano while bass and drums keep the pulse.[57]

Driving the change, perhaps at its root, was a set of social and even political circumstances. The wartime draft, combined with bans imposed by the American Society of Composers, Authors, and Publishers (ASCAP) and the American Federation of Musicians, had knocked the props from under the dance band business. Imposition of a 20 percent "entertainment tax" on establishments offering dancing only accelerated the process. Almost overnight, popular music belonged to the vocalists; jazz, whatever its style, was being played for listening in small nightclubs and bars.

Stripped of the need to lay down a strong pulse for dancers, all forms of the music—even, ironically, the older styles—became rhythmically more elastic. Drummers began toying with melodic ideas; pianists and guitarists kept their comping sparse, redirecting their efforts toward single-note melodic solo lines. Among the major casualties of such change was the rhythm guitar, once the very heartbeat of the timekeeping process: to hear Reuss, a year before the Arnold Ross date, strumming an explicit pulse on "Stuffy" and other records with Coleman Hawkins's "modern" quintet, as Sir Charles Thompson (piano), Oscar Pettiford (bass), and Denzil Best (drums) strain against it, is to realize that things were changing, and jazz would never again be the same.

Charlie Christian quickly became a trendsetter. Knowledge of his "Solo Flight" was as much a card of identity for a new generation as Beiderbecke's "Singin' the Blues" or Armstrong's "West End Blues" solos had been for brassmen a decade earlier. Aided by the high visibility of his job with Goodman, the young Oklahoman became the best-known and most influential of all electric guitarists.

But he was not the first to travel this road. A white Chicago teenager named George Barnes had been working with electric guitar since 1934, acquiring an impressive local reputation. His style seemed poised midway between the country accents of Shamblin and the lyric flights of Reinhardt, but with a stronger blues orientation than either.

Chicago Heights, where George Barnes grew up, is on the South Side. By the time the young guitarist, who claimed to have joined the musicians' union at age twelve, began to work around town, he'd heard or sat in with most major black players active in the city, including many bluesmen.

"Nobody knows who invented the electric guitar," he told producer-biographer Irving Townsend, "but there were a lot of homemade ones around when I began. My brother was an electronics expert, so he made a microphone out of a carbon container and a sheet of conical cardboard suspended on a coat-hanger over my guitar. That was 1931. There were no commercially made instruments available, but a lot of guys were experimenting."[58]

Son of musical parents, the boy had begun piano at age six and switched to guitar by the time he was ten. From the start, the possibilities in amplification appealed to him. "I desperately wanted to be heard," he said. "You take a Chicago-style band and put a guitar in it and you can't hear a thing. Pee Wee Russell used to say he'd been working with Eddie Condon for ten years and had never heard him yet."[59]

Barnes listened avidly to whatever he could find on the radio, including—on Chicago station WJJD—a country-accented electric guitarist billed as "Rhubarb Red." He soon found out that "Red" was actually Les Paul, who at the same time was fronting a jazz trio on another station.

"He came to visit me at the studio," Paul remembered. "He was just a kid, called me 'Mr. Paul.' We got to be good friends: he even started using a plain G-string, the way I did, instead of the wound ones everybody else was using at the time." The friendship grew and lasted. Indeed, some of the country inflections in Barnes's solo style may have come through Paul, who had absorbed the lessons of Shamblin, McAuliffe, and the others at first hand.

By 1938, when Barnes was seventeen, he'd worked with Billie Holiday at the Three Deuces, with Jimmy McPartland and various other jazz players around town. He'd also put his affinity for the blues to good use, recording with such stalwarts as Big Bill Broonzy, Washboard Sam, and Jazz Gillum. Inevitably, such versatility brought him to the attention of network executive Leroy Shield, who offered him $150 a week to become an NBC staff musician. At that time NBC maintained two parallel radio networks, the "Red" (with WMAQ as local outlet) and "Blue" (WENR). Barnes, as one of the few staff men who could play jazz, immediately took over as much work as he could handle.

It didn't stop him from heading for the South Side after hours to sit in with veteran New Orleans clarinetist Jimmie Noone. "I was through at NBC at 4:30 every afternoon and on South State Street every night with Noone and many others," he said. "I played with those groups so much that even though I never got paid the owner of the joint would bawl me out if I was late."

He soon became something of an attraction on the air as well. No edition of NBC's regular, country-flavored *Plantation Party* was complete without a snappy guitar feature from "Georgie" Barnes, usually backed by just a rhythm section. "You know, folks," says the announcer on one of the shows, "that guitar Georgie plays is a right modern contraption. It's electric. 'Course Georgie still has to do the work, but instead of all those fast notes coming out of the guitar, they come out of a little loudspeaker. So by the time they get to your loudspeaker, as I call it, they'll be twice as good."

Many of these feature spots have been preserved on off-the-air recordings. To ears accustomed to Christian, Barnes playing such numbers as "Ain't Misbehavin'," "Down in Jungle Town," and "There'll Be Some Changes Made" is a shock. Rhythmically and technically sure, he moves forward with poise and momentum. This is no acolyte, struggling to find a mode of expression within guidelines laid down by another; Barnes speaks with his own voice, and it is as individual as that of Christian.

One obvious, perhaps crucial, difference between them seems to rest in the models each has espoused. Every phrase Christian plays reflects his admiration for the fluid lines of Lester Young. Even his honking entrance on "Seven Come Eleven," with Goodman's Sextet, could well have issued from the bell of Pres's tenor saxophone.

In emulating Young, Christian positioned himself in the center of the new developments and refinements that shortly led to the emergence of bebop. His application of Young's precedent not only accelerated his instrument's departure from its acoustic role but established a new basic vocabulary. His long, hornlike lines, steeped in the blues, were natural antecedents to the explosion of complex solo playing embodied in the work of Dizzy Gillespie and Charlie Parker.

George Barnes went another way, embraced a different language. If anything, his clipped attacks and tight, strutting lines recall the western swing players, an affinity even more sharply etched when he incorporates the slides, squawks, and other effects so familiar in the work of Dunn, McAuliffe, and Shamblin.

The *Plantation Party* airchecks offer good representation. His phrasing on a medium-tempo " 'Deed I Do" is as "hornlike" as Christian's, but the "horn" is more a trumpet than a tenor sax, the rhythmic thrust almost evocative of Bunny

545

Berigan. On number after number, whether a fleet "Stumbling" or humorously delivered "Comin' Through the Rye," he concocts neatly turned little head arrangements within which his single-string lines flash and gleam like silver.

Barnes's vocabulary, particularly its western overtones, has not endeared him to jazz cognoscenti. It is as if the country inflections were a contaminant, placing the entire style outside some pale of acceptability. For all his mastery, imagination, and swing, George Barnes is regularly ignored when the development of jazz guitar is considered; his name seldom appears in lists of the important players who emerged in the pre–World War II years. Though recognized at first (Christian's 1939 Down Beat article lauds "Georgie Barnes, the 17-year-old Chicagoan, who, with an amplified instrument, set that town on its ear . . . last spring"), he remained something of a fringe figure, belonging neither to the older, largely chordal, tradition of the Lang disciples nor to the Christian-inspired wave. There is no entry for him, for example, in John Chilton's Who's Who in Jazz. Yet Barnes was a formidable presence: after moving to New York around 1950 he was readily identifiable on countless records, in bands led by Yank Lawson and Bob Haggart, Jimmy McPartland, Bud Freeman, and many others.

"You gotta remember," said guitarist Marty Grosz, "that anything Benny Goodman did in those days made big news. Every time he hired a vocalist, or added some guy to his band, it made headlines. So if he added Charlie Christian to his band, people were going to notice, and in a big way. You know—BENNY SCRAPS SEXTET, ADDS HARP. That kind of thing. Not that Christian wasn't good—he was. But guys like Barnes never had that advantage."[60]

Bucky Pizzarelli agreed. "Christian was in the right setting, the right place at the right time. What was George Barnes doing in 1939? Playing on a country-and-western radio program in Chicago. When I was a kid in New Jersey I used to tune in and hear him on this certain station. I marked it on the dial of my radio. Never missed it.

"Somebody recently sent me a tape of George's features from those Plantation Party shows, and I'm not exaggerating when I say that's the greatest single-string playing I've ever heard in my life. Unbelievable. Nobody—and I mean nobody—could touch that. If you want to talk pure music, he made more music on those shows than a lot of guys—and I'm not mentioning any names here—who are lots better known."[61]

Even Goodman apparently came to recognize this. "I'll tell you something," said Pizzarelli. "Many years later, when George and I were working as a duo at the St. Regis [Hotel, New York City], Benny used to come in now and then and sit in. Well, one day he called me and said, 'Hey, Pops, why don't you come over to the apartment, and we'll play a little?' I brought George with me, and we played together, and he was just all over Benny with that single-string stuff. Chased him in circles, all over the place. Benny couldn't get over it, and couldn't get enough of it."

In the early '60s Barnes teamed with Carl Kress in a guitar duo, touring widely and recording regularly. His single-note lines blended well with his partner's rich chordal accompaniments, and when they added Bud Freeman's tenor sax for a

1962 trio date issued under the title *Something Tender*, the results were extraordinary. When Kress died suddenly in 1965, young Pizzarelli stepped in.

"George was amazing," said Pizzarelli. "In all the time we were together I never once heard him make a mistake, even muff a note, put a foot wrong. I did a lot of studio dates with him, watched him in action, and I'll tell you, he was in disfavor with a lot of conductors. He'd just get up and walk over to the sax section and mark the dynamics and accents with a pencil, before the arranger could even stop him. He'd say, 'This is the way this is gonna pay off. Do it like this.' "

Barnes's natural affinity for meshing his talents with those of others found expression in an unorthodox quartet he led between 1973 and 1975 with cornetist Ruby Braff. Supported only by rhythm guitar and bass, the two soloists carried their musical communication to sometimes extrasensory heights; on *To Fred Astaire With Love*, perhaps their finest recorded effort, they use arrangement, interplay, and individual performance to achieve an eloquence equal to that of Venuti and Lang in the '30s and Kress and McDonough in the following decade.

Demanding and volatile personalities, Braff and Barnes were bound to clash sooner or later. It came as no surprise to colleagues—though an immeasurable disappointment—when the quartet split up amid anger and mutual invective. The Barnes-Pizzarelli association had also ended in acrimony, as did a brief partnership with Art Ryerson. "We actually got along fine," said Ryerson, "but with George it had to be his way or not at all. That was just the way he was." Barnes resettled in California, where he died in 1977 of a heart attack.

While working at NBC in Chicago, Barnes organized the first edition of his Octet, shortly to become one of the most inventive, musically refreshing of jazz chamber groups. He chose an unusual instrumentation: four symphony-quality woodwind players and a rhythm section of himself, a rhythm guitarist, bass, and drums. From 1939 through 1942 the Octet was a regular broadcast feature, but it never recorded commercially and remained known mostly to radio listeners.

Back in Chicago after World War II, Barnes reorganized, this time with slightly different personnel, and went back to regular broadcasting. Again, the group recorded only transcriptions; but fifteen titles found their way to LP in the late '70s, and they are astonishing.

Musically the group is a hybrid, related (if sometimes distantly) to such units as the John Kirby Sextet, the Raymond Scott Quintet, and the rather more ambitious Alec Wilder Octet. Like the Wilder unit, this eight-piecer is chiefly an arranger's vehicle, a canvas. The woodwinds achieve surprising textures; there are shifts of time signature, meter, harmony; contrapuntal passages, brilliantly conceived and flawlessly executed. But where the Alec Wilder group used no improvisation at all, lending its performances a static, viewed-under-glass quality, the Barnes Octet was built around a vibrant, hard-swinging improviser, capable of driving the whole enterprise ahead with irresistible momentum. Now and then there are also brief "improvised" solos for clarinet, flute, or bassoon—every note written out and choreographed by Barnes.

ABC, succeeding NBC's Blue Network, knew what it had inherited. "I had complete freedom on the network to play whatever I wanted, and we were very well received because the sound contrasted so much with the vanilla sounds of staff bands in those days," Barnes told Irving Townsend. "We were considered very far out. And at the station my group was an exclusive club. If a musician played with me, he was excused from playing the early-morning 'Breakfast Club' show, he got out of other rehearsals, was given preferential treatment and made extra money from our activities."[62]

Each performance offers a surprise. Little survives of the prewar Octet, but fragments of "Get Happy" and "Muskrat Ramble," recorded off the air in mid-1942, show the group tightly arranged and well rehearsed, with Barnes as its centerpiece. But even that is little preparation for the Octet of the 1946 transcriptions. By this time Barnes knew his men, and in writing for them let his imagination run free. The centerpiece of "South Side Blues," for example, is a kind of adagio dance, with guitar, clarinet, and bass clarinet moving in sinuous tandem, hi-hat swishing softly in support. "I wrote a bass line I used to hear Pinetop Smith play, a contrary-motion line for the clarinet," he said. "And then I just played the blues."[63]

Some selections are more complex. Guitar leads tightly voiced woodwinds through the first sixteen bars of "Smoke Gets in Your Eyes," then ushers in a series of variations reminiscent of Eddie Sauter's imaginative writing for Artie Shaw, Benny Goodman, and Ray McKinley. That's especially true of such Barnes originals as "Zebra's Derby," with its interlocking bass clarinets; "Straight Interlude," which turns Glenn Miller–type reed scoring deliciously inside out; and "Priority on a Moonbeam," with its hypnotic up-and-down chromatic movement.

It's obvious that Barnes regarded his group as a personal laboratory and enjoyed exploring its resources. The transcriptions were on sixteen-inch long-play discs, each side holding five three-minute selections, and recorded in direct-to-disc fashion, without interruption. In all fifteen of the Octet's issued performances there is never a slip, never a goof or misstep.

For a faux-dixieland version of "At the Jazz Band Ball," Barnes bought reedman Eddie Swan a bass sax and coached him in the style of Adrian Rollini, even writing out a Rollini-style "hot" solo which Swan executes in dutiful, if rather wooden, fashion.

The Octet has perhaps its finest moment on "Imagination," combining beautifully turned Barnes guitar phrases with writing of a high creative order. It opens with Phil Wing's oboe, leading the woodwinds as Barnes embellishes; at a later point the fabric parts to reveal two bass clarinets, and elsewhere drummer Frankie Rullo switches to vibes for a double-time unison duet with Barnes. Toward the end, unexpectedly, Tommy Miller emerges from the ensemble for a Syrinx-like unaccompanied flute passage.[64]

"George thought of the guitar entirely in single-string terms, and all upper-register," said Bucky Pizzarelli. "He had no chordal side to him at all. He was like a horn player, a clarinet or trumpet; in a sense the fact that he played guitar was just a coincidence. There was nothing particularly guitaristic about the way he played. He couldn't even play a regular guitar tremolo."

Les Paul explained why. "It was the way he held his pick. He held one edge with his thumb, the other with his first finger, and used the second finger to reinforce it, in the back. All this with the wrist turned over, holding the pick straight up. It was very strong that way, very powerful. It enabled him to really sting out those notes. But it was stiff, too, a kind of trap."

George Barnes left a plentiful and varied recorded legacy. "He could walk away with anybody," said Pizzarelli. "Any key, any tempo, anything. His single-line was as adept as George Van Eps's chordal playing; they just went in different directions. Both had faultless taste. Never a goof, never a slip. Taken together, they—and Lang and just a few other guys—set a standard for the instrument. As far as I can tell, it's never been surpassed. It may never be. But Barnes—well, I guess you could say he just didn't know how to deal with success."

The Big
Bands 2

At the Summit

22

Benny Goodman

With the obvious exception of Artie Shaw, few major jazzmen of the early years were verbally articulate, and fewer still took time and trouble to record their views and experiences with posterity in mind. As several have put it, "We just didn't think that way; we were too busy playing and making a living to bother what anybody would think." This is regrettable: seen in retrospect, their personal views were often of surpassing importance.

Most are gone now, and the extent of what has been lost through their silence is made all the more evident in the wide-ranging observations of one of the era's most significant players, Benny Goodman. Coming of age in the '20s and early '30s, Goodman brought to bear a flawless mastery of the clarinet with an implicit understanding of the emergent hot jazz idiom. The result was a synthesis, drawing on such diverse precedents as clarinetists Jimmie Noone and Leon Roppolo, brass innovators Armstrong and (especially) Beiderbecke, and even the aggressive energies of his Chicago coevals in forging a style which soon became an almost universal standard for his instrument. Goodman's career spanned six decades: at the time of his death, on June 20, 1986, he was still leading a band, still deeply affecting a brand-new generation of musicians barely into their twenties.

Late in 1980, *American Heritage* magazine commissioned a feature article based on informal conversations with Benny Goodman. At that time there was little in print that even attempted to penetrate the "King of Swing" façade that still formed the substance of his public image. Geoffrey Ward, editor of *American Her-*

itage, realized that and assigned the piece in hopes of getting at the man behind the clarinet.

Benny brought a surprising honesty to criticism of himself. He was keenly aware of the regard, for good and ill, in which he was held by colleagues, peers, and musicians who had worked in his many bands. He spoke of them without rancor, simply accepting that his relations with them were a result of who they were and, more important, who he was.

Goodman is often spoken of as a complex man. At the fundamental level he may be just the opposite, a man of simple, linear thoughts and emotions who early in life defined the direction in which he wished to travel and strayed little, if at all, from that course. There was in him little of the intricacy, the close-woven emotional and intellectual stitchwork, that characterized Shaw.

Goodman regarded himself above all as a player of the clarinet, and jazz as one of several options a virtuoso clarinetist could exercise. He differed in this regard from both Shaw, whose obsession was a broad musical *Weltanschauung*, and Pee Wee Russell, a single-minded jazz improviser for whom the instrument was chiefly a conduit, a means to an end.

He had his quirks. One of them was the clear and rigid line he drew between the way he dealt with people—in and outside music—whom he admired and viewed as peers, and his treatment of his employees, his sidemen. Since his death in 1986, the latter have come forward in ever greater numbers to tell bandroom tales about his parsimony, his sometimes cruel obliviousness to the feelings of others, his gaucherie. The truth of such accounts is not at issue here; rather, it is well to acknowledge that they represent only one part of the story, one way of viewing the man.

What follows is basically the text of the *American Heritage* article, with material deleted at the time of publication—due largely to the constraints of space—replaced.

Benny Goodman strolled down New York's Second Avenue one recent morning, covering the nine blocks between his apartment and a health club, where he swims each day, in about ten minutes. During that time no fewer than four strangers recognized him and vigorously shook his hand. They varied in age from near-contemporaries to youngsters clearly born long after Goodman's glory days. But all had much the same thing to say. "I just want to thank you," said one, who appeared to be in his late forties. "I can't imagine my life without you and your music." Indeed, it's difficult to imagine twentieth-century America—at least that part of it which had to do with entertainment—without Benny Goodman. No other jazz figure—not even Duke Ellington or Louis Armstrong—has come to mean so much to so wide a cross-section of the population as has this quiet-spoken, bespectacled jazz clarinetist.

Benjamin David Goodman was born in Chicago, May 30, 1909, ninth of twelve children of Russian-Jewish immigrant parents. His father worked hard; but it was clear from the outset that the Goodman siblings would have to learn quickly and well how to be self-sufficient in a tough, keenly competitive—and not always just—world. Young Benjamin received his first clarinet at age ten, and within four years he was playing it professionally around Chicago.

He couldn't have come along at a better place and time. Chicago in the early 1920s was full of a new music called jazz; its delirious charm spoke most forcefully to the young. Still in short pants, Goodman soon fell in with other youthful musicians who spent most of their time frequenting speakeasies and dance halls, listening to such jazz pioneers as the New Orleans Rhythm Kings and cornetist Joe ("King") Oliver, whose Creole Jazz Band included clarinetist Johnny Dodds and, on second cornet, a legend-to-be, Louis Armstrong.

Things moved fast thereafter. His reputation spread quickly, especially after he started making phonograph records; by the time he arrived in New York as a member of Ben Pollack's orchestra, the word was out—a new and revolutionary clarinet talent was on the scene. He played a hot style comparable to others of his time—Pee Wee Russell, Don Murray, and fellow-Chicagoan Frank Teschemacher among them—but there was a difference. Young Goodman was clearly a clarinet virtuoso, fusing his jazz influences in a concept that rode on—but never lost itself in—blinding, seemingly flawless technique. Passages that might have seemed feats of execution for other reedmen lay easily under his fingers. He had tone, control, pinpoint accuracy—yet the capacity to remain logical and melodically appealing even at roller-coaster tempos.

He worked through a number of bands, playing as a peer with most of the top white jazz names of the day and a few of the black ones—through jazz, like the rest of the entertainment business of the late '20s and early '30s, was still rigidly segregated, at least in public. Goodman performed and recorded with Bix Beiderbecke, Jack Teagarden, Coleman Hawkins, Fats Waller, Bud Freeman, Red Nichols, Ethel Waters—and even on the final recording of the legendary "Empress of the Blues," Bessie Smith.

When the Depression hit, Goodman was firmly established in radio and recording studio orchestras, able—though not always willing—to play expertly any music put in front of him. There he stayed, until a combination of ambition and circumstance began to place him in front of bands rather than in them. His ultimate success as a bandleader has been attributed to any number of causes: astute management, the advocacy of such influential figures as his brother-in-law and sometime manager, John Hammond, excellent sidemen, fine arrangements by Fletcher Henderson and others—even, as Goodman himself contends, a large measure of determination and plain old good luck.

He reached the zenith of his popularity between 1936 and 1940, though he led several notable and highly regarded bands after that. His January 16, 1938, concert at Carnegie Hall was a music landmark—the first time an evening in that concertgoers' shrine had been devoted entirely to jazz. His bands were collections of stars and stars-in-the-making, including drummers Gene Krupa, Dave Tough, and Sid Catlett; trumpeters Bunny Berigan, Harry James, Ziggy Elman, Cootie Williams, and Billy Butterfield; and pianists Jess Stacy and Mel Powell. He was among the first to successfully bridge the color line by hiring pianist Teddy Wilson and vibraphonist Lionel Hampton and by refusing to appear anywhere—even in the deepest South—without them.

His records still sell. Such Goodman anthems as "Let's Dance," "Stomping at the Savoy," "King Porter Stomp," "Roll 'Em," and, of course, "Sing Sing Sing" remain popular today, still found on jukeboxes, label-to-label with the latest rock-and-roll trifles.

Though Goodman's greatest triumphs are nearly half a century behind him, his name remains magic at the box office. A Carnegie Hall concert commemorating the fortieth anniversary of the 1938 triumph sold out within twenty-four hours. His influence on jazz clarinetists is unquestioned and universal: like Louis Armstrong on the trumpet, Goodman determined the very shape of a jazz approach to his instrument.

Perhaps the best question with which to start is the most obvious—and the hardest to answer. That is, why did it happen to you? Did you deliberately set out to become the most prominent popular musician and bandleader of your time?

Oh no, no. Not at all. Goodness no. I started out as a clarinetist playing around Chicago, making a living, listening to other people like many musicians did. I heard Dodds and Noone and the others, all with a great deal of love and passion for what went on, a lot of respect for them. I enjoyed playing—and I found myself really making money at age fourteen or so, around the time I was playing with those fellows who later were known as the Austin High Gang. You know, Jimmy McPartland and Bud Freeman and the rest. I was never at Austin High myself. I played in theatres, at the Midway Gardens, places like that.

Several of those musicians have said you always seemed to be on a track slightly different from theirs.

Well, that's a good point. Some of the guys I played with in those days didn't go around learning more about their instruments from an intellectual point of view. All they wanted was to play hot jazz, and the instrument was just a means. I'd imagine that a lot of them criticized me—said my technique was too good. Something like that. But I've always wanted to know what made music. How you do it, and why it sounds good. I always practiced, worked like hell. And I think it was kind of a defense with me, too, a way of getting away—especially later, from agents and business people and the rest. They couldn't talk to you if you were practicing.

So you were interested in the instrument for its own sake, not just in being someone who played hot jazz on it—Pee Wee Russell, for example.

Well, I was never a Pee Wee Russell kind of player. He was sort of a joke to me—although I appreciated what he did. Still, that that wasn't my point of view about music. Don't forget, the clarinet itself has a great history in classical music. You know, every one of the great composers—Brahms, Weber, Mozart—was associated with the clarinet and its players.

My teacher was Franz Schoepp, one of the best known in Chicago. I must have been about eleven. He had both colored and white students. I know Buster

Bailey, for one, studied with him. He had a habit of keeping the preceding pupil there when you came in and having you play duets. I think that's how I got to know Buster. Schoepp was German, and he used all German editions of his books. One day I said to him, "Mr. Schoepp, why do you have everything in German? Why don't you have anything in English? We're here now." And he said, "Dummkopf! Pretty soon *everything* will be in German."

How did you become interested in music in the first place?
We always had a Victrola in our home. It was hand-wound, and we had all sorts of records to go with it. Caruso and people like that—but also Ted Lewis, who was a big thing in those days, and even the Original Dixieland Jazz Band. My father was the one who was very much interested: he thought it was a very good idea for us to play music, whether we made a living out of it or not. He loved music himself; he discovered that the Kehelah Jacob Synagogue, not much more than a mile from where we lived, would lend instruments to youngsters and supply them with lessons, so they could play in the band at the synagogue. So we all went down, and my brother Harry, who was about twelve and the biggest of us, got a tuba. Freddy, who was a year older than I was, got a trumpet, and I wound up with the clarinet.

Where did you make your public debut?
At the Central Park Theater, a Balaban and Katz presentation house on Chicago's West Side. They tell me I imitated Ted Lewis. All I remember is that because of the child labor laws, I couldn't perform onstage. So I played from the pit. I was still playing a C clarinet then [most conventional clarinets are pitched a whole tone lower, in B♭], so the band had to transpose everything to my key.

You began working around Chicago, and on the Lake Michigan excursion boats, where you met the cornetist and pianist Bix Beiderbecke. He was a good six years older than you, an experienced pro of twenty. What do you remember about him?
I think my first impression was the lasting one. I remember very clearly thinking, "Where, what planet, did this guy come from? Is he from outer space?" I'd never heard anything like the way he played—not in Chicago, no place. The tone—he had this wonderful, ringing cornet tone. He could have played in a symphony orchestra with that tone. But also the intervals he played, the figures—whatever the hell he did. There was a refinement about his playing. You know, in those days I played a little trumpet, and I could play all the solos from his records, by heart.

How did you come to join the drummer Ben Pollack's dance orchestra?
That came about in a funny way. I had a job at the Midway Gardens, which was across from Washington Park on the Near South Side. Gil Rodin, who was playing saxophone with Pollack and who later had quite a hand in the success of Bob Crosby's band, came in to see me. He began talking about glamorous California; Pollack was working at Venice, outside Los Angeles, and it sounded so great. The more he talked about it, the better it sounded to me. Go west—the idea of going

out there on a train, seeing places like Santa Monica, all beautiful hotels and glamorous people and places. It sounded too good to be true.

All I could think was, "Gosh, I've got to get out there some way." Later in the summer—it was '26, I guess—as soon as I got word that Pollack had an opening, I quit my job. My parents, of course, weren't nuts about having me go so far away, but I told them, "Look, I lost my job at the Midway Gardens. This other one [meaning Pollack's] is the only one I've got." There was no way they could object. I'd be making decent money—and, of course, I always sent money home. So off I went.

And when you got there, all of seventeen years old?
Oh boy. It was the sleaziest place. Rides, roller coasters, and all that. I just looked around and I thought, "What the hell did I come here for?" But there I was—and the band was very good, after all.

What kind of a bandleader did Pollack turn out to be?
It's hard to say, but to me he always seemed to be doing something wrong. Instead of just letting things come his way in their natural order, he'd always be reaching for something that was inaccessible. He had the wrong managers. They were always telling him how great he was, encouraging him to make decisions which were just wrong. Mistakes. Like singing. Or ending his records in that silly, whiny little voice, saying, "May it please you—Ben Pollack."

He just wasn't the kind of guy to stop and reflect and ask himself, "What am I? Who am I? Where am I going and why?" No objectivity, no insight. And no sense of humor about himself. Wasn't able to think, "I'm doing well. I ought to treat these kids well"—meaning us—"accept ideas from them and encourage their confidence."

I'll give you an example of Pollack's capacity for going in the wrong direction—but one which actually wound up having a funny side to it. When the band came to Chicago from California, we were playing well, but in comparison with a lot of other bands of the day we didn't have a lot of instruments. Sure—saxophones and clarinets in our section, for instance, but nothing more. Now a band like Roger Wolfe Kahn's—they had a million instruments: all sorts of woodwinds, like oboes and flutes and things. And it looked sharp! Well, Pollack took one look at them and decided that we had to have all that stuff too. They cost a fortune at that time: a Loré oboe, for example, which probably costs about twenty-five hundred dollars now, was three hundred dollars then.

Well, being a kind of serious musician, I thought I'd better learn something about all this, so I went to a teacher named Ruckl, who used to play with the Chicago Symphony Orchestra. Nice guy—I went to him religiously for oboe lessons. After a couple of lessons, he sent me to buy the Loré method book. So I went and looked—and looked and looked. And I couldn't find any book for oboe by that name. So I went back and apologized and said, "I'm sorry, Mr. Ruckl, but all I could find was something for the 'hot-boy.' " Boy oh boy, did he laugh! *Hautbois*, of course, is French for "oboe." But I wound up playing it pretty well—even took a chorus on it on "Japanese Sandman."

You played New York for the first time with Pollack's band. What was that like?
When I first arrived, it seemed to me the most terrifying city in the world . . . all those big buildings. I remember walking on Broadway, looking up at this huge, mountainous place—and being so lonely. But things started to clear up when I met a few people on the street whom I'd met before—all of a sudden there got to be a certain familiarity about the place, and the terror kind of evaporated. There was a lot of playing going on, and the New Yorkers, of course, were a completely different crowd from what I'd known. Red Nichols, Tommy and Jimmy Dorsey, Miff Mole, Adrian Rollini—they came down to hear us, and there was this intermingling. It was quite exciting, with a lot of mutual respect. And within the band, we were all very close.

Glenn Miller was in that band, writing arrangements. Another trombonist, Jack Teagarden from Texas, joined the band after you did.
Jack wasn't an easy guy to know. He drank quite a bit. I, being a nice Jewish boy, didn't drink that much. Jack—well, he was a singular kind of guy. Had a vocabulary of about eight words and wasn't really interested in any more. But he was an absolutely fantastic trombone player, and I loved to listen to him take solos—although that almost got me into trouble with him at one point. The reed section used to sit in front, and the brass behind us, and when Jack would play. I'd hear these marvelous notes and I'd sort of wheel around in my chair to listen. He interpreted that wrong—he seemed to think I was giving him a look, putting him down. Well, one night he got a couple of drinks in him and came up to me and said, "What the hell are you turnin' around like that for?" He was ready for a fight—and it took me a little time, swearing on my word of honor, to convince him that I really meant well.

You and Pollack used to play clarinet and drum duets.
We did that on songs like—what was it—"I want to go where you go, Do what you do . . ." You know—"Then I'll Be Happy." Pollack had a fly swatter, and he'd lean over and be banging on the bass drum with it, yelling, "Take another one, take another one," and we'd keep on like that, generating a lot of steam. I must have enjoyed it, because I guess we did it a lot. Nobody else at the time was doing it.

How did you get started as a bandleader?
We were doing broadcasts somewhere in Brooklyn. Russ Columbo, the crooner, had a manager named Con Conrad, who had also written things like "Barney Google," "Margie," and "Ma, He's Makin' Eyes at Me." He heard about me, and told me Columbo wanted to get a band for a job up at the Woodmanston Inn. I got guys I knew—Gene Krupa on drums, Joe Sullivan on piano, Babe Russin on tenor sax—and we worked there for the summer, and I was the leader. Columbo sang and walked around with a fiddle under his arm, and everything seemed okay. It was a good little band—but Conrad wound up getting mad at me, because whenever we played for dancing, people seemed to really like it. I mean, we'd play "Between the Devil and the Deep Blue Sea," or some song like

that, and all of a sudden the joint was rocking. He'd say, "Hey, wait a minute—you guys aren't supposed to be the attraction here," and he meant it.

Did that experience spur greater ambition to lead your own band?
No, not really. I don't think so. All I knew was that I was bored as hell, playing in stupid little radio bands, playing for Pick and Pat and all sorts of other acts. I think the idea that was foremost in all our minds was that we wanted to play some kind of music. Good music. And we just grabbed any opportunity that presented itself.

You were then on the verge of great success, an extraordinary pattern of success and good judgment, even good luck. Still, a lot of people played good clarinet and a lot led good bands. But once things started happening for you, they never stopped. What's your explanation?
Well, you can call it luck if you want to. But I'd go a little further, and say that there are, always have been, people out there who have just a little bit more than everybody else has got. In musicianship, in stamina. You can even call it a certain kind of integrity if you want to. The important thing, to me, has always been setting an example: an orchestra's got to follow what you do. If you're playing five shows a day—that's five shows—and they see you're not complaining but are instead up there really giving everything, they're not going to complain either.

Some people run a good store and some don't. I remember Glenn Miller coming to me once, before he had his own band, saying, "How do you do it? How do you get started? It's so difficult." I told him, "I don't know, but whatever you do, don't stop. Just keep on going. Because one way or the other, if you want to find reasons why you shouldn't keep on, you'll find 'em. The obstacles are all there—there are a million of 'em. But if you want to do something, you do it anyway, and handle the obstacles as they come."

Didn't you also have doubts at the start? Weren't there times when you wanted to give up?
Well, in a way, I guess. After we got the job at Billy Rose's Music Hall on Broadway at 54th Street—it's now the Ed Sullivan Theater—I had moments. It was tough as a son of a bitch. I couldn't pay any money. I didn't know, night after night, who was going to be there and who was going to send in a sub. Sometimes I'd stand outside the front door and think, "Shall I go inside or not? Maybe I should just get out." But even then, after we'd been there six or seven weeks, I was listening one night and remember thinking, "Gee, this is a pretty good band!" I think it was right after that that we got our notice.

Was that about the time you got a job on that late-night NBC radio show, Let's Dance? That proved to be a turning point for you, didn't it?
You know what I remember about all that? I remember the fact that we had to audition for the job—well, really it was an audition to audition—and I was worried. We had to be heard by some people from the ad agency that was helping put the show together—McCann Erickson, I think—and if they thought we were the kind of band they wanted, then we'd be able to audition for the show. I kept after this one guy to find out what time they were coming to the Music Hall to hear us because I had to get hold of the players and make sure they'd be there

for that hour or so, nail them to their chairs if necessary. Think how it would have been if we'd had a band full of subs that night. Also, we had maybe fifteen special arrangements in the book—"Cokey," "Bugle Call Rag," "Nitwit Serenade," some of those. That meant we had to do our numbers and then get those people out of there, because we didn't have any comparable new material.

It went off fine. But toward the end of the set, I went over to the agency people and said, "Well, you know, nothing really happens after this." I have to laugh now—they were probably going home anyway. Anyway, to jump a little, when I got the call telling me we'd gotten the job, I didn't believe it. All I could think was "Well, this is the moment. Take advantage of it, because you're not gonna get too many chances like this."

As I recall, the show ran from 10:30 P.M. till 3:30 A.M. every Saturday night, sponsored by the National Biscuit Company. Your band alternated fifteen-minute sets with those of Kel Murray and Xavier Cugat, which meant that audiences in four time zones had a chance to hear the band several times on a given evening. During Daylight Saving Time the bands were broadcasting for six hours. On the strength of it, you made your first extended tour outside New York, a tour that would ultimately take you to the West Coast. Did you think history was about to be made?

History? I remember thinking, "Gosh, you sure have a lot of chutzpah. Lead a band, go on the radio . . ." And yet, if you have convictions, and a point of view, and all that energy, why not? If I have something I want to do, I make a business of doing it.

The tour had its share of disappointments—for example, a four-week run at Elitch's Gardens, in Denver, where the crowds wanted waltzes and the management demanded MCA withdraw the band at once.

You know, I remember thinking after Denver, "Oh well, that's the end of this goddamn thing." Meaning the whole business of leading a band. I was really down. Then we got to the Coast and were supposed to play at a ballroom in Oakland, across the bay from San Francisco. I remember walking in with Helen Ward, our singer, and seeing crowds of people, and saying to her, "Christ, Helen, we must be in the wrong place. What are all these people doing here?" Mind you, the place didn't hold all that many people—maybe fourteen or fifteen hundred tops—it was an intimate kind of place, really. But all the same, given my state of mind, I thought; "What's this? Is Benny Goodman really playing here?" But we went in and played, and my goodness, they really reacted. Went crazy. I suppose it prepared us for the Palomar Ballroom, outside Los Angeles.

What stays in my mind about the Palomar is just that we started quietly. Didn't know what to expect, and in any case I was trying not to take the whole business too seriously. Things went on kind of so-so for an hour, nothing much happening. All of a sudden I thought to myself, "Screw this—let's play. If we're gonna flop again let's at least do it our own way." I'd had enough by then. So we started playing Fletcher Henderson's arrangements of "King Porter Stomp" and "When Buddha Smiles"—some of those. Half the crowd just stopped dancing and gathered round the bandstand. I knew things would be all right from then on.

Bunny Berigan, the trumpet player, was a potent force in the band at that point, wasn't he?
Absolutely. You know, he drank—not so much then, or at least it wasn't getting to him yet. But—well, you put up with certain things in certain people because of what they are. People today who follow jazz seem to have forgotten about Bunny, about just how marvelous he was. His tone, his beautiful sound and range, everything. Most of all, he had this ability to stimulate a whole band: he'd take a solo, and wow! He was so inventive that he'd just lift the whole thing.

We were supposed to be at the Palomar only a month, but the engagement was extended, and we were doing radio broadcasts at night. They came and asked me, "What time do you want to be on the radio? Do you want an 11:30 slot, or 12:30?" I told them I thought 11:30 would be good. The earlier the better—largely because if it were any later Bunny would usually be wiped out.

Did the Palomar success make the going any easier for you when you finally headed back east?
I wouldn't say so. In those days, success was sort of local. You had to go out and make a hit, satisfy the patrons and the people, then do it all over again the next time. All bands started out that way—at first they'd always lose money.

Here's a question that's just a personal indulgence of mine. I've always wondered why Art Rollini always wound up playing fourth, and wasn't given more solo space. Any particular reason?
That was simple. The others just were better saxophone players, played with more fire. But Schneez—that's what we used to call him—was a nice player. But that reminds me about when we hired Vido Musso. He couldn't read a goddamn note, but I didn't know that. We were in California, and one afternoon I told Hymie [Schertzer], "Why don't you rehearse the saxophone section. Go over some of the arrangements with [Vido] so he'll get an idea what they go like, and so forth." That night I came to the job, and Hymie looked a little disconsolate. I said, "Well, how did it go? Did you get through it?" He said, "Yeah, we got through four bars. He can't read a note. He can't even read the newspaper." So I said, "Well, just let him play." So he did: when it went up, he went up, and when it went down, he went down. He had a good ear, thank heavens.

Success followed success, and for the next several years, you were the hottest thing in the music business. How did the 1938 Carnegie Hall concert come about? Were you nervous?
A publicity man dreamed it up, and my first reaction was, "You must be out of your mind." Looking back on it, I sometimes think that the thing really made that concert important was the album that came out. I don't know what would have happened if the concert hadn't been recorded. People would have remembered it, sure—but not like this.

Tell you one thing: Playing a job at a place like the Madhattan Room of the Pennsylvania Hotel, where we were then, or most anyplace, we'd usually start kind of quietly. Play dinner music, so to speak. Warm up a little bit. It wouldn't be until later that the band really got rocking. But in a concert you had to hit right from the top, bang! Then, too, in Carnegie Hall the acoustics are special. The Madhattan Room, for instance, was very dead. You'd just blow like hell in there all the time. Carnegie, as you know, is very live, so I insisted we go in about two or three days in advance to rehearse there, just to get used to it. By the time I gave the downbeat on "Don't Be That Way," we were pretty confident. Mind you, I'd had my doubts: I had even tried to get Bea Lillie, for pete's sake, to come on first and warm up the audience by telling jokes. Obviously, if I'd felt cocksure that we were going to be a big hit I wouldn't have thought up something as dumb as that. Stupidest thing I could have done—and she was smart enough to say no.

The Carnegie concert has been discussed to death, and it's not my intention to dwell on it here. The only question I'd ask is about Jess Stacy. How did you happen to give him a solo at that point, so late in the program?
Well, we used to let him play—sometimes when things were going a bit slow, it'd be "Jess, take one," and he would. But this was different. Here I was standing there, leading the band; and when Jess got maybe two minutes, two and a half, into his solo, with all this beautiful music coming out of the piano, I said to myself, "Of all the oddities, here's Jess playing with all these great stars sitting there—Harry James, Gene Krupa, Ziggy Elman—and in his quiet way he's stealing the show, taking the whole thing away from everybody, right before my eyes!" It was like Rachmaninoff was playing the piano. The *sound*, the touch, the tone quality.

Speaking of that, why didn't you give Jess more exposure, give him more to do? Seems you kept him under wraps a lot of the time.
Well, I thought he did a lot on records, behind vocalists and solos and things. He just—well, you know, there was Teddy. They were two different kinds of animals completely. Here was one, very facile and all over the keyboard, and— there was never any kind of competition between them. Jess wasn't insecure about Teddy, or anything like that. In fact, sometimes a vocalist would be singing, and I'd say to Jess, "Come on, play more, play louder." Jess—you could always depend on him.

Of all the bands you've led, was that one your favorite?
No. No—the Carnegie band had some stars, sure. And by this time the public was applauding solos and all that. They were aware who was playing what. Harry and Gene, Ziggy and others had public identities. But I think the band that played the Joseph Urban Room at the Congress Hotel, in Chicago, on our way back from the Palomar, was my favorite. The records we made then show it, too: that earlier band was more of a team effort. Less sensational. Everybody really pulling together. It had solidity, even some subtlety, the feeling of a small band. Not struggling: just playing to enjoy it.

Nate Kazebier played trumpet in that band, right? And Bunny had left by then?
Right. I remember Nate saying, "Jeez, I can't play Bunny's book." I said, "Sure you can. Don't worry about a thing; just play it. Forget whose book it was." But he kept protesting, saying, "I can't, I can't"—he had a great habit of doing that— and before you knew it he was playing it just fine. It's a matter of giving people

confidence in a band: it's all you need—providing your people have some kind of talent.

While we're talking about individuals, I've always wondered why Bud Freeman didn't work out in the '38 band.
Oh, I think it was a matter of mutual feeling, chemistry. In the first place, I don't think he really liked big bands. He liked Tommy Dorsey's band, I think, because Tommy favored him so much, gave him chorus after chorus. Then he came to my band, and it was just a different kind of band. Dave Tough was in the band then, and I think that's the reason I got Bud. I mean, he played well enough—took fine solos on "Lullaby in Rhythm," things like that. But you know Bud—he's kind of funny, with that laissez-faire way of his. You know, like it's all beneath him somehow. He wanted to go to London and act, or some damn thing. And he's still doing it, isn't he?

Was there ever any open strife between you? And anger? After all, you'd known one another virtually since you were kids.
No, no. No strife or bad feelings. As I say, it was just never the right chemistry. My band just wasn't the right place for him. And you know, there was no throwing him off the path he'd set for himself.

You mentioned Dave Tough. What was it like, having him come into the band right after Gene?
Well, it's funny. His time-playing was quite different from Gene's, and I never thought he was as good for the band as Gene had been; but some people thought he was better. Certainly for the Trio and Quartet he wasn't as—well, he wasn't a showman. Not that I gave a damn about that: when Gene left, I sort of said to myself, "Well, that chapter is over. I'm not going to get somebody like that." I remember Buddy Rich auditioned for me about then, and I thought, "Now that's the last thing I want, to have another Gene inside of three weeks." Dave Tough—you know, that was sad, the drinking and all. There we'd be, opening at the Waldorf—*opening night at the Waldorf*—and where was Dave? I'm sure that if it hadn't been for the drinking he'd have been another kind of person. More strength, everything.

A lot of people have expressed the view that the band you had in 1941 or thereabouts, with arrangements by Eddie Sauter—the band that recorded for Columbia—was one of your greatest. How do you feel about that one?
To tell the truth, I never liked that band as well as some others. To me it was—it was a rather affected kind of band. Good musicians—but with all respect to Eddie Sauter, he wasn't really a jazz man. Too involved, too fussy: you had to watch your P's and Q's so goddamn much you could never play.

Yet you have to admit that Sauter was a wonderful arranger, a fine craftsman.
Of course, of course. I always liked him. But listen to the arrangements: "My Old Flame," for instance. Some rather strange things about it. Did you know that some of those pieces that wound up as instrumentals were originally modulations? "Clarinet à la King," for example. It was a modulation in another arrange-

ment. And I said, "Eddie, what's this got to do with this piece? But I think it's so good: why don't you just take it out and make a piece out of it?"

"And Benny Rides Again"?
Awfully hard to play, and nobody could dance to it. It was edited a great deal, you know, but it was a very ambitious work, and a very good record, I thought. All those things he wrote—"Moonlight on the Ganges," "Smoke Gets in Your Eyes," "It Never Entered My Mind." Beautiful arrangements: it was always an event when a new one came, because you never knew what it was gonna be. It would be something provocative, or very interesting, or something, but it was never dull. That's a great asset for an arranger. But you had to have time to work all that out and decide what you were gonna cut, and so forth. And Eddie would get madder than hell if you cut *anything*

You had a high regard for Lester Young, didn't you?
Oh yes. You know, I gave him a clarinet. I'd just come back from Europe—you know, Selmers were only forty dollars apiece over there. Anyway, he came to see me when we were playing at the Waldorf, and I gave him this clarinet. Funny, you know: I always had the feeling that his playing was influenced by Bud Freeman.

Oh? He always denied that, citing Tram and Jimmy Dorsey.
Jimmy? No, I couldn't see that. I always thought it was Bud Freeman. The triplets, you know. The way he used his vibrato in those days. I loved playing with him: he was one with whom the chemistry was right, you know.

You'll pardon if I tread on some very familiar ground here, but there's one name I have to throw at you—for obvious reasons. Artie Shaw.
Well, why not? He was very talented, a very capable clarinet player. He had a quite different tone, you know, and idea, different from what other people had, but he was quite effective. And he really knew how to pick songs, musicians, things like that, very well. He had a hell of a band, but I don't think there was ever this competition that everybody talks about.

What about his playing?
Well, I always thought his tone was closer to a saxophone tone than a clarinet. But it was perfectly all right for him. I think it would have left you laughing if you were to play classical music with him, though he did play quite a bit of it, didn't he?

Speaking of classical music, why, at the height of your success as a jazz musician, did you begin to involve yourself heavily in playing classical music on the clarinet?
Well, it had actually started earlier. Somebody arranged for me to record the Mozart Quintet with a string quartet. I was playing somewhere in Wisconsin and drove to Chicago to do the recording. I got to the hotel about two or three in the morning, and to the recording studio at about nine. There were these four Frenchmen or Belgians who hardly spoke a word of English; well, we started to record the Mozart, and after playing for maybe five minutes, I started saying to

myself, "What the hell am I doing here? This is nuts. I don't know this piece." I just wasn't prepared. So I excused myself, saying, "I'm sorry, gentleman. Thank you, but this was my mistake. I hope I didn't inconvenience you—but some other time, perhaps."

You didn't give up, though: there were soon concerts and records with prominent classical musicians—Igor Stravinsky, Béla Bartók, the Budapest String Quartet, and original works were written for you by Bartók, Paul Hindemith, Aaron Copland, Malcolm Arnold, and others. This is not a common course for a jazz musician to steer. Can you account for it?
Well, sometimes I was just kind of overwhelmed with the greatness of some of that music. I'd ask myself, "How the hell can you improvise any better than that?" I mean, I've played all the choruses on "Lady Be Good" ninety million times. I'll always be able to play 'em, I think. I wanted something else to do, to give myself a challenge. It's a sense of—well, growing up, I guess. If I hadn't done it, I probably would always have regretted it, felt there was something I should have done. I mean, here we are on a stage and where is jazz? And what is jazz? What are you going to do, go out and play "Lady Be Good" again, forever and ever? How many times? Is somebody going to write the great jazz composition? I don't think so—and I never believed in that third-stream stuff. Either you play one thing or you play the other.

Is this a point of view you developed gradually, or did it happen all at once?
Hard to say. I was so brash in those days—I did things a more cautious head would never have done. One time, for instance, I decided, "Well, now I think I'll play with the New York Philharmonic." I wanted to do both the Mozart Concerto and the Debussy Rhapsody. And I prepared, worked very hard. When the time came, I was ready—played the Debussy then probably better than I do now. Sir John Barbirolli was conducting then, and the orchestra was giving him a hard time. They were a bunch of tough bastards, and Barbirolli had the misfortune of following Toscanini, so they really gave it to him. Well, we ran one of the works down, the Mozart I think. And at the end, you know how they go—tap-tap-tap with the bows, "very good," and all. All I said was, "All right, once more from the top." And we finished it, and the same business, "tap-tap-tap." And once again I said, "All right, now once again from the top." You know, thinking of it in retrospect, I think Barbirolli got a kind of vicarious kick out of it. He couldn't handle them that way at that point.

Did you ever entertain the possibility that you could have fallen on your face?
No, no. Not at all. Later you get wiser.

That's in keeping with the way you've always approached things professionally. No doubts or hesitations. You've never, in a figurative or real sense, thought poor?
No, never. I always wanted to do things with style. Don't care if it was clothes, or eating, or women. Or making music. Especially that. If you're going to do it, do it right. Don't take second class. You know—I'd rather have one or two good suits than a bunch of crappy ones. One of the things I think is wrong with a lot

of what you see today is that it doesn't have that sense of style, of elegance. I don't know where it's gone.

For instance?
In the days we've been talking about, a band had to be dressed correctly: shoes polished, suits clean and pressed. Even your horn shining. You don't want to look like a bunch of ragamuffins. Even to this day, I don't like people walking on stage not looking good. You have to look good. If you *feel* special about yourself, then you're going to play special. We used to wear tails at the Pennsylvania Hotel on Saturday nights—it was no problem to put 'em on. I can't stand, have always abhorred, seeing a musician walk in for a job wearing some damn Taj Mahal jacket or whatever they call them. Look, what I mean is this: if an individual allows his own personal standard to be eroded, something of what he does is going to be compromised. It's a matter of detail, sometimes. When you start losing detail, whether it's in music or in life—something as small as not sending a thank-you note, or failing to be polite to someone—you start to lose substance.

What about the newer developments in jazz? Do you listen to any of it—and do you like what you hear?
I've tried. It's hard to generalize, but it seems to me that a lot of the avant-garde music nowadays—maybe not the innovators, but certainly the copiers—is really kind of rough to listen to. I think one problem is very basic: they don't tune up. I don't see how you can play if you're out of tune. A while ago, someone I know who's very knowledgeable told me to listen to this girl flute player. Sure enough, when she started to play she was a quarter tone out—she just wasn't a musician. And tone—let's face it, the old-timers, like Louis, Bunny, Bix, Sidney Bechet, Johnny Dodds—they had lovely sounds. Individual, but beautiful. It seems to come with their talent for improvising, their overall musicianship.

Were things of that sort really priorities in those days?
Sure. How can you have a real ensemble otherwise? I mean, how can a string quartet play together if they don't have some similarity of tone and concept?

Those are pretty demanding standards. Are they responsible, I wonder, for some of the friction that has existed over the years between you and various musicians who have worked for you?
I think Gene Krupa expressed it as well as anybody. He always said about me— and I don't think he was being kind, but really rather critical—"Well, you know, Benny expects a hell of a lot out of himself, and just naturally expects it out of everyone else, too. To do the best they can." When they let me down, I get irritated—although I know that it doesn't do any good. Might as well just go along with it. Also, it all depends how I feel: if I'm not playing well myself, I might blame anybody. If I'm playing extraordinarily well, I think everybody else is wonderful, too—until daylight hits. Then I say, "Well, this guy really wasn't much good."

What do you think of today's popular music?
I don't really stay that much in touch with it. All I'll say is that I can't imagine someone forty years from now reminiscing fondly about having heard Blondie, or even the Rolling Stones, or—what was the name of that group the other day— Clash. What could they say about it? "Remember the volume, the flickering lights? Remember when we got high?" I kind of doubt it.

And a final word in self-evaluation. Where do you think you fit?
I think I've done a lot in this business, whether through screwball methods or not I don't know, that has helped other bands. I made a kind of road for them, you might say. If I raised my price, they found out about it and raised theirs. But somebody had to start it, to make the first move. You have to have the courage and confidence in your own ability. You have to know what the hell and who the hell you are in this business. Music may change, but I don't think that ever will.

23

Artie Shaw (I):
Matchless Music

*I should be sorry, my lord, if I have only succeeeded
in entertaining them. I wished to make them better.*
—George Frideric Handel, to his
English patron, after the 1743
London premiere of *Messiah*

In one of Artie Shaw's favorite illustrations of the difference between him and
Benny Goodman, the two are lunching together at a restaurant. Perhaps inevitably, conversation drifts into familiar territory.

"He kept insisting on asking me about other clarinet players" is Shaw's memory of it. "What did I think about this guy? How did I evaluate that guy? On
and on and on. Finally I said something like, 'Come on, Benny, quit it. You're
too hung up on the goddamn clarinet.'

"He looked at me really strangely. 'But that's what we play, isn't it?' he said.
And I said, 'No—I'm trying to play music.' Well, that seemed like a brand-new
thought to him, and for a moment I thought I saw a lightbulb flicker; but before
you knew it we were back to the clarinet."[1]

Shaw's account, if self-serving, is not without a certain ring of truth. To the
American public of the 1930s, these two were the "King of Swing" and the
"King of the Clarinet," monarch and pretender, locked eternally in a publicity
Totentanz manufactured by the popular music trade press.

Beyond the publicity the two men seemed quite different, even antithetical, personalities, driven by yet more disparate creative engines. Goodman, of course, emerged early as a peerless jazz clarinetist, able to play hot and fast, brightening even the dreariest studio ensemble. He recorded with Bix Beiderbecke, Red Nichols, Joe Venuti and Eddie Lang, the Teagarden brothers; the early, spiky energy of his teenage work quickly blossomed into a virtuosity unchallenged in the popular music world of the early '30s. There seemed little—in a jazz context, at least—he couldn't do.

Artie Shaw ripened more slowly and by a rather more circuitous route. His mature jazz clarinet style, achieved only toward the end of the decade, exemplifies a line of development that stresses the Apollonian ideals of logic, structural integrity, melodic balance, harmonic subtlety, introspection, emotional restraint, and great tonal beauty. It is the way of Beiderbecke and his musical foil, C-melody saxophonist Frank Trumbauer.

If understanding Goodman the clarinetist unlocks the man, understanding Shaw the clarinetist does little more than furnish clues, raise questions. Real insight comes only through patience and a broader view of Shaw's music-making as one expression of a diverse, probing, voracious, self-nourishing—and self-serving—intelligence.

"Artie was thirsty for knowledge, yes," one colleague has said, "but even more for acknowledgment by the world as a man who had that knowledge and who was above being just a musician. A man of intellect and erudition."

In mid-1939 Shaw recorded a popular song bearing the title "A Man and His Dream." That it was a rather undistinguished melody and lyric seems regrettable, in that the idea of it is a made-to-order Leitmotif, guiding an investigator through the labyrinth of Shaw's mind, utterances, and achievements.

The dream, a projection of how one man wanted things to be, is full and all-encompassing and limitlessly manipulative, shaping every band, every arrangement, every clarinet solo, in its image. An Artie Shaw orchestra, regardless of personnel, instrumentation, or repertoire, was from its inception—and for a long time thereafter—an expression of Shaw's mind and will.

That's quite different from the process of interaction, spontaneous chemistry, ceaseless give-and-take, that characterizes what we know as jazz: the process that formed the early Count Basie orchestras, with their succession of compulsively individual soloists. Even Duke Ellington, for all the discussion of the "Ellington vision," presided over, and provided context for, a collection of often unruly individuals; their personal expressiveness, both individually and in combinations within the whole, accounts in great measure for the orchestra's lasting fertility.

Benny Goodman's bands, especially in the '30s, were rooted firmly in collective chemistry. The arrangements, particularly those of Fletcher Henderson, were functional vehicles, catalysts, promoting coalescence between the leader's dynamic brilliance and that of Gene Krupa, Bunny Berigan, Harry James, Jess Stacy, and numerous others.

Artie Shaw's orchestras were different. Until the mid-1940s, when a combination of personal crises shook his faith in himself, it was Shaw alone who determined the overall design of his bands. There are few moments that do not in some way proceed from a characteristically well thought-out conception.

"If you're running a band," he has said, "and you have a strong idea, a strong notion, of what you're doing, you're going to try different things, and you *impose* that on the men, without killing them, without diminishing their egos."

And true to Shaw's comment in his lunchtime exchange with Goodman, it was a conception based on exactly what Shaw said it was: on music, not an instrument. The Shaw clarinet itself often seems part of the plan, in the way both choral and solo parts of a Handel oratorio, however eloquent on their own, belong to an overall whole.

A plan, it must be added, that may or may not have proceeded from any canon or set of rules readily identifiable as jazz. It is arguably this last which has made assessment of Shaw so problematic for writers: the idea that an ensemble could *incorporate* the expressive language of jazz improvisation as an ingredient within a larger context, one that was not necessarily the result of interaction, seems to trouble jazz chroniclers—and more than a few musicians as well.

Tenor saxophonist Jerry Jerome, who worked for Goodman and Shaw in quick succession, has spoken insightfully of their differences in conception. The 1940 Shaw orchestra, he has said, "wasn't ideal for the jazz soloist. Not only wasn't there enough space given to the jazz players, [but] the 'feel' wasn't really right for jazz. Unlike the Goodman band, *which was deeply into jazz* [emphasis added], Shaw had an almost symphonic approach during this period."[2]

Not that Shaw's clarinet was anything but a jazz voice—perhaps, at its peak, one of the most eloquent of all jazz solo voices. But the ways in which it spoke, the uses to which it was put, and most of all the concept that drove it represented something wider and more encompassing.

"To me," said Shaw, "listening to Benny talk about the clarinet was like listening to a surgeon getting hung up on a scalpel. He was totally tied up in it, to the exclusion of all else. He'd point at the horn and say, 'This thing will never let you down.' I found that very strange. 'Instrument,' after all, is a self-defining word. Something by means of which you define certain things. A medium, not an end: a way to get something done. A compass is an instrument, and so's a clarinet. Even mastery of the instrument is an incidental—a way to get to something, to realize a greater goal."

He was born Arthur Jacob Arshawsky, Jewish and poor, on New York's Lower East Side, on May 23, 1910, almost a year to the day after Goodman's birth in similar circumstances in Chicago (and, like him, the son of a tailor). When he was seven his family moved to New Haven, and it was there that the boy became seriously interested in music around age twelve, after hearing a saxophonist in a bright blue-and-white striped blazer play "Dreamy Melody," lyricist Ted Koehler's first published song, at a local theatre.

Shaw's description of the event, especially of the saxophone itself as "a glistening, golden gadget with mother-of-pearl keys stuck all over it," recalls a similar formative moment experienced by a teenaged Bud Freeman in a Chicago theatre, watching saxophonist Paul Biese in a spotlight, his instrument "shining and sparkling" (see chapter 11).[3]

Shaw has described his learning process often, including an account in his discursive autobiography, *The Trouble With Cinderella*. By his mid-teens he was in Cleveland, where he attracted attention with Austin Wylie's orchestra. Among those who heard about him was drummer Ben Pollack, then recruiting musicians for a brand-new band, to be headquartered in Venice, California.

"I could have gone with Pollack," said Shaw. "He called me in Cleveland to come out to the Coast. But I was having too much fun with Wylie—leading the band, gaining terrific experience. Wylie would let me chop up stocks, call out modulations. Besides, I was making a lot of dough—$175 a week plus extra for arrangements. [Pianist] Claude Thornhill and I had become friends, and I'd even gotten him into the band. Why should I leave?" Pollack, of course, ultimately hired fifteen-year-old Benny Goodman.[4]

Mostly just for the fun of it, "Art Shaw," as he now called himself, entered an essay contest, first in a series sponsored by the now almost forgotten *Cleveland Daily News*. The subject: how the forthcoming National Air Races, scheduled to be held in the lakeside city, would benefit Cleveland. Each contestant also had to submit an original song.

Young Shaw won handily, gladly accepting the first prize, an all-expenses-paid trip to Hollywood—where he promptly ran into two New Haven pals, trumpeter Charlie Trotta and saxophonist Tony Pestritto. They were with Irving Aaronson's Commanders at the Blossom Room of the Roosevelt Hotel and were about to begin a tour with the road company of Cole Porter's show *Paris*, in which they'd played Broadway that winter.

Between then and December 9, when they were scheduled to begin a week in Cleveland, Trotta and Pestritto promised to talk to Aaronson, get him down to the Golden Pheasant Restaurant to hear Wylie's young reedman. Ultimately he came, listened, and after some weeks cabled a job offer. Shaw jumped at it. His replacement with Wylie was twenty-one-year-old Clarence Hutchenrider, who joined with a friend and fellow-Texan, trumpeter Grady Watts. Both men, soon to find prominence with the Casa Loma Orchestra, remembered hearing Shaw on his last night as a Wylie sideman.

"I never heard anybody play so beautifully in all my life," said Watts. "Of course he was hot as hell at that time, and so many of the arrangements were built around him. Artie—well, he really had them applauding that night—and the next day he was gone."[5]

Now with Aaronson, Shaw played six weeks at Chicago's Granada Café. Every night after hours he made straight for the South Side, where he heard Jimmie Noone, sat in with Earl Hines, met and played with some of the young white jazzmen emerging there at the time, including clarinetist Frank Teschemacher and pianist Jess Stacy. Muggsy Spanier, in town with Ted Lewis, brought his horn around one night.

The Commanders moved on to Manhattan—and into one of the most painful episodes of Shaw's life. As he tells it in The Trouble With Cinderella, "I hit a man with my car. It couldn't have been helped, for he stepped off a curb right in front of my car in a way that it was utterly impossible to avoid hitting him. Anyone who happened to be driving in that place at that time would have hit him—it just happened to be me . . . He died almost instantly."[6]

The ensuing months of litigation and mental anguish left the young musician broke and demoralized. Because a damage suit was still pending he couldn't go back on the road with Aaronson; he stayed in New York, put in his local 802 card, and waited out the statutory six-month period during which he wasn't allowed to work.

Eventually he found his way uptown and began sitting in at Pod's and Jerry's with the house pianist, Willie "the Lion" Smith. "My boy Artie was a good student," said Smith, "and The Lion was proud of him when we went out to jam after finishing our nightly stint at P's & J's." On one of these after-hours jaunts they ran into Sidney Bechet, who (in the Lion's phrase) "was particular about clarinet players." From the Lion's account of that meeting, it's clear that the New Orleans master also liked what he heard.[7]

Shaw, too, has described those nights, and the friendships he made among Harlem musicians, in The Trouble With Cinderella. But his description lacks any real sense of his own participation; he is like a commentator at a sporting event, observing the interaction, the bonding process, reporting it. He tells us what happened, but in so doing all but extracts himself emotionally from the very events he describes.

Fortunately, Shaw is also a writer of fiction and has used that other, ultimately more liberating medium to describe many of these same events. His short story "Snow White in Harlem, 1930," for example, deals with his nights at Pod's and Jerry's. In it, through the third-person perceptions of the barely fictionalized character Al (later Albie) Snow, we get closer to Shaw the young musician, actually participating in—feeling—a remarkable moment.

By the time Snow got used to the pianist's "funny, choppy-sounding, semi-ragtime-y type of beat," he writes,

> he started trotting out a few slightly more complicated licks of his own—
> odds and ends of long-line phrases incorporating various combinations
> of passing notes and altered chords he'd been working on lately but
> hadn't yet had a chance to try out with other musicians up to now . . .
> Some twenty or more choruses later, he stopped playing. He was so high
> it took quite a while before he could even start to come back down again.
> Then he suddenly realized he had completely forgotten where he was,
> and even who he was playing with. And that there toward the end, in
> the last four or five choruses, he'd been putting out stuff he'd never

thought of before in his whole life, some of it so far over his head he had no idea where in the world it was even coming from.[8]

The 802 waiting period up at last, Shaw began to work. Word had spread: he was fast, versatile, could play lead alto *and* hot clarinet. With the Depression taking hold and the entertainment business much shriveled, radio and recording seemed the most promising—and lucrative—fields available.

But there were obstacles. "Benny had arrived before me, and he was dominating things at that time. Jimmy Dorsey had been there first, but Benny had come in and—well, thrown him right out. He had the clarinet thing sewed up. The way most dance band books were written then, first altos didn't play jazz, especially on clarinet," Shaw said. "The book was usually written for the jazz to come out of the second alto—or third alto, as we used to call it."

So Shaw concentrated, for the moment at least, on being a lead alto player. He worked for Fred Rich at CBS, for Red Nichols at the Park Central Hotel, for such leaders as Paul Specht and Vincent Lopez.

"I developed the kind of lead alto sound you needed to cut through in radio. It's a brighter sound than what I'd used in the Midwest. That sound was more stuffy, a little like the way you'd sound with a rag in the bell of your horn. More like [Frank] Trumbauer, I guess, or the French saxophonists, like Marcel Mule.

"I didn't much like that radio sound, as we called it then, at first—too blatant. Had to change mouthpieces, approach it differently. But you know, you always give up something to gain something: there's a price to pay for everything. You gain that extra volume, that cutting edge and you've lost a certain mellifluous sound."

Sometimes Goodman, a competent alto player at best, played second to him in a section. Not without a certain *Schadenfreude*, Shaw told of an arrangement of Rodgers and Hart's "Lover" which featured an especially attractive alto counter-line. Though it was in Shaw's lead part, Goodman asked to play it. After one runthrough, the conductor (Shaw remembered it as David Raksin, himself an able clarinetist and saxophonist, later to win lasting respect as composer of "Laura") stopped the band. Who, he asked, was playing the alto countermelody? Goodman raised his hand. "Give it to Shaw" was Raksin's immediate and peremptory reply.

Along came Roger Wolfe Kahn, son of millionaire banker and philanthropist Otto Kahn (and co-composer of the popular standard "Crazy Rhythm"), with plans to form a new band for an engagement at the Pennsylvania Hotel. Kahn's mid-'20s orchestra, resident at the Biltmore, had been the talk of New York, with Miff Mole, Joe Venuti, Vic Berton, and trumpeter Leo McConville among its stars. Jack Teagarden, subbing for Mole, took his first major recorded trombone solo on a 1928 Kahn session.

Now Kahn was building a brand-new band with a brand-new book—one that called for the lead alto to play the jazz clarinet solos. The socialite-leader's choice for that chair was Artie Shaw. But Shaw, his finances still shaky after the auto accident and its aftermath, was determined to be hired only on *his* terms, which started with the—for 1932—outlandish weekly salary of $500.

"I told him, 'I want ten weeks half-pay in advance, and the rest while I play.' He gave it to me. I changed the money into five-dollar bills and took it home. Claude [Thornhill] and his wife Polly were living in the same building; he'd come in from Cleveland and was waiting out his card. I knocked on their door, and when Polly opened it I went ZAP! tossed it all in the air. I don't know how many bills there were, but it was quite a pile. Claude stood there, stunned. He couldn't believe it. He kept yelling, 'Is this *real*? Is this *real*?' "

It was a good band, with Charlie Teagarden, Larry Binyon, and drummer Chauncey Morehouse among the sidemen and arrangements by Thornhill, Arthur Schutt, Bill Challis, and even a seventeen-year-old Eddie Sauter. They played Boston and Atlantic City, did six weeks at the Grill Room of the Pennsylvania Hotel ("Roger would leave and we'd play the blues—the waiters and the rest of them *hated* us"), after which most of Kahn's sidemen—but not the leader—signed on for the pit orchestra of the Gershwin show *Pardon My English*. After tryouts in Boston it opened in New York on January 20, 1933, and lasted only forty-six performances. Kahn reassembled his men that spring for a month at the swanky Club Forest, in New Orleans—but that was the end of the road. The leader, a new wife at his side (a brief marriage to singer Hannah Williams had come and gone in 1932), sailed for Europe on August 5, 1933.[9]

Shaw slipped right back into radio. That most broadcast work was surely, in his words, "boring, mind-numbing garbage" is more than substantiated by a photograph recently unearthed by the Institute of Jazz Studies, at Rutgers University. It shows an orchestra led by veteran saxophonist Bennie Krueger for the *Pick and Pat* radio show, a very youthful-looking Shaw sitting demurely among the reeds; but it's the brass, in the back row, that catch the eye. Trumpeters Charlie Margulis and Manny Klein and trombonist Jack Jenney are playing their horns backward, left-handed and perfectly deadpan, while Kreuger, none the wiser, stands in front, his back to them. The message comes across loud and clear.

Shaw was by then recording often. He's on records by Specht, Fred Rich, various of the ARC-Brunswick house groups—and a dozen Columbia titles by the Kahn band, recorded between May and September of 1932. He solos on two, his style as yet unfinished. His sixteen bars on "Fit as a Fiddle" are bright-toned, rhythmically fluid, not unlike Goodman of the same time, but with less heat. On "It Don't Mean a Thing (If It Ain't Got That Swing)," he runs into a momentary fingering glitch, then two bars later, apparently expecting an A-minor chord to resolve to A7 en route to a cadence (the key is C), he lands squarely on a C♯. Soon enough, he will purge such missteps from his work.

Shaw's first appearance on a strictly "hot" record date appears to be an August 15, 1934, session led by trumpeter Wingy Manone. It's a racially mixed band, with Wingy, Shaw, Bud Freeman, and trombonist Dicky Wells on the front line and bassist John Kirby, drummer Kaiser Marshall, and guitarist Frank Victor in the rhythm. Two pianists share the date, forming a fascinating polarity: one, Teddy Wilson, very much the newly arrived man of the hour; the other, Jelly Roll Morton, already slipping into obscurity, flamboyant relic of an earlier time. Shaw comes on vigorous and surprisingly hot on "Easy Like," displaying the kind of punchy attack and raspy tone more often associated with Matty Matlock or Sidney Arodin. The shape and execution of his half-chorus on "I'm Alone Without You" recalls Goodman of the same period.[10]

Shaw and Wilson came together again a month later as part of a hand-picked Red Norvo recording group also including Jack Jenney on trombone and Charlie Barnet on tenor. Artie contributes a thoughtful obbligato to Norvo's opening melody statement on "Old Fashioned Love," then turns in a nicely organized chorus on his own. His two buoyant choruses on Norvo's "Tomboy" (a melodyless original on a chord sequence fusing "I Got Rhythm" with the bridge of "Rosetta") are even better. It's good hot playing, but there's little here to distinguish Shaw from Matty Matlock, Johnny Mince, or any of the other good journeyman clarinetists then recording in the New York studios.

Shaw turns up increasingly on records with Frank Trumbauer, with the Boswell Sisters, with an all-star pickup group led by trumpeter Manny Klein, with Fats Waller sound-alike Bob Howard and studio contract singer Chick Bullock. Though he plays consistently well, there is as yet little indication of the searching imagination and surpassing beauty shortly to become his hallmarks.

(Once established as a clarinetist, Shaw seems to have restricted his alto playing to the radio studios—with at least one memorable exception. Trumpeter Manny Klein, one of Artie's early champions in New York, told of a night when Jimmy Dorsey sat in with the house band at the Famous Door. As Artie listened, said Klein, "he kept shaking his head. Finally he got up and said, 'Are you coming?' I stared at him: 'Where are we going?' He motioned with his hand: 'To get my horn.' So I drove him up to his apartment, somewhere on Central Park West in the 90s. When we returned to the Door, he got on the stand—and he played! You never heard such sax playing in your life. He was a demon!")[11]

The turning point—or at least the first clear glimpse of what lay in store— came with Shaw's appearance in the landmark Swing Music Concert held at New York's Imperial Theatre Sunday evening, May 24, 1936 (performances at this event by Bunny Berigan and the team of Red Norvo and Mildred Bailey are described in the chapters devoted to them). Announced as a benefit for Local 802 of the musicians' union, it was an ambitious undertaking. The sheer mechanics of shuttling nearly twenty acts, from solo pianists to big bands, on and offstage could have ended in chaos. But a combination of quick, efficient staging and smooth master-of-ceremonies work kept things moving.[12]

As Shaw remembered it, concert organizer Joe Helbock, proprietor of the Onyx Club and a powerful presence on 52nd Street, wanted him to play with a small group for about five minutes in front of a closed curtain while things were being set up for the next big band. "Since many of those groups were going to be fronted by friends of mine, guys I worked with daily around the radio studios, I could see no harm in it," he wrote.[13]

He soon discovered that most of his colleagues were planning to use standard horns-and-rhythm instrumentations in their groups. That made him think: he'd been getting together occasionally with a string quartet to play through concert literature. Why not use them, with guitar and drums added? Billed as "Arthur Shaw's String Swing Ensemble," it performed a quickly assembled Shaw composition, an essay in contrasts introduced as *Interlude in B-flat*.[14]

After a quiet opening string passage strongly reminiscent of Ravel's 1905 *Introduction and Allegro* (for harp, string quartet, clarinet, and flute), Shaw enters with a brief, and highly romantic, cadenza, then launches into a technically intricate theme based on the chord structure of the old standard "Shine." The introduction turns out to have been a phrase fragment belonging to an expansive middle section, now played with considerable tenderness by clarinet and strings. A return to the "Shine" section sees things home.[15]

When they started, said Shaw, the audience was still abuzz from the last brass-and-reeds *fortissimo* onslaught. Things hadn't gone far beyond the introduction when "I became aware of people shushing each other, and the whole theatre becoming very, very quiet. I was terrified—but when we went into the 'jazz' section, I realized that people were actually starting to applaud!"

The applause grew to a prolonged ovation, which kept swelling even after Shaw finished taking his bows. (At this point, his memory of what happened diverges slightly from press accounts published at the time. He states in *The Trouble With Cinderella* and elsewhere that the group had nothing else arranged or rehearsed, so they simply played the *Interlude* again. Yet a *Down Beat* article published the following week reports that the "second selection was 'Japanese Sandman' and proved that [the] idea could be adapted to [a] popular selection with plenty [of] guts").[16]

Interlude in B-flat was the critical sensation of the evening, "probably the only new creation in modern music within the past five years!" in *Down Beat's* breathless—and inaccurate—evaluation. "Shaw came in for some dynamic clarinet work that will probably keep Goodman awake for several nights to come."

Whether the *Interlude* ever disturbed Benny's sleep patterns will never be known. But without doubt its performance that night opened doors for Artie Shaw. Within days a major booker had phoned to ask whether he might consider leading his own band. Goodman and the Dorseys had done it, and seemed to be thriving. Red Norvo, too. Shaw, suddenly the man of the hour (and a handsome one at that), might just be next, a natural.

Little more than a fortnight after stepping onstage at the Imperial, "Arthur Shaw" strolled into Brunswick's tiny 57th Street studio, where he had recorded "I Can't Get Started" with Bunny Berigan that April. But now he was there to lead, for the first time, his own group. Again, the string quartet was at the core; but with the greater flexibility of studio acoustics and microphone balancing, he could expand the horns, adding trumpet, tenor sax, and trombone to the clarinet.

The moment, above all, was his, a watershed in his life. Before the *Interlude* and this first recording session, it doesn't seem to have seriously occurred to

Shaw that he could establish, then control, his own musical environment. That he could have the freedom to experiment, to realize ideas perhaps long held, perhaps suddenly chanced upon, through the agency of a group of musicians.

Predictably, the results of this first date were in spots shapeless, musically uneven. Here and there (as on "The Japanese Sandman"), he works the strings comfortably into the ensembles amid good, brief solos from tenor saxophonist Tony Zimmers and others. But Sam Weiss's drumming, a clattering recital of 1920s "dixieland" band gimmicks, compromises some of the nuanced quality that had made the *Interlude* performance so distinctive.

The leader's own solos stand up best, and there are signs of something new afoot. He's engagingly punchy on the minor-key "It Ain't Right"; elsewhere the phrases are longer, more unified, than in 1934. Such melody statements as the opening chorus of "I Used to Be Above Love" show a sensitivity of tone and dynamics that promises interesting things to come.

The next few Brunswick dates, running through year's end, found band and leader in an ongoing process of trial and error: Shaw shuffles combinations, voicings, tonal possibilities; he readjusts ensemble textures. Some things come off better than others: at one point Artie (who seems to be responsible for most of the routining, though arranger Jerry Gray appears as a violinist on the second date and every one thereafter) uses a three-horn "dixieland" front line against Stravinsky-esque writing in the strings.[17]

There is no point at which this Shaw ensemble sounds like a standard swing band. "I was so sick, bored to death, with all those riff things people were playing," he said. "Tommy and Jimmy [Dorsey] had done the same thing; and Benny, and the Casa Loma band before him. It was all so formulaic: apart from the soloists, I thought Fletcher Henderson's was one of the most boring bands in the world. You knew exactly what was going to happen unless somebody like Coleman [Hawkins] or Louis [Armstrong] was in there doing something."[18]

Though they often seem to grope for musical definition, these first Shaw records offer flashes of charm and even real surprise: a dixielandish reading of the movie song "Skeleton in the Closet," for example, gives way abruptly to a half-tempo announcement of the eerie, ominous theme that shortly became "Nightmare," Shaw's band signature.

Lee Castaldo (Castle), on trumpet, does frequent homage to Bunny Berigan, and Peg La Centra approaches her vocals with refreshing intelligence. "She sang the words as though she understood what they meant," Shaw said. "She was an actress, working at CBS. Came from Boston, I think. She heard me rehearsing the band one day, came in and said, 'Are you going to use a singer?' I said something like 'Sure, I suppose I have to.' So she said, 'Then I'd like to ask for the job.' "

Shaw's own clarinet solos were taking on distinctive shape and texture. "Darling, Not Without You" presages his "singing" ballad manner; "Take Another Guess" finds him exploring his clean, pitch-perfect upper register; on "There's Frost on the Moon" he struts handsomely for half a chorus.

But the feature that, from 1936 on, sets Artie Shaw apart is the tone. Centered in all registers, its sweetness balanced by a minty astringency of attack and warmed by a violin-like vibrato, it is almost from date to date ("My Blue Heaven" is particularly good) an increasingly personal expressive vehicle. Why the transformation? Just practice, it seems, and lots of it. "The clarinet is not an instrument to be put aside and picked up six months or a year later," Shaw has said. "It calls for total concentration. Its very name means 'clear.' I used up a large part of my life developing and honing my technique." Shaw, it seems, was not *always* above the sort of single-minded attention to his instrument for which he chaffed Goodman.

Others have identified the almost fanatic intensity, the focus and exactitude, of Shaw at work, as (in the words of *New Yorker* writer Robert Lewis Taylor) "the principal ingredient of Shaw's disposition—a deadly, dogged, skull-cracking determination. His singleness of purpose during any given phase of learning is frightening—verging, indeed, on the suicidal."[19]

Shaw's view is somewhat less dramatic. "I was never satisfied, even when I was on top," he has said. "I sought a sound which was distinctly my own, but I often felt I hadn't quite reached it. Even when I would vacation and go fishing in Canada . . . I'd go off in the woods and blow for at least an hour a day."[20]

Somewhat more problematical is Shaw's thinking in assembling this first band at all. Benny Goodman's Palomar Ballroom success the previous year had touched off a public craze for "swing bands"—which most often meant large, loud, high-voltage ensembles dominated by powerful brass sections. What could a new, untried leader hope to achieve in exposing this rather delicate flower of a band to the dancing public?

Yet here was Shaw, trying to market an ensemble whose dynamic range and tonal thrust seemed to defy the hot dance band format—and whose juxtaposition of stylistic and textural elements often appeared conceptually rooted in the late '20s. If anything, these first Shaw records recall the efforts of such arrangers as Bill Challis, Tom Satterfield, Matt Malneck, and Lennie Hayton, writing for the Paul Whiteman Orchestra of the vintage years 1927–30.

Those scores had regularly brought together disparate ingredients: excerpts from *Petrouchka* and Délibes's *Sylvia* used to launch a Trumbauer saxophone solo (Hayton, "Nobody's Sweetheart"); Bix Beiderbecke soloing with warmth and rhythmic kick over *tenuto* strings (Challis, "Love Nest"); a "front line" of two cornets and clarinet playing spirited "dixieland" counterpoint to a sweetly flavored "straight" melody statement (Malneck, "Mary").[21]

It's an orchestration method of great creative potential, and it seems to have deeply affected Shaw. The impression is strengthened by his choice of repertoire, including such 1920s chestnuts as "Copenhagen" and "Sobbin' Blues"; in his use of Franklyn Marks's imaginative, but definitely not fashionable, "Cream Puff"; even in Shaw's own impeccably executed virtuoso demonstration piece, "Streamline," with its strong echoes of Jimmy Dorsey's "Beebe," written nearly a decade before.[22]

Commenting on "Cream Puff" in 1993, Shaw revealed a bit more about himself and the forces driving him than he may have intended. "It's an interesting piece of music," he said. "Imaginative. Indicates that this is an attempt to do something musically different from what was going on. *It shows a kind of restless mind that's trying to do something. The fact that it didn't catch on with the public—well, join the crowd, from Mozart on* [emphasis added]."

Long life, a fruitful career, and an indefatigable ability to discuss himself have left posterity in no doubt as to the restlessness—and fertility—of Artie Shaw's mind. But his "join the crowd" pronouncement, with its condescending tone, its identification of himself with Mozart and other figures of like stature, is a momentary dissonance. Did Shaw seriously think he could defy what he knew to be popular taste with a band built on such musically idiosyncratic premises? Did he not foresee even the simple functional problem of his string quartet being heard in a crowded, noisy ballroom?

Shaw believed, and in some respects never stopped believing, that a musician's only real job was to make interesting and original music, with some faceless cadre of agents, publicists, and business types circling about like a wartime fighter escort, attending to packaging, promoting, and selling it to the public. However, the novice bandleader soon discovered that the term "music business" contained two words. A ballroom manager's angry rebuff left him in no doubt of that:

> You listen to *me!* My problem is to get the dough to pay you and your goddamn band and all the rest of the expenses I got to pay to run this joint. Your problem is to get people in here. And if you want to take your pants down on that goddamn bandstand every night and take a crap up there, and if people'll pay to come in here and see you do it— I'll pay you to take a crap up there every night. That's how much I give a good goddamn about what kind of music you're playing—you hear me?[23]

Shaw heard him. After particularly disastrous engagements at the Adolphus Hotel in Dallas ("You could've shot deer in the place") and Frank Dailey's Meadowbrook in New Jersey ("Musicians loved us, showed up all the time: but musicians don't pay the rent"), he disbanded. In later years he would speak of this first band with heartfelt regret, as though something besides a group of musicians, something emotional within himself, had ceased to exist.

"It broke my heart," he has said. "People kept telling me, 'Stay with it,' but I couldn't. There was no way. And Jerry Gray—poor little guy, he played lead fiddle in the [string] quartet. He was brokenhearted. We put a lot of love and care into those arrangements, even the junky pieces."

He reorganized with a more conventional swing instrumentation—and with more than a small degree of pique. "I thought, 'If that's what they want, I'll give 'em the loudest goddamn band in the world.' " He's made the statement on countless occasions, usually as preamble to a disquisition on the evils of the entertainment business.

Generally it goes more or less as follows: "I'm convinced that the major problem for the artist is the disparity between what he's trying to do and what the audience perceives. The very nature of an artist is that you are thinking of value; the very nature of an audience is that you are thinking of amusement. Entertainment vs. art. But art *was never meant to be entertaining* [emphasis added].''

Helen Forrest, whose vocals greatly enhanced the 1938–39 Shaw orchestra, tells of Shaw, the night he abandoned band and music business at the Pennsylvania Hotel, railing: "I hate selling myself. I hate the fans. They won't even let me play without interrupting me. They scream when I play, they don't listen. They don't care about the music."[24]

Yes, yes, an interlocutor longs to say. We know that. Know that Tobias Smollett could have been speaking for Artie Shaw when, in *The Adventures of Sir Launcelot Greaves*, he wrote, "I think for my part one half of the nation is mad—and the other half not very sound." Yet Shaw pressed ahead: the '30s, when all this began, was a time when the twin curves of American art music and popular entertainment intersected. As subsequent cultural history has shown, it was a nexus unique in twentieth-century America. In becoming a professional bandleader in 1936, Shaw—a highly intelligent man and seasoned musician—had to have known what awaited him; known that leading a dance orchestra at the height of a national craze was in no way comparable to membership in a chamber ensemble; that playing for thousands of dancers in a crowded ballroom had little in common with playing for a few hundred *cognoscenti* in a concert hall.

So whence the petulance, a *Leitmotif* of Shaw's career, during and since his days as a musician? From what does it proceed? Given the testimony of those who knew him off the bandstand, including several of the women to whom he was married, Shaw's contempt for his audiences, for the popular music business, for the various tyrannies under which professional entertainers must live their lives, seems little more than part of a behavioral whole. Basic to this man's nature seems to be a need to control, to order and shape his life circumstances, professional and private. To make the world at large—at least so far as it affected him—conform to his projection of how it ought to be.

Why this should have been is a subject dealt with, as Shaw himself has indicated on numerous occasions, in years of analysis. It has little place in a discussion of his musicianship and musical achievements, save to illuminate the shape and direction of Shaw's orchestras and his own personal style.

But as the story of those orchestras unfolds, it would be well to remember a description by Evelyn Keyes, far and away the most perceptive and articulate of Shaw's eight wives, of her realization of what marriage to him would require of her:

> The least I could do for my man, then, was to get things the way he liked them. (If they are to be done, why not the right way, he would say.) His morning egg the exact degree of hard/softness, the freshly squeezed orange juice without seeds or pulp, toast buttered to the edge and not a fraction less, coffee poured to the exact quarter-inch below the rim, no more, no less.[25]

*   *   *

"Art Shaw and His New Music" was rough at first, even slapdash, as its first batch of radio transcriptions, made for Thesaurus in early 1937, reveals. The sax section blend is often haphazard, and the brass has ragged moments. There is as yet no book. Many arrangements are obviously borrowed: one, on the Harry Warren–Johnny Mercer "Night Over Shanghai," even has the characteristically British sound most often associated with Ray Noble. Some just sound like heads, patched together for the date.

It was a *Zwischenzeit*, a "time between," band and leader casting about for a commercially viable collective identity. Shaw's Brunswick records continued to be an uneven lot: "Sweet Adeline" and "All God's Chillun Got Rhythm," for example, differ little from the things Fletcher Henderson and others were doing— except for Shaw's clarinet. He swings hard and brightly on "Just You, Just Me," ideas seeming to cascade effortlessly out of the horn. Critic-historian Max Harrison's declaration that "there is hardly a number which does not get its sharpest flavor from Shaw's unmistakable sound" begins to take on meaning.

Shaw has been forthright in discussing the evolution of his own playing, particularly his uncanny control of the clarinet's highest reaches. "I invented that register in jazz" is his way of explaining it. "In those days, clarinet went up effectively to a high G [concert F] or A [concert G], at the utmost. Most players thought, what would have been the point of going higher? It wasn't written in any of the literature, so you didn't have to learn it. There weren't even any fingerings for those notes, for a B♮ or a D♭ above high C. I found fingerings for those notes."

In a conversation with academician (and proficient amateur clarinetist) Henry Duckham, he added that in those days of haphazard miking and small loudspeakers, "I couldn't compete with trumpets playing high D's and E♭'s, so I had to play high G's and A's and B's and even C's to get above them . . . [but] if I were going to play up there it should sound like normal notes. I didn't see any reason for the tone to thin out. I worked at it until it came out."[26]

When it came out it was not only musical but often startlingly beautiful, even in the most vertiginous reaches; the altissimo notes *sang*, vibrato and all. Shaw's solo on Gray's May 1937 arrangement of "Blue Skies," for example, carries him up to his high C, but with no sense of effect or display; it's merely the logical culmination of a set of phrases.

His chorus on the jazz standard "Someday Sweetheart," made the same day, comfortably and naturally incorporates high A's and B's, leaving listeners blissfully unaware that anything out of the ordinary has occurred. It also illustrates quite graphically the degree to which Shaw's melodic concept—figure-shapes, points of emphasis, fondness for certain chordal intervals—was affected by his admiration for Bix Beiderbecke.

One has only to imagine the pickups and melody exposition of bars 1–3, or the cadential figure of bars 6–7, played on a cornet; or the way he plays with a simple figure in the bridge, varying it, building its intensity each time—and finally, gloriously, the declamatory figure of bars 28–29, where Bix's silver tone and attack seem to resound within Shaw's.

"Someday Sweetheart," Artie Shaw clarinet solo, 1937.

Shaw's solo on this band's first record of "Nightmare" illuminates another, quite unexpected, quality. Call it a Jewish flavor, an emotional predisposition, something cantorial: the catch in the voice, the certain keening, grieving, quality that distinguishes the *Kaddish* and *Kol Nidre* of Jewish liturgy. The manner in which Shaw, in his "Nightmare" solo, uses a rapidly alternating C♯ and B♮ combination, seems to connect with something distant, intimate, mysterious. Shaw himself offers no explanation, save that "often I was trying to sound like a violin, especially like [Jascha] Heifetz. He had a quality quite apart—you know, perhaps the best thing to say, the best way to explain it, is that what you play is what you are. Certainly I can't deny the influence of my Russian-Jewish-Austrian ancestry. But how it comes out, how it makes itself felt—that's a mystery."[27]

But above all else there is the tone, a sound which, in trumpeter Bernie

Privin's apt phrase, "remains in your mind." Artie Baker, who worked for Shaw in 1941 and is himself an exceptionally accomplished clarinetist, cited Shaw's prowess as a lead alto saxophone player as the root of his tonal conception on the clarinet: "The way I hear it, he's taken what he knows from the saxophone— the legato feel, the way of moving from note to note, the expressive vibrato— and applied it to the clarinet. His vibrato is very unusual in a clarinet: listen to any other clarinet player, even Benny, and you'll never hear a vibrato like that. It's pretty, but not just pretty: he knows how to use it, how to apply it to make it *express* something."[28]

"I worked hard on that," Shaw has said. "The thing was in my face seven, maybe eight hours a day. I wanted to make it an instrument that *sang*. I didn't listen much to anybody else, though there were people—Lester Young, Louis, Bix, Trumbauer—I enjoyed. But I always felt there had to be more to it, to making music, than just the jazz language."

Hank Freeman, who joined Shaw's band as second alto in time for the "Blue Skies" date, put the matter in better focus by suggesting that Shaw "wasn't as much a clarinetist as he was a *musician* [emphasis added] . . . The instrument disappeared. He became a voice that spoke to you on a variety of levels."[29]

In early 1938, Shaw signed with RCA Victor to make records for its thirty-five-cent Bluebird subsidiary. His very first effort under the new contract, coupling Rudolf Friml's old operetta favorite "Indian Love Call" with the unusually structured "Begin the Beguine," from Cole Porter's 1936 show, *Jubilee*, achieved the impossible: it became an instant and enormous hit.

Its success literally hurled the twenty-eight-year-old clarinetist into orbit as a national celebrity. It also thrust him into the very situation he'd dreaded most. He'd consoled himself with the thought that, once having earned and saved up decent money leading a dance band, he could return to making music as he wanted to, supporting himself on the proceeds of his commercial adventure and supplementing his income from time to time with the kind of studio work that had seen him through the early 1930s.

Now, beyond doubt or denial, he was a prisoner of his own commercial success. By the end of 1938 it was obvious that, like it or not, he was stuck in front of a six-brass, four-reed dance orchestra. His many disquisitions on finding a policy for that orchestra, on presenting quality songs with clarity and simplicity, seem, at root, to only state the obvious. What else, after all, would he have sought in shaping a band sound—particularly given his oft-declared aversion to "dumb, boring" riff numbers—besides quality repertoire, clarity, simplicity, directness, and the rest?

If this is the sort of band he has to lead, he seems to be saying, he will make it the best damn band of its kind in the field. Shaw had the means: a strongly thought-out vision, steady authority, his own instrumental mastery. The strength and force of will to recast his surroundings in whatever shape he chose.

A band, a group of musicians being paid to be the agency of one man's will, is arguably easier to alter, pound and pummel into shape, than is another human being. Certainly there is no gainsaying Shaw's success at turning a collection of potentially disparate individual players into a smooth and efficient team.

Max Harrison has referred to Shaw as "a tutelary spirit, combining Prospero and Ariel in one," and the formulation is a good one. Prospero, the poet, incarnation of wisdom and benevolence; Ariel, blithe, airborne spirit of lyric fancy. They coexist naturally and comfortably in Artie Shaw.

"I paid a lot of attention to each chair in that band," he reports. "Each chair and each section and the blend they got." That's especially obvious in the reeds: as Shaw has said, altos Les Robinson and Hank Freeman, and tenors Tony Pestritto (by now changed to "Pastor") and Georgie Auld, heard individually, had quite different tones and phrasing concepts. Yet Shaw managed, through intensive rehearsal and attention to detail, to turn them into a section that was the envy of the band business. The *soli* passages on "The Man I Love," "Lover, Come Back to Me," and "Out of Nowhere"—all 1939—are flawlessly matched, even down to speed and width of vibrato. Such passages seem to *sing*, much in the same way that Shaw's clarinet solos sing.

Shaw's way of fielding comments about Les Robinson's prowess as a lead alto player—the elegance of his phrasing, the sometimes astonishing beauty of his tone—is anything but self-effacing. "I taught him everything he knows," he has said. "The way he plays, even the sound he gets—that's an exact replica of the way I played lead alto." Robinson and others have enthusiastically agreed: Robinson's lead was especially pliant, particularly when compared to the stricter phrasing of such outstanding lead men as Nuncio "Toots" Mondello.

"I gave as much as I could," Shaw told Burt Korall, "considering that I was being pulled and torn by a lot of extraneous facts [sic] that come with success. I never put that much time into a band again."[30]

Much credit for the success of this Shaw orchestra must go to Jerry Gray. The diminutive violinist from Boston had grown swiftly into an arranger of range and depth, sometimes able to understand what Shaw was after even better than Artie himself did, and give it expression. "Jerry and I became practically alter egos" was Shaw's way of saying it. "We functioned in much the same way Duke [Ellington] and [Billy] Strayhorn did." This often involved, he said, Shaw writing a sketch, with lead lines and phrasing indicated, then turning it over to Gray to fill in and fill out.

But this way of doing things, the imposition of a single will on a group of as yet unformed musicians, comes at a price. Shaw's was the animating spirit, the presiding deity, the creative engine, that drove this band. And, by a wide margin, its most distinctive soloist. Not until the arrival of tenor saxophonist Auld and drummer Buddy Rich at the end of 1938 did the band gain musicians who in any way could be considered its leader's peers.[31]

Rich brought an irresistibly manic intensity to the rhythm numbers; the band meanwhile gained one outstanding singer and one great one, in Helen Forrest and Billie Holiday, respectively. By the time the Shaw band displaced Goodman's at the top of the annual *Down Beat* popularity poll, it was functioning at peak form. "We were playing all the time," said Shaw. "It got to the point where I could

585

do anything I wanted on the instrument. There was a real silkiness to my sound. I listen to some of those records today, hear myself play, and think, 'How did I ever do that?' ''

He's not exaggerating, as his work on any record of 1938–39, chosen at random, will attest. "Say It With a Kiss," a delightful and neglected Harry Warren–Johnny Mercer collaboration, opens with eight bars of simple melody, played by Shaw with a nuanced, highly vocalized tone. The reeds, scored low and voiced close, enter behind him in bar nine, sounding much like—no surprise, this—a string section. It is eerie, and quite magical.

The band also recorded "It Had To Be You" on this date, only a week after Benny Goodman had recorded the same song, in a Fletcher Henderson arrangement, for the same company and in the same studio. Each has an excellent, and typical, clarinet solo; a comparison is both irresistible and instructive.

Conceptually the two arrangements are similar, though Goodman takes things a bit slower ($\d = 142$ to Shaw's $\d = 165$): each begins with an ensemble in which brass state the melody for a half-chorus, answered by the saxes, then the position is reversed. Each has at least one tutti passage later on to show off the reeds, Les Robinson leading with rather more incisive attack than Goodman's Noni Bernardi, though both sections are light and dextrous.

The major difference emerges in the clarinet solos. Goodman's half-chorus, in concert B♭, is thoughtful, blues-tinged, a paraphrase of the melody. It is also harmonically conservative, using nothing more adventuresome than a momentary D♭ neighbor against a C9 chord in bars 5–6. In each case he resolves it so quickly that its effect is as little more than a passing tone or embellishment of the chordal voice.

Shaw, by contrast, strides into a full chorus (in concert C), using the melody as a point of departure in building an essay of wit and imagination. He uses upper chordal voices freely, even resolving his first eight bars, à la Beiderbecke, on a move from middle-line concert B down to E, the thirteenth and eleventh of the D9 chord. The solo brims with such attractive moments, sometimes only in points of detail, such as the upper-and lower-neighbor figure he plays against his C♯m7 (Em6) and F♯9 in bar 10:

"It Had To Be You," Artie Shaw solo (bars 9–11), 1941.

The band is at its most relaxed and exuberant on its (evening) broadcast recordings from the Blue Room of the Hotel Lincoln, the Café Rouge of the Pennsylvania, and Boston's Ritz-Carlton Hotel. Ensembles are tight, the reeds particularly well matched. Among the highlights: a Shaw solo on "Just You, Just Me" that comes close to topping the tearaway *brio* of the Brunswick; another "It

Had To Be You," with a solo even surpassing the studio version; and a "Carioca" that finds the entire band playing with a fire it seldom achieved in studio performances. Part of the visceral excitement of this and other 1939 radio performances lies not only in Rich's drumming but in Auld's saxophone solos, which seem to combine the virtues of Count Basie's two great tenor men of the time— the lighter-than-air reveries of Lester Young and the full-throated tone of Herschel Evans.

But there is no doubt, hearing the live performances and Bluebird studio recordings, that however catalytic Auld and Rich might have been, the chief inspiration remained Shaw himself. The sheer number of beautifully conceived, flawlessly executed clarinet solos can confound imagination; it certainly places him squarely in the ranks of the most creative improvising soloists of the era.

Examples from 1939 can be chosen almost at random: Shaw on the Bluebird "Rose Room" develops a chain of sinuously interrelated phrases which recall— and often surpass—Frank Trumbauer's C-melody saxophone inventions. He follows Helen Forrest's vocal on "Deep Purple" with a forest glade of a solo, endless patterns of light and shade, the tone transcending any sense of something produced on an instrument.

On Christmas Day 1938, Shaw joined Paul Whiteman's Orchestra in a Carnegie Hall concert, playing a lengthy essay on a B♭ blues which included various tempos, a long, cantorial central cadenza section, a paraphrase of "St. Louis Blues" and a clarinet-and-tomtom episode faintly reminiscent of Goodman's "Sing Sing Sing" party piece (though there's plenty of evidence that Artie favored this combination, independent of Benny, from the start), all of it winding up on a preternaturally vivid high C (concert B♭).

What's most striking is not the piece itself, which is a farrago, or even Shaw's effortless mastery of the instrument, but the fact that he has managed to sustain a listener's interest for eleven and one-half minutes: there are scarcely four bars anywhere in this performance when he is not playing. It is all Shaw.[32]

But his hostility to the mere fact of being a popular entertainer showed no sign of abating. "When America dances, it pays its pipers well," he declared in a magazine interview. "And yet, despite that [sic] I earn close to five thousand dollars a week, I'd think twice before advising anyone to follow in my footsteps . . . Unfortunately, popular music in America is ten percent art and ninety percent business. As a result, it boasts more than its share of charlatans and lacks its share of honest, intelligent critics."[33]

On another occasion he protested: "I'm not up here to look nice. I'm here to play music which I hope dancers and listeners will enjoy. If they like the music that's all I'm interested in. I don't give a damn what they think of me personally and I feel I needn't go out of my way to encourage their liking me. The music is all that matters."[34]

"Jitterbugs are morons," he told New York Post reporter Michael Mok in 1939. "Autograph hunters won't give you a chance to breathe." Such utterances, and many more, leave the almost palpable impression of a man on a collision course with himself. And, forever, the unanswered question: if he had so little use for the sort of diplomacy that, in those times at least, was a *sine qua non* of celebrity in popular culture, why was he in it?

Given that question, everything that happened in 1939, culminating in Shaw's abrupt departure from the bandstand at the Hotel Pennsylvania that November and subsequent flight from the music business and the country, makes its own kind of sense.

"When things didn't go right or suit him," one longtime acquaintance has put it, "Artie took off like some skittish bird." And take off he did. No defection, even at the height of the Cold War several decades later, has been as widely publicized—with so little attempt on the part of its chroniclers to understand what it was, what drove it, and what effect it had.[35]

But something about his flight, as with all such grand gestures, gripped the popular imagination; to many it seemed almost romantic. As the *New York Times* put it, "Any commentary that might occur to us would be lost in our sense of admiration at the Shakespearian sweep of Mr. Shaw's exodus; the kind of spectacularly irreverent farewell to his work and former associates that even the timidest soul must occasionally dream of, a beautifully incautious burning of all his bridges behind him."[36]

Paradoxically, the most telling effect of Shaw's 1939 absentation was to thrust him, after a brief hiatus, into the next phase of his own development as a musician—and to bring him a lot closer to making the kind of music he wanted to than had the band he left behind.

(The effect of his departure on that band can be measured precisely. In January and February of 1940, under Georgie Auld's leadership, what had been the Shaw orchestra recorded ten titles for the small independent Varsity label. Some major figures were gone: Buddy Rich had moved on to Tommy Dorsey's band, Helen Forrest to Goodman's. But most of the personnel remained intact.

(Among the most revealing performances are "Sweet Sue," in the same arrangement used on the Shaw broadcast of November 4, 1939, and "This Is Romance," recorded by Shaw and a reorganized band at the end of 1940. In both cases, and elsewhere on the Varsity titles, the band plays to its customary high standard of professionalism and discipline. Auld and Les Robinson do nicely with the leader's solo spots.

(But something is missing. It is as if the very essence of the Shaw orchestra had been removed, excised with the precision of a surgeon's scalpel. These performances, for all their skill, are without flavor or personality—devoid, it must be said, of the animating "tutelary spirit" of Artie Shaw. As Bernie Privin put it to Burt Korall: "Without Artie, it was like the Yankees without Babe Ruth . . . The guys felt pretty lost but did their collective best to carry on."[37]

(A front-page report in *Down Beat*, March 1, 1940, indicates that Auld's troubles were not confined to music. "Discouraged by lay-offs, and pessimistic over the band's future," it said, some key band members had given their notices, but Auld was determined to soldier on with new, even less experienced, replacements. "Several men in the band refused to cooperate with Auld," the item added.

"Having played alongside him for so long, they refused to pay him much respect as a leader. As a result, Auld couldn't maintain discipline.")

Artie turned up that spring in Los Angeles, and—filling out his Victor contract—organized a large studio orchestra for some records. "I wasn't deeply motivated musically at this point," he has said. "I just wanted to do a good, professional job." In fact he did rather more than that: the orchestra is superb, the records full of texture and color. Again, the Paul Whiteman precedent comes to mind, enhanced by the presence of Whiteman veterans Charlie Margulis (trumpet), Bill Rank (trombone), and Mischa Russell (violin) in the personnel.

Though "Frenesi," a tune by Mexican composer Alberto Dominguez, became a hit of epic proportions (astonishing, considering how greatly it differed from standard swing band treatments of the time), Shaw's real achievements with this unit lie elsewhere, mostly in his collaboration with yet another Whiteman alumnus, the respected composer-arranger William Grant Still.[38]

Still's treatment of "Gloomy Sunday," for example, turns the dirge-like Hungarian song into a tone poem, a multi-hued musical tapestry. Even singer Pauline Byrne's account of the lyric downplays its inherent mawkishness. From the first notes of its solo English horn opening, Still's score surprises with instrumental combinations and sonorities: French horn with trombones, Shaw over clarinet choir, oboe and flute played off against muted brass.

But his best effort lies in a recording which appears to have been considered too esoteric for issue in 1940, an orchestral projection of Edward MacDowell's "A Deserted Farm," eighth of the American composer's ten *Woodland Sketches*. Burt Korall is astute in praising the work's "sharp sense of yearning." He quotes the fifth (1954) edition of *Grove's Dictionary of Music and Musicians*, to the effect that MacDowell "believed in poetical suggestion and programmatic titles . . . he aimed at depicting the moods of things and the moods awakened by things rather than the things themselves."

The other two titles from this session, while perhaps less ambitious, have specific charms. "My Fantasy" is based on the same Borodin melody that later became "Stranger in Paradise," and Shaw brings a certain dry wit to his own "Don't Fall Asleep." It is his "movie song," his lyric replete with allusions to Gable, Hedy Lamarr, Greta Garbo, and—perhaps most memorably:

> I'm a girl who knows what love means,
> I don't need Lubitsch when I do my love scenes.[39]

By contrast, Shaw's second Hollywood date was a letdown, closer to the "good, professional job" referred to above, and with a noticeable lack of emotional involvement. He plays well on all these titles, particularly "Mister Meadowlark" and "April in Paris," but it could have been the work of any number of highly capable sidemen: there is little of him here, little of the essence that had shaped, sustained, and lit up the 1938–39 band. The impact of his non-involvement is not as great here as on the Auld Varsity titles, though, chiefly because the arrangements (by Bobby Sherwood and Gil Grau) are not specifically Shaw arrangements in the way each score in the earlier band's book emphatically *was* a Shaw arrangement.

These two dates brought Artie Shaw back into circulation and led him (especially after the success of "Frenesi") to form a new band. He inherited six men from a Benny Goodman unit that broke up in July after a month on Catalina Island, among them Les Robinson (who had been playing second to Toots Mondello with Benny), pianist Johnny Guarnieri, and jazz tenor man Jerry Jerome. Trumpeter Billy Butterfield had left Bob Crosby in June and was available. Trombonist Jack Jenney, whom Shaw had admired since the early '30s, had tried a band of his own, made some fine records, and flopped. After doing the soundtrack for the Fred Astaire film *Second Chorus* (with Butterfield and an imported Bobby Hackett sharing solo jazz trumpet duties), the new band opened in September at the Palace Hotel in San Francisco. In almost every way it brought Shaw's concept of a dance orchestra to fruition. And in Robinson, Butterfield, and Jenney it had men who could match the clarinetist's own "singing" quality, making it far and away the most *vocalized* of all Shaw orchestras.

It also had nine strings, enough to work effectively as a section while filling out and deepening the ensembles, and a book full of arrangements by Still, Lennie Hayton, and, a bit later, the gifted trombonist Ray Conniff. As Robinson told Burt Korall: "The dynamics of this ensemble were really outstanding, and ever so natural as well. When we recorded our first sides, the engineer out here in California said the band was no trouble at all, that it balanced itself."[40]

"Going directly from Benny's band to Artie's was quite an experience," said Jerry Jerome. "There's no comparing them, really—vanilla and chocolate. But I must say that, musical differences aside, joining Artie was truly enjoyable. For my wife and me it was like going on this wonderful extended vacation. Every gig was a good gig: we made the picture for six weeks, with nothing to do in the morning except pop in and work—and look at Paulette Goddard's legs. Working at the Palace Hotel, in San Francisco, and the Hollywood Palladium, was a treat. And Artie was—well, a very kind person. If he gave a guy a bad time, it wasn't with invective or anger or bile. He wasn't that way."[41]

A chief difference with Goodman, the saxophonist said, lay in the two leaders' methods of shaping a band. Shaw's band was the result of his vision, his temperament, his overall concept of ensemble sound. Removing it from the equation, as the 1940 Auld records demonstrate, left little more than a shell.

"He was never temperamental, always a gentleman," more than one ex-sideman has said. The volcanic temper, unpredictable and uncontrollable, reported by various of his wives never surfaced in Shaw's dealings with his musicians. Jerry Jerome remembered a night when tenor saxophonist Clarence "Bus" Bassey, usually quiet and reserved, blew up and left the stand. "Artie, real cool, walked after him, followed him, then took him into the kitchen, where they could talk privately, away from everybody, and thrash it out. That's the way he was."

Goodman bands, by contrast, were collections of individualists, some of them quite forceful and vivid; the chemistry among them, said Jerome, including clashes of temperament, helped determine the overall character and impact of a Goodman band.

"Take the sax section. A Shaw sax section was bound to be perfect. He knew just what he wanted: he could take such disparate guys and mold them into a unit that was close to perfect. By contrast, I don't remember Benny ever rehearsing the saxes to give us things to do. He never bothered with 'Hey, you ought to play a little less,' or anything like that. He never balanced a group—*we* did that. You could say that Benny's bands in general always had lots of musicians who were bitching and complaining about Benny—and not leaving the band, because they were happy to be there."[42]

Shaw worked carefully with his arrangers, particularly Still and Hayton, on balance, placement of solos, matters of key, texture, and ensemble density—even, he recalled, ways to voice each section. "I was an editor, too, and sometimes a very exacting one," he has said. "When a writer brought in a score, I worked with it the way an editor works with copy. I had a policy, a style, and knew what I wanted to do in achieving it."

That meant a somewhat less than ideal situation for jazz soloists. "You couldn't pig out blowing," said Jerome. "Not on sixteen bars here and a modulation there. It was the kind of situation in which, after you finished at, say, two in the morning, you'd be hightailing it to some joint, to blow with a five-piece group, and hear yourself. Artie rarely—when a guy got cooking, he wasn't the kind of guy who would say, 'Go on, take another chorus.' That wasn't his way."

"The band," Shaw might have said, "c'est moi." As Burt Korall has put it: "There was no equivocation regarding direction and goals. Not a jazz group or concert attraction but a creature of Shaw's more serious aspirations within the popular *dance* orchestra idiom, it gracefully combined provocative orchestral thinking—the mingling of a variety of colors, via the usage [sic] of creative and winning arranging devices—and the humanity provided by thoughtful and sometimes memorable solos."[43]

The concept finds its most masterful expression in the October 7, 1940, "Star Dust," arranged by Hayton and recorded at the band's second studio date. It is a study in equipoise, each element distinct from—yet complementing—the others, as evidenced by Billy Butterfield's glowing opening solo (and section lead) and the organic richness of Hayton's string writing, especially its reinforcement of the *tutti* passages.

Shaw's half-chorus solo, following a modulation from D♭ to F, is a stunning exposition of his melodic concept. "Melody and song are not at all the same thing" is his way of putting it. "A melody can exist without being a song. It doesn't need words to show you what its emotional content should be. In a way the words *narrow* the scope of a melody. What if you don't know the lyric? Does that mean you can't play a melody effectively, even eloquently? No, of course not. What makes Schumann's *Träumerei* the beautiful thing it is? There's no lyric: it's a beautiful melody. You don't even need a piano—I've heard 'cello alone play it.''

So is Shaw soloing here on "Star Dust," a popular song with an evocative (though hardly transcendant) lyric by Mitchell Parish, or is his sixteen-bar essay a response solely to Hoagy Carmichael's lovely melody, with its strong evocation of the composer's admiration for Shaw's hero Bix Beiderbecke?

Either way, it represents the full brilliance of his clarinet style. The long upward phrase uncoiling through bars 9–12, and the ascent to a masterfully played high concert A that follows, belong to a kind of melodic architecture found but seldom even in jazz. Its very perfection has prompted many listeners, among them more than a few clarinetists of stature, to assume that the solo can't have been spontaneous, must have been worked out carefully in advance.

Shaw's own testimony, and the evidence of his work on two late-1938 air-check performances of "Star Dust," indicate a slightly different reality. Many of the great recorded solos of jazz history appear to have been the result of an ongoing organic process. Over time, and repeated playings of both the song and improvisations on similar chord structures in the same key, a player evolves patterns, ways of dealing with melodic and harmonic situations. Through a gradual, sometimes piecemeal, process of refraction and refinement, of composition and editing, the soloist gets things about where he wants them—and seldom changes things in any substantive way after that.

So it seems to have been with Artie Shaw and "Star Dust." The 1938 broadcast solos, full choruses each, are not as rigorously constructed or edited as the half-chorus of 1940, but the components are finding their places. Here are the "stretched" phrases, the flawless ear dealing with the chords, even the inevitable culmination in a high concert A. Shaw's tone and vibrato, too, are at their warmest and most lyrical.[44]

The solo became one of the great set-pieces of the jazz canon, alongside Beiderbecke's and Trumbauer's "Singin' the Blues" choruses, Armstrong's "West End Blues," and Coleman Hawkins's epic transformation of "Body and Soul." Each, in its time, has been copied, emulated, incorporated into arrangements— almost to the point of becoming part of the common understanding of the song.

Similar honor has been accorded Jack Jenney's eight-bar solo. Following directly on Shaw's, it maintains the same high expressive level. A similar process seems to have brought the trombonist to this moment: almost exactly a year earlier, he'd recorded "Star Dust" with his own band as a showpiece for his solo style. Though issued by Columbia, the record was not widely circulated at the time and still is little reissued.

It is a striking performance, a two-chorus essay on melody and chord structure. Like Hawkins on "Body and Soul" (made, coincidentally, just a week earlier), Jenney never states the melody directly but refers to it obliquely from time to time. Unlike the Hawkins classic, Jenney's "Star Dust" exists in two takes; though his methods and the way he hears the song remain consistent, he never repeats an idea or construction in any but a general way. Though the key is different (1939 is in E♭, 1940 in F), the makings of the later solo—even the leap to high tone—is present in these two performances. Given that a trombone high F was not quite so rare in 1940, or considered so much a feat, as some have supposed (witness recorded performances by Billy Rauch, with the Casa Loma Orchestra, and Nat Lobovsky, with the 1938 Bunny Berigan band), its use by Jenney here is notable for the taste and musicality with which it is incorporated.[45]

By Shaw's own admission, *Concerto for Clarinet* was a fraud, a pasteup, slung together for use in *Second Chorus* and issued on two sides of a twelve-inch 78 rpm record. It's not a "concerto" in any formal sense, and anything but an integrated work: almost the entire first half is a series of jazz choruses on a medium-tempo B♭ blues, featuring Shaw, Robinson, Jerome, pianist Johnny Guarnieri, and trombonist Vernon Brown. Artie's entrance in the final ensemble is reminiscent of Goodman's in a similar place on his 1937 aircheck version of "Roll 'Em," but without the fevered, irresistible momentum of that earlier performance.

For part two, Shaw merely appropriated episodes—clarinet and tomtoms, cadenzas, closing "shout" ensemble—from the long "Blues" he'd played on the 1938 Whiteman broadcast. The cadenza passages are shorter, all the more striking for it, and reflect Shaw's "cantorial" side. The opening especially, played against a B♭m-E♭m-F7-B♭m sequence, is in attitude and effect a *Doina*, the heavily embellished minor-key lament common in the folk music of Romania and other Eastern European countries and in their Ashkenazi Jewish populations.

Perhaps in keeping with the fashion of the time for small bands within larger ones, Shaw also made four records, eight sides, with a sextet drawn from the main personnel. In a moment of whimsy he called it the Gramercy Five, after a popular New York City telephone exchange that survives today as the immeasurably less evocative "475."

Though ostensibly a jazz group, the Gramercy Five was no less an expression of its leader's conceptual and organizational mind than the large orchestra. Heard now, even such relatively free-wheeling performances as "Special Delivery Stomp" (basically "Diga Diga Doo" without the melody) and "My Blue Heaven" seem cut to plan, part of a concept. The group owes its distinctive flavor to the harpsichord, played by Johnny Guarnieri; he plays it well, extracting from its sometimes uncompromising sonority and attack (the strings are plucked, making control of texture and touch problematical) considerable drive.

But rather than blend, the harpsichord pervades; where elasticity might have been desirable, it is rhythmically stiff. Perhaps a number or two with Guarnieri playing on a conventional piano, the rhythm section able to loosen up a bit, might have afforded useful contrast—and freed the group from the harpsichord's rhythmic hammerlock.

All the same, the setting elicits from Shaw some of his most intense and spirited—even *hot*—playing, recalling Jerry Jerome's remark, "When Artie swung at his best it was because of what was going on behind him." Shaw's choruses on "My Blue Heaven," "Keepin' Myself for You," and the satirically titled "When the Quail Come Back to San Quentin" seem to bear him out. Yet for all its innovative touches (the unison heard on the blues "Summit Ridge Drive," for example, became a familiar bebop sonority), the Gramercy Five never quite achieves the free-wheeling urgency of a small jam group. It remains, *nach wie vor*, its leader's creation, a setting, within which Artie Shaw expresses another aspect of his musical consciousness.

After its San Francisco and Hollywood engagements the Shaw band signed on with the George Burns–Gracie Allen radio show, and when NBC moved the popular series to New York early in 1941, Artie and a few key sidemen went along, reconstituting the larger unit with New York men. But that was it: after a few weeks and one further record date, Artie Shaw orchestra number three entered the past tense.

For Shaw himself, the quest continued. A June 26 Victor session combined a large string section with a small ensemble featuring such prominent black jazzmen as Henry "Red" Allen, J. C. Higginbotham, and Benny Carter. The results are disappointing: only on "Confessin' " (ironically, the only one of the four titles not issued at the time) do these distinguished soloists get a chance to be heard at any length. Listening to all four titles in sequence makes clear that Allen, Higginbotham, and Carter are present more for the flavors they impart than for their gifts as improvisers. When, on "Love Me a Little," Carter states the melody over sustained strings, he contributes a sound, a texture, quite different from what would have been the case had Les Robinson played the part.

In a way that comes as no surprise: from the start, after all, Shaw's declared obsession had been with *sound*. The sound of the Jean Goldkette Orchestra, "the sound Bix and Trumbauer got out of their horns, the sound the whole ensemble made . . . Funny: I can't consciously remember much about Bix except the sound of his horn. That's what impressed me."

The idea of sound as an entity unto itself, then, seems to lie at the heart of Shaw's band-building exercises. And if sound is all, then individuals are ingredients, used where they can contribute most effectively to a tonal picture. If the sound of Carter, Allen, and Higginbotham fits some overall projection in Shaw's mind, then that is the role they will play.

Shaw seems fascinated with blends of individuals, sections, voicings, in search of sound, balance, some as yet unachieved aesthetic insight. In this he is comparable to Duke Ellington, though Ellington's fusion of individual and collective textures is rather more idiosyncratic and interactive, and ultimately more effective compositionally, than anything essayed by Shaw.

Yet Artie's Allen-Carter-Higginbotham experiment may constitute a tentative move in this direction—especially considering the personnel of the band he formed in late summer of 1941. Alongside Robinson, Jenney, Auld, Guarnieri, Conniff, and a few others from prior groups, he brought in a new sound and flavor: the dynamic, blues-saturated trumpeter and singer Oran "Lips" Page. Born in Texas in 1908, Page made his reputation in Kansas City with the great Bennie Moten band and came to New York in the mid-1930s as a kind of second-line Louis Armstrong. But he had qualities very much his own, among them a natural ebullience, which invariably proved a catalyst for musicians playing with him.

As a somewhat perfervid *Down Beat* story of the time indicates, an invitation from Artie Shaw to join a new band carried weight among fellow-musicians. "Les Robinson quit Will Bradley. Georgie Auld refused to accept big-money offers from others and went without work [for] six weeks until Shaw's rehearsals got under way. Lee Castle quit Bradley too, and Eddie McKinney toted his big bull fiddle right off Tony Pastor's bandstand [presumably with that leader's blessing] and into Artie's room. 'Lips' Page abandoned hopes to get his own jazz band clicking and made a beeline to Shaw's initial rehearsal." Similar circumstances attended the coming of Conniff, trumpeters Max Kaminsky and Steve Lipkins, saxophonist-clarinetist Artie Baker, guitarist Mike Bryan, and—most important of all—nonpareil drummer Dave Tough.[46]

"You just knew," said Baker, "that it was going to be interesting, and that Artie knew exactly what he wanted. He'd thought it out, and had all the pieces in place in his mind. The only thing left to do was call the guys."[47]

Page, who later told friends that his days in this band were the happiest of his career, is at the center of many of these performances. Whether singing ("Blues in the Night," "Take Your Shoes Off, Baby") or using his plunger ("Just Kiddin' Around"), he's a strong, vivid presence.

Just how vivid is clear in the recorded performance of *Nocturne*, a 1928 concert piece written by the now-obscure American composer Thomas Griselle (1891–1955) and arranged for Shaw by his old Roger Wolfe Kahn associate, Jerry Sears. It belongs to the same musical efflorescence that produced the *Rhapsody in Blue* and *Concerto in F*, applying the American vernacular to European forms, but without the lapses into stilted "jazzy" phrasing that mar the better-known Gershwin works. Page (functioning as sound and accent) plays a straightforward melody solo, using his singular tone, vibrato, and attack—and even an attractive rasp—to illuminate the theme.

Such material, arranged for this kind of band, was intended, said Shaw, to "show that any distinctions we draw between 'jazz' and 'concert music' are arbitrary and quite unnecessary. Music is music is music, after all. Think of jazz as a tributary to the main river that we call music."

But something new, and perhaps unanticipated, is beginning to happen here alongside such undertakings. Shaw's master-plan methodology is still dominant, but the combination of strong soloists and a widening, increasingly diverse cadre of arrangers is starting to create a countervailing force. Dave Tough is the engine behind a new sense of movement, an abandon unprecedented in Shaw bands. His cymbals—restless, propulsive, kaleidoscopic—incite the soloists and splash great swatches of color across the ensembles on such originals as Fred Norman's "Solid Sam" (Page sounding a bit like Roy Eldridge), Conniff's "Just Kiddin' Around" (written for Berigan's band as "Savoy Jump"), and Margie Gibson's "Deuces Wild."

"For my money," an enthusiastic George Frazier wrote in *Down Beat*, "the star of Artie's band—the one really indispensable man in it—is Dave Tough. His drumming is nothing short of stupendous, and without it the band would be a considerably less exciting affair than it is at the moment." Frazier went on to laud Tough's "enormous competence, impeccable taste, and one of the most miraculous beats in jazz."

Among others singled out for praise were trumpeters Page, Max Kaminsky and Lee Castle (strong indication that the band on the job featured a greater number of its star sidemen than its records indicate), Jenney, and Conniff. Frazier compares this thirty-two-member leviathan to Whiteman's late-'20s orchestra, then lauds Shaw for restraining any inclination he might have to show his men "how to play their instruments. That's an important consideration, because people like Kaminsky and Tough resent being reminded that the Budapest Quartet would have played it differently."[48]

Ellingtonian colors and textures permeate a two-part "St. James Infirmary"— in growling brasses behind Auld's Ben Websterish solo, in Conniff's Tricky Sam– like chorus, and even in the use of plungers behind Shaw. Page is the main event here, singing effectively (with nice, if distant, backing by Kaminsky) and ending the performance with a long cadenza that chooses, refreshingly, not to culminate in a bravura high note.

As usual, Shaw's playing is clean, consistently musical, often stirring. But he's at his most eloquent on the melodic material: his two solo passages in Vincent Youmans's "Through the Years," for example, are heart-breaking in their simple beauty. The tone—loving, intimate—caresses and consoles.

Shaw was obviously interested in this band and had no thought of relinquishing it. But on Sunday, December 7, 1941, destiny intervened. "We were playing a Sunday afternoon show at a theatre in Providence," said Max Kaminsky, "when the manager interrupted the performance to announce that the Japanese had bombed Pearl Harbor."

It was as good as a death sentence. Soon the draft would start plucking at Shaw's men, until it was impossible to continue. But before that began to happen, Shaw returned to Victor to record what may be the finest performances of this band's six-month existence, two works by Chicago-born composer-arranger Paul Jordan. Both *Evensong* and *Suite No. 8* create their own musical environments, drawing on the pastel harmonies and gauzy textures of the Impressionists, and with equal felicity on a largely Ellingtonian jazz vocabulary.

Evensong (listed in some discographies as *Dusk*) is a small tone poem, pensive and serene, illuminated by (and illuminating) Shaw's singing tone; with flawless control of orchestral texture, Jordan builds on a shifting tonal center, never quite going into strict rhythm, yet drawing strength and motive force from the jazz orientation of the players.

The orientation is more explicit in *Suite No. 8*. After an introductory passage featuring an unusual blend of strings and cup-muted brass, the performance shifts into up-tempo, Page (with Tough a dynamo behind him) bringing fierce energy to a plunger-muted solo, and Shaw playing like a man possessed.

Jordan's work as an arranger of more straightforward jazz material displays the same colorational facility. He bases his January 1942 "Two in One Blues" on a twelve-bar form, but much altered harmonically; from the clarinet-tenor octaves of the opening to the ghostly string tapestry behind Les Robinson's alto solo, the revelations never stop. His "Carnival" is an object lesson in integration of a large string section into the overall fabric of an ensemble.

That date also features a curiosity, in Ray Conniff's "Needlenose," a medium-tempo exercise—humorous? satiric?—in what appears to be the Glenn Miller manner. As if thematic echoes of both "Pennsylvania 6-5000" and "Tuxedo Junction" weren't enough, there's even a direct allusion to "A String of Pearls."

Then, finally, it was time to quit. The band played a few one-nighters, ending in Detroit. Shaw, onstage, spoke feelingfully about the war, ending with an emotional farewell both to his musicians and—uncharacteristically—the public. "I imagine that everybody was touched about a millimeter deep," he said later.

As usual, he underestimated his audience. The Pearl Harbor attack had stirred and united Americans as had nothing else in living memory. Not the Great War, not even the worst tribulations of the Depression. It might have been as mindless and superficial as some of the songs that shortly came pouring out of Tin Pan Alley music mills, but there's no questioning that the response was real, strong, heartfelt: a national groundswell.

And there is no denying that Artie Shaw, whatever was in his mind at that point about music, the American public or anything else, was himself swept up in it. Not long after that final Detroit evening, he rode with his brand-new fourth wife, Elizabeth "Betty" Kern—daughter of Jerome Kern—to an induction center on Church Street, in lower Manhattan, where he enlisted in the U.S. Navy.

24

Artie Shaw (2): Time and Change

In late spring of 1944 the word went out: Artie Shaw was back in circulation and thinking of putting together a band.

Shaw? No kidding. Last anyone had heard he was off somewhere in the Pacific, leading a U.S. Navy band called the Rangers. He'd had Maxie Kaminsky, Johnny Best, and a couple of other guys from his civilian bands; Claude Thornhill and two sidemen from his last prewar band—Tasso Harris on trombone and the amazing young lead trumpeter Conrad Gozzo; the extraordinary young tenor saxophonist Sam Donahue, who'd been leading his own civilian band. And, through some miracle of bureaucratic chicanery, he'd gotten Dave Tough, who all but defined the term "4-F."

They'd island-hopped throughout the whole Pacific theatre. In contrast to the far more glamorous Glenn Miller Europe-based unit, Shaw's navy band apparently traveled by the seat of its collective pants, forever vulnerable to all manner of misadventure, from tropical disease to Japanese attack. In Shaw's words, the navy "didn't have any conception of what to do with a band like mine . . . The brass considered our mission silly, and I heard a lot of 'You're not in Hollywood now.' "[1]

Kaminsky's account of Dave Tough's pre-induction physical is a small gem of understated humor. Barely more than five feet tall, weighing something like a hundred pounds, the drummer "looked like an emaciated imp. His wife, Casey, and I had fed him spaghetti night and day for two weeks in an attempt to put some weight on him."

To little avail. When Tough stripped for his examination,

the medical officer took one unbelieving look at him, and turning to Artie, he said incredulously, "Do you really need this man in your band?"

"This is the world's greatest drummer," Artie snapped.

"Then get him the hell out of here before somebody sees him," the officer snapped back. "This guy is not only an impossible physical specimen, he violates every basic requirement for size, weight, height and health," he snarled as he stamped his approval on Dave's papers.[2]

Tough went, and the tribulations that followed—bad quarters, worse food, constant crisis—nearly killed him. After five months billeted in Aiea, a small village just outside Honolulu, they boarded the battleship *North Carolina* bound for the South Pacific and brief tours on such islands as Nouméa, Espíritu Santo, and Guadalcanal, before heading for New Zealand and Australia. They were strafed, bombed, shot at by Japanese snipers, accosted by snakes, mosquitos, and fleas, weakened by dysentery, dengue fever, and a panoply of other tropical ailments. There was even an encounter—described with admirable restraint by Kaminsky— involving a tribe of headhunters.

They played for crewmen on battleships and carriers. For wounded in navy hospitals. For battle-weary troops in remote island stations too near the front lines for anybody's peace of mind.[3]

And, as Kaminsky told it, there was at least one of those rare, thrill-of-a-lifetime moments. They were on the carrier *Saratoga*. The crew, more than three thousand strong, were gathered on the bottom deck.

> We set up the bandstand on the huge aircraft elevator and began playing our theme song, "Nightmare," as we descended slowly into the midst of the wildly cheering men. It was like being back at the Paramount Theatre again, except that the bandstand there used to rise slowly from the pit, while on the *Saratoga* it descended into the audience.
>
> As I sat there looking out at those thousands and thousands of sailors and feeling the waves of homesickness flow out of them at the sound of the familiar songs, I began to fill up so much that when I stood up to take my solo on the "St. Louis Blues," I blew like a madman. On hearing me let loose, Dave [Tough] started to swing the beat, and when I picked up my plunger and started to growl, those three thousand men went stark, raving crazy.[4]

Shaw and his band came home sick, worn out, on the verge of breakdown. His marriage to Betty Kern was in ruins; there was a bitter custody battle over their son, Steve. There was a period of hospitalization for deep depression. Finally he went into analysis with Dr. May Romm, whose celebrated clients included producer David O. Selznick. With her, Shaw plunged into intense examination of his career, motives, direction, trying to make some sense of a life that, more and more, seemed a meaningless jumble of wrong turns, false starts. Contradictions.

"My feeling was that anything would be up from where I was," he told Burt Korall. "Absolutely immobilized, I had nowhere to go, nowhere I wanted to go.

599

I didn't need money. I was in a position where it just meant nothing to me. Life absolutely *stopped*."

After much agonizing and soul-searching came a decision to start playing again, to form a new band. "I didn't want to," he has said with some emphasis. "I didn't *want* to do anything. Organizing a band wasn't what I'd call my heart's desire, but it seemed my only realistic option."[5]

Like the one that had preceded his entry into the war, Shaw's new band turned out to be extraordinary. With the fighting still raging, and the pool of topflight talent much depleted, even finding men of the right caliber took hard work. Shaw gained an effective, perhaps unexpected, ally in Freddy Goodman, younger brother of Benny and himself a former trumpeter. Together they sought out young musicians, held auditions at Artie's Beverly Hills home. And slowly, painstakingly, a personnel took shape.

Trombonist-arranger Ray Conniff and trombonist Harry Rodgers were the only holdovers from earlier Shaw groups (though lead alto Les Clarke had been with the band briefly in 1941). The rest of the men were young, many of them attracted by and involved in the new jazz developments known, generally and generically, under the term "bebop."

Once a basic personnel was established, Shaw carefully set a jewel in his crown. By any standard, Roy Eldridge had been one of the most revered jazz trumpet soloists of the '30s. Born in Pittsburgh, he'd come to national prominence with Teddy Hill's band, starred with Fletcher Henderson and others, led his own bristling small group in Chicago. His work on records with Teddy Wilson, Billie Holiday, Benny Goodman, and a host of others had dazzled fellow-musicians with an unprecedented combination of speed, range, technical fluency, imagination—and, perhaps above all, a kind of high-wire risk-taking all the more thrilling for the apparent ease with which he brought it off. A bristling, sometimes fierce, competitor, he could crank up the voltage in any musical situation.

Eldridge's two years as featured trumpet soloist (and occasional vocalist) with Gene Krupa's band had brought his incendiary playing to a far wider audience than ever before. His impromptu vocal duet with Anita O'Day and trumpet solo had made "Let Me Off Uptown," from his first record date with Krupa, into a million-selling national hit.

Not long after that, Shaw had put together his great 1941 band, with the no less catalytic Oran "Lips" Page at its center. Had he been watching, listening? It's conceivable—especially in view of his hiring of Eldridge four years later. Roy had spent much of the war as a member of the staff orchestra Paul Baron led for Mildred Bailey's CBS radio show—a pioneer time, considering the difficulty black musicians had in those years breaking into radio.

Shaw and Freddy Goodman, working in tandem, had staffed the band with good men. As tenor soloists they had British-born Jon Walton, whose rocking, big-toned chorus had been a highlight of "Six Flats Unfurnished," recorded by Benny Goodman's band in mid-1942, and young Herb Steward, one of several young, light-toned players who had been shaped by their admiration for Lester Young.

It's often been written that this was the most fully jazz-oriented of all Shaw bands. Certainly it was the one whose style was most dictated by its arrangers—though, as lead trumpeter Paulie Cohen was quick to add, that didn't mean that Shaw surrendered control of the situation.

"He never lost his cool. Never yelled. Never gave us 'the ray' or anything like that. But there was never any doubt that he was in charge. When we did a new arrangement the arranger was never there—except for Conniff, of course, who played in the band. We'd run the chart down according to what Artie wanted. And he *always* knew what he wanted: it was a done thing; he always had it ready, was always prepared. It made working for him very easy."[6]

Trumpeter Bernie Glow, who joined in early 1945, concurred. "The band was essentially happy and homogeneous," he told Burt Korall. "Artie made the environment within the band challenging yet quite livable . . . Nineteen and relatively inexperienced, I could have gone any number of ways. Shaw and the band pushed me in a fortunate direction."[7]

For Artie himself it was a different matter. Though Cohen, Glow, and others remembered him, in Les Clarke's phrase, as "like a good music teacher" who knew and got exactly what he wanted, Shaw himself has confessed that "I didn't feel very dedicated, very invested, at this point." It was clearly a transitional period for him, a time of stock-taking and self-assessment, of finding out who he was and what he wanted to do.

The music business was changing: new circumstances, new music—and, for Artie Shaw, new ways of thinking even about playing the clarinet. It's hardly surprising that his playing, even on the most brilliant of the records made in this period, seems only fitfully to display the strong sense of self, the *presence*, that had made it so memorable before the war.

"It was kinda strange," said Cohen. "His playing on recordings was great, but when we went out to do a theatre date he was a little—well, he didn't seem to have the focus, or the intensity. It was as if his mind was somewhere else sometimes."

This inconsistency of personal involvement seems to have worked to the band's advantage, leaving more latitude for the arrangers. Conniff blossomed, in a way only hinted at in such 1941–42 arrangements as his "To a Broadway Rose" and "Needlenose." Eddie Sauter, whose 1939–42 arrangements for Benny Goodman often suffered from chronic overwriting, returned to form in working for Shaw. Harry Rodgers, who had played trombone in the 1938–39 band, contributed good arrangements, as did the young George Siravo and veteran Jimmy Mundy. Buster Harding, soon to distinguish himself arranging for Count Basie, contributed scores that gave Eldridge much maneuvering room (Shaw even commissioned him to write a feature for the trumpeter, appropriately titled "Little Jazz") and got things swinging hard and loose in a way unusual for a white band of the time.

Whatever was happening to Shaw internally, his skills as an editor remained unimpaired. He understood—and communicated to his arrangers—the idea of a band as a culinary masterwork, a blend and interaction of ingredients. Eldridge is perhaps the best example: rather than simply turning him loose on this number or that to "Blow, Roy, Blow!" in Anita O'Day's unforgettable phrase from "Let Me Off Uptown," the writers used his biting attack and swaggering rhythm conception to add dimension and drama to a musical tapestry full of color and textural nuance. Again and again, they create windows, frames for him, focusing and compressing the strong essence of his style. The effect is to harness and direct Eldridge, suppressing his penchant for grandstanding and high-note screeching. The result is some of the leanest, most pointed, emotionally concise Eldridge work on record.

He pops up often in 1945, as on "Easy to Love," "Time on My Hands," "I Could Write a Book," "Thrill of a Lifetime" and a splendid George Siravo arrangement of "Soon": eight bars here, half a chorus there, sometimes doing little more than embellishing the melody. The effect is never less than satisfying, and sometimes vastly more than that. His sixteen muted bars over trombone choir on the Shaw-Siravo original "Just Floatin' Along" (melodically a first cousin to "Jersey Bounce") are delicious enough to eat.

On "They Can't Take That Away From Me," another Siravo score, he presents the bridge in simple but startling variation:

"They Can't Take That Away From Me," Roy Eldridge trumpet solo (bars 17–24), 1945.

Predictably, he makes the most of Buster Harding's celebratory "Little Jazz," swaggering grandly over a solid, Krupa-like backbeat platform laid down by drummer Lou Fromm. The result is a tougher-minded musical environment than is generally found in Artie Shaw performances—and it's probably no accident that this is one of the very few Shaw records that does not include a clarinet solo.

But it's in performances of three Eddie Sauter arrangements that this band most approaches fulfilling its musical potential. His "Summertime" is a tone poem, its textures carefully layered, ever shifting. Among the highlights is a unison clarinet passage in Shaw's style, impeccably executed (and flawlessly in tune), ascending into the instrument's most supernal register while Chuck Gentry's baritone sax stalks about far below.

Eldridge, using a plunger, is vital, eloquent. But it almost didn't come to pass. "I can't use that thing, man," he protested to Shaw. "I don't want to sound like Bubber Miley or Cootie Williams." Artie stood his ground, coolly arguing that the plunger, the growl sound, was there for good aesthetic reason, and that any other way of playing the solo would disrupt the landscape Sauter (and Shaw) had laid out. At length, he prevailed: Roy played the solo with plunger, sounding not a bit like Cootie or Bubber or "Lips" Page, but like Roy Eldridge using a plunger—which was, after all, the point. "You know," said Roy when they talked about it years later, "you were right about that." A pause, and a chuckle. "At least in *that* case."

Equally impressive is Sauter's transformation of "The Man I Love." He begins his second chorus with a reed *soli* that seems to be consciously updating the lush Jerry Gray voicings of Shaw's 1939 record—only to hand over to Eldridge, whose eight bars have an urgent, coiled-spring intensity. The final *tutti* also echoes the earlier score, but only as an act of acknowledgment: the context is broader, fuller now.

"The Maid With the Flaccid Air," its title a spoof on Debussy's *Maid With the Flaxen Hair*, is a leisurely paced Sauter composition which seems, at first hearing, far simpler than it turns out to be. Its initial theme, stated in the reeds with Eldridge, harmon-muted, providing a commentary, opens out into a kind of mosaic, each episode returning in unexpected combinations with the others. At one point trombonist Ollie Wilson, playing open over closely voiced reeds, spins out what could be an allusion to Bix Beiderbecke's piano piece *Candlelights*. This is Sauter at his best, recapturing the clarity and almost translucent orchestral textures that made his early work for Red Norvo so impressive.

Ironically, the sole unsettling feature of these performances is Shaw's clarinet. Though technically impeccable and musically probing, it seems to have lost some of the sense of conviction that makes so many solos of the 1939–41 period shine so brightly. The distinction is subtle, but there are moments here of something like listlessness. It is perhaps too easy to read the circumstances of his private life—the analysis, the soul-searching, his impulsive marriage to yet another Hollywood sex goddess, this time Ava Gardner—into the music. Yet there *are* differences, and not merely attributable to maturation and musical change.

His clarinet solos on the 1939 and 1945 versions of "The Man I Love" seem to say quite different things about his sense of himself at two moments six years apart. The earlier solo is engagingly secure, and perhaps a trifle naive, in its tone-painting; the later "Man I Love," by contrast, *does* seem more vulnerable, product of a more complex awareness.

Pianist Dodo "Moose" Marmarosa, guitarist Barney Kessel, trombonist Ollie Wilson, and others were clearly fascinated by, and embracing, the new sounds and inflections being developed in those years by Charlie Parker, Dizzy Gillespie, Bud Powell, and others. Not only in the notes they play, the chromaticism and chordal substitutions now becoming standard features of their work, but in matters of delivery: beside them, the romantic tone and "singing" vibrato of Shaw's earlier work seem a thing apart, separated by time and circumstances. If a certain diffidence has crept into Shaw's work at this point, it could as easily be the first signs that he is groping for a new way, an altered vocabulary for an altered context.[8]

"Lament," a clarinet showcase written by Conniff, reaches back to the Shaw of *Concerto* days, even with a final cadenza that sends him spiraling up to his altissimo high C (concert B♭). But the very next title, Conniff's "Lucky Number," shows beyond doubt how carefully Shaw has been listening to what's going on around him. His phrases are more chromatically oriented, full of boppy triplet configurations. He almost seems to say: "Look—I've just figured it out. This is what you have to do."

For Conniff, too, "Lucky Number" is something of a situation report. His ensembles bristle with unusual voicings (the reharmonized bridge of Shaw's chorus, for example); he lets Eldridge crank up the tension over the first half of the final chorus, then uses the full ensemble to continue the upward trajectory.

Shaw seems particularly happy on six titles recorded between January and August 1945 by a second, overall more effective, edition of the Gramercy Five. As before, he shares the front line with trumpet (in this case Eldridge) and electric guitar (Kessel). He, Marmorosa, bassist Morris Rayman, and drummer Lou Fromm make a generally looser rhythm team than the harpsichord-encumbered Guarnieri-Hendrickson-DeNaut-Fatool combination.

The result, while not totally free of a certain sense of contrivance, occasions some of Shaw's most creative and free-wheeling solo work. His chorus on "The Gentle Grifter," a medium-tempo "blowing piece" with a bridge based on the chords of the old standard "Dinah," generates seductive intensity, while on Buster Harding's "The Sad Sack," he plays the blues with grit and conviction. But Kessel, following him directly, illustrates the stylistic gulf that still exists between them: the guitarist has adopted the long-lined precedent of fellow-Oklahoman Charlie Christian (and through him of Lester Young) and extended it yet farther.

Eldridge in this context is a force of nature. Seldom playing open, he exploits the colorational potential of his straight, cup, harmon, and plunger mutes to pointed effect. He's genially abrasive on the D-minor "Grabtown Grapple," which also sports a rather Bud Powell–like Marmorosa piano solo. The pianist is featured well on "Hop, Skip and Jump," which has some of Shaw's most intense playing of these sessions. Certainly there is nothing diffident or listless in Artie's work here: he knows his role, feels comfortable with it, and plays at top form.

The Gramercy Five date of August 2 was Shaw's last under his Victor contract. But there was still a bit more he wanted to do, material he felt should be recorded. At his own expense he took the big band into a Hollywood studio sometime in early autumn, recording six numbers. Four of these appeared on the small independent Musicraft label: Buster Harding's "The Hornet" and "The Glider"; an instrumental reassessment of Shaw's own "Love of My Life"; and "Let's Walk," a George Siravo arrangement of a blues sketched out by Shaw. The two Harding titles, strong and Basie-like, find Artie playing with a drive and tough attack not heard in his work since the middle '30s. His three choruses on "Let's Walk," especially, are outstanding.[9]

This band had surfaced at a relatively inopportune time to expect any real public acceptance: sentimentality and nostalgia, driven by relief at the end of the war, had swept the country, and "our audiences—well, you can imagine," said Shaw.

"They wanted to hear what they knew, what was comfortable. Familiar, reassuring things. As it happened, those were things I couldn't play any more with any conviction. That made it hard."

Also, as Shaw commentator Vladimir Simosko has written, "the distinction between creative jazz and popular music, which had overlapped and blurred together only during the peak of the Swing Era, was again becoming clearer." The old schism had reopened between the imperatives of musicians and those of the mass audience. That was increasingly on Shaw's mind as the Victor records racked up poor sales figures, and the band's public appearances did rather less than capacity business.[10]

In November 1945, little more than a year after assembling this new and exciting band, he broke it up. He did some recording for Musicraft in 1946–47 with Los Angeles studio orchestras organized by Manny Klein's brother Dave, himself a former trumpeter. Beautifully played, excellently arranged by Sonny Burke and veteran Dick Jones in collaboration with Shaw, they are among the most unfairly neglected performances of the clarinetist's career.

It's not hard to understand. The 1944–45 band had set a high standard; anything short of that, however good, was bound to suffer. As it is, there are fine accounts of several Cole Porter numbers, including a remake, with strings, of "Begin the Beguine" and an intentionally "Jewish" reading of "My Heart Belongs to Daddy," opening on a Harry Bluestone violin cadenza and interpolating "Nightmare" as a way of bringing on Kitty Kallen's vocal.

There is every indication that Shaw approached even these projects with the same intelligence that had won the respect of so many sidemen. Mel Tormé, who sang on "Get Out of Town" and other Musicraft selections at the time, remembered the clarinetist as "everything I had hoped he would be: friendly, helpful, thoroughly professional, full of great ideas, hugely intelligent, a voluble talker, and all in all, someone worth looking up to."[11]

Certainly the clarinet choruses on "Love for Sale" (documented as a pioneer studio overdubbing effort), which also featured Babe Russin's tenor sax, and a lovely account by Shaw and Tormé of the Gershwins' "For You, for Me, Forevermore," are fine work. The leader's own "When You're Around" is a reminder that, for all his denigration of popular songs, he was himself an adept at songwriting.[12]

If Shaw's own accounts of this period in his life stress its turbulence, there is also much evidence that, for all the analysis and soul-searching, his need to control, manipulate, his personal life remained unchanged. Otto Friedrich, writing of Hollywood in the '40s, remarks wryly: "No sooner had [Shaw] recovered sufficiently to start courting Ava Gardner than he wanted her to join him in consulting Dr. Romm. Miss Gardner dutifully began to prepare herself for analysis, but then Shaw began to worry that his own analysis might cure him of wanting to marry Miss Gardner, so he gallantly abandoned Dr. Romm."[13]

In *Ava: My Story*, the actress herself describes a very familiar Artie Shaw. "Artie was handsome, bronzed, very sure of himself, and he never stopped talking. It was a way of life with him. Artie could go on about every subject in the world, and for that matter, a few outside it as well. But he was full of such warmth and charm that I fell in love with him, just like that."[14]

Soon after they were married, Shaw—as was his pattern—undertook his new wife's "improvement." A sharecropper's daughter from Grabtown, North Carolina (lending added significance to the title of Shaw's Gramercy Five piece "The Grabtown Grapple"), Ava Gardner had never read much beyond *Gone With the Wind*. Now, abruptly, Shaw was thrusting such works as Freud's *The Interpretation of Dreams* and Thomas Mann's *The Magic Mountain* into her hands.

Artie Shaw's zeal for education and self-improvement had been a powerful driving force in both his professional and private lives. It is a quality at the very center of life among Jews who came to America from Russia and Russian-dominated Eastern Europe. Irving Howe has written movingly of its significance among Jewish immigrants in New York in the first days of the century:

> Uneducated, ill-educated, narrowly educated, or educated according to premises that seemed not to bear on American life, the immigrant Jews now wanted to learn at least a fraction of what had long been denied them. The hunger for knowledge was widespread, and among a few it rose to a fierce and remarkable passion.

Howe goes on to describe the Ashkenazi immigrant as not only "a proletarian searching for articulation and dignity, [but] also a Jew who had come to hope that by approaching Western thought he would both satisfy his own blossoming needs and help to remedy the disadvantages of the Jews as a people."[15]

For some, the very act of embracing Western thought and intellectual life (and by extension the social ways of the American gentile world) was itself a form of self-improvement. To music and literature, especially, attached a cultural cachet that transcended the meanness of everyday life. Moreover, this was America, land of dreams, where Louis B. Mayer, a poor Jew from Minsk, could rise from running a junkyard to controlling a multimillion-dollar entertainment empire. America, citadel of self-improvement; land of Horatio Alger and Henry Ford.

Among Jewish immigrants from Eastern Europe, and among their children, cultural assimilation became a compulsion. "What united them," Neil Gabler has written of the early movie moguls,

> was their utter and absolute rejection of their pasts and their equally absolute devotion to their new country. For immigrant Jews to want to assimilate . . . was nothing exceptional. But something drove the young Hollywood Jews to a ferocious, even pathological, embrace of America . . . [They] embarked on an assimilation so ruthless and complete that they cut their lives to the pattern of American respectability as they interpreted it.[16]

Arthur Arshawsky, in becoming Art Shaw, had taken a major step toward assimilation. His new name didn't even *sound* Jewish; handsome and assured, he didn't look Jewish in any stereotypical way. Music, and the very commercial success he later so deplored, had catapulted him into some of the most glamorous circles in American (i.e., gentile) society. And along with that came the trophy women, what he later called "the beautifully bedecked, powerful, fragrant-smelling girls who draw men like flies . . . If you're at a party and a woman like Ava Gardner comes up to you and says, 'Hey, I like you,' what are you going to do? Say no? Cut and run? That's stupid." In a sense, he said, they remained abstractions, part of the mystique, "these radiant, marvelous creatures" who represented yet another way in which Arthur Arshawsky had moved beyond the world of tenements and guttural accents, of being "a little Jewish kid who felt he didn't belong anywhere."

His approach to learning was voracious, often indiscriminate. Gerald Bordman, in his 1980 biography of Jerome Kern, describes the great songwriter's puzzlement at "Shaw's wide-ranging and probing fascination with all sorts of nickel knowledge."[17]

Shaw has made no attempt to deny that. "Very early," he told writer Merle Miller, "I had to decide whether to learn a lot about a little bit or a little bit about a great many things. I decided on the latter." Besides, he added, "I am impatient with details."[18]

Jerry Jerome, tenor saxophone soloist in the 1940 band, described an after-hours rehearsal at San Francisco's Palace Hotel when Shaw asked Jerome's wife, Eve, and singer Bonnie Lake to go up to his room and bring down a box of reeds. "When they came down they were all agog. 'Oh my God, he's got a book of physics open to a page dealing with the speed of light. He's got a telescope sticking out of his window . . .' They were like two high school kids. Everything was 'Wow! Did you see that?' Artie was so compulsive about knowledge, about learning. I still wonder whether part of it wasn't just some need to see himself as above being just a musician. He didn't want to be on the plane of ordinary people; he wanted to be an *intellectual*, in the worst way."[19]

When he socialized offstand, Shaw seldom sought out fellow-musicians, instead courting well-known intellectuals—composers, poets, painters, such writers as John Steinbeck and William Saroyan. "Musicians, generally, aren't very interesting people," he has said. "Most of what they think about—Benny, for instance—is technique: how many fingers you can move to get this or that effect. I can't relate to them much. Even now, so many years later, I'll go over to Beverly Hills and spend some time with old music business friends. We'll talk on the surface, about this one's heart attack, that one's marriage. But it's limited, doesn't lead anywhere."

Once in a while such sentiments—and his inability to mask them—got him into trouble. While filming *Dancing Co-ed*, Lana Turner wrote, he "never missed a chance to complain that it was beneath him to appear in a Hollywood movie. The crew plotted to drop an arc light on his head."[20]

However he might have felt about being a musician, there can be no doubting either the seriousness of Shaw's commitment to music or the intensity of his aspiration. Confronted with the musical ferment going on in the mid-'40s, it was natural that he should find it fascinating, want to study it, analyze it, understand it in depth—then pitch himself all-consumingly into finding a way to adapt to it.

In the meantime, he devoted himself to polishing his mastery of the instrument, performing and recording classical (Shaw always preferred to call them "long-form") pieces with symphony orchestras and chamber ensembles. His 1947 WOR broadcast recording of the Mozart Clarinet Quintet is something of an oddity: Shaw's playing, technically impeccable, bears traces of a light vibrato in some of his sustained tones. "I wanted to see what would happen to my sound," he has said, "so I developed a sound with a ripple, a very thin vibrato, rather than the full one I'd had. More than a few symphonic clarinetists have said to me, 'Why did you play the Mozart with a vibrato?' and I've answered by saying, 'Why not?' It's just a performance convention, after all.

"When you learn clarinet you're taught that it's not a vibrating horn. But that's an anomaly, isn't it? In a woodwind quintet you've got a flute that vibrates—you do it with your stomach—an oboe that vibrates, even a bassoon, to a certain extent. The only one that doesn't is the French horn, which is really a hunting horn anyway. So why should the clarinet stick out like a little foghorn among those people? I always tell them, 'I *want* to blend.' I'll bet Mozart, were he alive today and had he heard that performance, would have thought it was a good idea."[21]

Of all the pieces Shaw addressed in 1947–48, by far the most challenging was a concerto—a real one this time—by Russian-born Nicolai Berezowsky. Shaw had met him when they were both CBS staff musicians, and they had remained friends; told that Artie intended to spend a year or more honing his concert clarinet skills and was looking actively for repertoire, Berezowsky converted a piece he'd written some years earlier for violist William Primrose.

Shaw performed it first in concert with the Denver Symphony, then in Carnegie Hall, as guest soloist with the National Youth Symphony. "The last movement is one of the toughest things I have ever played on the clarinet," he said. "There's one segment of ten or eleven seconds that I spent almost three months practicing, just to get it right.

"Funny, the impression that work made on me. Even now, years after putting the clarinet down for good, I'll still wake up in the night sometimes and realize that I've been trying, in my sleep, to work out better fingerings for certain passages in that third movement."[22]

How profoundly the changes going on in music, and in the world around him, had affected Shaw became clear when, in early 1949, he undertook what seemed an eminently quixotic project: major recordings of pieces by Debussy, Ravel, Milhaud, Poulenc, and Morton Gould—and by Russian composers Dmitri Kabalevsky and Dmitri Shostakovitch. Attacked by Hearst newspaper columnists for including "Red" composers, Shaw shot back: "Anybody who plays a program of modern music and doesn't include the Russian composers is scratching his left ear with his right hand."[23]

Such outbursts—and the divorce testimony of his sixth wife, *Forever Amber* author Kathleen Winsor, that he had been, briefly, a member of the Communist Party—won Shaw a place in the notorious publication *Red Channels* and a summons to appear before the House Un-American Activities Committee.[24]

Under the headline SHAW SETS NEW CREW, a small item in the August 12, 1949, *Down Beat* announced that Artie Shaw was shortly to begin rehearsing a new band in preparation for a twelve-week autumn tour. It quoted Lenny Lewis, identified as contractor and road manager, as saying new band's book would combine familiar standards with new material written in "the modern groove . . . We won't call it bop."

But bop it most certainly was, to be played by a band full of young, bop-oriented jazzmen. Nor was Shaw the first leader to flirt with "the modern groove." Benny Goodman had tried some new ensemble sounds and textures, but half-heartedly, reluctant to make real change. "We had two books," said Buddy Greco, pianist with Goodman's 1948–49 "bop band." "We had the old Fletcher Henderson–style book made up of all his big hits, and we had the much smaller bop book by Chico O'Farrill, Tadd Dameron, and a number of other modern writers, including myself." On one-nighters, Goodman would spend most of the evening playing the "greatest hits" book, then leave the stage, turning the band over to Greco, who pulled out the "bop" book.[25]

Other bands, notably those of Woody Herman and Boyd Raeburn, had embraced the new ways with real commitment and determination and salutary musical results. Both had served as incubators for some of the outstanding young players and arrangers of the day. Stan Kenton's large and often flamboyant orchestra, with its ten-man brass section, had opened a wide range of possibility in timbre, depth, and dynamics. Duke Ellington, alert as ever to the creative possibilities of larger instrumentations and harmonic advance, had incorporated new sounds and flavors—though on his own terms. Dizzy Gillespie's own big band of the same period added yet another element: the energy and variety of Afro-Cuban rhythms.

Artie Shaw's newest band began rehearsing in mid-August, at Manhattan's popular Nola studio. "We'd start at ten in the morning, every day," said baritone saxophonist Danny Bank, "and would be scheduled to go all day, till about six, with just a break for lunch. Day after day, for a whole week, we'd just keep going."[26]

The personnel evolved a little at a time. At first it included musicians who had been part of Lenny Lewis's own band around Buffalo, New York, but by the time the band took to the road all but one, trombonist Angie Callea, had been supplanted by New York men. Though Shaw remained firmly in charge, he ran things with what for him was a far lighter touch. "I used to have too set an idea of what I wanted," he told Barry Ulanov in a *Metronome* magazine interview. "This band can't be a stylized band. At least at first it can't be." It would find its style, he added, rather than having that style imposed upon it.[27]

Still, said Danny Bank, his methods were thorough. The musical memory that had enabled him, back in his CBS staff days, to play through an entire broadcast without once looking at his parts served him well here. He came to each rehearsal thoroughly prepared, intimately conversant with even the most complex score.

"We used to talk among ourselves about how strong his kidneys must be," said Bank. "I mean, he never went to the men's room. Never left the stool he was sitting on in front of the band. He'd sit on that stool from ten in the morning until we quit for lunch. We agreed that he must be the world's champ. He was so into the music he couldn't even take a piss break."

By the time they headed for Boston to begin a tour that would take it as far west as Chicago, Shaw's band was tight, spirited, well rehearsed—and full of top-of-the-line musicians. Besides Bank, the sax section included Al Cohn, Zoot Sims, and Herbie Steward, all stars of Woody Herman's "Four Brothers" band of 1947–48. Steward, whose light-textured tenor also had been a feature of Shaw's 1945 band, was playing alto, leading the section. Second alto Frank Socolow had worked for Georgie Auld and Boyd Raeburn, among others, and had just returned from a European tour with bassist Chubby Jackson.[28]

"That was," said Danny Bank, "the greatest sax section I ever worked with. Al Cohn took most of the tenor solos, and—well, you know, Artie respected him so much he wouldn't follow him in the solo sequence. Whenever an arrangement came up that had tenor and then clarinet, he'd rearrange the solos so that he didn't have to follow Al. He understood how good Al was."

It was a reed section sound quite different from that of the great Shaw band of a decade earlier. Little vibrato, another way of phrasing, another blend. "It took a while for me to get used to it," Shaw has said. "But you can't stay rooted in the past forever. This was another time, another way of doing things. But God, they were good: played in tune, played together, even breathed together. Why should I try to change them?"

The style might have changed, but Shaw was no less exacting about what he wanted to hear from his reeds. "He was especially rough on the first alto player," said trombonist Sonny Russo. "He'd been a great lead alto player himself and knew how things should go: dynamics, phrasing, breathing."[29]

The rest of the band was no less illustrious: New England trumpeter Don Fagerquist had won praise with Gene Krupa's 1944–45 band; guitarist Jimmy Raney and drummer Irv Kluger were young and precocious. Shaw also brought with him a certain amount of continuity from past bands—in this case pianist Dodo Marmarosa and certain key arrangements by Paul Jordan, George Siravo, Ray Conniff, and even, from the 1940–41 period, Lennie Hayton.

"And why not?" he asked, going on to answer his own question in customarily expansive fashion. "If something is good it will always be good. We impose time on things. Why shouldn't a painting by van Gogh stand up to one by Picasso or de Kooning? This is human expression, after all, and time doesn't lessen its potency. Is the beauty of what Bix did any less potent because he played what he did more than sixty years ago?"

Rhetoric aside, the band managed to be comfortable facing both ways. Its interpretations of material from Shaw's past was fresh, enthusiastic, sometimes—

as on Conniff's " 'S Wonderful" arrangement—even outdoing the original performances.

Arrangers Cohn, Callea, Johnny Mandel, George Russell, Gene Roland, and
Tadd Dameron understood both where Shaw had been and how he had moved
and developed since the 1930s. Trade paper articles announced that Eddie Sauter,
Gerry Mulligan, Mary Lou Williams, and others would also contribute arrangements.

The tour culminated in a memorable stand at the Blue Note in Chicago. But
in general, response from the public had been somewhat less than Shaw had
hoped. "The people just didn't know," Shaw told Burt Korall. "They wanted bad
music, played in a mediocre way. And constantly it was the past. Play *Beguine*,
play this, that and the other that I had gone past years before."[30]

Sixteen selections made for a transcription service reveal an ensemble bursting
with ideas, creative possibilities—and the skill to realize them. And remarkably
polished, given the short time it had been in existence. It's a band with range,
able to give incisive, idiomatically appropriate accounts of Hayton's 1940 "Star
Dust" and Jordan's 1942 "Carnival," then dealing easily with Gene Roland's
boppy, linear "Aesop's Foibles," Mandel's lightly textured "I Get a Kick out of
You" or "So Easy," a Tadd Dameron blues bristling with altered chords.

Shaw's clarinet solos are revealing. In common with Red Norvo, he had
always heard far beyond the four- and five-voice chords underpinning most jazz
improvisation of the 1920s and '30s. Even Bix, Trumbauer, and other harmonically "advanced" early players had regarded upper voices and substitutions largely
as colorational devices, used for melodic effect in relatively simple harmonic
environments. Lester Young, aesthetically the driving force behind the styles of
Cohn, Sims, Stan Getz, and so many other soloists who emerged in the '40s,
seems also to have thought this way.

With a well-honed instinct for aesthetic implication, Shaw incorporated, assimilated, the conventions of modern jazz. In the manner of a writer absorbing
a vocabulary, matters of idiom, metaphor, and cadence, he found ways that neatly
bypassed simple eclecticism en route to an organic whole.

Easiest to spot are the mechanics, matters of execution: his melody statement
on the 1949 "They Can't Take That Away From Me" differs greatly from the
same passage on the same George Siravo arrangement recorded just four years
earlier. He has smoothed out vibrato and attack, introduced the small triplet
"turns" on which much bop playing depends for its linearity.

(Nothing illustrates the continuing duality in Shaw's life better than his par-
ticipation in a November 9 concert recital at Chicago's Temple Sholom, on Lake
Shore Drive. Accompanied by a full orchestra under radio conductor Alfredo
Antonini, he performed two selections: the Mozart Concerto and a *Fantasie on Three
American Songs*—in this case "Frenesi," "Star Dust," and "Begin the Beguine.")

Perhaps the most astonishing demonstration of this band's range and poten-
tial, and of the latitude Shaw was prepared to give his musicians, is George
Russell's "Similau." A charter member of the innovative Miles Davis–Gil Evans–
Gerry Mulligan circle of the '40s, Russell had experimented early with Afro-Cuban

rhythms, as demonstrated in "Cubana-Be" and "Cubana-Bop," written for Dizzy Gillespie's big band in 1947. He'd also developed a personal concept of orchestral writing; it found ultimate expression in a 1953 treatise, The Lydian Concept of Tonal Organization, which became a standard text for many college courses in jazz composition.

"Similau" itself is a rather straightforward 1949 pop tune, structured AABA; but Russell utterly transforms it through use of polytonal layering, superimposition of one tonal center on another, through canonic passages set in motion by Shaw's clarinet. It's a way of thinking that found strong expression in tenor saxophonist John Coltrane's seminal work of the early '60s. Russell even presents some challenging variations on the clarinet-and-tomtoms configuration used by Shaw (and Goodman) in the '30s.

By any standard, "Similau" is an ambitious undertaking, a valuable measure of Artie Shaw's musical reach. "I have a very low boredom threshold," he has said. "The interesting part of a band, to me, is forming it. Getting the book. Rehearsing it and adding and trying new things until you have an instrument. Reaching a point where you think, 'I've done all I can do with this group. Now let's get another one.'"

Regrettably, neither the band nor its leader ever had a chance to reach that point. Not long into 1950, a gallstone condition that had plagued Shaw for some time became critical enough to necessitate surgery. With great reluctance he gave the band its notice. What could have been the most creatively intriguing of all Artie Shaw orchestras, full of prodigious individual talents and able to reach comfortably across large gulfs of time and style, was over when it had barely gotten started.

When he returned, there was another band, even shorter-lived than its predecessor, returning to the old instrumentation of six brass and four reeds, with greater emphasis on old favorites. Shaw remembered it with a mixture of amusement and distaste: "I laughed, ogled, waggled my head—in general behaved like a mechanical wind-up doll. I even put the clarinet on my shoulder like a rifle and marched with it. And don't you know there were people who loved it, thought it was the best band I'd ever had?"

(Sonny Russo remembered it differently. "Sure, we played more of the old stuff, but we did a lot of the new things too. He had some of the George Russell and Gene Roland charts revoiced for the smaller instrumentation. We even played Bop City, the old Bop City at Broadway and 49th Street. We played the black circuit: the Apollo, the Howard in Washington, the Royal in Baltimore—even the Adams Theatre in Newark. It wasn't that bad a band. Not as good as the '49 one had been, but not bad.")[31]

Shaw has cited the failure of his 1949 band as the beginning of the end, the event that triggered his decision, midway through the '50s, to put away the clarinet and leave the music business. Certainly the ever-widening contrast between the music's excellence and the audience's lack of interest must have been hard to bear.

"Who was it—Dryden, I think—who said, 'He who lives to please, must please to live'? Money came from playing, and when it stopped coming, in quantitites large enough for me to hire and pay the men I wanted and needed, then it didn't work. Those people who provided the money wouldn't show up if I did what I wanted. I got sick to death of that, sick of people whose very *actions* said, 'We *made* you, so you'd better play what *we* want. You might say I didn't want to please to live any more."[32]

But then, he hadn't wanted to in the first place. What else besides ambivalence about the dance band business could have prompted Shaw's early experiments with the string quartet band, a group he must have known would be a non-starter in a field dominated by bigger, louder swing orchestras? It was certainly behind his well-publicized late-1930s outbursts against "jitterbugs" and impelled his end-of-1939 walkout. "Pearls before swine," a phrase frequently on his lips, seems an accurate summation of his attitude.

It also lies behind his decision, in 1954, to form one last Gramercy Five, a no-compromises jazz unit made up entirely of younger modern musicians. Pianist Hank Jones combined thorough grounding in Teddy Wilson and Nat Cole with keen understanding of bop pioneers Al Haig and Bud Powell; guitarist Tal Farlow had been part of Red Norvo's ground-breaking trio (alongside Charles Mingus) of 1950–53; vibraphonist Joe Roland had just left the high-profile George Shearing Quintet; Tommy Potter, one of the preeminent younger bassists, had recorded and toured with Charlie Parker; drummer Irv Kluger, before joining the 1949 Shaw big band, had been with Stan Kenton, Boyd Raeburn and other innovative groups and recorded with Dizzy Gillespie.

They worked at the Embers, and they worked in Las Vegas. They made two batches of records, first in New York and then, without Roland and with Joe Puma replacing Farlow on guitar, in Hollywood. As in 1949, the repertoire blended past and present. There are searching, musically astute reworkings of such earlier band landmarks as "Back Bay Shuffle," "Love of My Life," and even "Beguine" and "Frenesi." Shaw re-examines some specialties from editions one and two of the Gramercy Five, among them "Summit Ridge Drive," "When the Quail Come Back to San Quentin," "Scuttlebutt," and "Mysterioso." He addresses the bop anthem "How High the Moon" and brings an updated lyric sense to such ballads as "Tenderly," "Someone to Watch Over Me," and "Don't Take Your Love From Me." And, too, there is yet another magical reassessment of "Star Dust."

His playing had continued the process of evolution set in motion in the late '40s. He'd switched clarinets, forsaking his Selmer, instrument of choice for most jazzmen, for the darker, woodier-sounding Buffet, favored by classical and chamber music specialists.

"But that's what this was," he said. "It was chamber music. At least that's how I thought about it. I'd say to the band, 'Forget this is jazz.' I'd impressed on them that I didn't want to have the usual kind of jazz group. 'Let's play music here,' I'd say. And that's what happened.

"You know, I saw Hank Jones not long ago, and the first thing he said was,

'Hey, let's get together and do that again!' And after more than forty years! But he loved that band. We were playing stuff he's never done since. Same with Tal.''

The records are as musical, as thoughtful, as Shaw wanted them to be. The performances bristle with deftly turned ensembles, original backgrounds for solos, surprising uses of familiar material. Even the range of "quoting," a popular jazz-man's device in which a phrase from another composition is dropped into a solo or arranged passage, is vast: an alert ear can pick up allusions to Tchaikovsky, Brahms, Chopin, Stravinsky, Dvořák on the one hand, myriad popular songs and even jazz themes on the other.

Almost without exception (the disposable "Stop and Go Mambo" may be one such), these are supremely intelligent, finely honed performances, punctuated with moments of great beauty: Shaw's melody statement on "Someone to Watch Over Me"—alternately understated and heavily embellished—is but one. His two solo choruses on a well-considered "Dancing on the Ceiling," as saxophonist Loren Schoenberg has suggested, do bring Lester Young to mind in their conti-nuity and linear flow.

Shaw is playing softly, taking little of the mouthpiece, working close to the microphone, and what he loses in fullness and projection he gains in intimacy. Even the sound of the pads closing on the instrument's tone-holes is clear and distinct.

Writer Gene Lees has singled out this group's reexamination of "Star Dust" for praise. Musically it's an kind of exegesis, an informed commentary on a major earlier work—and, perhaps inadvertently, an argument against such reexamina-tion. Opening with a melody statement, Shaw refers obliquely to Billy Butter-field's exposition on the 1940 original: where the trumpeter afforded clarity of view into the very heart of the melody, though, Shaw's embellishments and commentaries seem almost to mask it.

But exegesis, after all, is in the nature of Artie Shaw's intellect—a mind ever driven by the need to question, to examine and explain. Actress Evelyn Keyes, to whom he was married for twenty-eight years, described her first meeting, in a Paris apartment, with a man who "dominated the room with his flow of ani-mated, inquisitive talk, wanting to know everything instantly, his vibrancy rich-ocheting around the ancient walls like sparks off a flint."[33]

Sometimes the process works to his advantage, as with "Begin the Beguine," a song possessed of depths and dramatic implications barely suggested by Shaw's 1938 hit record. Arguably, this is one of those instances in which the clarinetist's declared aversion to songs and their "banal" lyrics may be somewhat misplaced.

("Beguine" is less a song than a kind of psychodrama in miniature, with emotions of widely different natures clashing within the mind of the narrator. The song's epic 108-bar length carries an opening mood of affectionate nostalgia ["*a night of tropical splendor*"] into increasingly painful realms, as memory brings first regret ["*to live it again is past all endeavor*"], then self-castigation ["*And now when I hear people curse the chance that was wasted/I know but too well what they mean*"], then despair fading into something like resignation.)[34]

Though borrowing from the 1938 record (Farlow, for example, paraphrases—and consolidates—Tony Pastor's tenor solo), this performance establishes a hushed, ruefully introspective mood that which serves the song rather better than did the swingy ballroom arrangement of 1938.

Beyond argument, the best of these performances—and perhaps one of the jewels of Shaw's career on record—is an extraordinary account of Henry Nemo's 1941 standard "Don't Take Your Love From Me." "Goddamn, that's good!" was the clarinetist's own reaction during a recent hearing. "You listen to it quietly, hear it a few times, and you think, 'That isn't *jazz*, that's *music!*' Chamber music. Which is precisely what I was trying to do with that band in the first place."

There is no disputing him: the first-chorus dialogue between Shaw, stating the melody, and Jones, supporting and illuminating, displays rare unity of purpose. The pianist's locked-hands solo sounds like neither Milt Buckner (who brought the style into jazz) nor George Shearing (who popularized it); instead, it is entirely consonant with the presentation of the song, style subordinate to content.

Not all these last performances achieve this exalted plane. While some reexaminations of previous Shaw material ("The Sad Sack," "When the Quail Come Back to San Quentin") add new dimensions to the originals, others either sacrifice the focus of the earlier versions ("Cross Your Heart") or seem unable to escape the collision of the hermeneutic and the discursive in Shaw's own nature ("Yesterdays").

Evelyn Keyes, writing with an awe that transcends whatever rancor attended her marriage to Shaw, describes the totality that attended a cognition process unique in its energy, virtually limitless in its diversity:

> Then there was the daily chess game. Artie even made several chess boards himself, out of wood and cork. He designed a chess set out of two shades of silver, a modern flat affair that came apart, easily packed for traveling. He liked to use his hands. He carved, he painted, he made his own [fishing] flies, he fixed electrical appliances when they broke. There didn't seem to be anything he couldn't do, or didn't know the answer to . . . He bought books and charts of the stars and planets, and a big telescope. Nightly we gazed up at the heavens to find Venus, Saturn and its rings, Jupiter and its moons, and the worlds beyond.[35]

Elsewhere she describes her astonishment at watching her husband doing everything from ice-skating ("Artie, my God, could . . . even do figure-eights!") to teaching himself Chopin polonaises on the piano. At one point he became interested in firearms and before long was designing and building his own weapons and ammunition, demonstrating skill as nothing less than a crack marksman. Was there no end, she exclaimed, to his accomplishments?

The answer, in general, is no, not for this sort of restless, inquiring mind. It's not much of a reach to imagine Shaw "figuring out" the bop style, then applying his peerless musical skills to its mastery.

Listening to Shaw's work here in quantity and with concentration, it is hard not to see that process in action. There is a certain, not quite definable, sense that this mind of such formidable analytical and executive strengths has addressed a new way of playing music less as a matter of emotional experience than as a problem in applied mathematics. Make this adjustment, change that method of attack or tone production, reconfigure various shapes. The result, executed with Shaw's matchless ear, is a virtual reinvention of his style.

It only takes setting Shaw's work in this context beside that of his friend and onetime employer, Red Norvo, to understand that such methods of synthesis can exact a price. Unlike Shaw, Norvo had never found it necessary to *plan* an adaptation; the harmonic and melodic vocabulary of bop seemed little more than an extension of the way he'd been playing since the '30s—highly chromatic, long-lined, incorporating extended chords and substitutions.

As early as 1944–45, while working with Benny Goodman, Norvo was hiring such musicians as Gillespie and Parker for his own record dates; he fit in comfortably as soloist with Woody Herman's forward-looking "Herd" of 1946. Most notably, the Norvo trio of 1950–53, with Farlow and bassist Charles Mingus, has held its preeminence as one of the most innovative—and viscerally stimulating—units of its time.

The comparison is not drawn to slight Shaw but rather to understand why, even at their most exceptional, the records of the 1954 Gramercy Five operate most successfully on a purely intellectual level. "I was looking for a chamber music sound, a kind of transparency," he told Dan Morgenstern, and that is exactly what these performances represent. When they engage the emotions (*vide* "Don't Take Your Love From Me"), it is in much the way that a string quartet or Mozart wind serenade engages the emotions: with its inner perfection, an Apollonian sense of order and balance, a clarity and—yes—transparency of texture.[36]

What's missing is the sort of visceral stimulation, the sense of emotional engagement, and enlistment of the listener, that lies at the inspirational core of the Norvo Trio—and at the core of Shaw's own earlier playing, particularly in the 1938–41 period. It's the "singing" quality so apparent in so many Shaw solos of those years and collectively in the Jenney-Butterfield-Robinson "Star Dust" band of 1940-41.

Artie Shaw laid his clarinet aside, never to pick it up again, in 1955. Why he did it may never be known. More than once he has spoken of "a gangrenous right arm that was going to kill you; you cut it off to save your life." Such comparisons, while colorful enough to put the unwary interviewer off stride, seem mostly to address his oft-declared loathing for the music business, for the mechanics of being a professional musician and leading dance orchestras. But that is, as Shaw himself is wont to say, a thing apart from the intensely personal matter of playing an instrument.

(Evelyn Keyes, who married Shaw after he had abandoned the clarinet, tells of watching him in Toronto, rehearsing a specially organized big band for a TV special. "Artie only had to sharpen them up a little here and there. And he did it so easily, relaxed, knowing his stuff, doing the things he knew best. I had never seen this person before. I understood then, that when he had been worrying about losing a part of himself . . . he had already lost the biggest part of all when he'd given up his music.")[37]

At all events, the "why" is less important within this context than the fact of his having done it. Shaw lived on into the century's last decade, his intellectual powers undimmed, his ability to express himself unimpaired. It's easy to draw comparisons to the likes of Gioachino Rossini, who at age thirty-seven stopped writing the operas on which his considerable reputation was built, then lived on another nearly four decades, apparently enjoying himself immensely as a gourmand and bon vivant.

Shaw's may be a rather more complex case than that of Rossini, or even of Sibelius, who "retired" from composing at age sixty-two and lived another three decades, his mental faculties apparently unimpaired. Shaw's own explanation is that he transferred his expressive energies from music to the printed word. "I didn't stop playing, I began writing," he has insisted. "There's no room [in my life] for both." The Trouble With Cinderella, published in 1952, bears the subtitle "An Outline of Identity," and the phrase was well chosen: more an exercise in self-contemplation than an autobiography, it is often quite wry in tone. Two collections of short fiction, I Love You, I Hate You, Drop Dead and The Best of Intentions, show Shaw to be a skilled, if occasionally self-indulgent, writer.

His potentially crowning achievement in writing, some three decades in the making, was as of the late 1990s still a work in progress. Provisionally titled The Education of Albie Snow, it is—as would be expected of Artie Shaw—a hybrid, a form of his own devising, part Bildungsroman, part roman à clef, part straightforward autobiography. It is drawn on a grand scale, punctuated by shifts of structure and presentation worthy of Lawrence Sterne.

At one point Snow moves into verse—but here, too, the form and ground rules are the author's own. Covering more than two typewritten pages, the verse is entirely unpunctuated: Shaw relies on natural cadence, on weight, the inner rhythms of his words and phrases, to convey meaning and emphasis. It is a virtuoso turn.

When reading Albie Snow, it is easy to understand how its author, having taken both the clarinet and the ability to organize and shape bands to a zenith, might perhaps have decided to call a halt. Might have: but the question refuses to dry up and blow away. Were there no circumstances under which Artie Shaw might have remained a clarinetist? No musical terrain left to explore? No satisfactions as yet unperceived, unrealized? What follows is excerpted from a much longer discussion in Shaw's California home, beginning at midday and extending far into the night.

Question: Let's say you'd been free to organize ensembles, commission arrangements from whomever you pleased, do what you wanted—all without the pressure of having to sue for the acceptance of popular audiences. Would you have—

Shaw: You mean no "Beguine"? No "Frenesi" and the rest of it? No people tugging at me, reminding me, "We made you"?

Question: Just so. Just music. No obligations or compromises. And underwriting enough to allow you to do what you wanted, musically, on whatever scale.

Shaw: Tempting. I'd probably have stayed with music the rest of my life—and written, if only short stories.

Question: All the stuff about gangrenous limbs aside, aren't there times when you just plain miss making music? Not so much the physical act of playing the instrument: many people simply get tired of doing that after a long time. It's only human. I'm talking about the process of creating music, bringing something into being.

Shaw: You're talking about music in the abstract. But I don't think you can do that; when I talk about making music it's about playing for audiences—in fact, the very same audiences that wouldn't support me so I could do the things I wanted to do with the musicians I knew could do them.

Question: I think you're conflating two different things. Let's say, let's imagine, the option had been open to you, through grant funding or some form of subsidy, to—

Shaw: No, no! Look, Roger Wolfe Kahn was like that. He was a dilettante, a rich kid, and he got bored with it. I don't believe in dilettantism: the one nice thing about music not being supported is that either you make it work or you don't. That's part of the dues you pay. The guy who can afford to do it because he's subsidized doesn't really know the value of strife.

Question: But surely you've contradicted yourself here. On the one hand you don't want to have to deal with audiences and their ceaseless appetite for "Beguine" and the rest; on the other you profess not to be interested in being subsidized. What's left? How else can it possibly work?

Shaw: Look at Duke [Ellington]. He couldn't have kept his band going without the ASCAP money, the royalties from his songs. He was able to pay his men out of that, so he kept the band. I didn't have that—and worse yet, I didn't have the sense to think, "Well, buy up a bunch of copyrights to your stuff and you'll get paid." Jesus, I do wish I'd done something like that.

Question: Well, if Ellington did that, and if other organizations and individuals find funding (not without some struggle, I might add from personal experience) that enables them to go on making music without depending on filling seats or selling tickets, surely—

Shaw: Hold it. I can't talk about that. I can't hear music in the abstract. If I hear Beethoven I think of his life, about the Heiligenstadt Testament. If I think of Ravel, I think about his collection of little objets d'art. The music, the life, a picture—it all goes together.

Question: And what if I'm driving somewhere, or sitting on the beach, and the very sound and emotional ambiance of Paul Jordan's "Evensong," or your "Star Dust" solo, come unbidden to mind, nourishing whatever frame of mind I happen to be in at the time? Isn't that an abstraction, and doesn't it have its own validity?

Shaw: No. No. Music for me is a communicative language. Even in the example you've just cited it has communicated on some level. Without that it's just a form of masturbation.

Question: Isn't there an ideal audience, one that wouldn't think of pestering you for "Frenesi" or the other stuff? One that was interested only in what you had to say right *now*?

Shaw: That's a nice idea, but I don't think it exists. I own a book that says, "What if the moon didn't exist?" It's not hard to imagine, but if the moon in fact didn't exist you'd have a different world. A different system. Nothing would be the same.

Question: So what you're saying in the end is threefold. First, that music must have an audience, communicate with that audience, in order to justify itself. Second, that that audience is going to make demands on you that you couldn't—wouldn't—meet. And third, that you were no longer willing, if you ever were, to deal with what was required to be able to pursue real communication. As the guy in Potter's *The Singing Detective* puts it, am I right or am I right?

Shaw: You're right.

And here the story stops, incomplete, contradictory, still open. Safe to say that jazz, and perhaps all American popular music, has never seen a man, a being, comparable to Artie Shaw. One of the great jazz improvisers? Yes, no doubt of that: but within a frame of reference that is ultimately his and his alone. Leader, architect, and master-builder of extraordinary dance orchestras. Thinker. And, some would say, poseur.

There's little doubt that he could be a difficult, willful, self-centered, and at times even cruel man; that Shaw himself, above all, is his own trouble with Cinderella. His various wives have left vivid accounts of their lives with him; as much as they vary in tone and level of expression, they form a remarkably consistent composite portrait. As Ava Gardner put it, "he's impossible to live with, sometimes even to be friends with, but he is a worthwhile human being, an extraordinary man."[38]

The forces driving him, the need to learn and master, create and control, play show-and-tell with his mind and achievements, constitute a psychoanalyst's delight. Without doubt, they will one day be fertile subject matter for an ambitious researcher and a colorful, multi-layered biography. But it seems equally likely that such a work needs must be posthumous: were it otherwise, Artie Shaw's mind and voice—animated, erudite, free-ranging, self-serving and self-conscious, by turns illuminative and obfuscatory—would surely overpower all else. They have been his strength, and someday may also be seen to have been his undoing.

VII

**The Fine Art
of *Sui Generis***

25

Bobby Hackett: Making It Sing

Fellow-musicians still talk about the time Bobby Hackett was trying to sell one of his many cornets to a friend. "It's been played a bit," he said with real earnestness, "but the high register"—(here a small chuckle)—"that's unused, brand-new."

That was his way—wry, a little self-deprecating—of reminding people that he didn't often use his instrument's extremes of register, either upper or lower, preferring to work in its vocal middle range. Anyone who knew Bobby even slightly will recognize the humor, as characteristic of the man as the sound of his horn on hundreds, even thousands, of records, over four decades.

It may have been largely social rhetoric, a conversational device, an idiosyncratic way of telling those he met that he was, after all, just a modest guy who happened to do his own small thing well and would never think of letting it inflate his ego. But device or not, the gentle self-mockery may also be a clue to why Bobby Hackett—whose playing set a standard for discreet musicianship and inventiveness in jazz which has seldom, if ever, been challenged—remains forever a step or two outside the limelight.

It's difficult, in fact, to think of another musician so admired by his peers, so deeply beloved across borders of style, generation, and race, who remains so constantly undervalued by historians and opinion-makers. Louis Armstrong esteemed him above almost all others, spoke of him often, seized every opportunity to play with him. Such diverse fellow-jazzmen as Miles Davis, Dizzy Gillespie, Benny Goodman, Ruby Braff, Clark Terry, Vic Dickenson, Jonah Jones, Pee Wee

Erwin, and Joe Newman regarded him with a deference reserved only for a choice few, and never hesitated to say so.*

Yet Hackett has not made out well in the jazz history books. With the exception of an insightful 1972 profile by Whitney Balliett, which appeared first in the New Yorker, no chapter in a major jazz anthology has been devoted to him. When the names of the great brassmen of jazz are invoked, his is seldom among them.

Robert Leo Hackett, cornetist, of Providence, Rhode Island, may have been one of the most perfect and fully realized of all improvising soloists. His recorded performances constitute a primer in musical intelligence, logic of conception, unimpeachable taste, beauty of tone and execution, second only to those of his friend and hero, Louis Armstrong.

He sounds like no one else, though aspects of his playing at various times reflect admiration for both Armstrong and Bix Beiderbecke. He seems beyond category, above it, able to explore the subtlest melodic and chordal implications of a song without disrupting a near-perfect coherence.

His is a calm, ordered voice, of sometimes startling purity. His solos are logical in what Balliett has rightly termed a mathemetician's way, yet never abstract, never less than emotionally satisfying. He is not an overt swinger: there is seldom anything even remotely like swagger or bravado in his manner, yet he's capable of generating rhythmic intensity, even heat.

Hackett's chief strengths are lyrical and melodic. Saxophonist Ben Webster, himself a master melodist, was wont to cite Hackett in conversations about the deceptive simplicity of setting out a melody. Anyone, he said, can develop technique, learn harmony, run all over his horn. But who can play a song, varying the basic melody hardly at all, and bring a tear to someone's eye? That, the great tenor soloist said, was the special art of Bobby Hackett and precious few others.[1]

Hackett recorded in diverse circumstances, taking in everything from the sublime (small, hand-picked jazz units) to the grandiose (vast string orchestras) to the potentially absurd (ukulele bands, skating-rink pipe organs). Yet despite the surroundings, few will contend that he ever made a record that was anything less than excellent, and often more than that. In common with all superior improvisers, Hackett seemed able to elevate a situation simply by being part of it.

Balliett, in his New Yorker profile, described him as "imperishable," and it is the best of words. Poised, as precise as the movement of a fine watch, he goes his unhurried way, producing solos able to touch the heart while tantalizing the mind and seducing the ear.

The restraint and emotional layering in much of his work and especially in his early years—his tone and the shapes of his phrases have prompted quite a

---

*Davis, ending a diatribe about a Don Ellis record during a 1968 Blindfold Test, delivered himself of the opinion, "You can be black and no good, white and no good . . . A guy like Bobby Hackett plays what he plays with feeling, and you can put him into any kind of thing and he'll do it" (Down Beat, June 13, 1968).

few listeners to compare him to Beiderbecke. Bix, after all, was only a few years gone when Hackett came to wide notice, and those who had heard and cherished the ill-fated Iowan longed to find him again in the newcomer from New England.

For a while, Hackett went along with the comparison: he allowed himself, perhaps unwisely, to recreate the Beiderbecke "I'm Comin', Virginia" solo as part of Benny Goodman's 1938 Carnegie Hall concert. He was nervous and his performance showed it; worse yet, he never got a chance on that momentous night to show off his own, by then, distinctively personal style.

In general, the overall effect of Hackett's playing on the ear differs from that of Beiderbecke; there is little of the sense of melancholy that pervades every Bix solo. Instead, there is to Hackett a primness and a certain sunniness of outlook that from the start declared him his own man.

Hackett the soloist is like a gifted orator: he chooses his words carefully, delivering them with a tone—a voice—instantly, gently, recognizable. "That sound," said Ruby Braff. "It's the first thing that strikes you. It's what you hear before you hear anything—a pure and warm sound, very attractive. It kind of winds around notes which are themselves extraordinary: he had a genius for selecting the most marvelous notes of every chord in any song he played."[2]

A melodic line, after all, can be compounded out of any combination of notes, intervals, distribution of phrases. In that sense it is almost a random process: as a prose stylist fits words, phrases, together to form a coherent whole, so does the architect of a melody assemble its component parts. What distinguishes a great prose stylist from a mere compiler of words has to do with selection, with inner rhythm, with factors far transcending the simple mechanics of sentence construction.

The writer of prose understands instinctively that certain combinations of phrases and rhythms—the inflections, as it were, of the rhetor's inner voice—will produce strong and varied responses in a reader. It's equally applicable to the great melodists: Tchaikovsky among nineteenth-century composers, Jerome Kern among songwriters of the American twentieth century, knew the emotive power of certain intervals, certain combinations of notes and rhythms, and the contexts in which they could be presented most effectively.

The very word "melody" is compounded of two Greek words, *melos* and *ode*, both clear references to singing. A third Greek word, *harmonia*, is a near neighbor, dealing with the implications of a melodic line when expressed in terms of a regular rhythm or setting. Nicolas Slonimsky, writing in *A Lectionary of Music*, observes, "Aesthetically, a beautiful melody must have a perfect balance between the high and low registers and a symmetric alternation of ascending and descending tonal groups. The main body of the melody is in the middle register."[3]

The jazz improviser—at least the improviser of Hackett's sort—is in a very pure sense a creator of melodies. In common with any composer, he is constantly making decisions which will determine not only the outcome of a given line but its overall effect on the sensibilities of his listeners. All the criteria, including those set out by Slonimsky, apply directly to him. The critical difference lies in the fact that the improviser's decisions are extempore, made on the spot. There is little opportunity to try out a given pattern in a given situation, giving it a dry run, then perhaps rejecting it and moving on to another if it fails to please ear and sensibilities. The possibilites are all but limitless, as are the chances of a misstep, a choice which, though harmonically and technically sound, will break the spell, snap the thread, bring things irremediably to earth.

Granted, playing the same songs in the same keys in myriad situations over many years tends inevitably to take the fine edge off improvising. It's even been demonstrated that after a certain amount of this sort of repetition jazz improvisation evolves into a more finite selection process, the player consulting a supply of known phrases and formulae, knowing from experience which to place and where, for greatest effect.

Still, even the placement skill, while conceivably of a lesser order than wholly extemporaneous melodic invention, nevertheless enlists the melodist's instinct for the aesthetics of line, balance, and emotive power. The great jazz melodists of early years—Armstrong, Bechet, Beiderbecke, Lester Young, Artie Shaw, Benny Carter, Hackett—demonstrated a fingertip sensibility which allowed them to skirt wrong or ill-judged decisions. The overarching nobility of Louis's closing solo on "That's My Home," the inevitability and inner design of Bix's "Singin' the Blues" chorus, the balance of strength and vulnerability in Young's sixteen bars on the 1937 "I Must Have That Man" with Billie Holiday—these and others are extraordinary because they are the result of a basically extemporaneous process, even in those cases where matters of form and direction have been worked out in advance.

Ruby Braff, himself a player of scrupulously honed aesthetics, could have been talking about any of the great melodic improvisers in declaring: "There's no school of study anywhere on planet earth, not at any college, that will cause you to have the kind of ear [Hackett] had, that was that selective of the notes."[4]

Ernest Anderson, whose long career as a press agent and publicist included close associations with Armstrong, Eddie Condon, Pee Wee Russell, and other major figures, put it even more categorically: "I think Bobby Hackett is the greatest white jazz musician of our time," he said in a 1993 conversation. "He had a kind of genius, a musical intelligence, immaculate taste. He was in a class by himself. Totally."[5]

Born January 31, 1915, sixth of a railroad blacksmith's nine children, Bobby Hackett grew up in the rough-and-tumble part of Providence known as Beer Hill, took to music early, and by age fourteen was playing violin and guitar in a local band. He soon expanded his field of operation, playing guitar and banjo in bands around New England and picking up enough cornet along the way to contribute occasional solos. At first the going on that instrument seems to have been slow; the manager of the Onondaga Hotel in Syracuse is said to have threatened to fire Herb Marsh's entire band if "that kid"—the guitar player—didn't stop trying to take solos on the little horn.

626

On a 1933 summer job on Cape Cod, young Hackett's path crossed that of Pee Wee Russell, and things were never again the same. The clarinetist recognized what various Boston colleagues, among them pianist Payson Ré and multi-instrumentalist Brad Gowans, had also heard: here was an exceptional young musician, as yet not fully formed, but with an obvious and singular talent.

(Al Sudhalter was prominent in New England at the time as an alto saxophonist who often worked with Gowans, Arthur Karle, and other regional jazzmen. He heard Hackett frequently at this point and recalled that "Bobby fumbled a lot at first; sometimes he couldn't execute what he was hearing, didn't have much of an embouchure on cornet, and seemed to get tired fast. But listening to him, you could always hear what was in his mind, and you knew it was just a matter of time before he developed what he needed to express it.")

Russell and Hackett became friends, and there is little doubt that Pee Wee, vastly more experienced, profoundly affected the eighteen-year-old Rhode Islander. He got Hackett listening seriously to Bix, encouraged him to use chordal knowledge gleaned from his guitar in learning how to arrange. And, Bobby admitted many years later, Russell also "taught me how to drink."

That fall, despite problems with Boston musicians' union local 9 (solved, it seems, through some unspecified, but long-standing, Russell underworld connections), Pee Wee and Bobby wound up working as a trio with pianist Teddy Roy at Boston's Crescent Club, a local hangout which, until repeal, had operated as a speakeasy.

Once back in New York, Russell joined New Englanders Gowans, Max Kaminsky, and alto saxophonist Nuncio "Toots" Mondello in spreading the word about the little guy (he stood five feet, five inches and weighed, in his own words, "about as much as a sparrow") who "plays like Bix, only different."

By May 1936, when Bobby assumed leadership of the band at Boston's Theatrical Club (a group that also periodically included Gowans and Teddy Roy), musicians were showing up in growing numbers to find out what all the fuss was about. Among the after-hours visitors: Fats Waller, Benny Goodman, and Bunny Berigan.

George Frazier, ever a writer with an ear for a talented jazzman, was probably the first to hail the young cornetist in print. "It is difficult for non-Bostonians to grasp the significance of what Hackett has done for this stupid city," he wrote in a *Down Beat* dispatch. "He gave it, in a word, jazz, and that is the thing all of us had craved these many lean years." About the young man himself, Frazier had this to say: "Hackett, just past voting age, is an amazing cornetist. He has taste, tone, swing and interesting ideas. No one has ever caught Bix's eloquent tone quite so successfully . . . He plays with an amazing delicacy, avoiding meaningless technical displays and high notes."[6]

Reed Dickerson, a young jazz fan and sometime journalist on the threshold of a distinguished academic career, dropped in one night and published his findings in *Down Beat*. Boston nightlife, he wrote, "is officially supposed to end at the stroke of one and there must be some place to go for those who do not feel like turning in. Hence the Theatrical Club.'' Listening to Hackett, Gowans and friends for a few sets left him with the conviction that "with the caution one must use in evaluating a person he has heard only twice, you may still say that Bobby's trumpet [sic] sounds more like Bix than almost anyone else playing today . . . Whether he will turn out to be anything I can't say,'' Dickerson added. "A little listening will disclose whether or not he is a one-solo man. But even if he is, I want to congratulate him on his good taste, his fine tone, and a sound understanding of jazz essentials.''[7]

Such notices, fueled by the enthusiasm of fellow-musicians, made it an all but foregone conclusion that Hackett would soon depart for New York. So he did. But his first try turned out to be an abbreviated one: he took the train, and from Grand Central Station, he told Whitney Balliett, he went directly to the Famous Door, on 52nd Street, where Pee Wee Russell was working with Louis Prima. The New Orleans trumpeter, in Hackett's words, was "like a hurricane on the stand'' and so intimidated the young New Englander that "I got so scared I got drunk, and I went back to Boston the next day.'' Fortunately he tried again, and this time hooked up with vocalist-promoter Red McKenzie, Eddie Condon, Joe Marsala, and others in a position to help him get started.

Through McKenzie and Condon he landed steady work as house cornetist at Decca Records, part of a band that usually included veterans Al Philburn on trombone and Frank Signorelli at the piano. They provided backing for McKenzie, Dick Robertson, the Nicholas Brothers, the Andrews Sisters, and others on Jack Kapp's bustling young label.

In later years the cornetist tended to dismiss his early records, complaining— usually only half in jest—that "people keep listening to this stuff and think I haven't gotten any better. My wife, Edna, likes them, and keeps playing them on the tape recorder she keeps in the kitchen. Drives me nuts.''

All the same, these first efforts reveal much about what animated the cornetist's early champions. On "Roses in December'' (October 7, 1937), with Robertson, he delivers sixteen emphatic bars with a tone and attack indeed reminiscent of Beiderbecke. If the solo lacks Bix's sense of inner architecture, it nevertheless shows the same fondness for unusual intervals and impeccably chosen chordal voices.[8]

Probably Hackett's best-known early solo is a restrained half-chorus on the Andrews Sisters' hit record of "Bei Mir Bist Du Schoen'' a month later—sufficiently so that second pressings of the disc included the band personnel on the label, one of the first known examples of what was shortly to become common practice.[9]

By mid-1938, Hackett was recording extensively: on "That Da Da Strain'' done for Vocalion under his own name in February 1938, he opens his chorus matter-of-factly with a very Bix-like move from the tonic, a concert $B\flat$, half a step up to a $B\natural$, the thirteenth of the D7 chord. But for all their considerable charm, these are not yet fully realized efforts: the sudden exposure also threw into relief various technical deficiencies, problems in playing the horn which he'd not yet entirely worked out.

Recording for Milt Gabler's brand-new Commodore label in early 1938 with Russell, Condon, Bud Freeman, and others, Bobby contributes some fiery but rather forced ensemble playing to a fast blues, "Carnegie Jump," and a shapely conception of "Embraceable You," marred toward the end by flagging endurance and obvious mouthpiece pressure.[10]

He's stronger, more secure, on four titles recorded June 23, 1938, by a quintet under Adrian Rollini's leadership (and including a cocky young drummer named Buddy Rich). The cornet lines on "Ten Easy Lessons" and "On the Bumpy Road to Love" dart and shine, melting and melding with the ice-lolly pastels of Rollini's vibes. Hackett's final, cup-muted half chorus on "I Wish I Had You" floats, feather-light and graceful, above sustained chords by the Tune Twisters vocal trio.

But it's his half-chorus solo on Hoagy Carmichael's song "Small Fry" that affords a clear, unmistakable glimpse of the Hackett musical intelligence at work. With a lyric by Frank Loesser, "Small Fry" is a charming trifle, a simple melody built (like the Carmichael-Loesser "Heart and Soul," of the same year) on the familiar revolving chord pattern, I-VI-II-V. (The very simplicity of this pattern, which in the key of C can be expressed with triads in C, A-minor, D-minor, and G, has been a staple of every child's initial approach to the piano for generations. It's the foundation for Rodgers and Hart's "Blue Moon," the Harold Arlen–Ted Koehler "Between the Devil and the Deep Blue Sea," and hundreds of other popular songs.)

(continued)

"Small Fry," sixteen-bar Bobby Hackett solo, 1938.

The pattern's circularity poses a dilemma for jazz improvisers, imposing a tyranny of monotonously tidy two- and four-bar phrases. Hackett solves the problem in simple, stunningly effective, fashion: he actually begins his solo a bar *before* the song's down beat, against the dominant harmony (a B♭7 chord) which introduces the new chorus. He sustains the displacement throughout, building phrases of varying lengths which evade the repeating pattern without ever sounding unnatural or contrived.

In doing so, Hackett recasts Carmichael's melody along more adventuresome lines, full of choice intervals (as in bar 7, where he drops a minor sixth, then ascends through a whole-tone scale), unexpected voice leadings (bar 11, with its logical yet surprising move from the B♮ of a G7 chord to the B♭ of a C7), and exquisitely conceived phrases (such as the four-bar beauty occupying bars 14–17 and ending the solo).

Choice Hackett moments on record were becoming more and more frequent. He contributes an elegant sixteen bars and ensemble lead to "Let's Get Happy," with an all-star band assembled by recently arrived English critic-pianist Leonard Feather; a lilting half-chorus opening "You're Gonna See a Lot of Me" with Teddy Wilson, setting up a winsome Billie Holiday vocal; a thoughtful bridge toward the end of "Sunday," done for Commodore with Bud Freeman, Pee Wee Russell, and other kindred spirits—including trombonist Vernon Brown, who'd been with Russell and Beiderbecke in Frank Trumbauer's St. Louis band of more than a decade before.

Another date for Feather found Bobby in good form. As on the "Let's Get Happy" session, each participant began by doubling on another instrument. Alto saxophonists Benny Carter and Pete Brown are heard on trumpet, and Hackett picks up his guitar to solo, softly but effectively, on a slow blues titled "Feather Bed Lament."[11]

The session's easy highlight is a fast, straightforward B♭ blues titled "Twelve-

Bar Stampede." Carter opens on trumpet, followed by Brown on alto, soloing over strong rhythm laid down by Hackett, pianist Billy Kyle (then featured with John Kirby's sextet on 52nd Street), bassist Hayes Alvis, and drummer Cozy Cole. After solos by Kyle, Joe Marsala (on clarinet), and Carter (on alto), Bobby delivers two straight-muted cornet choruses which in their clarity and logic all but capture the performance from his better-known colleagues.

He was now in demand, his reputation growing. Given the times, it was probably inevitable that someone would take a look at him and declare, "Hey, this guy can play, he looks good on the bandstand. People seem to take to him. Why the hell isn't he leading his own big band?"

Everyone, after all, was doing it. Benny Goodman, the Dorsey brothers, Artie Shaw, Bunny Berigan, and numerous other former sidemen were now leading successful big bands. Jack Teagarden was about to take the plunge. Even such unlikely figures as Fats Waller and cornetist Muggsy Spanier were fronting larger units. In what he later called "the biggest mistake of my life," Hackett accepted an offer from agent Sidney Mills of the Music Corporation of America (MCA) and organized a thirteen-piece band built around his solo talents. It lasted six months and was, in the cornetist's own assessment, "a disaster."

Perhaps. But the disaster, it must be said, was less a matter of music than of poor business judgment, a trait which dogged Hackett all his life and was responsible for many bad breaks and fumbled opportunities. Instead of assembling a band of eager young players determined to make good, then shaping them into a disciplined unit that would show him off to best advantage, Hackett seems to have done little more than call together a baker's dozen of his pals and drinking buddies.

A cursory look at the personnel tells the story with dismaying clarity: cornetist Stirling Bose, trombonists George Troup and Brad Gowans, Pee Wee Russell, Eddie Condon—all champion drinkers, none known in those years for punctilious attention to matters of discipline.

All the same, things began promisingly. The band was loaded with talent and quickly built a library of serviceable arrangements, largely by Hackett, Gowans, and Buck Ram (later famed as a producer of '50s rock-and-roll hits and the architect of the million-selling vocal group the Platters). It also snared some choice work, including the 1939 World's Fair in New York, and the Trocadero, at 53 West 52nd Street, across the street from the Famous Door. Brothers Si (sometimes Sy) and Charlie Shribman, fans of the young cornetist since his Herb Marsh and Payson Ré days, booked the band on a tour of ballrooms they controlled around New England.*

---

*The Trocadero didn't last long. When it failed, owner-operator George McGough sold out to a friend he'd known since they were both summer lifeguards at New York City beaches. The friend was Jimmy Ryan, and, in partnership with his brother-in-law, Matty Walsh, he renamed "the Troc" after himself; as "Jimmy Ryan's," it soon became a focal point in 52nd Street jazz life and remained a Manhattan jazz landmark for the next four decades.

There was also one major plum: the Ben Franklin Hotel in Philadelphia, much valued by bands because its twelve live broadcasts a week reached a wide and enthusiastic listening audience throughout the Midwest. A small item in the May 1939 *Down Beat* announced the Philadelphia opening, noting that the band would move on to Boston's prestigious State Ballroom, presumably under the Shribmans' benevolent auspices, where it would continue to broadcast for CBS.[12]

Bassist Jack Lesberg, then twenty years old and working with Muggsy Spanier, visited the State during this engagement—and found Hackett fretting, visibly unhappy. "Harry James was getting big at that point," said Lesberg, "playing high and spectacularly, in that way of his. Bobby? Well, he was just playing quiet and pretty the way he did. But here he was, talking about changing horns, changing mouthpieces, changing his style, in order to sound more like Harry James. Muggsy and the rest of them—Vernon Brown, the trombonist, was with us—were saying no, no, you mustn't. Keep doing things the way you do 'em."[13]

The band's first record date for Vocalion, April 13, 1939, clearly shows its potential. "Ain't Misbehavin'," as arranged by Gowans, opens with a gliding cornet melody statement, followed by some light-textured reed section work before Bobby returns with eight very Bix-like bars. "Sunrise Serenade" (composed and popularized by fellow–Rhode Islander Frankie Carle) belongs to Pee Wee, who barges in on a sedate opening ensemble like Wyatt Earp invading a Dodge City saloon looking for the Clanton brothers.

The peak, however, comes last, on "Embraceable You." Compared to this, the Commodore performance of the previous year seems a warmup. The Hackett charms are in full early bloom: balanced phrasing, the melodic essence glowing through the embellishments; an unerring ability, as Ruby Braff observed, to select the most poignant intervals and chordal voices—all delivered with a heartwarming tone. From his lilting first phrase, an oblique allusion to the Harry Warren–Al Dubin "Shadow Waltz," he comes close to recomposing Gershwin's melody.[14] (See music example on next page.)

The auguries seemed good. But Hackett's chronic inability to manage or maintain any but a personal musical discipline doomed the enterprise from the start. Small lapses gave way to large ones, and the breaking point came late that summer, after a second Vocalion date. The late writer Mort Goode summed it up with admirable, terrible precision a few years ago:

> One of the major radio shows had reached a near-decision that the orchestra would have the regular spot for the coming season. An audition was necessary, however, for the sponsors, but the conclusion was foregone. All the band had to do was show up. Most of them did. A few didn't, for obvious reasons. Sammy Kaye and his Swing and Sway got the job. The Hackett band folded.[15]

"Embraceable You," thirty-two-bar Bobby Hackett solo, 1939.

For the brief period of its existence, said lead alto saxophonist Louis Columbo, it was an excellent band. "I'll bet nobody knows that during the New England tour, when we played all the way up through New Hampshire and Maine, we even had Lips Page as part of the trumpet section. Bobby didn't make a big fuss about it, the racial thing and all. But he loved Lips, and gave him lots of space to play. He was especially good on swinging things, blues, stuff with high notes."

By July, when the band did its second and last Vocalion record date, the personnel had changed considerably. Russell, Condon, Gowans, and most of Hackett's other New York jazz cronies were gone, and replacements hadn't yet been found. Columbo recalled Irving Goodman and Max Kaminsky among those filling in on an *ad hoc* basis.

633

"You've got to remember, everybody loved Bobby. There was something about the way he played—the sweetness, the beauty—that just won people's hearts. He'd go into the Hickory House, for example, and they'd bring him ribs, all kinds of food, anything he wanted. I was with him a lot: I was always broke, and guys who were with him knew that everybody would get a free meal, and Bobby would sign for it. That's just the way he was—and I'm sure it helped get him into heavy debt."[16]

By the time he called it quits, Hackett was indeed deeply in the red. He'd spent too much, exercised too little common sense. What counsel he'd received and heeded had not been wise. The Hackett big band had failed, but not for musical reasons. To help recoup his losses Bobby went to work playing third cornet for Horace Heidt's "Musical Knights." Looking back, he was wont to refer to Heidt's band as "a musical circus"; all the same, the leader clearly respected him and treated him well. His brief solos on such Heidt records as "Say It," "Good Morning," and on "I'm Just Wild About Harry"—a particularly crisp half-chorus—are lovely and diverting moments.[17]

The association with Heidt also produced one landmark record date. In January 1940, Hackett recorded four titles with a group of Heidt sidemen including Frankie Carle and the excellent Chicago drummer Don Carter, a member of the ill-fated Hackett big band. "Clarinet Marmalade" and "Singin' the Blues" are direct acts of homage to Bix, incorporating tasteful ensemble transcriptions of the 1927 Beiderbecke and Frank Trumbauer solos. If Bobby seems a bit intimidated by the precedent on "Singin' the Blues" (his solo on a version done for World Transcriptions the previous year is considerably less self-conscious), he rolls easily through two sixteen-bar episodes on "Clarinet Marmalade," casually quoting portions of the Beiderbecke solo along the way.

But it's on the other two titles that he shines brightest. Both "That Old Gang of Mine" and "After I Say I'm Sorry" were, by 1940, old songs, barbershop favorites; it's possible to guess that their use here was thought to be in keeping with the nostalgic flavor of the other two selections. Hackett's obbligatos and solos on both are clean, beautifully shaped, and delivered with more force than on the Bix material. He opens a full chorus on "After I Say I'm Sorry" with nine strongly attacked concert C's, riding the rhythm and establishing a modulation from F to A♭.

He stayed with Heidt nearly a year, then went to Hollywood, where he and friend Billy Butterfield recorded the soundtrack (along with Artie Shaw and his orchestra) for the Fred Astaire movie *Second Chorus*. At one point, where Astaire and Burgess Meredith (playing two trumpet players, friendly rivals in music and love) trade four-bar segments on "Sugar," the sounds of Hackett and Butterfield are instantly recognizable on the soundtrack.

Around this time Bobby hit a rough patch. Some long-deferred dental surgery left him all but unable to play, and work prospects for the immediate future looked dim. Abruptly, remarkably, Si Shribman called: would Bobby be interested in joining Glenn Miller's band as guitarist and, when things healed sufficiently, occasional cornet soloist? "Glenn really didn't need me," he told George T.

Simon. "He had four good trumpets, and I was just a luxury to him. But Glenn wanted to help me out. To me he was a very wonderful guy, and I always considered it a great honor to have played for him."[18]

The job was indeed a plum. The Miller band was riding high, capturing the best work, doing regular radio broadcasts for Chesterfield cigarettes, recording for Victor, and even making films. As a special bonus, Bobby's pal and drinking companion Ernie Caceres was also in the band, playing alto and baritone.

Gradually, Hackett solos became part of Miller records and live appearances; as with Heidt, they stand out as small gems amid the highly regimented, standardized swing band format. He can be heard, if briefly, on "Rhapsody in Blue," "Sweet Eloise," "Vilia," "April in Paris," and "Serenade in Blue." By far his best-known, most lasting contribution to a Miller performance is his twelve bars on the Jerry Gray original "A String of Pearls."

It's basically just a blues, dressed up with some ascending and descending triads on the tonic, subdominant and dominant degrees of the E♭ scale. In later years Hackett told interviewers he'd ad libbed the solo directly off a guitar part, following the chordal movement, and that's exactly how it sounds—yet it manages to extract a strong melodic statement out of what is basically a harmonic exercise.

"Hey, Hack, do you remember what you played there?" Miller reportedly asked him after the first rundown. Affirmative. "Well, I think you ought to play it that way all the time." And, with minor variations, that's what he did, not only during the rest of his year with Miller but at intervals throughout his subsequent career. It's a simple conception which, because of its balance and precision of execution, manages to sound relatively complex.

Perhaps the best indication we have of the regard in which Miller and his sidemen held Hackett is to be found not on this or any other commercial record but in a version of "Little Brown Jug" taken off the air during a broadcast of June 2, 1942. A slower, more rocking tempo than on the 1939 Bluebird record lends Bill Finegan's arrangement added weight and authority; Tex Beneke solos on tenor sax with a muscularity reminiscent of Count Basie's Herschel Evans, much admired among many white saxophonists.

Hackett, following him, disregards the swagger, laying out two unruffled choruses which manage to revise and sweeten the entire mood. Nor is the effect lost on his colleagues: after his first chorus, someone shouts, quite audibly, "Hit it, Bobby"—and he carries on. Easy, here, to believe George Simon's account of seeing the Miller band at an Ohio location date when fellow sidemen, "obviously as excited as the dancers, stopped to listen to Bobby solo."[19]

Hackett had moved to Miller's trumpet section when Simon caught the band one night in January 1942. It was less than a month after Pearl Harbor, and many musicians had been called up. Bobby, still not back to full playing strength, was filling in on fourth trumpet, coping as best he could until veteran Steve Lipkins arrived to take over the lead. It was not an experience the cornetist remembered with pleasure: more and more, it pointed up his technical shortcomings, showed him beyond doubt or denial that he had some work to do on his horn.

Miller's civilian band gave its last public performance on September 27, 1942, just before the leader joined the U.S. Army and organized his much-revered Allied Expeditionary Forces (AEF) Orchestra. Hackett, in a familiar show biz phrase, remained "at liberty." He toured with a reconstituted "Original Dixieland Jazz Band" organized by Brad Gowans for Katharine Dunham's dance troupe; worked with various pickup groups, including one led by Joe Marsala at the clarinetist's old stand, the Hickory House; filled in at Nick's, on Seventh Avenue in the Village. He also started to do staff work at NBC.

"I found myself suddenly a little too well known and not capable enough of backing it up," he said, recalling this period in his life. "It was after I left Glenn Miller and went to work at the National Broadcasting Company. I found I was over my head there, couldn't cut the parts. So I had to go to a teacher. Until then I'd done everything by instinct, and mostly wrong."[20]

In those years, said historian Henry A. Kmen, Hackett was a technically flawed player, who had trouble being heard above such robust colleagues as trombonist George Brunis. "For Bobby to be heard, Brunis would have to tone down," said Kmen—who as "Hank" Kmen played tenor sax in Hackett's big band. "Bobby just never could play loud; he didn't have the lip for it. He was just a guy with a lot of fine ideas for trumpet, not all of which he always was able to execute. But even his 'muffs' were awfully pretty."[21]

So in 1943, with the first American Federation of Musicians recording ban in effect, Bobby Hackett took to the woodshed. He devoted the year to studying and practicing, going to such highly regarded teachers as Boston's Fred Berman and New York symphony trumpeter Bernard "Benny" Baker, ironing out the technical inconsistencies which had plagued him since his New England days. He punctuated his reminiscence with a laugh. "Doc Severinson and I went to Benny Baker at about the same time," he said. "Only one difference between us—Doc kept practicing."[22]

Hackett learned a lot from Baker about mouthpiece positioning, breath control, diaphragm support, and the other basic physical features of brass playing. He began occasionally playing trumpet, which opened out his volume, range, and tonal amplitude, increasing his ability to blend in section work.[23]

He also took Muggsy Spanier's advice and joined Alcoholics Anonymous, a move which, he said many years later, "probably saved my life, though I didn't know it at the time." Heard now, the Bobby Hackett who returns to recording in early 1944 seems a far surer player: stronger, brighter, more assertive. He bites into "I Must Have That Man," recorded for Commodore April 28 under Miff Mole's name, with unaccustomed energy and decisive attack.

Between October 1944 and September 1946, he appeared as soloist with the Casa Loma Orchestra, then long past its prime as a seminal force in the dance band business and not far from the end of the road. Radio transcriptions, first issued on LP three decades later, feature Hackett soloing effectively on "If I Love Again" (also recorded about this time for Decca) and "After You've Gone" and contributing lilting moments to Gershwin's "Maybe" and the otherwise forget-table ballad "I Don't Care Who Knows It." His solo on "Savage," a Ray Conniff original, is quite fiery: it's hard to imagine even the Hackett of 1938–39 having played with such controlled force.

Arguably his best work of this period comes on a May 1945 date for the small, short-lived Melrose label. Only two of four titles done that day were issued. A slow, wistful "Pennies From Heaven" returns to the basic idea of the song as sung by Bing Crosby a decade earlier. "Rose of the Rio Grande" gets a straightforward jazz band treatment, Hackett slashing into his solo with particular vigor. The ease with which he negotiates bars 13–16, with their shift of tonal center, is particularly fetching.

But perhaps the session's most impressive playing is on one of the two unissued sides, a cornet feature on "Body and Soul." A couple of fluffs and some unsteadiness at the end probably account for its having been held back; but today's ear, hearing it fresh after nearly half a century, notes only a heart-stopping poignancy few besides Bobby Hackett could achieve. Returning in the bridge after a Dave Bowman piano solo, he turns the simplest figures into a *cri de coeur*. It's part of Hackett's magic: no other trumpeter or cornetist, possibly excepting the imaginative but ill-starred Johnny Windhurst, was able to so pull the emotional strings in a listener.

Hackett remained acutely conscious of the flaws, the blemishes, in his playing. It spurred a lifelong quest for the perfect combination of mouthpiece and instrument that would magically rid him forever of all imperfections. "You've got to understand," said Jack Lesberg. "He was never satisfied with what he did. Always walking away from something thinking of ways in which he could have done it better. Another mouthpiece, another horn. Always changing something." Among the personal effects found in Hackett's home following his death in 1976 was a large wooden box loaded with nearly two hundred mouthpieces, many made expressly for him by craftsmen all over the world.

By contrast, Bobby's basic approach to the aesthetics of what he did never changed. "It's got to be pretty," he told more than one interviewer. "Keep the melody in mind; people want to hear it and recognize it. And keep things simple. Never mind the home runs: just concentrate on trying to get on base."[24]

He remained categorical about the simplicity, asking of his pianists only the standard, published harmonies of a song, unembellished, without "improvements." His contention (as explained on countless occasions to anyone who would listen) was that growing harmonic complexity in jazz, particularly with the coming of bop, had shrunk, not expanded, expressive options for his kind of soloist.

If a pianist or guitarist backed him with chords more complex than the standard four or five voices (up to and including the ninth), he said, it left him fewer opportunities to use the upper voices—elevenths, thirteenths, chordal substitutions—as colorational or emotive elements, special events, within his own melodic constructions.

The contention has its logic. A pianist who brings more complex harmonies to accompanying a single-line soloist is effectively decreeing that the soloist also make use of the harmonies he, the pianist, has chosen. The result, when the

637

soloist's harmonic vocabulary is simpler than that of his accompanists, works to the former's detriment. "Who's taking the solo here, anyway," Hackett would ask, "him or me?"

Accordingly, Hackett demanded the simplest, most straightforward of accompaniments. It's the same thinking that lies behind Lester Young's exhortation to his pianists to "just play vanilla": keep it simple and neutral. Let me be the star when I take a solo.

"Bobby was very clear on what he wanted," pianist Chuck Folds has said. "Spoken or unspoken, it was 'Just lay the chords down. Stay out of the way. Don't comment, by playing little melodies against what I play. I just want to hear the chords.' "[25]

Dave McKenna, one of Hackett's favorite accompanists, concurred. "It wasn't that he *said* anything. There were never any orders from him. Not Bobby. A lot of the time I had to do it by instinct, do what my ears told me. Think to myself, 'What would he like here?' Lots of times that meant playing for him in not quite the way I ordinarily would."[26]

On his arrival in New York in 1937, Hackett had fallen in with the circle of jazzmen surrounding Eddie Condon. At that time it was a natural association: the guitarist was a center of gravity for white—and some black—musicians dedicated to playing small-band hot jazz. By 1940, the musicians around Condon included New Englanders Hackett, Gowans, and Max Kaminsky; midwesterners Bud Freeman, Jess Stacy, Muggsy Spanier, and George Wettling; southwesterners Jack Teagarden and Pee Wee Russell; and pioneer trombonists George Brunis and Miff Mole. And, too, a Hackett friend and frequent associate, the distinguished baritone saxophonist and clarinetist Ernesto "Ernie" Caceres.

From the moment of his arrival in New York in 1937, Ernie Caceres provided a vital and commanding alternative to Duke Ellington's longtime baritone master, New Englander Harry Carney. Easily Carney's technical equal, he was also no less eloquent as a soloist, with considerable emotional range.

Born in Rockport, Texas, November 22, 1911, Ernie Caceres first attracted attention as a member of a family unit with two brothers, violinist Emilio and pianist-trumpeter Pinero ("Pini"). Ernie's first records, made in New York November 5, 1937, in trio with Emilio and guitarist Johnny Gomez, are an auspicious debut, showing his command of both baritone and clarinet.

Several of the titles ("What's the Use?" and "Humoresque," for example) are clearly modeled on the Venuti-Lang Blue Four records of the previous decade, Ernie's baritone occasionally recalling Rollini's bass sax. The true star of these six titles, if by a narrow margin, is Emilio Caceres. His playing is technically secure and unflaggingly inventive: "Jig In G," based on a chord structure combining "Oh, Baby!" with the bridge of "Rosetta" in the manner of the Mound City Blue Blowers' "Hello Lola," would have been enough to rank him alongside Joe Venuti and very few others as a master of hot violin. That he did not record more widely, in the kind of challenging company New York could have offered him, is regrettable.

Ernie Caceres is best heard here on clarinet. If his sound and approach resemble those of any other player it is the New Orleans master Sidney Arodin: indeed, the fact that Arodin was active throughout the Southwest during the 1920s may not be irrelevant here. "Runnin' Wild" and "Who's Sorry Now?" contain excellent examples of this affinity.

Ernie's first year in New York brought a great boost in confidence, and in his fluency on the baritone. He shows it on a November 16, 1938, Vocalion date, going head-to-head with Sidney Bechet's declamatory soprano. Surprisingly, there's no sense of competition: baritone and soprano work comfortably together, Caceres slotting easily into an accompanying role and soloing briefly on each selection. His ensemble playing behind Bechet, particularly on the sprightly "What a Dream" and on "Jungle Drums" (which occasionally seems about to transform itself into "Caravan"), is percussive in the Rollini manner, yet with no loss of melodic continuity.

The Caceres baritone sound, if perhaps less plummy than Carney's, instead boasts a fine cutting edge and dense, mahogany-dark quality not unlike that achieved by Coleman Hawkins on tenor, but with no loss of dexterity: Caceres moves around his big horn with ease, and with his own unique range of dynamics and texture.

Clarinetist Kenny Davern, a lifelong Caceres admirer, adds an intriguing dimension. "Take an LP issue of 'What a Dream,' " he said in a 1993 conversation. "Speed it up to 45 rpm. Ernie sounds almost exactly, note for note, like Bechet, both in execution and in concept. It's not a matter of the mechanics of getting over the horn, though that's impressive enough. But he really *understands* Bechet and is playing *with* him." So much so, it must be added, that the fact that these two never recorded again in this configuration seems a pity. Their sound together is a complementary blend of two strong personalities.[27]

Caceres is heard more extensively, therefore perhaps more effectively, on a December 1938 radio transcription session led by Hackett and released by Thesaurus as "The Rhythm Cats." The repertoire is mostly ODJB-NORK mainline standards (though "Thinking of You"—not the 1927 Kalmar-and-Ruby hit—is an attractive newcomer), but they attack it with enthusiasm. The four horns are Hackett, Russell, valve trombonist Gowans, and Caceres, and perhaps because of the register spread (and because Gowans keeps his contributions simple), the blend is particularly coherent.

The baritonist delivers deep-voiced, rhythmically kicking solos on "Muskrat Ramble," "Jazz Me Blues," and "Love Is Just Around the Corner," yet on the slower material (an excellent "Singin' the Blues," for example) employs a feathery high register reminiscent of the open-throated tenor sax sound of Eddie Miller. An adept sight-reader, Caceres joined Glenn Miller's orchestra in 1940. It was the first time Miller had used a baritone doubler in his reed section (Caceres's book consisted mostly of alto and clarinet), and his arranger's mind must have been intrigued; little by little, ensembles anchored by Caceres's resonant baritone begin appearing on Miller performances.

By this time, Caceres and Hackett were close friends and drinking partners. Both became regulars at Condon's Town Hall concerts, broadcast over the NBC

"Blue" Network (later to become the American Broadcasting Company) throughout 1944. Caceres also begins to appear in the personnels of Commodore records, starting with an April 22 Muggsy Spanier date. His work is uniformly satisfying: light and restrained on the ballads, deep-toned and vigorous on the rhythm numbers. He adds breadth to ensembles and is expert at using stinging rhythmic anticipations in the Rollini mode to move things along.

He's particularly effective on a June 8, 1944, Condon Associated Transcriptions date. "That's a Plenty," "Ballin' the Jack," and "Cherry" have no trombone; the three horns are trumpet (Hackett on the first two titles, Butterfield on the third), clarinet (Russell), and Caceres on baritone. His ensemble work on "That's a Plenty," especially, is a primer in how to stay clear of the other horns, yet drive the collective passages hard. Sometimes he appears to parallel the bass lines, sometimes to play off the melodic swoops of the two other horns.

A ballad-tempo "Ja-Da" brings the conceptual affinity between Hackett and Caceres into sharp focus. They are the only two soloists: Ernie goes first, using his fluffy high-register texture to explore the lyric implications of the descending chromatic harmony. Then it's Bobby's turn, and he goes on to reconfigure Bob Carleton's simple old vaudeville tune into a ballad statement of surpassing beauty.

His method of doing it is a working illustration of his own philosophy. The band (including fellow-trumpeters Butterfield and Kaminsky) lays down a rich but harmonically simple chordal carpet, leaving Hackett free to employ his full vocabulary, including the altered upper voices that, in his hands, become evocative "color tones."

Caceres, too, speaks in his own voice. "He was a superb musician," said Ruby Braff. "When it came to taste—to understanding what notes to select and how to put them together, he was—well, you can call him the Bobby Hackett of the saxophone and not be far off. And don't forget—Bobby loved him."

Much the same evaluation has come from Kenny Davern, who heard Caceres often around New York during the early 1950s: "Ernie Caceres was probably the greatest improvising baritone player who ever lived, bar none" was his unequivocal assessment.

Jack Lesberg: "Harry Carney had his own sound and his own way, and was wonderful, of course. But so did Ernie. A wonderful way of swinging, marvelous ears, perfect intonation—and that fabulous, big fat old sound."

And, as historian James T. Maher has observed, Carney had "a great additional advantage—a fabled, high-visibility showcase for almost fifty years."[28]

The sheer force of Caceres's presence on baritone can sometimes distract attention from his no less excellent work on clarinet, and how little it sounds like that of anyone else: even the resemblance to Sidney Arodin, noted earlier, is at best occasional. Overall, he defies categorization, combining passages of great melodic grace with a hard-hitting, sometimes gritty delivery. His opening solo on the "Clarinet Chase," a blues, from the Condon Town Hall concert of August 26, 1944, provides astringent contrast to the efforts of Marsala and Russell.

He solos on clarinet on a December 7, 1944, "Rosetta," for V-disc, his Hackettish, almost offhand use of elevenths and thirteenths neatly stealing the spotlight from such heavyweights as trumpeter Charlie Shavers, trombonist Trummy Young, and tenor saxophonist Don Byas. A baritone feature on the Town Hall concert of September 23 also commands attention. Titled "Crickett Jumps," it's based on a chord sequence related to several standards, among them "Honey-suckle Rose," and shows Caceres at his most supple, tone full yet textured, as he negotiates a line reminiscent of some of Bud Freeman's serpentine creations.

Immediately before this, on a medium-tempo "Easter Parade," Caceres and Hackett solo in sequence, and the similarity in their conceptions is again striking. Though separated by register and timbre, the two solos could almost have been the work of the same mind. "They had a lot in common," Kenny Davern has recalled. "Both of them really knew music, from the inside out. Do I think both of them were jazz greats? Absolutely. Beyond a doubt. Bobby—well, he was the greatest tapestry weaver that ever was, a maker of fine, exquisite mosaics. Ernie's mind was like that, too."

Fortunately, both Hackett and Caceres recorded prolifically; evidence of what they were able to do is in ample supply. Why they have been so flagrantly neglected in recent years is less important to the purposes of this work than the simple fact that they have been, and should not be.

For a horn player, effective improvised accompaniment to a singer (or another soloist) is a marriage of exact science and exact instinct. The accompanist must know, or be able to hear, a singer's methods of phrase placement, customary breath points, patterns of emphasis. He benefits greatly from understanding the lyrics to a song and the ways in which words and melody fit together: he must know that there are certain situations—determined by tempo, lyric, number and shape of notes being sung—where the accompanist is best advised to remain silent. Not to play.

Some "fills," phrases played by the accompanist between (or in response to) a sung phrase, ask to be major declarations, strongly stated. Others require little more than a murmur, a consolation whispered, as it were, in the ear. In all, the accompanist must be able to subordinate his own ego, illuminating, limning the singer's phrases for the sake of overall impact, strengthening the whole. Contrary to the inferred belief of many jazz soloists, a relationship with a singer is rarely one of equals, rarely a duet or other form of self-display. It is, instead, a willing step back and to the side, out of the spotlight into a unique supporting role. Far from faceless, it is vital, indispensable to the effectiveness of the singer's performance.

Such self-effacement appears to work directly at cross-purposes to the kind of ego-driven expression lying at the heart of many jazz solo styles. Therefore it's hardly surprising that so few jazzmen have truly excelled at vocal accompa-niment. Lester Young, backing Billie Holiday on their matchless 1937–38 records; Stan Getz, among the later generation of tenor saxophonists who learned from Lester (hear him with singer Tony Bennett on the 1968 "Danny Boy"); Bunny Berigan, supporting Mildred Bailey on four memorable 1935 titles, discussed elsewhere in this volume; trumpeter Joe Smith, a constant marvel in his coun-terlines to blues singer Bessie Smith.

And, *primus inter pares*, Bobby Hackett. Is it possible to imagine, for example, another accompanist lending the glow to such vocal recordings as Bennett's 1962 "The Very Thought of You," Frank Sinatra's Columbia "Body and Soul" and "I've Got a Crush on You," or Lee Wiley's 1950 *Night in Manhattan* album?

On the 1944 V-disc date that produced the aforementioned "Rosetta," Hackett backs Jack Teagarden's vocal on "If I Could Be With You One Hour Tonight" with faultless taste in choice and placement of phrases. Again and again, he leaves a listener amazed: How did he *know*? What force impelled him to put *that* right *there*, in *that* way? For the duration of those eighteen bars, he is Teagarden's partner and amanuensis in one.

Outstanding examples of Hackett accompaniments on records are plentiful and easy to find. He was musical director of the band that backed Louis Armstrong in the memorable Town Hall concert of May 17, 1947, and is responsible for one of that evening's most sublime moments. "Rockin' Chair" opens with the band playing the last eight bars of the song, and what happens between Armstrong and Hackett has to be heard, savored, and heard again before it can be entirely believed.

Louis sets out a strong, commanding trumpet lead, tone brilliant. Bobby—lighter, more supple, on cornet—weaves a counterline which flatters and decorates, at once compliment and complement. The result, only eight bars, approaches perfection. Can we imagine any trumpet or cornet player other than Bobby Hackett choreographing so beautifully realized a *pas de deux*?

"Rockin' Chair," Hackett–Louis Armstrong duet (eight bars), 1947.

Hackett's friendship with Armstrong was close, long-standing, and built on a firm foundation of mutual admiration. "I'm the coffee, and Bobby's the cream," he once said, in a remark all the more interesting because it seems to operate both on musical and racial levels. The two men were near-neighbors in the New York borough of Queens (Bobby lived in Jackson Heights, Louis in Corona) and spent considerable time together, talking music and sharing Louis's marijuana of choice.

"It was less a friendship than a love affair," said photographer-archivist Jack Bradley, a longtime admirer and friend of both. "Every time someone would compare Bobby to Bix, which happened a lot, he'd go out of his way to remind them that Louis was the one who really changed his life. And Louis—well, for him it was 'My man, Bobby Hackett.' And he meant it."[29]

Hackett's career, ever more diversified, carried him well into the 1970s. His melody statements and obbligatos on the string orchestra albums Music for Lovers Only, Music to Make You Misty, and others issued under the nominal leadership of comedian Jackie Gleason sold in the millions. Hackett, with characteristic lack of business acumen, accepted one-time scale payments for his efforts, rather than hold out for a royalty agreement with Gleason or Capitol Records which might have netted more appropriate profit and even given him the financial security he always coveted.

The success of these LPs opened the way for countless others of the same sort, on a variety of labels. Other companies, hoping to cash in on what they perceived as a major trend in "mood music," engaged other lyrical trumpet soloists: Pee Wee Erwin, Billy Butterfield, Ruby Braff, Charlie Shavers. Even that most unlikely candidate, "Wild Bill" Davison, did two quite commendable horn-and-strings LPs for Columbia; now, long after his death, Pretty Wild and With Strings Attached are widely acknowledged as containing some of Davison's best ballad work.

Hackett recorded constantly. Among his best jazz efforts were Columbia's ten-inch LP Jazz Session, backed by a rhythm section including bassist Lesberg and drummer Cliff Leeman, two memorable twelve-inch Capitol albums, Coast Concert (1955) and Jazz Ultimate (1956), and the aforementioned 1957 Eddie Condon Columbia LP, Bixieland.

Each of these finds him in top form—decisive, fluent, melodically rich—and with verve to spare. The two Capitol sets team him with Jack Teagarden and supporting casts of excellent sidemen in an informal, "dixieland"-oriented context. His execution is flawless throughout: the technical problems of earlier days have evaporated; solos and ensemble passages roll out with ease and brio.

Coast Concert, in particular, sustains a consistent rapport among the players: it is as if the infallible Hackett-Teagarden chemistry has spread to fellow-trombonist Abe Lincoln, clarinetist Matty Matlock, and the rest. The rhythm numbers sing (witness the exultant final ensembles of "Fidgety Feet" and "Big Butter and Egg Man," with their witty Nick Fatool drum "tags"). Listening to Bobby and Jack tone-painting "I Guess I'll Have to Change My Plan," it's hard to imagine a more fully realized performance: though no one sings a word, the thought occurs: could any singer have interpreted the substance and meaning of the great Schwartz and Dietz classic more fully than this? Hackett is particularly empyreal, opening his chorus on a wistful, tumbling phrase which captures the song like a hand cupped gently over a radiantly hued butterfly.

He splits the Condon Bixieland set with "Wild Bill" Davison, each taking five of the ten titles. Bobby's lead on an up-tempo "I'll Be a Friend 'With Pleasure' " recalls Beiderbecke's almost ethereal sweetness; he puts his own authoritative stamp on "Singin' the Blues," in a way the 1940 effort never came near doing; his solo and breaks on "From Monday On" are, in Dave McKenna's enraptured phrase, "pure Bach, classical music."

But the gem of the collection is "I'm Comin', Virginia." Taking the lovely old standard at a slow, broad ballad tempo (underpinned by Walter Page's bowed bass), he uses the full range of his horn (in this case a trumpet) up to a concert high C, his written D, in shaping a solo of astonishing beauty. He draws on a bit of everything: Armstrong *rubato*, Bixian clarity, his own faultless instinct for intervals, choice and placement of notes. Here is Bobby Hackett at his expressive peak: if there be a need for proof positive of his stature as a jazz improviser, a singer of songs for any age, it lies in these bars.

"I think of music in vocal terms," Hackett said in a 1972 interview. "An instrument is an extension of yourself. You sing into it if you want it to sound musical." Simple—until you try it. What gives a Hackett solo its uniquely vocal quality? What makes "I Guess I'll Have to Change My Plan" a more purely *sung* performance than those of many singers? Various factors are at work here, some conceptual and some directly connected with the mechanics of playing the instrument.

Vibrato, for example. One of the most expressive of musical devices, vibrato can determine through its speed, breadth, and intensity the ways in which music is perceived by the listener. Many wind players have drawn their concepts of vibrato from the traditions of voice and string playing, a regular oscillation beginning with the tone and continuing throughout its entire duration. The playing of Harry James, for example, is illustrative, as is that of tenor saxophonist Chu Berry, whose primary tonal inspiration seems to have been the vibrato-saturated work of bandleader Freddy Martin.

Such methods of tonal and vibrato production were much admired in the early days of jazz. Vibrato—wide, fast, and steady—saturates the soprano sax tone of Sidney Bechet. Many jazz alto saxophonists of both races openly emulated the methods of Rudy Wiedoeft, who in turn drew inspiration from the violinistic concept of the conservatory-based "French school" of saxophone technique.[30]

Beginning in the 1920s, certain jazz soloists began to abandon this concept, opting instead for the more subjective, personal, terminal vibrato—that is, used only at the end of a given note or phrase. Both Louis Armstrong and Bix Beiderbecke made terminal vibratos key features of their styles. Saxophonist Jimmy Dorsey slowed this vibrato down and reduced its amplitude, wedding it to a harder, brighter tone than was common at the time. In doing so he caught the attention of Charlie Parker, thus foreshadowing the latter's execution of two decades hence.

That Frank Trumbauer's use of a light, shallow terminal vibrato on C-melody saxophone deeply impressed a youthful Lester Young is a basic article of the jazz canon. But so, too, is the misapprehension that either man played without vibrato entirely: they didn't, any more than Miles Davis did, despite the trumpeter's own widely quoted doctrine of "light, fast, and no vibrato." In both cases, the vibrato is indeed there, but only lightly, at the end of the tone, as an expressive (and sometimes rhythmic) medium like a growl, a half-valve effect, a sudden shift of dynamics or texture.

Bobby Hackett is a consummate practitioner of terminal vibrato. Often in his work it is a short burst of rapid oscillation, actually breaking the harmonic overtone in the equivalent of a cantorial crack, or "catch," in a singer's voice. It can have the effect of sob or smile, pleasure or pain, depending on where and how it's used. In a Hackett solo the "crack" is often a signature, underscoring and highlighting, enhancing.

Hackett seldom ventured into his instrument's upper register (though certain of his recorded work in the 1950s indicates that he was perfectly capable of doing so)—largely, it seems, for reasons that were more aesthetic than physical. "Anybody can play high notes," he said in 1972. "That's just a matter of having eight hours' sleep, keeping your body in good condition. But I've never really heard anybody play high notes that sounded musical to me except Louis Armstrong. He was the only guy who could play a melody way up high and still play musical notes. The only guy besides Louis who can play up high and always make it musical is Billy Butterfield."

Hackett warmed eagerly to the subject of Butterfield, a longtime friend and close colleague. "Pound for pound, Billy Butterfield is more than likely the best trumpet player in the world right now, bar none, and has been for quite some time . . . Not enough people realize what a beautiful player he is."[31]

Like Hackett, Butterfield is often overlooked by jazz opinion-makers; again, the neglect seems related to his versatility, an ability to fit comfortably into many musical contexts. The received message seems to be that no one who can do, and actually *enjoy* doing, so many things well can possibly be taken seriously as a major improvising soloist.

Briton Digby Fairweather, himself a trumpeter-critic of considerable gifts, got it right in terming Butterfield, along with Hackett, "the most artistic swing trumpeter of post-war America." A trained and disciplined musician, Butterfield was equally adept at playing powerful lead in a big band brass section, or delivering a solo ballad performance with the purest of sunlight-on-silver tones.[32]

Born in Middletown, Ohio, January 14, 1917, Charles William Butterfield originally studied medicine. That didn't last long: by the time he was twenty his range, sound, and general facility had won him a trumpet section chair in Bob Crosby's band, alongside Yank Lawson and Charlie Spivak. His solo on Bob Haggart's "I'm Free" (shortly thereafter outfitted with a Johnny Burke lyric and retitled "What's New") established Butterfield as an important young trumpeter, and in mid-1938, when Lawson left to join Tommy Dorsey, the newcomer inherited most of the hot trumpet work. He rose to it with enthusiasm and flair, his small-group leads on the Bobcats sessions rivaling his predecessor's for drive,

645

his ballad statements (the opening on "Embraceable You," for example) tonally exquisite. There was even the solo and ending of "What Goes Up Must Come Down," with its strong evocation of Bix Beiderbecke.

Butterfield starred with Artie Shaw's large orchestra of 1940; his soaring opening to "Star Dust" helped establish that record as a popular music landmark; it's still heard, half a century later, on jukeboxes and radio stations across the land. Bands playing the song at dances invariably begin with the trumpet taking the three–quarter-note pickup to the melody in deference, albeit largely unwitting, to the Butterfield model.

He also put in time with Benny Goodman and, for a while after World War II, led his own big band; like Hackett's bandleading fling it soon ended, leaving Butterfield disgruntled and in debt. By the 1950s he and Hackett, close friends, were on staff at ABC, the American Broadcasting Corporation.

Colleagues (and most ABC musical directors) came to regard them as a team, subbing for one another, sometimes playing side by side. Each spoke with unstinting admiration of the other. Upon being told of Hackett's evaluation of him as "the best trumpet player in the world right now," Butterfield snorted in disdain. "Listen," he said. "Hackett and I differ in one big respect. He's one of the really great players. I don't see myself as being anywhere near that category. But he sure as hell is."[33]

Now and then they recorded together. Their similarities and differences are obvious on the December 1944 Eddie Condon Decca record of "When Your Lover Has Gone": Hackett opens with a flowing, heart-tugging melody chorus in A♭, interrupted briefly by Ernie Caceres, all delicacy and restraint. After a Jack Teagarden half-chorus, Butterfield finishes it out.

For years, listeners simply assumed that Hackett had played both passages, so well matched were their tones and overall conceptions. Yet careful listening reveals key differences: Butterfield's variations are more in the manner of embellishments, where Hackett's are actual developments of Einar Swan's 1931 melody. In his ninth bar, Butterfield treats us to one of his personal trademarks, an octave slur on a concert E♭, done so smoothly, so effortlessly, that the upper note seems to begin sounding *before* the lower one has ended. The "Butterfield slur" became, among brass players, an industry standard; of the many who have tried to equal it, only the formidable (and much underappreciated) Don Goldie, son of longtime Paul Whiteman trumpeter Harry Goldfield, succeeded to any great degree.[34]

Butterfield's studio career was long and successful, thanks to his superior technical skills, note-perfect sight-reading, and his ability to play any chair in a section. Not a little wryly, Hackett told of being called upon, while subbing for Butterfield at a rehearsal for ABC's *Metropolitan Opera Auditions*, to read through portions of Benjamin Britten's opera *Peter Grimes*.

"So I, the wise guy, grab the third book, figuring it's the easiest one," he said. "Well, we're reading along, and all of a sudden I see a big black bunch of notes up ahead that look like a tornado's coming up. It was written in E and called for transposition, had all sorts of trilling and tremendous shenanigans up around high E and F♯ on the horn. Well, about four bars or so before it I just look up helplessly at Joe [Stopak, conductor] and he looks down at me and we both break out laughing. So we let it go—you know, there are just some things you can't lick.

"Comes the show, and in comes Billy—on the air, cold—and reads it all off perfectly. Bang! First time. Perfect. You can't beat that—and coming from a guy who plays the best jazz around, too."[35]

Choice examples of Butterfield's jazz playing on record are easy to find. The 1962 LP *Billy Plays Bix* is representative; he contributes forcefully to many Eddie Condon performances, including Columbia's highly regarded *Jammin' at Condon's* and many of the Town Hall concerts. Equally at home in other jazz settings, he appears, poised and confident, on a celebrated Savoy session of April 18, 1944, with Lester Young and pianist Johnny Guarnieri. His stabbing, harmon-muted trumpet drives "Exercise in Swing"; he plays broad-toned blues on "Salute to Fats" (Waller had died suddenly only four months earlier); and ends his chorus on "Basie English" with a jaunty, Rex Stewart–like upward sweep.[36]

Butterfield, too, was a favorite of Louis Armstrong, whom he and Bobby admired above all others, and who profoundly affected the playing of both. Asked once which of the two he preferred, Louis thought a long time. "Bobby," he said at length. "He got more ingredients." But the decision had obviously been a tough one.[37]

In later years Butterfield played often in jazz bands co-led by fellow-trumpeter Yank Lawson and bassist Bob Haggart. The association began in the '50s, when both men were staff musicians, and produced a series of splendid Decca LPs under the name of the "Lawson-Haggart Jazz Band." Butterfield's solos on "Ostrich Walk" and the "Original Dixieland One-Step," for example, on Decca Decca's LP *Hold That Tiger!*, are exemplary.

That association evolved, in 1968, into the World's Greatest Jazz Band, which despite the obvious hyperbole of its name (brainchild of Colorado millionaire and jazz party organizer Dick Gibson) was an outstanding unit. Its records, usually built around canny, spacious Haggart arrangements, gave all the soloists—reedmen Bob Wilber and Bud Freeman, trumpeters Lawson and Butterfield and sometimes Hackett, and a variety of trombonists—great latitude.

Butterfield's duets with Lawson were a highlight, pairing the former's sometimes gruff (and, in Digby Fairweather's apt word, "hectoring") phrasing with Butterfield's shining tone and airborne lyricism. "The Windmills of Your Mind," from their second album, and "New Orleans," from *Live at the Roosevelt Grill*, are striking examples of their compatibility. "Billy and I just seem to understand each other's playing," Lawson told Scottish writer Ken Gallacher. "It isn't a conscious thing. Both of us seem to realize what should happen and we fall into it together."[38]

In conversations with Whitney Balliett, which led to the *New Yorker* profile, Hackett talked at some length about the way he approached playing a song. "The hardest thing of all," he said, "is to play straight melody and make it sound like you. It's stripping the medium down to its bare parts . . . If it's a good tune, I don't change the composer's lines. Any player who edits Ellington or Gershwin

647

or Fats Waller implies that he knows more." He compared a fine song to the work of a great architect: to tamper with its basic structure was comparable to attempting to alter parts of the plan for a carefully designed building.

"Playing with him taught me to treat melodies very carefully, very reverentially," said pianist Chuck Folds. "He humanized songs. You could almost say he treated them like people. He made me concentrate on making everything *sing*, the way he did all the time. He had very subtle ways of doing that. It wasn't just the notes of a melody, but the subtle intervals between them, and the very subtle ways you can use to dramatize them. With Bobby you always knew a melody was headed somewhere, but he made you as aware of the journey as of the destination.

"He knew, instinctively, how to wait just that right amount of time—the spaces, the tensions, between the notes. The small variations on the way he placed a phrase, structured a melody. It's such a subtle thing—especially with a guy like Bobby, whose playing seems to stay on such an even emotional keel.

"But it could really get to you. I remember one time in Hyannis, on the Cape, when he was playing 'April in Paris,' and I realized, to my astonishment, that I was hanging on every note he played, dying for the next note, wondering what surprise he held in store. He could have that effect on you."[39]

Fans of traditional jazz tend to be quite unforgiving about what they view as defection from their own gnosis, or revealed truth. One prolific contributor to a leading genre periodical has been known to condemn a respected brassman, in language little short of vicious, for the perceived apostasy of reproducing a Bix Beiderbecke solo on a trumpet rather than a 1927 period cornet.

Though Hackett paralleled his commercial efforts with a succession of outstanding jazz albums, such writers (and many fans) have suggested that his activities in the commercial marketplace somehow call into doubt his *bona fides* as a jazzman. Yet throughout the 1950s and 1960s he continued to lead excellent groups. Perhaps the standout was the sextet he ran for two years in the mid-'50s, which played an extended run at the Voyager Room of the Henry Hudson Hotel, on West 57th Street in Manhattan.

Its original personnel boasted two reed players—Ernie Caceres doubling baritone and clarinet—and Virginian Tom Gwaltney on clarinet and, affording another ensemble color, vibraphone. Dick Cary was the pianist and principal arranger, picking up his E♭ alto horn or trumpet when needed; John Dengler, on tuba and bass sax, was also a good cornetist and could complete a three-man brass section. Various drummers, including New Englanders Tony Hannan and Buzzy Drootin, rounded out the personnel.

A strikingly creative group, it drew its repertoire from a wide range of sources. What other small band of the time could routinely follow "Cornet Chop Suey" with a Benny Golson arrangement of his own "Whisper Not," do justice to Ellington's "Lady of the Lavender Mist," and deliver a light-hearted adaptation of Django Reinhardt's "Swing 39," all with no lapse in skill or stylistic continuity? As more than one writer has noted, this was one of the first "jazz repertory" ensembles, but with a difference: rather than play its range of music as items of recreation, it did so as living, contemporary music, regardless of style.

The band attracted enough critical attention to win a regular WOR radio slot and a contract to do an LP for Capitol. But for reasons never entirely clear, the record that appeared in 1957 as *Gotham Jazz Scene* hardly represented the band on its live dates. The repertoire, though tastefully executed, was conservative: all familiar standards and "dixieland"-flavored arrangements. Better by far is a three-LP set of broadcasts issued by the California-based Shoestring label. The personnel evolves: Cary departs, replaced by pianist Pinero "Pini" Caceres; reedmen Dick Hafer and Bob Wilber supplant Ernie Caceres and Tom Gwaltney.

It's Wilber and Hafer, in fact, who on one broadcast turn Bud Freeman's little-known "The Seal" into a two-tenor romp, both soloists keeping the composer quite firmly in mind. Cary scores his original "Swiss Kriss" (a kind of peristaltic *hommage* to Louis Armstrong) for five closely voiced horns—Hackett and Dengler on trumpets, himself on E♭ alto horn, Wilber on tenor, and Hafer on baritone—leaving Drootin alone to carry the beat. It works handsomely.

Above all, Hackett plays at top form, reeling off solos full of deft, often arresting phrases. Now and then, as in "Cornet Chop Suey," high-register salvos take him all the way up to concert E♭, high F on his horn. The chromatic bridge of "I'm Beginning to See the Light" finds him firing off boppish double-time passages; two versions of "The Reverend's in Town," a stylish original by Cary and Bud Freeman, afford two similarly conceived but quite different Hackett choruses, tone pleasantly blunted in a bucket mute.[40]

"That band should have been a big success," said Tom Gwaltney. "It had everything you'd want musically, and Bobby was always a joy to play with. While we were there, the Voyager Room became very popular, celebrities coming in all the time. Willie 'the Lion' Smith would come by a couple of nights a week and play intermission piano, just for the hell of it. We rehearsed twice a week, always new stuff. Bobby was never a hard taskmaster—but at least two or three of us in the band were so damn thrilled to be a part of it that if he'd said to go jump in the river we would have done it.

"But Bobby—well, it seemed he never did much with the opportunities that came our way. He was a wonderful guy, but no businessman at all: everybody loved him, but he was the world's worst when it came to business. I sometimes think he needed a keeper—you know, someone to say, 'Bobby, take your medicine. Bobby, it's time to go to work. Bobby, call Mr. So-and-so about that contract.' That was what he needed."[41]

Gwaltney has a point, echoed by others who knew Hackett over the years. "He was a dreamer," said vocalist Maxine Sullivan. "He should have had someone else taking care of everything for him, so he could just get up on a bandstand and make music with his horn. That's what God intended for him to do."[42]

Indeed, Bobby Hackett's career was littered with near-misses, opportunities which never quite materialized—largely, in one way or another, through his chronic failure to attend to business. He was considered for the soundtrack

649

role in Hollywood's adaptation of *Young Man With a Horn*, for example, but lost out when someone mentioned his drinking history (he had long since stopped by that time) to a studio executive. Harry James, an unlikely choice for a film even indirectly based on the life and music of Bix Beiderbecke, got the job—and the big paycheck that went with it.

Hackett seems to have let the Henry Hudson job simply peter out, ending in mid-1958; with it ended the sextet. Bobby, as usual, simply carried on—making records, traveling, keeping to a full work schedule. He joined Tony Bennett as part of the singer's regular musical entourage; Bennett's "The Very Thought of You," with its quietly radiant Hackett obbligato and solo, is a particularly ambrosial reminder of this time.

During the 1960s he also began his last two regular musical associations, with Dave McKenna and trombonist Vic Dickenson. Teaming with Dickenson proved especially fruitful: both understood and appreciated songs; both were walking databanks of beautiful, sometimes quite obscure melodies (including some that Vic himself had composed). Personally they were natural foils: Hackett elegant, a bit earnest; Dickenson no less lyrical, but leavened with a sardonic wit, the eye and ear of the natural satirist. There's more than a touch of Bix and Tram in this union, in the endless lightening-and-darkening that results from interplay between the two forces.

Dickenson "does things on trombone nobody I can remember has ever done," Hackett told Toronto journalist Paul McKenna Davis. "He never does the same thing twice. Every night, every session we play, he shows me something new—but beautiful."[43]

They played together happily and well, most often backed by Dave McKenna. The pianist still chuckles when he recalls playing "Baubles, Bangles and Beads" with Bobby. "If we played it in A♭, he wanted a plain dominant seventh chord, in this case an E♭7, to start it, where most guys would play the II-V combination, the B♭ minor seventh leading to the E♭7. To my ear the song demands that B♭m7; but Bobby was Bobby, and he wanted that pure dominant sound, so I of course obliged him.

"Sometime later I made a record with Hall Overton, the very respected composer and arranger, and we played 'Baubles,' and I used that plain dominant chord to start. Hall didn't say anything, but I kind of knew he was amazed, thinking, 'Here's this real young guy, and he's playing these old-fashioned chords.' "[44]

Chuck Folds also played "Baubles, Bangles and Beads" with Hackett. "I had the music and knew that in A♭ it required you to begin that phrase with a straight E♭7, so that's what I did. And don't you know—in the break he came up to me and said, 'You're the only pianist I've ever played with who plays that right.' "[45]

A series of LPs issued in the 1970s on Hank O'Neal's Chiaroscuro label finds Hackett, Dickenson, and McKenna live at the Roosevelt Grill, in Rockefeller Center, supported by Jack Lesberg and drummer Cliff Leeman. "There were nights," said Lesberg, "when things really got going nicely. Bobby and Vic really enjoyed playing off one another. I think he was really most effective when he was playing off someone else, instead of just playing alone, as the only horn."

Dave McKenna expanded on the point: "To me he was at his best when he was leading an ensemble, other horns. Listen to the way he plays on the Condon *Bixieland* album, or on *Coast Concert* and *Jazz Ultimate* with Teagarden. He really knew where he wanted to take things, and I've never heard anybody do it better."

But even the Hackett-Dickenson *entente cordiale* came to an end—largely because Hackett, characteristically, just let it happen. "Dick Gibson called me," he said, "and asked if I'd mind if Vic went with Yank [Lawson] and Bob [Haggart] and the World's Greatest Jazz Band. Well, it meant better money than I could pay him, so I said okay." Benny Morton, a distinguished trombonist, came in as Vic's replacement, but things were never again the same. As usual, Bobby Hackett had done himself out of another musically rewarding situation: his "dream band" with Dickenson had lasted only a year.

Now, suddenly, time was no longer on his side. A combination of diabetes and other ailments affected the cornetist's general health more and more notice-ably as the 1970s got under way. He and Edna, his wife and childhood sweet-heart, finally left New York City, where they'd lived since the late '30s, and bought a neatly designed ranch house in Chatham, on Cape Cod. The effect was salutary, at least for a while. But the habits of a lifetime were beginning to take their toll: a chain smoker, Hackett had developed serious lung trouble, evidenced by increased raspiness of voice and a deep, rumbling cough.

He was in and out of hospitals with increasing frequency. A 1974 tour in England found him looking frail, his playing at times almost tentative. Only later did the word get around that he'd been gravely ill, spent one crisis time in a diabetic coma, his future uncertain. He never once mentioned it to his hosts.

A series of ill-conceived business ventures had left him deep in debt, with no choice but to take what work came along. As he entered his sixties, an age when a lifetime of musical achievement should have allowed him some leisure, Bobby Hackett found himself still scuffling. He continued to record: even now, decades after his death, his thoughtful statements on popular ballads are still heard floating out of the ceiling speakers of supermarkets, department stores, elevators, restaurants, and doctors' waiting rooms everywhere. He can stop a discerning listener in his tracks with some exquisite variation on "I Cover the Waterfront" or "My Funny Valentine." Tone, attack, vibrato, phrase shapes: immediately, unmistakably Hackett.

No other major soloist has been so widely heard, yet so seldom recognized. Why? What kept the name of Bobby Hackett, for all the excellence of his musi-cianship, from major public recognition?

Ruby Braff, for one, has strong convictions on the subject. "Bobby didn't give his heart to an audience," the cornetist said. "He gave it to his horn. He just wanted to play beautifully and wonderfully—but for himself and for other musicians, not for the people. I think he shared an attitude very common among musicians. You know—'here they come, the enemy is coming.' *Them. The enemy.* I think Bobby had a certain amount of that; he seemed to be afraid that other musicians would put him down if he fell in love with performing. Almost as if he had something against the idea of show business, performing for an audience.

"Audiences know that. They feel it when you've disconnected yourself from them. I've always felt that if Bobby had reached out a little more it would have helped him make that connection. Can you imagine what would have happened if he'd been able to open his heart and really give it to his listeners?"[46]

All the same, Hackett's effect on those who knew him, particularly on musicians who played with him, was lasting and profound. Bassist Frank Tate, for example, had particular reason to listen hard when he worked for Hackett on Cape Cod in the mid-'70s. "I'd started out as a trumpet player," he said recently, "and I guess I was still thinking like one, even though I was now playing the bass. The way he played melodies, chose his notes—I'd never really paid much attention to that, and at one point it just dawned on me what a total *master* he was. As other people will tell you, he knew just what he wanted from a rhythm section, even down to the bass notes; those were lessons you learned real fast with him. You just heard it.

"Well, that was nearly thirty years ago, and there are times, so help me, when I think the notes I play when I solo sound just like things I heard Bobby play. He got into your head, into your ears, that way. I just wish he'd stayed around longer. He had so much to teach everybody—things about taste and lines and how to choose the best notes that you can't learn from very many others."[47]

Bobby Hackett died at his Chatham home at 4:30 A.M. on Monday, June 7, 1976. The official cause of death was a heart attack; but those who knew him best saw his death as the culmination of an unraveling process which had been going on a long, long time. He'd gotten out of the hospital Friday, played that night and Saturday, said he'd never felt better. But by then it was far too late.

In one sense, Bobby Hackett's had been a life triumphant, a paradigm for all that is elegant, intelligent, ordered, and tasteful in music. But music apart, it had been something quite other—in Whitney Balliett's words, "an endless parade of small disappointments, missed chances, broken promises, poor advice."

He'd hoped to establish a club on the Cape, where he could spend most of the year playing, while living comfortably in Chatham. The deal fell through. He founded his own record company, Hyannisport, which issued a pair of ill-distributed LPs, went bankrupt, and folded. After he died, creditors and the Internal Revenue Service descended in a feeding frenzy; a lien was placed even on the Chatham house.

At some basic, subliminal level, Hackett may have known what was coming. Talking to British critic Max Jones in 1974, he remarked, "When Duke [in 1974] died and when Louis [in 1971] died, I felt that maybe a little bit of me went with them. Maybe I'm wrong; it's a crazy theory but I can't help suspecting it might be true. All those guys like Louis, they were part of my history and upbringing, and so a little of you goes with 'em each time; you can't help but feel that, and deal with it."[48]

Less than two years later Bobby Hackett, too, was gone. And as with Louis, Duke, and the others he so admired, we will not see his like again.

Red Norvo and Mildred Bailey (1): Early Careers

Otis Ferguson, whose commentaries on jazz and other lively arts for the mid-1930s *New Republic* can still surprise, wrote with particular insight about Red Norvo. "A special conception of music" was Ferguson's verdict in a 1938 review. "Balance, restraint, clean ensembles and no tricks . . . And under a complete delicacy of taste he had the urgent carrying beat without which music like this must be sick or pseudo."[1]

No tricks. How better to describe a musical orientation, an aesthetic, of such utter purity? Just how pure, in fact, becomes clear with the realization that Red Norvo's way of playing music on the xylophone (or, as later, the vibraharp) had no recognizable precedent—and, once formed, it never really changed. From 1933, when he made his first records, straight through to the 1980s, when physical infirmity finally put an end to his playing career, his basic concept remained firmly, radiantly, in place.

Fashions changed around him. Ways of dealing with harmony, melodic lines, laying down a beat, and, starting in the World War II years, even the inner aesthetic of music-making underwent startling transformations. But Norvo's musical sensibility seemed equal to all of it, able to acknowledge and absorb everything without compromising itself.

"All his music is its own signature" was Ferguson's way of putting it—and that is a statement of incontrovertible fact. It also places Norvo in the small and ultra-select circle of jazz innovators, true originals.

At this point it's useful to draw a distinction between the often conflated ideas of innovation and personal creativity. Though both qualities may be embodied in one musician—Louis Armstrong is, in jazz at least, the paramount example—the latter does not necessarily encompass the former.

Few will dispute, for example, that Lester Young, at least before World War II, was a soloist of great originality. But on the evidence of his first records, made in 1936, Young was not exactly an innovator; he was, rather, working within an established tradition, which had begun with Frank Trumbauer and Jimmy Dorsey (and, conceptually, Bix Beiderbecke) and continued on through Bud Freeman and a number of other white saxophonists.

Coleman Hawkins, by contrast, was a ground-breaking force: before his emergence in the mid-1920s, there was no focused, consensual way of playing hot jazz on the tenor saxophone. He formed that himself, developing it into his instrument's first industry standard. Others had played "hot" tenor solos, some quite well: Prince Robinson, best known through his work with McKinney's Cotton Pickers, was one. Others included white saxophonists Don Murray, Fud Livingston, and, later in the decade, Bud Freeman.

This was not the case with Red Norvo. For him there was no precedent: mallet instruments were virgin territory as vehicles for "hot" improvisation. By what alchemic process, then, did he transform the xylophone (and, shortly, the marimba) into an effective, often eloquent, solo voice?

Fortunately, Norvo has been a frequent, accessible, and unfailingly clear-minded interview subject, with the result that details of his life and career are plentiful and well documented.

Born March 31, 1908, in Beardstown, Illinois, Joseph Kenneth Norville Jr. began piano lessons at six and spent summers listening to dance orchestras on the great excursion boats that plied the Illinois River. He remembered little of that time, he has said, save a continuing fascination with the music. But when he was thirteen the river overflowed its banks, flooding the Norville home. Off went the boy to Rolla, Missouri, where his brothers Howard and Glen were at mining school—and where he heard a man with the improbable name of Wentworth Woodworth playing the marimba in a local theatre pit band.

Woodworth, it turned out, was one of the elder Norville boys' fraternity brothers. Within days, young Joseph had been seduced by the sounds and textures of mallet instruments and was importuning his father, a dispatcher for the Chicago, Burlington, and Quincy Railroad, to buy him a xylophone.

Norville senior was a quiet, practical Scotsman who championed the virtues of hard work. He'd watched his two elder sons take music lessons, then lose interest and wander off; even Joe junior—or Kenneth, as his mother had taken to calling him—had only stuck with the piano a short while, until his teacher discovered he was memorizing his lessons by ear instead of actually reading them.

All right, said Norville père; you can have your xylophone, but only if you're willing to work for it. With a lack of fuss which was to characterize him all his life, Kenneth responded by taking a summer job for the CB & Q, picking up railroad ties and jacking up freight cars. As biographer Don DeMicheal reports, he even sold his pet pony to help raise the $137.50 price of a Deagan table-model xylophone.[2]

He got it, and went to work learning to play it. Fortunately for him, the early 1920s was a time of wide popularity for mallet instruments, particularly xylophone. Soloists on the instrument were featured regularly on theatre bills, in popular concerts, and even on the emerging wonder of phonograph records. The young man listened, imitated, and just figured out the rest of what he had to know.

Sporting such names as Crippled Ernie Woods, Signor Frisco, and "Professor" Lamberto, many xylophonists seemed also to be vaudeville performers—dancers, comedians, and showmen. Their musical bill of fare stressed light novelties, written to showcase the player's dexterity and often stressing velocity at the expense of content. One latter-day columnist remembered vaudeville xylophonists who "climaxed their acts by proudly displaying both hands full of mallets and tearing off the 'Lone Ranger' movement from the *William Tell* overture while doing a tap dance."[3]

But a few players, notable among them the respected George Hamilton Green, were working to change that, to win acceptance for the xylophone as a "serious" solo instrument. Beginning in 1919, Green and his brother Joe were among the most frequently recorded of popular artists; often billed as the "Green Brothers Novelty Orchestra," they handled a wide-ranging repertoire, from mallet novelties through "treatments" of popular songs and no-nonsense adaptations of light classical works. (They continued to do so throughout the 1930s. The two brothers also maintained separate, equally prolific recording careers: Joe Green, for example, began making records with his own groups in 1925 and for the next decade.)

Young Norville took heed, secretly resolving that someday he'd meet the one and only George Hamilton Green. When he did, some years later, the older man turned the tables on him by confessing that there was nothing he knew that the newcomer didn't already know—and do—better.

The youth worked a summer on the Chautauqua tent circuit, touring with a marimba octet billed as "the Collegians," and, much to his family's alarm, found he actually enjoyed it. Though his parents were themselves musical—Joseph sang and played some piano, his wife, Estelle, the trumpet—they shared a disapproval of professional music common among white middle-class families of the time. It was one thing to play for enjoyment in the home, they seemed to say, but quite another to be perceived by the public as someone who made his living at it.[4]

As Norvo recalled later, his brother Glen even turned up at one of the Collegians' engagements to entreat his brother to come home. "Only drunkards and dope fiends are musicians!" was his none-too-tactful way of putting it. The entire scene could have been lifted bodily out of the lives of any number of other young white musicians of the time, Bix Beiderbecke included; as so often in such cases, the parents prevailed, at least temporarily. Kenneth left the Collegians and returned to school, enrolling at the University of Illinois at Champaign—just as Beiderbecke, around the same time and for much the same reason, was trying the University of Iowa.

The truce was short-lived: Norville had been at Champaign less than three months when a telegram arrived, offering a vaudeville tour with the Collegians. "I split, just like that," he told DeMicheal. "My father sent me my allowance for that month and I was gone."[5]

That tour, which presented the octet on a bill with a female impersonator, a song-and-dance act and a soft-shoe team, had two lasting effects on the young xylophonist: first, he emerged a more polished musician, technically sure and able to read music with the speed and accuracy of a veteran. Second, somewhere in his travels he acquired a wind-up phonograph and a stack of records, most of them examples of the new, exciting music known as jazz.

In later years he couldn't remember which records they were, only that "I drove everybody crazy playing them backstage." But it's more than likely that in 1925 they may have included performances by the seemingly ubiquitous Original Dixieland Jazz Band and the Chicago-based Friars Society Orchestra, perhaps even by King Oliver's Creole Jazz Band and by the Wolverines, with Bix.

He was aware very early of Beiderbecke and Frank Trumbauer. The two had met in 1923, when the popular Benson Orchestra of Chicago played a date at the Coliseum, a dance hall in Beiderbecke's home town of Davenport, Iowa; by autumn 1925, they were working together at the Arcadia Ballroom in St. Louis. And, sometime around then, Kenneth Norville heard them, either in St. Louis itself or on a Mississippi river excursion boat. What remained with him was "the intonation, the flow. Everything they did sounded so easy and flowing."

To him, as to so many others, hearing Beiderbecke live was something quite different from hearing Beiderbecke on a record. "That sound he got: I don't think Bix ever made a record that sounded as good as he did in person. Live—I don't know—he just sounded better: more fluent, and the sound of his horn just rang. On the records there was always something missing from what I originally remember him in my ear sounding like.

"Trumbauer, too. I can't figure out why [people] don't talk about Trumbauer any more. They talk about so many players—and yet, nobody ever played the way he played. Later, when I was with [Paul] Whiteman, I got to know him very well. He was one of my favorite people."[6]

Norville may have been listening to hot music on his Victrola backstage, but as far as the public knew he was a vaudeville performer, tossing off H. H. Booth's "Xylophone Rag" and other similar mallet specialties, garnishing his solo spots now and then with deftly executed dance turns. He wound up in Chicago and before long was working for orchestra leader and impresario Paul Ash.

It was Ash who, quite unintentionally, was responsible for changing Kenneth Norville into Red Norvo. "He couldn't remember my name: One night he'd call me 'Norvin.' Another, 'Norvox.' Or 'Norvick.' You can't imagine. He really mangled it. Not on purpose, you understand: he just couldn't remember. One night it was 'Norvo': I kind of liked the sound, especially after it wound up that way in *Variety*. After that I was Norvo, and that was that."

The "Red" part is self-evident: red hair, blue eyes, pale skin; a textbook Scottish redhead. Red Norvo he became, and Red Norvo he stayed. Very few persisted in addressing him as Kenneth.

He was earning good money in vaudeville, sometimes as much as $650 a week. But the music he was hearing in Chicago, and the effect it was having on him, made it obvious this couldn't go on forever. The late 1920s found him vacillating between the security of stage work and a few tentative stabs in new directions. He led a band at the Eagle Ballroom in nearby Milwaukee; spent four months at the University of Detroit in one final fling at education; camped for nearly a year in Minneapolis, leading a band at the Marigold Ballroom and working as a staff musician at local radio station KSTP.

It was an unsettled time, a learning time. He began to compose, crystallizing ideas that were evolving out of his rapidly developing mallet facility. And he began working seriously at solving the problems of playing improvised solos on an instrument with a piano-like keyboard, but no ability to sustain a note beyond the sound it makes when struck.

Taking some time off in Chicago, he ran into an old friend. Victor Young was a violinist, Chicago born, who had studied abroad, toured the country as a concert artist, worked extensively in theatres. He'd played on Ben Pollack's first record dates for Victor, alongside Benny Goodman and Glenn Miller, and in 1928 had broken through as a songwriter with "Sweet Sue (Just You)." Now he was on his way to comparable success in radio as an orchestra conductor.

Ah, he said as he greeted Norvo, with whom he'd shared more than a few theatre jobs. "Just the guy I want to see." He was putting together a band for a brand-new National Broadcasting Company (NBC) radio show, to be sponsored by the Maytag Company, and needed a xylophone player. Could Red come in and do it? He said yes, returned to Chicago, went to work on the weekly Maytag show—and soon thereafter joined Ben Bernie's orchestra at the popular College Inn, playing intermission solo features.

At this point, he was exclusively what musicians call a "wood" player, specializing in xylophone and marimba, both instruments with keyboards made of hardwood. The xylophone keyboard is set up like that of a piano, with the accidental (or "black") notes slightly higher than the natural (or "white") keys. The underside of each key is hollowed out (or, in the case of the marimba, simply thinned), the amount of hollowing determining its pitch.

The xylophone has a normal playing range of three and one-half octaves, the marimba four, its top note an octave lower than that of the xylophone. Both are thought to have been of African origin (the name "marimba" is African), although similar percussion instruments existed in pre-Columbian Mexico and neighboring countries. The marimba was already popular throughout Central America by 1910, when it was introduced in the United States. The J. C. Deagan Company, pioneer in the manufacture of mallet instruments, also developed a bass marimba, whose very low range (down to a 'cello C) and pellucid, almost ghostly, tone made it particularly appealing as a color instrument.

Extending down from the keys (or "bars") of both instruments are vertical metal tubes called resonators, each designed to vibrate sympathetically in the pitch of the key to which it's attached. At the time Red Norvo joined Ben Bernie he was playing a custom-built Deagan marimba-xylophone, a five-octave hybrid more than seven feet long, which afforded both the *mysterioso* tonal possibilities of the former and the high-register brightness of the latter.

The third member of this family, of course, is the vibraphone—or, as manufactured by Deagan, vibraharp. Its bars are of metal, usually aluminum (attached to resonators), and ring longer when struck, giving a player the option of sustaining tones. Xylophone and marimba players, faced with the necessity of playing longer notes, had developed a method of "rolling," rapid alternation of mallets—either on the same note or in octaves, or in small intervals such as seconds or thirds—for as long as the note needed to be sustained.[7]

"Vibes," as the instrument quickly came to be called, eliminated the need for such techniques. But there was a drawback: in early models there was no way to *stop* notes from ringing—save to block the keys with elbow, forearm, or hand. Until the introduction of a damper pedal in the early 1930s, this singular disadvantage restricted the vibraphone (the word has become more or less generic) to a subordinate role as a color agent: it could add a shimmering effect to *tutti* passages, and its characteristic "ping!" ends many a mid-'20s dance band record.

But what chiefly set the vibraphone/vibraharp apart from other mallet instruments was an electric device, a set of revolving discs mounted on a shaft inserted through the open top of each resonator pipe and attached to a small motor. The motor spun the discs, which set an air column in the tubes pulsating, producing an effect like a wind player's vibrato. Early motors were primitive, operating at only one speed. More sophisticated, variable-pitch motors soon corrected this deficiency.

If the vibraphone had to await the pleasure of technology for its debut as a solo instrument, the xylophone was an attraction from the start. Its only major problem besides sustaining was volume: neither it nor its cousin the marimba could play very loudly. Though some volume was possible through use of harder mallets, both instruments were easily swamped in orchestral passages, and even solo turns had to be accompanied with keen attention to dynamics.

Multi-instrumental prodigy Adrian Rollini, originally a pianist, had played xylophone regularly since the early 1920s and from all reports was quite adept at mallet techniques; but no recorded evidence exists of his work before 1933, when he started using vibes on records with his own groups and those led by Joe Venuti. Ever-versatile drummer Victor Berton whacked out a xylophone break on a Red Nichols record or two; others dropped in vibes touches here and there. At Louis Armstrong's urging, drummer Lionel Hampton played a rather faltering vibraphone intro to the trumpeter's 1930 recording of "Memories of You."

That apart, in 1930 Norvo was alone in the field. Ben Bernie, ever the showman, encouraged him to wheel his huge marimba-xylophone (which wouldn't fit on the bandstand) from table to table at the College Inn, serenading customers in the manner of a strolling violinist. He could play popular hits, such specialties as Debussy's "Golliwog's Cakewalk," even answer requests; but, said the leader, "play that other stuff you play, too."

The "other stuff" was material Norvo had been working up, including his adaptations of Bix Beiderbecke's four piano pieces. In a Mist, in fact, captured the attention of what Norvo remembered as a very drunk Paul Whiteman, who had come in with a large party. "They were really havin' a ball," said Norvo, "laughing and carrying on. And I'm thinking, 'Oh-oh, this is gonna be something.' I played, played all kinds of things, and they're not payin' any attention to the music. So I did In a Mist, and the big guy, whom I recognized as Whiteman, calls out, 'Hey, did you hear that kid? He just played one of Bix's things.' ''

Whiteman came back, sober, several days later to find out about the "kid" who had played In a Mist. As a result of that encounter, Norvo soon found himself working staff radio jobs at NBC for vice president and musical director Jules Herbuveaux. Whiteman, consolidating his power base at the network, installed two lieutenants, composer-arrangers Ferde Grofé and Roy Bargy, as staff orchestra leaders; within a short time he supplanted Herbuveaux as head of music at NBC Chicago and established his orchestra at the Marine Room of the swank Edgewater Beach Hotel, where it broadcast regularly over station WEBH, one of two local NBC outlets.[8]

Norvo remembered his NBC time with affection. A highlight of each day was a daily morning show, from seven to eight A.M., with a little group led by Herbuveaux, who played tenor sax, and also featuring pianist David Rose and hot clarinetist Voltaire "Volly" De Faut. Some reports have also placed Wingy Manone in this band, but from available evidence (and considering Manone's inability to read music) it seems unlikely. Trumpeter Stirling Bose, an accomplished reader, was on staff at NBC station WGN around this time, and it may have been he who did the broadcasts.

And, three afternoons a week, there were fifteen-minute shows backing one of Whiteman's singers, a heavy, tart-tongued, short-tempered woman, part American Indian, who sang in a surprisingly clear, rounded voice and phrased like no one Red had ever heard. Her name was Mildred Bailey.

Born Mildred Rinker in Tekoa, Washington, on February 27, 1907, she was the elder sister of Alton Rinker, one of Whiteman's three singing "Rhythm Boys." She had worked as a song demonstrator in a five-and-dime store (where she also first heard records by Bessie Smith and other blues artists) and been through an unsuccessful marriage to a man named Bailey, whose name she kept because she thought it sounded better professionally than Rinker.

Hooking on with the Fanchon and Marco stage revue, she'd come down to Los Angeles in 1929 and landed some work right away on radio station KMTR. But regular employment was scarce. She remarried and settled down to what looked like a steady, if unexciting, domestic life, in which singing would play a secondary role.

Al Rinker, meanwhile, had been touting his sister to Paul Whiteman but getting nowhere. The "King of Jazz" had heard more than his share of aspirant vocalists, sisters of friends and friends of friends, all looking for the big break, and had long since adopted a "sorry, not interested" policy in dealing with them all.

A bit of strategy was called for. The Whiteman orchestra was in Hollywood to begin filming Universal's first Technicolor musical, The King of Jazz. But there had been delays, and the musicians found themselves with a lot of free time. Rinker, fellow Rhythm Boy Bing Crosby, and several other Whiteman musicians decided that the best solution would be a party, to be held at Mildred's home. Their strategy was simple: invite the whole band—_except_ its leader. "Don't worry," Crosby told her on the phone. "He can't _stand_ being left out. He'll be here."[9]

It came off exactly as planned. Whiteman showed up halfway through the party, and as he stood in the kitchen, chatting with Beiderbecke, clarinetist Irving Friedman, and several of the others, Mildred sang "What Can I Say, Dear, After I Say I'm Sorry?," backed by Eddie Lang on guitar and Lennie Hayton at the piano. "Who is _that?_" Whiteman bellowed.

Three days later Mildred Bailey was a member of Paul Whiteman's orchestra, the first woman to sing regularly with a band, just as Crosby had been the first man. She made her official debut on the Old Gold network radio show of Tuesday, August 6, 1929, singing "Moanin' Low" in an arrangement written for her by Roy Bargy and featuring solos by Bix and Frank Trumbauer.

Whiteman, in a move rare for him at that time, grabbed the microphone during that show to report that a fan had phoned KMTR to rave about "the best number he'd ever heard us do. Listening to this girl's voice myself, I'm tempted to agree."[10]

As trombonist Bill Rank remembered her, "she was like one of the guys" and could be as salty or profane as any of her colleagues. When she blew off at someone, the billingsgate could make a sailor blush; she could be, in Rank's phrase, "one tough customer."[11]

But somehow it was different when she dealt with Bix Beiderbecke. By 1929, Whiteman's star cornetist was clearly a man in trouble: his drinking had worsened, and there were lapses in performance, only partly compensated for by the presence in Whiteman's brass section of a Bix admirer and sound-alike, the far more reliable Andy Secrest.

At such a remove it's hard to say how it worked, and why, but Whiteman musicians testified that when Mildred was around Bix she became another person—soft, affectionate, chiding him if he didn't take care of himself, scolding him if he showed up drunk or hung over, and ready with a hug and motherly kiss when he played well.[12]

Two years to the day after Mildred's Old Gold debut, Bix Beiderbecke died in a squalid apartment in Queens, his body devastated by pneumonia and the effects of alcoholism. She mourned him deeply, said Norvo. The image that lasts, as reported by several musicians, is of a late-evening party in Bix's New York hotel room: Mildred, a massive arm around Bix's shoulders, singing the blues to him as she pillows his head on her bosom.

Norvo, playing for her three times a week in Chicago, took to her at once. "She gassed me as a singer" is his standard way of putting it to interviewers. "I really dug her. We started having a bite together now and then." Mildred (or "Bails," as Whiteman was fond of calling her) was hep: she knew good music from bad, knew where to find the good stuff. And in common with Norvo, she drew no color lines when it came to appreciation.

Soon the two of them, as visually unlikely a couple as could be imagined, were making the rounds of Chicago's after-hours joints together. Among their favorites was clarinetist Jimmie Noone, still working around town with a six-piece group showcasing his clarinet against an alto sax, played at this time by fellow–New Orleans emigré Eddie Pollack.

On January 12, 1931, Mildred joined Noone and friends in recording two titles for Vocalion. She'd recorded before, doing a chorus on an Eddie Lang record ("What Kind o' Man Is You?," in 1929) and another, in an almost Betty Boopish mode, on a date with Trumbauer the following year. But these Noone sessions are the first recorded performances that give her any room to be heard on her own.

A strong vein of sentimentality runs through her singing here, expressing itself through phrasing, vibrato, and frequent use of portamento, a way of sliding into notes from below, equally popular with string players and singers of the day. She also has a barroom-ballad way of "shaking" downward at the end of a note, which can be heard in the work of Red McKenzie (and, later, in the young, jazz-oriented Ella Logan, and even in Billie Holiday).

Later these various devices were absorbed into Mildred's more rounded, mature style. But here they dominate—largely because the same kind and degree of sentimental excess saturates Noone's own ballad playing. His opening melody statement on "Trav'lin' All Alone" establishes the climate, and Mildred responds, her vocal "milking" an already loaded lyric: the way in which she deals with the word "misery" alone veers perilously close to mawkishness.*

The second title, "He's Not Worth Your Tears," offers more of the same. With the exception of a Hines-like eight bars by pianist "Zinky" Cohn, these are straightforward "sweet" performances in the style of the day. While they show Mildred Bailey to be a polished and musicianly singer, in control of tone production, intonation, and phrasing, the lack of any counterbalance to the sentimental bias makes them ultimately disappointing.

The Norvo-Bailey courtship didn't last long. In May 1931, they were married during a brief band visit to upstate New York (with Trumbauer as best man), and for about a year they performed together as members of Whiteman's entourage. "You had a feeling with that band, that you were with the best," Norvo said. "Kind of like being on a championship basketball team. We had real confidence in ourselves."

A photo taken slightly later, in 1934, and published widely, illustrates the point. Mildred, her shoulders draped in a fur-trimmed coat, stands at the center, flanked by Norvo, Jimmy Dorsey, Fud Livingston, Red McKenzie, and pianists Bobby Van Eps and Bob Laine. In the relaxation and easy geniality they exude self-confidence, as if to say, "Yes! We know what's happening, because we *are* what's happening."

*   *   *

*Such material has always posed problems for singers. Billie Holiday avoided the pitfalls by taking "Trav'lin' All Alone" at a brisk, unsentimental tempo in her 1937 recording; in doing so she and Lester Young created a jazz classic—but missed most of the lyric's expression of pain and world-weariness. Only Ethel Waters, recording in 1947, seems to have found her way to the song's emotional core through a restraint which leaves equal room for despair and anger, tough-mindedness and vulnerability.

Toward the end of 1931, the Whiteman orchestra finally left Chicago and headed east, with Norvo featured as a kind of combination solo virtuoso and one-man novelty act. Part of his routine involved playing the marimba with a pair of mallets of his own devising, which he called "slap hammers." With rectangular, flat heads the size of a standard tablespoon, they struck the keys with a dull "thwack," adding emphasis and projection to his instrument's ordinarily dulcet tone.

Made of cork and covered with a layer of felt, the slap hammers were then encased in hand-stitched buckskin. Not surprisingly, they often succumbed to simple wear and tear, splitting and even flying apart in mid-performance. And who should be on hand with needle, thread, and pieces of buckskin, to repair them with dexterity and enviable speed, but saxophonist Frank Trumbauer.

Norvo's reputation had already preceded him. "Thanks to the musical grapevine," said Rex Stewart, "Red did not arrive in New York as a stranger." The cornetist described taking an interurban streetcar, in a snowstorm, out to Paterson, New Jersey, in company with guitarist Bernard Addison and several other Fletcher Henderson sidemen, just to check out the newly arrived innovator.

"Red was only given the solo spot on one or two numbers in the stage show, as I recall, but that was enough to set our hearts thumping and our heads nodding in agreement. This cat had it!" The word spread fast, said Stewart, and "once we were convinced, we always brought up Norvo's name whenever somebody said ofays [i.e., whites] couldn't swing."[13]

The band finally reached New York—to discover that only musicians holding local 802 cards could work steady engagements there. When Whiteman opened at the Cascades Roof of the swank Biltmore Hotel, it was without his star mallet soloist. "I couldn't even be a guest," Norvo said. "Paul tried to fix it up so I could come out and do some numbers . . . [but] the union wouldn't stand for it. So I put my card in and just had to wait."

That meant a year of strictly casual employment, including a numbing succession of society jobs with Meyer Davis and the Lanin brothers, and one-night ordeals with accordion players. "In a way it wasn't that bad," he said. "That stuff at least paid pretty well, and I started to pick up a lot of substitute work from Sammy Herman, who was the top xylophone player in New York at the time. He was working so much in radio that he didn't want to do a lot of the other things. So he'd throw 'em my way, which was very nice. I'd say that I got through the year all right."

His union status didn't keep him from recording, both with Trumbauer and as part of a group backing Mildred. She'd been active since the Noone date, doing four titles for Brunswick with the popular Casa Loma Orchestra, recording with both the full Whiteman ensemble and smaller units. As might be expected, they show off a wider emotional range than is apparent on "Trav'lin' All Alone" and its companion title with Noone.

On the Casa Loma date she handles Benny Carter's "Blues in My Heart" with an engaging grittiness, a bit reminiscent of Ethel Waters, and even exchanges scatted four-bar phrases with clarinetist Clarence Hutchenrider. Her approach to "Wrap Your Troubles in Dreams" is not unlike Crosby's, direct and rather rhythmic. But the most revealing of these four selections is "When It's Sleepy Time Down South," which she recorded again with Whiteman only two weeks later.

The two performances couldn't be more different. Where her singing on the Whiteman record plays to the song's inherent sentimentality, with the Casa Loma Orchestra she takes a tougher-minded view, enhanced by a faster tempo and a more rhythmic approach by the band. Her phrasing is Armstrong-like; indeed, she even scats sixteen bars over Gene Gifford's rather prominent banjo.[14]

For a while she seems a singer divided. On such irredeemable banalities as " 'Leven Pounds of Heaven" and "That's Why Darkies Were Born," she returns to the *portamenti* and swoops. But on "Home," "Georgia on My Mind," and Fats Waller's delightful "Concentratin'," made in November and issued under her own name, her tenderness is quite winning. But she's not yet been stretched enough to find a balance between the saccharine excesses of some of her White-man vocals and the muscularity implied on the Casa Loma date.

Then came "Rockin' Chair." Contrary to some reports, Hoagy Carmichael did not write this elegiac song expressly for Mildred. He'd recorded it, as "When Baby Sleeps," for Gennett on the 1927 date which also introduced "Star Dust" (as yet without lyrics) to the world. He had recorded it again, this time as "Rockin' Chair," at a February 1928 Victor session, using lyrics different from those eventually published by Mills Music. He'd sung it in duet with Louis Armstrong on a 1929 record, then recorded it a fourth time the following May, this time with Bix among his accompanists.[15]

But on August 18, 1932, Mildred Bailey made "Rockin' Chair" her own. Her Victor record, backed by Norvo and what sounds to be a small group of White-man musicians, is a gem: strong, balanced, her passionate treatment of melody and lyric sounds as though the song might just as well have been written for her.[16]

Apart from a four-bar introduction, Norvo takes no solo here or on the companion piece, "Love Me Tonight," remaining discreetly in the background. But his two-mallet obbligatos on both titles make clear that he's a formidable player, relaxed and melodically resourceful.

Despite its overall excellence, and despite Mildred's subsequent reputation as the "Rockin' Chair Lady," this first, superlative Bailey performance has gone all but unreissued through the years. It's all the more inexplicable in that, along with the Casa Loma recordings (also neglected), it establishes Mildred Bailey beyond dispute as one of the strongest vocal presences of the early '30s. Without these key recordings available for study, much critical assessment of her at this early stage of her career has been badly skewed.

On "I'll Never Be the Same," made with Whiteman a week before the "Rockin' Chair" date, she recasts the melody (by violinist Matt Malneck and jazz pianist Frank Signorelli), smoothing out some of its hill-and-dale awkwardness. Her chorus is in perfect balance, emotionally direct yet controlled, and displaying a rhythmic elasticity that keeps it fresh and poignant even after repeated hearings. Here, as with "Rockin' Chair" and the Casa Loma "Sleepy Time," it is possible to discern that waiting inside this very good singer is a potentially great one.

By the beginning of 1933, both Mr. and Mrs. Norvo—already unofficially, as George T. Simon would soon dub them, Mr. and Mrs. Swing—were Whiteman alumni, out on their own. "I hate to say these things," said Norvo,

> but that all happened because Whiteman didn't pay her well. He was making $1,500 a week for her and paying her $250. Why? I guess he figured he'd discovered her and that's the way it should be. Funny thing was, he was crazy about her, adored her singing. Adored her as a person. They were a lot of fun together. She was the first one to call him "Pops." They had a lot of laughs, used to laugh together all the time.
>
> But there were no laughs when it came to asking her boss for a raise. "She told him, "Paul, I can't buy gowns and stuff and live on what you're paying me. I've got to have more, and I don't think I'm asking for anything that's unreasonable." All she was praying for was, say, $350 or $400. Not a helluva lot. But he wouldn't talk to her, and it ended up with her leaving.
>
> When she did, he really turned on her. He didn't want it known that he was getting so much for her and paying her so little. So he started putting it about that she was uncontrollable, temperamental, couldn't get along with anybody, not even her brothers. She bore that stigma all the years that we worked. Everybody had their dukes up whenever she walked in. If she tried to correct anything she knew was wrong, it was uphill all the way.
>
> The pity was, she missed a lot of things because of all that. Doors that just closed. She could have had that [promotion] that Kate Smith had—but she wasn't ever really bitter about it. Later, in the '40s, when Paul and Margaret Livingston had a place over in Bucks County, Pennsylvania, we used to see him over there once in a while. We'd meet him at Hurley's, on Sixth Avenue, and go out there and have steaks and things—even during the war when things were scarce—because he had Angus cattle.[20]

Given Norvo's own accounts of their often stormy marriage, and the reminiscences of musicians associated with them when they were "Mr. and Mrs. Swing," it seems unlikely that the reality was that simple. Mildred could be difficult and often demonstrated a temper of awesome violence. Reactions varied widely. Those who knew her best, who knew the warm, funny, and affectionate side of her, tended to suffer her rages more patiently than those (particularly sidemen in Norvo's later bands) who saw only that aspect of her.

Leaving Whiteman soon proved beneficial for both performers: April 8, 1933, found them both at the American Record Co. studios at 1776 Broadway, Mildred to do two titles with an all-star pickup group led by Tommy and Jimmy Dorsey, Red to record two solo xylophone specialties. With the Dorseys, tenor saxophonist Larry Binyon, and Bunny Berigan's trumpet spurring her on, Mildred charges into "Is That Religion?" with revival-meeting exuberance and no little wit. Berigan is all fireworks, and the rhythm section—pianist Fulton "Fidgy" McGrath, guitarist Dick McDonough, bassist Art Bernstein, and veteran drummer Stan King—pushes her harder than Whiteman's ever did.

If anything, Willard Robison's "Harlem Lullaby" is even more startling for what it shows of Mildred's ballad style. Gone almost without trace are the sentimental trappings and exaggerations of line and lyric so apparent on the Noone and early Whiteman performances; in their place is an even attack and a tight, fast vibrato which seems to balance the sweetness of her vocal quality.

Here, too, it's possible for the first time to really hear Mildred Bailey's unique vocal sound. Hers is a small voice, which has led many listeners to refer to it, erroneously, as high-pitched, in the manner of a little girl. It is, in fact, not particularly high at all: she takes "Harlem Lullaby," for example, in the key of C, beginning on a full, rounded middle C and dropping to a G below that at the end of the first eight bars. If the voice has to be labeled, it can be called a mezzo-soprano with something of a contralto range.

What sets the Bailey sound apart—and accounts for all the "little high voice" mislabeling—is a technical phenomenon, a matter of pure vocalism. In the world of concert and opera singing, a singer is recognized as possessing two voices in one: a lower voice, resonating in the chest cavity, and an upper one, whose sounding board is the bone structure of the face and skull (some theorists also speak of a "middle" voice, combining the two). Formal instruction trains singers to carry the "chest" voice, with its fuller and darker sound, as high as breath control and technique will permit, easing over the "break" as smoothly as possible into the more penetrating "head" resonance.

Mildred reversed the procedure, slipping into head voice relatively low in her range—or, expressed another way, bringing her head voice down to a point much lower than is ordinarily the case. As a result, even her middle notes possess the thinner, purer, and more focused upper-voice quality. Other singers had made relatively low breaks before her: but in such performers as Ethel Waters, for example, the tonal difference between the two voices is obvious, sometimes jarring, the upper coming across as a falsetto.

A possible, and intriguing, explanation for this quality in Mildred's singing comes from the singer herself. In an interview with Metronome's Barry Ulanov, she described going with her mother, a Coeur d'Alene Indian, to a reservation outside Spokane and hearing singing there.

> I don't know whether this music compares with jazz or the classics, but I do know that it offers a young singer a remarkable background and training. It takes a squeaky soprano and straightens out the clinkers that make it squeak; it removes the bass boom from the contralto voice, this Indian music does, because you have to sing an awful lot of notes to get by, and you've got to cover an awful range.[18]

Once the Bailey-Dorsey session was finished, it was Norvo's turn. Borrowing Jimmy Dorsey, plus McDonough, McGrath, and Bernstein, he recorded two original xylophone compositions, his own "Knockin' on Wood" and "Hole in the Wall."

Both are rightly identified, in the language of the day, as "rhythmic novelties" (Norvo himself referred to them as "little tinkly things"), their roots as much in the instrumental vaudeville tradition as in hot jazz. They also have much in common with some of the material being recorded around the same time by groups led by Norvo's friends Joe Venuti and Eddie Lang.

"Knockin' on Wood" and "Hole in the Wall," with their alternation of tempos, passages of swing punctuated with moments of technical display, also fit firmly into the style of such Jimmy Dorsey specialties as "Oodles of Noodles" and "Beebe," recorded by the saxophonist the previous summer. The first sixteen bars of "Knockin' On Wood," in fact, are built on an ascending chord sequence similar to that which opens "Beebe," heightening the sense of kinship. A second take of "Knockin' on Wood," moreover, reveals its careful structure; as with "Beebe" and "Oodles" there is little variation from take to take.

Brunswick recording director Jack Kapp clearly liked the "little tinkly things" and quickly offered the young xylophonist a return date. This time, however, Norvo had other things in mind. He asked Kapp's permission to do a couple of more ambitious numbers, including his adaptation of Beiderbecke's In a Mist. Kapp, whose record business instincts were defined by a sign in his office reading WHERE'S THE MELODY?, wasn't interested. He was all for another Norvo date—but only if it resulted in another pair of "tinkly things."[19]

Kapp's thinking was commercially sound. This was the Depression, after all, and recording had been among the hardest-hit of all businesses. There was little enough money around, Americans by the millions seemed to be saying; why spend it on records when you could stay home and hear all the music you wanted on the radio, and at no cost? Anybody making records for a living *had* to think sales, and records, for better or worse, were the living that Jack Kapp and his brother Dave had chosen.

In later years, such artists as Bing Crosby and Connie Boswell remembered Kapp as quite categorical on the subject of commercial potential. Many of the Boswell Sisters' most creative arrangements never found their way to record because Jack Kapp thought them too esoteric for the everyday record buyer. "He'd never had any musical training," his wife Frieda (or "Fritzie," as she was more familiarly known) said. "But he had instincts for what the public would accept. Not that he never made a mistake: but he could tell a good deal of the time."[20]

And perhaps, by his lights, he was right. From all reports, some of the Boswell Sisters' arrangements were, in the context of 1931–32, rather "far out," with shifting tonal centers and even more audacious readjustments of melody and harmony than found their way on to records. It's possible that such performances would not have sold. The conflict between the imperatives of creativity and those of the marketplace is, after all, eternal.

Red Norvo's plea for more latitude didn't fall entirely on deaf ears. He found a willing listener in Mortimer "Morty" Palitz, who had supervised the "Knockin' on Wood" session. What, precisely, did Red have in mind, he wanted to know.

Morty Palitz was as different a character from Jack Kapp as could be imagined. A formally trained and apparently proficient violinist, he was the nephew of Richard Altshuler, head of the American Record Company; ARC had brought Brunswick in 1931 from Warner Brothers, who had acquired it from the failing Brunswick-Balke-Collender Co. the previous year.[21]

Palitz spent evenings at Norvo's Forest Hills home, listening to the mallet compositions. "I want to record some of this," Norvo told his visitor. "You should," came the reply, "and we will." They did it, with all the trappings of an elaborately planned burglary, shortly after midnight on Tuesday, November 21, 1933. Sneaking in for the date, they must have made an unlikely-looking bunch, reminiscent of Alec Guinness and his ill-matched cronies in *The Ladykillers*: Palitz, in the lead, helping Norvo wheel in the giant xylo-marimba, and followed by bespectacled Benny Goodman, lugging a big bass clarinet, borrowed for the occasion, Art Bernstein groaning under the weight of his bass, and McDonough cradling his guitar like a baby.

The result was a pair of performances that even now, more than six decades later, sound fresh and musically challenging. If there is a standard by which timelessness in music can be measured, it's imbedded in these records. *In a Mist* is ideally suited to the sound of the big marimba, which draws from it a range of mood and tone color barely hinted at in Bix's own 1927 solo record. A more leisurely tempo allows Norvo to dig beneath its surface, mining an emotional complexity familiar from the composer's best-known cornet solos. Norvo uses his accompanists wisely and sparingly: a chordal underpinning here, a touch of rhythmic reinforcement there. At no time do their contributions intrude or in any way alter the character of the interpretation.

Perhaps the most creative feature of this reading lies in the fact that, using four mallets, he is only able to strike four notes at a time, whereas the original music regularly uses five- and six-note spreads to achieve its harmonic and melodic textures. Norvo obviously has thought long and hard about how to condense such passages into four voices without sacrificing color, weight, depth.

"It was just a matter of taste and common sense," he said in explanation. "All chords in certain positions on the instruments, no matter how complex, have four prominent notes, the ones the ear remembers. Those were the ones I chose. The ear retains a lot more than you might give it credit for: you have to know *what* it hears and *how* it hears, and try to work from that."

If any solo recording of *In a Mist* can be regarded as definitive it is this— making it all the more regrettable that this same combination of musicians didn't record the other three of Beiderbecke's four piano pieces, especially *Candlelights*, thematically and structurally the most ambitious.

If *In a Mist* is a revelation, Norvo's own "Dance of the Octopus" is a marvel. Its opening bars evoke a striking visual image, Jules Verne's *20,000 Leagues Under the Sea* set to music; Goodman's bass clarinet trills ominously while the marimba-xylophone introduces a four-mallet vamp based on open-voiced fourths and fifths. By drawing a felt-covered pick across his strings behind the bridge, McDonough meanwhile produces the effect of suffused light, glimpsed fitfully through stygian darkness.

It then opens out into an essay rich in thoughts, a musical octopus whose tentacles seem to reach in all directions at once: sections in and out of tempo, use of whole-tones and melodic passages with intriguing harmonic implications; contrapuntal contrary motion, unexpected turnings this way and that—with Goodman, McDonough, and Bernstein's bowed bass reinforcing, filling out, emphasizing.

As Gunther Schuller observes, if "Dance of the Octopus" is not quite atonal it is certainly tonally uncentered: "It is clearly the most advanced composition of the early thirties, falling almost outside the realm of jazz, and being in no sense a dance or 'entertainment' music."[22]

The following is a portion of Norvo's own transcription of "Dance of the Octopus," committed to paper sometime between 1960 and 1985. It represents the marimba's entry after an eight-bar introduction and carries through until the beginning of an interlude featuring the bass clarinet.

"Dance of the Octopus," marimba solo (bars 17 etseq.), 1933.

Perhaps most extraordinary, Norvo has said, the record represents only half of "Dance of the Octopus" as he wrote it. "Don't forget, we only had three minutes in those days, and when I got the signal that we were running out of time I just improvised an ending. Never even got into the next theme. And when the piece was published, Robbins [Music Co.] wanted it exactly as it had been on the record, so that was that."

Norvo was soon summoned to Kapp's office. "So we're sitting there, and he says, kind of calmly, 'So what are those things you made?' And I said, 'Well, it's a different kind of playing. It's four-hammer playing. I think it's a little more interesting than what we've been doing, and I thought it would be nice to do.' And he looks at me and says, 'I couldn't sell five of those records'—and while he's saying it, real slow, he's sitting there tearing up my contract. Tearing it up into little pieces. And then he hands it to me and says, 'Here's your contract. That's it, buddy. That's all.' It's funny how you react at times like that. I just said, 'Okay, thanks,' and left—and went home and cried."

Then, sheet by sheet, he flung into the fireplace the rest of the compositions he'd worked out for the xylophone-marimba during his KSTP days. Among them, he said, were adaptations of the three other Beiderbecke pieces and the original manuscript of "Dance of the Octopus," with its unrecorded second theme.

"Mildred came in and said, 'My God, what are you doing?' She tried to get it all out, but it burned. Thank God she was there: if it hadn't been for her I think I'd have gotten on a train and gone back to Chicago. I thought I'd remember the pieces. I remember thinking, 'Gee, I'll never forget those.' But you know, you get to doing other things, and your mind gets away. Those things just dis-integrated in my mind: in a couple of years I tried to remember them, but I'd forgotten them entirely."

Enter, at this point, John Henry Hammond. Young, aristocratic, not long out of Yale, he'd heard about Norvo's "Dance of the Octopus" record date from Artie Bernstein, who played 'cello as part of a once-a-week amateur string quartet in which Hammond played the viola. On a trip to England, where his sister Alice (later to become Mrs. Benny Goodman) was married to an English lord, he'd bought about twenty copies, which he distributed to strategically placed friends.

Widely known for his enthusiasms, Hammond had been producing records for more than a year, organizing dates with American jazzmen for issue on the English Parlophone label. Energetic, vocal, he seemed to be everywhere at once—especially in those places where jazz was being played. As Otis Ferguson has described it:

> You can tell him by the crew haircut, which bobs approximately in time to the music . . . Go forward to meet him and his head juts forward at you, slightly lowered as if to charge, but belying any seeming truculence by the open heartiness of his greeting. He is either spilling over with enthusiasm (Isn't it *swell?*) or only partly concealing his disgust (It's a *crime*, it stinks) . . . He slaps his knee, he clasps his head in his hands, he strides out of places or sits with his head too far back and claps too heavily.[23]

Hammond's passions included a keen sense of social justice, which found expression in a strong, often outspoken partiality for black jazzmen. But such convictions also left of room for appreciation of certain white musicians, among them Goodman, Bunny Berigan, Bud Freeman, Jack Teagarden—and Red Norvo and Mildred Bailey. On February 2, 1934, Hammond added Mildred to a session led by Goodman and featuring Coleman Hawkins on tenor. Then, that September 26, he put Norvo together with some like-minded colleagues for a straightforward, no-frills jazz date.

Red had been doing all right on his own. That March he'd recorded with Hoagy Carmichael and the Dorseys, playing a xylophone on "Moon Country" and vibes on "Judy." He'd become friends with Charlie Barnet, like Hammond a young man from a background of great wealth—but unlike Hammond a talented, highly capable musician. Barnet and Norvo had formed a band together: on those occasions when it worked, whichever of them had landed the job was the leader, the other taking his place in the ranks. On Barnet-led jobs, Norvo was the pianist: it beat lugging a xylophone from city to city.[24]

"Red Norvo and His Swing Septet," as Hammond billed the impromptu recording group, included Barnet on tenor sax, pianist Teddy Wilson, Artie Shaw on clarinet—and, on trombone, a short, dapper Iowan named Jack Jenney. He'd been with a number of good bands, including Isham Jones and Mal Hallet, and was with Phil Harris at the Hotel Pennsylvania Roof when Norvo heard him.

"That was a good band," he said. "They had a jazz trombone player, another guy. You know how bands will have regular guys who get the jazz book, but on the last set, when they're playing tunes, they'll let another guy play who plays pretty good. Well, during one of those things I'm sitting there and this other trombone player stands up and plays—and he completely *smeared* me. I didn't know what to make of this guy—thought he was much better than the guy who'd been playing all the jazz. So I got him for the date."

Jack Jenney was a stylistic original, who followed neither the calisthenic Miff Mole approach nor the richly blues-tinged Jack Teagarden way. Nor did he sound like J. C. Higginbotham, Benny Morton, Dickie Wells, or any of the other influential black players. His serenely lyrical style seemed anchored in his tone: dark, veiled, richly textured, it was at its best on brooding, introspective ballad material. Yet it had little in common with the ballad playing of Tommy Dorsey, which, however seamless, rarely approached the evocative depths that were Jenney's native habitat.

Jenney led his own band for a time at the end of the 1930s, and when it collapsed—inevitable consequence of mismanagement and lack of discipline—he joined Artie Shaw. For many, his rhapsodic eight-bar solo was the high point of Shaw's 1940 record of "Star Dust," surpassing even the leader's solo efforts and those of trumpeter Billy Butterfield.

Fellow-musicians admired Jenney for the ease with which he moved through the full range of his horn, including an unusually full and effortless high register. Frank Black, a respected arranger and, for a time, head of music at NBC, was widely quoted as telling colleagues he thought four musicians had "transformed American trombone playing." They were Dorsey, studio men Jack Lacey and Will Bradley, and Jack Jenney.[25]

Jenney opens "I Surrender Dear," on the first Norvo session, without introduction or preamble, and seems to be singing words rather than playing the notes of the melody. At one point in his second eight bars, he leaps the major seventh from C to his B♮ above with particular grace, resolving the phrase over the sixth to the third, then ending the entire episode on the fifth.

He gets "The Night Is Blue" (which he recorded again, with his own band, four years later) rolling with another richly hued melody statement, his sound similar to that of Duke Ellington's Puerto Rican–born valve trombonist, Juan Tizol (who was not, unlike Jenney, an improviser). What wonderful uses could Ellington have made of Jenney's ability to evoke so great a range of color and texture out of such simple material?

"The Night Is Blue" isn't Jenney's alone. Norvo, following him, uses a variety of trill patterns to construct sixteen wistful, yearning bars; so delicate is the mood that Charlie Barnet's entry in the bridge, however restrained, sounds bumptious by comparison.

Jack Jenney was only thirty-five when he died, in 1945, of peritonitis brought on by a ruptured pancreas. His death robbed jazz history of a uniquely expressive soloist.[26]

Hammond's investment in Mildred Bailey had also paid off handsomely. She contributes relaxed, confident vocals to three titles at Goodman's February 2 date: Hawkins spurs her on with some nudging, agitated obbligato playing on "Junk Man," but it's on the pop songs "Ol' Pappy" and "Emaline" that the singer really comes into her own. She sings Mitchell Parish's "Emaline" lyric unaltered— that is, without adapting its boy-proposing-to-girl format—but still manages to make it credible. Trombonist Sonny Lee, who'd played with Beiderbecke and Trumbauer in the 1920s, provides sixteen neatly turned bars reminiscent of his friend and fellow-Texan Jack Teagarden. Mildred overcomes the faux-primitive conceit of "Ol' Pappy" to deliver a lyric statement of some little tenderness; Hawkins, in response, follows with a chorus in his most rapturous vein.[27]

If Red Norvo's first date for Hammond produced memorable music, it was soon eclipsed by a second, on January 25, 1935. Fresh back from New Orleans, where he'd spent three weeks playing piano with Charlie Barnet at the Roosevelt Hotel, Norvo now had the distinctive presence of Bunny Berigan. They had met in Madison, Wisconsin, back in the '20s and had renewed the friendship in New York; with his trumpet added, the Swing Septet became an octet, Johnny Mince replacing Shaw on clarinet and Leon "Chu" Berry in for Barnet on tenor. At Hammond's urging, Red had substituted Gene Krupa for drummer Billy Gussak (later to win a kind of fame with Bill Haley's Comets on their hit record, "Rock Around the Clock").

But most significant, next to Berigan, was the replacement of Dick Mc-

Donough with the twenty-one-year-old guitar whiz George Van Eps, destined to become one of the most innovative figures in the history of his instrument (see chapter 21).

Norvo's all-star personnel delivered handsomely. Berry, a Hawkins disciple, had developed a fluid, rolling way of playing which could ignite any ensemble. Jenney, Mince, and Wilson were in fine form, and Krupa was indeed a rhythm section improvement. But above all there was twenty-five-year-old Berigan, playing at the peak of his powers: facility in all registers, power to spare, a fertile mind, and an innate sense of drama—all carried on a tone whose size and amplitude were nothing short of majestic. The sheer energy with which he tears into the intro and opening bars of "Honeysuckle Rose" imparts to the performance—and the entire date—a supercharged quality.

Where Bunny pushes the beat, Red seems to dance around it, at once percussive and delicate. Mince, taking over, reminds everyone that Benny Goodman was by no means alone in the hot clarinet field: he's fast, fluent, and incisive. Jenney and Berry split an equally intense chorus, the saxophonist dropping in one of his favorite little chromatically based tricks as he swings into his last eight bars.

But easily the highlight is the sixteen-bar Norvo–Van Eps duet that follows. Even the most faithful transcription will miss the delight of this few seconds of music, the faultless synchronization of intent and execution, between guitar and xylophone. It is joint music-making of a high order, seldom equaled in the history of jazz on record.[28]

"With All My Heart and Soul" is similar in mood and texture to "The Night Is Blue," opening with some Jenney ruminations and carrying through decorative Norvo, decorous Wilson, and flamboyant Berry to a supernal Berigan ending. On another date it might have been a peak, but on this session it serves largely to maintain an overall standard of performance.

"Bughouse," a Wilson-Norvo collaboration, is straightforward and fast, Berigan alternately swaggering and flashing, and the others in suitably muscular form. Indeed, if the session had stopped here, with just the three titles completed, it would still have been an important and memorable one. But there is also the transcendent "Blues in E Flat." No arrangement: just a string of solos, starting with a Norvo chorus over Bernstein's bowed bass. When Mills Music, for which John Hammond was working at the time, published this "Blues" (along with "Bughouse") as a stock orchestration, the first two and last two bars of Norvo's chorus appeared, in faithful transcription by leader-arranger Russ Case, as a four-bar piano introduction marked *solo quasi xylo*, "solo in the manner of a xylophone." Solos by Berigan, Berry, and Wilson follow, all leading into a stately and eloquent final ensemble.

The mood is cumulative, each twelve bars adding something—some insight, some new dimension—to the chorus preceding it. In that sense it's the very best that jazz as a shared language has to offer: a colloquy, in which each speaker grasps a central idea and carries it a step further by adding thoughts of his own.

The result is a performance rich in what B. H. Haggin has called "the immediacy of relation."[29]

Otis Ferguson, as usual, expressed it best: "I recommend for your pleasure and for posterity the 'Blues' . . . as being perfect in the collective feeling and very high and strange in the interludes of Norvo and Wilson, whose instruments come up through the pattern with the renewing sweetness of fresh-water springs."[30]

Mildred Bailey, meanwhile, seems to have been absent from recording studios for more than a year after her February 1934 Goodman session. But for her, as for her husband, it was a musically fertile period all the same. The Norvo home, on Pilgrim Circle in the Forest Hills section of Queens, had become something of a hot music *salon*: the couple entertained constantly, and impromptu sessions were frequent. Regular guests included Goodman and Berigan; singers Bessie Smith and Lee Wiley; pianists Teddy Wilson, Fats Waller, and Jess Stacy. Hammond and composer Alec Wilder were habitués, as were Joe and Sally Venuti, close friends; no surprise that the violinist included Red on a December 1934 band date for Muzak which also included New Orleans trumpeter Louis Prima.

It was at a Norvo-Bailey soiree, in early summer 1935, that Goodman and Wilson played a particularly rewarding set together, Mildred's cousin Carl Bellinger whacking out the rhythm with wire brushes. Hammond, hovering over the proceedings, waxed particularly enthusiastic, and for good reason; by common agreement, that evening marks the beginning of the Goodman Trio.

Bessie Smith seemed particularly fond of Mildred. They "used to laugh at each other and do this routine," Norvo told Whitney Balliett. "They were both big women, and when they saw each other one of them would say, 'Look, I've got this brand-new dress, but it's got too *big* for me, so why don't *you* take it?' And they'd both break up."[31]

In general, said Norvo, there was great closeness between white and black musicians, based on affection and mutual respect. He told of evenings spent at Fats Waller's Harlem home, with epic banquets prepared by the pianist's wife and mother-in-law. "Mildred's popularity at that time was enormous," he said. "She was a favorite of all the black singers, especially. They were crazy about her." One journalist, writing in a Pittsburgh newspaper, even asked in print, "Is Mildred Bailey colored or white?"—loosing a controversy which at one point threatened to take on major proportions.[32]

Mildred, said Norvo, was a quick and perceptive judge of music and musicians. After listening to Benny Goodman's newly formed band during one of its early broadcasts, she remarked to the clarinetist that the ensemble still lacked a sense of strong identity and suggested that he seek out more distinctive arrangements. "Go get a Harlem book" was her recommendation on one occasion. It was her prodding, said Norvo, that goaded Benny into buying scores from Jimmy Mundy, Edgar Sampson, and, perhaps most important, Fletcher Henderson.

Such keenness also extended to other singers. "John Hammond used to come over on Thursday nights and have dinner, then we'd all drive into town and catch the amateur shows at the Apollo Theatre," Norvo said. "After that we'd go round to different clubs. At one of them, just a little corner place, we heard this singer.

"We were sitting up on a little balcony. They had a piano, and this girl started to sing. Now we didn't know this girl from the man in the moon, and neither did John. But she sang one song, then started something else, and Mildred said, 'John, that girl's got it.' He says, 'What do you mean?' and she repeated it: 'I said, that girl can sing.' So he immediately got up and ran downstairs to find out who it was. Turned out her name was Billie Holiday."

Norvo's account differs from many others in its insistence that Hammond had never heard Billie before. If this is true, the encounter described above would have to have taken place early in 1933, before Hammond arranged for the singer, barely eighteen, to record two numbers with Goodman for Columbia, which throws a slightly different light on his claim to have "discovered" her. Additionally, Norvo said, once Hammond was aware of Billie Holiday, she became a passion with him—though the passion, from all accounts, was not reciprocated. Some have suggested that she actively disliked him.[33]

Perhaps even more telling is Norvo's version of a series of events concerning Billie Holiday's mother. It has been suggested, even by such reputable chroniclers as John Chilton, that Mildred's early appreciation of Billie quickly curdled into jealousy. Holiday, goes the story, was not only talented but beautiful as well, and Mildred felt it.

As Chilton tells in his book Billie's Blues, an urge to cut Billie down a bit drove Mildred to hire Sadie Fagan, her mother, as cook and maid at the Pilgrim Circle house. "Soon afterwards," said Chilton, "Mildred began telling anyone who would listen that she had hired a woman who was the laziest maid and the worst cook in the world combined—inevitably, the name of Sadie's daughter was mentioned in the tirade." Chilton goes on to assert that the two singers "never achieved any degree of friendship, but Red Norvo retained a lifelong admiration for Billie's singing."[34]

It seems curious that Chilton (unlike Stuart Nicholson, author of a 1994 Holiday biography) seems never to have solicited Norvo's account of these events, which affords a different perspective on the characters and behavior of those involved:

Every Thursday, when John would come out, he'd tell us how bad off Billie and her mother both were. So we finally took her mother on as a second maid—really just to give her some work. Remember, Mildred was doing very well at that time. She had a good radio show. She was making something like thirty-five hundred dollars a week, so she could afford to take Sadie on, just to get her over the rough parts. And it went on like that for a while. But finally something happened. It was the [regular] maid's day off, and we were having somebody—I forget who it was—out for dinner and wanted to prepare a turkey.

So we came home from New York and here she was—Sadie—out cold on the floor, and the turkey burned down to about the size of a squab. Just burned to nothing. She'd gotten into the booze. She'd done that a few times, but this was the worst. So I said, "Mildred, this is it. You can't keep doin' this. You have a maid and everything. You're trying to be kind to Billie, but it just won't work."

So I picked up Sadie, made some coffee for her, then got her in the car and drove her up to her place in Harlem. I let her out and she said, "I can make it from here." Nobody was home. So I left her there, and that was it. She knew she was fired. I'd told her so.

Yet from that instant Billie never liked Mildred, because her mother had told her a story. She'd say, "My mother used to love you, but she hated Mildred." And I'd say, "Billie, you've got it all wrong. You've gotta listen to me: I was the one who fired your mother, and I was the one that brought her home. If you're gonna hate someone it should be me." But she'd never do it: she always directed it at Mildred. Her mother told her, and that's what she believed.

I guess it was only natural. They were just starting to get their heads above water, you know, and then this happened. And her mother—well, I guess she'd had this spree, and was embarrassed. So she made a big thing about it, a big scene. And Billie never forgave or forgot. Mildred? She just accepted it. There was nothing she could have done, because she hadn't done anything wrong in the first place.

Norvo scoffed at any suggestion that Mildred was professionally jealous of Billie Holiday. "Jealous? Why? Of what? Mildred was making all this money. Billie? Well, what happened to her in her life, her career, hasn't got anything to do with the 'system' or 'discrimination' or any of that stuff. Billie simply never followed through on anything, never upheld anything that she started. She could only work on 52nd Street, mostly because she wasn't dependable for anything else."

In writer Dave Dexter's phrase, Mildred seemed to be the "first of the truly all-knowing hip chicks, blessed with an unerring ear and astonishing good taste in jazz." She was also apparently one of the first to employ the now-common musicians' device of turning language around—expressing approval, for example, by referring to something or someone as "bad."

"Mildred was good company," Dexter wrote. "She had a wild, unbridled sense of humor . . . [and] horrible, frightening periods of depression as well, and many a musician withered before her profanity when dark moods beset her."[35]

Stories of her outbursts, and of some of her more colorful domestic clashes with Norvo, are legion. In the most famous of them, Red returns from a fishing trip with Benny Goodman to find Mildred seething, her fury at his protracted absence barely controlled. A battle-royal soon ensues, each of them (Norvo's temper, though steadier, had its moments as well) throwing the other's prize possessions—a new hat, a mink stole, even pieces of furniture—into a roaring fireplace. "Damn it," she flings at him, a smirk starting to play about her mouth, "if you'd make my weight, I'd lick you."

"They fought," said George T. Simon. "No doubt about that. She could be tough. I remember one time, driving down with her from Syracuse or someplace, I made some mistake—I no longer know what it was—and she really let me have it. But Red was no patsy: he could be just as stubborn as she was, and wasn't afraid to let her have it if the situation called for that."

But basically, said Simon, "she was a warm, very caring person. Everything, I'm convinced, had to do with her weight. It made her feel very inferior, very insecure. And it wasn't a matter of eating: none of her brothers, and I knew them all, was heavy. It was glandular."[36]

Now, with all available evidence in, there's every indication Simon was right: that Mildred's extremes of temperament, as well as her problems with weight, were physiologically based, and that today's medicines and techniques might well have been able to bring both under control. But in 1935 such concepts were in their research infancy. Mildred Bailey, for all practical purposes, was on her own.

"When I first knew her with Whiteman she wasn't nearly as big as she was later," Norvo said. She went to early thyroid specialists, without much effect. She tried crash dieting—only to turn around and go on epic eating binges. Norvo remained convinced that the diabetes Mildred developed later, which contributed greatly to her early death, was a direct result of these extremes.

The problems of being an overweight and not particularly glamorous woman in a business dominated by superficial glamour is neither new nor particularly hard to understand. Kate Smith, who encountered similar difficulties early in her career, wrote with poignant candor of her desperation at having to play fat-girl roles on Broadway, forever the butt of comedians' jokes.

Fortunately, her path crossed that of Columbia Records executive Ted Collins in 1931; he became manager, friend, surrogate father, and cheerleader. "I'll pick your songs," she quoted him as saying, "and you sing 'em. You won't have anything else ever to worry about but just singing . . . We'll be millionaires before you know what to do with a million dollars. And all you'll have to do is sing— and follow my instructions."[37]

From the perspective of a later age, such an arrangement invites vilification. Worth noting is only that the relationship was acceptable to those affected by it, and that it worked. In Kate Smith's case it all but neutralized a sense of herself as an unwanted outsider; if now and then the demons came pounding on the walls, as inevitably they must have, the practical Collins was there to help fend them off.

Mildred Bailey had no comparable protector, and seems to have realized that at a very early point. Friends knew her as a remarkably capable and independent woman, able to speak her mind and exercise her will quite forcefully. "She could do everything," Norvo said. "She could keep house, she was a great cook. She could drive. She did all these things and lots more. What I mean to say is, she could take care of herself."

What she couldn't always take care of was her emotions—and that included her feelings about her husband. Red Norvo in those years was an exceptionally attractive man. Trim and genial, he radiated an impish charm which, coupled with good looks, made him all but irresistible to many women. When, in early 1935, he began working regularly on 52nd Street, first at the Hickory House and then at the Famous Door, he wasn't long in being noticed.

Mildred was only too aware of that. "Make no mistake," a woman who knew them both well in those years said on condition of anonymity, "Red had his women, and she was aware of it. But she couldn't compete. Not that way, anyway. I mean, how do you think she felt, carrying around all that weight, but unable to do anything about it?"

All the same, the relationship appeared to work, and for many friends and music business onlookers it seemed only a matter of time before Red Norvo and Mildred Bailey joined forces professionally as well as privately and began working together as a performing unit.

It did happen, and as is so often the case, it happened almost by accident, in a way neither Red nor Mildred could have foreseen.

27

Red Norvo and Mildred Bailey (2): Mr. and Mrs. Swing

"I was always impressed that [Mildred] sang a song without any seeming concern for the bar line. The phrase was the point. She had such a built-in sense of rhythm that she didn't have to announce the bar line to the audience. She had marvelous diction and . . . a quality of utter innocence. She always had this, no matter how she would imply other, less childlike things in some of her songs."

—Alec Wilder,
statement on National Public Radio, 1978

To hear Red Norvo tell it, he never had the slightest intention of leading his own band. "I didn't want to be a leader," he has insisted. "Never thought of myself that way; never had the slightest aspiration in that direction."

One of Norvo's many endearing traits, however, is a practical nature. "I did realize," he is wont to add, "that [leading a band] was a means for me to play what I wanted to play. To do things the way I wanted to do them. "So," he says with a characteristic shrug, "I did it."

In 1935 a mallet player whose specialty was jazz, no matter how gifted, had a limited selection of career choices. He could make a comfortable living as a radio percussionist, getting to do a hot solo now and then alongside his colorational function in orchestras led by Andre Kostelanetz, Victor Young, and other major names. He could work in Broadway pit orchestras; if he played good piano, as Norvo did, he could have all the society work he desired.

But most of that was faceless, anonymous, and—as many musicians have attested—often mind-numbing in its tedium. If you wanted to play things your own way, control your musical environment and *reach* people, there was nothing for it but to take the plunge with your own band. Large band, small band, whatever—just so it was yours.

Thus it came to pass that in the summer of 1935, after leading a series of extraordinary record dates under his own name, Red Norvo took his first band out on a location job, to the fashionable summer retreat of Bar Harbor, Maine.

It was a patched-together group. He'd kept a few arrangements from his co-leading days with Charlie Barnet, borrowed a few more from Harlem bandleader Teddy Hill. One of the trumpets, a twenty-one-year-old Juilliard alumnus named Eddie Sauter, had done some scoring; Red encouraged him to do more.

It was a good, young band, including such budding talents as trumpeters Chris Griffin and Salvador "Tutti" Camarata, trombonist Neil Reid, and saxophonists Tony Zimmers and Herbie Haymer. They were billed as "Rudy Vallee's New Yorkers": the famed crooner and radio star had most likely landed the job and taken a cut of the contracting fees.

"I swear," said Norvo, "the people in Bar Harbor had no idea what we were doing. None. But we didn't mind. We just enjoyed the band." They lived in two rented houses; sometime in June Mildred Bailey came up, the couple moved into a cottage not far away, and for a while at least it was a summer idyll, full of swimming, clambakes and horseplay on the beach, and lots of good music.[1]

Vallee himself arrived in person for the July 4 holiday weekend, leading a New York society band that included trumpeter Mickey Bloom and pianist Walter Gross, famed in later years as composer of the popular hit "Tenderly."

"Naturally, with him there, we had to go on first," Red said. "And I tell you, we just *barrelled*—that band really played. Herbie and Tony were really blowing. I mean *stomping!* Everything was ticking over just fine. But when we finished there wasn't too much applause. The audience, as I said, didn't have a clue what we were up to.

"As I came walking off the stage, there were Mickey and Walter talking to Vallee. Walter's jabbing his finger in Rudy's face, saying something like, 'If you think I'm going to go up on that stage after that band, you got another think coming!' That, at least, made me feel good."[2]

The Vallee band eventually went on, and of course carried the audience. Some things, as musicians well know, never change.

After that weekend, perhaps in part because of it, relations with the Bar Harbor management began to sour. The atmosphere deteriorated; often the band wasn't paid. For a while the men got by on their wits, fishing for flounder, digging clams at the beach, Neil Reid baking pies with apples stolen from a nearby orchard. But that couldn't last: eventually there was a showdown, and Red broke up the band, most of the sidemen returning to New York. He and Mildred stayed on a while, savoring what he later called "one of the nicer times of my life."

In the end he, too, went back—and right into a major bonanza. Hot music had found a home along West 52nd Street, or at least the block of it between Fifth and Sixth avenues lined with brownstones: during Prohibition their ground-level flats, usually entered under the front staircase, had provided ideal layouts for speakeasies. With repeal at the end of 1933, quite a few of them transformed themselves hastily into little clubs, usually featuring small live bands.

All accounts of those days agree that the first successful operation on "the Street" was the Onyx Club, originally located at number 35. Joe Helbock, its manager and guiding spirit, made it a popular hangout for musicians, especially the studio men who came around for drinks and after-hours jamming. It was hardly surprising to find quite a few of them among investors in the Onyx and other 52nd Street clubs.

In March of 1935, after the Onyx moved across the Street to number 72 (and survived after a potentially ruinous fire, thanks in no small measure to an infusion of capital from guitarist Carl Kress), a group of studio musicians took over the old location. Pianist-arranger Lennie Hayton was the main contributor, kicking in a thousand dollars, trailed by Jack Jenney, Manny Klein, Artie Bernstein, violinist Harry Bluestone, Jimmy Dorsey, Glenn Miller, and others. They called it the Famous Door.*

Flamboyant trumpeter Louis Prima, fresh in from New Orleans, was the lead-off attraction, with a little band that included Pee Wee Russell on clarinet. Newspaper columnists Louis Sobol and Ed Sullivan started touting the place, and by autumn competition was heating up. Every little joint on "the Street" had a band, and in order to keep its edge the Door would have to come up with something new and different.

It did, in the person of Red Norvo. He opened on September 29, leading a sextet: three horns, xylophone, bass, and guitar—no drums. It was something brand-new—tasteful, shapely, original. Above all, it was by 52nd Street standards remarkably subtle.

"All the other bands in the Street at that time were playing some form of 'dixieland,' jamming on tunes," Norvo has recalled. "That was fine, and people liked it. But it wasn't the way I wanted to go. There had to be a different way.

"I thought about it. Why have drums? Why have piano? We didn't need it. Maybe the horns could supply enough harmony. So we played a lot of riff things, swinging and close-harmony things—and all of it very soft."[3]

It was a band of colors and textures. Trumpeter Stew Pletcher, for example, worked much of the time with a felt hat over the bell of his horn, allowing him to blend more closely with tenor saxophonist Tony Zimmers (soon replaced by Herbie Haymer) and Don McCook's clarinet. Often they'd play quiet three-way backgrounds to the leader's xylophone and occasional piano solos. "I'd sing them

---

*According to several commentators there actually was a "famous" door, inscribed with many musicians' signatures. But it was nowhere to be found in the club itself, and there is now no clue as to its ultimate whereabouts.

a lead," Norvo has said, "and they'd find three parts real quick. They were good at that."

Pletcher, in particular, was a fast, heads-up musician. Child of wealth (his family owned the QRS company, makers of piano rolls and records), he'd been to Yale and had forsaken far more profitable career opportunities for the sake of playing hot trumpet. Records made by Yale-based groups in 1930 (some of them for QRS) show him to be firmly under the spell of Louis Armstrong, by this time a personal friend. His choruses on "Puttin' On the Ritz" and "Blue Again" are notable.

"He had a tremendous mind, very sharp," said Norvo. "You'd be riding with him in a bus—this was later, of course—and guys were reading. They'd get to a word they didn't know and they'd say, 'Hey, Stewie, what's this word?' Spell it for him. And he'd tell you what it was, derive it, tell you where it was from, how to pronounce it, everything. He was amazing."

The Famous Door job was an unqualified success. Teddy Wilson was the intermission pianist, and according to Norvo they did capacity business.[4]

"It wasn't long before all the kids from the East Side, the society kids, from the Stork Club and everything, 'discovered' the Famous Door," he said. "We were packed all the time, a big hit on the Street." It was the same all over again when they moved further west to John Popkin's Hickory House, then down to Jack Dempsey's Broadway restaurant.

The "swing sextet" was showing signs of catching on with a potentially lucrative audience; pianist Eddy Duchin, then leading the favored society and prom band, even took them along to play intermissions on his college dates. But such attention also led Norvo into a misstep that almost ended in disaster. Johnny Hyde, an agent with William Morris (and destined for a footnote in show business history through his romantic liaison with Marilyn Monroe), used the band's popularity with the East Side crowd to generate a booking at the Versailles, chief rival to El Morocco for the smart set.

"Well, we did it," Norvo said wryly. "And the minute we opened there I knew it was a mistake. The head waiter came up and kind of commanded us, 'Play a rhumba!' Just to show how stupid it seemed to us, Dave Barbour, our guitar player, said, kinda wide-eyed, 'What's that? What's a rhumba?' The guy said, 'Play a waltz!' Like a military officer, you know. And Dave says, 'Oh, is that the one that goes one, two, three?'

"I wound up playing mostly piano with it—you know, society style. Finally Johnny Hyde came around, and we settled things and got out of there."

Two batches of records, made in early 1936, give some idea what this remarkable little band must have sounded like on the job. Perhaps the best of them is the first, an otherwise forgotten pop item called "Gramercy Square." From the opening bars, arranger Sauter makes it plain that he's been listening—to Duke Ellington and to such other pioneer orchestrators as Bill Challis, Fud Livingston, and the underappreciated Bobby Van Eps.[5]

He shifts colors frequently, beginning with an episode in which his own mellophone seems to have the lead over the horns of Pletcher, Haymer, and

McCook, with Norvo providing spare, telling xylophone accompaniment. The variety continues: reed unisons with muted trumpet obbligato, xylophone over a four-horn chordal carpet, which in its close voicing and restrained sound seems to foreshadow the reed section of the soon-to-be-unveiled Norvo big band.

Several of the numbers ("Polly Wolly Doodle," "Decca Stomp," "The Wedding of Jack and Jill") include tight ensemble writing that anticipates the John Kirby Sextet, an Onyx favorite later in the decade—though 1936–37 recordings by trumpeter Frank Newton, vocalist Midge Williams, and others also seemed to be working in this direction.

Norvo's solos are lightly rhythmic, sometimes quite witty—as in "Decca Stomp," where he plays around engagingly with minor ninth chords. On six titles made February 26, he plays piano—and quite well. His full-chorus solo on "You Started Me Dreaming," for example, displays the notes-on-springs quality characteristic of Jess Stacy.

Pletcher shows himself very much his own man on trumpet, shaped by both Louis and Bix but speaking in his own voice. His full chorus on an up-tempo "Let Yourself Go" is steady and hot, riding confidently, and he's equally emphatic on "Oh! Lady Be Good," both from the March 16 session.

Best of all is a March 6 appearance on a radio show hosted by Paul Whiteman. They tear through "Clarinet Marmalade" and "I Never Knew" with a swing that's light yet driving, a wonder to hear. Red's solos, impeccably executed, spill out of him in a torrent; Sauter uses a wide textural palette—band riffs, reeds in octaves, brief but effective jam ensembles, xylophone-and-horns antiphonal passages. And the rhythm—just bassist Pete Peterson and guitarist Dave Barbour—seems to fly, to soar. Whiteman called it "seductive swing," and he was right on the mark.

Stew Pletcher's value to this mix can't be underestimated. "I always liked what Stew was thinking" was Norvo's way of putting it. Eddie Sauter thought Pletcher less an accomplished trumpet player in any technical sense than a talented and original jazz improviser. "I think I learned more jazz from Stewie," he told musician-interviewer Bill Kirchner, "because he would always try for things and [sometimes] miss, but it was his regrouping that made the thing [interesting] . . . To me most of the fun is reaching for something, not quite knowing where you're going, and if you miss, use it. I learned that from Stew, and I think that's an artistic precept."[6]

The Norvo band recorded again March 27, 1936, this time for RCA's low-priced Bluebird label and under Pletcher's nominal leadership. The trumpeter sings on each of the six titles, in a warm but unpolished manner, and delivers some engaging Armstrong-flavored playing on "Will I Ever Know?" Norvo's solo on "I Hope Gabriel Likes My Music" is particularly attractive, the band playing the melody lightly behind him.*

---

*Pletcher, in and out of music often, spent much of World War II working in the production department of the Douglas Aircraft Co. plant in Santa Monica, California. Later he played with a Los

* * *

Mildred Bailey, meanwhile, had been busy. She'd done a Columbia record date under her own name for John Hammond in September of 1935, backed by a racially mixed band: Chris Griffin (trumpet) and Chu Berry (tenor sax) the horns, a rhythm section of Teddy Wilson, Dick McDonough, Artie Bernstein, and drummer Eddie Dougherty, plus Norvo as guest soloist on one title, a somewhat too-fast reading of the old '20s favorite "When Day Is Done."

She's crisp and alert on "I'd Rather Listen to Your Eyes" but really comes into her own on "Someday Sweetheart." Teddy Wilson remembered engineers placing the singer ten to fifteen feet from the musicians, so the band would not swamp her voice. As a result, the pianist said, he hardly heard what she sang. "It's not as hard as it seems," he said years later. "You just go ahead and play but avoid important melody notes that you know the singer is doing. You didn't have to hear the singer to do that. You just had to know the song and where the openings were."[7]

(Mildred's phrasing, conception of the beat, placement of lyrics, all seem to bring up the old, ever frustrating question, "What is a 'jazz singer?' " Like Billie Holiday, recording at the same time under Hammond's aegis, and with Wilson and many of the same sidemen, Mildred works easily here as part of the band, the degree of interaction remaining consistently high. So, too, was the case on records by Connie Boswell [see chapter 15]. Yet chroniclers continue to hail Holiday as a "jazz singer," relegating Bailey and Boswell to secondary status with the grandly condescending phrase "jazz-influenced." What, if anything, is the difference? If recorded performances are any evidence, the answer is an emphatic "not much.")

In December 1935, Hammond tried an audacious move, recording Mildred Bailey backed by just four musicians: Bunny Berigan and alto saxophonist Johnny Hodges (the two had never worked together), Wilson, and bassist Grachan Moncur, half-brother of Al Cooper, with whom he co-founded the popular Savoy Sultans, house band at the famed Harlem ballroom. There was no drummer.

"Mildred thought I was crazy," Hammond said in his autobiography, *John Hammond on Record*, "but she went along with it." They did "Downhearted Blues" (which had been Bessie Smith's first issued recording) and three Fats Waller numbers, "Squeeze Me," "Willow Tree," and "Honeysuckle Rose."

Hammond was still making American records for English Parlophone, which was contractually linked with American Decca. "So I had to use what we called the broom closet, the tiny studio at 799 Seventh Avenue that Decca had already all but abandoned. It was an awful place—stuffy and cramped, with awful sound.

Angeles–based "dixieland" group led by guitarist-banjoist Hilton "Nappy" Lamare, featuring Brad Gowans on valve trombone, Zutty Singleton on drums, and clarinetist Johnny Costello, veteran of the Original Memphis Five–Indiana Five Circle in early-'20s New York. Stew Pletcher died in 1978, but his son Tom, an adept cornetist in the Bix Beiderbecke manner, carries on the family legacy.

But we were stuck with it." He'd been there with Berigan two days before to record four sides under Bud Freeman's leadership: bad acoustics or not, they had turned out magnificently; so, too, did these.

"Everybody did it for scale," Hammond said. "Mildred bitched like mad, because there were no royalties. But not for long, after she heard the results. It was a completely happy session. In fact Bunny told me it was one of the greatest sessions he'd ever played in."[8]

Mildred's singing on "Willow Tree," especially, seems to underscore Norvo's statement (to critic Whitney Balliett) that "she made you feel that she was not singing a song because she wanted you to hear how she could sing but to make you hear and value that song."[9]

Without drums or even guitar to firm up the rhythm, Wilson and bassist Moncur provide a loose, elastic accompaniment on all four titles. Berigan and Hodges respond in kind: neither feels compelled to pitch to the back row. Result: some of the most thoughtful, communicative, and utterly selfless playing either man ever put on record.

Mildred glides along easily, singing with her accompanists as well as over them, as comfortable and effective in such surroundings as was Holiday. The interaction between voice and trumpet on "Willow Tree," especially, is extraordinary. As she sings, Bunny answers with sympathetic comments, framing, outlining, deepening the effect, shaping phrases and even just individual notes to her inflections. When she sings the line "For me it rains and rains," he's right with her, in the same register, speaking in the same voice, and when, in her final eight bars, she brings that episode to its logical climax, Bunny's playing also takes on greater urgency and depth of feeling.[10]

"As to the whiteness or the blackness of this kind of jazz," critic Irving Kolodin wrote in 1980, when the "whites can't play the blues" argument was gaining ground in some quarters, "both colors are subordinate to the redness of the blood in them."[11]

In mid-1936, following the Versailles debacle, Norvo got an offer too good to overlook: a summer season in the Palm Room of New York's high-profile Commodore Hotel. It meant expanding the band to thirteen pieces, adding two trumpets, trombone, two alto saxes, piano, and drums, and it meant getting Eddie Sauter to generate scores for the new instrumentation.

"Don't use the full band all the time," Norvo told him. "Just what you need. We're going to study the men; we're going to find out what one does better than, say, some other saxophone player or some other trumpet player, and we'll use those qualities."[12]

It was a concept not unlike that of Duke Ellington—and, for many listeners, with no less satisfying results. From the start, Norvo seemed to have a firm idea of what kind of band he wanted, and the ability to enlist his young arranger in achieving it. "The xylophone didn't have the loud, screeching potential that a trumpet would have, or a trombone or clarinet or even a tenor or alto," he said. "I'd have to approach the music in an entirely different way." So he carried over to the larger instrumentation the balance, the sense of color and dynamics, that had characterized the Famous Door band.

Playing nightly at the Commodore allowed Norvo and Sauter to work on the sound, shape it, assess its strengths and weaknesses. One factor, for example, was Frank Simeone's lead alto sax sound. Norvo called it a "jug" tone: soft, breathy, almost introverted, it lent a kind of *sotto voce* quality to the reeds, ideal accompaniment for the xylophone solos.

"If there is a better white band than Red Norvo's in New York," George Frazier proclaimed in *Down Beat*, in a roundup of the New York jazz scene, "I didn't get around to hear it." He praised its "perfect taste" and "absolutely original style," Pletcher's trumpet solos, Russ Jenner's trombone, and Maurice "Moe" Purtill's drumming. But, he added, "the real thrill of Norvo's band is its complete ease. Not even Benny Goodman has it."[13]

One of the first lessons Norvo learned at the Commodore was that Sauter, given too much time to fool around with an arrangement, tended to overwrite. (It was a weakness which developed into a real liability in his work several years later for Benny Goodman and reached fullest flower in some of his scores for the large orchestra he co-led with fellow-arranger Bill Finegan in the '50s.)

Norvo soon found an antidote. "I made him work fast," he has recalled. "Pushed him. Made him work at short notice. Gave him deadlines, so he wouldn't have time to mess with a score and fiddle with it and change it. Otherwise, if he took much time, he'd overdo it. But if he worked fast, against the clock, there was no time—he had to keep things simple. Eddie was a great talent, but he just needed that supervision."

Norvo's idea for the band, shared by Sauter, was "strictly contrapuntal. When he started to write, I said, 'I want every part to be as interesting as the lead part. I don't want a [Fletcher] Henderson thing where it goes right down the line, three lead lines and parts filled in. Use the clarinet. Use mutes. Use voicings, different colors together. Write for the guys, not for yourself.'"

It took time, and several personnel shifts, for all the pieces to fall into place. But even that first summer at the Commodore, as big band historian George T. Simon has written, the band "underplayed its music, injecting into the unique Eddie Sauter scores a tremendous but subdued excitement—the sort of excitement one experiences not during the culmination of something great but in *anticipation* [emphasis added] of something great. It would swing so subtly and so softly and so charmingly through chorus after chorus of exquisite solos and light, moving ensembles, always threatening to erupt while holding the listener mesmerized, until at long last, when he was about ready to scream, 'Let me up!' it would charge off into one of its exhilarating musical climaxes."[14]

Even the genteel John Hammond, who had judged the Famous Door group "too genteel for comfort," had to vouchsafe that the Commodore band was "surprisingly satisfactory." He singled out as particularly noteworthy a couple of broadcasts they'd done with Bunny Berigan sitting in as guest soloist—and scolded Norvo for failure "to feature his xylophone enough to stamp his band as the unique group it is."[15]

The sound at this early stage is preserved on four titles recorded for Brunswick on August 26, 1936. The charm and subtlety Simon remembered so vividly are present above all on a Sauter arrangement of James P. Johnson's "A Porter's Love Song to a Chambermaid." It's quite original—and rather subversive, for being so creative within what appears to be a standardized form. To the unwary ear this can sound like little more than a good, disciplined band and capable vocalist (Mildred) working through an engaging pop tune. But more careful listening yields riches.

From the opening, with Pletcher's muted trumpet carrying the melody over a reed section that sounds (thanks to Simeone's distinctive lead) as though it's playing underwater, and Norvo embellishing discreetly, it's clear that great care has gone into sound and tonal balance. Norvo works freely behind Mildred, as Sauter's reed scoring pulls things together into a unified compositional whole.

In the following chorus, unison reeds carry the melody for eight bars, with straight-muted trumpets playing a complementary riff; then Slats Long, a capable (and alas, all-but-forgotten) clarinetist, solos over saxophones, with Norvo commenting sparely; Herbie Haymer's tenor takes the next eight, with kicks from the brass and Moe Purtill's drums; the last episode is a tutti—but instead of boosting things to a climax it throttles back gradually to bring on Norvo. His solo, over clarinets and cup-muted brass, winds things down to a quiet, elegant little resolution punctuated by a two-note "that's all" played by xylophone and reeds.

Though none of the other three sides made that day comes up quite to the level of "A Porter's Love Song," moments of grace abound. The interplay between xylophone and band in the first chorus of "It All Begins and Ends With You" is striking, as is Mildred's relaxed vocal. "I Know That You Know," taken very fast, features Red in a fleet solo which could have been transferred to Benny Goodman's clarinet without alteration; on "Picture Me Without You" (not to be confused with Cole Porter's "A Picture of Me Without You"), the xylophone adds droll comments as Mildred phrases easily over a Simeone-led reed cushion.

After finishing at the Commodore they hit the road, doing one-nighters in New England and an extended run in Syracuse, New York. Slats Long saw no reason to travel: he was doing nicely as a New York freelancer, and his wife worked at the Roxy Theatre. They replaced him with a clarinetist who would shortly become one of the band's true assets. Hank d'Amico was from Rochester, had worked around Chicago in the early '30s, and at the time he joined Norvo had just been with Paul Specht's orchestra. He brought technique, purity of tone, and an approach whose inner delicacy was very much its own. Lead trumpeter Bill Hyland, said Norvo, "could play a high C *pianissimo*, which was an amazing feat in those days. No trumpet player then could do that. So Sauter incorporated that, just as he incorporated d'Amico's sound."

Though Mildred sang on the August 26 record date and again on October 19 ("It's Love I'm After," "Now That Summer Is Gone"), she was not yet working with the band. Norvo's nominal female vocalist at the time, in fact, was Nancy Flake (who soon married drummer Purtill). Norvo and his wife became "Mr. and Mrs. Swing" in the eyes—and ears—of the public largely through a chain of circumstances set in motion by Don Roth, owner of Chicago's Blackhawk Restaurant.

The Blackhawk in the 1920s had been home for a procession of bands, including that of Ben Pollack. It had a radio wire and got regular coverage in the press. "Roth had first heard us on the air, broadcasting from Syracuse," said Norvo. "He came east, came in to hear us on a Saturday night. The place was packed, and people were just crazy about the band." So too, apparently, was Roth. To his ears, this controlled, modulated ensemble sound would be perfect for the restaurant's main dining room. The Norvo band opened at the Blackhawk in October 1936, doing seven nights a week and Sunday matinees.

Mildred, said Red, "was determined to go with me one way or the other." After some wrangling, the Chicago-based Music Corporation of America (MCA), handling the Blackhawk booking, agreed to slot her into the floor show, along with actor-comedian Rollo Vincent and a dance team.

She'd been on the radio in Chicago a lot during her Whiteman days and still had a large and loyal following, which now began agitating to hear her. Before long, station WGN was pressuring MCA and the Blackhawk management to include her in broadcasts from the restaurant. They finally agreed, and from the very first song on the very first night she was a hit.

"That's how it started, this thing of working together regularly," Norvo said. "Just being on the air. People started expecting it, I guess. It just—well, it just happened." They wound up doing twenty-eight radio shows a week, and attracting national attention. Things got so comfortable that the couple made themselves at home in Chicago, eventually selling their Forest Hills house.

Their second Tuesday night *Swing Concert* broadcast from the Blackhawk, aired February 9, 1937, has been preserved on acetate discs. Mildred sings Willard Robison's " 'Round My Old Deserted Farm" in a richly textured setting, evoking the twin themes of loneliness and rural life with touching simplicity. After a two-chorus Herbie Haymer feature on "Indiana," Mildred returns with Robison's "Harlem Lullaby." As usual with a Sauter score, the impression is of a carefully sculpted musical environment, components meshed easily and precisely. The show ends with a loosely swinging instrumental version of "Love Me or Leave Me," Norvo's solo dancing over the rhythm; Haymer, Pletcher, and d'Amico are strong and assured, the final ensemble a model of how to generate intensity without the loud flagwaver endings that had become a swing band cliché.

Mildred's choice of two songs by Willard Robison was no accident but a gesture of respect and real affinity. Born in the small town of Shelbina, Missouri, September 18, 1894, Robison was one of a handful of songwriter-performers who evoked American life outside the big cities with an eloquence often comparable to fellow-Missourian Thomas Hart Benton's paintings of the same years.

His most memorable songs are those on small-town and rural themes— " 'Round My Old Deserted Farm," "Guess I'll Go Back Home This Summer," or the haunting "Deep Summer Music." His "Old Folks" describes a venerable and beloved small-town character. Even the near-bathos of "A Cottage for Sale" is a portrait of a bucolic idyll gone wrong. "Harlem Lullaby" and "Don't Smoke in

Bed," though set in the city, seem saturated with longing for simpler places and ways.

Without stretching the point, there is something not only of Benton but of Edward Hopper to Robison—as if *Early Sunday Morning, Drug Store,* or even the loneliness of *Room in New York* or *Nighthawks* had been redistilled as a thirty-two-bar popular song. Only Hoagy Carmichael and Johnny Mercer, products of similar environments (though in different parts of the country), compare to Robison in this regard. But there are differences: "Moon Country," a Carmichael-Mercer collaboration, is evocative of small-town America, but with more affection than pain—reminiscent, it might be said, more of Norman Rockwell than of Hopper.

Unlike Mercer and Carmichael, moreover, Robison was not in any but a marginal sense a jazz musician; but his songs lent themselves to, and have been favored by, many outstanding jazz instrumentalists and vocalists through the years, among them Jack Teagarden, Lee Wiley, and, latterly, the elegant and much-underappreciated Barbara Lea.

Willard Robison came to New York in the mid-1920s and, with Paul Whiteman's assistance, soon established himself as a radio entertainer. Accompanied by his "Deep River Orchestra" (arrangements by Whiteman alumni William Grant Still and Bill Challis), he played the piano and sang in an unaffected style which soon won him a large and faithful listenership.

But bad judgment, reinforced by alcohol, soon unraveled what success he'd achieved. In later years, despite the efforts of admiring colleagues to help him, he drifted gradually into obscurity. Often he'd sell the same song to two publishers, raising enough money to keep the whiskey flowing. Every now and then he'd try to cash in on a prevailing trend and turn out a song meant for the hit parade. It never worked, and he'd return to the pastoral visions which were his true strength.

Willard Robison died, broke and forgotten by all but a few loyal friends, in 1968. Of the entire music community in which he had spent his lifetime, only a handful of musicians, including Eddie Condon, Pee Wee Russell, and Lee Wiley, attended his funeral. Johnny Mercer, unable to come, sent flowers and a note, which summed up the feelings of many: "Thanks for all the Deep Summer Music. Sweet dreams."[16]

Mildred Bailey remained a major Robison cheerleader, performing and plugging his songs at every opportunity. Her 1938 record of his "Barrelhouse Music" remains unsurpassed. She brought to him—as to Carmichael, whom she also favored—a warmth and unaffected directness that allows them to breathe, to be what they are without apology. However easy it would be to condescend to a line such as "The pray'r-meeting bell lends a heartache to the spell,/'Round my old deserted farm," Mildred never does. Instead, she trusts its honesty and sincerity—and her performance vindicates that trust handsomely.

She sang Robison's and Carmichael's songs, Johnny Mercer said, "because they were absolutely the best jazz composers writing at that time. She recognized that."[17]

The band, meanwhile, continued to evolve. Sauter began taking theory and composition lessons from Louis Gruenberg at Chicago Music College. In Norvo's words, he "really took to it. Absorbed like a madman." Red kept playing with the sound, even trying the marimba on some numbers. But its lower pitch put it right in the middle of the reed section's most frequently used register, and it tended to be lost in all but the most lightly scored passages.[18]

The combination of Norvo's virtuosity, Sauter's arrangements, Mildred's vocals, and the restrained ensemble swing began to pay off. The Norvo band's popularity grew, its reputation spreading apace. Musicians, alerted, went out of their way to listen. "Even as late as the '60s, guys would come up to me and say things like 'Oh, that band—I used to lie awake at night and listen to it on the radio.' Things like that," Norvo said. "Made me feel good."

His sidemen shared the enthusiasm. "That was the greatest musical band there ever was," drummer Maurice Purtill told George T. Simon. "It was the only band I ever heard of where, after work, the guys would ask to rehearse."[19]

Records made during the Blackhawk run more than justify such superlatives. For example there's Sauter's arrangement of "Smoke Dreams," from their first date, January 8, 1937. One of the lesser fruits of the songwriting partnership of Arthur Freed and Nacio Herb Brown, the tune had appeared on the soundtrack of *After the Thin Man*, MGM's first of several sequels to the popular William Powell–Myrna Loy detective thriller. But Sauter's arrangement is a makeover, a complete transformation.

Why did they choose this song for such treatment? There have been lots of guesses, but in the end only the arrangement matters: it's truly a curio, and something of a curate's egg besides. Norvo refers to it as an exercise in polytonality. It's not: as Gunther Schuller correctly observes, that aspect is little more than a layering of harmonic elements.

Sauter's introduction, for example, is built around a descending series of momentary dissonances—seconds, mainly—with a general tonality of A♭, while Norvo juxtaposes a simple eight-note figure in G-major. But Sauter so manages to blur the passage's tonal center that pianist Joe Liss has to "feed" Mildred the F♮ on which she begins her vocal.

(Sauter echoes some of the same textures and tonal effects, albeit in more coherent form, in arrangements for Benny Goodman and Woody Herman in the '40s. His "Time Waits for No One," written for Herman but unrecorded until a 1987 performance by tenor saxophonist Loren Schoenberg's orchestra, is a fine representative example.)

The second Chicago date, on March 22, 1937, was even better; among its riches were, in the words of the late publisher Neil McCaffrey, "three of the most precious minutes from the Swing Era." He referred to "Remember," arrangement and performance, and he was right on the mark. From Frank Simeone's opening concert G♯ to the major ninth (an E♭ in the key of D♭) on which it ends, it is its own kind of perfection: a balance of tonality, execution, structure, and tempo which suits the Berlin song, establishes an atmosphere, and delivers on its promises.[20]

By writing his saxophones (augmented to four with the addition of Charles

Lamphere) low, the arranger emphasizes warmth rather than brilliance. His arrangement of "It Can Happen to You," recorded before the band left New York, has Simeone beginning his opening melody statement on a G below middle C; that's the alto saxophone's first-line low E♮, only a tritone (augmented fourth) above its lowest note.

"Remember" opens with the reeds stating the melody in the key of D. Stew Pletcher, taking the first chorus bridge on trumpet, resolves his solo to a provocative concert G♯, the ninth of the F♯7 chord leading into the final eight bars. It's a felicitous and appropriately Beiderbeckian touch.

Norvo plays his full-chorus solo in F, over a series of background figures which suggest darker, more dissonant textures without actually entering them. The result is consonant with the song's bittersweet quality ("but you forgot to remember"), and when the key shifts again, this time down a major third to D♭, the effect only broadens.

The other three titles done that day also show the Norvo orchestra in top form. "I Would Do Anything for You" is as close as Sauter seemed interested in getting to the standard section-against-section formula of Fletcher Henderson–type arranging. But even this has its moments: a considered Pletcher half-chorus; Norvo and Hank d'Amico together in a clarinet-and-mallet tandem that owes not a thing to Goodman and Lionel Hampton; Norvo over a series of band riffs, each episode ending with a zany, not-quite-over-the-top xylophone break.

"Jivin' the Jeep" is based on the chords of "Nagasaki" without the melody and is basically an up-tempo xylophone feature. Red sets the pace with two flashing, cascading choruses, their technical mastery, harmonic sophistication, and rhythmic assurance leaving no doubt as to his supremacy in the narrow world of jazz mallet playing.

Some discussion of Lionel Hampton is useful here. Both men were at an early peak, Norvo with his own band and Hampton as a member of Benny Goodman's Quartet. It was also around this time that the latter began making records under his own name for Victor. The fact that they played different instruments (Norvo didn't take up the vibraharp on a full-time basis until the following decade) is in itself a distinction between them. But more significant, Hampton came to mallet playing from a background as a drummer, where Norvo was a pianist. The emphasis in Lionel's solos, even on such melodic material as his August 16, 1937, "I Surrender Dear," tends to be rhythmic, leaning heavily on repeated-riff patterns and incisive attack. Norvo, by contrast, is always thinking melodically and is harmonically by far the more venturesome of the two. That he could also play with great swing is beyond question, as countless records will attest.

"Jivin' the Jeep," however fast ($\quarternote = 276$), finds him fashioning coherent, attractive melodic shapes. The long phrases spanning the bridges of both his choruses could be transferred easily to clarinet with no loss of content or character. Pletcher also delivers a shapely muted chorus.

If "Remember" is the main course in this musical banquet, Sauter's arrangement of "Liza" must be adjudged the master chef's exquisite dessert. Its tonally dense opening ensemble is in E♭, with middle-register brass and reeds achieving a rounded warmth virtually unknown in larger bands of the time. Sauter keeps his saxes low and dark in providing a chordal carpet well out of Norvo's way during the xylophone solo.

Red mines an especially rich melodic lode here; even the eighth-note triplet passages of the second and last eight bars, perhaps vaudevillian in other hands, make sense. Things move up to the brighter key of G, where brass "kicks" elicit a particularly avid solo from Haymer—then back down to F (itself an unusual move away from coloristic intensity) for a well-realized final tutti.

Part of the rounded ensemble sound, Eddie Sauter later observed, may have had to do with the small, dead Chicago studio in which the band recorded. But these musicians also knew how to use dynamics. "People wanted to talk [in restaurants and clubs]," Sauter told saxophonist Bill Kirchner, "so the emphasis was on playing softly, and we really did play soft whether you did it on a clarinet or a saxophone didn't make very much difference. It was more difficult to play soft on a trumpet. But that was a specialty of Red's: they used to call us the subtle swing."[21]

But George T. Simon, writing in Metronome, noted a change in the band over its months at the Blackhawk. It was a large room, he added in recollection, and "gradually the band was forced to blow more blatantly and obviously for the larger and generally squarer customers. 'Red is offering,' I wrote rather sadly in 1937, 'more and more slam-bang arrangements with much gusto and forte.' "[22]

His concern was premature. Records made back in New York that July, especially after Louis Mucci took Hyland's place as lead trumpet, show the ensemble tonality to be, if anything, richer and more subtle. Mucci, a remarkable player, imparted to the brass a velour quality, much like what might have resulted had the trumpets all been playing fluegelhorns.

By the time the Blackhawk job ended, Red and Mildred were a performing team. Her vocals enhanced the band both musically and commercially—and there's every indication that, for a while at least, the Norvo-Bailey-Sauter triumvirate was on to something precious and rare.

"When I hear a new song I immediately get a definite idea of how I want to sing it and how the entire arrangement should sound," Mildred told Simon. "And without fail, Eddie comes through with just the kind of arrangement I'd been dreaming of—only better!"[23]

However, from the start there was personal friction within both the leadership and the band. With the perspective conferred by hindsight, it now seems likely that they were all results, direct or indirect, of storms that had raged within Mildred Bailey all her life.

Musicians who worked for "Mr. and Mrs. Swing" between 1937 and 1939 varied in their assessments of what they saw and heard. Some saw Mildred as temperamental, meddlesome, constantly fomenting discord. "She was a disrupting influence," said saxophonist Maurice "Hawk" Kogan, who worked with the band for several months in 1938. "Always interfering. Never made any attempt to be friendly."[24]

Tenor saxophonist Jerry Jerome, who joined in early 1938, during the second Hotel Commodore engagement, described flare-ups at rehearsals, where "they sure would chop each other up a bit. There really wasn't much public display, at least not that I saw. But Mildred—she could be tough sometimes."[25]

Even George T. Simon, forever her fan, admitted that the singer "often asserted herself too emphatically, creating tensions that were anathema for a band that relied so much on a relaxed approach."[26]

Mildred Bailey's musicianship and musical taste were beyond question. Of all the singers, black or white, working in the 1930s, few could even approach the balance of phrasing, rhythm, intonation, and overall musical intelligence she brought to each performance, however modest the song. As trumpeter Lyle "Rusty" Dedrick, a later Norvo sideman, put it: "She had a magic. So many people down the line, so many singers, benefited from her, owe debts to her—and they don't even know it."[27]

From all indications a sense of deep personal insecurity, disgust at her weight and lack of physical appeal, often transformed her expressions of musical will into extreme behavior. "Red Norvo was convinced that she was a genius and treated her like one," their friend novelist Bucklin Moon wrote in a perceptive eulogy. But he, too, remembered "too many tantrums, too many little betrayals, and on her part probably the feeling that no man, not even Red, liked her appearance any more than she did."[28]

"She wanted children," said Norvo, "and couldn't have them. I've always thought that was a shame. She was so good with them. We even talked about adopting a child, but it never came to anything. And by then it was—well, kind of too late. It should've been done earlier."

But earlier Mildred was still hoping she could bear a child of her own—until a doctor told her that the glandular condition at least partly responsible for her weight also made that impossible. "I've often wondered," Norvo has reflected, "whether if we'd gone ahead and adopted, the way other people we knew did, it might have been different."[29]

Mildred's natural maternal instinct asserted itself in lavish displays of affection for Red, for friends and even for her two pet dachshunds, Hans and Fritz. Trombonist Eddie Bert remembered with both sympathy and incredulity Mildred's inconsolable grief when one of the dogs ate some rat poison at a theatre in Fort Wayne, Indiana, and died.

And, all agreed, she truly loved Red Norvo. Even later, when the marriage had, in one writer's words, "run out of options," her passion for him remained undimmed. But by then it was far too late. "She never got the family, the home life, the security, the man she loved, the kids," said Bert's wife, Mollie, a close friend.[30]

"Mr. and Mrs. Swing" carried on together throughout 1938. The records, if never quite up to the standard of "Remember," remained nonetheless excellent. Sauter's introduction to "I Kiss Your Hand, Madame," unissued until 1993, spotlights contrary reed motion against the brass, underpinned by George Wettling's rat-a-tat drum ostinato.

In late summer the band opened at the Palomar Ballroom in Los Angeles, where Benny Goodman's smash engagement of 1935 had ushered in what had soon come to be known as the "Swing Era." Goodman had just finished a run there and had arranged to make some Victor records before moving on to Dallas. John Hammond was also in town and, as usual, had wasted no time cobbling together a Brunswick record date under Teddy Wilson's leadership, including some of Benny's men.

According to at least one account it was to be a debut session for a new, unknown vibraphonist who, Hammond assured everyone, was "simply mahvelous, even better than Lionel." But the man never showed up, and Hammond importuned Norvo, newly arrived in town, to fill in. Ever-affable, Red agreed—though he hadn't played vibes in a recording studio since doing "Judy," with Hoagy Carmichael, more than three years before.

At the end of the August 29 Wilson band date, Norvo joined the pianist, trumpeter Harry James, and bassist John Simmons for an impromptu quartet performance of "Ain't Misbehavin'." It wasn't issued, but a test pressing found its way into an early '80s Time-Life *Giants of Jazz* package. Predictably, he sounds a little less than totally sure of his ground: by this time vibes were being manufactured with a damper pedal to keep a struck note from ringing indefinitely, but Norvo still hadn't used the device enough to be completely at home with it. Also, the slightly different layout of the keyboard (discussed at length in the preceding chapter) promoted caution.

He solved most of the problems by playing the vibraharp as if it had been a xylophone: he didn't use the motor that produced the instrument's vibrato, ignored the damper pedal; his lines, behind James and in solo, are light and spare.

Playing with Norvo and Wilson seemed to draw from James some of the most restrained and balanced playing he'd committed to record. The trumpeter, whose solos with Goodman too often veered toward bravura display, brought to this first "Ain't Misbehavin' " a sense of line and a feel for team interplay.

A week later they were back, this time with Red playing xylophone, for a session featuring two excellent performances of Waller tunes (a buoyant "Honeysuckle Rose" and a solid final take of "Ain't Misbehavin' ") and one great one, the two-sided slow D♭ blues issued as "Just a Mood."

It's hardly excessive or controversial to note that none of these three men had shown any particular affinity for the blues. James, product of the Southwest, was perhaps most at home in the idiom; but Wilson, though born in Texas, was if anything rather closer to the more melody-oriented approach of Bix, Red Nichols, Miff Mole, and the other white New Yorkers. One of the profound experiences of his early career, he said in later years, was hearing the Beiderbecke-Trumbauer "Singin' the Blues," with its nuanced emotions, sense of restraint, and almost classical orderliness of structure.[31]

Norvo could play the blues effectively, as he had demonstrated on the 1935 "Blues in E Flat," but from a largely melodic approach, as though the twelve-bar structure were the vessel in which a particularly interesting song was housed. Indeed, there is little conventional "blues feeling" to "Just a Mood"—at least not in the sense of what Louis Armstrong or Jack Teagarden, Johnny Hodges or Bunny Berigan, brought to their blues performances. Instead there is something equally effective, just what the number's parenthetical subtitle implies: a "blue mood." James and Wilson take four choruses each, and Norvo three, before they come together for a final ensemble.

James handles his opening solo with authority, building a statement at once earthy and fanciful; it's interesting to note that his fourth chorus begins with a familiar James D♭ blues figure, used elsewhere to generally flamboyant effect (such as in his "One O'Clock Jump" solo in Goodman's 1938 Carnegie Hall concert). Here, admirably, it proceeds as a logical and gripping development of what precedes it. Harry James may lack the majesty and emotional depth of Bunny Berigan (compare his work here with Berigan's contributions to "Blues in E Flat," or the 1935 "Nothin' but the Blues," under Gene Gifford's leadership), but he achieves his own kind of grace.

Most compelling is the melodic kinship between Wilson and Norvo. Again and again on this date, the work of one seems to meld into that of the other—as if, in Don DeMicheal's phrase, "a single mind had been guiding both sets of hands." From that viewpoint Norvo's three choruses seem an extension and further development of Wilson's four. Both are technically assured, balanced, modestly decorative, the melodic core always discernible.

Norvo's notes hang on the air, Japanese lanterns strung above the placid surface of a lake on a hot summer night. Particularly arresting moments include the ascending phrase with which Norvo climbs out of the D♭7 chord in bars 3–4 of his second chorus, and the declarative passage in octaves, almost Hines-like, which opens his third. Anyone seeking an index to Red Norvo's creative supremacy in those years need look no further than this sublimely realized thirty-six bars.

"Honeysuckle Rose" is only slightly less impressive. In eloquent corroboration of DeMicheal's "one set of hands" remark, there's a fleeting moment, at the beginning of the first solo coming out of James's opening statement, when the ear is not sure whether the player is Wilson or Norvo. So perfectly matched are their manners of conception and execution, so crystalline the touch of each, that the sounds seem to proceed from the same source. In this case it's Red, who has been playing counterlines to Harry's lead in much the manner often employed by Wilson in partnering Benny Goodman in the Trio and Quartet. It doesn't take too great a leap to imagine the xylophone line as the pianist's right hand, with the left providing solid rhythmic support.

The Norvo band continued making excellent records throughout 1938, with "Russian Lullaby," "Just You, Just Me," and "Nuances by Norvo" among the standouts. Mildred contributes superior vocals to "There's a Lull in My Life," "Please Be Kind," and an affecting reading of Irving Berlin's "I Used to Be Color Blind."

But there was trouble in view. A series of performances done for World Transcriptions in the latter part of the year hints at disruption of the extraordinary inner balance of a year earlier. The band seems ill at ease, even on such intriguing scores (mostly by pianist Bill Miller) as "Tea Time," "I'd Climb the Highest Mountain" (with an especially good tenor solo by "Hawk" Kogan), and "Uptown Conversation," a colloquy which, judging by its chord structure, must have taken place on the corner of 141st Street and Lenox Avenue, outside the Savoy Ballroom, the "Home of Happy Feet."

Though Norvo solos, as ever, excellently, and Mildred's vocals range from genial ("Step Aside, Jump's Here") to truly moving ("A Cigarette and a Silhouette"), there's something rather too brash, something a bit off center, about these performances. Some of it may have to do with George Wettling: during these very months, the drummer was recording often for Milt Gabler's fledgling Commodore label, in company with Bud Freeman, Pee Wee Russell, and other old pals. The records established him beyond challenge as a master of the free-wheeling "Chicago style" hot music in which Commodore specialized.

He'd been just as effective playing for Bunny Berigan's new band, driving hard on "Frankie and Johnny," "The Prisoner's Song," and other spirited records. But in the more restrained context of Norvo's band he sometimes seems over-bearing, his use of rims, cymbals, and snare drum rimshots inappropriate. When they played Frank Dailey's Meadowbrook in September, George T. Simon scarcely hid his concern in remarking that "This band used to be noted for its 'soft, subtle swing.' Remember? Well, during the past couple of years the 'soft' has disap-peared almost completely, the 'subtle' has been minimized, but the 'swing' re-mains—and how!" It was understandable, he said: you could play softly and with restraint in hotel dining rooms, but out on the road, where you had to be heard across a crowded ballroom, it was impossible not to lose the fine edge in matters of dynamics and ensemble balance.[32]

Norvo seemed to feature himself less and less—which some have read as a sign that the ensemble balance no longer favored the lighter sound and texture of the xylophone. By October most of the original sidemen had jumped ship, leaving only bassist Pete Peterson, and around year's end Norvo announced he was breaking up the band.

"Some of the boys were ill with colds and flu," he said in a Down Beat item, "and I let them take a rest—a sort of winter vacation—while Mildred and I worked solo at the Famous Door . . . There is absolutely no truth in the story that there was any trouble among the boys." But the article also mentioned that Mildred Bailey would not be appearing with a reorganized Norvo band when it opened January 13 at Philadelphia's Ben Franklin Hotel.[33]

On the same page, Down Beat ran the full text of a letter from former Norvo band manager Irv Tonkin, blaming the breakup squarely on the singer. He de-scribed tension and barely suppressed anger among sidemen at Bailey's constant interference with her husband's running of the band. "If I were really to give my opinion and the opinion of the others about her, it would not be fit to print," Tonkin wrote. "In my estimation, she is one of the most unreasonable persons in the band business today."[34]

Saxophonist "Hawk" Kogan concurred. "I was with that band for months, and she never once said hello to me," he said. "I know [pianist] Bill Miller hated her. I heard that after I left, when they went into the Famous Door, George Wettling had enough one night and got up, spit in her face, and walked out."[35]

(In an unpublished memoir, Kogan held Bailey and Norvo equally responsible for the band's internal tensions. As featured tenor soloist, "Hawkie" was a favorite with the crowds. "Whenever I got up and played a jazz solo, the resultant applause was thunderous, dwarfing everyone else's," he wrote. But "they"—by which he clearly means Mildred and Red—were not pleased, and after George Berg took over the second tenor chair, he inherited more and more of Kogan's solos. Things reached critical mass at a ballroom in Chicago, when a black customer came to the stand expressly to praise Kogan—only to be turned away rudely by Norvo. "The guy's face fell, and with a look of disgust he turned and walked away," the saxophonist wrote. "I resolved then and there to get the hell out of this revolting scene the first chance I got.")[36]

Norvo stubbornly denied such accusations. Mildred was a musical perfectionist, he said; friction only arose because "she wanted things right—anybody does who really tries. You can find fault with anything. You work seven days a week for a couple of years, knocking your head against the wall, you can be unhappy with everything."

Irv Tonkin may have been accurate in singling Red out as "more wrapped up in his playing than in his organization . . . Personally, he's a swell guy and would make a real leader if it were not for the continual harassing he receives from Mildred." She may have been an asset, he wrote, but "Red could have accomplished more if he had had the organization to himself and completely forgot [sic] Mildred."[37]

His appraisal, however plausible, fails to address what is surely the real dilemma: an intelligent and discerning man, Red Norvo was well aware of his wife's conflicts and must have seen their disruptive influence on the day-to-day life of his band. Moreover, his own personal courage and artistic integrity, demonstrated countless times over many years, make it obvious that this was no preoccupied, henpecked husband.

At the outset, beginning with the enchanted months at the Blackhawk, it actually seemed that he could keep all the potentially unstable elements in balance. But Mildred was proving too volatile, and it is not hard to imagine her agitating for an ever-greater piece of the featured time. Of thirty-three Brunswick titles recorded by the band under Norvo's name between January 21 and September 12, 1938, only five are instrumentals. Mildred sings on twenty-four, male vocalist Terry Allen on four. This tally doesn't take into account nineteen additional titles done with the band in the same period but issued on Vocalion under her name.

Compared with just about any other band (except, of course, those led by singers), that's a lot of emphasis on vocals, leading to the conclusion that, in the public perception at least, the Norvo orchestra had become a showcase for Mildred Bailey. To be sure, the book contained many instrumentals which were played on the job; but the very fact that they were not recorded, while so many vocals were (the split in 1937 had been almost exactly fifty-fifty), attests to the role Mildred Bailey had come to play.

Had she been a lesser singer, it might have been easier to challenge her prominence on artistic grounds. But with the exceptions of Lee Wiley and Connie Boswell, who operated in slightly different contexts (and neither of whom appeared regularly with a dance band), there was not another white singer of the era—and only a handful among black vocalists—to rival her. Few of the Norvo-Bailey records of 1937–38, moreover, are less than superb.[38]

But this is the band that had recorded "Remember," one of the most memorable performances of its age. With that in mind, allocation of so much recorded space to Bailey vocals, no matter how good, must be viewed as a sacrifice. Without stretching the point too far, it's useful to imagine what would have happened if twenty-four out of thirty-three titles recorded by Duke Ellington's Orchestra in a like period had been devoted to vocals, however excellent, by Ivie Anderson, leaving only five instrumentals. The results might have been musically satisfying, but the loss to music history would have been incalculable.

It's arguable, too, if ironic, that the best Bailey vocals of the time are to be found on records with groups other than the Norvo band. She's close to her peak on "Thanks for the Memory," "Lover, Come Back to Me," and two other titles made in January 1938, with a small group including d'Amico, Peterson, and trumpeter Jimmy Blake from the Norvo band, plus Teddy Wilson, tenor saxophonist Chu Berry, guitarist Allan Reuss, and the nonpareil Dave Tough on drums.

A series of dates later that year with the John Kirby Sextet, plus Norvo, was also successful, with a fast-paced "St. Louis Blues" a highlight. Just how good Mildred could be is obvious on "What Shall I Say?," recorded with this group on January 18, 1939. Sidestepping the song's potential for self-pity (Billie Holiday's version, made two weeks later, all but drowns in it), she delivers the lyric as a declaration of stoic faith, heartbreaking in its simplicity.

If a remake of "Downhearted Blues" misses the immediacy of her 1935 version, a group of blues titles made March 16, 1939, with a rhythm section dominated by pianist Mary Lou Williams, gets right to the heart of the matter. Both "Gulf Coast Blues" and "You Don't Know My Mind Blues" show Mildred quite at home in the idiom, dealing easily with its melodic and rhythmic language. When she sings, in the former title, "The mailman passed me by/But he didn't leave me no news," the effect may not be as grave as that left by Bessie Smith's reading of the line, but it speaks powerfully nonetheless. Mildred, in singing the blues, slips easily into the persona of the genial hot mama, the woman who's been around, cautioning all and sundry that a man's got "a mouth full of 'gimme,' and a hand full of 'much obliged.' "[39]

Mildred Bailey probably never made a bad record; she made many that were excellent and quite a few considerably better, even, than that. Norvo remained steadfast in his belief that she was the preeminent singer of her time. "Billie? She wasn't even near in the same ballpark as Mildred. Took her forever to learn a tune; she only had a six-note range, and all she sang was a minor third, and she sang that flat. When it came to singing, really singing, Ethel Waters cut the shit out of her—and Mildred did, too."

But as the '30s came to a close, her personal life—and her increasingly precarious health—seemed to hamper her fortunes as a performer. Though apparently not a regular member of Norvo's 1939 band, she was on some of its records, including an excellent "There'll Never Be Another You"—not the similarly titled and better-known Harry Warren standard but an appealing and undeservedly obscure ballad by with a lyric by Russian-born Peter Tinturin, composer of the Billie Holiday favorite "Foolin' Myself."

That band broke up in late 1939, and Norvo tried again the following year, this time with a young personnel sparked by the dynamic lead trumpet of eighteen-year-old Conrad Gozzo, with Lyle "Rusty" Dedrick handling the jazz solos. For a moment, listening to the youngsters playing the Eddie Sauter arrangements (and some new ones in a similar vein by Dedrick and guitarist Allen Hanlon), quite a few fans—George T. Simon among them—found themselves hoping that Red had returned to the "soft, subtle swing" concept of three years before.

"It was really a gas," said the leader. "We'd go into Atlantic City opposite some of those Mack trucks, the big sissy [fancy] bands with singers and all, and gosh! They'd be over there and they'd see this little band of ours, about ten-eleven pieces, and we'd get swinging—and by God, they'd be over on our side before the night was over!"

That group had started larger, but the economics of running a band at that precarious time had quickly forced Norvo to scale down. "With Red you learned by example," Dedrick said. "His playing, his onstand demeanor—he was my first teacher. He taught me, all of us, to swing. He gave you a freedom, allowed you to develop a self-confidence. Not consciously: they just happened. You know, we'd get to an out chorus and he'd just half-turn and say, 'Walk it!' and by his very gestures—his head, his feet, everything—we knew what he meant. And you'd better know—we *walked* it."

Dedrick at that time was living at the Century Hotel in midtown Manhattan, and often went to the Norvos' apartment at number 1 Horatio Street, in the Village, to use their piano. "They were always fighting, in their personal life and on the bandstand, too. Red—well, it's true that he treated her with kid gloves. Things got pretty fierce sometimes, but it seemed that he'd sooner back down in a conflict than challenge her. It was as if he were somehow in awe of her, though there was no need to be.

"But I'll tell you: when she started to sing—well, it just resolved all problems, forgave all sins. However trite this sounds, she sang like an angel."[40]

Writer Dave Dexter, hearing the band in mid-1940, declared in *Down Beat* that the record companies "are to be blamed for being so blind to an outfit with tremendous possibilities."[41]

Though full of young, and as yet unknown, men—Dedrick and Gozzo, saxophonists Ray Anderson and Ted Goddard, pianist Lionel Prouting—it played with cohesion and authority. "It was all the more surprising," said Dedrick, "because we didn't rehearse. We just *sounded* as though we did.

"It was that way in [Claude] Thornhill's band, too. I remember once going into the Forrest [Hotel] bar and somebody saying, 'You guys sounded sensational on the radio last night, but I wouldn't want to play with that band.' And I naturally asked why, because it was wonderful and I loved it. And he said, 'Because you guys must rehearse all the time.' Because the band *sounded* so rehearsed. But that's the thing—it didn't. Well, that's the way it was with Red's band, too.

"We had the charts, but we also did a lot of head arrangements. Above all it was Red: I don't recall him ever saying, 'Well, this should be that way,' or whatever. It was by example. He was Mister Swing, and he inspired you."[42]

But it didn't last long. Norvo maintained that he dissolved this band to break a contractual stranglehold the Music Corporation of America had on him. Characteristically, he channeled several of his best men, Dedrick and Gozzo and trombonist Bob Jenney (brother of Jack) among them, into a brand-new band being formed by an old pal, pianist Claude Thornhill. Like the Norvo band, Thornhill's was an ensemble based not on power but on taste and subtlety, with a musically interesting book written by the pianist himself, his close friend Bill Borden, and a talented young Californian named Gil Evans.

In late 1941, refusing to concede defeat, Norvo fielded yet another band, his largest (six brass, five reeds) yet, with an all-new book by Johnny Thompson. Again, he used Mildred on recordings and an assortment of other singers on one-nighters.

They made just two commercial records, four sides, before the American Federation of Musicians (AFM) recording ban went into effect. But a collection of live performances, recorded off the air the night of January 4, 1942, and preserved on acetate discs by trombonist Eddie Bert, shows this band at the peak of its brief life.

The larger instrumentation, including a full compliment of woodwind doublers, gives arranger Thompson a wide tonal palette, and he makes abundant use of it. Linear and contrapuntal writing for English horn, flute, and bass clarinet lend color and textural variety to ballad readings of "Star Dust" and "Don't Take Your Love From Me." Trumpets and trombones exploit the Shastock, an adjustable cup mute which allows the player to achieve an unusually tight sound, compact and non-penetrating. On a magnificent "April in Paris," Norvo solos over *sotto voce* baritone sax, as the woodwinds weave gossamer strands of countermelody around him.

These recordings constitute a watershed—both for Norvo, in that they bring to an expressive peak a process begun with Sauter in 1936, and for big band scoring in general. They are an antidote to the monolithic, riff-based writing still dominant in the dance band field and point the way to later exploitations of timbre and texture by Gil Evans, Gerry Mulligan, John Carisi, and others.

One of this band's commercial records, a performance of Alec Wilder's "I'll Be Around," enjoys the added benefit of a vocal by Mildred. By any measure it is a classic: that it went unissued for more than three decades remains inexplicable. "When I was a young man," Wilder said on a 1978 radio program, "the first singer I was aware of was Ethel Waters, and all the songs I wrote were for her, though I never knew her and only met her formally years later." Then he met Mildred, he said, "and I began to think of her when I wrote songs."[43]

The marriage, meanwhile, was disintegrating by stages. As Norvo put it to Whitney Balliett, "the car skids a little before it stops, the carburetor skips a little before it quits. I'd move out and we would go back together and I'd move out again. It lasted twelve years before we were divorced."[44]

Their careers traveled increasingly separate paths, but paths that kept crossing. Mildred continued to record and play major theatre and hotel jobs with Red; when she landed her own regular radio show, Friday nights on CBS, he was a frequent guest, along with Teddy Wilson, Roy Eldridge, and other notable jazzmen.

An Armed Forces Radio Service *One Night Stand* broadcast of January 17, 1945, reunited the couple with Wilson and Benny Goodman for a "Downhearted Blues" which perhaps surpasses even the 1935 effort as evidence of what can happen when superior jazz minds blend in common effort.

Norvo continued to go from strength to strength as a soloist and creative force. Every time he led a band, however short its life, its members remembered it with a respect and affection rare among the generally cynical, seen-it-all work-a-day musicians. "He could take even the most raw material and get it going," said trombonist Eddie Bert. "He could mold any band into a good-sounding unit, and do it with the lightest touch."[45]

"What's the difference between a bull and a band?" goes a popular musicians' joke still making the rounds after more than half a century. Answer: "With a bull the horns are in front and the asshole is in the back." Many leaders, even top ones, fit that general description in the eyes of their sidemen.

But not Red Norvo. "Red's was a wonderful band to be in," said saxophonist Jerry Jerome. "You could play and be heard without playing hard. He had one of the most interesting tenor books I'd ever seen, if not the most interesting: modulations, introductions, all kinds of devices that I hadn't seen in my playing up to that point.

"And Red would open things up on the job. If a guy was really blowing, he'd let him blow. The whole band swung in a restrained, seductive way. A good, kind of coochie [sexy] feel. A dance feel. And Red—well, it was his personality, his way of doing things, that made it that way. He was unique."[46]

Otis Ferguson, once again, found the right words to describe Norvo's leadership style. For that most perceptive of writers, Red was

> sunny, patient and almost shy; yet confident enough and flexible enough of mind so that he would rather hire an unknown kid with talent than the Best Man In The Field, even on the same terms, and when he got the men, he would hold his own way with deference, leading and bringing

out rather than shoving around—add this and you may see why the Norvo style is always evident no matter who plays with him, men more famous or men not famous at all.[47]

Rusty Dedrick concurred. "I think my time with Red Norvo was the best thing that ever happened to me professionally," he said. "If my being a trumpet player in this life was inevitable, preordained, then it follows that working with and for him was part of that destiny. It certainly did me greater benefit than any other single experience I've had in the field."[48]

The early months of World War II made it clear that running a big band wasn't going to get any easier: not only were economic circumstances against it, but Norvo, in common with many other leaders, kept losing bright young players to the draft. It was harder all the time to find appropriate replacements.

So, ever-practical, and with a reported five-thousand-dollar loan from Joe Glaser (astonishing, considering the agent-manager's reputation for tight-fistedness), he bought his contract back from the William Morris Agency, broke things down to an octet and opened again at the Famous Door, spotlighting such young talents as Eddie Bert, trumpeter Milton "Shorty" Rogers, reedman Aaron Sachs, and, as pianist, a young man from the Boston suburbs with a fine arranging touch. Within a very short time Ralph Burns would be a leading force in his field, arranging for Woody Herman's big and exciting band—a band which would, for a while at least, feature Red Norvo.

Norvo's career, which had already peaked higher than those of many of his peers, was in a major sense just beginning. His switch to vibes, his time in the '40s with Herman and as a member of perhaps the most exciting of all Benny Goodman Sextets, constitute a story in themselves. Perhaps even more, the great Norvo Trio of postwar years, with Tal Farlow and Charles Mingus, propelled the concept of small-group improvised music to new and vertiginous heights.

His later work merely confirms his preeminence as one of the most consistently original and creative of all jazz soloists. Gunther Schuller puts it bluntly: he was "among the very best artists jazz has had to offer." Listeners today still marvel at the harmonic sophistication which enabled Norvo to absorb the complexities of bebop with no apparent effort. Unlike Artie Shaw and others who went at the transformation with sometimes fevered determination, Norvo's concepts of rhythm, harmony, and melody seemed universal, unbound by time, place, or fashion.[49]

Mildred Bailey's story is, alas, quite different. Things went well enough professionally during the war years: regularly featured on radio, she recorded with Benny Goodman's band, made a series of excellent twelve-inch V-discs for U.S. servicemen, and was reunited from time to time with Norvo. But ill health—diabetes, liver and heart trouble, and a variety of lesser ailments—continued to plague her.

She was Goodman's first guest after he recaptured the NBC *Camel Caravan* radio series in 1939, and started recording regularly with his band shortly thereafter—

often singing on arrangements by her old friend Eddie Sauter. The records cast her in the role of band singer and are all the more remarkable for it: her single choruses on "I Thought About You" and "Darn That Dream," for example, elevate the band-singing genre in a way equaled only by Billie Holiday's contribution to the 1938 Artie Shaw record of "Any Old Time."

Mildred's chorus, like Holiday's on the Shaw record, is so well conceived and executed, and so effectively transfigures the substance of the song, as to constitute an independent artistic statement. (It's a small irony that both singers were replaced by Helen Forrest, respected among band vocalists of the time, but a player, as it were, in another artistic ballpark.)

She gets things moving right from the start of "Peace, Brother!" (arrangement by Sauter): her rhythmic placement of the two title words is like a three-note phrase snapped out by a particularly swinging trumpet player, galvanizing the whole band into action.

But Mildred's doctor was adamant: if she didn't limit her musical activities she'd be in real danger. Her last appearance with Goodman was on an October 7 *Camel Caravan*: she contributed a spirited revival of "Shoutin' in That Amen Corner," which she'd recorded with the Dorseys in 1933, and a reading of "The Lamp Is Low," based on a theme from Maurice Ravel's *Pavane pour une infante défunte.*[50]

It is music to stop the heart—spiritual, transcendent, combining vocal and arrangement to achieve a texture richly layered with yearning, hope, and eternal faith. It affords the briefest of hints of what treasures Mildred Bailey could have found within herself had she survived.

"There were lots of times when it seemed she'd have been happier with the life of a housewife than being Mildred Bailey," Mollie Bert has said. "You know—children, a regular life, a loving husband. She loved just watching the way Eddie and I were with each other. She was the most maternal woman I've ever met."[51]

There were moments of happiness, bursts of impulsive generosity—toward friends and total strangers alike. But more frequent, Mollie has recalled, were those moments when illness, despair, or both all but overwhelmed her.

Through it all she continued to perform. "She was usually working," said Bucklin Moon, "though not always when and where she ought to have been, and she never lacked for a tight little following who loved and admired her. But somehow just about the time you figured she had it made finally, it all started to come undone again."[52]

She made more records, some of them superb. An outstanding example is a March 1, 1947, broadcast version of the Buddy Kaye–Billy Reid ballad "I'll Close My Eyes," accompanied by pianist Ellis Larkins and a trio and released on a V-disc. It's not stretching a point to hear in Mildred's simple, unaffected delivery of the lyric an echo of Mollie Bert's contention that she "never stopped loving Red."

I'll close my eyes to everything that's gay,
If you're not there to share each lovely day.

And through the years,
Those moments when we're apart,
I'll close my eyes and see you with my heart.[53]

Mildred and Red were divorced in 1945 but remained friends even after Norvo remarried, this time to Eve Rogers, sister of trumpeter Shorty. Mildred became devoted to the couple's two children, playing the doting aunt with a passion and showering them with gifts. Now and then she'd seem to fade from view, as exhaustion and illness took their toll; but just as quickly she'd be back, winning new admirers with singing which seemed deeper and more meaningful at each hearing.

She opened at Barney Josephson's Café Society Downtown, to glowing reviews—including a near-ecstatic piece in Time magazine. At such times she seldom had very far to look for courtiers and acolytes, ever ready to fawn and flatter. Real friends, however, seemed in shorter supply.

"Everyone used her," Mollie Bert told the author. "Believe me when I say that people, those people who hung around her in those days, took her for whatever they could get. All that hugging and kissing. But when she needed them, needed love and affection and true friends, where were they?"

There were nights, the trombonist's wife added, when Mildred was sick enough to have no business performing. But she went on anyway. "One time at Café Society—Uptown, I think this was—she was running a 103° fever, and could hardly stand, let alone sing. And there was this heckler right in front of her, a drunk, saying really awful things to her.

"She was lying down between shows, and I was putting cold compresses on her head and the back of her neck. I think she'd done two shows and just wanted to skip the third, the late one. So she said to the manager, I forget his name, 'Can I please go home?' And what did he say? 'You can talk, can't you?' If she could talk she could go on. So she did the show—I don't know to this day how she got through it."[54]

Perhaps leaving Manhattan for a more relaxed rural environment would help. She bought an old farm in Stormville, New York, about ten miles southeast of Poughkeepsie. Though heavily mortgaged, it provided a real retreat, much-needed tranquility for her and her beloved dachshunds.

"She loved the farm," record producer Irving Townsend wrote, "and struggled to keep it when everything seemed to be collapsing around her, and long after she could no longer sing, she lived there with the puppies, alternating between rage that so many she had helped could forget her so easily and bewildered delight that a neighbor who hardly knew her had befriended her."[55]

Her illnesses became more serious. In 1950, by now weakened and only a shadow of her former size, she contracted pneumonia and was rushed to St. Francis Hospital in Poughkeepsie. Alec Wilder, Eddie Sauter, and Morty Palitz drove up to see her and were appalled at what they found.

"She was in a public ward, full of depressing old ladies," Wilder said. "She couldn't stand it, but she had no money for a private room. Word must have reached [Frank] Sinatra, who had never even met her, but [who] had such an enormous respect for her that within two hours she was out of that ward and in a private room, with everything she wanted."[56]

She seemed to improve, and soon was on her way home. In the meantime, said Wilder, Bing Crosby had quietly picked up the mortgage on the farm, so she could live there securely, free of anxiety about money.

Back on her feet, she went to California for an April 12, 1950, appearance on Bing's network radio show. There's real affection in the tone of their remarks to one another, and when she sings "Georgia on My Mind," backed by John Scott Trotter's orchestra, the years seem to roll away. No illness, no bitterness, no heartbreak: "Bails" is home at last.

Crosby joins her for "I've Got the World on a String"—and Trotter's arrangement secures the common bond between them with a richly scored quotation from Bix's In a Mist. The two singers toss phrases and quips back and forth like two old pals, once again playing catch in the Rinker family back yard.

While in Los Angeles, and probably thanks to Crosby, she made what were to be her last records: two sides for Decca backed by a studio band led by Vic Schoen. The second of these was "Blue Prelude," a 1933 standard with an eerily prescient lyric by Gordon Jenkins:

Won't be long till my song will be thru',
'Cause I know I'm on my last go-round.
All the love I could steal, beg or borrow
Wouldn't heal all this pain in my soul.
What is love but a prelude to sorrow,
With a heartbreak ahead for your goal?[57]

Shortly after arriving home, Mildred appeared on another network show, Refreshment Time, hosted by singer Morton Downey, who had also gotten his professional start with Paul Whiteman. After a thoughtful reading of "Lover, Come Back to Me," she talks to Downey about the farm, about her four new dachshund puppies—"Linda, Spotty, Susan, and Pocahontas, the Indian puppy"—and unveils Alec Wilder's brand-new "It's So Peaceful in the Country."

Wilder had written it for her one summer a few years before, when there was not yet a farm, and Mildred had been stuck in her East 31st Street apartment, longing to get away but held prisoner by work. "I wrote it in the back room of the Algonquin," he said, "on a piano that produced so much dust when I sneezed that I couldn't see the keys."[58]

When, in the last eight bars, she sings "The only place to be/The place for you and me," her conviction is obvious and touching. But by this time her health was so precarious, body and mind so tired from fighting illness and personal demons, that she had little resistance. While working in a club in Detroit she collapsed and returned home, and on Wednesday, December 12, 1951, during a hospital checkup in Poughkeepsie, she suffered a heart attack and died in her sleep.

All her life Mildred Bailey had been a woman in conflict: conflict with herself about her looks, her weight. Conflict with a world in which the success and security she sought could come so close, only to crumble in her grasp. Conflict with colleagues who failed to understand the artistic standard to which she worked.

There is little doubt that Mildred's inability to curb the more extreme expressions of her frustration cost her dearly. As Bucklin Moon put it: "To the bitter end she was in revolt against something. But no one destroyed her. She destroyed herself."

But in so saying, Moon also recognized the life-affirming nature of Mildred Bailey's artistry. "Whatever she sang, and on the surface much of it was trite, she gave validity and dignity; and where respect was due it was granted, without fanfare, by a subtle warm overtone in the voice or by a gesture of that ample body."[59]

And it is that, above all, for which she is remembered and loved. How sad, how tragic, that everyone seemed to know it but her.

28

Pee Wee Russell
and Jack Teagarden

It was in Houston, Pee Wee Russell always said, that he first ran into Jack Teagarden.

He'd come south to audition for a summer band job at the nearby resort of Sylvan Beach, on Galveston Bay. The leader, pianist John "Peck" Kelley, met his train, and together they took a cab downtown to Thomas Goggan's Music Store.

Even at eighteen Russell was already a bit of an old pro in the dance band business. Born March 27, 1906, in the St. Louis suburb of Maplewood, he'd played clarinet and alto sax around town, worked the Mississippi riverboats, even done some touring, ranging as far as Juarez, Mexico.

Kelley, widely admired among musicians in the Southwest, had wanted Frank Trumbauer, a hero among St. Louis musicians; but the C-melody saxophonist, his national reputation growing, had gone east to join Ray Miller's band. A Kelley associate, trombonist Thomas "Sonny" Lee, quickly recommended Russell.

The way Pee Wee remembered it, they got to Goggan's, and without pre-amble Peck sat down at the piano and started a slow blues, Russell joining in. And that was the scene when a stocky guy with shoe-polish hair, whose broad, high-cheekboned face made him look a little like an Indian, wandered in, stood and listened a while, then casually reached up and lifted a trombone off a coat-hook on the wall.

He blew a phrase, and Russell, who only an hour before had felt "like a big shot arriving in a hick town," almost fainted: he'd never heard a hot trombone with that kind of sound and fluency, and so deeply flavored by the blues. Who *was* this guy, and why hadn't anybody in St. Louis ever said anything about him? Every phrase just deepened his astonishment and bewilderment.

"Look," Russell burst out when it was over. "I'm a nice guy a thousand miles from home and I think I'm out of my class . . . Why not let me work a week and make my fare home?" As things turned out, he stayed the summer, in a band that also included, for a while, clarinetist Leon Roppolo, revered among musicians for his pioneering work with the New Orleans Rhythm Kings.

The Sylvan Beach job over, Russell and Teagarden went their separate ways, at least for the time being. But they soon met again, and the kinship established with that first encounter lasted the rest of their lives.[1]

Historically the meeting is just a footnote, even a romantic conceit—but symbolically it's a richly fateful event, bringing together two of most resolute individualists to emerge from the early jazz years. Both soon became stylists as easy to recognize as they were difficult to imitate, and their very inimitability presents students of jazz history with an intriguing conundrum.

Neither Russell nor Teagarden left a major stylistic progeny. Neither exerted the kind of direct and diversified influence on subsequent jazz players so notable in Coleman Hawkins, Lester Young, Benny Goodman, Charlie Parker, Roy Eldridge—and, above all, Louis Armstrong.

Standard jazz histories have consistently favored these widely emulated figures, as if to suggest that the degree to which an individual style affects those of others is a measure of its importance and, by implication, its stature. The Armstrongs, Hawkinses, Youngs, and Goodmans set great trends in motion: does it not follow, then, that they are the major markers, the ones who *matter*?

Well, yes and no. Influentiality most often depends on accessibility and, by implication, on imitability. That, in turn, hints at a consistency of method that can be addressed, absorbed, parsed, replicated, developed further by others; that moves easily from the specific to the general, from idiosyncrasy to convention.

Hawkins, achieving his first maturity at the end of the 1920s, brought an assortment of commanding qualities to his improvising on the tenor saxophone: power, variety, virility, tonal majesty, a broad, probing harmonic imagination. Younger players, dazzled, fastened eagerly on one aspect or another: Chu Berry, Ben Webster, Budd Johnson, Herschel Evans, George "Buddy" Tate, and Dick Wilson were but a handful among many who shaped distinctive musical voices out of elements they first heard in Hawkins.

But such conflation of influentiality with importance inevitably scants those who have sailed into the wind, applying unconventional concepts and methods in the service of creativity—and utter inimitability. And, somehow, it relegates such individualists to secondary rank. Even the vocabulary often used to identify them—maverick, idiosyncrasy, rebel, nonconformist—implies anomaly, departure from a norm. A benign judgment, perhaps, but a judgment nonetheless.

Examples are easy to find. If Charlie Parker became a pivotal, endlessly influential force in post–World War II jazz, what does that make of Paul Desmond or Lee Konitz? With subsequent generations of electric guitarists paying homage to Charlie Christian, what is to be said of George Barnes?

Or, for that matter, of Jack Teagarden or Pee Wee Russell? In John McDonough's words, Russell "made the clarinet sound like something he had invented for the purpose of expressing himself with sounds all his own." The same could be said for Teagarden and the trombone. Surely there is no better index for creativity.[2]

Superficially, at least, the two men couldn't have been more different. Pee Wee, pencil-thin, just short of six feet tall, was a nervous, often painfully shy man, given to epic bouts of melancholy. New Yorker critic Whitney Balliett described his

> parenthesis-like stoop, spidery fingers, and a long, wry, gentle face governed by a generous, wandering nose. When he plays, this already striking facial arrangement, which is overlaid with an endless grille of wrinkles and furrows, becomes knotted into unbelievable grimaces of pain, as if the music were pulling unbearably tight an inner drawstring.[3]

Jack Teagarden, by contrast, seemed placid, even lazy, a river flowing broadly and inevitably to rendezvous with some far-off sea. Born Weldon Leo Teagarden August 20, 1905, in Vernon, Texas, ten miles south of the Oklahoma border, he grew up the eldest of four children in a close-knit family. A gift for music, including perfect pitch, showed itself early—as did a mechanical aptitude inherited from his father. By age eight he had moved from the baritone horn to a mail-order trombone. Even his short arms, which kept three of the new instrument's seven slide positions permanently out of his reach, proved no obstacle: he simply found other, sometimes homecooked, ways of playing the notes.

Charles Ellsworth Russell III was a change-of-life baby and an only child. His parents, dutiful and attentive, also were quick to recognize a flair for music and steered the boy first to the piano, then the drums, then violin—all to little avail. But one night, after the family had resettled in Muskogee, Oklahoma, Russell père took twelve-year-old Ellsworth to a dance run by the Elks Club, for which he worked as a steward and bartender. The music was by an instrumental quintet from New Orleans, the Louisiana Five, headed by clarinetist Alcide "Yellow" Nunez.

A regular member of "Papa" Jack Laine's elite circle of New Orleans musicians, Nunez had come north with the Original Dixieland Jazz Band in 1916 but soon fell out with the temperamental cornetist Nick LaRocca and went his own way. With trombonist Charlie Panelli he formed the Louisiana Five, which began recording in late 1918. Unlike all the other "Fives" of the rapidly burgeoning jazz band craze, the Nunez-Panelli quintet used no cornet. That cast the clarinet as an assertive and rhythmic lead, with less of the decorative fluidity of the instrument's early ensemble role.

(With "Heart-Sickness Blues" of December 1918, opening title on the Louisiana Five's first recording session for the Emerson label, it's clear that Nunez is breaking new ground. As Panelli fills in *portamenti* and sustained tones in concert-band trombone fashion, Nunez creates a part that is at once lead line and solo. He lays out the melody firmly, on the beat, while also reaching into his high register with the swooping elegance of the ODJB's Larry Shields. On the other side, "Orange Blossom Rag," he's as punchy as a cornet without losing the clarinet's suppleness.)

With Russell's own mature style in mind, it's easy to imagine the impact hearing Nunez must have made on him. Before long, he began clarinet lessons with a local theatre musician named Charlie Merrill, and by summer of 1919 he was working with a little band at Ray Stem's dance pavilion, out at the Muskogee reservoir. A job on an Arkansas River excursion boat (he wore long pants "borrowed" from his father) came to an abrupt end when, on the very first night, Russell senior turned up in the audience to rein the boy in.

The Teagarden family was of German extraction, and (contrary to various journalistic efforts to explain young Weldon's affinity for the blues) without any admixture of either black or American Indian blood. The boy's grandfather, Johann Heinrich Gienger, had left Baden-Württemberg in the early 1870s and, changing his given name to Henry, stayed long enough in Pennsylvania to marry a local Dutch girl, then moved to Texas, where he went to work for the Fort Worth and Denver Railroad. Helen Gienger, one of the couple's five daughters, married a local youth named Charles Teagarden, an inspector for a cotton-gin company.[4]

Charles played what Balliett calls "weak but industrious" cornet in the town concert band; Helen, more solidly gifted, was proficient on several instruments, including the piano, and made sure all her children could read music.

The great influenza epidemic of 1918 took Charles Teagarden at age thirty-nine, leaving his twenty-seven-year-old widow to fend for herself and the children. They relocated in Oklahoma City, then moved to Chappell, Nebraska, where Helen Teagarden gave music lessons, played movie-theatre piano for four dollars a night (sometimes with young Weldon joining in, reading the melodies from the song sheets), and somehow got the family through a particularly harsh winter. With the spring they returned to Oklahoma, thence eventually back to Vernon.

It was, in Richard Hadlock's succinct phrase, "a strange and rather melancholy childhood for a robust western kid" and left young Weldon with an inner solitariness strangely consonant with that of Russell. Let me amble through life at my own pace, he often seemed to be saying, and I'll let others deal with the complications.[5]

His fascination with things mechanical found its most lasting expression in the unique way he played the trombone, particularly the solutions he devised to its technical problems. His early experience with the baritone horn had taught him mouthpiece placement, tone production, valve fingerings. A trombone slide works on the same principle as the baritone's three valves: in both cases, a vibrating air column moves through a given length of brass tubing; the simplest explanation for this ultimately rather complex bit of applied physics is that shortening the tube raises the pitch, lengthening lowers it.

Then things get complicated. Each length of tubing produces not just one pitch but a veritable pyramid of tones called an overtone series. It is what allows a bugler to play sometimes rather complex calls without any apparatus to physically alter the length of tubing. In its first, or "closed" (unaltered) position, for example, a B♭ trombone can play the following notes:

(pedal)   (false)   (false)

Bb trombone overtone series (closed position).

Moving the slide out one position does what use of the baritone's middle valve would do: lengthens the tubing just enough to drop each pitch in the pyramid by a half step. A two-position extension yields a drop of a whole step (as does the baritone first valve), and so on down the line. To play lower pitches, a trombonist must extend his slide to its sixth or seventh position. A youngster with short arms (Teagarden, after all, was only eight when he started the instrument) will find these outer positions difficult, if not impossible, to reach.

He found a solution, based on an intuitive understanding of how brass instruments work. The higher a trumpet or trombone plays, the closer together the notes in the "pyramid," and the more options it offers for producing a given note. Some such alternatives are so naturally out of tune that (on a valved instrument especially) they can't be used at all. A trombone slide offers a chance to correct such pitch anomalies with often finely calibrated adjustments.

Multiplying this by all the levels of the overtone series makes clear what young Weldon discovered very early: with diligent practice, and relying on an unusually acute ear to adjust intonation, he could play almost any note he wanted (save the very low ones) by favoring positions which kept the slide close to his face.[6]

Jazzmen who heard Teagarden throughout his career were often amazed that such a musical torrent could come of so little apparent slide movement. British trumpeter Humphrey Lyttelton, for one, "marveled at the way in which [Teagarden's] huge, square right hand seemed to wave languidly an inch or two in front of his face while the notes tumbled out."[7]

Even in the 1920s, when Teagarden first began attracting attention, such unconventional methods were far from new or unknown among top "legit" trombone virtuosi. Research by the indefatigable Steve Dillon, for example, has found much evidence of such "false" slide positions in the work of the great turn-of-the-century soloist-bandmaster Arthur Pryor. Later jazz trombonists, too, became adept at such usage, and even mastered a kind of *trompe d'oreille*, false notes "lipped" into correct pitch, to facilitate daring runs and arabesques. But there is no disputing that such methods, and the principles behind them, entered the jazz vocabulary with Weldon Leo Teagarden.

By the time he'd reached his mid-teens, the young man had forsaken "Weldon" for the more collegial "Jack" and was working throughout the Southwest with an ever-widening circle of musicians. Billed on more than one occasion as "the South's Greatest Sensational Trombone Wonder," he won the admiration of such regional colleagues as Kelley, New Orleans clarinetists Roppolo, Sidney Arodin, and Charlie Cordilla, trumpeter Joe "Wingy" Manone—and, of course, Pee Wee Russell.

Apprenticeship in the Southwest, moreover, brought both Teagarden and Russell in contact with racial and ethnic cultures that might not have been so readily available to them up north. As a boy of seven or eight, Teagarden regularly attended black revival meetings in an open field at the end of his street. "I used to sit out on the fence and listen to the spirituals, and I knew right then and there that [that] was when I could hear my heart . . . that I loved them and I liked the stories they told." Drummer Tom Joyner, who worked with the young trombonist in 1921, recalled that "when we would get through at night, he would want me to go with him to hear one of the colored orchestras play."[8]

But even such testimony hardly explains the affinity that Teagarden and Russell shared for the blues, and any suggestion that a white musician could "pick up" blues feeling strictly from listening to black musicians seems simplistic and implausible. It remains, for all practical purposes, a mystery.

If any single figure helped shape Russell's musical outlook directly in those early years it was Bix Beiderbecke, a musician clearly *without* much noticeable affinity for the blues. They met in mid-1925, in a band assembled by Frank Trumbauer for an engagement at the Arcadia Ballroom, in downtown St. Louis. "We hit it right off" was Russell's memory of it. "We were never apart for a couple of years—day, night, good, bad, sick, well, broke, drunk."[9]

They soon discovered a shared passion for modern concert music, and sometime that November, Pee Wee began going along with Bix and saxophonist Damon "Bud" Hassler to Friday matinee "winter weekend" concerts by the St. Louis Symphony Orchestra, under Rudolph Ganz. Through Hassler's connections, and those of Arcadia bassist Anton Casertani, they were able to meet the symphony musicians. Perhaps as a result of all this activity, Bix went to trumpeter Joe Gustat for lessons in "legit" technique, and Russell began irregular sessions with clarinetist Anthony Sarlie. "I used to try to get him to teach me," Pee Wee said in later years. "I wish I had studied more."

The Arcadia closed for the summer on May 3, 1926. Within weeks, Bix,

Russell, and others from the St. Louis band were working under Trumbauer's leadership at the Blue Lantern Inn in Hudson Lake, an Indiana resort community on the Lake Michigan shore ninety miles east of Chicago. Stories of their escapades, particularly of their "bohemian" existence in a little cottage behind the hotel where the rest of the band stayed, now belong to the more colorfully anecdotal side of early jazz lore.

The Hudson Lake band quickly became a team, integrating "modernistic" arrangements first worked out at the Arcadia, and attracting groups of young white Chicago jazzmen, who eagerly made the drive on their nights off to hear Bix in such congenial surroundings. Russell clearly found something compelling in Bix, a set of governing aesthetic principles that stayed with him, and in later years he called the short-lived cornetist "one of the greatest musicians who ever lived. He had more imagination and more thought than anybody else I can think of . . . Everything he played I loved."[10]

New York, traditionally a magnet for young artists of all disciplines, drew both Teagarden and Russell beginning in mid-1927. For Pee Wee, entree came with an invitation from cornetist Ernest Loring "Red" Nichols, an influential and well-connected member of New York's hot dance music elite. Nichols commanded an ever-expanding range of work opportunities, for which he needed a large pool of musicians, preferably musicians not already overcommitted with other jobs. When the seemingly ubiquitous trombonist Sonny Lee started talking Russell up to Nichols, the cornetist, intrigued, shot off a cable to St. Louis with a firm offer; Pee Wee was quick to accept.

En route he stopped off to see various hot music friends in Chicago, crossing paths briefly with a clarinetist to whom he has often been compared. Superficial resemblances between Russell's style and that of Frank Teschemacher have even led some writers to suggest that one "influenced" the other. To be sure, both men phrased in an angular manner, often favoring a gritty, "non-legit" tone and technique (though at this stage Teschemacher did this far more than Russell), and used pitch in unconventional ways.

But recorded evidence suggests that any similarity between them is no more than a nexus, an intersection of two individual trajectories. By the time of Teschemacher's death, in 1932, his clarinet style had evolved far beyond its wild-and-woolly 1927 incarnation. Records made between 1928 and 1930 (such as "Farewell Blues," with Ted Lewis, and "Prince of Wails," with Elmer Schoebel) show more polished technique, introduction of a liquid, almost Jimmie Noone–like tone, increased regularity of phrasing, more "conventional" pitch sense.

Russell, by contrast, seems in the same years to be moving in the opposite direction. Where his sound and approach on his first records are balanced, even Bix-like, in their symmetry and sense of order, he very soon begins a process of what can almost be termed deconstruction. His work on records from 1928 on, in fact, conveys the sense that he is systematically dismantling that sense of order, then reassembling the pieces according to some new, inner imperative.

Russell's first appearance on records, an August 15, 1927, Brunswick session with Nichols, gives him a full chorus on Hoagy Carmichael's "Riverboat Shuffle," written for Bix in 1924 and recorded by him twice. Nichols takes it at a leisurely, even lilting, $\downarrow$ = 77 (compared to the Wolverines' $\downarrow$ = 92 and the headlong $\downarrow$ = 104 of the Bix-Trumbauer performance). Pee Wee, first soloist out, fashions a full chorus out of the kind of "correlated"—i.e., paired—phrases Beiderbecke favored. An alternate take, issued at the same time, affords a look at the young clarinetist's mind at work: once having established a phrase or pattern, he seems to scatter it on a tabletop like a deck of cards, then gather it back together in new orders and shapes.

The same session also produced "Ida, Sweet as Apple Cider," written in 1903 and already a "golden oldie" by the time Nichols got around to it. Commentators through the years have fastened on Russell's impetuous break and eight-bar solo as evidence of his unconventional style; and in contrast to the rather foursquare approaches of Nichols and trombonist Miff Mole, it can seem that way. But he sounds, overall, as nervous and unsettled as his own recollections indicate he was.

Even at this relatively inchoate phase of his development, Pee Wee clearly impressed the New York musicians—though not quite yet as a revolutionary. Reedman-arranger Joseph "Fud" Livingston had played in Chicago and the Midwest earlier in the decade and developed a clarinet style along lines that were, for a time at least, comparable. On the February 1928 Nichols record of "Nobody's Sweetheart"—taken, like "Riverboat Shuffle," at a stately tempo—Livingston manages to evoke both Russell and Teschemacher.

A major factor uniting all three—and dozens of other musicians, white and black, besides—was still a shared admiration for Beiderbecke. On "Crying All Day," recorded for OKeh October 25, 1927, with Frank Trumbauer's Orchestra, Russell follows Bix's sixteen-bar cornet solo with one of his own, maintaining and even developing its architecture and emotional content. So similar are the two passages in conception, so consonant in stance, that they could have sprung from the same mind. (For transcription and further discussion of both, see chapter 17.)

The clarinetist is equally Bix-like on the Nichols record of the Yellen-Ager song "Sugar," made the next day and with many of the same musicians. Bix is not present, but he might just as well have been, so pronounced is his effect on Trumbauer and trombonist Bill Rank, Nichols, Adrian Rollini—and Russell.

Pee Wee's full chorus, in fact, seems driven by the same undercurrent of melancholy that makes "Crying All Day" so memorable. Listeners used to his later vocabulary of squawks and growls, cries and whispers, can only be startled by his clear tone and poised phrasing here. He comes closer to capturing the inner spirit of Bix than does even Nichols, whose eight-bar trumpet solo is a careful simulacrum.

713

"Sugar," Pee Wee Russell clarinet solo (thirty-three bars), 1927.

*   *   *

Within a few days of Russell's "Sugar" recording with Nichols, drummer-bandleader Edward "Doc" Ross, and several other musicians set out by car from Houston, bound for New York City. Riding along with Ross, who had been promised a hotel job in Larchmont, north of the city, were pianist Cecil "Snaps" Elliott, banjoist "Red" Hawn, reedmen Bob McCracken and Bob Muse—and, snoring softly in the back seat of Hawn's car, Jack Teagarden.

Things didn't work out quite as anticipated. Ross and Elliott got the Larchmont job, but not Hawn, Muse, and McCracken, who found work with society bandleader Johnny Johnson at Manhattan's Pennsylvania Hotel. Teagarden, just happy to be there, began doing casuals, subbing, filling in here and there as word of his prowess began to get around.

Accounts of this part of his career have taken on an almost bardic quality. The affable, slow-talking young Texan arrives in the big city, playing hot trombone in a manner that upends, overnight, all prevailing orthodoxies. Colleagues, rapturous, spread the word. Black musicians, chronically skeptical of white jazzmen in those musically segregated times, welcome him into their midst, a few even hinting that no one outside "the race" could play the blues that well. Teagarden unseats Miff Mole at the top of the New York heap, joins Ben Pollack, records with Bix and Louis, Fats Waller and Joe Venuti. Everywhere he goes, it's love at first hearing.

Filling in for Mole on a March 1928 Roger Wolfe Kahn record date, Teagarden played a 32-bar solo on a Harry Woods tune called "She's a Great, Great Girl." In its unassuming way it's little short of startling: where Miff's choruses were most often witty, carefully crafted miniatures, Teagarden's (with Vic Berton's buoyant tympani lifting the rhythm) is a relaxed, genial narrative. Its almost offhand ease makes even a Joe Venuti–Eddie Lang outing in the same performance seem stodgy.

Again, two takes exist. Unlike Russell, Teagarden seems happy to define the overall outline of what he wants to play, then just vary the details. His two "She's a Great, Great Girl" solos share the same figure-shapes and general feel, and the same mid-chorus break, built around "lipped" triplets.

Even at this early stage it's clear that Teagarden's trombone playing proceeds from a largely vocalized concept. He sings through the instrument, and when his vocals begin appearing on records (the first seems to have been the blues "Makin' Friends," issued under Eddie Condon's name), they seem exact cognates to the trombone solos in conception, phrasing, even tone. It is hard to think of another singer-instrumentalist—not Wingy Manone or Louis Prima, not Bunny Berigan or Lips Page, and perhaps not even the incomparable Louis Armstrong himself—leaving so vivid an impression of matched vocal and instrumental expressions of the same sensibility.

It is really a tripartite mode. In addition to trombone and voice, Teagarden also achieved considerable expressive range in a personal, typically homemade way: by playing only the detached slide section of his instrument, holding an empty water glass over its nether end as a primitive sounding-box. The resulting sound—distant, plaintive, even spectral—was particularly effective on the blues and on such minor-key vehicles as the traditional "St. James Infirmary," which later became a Teagarden feature specialty.[11]

When Gunther Schuller cites Teagarden's vocalization of his instrument as a key factor setting him apart from the black trombonist Jimmy Harrison, he's identifying a crucial distinction. Harrison's name often comes up in discussion of Teagarden's early impact, sometimes seemingly as a way of finding a black antecedent for so original a style. But testimony of colleagues, and the subsequent course of his development, indicate that the Texan's way of playing jazz trombone was firmly in place by the time he arrived in New York.

Even Harrison's best work on records—and there's more than is generally acknowledged—fails to support claims for him as a stylistic Vorbild for Teagarden. His solos on "Hop Off" (Fletcher Henderson, 1927), "King Porter Stomp" (Henderson, 1928), and "Walk That Thing" (Charlie Johnson, 1928), while vigorous, display little of the ease that makes even Teagarden's earliest recorded efforts so attractive. There's a tension in Harrison's playing which, at its best, lends his

715

solos an undeniable urgency; but just as often (as on "Oh, Baby!," Dixie Stompers, 1928), he simply sounds tense.

All, moreover, are unmistakably _trombone_ solos, played by a man who is thinking as a brass player. At some moments (his eight bars on "Come On, Baby," with Henderson, is an example) Harrison's tongued eighth notes even seem to recall Miff Mole.

By the end of 1930, and a date for OKeh issued under the generic house name "Chocolate Dandies," Harrison had changed greatly: many of his note choices on "Dee Blues"—his inflections, tonal characteristics, even the solo's overall _shape_—now seemed to echo Teagarden. Here is a comparison of Harrison's single "Dee Blues" chorus with a twelve-bar Teagarden blues on a Red Nichols record ("Basin Street Blues," issued as the "Louisiana Rhythm Kings").[12]

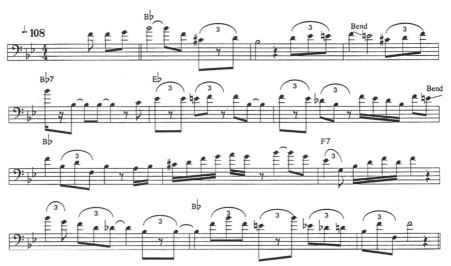

1: "Basin Street Blues," Jack Teagarden trombone solo (twelve bars), 1929.

2: "Dee Blues," Jimmy Harrison trombone solo (twelve bars), 1930.

By this time Harrison was terminally ill with cancer and would live only seven months more. His solo on Benny Carter's "Goodbye Blues," from the same session, shows him struggling with his horn, though here, too, the conception is more spacious, even vocalized.

Given Harrison's 1927–28 recorded work, only one conclusion is possible: listening to Teagarden had changed Jimmy Harrison's solo style rather more substantially than listening to Harrison had affected Teagarden. That is not to scant Harrison's eminence, or his role in separating the trombone from its novelty function in earlier jazz bands. But Harrison must share this distinction with Mole, Tommy Dorsey, Claude Jones, Benny Morton, and the often astounding J. C. Higginbotham, among other contemporaries.

Weldon Leo Teagarden had become a force in hot music, his every recorded solo doted over by fellow-musicians. Whether making gold out of Tin Pan Alley dross ("Buy, Buy for Baby," with Ben Pollack, 1928), swinging out on a hot instrumental ("Whoopee Stomp," Harmony label version, 1928), or playing and singing the blues ("That's a Serious Thing," 1929, under Eddie Condon's name), he simply sounds like no one else.

Where Teagarden's basic sound and concept seem to have been in place when he arrived in New York, Russell's were apparently in flux. His biographer, Robert Hilbert, suggests that major change set in during a 1928–29 cross-country tour with the New York-based Cass Hagan orchestra. The itinerary included stops in Kansas City and St. Louis—and it was in his home town that Russell got off the bus for a six-month stay. Revisiting the Southwest, Hilbert suggests, may have worked a metamorphosis in the clarinetist:

> The Beiderbecke influence, though it would always remain strong, was less obvious. Pee Wee's playing had become much more assertive and individualistic. By the time Red Nichols called him to return to New York in the summer of 1929, Pee Wee had developed a new, and instantly identifiable, jazz voice.[13]

At first examination, such reasoning suggests what James T. Maher calls "the tooth-fairy theory" of jazz evolution: the notion that a style, in all its particulars, could be delivered mysteriously intact to a player within one closely defined period of time. But the organic way in which style develops seems to militate against such theorizing. The idea that Russell spent a few months on the road and returned to New York with what was, in its contours, a brand-new way of playing hot clarinet and saxophone strains plausibility.

Still, his solo on the same "Basin Street Blues" cited above, this time on the sixteen-bar refrain of the song, is a departure from his earlier, orderly, more Bix-like efforts. John S. Wilson, writing in 1979, referred to it as a "halting, piercing, astonishing piece of Chicago surrealism." Wilson's geography may be open to question, but he has the rest of it right: punching, trumpet-like attacks alternating with *sotto voce* mutterings; rasps and growls; lightning shifts of dynamics and tonal texture; a rubber-band stretching of pitch and rhythmic emphasis; and, perhaps above all, a keening quality rare in hot solo work of the time, white or black, as different from the majesty of Bechet and Armstrong as from the thoughtful symmetry of Beiderbecke.

717

The mystery remains: where did all this come from? It's not in evidence on earlier Russell solos, however excellent: now, with this 1929 performance, the stylistic "voice" of Pee Wee Russell is emerging. "Rose of Washington Square," recorded the following day by an augmented version of the same group and issued under Nichols's name, shows that the "Basin Street" clarinet solo was no fluke. Russell's chorus, at a faster tempo, contrasts dramatically with his 1927 work on such up-tempo numbers as "Honolulu Blues" (Mole's Molers) and four distinct versions of the original "Feelin' No Pain," all with Nichols-led groups. In each of those, Russell plays fluidly, solidly on the beat.[14]

But no more: for "Rose of Washington Square," he has field-stripped his style and reassembled it in new, less regular, shapes. Jack Teagarden is also present, and the occasion represents a kind of grand reunion, the first time the two men, friends since their Peck Kelley days, were recording together. They seem to energize one another. (For discussion of Bud Freeman's solo on the same record, see chapter 11).[15]

Jack Teagarden's classic blues "Makin' Friends" was aptly titled. "Everybody liked him," Jimmy McPartland said simply. "And when you heard him play, you just had to love him." As Len Gutteridge, writing for a Time-Life collection in the 1980s, put it, "nobody could resist the big, bearlike trombonist (he stood nearly six feet tall and weighed close to 200 pounds) with his shy grin, rumpled clothes and dowdy cap." In bassist Harry Goodman's words, "His hair was always well-groomed, but his pants were never pressed."[16]

"He was a country-type boy," said trumpeter Don Goldie, who worked with Teagarden in later years, "in some ways an unsophisticated man, a very personal man . . . a shy man, who found small talk difficult and who hated the telephone. He was gentle and kind. If he couldn't say something nice about someone, he didn't say anything."[17]

But in the end it was the way he played and sang that won the hearts of fellow-musicians and laymen alike. Many writers have attempted, with varying degrees of success, to define the qualities that set Jack Teagarden apart, that gave his every appearance on record, regardless how brief, the air of an *event*.

Writer-musician Richard Hadlock hears even in Teagarden's early work "an ear for melodic, rhythmic and harmonic subtleties that few jazzmen could match . . . [often] building a melodic line with sixths and diminished, major and minor sevenths, and ninths."

Or Humphrey Lyttelton: "It is hard to find a single Teagarden record which he did not enhance with his beautiful, curiously blunted tone, his marvelously fluent articulation, his perfect rhythmic poise and the sheer elegance of his musical thought." Another Briton, trumpeter Digby Fairweather, hears "a delicately contoured tone in which every note sounded as if it were gift-boxed . . . above all, an ability to make whatever he played sound naturally right."[18]

Teagarden, says Whitney Balliett, "had several different tones: a light, nasal one; a gruff, heavy one; and a weary, hoarse one—a twilight tone he used for slow blues, and for ballads that moved him."[19]

Certainly the tone (or tones) is distinctive, as is Teagarden's use of close-to-the-face "false" slide positions, "lipped" triplets, seemingly improbable glisses (apparently seamless passage from one note to another, as far as an octave away), the *gruppetto* (a form of ornamentation also known as a "turn," consisting of a group of four or five notes "turning" around a central one), and other devices.

Trombonist and music historian Steve Dillon, closely conversant with Teagarden's way of addressing his horn, recently demonstrated some of the Texan's execution of these devices. "Above all," said Dillon, "what he did depended on relaxation and a strong, easy-flowing air column. Remember, he wasn't a particularly loud player: if he had been, he'd have had to use more mouthpiece pressure, and it would have restricted his flexibility, all those turns and things he did."[20]

For corroboration, a listener has only to compare the work of the late, highly regarded trombonist and Teagarden admirer Lou McGarity. A far more forceful player, with a brassy tonal edge, McGarity's occasional use of Teagarden-like glisses and *gruppetti* often seems forced, even clumsy.[21]

Teagarden solos on record display characteristic figures. While they make him easy to recognize, they don't begin to explain the *immediacy*, the sense of humanity, that reaches out to touch every listener. Other trombonists, after all, had their own devices and designs: J. C. Higginbotham used machine-gun chromatic triplets, lip-trills, and other embellishments in solos that are still exuberant marvels; Duke Ellington's trombone soloist Joe "Tricky Sam" Nanton developed use of the plunger into a kind of fine art; Lawrence "Snub" Moseley brought a zany, acrobatic humor to his solos with Alphonso Trent's Southwest-based territory band; Jack Jenney, another "soft" player coming along in the early '30s, refined trombone lyricism to an almost poetic delicacy.

But Teagarden was different, and defining what made him different calls for a brief digression. Creative jazz soloists seem to fall into two general types. There are the proteans, endlessly questing, discovering, reinventing, reshaping—all in pursuit of some half-glimpsed, fugitive perfection. Among these, Coleman Hawkins springs readily to mind: over four decades his basic style took various forms, from silken smoothness to something occasionally approaching brutality. Like composer Igor Stravinsky, he seemed to devise and perfect a given mode or approach only to desert it, again *auf der Suche*.

Others, by contrast, arrive relatively early at an effective mode of expression, then spend the rest of their days adjusting, refining, polishing their creation to a high luster. Beyond argument, Jack Teagarden belongs to, exemplifies, the latter group: his style "set" quickly, and thereafter changed only subtly. It included not only recognizable patterns but entire "master choruses" on familiar numbers, delivered often enough to become trademarks. There were certain blues solos, all the more beloved for their familiarity; pet cadenzas, richly decorated with lightning triplets and *gruppetti* of impeccably executed sixteenth notes; set routines on such standards as "Basin Street Blues," "The Sheik of Araby," "Rockin' Chair," and the aforementioned "St. James Infirmary."

Yet none of this even begins to approach playing by rote. The examples of countless other players, some of them discussed throughout this volume, have made it clear that some of the most celebrated "improvisations" of jazz history were set-pieces, carefully worked out by their creators. Yet they are no less masterpieces for that. The glory lies both in their intrinsic perfection (Berigan on "I Can't Get Started" is one example among many) and in the manner of their delivery.

Each Teagarden phrase, each passage, each chorus, somehow sounded fresh-minted each time out: if anything, familiarity enhanced their eloquence—as, too, was the case with the trombonist's lifelong friend Louis Armstrong. It didn't take much, moreover, to alter the face of even an oft-repeated solo: the difference lies in the details.

Among the best, even defining, records of Teagarden's early years are those he made with Red Nichols between early 1929 and early 1931. While good, even eloquent Teagarden solos will be found on performances by the Ben Pollack Orchestra ("Sentimental Baby," "My Kinda Love," "From Now On"), Red McKenzie's Mound City Blue Blowers ("Tailspin Blues," "Never Had a Reason to Believe in You"), and various other small units, the Nichols titles constitute a defining musical peak.

Nichols recognized and respected exceptional talent: both Teagarden and fellow–Pollack bandsman Benny Goodman get generous solo exposure on these records. Most of the arranging is by trombonist Glenn Miller; whatever his feelings about being supplanted by Teagarden in the Pollack orchestra, Miller understood the Texan and showcased him well.

Teagarden's debut session with Nichols, on April 18, 1929, was especially auspicious. Two issued takes of "Indiana" offer punchy, bright-toned Goodman, a carefully devised Nichols chorus (played into a derby in the Bix manner), and, after a modulation from G to B♭, two masterful sixteen-bar Teagarden solos. The trombonist's phrases are short, economical, delivered in an almost brusque manner; but their overall impact reduces even Goodman's admirable efforts to the level of simple competence.

Teagarden's "natural tendency to transform popular songs into the blues," cited by Hadlock in *Jazz Masters of the Twenties*, is the motive force behind "Dinah," recorded at the same session. The song itself, a straightforward scalar melody strung across a simple chord sequence, has been a musicians' favorite since being introduced by Ethel Waters in 1925. By taking it at a bluesy *allegretto* ($\downarrow = 128$), Miller's arrangement leaves maximum latitude for the transformation. Goodman's solo, over a rhythm section shuffle, is one of his best of the period, blending the stabbing accents of his Chicago background with an emergent, and characteristic, fluidity.

But Teagarden, entering on a paraphrase of "A-hunting we will go," again trumps him, fusing blues inflections and poised double-time phrases into an intensely subjective utterance. It culminates, in the bridge, with four upward rips, from concert F to the C above it. There is much darkness here, a *gravitas* not hinted at either in the original song or in the solos of Goodman or tenor saxophonist Irving "Babe" Russin.

Other Teagarden appearances with Nichols are no less rewarding. His opening and closing cadenzas on "China Boy," obbligato to Scrappy Lambert's "On the Alamo" vocal, full chorus on "The Sheik of Araby" (over Miller's straight melody), elegiac solo and cadenza on "Tea for Two"—these are sublime moments. His entry on "I'm Just Wild About Harry" is even more than that: after good, thrusting solos by the Russin brothers, Babe and pianist Jack, Teagarden waits a beat, then tosses off a four-note melody paraphrase which at once sums up the song and declares a change of lighting and temperature. While never straying far from the melody, he recasts it, darkens and weights it with new meaning.

"I'm Just Wild About Harry," Jack Teagarden solo (eighteen bars), 1930.

Teagarden's vocal and instrumental contributions to "After You've Gone," by contrast, brighten a song whose basic character is dark, aggrieved. He's first out of the gate on "I Want to Be Happy," riding jauntily on Krupa's choke cymbal backbeats. Toward the end of a Nichols "production" treatment of "Sally, Won't You Please Come Back?" Teagarden uses the title as the basis for an impromptu vocal blues, its depth contrasting sharply with the sentimental frivolity of what's preceded it. One of the other trombones on the date, either Miller or Bill Trone (both capable improvisers) plays some decidedly Teagardenish licks behind him.

"Peg o' My Heart" begins with a melody statement by Jack's trumpet-playing younger brother Charles, and the similarity between their phrasing methods is striking. The opening two bars include a variation that could as easily have been

721

played on the former's trombone; Charles even shows an affinity for the sorts of embellishments that distinguish his elder brother's ballad style. Jack Teagarden's muted choruses on both issued takes are measured, judicious summings-up, again converting the song's inherent sentimentality into the blues.[22]

Listening to Teagarden records made in this period, it is possible to conclude that he seldom, if ever, turned in a performance that was less than superb, even inspiring. His blues (including the 1929 "That's a Serious Thing," with its adumbration of "Stormy Weather") rhythmic "hot" solos (the Venuti "Dancing With Tears in My Eyes"), "glass and a half" essays (several versions of the blues, "Makin' Friends"), and cameos on otherwise uneven Pollack records ("Keep Your Undershirt On" is among the best) are moments to cherish.

It's unlikely that Red McKenzie and Eddie Condon thought much about posterity in bringing Pee Wee Russell and Coleman Hawkins together for a late-1929 Mound City Blue Blowers date. But posterity, it turned out, was their beneficiary.

Hawkins, tenor sax star of the Fletcher Henderson orchestra, had made few small group records, and none outside the company of fellow–Henderson musicians. Russell, who had reacted so brilliantly to the company of Teagarden, Freeman, and drummer Dave Tough that June on "Rose of Washington Square," had seldom recorded outside the Red Nichols circle.

This occasion backed the two reedmen with a pianoless rhythm section: Condon (banjo) and Jack Bland (guitar), Krupa on drums, and, on bass, the hard-driving George "Pops" Foster, from Luis Russell's orchestra. McKenzie's comb took on the trumpet role, and Glenn Miller, on trombone, filled out the four-"horn" front line.[23]

The up-tempo "Hello Lola" (named, according to some reports, after a particularly tempestuous Russell girlfriend) is clearly a "blowing tune," its chords fusing the first eight bars of the currently popular "Oh, Baby!" with a minor-key bridge later used in Earl Hines's "Rosetta." McKenzie swings out forcefully for two choruses, sustaining melodic interest throughout (relatively few "hot" trumpet players of the day could have done this as well). Pee Wee takes a single chorus, then jumps clear as the Hawkins juggernaut bears down. The saxophonist is still tonguing his notes, slapping out staccato phrases on the beat, and not always with melodic continuity. Russell, also working with fragmentary phrases and from a similar rhythmic conception, does better at staying coherent.[24]

The two men were already friends: Pee Wee, who doubled on tenor in those days, had even subbed for Hawkins in Henderson's reed section, an experience he recalled with some terror:

> My God, those scores! They were written in six flats, eight flats. I don't
> know how many flats. I never saw anything like it. Buster Bailey was in
> the section next to me, and after a couple of numbers I told him, "Man,
> I came up here to have a good time, not to work. Where's Hawkins?"[25]

The session's undisputed apex is the second title, a reading of James P. Johnson's "If I Could Be With You One Hour Tonight" without its melody, retitled

"One Hour" and credited to McKenzie and Krupa. McKenzie again opens, "blue-blowing" through his comb with the ardency of an Irish tenor—which, in a sense, is just what he was. Hawkins, up next, unveils his evolving ballad style: rhapsodic, smoothly executed, it's a total departure from the staccato *attack* mode of "Hello Lola." Where the former fell away rapidly after the '20s, this latter Hawkins manner was to be the defining one for most of the coming decade. His solo is full of harmonic probings and irregular phrase shapes quite audacious even in the richly experimental context of 1929.[26]

Russell, following Hawkins, is no less exploratory, but the contrast between them is striking. He delivers his five annunciatory concert B♭'s—two as pickups, three inside the first bar—tersely, with a tone as dry and acidulous as Hawkins's was lush. With the blues as a point of reference, he seems to *pop* his phrases out, in a narrative voice comparable to none in hot music at the time. Schuller calls him "an Edgar Allan Poe, a Wilhelm Busch, and Charles Schulz all rolled into one"—the grotesque and the satiric, whimsy and high seriousness, the affectionate and the macabre, all housed in one sensibility.[27]

This marks the decisive beginning, on record at least, of the mature Pee Wee Russell. From here on, there is never a solo that could be called routine, never a descent into cliché, seldom even a perfunctory moment. Not to say that characteristic Russell phrases do not appear: certain patterns, including a fondness for the tritone (this many years before the flatted fifth became an emblem of the emergent bop movement), a manner of attack—and, perhaps above all, an astonishing variety of tonal timbres and textures—readily identify Pee Wee, no matter what the context.

Eddie Condon, who had appointed himself Russell's advocate-in-chief, hired him for a series of 1932 record dates organized by publisher Irving Mills for the nominal purpose of featuring singer (and female impersonator) Billy Banks. On trumpet was Henry "Red" Allen, then still working alongside Pops Foster and other New Orleans expatriates in Luis Russell's band.

The pairing was inspired. Allen, like Russell, was an architect of wonderfully asymmetrical musical structures, often in defiance of rhythmic and melodic convention. He'd grown up in much the same environment as Louis Armstrong, and they shared some superficial similarities; but Allen's exaggerated flair for *rubato*, and a penchant for irregular, across-the-bar-line phrases, set him emphatically apart from Armstrong's declamatory ways.

Allen and Russell seem to have recognized one another instantly as twinned spirits. On four dates by the "Rhythmakers," between April and October, the two musicians whirl and frolic, cavort, challenge, and carom gleefully off one another, backed by a shifting personnel which includes Condon and Bland, Krupa and drummer Zutty Singleton, pianists Fats Waller, Joe Sullivan, and Frank Froeba, bassists Foster and Al Morgan, trombonist Tommy Dorsey, saxophonist Happy Caldwell, and others.

Each performance strikes its own sparks, whether in the whirligig trumpet-clarinet volleying of "Bugle Call Rag," Russell's low-register musings on the various takes of "Oh, Peter," his tart counterline to Allen's sustained high concert

A in the last moments of the blues "Spider Crawl," or even his gutty tenor solos on "Mean Old Bed Bug Blues" and "I Would Do Anything for You."

But even in this charged environment two moments stand out. Russell lets the rhythm, especially Morgan's percussive bass, propel him through sixteen bars on "Who's Sorry Now?" (he opens the performance with a full-chorus tenor solo)—only to have Allen one-up him with a supremely conceived full-chorus study in rhythmic displacement; the pair of them, the only horns on this date, go darting and flashing into the final ensemble chorus, the ear "watching" them with astonished delight.

Slightly less fevered, but no less thrilling, is the sequence of blues choruses making up "Bald-Headed Mama." Allen bustles in after a good, rolling Joe Sullivan piano chorus, alternating double-time flurries with sudden, pregnant silences, courting the beat without ever stating it. Russell, out of some divine contrarian instinct, strides to center stage with a determined three-note figure, two concert A's and an F above, that incarnates the very pulse which Allen has flouted so outrageously. He underlines the phrase before moving on to a solo that flirts with its own kind of asymmetry. The two final ensemble choruses, obviating a weightless Banks vocal, leave all frenzy behind in a good-natured conversation between two friends, comparing notes on what great fun they've just had.

By 1931 Jack Teagarden had achieved a unique and unquestioned stature among New York musicians. Fellow-trombonists, far from displaying jealousy, flocked to hear him, meet him, play with him. Even the fiercely competitive Tommy Dorsey, already acknowledged as one of the most versatile and accomplished men in the field, played the votary—if in his own way. During the weeks Teagarden was in a band led by trumpeter Tommy Gott at Manhattan's Silver Slipper, said drummer Jim Wilson, Dorsey would "sneak in and sit in the back by himself, never saying hello, and dig Jack like crazy." Fletcher Henderson first heard Teagarden at Roseland and took to him at once. As one fellow-bandsman recalled, "Fletcher would take Jack all over Harlem at the end of our evening, showing him off as if he were a man from Mars." As Hawkins, who jammed with him often in after-hours sessions uptown, said in an interview many years later, "He must have never slept, playing horn night and day."[28]

All the playing, all the attention—and, it must be added, some prodigious drinking—wrought havoc in the Texan's private life. His first marriage, which produced two sons, quickly fell apart. (His second wife, Clare Manzi, was later widely quoted among musicians as commenting "Jack loves music, liquor and me, in that order.")

Even with the Depression taking hold and many musicians scuffling to make a living, Teagarden was doing comfortably. During the dry spells, when the Pollack band wasn't working, something always came along—including, in 1931, a few weeks in the pit orchestra for Everybody's Welcome, a Broadway show remembered today only for having introduced the standard "As Time Goes By."

Two record dates that fall, a month apart, teamed him, happily, with Fats

Waller and such other cronies as brother Charles, cornetist Stirling Bose, bass saxophonist Adrian Rollini—and, on clarinet, Pee Wee Russell. Though this band of jazzmen seems to be playing stock arrangements on all but one title of the first date and sounds a bit top-heavy (probable result, given the strong rhythm section, of the studio miking setup), Teagarden and Waller make an engaging team. They play superbly together, and trade spirited vaudeville-style quips on "You Rascal You" and "That's What I Like About You." Charles, Bose (very Bix-like), Rollini, and Russell all have good solos here and on the fourth title, the long-lost "I Got the Ritz From the One I Love." The second session includes a genial "China Boy" and "Tiger Rag," with solos along the way for Fats, Jack (in a take-charge mode), Bose, Charles, Pee Wee (a bit subdued), and Rollini.

Teagarden left Pollack's dissension-ridden troupe in 1933 ("Two Tickets to Georgia," the last title recorded before his departure, contains an exceptionally good half-chorus solo), spending most of the rest of the year in the New England–based band of Mal Hallett. At one point, the trombone section consisted of Teagarden and Jack Jenney; imagination leaps at the very idea of these two premier melodists soloing side by side.

Finally, at year's end, Jack Teagarden signed a five-year contract with Paul Whiteman's orchestra. Was it truly "one of the most unfortunate decisions of his professional life," as Hadlock and others have suggested? Did his tenure as a Whiteman employee really keep him on the sidelines when the big reputations of the emergent "swing era" were being made; make him, in Otis Ferguson's phrase, "tired and cynical, his creation a bit shop-worn?" Was it, as record producer John Hammond later insisted, little more than a form of indentured servitude, sapping the trombonist of his creative vitality? Were his recordings in this period really, as critic Rudi Blesh charged, little more than "sad memorials to security?"[29]

The answer, in general, seems to be a resounding no. Whiteman offered Teagarden a handsome form of job security, with a weekly paycheck that often climbed to just short of five hundred dollars. He treated the trombonist well, featured him often, suffered his alcoholic lapses with good grace, allowed him considerable latitude in recording, and even bankrolled a small-group engagement at New York's Hickory House featuring the Teagarden brothers (Charles, as ever, had followed Jack into Whiteman's brass section) and C-melody saxophonist Frank Trumbauer.

Whiteman still takes a drubbing from the jazz faithful. Regularly accused of having "stifled" Bix and, later, Bunny Berigan, of cynically crowning himself "King of Jazz"—a sobriquet bestowed by a zealous press agent—of having prof-ited at the expense of (presumably more deserving) black artists, he has also been accused of holding Jack and Charles virtual prisoner at a time when stardom could have been theirs.

A look at the facts tells another story. Yes, Teagarden found much of his work with the Whiteman orchestra—playing for greyhound races, circuses, movies, even the immense Billy Rose extravaganza Jumbo—tedious. But no more so, it must be remembered, than the routine stuff that such presumably more enlight-

725

ened colleagues as Benny Goodman, Artie Shaw, Berigan, Manny Klein, and the Dorseys faced every day as part of their cushy network radio jobs.

"Contrary to speculation," Helen Oakley noted in a *Down Beat* column of the time, "I believe Jack enjoys his association with Whiteman, he gets to 'swing' occasionally, and he is certainly proving himself of commercial value to the band." She described a date in Milwaukee, "one of the greatest thrills of my life," during which Whiteman featured the trombonist on "Basin Street Blues," "Fare Thee Well to Harlem," "Way Down Yonder in New Orleans," and several other numbers, with Charles playing excellent trumpet behind his elder brother's vocals.[30]

What if, as so many fans have wished, Teagarden had not signed on with Whiteman? When the "Pollack Orphans," as the jazz-oriented nucleus of the drummer's now-defunct band came to be called, decided to form a group of their own, Jack was their candidate for leader. They loved him, esteemed his musicianship, relished his easy company. But what sort of leader would he have made, having to deal with the day-to-day stress of running an orchestra? On the basis of his later misadventures with his own band, the answer has to be: not such a good one.

The leap from sideman-colleague-pal to leader is roughly comparable to the elevation of a corporate worker to management, or surrender of a military non-com's stripes for an officer's bars. It requires a little iron in the soul, an ability to put *Abstand* between one's self and one's men—above all to establish an authority, no matter at what cost, that makes a change in the basic relationship clear beyond misunderstanding.

Tommy Dorsey and Benny Goodman did it successfully, as did Artie Shaw, Harry James, and, in a rather gentler way, Gene Krupa. But Bunny Berigan, Bobby Hackett, and Teagarden, among others, never did. In this context it's likely that working for Whiteman between 1933 and 1938 was the best thing that could have happened to Jack Teagarden at that time. As Blesh himself averred, Teagarden

> was cut out by God or nature and shaped into an artist designed to play free, creative music . . . to astonish the silence with a wonderful sound. God or nature did not design him to be a big-name bandleader or a business man.[31]

By 1933, too, the nascent Depression had deeply affected the record business, and major companies drastically throttled back their popular music policies. Columbia, shaky since the late '20s, finally tumbled into bankruptcy.

Enter, around this time, John Hammond. An avid, crewcut young man with a Vanderbilt and Sloan pedigree and an education that included Hotchkiss and Yale, he pursued social justice for American blacks—and hot music, which he clearly viewed as a branch of the same cause. Among the relatively small number of white jazzmen on Hammond's list of favorites were Benny Goodman and Jack Teagarden.

During a visit to England Hammond was introduced to Louis Sterling, the American-born record mogul who had owned English Columbia since the early '20s. Though the Depression hit British record firms with nothing like the severity felt in the United States, Sterling and other executives nevertheless took action. In early 1931, Columbia went into partnership with its chief rival, the Gramophone Company, manufacturers of the "His Master's Voice" line; the resultant conglomerate, Electric and Musical Industries Ltd., or EMI, remains one of the media industry's giants.

Sterling realized that the sort of hot jazz which had done so well on Parlophone and English Columbia might still have a significant market in Britain. It was worth an experiment, at least, and this wealthy, enthusiastic young man, who seemed to know his way around musician circles (and was sufficiently well-off not to demand a large fee), could be just the one to implement it.[32]

Hammond returned with Sterling's commission to record several groups for both Parlophone and English Columbia. Among the musicians he approached was Benny Goodman, who in turn hired Teagarden. The trombonist and drummer Gene Krupa were working with Hallett, who immediately agreed to let them off, against Hammond's promise to pay their train fares to New York. Teagarden's only condition: hire his brother Charles as one of the trumpet players. Others on the first date included versatile trumpeter Manny Klein, guitarist Dick McDonough, and pianist Joe Sullivan.

Six more sessions followed, with some variations in personnel; on the one Teagarden did not attend (a pity, in that it included Hawkins and Mildred Bailey), fellow-Texan Sonny Lee was a more than capable deputy. The records find Teagarden soloing often, singing regularly. Some performances, the punningly titled blues "Texas Tea Party" among them, are basically his features.

His singing of "I Gotta Right to Sing the Blues" makes the Harold Arlen–Ted Koehler classic sound as if it had been written just for him (it later became his theme). His accentuation and placement of the word "misery," capping the two-bar ascending phrase in mid-chorus, suggests pathos without mawkishness. Striking, too, is his rugged delivery of arpeggiated triplets in the final chorus, in response to a similar figure in the trumpet lead. He's upbeat all the way on McDonough's "Dr. Heckle and Mr. Jibe," and his vocals on Fats Waller's "Ain'tcha Glad" and "Keep On Doin' What You're Doin' " (the latter despite an obvious head cold) direct and surprisingly romantic. "Texas Tea Party" has a feathery Goodman intro and some of the clarinetist's best blues playing, alongside top-drawer Teagarden. "Your Mother's Son-in-Law" and "Riffin' the Scotch" (the latter an amplification, with lyrics, of Goodman's reflective opening phrase from "Texas Tea Party") spotlight a young, and none too self-assured, Billie Holiday.

But Teagarden's performance on the May 14, 1934, Goodman date is perhaps his most telling, warranting closer examination. Taken on its own, "I Ain't Lazy— I'm Just Dreamin' " is a pop song of ineffable mediocrity: it's hard to imagine any adult, let alone a Jack Teagarden, singing such lines as

Always tell the daisies everything I've planned;
When they nod their heads I know they understand . . .

without having to suppress at least an indulgent chuckle. Teagarden doesn't laugh: he sings the words with obvious sincerity, and in so doing elevates them to

727

something like eloquence. The effect is comparable to Louis Armstrong's heartfelt delivery of the equally wretched "That's My Home," with its references to "Mammy's love," the Swanee River, and a "little shack [that's] home, sweet home." By not condescending, Louis ennobles: his vocal and trumpet solo make the 1931 record, and the song, an enduring testament to his artistry.

So, too, with Teagarden and "I Ain't Lazy." His reading of, "Funny when you're dreamin', how the time goes by," for example, exemplifies the point. Rather than follow the dotted-eighth-and-sixteenth pattern of the original, he compresses the first six syllables into something closer to sixteenth notes, letting the word "dreamin'" float a bit before delivering the rest of the line with the word "time" stretched for emphasis.

His sixteen-bar trombone solo, following directly, is perhaps an even greater wonder, freed of the lyric's specifics in extending both thought and emotional positioning. The effect broadens, deepens, and generalizes the idealism and sense of innocence and, as with Louis on "That's My Home," universalizes them.

For Pee Wee Russell, too, 1933 was a watershed year. He spent the summer on Cape Cod, working with a band led by Boston pianist Payson Ré and including, on guitar, violin, and cornet, a dapper eighteen-year-old from Providence, Rhode Island, named Bobby Hackett. The kid's cornet embouchure was still weak, his technique unformed; but his singing tone, lyrical turn of phrase, and—perhaps most of all—understanding of harmonic subtlety instantly reminded Russell of his friend Bix, then less than three years gone. Once back in New York, Pee Wee spread the word, returning to Boston that winter to work some more with Hackett.

Eddie Condon, meanwhile, had been hustling work. Among his prizes was an October 21 date for Brunswick, now owned by the low-priced (and low-paying) American Record Corp. The band, hand-picked from his current roster of favorites, included Russell, Bud Freeman, Boston trumpeter Max Kaminsky, Chicago trombonist Floyd O'Brien, bassist Artie Bernstein, pianist-arranger Alex Hill, and, on drums, the beloved "Big Sid" Catlett.

Each of the four titles is significant in its own way. Freeman's up-tempo "The Eel" (see chapter 11) was both summation of and showcase for his unique, evolving style. Pee Wee's contribution to the originally issued version: two charging, economically phrased blues choruses, delivered in a particularly "dirty," strangulated tone—part of what Gunther Schuller, in The Swing Era, calls "a timbral zoo of sounds that could never have come out of a conservatory clarinet studio" but "formed the substance, the guts, of his musical vision as much as the notes and melodic lines themselves."

Hill's "Madame Dynamite" is a crisply arranged original in the emergent small-band swing style, with brief, effective solos all around. Pee Wee begins the solo sequence on "Home Cooking," a leisurely E♭ blues, in the catacombs of his lower register, an intensely private place which he was to explore again and again.

Inexplicably, the same band (with Joe Sullivan replacing Hill) returned to the same studio, at Broadway and West 57th Street, less than a month later, apparently for the purpose of re-recording both "The Eel" and "Home Cooking." In later years no one, not even Condon himself, could remember why: all takes of all titles were released on various labels, with three versions of the Freeman original and two each of "Madame Dynamite," "Home Cooking," and "Tennessee Twilight" in relatively wide circulation.[33]

Russell's second "Home Cooking" brew draws on a recipe quite different from the first. Though the tempo is marginally faster, the change seems to be one of mood, with his frequent use of the flatted fifth much in evidence. But however eloquent these blues choruses, Russell's most effective vehicle here is Hill's "Tennessee Twilight." Richly atmospheric, it's a skillfully arranged, twenty-bar song form with an unusual structure: A (4 bars), B (4), A (4), B¹ (2), C (6). Its chord pattern, also deceptively simple, begins on the evocative "German sixth" (A7 in the performance key of D♭) and uses augmented chords with particular effectiveness.

After a rolling four-bar intro by Freeman, Russell sets out the melody in a contemplative, even elegiac manner, over sustained chords by the other horns. His last two bars are a break: in one version he tosses out an exclamatory double-time figure; in the other, rather more satisfyingly, peers quietly inward.

While Jack Teagarden was getting settled with Whiteman, Russell was still picking up work where he could: a few weeks in Boston (again with Hackett), some Condon casuals. Most of the time, however, he was just around, drinking more than he ought, and deepening his reputation, already widespread, as a jazz eccentric. Naturally nervous, shy with strangers, he often went to extremes to avoid socially taxing situations. As cornetist Ruby Braff, a lifelong admirer and, much later, a friend, remarked:

> He had a lot of trouble communicating with most people, so he played the dumb character that they seemed to want—the drunken, grumpy boozer—and he wasn't that at all. He was very smart, very intelligent, far more intelligent than most of the people he had to work with.[34]

Then, in early 1935, Russell found his own version of the kind of job security Teagarden had achieved with "Pops" Whiteman. New Orleans trumpeter Louis Prima was due to open at the Famous Door, a tiny nightspot at 35 West 52nd Street, owned jointly by a group of New York studio musician "investors," including pianist Lennie Hayton, trombonists Jack Jenney and Jerry Colonna, and trumpeter Klein. Sidney Arodin was to have been his clarinetist but had instead joined fellow-hometowner Wingy Manone on another job. Prima, who had known Pee Wee since Texas, hired him for forty dollars a week, not bad money at the time.

From the start, the Door was intended as a musicians' hangout. According to 52nd Street historian Arnold Shaw, it seated fifty-five, "sold Scotch at 55¢ a shot, whiskey 50¢, and beer 35¢ a brimming glass." More than a few habitués shared columnist Robert Sylvester's opinion that the entire concept of West 52nd Street as "Swing Street" was born with this little room.[35]

Prima's showmanship, extrovert singing, and flamboyant, Armstrong-inspired trumpet "broke the Street wide open," in one veteran's words. He also admired Pee Wee to the point of idolatry, giving him wide latitude both on and off the bandstand—though he was no more adept than anyone else in keeping the clarinetist's alcohol intake down to tolerable levels.

The leader's onstage antics may have angered such purist critics as Hammond,

729

who found him "tiresome," but they hardly seemed to bother Russell. He was happy to be playing regularly, in circumstances where he was appreciated, and his work on records of the time shows it. He'd never had more fun, he told friends in later years, adding (in a conversation with writer-historian Dan Morgenstern) that "I looked forward to going to work every night."

Russell solos on some forty Prima performances between "The Lady in Red" in May 1935 and "Mr. Ghost Goes to Town" in November 1936, never less than interestingly and sometimes far more than that. A few of the many highlights: his gargling, thrusting half-chorus on the first title; still hotter up-tempo demolition of the otherwise reflective "Chasing Shadows"; gentle obbligatos to Prima vocals on "Plain Old Me" and "Weather Man"; plaintive half-time chorus on an otherwise mile-a-minute "I Love You Truly"; Lester Young–like false fingering licks on "At the Darktown Strutters' Ball."

On "Lazy River," Prima brings him on with an ebullient "Oh, Pee Wee, la-de-la-de Pee Wee!" and the clarinetist promptly reverts to his thoughtful "Tennessee Twilight" mode; Louis himself is the highlight of "Alice Blue Gown," playing an understated, Berigan-like chorus into a hat.

(Prima deserves a separate word. His latter-day career, with its brash Las Vegas overtones and relentless showmanship, has made him a virtual non-person to jazz fans. But among these titles with Russell there is hardly one that doesn't feature a dramatic, superbly executed, sometimes quite poignant trumpet solo. Prima often plays to the grandstand in showy endings and Armstrong-like high-register flourishes; but his musicianship, fluency, command of his horn, and sheer swing more than compensate. His records of the period, some with such New Orleans clarinetists as Arodin, Eddie Miller, and the excellent, all-but-forgotten Meyer Weinberg, warrant serious reexamination. As Russell said of him, in conversation with Dan Morgenstern, "Hell of a trumpet man.")

The clarinet-trumpet ensemble on several of these titles frequently recalls Pee Wee's 1932 pairing with Henry "Red" Allen; he gleefully shatters the sentimentality of "The Stars Know" and more than lives up to the title of "Let's Have Fun," wielding his horn like a scythe cutting through heavy grass.

But perhaps most amazing of all is "Cross Patch," done with an augmented group in generic swing band style. Pee Wee, unintimidated, erupts with (in John McDonough's good phrase) "a shrill, stinging blast that suddenly elevates the record to a different level." But it's even more than that. No attempt to transcribe his twenty-four bars on a printed staff could approach doing justice to the squashed, mangled, stabbing, spit-filled tone, the bends and eldritch distortions of pitch, the rhythmic drive and displacements, that propel this solo. Not even Joe Catalyne's rather mucilaginous tenor in the bridge can stay Pee Wee's hurtling momentum. It is a master affirmation, morning-fresh even after thousands of hearings.

It's also a favorite record of fellow-clarinetist Kenny Davern, who fell hard for Russell when, late one night, he first heard him on a live radio broadcast:

> I heard this—I didn't know what it was—this spittle, and growl. This sound just came over the radio, and I stood there, transfixed, staring at the

speaker. I was transported—it was an experience, emotional and musical, that up to that point I hadn't had, not from any of the players I'd heard. I'd liked the way they played—liked their sounds, liked Fazola, Benny, Artie Shaw, and the way they approached the instrument. But none of them really went FLOCK! right between the eyes. I listened, and thought, "What was *that*, and *who* was that?" It was Pee Wee Russell, playing two choruses on "Memphis Blues," with a band led by Muggsy Spanier—and I thought, "That's it. That's what I want. I want to express myself that way for the rest of my life . . ." I knew [from that moment] that the instrument as a medium was something I was going to take very seriously.[36]

Davern and Russell became friends toward the end of the older man's life. One night in 1961 they listened together to "Cross Patch." "He'd sit there and go 'oooh' at a good turn of phrase. He'd leap up and say, 'Wow!' Then he'd sit [back down] and sock his ear"—Pee Wee's typically singular way, presumably, of telling his admirer, "not bad, eh?"[37]

Prima did turnaway business at the club, and his records sold well. But when manager Jack Colt turned down his request for a raise, he headed for California, where he'd already rounded up backing for a Los Angeles Famous Door. Opening night at the rather larger Vine Street location was no less a sensation than in New York, and at the heart of it was Pee Wee Russell.

"That man is a genius," Prima told an interviewer. "He never looked at a note. But the second time I played a lick, he'd play along with me in harmony, seemed to read my mind. [He was] the most fabulous musical mind I have ever worked with or known. We had a ball on the bandstand every night."[38]

Jack Teagarden's contract with Paul Whiteman ended in 1939. Still the most popular hot trombonist in the business, he even won one of *Metronome* magazine's all-star polls, appearing alongside Tommy Dorsey on the magazine's first "All-Star band" record. While with Whiteman he'd made outstanding records, many with small units fronted by Trumbauer, and emerged as a warm and appealing singer of ballads, as such records as "Stars Fell on Alabama," "A Hundred Years From Today," and the rarely heard Victor Young–Ned Washington "Love Me." He'd contributed ebulliently to "I Hope Gabriel Likes My Music," "I'm an Old Cowhand," and other Trumbauer-led performances of current pop tunes, usually also with good trumpet solos by brother Charlie. He's featured, singing and playing, on a 1935 Whiteman version of "Nobody's Sweetheart," duets pleasingly with Johnny Mercer on "Fare Thee Well to Harlem" and "Christmas Night in Harlem" (though their quasi-blackface banter hasn't worn especially well), and dominates "Aunt Hagar's Blues," by Whiteman's band-within-a-band, the "Swing Wing."

He'd also been watching and listening as various of his friends and colleagues began forming their own big bands. Why, then, not him? Once free of his Whiteman contract, that's just what he did, and with generally disastrous results.

Musically, the Teagarden band impressed critics (*Metronome's* George T. Simon, with some hyberbole, declared it potentially "one of the greatest outfits jazz has ever known"), made some good records, appeared in a few film shorts. But however superb his playing, however genial his onstage demeanor, Jack Teagarden succeeded only in running himself and his band deep into debt. He somehow managed to keep a regular unit together until 1946, but by common agreement his most memorable efforts of these years, at least on records, were in small groups, many of them organized specifically for recording dates.

April 30, 1938, proves the point. Milt Gabler had succeeded in getting his brand-new Commodore label off the ground with a half-dozen sessions, most featuring Condon, Bud Freeman, Jess Stacy, and other favorites. He'd wanted Teagarden as well, but schedules hadn't meshed until the last Saturday in April.

Even then, there were problems. Gabler had all but exhausted his (and his shop's) cash reserves, and there might not have been funds enough for this date had Eddie Condon not prevailed upon a friend, *Life* magazine editor Alexander King, to do a photo feature at the next Commodore session. King cooperated, *Life* came up with some money, and the session went ahead. Photos taken that day show Teagarden happy and at ease alongside Russell, Hackett, Freeman, Stacy, Condon, and George Wettling. The music, too, was as friendly and relaxed as could be imagined.

"Diane," Teagarden's feature (also see chapter 12), was an appropriate choice: according to the "received" account, Erno Rapée's newly published waltz was the melody the trombonist chose when, one night in 1928, Freeman, Russell, and cornetist Jimmy McPartland cornered him in a speakeasy and asked him to "play something." He accords "Diane" all the affection due an old flame, Stacy supplying filigree and solid chording behind him. A second take, issued later, is no less heartfelt, but the tempo is too fast, and the more rhythmic emphasis sacrifices some of the ballad quality.[39]

An up-tempo "Meet Me Tonight in Dreamland" is largely Freeman's show— and perhaps inadvertently highlights one of Jack Teagarden's few significant weaknesses, in the matter of ensemble playing.

A standard jazz front line works on specific principles: the trumpet or cornet lead generally centers on what Whitney Balliett has called the "bourgeois" middle register, the two octaves centered on the treble staff. Clarinet, though sometimes active in the upper of these two octaves, can also soar higher, keeping clear of any clash with the lead. Tenor sax, when present, works the lower octave of the lead register but can also go lower—and offset its phrases rhythmically to avoid collision (Freeman is a master of such skills). Trombone, traditionally, can use its outer (fifth, sixth, seventh) positions for foundation notes which reinforce ensemble texture while keeping out of the trumpet's way.

How well an ensemble works, especially at medium and up tempos, depends entirely on its mixture of elements. The tutti portions of "Love Is Just Around the Corner," from Commodore's maiden session, are close to perfection, largely because trombonist George Brunis plays relatively simple foundation figures, often in his lower register, counterbalancing the frequently decorative arabesques of Freeman and Hackett. Here, and on the driving final choruses of the blues "Carnegie Jump," things remain clear, well defined, even Hackett stripping his lead to essentials.

Teagarden, replacing Brunis, is an infinitely better soloist. He and Russell dominate the blues "Serenade to a Shylock," its title an apparent reference to Pee Wee's tribulations in getting his clarinet out of hock. Jack sings, and Pee Wee, in McDonough's words, "maintains a dialogue with him all the way, answering, reproaching, disputing, denying." He leaps to the fore when they double the tempo, scattering the competition with a spectacularly "raunchy" solo, to borrow Dan Morgenstern's word.

But things go astray somewhat in the two closing choruses of "Meet Me Tonight in Dreamland." Teagarden's self-devised manner of playing trombone, with its numerous "false" and invented ways of finding notes without extending his slide, also sites both his ensemble and solo playing in his upper middle register. Nor is his way of playing in collectives particularly economical. With Hackett's rather busy lead and without a Brunis to anchor and define, ensemble coherence disappears into a Babel that makes the lineaments of the song hard to discern.[40]

Freeman's Columbia session of July 23, 1940, by contrast, pairs Teagarden with trumpeter Max Kaminsky, whose direct, spare lead allows the trombonist ample room to move around. The happy result is obvious on all eight titles, particularly "Shimme-Sha Wabble," "That Da Da Strain," and a particularly spirited "At the Jazz Band Ball."

(This last contains one delectable point of detail. Opening his chorus, Teagarden leads strongly into a solidly played concert B♭, which clashes—in theory, at least—with the B♮ in the G7 chord played by the rhythm section. Yet the strength and authority with which he plays it, and in which the phrase flows from there, create a sense of inevitability quite transcending any "right" or "wrong." Bunny Berigan's solo on "Sometimes I'm Happy" and Bix Beiderbecke's on the originally issued take of "Lonely Melody" are other examples of such exquisitely right "wrong" notes.)

Teagarden's best moments at this session are on two blues, both recorded while the band was waiting for Kaminsky to show up. Teagarden opens the slower "Jack Hits the Road" with two well-turned choruses, the second using repeated major sevenths against a tonic chord, one falling (in Humphrey Lyttelton's words) "further behind the beat, successively defusing the threat of rhythmic squareness inherent in the notes themselves." More intriguingly still, the figure implies a constant back-and-forth seesawing between tonic and subdominant, something not picked up by the rhythm section; the result is not a clash, but a fascinating buildup of inner tension.

"Jack Hits the Road," Jack Teagarden first solo (four bars), 1940.

"Big Tea" then brings infectious good humor to a vocal (hear Russell's wry clarinet "comments" behind him) describing his tribulations in leading his own band and the money he owes its booking agency:

Oh I started up to see Bud Freeman,
But I lost my way;
I started up to see Bud Freeman,
But I lost my way;
An' I thought for a minute
I was on the road for MCA.[41]

But even these delights fail to prepare the unsuspecting listener for the trombonist's closing solo, a single chorus of stark emotive power. It begins, unusually for Teagarden, with a slide into a low B♭, a distant echo of George Brunis's entry on "Tin Roof Blues" with the New Orleans Rhythm Kings.[42]

Four bars of quiet, gently disconsolate rumination give way to what Lyttelton calls "a great cry of anguish, of such uncharacteristic volume that it causes a perceptible tremor of distortion in the recording." This is emotion laid bare, personal and private, unmodulated by guile or finesse.

Even by the standards of Teagarden's own work, the passage in bars 7–8 is a masterpiece of complexity, in both conception and execution; somehow it expands, explains, qualifies the outburst preceding it, while balancing it compositionally. Lyttelton compares its intensity, and its "complicated and yet logical pattern," to Louis Armstrong's opening cadenza on "West End Blues."[43]

"Jack Hits the Road," Teagarden closing solo (twelve bars), 1940.

* * *

Unlike Teagarden, Russell is nearly impossible to capture on paper. It is hard, in fact, to think of another jazz style in which content, tone, and execution are of such equal importance. *How* Pee Wee Russell plays, in other words, defines him at least as much as *what*. This creates diabolical problems in transcribing his solos: how can formal notation represent the bends, twists, distortions of pitch; the strangulated, growling, gargling sounds; the rhythmic freedom, with its idiosyncratic uses of *rubato*, which characterizes a Russell solo?

Nor are annotators the only ones nonplussed by Russell's ways. Many fellow-clarinetists, too, regarded him with emotions ranging from bafflement to mockery to outright hostility—particularly after a Conn Instrument Co. advertisement touted him as "the greatest swing clarinetist of modern times." For the classically trained Benny Goodman he was "a joke." Artie Shaw averred that he did "some interesting things" but sounded like a "leaky bicycle pump." New Orleans–born Barney Bigard, clarinet soloist with the Duke Ellington orchestra, remarked in his autobiography:

> I used to buy *Downbeat* [sic] magazine all the time but once I read that Pee Wee Russell had won a *Downbeat* poll. That did it. I never read that magazine again. Guys like him and that Frank Teschemacher aren't clarinet players to me.[44]

By contrast, Milt Gabler recalled more than once seeing Lester Young, himself the proprietor of a highly unconventional—and never successfully imitated—clarinet style, standing beside the bandstand at Jimmy Ryan's, listening intently to Russell, his face closed in around one of his own private little smiles.[45]

By the end of the '30s, Russell had gained a following outside the immediate ranks of fellow-musicians, and especially with the fans who showed up every night when he played at Nick's. He, in his turn, seemed to realize that his status as a jazz "character" was at least part of his appeal. "When Russell played," said John McDonough, "his face seemed to fold itself into a hundred different expressions of physical and emotional stress."

The author's own visual recollections are of a man perpetually in mortal combat with his horn, the song, and often some musical *cul-de-sac* into which his ceaseless exploration had driven him. "Between phrases that appeared to be wrung from the clarinet under protest," Dan Morgenstern has written, "Pee Wee would make faces and mutter Fieldsian asides to himself." Russell knew the power of such toils to hold audiences rapt. "It was the music they loved," said Milt Gabler, "but the facial thing made him seem even more of a character. He was all musician, but he knew he had that face."[46]

Trumpeter Max Kaminsky, a frequent associate, remembered Russell's conversation as "the same as his playing—he'd talk in sudden, swooping little bursts and slide in a wry remark with a shrug, crossing and uncrossing his long, nervous legs and hunching his bony shoulders or screwing up his long, sad face."[47]

In the absence of an accurate transcription method, it seems best to select a representative handful out of the many outstanding Pee Wee Russell solos of the 1938–44 period. His two choruses on the Commodore "Love Is Just Around the

735

Corner'' pick and worry ceaselessly at the tonal relationships between minor third and flatted fifth; his thirty-two *sotto voce* bars on ''Fidgety Feet,'' with the 1940 Summa Cum Laude band, generate intense momentum, without leaving his low register or carrying the dynamic level above a *mezzo-piano*; and his two unsurpassed closing choruses on the 1941 Commodore blues ''The Last Time I Saw Chicago,'' backed to perfection by Joe Sullivan and Zutty Singleton, are a thesaurus of everything that sets Pee Wee Russell apart. After a powerful Sullivan solo, Pee Wee enters low, backed by rolling piano tremolo:

"The Last Time I Saw Chicago," Pee Wee Russell solo (twenty-four bars), 1941.

Here are the intervals, the calculated dissonances, the vocalized mid-range figures, the leaps to a keening upper register, the mixture of tension and release.

736

But even such use of the cryogenic vocabulary of analysis conveys almost nothing of the passion, the sense of personal *presence*, that illuminates these choruses.

Russell bursts resolutely out of the sedate opening ensemble of "Sunrise Serenade," recorded in 1939 with Bobby Hackett's short-lived big band, saturating Frankie Carle's tune with gritty lyricism; he tosses off two agitated choruses on Davison's Commodore "That's a Plenty" and delivers an even better one on a transcription version of the same tune with Bobby Hackett and Ernie Caceres.

Then, too, there are the four extraordinary quartet titles of September, 1944, also on Commodore, with Jess Stacy, Sid Weiss, and George Wettling. "Take Me to the Land of Jazz" and "Rose of Washington Square" (the latter at a far more relaxed tempo than the 1929 version) exist in three takes each, riding comfortably on Stacy's buoyant keyboard touch. Russell keeps probing, investigating, following his instincts; each solo is a fresh conception, reflecting a mind ceaselessly, restlessly at work. "We were equal partners in an ensemble," Stacy told John McDonough. "I could get behind Pee Wee and really push . . . get in and counterpunch and play creatively."

Pee Wee is also a superb ensemble player, custom-tailoring how much he plays, how he plays it and where, to the lead and texture established by the other horns. On the early-'30s records with Allen and Prima he can be heard waiting, listening, placing his figures to complement these rather extravagant trumpeters. With Hackett, as on the Commodore version of the ODJB standard "Skeleton Jangle," he uses longer notes, and fewer of them, often resolving his phrases in the cornetist's breath points. Less discursive lead players, Muggsy Spanier and Max Kaminsky among them, prompt him to play more. The last two choruses of "Strut Miss Lizzie," with Kaminsky and valve trombonist Brad Gowans, find him downright garrulous.

Sometimes, when the ensembles are simply too busy and too thick for Russell to play any meaningful role, he retreats into his upper register, chops his phrases into bits, and sprinkles them into openings in the texture. The closing "Impromptu Ensemble" jam session numbers that usually ended Eddie Condon's weekly Town Hall concerts provide countless examples of this unique art.

If Pee Wee's throaty solo on "St. Louis Blues" with Miff Mole in April 1944 is like a cubist painting, as has been suggested, his end-of-chorus break in the final ensemble spills over into outright surrealism. Yet for "Peg o' My Heart," on the selfsame session, he turns strictly representationalist, honoring Fred Fisher's old (1913) melody with surpassing tenderness.

Not surprisingly, Russell was among the musicians featured most prominently on the Condon concerts, broadcast on NBC's "Blue" Network. But a worrisome element had entered the relationship: whether out of habit or because he thought the more bizarre aspects of Russell's playing and stage demeanor would entertain audiences, Condon began to play the clarinetist for laughs. Many a spoken introduction would refer to Pee Wee as "the strong-arm man of jazz," or otherwise allude to his frailty or overall air of melancholy.

Condon meant no harm—his affection and respect for the clarinetist were deep and long-standing—but the constant jokes, the one-liners and asides, found a vulnerable target. Despite the long friendship, a resentment grew between them, and not only on a personal level. Years of catering to the customers at Nick's (and, later, at his own club) had nudged Condon's musical leadership into the kind of formulaic rigidity deplored by Artie Shaw in describing his post–"Begin the Beguine" band as "about as creative as a bunch of stockbrokers . . . a band capable of remarkable performances and taking major strides . . . caught in a trap created by success."[48]

For a great number of its lay fans, "dixieland," as played by Condon's bands and others, had come to mean little more than overcooked reprises of "At the Jazz Band Ball," "That's a Plenty," "Tin Roof Blues," and the rest. Quietly, tentatively, Pee Wee Russell began to rebel. His wife Mary, whom he'd married in 1943, campaigned tirelessly to expand his horizons; to make him eat regularly, reduce his alcohol intake. She had little time for those among her husband's old cronies who seemed to delight in making a drunken caricature of him. More than a few times Condon's gibes drove her into a fury.

But after a time even she threw up her hands: in 1949 the couple separated—and Russell promptly ran himself into the ground. He fell off the wagon, ate next to nothing, as his weight plummeted well below a hundred pounds. On New Year's Eve 1951, he collapsed in San Francisco and was taken to the charity ward of a local hospital.

His illness stirred the entire jazz community. A *Life* magazine photo, widely circulated at the time, shows Louis Armstrong and Jack Teagarden, concern etched on their faces, bending over the bedside of an emaciated, grievously ill Russell. What millions of *Life* readers didn't see was what editors had discreetly cropped out: a lit, half-smoked cigarette in the sick man's hand. Illness or no, some things never changed.[49]

Benefit concerts in several cities, including one in San Francisco featuring Teagarden and Armstrong, raised close to five thousand dollars, and by early spring, Pee Wee Russell—minus some surgically removed stomach cysts—was well on the way to recovery. But his close brush with death had changed him: he seemed more outgoing, talked more ("as if," said Mary, with whom he was soon reunited, "he were trying to catch up"); and, perhaps most remarkable, he began reaching in new musical directions.[50]

Jack Teagarden, meanwhile, was treading quite another path. Tired and deep in debt, drained by alimony payments to his third of four wives, he finally abandoned bandleading in late 1946. The next months were a time of recurrent illness, little work, less money. Though never one to discuss his troubles, Teagarden must have wondered more than once whether he had a future at all.

An answer came on Saturday night, May 17, 1947, when New York ad executive and press agent Ernie Anderson (with a musical assist from Bobby Hackett) presented Louis Armstrong and a hand-picked sextet in concert at New York's Town Hall. The evening was a sellout, reestablishing Armstrong in a small-band context—and reuniting him happily with Teagarden.

"I've been waiting a long, long time, about twenty-three years, for this op-portunity," the trombonist told master of ceremonies Fred Robbins in a brief onstage interview. "I'm really in heaven tonight." That he wasn't exaggerating is clear from his amiable banter with Louis on "Rockin' Chair," and even more from the first notes of his feature, "St. James Infirmary." He'd performed it countless times since his Ben Pollack days, recorded it at least once. But this one was different: intensely, deeply felt, it is a spellbinding moment.[51]

He begins open horn, sings a pair, then, as a hush falls over the hall, finishes with just his slide and a water glass. All but encrusted with rococo embellishment, these two choruses seem as much a visual as an auditory experience. The eye longs to peer more closely, admiring the finely carved scrollwork, the gold leaf, the inlay of precious stones.

Max Harrison, perceptive as ever, identifies this moment as "in both instru-mental and vocal terms quite simply one of the trombonist's greatest recordings," adding that Teagarden's phrases "are highly detailed yet have an inevitability that only a master could impart."[52]

The Town Hall concert led to formation of Louis Armstrong's All-Stars, a loosely organized sextet which, at first, boasted such members as pianist Earl Hines, clarinetist Bigard, drummer Sid Catlett, and, of course, Teagarden. That the group in its entirety never quite added up to the sum of its illustrious parts in no way dims the brilliance of many individual performances.

The trombonist stayed with Louis four years, then put together a small touring band of his own; by late 1953 it included sister Norma Teagarden at the piano and an old comrade, New Orleans–born Ray Bauduc, on drums. But Teagarden himself had by now retreated into what often seemed a mysterious private for-tress, ringed by a moat of alcohol and seeming to contain little save his trombone and whatever bit of gadgetry captured his fancy at the time.

"I found him warm but distant," said clarinetist Kenny Davern, who joined the group in 1954. "There, but not there. Emotionally closed off. Sometimes it seemed that his idea of spending an afternoon was to come into a place where we'd be playing and tune the piano. Or make brass mouthpieces on a lathe he had in his garage. I got the idea sometimes that all that tinkering was his way of putting something between him and the world, so he wouldn't have to deal with it."[53]

In his playing, too, a schism had opened. Richard Hadlock gets right to the point, noting that Teagarden "always performed best when supported sympa-thetically by his musical equals." The trombonist himself expressed similar thoughts to Down Beat's John Tynan in 1957: "Guess you could call me an inspi-ration man. Unless I've got good guys around me, I'm no good."[54]

Teagarden's records with his own groups of the '50s are never less than good but seldom rise to real heights of inspiration. Yet on two LPs with Bobby Hackett, in 1955 and 1957, he shines with all the old brilliance; there is even a "St. James Infirmary" which comes within hailing distance of the great Town Hall version of 1947.

But shadows were closing in. Connie Jones, who played cornet in the last edition of Teagarden's traveling sextet, remembered meeting his new boss one Sunday afternoon at a club in Cherry Hill, New Jersey, outside Philadelphia. "He was sitting at the back of the room, at a table all by himself, drinking a cup of coffee," said Jones. "No mistaking him. But I remember thinking that in that moment he looked to me like the loneliest man I'd ever seen."[55]

The late trumpeter Don Goldie, who spent four years in Teagarden's band and had known him since childhood, "always got the feeling that a lot of happiness was locked away inside Jack, really padlocked, and never came out . . . Just this feeling of sadness. It was always there."[56]

Jack Teagarden died, alone, in his room at the Prince Conti Hotel in New Orleans on January 15, 1964. He was only fifty-eight. "I sometimes think people like Jack were just go-betweens," Bobby Hackett told a friend. "The Good Lord said, 'Now you go and show 'em what it is,' and he did. I think everybody familiar with Jack Teagarden knows that he was something that happens just once. It won't happen again. Not that way."[57]

Pee Wee Russell's later career, unlike Teagarden's, was a time of fulfillment, exploration, and, for many critics and fans, rediscovery: enough so to almost warrant a chapter of its own. Reluctant to spend the rest of his days in the lockstep of "That's a Plenty" and "Royal Garden Blues," the clarinetist reached into new areas—new repertoire and, in many cases, new musical companions.

"We just made a record," he told Dan Morgenstern during a chance meeting in 1960. "It was modern. And the piano player was one of the best I've ever played with." He was Tommy Flanagan, widely esteemed for his work with Miles Davis, Sonny Rollins, and other contemporary figures, and as accompanist to such top singers as Ella Fitzgerald.

Suddenly, it seemed, Pee Wee Russell was the man of the hour, who had always been "modern." For the 1957 TV show The Sound of Jazz, he played the blues in duo with Jimmy Giuffre, whose low-register clarinet style owed much to Russell but lacked its unpredictability and complexity. He recorded such numbers as Billy Strayhorn's "Chelsea Bridge," John Coltrane's "Red Planet," and the old bop standard "Good Bait."

The new Pee Wee mania reached a peak of sorts in 1963, when jazz impresario George Wein paired the clarinetist with Thelonious Monk at the Newport Jazz Festival. A quartet with arranger and valve trombonist Marshall Brown aroused interest, though Pee Wee quickly tired of Brown's controlling ways: "I haven't taken so many orders since military school," he commented acidly. At one concert he played a clarinet duet with Gerry Mulligan, who afterwards commented that Russell "was inclined to be further out—harmonically and melodically—than I am . . . He was fearless. I never thought of him [strictly] as a clarinet player—it was more like a direct line to his subconscious."[58]

Another object of newfound attention was Russell's old friend and soulmate, trumpeter Red Allen. Both suddenly found themselves hailed (much to their amusement, surely) as men ahead of their time, even—as in trumpeter Don Ellis's widely quoted paean to Allen—truly "avant-garde" musicians. But colleagues who had known both for years tended to dismiss the hoopla. As Coleman Hawkins said of Russell after their 1961 *Jazz Reunion* record session, "for thirty years I've been listening to him play those funny notes. He used to think they were wrong, but they weren't. He's always been 'way out,' but they didn't have a word for it then."[59]

(An NBC television special, *Chicago and All That Jazz*, also provided "jazz reunion," but of another sort—and with vastly different results. Russell and Teagarden, neither of whom had ever had much to do with Chicago, appeared with old Chicagoans Condon, Freeman, Joe Sullivan, cornetist Jimmy McPartland, and drummer Gene Krupa playing such anthems as "Nobody's Sweetheart," "Sugar," and "China Boy." Viewed now, Teagarden seems to be functioning on automatic pilot, Russell going through well-worn and perfunctory routines. A dispirited air hangs over the proceedings, both on the TV soundtrack and on an LP done for Verve at about the same time.)[60]

His own "Pee Wee's Blues," oft-played and oft-recorded, shows his thinking well. Though based on a standard twelve-bar structure, both melody and changes make free and natural use of chromaticism and chordal extensions. Perhaps the most ambitious version is an orchestral setting devised by composer-arranger Oliver Nelson for the *Spirit of '67* LP, which featured Russell in front of a big band that included such jazz stars as trumpeters Clark Terry and Thad Jones, trombonists Jimmy Cleveland and Urbie Green, and fellow-reedmen Phil Woods and Jerry Dodgion. "I don't think I'd ever realized before what a visionary he was," said Dodgion. "I'd never heard him in person before that. He was so quiet, unassuming: yet what he played sounded like nobody else I'd ever heard. It was a real discovery for me."[61]

Admiration of Russell's work centered on three qualities: his highly expressive and frequently un-clarinet-like tone; his rhythmic sense, as free and defiant of strict analysis as Allen's; and, perhaps above all, his ceaseless daring. All three qualities come triumphantly together in the hushed intimacy and inevitable logic of his choruses on "Mariooch," a slow B♭ blues recorded in 1961 and named after his beloved Mary.

Drummer-journalist Don DeMicheal, reviewing the record in *Down Beat*, found its introspection "almost embarrassing, for what he plays is so personal." And no wonder: these five choruses, sixty bars, constitute a guided tour of Pee Wee Russell's imagination. All the "funny notes" are there: chromatic upper and lower neighbors, elevenths and thirteenths, flatted fifths and major sevenths. Again, execution is as important as content: it is hard to imagine any other clarinetist, even the prodigiously accomplished Kenny Davern, capturing the *rubato*, the pregnant pauses, the hurry-up-and-wait flurries, even the urgent, wholly organic inner drive of Russell's vibrato. Whitney Balliett has praised "Mariooch" as "a five-chorus edifice of melancholy and triumph," in which the ear finds itself "wholly caught up by . . . a singing, strange, solitary voice that had never been heard in jazz before."[62]

Through "Mariooch," as neighbors in their largely Italian section of Greenwich Village called her, Russell also came to the other great artistic outlet of his later life. Bridling at the sight of her husband sitting idle between jobs, watching TV, she bought him a painting set at Macy's, all but hurling it at him with the command, "Here! Do something with yourself! Paint!"

He did just that and, on November 30, 1965, completed his first oil. Over the next year he turned out more than sixty canvases, gaining skill, assurance, and subtlety with each one. Unlike the paintings of his friend George Wettling, pupil and disciple of abstractionist Stuart Davis, they were derivative of nothing and no one, as original as his clarinet. "His style, if one had to classify it, at first glance looked like geometric abstraction," said Dan Morgenstern, "but closer inspection usually revealed representational elements. The colors were bold and beautifully harmonized, and there was a fey humor in his work that reminded one of his playing."[63]

One of Russell's own descriptions of his painting technique, in fact, sounds exactly like the process by which he made music on the clarinet: "I start with certain colors and when it starts getting too dull for me, I say how will I get out of this and what color will I use?"[64]

Mary Russell died of cancer in 1967; her passing, viewed in restrospect, signaled the beginning of the end for Pee Wee as well. He stopped working, stopped eating regularly, resumed heavy drinking. Never touched a paintbrush again.

"It's my fault," he told Phyllis Condon, tears coursing down the seamed face. "I killed her." Despite the efforts of friends, Davern and fellow-clarinetist Tom Gwaltney prominent among them, to look after him, Pee Wee Russell died at a hospital in Alexandria, Virginia, on February 15, 1969. He is buried next to his "Mariooch" at a New Jersey cemetery.

Similar in eloquence, strikingly dissimilar in method, Pee Wee Russell and Jack Teagarden, considered together, often seem two halves of a whole. Both were intensely personal storytellers: if Teagarden, with his emotional directness and mastery of often subtle language, was Mark Twain, Russell's locutions and conceits invite comparison with the fabulist E. T. A. Hoffmann. Both were immediate, warm, musically intelligent, naturally swinging. Both were singular blues players who found powerful, personal expression in the feelings, flavors, and accents of the form.

It hardly seems excessive to suggest that these two, in their inimitable ways, represent the highest form of creativity available to a jazz improviser. Far from "eccentric," "maverick," or "idiosyncratic," they belong at the very center of stylistic distinction.

Perhaps the ultimate tribute is simply to try to imagine jazz without them. Such indispensables form a small, ultimate elite, one equally singular for the names it includes and those it does not. Yes, the influences, the trendsetters, are there; but so, too, no less reverenced, are the one-in-a-million, once-in-a-lifetime Teagardens and Russells.

Connie Jones, the New Orleans cornetist working with Jack Teagarden at the time of the trombonist's death, was a pallbearer for the wake, held at a funeral parlor on leafy St. Charles Avenue: "I remember seeing him there in a coffin, a traveling coffin. They were going to fly him to Los Angeles for burial right after that. The coffin was open, and I remember thinking, 'Boy, he really looks uncomfortable in there.'

"Not that he was that tall. Maybe five foot ten or so, at the most. But he was kinda wide across the shoulders—and most of all he just gave you the impression he was a big man, in every way. In that coffin—well, I can't really explain it, but he seemed to be scrunched up into a space that was too small to contain him."[65]

Jack Teagarden and Pee Wee Russell will ever remain so, their spirits unconfined even by death and slow time. In Charles Kingsley's tender exhortation,

> Do lovely things, not dream them, all day long;
> And so make Life, and Death, and that For Ever,
> One grand sweet song.[66]

Epilogue

Beyond dispute, white musicians have been an integral force in jazz from its earliest days. But what other conclusions can be drawn from this vast and sprawling chronicle? Surely that much "received" history, for various reasons, has promulgated a distorted version of the facts. That the first, formative jazz criticism of the Depression years was shaped—and skewed—by ideas that were ideological before they were musical. Above all, that the idea of jazz as an exclusively black cultural preserve does not stand up to close scrutiny.

Such matters have been loudly argued, even fought over, and doubtless will continue to be hot subjects for some time to come. More relevant, at least to this survey, is the question of the music itself: Does any evidence support the idea of identifiable "black" and "white" styles? Did it ever? Roy Eldridge, at the outset of a long-ago "Blindfold Test," boasted to critic Leonard Feather that he could tell right away whether any record featured a white or a black band. He then proceeded to get almost every example Feather played for him wrong. By that time, in the 1950s, there had been too much blending of musical elements, too much mutual influence among musicians, for Eldridge to be able to make such distinctions.

Earlier, however, especially in the 1920s and '30s, there *were* differences. As this history has shown, they came about chiefly because musicians of different races were separated in their day-to-day and professional lives. And it was separately that black and white musicians grappled with the same problems of rhythm, harmony, melodic construction, interaction.

Some of his more extreme views may make Amiri Baraka (a.k.a. Leroi Jones) an unlikely source of valuable insight into such matters. Yet he seems right on target when he remarks, in *Blues People*:

> Jazz as played by white musicians was not the same as that played by black musicians, *nor was there any reason for it to be* [emphasis added]. The music of the white jazz musicians did not issue from the same cultural circumstances.[1]

In the context of the early years, the distinction is important. Differences in upbringing, environment, and musical training left white jazzmen (especially those who had little personal contact with black culture and its traditions) more likely to intellectualize, emphasizing matters of harmony and structure. The almost hermetical music of the Original Memphis Five, and of the Georgians, seems to underscore the point.

Performances by black ensembles, above all those of the South and Southwest, possessed, in general, a degree of rhythmic freedom, personal interaction, and often a blues feeling and melodic vocabulary rarely found in music by corresponding white bands. Again, Baraka gets it right:

> The white musicians understood the blues first as music, but seldom as an attitude, since the attitude, or world-view, the white musician was responsible to was necessarily quite a different one.[2]

But, along with other scholars who follow this line of reasoning, he fails to account for those many major black jazzmen who feel, and display, little or no affinity for the blues and its "attitude." The exceptions they present, in their very numbers, are a counterargument, which cannot be explained, as Baraka tries to do, only as a matter of "Negroes trying to pretend that they had issued from [white] culture."

More likely, it seems, is an interpretation suggesting that mastery of what came to be called jazz was not a matter of racial or genetic affinity (always a dangerous hypothesis) but of choice. It has been widely demonstrated here that jazzmen of the pre–World War II decades, black and white, paid careful attention to each other's work, and that the degree to which such mutuality affected individuals varied immensely.

Some players, as would be expected, retained a greater insularity of approach than others. Comparison of two pairs of cornetists—Louisiana-born Tommy Ladnier and his northern colleague Joe Smith, and Red Nichols and Muggsy Spanier—provides graphic illustration. Ladnier, sitting alongside Smith in Fletcher Henderson's mid-'20s orchestra, is deeply rooted in the special emotional urgency of the blues, whereas his sectionmate seems drawn to *song*, with its consciousness of form, tonal purity, precision of execution.

So, too, with Nichols and Spanier. The former's clean, careful lines never lose an aura of calculation, almost as if he has the last note in mind as soon as he plays the first; Spanier, more visceral, has listened hard to Oliver and Armstrong, absorbed the blues—and blended it all with an endearingly hand-on-heart Irish sentimentality.

Beginning in the 1920s, individual musicians (and sometimes entire ensem-

745

bles) made choices based on what they liked, even admired, incorporating the results in their emergent solo styles. Choice, above all, quickly became the determinant of what and how a man played, how he constructed and developed a solo, addressed the beat. In this context, as noted earlier, certain traits—tendencies and attitudes—can be identified as "white" and "black" contributions to the mix.

Once identified, they must also be qualified. Within this frame of reference there is obviously more than a merely semantic difference between the concept of "white" or "black" jazz tendencies and that of jazz as played by black and white musicians. In the clear majority of cases, one played as one played; Benny Carter's elegant, highly sculpted approach to the saxophone occasioned no censure from his peers because it was "white"—any more than did the Armstrong-inspired rubato flourishes of Jack Purvis because their source of inspiration was "black." A black-white symbiosis was under way, and out of it emerged the modern language of jazz.

Today, so many decades later, with jazz having conquered the world and absorbed musical dialects from Rio to Rawalpindi, Hokkaido to Harare to Havana, it's hard to say whether "white" and "black" traits or methods of approach can still be discerned. A more pressing matter concerns the ways in which we look at and evaluate the past. If understanding of jazz, in all its endless variegation, is to survive, there must be acknowledgment of all its contributory forces, free of the distortions of political or racial bias. We must understand that no one quality is intrinsically more echt than any others; that the "blacks invented, whites appropriated" canon is based on either ignorance or willful misreading of the historical record. The very idea of establishing critical litmus tests for jazz "authenticity," based on the blues, some concept of swing, or any other arbitrary criterion, is both irresponsible and short-sighted. Rather than enrich, it impoverishes by exclusion, and its victims are those who will inherit the music's cultural legacy.

Throughout most of its history, jazz has been profoundly pluralist. It is within this pluralism that its musicians created (and for many decades preserved) an environment in which stylistic difference led not to strife but to cross-fertilization, respect, and artistic growth. Very often, such unity was strong enough, elastic enough, to thrive against countervailing pressures from the society at large.

Cultural and racial politics in the last decades of twentieth-century America have brought a divisiveness into jazz. Whatever its motives—and there is no impugning the integrity, even altruism, of some of those responsible—its results have been fractiousness and fracture, rivalry and mutual suspicion, elevation of some figures and exclusion of others; a revisionist interpretation of jazz history as a dynasty of black masters, with whites either absent or, worse, vilified as thieves and exploiters.

The music, meanwhile, seems to have come to a creative impasse. Such cultural institutions as Lincoln Center in New York and the Smithsonian in Washington have created "official" ensembles whose major purpose seems to be presentation of jazz as a kind of anthropological orthodoxy, existing in a cultural vacuum, no more relevant to these times than a Puccini opera or Palestrina motet.

Glenn McNatt, writing in the *Baltimore Sun* (December 24, 1995) sees this transformation as evidence of a decline in creative ferment, which "seems to come from deeper changes in the social attitudes and modes of behavior that underlie the way of life represented by the jazz art." If this is so, it is cause for regret, in that it signals extinction of a way of life based on a communality felt by all jazz musicians, white and black.

New generations of players, arriving in waves since the 1950s, have drawn on a far wider range of stylistic antecedents than were available to their predecessors. If many younger whites are attracted to the '20s and '30s, while large numbers of blacks espouse the hard bop of the '50s, is one group to be deemed more "authentic" than another?

If jazz with its attendant traditions—white and black, African and European, regional and universal—is to survive as a creative entity, and someday even flourish again, there must be a coming together, a rejection of fragmentation, a revival of real pluralism and shared curiosity. A return, in brief, to what one writer lauded recently—if a little wistfully (and with a deliberate nod to Dr. Martin Luther King)—as "a safe haven from the storms of ideology, a meritocracy of comrades in which . . . players are judged not by the color of their skin but the content of their choruses."[3]

Then, and only then, will "white jazz" and "black jazz" become the simple, neutral, and essentially innocuous descriptive phrases they should have been all along.

Notes

Preface

1. George T. Simon, "Barnet's—Blackest White Band of All!" *Metronome*, August, 1939, anthologized in *Simon Says: The Sights and Sounds of The Swing Era* (New Rochelle, N.Y.: Arlington House, 1971), p. 138.

Introduction

1. Barbara Tuchman, lecture to National Archives Conference on research in The Second World War, June 1971. First published in *Maryland Historian*, fall 1971, anthologized in *Practicing History* (New York: Ballantine, 1982).

2. Arthur M. Schlesinger Jr., *The Disuniting of America*. (New York: W. W. Norton, 1992), p. 47.

3. Adolphus "Doc" Cheatham, conversation with the author, February 18, 1993.

4. Bob Wilber (with Derek Webster), *Music Was Not Enough*. (New York: Oxford University Press, 1987), p. 43.

5. Paul Whiteman and Mary Margaret McBride, *Jazz*. (New York: J. H. Sears, 1926), p. 116.

6. Albert Murray, *Stompin' the Blues*. (New York: McGraw-Hill, 1976), p. 214.

7. André Hodeir, *Jazz: Its Evolution and Essence* (New York: Grove Press reprint, 1956), translated from the French by David Noakes, p. 156. In this connection, the author also remarks that even characteristic inflections of the blues are conspicuous by their absence from Hawkins's famed performance.

8. In this context it is also useful to address the belief, widely held but thinly doc-

umented, that the true roots of jazz lie in Africa. Writing in *The Siege on Modernity* (Buenos Aires, 1991, pp. 259–60, translated from the Spanish by Carol Sudhalter), Argentine essayist and social historian Juan José Sebreli observes that black Africans historically have "seemed not to feel the least bit of identification with a music that was supposedly of African origin. Paul Morand in his trip to Africa in 1928 . . . found that in Dakar a jazz group had been formed of white musicians because they found no blacks to play; and the blacks to whom they played records seemed more enthused by Russian melodies than by jazz." American researcher Jerome S. Shipman suggests that even if identifiable sources of jazz were to be found in Africa, "those sources would have been current in a time a hundred or a hundred and fifty years before there were any recordings (or even transcriptions) of African music, and although the music may be presumed to have changed relatively slowly, who really knows what it was like in the eighteenth century? The diversity of African music not only from region to region, but from tribe to tribe within a region, poses further problems, and [renders] the difficulties of establishing a causal link between some African practice and a similar jazz practice virtually insuperable" (*IAJRC Journal*, October 1979).

9. Carol Muske, "Laura Riding Roughshod," *New York Sunday Times Book Review*, Nov. 28, 1993.

Chapter 1

1. Evidence suggests that southern white ragtime musicians, individually or even in groups, may have come north at earlier dates. The great World's Columbian Exposition of May-November 1893, for example, is known to have attracted numerous black ragtime pianists, probably including pioneers Scott Joplin and Ben Harney. But as Edward A. Berlin points out in *Ragtime: A Musical and Cultural History* (Berkeley: University of California Press, 1980), no contemporary documentation has been found of any direct participation on the fairgrounds. It is similarly unclear whether any whites were among those "professors" who performed in Chicago music halls and cabarets at this early time. But older Chicago musicians, talking to historian John Steiner, recalled "no jazz hornmen or anything like Dixieland jazz in Chicago before 1911." Quoted in Leroy Ostransky, *Jazz City: The Impact of Our Cities on the Development of Jazz* (Englewood Cliffs, N.J.: Prentice-Hall, 1978), p. 62.

2. Steve Brown, interview with William Russell and Richard B. Allen, New Orleans, April 22, 1958; tape and transcript on file at William Ransom Hogan Jazz Archive, Tulane University, New Orleans.* Also relevant here is the distinction drawn in New Orleans, as elsewhere, between reading musicians, able to adapt to a variety of situations, and those who "faked"—i.e., played by ear. Employment options for the latter group were limited: even admission to the musicians' union was contingent on sight-reading abilities. For this reason alone, many early jazz names do not show up on federation rolls. There is every indication that the "readers" among early jazzmen (cornetist Johnny DeDroit and trombonist Eddie Edwards were two of many) had less trouble finding work, whatever the season, than did the "fakers."

3. Ray Lopez (as told to Dick Holbrook), "Mister Jazz Himself," *Storyville*, April-May 1976, pp. 135–51.

4. St. Clair Drake and Horace R. Cayton, *Black Metropolis* (New York: Harcourt Brace, 1945).

5. Studs Terkel, *Division Street: America* (New York: Pantheon, 1967), p. 379.

*Hereafter referred to as Hogan Archive.

6. S. Frederick Starr, "Der Fruehe New Orleans Jazz: Legende und Wirklichkeit" (Early New Orleans Jazz: Legend and Reality), essay accompanying exhibition That's Jazz: The Sound of the 20th Century, in Darmstadt, West Germany, 1985 (translated by the author).

7. Lopez, as above, note 3.

8. Ibid.

9. This photograph has been the subject of some dispute. At various times the man in front has been identified as vaudevillian Joe Cook (real name Joseph Lopez, no relation). Cook is apparently in the photograph, but toward the rear. Joe Frisco (real name Louis Joseph) had heard Brown's band in New Orleans, where he was appearing as part of a ballroom dancing act billed as "Francisco and Loretta." He had also encouraged them to come north: in later years he claimed to have personally set up the deal with Gorham, but there is no evidence to support this. At the left of the photo, leaning on Brown's trombone case, is a figure in a cap whom some (see Rose and Souchon, New Orleans Jazz: A Family Album) have identified as future mob czar Alphonse Capone. Various historians have established that the earliest "Scarface" could have been in Chicago was 1919; an even more likely date of his arrival, according to Laurence Bergreen in Capone, is 1921. Finis Farr, in Chicago, puts it at 1922.

10. Brown, as above, note 2.

11. Arnold Loyocano, interview with Dr. Edmond Souchon, New Orleans, September 29, 1956, tape Hogan Archive. Betty Jane Holder, "Libretto—The Story of Arnold Loyocano," Second Line, January 1951.

12. Dick Holbrook, "Our Word JAZZ," Storyville, December 1973–January 1974, pp. 46–58. Starr reference from New Orleans UnMasqued (Édition Dedeaux, 1985). Jacobson quoted in "Origin of Term JAZZ," Jazz Session, July-August 1945.

13. Some doubt surrounds Lopez's account of this switch. According to the cornetist, "Gussie" was a proficient sight-reader and versatile bandsman, an asset for section work as well as small extempore combinations. Yet Paul Whiteman, for whom Mueller worked in the early 1920s, declared (in Jazz, p. 241) that Mueller was "wonderful on the clarinet and saxophone, but he couldn't read a line of music. I tried to teach him, but he wouldn't try to learn, so I had to play everything over for him and let him get it by ear."

14. Loyocano, as above, note 11.

15. William Howland Kenney, Chicago Jazz: A Cultural History, 1904–1930 (New York: Oxford University Press, 1993). Ostransky, as above, note 1. According to historian Lawrence Gushee (notes to The Legendary Freddie Keppard, Smithsonian LP R-020, 1979), the Creole Orchestra played an engagement of unknown length at Chicago's Grand Theatre in early February 1915. It is even possible, he adds, that this ensemble worked at the North American Café, in the downtown Loop area, around the time Tom Brown's band went to work at Lamb's. No documentation, alas, has been unearthed. What is known is that on August 16 the Original Creole Orchestra began a thirteen-week tour of theatres in Iowa and Illinois, then headed east for engagements in New York.

16. This event seems doomed to inspire controversy. Some writers have even argued that it was simply not appropriate that a white band be the first to record the new music. As Paul Eduard Miller and George Hoefer wrote in The Esquire Jazz Book in 1946, "the Negro jazzmen were just better, that's all—more mature, more confident . . ." ("Chicago Jazz History," p. 124). It should be noted in this context that white bands, too, missed a chance to record; often it seems less a matter of bias on the part of record firms (who were interested chiefly in making money) than a certain conservatism on the part of the musicians. Most of the southern players were unsophisticated men, who had neither interest

nor trust in the emergent wonders of technology. Offers were reportedly made to, and refused by, bands of both races. As Lawrence Gushee further observes, many vaudeville artists of the day "were fearful of and resentful about the pirating of their best routines ("How the Creole Band Came to Be," *Black Music Research Journal* 8, no. 1 [1988], p. 90). The situation only began to change when sales of records by the Original Dixieland Jazz Band proved that money could be made through recording.

17. Musical and cultural scholar James T. Maher has discussed, in this connection, what he terms "American syncopation." Beginning in the mid-nineteenth century, says Maher, the very nature of syncopation in popular music forms displays an indigenously "American" character distinct from its usage in European forms. Brahms, Dvořák and others heard it, recognized it as something new, and in some cases attempted to incorporate it. Its use in an American context carried syncopation from the role of device, as it had been in Europe, to that of "a basic rhythmic (propulsive) element in American dance music and dancing." Maher views this transformation process as a "gray area, a phenomenon that has yet to be seriously explored by jazz researchers" (conversation with the author, April 20, 1996). Scholar-historian Lawrence Gushee is reportedly at work in this important area.

18. Details of these events, predictably, have varied from account to account. Drummer Anton Lada, for example, has been quoted as saying it was he, LaRocca, Nunez, Edwards, and Ragas who answered Harry James's summons, that they worked first at Casino Gardens, and that they broke up in a dispute over money. LaRocca then reorganized, sending for Stein as Lada's replacement. The activities of such entrepreneurs as James would appear to support James Lincoln Collier's hypothesis that, for all the opposition of pedagogues, clergymen, and other putative upholders of the public morality, jazz had a following among middle-class white Americans from the start, a novel, highly saleable commodity. And, Collier asserts (in "The Faking of Jazz," *New Republic*, November 18, 1985), it was through the efforts of such businessmen as James, Gorham, and others that jazz bands began to be heard in the big cities of the North.

19. H. O. Brunn, *The Story of the Original Dixieland Jazz Band* (Baton Rouge: Louisiana State University Press, 1960), pp. 37–38.

20. Ibid.

21. According to Brunn, Nunez returned briefly to New Orleans, only to reappear in Chicago with a band including Stein, Behrenson—on trombone this time—Emile Christian on cornet, and Eddie Shields, clarinetist Larry's kid brother, at the piano. It appears to have been typical of New Orleans bands that many players were skilled on several instruments: Behrenson, for example, was also an excellent clarinetist, who recorded in New York with trumpeter Phil Napoleon and others.

22. Bert Lopez, letter to Dick Holbrook, c. 1972.

23. Erik Blom, ed., *Grove's Dictionary of Music and Musicians*, 5th ed. (New York: St. Martin's Press, 1954), vol. 2, pp. 464–65.

24. New Orleans scholar-musicians John Chaffee and John Joyce, who worked with Brown in the 1960s, report (conversations with the author, 1996) that his sound and style remained consistent and resembled that of Emile Christian in its balance between band ragtime and small-band hot jazz.

25. Bruce Boyd Raeburn, "Jazz and the Italian Connection," *Jazz Archivist* 6, no. 1, published by the Hogan Archive (May 1991), pp. 3–4.

26. Eddie Edwards, interview with Richard B. Allen, July 1, 1959, Hogan Archive.

27. Lopez, as above, note 3.

28. Research by Lawrence Gushee indicates that a surprising number of New Orleans musicians of both races played engagements in California during these years. Gushee re-

cords that Merritt and Henry Brunies deposited their transfers in Los Angeles union local 47 in late 1920; that Bill Lambert went there around the same time; that clarinetists Achille Baquet, Larry Shields, and Gus Mueller were all working or present in Los Angeles in 1921–22. He suggests, with apparently strong justification, that California in general played a far greater role in the early evolution of jazz than has thus far been documented or popularly supposed. The Creole Band (or Orchestra), referred to earlier, seems to have played Los Angeles before coming to Chicago. Gushee marshals evidence that another, earlier, "Creole Band" of New Orleans musicians traveled to California before 1910. "How the Creole Band Came to Be," as above, note 16, and "New Orleans–Area Musicians on the West Coast, 1908–1925," *Black Music Research Journal* 9, no. 1 (1989), pp. 9–14.

29. Rudi Blesh, notes to *The Original Dixieland Jazz Band*, RCA Vintage LP LPV-547.

30. "Our music is strictly a white man's music," he fulminated in an early article. "We patterned our earlier efforts after military marches, which we heard at park concerts in New Orleans in our youth. Many writers have attributed this rhythm that we introduced as something coming from the African jungles, and crediting the negro race with it. My contention is that the negroes learned to play this rhythm and music from the whites, and I'm sure that you could go all over Africa and never hear anything remotely resembling our music, unless it were from a phonograph recording of some American or foreign band playing American music. Nick LaRocca, "Jazz Stems From Whites Not Blacks, Says La-Rocca," *Metronome*, October 1936.

31. James T. Maher, conversation with the author, July 1993.

32. Much of the available evidence is contradictory. The published "stock" orchestration of "Smoke Rings," arranged by Gene Gifford for the Casa Loma Orchestra, contains an extra 1½ ensemble choruses, which do not appear on the band's various records. Played in its entirety, it seems discursive, diluting the number's effectiveness and reducing trombonist Billy Rauch's final reentry almost to anticlimax. If this is a faithful reproduction of the original, and if it was cut for recording purposes, the cut has the effect of sharpening and focusing the performance, in effect transforming a good arrangement into a great one. Yet there also exists the possibility that the extra chorus was added at the publisher's request to purposely lengthen the arrangement, prolonging the mood. Did simple physical imperatives determine that fast, rhythmic arrangements be shorter than slow, romantic ones? A similar instance occurs in the genesis of "In the Mood," one of the major swing anthems of the '30s. In its original form, Joe Garland's composition ran more than five minutes and (on the evidence of several "aircheck" performances) easily bogged down in tedium. As edited for Glenn Miller's orchestra, it not only fit neatly within the 78 rpm time limits but also became a major—and enduring—dance-floor favorite.

33. "Eddie Edwards Gives," *Second Line*, September-October 1955. Allen, as above, note 25.

34. Bruce Boyd Raeburn, "New Orleans Style: The Awakening of American Jazz Scholarship and Its Cultural Implications," diss., Tulane University, 1991.

35. Raeburn, as above, note 24.

36. In Frederick Lewis Allen, *Only Yesterday* (New York: Harper and Brothers, 1931), pp. 78–79, quoted from *Atlantic Monthly*, September 1920.

37. The tempos of the English records are clearly dictated by the forms of dancing for which the band was providing music. The ODJB repertoire falls consistently into three discernible tempo slots, which could be defined as slow ($\sqrt{} = 88$–90), medium ($\sqrt{}$=96–100), and fast ($\sqrt{} = 15$–30). It's no accident, for example, that such numbers as "Tiger Rag," "At the Jazz Band Ball," "Dixie Jass Band One-Step," and "Sensation Rag" all come down solidly at around ($\sqrt{}$=127). This subject, never sufficiently explored in standard jazz

histories, seems fertile ground for scholars of vernacular dance and popular music forms. For example, by 1923, when the ODJB gets around to recording "Tiger Rag" for OKeh, the tempo has slowed to ($\downarrow$ = 110), but the rhythmic spelling has changed: the basic unit of metric measure has become the quarter note.

38. ODJB devotee Brad Gowans recorded "The Sphinx," as leader of his own group, for ARC in 1934. It was not released at the time; but a test pressing, recovered in the '70s and issued on a limited-circulation collectors' label, indicates that Gowans (who is probably the clarinetist) was quite familiar with the number as the ODJB had played it. The rest of his personnel is unidentified, though the cornetist seems to be Stirling Bose, who spent much of his youth in New Orleans.

39. Brunn, as above, note 19, p. 134.

40. Harry Shields, interview with Johnny Wiggs and Bill Russell, New Orleans, May 28, 1961, Archive.

41. Gunther Schuller, Early Jazz (New York: Oxford University Press, 1968), p. 182.

42. Humphrey Lyttelton, The Best of Jazz: Basin Street to Harlem (New York: Taplinger, 1982), p. 14. In this connection, it is also relevant to note Bechet's ill-disguised and lifelong resentment of the attention paid Louis Armstrong. As a Creole, and a product of the middle class, he appears to have regarded himself as in every way the social superior of an "uptown" black boy who had grown up poor. Morton, too, was often at pains—contrary to the assertions of latter-day scholars and playwrights—to emphasize the "French" and "Spanish" sides of his Creole heritage.

43. Adolphus "Doc" Cheatham, conversation with the author, February 18, 1993.

44. Richard M. Sudhalter and Philip R. Evans, Bix: Man and Legend (New Rochelle, N.Y.: Arlington House, 1974), p. 324.

45. Paul Whiteman and Mary Margaret McBride, Jazz (New York: J. H. Sears, 1926), p. 104.

46. Chicago jazz scholar William Howland Kenney (Chicago Jazz: A Cultural History, 1904–1930) describes the Auto Inn as "a particularly notorious, segregated, whites-only cabaret where Dapper Dan McCarthy had shot Steve Kelleher to death." The address is best known as the site of the Plantation Café, where King Oliver's "Dixie Syncopators" played in 1925.

47. Lopez, as above, note 3.

48. Ibid.

49. At one point the troupe shared a bill with dancers Vi Quinn and Frank Farnum, accompanied by the Original Memphis Five. According to Lopez, trumpeter Phil Napoleon promptly asked his fellow-cornetist to take part in a Memphis Five record date—something Miss Seeley blocked, claiming she, the vaudeville trio, and the band were about to make records of their own. The date of this encounter, if it happened, is uncertain. Available evidence seems to point to 1918–19. Yet the Original Memphis Five began recording only in 1921. With all principal characters now departed, it is virtually impossible to know what happened—whether, for example, Lopez confused this incident with another, later, meeting.

50. Lopez, as above, note 3.

51. Ray Lopez is easily recognizable, and featured often, in two newly discovered sound film shorts by Gus Arnheim's orchestra. In the first, he takes an eight-bar muted "hot" solo on the 1927 pop song "Who-oo? You-oo, That's Who!" In the second, he has twenty-four bars in "If I Can't Have You" (recorded at Arnheim's debut record date for OKeh in early 1928); he takes a half-chorus in a spirited "Tiger Rag," then plays on in a derby over the ensemble, all in a ragtime-based, early-1920s manner. Two points of added interest: the lead trumpet is Colorado-born Roy Fox, shortly to gain stardom in

Britain as "the Whispering Cornetist" leading his own band. Also prominent, singing with a band trio and playing creditable "hot" violin solos, is a youthfully suave Russ Columbo.

Chapter 2

1. George Brunis, interview with William Russell, New Orleans, June 3, 1958, Hogan Archive. As the reader will note, this family name is spelled two ways throughout this and other chapters. Its original spelling was, of course, "Brunies." Trombonist George dropped the final *e* later in life (also trying, less successfully, to change his given name to the German "Georg"). In the interests of consistency, the original spelling will be used most often, particularly in reference to those family members less given to orthographic (and numerological) caprice. The variant "Brunis" will appear in latter-day references to George—or, if called for, Georg.

2. Ibid.

3. Santo Pecora, interview with Richard B. Allen and Lars Erdegran, Metairie, La., November 9, 1972, Hogan Archive.

4. Esten Spurrier, quoted in Richard M. Sudhalter and Philip R. Evans, Bix: Man and Legend (New Rochelle, N.Y.: Arlington House, 1974), p. 49.

5. Tony Catalano and Phyllis Humphrey, "Days When Musicians Couldn't Read a Note," Down Beat, May 1938. John Steiner, "Chicago," In Nat Hentoff and Albert J. McCarthy, eds., Jazz, (London: Quartet Books, 1977).

6. Joe Mares, interview with William Russell, New Orleans, April 8, 1960, Hogan Archive. George W. Kay, "Joe Mares and His New Orleans Memories," Mississippi Rag, January 1980. Harrison's relationship with the trumpeter took on a more personal side when Mares met and married his sister, Marie.

7. Ben Pollack, "Ten Years of Good Bands and Bad Breaks," Down Beat, October 1936.

8. Marshall Stearns, "The History of Swing Music," chapter 4, Down Beat, September 1936.

9. Arnold Loyocano, interview with Dr. Edmond Souchon, New Orleans, September 29, 1956, Hogan Archive. Inevitably, there are points of disagreement, even contradiction, in various accounts of these events. Chicago jazz historian John Steiner, for example, cited testimony from Frank Snyder that he and Pettis landed the Friars job, and that Mares and Brunies had worked for Fritzel at the Arsonia (letter to the author, July 9, 1992). All participants agree, however, that the band came together through a gradual process of interaction. Also, around this time—the exact date is uncertain—Fritzel moved his cabaret to larger quarters in a basement at 60 Van Buren, on the northeast corner of its intersection with Wabash. It was there that the new band went to work.

10. Loyocano, as above, note 9.

11. Later in his career Schoebel moved to New York, where he did much the same thing for the Music Publishers' Holding Corp., a Warner Brothers subsidiary, while playing around town with dixieland groups. Clarinetist Kenny Davern (in conversation with the author, 1980) remembered him as "very good, very polished, and with a million stories about the old days." It is only regrettable that some enterprising chronicler did not take some of those stories down. Schoebel died in Florida December 14, 1970.

12. Hoagy Carmichael, Sometimes I Wonder (New York: Farrar, Straus and Giroux, 1965), pp. 89–90.

13. Warren K. Plath, "Don Murray–The Early Years," Storyville, December 1985–January 1986.

14. According to Ben Pollack (as above, note 7), the name of Chicago booker and

contractor Husk O'Hare appears on the labels because he helped set up the recording date; there's no sign of any other connection between him and either the band or the Friars' Inn engagement. In a supremely ironic coincidence, Mares, Brunies, Roppolo, and Brown, who made these first records within days of a New Orleans city decision authorizing construction of a new seawall, extending the Lake Pontchartrain shoreline out several hundred feet into the lake. The move effectively signaled the end of the resort communities of West End, Milneburg, and Spanish Fort, where all three had learned their craft playing in the local pavilions, gazebos, and restaurants.

15. Inevitably, perhaps, various chroniclers have attempted to represent the music of the Friars ensemble as little more than a thin and superficial echo of Oliver's Creole Band. The prejudice behind such assertions, based on a conceptual foundation of black-as-creator, white-as-imitator, has made easy to accept—for example—trombonist Preston Jackson's "recollection" of seeing clarinetist Roppolo at the Lincoln Gardens, scribbling feverishly on his cuff while listening to the Oliver band. Not only would the long Friars' Inn hours have made such pilgrimages all but impossible, but Roppolo in any case neither read nor wrote music. Jackson quoted in Nat Hentoff and Nat Shapiro, eds., Hear Me Talkin' to Ya (New York: Reinhart, 1955) p. 99; original source Down Beat, November 1, 1942.

16. Stearns, as above, note 8. In this connection it may be revealing that white New Orleans men of this generation, among them Johnny Wiggs, Emile Christian, "Chink Martin" Abraham, and many others, most often used the adjective "pretty" to describe particularly exciting numbers. Such words as "hot" and "driving," or even "swinging," occurred less often in their standard vocabulary of approbation.

17. James "Rosy" McHargue, conversation with the author, Los Angeles, April 19, 1988.

18. Loyocano, as above, note 9.

19. Ibid.

20. Brunis, as above, note 1.

21. Quoted in Hentoff and Shapiro, as above, note 15, p. 122.

22. Pollack, as above, note 7.

23. Brunis, as above, note 1. Hogan Archive, Tulane. It is hard to know whether Brunis's use of the word "dixie" actually belongs to the usage of the times or is the trombonist's 1958 interpolation.

24. Pollack's recollection (as above, note 7) of fifty dollars a week is at variance with the figure of ninety dollars cited by Brunies. It is hardly beyond supposing that the New Orleans men simply paid the newcomer less than they were making, dividing up the difference; fifty dollars, after all, was still respectable money for a twenty-year-old to be earning in 1922–23.

25. The Midway Gardens, along with the White City Casino (63rd and Cottage Grove) and Paddy Harmon's Dreamland (Paulina and Van Buren), had the approval of the influential Juvenile Protective Association (JPA), active since 1904 to protect Chicago's youth from the blandishments of commercialized vice. In 1921, owners of several major ballrooms, the Midway Gardens among them, had joined forces in the National Association of Ballroom Proprietors and Managers and—together with the JPA—had undertaken a program of reform to make their establishments more "respectable" in the reformers' eyes. One of the products of these early negotiations involved a general "speeding up" of the music—the idea being that slower tempos promoted less reputable activities. As a September 1, 1926, Variety article on the subject attested, "the toddle, the shimmy and kindred slow syncopated motions were impossible at the brisk pace the music set." Quoted in

William Howland Kenney, *Chicago Jazz: A Cultural History, 1904–1930* (New York: Oxford University Press, 1993), p. 71.

26. John Steiner, letters to the author, 1992.

27. Quoted in Sudhalter and Evans, as above, note 4, p. 84.

28. Ben Pollack, "Long-Hair Stumps Rhythm Kings on Reading," *Down Beat*, November 1936, p. 11.

29. Mares, as above, note 21.

30. Ibid.

31. John T. Schenck, "Life History of Volly De Faut," appeared in both *Jazz Information* and *Jazz Record*, exact dates unknown, 1946; copies on file at Institute of Jazz Studies, Rutgers University.

32. David A. Jasen, *Tin Pan Alley* (New York: Primus Books, 1988).

33. John Steiner, conversation with the author, March 1990.

34. Kenny Davern, conversation with the author, January 5, 1994.

35. Brunis, as above, note 1. Various other accounts exist, placing the Tin Roof Café at other New Orleans locations. It is even possible that more than one establishment bore the name at one time or another.

36. Because the melody bears some resemblance to one strain of Richard M. Jones's "Jazzin' Babies Blues," as recorded by Oliver, it has been suggested that the New Orleans Rhythm Kings stole the number. Jazz scholar Lawrence Gushee (notes to *King Oliver's Jazz Band*, 1923, Smithsonian Records, LP R-001) rejects the contention, pointing out that the Rhythm Kings recorded their tune first and that Jones did not copyright "Jazzin' Babies Blues" until early 1924. He is quite right in labeling the whole matter "some kind of red herring, straw man, or dead horse." The story (which first appears in print in Ramsey and Smith's 1939 *Jazzmen*) seems to have survived only because it supports the notion of the Rhythm Kings as imitators and copyists. In any case, "Tin Roof" and "Jazzin' Babies Blues" are melodically quite dissimilar.

37. Lawrence Gushee remarks in his notes to the 1975 Smithsonian Oliver two-LP set that most of the Oliver band performance "sounds as though it is being read." Comparison of the two groups' treatments of "London (Café) Blues" and "Sobbin' Blues" is difficult, owing to the presence (and prominence) of the saxophones on the New Orleans Rhythm Kings versions, as well as some obvious differences of intent. In general, the Creole Jazz Band handles the Morton blues with deeper affinity, and the NORK generally seems more comfortable dealing with Kassel's pop song. Roppolo's melody statement of the verse is particularly lovely.

38. Quoted in Kay, as above, note 6.

39. Quoted by Donald M. Marquis in interview, *Second Line*, fall 1979. Quoted by George W. Kay in interview, *Jazz Journal*, April 1972.

40. "Chink Martin" Abraham, interview with Richard B. Allen, William Russell, and Leonard Ferguson, New Orleans, October 19, 1966, Hogan Archive.

41. Another version of "She's Cryin' for Me," done two months later (March 26, 1925) by essentially the same band, substitutes the talented Charlie Cordilla for Roppolo. Though far better recorded (the electric microphones pick Mares up particularly well), the performance never quite comes to life. Cordilla's two blues choruses, while bright-toned and well executed, illustrate the great distance between Roppolo and even his most skilled admirers. According to "Monk" Hazel (interview of July 16, 1959), Roppolo was on this session as well. "Every time Rap would get a chorus, he'd get up there and hit one of those pea-whistle notes and . . . he'd blow the needle off the wax. Old man [Eddie] King

kept telling him to quit playing those high notes, [but] to tell Rap to quit doing anything—well, you might just as well talk to the King of England." In the end King dismissed Roppolo, said Hazel, and Cordilla did the date. Jelly Roll Morton uses the chord structure of the non-blues section of "She's Cryin' for Me" as the basis for his "Georgia Swing" of June 11, 1928. Such borrowing appears to have been common, especially among the New Orleans musicians.

42. Max Harrison, Charles Fox, and Eric Thacker, *The Essential Jazz Records, Vol. I* (London: Mansell, 1984).

43. From all reports, Roppolo's personal life was as dark—and as mercurial—as his clarinet playing. More than a few visitors to the Friars' Inn described behavior ranging from trance-like reverie (induced to no small measure by a more-or-less constant indulgence in marijuana) to more violent behavior. In a letter to writer Otis Ferguson, Bix Beiderbecke's Davenport friend Larry Andrews said "it was common knowledge that [Roppolo] used to make a mistake now and then on the gob-stick and he would let loose his violent temper by flinging his clarinet against the wall and sitting there glowering at the dancers. A little while later he would walk over and pick up the instrument again, and patch up the broken parts and tear into it again" (letter in author's possession). Oral history interviews with New Orleans veterans, on file at the Hogan Archive, contain accounts of similar behavior.

Chapter 3

1. Wilfred Owen, "Futility," 1918; widely anthologized, but to be found, with annotations, in *The Poems of Wilfred Owen*, Jon Stallworthy, ed. (New York: W. W. Norton, 1985).

2. Various accounts of Hardy's life spell his first name both as "Emmet," with one t, and "Emmett," with two. The cornetist's own letters to Martha Boswell, in the possession of her niece, Vet Boswell Minnerly, spell it "Emmett," as did various Boswell and Hardy family members. In this volume, therefore, he will be Emmett Hardy.

3. Karl Koenig, *The Mother of All Jazz Waters: The Music History of the South and North Shore of Lake Pontchartrain*, monograph (Abita Springs, La.: Basin Street Press, n.d.).

4. Harry Shields, interview with William Russell and Johnny Wiggs, New Orleans, May 28, 1961, Hogan Archive.

5. Dave Dexter Jr., "Hardy Welcomed Death by Playing the Blues," *Down Beat*, June 1, 1940.

6. Dave Dexter Jr. "White Kid Who Taught Bix Died at 22 and Was Forgotten," *Down Beat*, May 15, 1940.

7. Shields, as above, note 4.

8. Horace Diaz, conversation with the author, New York City, August 14, 1990.

9. Santo Pecora, interview with Richard M. Allen and Lars Edegran, Metairie, La., November 9, 1972, Hogan Jazz Archive.

10. Abel Green and Joe Laurie Jr., *Show Biz: From Vaude to Video* (New York: Henry Holt, 1951).

11. Quoted in Richard M. Sudhalter and Philip R. Evans, *Bix: Man and Legend* (New Rochelle, N.Y.: Arlington House, 1974), p. 49.

12. Ibid. There may have been other reasons as well. Riverboat trumpeter Tony Catalano, who knew the New Orleans men well, quoted Roppolo as saying the entertainers owed their musicians about four hundred dollars apiece at the time they dispersed.

13. Sudhalter and Evans, as above, note 11.

14. Pecora, as above, note 9.

15. Esten Spurrier, letter to Philip R. Evans, February 22, 1973.

16. Bocage quoted in James Lincoln Collier, *Louis Armstrong: An American Genius* (New York: Oxford University Press, 1983), p. 78. Wiley in "Drummer From Chicago," quoted in Art Hodes and Chadwick Hansen, eds., *Selections From the Gutter* (Berkeley: University of California Press, 1977).

17. Arthur "Monk" Hazel, interview with William Russell, New Orleans, July 16, 1959, Hogan Archive. Frank Mackie, quoted in *Coda* magazine, May 1962. George Brunis, interview with William Russell, New Orleans, June 3, 1958, Hogan Archive.

18. Steve Brown, interview with William Russell, New Orleans, April 22, 1958, Hogan Archive.

19. Hazel, as above, note 17.

20. Dexter, as above, note 6.

21. Wiggs quoted in Myra Menville, "Wiggs—Self-Explained," *Second Line*, Spring 1977. Material about "correlated" phrasing in conversations with John Joyce, New Orleans drummer and scholar, who worked frequently with Wiggs in the early '60s.

22. John T. Schenck, "Life History of Volly De Faut," appeared in both *Jazz Record* and *Jazz Information*, exact date unknown, 1946; copies on file at Institute of Jazz Studies, Rutgers University.

23. George W. Kay, "Raymond Burke—New Orleans Living Legend," *Second Line*, winter 1982.

24. Gary M. Horbar, M.D., conversation with the author, July 1991.

25. Hazel, as above, note 17.

26. Ibid., and quoted in Dexter, as above, note 5.

27. Hazel, as above, note 17.

28. Ibid.

29. Quoted in Dexter, as above, note 6.

30. Ibid.

Chapter 4

1. William Ivy Hair, *Carnival of Fury: Robert Charles and the New Orleans Race Riot of 1900* (Baton Rouge: Louisiana State University Press, 1976).

2. S. Frederick Starr, "Der Frühe New Orleans Jazz: Legende und Wirklichkeit" ("Early New Orleans Jazz: Legend and Reality"), essay accompanying exhibition *That's Jazz: The Sound of the 20th Century*, Darmstadt, West Germany, 1985, (translated by the author), and conversation with the author, July 4, 1990.

3. Lakefront information from Karl Koenig, *The Mother of All Jazz Waters: The Music History of the South and North Shore of Lake Pontchartrain*, monograph (Abita Springs, La.: Basin Street Press, n.d.). Danny Barker, quoted in Nat Shapiro and Nat Hentoff, eds., *Hear Me Talkin' to Ya* (New York: Reinhart, 1955). DeDroit information from S. Frederick Starr interview, cited in conversation with the author. Laine from interview, Hogan Archive, and cited by Koenig in "Papa Laine, 1873–1966," *Mississippi Rag*, March 1984.

4. Peer eventually went to work for Victor and returned in 1927, recording bands led by cornetists Louis Dumaine (black) and John Hyman ("Johnny Wiggs," white). His career has been widely, if superficially, documented: Bruce Boyd Raeburn referred to articles by Alan Ward, Mike Hazeldine, and James S. Griffith, all published in 1989, in assembling the information on this seminal recording executive which appears in his doctoral dissertation ("New Orleans Style: The Awakening of American Jazz Scholarship and

Its Cultural Implications," Tulane University, 1991). Still, a void remains for some ambitious scholar to fill: chronicling the indispensable role played by such men as Peer, Tom Rockwell of OKeh, and others like them, who recognized great potential (both for music's sake and for profit) in the new music and were willing to create opportunities for it to be widely heard.

5. Quoted in Dixon Gayer, "There Is a Chicago Style—Mares," *Down Beat*, February 15, 1943, and reprinted in Shapiro and Hentoff, *Talkin'-to-Ya* as above, note 3.

6. "Jass and Jassism," *New Orleans Times Picayune*, June 20, 1918.

7. Myra Menville, "An Impression of Johnny DeDroit," *Second Line*, fall 1976, pp. 3–8.

8. For one reference to "Tiger Rag" as "Number Two" see Arnold Loyocano interview of September 29, 1956, Hogan Archive.

9. Like the Brown brothers and others of their circle, Bayersdorffer was a part-time musician, working days for the U.S. Civil Service as a stenographer and clerk. In a letter dated September 1, 1960, he describes Spanish Fort as "a summer resort similar to Coney Island in New York." After the band's summer 1924, engagement there, he "decided that the band was ready for the big time" and resigned his day job—only to be informed by his musicians that they had decided *en masse* to stay in New Orleans. He quickly recruited some replacements, including seventeen-year-old Ray Bauduc on drums, and headed for Chicago. Not all the anticipated "big time" work materialized, though there were such plums as a stint at the Rainbow Casino Gardens in Indianapolis, playing opposite Bix Beiderbecke and the Wolverines. By early 1925 Bayersdorffer and his musicians were back in New Orleans; over the next several years he played engagements in Los Angeles, Detroit, and Chicago, with mixtures of sidemen that included trombonist Santo Pecora, guitarist Hilton "Nappy" Lamare, and Lester Bouchon on clarinet and tenor sax. Letter published in *Storyville*, June–July 1967.

10. Max Harrison, Charles Fox, and Eric Thacker, *The Essential Jazz Records, Vol. I* (London: Mansell, 1984). Bayersdorffer, a talented cornetist and even better businessman, reorganized his band in mid-1924, adding drummer Ray Bauduc and, the following year, banjoist Hilton "Nappy" Lamare. This group appears to have recorded three titles for Gennett early in 1925. They were never issued. Was Scaglione present? Is it possible that test pressings of this date still exist? In late '25 this band traveled to California, where Bauduc met drummer Ben Pollack, then getting started with his own band. When Pollack, in 1928, decided to front his own band, he brought in the kid from New Orleans (by that time resident in New York) to take over behind the drums.

11. In a 1961 interview, pianist-leader Norman Brownlee said the younger Shields was the first clarinetist he'd heard play a solo in the low-register style that became associated with Roppolo. Cornetist Johnny Wiggs, also a Harry Shields admirer, found his style "completely different" from that of his better-known elder brother. It was "lyrical," Wiggs said, almost Bix-like in its phrase construction. Drummer-scholar John Joyce worked with Harry Shields in the 1960s and "found his drive and intensity nothing short of awesome."

12. John V. Baiamonte Jr., *Spirit of Vengeance: Nativism and Louisiana Justice, 1921–24* (Baton Rouge: Louisiana State University Press, 1986). Humbert S. Nelli, *The Business of Crime* (New York: Oxford University Press, 1976).

13. Margaret Hindle Hazen, "The Band Movement," in S. Frederick Starr, ed., *The Oberlin Book of Bandstands* (Washington, D.C.: Preservation Press, 1987).

14. Ronald L. Davis, *A History of Music in American Life*, vol. 2. (Malabar, Fla.: Robert Krieger, 1980).

15. Jerome S. Shipman, record review, *IAJRC Journal*, January 1979.

16. See entry under "Music: Spirituals," in W. Augustus Low and Virgil A. Clift, *Encyclopedia of Black America* (New York: McGraw-Hill, 1981).

17. Drummer-mellophonist Arthur "Monk" Hazel told interviewers in 1959 that Bill Creger, clarinetist with Oliver Naylor's New Orleans–based Seven Aces, took the stock orchestration of "High Society" from the Library of Congress, while the band was appearing in Washington, D.C. It was scored for full military band, he said, and included the passage now traditionally played as a clarinet solo—but as a piccolo countermelody, similar to (and perhaps inspired by) that featured in the trio section of John Philip Sousa's 1897 favorite, "The Stars and Stripes Forever." It is worth noting that "High Society" was the first number recorded by the Naylor band at its first Gennett session, February 1, 1924. "I got to laugh" was Monk Hazel's reply when asked about Alphonse Picou, the Creole clarinetist generally credited with originating the solo. "I saw the thing with my own eyes, where it was a piccolo part" (interview, Hogan Archive). As recorded for Columbia by Prince's Band shortly after publication in 1911, however, "High Society" has no such countermelody, for piccolo or any other instrument. As various scholars have suggested, the original arrangement may have been cut to fit the three-minute time limitation of the 78 rpm disc.

18. William J. Schafer, "Hot Dancing in New Orleans," *Mississippi Rag*, August 1980.

19. Frederic Ramsey Jr., "Friends of Music in New Orleans," notes to Folkways LP FP-60.

20. Schafer, as above, note 18.

21. It is instructive to compare these titles with four recorded the previous day by Sam Morgan's New Orleans Jazz Band. From the opening bars of "Steppin' on the Gas" the emphasis is on the ensemble, driven along by Sidney Brown's four-to-the-bar string bass. Soloists rarely emerge from the energetic but rather muddled ensembles (alto saxophonist Earl Fouche has some good moments); but even when they do, it is as if the individual has stepped forward only a pace. The ensemble churns on behind him. The Halfway House soloists, particularly the clarinet, play a far more clearly defined role, and the texture remains clear. It may not be an exaggeration to say that if the overall outline of the far more organized Luis Russell band is discernible in the Morgan records, the general shape and direction of the later Bob Crosby ensemble emerges from the Halfway House efforts.

22. Arodin also claimed to have been present on a June 1922 Original Memphis Five date for the newly formed Cameo label issued under the name "Jazz-Bo's Carolina Serenaders." German scholar Horst H. Lange insists that on aural evidence the man who plays the clarinet solo on "Lonesome Mama Blues" is the group's regular man, Jimmy Lytell. Repeated listening to the two choruses, one in the upper register, one in the lower, throws some doubt on Lange's case. The resemblance between this clarinetist and the man who solos on "Down Where the South Begins" is too strong to be so easily dismissed. His phrase shapes and fast vibrato resemble those of Roppolo: because the Friars Society Orchestra had not yet recorded, Lytell could not have been familiar with this way of playing; Arodin, by contrast, was a friend and admirer, who knew Roppolo's style well.

23. Armand Hug, interview, July 14, 1960. Harry Shields, interview, May 28, 1961. Both, Hogan Archive.

24. In an oral history interview on file at the Hogan Archive, Benjie White contends that the "stock" arrangements were forced on the group by Columbia recording executives in the interests of "commercial" appeal. It is a credible assertion, in view of prevailing

company policies of the day, especially in dealing with a new and as yet unproven band. Unfamiliarity with the arrangements could also explain the ungainliness of the saxophones in their soli passages.

25. Curiously, only two of the six numbers were released in the United States at the time, a third in Australia, where it sold poorly. Not until the '70s, when all six appeared on LP in Britain, were they made generally available.

26. Arthur "Monk" Hazel, interview with William Russell, July 16, 1959, Hogan Archive. As an interesting sidelight, four major white New Orleans cornetists of those days—LaRocca, Ray Lopez, Sharkey, and Lawrence Veca—played the cornet left-handed, fingering the valves with their left hands instead of the customary right. Coincidence?

27. The activities of itinerant white bands active throughout the South, Southwest, and middle Atlantic states in the '20s and early '30s constitute one of the great underdocumented areas of early jazz history. Bands such as those of Britt, Clapp, Blue Steele, Slim Lamar, Doc Daugherty, and others were known and respected among musicians and recorded enough to show their often impressive musicianship. Like their black counterparts, they were often incubators for major hot jazz talent. Yet in most jazz histories the very phrase "territory band" has come to identify the black units only. The inquiring listener need only seek out Britt's "Goose Creek Stomp" (a.k.a "Weary Blues"), with its excellent Arodin solo, Lamar's "Memphis Kick-up" ("Panama" in mufti), or—even better—Daugherty's driving "Alcoholic Blues" and "Ninety in the Shade," with a strong, unidentified bass sax soloist, to realize the quality and jazz strength of these neglected ensembles. What little information has come to light points to a pool of musicians, generally working out of New Orleans, Dallas, San Antonio, and other regional cities. Saxophonist Drew Page, in his autobiographical *Drew's Blues* (Baton Rouge: Louisiana State University Press, 1980), furnishes some tantalizing information about these bands and their relationship to the better-known currents of early jazz development.

28. These latter remarks appeared first in "Lee Collins' Story—as told to Mary Collins and John W. Miner," *Evergreen Review*, no. 35, n.d. Subsequently incorporated in Mary Collins, *Oh, Didn't He Ramble*, ed. by Frank Gillis and John W. Miner (Urbana: University of Illinois Press, 1974).

29. John Chilton, *Stomp Off, Let's Go* (self-published, 1983).

30. According to Lee Collins (interview, June 2, 1958, Hogan Archive), Arodin "used to play it and mug it every time he got drunk." The clarinetist, he said, "used to go sit, sit on the river every morning and blow his clarinet and look at the river . . . and he used to play that piece . . . and I used to play it with him." In the *Evergreen Review* article (see above, note 28), which (unlike the Tulane material) reveals an editor's touch, he's quoted as saying, "Sidney loved to go down to the river and sit for hours, just watching the water. I happened to have my cornet with me there the time he was making up 'Lazy River,' so I know I was the first musician to ever play that tune." Reedman Drew Page recalled Arodin's "ballad-style clarinet solo, which some of us clarinetists played before it was published. The tune had no lyrics yet, and Sid called it, simply and affectionately, 'Lazy Nigger.' Later, in collaboration with Hoagy Carmichael, the solo became 'Lazy River.' Sid got only eight hundred dollars of all the money that song made, according to a newspaper report when he died." (Page, as above note 27.) Eddie Miller, who knew Arodin well in those days, corroborated the "unofficial" title but assured the author that the word in this context was neither condescending nor hostile. It was, he said, just New Orleans usage, closer to the rich range of tone and meaning characteristic of its use within black social circles.

31. Clarinetist Joe Dixon, describing his time as a sideman with Bunny Berigan,

complained that "I had to change mouthpieces on clarinet to play with this band . . . Bunny's idea of a clarinet player was to get out there and wail and scream while the brass went doo-wah, doo-wah. You had to pierce through all that like a piccolo in a marching band, otherwise you wouldn't be heard." On the evidence of these records, working with the extrovert, high-energy team of Prima and Brunies may have forced Arodin into a similar role.

32. Meyer Weinberg belongs to a small, but respected, cadre of Jewish musicians active in New Orleans during the formative jazz years. Other names mentioned by chroniclers include cornetist Mike Caplan, violinist-leader Charlie Fischbein, drummer Bob Stein, pianist Joe Wolfe, and the brothers Marty (or Monty) and Marcus Korn, clarinet and trombone, respectively. Bruce Boyd Raeburn suggests that most of these men were legitimately trained "readers," who could "make excursions into jazz on occasion without actually having to rely on it" ("Jewish Jazzmen in New Orleans, 1890–1940: An overview," paper presented to the annual conference of the Southern Jewish Historical Society, Monteleone Hotel, New Orleans, October 28, 1995).

33. Max Jones and John Chilton, *Louis* (London: Studio Vista, 1971).

Chapter 5

1. Thompson's successor, pro-Prohibition Democrat William Dever, lasted just one term. Big Bill was back in 1927, and among those who welcomed his return were club proprietors and the entertainers who worked for them. According to the *Chicago Defender*, a Victory Ball held at the Eighth Regimental Armory on the South Side included performances by the entire casts from the Casino de Paris (a renamed Lincoln Gardens) and the Sunset Café, including Louis Armstrong's Orchestra.

2. Humbert S. Nelli, *The Business of Crime* (New York: Oxford University Press, 1976), pp. 148–49.

3. Lloyd Wendt and Herman Kogan, *Big Bill of Chicago* (New York: Bobbs-Merrill, 1953), cited in William Howland Kenney, *Chicago Jazz: A Cultural History, 1904–1930* (New York: Oxford University Press, 1993).

4. Kenney, as above, note 3, p. 62.

5. Like Mares, Steinberg has not yet learned how to shake free of the beat and of the conventions of ensemble playing. Both Louis Armstrong and Bix Beiderbecke would shortly demonstrate more vocalized approaches to solo phrasing, which rode the pulse without being confined by it. But Mares, in common with Oliver, still conceived of a melodic line only in terms of a functional embellished lead. Muggsy Spanier's Bucktown Five records, discussed at the end of this chapter, clearly show the young cornetist seeking to adapt his Oliver-inspired ensemble style to the new requirements of solo playing. The distinction between these two conceptions is critical: recognition of it helps the listener avoid the judgmental trap into which the otherwise insightful William Howland Kenney (as above, note 3) falls in stating (p. 77) that none of the Midway Gardens horn players, "not even Murph Steinberg, who hung around with jazz musicians, had advanced rhythmically as far as the musicians who had come over from the New Orleans Rhythm Kings."

6. Inexplicably, the records made at these dates were issued not under the Midway Gardens name but a variety of pseudonyms instead. On Gennett, they were the "Original Memphis Melody Boys," while Columbia opted for the "Chicago Blues Dance Orchestra." Not until October were they permitted the luxury of appearing on a record label as "the Midway Dance Orchestra" (Columbia) or "the Midway Garden Orchestra" (Paramount/Claxtonola).

7. Quoted in Larry Gara, The Baby Dodds Story (Pasadena: Castle Press [Grant Dahlstrom], 1959), cited in Whitney Balliett, New Yorker, October 14, 1991.

8. John Steiner, conversation with the author, Chicago, April 1990.

9. Quoted in Samuel Charters and Leonard Kunstadt, Jazz: A History of the New York Scene (Garden City, N.Y.: Doubleday, 1962), p. 78.

10. When Abbe Niles, writing on W. C. Handy, refers to "breaks" as an integral part of such early Handy compositions as the "Memphis Blues," he is using the term in a different sense. As is clear from the context, he identifies a "break" as a between-phrases gap in a melodic line, filled by one or another of the ensemble players. He never once implies the actual interruption of the rhythm, for two or even four bars, which is the "break" as practiced by Hickman's two saxophonists and later by Oliver and Armstrong, as well as numerous jazz soloists. Edward Abbe Niles, "The Story of the Blues," in W. C. Handy, ed., Blues: An Anthology (1949, New York: Macmillan, 1972).

11. Further exposition of James T. Maher's invaluable work in this field will be found in two books: James Lincoln Collier, Benny Goodman and the Swing Era (New York: Oxford University Press, 1989); Gene Lees, Leader of the Band: The Life of Woody Herman (New York: Oxford University Press, 1995). His scrupulous blend of scholarship and anecdotal evidence has made possible at last an accurate picture of how what later became known as the "big band" evolved.

12. James T. Maher, conversation with the author, 1991, and notes to The Great Isham Jones and His Orchestra, RCA LPV-504, 1964. Whiteman flopped at the Trianon, said Maher, largely because his band couldn't supply the kind of steady, danceable rhythm Chicago dancers were used to hearing. "My God, they just wouldn't dance to our music," he quoted reedman Ross Gorman as saying. As British historian Albert McCarthy has put it (in The Dance Band Era, as below, note 14), the dancers seemed to have felt that Whiteman "substituted showy effects for solidity of rhythm."

13. Benson was easily the reigning power in Chicago's dance band business in the early '20s, working with publishers, retailers, and record companies to consolidate his hold on the city's prestige locations. This way he could easily control which bands worked, where they worked, and for how much. His methods, and their effect on the employment of musicians, are dealt with in detail in Kenney, as above, note 3. Only the emergence of Jules Stein, who went into partnership with veterans Ernie Young and Fred Hamm in founding the Music Corporation of America, brought Benson's stranglehold to an end. When, later in the '20s, veteran independents Joe Kayser and Husk O'Hare came in with Stein, MCA's hegemony was complete. With radio spreading the word, the agency branched out into national management, tours, and representation of groups passing through the Chicago area. This and other similar organizations soon came to dominate the music industry.

14. Albert McCarthy, The Dance Band Era (London: November Books, 1971), pp. 70–71.

15. James T. Maher, letter to the author, April 23, 1996.

16. Ibid.

17. John Steiner, as above, note 8.

18. Adolphus "Doc" Cheatham, conversation with the author, September 1991.

19. Jess Stacy, conversation with the author, April 21, 1988.

20. Steiner, as above, note 8.

21. S. Frederick Starr, conversation with the author, July 4, 1990.

22. Richard M. Sudhalter and Philip R. Evans, Bix: Man and Legend (New Rochelle, N.Y.: Arlington House, 1974), p. 71.

23. Quoted in McCarthy, as above, note 14.

24. Jack Bland, "The Kazoo Comes On," *Jazz Record*, anthologized in Art Hodes and Chadwick Hansen, eds., *Selections From the Gutter* (Berkeley: University of California Press, 1977), pp. 143–46.

25. Jones similarly boosted the black "stride" piano master James P. Johnson, then scuffling in Chicago. Johnson played his song "Ivy (Cling to Me)" for Jones, who proposed adding his name as co-composer. "That way," Jones said, "you'll get a lot of recordings." And so it came to pass: Jones, Paul Whiteman, and others soon recorded it, and Johnson's royalties—all of them—began coming in; Jones had taken no cut, insisting the pianist receive 100 percent of the profits. Source: James Breyley, as told to James T. Maher.

26. Bland, as above, note 24.

27. Some later listeners have heard the Mound City Blue Blowers as an outgrowth of the "down-home mountain music" of the white Appalachian South, a hypothesis that seems to have occurred to some of their contemporaries as well. Two 1929 Vitaphone movie shorts, *Opry House* and *Nine O'Clock Folks*, show them in small-town "hillbilly" settings, dressed as hayseeds. The antics (and appearance, with blacked-out teeth) of Frank "Josh" Billings, playing on a suitcase with a pair of whisk brooms, go far toward promoting the image. But the music, including a rousing "St. Louis Blues," with Eddie Condon replacing Lang on guitar, is hot, driving, and unmistakably jazz.

28. George Brunis, interview with William Russell, New Orleans, June 3, 1958, Hogan Archive.

Chapter 6

1. Burt Goldblatt, *Newport Jazz Festival: An Illustrated History* (New York: Dial Press, 1977).

2. Dan Morgenstern, conversation with the author, December 4, 1992.

3. Jack Bradley, conversation with the author, December 5, 1992.

4. Richard DuPage, "Miff Mole, First Trailblazer of Modern Jazz Trombone," *Record Research* 34, April 1961.

5. Bob Hilbert, "Long Live the Emperor! Memories of Phil Napoleon," *IAJRC Journal*, winter 1992, pp. 1–10. In April 1922, a band billed as the "Original Dixieland Jazz Band" recorded two titles for the obscure Arto label with Napoleon leading an entirely Memphis Five personnel. They are among the rarest of early collector's items. The association also had something of a social dimension: Napoleon, Signorelli, and ODJB members LaRocca, Edwards, Larry Shields, and Sbarbaro were among twenty-five persons arrested for disorderly conduct at a May 15, 1921, party celebrating the return of the Dixielanders from abroad.

6. Al Sudhalter, conversations with the author, 1955–75.

7. *Variety*, February 22, 1924, quoted in Samuel Charters and Leonard Kunstadt, *Jazz: A History of the New York Scene* (Garden City, N.Y.: Doubleday, 1962).

8. Garvin Bushell (with Mark Tucker), *Jazz: From the Beginning* (Ann Arbor: University of Michigan Press, 1988). For an example of a black band emulating the ODJB, the author suggests "Truly," recorded for the obscure C & S label in mid-1922 by a group called Bobby Lee's Music Landers and available through collector channels.

9. Hilbert, as above, note 5.

10. Interview with Ted Grossman, on *Night Train* program, broadcast on WLRN-FM, Miami, Fla., quoted by Hilbert, as above, note 5.

11. Phil Napoleon, conversation with the author, 1989.

12. Pat Harris, "Miff Rated One of Trombone Greats," *Down Beat*, October 5, 1951.

13. Laurie Wright, conversation with the author, January 1, 1993.

14. Joe Tarto, conversation with the author, c. 1981.

15. DuPage, as above, note 4. Clarification of this period presents many difficulties. With all the principals long dead and little early documentation, it is hard to pinpoint dates and places with certainty. Mole, for example, told DuPage he remembered recording the "Original Dixieland One-Step" and at least one other number for OKeh shortly after returning to New York. The records were never issued and have never been found. Similarly, the Memphis Five's many disbandings and reorganizations of the time present a nightmare to historian and discographer alike. Horst H. Lange addresses this immense jigsaw puzzle in The Fabulous Fives (London: Storyville Publications, 1978). The Southern Serenaders' records are a case in point: around the same time, perhaps within days of the Emerson session, much the same band recorded the same titles for Gennett (as Ladd's Black Aces) and yet again for Paramount and Pathé under an alphbet soup of pseudonyms. Which was first? In what sequence? It is impossible now to tell: all that is certain is Lanin's connection to the entire operation and Napoleon's presence on all the dates. Some discographers, Lange among them, have questioned Mole's presence, though Miff himself confirmed to DuPage that he was present. Similarly, Lange and Brian Rust have identified Jimmy Durante as the pianist. But Napoleon told Bob Hilbert that, though he knew the comedian in those days, they'd never recorded together, and he "was a terrible piano player, [who] could only play in one key—but he was a good friend." Overall, Signorelli seems a more likely choice, just as Jack Roth, the OM5's regular drummer, seems a more plausible percussionist than Lanin himself.

16. It's easy to discern in his work the roots of '20s saxophone playing in European string traditions, as exemplified by the work of violinist Fritz Kreisler. This line of investigation has been very little pursued by jazz scholars: it is surprising how many reed players of the generations which came of age in the '20s and '30s began their music studies as violinists and carried that instrument's conceptual principles over to the saxophone. The "French school" of alto saxophone tone, vibrato, and technique, the industry standard of the period, shaped the tonally rich ballad playing of Rudy Wiedoeft, Clyde Doerr, Andy Sannella, and other popular saxophonists of the time. It stems directly from string practices of the late nineteenth and early twentieth centuries. The playing of Otto "Toby" Hardwick, with Duke Ellington's orchestra, belongs to this tradition, as does Chester "Chet" Hazlett, perhaps the most emulated lead saxophone of the period; its influence is also discernible, if less directly, in the tonal conceptions of such jazzmen as Johnny Hodges, Charlie Holmes, and Benny Carter.

17. James H. S. Moynahan, "Ragtime to Swing," Saturday Evening Post, February 13, 1937. Further information on McMurray supplied by Jerome Shipman.

18. Letter in the possession of Horst H. Lange, quoted in notes to Ladd's Black Aces: Pioneers of recorded Jazz, Fountain LP FJ-102.

19. Mole told Down Beat interviewer Pat Harris in 1951 that pianist-songwriter Clarence Williams sold them the tune, claiming he'd written it with New Orleans violinist-bandleader Armand J. Piron. Williams's wife, singer Eva Taylor, remembered broadcasting with the Memphis Five in the early '20s on New York radio station WEAF. In a 1968 conversation with the author, she said that although her voice sounded "white" enough to be acceptable to the station's listeners, studio executives took no chances: they set up a scrim curtain between her and the band as protection against any possible charges of racial "mixing."

20. The term bel canto is used several times in this volume, particularly in connection

with the playing of Italian musicians. Translated variously as "beautiful singing" and "beautiful song," it refers to the achievement of vocal perfection. But attempts to define the tradition, which flourished in Italy in the seventeenth and eighteenth centuries, are often contradictory. *The Harvard Dictionary of Music*, for example, states that *bel canto* emphasizes "beauty of sound and brilliance of performance rather than dramatic expression or romantic emotion." Such a polarity can lead to the impression that the tradition values form and execution over content, which is not, strictly speaking, accurate. Rather more balanced is Pratt's *New Encyclopedia of Music and Musicians*, published in 1924, which defines bel canto as "the vocal method or style associated with the singing of the Italian school, especially of the 17th and 18th centuries, in which beauty and finish of tone and delivery were more prized than declamatory or dramatic effect." Even there it remains something of an intangible, a quality of innate *melodiousness* more easily recognized than defined. The vocalized playing of many jazzmen of Italian ancestry, Roppolo and Lytell among them, abounds in this quality.

21. Cited by Hilbert, as above, note 5.

22. Otis Ferguson, "The Five Pennies," in Charles Edward Smith and Frederick Ramsey, eds., *Jazzmen* (New York: Harcourt, Brace, 1939), reprinted in *The Otis Ferguson Reader* (Chicago: December Press, 1982).

23. The major source for much of the information in this section is "Frank Guarente, a Forgotten Pioneer," an article by Italian researcher Giuseppe Barrazzetta which appeared first in the magazine *Discoteca* and was reprinted, in translation, in *Jazz Monthly*, December 1966. Mr. Barrazzetta draws on a diversity of well-authenticated sources, including an article by Paul Specht, published in the French magazine *Jazz Hot* for autumn 1951. He also enlisted the cooperation and assistance of the respected Italian jazz historian Liberio Pusateri. The author is in their debt for having unearthed invaluable information about the otherwise all-but-undocumented Georgians and Frank Guarente. Subsequent references, direct and indirect, to Barrazzetta's lengthy piece will be labeled where possible. Another Italian researcher, radio-TV executive Adriano Mazzoletti, has reportedly completed a Guarente biography based in part on the trumpeter's private papers and diaries; its appearance is eagerly awaited.

24. Ken Farnsworth, "Specht's 'Jass' Played a Big Part in Progress of Swing," *Down Beat*, September 1, 1940.

25. Sources for material in this section: Horst H. Lange, "Die Frank Guarente Story," *Jazz Podium* (Germany), three issues in 1957–58, translations by the author. Barrazzetta, as above, note 23. Paul Specht, "L'Histoire des Georgians," *Jazz Hot* (France), October 1951; in English, *Jazz Music*, May-June-August 1960. Les Erskine, "Frank Guarente: The Forgotten Man in New Orleans Jazz History," *Second Line*, fall 1980. Farnsworth, as above, note 24. In numerous instances, authors of the various articles appear to draw freely from one another, sometimes with attribution, sometimes not. Where possible, I have indicated a specific source for accounts of specific events or statements.

26. Lange, as above, note 25. German passage: "Guarente konnte seinerseits King Oliver mit den fundamentalen Begriffen der Notenlehre bekanntmachen, und unterrichtete ihn in der Handhabe des Kornetts im Sinne europäischer klassischer Schule und der diesbezüglichen korrekten Spielweise." Passage also cited, in slightly different translation, by Barazzetta, as above, note 23.

27. Erskine, as above, note 25. Tony Parenti, "Early Years in New Orleans," *Second Line*, October 1951.

28. It's worth noting that the nucleus of Specht's band, including the leader himself, consisted of musicians from Pennsylvania. Morehouse grew up in Chamberburg, pianist

Arthur Schutt in Reading. Trombonist Stillwell was from East Liverpool, Ohio, hard on the Pennsylvania state line. His ultimate replacement was Russ Morgan, from Scranton. Banjoist Deppe was also a Pennsylvanian. Later products of this fertile musical territory included Jimmy and Tommy Dorsey, arranger Bill Challis, trumpeter Fred "Fuzzy" Farrar, pianist Irving "Itzy" Riskin, and others. See discussion elsewhere in this volume of the leading regional band, the Scranton Sirens.

29. Lange, as above, note 25.

30. Articles as above, notes 23 and 25, plus Jim Godbolt, *A History of Jazz in Britain, 1919–50* (London: Quartet Books, 1984).

31. This operation was based on an audacious and forward-looking plan: Specht would handle dozens of bands, using the growing potential of radio as a sales medium to sponsor and promote them. It was this scheme that enabled Harl Smith, a drummer who managed Specht's New York office, to bring Bix and the Wolverines east and book them at the Cinderella, center of the new "Charleston" craze, opposite the popular "straight" band of Willie Creager. Specht's office was also, according to writer Ken Farnsworth (as above, note 24) responsible for the band's first New York radio broadcast, on station WHN.

32. *Neue Zürcher Zeitung*, April 12, 1926. "Man mag sich zum Jazz stellen wie man will, man wird diesen Georgians das Zugeständnis machen müssen, dass sie famose Vertreter ihrer Kunst sind . . . jeder ist hier auf seinem Instrument ein Meister, und Trompeter, wie diese Truppe einen hat, gibt es nicht überall." Translation by the author. Recent research by Swiss collector Hans Peter Woessner (and published in *Storyville* magazine, September 1, 1991) indicates that this band recorded in Geneva October 7, 1926, for the obscure Kalophon label. Among the personnel were trombonist Ben Pickering, later with Tommy Dorsey's orchestra, and drummer Ted Noyes, who had replaced Morehouse with Specht.

33. Dick Hill, *Sylvester Ahola: The Gloucester Gabriel* (Metuchen, N.J.: Scarecrow Press and Institute of Jazz Studies, Rutgers University, 1993).

34. According to Lange and others, Guarente is the muted trumpet soloist on Crosby's 1931 "Dinah," with the Mills Brothers, and is also heard, again muted, on the Nov. 11, 1933, Jack Teagarden date for Brunswick that produced "One Hundred Years From To-day," "I Just Couldn't Take It, Baby," and two other titles.

35. Lange, as above, note 25. German passage: "Obwohl Guarente längst US-Amerikaner geworden war, sorgte der mächtiger Manager Salter dafür, daß Guarente zunächst ohne Arbeit blieb."

36. During the mid-'20s Miller worked out of Chicago, where he drew regularly on the new generation of hot players just coming of age there. Such Miller records as "Sorry," "Weary Blues," "Angry," and "That's a Plenty" feature jazzmen Volly De Faut and Muggsy Spanier, with excellent arrangements by pianist Art Gronwall.

37. Gunther Schuller, *The Swing Era* (New York: Oxford University Press, 1989).

38. DuPage, as above, note 4.

39. Nichols's brief 1925 hitch with the California Ramblers is instructive in this connection. Though founder-manager W. T. "Ed" Kirkeby paid him a higher salary than any other band member, Red kept making records on his own, in violation of the terms of his contract. Kirkeby, having no patience for such shenanigans, soon let him go. By contrast, bass saxophonist Adrian Rollini, though equally in demand for freelance recording, held to his contract until his 1927 resignation from the band. It's for this reason that he appears to burst into view in early summer, recording with Nichols, Mole, Bix, Trumbauer, Venuti, and Lang, and others, on an almost daily basis.

40. As an intro on "Five Foot Two," Red borrowed the opening of his own "Nervous Charlie," then went on a week or so later to record the piece itself for Pathé. The other

side, a pop tune called "I'm 'Gonna' Hang Around My Sugar," features a full-chorus solo by an unidentified (and skilled) hot violinist. Discographers have suggested that one of the reed players present might have doubled; a more plausible notion is that Mole, who had worked on violin around New York before emerging as a trombonist, is himself the mystery fiddler.

41. Ferguson, as above, note 22.

42. Max Harrison, "Miff Mole's OKeh Recordings," *Jazz Monthly*, 1973; anthologized in *A Jazz Retrospect* (Newton Abbot (UK): David & Charles, 1976).

43. Ferguson, as above, note 22.

44. Harris, as above, note 12.

45. The treatment of the blues here is remarkably like that of "Shirt Tail Stomp," as recorded by various groups from the Ben Pollack band in 1928, and featuring Benny Goodman (also doing a Ted Lewis impersonation), Jimmy McPartland (somewhere in Clyde McCoy territory), and Glenn Miller. The similarity is striking enough to prompt the thought that certain aspects of the blues, far from being defining elements of jazz (as Albert Murray and other latter-day scholars contend), may have been regarded by these "modern" musicians of the time as corny, holdovers from the days of vaudeville and novelty ragtime. On those records, moreover, where Mole and the others play the blues without humorous intent ("Brown Sugar," "Hurricane") they clearly regard it as little more than a song form, without an indigenous flavor or aesthetic. Yet their playing is unmistakably jazz, leaving open the entire question of the blues as any *sine qua non* of jazz style.

46. As Richard DuPage (as above, note 4) reports, when the Columbia Phonograph Co. jumped into radio by presenting *The La Palina Cigar Program* on WOR and twenty other stations, it was laying the foundation for what shortly became CBS, the Columbia Broadcasting System.

47. Johnny Blowers, conversation with the author, December 31, 1992.

48. Bill Rank, one of the most accomplished of Mole disciples, underwent similar changes in later life. At a 1967 recording session in London, he astonished the author and other participants with smooth-toned, legato solos in a Teagarden manner. Rank reminded his companions that he had sat beside the Texan in Paul Whiteman's trombone section for the better part of four years, listening to him night after night. "I couldn't get enough of him" was his explanation.

49. Max Harrison, essay on Mole in Harrison, Charles Fox, and Eric Thacker, *The Essential Jazz Records, Vol. I* (London: Mansell, 1984).

50. Due to the American Federation of Musicians recording ban, Goodman's 1943 band never recorded commercially. Transcriptions and airchecks exist, however. Mole is visible onscreen during Goodman's "Minnie's in the Money" feature in the 1943 Hollywood movie *The Gang's All Here*. With Miff in the trombone section, Joe Rushton's bass sax anchoring both reeds and brass, and stalwarts Jess Stacy and Allan Reuss back in place, it was a strong and unusual band. The circumstances surrounding Miff's departure are unclear: one story persists that Benny took offense when the trombonist praised Whiteman's longtime alto sax virtuoso Al Gallodoro in his presence, and that relations went downhill from there. Whatever the case, Mole, Rushton, and fellow-trombonist Joe Harris left Goodman in August of 1943.

51. Harris, as above, note 12.

52. Jack Lesberg, conversation with the author, January 5, 1993.

53. Harris, as above, note 12.

54. Blowers, as above, note 47.

Chapter 7

1. Nicolas Slonimsky, *The Concise Baker's Biographical Dictionary of Musicians* (New York: Schirmer-Macmillan, 1988).

2. Milton Mezzrow (with Bernard Wolfe), *Really the Blues* (New York: Random House, 1946).

3. Quoted in Nat Shapiro and Nat Hentoff, eds., *Hear Me Talkin' to Ya* (New York: Reinhart, 1955).

4. Stanley Dance, notes to *The Jazz Trumpet, Vol. I: Classic Jazz to Swing*, Prestige double-LP R-24111.

5. Gunther Schuller, *Early Jazz* (New York: Oxford University Press, 1968) and *The Swing Era* (New York: Oxford University Press, 1989).

6. Benny Goodman, *The Kingdom of Swing* (New York: Stackpole, 1939; rpt. New York: Frederick Ungar, 1961).

7. Bud Freeman (as told to Robert Wolf), *Crazeology: The Autobiography of a Chicago Jazzman* (Chicago: University of Illinois Press, 1989).

8. Mezzrow, as above, see note 2. Condon quote from *Eddie Condon's Scrapbook of Jazz* (New York: St. Martin's Press, 1973). Max Kaminsky (with V. E. Hughes), *My Life in Jazz* (New York: Harper and Row, 1963).

9. Martin Williams summed up the situation brilliantly in *The Jazz Tradition* (New York: Oxford University Press, 1983) by observing that "our liberal clichés long ago put us in the position of assuming that differences imply an innate moral or intellectual superiority on the one hand and inferiority on the other. We cannot allow for differences or allow them to be differences. And we assume thereby, surely without realizing it, that all men are equal only if they are the same."

10. Marshall Stearns, review of Columbia's four-LP *Thesaurus of Classic Jazz*, in *Down Beat*, 1961, anthologized in *Down Beat's Jazz Record Reviews*, vol. 6 (Chicago: Maher Publications, 1962), p. 278.

11. Ibid.

12. Joey Nash, conversation with Michael Brooks, c. 1970. Used by permission.

13. Joe Tarto, conversation with the author, c. 1975.

14. Not surprisingly, other drummers and percussionists have laid claim to some of these innovations. Ben Pollack, for example, also claimed the "sock cymbal." As drummer-researcher Hal Smith has noted, others claiming credit for these and other devices have included Kaiser Marshall, A. G. Godley, and William Ludwig Sr., patriarch of the drum equipment company which bears his family name. Given the absence of reliable documentation and the laxity of early musicians about patents, the facts may never be known.

15. Ralph Berton, *Remembering Bix: A Memoir of the Jazz Age* (New York: Harper and Row, 1974).

16. Schuller, *The Swing Era*, as above, note 5.

17. According to a story widely circulated among musicians at the time, "Dinah" was actually written by a drummer named Frankie Warschauer, who worked for society bandleader Emil Coleman. Singer Joey Nash told Michael Brooks in 1970 that the tune was familiarly known as "Dirty Nellie" and that songwriter Harry Akst stole it and claimed it as his own. According to Nash, Warschauer threatened to bring suit, and Akst bought him off by paying him $150 a week for the rest of his life.

18. Miller's use of ensemble backbeats in the introduction to "I Want to Be Happy" seems to have been lifted bodily from his entr'acte music to *Girl Crazy*, for which, according

to the show's ledgers, he was paid a far from princely $211.25. Two versions of the same arrangement of "Sweet Georgia Brown" are revealing on several levels: for a capsule lesson in what was happening to jazz piano, for example, compare Schutt's chorus on the transcription, rich in subtleties and cross-rhythms but never quite finding its feet rhythmically, with Joe Sullivan's rocking solo on the issued Brunswick version.

19. Without stretching a point, it may be suggested that the ways in which black impulses, flavors, and sounds moved to the center of American popular culture starting in the 1960s had more than coincidentally to do with the crisis of confidence experienced by the nation's white majority in that time. Tangled threads of envy, fear, jealousy, self-doubt, guilt, and ambition that historically have characterized American race relations can be seen to have played a major role in the shift, so clearly articulated by Albert Murray in *The Omni-Americans*. While such social dynamics lie, strictly speaking, beyond the range of this study, it is important to bear them in mind in assessing the ways in which white and black jazz traditions fused, coalesced, and blended beginning in the late 1920s.

20. A 1971 statement by trumpeter Miles Davis, as quoted by Amiri Baraka, has bearing here: "White musicians are overtrained and black musicians are undertrained," the trumpeter is quoted as saying. "You got to mix the two. A black musician has his own sound, but if you want it played straight, mix in a white musician and the piece will still be straight, only you'll get feeling and texture—up, down, around, silly, wrong, slow, fast—you got more to work with." Amiri Baraka (Leroi Jones), *The Music: Reflections on Jazz and Blues* (New York: William Morrow, 1987). Davis may simplify, and even mistake a regional ethos for a racial one: after all, New York at the height of the Harlem Renaissance of the 1920s was full of educated, self-consciously "highbrow" black musicians, who brought the supposedly "white" or "European" qualities of discipline, restraint, and technical exactitude to their efforts. Not that differences, even those defined by race and upbringing, did not exist—but it is best to look outside the crucible of New York artistic life in defining them. Also, in view of the fertility and variegation of activity going on in white New York jazz circles of those years, Ann Douglas's statement in *A Terrible Honesty: Mongrel Manhattan*, (New York: Farrar, Straus and Giroux, 1995) that "the white jazz world, better organized, better publicized, was vastly less innovative than the black one" seems at best woefully ill-informed and in any case naive.

21. Before the arrival of Coleman Hawkins and Bud Freeman, the Pettis style was, generally, the way white jazzmen played tenor sax. It finds its echoes in the early tenor solos of Pee Wee Russell, Larry Binyon, and even the young, half-formed Arthur Rollini. It seems to have been played as an extension and amalgam of both clarinet and alto sax, with the former's arpeggiated figures and legato attack and the latter's creamy tone and vibrato. The solos of George Johnson on 1924 records by the Wolverines, of Don Murray with Jean Goldkette's Orchestra (even as late as "Blue River," in 1927), and even Bostonian Perley Breed on his 1924 "Tell Me, Dreamy Eyes/Where's My Sweetie Hiding" (Gennett) seem to vouch for the concept's universality. Livingston's own solo on Pollack's " 'Deed I Do" is typical, as is the tenor chorus, whoever takes it, on Goldkette's 1926 "Just a Bird's Eye View of My Old Kentucky Home."

22. Michael Aloysius Philburn, conversation with Michael Brooks, 1970.

23. Boston reedman and sometime journalist Jim Moynahan contended that a "hot" cornet break played by his friend Brad Gowans on the Red Heads' (Red Nichols) December 1926 record of "Heebie Jeebies" was the true source for "Humpty Dumpty." He may have been right: the figure is the same.

24. Livingston himself was in London at the time "Oh Baby" was recorded, working

for Fred Elizalde. But he later recycled the arrangement for Paul Whiteman: a score and parts, in his own hand and bearing his name, are on file in the Whiteman collection at Williams College, Williamstown, Massachusetts.

25. S. Frederick Starr has drawn attention to the great and central involvement of Italo-American musicians in jazz since its earliest days, in New Orleans and elsewhere. Citing Rollini, Venuti, Lang, Napoleon, LaRocca, Roppolo, and others, he asks why Italo-American musicians, "almost surely steeped in Italian *melos*, are not recognized as bringing a pertinent musical-cultural heritage [to jazz], whereas blacks are." The Italian contribution, when it is recognized at all, seems to be treated only as part of a wider, more generalized, and in most ways quite insupportable "European" approach.

26. Norman Gentieu, "Viva Venuti!" *IAJRC Journal*, April 1979.

27. Missouri-born Eddie South, who came of age musically in the great South Side bands of mid-1920s Chicago, is often mentioned as Venuti's opposite number among black musicians. Of South's consummate technical mastery there is no doubt, as his records—including six titles made under his own name in 1927–28—more than attest. Critic Leonard Feather and bassist Milt Hinton number among his ardent champions. But Feather also makes the point that "the dark angel of the violin" played in a hot style which often seemed close to the figure shapes and rhythmic concept of a country fiddler, while Venuti's "have always been unmistakably jazz and have never been outswung." Cited by Richard DuPage in notes to *Stringin' the Blues*, Columbia LP boxed set.

28. Quoted in Shapiro and Hentoff, as above, note 3.

29. He had numerous disciples, among them the excellent Al Duffy, Matty Malneck, and various others, at home and abroad. None, however adept, ever mastered Venuti's "four-string Joe" chordal bowing technique.

30. Quoted by Venuti in conversation with Steve Calt, 1973.

31. Joe Venuti, interview with Steve Calt, quoted in sleeve notes to *Eddie Lang, Jazz Guitar Virtuoso*, Yazoo Records LP 1059.

32. Jack Bland, "As I Knew Eddie Lang," *Jazz Record*, 1945, anthologized in Art Hodes and Chadwick Hansen, eds., *Selections From the Gutter* (Berkeley: University of California Press, 1977).

33. "Working with Lang Rated as 'Greatest Thrill' by Johnson," *Down Beat*, May 1939.

34. Artie Shaw, conversation with the author, February 1992.

35. Richard DuPage, notes to *Stringing the Blues*, Columbia boxed set C2L-24, two LPs, issued 1962.

36. Richard Hadlock, *Jazz Masters of the Twenties* (New York: Macmillan, 1965).

37. Marty Grosz (with Lawrence Cohn), notes to *The Guitarists*, boxed set issued by Time-Life Records as part of the *Giants of Jazz* series (TL J-12), 1980.

38. Leonard Feather, notes to *A Jazz Holiday*, MCA double album 2-4018, issued 1973.

Chapter 8

1. Michael Brooks, notes to *Hallelujah! Here Comes the California Ramblers*, Biograph BLP-12021.

2. James T. Maher, conversation with the author, 1991. Saxophonist Harold Marcus, who worked with the Ramblers and numerous other New York–based dance bands in the early '20s, noted in a letter to George W. Kay that his first exposure to "serious sax arranging" came around 1921 and was the result of "Ferde Grofé's knowledge of voicing for reeds." Grofé, for his part, denied the distinction. Evidence now suggests that pioneer dance band leader, arranger, and theorist Arthur Lange may have been an equally important

influence. It was Lange, for example, who first supplied saxophone parts for "stock" arrangements, which hitherto had been scored only for clarinets and various woodwinds. After Lange's innovation, a saxophone trio (alto-alto-tenor) quickly became an integral part of every published arrangement and a key force behind the "modern" saxophone section.

3. Undated clipping from scrapbook of W. T. Kirkeby, on file at Institute of Jazz Studies, Rutgers University.

4. W. T. "Ed" Kirkeby, "The Rise and Fall of the California Ramblers," *Melody Maker*, August 27, 1938, p. 8.

5. Arnold Brilhart, conversation with the author, January 13, 1992.

6. Arthur Rollini, conversation with the author, March 6, 1992.

7. Brilhart, as above, note 5.

8. *Yonkers Herald* clipping from Kirkeby scrapbook, as above, note 3.

9. Gunther Schuller, *Early Jazz* (New York: Oxford University Press, 1968), footnote, p. 255.

10. Here, as elsewhere, the Arnold Bopp tape collection is of inestimable value. It makes clear beyond contest that the Ramblers of 1923 were no more or less disjunct in their phrasing, choppy in their concept of the beat, than all other dance orchestras, regardless of race, working in New York at the time. To single out and stigmatize the Califonia Ramblers on these grounds, without reference to the context within which they worked, is to foreclose any possiblity of objective assessment.

11. Bill Moore is a tantalizing figure. Born in Brooklyn of mixed parentage, he appears to have spent his entire career playing with white bands. In addition to the Ramblers, he worked for a long period with Ben Bernie and recorded prolifically, often in small jazz groups led by saxophonist Jack Pettis. In later years he forsook jazz altogether for the financial security of radio studio orchestras. Well liked by fellow-bandsmen, he appears to have been referred to familiarly as "Nigger" Moore and to have chosen to accept the sobriquet in an affectionate light. He died in 1964.

12. Kirkeby scrapbook, as above, note 3.

13. Bill Priestley, conversation with Michael Brooks, c. 1970. Used by permission.

14. Spencer Clark, conversation with the author, February 22, 1992.

15. Arnold Brilhart, statement to *Saxophone Journal*, January-February 1990. In this connection it is also useful to note that Rudy Wiedoeft, far and away the most prominent popular saxophonist of the era, used an alto saxophone mouthpiece on the lower C-melody. The result, as with Rollini, was a combination of the smaller instrument's flexibility and its larger cousin's depth and fullness of tone.

16. Brilhart, as above, note 5.

17. Allen reference in *Hendersonia* (self-published, 1973). Pianist Dick Hyman, reproducing Rollini's goofus solos in a 1993 concert, used a melodica, which substitutes a miniature piano keyboard for the spring-driven hole-covering keys of the original instrument. The result was nonetheless an accurate simulacrum of the Couesnophone.

18. Percy A. Scholes, *The Oxford Companion to Music*, 10th ed. (London: Oxford University Press, 1938; 7th corrected rpt., 1980), p. 415.

19. Four different versions of the Yellen-Ager pop trifle "Vo-Do-Do-De-O Blues" make the point. As is the case with Ellington's recordings of such originals as "Black and Tan Fantasy" (or "Fantasie") and "The Mooche," the Ramblers manage to mine some rather simple material for a variety of textures and effects. On the Columbia version, Kirkeby sings (never a particularly good idea) the foolish lyric, the reeds turn in a good clarinet trio passage, and Bobby Davis solos genially if uneventfully for sixteen bars. On Pathé, there is another Kirkeby vocal, but better solo spots for Quealey, Davis, and pi-

anist Jack Russin. The Broadway-Cameo label version (as "the Varsity Eight") does away with the vocal and adds solos by Al Philburn on trombone and Rollini on his goofus. Finally, the Goofus Five performance on OKeh gives Davis an elegant chorus, Quealey some nice moments, the "goofus" itself sixteen bars, and even opens a brief solo for tenor saxophonist Sam Ruby.

20. Quealey's having reproduced the Beiderbecke solo is a curiosity. The Wolverines' "Tiger Rag" was not issued in the United States in the '20s, appearing only later on an English Brunswick issue, thanks to the efforts of pianist Dick Voynow and collector Edwin M. "Squirrel" Ashcraft. At that time only two test pressings, one of them seriously cracked, were known to exist. How, then, had Quealey, in New York, heard this performance? It is conceivable that Beiderbecke or another of the Wolverines had a copy and played it for him—but Quealey's performance here betokens careful listening and imitation.

21. Clark, as above, note 14.

22. Brooks from notes to Swing Time, Columbia CD boxed set 52862. Weil quoted in Herb Sanford, Tommy and Jimmy: The Dorsey Years (New Rochelle, N.Y.: Arlington House, 1972).

23. Stanley Dance, The World of Duke Ellington (New York: Charles Scribner's Sons, 1970). For indication of the extent of Carney's admiration for Rollini, attention is drawn to his opening baritone solo on "Why Do I Lie to Myself About You," recorded for Brunswick under Teddy Wilson's leadership June 30, 1936.

24. Quoted in Richard M. Sudhalter and Philip R. Evans, Bix: Man and Legend (New Rochelle, N.Y.: Arlington House, 1973).

25. The name of Tom Rockwell, like those of record company talent scout Ralph Peer, New England ballroom owners Si (or Sy) and Charlie Shribman, and even bandleader Isham Jones, belongs in the pantheon of behind-the-scenes heroes of the early jazz years. Born in Minnesota, he went to work for the OKeh Company in Chicago in the early '20s; it was through his efforts that Louis Armstrong was able, starting in late 1925, to make records with his hand-picked "Hot Five" and, later, "Hot Seven." It was through Rockwell's foresight, in late 1927, that "McKenzie and Condon's Chicagoans" made their four landmark titles for OKeh. Relocating in New York, Rockwell continued his pioneering efforts: at his suggestion, for example, Bix recorded his piano solo "In a Mist" for OKeh. Soon after the start of the 1930s, Rockwell left the record business, teaming with Francis "Cork" O'Keefe to launch a successful booking operation. Their efforts were responsible for the success of the Casa Loma Orchestra, easily among the most popular and influential dance bands of the era. Rockwell and others like him have been badly slighted by the chroniclers and opinion-makers of jazz. In latter years, especially, they have too often been vilified as little more than predators, who realized there was money to be made by exploiting hot jazz. Such assessments are, to say the least, mean-spirited: Rockwell, Peer, and the rest may indeed have been businessmen, but if they had not believed—unwaveringly, and often directly in the face of "conventional wisdom"—in the value of the music, they would never have taken the risks they took on its behalf. As James T. Maher might put it, the tooth fairy didn't bring opportunities for early jazzmen: the Tom Rockwells, Ralph Peers, Ernie Youngs, and Si Shribmans did.

26. Stranger still, a second cornet is heard distantly in the final few bars of this selection, as if standing far off mike. Nichols furnished a clue, in a statement to Philip R. Evans used in Bix: Man and Legend (p. 220, as above, note 24). Nichols apparently had gone to the OKeh studios intending to do the date, and run into trouble in the person of Tom Rockwell.

I gathered [Rockwell] didn't like me because he objected to Tram using me. He said he would honor the recording date but Tram had to use Bix. Tram argued that Bix was in bad shape that day. Tommy said either Bix or no date. I left the studio. As I understand it, Tram found Bix in a speakeasy and he was plastered. He brought him to the studio to show Tommy. Made no difference to him. Bix had to do the date. When Tram heard the playbacks he was furious, and stomped out of the studio.

Who, then, is the halting, thin-toned soloist? Trumbauer, who played some cornet, or another of the reed players? And can it be Bix, present but under the weather, noodling in the last ensemble? The mystery remains.

27. George Hurley, conversation with the author, 1974.

28. Stanley Nelson, "Fred Elizalde and His Savoy Hotel Music," *Eye Witness Jazz*, no. 1 (London), 1947.

29. As quoted in Albert McCarthy, *The Dance Band Era* (London: November Books, 1971).

30. Nelson, as above, note 28.

31. American musicians, particularly from Boston, had been a fixture in London dance band circles since the start of the decade. Saxophonist Bert Ralton, who had helped pioneer the modern dance band sound as part of Art Hickman's California reed team, took over direction of the Savoy Orpheans. Brothers Al, Ray, and Rudy Starita and pianist-songwriter Carroll Gibbons, all Bostonians, were popular figures, as was "whispering cornetist" Roy Fox, a native of Colorado. Clarinetist Danny Polo, pianist Leo Kahn, and trumpeter Henry "Hot Lips" Levine (who though born in London grew up in New York) were among other Americans active in London in the late '20s. Sylvester Ahola, who had played with Paul Specht, Cass Hagan, and others and had the lead book in the Rollini New Yorker band, blossomed in England as a "hot" man in a manner reminiscent, by turns, of Nichols, Quealey, and Bix. His emphatic solos on the Night Club Kings' "Someone" and "In the Moonlight," recorded January 21, 1930, are representative. Among other Bostonians approached by Joe Brannelly was alto saxophonist Al Sudhalter, father of the author. Swayed by family objections, Sudhalter turned down the Ambrose offer, which he recalled as generous and quite tempting. Fellow-Bostonians Perley Breed and Johnny Helfer went instead, quickly becoming two of the most sought-after reedmen on the British dance band scene.

32. Pianist Jack Russin had joined at the end of July, after playing his way across the Atlantic in George Carhart's band, as mentioned earlier.

33. Kirkeby scrapbook, as above, note 3.

34. Early neglect of the vibes was far from inadvertent but the result of inherent limitations in the technology of the instrument: until the introduction of a damper pedal in the early '30s, for example, there was no way to keep each tone from ringing except with the arm or hand. This and other specific points are discussed more fully in the chapters on Red Norvo.

35. Rollini also made good use of his skills on other instruments, including piano and drums. He plays piano with surprising fluency on a February 28, 1936, date led by trumpeter Louis "King" Garcia: "Christopher Columbus" and "Swing Mister Charlie" find him rhythmic, fully chorded, and sparkling in both ensemble and solo.

36. Charles M. DiCarlo, "Public Doesn't Appreciate Rollini!!" *Down Beat*, April 1939.

37. Norman Gentieu, "Was Adrian Rollini Murdered?" *IAJRC Journal*, January 1988. Letter from Bob Hilbert published in next issue (April 1988) of same journal.

Chapter 9

1. Eddie Condon (with Thomas Sugrue), *We Called It Music* (New York: Henry Holt, 1947).

2. Adolphus "Doc" Cheatham, interview with Whitney Balliett, *New Yorker* anthologized in *American Musicians* (New York: Oxford University Press, 1986).

3. Milton "Mezz" Mezzrow (with Bernard Wolfe), *Really the Blues* (New York: Random House, 1946).

4. Quoted in Max Jones, *Talking Jazz* (New York: W. W. Norton, 1988).

5. Catherine Jacobson, "The Story of Dick McPartland," *Jazz*, n.d. 1945.

6. Quoted by Catherine Jacobson, "Facts About Bud Hunter," *Jazz* 1, no. 7 (autumn 1943), p. 20.

7. Freeman comment from *Crazeology: The Autobiography of a Chicago Jazzman* (as told to Robert Wolf) (Chicago: University of Illinois Press, 1989). McPartland remark from conversation with the author, 1989.

8. Quoted in Dave Dexter Jr., "Tesch Quit Banjo to Become a Jazz Immortal," *Down Beat*, November 15, 1939.

9. Quoted in Jones, as above, note 4.

10. William Howland Kenney, *Chicago Jazz: A Cultural History, 1904–1930* (New York: Oxford University Press, 1993).

11. John McDonough, notes to *The Original Dixieland Jazz Band*, Bluebird CD BB-61098, 1992.

12. Condon, as above, note 1.

13. Jess Stacy, conversation with the author, April 21, 1988.

14. Art Hodes, "Wingy, Louis and Me," in Art Hodes and Chadwick Hansen, eds., *Selections From the Gutter* (Berkeley: University of California Press, 1977).

15. Jones, as above, note 4.

16. Dexter, as above, note 9.

17. Jones, as above, note 4.

18. Quoted in Chip Deffaa, "Bud Freeman—The Early Years," *Mississippi Rag*, December 1986.

19. In addition to providing employment for a succession of outstanding bands, Patrick T. "Paddy" Harmon enjoys another, quite different, jazz distinction. It was reportedly at his order that the metal mute which today bears his name was designed, perhaps for trumpeters Freddie Keppard and Elwood Graham of the Doc Cooke Orchestra, long in residence at the Dreamland. Built in two sections, a squared-off hollow body and a sliding cylindrical stem with a small horn at one end, it enabled players to achieve a range of effects, from the crying "wah-wah" so beloved of early dance bands to a penetrating, yet curiously intimate, buzzing quality.

20. Quoted in Ralph J. Gleason, "Muggsy Picks Some Roses," *Down Beat*, June 26, 1958, p. 15.

21. Quoted in Steve Voce, "Lawrence of Arcadia," *Jazz Journal*, June 1975.

22. Benny Goodman, *The Kingdom of Swing* (rpt. New York: Frederick Ungar, 1961.

23. Al Sudhalter, conversation with the author, 1973.

24. Jones, as above, note 4.

25. Jimmy McPartland, conversation with the author, 1986.

26. Johnson, George L. "Wolverines Had Tough Luck After Beiderbecke Left Band," *Down Beat*, December 1938.

27. Stacy, as above, note 13.

28. Quoted in Jones, as above, note 4.

29. Arny Freeman, "Bad Times, Good Tempos," *Jazz Journal*, July 1975.

30. Jimmy McPartland, conversation with the author, 1987. Mezzrow's attitudes emerge most strongly in his 1947 autobiography, *Really the Blues*, including an almost bar-by-bar analysis of records by the young white Chicagoans, upbraiding them with Marxist-Leninist rigor for alleged deviations from the "correct" line of Oliver, Dodds, Noone, Bechet, Morton, and others. In this connection it is perhaps not altogether surprising to learn that the clarinetist's gifted literary "ghost," novelist Bernard Wolfe, had been secretary to Leon Trotsky during the famed Bolshevik's exile in Mexico. Mezzrow's kind of racially determined jazz orthodoxy reached almost canonic status in the 1990s as a result of several factors, most of them more directly related to American sociology and racial politics than to music.

31. Quoted in "Chicago Style All Bunk," *Down Beat*, December 1, 1942.

32. Mezzrow, as above, note 3, p. 94.

33. Keith Keller, *Oh Jess! A Jazz Life* (New York: Mayan Music, 1989), p. 91.

34. Kenney, as above, note 10.

35. *Rhythm*, November 1927, p. 18.

36. Paul Eduard Miller and George Hoefer, "Chicago Jazz History," *The Esquire Jazz Book*, 1946.

37. Condon, as above, note 1.

38. Humphrey Lyttelton, *The Best of Jazz, Vol. I* (New York: Taplinger, 1982), p. 154.

39. Benny Goodman (1981) and Max Kaminsky (1991), conversations with the author.

40. Mezzrow, as above, note 3.

41. Stacy, as above, note 13.

42. Hugues Panassié, *Hot Jazz: The Guide to Swing Music*, trans. Lyle and Eleanor Dowling (London: Cassell, and New York: Witmark, 1936), originally published in France as *Le Jazz Hot* (1934).

43. Hugues Panassié, *The Real Jazz*, trans. Anne Sorelle Williams, adapted by Charles Edward Smith (New York: Smith and Durrell, 1942).

44. Albert Murray, *The Omni-Americans* (New York: Outerbridge and Dienstfrey, 1970), pp. 172–73.

45. Richard Hadlock, notes to Time-Life *Giants of Jazz* Joe Sullivan set (STL-J27).

46. Max Kaminsky (with V. E. Hughes), *My Life in Jazz* (London: Andre Deutsch, 1964).

47. John Steiner, conversation with the author, May 1990. Lyttelton, as above, note 38.

48. Bill Esposito, "Muggsy—An Appreciation," *IAJRC Journal*, October 1988.

49. John Mehegan, *Jazz Rhythm and the Improvised Line* (New York: Watson-Guptill, 1962).

50. Eddie Condon and Hank O'Neal, *Eddie Condon's Scrapbook of Jazz* (New York: St. Martin's Press, 1973).

51. Benny Goodman, conversation with the author, April 1981. This interview, which first appeared in *American Heritage* magazine, is reprinted in its entirety in chapter 22.

52. Stacy, as above, note 13. Joe Venuti, according to Red Norvo, recalled a very young Goodman taking the bus from Chicago to Detroit to hear the Jean Goldkette Orchestra at the Graystone Ballroom and standing in front of clarinetist Don Murray for number after number.

53. Bee Palmer emerges again and again as an influential ally to jazzmen—and apparently those of both races. In mid-1928, the vaudevillian hired Eddie South, "dark angel

of the violin," to lead her backup band for an engagement at Chicago's College Inn (Kenney, as above, note 11, p. 34). Four years earlier there had been plans to have Fletcher Henderson's Orchestra accompany her in the Broadway musical *The Passing Show* at the Winter Garden, but it never materialized (Walter Allen, *Hendersonia*, p. 115).

54. Sullivan quoted in Hadlock, as above, note 47.

55. Whiteman, ever in search of jazzmen to strengthen his "King of Jazz" billing, had offered to hire Nichols and his "Five Pennies"—Miff Mole, Jimmy Dorsey, Arthur Schutt, and drummer Vic Berton—*en masse* in the spring of 1927. Only Nichols, Dorsey, and Berton accepted the offer: the cornetist stayed awhile and left, convinced he could do better as a freelancer. Berton clashed personally with Whiteman and quit (or was fired) amid great acrimony. Dorsey, milder of temperament, stayed on until early 1928.

56. Marty Grosz, notes to Time-Life *Giants of Jazz* Frank Teschemacher set, STL-J23.

57. The ever-alert pianist-arranger-archivist Dick Hyman seems to have been the first to point out that the personnel on "One Step to Heaven" is somewhat larger than has been assumed. At various points in the ensembles, at least four horns are clearly audible. In the coda, for example, after Nichols and Teschemacher play a two-bar figure together they're answered by Mole and another tenor-register horn, playing a descending figure in sixths. Research by Vince Giordano in the Red Nichols papers at the University of Oregon yielded a set of parts which appear to be those of the recording arrangement, scored for two trumpets, trombone, mellophone, and clarinet. Dudley Fosdick, a regular member of the Nichols-Mole circle, took part in the next Molers date, done three weeks later, so it seems reasonable to assume that he played the mellophone part. "Shimme-Sha Wabble," by contrast, seems to involve only the trumpet-trombone-clarinet front line and piano-banjo-drums rhythm section.

58. Quoted in Voce, as above, note 21.

59. Stacy, as above, note 13.

60. Quoted in Whitney Balliett, "Little Davey Tough," in *New Yorker*, November 18, 1985.

61. Kaminsky, as above, note 46.

62. Mort Goode, notes to *The Complete Benny Goodman, Vol. V*, (Bluebird twelve-inch LP set AXM2-5557.

63. Burt Korall, *Drummin' Men* (New York: Macmillan-Schirmer, 1990), pp. 212–13.

64. Quoted in Bill Gottlieb, "Dixieland Nowhere, Says Dave Tough," *Down Beat*, September 23, 1946.

65. Gene Lees, *Leader of the Band: The Life of Woody Herman* (New York: Oxford University Press, 1995), p. 107.

66. Among the many records that best demonstrate Dave Tough's qualities are the unusually well recorded *Comes Jazz* titles of July 23, 1940, issued under Freeman's name; such Tommy Dorsey performances as "Milenberg Joys," on which he can be heard energizing trumpeter Yank Lawson, clarinetist Johnny Mince, saxophonist Babe Russin, and Dorsey himself; such Benny Goodman radio performances as the Quartet's "Benny Sent Me," on which Tough cranks both Goodman and Lionel Hampton to something approaching a state of frenzy; and, of course, such records as "Apple Honey" and "Caldonia," by Woody Herman's 1945 "Herd," with Tough adrenalizing bassist Chubby Jackson and the rest of Herman's young rhythm section.

67. Quoted in Alma Hubner, "Muggsy Spanier," *Jazz Record*, April 1944.

68. Kenney, as above, note 11.

69. Lewis's reputation has taken something of a pounding at the hands of jazz fans and critics, due in equal measure to his vaudevillian antics and his truly dreadful "gaspipe"

clarinet playing. But another, surely more balanced, view comes from trombonist George Brunis, who in 1958 emphatically reminded an interviewer that Lewis was "a great showman; he gave me a great schooling for talking to an audience" (June 3, 1958, Hogan Archive). Lewis paid both Brunis and Spanier well, even in the darkest days of the Depression, and gave them plenty of chances to solo. Spanier's choruses on such Lewis records as "Dinah" and "Headin' for Better Times" number among his finest. Lewis also employed Goodman, Jimmy Dorsey, and, for two memorable record titles in mid-1929, Frank Teschemacher.

70. Dempsey J. Travis, *An Autobiography of Black Jazz* (Chicago: Urban Research Institute, 1983), p. 91.

Chapter 10

1. Charles Edward Smith and Frederic Ramsey Jr., *Jazzmen* (New York: Harcourt Brace, 1939).

2. Milton "Mezz" Mezzrow (with Bernard Wolfe), *Really the Blues* (New York: Random House, 1946).

3. Jess Stacy, conversation with the author, April 21, 1988.

4. Quoted in Keith Keller, *Oh, Jess! A Jazz Life* (New York: Mayan Music, 1989).

5. Otto Harbach, lyric to "Yesterdays," written with Jerome Kern for *Roberta*, 1933.

6. Don Watt, conversation with the author, Dec. 19, 1991.

7. It is impossible to resist comparing the sort of music Weems and other bands were called upon to play at the Muehlebach with what was going on around this time in the black area centered around 18th Street. This was the heyday of black Kansas City, with the bands of Bennie Moten, Walter Page, and Andy Kirk at full tilt. It is unlikely that the customers at the Muehlebach, for whom the Coon-Sanders Nighthawks playing "Roodles" or "Little Orphan Annie" was hot stuff, would have found their way to the Sunset, the Subway, the Cherry Blossom, or the Reno. On all available evidence, the Weems band was capable of heating things up quite respectably—but as Don Watt (ibid.) put it, that was "not what the folks came expecting to hear."

8. Ibid. Washburn's name has sometimes appeared with a final *e*, as "Washburne." Musicians' union directories and early periodicals list him as Washburn, as will this volume.

9. Ibid.

10. James "Rosy" McHargue, conversation with the author, April 19, 1988.

11. Warren Vaché, "Joe Haymes, Leader and Arranger," notes to *Joe Haymes and His Orchestra*, Bluebird LP set AXM2-5552.

12. Richard M. Sudhalter and Philip R. Evans, *Bix: Man and Legend* (New Rochelle, N.Y.: Arlington House, 1974).

13. Watt, as above, note 6.

14. Quoted by Marty Grosz in his notes to Frank Teschemacher record set in Time-Life *Giants of Jazz* series, STL-J23. During this time Teschemacher also worked for Jan Garber, in a band that included trumpeter Dale McMickle and saxophonist-arranger Lyle "Spud" Murphy. The rhythm section, Murphy recalled, was particularly inept, and "to overcome that I started writing arrangements. I went a little further and a little further until it got to be damn good. Until Garber said, 'Hey, you're changing the style of this band!' I said, 'I hope it's for the better,' and he said, 'I don't think so. I'm out to make money.' That was in New Orleans. A few days later, in Philadelphia, we were all fired; that's when he got the cornball imitation of Lombardo." (From Murphy conversation with Ray Hoffman, c. 1983. Used with permission.)

15. Bud Freeman, conversation with the author, 1988.

16. Quoted in Ross Russell, *Jazz Style in Kansas City and the Southwest* (Berkeley: University of California Press, 1971).

17. John Steiner, "Kansas City Frank," *Jazz*, mid-1943, reprinted in English magazine *Piano Jazz*, 1945.

18. Harvey Lebow, "Modest George," *Jazz Record*, anthologized in Art Hodes and Chadwick Hansen, eds., *Selections From the Gutter* (Berkeley: University of California Press, 1977).

19. Ibid.

20. Earl Wiley, "Drummer From Chicago," *Jazz Record* 29, February 1945.

21. Jimmy McPartland, conversation with the author, 1988.

22. Some uncertainty surrounds this session. A November 1934 *Down Beat* item, "Paul Mares Orch. Signed to Record for Brunswick," describes a visit to Harry's by impresario-publisher Irving Mills. The personnel, as described in the article, is Mares, two trombones, Boyce Brown, an unidentified clarinetist, and the rhythm section. Mention of Mills may lend credence to a later account by Joe Mares, the trumpeter's brother, suggesting that Hoagy Carmichael (who worked for Mills) had a hand in getting the band recorded. According to Joe Mares, Irving "Fazola" Prestopnick was supposed to be the clarinetist, but for reasons now lost to recollection was unable to attend.

23. Stacy, as above, note 3.

24. Hugues Panassié, *Hot Jazz: The Guide to Swing Music*, trans. Lyle and Eleanor Dowling (London: Cassell, and New York: Witmark, 1936), originally published in France as *Le Jazz Hot* (1934).

25. Priscilla Rushton, notes to *Informal Sessions At Squirrel's, Vol. 1*. MIS LP 3, privately distributed.

26. Eddie Condon, and Hank O'Neal, *Eddie Condon's Scrapbook of Jazz* (New York: St. Martin's Press, 1973).

27. Quoted in Max Jones, *Talking Jazz* (New York: W. W. Norton, 1988).

28. George Simon, *Simon Says: The Sights and Sounds of the Swing Era* (New Rochelle, N.Y.: Arlington House, 1971).

29. George Avakian, "Critic, on U.S. Tour, Rates Kaycee Ork Tops," *Down Beat*, October 15, 1939.

30. Gordon Darrah, "Boyce Brown and Floyd Bean," *Eye Witness Jazz*, July 1946.

31. Ibid.

32. Dave Dexter Jr., *The Jazz Story* (Englewood Cliffs, N.J.: Prentice-Hall, 1964), pp. 40–41.

33. According to Jacobson's wife Catherine, one of the most prolific chroniclers of early Chicago jazz, this was a lifelong practice. As a fourteen-year-old, Boyce had named his first alto sax "Clementine."

34. *Down Beat* clipping, n.d., on file at Institute of Jazz Studies, Rutgers University.

35. George Avakian, conversation with the author, January 8, 1992.

36. James T. Maher, conversation with the author, April 26, 1996.

37. "Earl Hines and Old Dixieland Gang in Jam Session," *Down Beat*, February 1937.

38. Avakian, as above, note 35.

39. Ibid.

40. Gerry Mulligan, conversation with the author, June 1992.

41. Another title, Jacobson's boogie-based "Opus I Sans Melody" (otherwise known as "Blue Slug II" or "Love at Sight") afforded Avakian a chance to apply his literature studies. Taken with Rinker's first-chorus counterline, he added a text adapted from the opening of John Donne's "On His Mistress": "By our first strange and fatal interview,/By

all desires which thereof did ensue . . ." They dedicated the result to singer Anita O'Day, who had worked with Jacobson around town before joining the big band of fellow-Chicagoan Gene Krupa.

42. John Steiner, "Kansas City Frank," Jazz, Magazine spring 1943.

43. "Frank Melrose, Chi Pianist, Is Found Fatally Injured," Down Beat, September 15, 1941.

Chapter 11

1. John Bainbridge, "The Diamond-Studded Saxophone," New Yorker, April 2, 1979.

2. Bud Freeman (as told to Robert Wolf), Crazeology: The Autobiography of a Chicago Jazzman (Chicago: University of Illinois Press, 1989).

3. Compounded from various Freeman accounts, including Crazeology (see note 2 above), and Chip Deffaa, "Bud Freeman—The Early Years," Mississippi Rag, December 1986. Freeman told this story, with minor variations in wording, often in later life—including, on more than one occasion, to the author.

4. His early love of the "dancer" image, especially, stayed with him. His first idol was Joe Frisco, who often billed himself as an "American Apache" and appeared (with Loretta McDermott) as part of the team of "Francisco and Loretta." It was while they were performing in New Orleans, in 1915, that Frisco first heard Tom Brown's band and subsequently played a role in bringing them to Chicago (see chapter 1).

5. Freeman, as above, note 2.

6. Quoted in Max Jones, Talking Jazz (London: Macmillan, 1987).

7. Ira Gitler, "Saga of a Saxophone Sage," Down Beat, May 24, 1962. Deffaa, as above, note 3.

8. Steve Voce, "Lawrence of Arcadia," Jazz Journal, June 1975.

9. Jones, as above, note 6.

10. Freeman, as above note 2.

11. Russin solos with great suppleness and drive on one of the rarest small-band records of the '30s, a version of the 1924 favorite "Where's My Sweetie Hiding?" made for Variety under the leadership of drummer Johnny Williams on June 15, 1937. Besides Russin, the sidemen include trombonist Jack Jenney, showing off a seldom-heard aggressive side, and Charlie Spivak, respected as one of the top lead trumpet men of the time. Here, and on "Little Old Lady," he returns to the role of hot soloist, which he played with some flair during his mid-'20s time with Paul Specht's Orchestra. Williams, best known for his work with the Raymond Scott Quintet, is the father of John Williams, who became a world celebrity in the late twentieth century as a composer of movie soundtracks (Superman, Raiders of the Lost Ark) and as conductor of the Boston Pops Orchestra.

12. Al Philburn, conversation with Michael Brooks, c. 1969.

13. Letter to Metronome, July-August 1937.

14. Freeman, as above, note 2.

15. Jimmy McPartland, conversation with the author, c. 1985.

16. Keith Ingham, conversation with the author, May 18, 1992.

17. Loren Schoenberg, conversation with the author, April 27, 1992.

18. On clarinet, too, Zimmers was capable of balanced, quite introspective playing. His solos on Decca sessions led by singer Dick Robertson in spring 1938 ("Goodnight Angel," "Let's Sail to Dreamland"), show this side of his work to good advantage.

19. Clinton quoted in George T. Simon, Simon Says (New Rochelle: Arlington House, 1971). Simon remark in conversation with the author, May 3, 1992.

20. George Avakian, conversation with the author, 1992.

21. Marsala is also heard on tenor on "Let's Get Happy," recorded for Commodore March 10, 1938, by an all-star group led by critic Leonard Feather.

22. To be sure, there were many white jazz tenor players who chose not to go his way. Charlie Barnet, Vido Musso, Herbie Haymer, and various others found the examples of Hawkins and/or Chu Berry more seductive and chose to emulate them. Canadian-born Georgie Auld heard Basie's Herschel Evans and recast his style along those broad-toned lines. Jerry Jerome, Joe "Flip" Phillips, and Sam Donahue, arriving at decade's end, seemed to combine elements of Hawkins and Young in finding their voices, as did Don Lodice. But none of these, ironically, seemed able to transcend his sources, to develop a distinctive solo identity out of his antecedents. Until the late '40s, and the emergence of Stan Getz, Zoot Sims, Al Cohn, and the rest of a generation inspired by Lester Young, the only white tenor stylists of real and demonstrable originality seem to have been Freeman and Eddie Miller.

23. One exception to this *idée fixe* is Gunther Schuller, who goes to great lengths in praising Miller in *The Swing Era*, while ignoring Freeman. The omission is inexplicable and regrettable, in that it distorts perception of an important chain of development. Schuller makes much of what he hears as a stylistic kinship between Miller and Frank Trumbauer, and even draws comparisons between Miller and Lester Young. "Miller was, to be sure, not as spontaneously creative and rhythmically loose as Young," says Schuller, "but he certainly aspired to the same kind of clean, incisive, intelligent, melodically linear approach." This line of thinking is astonishing in its failure to acknowledge Freeman's role as principal link in this stylistic chain—and indeed, along with Trumbauer, a key progenitor of the very clean, linear approach Schuller so warmly lauds.

24. Quoted by Dan Morgenstern in notes to *The Commodore Story, Vol. I*, Mosaic Records limited edition boxed set.

25. Joe Muranyi, conversation with the author, May 8, 1992.

26. George T. Simon, conversation with the author, April 29, 1992.

27. George Hoefer, "Freeman Big Influence on Saxists," *Down Beat*, March 21, 1952. John Chilton, *Song of the Hawk* (London: Quartet, 1990), p. 91. Coleman Hawkins, ever astute, heard similarities between the two. "Lester Young is great on phrasing," he said in an article for the Chicago magazine *Music and Rhythm* (August 1941). "For originality of ideas I would rank him first . . . Bud Freeman has a lot in common with Les Young; he phrases well and puts a lot of thought into his playing."

28. Late in life Young told several interviewers he'd never paid much attention to Freeman. That's understandable: by that time Lester had become something of a cult figure, revered and widely emulated. An entire generation of saxophonists, most of them white, had gained international reputations—and in some cases made very good money—with styles based almost entirely on his. Young's feelings toward them and their success are known to have been ambivalent. In view of this, it would have been only human to play down any debt to anyone except Trumbauer, who by that time was long gone from professional music (he died in 1956), for all practical purposes a figure of the distant past. Recent years have brought increasing emphasis on the black role in American popular culture, and with it long-overdue recognition to a cadre of veteran black musicians. Not unexpectedly, several of these have become quite circumspect in admitting to any but black influences in their formative years. While understandable in terms of political fashion, this is nonetheless to be regretted. The late saxophonist and arranger Eddie Barefield may have come closer to an accurate assessment in declaring to the author, "Black, white, hell! Everybody got something from somebody back then. You listened to whoever you could, and if you liked it, you took it. That's the way we all learned."

29. Hoefer, as above, note 27.

30. George T. Simon, Notes to *Ray Noble*, RCA Vintage series, LPV-536, 1967.

31. Freeman's efforts to use the clarinet in an ensemble with Berigan on the fourth title, "What Is There to Say?" are less successful, exposing his technical limitations on the instrument. This seems to have been Freeman's final appearance as a clarinetist. As far as can be ascertained, he never again used the instrument in public.

32. John Hammond, conversation with the author, c. 1983.

33. Freeman, as above, note 2.

34. Arthur Rollini, *Thirty Years with the Big Bands* (Chicago: University of Illinois Press, 1987).

35. Carmen Mastren, quoted in radio interview with the author, broadcast on WBAI-FM, New York, 1978.

36. Freeman, as above, note 2.

37. Dave Tough was the scheduled drummer on this session but came to work in a state of alcoholic collapse. He got through two numbers, then was unable to continue. Cornetist Marsala, an invited guest, had begun his career as a drummer and stepped in to finish the date. His playing, while rudimentary, was solid enough to keep things moving. Gabler, recalling the session, lamented that he'd had consistently bad luck with Tough. He tried again on November 12, 1938; the drums showed up, but without their owner, who'd again gone AWOL. This time the last-minute replacement was Lionel Hampton, who was staying at the same hotel. But by the time they got him, half the allotted session time had run out; they did only two of four scheduled titles that day.

38. When Teddy Wilson left Goodman in early 1939, Jess Stacy took over piano duties in both big band and small groups. His occasional solos with the full band ("My Honey's Lovin' Arms" of November 23, 1938, is typical) had seldom been less than outstanding—certainly his impromptu A-minor excursion on "Sing Sing Sing" near the end of the Carnegie Hall concert is one of the band's great moments. Now, however, he could also be heard in the more pellucid small-band context. He's relaxed and buoyant on "Opus 3/4" (April 6, 1939), a minor-key creation which opens with Benny remembering a melodic fragment from "Georgia Jubilee" and even manages to quote Bix Beiderbecke's famed "Jazz Me Blues" solo break along the way. Needless to say, Stacy blossomed in the more relaxed atmosphere of the Commodore sessions; Milt Gabler's ability to get the best out of his musicians through a combination of relaxation and canny studio setup is discussed elsewhere, but it's worth noting here that when Stacy brought in Eddie Miller for a November 30, 1939, date, the "Little Prince" played one of his warmest and most coherent solos on the Jimmy McHugh favorite "I Can't Believe That You're in Love With Me."

39. Max Kaminsky (with V. E. Hughes), *My Life in Jazz* (London: Andre Deutsch, 1964).

40. In quick succession, there were two other record dates. The four Decca titles recorded August 11 under Eddie Condon's name were part of a *Chicago Jazz* commemoration album dreamed up and organized by fledgling producer George Avakian. Discussion of this date will be found elsewhere. On September 18 Brunswick session they recorded Freeman's "The Sailfish," as well as loosely structured Gowans arrangements on "Sunday," "As Long as I Live," and the Original Dixieland Jazz Band standard "Satanic Blues." A laggard rhythm section, with society drummer Al "Zip" Seidel filling in for Morey Feld, keeps these performances relatively earthbound.

41. Eddie Condon (with Thomas Sugrue), *We Called It Music* (New York: Henry Holt, 1947).

42. One pleasant surprise is the drumming of Bostonian Fred Moynahan, an old

783

Gowans crony. Fred's clarinet-playing elder brother Jim Moynahan was known in those years as a tireless chronicler and advocate of such early groups as the Original Dixieland Jazz Band and the Original Memphis Five. Fred Moynahan outlived his brother by several years, remaining active around Boston throughout the 1950s. The author can attest through personal experience that, even in those late years, he was a deft and knowing drummer, able to drive a rhythm section hard yet unobtrusively.

43. Haggart quoted in Burt Korall, *Drummin' Men* (New York: Schirmer-Macmillan, 1990). Korall's chapter on Tough, enriched through the author's own hands-on knowledge of jazz drumming, is strongly recommended. For understanding of its subject on all levels it is unlikely to be surpassed.

44. Johnny Mince, conversation with the author, broadcast on WBAI-FM, 1976.

45. Ruby Braff, conversation with the author, May 14, 1992.

46. Gitler, as above, note 7.

47. His melody statement on the title track, for example, displays a direct, even solemn earnestness quite removed from the arched eyebrow of decades past. He intones the old Crosby favorites "Please" and "It Must Be True" with the ardor of a '30s crooner and approaches his own "Eel's Nephew" and "Disenchanted Trout" in gently ironic mien. He's capricious, even mischievous, on another original, "Doctor Paycer's Dilemma," named (with slight respelling) for one of his many analysts, a prominent New York psychiatrist—and, coincidentally, husband of Joan Peyser, musical scholar and author of biographical studies of Leonard Bernstein and George Gershwin.

48. Braff, as above, note 45.

49. Hugues Panassié, "Bud Freeman One of the Finest Hot Musicians," *Down Beat*, August 1936.

50. Ben Webster, conversation with the author, Copenhagen, summer 1973. Reconstructed from notes taken at the time and used by the author on sleeve essay for Commodore LP XFL 14941.

51. Kenny Davern, conversation with the author, May 12, 1992.

52. Bob White, "Saxophone or Shakespeare?" Article from unidentified magazine, on file in the archives of the Institute of Jazz Studies, Rutgers University.

Chapter 12

1. Ian Whitcomb, *After the Ball* (New York: Simon and Schuster, 1973).

2. Isabel Colegate's *The Shooting Party*, with its bucolic portrait of England on the eve of the "Great War," captures something of the same flavor. For all its flaws—class inequities, the self-indulgences of privilege and empire—this Edwardian time takes on the roseate glow, within Colegate's vision, of one last moment of innocence before the conflagration shortly to come. A 1984 film based on the book pointed up the attendant ironies of the situation handsomely.

3. Readers wishing a particularly American slant on this subject are invited to seek out *Looking Forward: Life in the Twentieth Century as Predicted in the Pages of American Magazines From 1895 to 1905*, compiled by Ray Brosseau and Edited by Ralph K. Andrist (New York: American Heritage Press, 1970). A remarkable volume, it assembles turn-of-the-century writings on such subjects as technology, urban living, women's rights, fashion, race, education, class, nutrition, physical culture—and even the end of the world. At once prophetic and self-deceiving, the various pieces foster great understanding of subsequent events in America and abroad.

4. "There Ain't No Land Like Dixieland To Me," words and music by Walter Don-

aldson, 1927. "Deep Down South," words by Monty Collins, music by George Green, 1930. "(They Made It Twice as Nice as Paradise) And They Called It Dixieland," words by Raymond Egan, music by Richard Whiting, 1916.

5. Regrettably, Armstrong does not sing the verse to "When It's Sleepy Time Down South," which frames the sentiments exactly:

> Homesick, tired,
> All alone in a big city,
> Why should everybody pity me?
> Night time's falling,
> And I'm yearning for Virginia;
> Hospitality within ya calls me

A few black songwriters dealt with conditions up north in a rather more direct, considerably less affectionate, manner. "Pickin' on Your Baby," a 1924 effort by a team identified only as James and Reynolds (the composer may be the pianist Richard M. Jones), is still remarkable for its forthright—even heartbreaking—treatment of racial hatred among children. Its lyric is topical enough, in fact, to include a pointed, if oblique, reference to the Doctor Feelgood of his day, Dr. Emil Coué:

> Day by day, in every way, when they get together,
> They go from bad to worse instead of gettin' better

6. Bix's admiration of the Dixieland band veers close to obsession. He had recorded their "Fidgety Feet," "Tiger Rag," "Lazy Daddy," and "Sensation" with the Wolverines, as well as "Jazz Me Blues" and "Royal Garden Blues," which were prominent in the band's repertoire at the time, he first heard them in person in 1921. After leaving the Wolverines he'd recorded the ODJB's "Toddlin' Blues" at his Gennett "Rhythm Jugglers" session of January 26, 1925; their "Clarinet Marmalade" and "Ostrich Walk" had been among the first records of his association with Frank Trumbauer. Even "Singin' the Blues," on which the cornetist took perhaps his greatest and most widely imitated solo, was the work of ODJB pianist J. Russel Robinson. A similar situation would have been unthinkable among black jazzmen: a parallel might have had Louis Armstrong devoting a large chunk of the repertoire at his Hot Five and Seven dates for OKeh to "Mabel's Dream," "Snake Rag," and other numbers associated with his mentor, King Oliver.

7. Jack Lesberg, conversation with the author, September 9, 1993.

8. Digby Fairweather, entry on Condon in Jazz: The Essential Companion (Englewood Cliffs, N.J.: Prentice-Hall, 1987).

9. Bud Freeman, quoted in Burt Korall Drummin' Men (New York: Schirmer-Macmillan, 1990).

10. Eddie Condon, We Called It Music (New York: Henry Holt, 1947).

11. Eddie Condon and Hank O'Neal, Eddie Condon's Scrapbook of Jazz (New York: St. Martin's Press, 1973).

12. Others following Gabler's lead included Bob Thiele (Signature), Dan Qualey (Solo Art), and, after a time, Nesuhi and Ahmet Ertegun (Atlantic). It's no exaggeration to say that the small independents have played—and still play—a major role in guaranteeing the survival of those jazz styles neglected by the larger companies. Such latter-day enterprises as Bob Erdos's Stomp Off and media entrepreneur George Buck's ever-shifting array of labels (Audiophile, Jazzology, Circle, Progressive, GHB) and, in the '90s, Mat Domber's Arbors and a host of labels based in other countries have furnished valued outlets for the efforts of jazz traditionalists. Similarly, the Commodore shop itself played an indispensable

role as a headquarters, hangout, rendezvous, and employment agency for hot music players, fans, and followers. More than one jazz magazine was born of avid conversations carried on among the store's record shelves.

13. Dan Morgenstern, "The Commodore Story," notes to vol. 1 of three-volume Mosaic boxed set covering the entire Commodore catalogue. Morgenstern's balance, fairness, and attention to detail, and the wealth of photos, many hitherto unpublished, illustrating his text, make this recommended, nay required, reading for anyone seriously interested in accurate (and refreshingly apolitical) historical coverage of pre-bop hot music.

14. Black bands had played and even recorded many of these same songs, particularly in the late '20s, but the decision to do so seems to some degree a result of record company desire to spot, then cash in on, trends and fads. When a contingent from Fletcher Henderson's Orchestra jams outright on Owen Murphy's "Oh Baby" on an April 1928 session, it's hard to tell whether they're working in response to some executive's idea (the song was featured in the Broadway revue *Rain or Shine* that year) or to Henderson's chronic failure to provide alternative material in time. In 1927–28 alone, Henderson units recorded Dixieland Band holdovers ("Fidgety Feet," "Sensation"), "jazzy" pop material by white writers ("Wabash Blues," "Wang Wang Blues"), and even such relatively intricate "symphonic jazz" items as "Whiteman Stomp" and trumpeter Donald Lindley's *A Rhythmic Dream*. But the "dixieland" title did not affix itself to his musicians.

15. Among the Whiteman Liederkranz Hall recordings are "Louisiana," "Dardanella," and the masterful "You Took Advantage of Me," all notable for an immediacy and ensemble warmth. Located on East 58th Street near Lexington Avenue, Liederkranz Hall continued to be used for recording until it was pulled down in the early '50s. Wettling's four-bar drum "tag" at the end of "Strut Miss Lizzie," played entirely without cymbals, affords the listener a chance to hear the Liederkranz "room sound" with unusual clarity. This was something of a rarity in the '30s, when tight, carefully damped recording studios were the general rule. This Liederkranz date, especially, seems to foreshadow the techniques of the '70s and '80s, particularly in classical music, where the natural resonance of a room became an indispensable component of the way a solo or ensemble sound was perceived.

16. Richard DuPage and Frank Driggs, notes to *A Thesaurus of Classic Jazz*, Columbia four-LP boxed set C4L 18, issued 1959.

17. Max Kaminsky, conversation with the author, November 18, 1991.

18. Toots Mondello, conversation with the author, April 1992, and ibid.

19. James H. S. Moynahan, "Ragtime to Swing," *Saturday Evening Post*, February 13, 1937.

20. George Frazier, "Amazing Trumpeter Has Bix' Tone and Taste," *Down Beat*, July 1936.

21. Orrin Keepnews, conversation with the author, August 21, 1995.

22. Moynahan, as above, note 19.

23. Jack Lesberg, conversation with the author, summer 1992.

24. Valide description from "Really Doubling in Brass," *Popular Science*, May 1946, p. 81. Drummer Ray McKinley, in whose big band Gowans worked briefly in 1942, remembered the parlor baseball game vividly. "It could be played by two people, or two teams, on a large table. Some of the Boston ballplayers—I no longer remember whether it was the Red Sox or the Braves—used to come out to his place on the outskirts of Boston, a little house he built on a lake, in the wee hours of the morning, just to play this game. He never patented it. But he was like that—brilliant, an all-round talented guy in a lot of ways. Very sharp mind, and very quick with the repartee. He was the only guy I ever saw

stand up to Eddie Condon in that department" (conversation with the author, December 2, 1991).

25. Kaminsky, as above, note 17.

26. Joe Dixon, conversation with the author, September 14, 1993.

27. James "Rosy" McHargue, conversation with the author, April 19, 1988.

28. Korall, as above, note 9.

29. Dick Hyman quote from conversation with the author, summer 1993.

30. George Frazier, notes to *Lee Wiley Sings Rodgers and Hart*, Storyville LP 312, 1953. Stanley Green, notes to *Lee Wiley Sings Rodgers and Hart and Harold Arlen*, Monmouth-Evergreen LP MES 6807.

31. Quoted in Robert Dupuis, *Bunny Berigan: Elusive Legend of Jazz* (Baton Rouge: Louisiana State University Press, 1993).

32. New Bedford, Massachusetts, *Mercury*, July 15, 1931, quoted in Paul Charosh, "The Leo Reisman Story," *Record Research*, April 1964.

33. Larry Carr, from *Lee Wiley Sings the Songs of George and Ira Gershwin and Cole Porter*. Audiophile double-LP set, AP1.

34. Fairweather, as above, note 8.

35. The records were issued under the auspices of the Liberty Music Shop, a Madison Avenue record store favored by music lovers of wide tastes. Condon and friends made similar history around the same time when they recorded for Decca (under George Avakian's supervision) as part of an album devoted entirely to Chicago jazz. This first "theme" album, featuring three separate bands, has been fully discussed in previous chapters.

36. Richard Hadlock, notes to *Lee Wiley, Early Recordings*, Philomel LP 1000, October 1977.

37. The single-composer idea and choice of Lee Wiley to implement it were the doing of adman John De Vries, a Condon crony who wrote lyrics to "Wherever There's Love" with Eddie and "Oh, Look at Me Now" with Joe Bushkin. De Vries got Liberty Music Shop owner William Hill to underwrite the project—but not without some shaky moments. "Bill Hill was more than a little dismayed at the way the sessions were run," he told the author in a 1989 conversation. "He was used to people like Bea Lillie, Ethel Merman—real pros. At our sessions—well, everybody was good and loaded. They were in it for kicks. Bottles everywhere. They didn't know it was going to be a historically important occasion. Lee just took off her shoes and sang. Bill was absolutely—well, he didn't know what to think. But he was into it, so we just went ahead."

38. Roy Hemming and David Hajdu, *Discovering Great Singers of Classic Pop* (New York: Newmarket Press, 1991). Garroway from notes to *The Wide, Wide World of Jazz*, RCA Victor LPM 1325.

39. As quoted by John S. Wilson in Lee Wiley obituary, *New York Times*, December 13, 1975.

40. Even that success was not without dissonant notes in a musically and, increasingly, politically polarized climate. In an otherwise rhapsodic account of opening night, a *Time* magazine reporter (or his copy desk editor) felt compelled to inform readers that "twelve blocks away, Manhattanites could hear the far more virile and exciting New Orleans *Negro* jazz [emphasis added] of cornetist Bunk Johnson." Listening now to Condon records of the period and those of Johnson and his cobbled-together band of second-tier New Orleans veterans, it's hard to credit such a conclusion, except in a context involving racial bias. Given the many errors of fact and usage saturating the rest of the *Time* piece (a reference to cornetist "Wild Bill" Davison, drummers George Wettling and Dave Tough,

and others as members of "ragtime's Valhalla" is especially piquant), and its generally uninformed tone, there is room for doubt that the writer had actually heard the Johnson band and known what he was hearing. More likely, whoever inserted the "virile and exciting" comment was playing variations on the "if it's black it has to be more genuine" theme, taking the primitive trombone of Jim Robinson and out-of-tune clarinet of George Lewis as hallmarks of authenticity.

41. Leonard Feather, *The Encyclopedia of Jazz*, rev. ed. (New York: Horizon Press, 1960).

42. Barbara Lea, conversations with the author, 1992–93.

43. Quoted in *Second Line*, winter 1983.

44. Philip Larkin, introduction to *All What Jazz: A Record Diary* (London: Faber and Faber, 1985; first published, in somewhat different form, in 1970).

45. George Frazier, "Someday Nick's Might Be 'Hallowed' Home of Jazz, Says Frazier," *Down Beat*, November 15, 1941.

46. Bob Wilber (with Derek Webster), *Music Was Not Enough* (New York: Oxford University Press, 1987).

47. Jack Maheu, conversation with the author, New Orleans, April 19, 1996.

48. Glen McNatt, "The Downbeat of Traditional Jazz," *Baltimore Sun*, reprinted in *Jazzletter* 15, no. 2 (February 1996).

Chapter 13

1. Jimmy McPartland, conversation with the author, 1988.

2. Newell "Spiegle" Willcox, conversation with the author, 1975.

3. Rex Stewart, *Jazz Masters of the Thirties* (New York: Macmillan, 1972). White bassist-arranger Joe Tarto later recalled arranging a "roses" waltz medley for Henderson; it was an immediate and lasting favorite with the dancers at Roseland and elsewhere, he said.

4. Richard M. Sudhalter and Philip R. Evans, *Bix: Man and Legend* (New Rochelle, NY: Arlington House, 1974), p. 187.

5. Stanley "Doc" Ryker, conversation with the author, 1967. Used in "A Band Like Nothing You've Ever Heard," *Storyville* August-September 1967.

6. Jean Goldkette, letter to Steve Brown, December 21, 1955.

7. In conversations with scholar James T. Maher, Redman rejected claims made for him by jazz writers as the supposed pioneer of clarinet trio scoring in hot dance bands. "Oh, we stole those from the polka bands" was his explanation. He also denied any innovative role in voicing saxophone sections. Yet the myths persist.

8. Bill Challis, conversation with the author, summer 1958.

9. Al Sudhalter, letter to the author, 1973.

10. Sudhalter and Evans, as above, note 4, p. 185. See also Rex Stewart's account in *Jazz Masters of the Thirties* (as above, note 3), and Walter Allen's in *Hendersonia* (self-published, 1973).

11. Bill Rank, letter to Philip R. Evans, May 25, 1960. Originally used (but not quoted) as source material for *Bix: Man and Legend*.

12. Artie Shaw, letter to John Hasse, Smithsonian Institution, November 25, 1989. Used by permission of the writer.

13. Red Norvo, conversation with the author, April 19, 1988.

14. Quoted in Sudhalter and Evans, as above, note 4, p. 193.

15. Between 1974 and 1990, the author led bands of top musicians in England, America, and Germany in concert performances of many of these arrangements. Perhaps their outstanding feature is their blend of scored and improvised elements, yielding a

texture that retains the elasticity of small-band hot jazz within a more formal context. "St. Louis Blues," obviously designed to showcase Beiderbecke, is a superb instance.

16. Milt Hinton, conversations with the author, 1975–85. On February 5, 1931, Henderson's orchestra recorded its own arrangement of "My Pretty Girl," with good solos by Hawkins and trumpeter Bobby Stark. Early in the performance, in salute to the Goldkette record, Claude Jones reproduces Willcox's "straight" trombone solo, and Benny Carter plays the Danny Polo clarinet obbligato note for note.

17. Steve Brown, conversation with William Russell, April 22, 1958.

18. Sudhalter and Evans, as above, note 4, p. 212. *Storyville* article, as above, note 5.

19. Sheasby, it later emerged, was not only a heavy drinker but one with a violent temper. Such explosions created tension between him and his charges—especially when, days after such an outburst, he seemed unable to recall what he'd done and said. "Sheasby, plain and simple, was a drunkard," Goldkette later told the authors of *Bix: Man and Legend.* "I first saw him again six or seven years later, and predictably he had no explanation to offer." Goldkette office executive Fred Bergin added that Sheasby may have "reasoned that in some way he had been 'put upon' and decided to take 'his' arrangements with him when he made his exit. Actually only a few numbers in the library were his. I don't know whether or not the books were ever recovered." Sudhalter and Evans, as above, note 4, p. 203.

20. Amy Lee, "Jan Garber Cut Goldkette's Band!" *Metronome*, August 1940.

21. Newell "Spiegle" Willcox, conversation with the author, 1989.

22. Eddie Barefield, conversations with the author, 1980–85.

23. Neil Leonard, *Jazz: Myth and Religion* (New York: Oxford University Press, 1987), pp. 25–26.

24. Ben Pollack, "Ten Years of Good Bands and Bad Breaks," *Down Beat*, October 1936.

25. Ben Pollack, "Long-Hair Stumps Rhythm Kings on Reading," *Down Beat*, November 1936.

26. Benny Goodman, conversation with the author, May 7, 1981. A fuller version of these remarks appears as part of interview article first published in *American Heritage* magazine, October-November 1981, and reprinted, in expanded form, in chapter 22 of this volume.

27. George T. Simon, *Glenn Miller and His Orchestra* (New York: Thomas Y. Crowell, 1974), p. 47.

28. Benny Goodman, *The Kingdom of Swing* (New York: Frederick Ungar, 1936).

29. Harry Goodman, conversation with the author, 1991.

30. Quoted in Max Jones, *Talking Jazz* (London: Macmillan, 1987), p.162

31. Quoted in ibid.

32. Jimmy McPartland, conversation with the author, 1988.

33. Perhaps because they were recorded in Chicago, neither of these performances adheres to the "hot dance" formula so familiar on records made in New York. Compare them to "Buy, Buy for Baby" and "She's One Sweet Show Girl," made nearly a year later in New York.

34. H. Goodman, as above, note 29.

35. Quoted in "A Visit to Smith Ballew," *Storyville*, June-July 1975, p. 170.

36. Even had that not happened, the Broadway job would have been a disaster. *Say When* ran only twenty-four performances and closed. Its most enduring legacy is the song, "One Step to Heaven," recorded July 6 by Red Nichols and Miff Mole, augmented by Chicagoans Teschemacher, Eddie Condon, Joe Sullivan, and Gene Krupa.

37. Horst J. P. Bergmeier, "The New Yorkers," *Storyville*, March 1991.

38. Trevor Tolley, "Teschemacher and the Chicagoans in New York," *Storyville*, February-March 1984, pp. 84–88. Both Teschemacher and Teagarden are faintly but unmistakably audible behind Smith Ballew's vocal on " 'Round Evening," but no sign of either on "Out of the Dawn," the other title made at the September 29 Dorsey Brothers date. Another version of "Out of the Dawn," recorded at Brunswick for the English Duophone label later that autumn (and labeled only as the "Duophone Dance Orchestra"), seems to be by a similar personnel—and features solos by Teagarden and a clarinetist, probably Jimmy Dorsey, playing in a strongly Tesch-like vein.

39. Jimmy McPartland, conversations with the author, 1985–90.

40. Ibid.

41. Ruby Weinstein, All quotes in this chapter are from letter to the author, 1977.

42. H. Goodman, as above, note 29.

43. McPartland, as above, note 39.

44. George T. Simon, "Crosby Band Was Pollack's All Over Again," *Metronome*, October 1941.

45. McPartland, as above, note 39.

46. B. Goodman, as above, note 26.

47. Benny Goodman, conversation with the author, December 1, 1980. Not used in *American Heritage* article.

48. Irving Mills was quick to capitalize on what looked like the success of *Hello, Daddy*. He flooded the market with records of "Futuristic Rhythm," "Out Where the Blues Begin," and other songs from the score, many of them by small Pollack units. The show ran a respectable 198 performances, about the same as Cole Porter's *Paris* and more than Rodgers and Hart's *Present Arms*.

49. The band's August 15 Victor date is notable for the presence of Chicago trumpeter Arthur "Murphy" Steinberg, a temporary replacement for McPartland. Veteran of the Midway Gardens Orchestra, Steinberg turns in solos of surprising emotional urgency on "Where the Sweet Forget-Me-Nots Remember," "Song of the Blues," and "True Blue Lou," on which he manipulates a hand-held solotone mute with an expressive skill rivaling that of Ellington's plunger specialist, "Bubber" Miley. It seems a pity that this excellent trumpeter, so highly valued in Chicago, did not record more widely at this point in his career.

50. H. Goodman, as above, note 29.

Chapter 14

1. Clarence Hutchenrider, conversations with the author, 1985.

2. According to violinist Fred Culley, who led the house band at Toronto's Royal York Hotel (and later worked as musical director for Fred Waring), at least part of Pellatt's original intention in building the "castle" was to provide a residence for the Prince of Wales when the future King Edward VIII visited Canada. Protocol, alas, forbade such use of a private residence by the royal family. Source: Files of James T. Maher.

3. Gunther Schuller, *The Swing Era* (New York: Oxford University Press, 1989), p. 633.

4. Ibid., p. 317. It is useful here to note that no Nesbitt arrangement, at least among those recorded by the McKinney or Henderson bands, displays even a trace of the antiphonal, call-and-response patterns which became hallmarks of Gifford's up-tempo scores. Any but the most general resemblances between the work of the two men are hard to

find. If anything, some of Nesbitt's work (see "I Found a New Baby" as recorded for Victor April 8, 1929) seems to derive from Challis.

5. Marshall Stearns, *The Story of Jazz* (New York: Oxford University Press, 1956), p. 204. Eddie Barefield, conversations with the author, 1980–85.

6. Schuller's assertion that the band muffs the coda seems idiosyncratic: throughout the four bars the sections play in perfect concert—no sloppiness, no uncertainty or disagreement of attack. A listener can only conclude that if Schuller is right, and the Casa Lomans did muff things, they did even that with admirable precision. The identity of the trumpet soloist, on a date known not to have included Schoefner, has never been firmly established. But trumpeter Sylvester Ahola, who heard the Casa Loma Orchestra in person in 1930, told his biographer Dick Hill that Bobby Jones was playing lead and Joe Hostetter the "hot" solos. Impressed with the band, Ahola took several of their records back to England, where he was working for Bert Ambrose, and gave them to arranger Lew Stone, who copied the arrangements off note for note. Stone's own band later did much to popularize the Casa Loma style in England.

7. Glen Gray, "Casa Loma's Three Years of Barnstorming . . . ," *Down Beat*, December-January, 1935–36.

8. Grady Watts, interview with Ray Hoffman, December 30, 1983. Used by permission.
9. Billy Rauch, interview with Ray Hoffman, December 23, 1984.

10. Frank Driggs, "Glen Gray," in booklet accompanying *The Swing Era*, 1937–38, Time-Life Records, 1971, pp. 40–47.

11. Rauch, as above, note 9.

12. Stearns, as above, note 5, p. 206.

13. James T. Maher, conversation with the author, 1991.

14. Hutchenrider, as above, note 1.

15. Will Hudson (1908–81) surely ranks as one of the best, and least appreciated, of the first-rank arrangers working in the '30s. He grew up in Detroit, where he arranged for McKinney's Cotton Pickers and for Cab Calloway, with whose help he moved to New York and went to work for the Irving Mills Music Publishing operation. He wrote in two basic styles: spare, clean-lined and riff-based on the medium and fast specialties, thicker-textured on the ballads. To say, as does Stanley Dance (notes to *The Complete Fletcher Henderson*, Bluebird LP set AXM2-5507, 1976), that Hudson "had an ear for uptown riffs, knew what and where to borrow, and sometimes came up with listenable concoctions" manages to slander Hudson in three distinct ways, even while appearing to praise him. As his work for a wide variety of bands illustrates, his concoctions were considerably more than just "listenable." Hudson was also an accomplished songwriter—and herein lies what may be the reason for Dance's animus toward him. Though he wrote such '30s favorites as "Sophisticated Swing," "Organ-Grinder's Swing," and "With All My Heart and Soul," he is best known for "Moonglow," on which he collaborated with lyricist Eddie DeLange. Musical evidence is strong that Hudson borrowed heavily from Ellington's 1934 "Lazy Rhapsody" (and perhaps less directly from an interlude in "It Don't Mean a Thing") in constructing the melody of "Moonglow." Both Hudson and Ellington were working for Mills at the time. In this context, Dance's remark about Hudson knowing "what and where to borrow" finds its resonance. All the same, Hudson's achievements as an arranger are genuine, and "Moonglow"—whatever its provenance—remains a superior popular song. Hudson co-led a band with DeLange in the late '30s, later returning to arranging.

16. Quoted in John Chilton, *The Song of the Hawk* (London: Quartet Books, 1990), pp. 111, 142.

17. Rauch, as above, note 9.

18. Clarence Hutchenrider, conversations with the author (1985–88) and Ray Hoffman (1983).

19. Clarence Hutchenrider, interview with Ray Hoffman, c. 1983.

20. Spud Murphy, like Will Hudson, is one of the great neglected heroes of early jazz arranging. Widely respected among musicians, he never achieved the critical attention accorded Gifford or Fletcher Henderson. Yet his scores, more than fifty of them, for the *Let's Dance* radio show helped shape the sound and style of Benny Goodman's orchestra even before the leader began buying arrangements from Henderson. When Grady Watts said he "could play Spud's music all night long," he was speaking for many colleagues. He also played and arranged for the widely admired Jimmie's Joys Orchestra, active in Texas, which at various times included such jazzmen as clarinetist Matty Matlock, Indiana alto saxophonist Chauncey Goodwin, and pianist-songwriter Terry Shand.

21. George Piersol, "We Liked It Hot—Strike up The Band," *Jersey Jazz*, Autumn 1985.

22. Maher, as above, note 13.

23. Clarence Hutchenrider, conversation with the author, May 31, 1988.

24. Ibid.

25. Leonard Feather, notes to *Glen Gray, 1907–1963*, Epitaph LP E-4005.

26. Quoted in Mel Tormé, *Traps: The Drum Wonder* (New York: Oxford University Press, 1991).

27. Kirk De Grazia, notes to *Glen Gray and the Casa Loma Orchestra*, Bandstand LP 7126.

28. Watts, as above, note 8.

29. Driggs, as above, note 10.

30. Ibid. Watts, as above, note 8. Ralston quoted in Driggs, as above, note 10.

31. Albert McCarthy, *Big Band Jazz* (New York: Berkley Windhover, 1972), p. 192.

32. George Frazier, "Critic Scores 'Goops' Who Interpret Casa Loma," *Down Beat*, April 1936, p. 1.

33. Nat Hentoff and Albert J. McCarthy, eds., *Jazz* (London: Quartet Books, 1977). Hughes Panassié, *The Real Jazz* (New York: Smith and Durrell, 1942).

34. Albert McCarthy, *The Dance Band Era* (London: November Books, 1971), p. 58.

35. James T. Maher, letter to the author, April 21, 1996.

36. Bob Haggart, conversation with the author, September 28, 1991.

37. Larry Wagner, conversation with the author, 1983.

38. Driggs, as above, note 10.

39. Wagner, as above, note 37.

40. McCarthy, as above, note 34, p. 56.

41. George T. Simon, conversation with the author, 1983.

42. Hutchenrider, as above, note 23.

43. McCarthy, as above, note 31, p. 193.

44. Schuller, as above, note 3, p. 645.

Chapter 15

1. As proof of Tommy Dorsey's alleged inadequacy, many writers have cited his refusal to solo on a 1939 Metronome All-Star date because the universally revered Jack Teagarden was also in the band. Seen objectively, his action seems less a commentary on his own gifts than a simple gesture of deference. It is also significant that fellow-musicians persuaded him to relent: his blues duet with Teagarden is a highlight of the session. At a similar date the following year, trombonist Jack Jenney, a superb jazzman, also declined

to solo, again because Teagarden was present. Such gestures are common in jazz: trumpeters Bobby Hackett and Billy Butterfield, though asked, declined to solo on a 1944 V-disc because Louis Armstrong, whom they esteemed beyond all others, was the featured guest.

2. Amy Lee, "The Dorsey Brothers Played for Pennies!," *Metronome*, September 1940.

3. Arnold Brilhart, conversation with the author, 1992.

4. Jimmy McPartland, conversation with the author, 1983.

5. Amy Lee, "Jimmy Was Worse Than Tommy Dorsey!," *Metronome*, October 1940.

6. Eddie Barefield, conversations with the author, 1975–85.

7. It's always been assumed that the early hot trombone tradition was carried forward exclusively by the black soloists—Charlie Green, Jimmy Harrison, Claude Jones, Benny Morton, J. C. Higginbotham—with only marginal white contribution until the arrival of Teagarden in the late '20s. This is an oversimplification: running parallel to the black trombone line, and frequently intersecting it, was what can be identified as a white approach, pioneered by Mole. He and his legacy are discussed at length in chapter 8. Tommy Dorsey belongs to this continuity, as does the comparably skilled, but far less known, Charlie Butterfield. His strong, well-turned solo on "Stack O'Lee Blues," recorded for OKeh May 3, 1928, with the novelty clarinetist Boyd Senter, displays elements of both Dorsey and Mole.

8. Gunther Schuller, *The Swing Era* (New York: Oxford University Press, 1989).

9. It has been suggested that the climactic high F at the end of the "Hot Heels" solo is in fact played by Jimmy on clarinet. No amount of close listening bears this out conclusively.

10. Ray McKinley, conversation with the author, April 10, 1992.

11. Dorsey's adoration of Armstrong, however, continued unabated. He winds up his trombone chorus on his July 11, 1938, Clambake Seven record of "Chinatown, My Chinatown" by reproducing the last eight bars of Armstrong's revered "Potato Head Blues" solo of 1927, in the same key of F, and beginning with the same descending phrase Hoagy Carmichael "borrowed" for use as bars 3–4 of "Star Dust."

12. As quoted by James T. Maher, conversation with the author, April 21, 1996.

13. George "Pee Wee" Erwin, Carmen Mastren, and Johnny Mince, conversation with the author broadcast on WBAI-FM, New York City, 1978.

14. Schuller, as above, note 8.

15. Like Goodman and so many others, Dorsey appears on dozens of commercial records made during this time under various leaders. His clarinet and alto solos on "Let Me Sing—and I'm Happy," recorded March 3, 1930, for Ben Selvin (and also featuring a cheerful Adrian Rollini bass sax chorus) are typical. He also contributes effectively to the Mound City Blue Blowers' "At the Darktown Strutters' Ball" (June 30, 1931), more than holding his own alongside Coleman Hawkins and cornetist Muggsy Spanier.

16. Such respected saxophonists as Chester Hazlett, Clyde Doerr, Larry Abbott, Jack Mayhew, and Andy Sannella performed and composed within this varied idiom, only a small percentage of which involved the acrobatics cited by Schuller. Rather more common was a fondness for poignant, often sentimental salon melodies, as typified by Oley Speakes's popular "Sylvia" and Wiedoeft's own fetching waltzes "Marilyn" and "Llewellyn." His elegiac "Dans l'Orient," moreover, displays not a trace of for-its-own-sake saxophone technique but is closer in feeling and evocation to such violin miniatures as Fritz Kreisler's sentimental *Liebesfreud*. It is perhaps no accident that a significant number of saxophonists of the early years began their careers as violinists. Concepts of tone, phrasing, even vibrato borrowed from the violin characterized the standard approach to the alto saxophone

throughout the '20s and well into the '30s. The style reached perhaps its last flowering in the virtuosity of Alfred Gallodoro, featured with Paul Whiteman in the mid-'30s. New Orleans born, Gallodoro elevated the alto saxophone to considerable heights as a solo vehicle: his 1949 recording of "Oodles of Noodles," for example, extends his instrument's compass through frequent and easy use of "false-fingered" high-register harmonic notes.

17. Eddie Barefield, conversation with the author, 1978.

18. Stephens, in common with Ralph Peer and other visionaries, was a force for good in the early years of jazz recording. At Okeh, and later at Brunswick and Decca, he was responsible for many far-reaching policy decisions. As part of OKeh's mobile crew, he helped discover and record bluesman Mississippi John Hurt during a swing through the Deep South. Later, working for Decca, he recorded the Count Basie Orchestra for the first time. According to an oft-repeated account, he noticed that Lester Young kept going off mike during his solos, largely because of the angle at which he held his tenor sax. Rather than tamper with the saxophonist's way of doing things, Stephens simply had him change places with the band's other tenor man, Herschel Evans. This way, the rest of the reed section microphones were now to Young's right and functioned as backups to his own. Posterity is his debtor.

19. Joey Nash, conversation with Michael Brooks, c. 1970.

20. Herb Sanford, Tommy and Jimmy: The Dorsey Years (New Rochelle, N.Y.: Arlington House, 1972).

21. Steve Lipkins, conversation with the author, c. 1979.

22. Arthur "Monk" Hazel, interview with William Russell, July 16, 1959, Hogan Archive.

23. Helvetia "Vet" Boswell, conversation with Rich Conaty, 1982, quoted in Will Friedwald, Jazz Singing (New York: Scribner's, 1990).

24. Quoted in Jan Shapiro, "The Inventive Vocal Style of Connee Boswell and the Boswell Sisters," Collected Papers of the National Association of Jazz Educators, 1989, pp. 225–38.

25. Composite Connie Boswell quote from George T. Simon (and Friends), The Best of the Music Makers (Garden City, NY: Doubleday, 1979), and Chris Ellis, "Connee Boswell: 3 December 1907–11 October 1976," Storyville, June-July 1977. Source for Ellis quotes: Michael Brooks interviews.

26. In the early 1940s Connie Boswell changed the spelling of her name to "Connee." It came about, she said, because in signing a photograph for a fan she had neglected to dot the letter i. The fan, misreading her signature, addressed a thank-you letter to "Connee" Boswell. "I liked the way it looked in print," the singer told writer John Lucas, "so when I left the [Bing] Crosby show and started making public appearances, I decided to go it with the two e's." Lucas, John. "Another Boswell Chronicle," Jazz Journal, January 1974. Chris Ellis (as above, note 25), suggests that Martha Boswell persuaded her sister to change the spelling in the belief that it would bring good luck. Because the present book deals with the Boswell Sisters in the '30s, it has retained "Connie," the name's original spelling.

27. Connie Boswell, conversation with Michael Brooks, quoted in sleeve notes to The Boswell Sisters, Biograph BLP-C3, issued 1972. Mildred Bailey and Bing Crosby were among other performers who seemed to loosen up rhythmically when they worked with the Dorseys. Certainly there's a new freedom in Bailey's "Is That Religion?," "There's a Cabin in the Pines," and other Dorsey-backed titles of April-October 1933; Crosby, too, seems loose and happy on "Someone Stole Gabriel's Horn" and "Stay on the Right Side of the Road" (March 14, 1933) backed by the Dorseys, Berigan, et al.

28. "I'd make the arrangement and Glenn would come in," Connie Boswell told

New York radio personality Rich Conaty. "It was just like if you wrote a story and called a secretary in and she took out her shorthand book and took down everything you said."

29. The reason for the breakup remains vague. The official version, repeated over six decades, is that Martha and Vet got married and preferred to settle down, away from the pressures of professional music. No one seems to have questioned this until Will Friedwald, writing in *Jazz Singing* in 1990, pointed out that both Martha and Connie married men within the music business, and that even when Vet became pregnant, the original intention was to suspend trio activities only temporarily. But just as Bing Crosby left the Rhythm Boys principally to launch a solo career, Friedwald suggests that Connie Boswell had something similar in mind. According to Helvetia Boswell's daughter, Vet Boswell Minnerly, it "was a lot more complicated than that." Ms. Minnerly's projected book on the Boswells, written in conjunction with historian David McCain, is expected to deal with the matter in detail.

30. When she was three, she told *Down Beat* in 1938, she was flung from a playmate's toy wagon, struck a telegraph pole and injured her spinal cord. But "I can move my feet, you know. I can stand, too. When I go to a night club and I'm asked to take a bow, I rise as pretty as you please. My legs are just too weak to carry me around, that's all." "Boswell Would Refuse Cure for Paralyzed Legs to Help Economic Cripples," *Down Beat*, August 1938.

31. Ellis, as above, note 25.

32. Artie Shaw, conversations with the author, 1990–92.

33. Quoted in George T. Simon *The Big Bands*, 4th ed. (New York: Schirmer-Macmillan, 1981). Also: McKinley conversation with the author, April 10, 1992.

34. Quoted in Burt Korall, *Drummin' Men: The Swing Years* (New York: Schirmer-Macmillan, 1990).

35. Simon, as above, note 33.

36. McKinley, as above, note 10.

37. Simon, as above, note 33. Maher comment from letter to the author, April 21, 1996.

38. Bonnie Lake, conversation with the author, April 10, 1992.

39. McKinley, as above, note 10.

40. Ibid.

41. Sanford, as above, note 20. Perhaps under pressure from O'Keefe, and perhaps as a favor to Bing Crosby, their old friend from Whiteman days, the siblings did reunite in August for a pair of final joint record dates, one of them backing the singer on six songs from his new film, *Two for Tonight*. Tommy plays a brief, unmistakable solo on "Without a Word of Warning." Bobby Byrne offered a piece of surprising additional information, confirming an item in *Variety*, that Tommy actually returned to front the Dorsey Brothers Orchestra, again at Glen Island Casino, at the end of August. Contrary to some accounts, he spent more than an hour on the stand each night, and at least a few times played the entire evening. Robert L. Stockdale, *Tommy Dorsey on the Side* (Metuchen, N.J.: Scarecrow Press and Institute of Jazz Studies, Rutgers, 1995), p. 366.

42. Schuller, as above, note 8.

43. McKinley, as above, note 10.

44. Quoted by Gino Falzarano in notes to *The Kitty Kallen Story*, Sony CD set A2K 48978, 1992.

45. Jean Bach, conversation with the author, 1983.

46. Irvin "Marky" Markowitz, conversation with the author, 1984.

47. Pee Wee Erwin and Johnny Mince, as above, note 13.

48. Writer Chip Deffaa captured the latter-day dynamic between the brothers nicely in an interview-profile on Lee Castle, published in *Swing Legacy* (Metuchen, N.J.: Scarecrow Press, 1989). In it, Castle dwells on Jimmy's unwillingness to confront his brother directly on matters in which they differed, preferring to work through intermediaries. It also includes the following exchange. Jimmy, said Castle, had called a band meeting, but Tommy summoned the trumpeter to go with him on some errand. Returning, they encountered an obviously miffed Jimmy.

> He says, "Where were you at the meeting?" I said, "I had to go somewhere with Tommy."
>
> "And if Tommy was having a meeting, could I take you somewhere with me?"
>
> I said, "Jim, what do you want? What do you mean? I don't understand."
>
> "No! You mean with me it's all right if you don't show up! But with *the brother*, you better be there, is that it?"
>
> I said, "No, it's not it. He insisted I go with him and I went with him. Take it up with him—*Jesus*." But that's the way it was, you know.

49. Lake, as above, note 38.

Chapter 16

1. George T. Simon, *The Big Bands*, 4th ed. (Garden City, N.Y.: Doubleday, 1981).

2. Joe Darensbourg (with Peter Vacher), *Jazz Odyssey: The Autobiography of Joe Darensbourg* (Baton Rouge: Louisiana State University Press, 1987).

3. Foster from George "Pops" Foster (with Tom Stoddard), *Pops Foster: New Orleans Jazzman* (Berkeley: University of California Press, 1971). Allen from Martin Williams, *Jazz Masters of New Orleans*, (New York: Macmillan, 1967). Holmes from Stanley Dance, *The World of Swing* (New York: Scribner's, 1974).

4. Foster, as above, note 3.

5. Pops Foster's and other, similar, declarations make clear his belief—shared widely—that if the Luis Russell band had lasted in its 1929–30 form, and not been taken over and recast as a prop for fellow-homeboy Louis Armstrong, it might have made a far deeper footprint in jazz history than it did. Such OKeh records as "Jersey Lightning," "Louisiana Swing," and an incomparable "Panama" make the case with eloquence. In its blend of declamatory solos and pliant ensembles, all on a rhythm as broad as a highway, the Russell orchestra sounded like none other of its time. Certainly no other, with the possible exception of the short-lived Jean Goldkette ensemble of 1926–27, played *together* so compellingly: Russell's December 17, 1930, "Case on Dawn" (a typographically butchered "Ease On Down") on Brunswick can still startle a listener with its concentration of energy.

6. Nappy Lamare, "Our Music Was Born in N'Orleans," *Down Beat*, June 1, 1940.

7. Bill Esposito, "Eddie Miller," *Jazz Journal*, April 1973.

8. Early chroniclers of this band subscribed to the notion that "Clark Randall" was a pseudonym for Alabama-born radio tenor Frank Tennille, considered briefly as a possible front man. Matty Matlock set the record straight, telling trumpeter-historian John Chilton the name was a fiction. Tennille himself (the "Captain" in a '70s pop act with his singing daughter, Toni) confirmed that "Clark Randall" was "the name of whoever fronted the band" (John Chilton, *Stomp Off, Let's Go* [self-published, 1983]).The "Randall" group's chief

distinction may be as the group with which Glenn Miller first tried out the arranging exercise that ultimately became "Moonlight Serenade." The musicians, said Eddie Miller, liked it, played it now and then—but thought it too far from their conception to be of real use (conversation with the author, 1981).

9. Each rejection carried its own logic. Goldfield, however well liked, conveyed an older image and was associated with a musical orientation (he had taken over Henry Busse's chair with Whiteman) quite different from that of the Pollack alumni; "Scat" Davis, shortly to become something of a movie personality, was perhaps too much the cutup—though as O'Keefe recalled, he'd done well filling in as pro tem leader of Smith Ballew's band. Teagarden was with Whiteman, and that was that—though it must also be noted that the trombonist, always easy-going, was far more at home playing his horn and singing than taking on the disciplinary and public relations duties required of a leader. The musicians liked, even argued for, Frank Tennille, who had the necessary charm and good looks; but apparently Rockwell and O'Keefe felt his name lacked widespread identification value.

10. The preceding section and others throughout this chapter owe considerable debt to John Chilton's outstanding and well-researched Stomp Off, Let's Go (self-published, 1983). He had the good fortune to know and interview in depth many Crosby alumni, now deceased. George T. Simon also has written widely about the band, including a series of articles which first appeared in Metronome magazine in 1941 and have been anthologized in Simon Says (New Rochelle, N.Y.: Arlington House, 1971). A similar series, covering much the same territory, had appeared in Down Beat in 1940 and may have prompted the Simon pieces. Those have been drawn on where cited.

11. John Hammond, "Pollack Veterans With Crosby's New Band," Down Beat, August 1935.

12. Versions of this statement included both in Chilton (see above, note 10) and conversations with the author, 1993–94.

13. Quote from Simon, as above, note 1. Review from Metronome, reprinted in Simon, as above, note 10.

14. Bob Haggart, combination of conversations with the author (April 30, 1992); Ken Gallacher, Jazz Journal, December 1971; and Chilton, as above, note 10.

15. Bob Haggart, conversation with the author, December 1, 1993.

16. Ibid.

17. Interview in Metronome, July 1936, reprinted in Simon, as above, note 10.

18. Review in Metronome, April 1936, and reprinted in Simon, as above, note 10.

19. Counterpoint definition in Don Michael Randel, The Harvard Concise Dictionary of Music (Cambridge: Harvard University/Belknap Press, 1978). One of the most characteristic and defining features of early jazz, the contrapuntal texture was also one of the earliest to be lost, first with the spread of sectional large-band writing in the '30s, then with widespread adoption of homophonic riff textures in small groups. In standard bloc-based swing arranging, one section predominates and the others support, often at the expense of melodic content. Such early Gene Gifford efforts as "Maniac's Ball" and the eponymous "Casa Loma Stomp" suffer from this weakness, as do most of the riff vehicles associated with the Count Basie Orchestra. Fletcher Henderson's arrangements for his own orchestras and for Benny Goodman often assign arbitrary, static roles to brass and reeds, leaving only the soloists to provide variations in texture. The Crosby orchestra, in keeping with its New Orleans roots, lent equal weight to ensembles and solos.

20. Gunther Schuller, The Swing Era (New York: Oxford University Press, 1989).

21. In spring of 1937, the Crosby band had joined brothers Johnny and Baby Dodds,

Roy Eldridge, and various others (including a ten-year-old piano prodigy from Danville, Illinois, named Bobby Short) in a giant benefit to raise money for Sullivan's care. Broadcast coast to coast on NBC, it ran three hours, and raised $1,550.

22. Asked whether this sort of thinking also helped determine the choice of Lou Stein, a (latterly) bop-oriented pianist, for the Lawson-Haggart records of the '50s, at a time many more stylistically compatible pianists were available, Haggart nodded vigorous agreement. "Lou never played bass lines, never fooled around down there. He left things open, giving the bass line a kind of freedom you couldn't get from a pianist with a strong left hand. That's what I liked about him."

23. Bob Haggart, conversation with the author, April 30, 1992.

24. Quoted in Chilton, as above, note 10.

25. Haggart, as above, note 23.

26. Carmen Mastren, conversations with the author, 1978.

27. Kincaide's departure from the Crosby band, result of an apparent disagreement over money, provides another insight into the insular nature of that organization's rapport. To take up the slack, Rodin tried commissioning arrangements by such highly regarded figures as Mary Lou Williams, Fud Livingston, and Franklyn Marks, who had contributed the attractive "Cream Puff" to Artie Shaw's short-lived 1936 band. None seemed able to grasp the unique timbre and flavor of the Crosby band: in Haggart's phrase, "they just made us sound like everybody else." So he and Matlock simply closed ranks and stepped up their output.

28. Yank Lawson, conversation with the author, December 1, 1993.

29. Ibid.

30. Haggart, as above, note 23.

31. Crosby quoted in Chilton, as above, note 10.

32. Quoted in ibid.

33. Ted Toll, "Zurke Happy Playing Solo Piano in Hotel," *Down Beat*, September 15, 1940.

34. Richard B. Hadlock, notes to Joe Sullivan, set in *Giants of Jazz* series, Time-Life Records, 1982.

35. Ibid.

36. Ibid.

37. Bob Crosby, quoted in "Crosby Interviews Crosby," *Down Beat*, June 1, 1940.

38. Quoted in Keith Keller, *Oh Jess! A Jazz Life* (New York: Mayan Publishing, 1989).

39. Spanier, Haggart recalled, "did things his own way, and we had no choice but to go along with him." His full chorus on "The Mark Hop," for example, makes no concessions to the background figures which seem to be trying to lift its emotional trajectory. Muggsy takes his time: the solo, while jaunty enough, sounds almost as if it had been borrowed from some other performance by some other band, perhaps the cornetist's own "Ragtimers."

40. Gil Rodin, quoted in undated 1940 *Metronome* clipping on file at Institute of Jazz Studies, Rutgers University.

41. Haggart, as above, note 23.

42. Yank Lawson, quoted in Chilton, as above, note 10.

43. Bob Haggart, notes to an exhibition of his painting at Wilkes College, Wilkes-Barre, Pa., March 11–April 8, 1984.

44. Haggart, as above, note 23.

45. Yank Lawson, letter to Ken Gallacher, 1983.

Chapter 17

1. Jimmy McPartland, conversations with the author, 1981–85.

2. Even in the late 1990s, scholars and musicians were still grasping at the possibility of recovering "lost" Beiderbecke compositions. A concert staged in New York in summer 1997 under the auspices of the giant JVC Jazz Festival presented fragments "recalled" by Joe Venuti and Indiana bandleader Charlie Davis as part of a program billed as *The Unknown Bix*. Needless to say, the pedigree of such "discoveries" was uncertain at best. A song listed in the archives of the Peer-Southern music publishers as "Someday Soon," and giving part composer credit to Beiderbecke and lyricist Paul Francis Webster, appears to have been an attempt to adapt one theme of "In a Mist" as a popular song.

3. Ann Douglas, *A Terrible Honesty: Mongrel Manhattan in the 1920s* (New York: Farrar, Straus and Giroux, 1995).

4. For further exploration of this subject, see the author's own "Faery Tales and Hero Worship," *Baltimore Sun*, May 26, 1996, reprinted in *Jazzletter*, August 1996.

5. His "China Boy" and "Oh, Miss Hannah" solos with Whiteman, for example, are among his most succinct efforts. But they are counterbalanced by the lapses: breakdown of imagination on "I'm in the Seventh Heaven," of execution on "Futuristic Rhythm," of intonation on "Louise," the latter two with Trumbauer units.

6. All the same, various critics and historians through the years—and some fellow-musicians—have attempted comparison on this basis, and inevitably found Bix wanting. The senselessness of such judgments is unmistakable when applied to another instrument—for example, the clarinet, and its role in the styles of Benny Goodman and Pee Wee Russell. Goodman is clearly, gloriously, a virtuoso clarinetist, who has turned his flawless command to jazz improvisation, emerging with a style of unsurpassed fluency and polish. Russell, in stark contrast, often seems not to be playing the clarinet at all but some pliable and often twisted extension of his innermost self. His technique is erratic at best (though far from inept, as some have claimed), this tone and intonation idiosyncratic, all of it combined with a lexicon of effects—growls, squeaks, gargling noises, whispers and whimpers and great keening cries—that belong only to him. Evaluated simply as a player of the clarinet, he emerges as (in Goodman's word) "a joke." Yet there is an eloquence, an emotive force, a complex inventiveness to his work that can capture the imagination more thoroughly, and on more levels, even than Goodman's.

7. Ryker quoted in Art Napoleon (Richard M. Sudhalter), "A Band Like Nothing You Ever Heard," *Storyville* August-September 1967.

8. Humphrey Lyttelton, *The Best of Jazz, Vol. I* (New York: Taplinger, 1978), p. 130.

9. Ibid. Benny Green, *The Reluctant Art* (London: MacGibbon and Kee, 1964).

10. Richard M. Sudhalter and Philip R. Evans, *Bix: Man and Legend* (New Rochelle, N.Y.: Arlington House, 1974), pp. 87–89.

11. James Lincoln Collier, *The Making of Jazz* (Boston: Houghton Mifflin, 1978).

12. Sudhalter and Evans, as above, note 10, p. 195.

13. Ibid.

14. Conversely, by 1923, when the ODJB remade "Tiger Rag" for OKeh, LaRocca was playing a far more supple, almost Bix-like lead, an effect heightened by the band's rhythmic approach, which seems to have embraced the more relaxed four-to-the-bar "feel" shortly to be associated with the Wolverines. The master-disciple relationship is even more discernible in LaRocca's work on the ODJB's May 1921 "Jazz Me Blues." The cornet lead, chiming and on the beat, prefigures Bix's own 1927 record of the same number.

15. Jay Arnold, *Bix Beiderbecke Trumpet Transcriptions* (New York: Robbins Music, 1944).

16. Ibid.

17. Two of these, "Royal Garden" and the Fletcher Henderson–Jo Trent "Goose Pimples," are blues. Bix's blues choruses on records are few and far between: besides these two, there is the Wolverines version of "Royal Garden," mentioned earlier, "Toddlin' Blues" (another ODJB creation), with Bix's own "Rhythm Jugglers" on January 26, 1925, a solo on the verse of "Can't Help Lovin' Dat Man" from the Paul Whiteman "*Show Boat* Medley" of May 1, 1928, and the opening chorus on "Deep Harlem," from an Irving Mills Brunswick date of mid-1930. As suggested earlier, none of these is a blues in any atmospheric or emotional sense: each is a song improvisation on the twelve-bar blues structure.

18. Green, as above, note 9.

19. Gunther Schuller, *Early Jazz* (New York: Oxford University Press, 1968).

20. Despite Schuller's endorsement, the opprobrium attached to Whiteman's name, especially among jazz critics, has persisted. This became painfully obvious in 1990, when the centenary of the leader's birth occasioned not a single event—concert, television program, even newspaper or magazine feature. It was as if a world which had come to understand "jazz" as synonymous with "African-American" music were holding Whiteman hostage to his long-ago "King of Jazz" billing. It hardly needs explaining that, to the public of the 1920s, "jazz" had a much more generalized meaning, one within which the "King" title had some relevance. Whiteman's domination of the light music world of his times was beyond dispute: and if, for most Americans, this was indeed the "jazz" age, he had more than passing claim to its rulership.

Whiteman understood that hot music, or at least a good simulacrum of it, had to be part of his regular presentation. Though his orchestra became quite adept at jazz-inflected performances, he never intended it to be (Schuller is right on target here) a jazz ensemble in the sense that Duke Ellington's was. Whiteman's achievements, whether as a popularizer (whose product, however alloyed, reached a far wider audience than did the purer hot music forms) or discoverer and promoter of talent, are real and lasting. The reverence in which he was, and continues to be, held by older musicians is summed up excellently in Red Norvo's remark: "Don't you dare ever bad-mouth Whiteman. We all owe him plenty."

Paul Whiteman's record as an employer of first-class jazz musicians is exemplary, and so is the wide latitude he allowed them within the context of his orchestra's varied musical menu and the heterogeneous audience it served. His musicians walked into their jobs with eyes and ears open: they knew what to expect, and the decision to accept or reject employment with Whiteman was theirs. Even Bunny Berigan, who from all reports did not share Beiderbecke's passion for the quasi-symphonic side of Whiteman's activities, was treated well: broadcast material recently brought to light shows him featured at every opportunity, even shoehorned into arrangements which had no trumpet solos—something which must be read as an effort to keep him happy. It is also well to remember that "Pops" Whiteman hired (and paid well) both Bing Crosby and Mildred Bailey, at a time long before bands regularly carried singers; he recognized and promoted songwriters Hoagy Carmichael, Johnny Mercer, and Willard Robison; he easily broke the color line in engaging William Grant Still as a staff arranger and opening the way for him in radio. Whiteman paid Don Redman a princely two thousand dollars in 1927 for twenty arrangements, the best known of which were "Sensation Stomp," "Whiteman Stomp," and "Henderson Stomp."

21. An interesting corollary lies in the so-called novelty piano style of the '20s, shortened from "novelty ragtime." Throughout the decade the term gradually expanded to

identify a variety of keyboard sounds and textures related to, and even overlapping, the hot jazz idiom. The harmonic, melodic, and rhythmic vocabulary of "Zez" Confrey's "Kitten on the Keys," for example, is essentially the same as for James P. Johnson's "Carolina Shout" and Fats Waller's "Handful of Keys."

But "Carolina Shout" and "Handful of Keys" have long been reverenced as landmarks of jazz piano, while "Kitten on the Keys" occupies a kind of period no-man's-land as a lightweight pianistic amusement. All three are composed, formal works. What, then, is the difference? That the Confrey pieces began with notation, the Johnson as improvisations? Has that been documented? And what is to be made of such pieces as Confrey's "High Hattin'," with its resemblance to the pianistics of Jelly Roll Morton? Echoes elsewhere in Confrey's work of Willie "the Lion" Smith, James P. Johnson (especially in "You Tell 'Em, Ivories"), and even Bix Beiderbecke's four published piano miniatures only emphasize the points of overlap between the "novelty" and "jazz piano" idioms. Conversely, more than one scholar has noted the effects of Confrey's pianistics in the jazz style of Earl Hines.

Reliable distinctions between the two are often difficult to draw, even harder to sustain. Pianist Dick Hyman, whose study of both the "novelty" and jazz piano idioms has lent him unquestioned authority in the field, suggests that "novelty" piano was functionally little more than a term music publishers began using shortly after World War I "to identify piano solos sold to the popular market as opposed to the 'serious,' or classical, market." In his view, the category was useful more for merchandising than for aesthetic purposes, since various genres of music were included in what was clearly an omnibus category.

" 'Novelty piano'," says Hyman, "is now often used in a more particular sense as referring to pieces employing an attractive, if deliberately unsettling, syncopation . . . a somewhat demanding keyboard technique, and a fanciful, programmatic title." As used this way, he adds, it is to some degree pejorative, systematically excluding the work of composer-players such as Waller, Johnson, Morton, Willie "the Lion" Smith, and even Eubie Blake, however much in common their work has with the genre. From a strictly musical standpoint, however, the distinction is artificial.

And what of Gershwin, himself reportedly a gifted improviser? "His approach," says Hyman, "was busy and full, with an active left hand and octaves in the right. Syncopated attention-getting devices place him with Confrey's influential school of novelty piano. However, the line between this style and those of, say, Frank Signorelli and Lennie Hayton . . . is impossible to draw, although Signorelli and Hayton probably improvised more than Confrey did. In the company of such colleagues—and we might add to the list Rube Bloom and Arthur Schutt—Gershwin was certainly playing jazz piano, however obsolete our ears perceive his style to have been."

It remains, to borrow the title of one of Arthur Schutt's best-known novelty pieces, a "Piano Puzzle," awash in contradiction. As Hyman has remarked, a practical—if neither strictly accurate nor ultimately satisfying—working hypothesis may be to regard the composers of "novelty" solos according to what they customarily did when not writing such pieces. (Dick Hyman, conversations with the author, December 21, 1991, and February 2, 1992, and "George Gershwin: Re-evaluating His Legacy in Jazz," *Keyboard*, July 1967).

22. Duke Ellington, on the strength of "Black and Tan Fantasie [or Fantasy]," "East St. Louis Toodle-oo," "The Mooche," and other works, seems to have been successful—as, on quite another level, was Jelly Roll Morton—at blending improvisation with formally written structures drawn from the improviser's language. It is essential, however, to avoid the conclusion that they were alone in the field. Composition within the hot music idiom took many forms, from Jimmy Dorsey's alto saxophone showpieces "Beebe" and "Oodles

of Noodles'' through the efforts of saxophonist Fud Livingston, whose "Imagination" and "Humpty-Dumpty" incorporate improvised solo passages with notable success. Particularly surprising are four selections recorded for Columbia in 1929–30 by saxophonist Merle Johnston, best known as a teacher and studio musician. They are actually settings of popular songs for saxophone quartet; but their imagination, balance, and beauty of execution carry them further. There is no improvisation, but the individual parts have the feel and function of improvised lines. The writing successfully combines melodic and rhythmic functions, even while achieving a sometimes dense harmonic texture. Even without benefit of rhythm section, "Baby, Oh Where Can You Be?" (July 26, 1929) and the others generate admirable momentum, and all four titles have the heft and strength of a jazz ensemble. Even as saxophone section scoring, Johnston's writing is remarkably forward-looking.

23. Sudhalter and Evans, as above, note 10.

24. Norman Gentieu, "Eastwood Lane," Rutgers University Journal of Jazz Studies, spring 1976.

25. Ibid.

26. Wingy Manone (with Paul Vandervoort II), Trumpet on the Wing (Garden City, N.Y.: Doubleday, 1964).

27. Milton "Mezz" Mezzrow (with Bernard Wolfe), Really the Blues (New York: Random House, 1946; rpt. Garden City, N.Y.: Doubleday, 1972).

28. Ralph Berton, Remembering Bix (New York: Harper and Row, 1974).

29. Ibid.

30. William J. Schafer, "Revising Bix," Mississippi Rag, March 1991.

31. Perhaps understandably, the homosexuality theme has not become popular with the rank-and-file of Beiderbecke admirers; it may even be responsible for an often disproportionate vilification of Berton's memoir in some quarters. But what if there were, indeed, some substance? Within this context, it is useful to consider a few abiding Beiderbecke mysteries:

(a) A father's wrath: Even given a certain amount of Teutonic rigidity, Bismarck Beiderbecke's obvious and growing coldness toward his younger son seems curious. It is certainly out of proportion to any imagined chagrin at the boy's failure to do well at school or at his having become a dance band musician. When Bix telephoned home in 1927 with news he'd joined Paul Whiteman, his father cannot have misunderstood the import of a solo chair with the highest-paid, most prestigious popular orchestra in the country. Yet his reported response was cool, distant. What, too, could have made him sufficiently bitter to have refused to open or play his son's records when they arrived, regularly, in the mail—and even prevented other family members from doing so? This is especially puzzling in view of the fact that Bix was regularly sending part of his two-hundred-dollar weekly salary home. And, finally, when news arrived that Bix was mortally ill, it was the mother who sped east; there is no indication of any paternal grief at his son's illness and death. Simple disappointment with choice of profession cannot begin to account for that.

(b) Banishment from Davenport: Even a wayward academic record seems slight reason to have removed Bix precipitantly from Davenport in mid-1921, enrolling him at an academy outside Chicago, a school notable for rigorously enforced military-style discipline. Had something happened, something serious enough to require immediate and summary action? Surely, too, the Beiderbeckes knew about Chicago: if the boy was too involved in hot music, as the family thereafter contended, why send him (presumably at no little expense) to a city well known as a center for revelry, fast living, and the very music cited as the reason for his exile? Were other, more pressing, imperatives at work?

(c) The protective attitude: Almost to a man, Bix's colleagues in the Goldkette and Whiteman orchestras adopted an affectionate, even paternal, tone in discussing Bix. What a fine musician he was, what a gentle soul! Everybody loved him (even Whiteman, who kept him on the payroll long after his departure). All such utterances, including those of his sister, Mary Louise Shoemaker, share a protective, almost defensive, quality—as if preempting criticism or censure. But of what? Bix's alcoholism? Unlikely, in the social drinking context of 1920s professional dance music. What were they defending?

(d) *Beatings, including the "bottle injury" incident of February 1929*: Accounts of these events remain slight, contradictory. When the Goldkette ensemble left Detroit by train for an Atlantic City engagement in the first week of August 1927, Bix was missing. He also missed an early-morning ferry. Bill Challis found him back at his hotel, beaten and bruised. He had been set upon by thugs, he said, and robbed at gunpoint. Then, in February 1929, he eluded a male nurse assigned to him in Cleveland after a delirium tremens attack, made his way to New York, and was badly beaten and cut up under circumstances never clearly explained. Some accounts speak of a run-in with sailors, others a fight with a gangster over a girl. Some versions of the story have the attacker ramming the jagged end of a broken bottle into Bix's gut; but rumors persist that the injury was not in the abdomen, as widely reported, but the groin or even rectum. Again, he goes out of focus: Where did he go after leaving Cleveland? How did he explain an injury severe enough to leave him limping, using a cane?

(e) *The last letters*: Bix, writing home in early 1931, seems determined to convince his parents that he is living and working in *respectable* places, has a nice girlfriend, is at last amounting to something in which they can take pride. A large cache of correspondence, now in the possession of Bix scholar Philip R. Evans, strikes this note again and again, as if petitioning for approval, in a way and to a degree which hints at a need to reclaim parental regard and affection somehow lost.

Other, similar, conundra persist. In the absence of information, speculation has remained unresolved, firmly in the realm of hypothesis. But some documentation indeed exists: carefully husbanded, withheld from public view, it records an event deemed serious enough, at least in the context of the early '20s, to have kindled Bismarck Beiderbecke's indignation; prompted the family to ship the boy off to Lake Forest in disgrace; driven friends to circle the wagons when historical inquiry began to get too close; kept Bix, even as a grown man, desperately seeking parental approbation and forgiveness. Above all, it begins to explain a sense of conflict and deep shame that could plausibly have driven Bix Beiderbecke to disparage his own achievements, seek the "respectability" of formal music—and find unjudgmental consolation in alcohol and early death. Will the specifics ever be made public? Perhaps not: the facts remain closely guarded and cannot be discussed here without betrayal of confidences. But information exists, and knowledge of its existence begins to make sense of the contradictions surrounding Bix Beiderbecke's short life. It is to be hoped that persistent research will at last bring the facts to light.

32. Alexander Waugh, "Learning More From the Notes," *Spectator*, October 14, 1995.

33. Teddy Wilson, conversation with the author, Nice, France, 1975.

34. Otis Ferguson, "Young Man With a Horn Again," *New Republic*, November 18, 1940.

35. Letter to the author, December 1992.

36. Berton, as above, note 28. McHargue quote from conversation with the author, April 19, 1988.

37. Hoagy Carmichael (with Sidney Longstreet), *Sometimes I Wonder* (New York: Farrar, Straus and Giroux, 1965).

38. Duncan Schiedt, *The Jazz State of Indiana* (Pittsboro, Ind.: Duncan Schiedt, 1977), introduction.

39. Such later Carmichael songs as "Skylark" and "Blue Orchids," played at the same

medium tempo, reveal the degree to which Beiderbecke's methods and very sensibility had helped shape his own. Herb Sanford, in his *Tommy and Jimmy: The Dorsey Years* (New Rochelle, N.Y.: Arlington House, 1972), traces the origins of "Skylark" to a four-bar motif Hoagy wrote in 1939 for what was to have been a Broadway production of *Young Man With a Horn*. His working title for it at that time: "Bix Lix."

40. Each recording unit varied the arrangement just a bit. McKinney's Cotton Pickers, recording for OKeh October 13, 1928, under the name of the Chocolate Dandies, drop Hoagy's piano solo, substituting a far less thematically related one by Todd Rhodes; the Mills Merry Makers Brunswick of November 8, 1928, the first to slow the tempo down drastically, bookends its performance between two statements of the final, clarinet-led, paraphrase; another Mills Brunswick, this time by a "Hotsy-Totsy Gang" contingent including the composer, on September 20, 1929, rescores the Carmichael piano solo for horns led by Jimmy Dorsey's alto and converts the last chorus theme into a piano solo. Hoagy returned to his keyboard paraphrase one last time during a piano solo recording made for Victor December 6, 1933. Neither it nor the early arrangement ever appeared on record again.

41. Rick Kennedy, *Jelly Roll, Bix, and Hoagy* (Bloomington: University of Indiana Press, 1994).

42. Schiedt, as above, note 38, p. 151.

43. This minor but noisy controversy rattles on among collectors. *Bix: Man and Legend*, appearing in the '70s, identified the soloist as Beiderbecke. The late Warren Plath, tireless researcher and chronicler of midwestern bands, presented what he felt to be proof positive that it was Morris. But Philip R. Evans, whose research for *Bix* spanned two decades, insisted he had further evidence of Beiderbecke's participation in the McKay date. Though aural evidence seems to work against identification of Beiderbecke with the solo, disagreement continues.

44. Hoagy Carmichael, conversation with the author, October 1979.

45. Sharp ears have discerned what may be a second cornet playing a simple inner line in the opening ensembles of "Riverboat Shuffle." Asked in 1997 if his father, who played some cornet (see "Walkin' the Dog" in this chapter), would have insisted on being present at the first performance of his debut compostition, Hoagy Bix Carmichael replied, "You couldn't have kept him away." In that case, might Bix have drafted the fledgling composer and his battered horn to fill out the ensemble? "Absolutely."

46. Hoagy Carmichael, *The Stardust Road* (New York: Rinehart, 1946). Kennedy, as above, note 41.

47. Cornetist Dant, later a successful artists-and-repertoire director for Decca Records, remembered the Gennett date clearly and insisted that Carmichael had taken home a test pressing of this "Star Dust." It was not among the composer's possessions at the time of his death, on December 28, 1981. Dant quoted Hoagy's lyric for Duncan Schiedt, who reproduced it in *The Jazz State of Indiana* as follows:

Stardust melody, you hold a charm
Through the lonely years;
Stardust strain, beautiful refrain
I hear you ringing in my ears.
But the world goes by, paying no attention to you;
To me you're everything in life and love
I know, 'deed it's so;
(vocal "doodling" for eight bars)

Oh, stardust strain, in my heart you will remain,
Stardust melody, I love you heart and soul I do-o-o
'Deed I do

48. Kennedy, as above, note 41.

49. Duncan P. Schiedt, *The Jazz State of Indiana*, as above, note 38, and "The Scrapbook of a Big Band Sideman," parts 1 and 2, *Second Line*, summer and winter 1973.

Chapter 18

1. Several Wiedoeft experts, among them veteran saxophonist–mouthpiece maker Arnold Brilhart and scholar-musician Ted Hegvik, attest that Wiedoeft escaped the C-melody's tonal difficulties by using the smaller, more compact alto mouthpiece. Among the results were increased agility and more centered tone and intonation.

2. Philip R. Evans and Larry Kiner (with William Trumbauer), *Tram: The Frank Trumbauer Story* (Metuchen, N.J.: Scarecrow Press and Institute of Jazz Studies, Rutgers University, 1994).

3. Mentioned and quoted in Herb Sanford, *Tommy and Jimmy: The Dorsey Years* (New Rochelle, N.Y.: Arlington House, 1972).

4. Ted Hegvik, notes to *The Legacy of Rudy Wiedoeft* (LP CRS 4155) and *Saxophone Nostalgia of the '20s* (LP CRS 4183), Golden Crest Records.

5. Rudy Wiedoeft's career seemed to wane quickly after the 1920s. By the mid-'30s his radio appearances had dwindled. His alcoholism worsened, and he found frequent sanctuary at the East Side apartment of his friend and musical disciple, Rudy Vallee. On March 24, 1937, he was badly injured when his wife, with whom he was quarreling, stabbed him with a kitchen knife; hospitalized for several weeks, he emerged unable to walk without the help of a cane. Stories about his reported involvement in oil drilling and prospecting schemes have never been substantiated. Rudy Wiedoeft died February 18, 1940, of "oesophageal varices" and the effects of cirrhosis.

6. Kenny Davern, conversation with the author, January, 1993.

7. Challis's projection of the Trumbauer chorus can be heard both on the extremely rare Bee Palmer session of January 10, 1929, and on recordings of the complete "Singin' the Blues" arrangement made in the early '70s by the author's short-lived New Paul Whiteman Orchestra, based in London.

8. New Orleans multi-instrumentalist Arthur "Monk" Hazel (interview, July 16, 1959, Hogan Archive) remembered working for Pettis about this time in a band that also included clarinetist Tony Parenti, trombonist Charlie Butterfield, and bassist Bennie (sometimes Bonnie) Pottle. It was a large band, he said, working mostly for Irving Mills. On one record date, Pettis hired Ken "Goof" Moyer to play mellophone. "But Goof didn't play anything but straight," he said, "just the straight lead." Despite Pettis's entreaties to "take off" (play a hot solo), Moyer continued to play the melody. "So Jack said, 'Hey Monk, where's your mellophone?' I said, 'It's at the house' . . . so he said, 'Go home and get your mellophone' . . . so he goes out to whoever the guy was that was director for the date, and he told him, 'Man, I got a drummer plays more mellophone than that guy.' So I went home and got the mellophone and I wound up making the date."

The story is intriguing on several counts: according to Hazel, while the date was in progress, Red Allen and two or three other black musicians came in to listen. "They were making a record with Ethel Waters . . . they heard me, and Red says, '[As] soon as I heard the beat I knew it had to be somebody from down home' . . . so I wound up going with the mellophone, finishing up on our date and then going over there making a date with Ethel Waters with them." Over where? Only two Pettis dates have been documented in 1929, one in February, the other in May (he left Bernie's band sometime between them), with no sign of a mellophone on either. There is nothing in 1930. Ethel Waters at this point was recording for Columbia, not Victor, and mostly with white studio musicians; no Waters record of the period includes any solo by a mellophone. On October 1, 1929, Allen and a contingent from the Luis Russell orchestra accompanied Victoria Spivey at Victor: but discographies list no Pettis or Irving Mills session anywhere on that date. Yet it seems unlikely that Hazel, whose memory of events far earlier than these has been proven clear and accurate, would have fabricated the story. Something of this sort must have happened, but when and where? In all, fertile ground for investigation.

9. James Eugene "Rosy" McHargue, best known as a clarinetist, stuck with C-melody throughout many decades after the '20s, and by the late '40s had evolved a strongly personal style on it. Rhythmically more vigorous than Trumbauer's, his conception seemed to draw on the clarinet in its overall thrust; tonally it remained quite recognizably a C-melody sound. McHargue is discussed in detail elsewhere in this volume. Still later, in the late '70s, Kenny Davern, also best known as a clarinetist, flirted briefly with the C-melody. As various records show, he chose to regard it not as a low alto but as a C-tenor. His feature on "Sweet Lorraine," from the 1977 LP John and Joe, done with Flip Phillips (Chiaroscuro CR-199), achieves a remarkably tenor-like quality, much in the manner of Ben Webster.

10. Webster's New International Dictionary of the English Language, 2nd ed. (New York: G. and C. Merriam, 1958).

11. The process was repeated and developed on a 1934 record, made in England, by veteran American vaudevillian Marion Harris. That performance set special lyrics to both the Trumbauer and Beiderbecke solos; Miss Harris, a more confident singer than Miss Palmer, brings it off handsomely. But a question remains: what prompted Marion Harris, whose long career—at least as far as is known—had only marginal connection with hot jazz musicians, to devote her final record date to this piece of material?

12. Some documentation has placed Bix in the personnel for these selections, but though what may be a cornet or trumpet is audible here and there playing sustained background tones, it is not recognizable as Bix or anyone else.

13. Evans and Kiner, as above, note 2.

14. Readers will note a departure, here as in other chapters, in the spelling of Bose's first name. This is the result of research done mainly in New Orleans by a number of historians and first appeared in the Al Rose–Edmond Souchon collaboration, New Orleans Jazz: A Family Album, rev. ed. (Baton Rouge: LSU Press, 1978).

15. Andy Secrest, statement to Philip R. Evans, quoted in Richard M. Sudhalter and Philip R. Evans, Bix: Man and Legend (New Rochelle, N.Y.: Arlington House, 1974).

16. "My Sweeter Than Sweet" presents a small puzzle to Beiderbecke sleuths. Secrest, taking the bridge of Tram's chorus, plays a seven-note figure (bars 3 and 4) that almost exactly replicates one that occurs in the same place and harmonic circumstances on Whiteman's "Waiting at the End of the Road." As a matter of convention, the latter solo has always been attributed to Bix, in line with accounts of his collapse at the Whiteman Columbia session of September 13, 1929. But there is no other known instance on records where a Secrest solo contains a figure or figures so similar to one played by Bix. Even their sixteen-bar solos on the Trumbauer "Baby, Won't You Please Come Home?," while Bix-like in nature, do not overlap in specifics. The two men construct essentially different figure-shapes and are readily distinguishable from one another. The similarity between the incidents on "My Sweeter Than Sweet" and "Waiting at the End of the Road," the fact

that they are both played against a B-minor chord, and the atypicality of the latter solo among other Bix efforts prompt speculation that Secrest may have been the soloist in both instances.

17. Humphrey Lyttelton, The Best of Jazz, Vol. II (New York: Crescendo-Taplinger, 1981–83).

18. "Pres," an interview with Lester Young, Down Beat, March 7, 1956, anthologized in Lewis Porter, ed., A Lester Young Reader (Washington: Smithsonian Institution Press, 1991).

19. Despite an infusion of such movie talent as Gloria Swanson and Noah Beery, the arrangement lasted scarcely more than a year. Warners peddled Brunswick to the American Record Co., which already had taken over producing the Plaza Group labels (Cameo, Romeo, Banner, et al.) for the five-and-dime stores. Brian Rust, The American Record Label Book (New Rochelle, N.Y.: Arlington House, 1978).

20. James "Rosy" McHargue, conversation with the author, April 1988.

21. Gunther Schuller, The Swing Era (New York: Oxford University Press, 1989).

22. The "One-Step Medley" also introduces a talented newcomer. Johnny Mercer was twenty-three, fresh in from Georgia; he'd landed a job working for a music publishing house and had written a couple of good songs, among them "Would'ja for a Big Red Apple?" and "Spring Is in My Heart Again"—the latter in collaboration with banker William Woodin, shortly to become Treasury Secretary in the brand-new Roosevelt administration. Just on a whim, he auditioned for one of Whiteman's radio talent contests; "Pops" spotted him at once, signing him to write and sing special material for the orchestra at a salary, quite respectable by Depression standards, of seventy-five dollars a week. He sings it straight on "Dinah," then unleashes some manic, but quite competent, scatting on "My Honey's Lovin' Arms."

23. Evans and Kiner, as above, note 2.

24. McHargue, as above, note 20.

25. Frank Trumbauer, Frank Trumbauer's Saxophone Studies (New York: Robbins Music, 1935).

26. Martin Williams, The Jazz Tradition, new and rev. ed. (New York: Oxford University Press, 1983), p. 72.

27. John Hammond, "Three T's Opening on Pins and Needles!" Down Beat, December 1936.

28. Charles Teagarden, "Little 'T' Flies High," Melody Maker, August 28, 1937.

29. Otis Ferguson, "John Hammond," HRS Society Rag, September 1938, reprinted in The Otis Ferguson Reader (Highland Park, Ill.: December Press, 1982).

30. Ibid. Hammond apparently also harbored an animus for Duke Ellington. On one occasion he criticized the latter's "Reminiscing in Tempo" in print because Ellington did not imbue that landmark work with enough "black suffering." Ellington, as one veteran musician who knew both men put it, "didn't have much time for John and his bleeding-heart politics. To him, if you weren't suffering and downtrodden you weren't really black. Duke had pride, real self-respect: he didn't need John, and he didn't mind showing it. John never forgave him for that."

31. Advertisement appearing in Down Beat, May 1938.

Chapter 19

1. Jim Goodwin, conversations with the author, March 29 and April 1, 1992.

2. Harold S. Kaye, "Jack Purvis and the New Yorkers in Europe," IAJRC Journal, January 1988, p. 15.

3. Quoted in Duncan Schiedt, The Jazz State of Indiana (Pittsboro, Ind.: Duncan Schiedt, 1977).

4. "Music Jottings," Billboard, October 30, 1926.

5. Spencer Clark, conversation with Michael Brooks, c. 1970. Unpublished. Used by permission.

6. Ibid.

7. A story persists that it was Bob Stephens, the former Scranton Sirens trumpeter who had become Rockwell's assistant at OKeh, who heard Purvis and got his boss interested. According to this account, Purvis and Stephens wound up rooming together in an apartment filled with records, among them test pressings of many alternate takes of Armstrong Hot Five and Seven performances. At one point, the story goes, they couldn't make the rent (though this seems curious in view of Stephens's position as a salaried employee) and had to desert the flat at short notice—leaving hundreds of potential collector's items to an uncertain fate.

8. Ballew's association with, and partiality for, jazzmen of this period is amply documented but little credited (he is responsible, for example, for what was clearly an effort to rehabilitate Bix Beiderbecke, at a time when few colleagues were doing much to look out for his welfare). Drummer and Purvis researcher Hal Smith has suggested that in organizing the band for the Febrary 25 date, Ballew may have "borrowed" (perhaps at Purvis's instigation) Luis Russell's rhythm men Will Johnson (guitar), George "Pops" Foster (bass), and Paul Barbarin (drums). Smith's suggestion may not be as implausible as first appears: certainly the broad 4/4 achieved by the rhythm on this title is strikingly reminiscent of the sound of Russell's rhythm section; and, too, by early 1930 mixed sessions—especially for OKeh—were by no means a rarity. Additionally, the A-and-R man for the date was Bob Stephens, a friend and admirer of both Purvis and the Russell band. Russell, moreover, worked at OKeh in this period as a "plate man," delivering metal stampers for pressing. Unfortunately, the two other songs recorded that day provide little corroboration. Both are ballads, performed in straightforward but unexceptional manner, the rhythm section keeping dutiful time.

9. Charlie Barnet, Those Swinging Years (Baton Rouge: Louisiana State University Press, 1984), p. 23.

10. Rex Stewart, "In My Opinion," conversation with Sinclair Traill, Jazz Journal, July 1967, p. 8.

11. Ibid. It is worth noting here that with very few exceptions, stock arrangements published in the 1920s were scored for only three brass—two trumpets and one trombone. If Stewart's story is true, anyone filling in a third trumpet part would have had no choice but to improvise it.

12. George "Pops" Foster (with Tom Stoddard), Pops Foster: The Autobiography of a New Orleans Jazzman (Berkeley: University of California Press, 1971), p. 140.

13. Al Philburn, conversation with Michael Brooks, c. 1970. Unpublished. Used by permission.

14. Mickey Bloom, Ben Williams, Gus Mayhew: quoted by Bozy White and cited in letter to IAJRC Journal, April 1988. Elaborated upon by White in conversation with the author, April 1, 1992. Barnet, as above, note 2, p.25.

15. Philburn, as above, note 13.

16. As quoted by Bozy White in letter to IAJRC Journal, April 1988, pp. 4–5.

17. Bill Priestley, conversation with Michael Brooks, c. 1970.

18. Barnet, as above, note 9.

19. The identity of "Eddie Droesch" remains a mystery. Brian Rust, in The American

Dance Band Discography, lists him as an alto saxophonist, but the local 802 directory for 1931 yields no such name listed on *any* instrument. An OKeh issue lists the title by "Buddy Campbell and His Orchestra," usually a Ben Selvin pseudonym. But on the basis of aural evidence this would appear not to be a New York–based band.

20. George Van Eps, conversation with the author, June 23, 1992.

21. Bonnie Lake, conversation with the author, March 1992.

22. Philburn, as above, note 13.

23. Helen O'Brien Griffin, conversation with the author, 1992.

24. Harry Leedy, conversation with Michael Brooks, c. 1969. Unpublished. Used by permission.

25. Texas musicians' stories cited in letter from Bruce Baker Jr. to George Hoefer, of *Down Beat,* dated April 15, 1946. Date of entry into Huntsville from Bozy White, quoting letter from J. C. Roberts, Texas Prison System, dated September 25, 1952, and published in *IAJRC Journal,* April 1988.

26. Dick Hall, "An Unusual Story of the Life of Musicians Behind Prison Walls," *Down Beat,* October and November 1938.

27. William Jolesch, "Thirty Minutes Behind the Walls," *Rural Radio,* May 1939, pp. 4–5.

28. Correspondence between Betty Lou Purvis and George Hoefer is on file in Hoefer Collection, Institute of Jazz Studies, Rutgers University. dated March 4, 1947.

29. White, as above, note 16.

30. Clark, as above, note 5. Same material covered in conversation with the author, 1992.

31. Betty Purvis, letter to Paul Larson, dated November 30, 1974. Supplied courtesy of Chris Tyle.

32. Paul A. Larson, "Final Curtain," *Storyville,* February-March 1972.

33. Purvis, as above, note 31.

Chapter 20

1. Joe Dixon quotes in this chapter are from conversations with the author, 1982–83, 1985, unless indicated otherwise.

2. Pee Wee Erwin, conversation with the author on WBAI-FM radio, New York, c. 1977.

3. Steve Lipkins, conversation with the author, 1982.

4. Louis Armstrong, " 'Berigan Can't Do No Wrong,' says Armstrong," *Down Beat.* September 1, 1941.

5. Composite quote: John Chilton, notes to Bunny Berigan volume in Time-Life *Giants of Jazz* series, 1982; James T. Maher, recorded interview with Trotter.

6. Robert Dupuis, *Bunny Berigan: Elusive Legend of Jazz* (Baton Rouge: Louisiana State University Press, 1993). Material from interviews gathered by "Bozy" White.

7. A story persists that Hughes, excited by what he heard of "one of the nicest kids in the profession," set up a recording date at English Decca for Friday, May 23, 1930, inviting Berigan to join regulars Norman Payne (cornet) and Phil Buchel (alto sax) and some other visiting Americans, including Jimmy Dorsey, in town with Ted Lewis, and Max Farley, then playing with Fred Elizalde's band at the Savoy Hotel. Berigan, whatever his reasons, never showed, and as a last-minute replacement Hughes reportedly hired Muggsy Spanier, also traveling with Lewis. One of four titles done that day was the Milton Ager–Jack Yellen "I Like to Do Things for You," featured by Paul Whiteman on the

soundtrack of The King of Jazz. Unissued at the time, it appeared in the 1980s on a Spike Hughes LP collection, thanks to a test pressing long in circulation among British collectors. But there's no Spanier: the only cornet heard is Payne. Berigan did play on one London date with Dorsey: a Columbia session led by Van Phillips, an American working in Britain, and also including some other Kemp musicians, a local rhythm section, and strings. They recorded medleys from two current shows, Song of the Flame and The Cuckoos. Dorsey solos recognizably and well on the latter title, but apart from some punchy ensemble lead in the bridge of his chorus, there's no sign of Berigan.

8. Eddie Miller, conversation with the author, 1983. According to available documentation the only Yale date played by such a group was a May 15 dance at Beta Theta Phi fraternity house. Berigan and Bix were the trumpets; Bill Moore was not present. Nor was he in the band that appeared at Princeton May 8. Moore was present, however, for an earlier college date, a March 14 Senior Hop at Amherst. Miller, speaking at a remove of four decades, may have simply mixed details of one engagement with those of another. (Source: Richard M. Sudhalter and Philip R. Evans, Bix: Man and Legend (New Rochelle, N.Y.: Arlington House, 1974).

9. Sudhalter and Evans, ibid.

10. Dupuis, as above, note 6, p. 59.

11. A week later, on March 8, he was part of the orchestra that recorded a two-part medley from Irving Berlin's show Face the Music. Part one, often reissued, features Bing Crosby singing a chorus of "Soft Lights and Sweet Music." Part two, unknown and unlisted in standard discographies (bx 11418, issued on Brunswick 20106), includes a scorching sixteen bars by Berigan, straight-muted, on "I Say It's Spinach." Those seeking further, still rarer, examples of 1932 Berigan are invited to sample "Sing a New Song" (February 17) and "Gosh Darn!" (April 5), both by ARC-Brunswick house orchestras and issued under various pseudonyms. Journeyman dance band performances, both include vigorous, even abandoned, Berigan solos.

12. Edgar Allan Poe, review of Hawthorne's Twice-Told Tales, quoted by W. Somerset Maugham in his introduction to Tellers of Tales (New York: Doubleday, Doran, 1939).

13. Eddie Barefield, conversations with the author, 1975–85.

14. Singleton and D. Berigan, quoted in Dupuis, as above, note 6.

15. Bill Rank, quoted in Chilton, as above, note 5.

16. Quoted in Dupuis, as above, note 14, p. 67.

17. Manny Klein, conversation with the author, c. 1981.

18. Art Drelinger, conversation with the author, c. 1982.

19. Erwin, as above, note 2.

20. Jim Maxwell, conversations with the author, 1975–80.

21. Klein, as above, note 17.

22. Some confusion attends the spelling of this trombonist's name. He was listed in discographies and other works as "Morey Samuel" until the early '80s, when a Time-Life researcher came up with evidence that the name was actually "Samel," without the u. The author checked further and found a local 802 directory for 1931 listing him as "Morey Samel." So Samel it remains. He was an excellent and often overlooked trombonist, who saw service in many top bands of the '30s, including Berigan's own.

23. Bud Freeman, conversation with the author, 1982.

24. Certain other soloists—Henry "Red" Allen comes quickly to mind—share this ability to elasticize a phrase to great expressive effect. Any attempt to transcribe Allen's solos on the two versions of "Queer Notions," with Fletcher Henderson's Orchestra, or Billie Holiday's phrasing of the five eighth notes that make up the phrase "How do you

do, you fool" in her 1937 Brunswick recording of "Foolin' Myself," with Teddy Wilson, brings immediate—and sobering—understanding of the intangibility of this phenomenon.

25. All Benny Goodman quotes in this chapter are from conversation with the author, 1981; portions used, in slightly altered form, elsewhere in this volume and in *American Heritage*, October-November 1981.

Berigan's presence in the band carried its own hazards. In a conversation with James T. Maher (related in note to the author, May 3, 1996), trombonist Jack Lacey recalled a night during the band's disastrous engagement at Elitch's Gardens, a ballroom outside Denver. Goodman, painfully aware that his musicians were not bringing in crowds and could be fired at any moment, accepted a sip from Berigan's Coca-Cola bottle one night just before the downbeat of "Let's Dance," "to wet his whistle." The clarinetist, a teetotaler, gagged, said Maher, and for a few moments was unable either to talk or play. The bottle was full of straight whiskey.

26. *Down Beat*, August 1, 1935.

27. Such instances, familiar in contemporary music, are relatively rare in early jazz. Harmonies, laid out simply and clearly, were there to be followed. But occasionally a solo would achieve so compelling an inner logic that it seemed to make its own rules as it went. A notable example among many is Bix Beiderbecke's chorus on the originally issued take of "Lonely Melody," with Paul Whiteman's orchestra. He resolves a particularly emphatic phrase on a concert A♭, though the song harmony has by that time shifted to an F7 chord. Yet for Bix to have altered his figure to resolve to the A♮ demanded by the chord would have weakened it badly, compromising its considerable emotive power.

28. An alternative, somewhat less dramatic, account has him mailing the instrument to CBS contractor (and bassist) Lou Shoobe.

29. Maxwell, as above, note 20.

30. Chris Griffin, conversation with the author, 1983.

31. Freeman, as above, note 23.

32. Marsala, whose role in quietly breaking down racial barriers in jazz has never been fully acknowledged, filled the trumpet slot with Henry "Red" Allen. With Eddie Condon and Joe Bushkin in the rhythm section it was a solid group, which, alas, never recorded. John Hammond, reviewing in *Down Beat*, hailed the band's "superlative music making."

33. The evocative charm of Berigan's singing—and of his stage presence in general—is obvious in a 1936 film clip of Bunny performing "Until Today," with a Fred Rich orchestra which includes Adrian Rollini, Babe Russin, and other top jazzmen. He comes across as quite professional but with an engaging shyness, notably in the vocal. The performance, though brief, affords valuable insight into Berigan's hold over audiences and colleagues. In the short feature *Mirrors*, also with a Rich-led ensemble, Berigan and Jimmy Dorsey are featured on a lively "China Boy." As would be expected, Bunny's half-chorus is the performance's highlight.

34. It should be noted that Armstrong's remarks appeared in *Down Beat* in 1941, when Berigan was on the skids and past his playing peak. Though it's quite likely that Louis, in common with many fellow musicians, was motivated by a desire to help an admired colleague who had fallen on hard times, there's no reason to doubt the sincerity of his praise. He was still expressing it in the mid-'40s, long after Bunny's death, when he told Baron Timme Ronsenkrantz that he'd never record "I Can't Get Started" because "that's Bunny's. It belongs to him. You just don't touch that one since he made it."

35. Bunny Berigan, "This Thing Called Swing," *Metronome*, September 1937.

36. Berigan was not without his competitors, self-styled challengers to his preemi-

nence. One of the more intriguing was trumpeter Louis "King" Garcia, born in Puerto Rico in 1905, who arrived in New York at the end of the '20s and recorded in 1930–31 with the Dorsey Brothers. Though he spent most of his career in society bands led by Emil Coleman, Richard Himber, and others, Garcia enjoyed a reputation among colleagues as a powerful jazzman who, in the words of historian Frank Driggs, "never hesitated to let anyone know how good he was, and as a result made few friends and fewer records." That Garcia was good is beyond doubt: his playing on five selections made under his own name for Bluebird February 28, 1936, is indeed strong and sure, at times resembling that of Berigan. His opening breaks and first-chorus fills on "Christopher Columbus," for example, are quite compelling; on "Swing, Mister Charlie" (recorded by Bunny four days earlier), Garcia plays with swagger and swing, but his half-chorus solo betrays a conception far less fully realized than Berigan's. Cut loose from the security of phrasing the melody, he seems at times not to know what's expected of him: rather than build phrases into statements, he often sets them out and allows them simply to trail off. Late in life Garcia moved to California, where illness eventually forced him to give up playing entirely.

37. Review and John Hammond, "New York Swing Concert Proved Headache . . . ," *Down Beat*, June 1936.

38. Gene Traxler, conversation with the author, 1982.

39. For an especially accurate transcription of the "Marie" solo see Gunther Schuller, *The Swing Era* (New York; Oxford University Press, 1989), chapter 7, part 2, p. 683.

40. Quoted by Ian Crosbie in article on Berigan, *Jazz Journal*, September 1974.

41. Quoted in ibid.

42. Erwin, as above, note 2.

43. Benny Goodman's discomfiture at having Bud Freeman and Dave Tough, friends and peers of his Chicago youth, in his band in 1938 is a case in point. Though their presence had a positive effect on his playing, personal relations remained tense. Both Goodman and Freeman remembered the time with marked displeasure.

44. Johnny Blowers, conversation with the author, 1983.

45. Arnold Fishkind, conversation with the author, 1982.

46. Joe Lipman, conversation with the author, 1982.

47. Joe Bushkin, conversation with the author, 1983.

48. Texas-born trombonist Thomas "Sonny" Lee was one of those jazzmen who, while respected by his peers, never gained much of a name with the public and has now been all but forgotten. Active around St. Louis in the '20s, he played alongside Bix Beiderbecke with Frank Trumbauer's much-praised Arcadia Ballroom band in 1925 and recorded the same year with black trumpeter Charlie Creath in what is surely one of the first racially mixed record sessions. He worked for various major leaders, including Isham Jones, and spent time in the bands of Artie Shaw and Jimmy Dorsey as well as with Berigan. His direct, blues-accented playing, while in no way imitative of Jack Teagarden's, has many points in common with that of his fellow-Texan.

49. Berigan's affinity for the blues, his effectiveness within that aspect of the vocabulary, is well represented in the inventory of his notable recorded performances: the two with Gene Gifford, "Nothin' but the Blues" and "Squareface"; the "Blues in E Flat" with Norvo; a "Blues" from the "Jam Session at Victor" date; another at the December 13, 1935, date for Hammond; "Downhearted Blues" with Mildred Bailey (and the blues-flavored "Willow Tree"). Also worth noting are such records with his own band as "Frankie and Johnny," "Livery Stable Blues," and, of course, "Jelly Roll Blues."

50. Drelinger, as above, note 18.

51. Ray Conniff, conversation with the author, 1985.

52. Bushkin, as above, note 47.

53. Bernie Privin, conversation with the author, 1982.

54. Quoted in Dupuis, as above, note 6, p. 187.

55. Gus Bivona, conversation with the author, 1985. Portions of this passage have appeared, in slightly different form, in the author's sleeve essays for Berigan sets in the Time-Life *Giants of Jazz* and Bluebird *Complete Bunny Berigan* reissue series.

56. Conniff, as above, note 51.

57. Bivona, as above, note 55.

58. According to Joe Bushkin the band hadn't been paid in six weeks. Bunny, he said, had been borrowing money from MCA to pay his sidemen; every cent he earned at the Sherman went to the agency, which instead of passing it on to him kept it in repayment of his outstanding debt. As a result, no money was coming to Berigan or his band. Petrillo, said Gus Bivona, ordered MCA to come across with the money Berigan owed his sidemen and pay it to the union, which would make sure the men got it. The sidemen, meanwhile, chipped in to help their leader with operating funds. "We were mad at MCA," Bushkin told John Chilton, "not Bunny. We loved Bunny."

59. "Says He's Broke," *Down Beat*, September 1939.

60. George T. Simon, conversation with the author, 1981.

61. Bushkin, as above, note 47.

62. Blowers, as above, note 44.

63. Bushkin, as above, note 47.

64. Joe Bushkin, conversation with the author, 1982.

Chapter 21

1. George Van Eps, conversation with the author, June 23, 1992.

2. Marty Grosz, conversation with the author, September 15, 1992.

3. According to a statement by George Van Eps in *Guitar Player* magazine, Lang played an adaptation of the Rachmaninoff *Prelude in C♯ Minor* for his young admirer before handing over the L-4. Also, some latitude must be left in describing the elder Van Eps's corn whiskey as "200 proof," which would make it pure alcohol. Still, there is little telling what a man of such prodigious technical skills might have devised.

4. Van Eps, as above, note 1.

5. Paul Whiteman, statement in notes to album of Kress guitar solos issued by Decca, 1940; also quoted in booklet to *The Guitarists* boxed set in Time-Life *Giants of Jazz* series, 1980. Whiteman's recollection of talking to Bargy appears to be in error. According to all available information, the pianist joined around February 1, nearly three weeks after this date. Bill Challis remembered no pianist at all being booked for "San," making it necessary for him to play the piano ("strictly oom-cha stuff") himself. Perhaps Whiteman voiced his reservations to—and was reassured by—Challis.

6. A standard six-string guitar is tuned (reading from lowest string to highest) E-A-D-G-B-E, beginning an octave and a sixth below piano middle C. This gives it an open-string compass of two octaves, which can then be extended upward by use of the fretboard. Kress retained the tenor banjo's C-G-D-A strings-in-fifths configuration in his top four strings but made two important modifications: he added two lower strings in fifths and dropped his top A an octave, giving him great middle-register flexibility. His tuning, then,

read, bottom-to-top, B♭-F-C-G-D-lowered A). While all but eliminating any possibility of playing dextrous single-line solos in the Lang manner (the fingerboard jumps were simply too great and too awkward), this setup gave Kress a sometimes astonishing number of chordal voicing options and opened myriad possibilities in his low register.

7. As historian James T. Maher observes (letter to the author, 1995), "another great Spanish musician,[cellist Pablo] Casals, was also having a profound, though perhaps 'hidden,' impact on jazz at about the same time. [Tenor saxophonist] Coleman Hawkins, for example, had played the 'cello in his youth, and came under the spell of Casals's historic 'singles,' recordings of short 'encore' works widely circulated in the late '20s." In Amsterdam in the mid-1930s, Hawkins astonished visitors by playing them records of the nonpareil trio of Casals, pianist Alfred Cortot, and violinist Jacques Thibaud performing a Schumann trio. Casals remained a Hawkins musical idol until the saxophonist's death.

8. Nicolas Slonimsky, *The Concise Baker's Biographical Dictionary of Musicians* (New York: Schirmer-Macmillan, 1988).

9. Lonnie Johnson, "Working With Lang Rated as 'Greatest Thrill' by Johnson," *Down Beat*, May 1939.

10. It is stating the obvious that by the time Johnson met Lang in a recording studio, the latter was already an established, widely respected figure. As early as January 26, 1925, Lang had provided both accompaniment and single-string solo for "Best Black," by the Mound City Blue Blowers (billed as "McKenzie's Kandy Kids" on the Vocalion label). It shows the essentials of his style already defined and may in fact be the first example of fully realized jazz guitar playing on record. In early 1925, by comparison, Lonnie Johnson was still in St. Louis, where, later that year, he made his first records as a violinist and vocalist with Charlie Creath's Jazz-o-Maniacs. Even chronologically, then, any suggestion that Johnson helped shape Lang's guitar style remains unsupported by documentation.

11. With sketches by Ring Lardner, Anita Loos, Eddie Cantor, and others, and music by the Gershwins, Kay Swift, Vincent Youmans, Harold Arlen (including "Get Happy"), and others, the *Revue* looked like a winner. After the Boston tryout it opened February 11, 1930, at Broadway's George M. Cohan Theatre—only to close after seven performances. McDonough, meanwhile, had ripened, as his solos on several Ballew records indicate. One of the best is "Funny, Dear, What Love Can Do" (January 16, 1930), recorded for OKeh and featuring nearly a full chorus of easily recognized McDonough guitar.

12. Van Eps, as above, note 1.

13. Ibid.

14. The idyll didn't last long. In what appears to have been an attempt to help, Ballew's bassist Rex Gavitte talked Bix into moving out of the 44th Street Hotel and into his apartment in Astoria, just across the East River in Queens. While there, Bix found a flat of his own nearby. But it was already too late: the cornetist died, screaming, in the throes of delirium tremens, the night of Thursday, August 6, 1931.

15. Even more than sixty years later, the full extent of everyday commercial recording that continued throughout the Depression has not yet been fully chronicled. Nor have band personnels been documented. The ARC-Brunswick "house bands," for example, are known to have included, on occasion, Bunny Berigan, Artie Shaw, Jack Teagarden, the Dorsey brothers, and many more, as well as guitarists Lang, McDonough, Kress, Botkin, Felline, and Tony Sacco. For the year 1931 alone, Brian Rust (in *The American Dance Band Discography*) lists 113 known titles.

16. The classical duo format has been much and successfully exploited in recent years, and the available literature greatly enlarged, by various guitar teams, including the pairing of Julian Bream and John Williams, both widely respected as soloists. The jazz and popular field had its share as well, including the team of Harry Volpe and Frank Victor, who recorded four duets for Decca in 1936, and Tony Mottola, who worked with Kress in the early '40s.

17. Art Ryerson, conversation with the author, October 13, 1992.

18. Drew Page, Drew's Blues: A Sideman's Life With the Big Bands (Baton Rouge: Louisiana State University Press, 1980).

19. Ross Russell, Jazz Style in Kansas City and the Southwest (Berkeley: University of California Press, 1971).

20. Charles R. Townsend, San Antonio Rose: The Life and Music of Bob Wills (Urbana: University of Illinois Press, 1976).

21. Les Paul, conversation with the author, October 7, 1992.

22. Townsend, as above, note 21.

23. Gary Ginell (with Roy Lee Brown), Milton Brown and the Founding of Western Swing (Urbana: University of Illinois Press, 1994).

24. Kevin Reed Coffey, "Steel Colossus: The Bob Dunn Story," Journal of Country Music 17, no. 2.

25. Bill Malone, Country Music USA (Austin: University of Texas Press, 1968). Thomason as quoted in Ginell, as above, note 24.

26. One latter-day musician who has done much to emphasize the affinities between the two musics is David Grisman, a mandolinist who recorded in the '70s with violinist Stephane Grappelly. Wary of labels imposed by critics, Grisman took to calling his hybrid efforts—which also incorporate elements from rock and the bluegrass music of the southern Appalachians—"Dawg Music."

27. Those wishing to investigate this fertile music further will find a wealth of recorded material, much of it recognizably jazz and featuring a variety of highly accomplished musicians. Among many recommended issues: The Golden Era: Bob Wills and His Texas Playboys, Columbia two-LP set C2-40149. The Bob Wills Anthology, Columbia two-LP set KG-32416. OKeh Western Swing, Epic two-LP (Contemporary Masters) set 37324. Leon McAuliffe, Columbia LP FC-38908. Tiny Moore Music, Kaleidoscope LP F-12. Back to Back: Tiny Moore and Jethro Burns, Kaleidoscope LP F-9. 'S Wonderful: Four Giants of Swing, Joe Venuti, Eldon Shamblin, Jethro Burns, et al., Flying Fish LP FF-035. Western Swing (anthology), vols. 1–3, Old Timey (Arhoolie) LPs 105, 116, 117. Under the Double Eagle: Great Western Swing Bands of the 1930s, RCA Heritage Series CD 2101-2-R.

28. John Hyman (Johnny Wiggs), "Snoozer Quinn, a Musician's Musician," Playback, 1948, on file at Hogan Archive. As Wiggs described it, one of Quinn's favorite "party tricks" involved using his left, or fretting, hand to keep a melodic line going, freeing the right altogether. He apparently chose the middle of a particularly impressive passage to pull it on Whiteman, shaking the leader's hand while continuing to play. In a 1959 interview, drummer-cornetist Arthur "Monk" Hazel confirmed that Quinn was equally adept with left and right hands.

29. Philip R. Evans and Larry Kiner (with William Trumbauer), Tram: The Frank Trumbauer Story (Metuchen, N.J.: Scarecrow Press and Institute of Jazz Studies, Rutgers University, 1994).

30. Tor Magnusson and Don Peak, "The Recordings of Snoozer Quinn, Legendary Guitar Player," Jazz Archivist 8, nos. 1–2, (newsletter of the Hogan Archive), December 1992.

31. Evans and Kiner, as above, note 30.

32. Magnusson and Peak, as above, note 31.

33. Page, as above, note 19. Arthur "Monk" Hazel, interview with William Russell, July 16, 1959, Hogan Archive.

34. Paul, as above, note 22. According to Monk Hazel (as above, note 34), Quinn's deformity was the result of a clumsily executed forceps birth. "His head came almost to a point; he was a funny-lookin' guy."

35. Page, as above, note 19.

36. Al Rose, notes to *The Legendary Snoozer Quinn*, Fat Cat LP 104.

37. Ryerson, as above, note 18.

38. Frank Vignola, conversation with the author, 1989.

39. Quoted in Charles Delaunay, *Django Reinhardt* (London: Cassell, 1963). A similar account appears in Max Abrams, *The Book of Django*, published privately in Los Angeles, 1973; it lists Delaunay as a key source.

40. Stephane Grappelli, quoted in notes to *The Guitarists*, as above, note 5. In later life the violinist changed the spelling of his surname to "Grappelli," substituting an i for the original y. This discussion has retained the original spelling.

41. Vignola, as above, note 39.

42. One less well known Reinhardt treasure is a group of four titles recorded February 22, 1940, and featuring alto saxophonist André Ekyan with Django, rhythm guitarist Pierre Ferret, and bassist Emmanuel Soudieux. "Sugar" offers a lilting Reinhardt solo, while both the guitarist and Ekyan drive hard on an excellent "Rosetta." The intense, assured saxophonist who comes tearing out of the guitar solo with an exhilarating modulation to A♭, is a far cry from the nervously incoherent tyro who had led off the solo sequence in "Crazy Rhythm" three years before. Both he and Reinhardt are in superb form on "Margie," final title of the date. Such performances furnish superb reminder that by 1940 an increasing number of European musicians had become polished, even eloquent, jazz stylists. Among the most prominent were Ekyan and tenor saxophonist Alix Combelle in France, clarinetist Ernst Höllerhagen and pianist Fritz Schulze in Germany, and trombonist George Chisholm, trumpeter Nat Gonella, and saxophonist Freddy Gardner in England. All, however, built their styles solidly on American models. Reinhardt, by contrast, stands out as the only indisputably original voice: he sounds like no one but himself.

43. John Lucas, "Rating the Gitmen Who 'Git Wit It,' " *Down Beat*, September 1, 1943.

44. Abrams, as above, note 40.

45. This is an avenue not yet adequately explored, even by Reinhardt's biographers— as the author's own experience attests. Traveling with a band of German musicians in early summer of 1961, he stopped for a late-night snack in a rural *Gaststube* outside Mannheim. While they were eating the door burst open and a troupe of perhaps a dozen gypsies strode in, installed themselves around one large round table, and ordered food and drink. Before long several of them produced guitars and a violin, and soon were jamming away in much the manner of the Quintette of the Hot Club of France, but with a more rhapsodic quality and quite engaging rhythmic wildness. Several of the guitarists soloed, all reminiscent in tone, attack, rhythmic thrust, of Reinhardt. One of the German musicians, saxophonist (now international jazz scholar) Joe Viera, smiled broadly and directed a question to the author. "Chicken or egg?" he said. It seems improbable that they could have developed as they did by listening to Reinhardt's records. The recent popularity of "the Gypsy Kings," playing a music not unrelated to that of Reinhardt and to what went on in that long-ago *Gaststube*, may furnish a clue.

46. Teddy Bunn, one of the outstanding black guitarists of the '30s, is an anomaly—a blues man born not in the South but in the Long Island town of Freeport, New York. As a member of the Spirits of Rhythm, he was a favorite on 52nd Street and made records with Duke Ellington (including the magnificent "Haunted Nights" in 1929), Red McKenzie, Mezz Mezzrow, John Kirby, and others. His single-string solos are widely admired for their ease and fluency. Unlike Alemán, who employed the classical "finger" technique, or most of the others, who used the pick, Bunn did all his articulation with his right thumb, foreshadowing Wes Montgomery by two decades. Bunn's way of mixing single-string and chordal passages occasionally recalls that of New Orleans guitarist Snoozer Quinn. The resemblance is especially pronounced on four titles Bunn recorded for the fledgling Blue Note Label on March 28, 1940. He approaches a medium-tempo "King Porter Stomp" much as Quinn might have—though the possibility that either man ever heard the other is remote at best. The work of Bunn's colleague Bernard Addison was closer to the chord-supported style of the white guitarists, though there seems to have been little mutual influence. Addison, who died in 1991, cited the Harlem "stride" pianists as his chief inspiration, and his sometimes ragtimey rhythmic concept seems to support this. Al Casey, as one of Fats Waller's supporting players on countless Victor records, seldom got a chance to shine until later in life. When he did (as on "Buck Jumpin'," in 1941), he showed himself to be adept at both single-string and chordal techniques.

47. Paul is also an acknowledged pioneer in the recording field, having devised and perfected the first multi-tracking techniques and the machines to go with them. He and his wife, singer Mary Ford, were immensely successful in the '50s as a popular music team, their sound built entirely on Paul's exploitation of his instrument's (and through it her voice's) electronic potential. The latter-day rock music industry, built on the sound of amplified guitar, has made an icon of Les Paul, pressing him to its bare, rather sudorous breast. Behind the hype is a home truth: if his stature as a jazzman is open to some dispute (his solos seem too often contrivances, stressing effect over content or coherence), he is beyond question a visionary, whose contributions to his instrument and its uses are unique and irreplaceable.

48. It ran in the family. In the '40s, his brother Bob solved a problem which had long frustrated manufacturers of phonograph records. On an ordinary disc recording, tracking a groove successfully becomes more difficult toward the inside, as the spiral tightens. A standard tone arm, moving along an arc from a fixed base, is subject to "pinch effect," a noticeable loss of fidelity, as it reaches the end of a 78 rpm disc. Bob Van Eps worked to reproduce the lateral motion of the original cutting head as it moved across the surface of a blank disc. He achieved his end with a dual arm, on very sensitive, finely ground bearings, which crossed the record, never having to swivel, never creating friction with the groove wall. "As a matter of fact," George said with obvious fraternal pride, "with his [tone] arm you could take an old record, play it half a dozen times and actually improve it, because the playing, instead of wearing down the groove walls, would burnish them. The stylus was no longer binding and trying to climb out of the groove because the turns were so tight. It was resting comfortably in the groove where it should. With Rob's arm you were playing the record back exactly the way it was cut."

49. Quoted in booklet for *The Guitarists*, as above, note 5.

50. Bucky Pizzarelli quote from conversations with the author, October 7, 1992, and July 1995.

51. Guitarist Howard Alden, who has studied Van Eps's style in minute detail and

often worked in duet with him, adds some illuminating detail. "The thing that Van Eps did more than anyone, and certainly more fluently than anyone else, is to sustain part of a chord and then play a melodic figure above it—again, a more pianistic effect than what other guitarists were doing. He also would sustain the outer part of a chord and move a voice in the middle of the chord around as a countermelody." This ability, said Alden, evolved into a mature style characterized by "control of the bass line, melody and inner voices all moving more or less independently; when you listen to some of his solo renditions it sounds almost like a string quartet, rather than the block chord style still favored by most guitarists today. He can also do an uncanny impersonation of a stride pianist, with the melody supported by the classic stride accompaniment patterns—rolling tenths alternating with chords in the middle register and the melody (sometimes supported by more harmonies) singing out on top." Letter to the author, March 11, 1996.

52. Howard Alden, conversations with the author, August 23, 1995, and March 10, 1996, and ibid.

53. In a conversation with Goodman, James T. Maher remarked casually that he "never knew how important Allan [Reuss] was to the band until he left." Goodman made a wry face: "Neither did we," he said. (Maher, letter to the author, May 2, 1996).

54. So implicitly did Van Eps trust the younger man (Reuss was born in 1915) that when Freddy Green, guitarist of the Count Basie Orchestra, approached him for lessons, he seconded the applicant to Reuss. Green had to learn, he said, how to voice rhythm chords so the broad, fat sound of the lower strings would predominate, rather than the thinner, ukulele-like texture of the upper ones. It is perhaps ironic that while Green has been so widely lionized as the custodian of the Basie rhythm section's steady heartbeat, Reuss's similar role in the Goodman band has gone all but unrecognized. A hearing of the first Basie records, the guitarless "Jones-Smith Incorporated" Vocalion date of October 9, 1936, makes clear that Basie, Walter Page, and Jo Jones were already keeping time in their distinctive four-to-the-bar fashion; the addition of Green merely enhanced an already established sense of unity. In Goodman's band, by contrast, the problems were more severe. As pianist Jess Stacy has said, both Krupa and bassist Harry Goodman were often quite random timekeepers: Reuss laid out what Pee Wee Erwin once called a "hard-hitting" pulse.

55. Guitarists of this school seem to have had a large supply of effective devices, ready to drop into situations as occasion demanded. On "New Orleans Twist," recorded for Victor (May 13, 1935) under arranger Gene Gifford's leadership, McDonough supplies a four-bar interlude, a self-contained, finely wrought miniature, setting up Bud Freeman's tenor sax solo. Its shape and content, and the casual assurance with which it's delivered, make plain that it is no spur-of-the-moment invention.

56. Charlie Christian, "Guitarmen, Wake Up and Pluck!" Down Beat, December 1, 1939.

57. In recent years, the acoustic guitar has enjoyed something of a revival, spearheaded by the extraordinary Marty Grosz. Son of the painter George Grosz, he was born in Berlin in 1930, was brought up in New York, and has remained an uncompromising champion of the idiom. His chord-supported style displays agility and great rhythmic power—and can generate remarkable volume levels in larger groups, without recourse to amplification. Grosz is also an erudite, outspoken scholar of his instrument who knows, and has written often about, its history.

John "Bucky" Pizzarelli, who spent most of his early career as a studio musician, replaced Carl Kress in duo with George Barnes [q.v.] after Kress's death in 1965. A friend and admirer of Van Eps, Pizzarelli plays a seven-string instrument (as does his son, guitarist-singer John Pizzarelli) and works comfortably within both the acoustic and electric idioms.

The late '80s and early '90s witnessed the arrival of a new generation of guitarists—among them Howard Alden, Frank Vignola, and James Chirillo—equally skilled in both acoustic and electric guitar techniques. Alden, playing a seven-string instrument, has toured and recorded with Van Eps; the two together, with their fourteen-string capacities for bass lines, widely voiced chordal passages, and combinations of textures, have opened an entire lexicon of new possibilites within the jazz guitar field.

Vignola, beginning as a disciple of Django Reinhardt, has grown into an accomplished acoustic stylist, who will play into a microphone, at carefully modulated volume levels, rather than use an electric pickup.

58. George Barnes, quoted in Irving Townsend, notes to *George Barnes and His Octet*, 1946, Hindsight LP HSR-106.

59. Many associates have praised Condon's rhythm section work, and a large amount of recorded evidence is readily available to back them up. The remark quoted by Barnes (if Russell made it at all) is meant to illustrate the former's strong belief in the importance of guitar amplification. Barnes conceived of his instrument *exclusively* as a single-string vehicle, and that is bound to have influenced his views on the entire matter of acoustic and chordal playing. Condon, who scrupulously avoided taking solos, seemed content to consider himself no more than part of a rhythm section—quite the opposite of the boy who "desperately wanted to be heard."

60. Marty Grosz, conversation with the author, September 23, 1992.

61. Pizzarelli, as above, note 51.

62. Barnes, as above, note 59.

63. The 1942 performances were recorded off the air by the author's father, Boston saxophonist Al Sudhalter. Conversations with him and other older musicians made clear the regard in which the Barnes Octet was held among colleagues. Its failure to record commercially was viewed with near-universal regret. "They were," the elder Sudhalter said often, "just the best thing we'd heard."

64. Many Barnes admirers compare his talent to that of Joe Mooney, a blind singer and multi-instrumentalist (piano, organ, accordion) who for nearly four decades, beginning in the late '20s, was something of a musical insiders' legend. Possessor of a startlingly original mind, Mooney was all but unknown to the general public, working mostly around New Jersey before moving to Florida in the '60s. He played some major New York rooms, where his quartet (including clarinetist Andy Fitzgerald and the sadly underappreciated guitarist Jack Hotop) won admiration for its inventive arranging and faultless musicianship. Mooney finally broke through to a kind of fame in the early '50s as vocalist on his own "Nina Never Knew," recorded by the Eddie Sauter–Bill Finegan Orchestra. But he remained, as more than one agent insisted, all but unbookable: "They didn't know how to sell him," said Bucky Pizzarelli, who worked with him in New Jersey.

Chapter 23

1. Artie Shaw, conversation with the author, May 7, 1995. All subsequent Shaw statements in this chapter, except where otherwise indicated, are drawn from this conversation and another, on February 11, 1993.

2. Jerry Jerome, conversation with Burt Korall, quoted in notes to *The Complete Artie Shaw, Vol. IV*, RCA Bluebird two-LP set AXM2-5572, copyright 1980.

3. Shaw from Robert Lewis Taylor, "Middle-Aged Man Without a Horn," *New Yorker*,

May 1962. Freeman from John Bainbridge, "The Diamond-Studded Saxophone," New Yorker, April 2, 1979.

4. In The Trouble With Cinderella (New York: Farrar, Straus and Young, 1952), Shaw also mentions receiving an offer to join the California Ramblers shortly before leaving for Cleveland but says he turned it down because "I wasn't sure I was good enough." He also describes, amusingly, the trial-and-error process by which he learned to arrange while playing with Wylie's and other Ohio bands.

5. Grady Watts, conversation with Ray Hoffman. Vero Beach, Fla., December 30, 1983. Used with permission.

6. Shaw, as above, note 4.

7. Willie "the Lion" Smith (with George Hoefer), Music on My Mind: The Memoirs of an American Pianist (New York: Doubleday, 1964).

8. Artie Shaw, "Snow White in Harlem, 1930," in The Best of Intentions and Other Stories (Santa Barbara, California: John Daniel, 1989).

9. This information thanks to Kahn's meticulously detailed scrapbooks, now on file at the Institute of Jazz Studies at Rutgers University. The Kahn orchestra also made a one-hour Vitaphone short in 1932, released as Yacht Party. Shaw is visible in several shots of the band and solos on several numbers, notably a lively "Way Down Yonder in New Orleans."

10. The rationale behind this oddly assorted personnel becomes clear when, on "Never Had No Lovin'," Wingy introduces the band. He singles out Freeman, Victor, Morton, and "Li'l Artie Shaw," then greets "John Hammond sittin' over there." It figures: Hammond had arranged to produce American hot records for English Columbia and Parlophone. He was actively engaged in promoting Wilson and was trying to rescue Morton from oblivion; Freeman was a Hammond favorite. The records remained unreleased until 1948, when American Columbia bought, and briefly issued, the two titles with Morton.

11. Quoted in Arnold Shaw, The Street That Never Slept (New York: Coward, McCann and Geoghegan, 1971).

12. Shaw disclosed in 1995 what press accounts of the day had overlooked: in addition to his own feature number, he appeared with the Bunny Berigan group playing, inter alia, "I Can't Get Started." On April 13, he'd been part of essentially the same personnel when it recorded the new Vernon Duke–Ira Gershwin song for Vocalion.

13. Shaw, as above, note 4.

14. The personnel, according to the night's printed program, included Harry Bluestone and Emanuel "Mannie" Green (violins), "Izzie" Zir (viola), Rudolph "Rudy" Sims (cello), Carl Kress (guitar), and Arthur Stein (drums).

15. Fortunately, and not a little mysteriously, the Interlude was recorded. It came to light years later, in a ten-dollar pile of old acetate discs bought by a Seattle collector from a studio that specialized in demo (i.e., demonstration) recordings. After much negotiation, Shaw arranged for it to be copied and issued by the Book-of-the-Month Club as part of a well-chosen—and now, alas, quite rare—LP boxed set). But the mystery doesn't end there. Shaw's assumption, that the Interlude had been recorded live, much as Benny Goodman's Carnegie Hall concert of two years later was recorded live, seems unlikely. The acetate is obviously of a studio recording, without any trace of an audience or of concert-hall acoustics or ambiance. But where, and when? Shaw himself disclaimed all knowledge. "I must have taken the group into a studio, perhaps right afterwards, and recorded it," he said. "But I don't remember doing that. Not the faintest memory."

16. " 'Jitter-Bugs' Thrill at N.Y. Jam Session," Down Beat, June 1936.

17. Shaw mentions, with some pride, that the great drummer Zutty Singleton was a

member of this group, though not on records. "He toured with us, came out to Atlantic City with us. He was perfect for that band—knew what to put in, what not to. Didn't obtrude. Very bright: all I had to do was look at him and nod, and he knew what to do. But the black-white thing was too tough: he couldn't stay where the others stayed, and there were all sorts of problems. This was 1936, after all. We got along beautifully, but at that time—well, there was no place to go with it." Only when the Benny Goodman Trio and Quartet, bearing the imprimatur and public endorsement of the influential John Hammond, got rolling later that same year did the wall of band-business segregation begin to crack.

18. It is worth noting that Red Norvo and bassist Bob Haggart have made similar statements describing their feelings at the time. In both cases, the bands resulting from such views were highly original, free of adherence to standard "riff" formula.

19. Taylor, as above, note 4.

20. Artie Shaw, statement to Jeff Scott, used in notes to Free for All, Epic LP EE 22023.

21. In this connection it is perhaps revealing that, returning to the band business in 1940 after his "escape" to Mexico, Shaw organized two successive large orchestras and turned for arrangements to Hayton and William Grant Still, both alumni of this very Whiteman ensemble. What Gunther Schuller has labeled the "Third Stream" efforts of various Shaw orchestras, blending jazz and other, more disparate, ingredients, can be traced directly to the Whiteman orchestra, Jahrgang 1927–30. Exhaustive research in the Whiteman Collection of arrangements, housed at Williams College in Massachusetts, has shown that the scores recorded by the orchestra in that four-year period represented only a fraction—and not necessarily the most creative fraction—of work being done by its arranging staff. A major assessment of this orchestra's achievements and its influence on the popular music world of its own and subsequent times (an assessment uncontaminated by latter-day racial politics) is long overdue. Though Schuller brought great insight to his discussion of the Whiteman orchestra in Early Jazz (New York: Oxford University Press, 1969), his chapter on Shaw in The Swing Era (New York: Oxford University Press, 1989), misses the link to Whiteman entirely.

Shaw himself, moreover, has often expressed admiration for the Jean Goldkette Victor Orchestra of 1926–27, whose stars—Challis, Bix Beiderbecke, and Frank Trumbauer— moved directly to Whiteman's far larger ensemble and utterly transformed it. In such Goldkette scores as "I'm Gonna Meet My Sweetie Now," "On the Alamo," and the masterful "Blue Room," Challis effectively combines the more limited textures and colors of the smaller group in ways which clearly presage his best work with Whiteman.

22. Several critics, Max Harrison among them, have speculated that Eddie Sauter may have written the "Sobbin' Blues" arrangement. Certainly Sauter, who wrote several scores for Roger Wolfe Kahn while Shaw was in the band, was by 1936 an established craftsman. But Shaw has stated categorically to the author that he and Jerry Gray worked on "Sobbin' Blues" together, and that the latter was responsible for the dramatic "train" effect, used as an end-of-performance diminuendo. The device is present in a Shaw aircheck performance of "Sobbin' Blues," broadcast from the Blue Room of New York's Hotel Lincoln in late 1938 and issued by RCA Victor in 1954 as part of a two-LP boxed set (LPT-6000).

23. Shaw, as above, note 4.

24. Helen Forrest (with Bill Libby), I Had the Craziest Dream (New York: Coward, McCann and Geoghagan, 1982).

25. Evelyn Keyes, Scarlett O'Hara's Younger Sister (Secaucus, N.J.: Lyle Stuart, 1977).

26. Henry Duckham, "A Master Class with Artie Shaw," Clarinet (publication of the International Clarinet Society) 12, no. 3 (Spring 1985).

27. Shaw's "cantorial" quality is found in few other jazz soloists, and none in quite this way or to this degree. It has little relation, in any but a general sense, to the *freilach* flourishes of Ziggy Elman or (upon occasion) Manny Klein. What "Jewish" textures exist in Benny Goodman's work seem to have their roots more in folklore than in liturgy and are in any case filtered through the mechanics of formal clarinet technique. Those moments of Goodman's widely admired A-minor essay on the Carnegie Hall version of "Sing Sing Sing" that sound "Jewish" (if the term can be so applied) relate more to the social activities of East European Jewry—the world of so-called Klezmer dance music—than to any liturgical or religious context. In general, it might be concluded that Shaw's "Jewish" quality is of the *shul*, where Goodman's evokes the festivities afterwards.

28. Artie Baker, conversation with the author, June 20, 1995.

29. Hank Freeman quoted in Burt Korall, notes to *The Complete Artie Shaw, Vol. I*, Bluebird two-LP set AXM2-5517.

30. Burt Korall, notes to *The Complete Artie Shaw, Vol. II*, RCA Bluebird two-LP set AXM2-5533.

31. Fellow-musicians expressed high regard for trombonist Les Jenkins, who also had worked for Tommy Dorsey. His bluesy, Teagardenish style had so charmed the leader that often, late at night, Dorsey would give him a chance to solo. Jenkins even takes a solo on a Dorsey record, the February 27, 1938, " 'Deed I Do." More than one former sideman has testified to Dorsey's admiration for Jenkins, and Shaw's as well.

32. For all the thousands of words written about this band—and about Shaw himself—only Gunther Schuller, writing in *The Swing Era* (as above, note 25), approaches his subject from a chiefly musical point of view. His chapter is a curious mixture of celebration and complaint: he refers at one point to Shaw's alleged discovery of "the pre-eminence of black composers, arrangers and bandleaders" and the "relative superiority of such black creative innovators as Benny Carter, Fletcher and Horace Henderson, and later, of course, Duke Ellington." He returns to that theme repeatedly, taking arranger Jerry Gray to task because what Gray was writing "had all been done before by any number of major [i.e., black] bands." Shaw's reply: "Pure horseshit." As the clarinetist has said on many occasions, he was working from quite another musical vision, one that did *not* emulate the riff tunes and call-and-response arranging conventions of the standard swing bands, black or white.

33. Artie Shaw (with Bob Maxwell), "Amazing American Dance Music Business," *Melody Maker*, January 13, 1940.

34. Artie Shaw, "I'm Not Mad at Anyone," *Music and Rhythm*, August 1941.

35. Shaw's itinerary after leaving New York is something of a mystery in itself. He has spoken of the time he spent in Acapulco, Mexico, seemingly doing little besides fishing and thinking. But Helen Forrest, in *I Had the Craziest Dream* (as above, note 30), added a further dimension. Shaw, age twenty-eight, had fallen in love with sixteen-year-old Judy Garland and dated her a few times—until the young star's mother stepped in. According to Forrest, Shaw phoned Garland from a motel in Little Rock, Arkansas, to ask what she thought he should do. She reportedly told him "the world was going nuts because he was among the missing and maybe he better [sic] cool it for a while." Other accounts, including that of David Shipman in *Judy Garland: The Secret Life of an American Legend* (New York: Hyperion, 1992), indicate that by the end of 1939 the Garland episode was finished, and Shaw had turned his romantic attentions to Betty Grable.

36. Quoted in Taylor, as above, note 4.

37. Quoted in Burt Korall, notes to *The Complete Artie Shaw, Vol. II*, RCA Bluebird two-LP set AXM2-5533.

38. The success of "Frenesi" turned out to be something of an embarrassment for Shaw. He'd heard some local musicians play it on a wharf in Acapulco and assumed it to be a folk song. Only after it became popular did he realize the financial implications of his miscalculation. "That little error cost me approximately half a million dollars," Shaw said later. "Under the usual system, I could have made a deal with the composer for fifty percent of the take in return for recording the tune. As it was, he got the money."

39. The same sense of humor informs Shaw's lyric to his "Any Old Time," sung so memorably by Billie Holiday on the band's first Bluebird date in 1938. This time the game is allusion to names of other songs, among them "Stormy Weather," Vincent Youmans's "Through the Years," and the Nacio Herb Brown–Arthur Freed "Yours and Mine," recorded by Holiday on a Teddy Wilson date in 1937. "I did that as sort of a stunt," said the clarinetist. "Billie was joining the band, and I wanted to give her a song she could sing. You'd be surprised—or maybe not—how few people caught it."

40. Quoted in Burt Korall, notes to *The Complete Artie Shaw, Vol. II*, RCA Bluebird two-LP set AXM2-5556.

41. Jerry Jerome, quotes in this chapter, unless otherwise indicated, are from conversations with the author, June 24–25, 1995.

42. Pianist Johnny Guarnieri, one of those who worked for Goodman and Shaw in quick succession, once described the difference between their methods, and the effect thereof, as follows: "Let's say we're in Milwaukee and the first alto man has to be replaced. He might have a terrible cold. We can't send back to New York or Los Angeles for a lead man, so what we do is call the best local fella and get him to play with the band. If it's Artie Shaw's band, by the end of the week everybody's all smiles, the man will have been paid very well, we shake hands all around, and that's the last you see of him. Now Benny comes into the same theatre under the same conditions, hires the same man. At the end of the week, the saxophone player is very unhappy. He hates Benny. He hasn't made much money. But he's rehearsing his own band. Playing with Benny made you think that way." Conversation with the author, Vineyard Theatre, New York City, January 6, 1985).

43. Korall, as above, note 2.

44. In an interesting bit of detail, Shaw revealed some years ago that he'd recorded his "Star Dust" solo using a plastic reed. In contrast to most other clarinetists (Goodman included), who will go through box after box of standard cane reeds looking for one that plays and feels "right," Shaw apparently just fixed the plastic reed in place and gave it no further thought. "It took an exceptionally strong embouchure," said clarinetist Artie Baker (as above, note 28), alumnus of both Goodman and Shaw bands. "It doesn't *give* like a cane reed does. It stays stationary, and it's up to you to learn to play it that way. I was using one when I was with Benny—probably because I'd seen Artie do it—and one day Benny tried to play on it. He couldn't get a sound out of it. He just turned away in disgust and said, 'Aw, you're not a clarinet player.' " Baker also commented on another feature of Shaw's playing. "He lifted his fingers very high over the keys, and *slapped* them down much more than most clarinet players do. Benny certainly didn't do that. When you do that it gives you a strong attack, decisive. Very effective. And it didn't compromise his speed at all."

45. Singer-songwriter Bonnie Lake, married to Jenney during this period, claimed to have had in her possession several other, unissued, takes of "Star Dust" from the 1939 Jenney band session. Each, she insisted, was totally different from the others. "One of these days," she promised the author on several occasions, "I'm going to go in that closet and pull them out." Alas, she never did, and when, after her death, her midtown Manhattan apartment was cleaned out, the reputed tests were not among her possessions. Yet she was

not a woman given to exaggeration or prevarication. On the basis of the two issued takes, there is every reason to believe the missing versions existed and were what she said they were: the trombonist's inventiveness on this kind of material seems to have been limitless.

46. Dave Dexter Jr., " '$1,000,000 Talent' in Shaw Band: Artie's Should Be Greatest Dance Combo Ever Assembled," Down Beat, September 1, 1941.

47. Baker, as above, note 28.

48. George Frazier, "Frazier's Thumbs Go Up for New Shaw Band," Down Beat, September 15, 1941.

Chapter 24

1. Robert Lewis Taylor, "Middle-Aged Man Without a Horn," New Yorker, May 1962. Other Shaw quotes in this chapter, unless specifically attributed, are from conversations with the author, February 11, 1993, and May 7, 1995.

2. Max Kaminsky (with V. E. Hughes), My Life in Jazz, (New York: Harper and Row, 1963).

3. The strains were internal as well. Dave Tough's alcoholism, which had shadowed his life since the early '30s, remained a constant hazard. "You had to be a very tough taskmaster with Davey," said Shaw. "I'd plead with him, 'Jesus Christ, Dave, I know you have this problem, but you're leaving us in limbo here. We can't go anywhere unless this band has a drummer, and you're it.' He couldn't help himself: one drink and he'd be gone. One night, on some desert island, he just fell off the bandstand. Out cold. I had to assign one of the men from the band to be with him all day on the day of a concert, taking turns watching him. We'd be in some goddamn jungle, on an island far from anywhere, no booze to be found for a thousand miles. But trust the American Seabees to put up stills and make what they called 'jungle juice.' It wasn't that he found his way to them: they found him. Before the concert they'd get to him, get him loaded, and that was that."

4. Kaminsky, as above, note 2.

5. Quoted in Burt Korall, notes to The Complete Artie Shaw, Vol. VI, RCA Bluebird two-LP set AXM2-5579, copyright 1981.

6. The two Paul Cohen quotes in this chapter are from conversation with the author, July 31, 1995.

7. Quoted in Korall, as above, note 5.

8. Shaw's dilemma has to have been something like that experienced by Woody Herman, a clarinetist of rather more limited technical means, around the same time. More and more, Herman's own solos and those of his young sidemen seem located on opposite flanks of a high mountain. This situation reached its peak with the "Four Brothers" band of 1947–48. While Stan Getz, Zoot Sims, Serge Chaloff, Al Cohn—and, significantly, Herbie Steward—were carrying forward a vocabulary developed out of Lester Young and Charlie Parker, Herman's basic lexicon and manner of delivery remained firmly rooted in the 1930s and even earlier. Shaw, with his acutely tuned ear and questing intelligence, seemed determined to find a way to adapt his own playing to the new conventions so clearly in evidence around him. How well he succeeded becomes increasingly apparent after 1945, culminating in the extraordinary small-group recordings of the early 1950s.

9. As might be expected, documentation of this date has been somewhat less than complete. Shaw himself has spoken of Roy Eldridge's participation, and the trumpet solos on "The Hornet" and "The Glider" have something of his aggressive bite. But the tone and rhythmic feel are quite different, bringing to mind such other high-voltage soloists as

Charlie Shavers, Jimmy Nottingham, or even the late Ray Linn, who had been with the band in its first weeks, before being replaced by Paul Cohen. Some evidence suggests that the session took place in November, after Eldridge had left, and shortly before Shaw disbanded. There's a logic to the idea that before breaking up an ensemble he obviously held dear (but which had been together little more than a year), Shaw wanted to record it just once more. Also to be considered is the question of the two "lost" titles. In mid-1995, Shaw withheld permission for the Smithsonian Institution to use either available take of the Victor "Summertime," citing what he said was a better version recorded at his own expense after expiration of the Victor contract. It has never surfaced.

10. Vladimir Simosko, notes to CD compilation *Artie Shaw Mixed Bag*, MusicMasters 01612-65119-2, issued 1994.

11. Mel Tormé, *It Wasn't All Velvet* (New York: Viking, 1988).

12. A listing of Shaw's own songs would include "Moon Ray," "Any Old Time," "Love of My Life," "Easy to Say," "Without a Dream to My Name," "Love Is Here," "Don't Fall Asleep," "If It's You," "I Ask the Stars" (also known as "Swing by Any Other Name"), "No One but You," and "Natch," as well as such jazz instrumentals as "Who's Excited," "Just Floatin' Along," "Summit Ridge Drive," "Special Delivery Stomp," "Non-Stop Flight," "One Foot in the Groove," "Pastel Blue" (with Charlie Shavers), "Comin' On," and, of course, "Nightmare." Many of these are singularly attractive melodies; that they are not performed more often is regrettable.

13. Otto Friedrich, *City of Nets: A Portrait of Hollywood in the '40s* (New York: Harper and Row, 1986).

14. Ava Gardner, *Ava: My Story*, (New York: Bantam Books, 1990).

15. Irving Howe, *World of Our Fathers*, (New York: Simon and Schuster, 1976).

16. Neil Gabler, *An Empire of Their Own: How the Jews Invented Hollywood* (New York: Crown, 1988). Gabler also makes the point that, with the exception of Hungarian-born Adolph Zukor, each of Hollywood's Jewish founding fathers had a *Luftmensch*, a luckless dreamer, as a father. So, too, did Arthur Arshawsky. As Gabler puts it, "One hesitates getting [sic] too Oedipal here, but the evidence certainly supports the view that the sons, embittered by their fathers' failures, launched a war against their own pasts—a patricide, one could say, against everything their fathers represented." In one of the most emotionally forceful passages in *The Trouble With Cinderella* (New York: Farrar, Straus and Young, 1952), Artie Shaw speaks of his half-remembered father as "a surly, disgruntled, and, on the whole, miserable man" who abandoned his family—and wound up, ironically, in Hollywood. One of his most starkly imprinted memories of his early Lower East Side childhood is of playing in the street with some friends and seeing his father approaching. "I made some excuse to hide myself till he had gone by. I was so ashamed of his guttural accent that I didn't want these other kids to hear him talk to me, to have further reason to despise me for 'being Jewish.' For by that time I had already been conditioned to believe that there was only one possible attitude *any* gentile could have toward *any* Jew."

17. Gerald Bordman, *Jerome Kern, His Life and Music* (New York: Oxford University Press, 1980).

18. Merle Miller, "Jazz and Jabberwocky," *Esquire*, September 1954.

19. Jerry Jerome, conversation with the author, June 24, 1995.

20. Lana Turner, *Lana: The Lady, the Legend, the Truth* (New York: E. P. Dutton, 1982).

21. An oddity in this context is Shaw's failure to credit English clarinet virtuoso Reginald Kell (1906–81), who in the 1930s and '40s, with the Royal Philharmonic, Philharmonia, and other major British orchestras, pioneered use of vibrato in "classical" clarinet playing. "I do not play the clarinet," he was quoted as saying, "I play music on it. I

use it to express my personal feelings in sound. Can you imagine [violinist] Fritz Kreisler, [Pablo] Casals or any of the finest singers in the world performing on their chosen instruments without that warmth which listeners and players alike so loosely call 'vibrato,' that same personal expression and vibrant glow so readily disregarded by the majority of clarinetists?" (" 'Dead Pan,' or the Simple Art of Blowing a Clarinet," *Woodwind*, January 1949.) In 1948, Reginald Kell came to the United States, where he was active in chamber ensembles and as a teacher. Among his students was Benny Goodman, who sought (in the words of Goodman biographer Ross Firestone) "to incorporate some of Kell's ease and expressiveness into his own playing." The teacher's verdict after several months of study: "He's doing fine . . . His playing has developed character, which it didn't have at the beginning." (Ross Firestone, *Swing Swing Swing: The Life and Times of Benny Goodman*, [New York: W. W. Norton, 1993].) What is striking, of course, is the similarity of Kell's views and methods with those so often expressed by Artie Shaw. Why, then, no acknowledgment? Simple pique, that Goodman had studied with him?

22. Nicolai Berezowsky (1900–53) was born and educated in St. Petersburg, played briefly with the Bolshoi Theatre Orchestra, and escaped from the newly formed Soviet Union in 1920, arriving in the United States two years later. After six years as a violinist with the New York Philharmonic, he began composing in earnest, conducting his own first and fourth symphonies with the Boston Symphony Orchestra. He also appeared as guest conductor with the Philadelphia and Cincinnati symphonies and was a member of the respected Coolidge String Quartet at the Library of Congress. Berezowsky's many works include a violin concerto (premiered by Carl Flesch), a viola concerto, a *concerto lirico* for 'cello and orchestra, premiered by Gregor Piatagorsky, and numerous others. Nicolas Slonimsky has commented that Berezowsky's work "possesses a Romantic quality, ingratiatingly Russian in color," *Grove's Dictionary of Music and Musicians* lists his viola concerto as opus 28 and his clarinet concerto as opus 29, both dated 1941.

23. Shaw statement on Leonard Feather's *Jazz at Its Best* radio program, quoted by Loren Schoenberg in notes to *Artie Shaw and His Orchestra, 1949*, released as MusicMasters CD CIJD6-0234M.

24. It came to little. Part of his psychotherapy, he explained, was to join a wide range of organizations, some of them Communist-inspired. "I *was* in favor of a 'World Peace Congress,' " he said later, and "put my name to any group identified with words I was interested in, like 'democracy' and 'peace,' but I never even got close to Communism. Out of curiosity, I attended a couple of Communist meetings under the name of Witherspoon, but I asked so many impertinent questions that they told me, 'Witherspoon, you aren't Communist material.' "

25. Quoted in Firestone, as above, note 21.

26. All Danny Bank quotes in this chapter are from conversation with the author, August 1, 1995.

27. Barry Ulanov, "Elder Statesman Returns," *Metronome*, September 1949.

28. A strong, if unspoken, motive force here was Lester Young, whose light-toned, witty approach to the saxophone provided the aesthetic foundation for the work of all these young reedmen. Shaw and Young had been friends and played together "a lot" in the late '30s. "Whenever I had to get my chops together to go out of town," the clarinetist told writer Kirk Silsbee in 1994, "when I was living in the lap of Beverly Hills luxury, I used to go and sit in with Basie's band when they came to town and played on Central Avenue. I'd sit between Lester and (alto saxophonist) Earle Warren. Lester and I developed a great friendship, we felt very much the same way about music. But I was playing in this

highly commercialized stratosphere and he was playing in a band that never hit that kind of commerce. So he had a lot more musical leeway."

29. Santo "Sonny" Russo, conversation with the author, August 2, 1995.

30. Quoted in Burt Korall, notes to *The Complete Artie Shaw, Vol. VII*, RCA Bluebird two-LP set AXM2-5580, copyright 1981.

31. Russo, as above, note 29.

32. The quotation is not from Dryden but from Dr. Samuel Johnson, who in his 1747 *Prologue at the Opening of the Drury Lane Theatre* wrote, "For we that live to please must please to live." Dryden, in 1681, wrote of a character in the satirical poem *Absalom and Achitophel*, "Whate'er he did was done with so much ease/In him alone, 'twas natural to please." Which might, for all Shaw's protestations to the contrary, apply as well to him and his music.

33. Evelyn Keyes, *Scarlett O'Hara's Younger Sister* (Secaucus, N.J.: Lyle Stuart, 1977).

34. In this connection the author is indebted to Barbara Lea, a singer of a rare intelligence and aesthetic judgment. It was she, in working out a way to perform the Porter song as something more than merely a test of endurance, who first realized its dimensions. She has performed "Beguine" often, each time seeming to find something new and hitherto unrealized.

35. Keyes, as above, note 33.

36. Quoted in Dan Morgenstern, notes to *More Lost Recordings*, MusicMasters two-CD set 01612-65101-2.

37. Keyes, as above, note 33.

38. Gardner, as above, note 14.

Chapter 25

1. Ben Webster, conversations with the author, Copenhagen, summer 1973.

2. All Ruby Braff quotes in this chapter are from conversation with the author, June 23, 1993.

3. Nicolas Slonimsky, *A Lectionary of Music* (New York: McGraw-Hill, 1989).

4. Braff, as above, note 2.

5. Ernie Anderson, conversation with the author, June 23, 1993.

6. George Frazier, "He Plays the Righteous Jazz," *Down Beat*, n.d. 1936, and "Amazing Trumpeter Has Bix' Tone and Taste," *Down Beat*, July 1936.

7. Reed Dickerson, "He's No Rhythm Sissy!" *Down Beat*, October 1936.

8. Other Robertson records containing excellent Hackett solos include "Toodle-Oo" (April 30, 1937), "Ten Pretty Girls" (December 6, 1937) and "My Gal Sal" (November 25, 1937). Many of these have been collected in a useful CD issue, *Dick Robertson and His Orchestra*, on the Netherlands-based Timeless label (CBC 1-008).

9. Contrary to some assertions, that was not the first time it was done. The original issue of "Singin' the Blues," in 1927, bore the credit "Frankie Trumbauer's Orchestra with Bix and Lang."

10. There is strong evidence from photographs, and from the sound of his early recorded solos, that Hackett—never a powerful player—at this point strove to achieve both volume and high register by pressing his mouthpiece into his upper lip. While effective as a short-term measure, it causes swelling and soon cuts off circulation. Brass teachers discourage such practices, preferring that breath support carry the pitch aloft and control matters of volume. Trumpeter Frank Newton, a hero of 52nd Street in the late 1930s, was

another who appears to have relied on mouthpiece pressure: his sound and execution in the final ensembles of quite a few of his records display the forced, overpercussive attack characteristic of this practice.

11. His guitar, seldom recorded, is heard to considerably better advantage on "Hackett Picking Blues," made in New York in October 1938 and issued in England under the name of British guitarist-bandleader-impresario Vic Lewis. A flamboyant character who later laid claim to the title of "Britain's Stan Kenton," Lewis in his early years was a devoted fan of the Eddie Condon circle and appears to have visited New York that October expressly to hire a studio and record his heroes. Among the participants on the two quite informal sessions (suggested dates are two Wednesdays, October 9 and 17) are Hackett, Russell, Condon, Marsala, Gowans, Ernie Caceres, pianist Dave Bowman, and drummer Zutty Singleton, who also contributes several vocals. On "Hackett Picking Blues," Bobby's single-string lines strongly resemble his cornet phrases in their choice of intervals and voice leadings.

12. "Hackett's New Band Opens in Philly," Down Beat, May 1939.

13. All Jack Lesberg quotes in this chapter are from conversation with the author, August 4, 1993.

14. Musicians of all persuasions loved it, as the following personal reminiscence indicates: shortly after arriving in New York in the mid-'70s, I was part of a pickup band playing a society engagement for the Meyer Davis office. Among the sidemen was the respected pianist Freddy Jagels. "Embraceable You" was called, and after setting out the melody on cornet, I was astonished to hear Jagels play a fully chorded paraphrase of Hackett's solo from the Vocalion record. Turning to him in astonishment, I started to ask something tactless along the lines of "How did you know that?" He cut me off with a broad grin. "Do you think," he said, "you jazz guys are the only people in this business who have ears?"

15. Mort Goode, notes to The Hackett Horn, CBS/Epic LP EE-22004.

16. Louis Columbo, conversation with the author, August 6, 1993.

17. These short passages, and others on such Heidt records as "My My" and "Give a Little Whistle," produce an effect not unlike that generated by Beiderbecke's solos on Paul Whiteman records of the decade before. Their logic, conciseness, and emotional involvement seem all the fresher emerging from surroundings of such bland neutrality. This is also the key to the spellbinding effectiveness of records made by Louis Armstrong in the late '20s and early '30s: Armstrong's Lombardo-style supporting bands, their stodgy rhythm sections and mooing saxophones so often decried by jazz commentators, provide a context within which Louis, both singing and playing, comes across vividly and forcefully. It is an infallible way of highlighting a soloist's work, comparable to the role of mat and frame in displaying a great painting.

18. George T. Simon, Glenn Miller and His Orchestra (New York: Thomas Y. Crowell, 1974).

19. George T. Simon, review, Metronome, August 1941.

20. Bobby Hackett, quoted in Art Napoleon (Richard M. Sudhalter), "A Conversation With Bobby Hackett," Jazz Journal, January 1973.

21. Henry A. Kmen, interview, February 13, 1963, Hogan Archive.

22. Napoleon, as above, note 20.

23. The trumpet-vs.-cornet dispute remains a hotly argued issue among adherents of traditional jazz. There are some who assert that the cornet's suppleness and more vocalized sound make it a superior jazz solo vehicle. Musicians such as Ruby Braff and Warren Vaché Jr. began as trumpeters but found the cornet more congenial to their conceptions. Bix

Beiderbecke, of course, remained a cornetist all his brief life (though a recent account has him, tantalizingly, discovering the fluegelhorn as a medium for playing ballads and the blues). Hackett seemed to vacillate: at times he told friends, the author included, that comparing trumpet to cornet was "like comparing a loudmouth to a real soft-spoken guy. The smoothie would be the cornet . . . It seems more lyrical, more sonorous." But at other times, particularly when he was strongly under the spell of Louis Armstrong, he was wont to remark, "Well, if the trumpet's all that bad, how come so many people play it?" For an example of Hackett's work on trumpet, try the 1955 Eddie Condon Columbia LP *Bixieland* (CL 719), recently reissued as part of a Mosaic boxed CD set, on which he's billed as "Pete Pesci" (a name borrowed from one of the managers at Eddie Condon's West 3rd Street club). His solos, notably a reading of "I'm Comin', Virginia," exhibit a ranginess and sense of drama not present in his more introspective cornet work.

24. Bobby Hackett, conversation with the author, 1974.

25. Chuck Folds, conversation with the author, August 3, 1993.

26. Dave McKenna, conversation with the author, August 4, 1993.

27. All Kenny Davern quotes in this chapter are from conversation with the author, July 5, 1993.

28. James T. Maher, letter to the author, May 5, 1996.

29. Jack Bradley, conversation with the author, August 7, 1993.

30. *The New Oxford Companion to Music* (vol. 2, p. 1912) offers a refreshingly objective view of vibrato, defining it as "the slight wavering of pitch used to enrich and intensify the tone of the voice and of many instruments, especially stringed. *Vibrato* on notes of reasonable length is now taken for granted . . . [but] this has not always been the case. Violinists, for example, from the Baroque period through [Fritz] Kreisler, have generally regarded *vibrato* as an ornament to be used for particularly expressive moments."

31. Napoleon, as above, note 20. It is perhaps worth noting in passing that this interview was conducted in 1973, after Louis Armstrong's death.

32. Digby Fairweather, *The Rough Guide to Jazz* (London: Penguin, 1995).

33. Billy Butterfield, conversation with the author, London, 1972.

34. Failure to notice and credit Butterfield on "When Your Lover Has Gone" does not lie entirely with unsuspecting or inattentive listeners. The label of the original 78 rpm record (and of a ten-inch LP after that) bears the legend "Instrumental fox trot with trumpet solo by Bobby Hackett."

35. Quoted in Napoleon, as above, note 20.

36. J. R. Taylor's notes to an LP reissue of this material are typical of Butterfield's treatment at the hands of jazz writers. In one place, "Butterfield's attempt at the Cootie Williams style is tense," or "Butterfield is at ease in a Buck Clayton manner." Objective listening yields a different, less condescending, interpetation: as his work on other records (including "Special Delivery Stomp, "Summit Ridge Drive," and others by Artie Shaw's Gramercy Five) shows, Butterfield was always at ease and always himself, whether open, with plunger, or with other forms of muted playing. His use of the devices, though perhaps influenced by others (and who, black or white, is impervious to the influences of admired colleagues?), was his own. It's entertaining to imagine the positions (or, more exactly, the racial politics) reversed: a writer, Taylor or any other, commenting on Rex Stewart's "nervous, imperfect attempts to emulate Beiderbecke," or Lester Young playing a ballad "much in a Trumbauer manner." In the end, Butterfield, like Hackett, was his own man.

37. From a 1972 *New Yorker* Hackett profile by Whitney Balliett, which has been anthologized several times, including in *American Musicians II: Seventy-two Portraits in Jazz* (New York: Oxford University Press, 1996).

38. Ken Gallacher, "The World's Greatest Jazz Band," *Jazz Journal*, November 1971.

39. Folds, as above, note 25.

40. An article on Hackett by Steve Voce in the August 1976 *Jazz Journal* notes that the British Broadcasting Corporation's Foreign Recordings Unit taped the Henry Hudson band during a concert appearance at the 1957 Newport Jazz Festival. This material has never been issued and presumably still exists in the BBC archives. It would be well worth seeking out.

41. Tom Gwaltney, conversation with the author, July 31, 1993.

42. Maxine Sullivan, conversation with the author, 1983.

43. Quoted in Martin Williams, "Bobby Hackett—Everything With Feeling," *International Musician*, November 1968.

44. McKenna, as above, note 26.

45. Folds, as above, note 25.

46. Ruby Braff, conversation with the author, June 23, 1994.

47. Frank Tate, conversation with the author, August 5, 1993.

48. Max Jones, *Talking Jazz* (New York: W. W. Norton, 1988; originally published in the UK: Macmillan, 1987).

Chapter 26

1. Otis Ferguson, "Red and Mildred," *New Republic*, August 17, 1938, and anthologized in Dorothy Chamberlain and Robert Wilson, eds., *The Otis Ferguson Reader* (Chicago: December Press, 1982).

2. Don DeMicheal, notes to Red Norvo album in Time-Life *Giants of Jazz* series, 1980.

3. Charles Emge in *Down Beat*, as quoted in J. Lee Anderson, "Mr. & Mrs. Swing," *Mississippi Rag*, April 1992.

4. Noël Coward's 1939 short story "Aunt Tittie," though set in England and Paris, offers a moving, often brilliant dissection of these attitudes and their often catastrophic psychological effects on all concerned.

5. DeMicheal, as above, note 2.

6. All subsequent Red Norvo quotes in this chapter, unless otherwise indicated, are from conversations with the author in 1982, 1988, and 1992.

7. What determined which roll was used in a given instance? "Doesn't make a lot of difference, really," Red said. "Sometimes it's whatever seems suitable harmonically. Sometimes it's just where your hands are positioned. The speed is another thing: South American mallet players, or the Guatemalans, have only one roll, and it's real fast, no matter what the tempo. I could always roll very evenly at any tempo, so I varied the speed to suit the tempo and character of what I was playing."

8. References in taped memoirs of Jules Herbuveaux, December 8, 1984, in conversation with John McDonough.

9. Quoted in Richard M. Sudhalter and Philip R. Evans, *Bix: Man and Legend* (New Rochelle, N.Y.: Arlington House, 1974).

10. Whiteman's considerable role in recognizing and encouraging new talent has never been fully acknowledged. Among those whose careers began with, or in some cases received large boosts and support from, Whiteman are Norvo, Bailey, Crosby, Beiderbecke, Trumbauer, Venuti, Tommy and Jimmy Dorsey, Johnny Mercer, Peter De Rose, Hoagy Carmichael, songwriter Willard Robison, Jack and Charlie Teagarden, arranger-composer William Grant Still, and, perhaps chief among them, George Gershwin. According to his-

torian James T. Maher, Whiteman while at NBC Chicago also gave a valuable career boost to jazz piano pioneer Earl "Fatha" Hines.

11. Sudhalter and Evans, as above, note 10.

12. Ibid.

13. Rex Stewart, *Jazz Masters of the Thirties* (New York: Macmillan, 1972). Stewart, articulate and highly intelligent, was among the first black musicians to range freely back and forth across the color line in his offstand assocations. His admiration for Bix Beiderbecke has been exhaustively documented. He was also one of the first friends Bunny Berigan made on arriving in New York at the end of the 1920s. One Norvo memory of the trip east was of driving from Detroit to Cleveland, just for the sake of hearing Art Tatum play the piano.

14. According to Norvo, Mildred recorded these titles during one of her frequent clashes with Whiteman over salary. "We were in Chicago," he said, "and she was trying to get more money from Paul, which she deserved, what with her radio show and all. Everybody in the band knew it. Well, she pulled away for a couple of weeks and came east and did these recordings. When she came back I said, 'Who'd you record with?' She told me it was just some band, a big band or something. She said she didn't know who it was."

15. Additionally, an unknown Indiana group, billed as "Bud Richie and His Boys," snapped up the Carmichael record arrangement note-for-note and recorded their own version for Gennett that October.

16. Strictly speaking, this is not Red Norvo's recording debut. A solo marimba can be heard clearly introducing "Swinging Down the Lane" on a "Medley of Isham Jones Dance Hits," recorded for Columbia April 5, 1932, by a band led by Frank Trumbauer. According to Philip R. Evans and Larry Kiner in *Tram: The Frank Trumbauer Story* (Metuchen, N.J.: Scarecrow, 1994) it is a Whiteman unit, with Norvo in the personnel.

17. Norvo, conversations with the author as above, note 6, and with Helen Oakley Dance, on file at the Institute of Jazz Studies, Rutgers University.

18. Barry Ulanov, *A History of Jazz in America* (rpt. New York: Da Capo, 1972).

19. According to some reports, the sign hung around the neck of a wooden statue of an Indian woman, not in Kapp's office but in the Brunswick recording studio.

20. Frieda "Fritzie" Kapp, conversation with the author, June 8, 1992.

21. In common with sometime songwriter Bernie Hanighen and other now nearly forgotten figures, Morty Palitz was a behind-the-scenes force for artistic good in the record industry, particularly in his willingness to take chances on new artists and innovative music. He was responsible, for example, for recording the highly unorthodox Alec Wilder Octet in the early '40s, harpsichord and all, and for getting some of Wilder's songs performed and recorded. The two men collaborated on a pair of standards, "While We're Young" and the evocative "Moon and Sand."

Many musicians, including Wilder, found in Palitz that record business rarity, a true kindred soul. George T. Simon (conversation with the author, 1992) remembered him as "very talented and very bright. Very opinionated, too: when he thought something was right, that was it. One thing not many people know: he was the inventor of the echo chamber. It was at that same Broadway studio, driest in the world. He came up with the idea of putting a mike in the men's room, then feeding the sound in there and bringing it back again."

Palitz's sudden death of a heart attack on November 17, 1962, on the eve of a new job as recording director for Frank Sinatra's fledgling Reprise record company, occasioned considerable grief and robbed the music business of a knowledgeable and much-loved figure.

22. Gunther Schuller, *The Swing Era* (New York: Oxford University Press, 1989).

23. Otis Ferguson, "John Hammond," *HRS Society Rag*, September 1938, anthologized in *The Otis Ferguson Reader*, as above, note 1.

24. Norvo has told the author that he also used a studio glockenspiel on one of these titles. Aural evidence does little to clarify the situation: the solo verse on "Moon Country" is clearly played on an instrument with wooden bars—in other words, a xylophone. The mallet counterline to Carmichael's vocal on "Judy" is on a metal keyboard: while it sounds like a vibraharp, the possibility remains, given the narrow range in which he plays, that it could be the glockenspiel, with a playing span of only two and one half octaves.

25. Pennsylvania-born Lacey (1911–65), highly respected during the 1930s, spent a year in Benny Goodman's orchestra, then devoted most of his remaining career to studio work. Possessor of a smooth, polished jazz style, he may be viewed, from a latter-day perspective, as a 1930s equivalent to Urbie Green. Will Bradley (1912–95) was born Wilbur Schwichtenberg in New Jersey and spent a long career moving back and forth between studio work and dance bands, including the all-star group with which Ray Noble opened New York's Rainbow Room in 1935. In the admiring words of his sectionmate Glenn Miller, "He can do more things better than any trombone player I've ever heard." For three years, beginning in 1939, he co-led a successful big band with drummer Ray McKinley, capitalizing on (and perpetuating) the boogie-woogie craze of the time with such hit records as "Beat Me, Daddy, Eight to the Bar" and "Strange Cargo," which became the band's theme. In later years, Bradley devoted much of his energy to "classical" composing, including a trombone sonata and several large string works. His jazz trombone style blended much of Tommy Dorsey's smoothness with a warm, more personal approach occasionally reminiscent of Jack Teagarden. A man of considerable gifts, Bradley was also skilled at painting, wood sculpture, and gemstone-cutting and silversmithing. His son, Bill Bradley, won respect as a jazz drummer.

26. Traces of Jenney's quiet, eloquent approach remain today in such players as Urbie Green and Carl Fontana, but perhaps most explicitly in big band veteran Bobby Pring, whose ballad playing reflects keen, oft-expressed, admiration.

27. "Ol' Pappy" is among several titles recorded by Mildred Bailey in these years which appear patronizing, even racially offensive, when judged by later political standards. Certainly Carmichael's "Lazy Bones" and "Snowball," done with the Dorseys in 1933, fall under this heading. Since the rise of the American civil rights movement in the '50s, such material has presented a problem for artists and for record companies. Many, unsurprisingly, have preferred to duck the whole issue: one company, reissuing a 1928 record of "Mississippi Mud," simply excised the vocal with its reference to "darkies," splicing from band modulation to final ensemble chorus. In the case of predominantly vocal performances this is, of course, not possible. Quite a few artists, Louis Armstrong included, recorded "Snowball" in 1933. His record has been widely reissued—in part, one suspects, because he omits the verse and "customizes" the rest of the lyric to the point of near unintelligibility. Not so Mildred Bailey, with her pristine diction. "Snowball" is a "character song," in the manner of "Mighty Lak a Rose," a lullaby sung by a black mammy to her sleeping child. She sings it with neither apology nor condescension: she doesn't declare herself superior to her material; neither does she distance herself from it. The result is a deeply compassionate performance, in which a mother's love for her child transcends all other particulars.

28. Among parallels that spring to mind are the surpassing Armstrong-Hines interplay

on "Weather Bird," the elegant Beiderbecke-Trumbauer duet on "You Took Advantage of Me," and, nearly three decades later, the uncanny five-chorus colloquy between trumpeter Clifford Brown and tenor saxophonist Harold Land on "The Blues Walk." In each case, it is as if one mind had been able to split itself into two complementary entities.

29. Berigan's solo, those of Berry and Wilson, and the trumpet lead line in the closing ensemble were also transcribed and published as part of the orchestration. This practice was widespread in the '30s, a time when instrumental records became popular as much because of outstanding soloists as because of the arrangement used. Occasionally, when a well-known solo presented technical challenges thought to be beyond the skills of most players (Berigan's solos on "Marie" and "Song of India" with Tommy Dorsey are examples), the transcription was modified accordingly. Sometimes the publishers of "stocks" went overboard in their quest for novelty: a mid-'30s Fud Livingston arrangement of the early standard "High Society" contains solos (whether transcribed or invented is not clear) in the styles of Frank Trumbauer, Louis Armstrong, and Benny Goodman.

30. Ferguson, as above, note 1.

31. Whitney Balliett, "Music Is More Important," New Yorker, anthologized in Improvising: Sixteen Jazz Musicians and Their Art (New York: Oxford University Press, 1977).

32. It found a curious, distant echo in 1994, with a U.S. Postal Service issue of stamps commemorating jazz and blues singers. Initially flattered that Mildred Bailey was among those represented (others included Bessie Smith, Jimmy Rushing, and Billie Holiday), Norvo soon discovered that the panelists making the choices had been under the mistaken impression that she was black. "I wonder whether they would have chosen her if they'd known she was white" was Norvo's amused reaction.

33. There are even accounts, some in print, which strongly suggest—without naming names—that Hammond's ardor for Billie eventually spilled over into sexual advance. According to one record business informant, such attentions were decisively and scornfully rebuffed, and Hammond's fury at the rejection helped precipitate Billie's abrupt (and never adequately explained) departure from the Count Basie Orchestra in 1938. In the absence of any documentation, the story remains well within the realm of post facto conjecture.

34. John Chilton, Billie's Blues (London: Quartet Books, 1975).

35. Dave Dexter Jr., The Jazz Story (Englewood Cliffs, N.J.: Prentice-Hall, 1964). Dexter's omission of Connie Boswell from the "hip chicks" roster is, to say the least, curious and contravenes the testimonies of many musicians active in the early 1930s.

36. George T. Simon, conversation with the author, June 9, 1992.

37. Kate Smith, Upon My Lips a Song (New York: Funk and Wagnalls, 1960).

Chapter 27

1. Red Norvo, conversation with Helen Oakley Dance, on file at Institute of Jazz Studies, Rutgers University.

2. Red Norvo, composite quote derived from conversations with Helen Oakley Dance and with the author.

3. All Red Norvo quotes in this chapter, unless otherwise indicated, are from conversations with the author in 1982, 1988, and 1992.

4. The Norvo group, with Mildred Bailey as vocalist, was among the highlights of the memorable (and very long) "Swing Concert" staged at New York's Imperial Theater on Sunday, May 24, 1936. Starting at nine P.M., organizer Joe Helbock presented virtually anybody who was anybody in the New York hot music world, beginning with the Casa Loma Orchestra. Among those who followed: Wingy Manone and clarinetist Joe Marsala;

the resident Onyx Club group co-led by violinist Stuff Smith and trumpeter Jonah Jones; Bunny Berigan and a small band (with Artie Shaw sitting in, and "I Can't Get Started" a standout); the guitar duo of Carl Kress and Dick McDonough; Tommy Dorsey's Clambake Seven, with Max Kaminsky and Bud Freeman; Louis Armstrong and his current big band; Bob Crosby's Bobcats, with Yank Lawson on trumpet and Eddie Miller on tenor; a Paul Whiteman unit featuring the "Three T's"—Jack and Charlie Teagarden and Frank Trumbauer; harpist Casper Reardon and a group; Chick Webb's band; Adrian Rollini and his Tap Room Gang; boogie-woogie pianist Meade "Lux" Lewis. Artie Shaw won great applause and equally lavish press coverage for his performance of his own "Interlude in B-Flat," specially written for the occasion and featuring the clarinetist backed by a string quartet. But Mildred, backed by Red's Famous Door group with Wilson added, "tore down the house and got the biggest sendoff of the night," in the words of a *Down Beat* report. "If for nothing else the price of admission was well repaid for her appearance." Red's xylophone chorus on a ballad-tempo "I Surrender Dear," the reviewer added, "was scented by cherubs and guarded by angels."

5. The band normally worked without either piano or drums. Why, then, add drummer Bob White for the "Gramercy Square" date? "That was Decca," said Norvo. Jack Kapp's brother Dave had become something of a fan and arranged for the band to record— on condition they add drums. "They didn't know what to do with just bass and guitar," Norvo said. "Thought it would sound too thin, too light. Thought the four horns would make it top-heavy. That was the way people thought then. Even later, when I had the trio with Tal [Farlow] and [Charles] Mingus, we had the same problem: they didn't know what to do without piano and drums. So on those early dates we added guys—Moe Purtill for some, Howard Smith on piano. Did a lot of dates that way." Norvo as above, note 2.

6. Eddie Sauter, conversation with Bill Kirchner, on file at Institute of Jazz Studies, Rutgers University.

7. Teddy Wilson, quoted in John McDonough, notes to Time-Life *Giants of Jazz* Teddy Wilson boxed LP set, STL-J20, copyright 1981. "I'd Rather Listen to Your Eyes," and the equally undistinguished "I'd Love to Take Orders From You," provide emphatic rebuttal to a notion, widely held among those who view the jazz past through the prism of racial and political conflict, that Billie Holiday was the only singer of the time burdened with mediocre songs on record dates. The simple reality was economic: labels such as Vocalion, selling at thirty-five cents a copy (or occasionally three for a dollar), provided an easy, cheap outlet for music publishers hawking their latest wares. Singers such as Bailey and Holiday, though they had followings, were not considered major sellers; accordingly, they often drew second-and-third-line songs, the pick of the crop going to performers with bigger and more marketable names.

8. John Hammond (with Irving Townsend), *John Hammond on Record* (New York: Summit Books, 1977); and conversation with the author, 1981. In later years, Norvo suggested that drummer Eddie Dougherty, a Bailey favorite, was supposed to make the date playing only brushes but had canceled at the last minute, leaving the band to record as a quartet. Hammond stuck to his story that it had been his intention from the start to record *sans* drums, to recapture the feel of an early Bessie Smith session.

9. As quoted in Whitney Balliett, "The Music Is More Important," *New Yorker*, anthologized in *Improvising: Sixteen Jazz Musicians and Their Art* (New York: Oxford University Press, 1977).

10. This passage is adapted from the author's own notes to the Time-Life *Bunny Berigan* LP reissue package.

11. Irving Kolodin, *In Quest of Music* (Garden City, N.Y.: Doubleday, 1980).

12. As quoted by the author in notes to *Benny Goodman, Vol. II* in Franklin Mint set *The Greatest Recordings of the Big Band Era*.

13. George Frazier, "Satchelmo's Band Is World's Worst; Norvo Excels," *Down Beat,* June 1936.

14. George T. Simon, *The Big Bands,* 4th ed. (New York: Schirmer-Macmillan, 1981).

15. John Hammond, "N.Y. Swing Concert Proved Headache," *Down Beat,* June 1936.

16. As one of his first major projects after helping found Capitol Records in the early 1940s, Mercer hired Robison and enlisted arranger Paul Weston and an all-star cast in producing what is still the definitive Robison album. For those who have heard it, the sound of Loulie Jean Norman's high voice, clear as a Kansas summer morning, singing "Deep Summer Music" is a rare and precious experience. There is a Decca LP, made in the early '50s, featuring Robison backed by an orchestra directed by another old admirer, trumpeter-arranger Russ Case. Jack Teagarden's 1962 album, *Think Well of Me,* was devoted to heartfelt performances of Robison songs. In recent years, Barbara Lea has made Robison a specialty, unearthing and performing little-known songs of sometimes striking beauty.

17. Johnny Mercer, recorded statement broadcast on Mildred Bailey tribute program presented by National Public Radio, August 1978.

18. Born in Russia, Louis Gruenberg (1884–1964) was already famous as a concert pianist when, at the beginning of the '20s, he turned exclusively to composing. One of the organizers of the League of Composers, he was an early champion of modern music, particularly jazz. His works in the '20s were among the first to successfully incorporate jazz rhythms and accents in symphonic settings. He taught in Chicago from 1933 to 1936, thereafter moving to Santa Monica, California, which also ultimately became Norvo's home.

19. Quoted in George T. Simon, *Glenn Miller and His Orchestra* (New York: Thomas Y. Crowell, 1974).

20. Neil McCaffrey, notes to Red Norvo set in Franklin Mint series *The Greatest Recordings of the Big Band Era,* vol. 81. Saxophonist-arranger Bill Kirchner, talking with Sauter in 1980 for the Smithsonian oral history project, likened the Norvo band's overall sonority here to that of the Gerry Mulligan "Concert Band" of the 1960s. The arrangements, by Mulligan, Gary McFarland, and Bob Brookmeyer, explored the same lightness and variety of texture pioneered two decades earlier by Sauter.

21. Eddie Sauter, Smithsonian Institution oral history interview, 1980.

22. Simon, as above, note 14.

23. Ibid.

24. Maurice Kogan, conversation with the author, June 11, 1992.

25. Jerry Jerome, conversation with the author, May 12, 1992.

26. Simon, as above, note 14.

27. Lyle "Rusty" Dedrick, conversation with the author, August 20, 1992.

28. Bucklin Moon, "Portrait," published as part of the notes to *Mildred Bailey: Her Greatest Performances, 1929–46,* Columbia three-LP boxed set, 1962.

29. Norvo, as above, note 2.

30. Mollie Bert, conversation with the author, June 8, 1992.

31. Teddy Wilson, conversation with the author, Nice, France, July 1975.

32. George T. Simon, review, *Metronome,* September, 1938.

33. " 'Illness Split Ork,' Says Norvo; Bailey Goes Out," *Down Beat,* January 1939.

34. " 'Real Story of Norvo Split-Up Never Told,' says Ex-Manager," *Down Beat,* January 1939.

35. Kogan, as above, note 24.

36. Maurice "Hawk" Kogan, unpublished memoir, 1994. Used with permission.

37. Tonkin, as above, note 34.

38. Edythe Wright, heavily featured with Tommy Dorsey's band, was at best an adequate singer, and sometimes rather less than that. But musicians knew what the public did not: that Miss Wright was the leader's paramour. As saxophonist Bud Freeman put it, in an interview with John McDonough, "She was Tommy's lady and that was that . . . There are certain things you can't say to a person who's going with your boss." After the Dorsey Clambake Seven played "Rhythm Saved the World" at the 1936 Imperial Theatre concert, a dispirited *Down Beat* reviewer asked, "Who can save Tommy from Wright?"

39. Perhaps coincidentally, the only other white singer of the time effective on such material was the now all-but-forgotten Teddy Grace; she recorded "Gulf Coast Blues" later that spring, backed by members of the John Kirby Sextet. Born Stella Gloria Crowson in Arcadia, Louisiana, she arrived in New York around 1933 and joined Mal Hallett's New England–based band; beginning in 1937 she recorded periodically for Decca, most often backed by small jazz groups. Decca recording supervisor Bob Stephens was sufficiently impressed to call her, in a letter, "the outstanding soldier of them all" and predict that "you can't miss being a big star." Her approach to the blues was tougher-minded than Mildred Bailey's and used a falsetto effect much akin to the kind of country yodel found in the work of the popular '20s recording artist Emmett Miller. On the basis of these recordings and her readings of such pop material as "Over the Rainbow" (with Bob Crosby), "The You and Me That Used to Be" (with Hallett), and "I'm the Lonesomest Gal in Town" (with Bud Freeman's Summa Cum Laude Orchestra), the brevity of her career and the scarcity of her recordings seem regrettable. She joined the Women's Army Corps (WACs) in 1943 and performed widely for bond rallies and recruiting shows—which apparently cost her her singing voice. In any case she never returned to the music business, and dropped out of sight. By 1991, when researcher David McCain traced her to a Los Angeles nursing home, she was already terminally ill with cancer; she died the following year.

40. Dedrick, as above, note 27.

41. Dave Dexter Jr., "Red Norvo Hits Comeback Trail With Fine New Band," *Down Beat*, October 15, 1940.

42. Dedrick, as above, note 27.

43. Alec Wilder, statement on PBS program devoted to Mildred Bailey, broadcast 1978. Transcribed by the author.

44. Red Norvo, quoted in Balliett, as above, note 9.

45. Eddie Bert, conversation with the author, June 8, 1992.

46. Jerome, as above, note 25.

47. Otis Ferguson, "Red and Mildred (Cont'd)," *New Republic*, August 17, 1938, anthologized in Dorothy Chamberlain and Robert Wilson, eds., *The Otis Ferguson Reader* (Chicago: December Press, 1982).

48. Dedrick, as above, note 27.

49. Gunther Schuller, *The Swing Era* (New York: Oxford University Press, 1989).

50. She'd recorded it that April 24, backed by the Kirby Sextet with Norvo clearly audible, though discographies regularly omit him from the personnel. Though Sauter is not credited with the arrangement, his is surely the guiding hand: the chromaticism of the introduction and various of the harmonic devices—the descending whole-tone figure behind the vocal concert C in the phrase "we'll never know" is an example—point strongly in his direction. Who else but Sauter would have found a way to work in the other main theme of the *Pavane* as an interlude between vocal portions? The writing on "And the Angels Sing," also recorded that day, is unlike anything done for the group by any of its

regular contributors; "Tit Willow" and "That Sly Old Gentleman," by contrast, bear Charlie Shavers's unmistakable musical signature.

51. Bert, as above, note 30.

52. Moon, as above, note 28.

53. "I'll Close My Eyes," music by Billy Reid, lyrics by Buddy Kaye, copyright 1947 by Maurice Peter Music Ltd.

54. Bert, as above, note 30.

55. Irving Townsend, notes to Columbia boxed set, as above, note 28.

56. Wilder, as above, note 43.

57. "Blue Prelude," music by Joe Bishop, lyrics by Gordon Jenkins, copyright 1933 by Isham Jones, Inc.

58. Wilder, as above, note 43.

59. Moon, as above, note 28.

Chapter 28

1. This meeting has been recounted in many places, by various authors, always with slightly different details. The quote, too, exists in several forms. It is in Robert Hilbert, *Pee Wee Russell: The Life of a Jazzman* (New York: Oxford University Press, 1993), in Whitney Balliett, "Even His Feet Look Sad," anthologized in *American Musicians II* (New York: Oxford University Press, 1986), and in notes to two volumes of the Time-Life *Giants of Jazz* LP series: Teagarden, written by Leonard E. Gutteridge (1979), and Russell, written by John McDonough (1981). Elsewhere as well. The version used here is a composite, drawn from these and other, similar, sources.

2. McDonough, as above, note 1. Unless otherwise indicated, all McDonough quotes in this chapter are from this source.

3. Whitney Balliett, "P. W. Russell, Poet," *New Yorker*, February 21, 1959.

4. Heiner Mückenberger, *Meet Me Where They Play the Blues: Jack Teagarden und Seine Musik* (Gauting-Buchendorf, Germany: OREOS Verlag, 1986). Jay D. Smith and Len Guttridge, *Jack Teagarden: The Story of a Jazz Maverick* (London: Cassell, 1960).

5. Various sources, including Richard Hadlock, *Jazz Masters of the Twenties* (New York: Macmillan, 1965). Account of young Teagarden playing with his mother at the movie house from Maurice Grupp, "How Jack Teagarden Got His Flexibility," *Metronome*, November 1938.

6. Gunther Schuller, in *The Swing Era* (New York: Oxford University Press, 1989), explains and analyzes these principles in exhaustive and accurate detail, applying them to examples from Teagarden's recorded solos. It is superb musicological scholarship and, for those who would truly understand Teagarden's unique use of his instrument, required reading.

7. Humphrey Lyttelton, *The Best of Jazz, Vol. II* (New York: Taplinger, 1983).

8. Joyner quoted in Howard Waters, *Jack Teagarden's Music* (Stanhope, N.J.: Walter C. Allen, 1960). Teagarden "spirituals" reminiscence tape-recorded in Cleveland, June 11, 1958, and used by permission of Joe Showler.

9. Quoted in Hilbert, as above, note 1, p. 34.

10. Radio interview, date unspecified, quoted in ibid., pp. 43–44.

11. The vastly shorter length of tubing also meant total loss of anything resembling a basic harmonic series. In first, or closed, position, trombone scholar Steve Dillon has identified the notes produced as, from the fundamental up, E, C, F, A, (false) C♯, and F. As would be expected, so irregular a basic pattern requires an entirely different set of slide

837

positions, as well as drastic simplification of what is played. Teagarden, as always, worked out a system by ear: he used the "glass and a half" configuration largely in the keys of F-minor and D-minor, presumably because those keys allowed him maximum latitude in so tonally skewed an environment.

12. It is in essence the same as Teagarden's first of two choruses on "Knockin' a Jug," recorded three months earlier with Louis Armstrong, one of many generic choruses Teagarden developed over several decades (q.v.). Curiously, and perhaps because of the circumstances of recording, the "Basin Street" interpolation is more cleanly and accurately executed than either of Teagarden's choruses on "Knockin' a Jug."

13. Hilbert, as above, note 1.

14. The four "Feelin' No Pain" performances, all featuring Russell solos, are Red Nichols and His Five Pennies (8/15/27, Br 3626), Miff Mole's Little Molers (8/30/27, OKeh 40890), the Charleston Chasers (9/8/27, Col 1229-D), and Red & Miff's Stompers (10/12/27, Vi 21183).

15. Standard discographies list Russell in the personnel for the blues "It's So Good," recorded by Teagarden on June 6 with a combination of freelancers and musicians from Pollack's band. But there is no audible sign of him. Bud Freeman takes the tenor sax and clarinet solos and is instantly recognizable on both. "Twelfth Street Rag," recorded the same day, is a "gag" version: the clarinet heard exchanging intentionally corny phrases with a Clyde McCoy–like trumpet could as well be Jimmy Dorsey, also in the band. "It's So Good" is interesting chiefly for Teagarden's two choruses of blues on trumpet, full of phrases typical of his trombone style.

16. Jimmy McPartland quote from conversation with the author, c. 1981. Gutteridge, as above, note 1. Harry Goodman from ibid. and conversation with the author, c. 1981.

17. Quoted in Whitney Balliett, "Big T," New Yorker, anthologized in American Musicians, II, as above, note 1.

18. Hadlock, as above, note 5. Lyttelton, as above, note 7. Digby Fairweather (with Ian Carr and Brian Priestley), Jazz: The Rough Guide (London: Penguin, 1995).

19. Balliett, as above, note 17.

20. Steve Dillon, conversation with the author, July 9, 1997.

21. An excellent example of the similarities and dissimilarities in their styles will be found on the December 7, 1944, V-disc version of "Jack-Armstrong Blues," in which the two men alternate first vocal, then instrumental, four-bar phrases.

22. Charles Teagarden (1913–84) enjoyed a long and successful career, much of it in the Hollywood film studios. His records show a solid, often eloquent jazz soloist, whose style became more florid over the years, with a broad legato and generous vibrato. Numerous quoted endorsements make it clear that Jack Teagarden took great pride in Charles's work and regarded it highly. Yet critical recognition for the younger Teagarden has always fallen short of expectation. Digby Fairweather suggests that "Jack Teagarden, in the last analysis, was an innovator, where Charlie was simply a very good and adaptable player." Still, the trumpeter's work on the George Wettling Decca date of January 16, 1940 (see chapter 10) and the Venuti-Lang All-Stars session of October 22, 1931 (chapter 7) shows him to be rather more than the competent journeyman described by Fairweather. Overall, the most probable explanation is the simplest one: Jack Teagarden's kid brother will always suffer from an implied comparison. Their sister Norma (1911–96), herself a forceful and versatile jazz pianist, met a similar fate. Both lived out their careers in Jack Teagarden's capacious shadow.

23. Condon, especially, emerged in the late '20s as a pioneer in organizing racially mixed record dates. His efforts resulted, among others, in the Louis Armstrong "Knockin'

a Jug" session of March 5, 1929 (also with Teagarden present); his February 8, 1929 Victor date under his own name, which produced "That's a Serious Thing" and "I'm Gonna Stomp Mr. Henry Lee," teamed such Harlem standouts as trumpeter Leonard "Ham" Davis and drummer George Stafford with Teagarden and Chicago pianist Joe Sullivan; Condon set up, then got Fats Waller to the studio in time for, the pianist's March 1, 1929 "Minor Drag" session. Nor are these all. Even in later years, Condon's regular circle of associates often included such musicians as clarinetist Edmond Hall, trombonist Vic Dickenson and cornetist Rex Stewart.

24. John Chilton, writing in *The Song of the Hawk* (London: Quartet, 1990), cites a 1935 *Down Beat* report that Joe Sullivan was to have played piano on the session but didn't show up. McKenzie and Condon therefore drafted Mound City Blue Blowers veteran Bland to fill out the rhythm. In another item cited by Chilton, Hawkins refers to the eponymous Lola as a girlfriend of Gordon Means, scion of a well-to-do Oklahoma family, who doubled as benefactor and occasional "hot suitcase" player to the Blue Blowers. Inclusion of Means's name as a co-composer for "Hello Lola" lends some credibility to his account.

25. Quoted in Balliett, as above, note 1.

26. Far from being an attempt to defraud, the practice of playing a pop song without its melody and retitling the result was already well established among jazzmen of both races. "For No Reason At All in C," as recorded in 1927 by Frank Trumbauer, Eddie Lang, and Bix Beiderbecke, was merely "I'd Climb the Highest Mountain" without its melody; "Moten Swing," as first recorded in 1932 by the Bennie Moten Orchestra, was Eddie Barefield's arrangement of "You're Driving Me Crazy" with its melody chorus lopped off. The practice soon became even more widespread: the Lester Young–Count Basie vehicle "Taxi War Dance" is "Willow, Weep for Me"; Charlie Parker's "Ornithology" is "How High the Moon"; "Donna Lee" is "Indiana." On and on, the performer (or creator) of the variant taking composer credit in each case.

27. Schuller, as above, note 6. Little has been said, either here or elsewhere, about the role played by Glenn Miller in these proceedings. It is well known that Miller sought respect as a "hot" trombonist but invariably found himself instead in the role of arranger, which he discharged with skill. Nevertheless, he welcomed opportunities to play jazz trombone and gives good account of himself on Red Nichols–led "Louisiana Rhythm Kings" sessions of early 1930, and elsewhere. While his twenty-four bars on "Hello Lola" barely afford him a chance to get rolling, his equally brief outing on "One Hour" is lyrical and well executed. Both his warm, burry tone and shake-like terminal vibrato sound less like Teagarden or even Miff Mole than such black trombonists of the time as Benny Morton and even Jimmy Harrison. It is not unreasonable to suggest that, had Teagarden not arrived when he did, Miller might have made more substantial impact as a trombonist.

28. Gutteridge, as above, note 1. Howard J. Waters Jr., *Jack Teagarden's Music* (Stanhope, N.J.: Walter C. Allen, 1960).

29. Rudi Blesh, "Big T," in *Combo USA* (New York: Chilton, 1971). Otis Ferguson, "The Man With the Blues in His Heart," *New Republic*, July 14, 1937, anthologized in Dorothy Chamberlain and Robert Wilson, eds., *The Otis Ferguson Reader* (Chicago: December Press, 1982).

30. Helen Oakley, "Ladies and Gentlemen—Teagarden and Teagarden," *Down Beat*, n.d., on file at Institute of Jazz Studies, Rutgers University.

31. Blesh, as above, note 29.

32. Information from Brian Rust, *The American Record Label Book* (New Rochelle, N.Y.: Arlington House, 1978), and John Hammond, *John Hammond on Record* (New York: Summit, 1977).

33. Too often dismissed as a journeyman pianist, Joe Sullivan was in reality a quite original stylist, who blended and transfigured the examples of Earl Hines and the Harlem "stride" players to suit a particularly hard-hitting approach. That he could also play with great delicacy is obvious from his work on such records as "Night and Day" and "The Man I Love" (December 13, 1939) with Billie Holiday. Deeply admired by fellow-musicians, he also pioneered the idea of independent motion in left and right hands. That included, as Richard Hadlock once put it in a record sleeve essay, "an array of off-tempo surprises, unexpected pauses and daring attacks in octaves and tenths that tended to keep his listeners in a constant state of delightful imbalance." A particularly thrilling example, one of many, comes in Sullivan's half-chorus on "Rose Room," recorded in 1951 with an Eddie Condon unit under drummer George Wettling's name. For twelve of the sixteen bars he weaves an intricate musical braid, its strands intertwining ever more tightly until, with a mighty upward gliss, he bursts out and stomps the solo to its finish. The late pianist Dick Wellstood, making his way around the Greenwich Village jazz scene of the early '40s as an avid seventeen-year-old, passed out cards to all and sundry bearing the question "Will someone please introduce me to Joe Sullivan?" A discerning and perceptive jazzmen, Wellstood knew just what he was looking for. Sullivan, plagued throughout most of his life by ill health (including chronic tuberculosis) and an often morbid sense of his own mortality, died in 1971. Hadlock's biography of him in the booklet to the early-'80s Time-Life *Giants of Jazz* record series is both sympathetic and perceptive, and highly recommended.

34. Quoted in Hilbert, as above, note 1.

35. Arnold Shaw, *The Street That Never Slept* (New York: Coward, McCann and Geoghegan, 1971).

36. Kenny Davern, conversation with the author, January 15, 1984.

37. This paragraph has three overlapping sources: McDonough, as above, note 1; same events quoted in Hilbert, as above, note 1; and author's own conversation with Davern, 1996.

38. Composite quote, also involving McDonough and Hilbert, ibid. Because Hilbert's book has neither notes nor index, the source of the Prima interview (a *Down Beat* article?) remains a mystery. It is in neither the Russell nor Prima files at the Rutgers Institute of Jazz Studies. Hilbert's early death makes it all but impossible to trace further.

39. The "Diane" story appears, in various forms, in Smith, and Guttridge, as above, note 4, in Guttridge, as above, note 1.

40. The ensemble portions of "Diane" suffer from no such difficulties, perhaps due to the slow tempo. But a "jam session," broadcast that October 19 on New York radio station WNEW, shows the problem at its worst. Again it's Teagarden and Freeman, but with Louis Armstrong leading this time and Fats Waller in the rhythm section. Armstrong appears so used to being the featured soloist that he makes little more than a perfunctory effort to play with his companions, instead addressing the *tuttis* as if soaring over one of the big band backings that were his most usual setting at the time. On "I Got Rhythm," for example, Louis goes for the grandstand, leaving Teagarden and Freeman behind in a rolling, roiling muddle.

41. From "Jack Hits the Road," originally issued as Co 35854.

42. Even by 1940 (a mere seventeen years after the original was recorded), the Brunis "Tin Roof" trombone chorus had become one of several jazz set pieces, *de rigueur* for bands playing the number. Others included Joe Oliver's three-chorus cornet solo on "Dipper-mouth Blues" (usually followed by a cry of "Oh, play that thing!") and Bix Beiderbecke's mid-chorus solo break on "Jazz Me Blues."

43. Lyttelton, as above, note 7. This two-volume work, long out of print, secures

the British trumpeter-commentator's place among a small and distinguished circle of jazz musician-critics. Like Richard Hadlock, Digby Fairweather, John Chilton, Bill Kirchner, and very few others, he writes with perception and skill from *inside* the music, his every word and phrase informed by firsthand knowledge of how jazz is made. The excellence of the result underscores an ongoing need for a cadre of musician-critics, able to work from a level of understanding that few non-musicians, however skilled, even begin to approach.

44. Shaw quote from conversation with the author, May 7, 1995. Goodman quote from conversation with the author, 1981. Barney Bigard (with Barry Martyn), *With Louis and the Duke* (New York: Oxford University Press, 1980). Bigard's statement is particularly interesting when juxtaposed with Jack Teagarden's oft-quoted declaration, from a *Down Beat* "Blindfold Test," that "I never did like anything Ellington ever did. He never had a band all in tune, always had a bad tone quality and bad blend."

45. Described in various places, among them Gabler's 1979 notes to *That's a Plenty: Wild Bill Davison and His Commodores*, CBS/Commodore LP XFL-14939.

46. Dan Morgenstern, text to *Jazz People*, photos by Ole Brask (New York: Harry N. Abrams, 1976). McDonough and Gabler quotes from McDonough, as above, note 2.

47. Max Kaminsky (with V. E. Hughes), *My Life in Jazz* (London: Andre Deutsch, 1963).

48. Quoted in Burt Korall, notes to *The Complete Artie Shaw*, Vol. III, RCA Bluebird two-LP set AXM2-5556.

49. Photo in *Life* magazine, February 12, 1951.

50. Mary Russell quoted in Barth Mackey, "A Chat With Mary," unidentified magazine clip, n.d., on file at Institute of Jazz Studies, Rutgers University.

51. Teagarden's mention of "twenty-three years" is puzzling. The reference would be to 1924, the year Armstrong came to New York City to join Fletcher Henderson. Teagarden did not arrive in New York until 1927, and there is no indication of his having met Armstrong earlier. But word of Louis's effect on fellow-musicians got around fast and perhaps reached Teagarden, who had joined Peck Kelley that summer. Certainly the two men performed together on many occasions through the years, so the reference cannot have had anything to do with a reunion. With admirable foresight, Anderson also saw to it that the Town Hall concert was recorded on acetate discs. Six selections, "Rockin' Chair" and "St. James Infirmary" among them, were released at the time and often reissued thereafter. But after extensive remastering work, the entire concert appeared in 1983 as a two-LP set (French RCA PM-45374).

52. Max Harrison (with Charles Fox and Eric Thacker), *The Essential Jazz Records*, Vol. I. (London: Mansell, 1984).

53. Kenny Davern, conversation with the author, September 10, 1997.

54. Hadlock, as above, note 5. John Tynan, "Teagarden Talks," *Down Beat*, March 6, 1957. Some of this material appears, in somewhat different form, in the author's own notes to *The Complete Capitol Fifties Jack Teagarden Sessions*, Mosaic boxed CD set MD4-168.

55. Connie Jones, conversation with the author, June 10, 1996.

56. Don Goldie, conversations with the author, 1983 and 1988.

57. Bobby Hackett, conversation with the author, Chatham, Mass., April 8, 1972.

58. Quoted in Hilbert, as above, note 1.

59. Quoted by Nat Hentoff in album notes for *Jazz Reunion* LP, Candid 5018, 1961.

60. A number of Chicago "revival" record sessions during the '50s found Russell cast in the Teschemacher role, even to the point (in one instance) of re-creating the four "McKenzie-Condon Chicagoans" OKeh titles of 1927. The clarinetist's thoughts on such exercises are not hard to imagine.

61. Jerry Dodgion, conversation with the author, September 20, 1997.

62. Whitney Balliett, "Man of Letters," *New Yorker*, n.d., on file Institute of Jazz Studies at Rutgers University. Don DeMicheal, *Down Beat* review of *Jazz Reunion*, anthologized in *Down Beat's Jazz Record Reviews*, vol. 6 (Chicago: John Maher, 1962).

63. Morgenstern, as above, note 46. Some of Russell's approximately one hundred paintings, bearing such titles as *Twins From Mars*, *Parisian Sewers*, and *The Inner Man*, have fetched quite substantial prices since his death. Several, gifts to the ever-faithful Morgenstern, hang at the Institute of Jazz Studies, Rutgers University. Russell biographer Bob Hilbert was especially diligent in defining the role of Mary Russell in the clarinetist's life. His Russell biography also makes good use of Pee Wee's correspondence with various friends (usually typed by Mary), among them Briton Jeff Atterton.

64. Quoted in Hilbert, as above, note 1.

65. Jones, as above, note 55.

66. Charles Kingsley, (1819–75), *A Farewell to C.E.G.*

Epilogue

1. LeRoi Jones (Amiri Baraka), *Blues People*, (New York: William Morrow, 1963), p. 153.

2. Ibid.

3. Terry Teachout, "The Color of Jazz," *Commentary*, September, 1995.

Acknowledgments

Many persons contributed, in ways great and small, to the making of this book, and over a long period of time. Without their help, their support and encouragement, none of it would have been possible. I salute them all—and hope that this, the result, vindicates, makes it all worthwhile.

Acker, Clive†
Alden, Howard
Anderson, Ernie†
Avakian, George
Bach, Jean
Baker, Artie
Bank, Danny
Barefield, Eddie†
Barrett, Dan
Beller, Alex†
Berger, Ed
Bert, Eddie
Bert, Mollie
Bivona, Gus
Blowers, Johnny
Borsetti, Enrico (Italy)

Boughton, Joe
Bradley, Jack
Braff, Ruby
Brilhart, Arnold†
Brooks, Michael
Burness, Les
Bushkin, Joe
Campbell, Charlie "Duff"
Carmichael, Hoagy Bix
Cathcart, Dick†
Cerruti, Dr. Jorge
Challis, Bill†
Cheatham, Adolphus "Doc"†
Chirillo, James
Clark, Spencer†
Cohen, Fred

† = deceased

Cohen, Paul "Paulie"
Columbo, Louis
Conaty, Rich
Conniff, Ray
Crump, Charles (UK)
Davern, Kenny
Davies, John R.T. (UK)
Dedrick, Lyle "Rusty"
Dillon, Steve
Dixon, Joe†
Dodgion, Jerry
Drelinger, Artie
Driggs, Frank
Dunham, Elmer "Sonny"†
Erwin, George "Pee Wee"†
Evans, Philip R.
Fishkind, Arnold
Folds, Chuck
Francis, David "Panama"
Freeman, Lawrence "Bud"†
Garment, Leonard
Gioia, Ted
Goldie, Don†
Goodman, Benny†
Goodman, Harry†
Goodwin, Jim
Griffin, Chris
Griffin, Helen
Grosz, Marty
Guarnieri, Johnny†
Gwaltney, Tom
Hackett, Bobby†
Hagert, Thornton
Haggart, Bob
Hammond, John†
Hilbert, Robert†
Hinton, Milt
Hoffman, Ray
Horbar, Gary M.D,
Hutchenrider, Clarence†
Hyman, Dick
Ingham, Keith
Jasen, David A.

Jerome, Jerry
Jones, Conrad "Connie"
Kaminsky, Max†
Kapp, Frieda "Fritzie"
Kelleher, Mary
Kieffer, Michael
Kiner, Larry†
Kirchner, Bill
Klein, Manny†
Kogan, Maurice "Hawk"
Lake, Bonnie†
Lawson, John "Yank"†
Lea, Barbara
Lesberg, Jack
Levey, Stan
Levinson, Dan
Lipkins, Steve
Lipman, Joe
McDonough, John
McHargue, James "Rosy"
MacKenzie, Scott
McKenna, Dave
McKinley, Ray
McPartland, Jimmy†
McPartland, Marian
Maher, James T.
Maheu, Jack
Mastren, Carmen†
Maxwell, Jimmy
Mazzoletti, Adriano (Italy)
Mince, Johnny†
Minnerly, Vet Boswell
Mondello, Nuncio "Toots"†
Morgenstern, Dan
Morrow, George
Muranyi, Joe
Nelson, Al†
Nichols, Keith
Norvo, Red
O'Neal, Hank
Paul, Les
Pelote, Vince
Phillips, Gary

† = deceased

844

Pizzarelli, John "Bucky"
Privin, Bernie
Raeburn, Bruce Boyd
Reynolds, Ed
Rollini, Arthur†
Ruff, Willie
Russo, Santo "Sonny"
Ryerson, Art
Saunders, Tom
Schiedt, Duncan
Schoenberg, Loren
Shaw, Artie
Shepherd, Jim (UK)
Sherman, Daryl
Shipman, Jerome
Showler, Joe
Simon, George T.
Smith, Hal
Spedale, Rhodes
Stacy, Jess†

Starr, S. Frederick
Steiner, John
Sudhalter, Albert†
Sudhalter, Vivian
Tate, Frank
Teachout, Terry
Traxler, Gene†
Tyle, Chris
Vaché, Warren Sr.
Van Eps, George
Vignola, Frank
Watt, Don†
White, Bozy
Weinstein, Ruby†
Weston, Paul†
Wexler, Jerry
Wiener, Dave
Willcox, Newell "Spiegle"
Wright, Laurie (UK)
Youngren, William H.

† = deceased

Credits

Index of Names

Index of Musical Titles